DICTIONARY OF
AMERICAN HISTORY

DICTIONARY OF
AMERICAN HISTORY

with the complete text of
The Constitution of the United States

by
MICHAEL MARTIN
and
LEONARD GELBER
Revised and Enlarged Edition
Edited by
Leo Lieberman, Ph.D.
Fordham University

DORSET PRESS
New York

PREFACE

In this volume the authors have attempted to provide a ready reference source of the subject matter of American history. In keeping with contemporary thinking they have been careful to cover the significant developments in economics, finance and banking, labor relations, constitutional and administrative law, social welfare, literature, industry, science, religion, commerce, international relations, foreign policy, education, and the arts, while not eschewing the traditional political and military events.

It is obvious that a work of this scope presents many serious problems of selection and emphasis. The limitations of a one volume dictionary of American history prohibited an extensive, encyclopedic treatment. It was decided, rather, to encompass a range of materials that would be useful and interesting to the student and lay reader alike. The biographical studies have, for example, been restricted, in the main, to those prominent personalities who, in the authors' opinion, have most notably distinguished themselves. Succinctly outlined, these biographies furnish the essential data in capsule form of their contributions to American life. In the other items it was necessarily left to the authors' judgment to treat specific entries briefly or at length in terms of their evaluation of the significance of these items.

It will be easy for the reader to question the omission of a given entry. The only plea offered is the lack of space, a perpetual inhibition against every effort to widen the book's scope.

The reader should be made aware of certain forms employed Words or phrases, within the text in small capital letters, indicate that they appear as separate articles elsewhere in the volume. The names of familiar institutions, universities, museums, libraries and the like, however, have not been thus cross-referenced, but are included as separate entries. The same is true of Congress, the President, members of the cabinet, the states, the federal Constitution, religions, the Departments of Defense, War, Army, and the Navy, and the important wars fought by the United States. These cross-references have been liberally employed, and readers will find the book most useful by checking them for the fullest data on any matter.

The authors wish to acknowledge their indebtedness to many who aided in the preparation and development of this volume. Professor Geoffrey Bruun of Cornell University was kind enough to offer valuable suggestions as to format and content. Professors William J. Ronan, Sterling D. Spero, and Emanuel Stein of New York University generously read portions of the manuscript and, by their wise counsel, rescued the authors from many pitfalls. Thanks are extended to Professor Warren Bower of New York University, Dr. James L. Dixon of the Kew-Forest School, and Mr. Eugene F. Martin for their assistance and cooperation. To Edith Gelber, who stinted neither time nor effort, a great debt is owed for her unremitting toil in typing, arranging material, and engaging in research.

MICHAEL MARTIN
LEONARD GELBER

DICTIONARY OF
AMERICAN HISTORY

A

ABBE, Cleveland. 1838-1916. Meteorologist. b. New York City. Important for having inaugurated the first daily weather forecasts, he was director of the Cincinnati Observatory (1868); influenced the establishment of a government weather service which he joined (1871); served in the UNITED STATES WEATHER BUREAU after its organization under the DEPARTMENT OF AGRICULTURE (1891); retired (1916).

ABBEY, Edwin Austin. 1852-1911. Artist. b. Philadelphia, Pa. Illustrator for *Harper's Weekly;* went to England to illustrate *Herrick's Poems;* famous for pen drawings for an edition of Shakespeare; commissioned by King Edward VII (1902) to paint the official coronation picture; exhibited at the Royal Academy and the Metropolitan Museum, N.Y.

ABBOTT, Charles Greeley. 1872-1973. Astrophysicist. b. New Hampshire. Director of the Smithsonian Institution Astrophysical Observatory (1907), where he perfected various instruments for measuring the sun's heat; interest in devices utilizing solar energy; completed mapping of infra-red solar spectrum; studied nature of atmospheric transmission and absorption; became secretary of the Smithsonian Institution (1928); resigned to become Research Associate (1944).

A.B.C. Powers. Argentina, Brazil, and Chile, three major South American nations which have acted as mediators in disputes involving Latin America. They mediated the dispute between the United States and Mexico at NIAGARA FALLS in 1914, the first conference of its kind in the Americas. In 1915, by the ABC Treaty, a permanent mediation commission was established which, in that year, settled a dispute between Colombia and Peru. In 1935 these powers mediated the GRAN CHACO DISPUTE between Bolivia and Paraguay.

ABEL, John Jacob. 1857-1938. Pharmacologist and physiological chemist, known chiefly for his analysis of internal secretions of the body. b. Cleveland, Ohio. First to obtain insulin in crystalline form; isolated compound known as *Epinephrine;* modern conception of protein metabolism based on his research.

Abolitionists. Those who wanted the immediate emancipation of the slaves. Protests against SLAVERY are recorded in America as early as 1624 although no specific action was taken until the QUAKERS conducted a poll in 1688 in Germantown, Pa. On the eve of the Revolution abolitionist sentiment had become widespread throughout the British colonies. JEFFERSON's first draft of the DECLARATION OF INDEPENDENCE had included an attack against the institution. Anti-slav-

1

ery societies were founded during and after the Revolution, exercising a sufficient influence to bring about emancipation in most of the northern states. The AMERICAN COLONIZATION SOCIETY was established in 1816 as the first abolitionist organization. As a result of the work of WILLIAM LLOYD GARRISON in 1828 the AMERICAN ANTI-SLAVERY SOCIETY was founded in 1833 as a coalition of regional organizations dedicated to abolition. Simultaneously, in the South, such men as JAMES G. BIRNEY, Cassius M. Clay, John G. Fee, Hinton Helper, and John Rankin carried on abolitionist work. Garrison, BENJAMIN LUNDY, ELIJAH LOVEJOY, and the New England group of THEODORE PARKER, HENRY WARD BEECHER, WILLIAM ELLERY CHANNING, WENDELL PHILLIPS, and JAMES G. WHITTIER demanded the immediate, uncompensated emancipation of all slaves. Although schisms among them prevented unified programs, their influence was potent enough to bring about political action in the formation of the LIBERTY and FREESOIL PARTIES. Politics thereafter became abolition's strongest weapon. The contribution of HARRIET BEECHER STOWE'S *Uncle Tom's Cabin*, the personal liberty laws, and the polemics of abolitionist congressmen served to highlight the problem on the eve of the Civil War.

Abolition of Slavery. The 13th amendment to the Constitution of the United States provides that neither slavery nor involuntary servitude, except as punishment for a crime for which the party has been convicted, shall exist within the United States or any place under its jurisdiction. The Congress is given the power to enforce the above by appropriate legislation. This amendment was adopted in 1865.

abortion. Despite the efforts of the Catholic Church and the "Right to Life" movement, there has been seen in recent years a definite trend to liberalizing abortion laws. In-

deed, on January 22, 1973, the Supreme Court in a 7-2 decision overturned all state laws that limited a woman's right to an abortion during the first three months of pregnancy. The Court left the states free to place increasing restrictions on abortion as the term of pregnancy increased. Opponents of abortion won a victory in 1977 when the Supreme Court ruled that although the state may not forbid abortions, it does not have to pay for them. As a result, women who cannot afford to pay for abortions will find it very difficult to get them.

Absentee Ownership. In business organization it is that situation in which ownership is divorced from management. Although this system has existed throughout history it became economically important after the Civil War with the growth of the corporate form of business organization. In the first half of the 20th century absentee ownership developed in AGRICULTURE. The phenomenon of BUSINESS CONSOLIDATION has provided data illustrating this movement.

ACHESON, Dean Goodeshan. 1893-1971. Statesman. b. Connecticut. Graduated, Yale University (1915) and Harvard Law School (1918); private secretary to Associate Justice, LOUIS D. BRANDEIS; practiced law; appointed Undersecretary of the Treasury (1933); resigned; appointed Assistant Secretary of State (1941-45) and Under Secretary of State (1945-47); favored aid to England; after World War II was a strong supporter of the UNITED NATIONS; international relief programs, and the TRUMAN DOCTRINE; vice-chairman, HOOVER COMMISSION (1947); appointed Secretary of State by TRUMAN (1949-1953); he was a constant target of attack by Senate investigating committees, and for his policy toward the Soviet Union.

ACHESON, Edward Goodrich. 1856-1931. b. Pennsylvania. Inventor; Assistant to THOMAS EDISON (1880-81); discovered silicon carbide; discovered carborundum, one of the best abrasives known; *Acheson graphite* has important industrial uses.

Act of 1651. See Navigation Acts.

Act of 1660. See Navigation Acts.

Act of 1663. See Navigation Acts.

Act of 1696. See Navigation Acts.

Acts of Trade. See Navigation Acts.

ADAIR, James. 1710?-1780?. Pioneer and author of *The History of the American Indians* (1775), which is valuable as a source book on frontier history and the life and customs of the Indians.

ADAMS, Abigail. 1744-1818. Wife of JOHN ADAMS, second President of the United States. b. Massachusetts. Mother of JOHN QUINCY ADAMS, sixth President; leading figure of the social life of the capital after 1787; famous for letters written to her husband and published by her grandson, CHARLES FRANCIS ADAMS.

ADAMS, Charles Francis. 1807-1886. Lawyer, diplomat and author. b. Boston, Mass. Son of JOHN QUINCY ADAMS. Member, U.S. House of Representatives (1858-61); minister during the Civil War to Great Britain (1861-68); one of five arbitrators at Geneva Tribunal which settled the ALABAMA CLAIMS (1871-72); edited 2 volumes of letters of ABIGAIL ADAMS, the *Works of John Adams* in 10 volumes, and *Memoirs of John Quincy Adams* in 12 volumes.

ADAMS, Charles Francis. 1835-1915. Economist and historian; son of CHARLES FRANCIS ADAMS. b. Boston, Mass. Served nearly four years in Union army during the Civil War; brigadier general; wrote an expose of Erie Railroad financing, *Chapters of Erie* (1871); chairman, Massachusetts Board of Railroad Commissioners (1872-79); appointed chairman of government directors, (1878) and president (1884) UNION PACIFIC RAILROAD; forced out by JAY GOULD (1890). Known for reforms in public school EDUCATION in Massachusetts; member of Board of Overseers of Harvard University for 24 years, being responsible for the modernization of the curriculum and methods of the university. Author of *Railroads: Their Origin and Problems* (1878); *Biography of Richard Henry Dana* (1890); *Life of Charles Francis Adams*, his father (1900), and his autobiography.

Adams Express Company. A transportation company founded in 1840 by Alvin Adams and Ephraim Farnsworth. Under its original name of Adams & Company it conducted an express service between New York and Boston. By 1843 its business extended as far west as New Orleans and St. Louis. In 1854 the company bought out a rival organization, Harnden and Company, being reorganized as the Adams ·Express Company. The company had a virtual monopoly of the transportation service in the Northeast for a number of years thereafter. In 1918 it was merged with the American Express Company, the Southern Express Company, and the WELLS FARGO Express Company into the AMERICAN RAILWAY EXPRESS COMPANY. Since then Adams has become an investment TRUST.

ADAMS, Henry Brooks. 1838-1918. Historian, son of CHARLES FRANCIS ADAMS (1807-1886). b. Boston, Mass. Secretary to his father in Washington (1860-61) and London (1861-68). Taught history at Harvard University, and edited *North American Review* (1869-76). Author of *History of the United States* (9 vols. 1889-91), covering the JEFFERSON and MADISON administrations; *The Life of Albert Gallatin;* the *Writings of Albert Gallatin* (3 vols. 1879); and *The Education of Henry Adams* (1906) a brilliant autobiography.

ADAMS, John. 1735-1826. Second President of the United States. b. Braintree (now Quincy), Mass. Graduated, Harvard (1755) and was admitted to the bar (1758). Elected Massachusetts delegate to the first CONTINENTAL CONGRESS (1774), where he aided in drafting a petition to the king and a declaration of rights; proposed WASHINGTON for commander of the army; aided in the drafting and was a signer of the DECLARATION OF INDEPENDENCE; in Congress until appointed as Commissioner to France (1777-78); made Minister to United Provinces (1780); negotiated, after difficulties, a loan from Dutch bankers (1782). He joined JAY and FRANKLIN in Paris to negotiate a treaty with Great Britain. He was envoy to Great Britain (1785-88), returning just in time to be chosen the first Vice-President of the United States; elected Vice-President (1788, 1792) and President (1796). He had a difficult administration because of the strong opposition of HAMILTON and was defeated by JEFFERSON for re-election. He retired to private life. Author of *Thoughts on Government* (1776); *A Defence of the Constitutions of the Government of the United States of America* (2 vols. 1787-88).

ADAMS, John Quincy. 1767-1848. Sixth President of the United States. b. Quincy, Mass. Son of JOHN and ABIGAIL ADAMS. Graduated Harvard (1788); admitted to the bar (1791); elected state senator (1802); U.S. Senator (1803), supporting JEFFERSON's embargo and the aquisition of Louisiana in opposition to the FEDERALISTS; resigned (1808). He was appointed Minister to Russia (1809) during Napoleon's invasion; head of the United States delegation to conclude the TREATY OF GHENT (1814); Minister to Great Britain (1815); Secretary of State under MONROE (1817-25); evolved principles of the MONROE DOCTRINE; negotiated treaty with Spain securing Florida (1819); President of the United States (1825-29); defeated by ANDREW JACKSON for re-election. He served as a Representative in Congress (1831-48), playing a major role in opposition to the extension of SLAVERY; contested the "GAG RULE" and opposed the Mexican War. He was interested in science and was largely responsible for the establishment of the SMITHSONIAN INSTITUTION as a government undertaking. Author of *Memoirs* (12 vols. ed. by C. F. Adams; published 1874-77); *Writings* (7 vols. ed. by W. C. Ford; published 1913).

ADAMS, Samuel. 1722-1803. Revolutionary patriot. b. Boston, Mass. Agitated against the SUGAR ACT (1764) and STAMP ACT (1765); drafted many important Revolutionary documents while member from Boston in the Massachusetts House of Representatives (1765-1774); instituted system of town COMMITTEES OF CORRESPONDENCE; helped organize Boston SONS OF LIBERTY; drew up Boston Bill of Rights; managed BOSTON TEA PARTY; led opposition to the BOSTON PORT BILL. Delegate to CONTINENTAL CONGRESS; signer of the DECLARATION OF INDEPENDENCE; member of Congress (to 1781); Lieutenant Governor of Massachusetts (1789-93); Governor (1794-97).

Adamson Act. Passed by Congress in 1916. The law established an EIGHT HOUR DAY for trainmen on interstate RAILROADS. It was enacted to prevent a threatened railway strike in the period of national defense preparation prior to the entry of the United States into World War I. As claimed by railway management, the law increased wages rather than reduced working hours, inasmuch as premium rates were paid for hours worked after eight hours per day.

ADDAMS, Jane. 1860-1935. Social settlement worker and peace advocate. b. Illinois. Graduated, Rockford College

(1881); with Ellen Gates Starr, founded Hull House in Chicago (1889), a social settlement which wielded influence in civic affairs; resident head (1889-1935); considered leader of social settlement work in the United States. President, International Congress of Women (1919); presided at Conventions at The Hague (1915, 1922), Zurich (1919), Vienna (1921) and Washington (1924). Shared NOBEL PEACE PRIZE with NICHOLAS MURRAY BUTLER (1931). Author of *Democracy and Social Ethics* (1902), and *Twenty Years at Hull House* (1910).

ADE, George. 1866-1944. Humorist. b. Indiana. Famous as the author of *Fables in Slang* which appeared in the Chicago *Record* (later the *Record-Herald*) (1899) and are examples of sophisticated wit and humor; he also wrote plays, comic operas, and movie scripts.

Ad Hoc Committee. A special committee of either house of Congress or of both houses, established for the purpose of investigating, examining, reporting, or otherwise dealing with a specific matter. It is not a standing committee and the resolution creating it ordinarily designates a terminal date when it gives up its existence. The importance of the committee's work or newly developed significant problems sometimes causes the extension of an *ad hoc* committee's life for years. Occasionally, the chamber or the Congress may establish such a committee as a permanent body. Generally an *ad hoc* committee is created as a sub-committee of a standing committee. Well known *ad hoc* committees have included the original COMMITTEE ON UN-AMERICAN ACTIVITIES, the Truman Committee to investigate war production, and the Tolan Committee on migratory labor during World War II.

ADLER, Cyrus. 1863-1940. Scholar, educator and author. b. Arkansas. Graduated University of Pennsylvania and Johns Hopkins University. With SMITHSONIAN INSTITUTION and the United States National Museum (1892-1908); founder, American Jewish Historical Society; president, Jewish Theological Seminary of America, New York (1924-40); editor, *Jewish Encyclopedia;* editor of *American Jewish Year Book* (from 1899).

ADLER, Felix. 1851-1933. Founder of the Ethical Culture Movement; educator and leader in social welfare. b. Germany; came to the United States (1857); graduated Columbia (1870). Founded New York Society of Ethical Culture (1876); professor of political and social ethics, Columbia University (from 1902); member of first tenement house commission of N.Y. state, and initiated the first tenement house law. Chairman, National Child Labor Committee for 25 years. Author of *Creed and Deed* (1877), and *An Ethical Philosophy of Life* (1918).

Administrative Law. Those elements of public law which govern the activities of administrative agencies and officials. They include the statute law which establishes the agencies and provides for their powers, the body of law created by these agencies in the course of their work, and the judicial doctrines laid down by the courts in interpreting the foregoing. Among the elements of administrative law developed by the administrative bodies are their rules and regulations and their administrative orders and decisions.

Admission to the Union. Refers to the policy of enlarging a nation by admitting TERRITORIES on equal status with states already in the Union. This policy was originally established by the NORTHWEST ORDINANCE OF 1787. Territorial constitutions must be approved by Congress as a condition for admission.

Adult Education. A movement for bringing organized educational opportunities to the adult population. In the United States its origins stem from the mechanics' institutes of the early 19th century. The LYCEUM movement of the Jacksonian era reflected a widespread public desire for the extension of education to organized groups of adults. Subsequently, the growth of the free public library and university extension movements carried these opportunities to even greater numbers of adults. The term itself was not in general use until 1924 when the Carnegie Corporation of New York began a series of studies to consider this need. In 1926 the American Association for Adult Education was established at Chicago. It acts as a clearing house for information, and carries on experiments, demonstrations, researches, and the publication of materials on the philosophy and methods of adult education. It publishes the quarterly *Journal of Adult Education*. It is estimated that over 30,000,000 Americans, roughly one-third of the adult population, participate annually in some form of organized educational activity. Today the various forms of adult schooling includes lyceums, Chautauquas, extension work, evening public schools, correspondence courses, indoor recreation groups, lecture courses, open forums, church groups, labor union courses, museum courses, settlement work, little theatre organizations, and university extension work. Among the latter are the famous adult education programs conducted by the Division of General Education of New York University, the School of General Studies of Columbia University, the New School for Social Research, and others.

Ad Valorem Tariff. Refers to a method of collecting customs. This form applies a percentage figure to the value of imported commodities, e.g. 80 per cent of the value of an automobile worth $1500. The collection in this instance would be

$1200. It is a Latin phrase whose English meaning is "according to value."

A.E.F. See American Expeditionary Force.

AFL-CIO. Two of the country's largest labor organizations, the American Federation of Labor and the Congress of Industrial Organizations effected a merger on Dec. 5, 1955. George Meany, pres., AFL, became pres. and Walter Reuther, pres., CIO, became vice pres. in charge of the Industrial Dept. The new labor organization started operations with $3,800,000 in the treasury and with a membership of about 15,000,000.

AGASSIZ, Alexander. 1835-1910. Zoologist and deep sea explorer. Son of LOUIS AGASSIZ. b. Switzerland. Came to the United States (1849); studied zoology at Harvard University; MINING at Lawrence Scientific School; mine superintendent at Calumet, Michigan; president, Calumet Mining Company. With the wealth he obtained from his copper mines, which were then the largest in the world, he endowed the Museum of Comparative Zoology at Harvard. He made many zoological exploration trips to the west coast of South America, U.S. coastal waters, and the Bahamas. Author of *North American Starfishes* (1877).

AGASSIZ, Louis. 1807-1873. Naturalist. Published many important works in Europe including papers on glacial action before coming to the United States (1846). Lectured at Cambridge; professor of natural history, Lawrence Scientific School, Harvard University (1848-73). Began collections now in Harvard Museum of Comparative Zoology (1859). Naturalized citizen of U.S. (1861). Finished four volumes of planned 10 volume work, *Contributions to the Natural History of the United States*. His wife, Elizabeth Cabot, *nee* Cary (1822-1907) was a founder of Radcliffe College (1879) and its president (1894-1902).

Age of Reform. See Progressive Era.

AGNEW, Spiro Theodore. 1918- Vice President of the U.S. 1969-1973. b. Maryland. He was the son of a Greek immigrant. He served in the Army in World War II. Graduated from University of Baltimore Law school in 1947. He was elected Governor of Maryland in 1964 and served as Vice President under Nixon. The Justice Department conducted a criminal investigation into his alleged acceptance of kickbacks during prior years. On October 10, 1973 he resigned from the Vice Presidency. He pleaded "no contest" to charges of failing to report close to $30,000 of income in 1967.

Agrarian Democracy. Expresses hope of THOMAS JEFFERSON that the United States would develop politically with widespread farmers' control over state and local governments. Reflects states rights doctrines of the DEMOCRATIC-REPUBLICAN PARTY in early 19th century. Based on Jefferson's vision of the national growth of small homesteading FARMERS.

Agrarian Imperialism. The name applied to the expansionist movement of the 1830's and 40's of the southern plantation proprietors seeking additional cotton land beyond the Mississippi. Spurred by the expanding European market for cotton and the exhaustion of existing land because of intensive cultivation these groups sought to acquire Mexican-owned and other TERRITORY in the far west. Justifying their imperialist aims by the slogan of "MANIFEST DESTINY" they pressed claims upon Texas, California, Oregon, and the area later to be known as the MEXICAN CESSION. Their greatest strength lay in the Democratic party which captured the government in 1844 and which, through the Mexican War and treaties with Great Britain, successfully obtained these territories.

"Agrarian Revolt." The term applied to the farmers' movement of the post-Civil War period designed to obtain favorable federal and state legislation regulating TRANSPORTATION, maintaining high prices, securing financial relief, aiding migratory labor, and barring foreign farm competition. The specific aims of this "revolt" were public regulation of RAILROADS to control rates and to eliminate abuses, an inflation of the CURRENCY through the issuance of GREENBACKS and/or silver certificates, reduction of the tariff on manufactured goods, public aid in foreclosures, assistance to homeless migratory farmers, and tariff protection on agricultural products to combat foreign competition. The movement took the form of lobbying activities by farm organizations, and the establishment of POLITICAL PARTIES representing the interests of the farmer. Among such organizations were the NATIONAL GRANGE, FARMERS' ALLIANCES, the GREENBACK PARTY, the GREENBACK-LABOR PARTY, and the POPULIST PARTY. In the election of 1896 this movement supported the Democratic party on the basis of the latter's FREE SILVER program.

Agricultural Adjustment Act, 1933. A law of Congress designed to raise the prices of wheat, corn, cotton, milk, and other farm crops and to restore the farmers' purchasing power to the level before World War I. The principle underlying the act was the restriction of production by the grant of a SUBSIDY or bounty to the farmer. The production of STAPLE CROPS was to be reduced by the withdrawal from production of these crops or their destruction after planting. The Secretary of Agriculture was authorized to levy a processing tax on the first domestic processing of a commodity and to enter into individual contracts by which sums were paid to the farmer for accomplishing these aims. By 1934 more than 40,-000,000 acres of farm land had been withdrawn from production for which farmers received several hundred millions of dollars in benefit payments. The income from the processing tax was roughly equal to the benefits paid. By 1936 farmers' per capita share of the national income had increased from 60 percent of the pre-World War I level to 80 percent. By 1939 more than 3,000 county associations and 24,000 community committees had been established as voluntary organizations to administer the program on a local basis. These remained in existence after the law was declared unconstitutional in 1936 in the case of UNITED STATES VS. BUTLER.

Agricultural Adjustment Act, 1938. Popularly known as the Second AAA. Replaced the AAA, 1933 and supplemented the SOIL CONSERVATION AND DOMESTIC ALLOTMENT ACT OF 1936. Established programs of crop insurance, PARITY PRICE payments, production quotas, and the "EVER NORMAL GRANARY". The objectives of the Act were to maintain farm commodity prices and to establish food reserves for periods of shortages.

Agricultural Credits Act. A law of Congress passed on March 4, 1923 to provide credit facilities for financing purchases of farm equipment and live-stock. It established 12 FEDERAL INTERMEDIATE CREDIT BANKS, one in each of the 12 districts created by the FEDERAL FARM LOAN ACT of 1916. These banks were empowered to extend loans to FARMERS for periods from six months to three years. They could also make loans to cooperative marketing associations in sums up to 75 percent of the value of crops or livestock held by these associations. The Intermediate Credit Banks were authorized to discount commercial paper representing loans made by banks, livestock companies, co-operative marketing companies, or agricultural credit associations. Their capital was obtained by Congressional appropriations and by the sale to the public of short term debentures.

Agricultural Machinery. See agricultural Revolution.

Agricultural Marketing Act. Also known as Cooperative Marketing Act. Passed by Congress in 1929. It created the FEDERAL FARM BOARD of eight members with the power of supervising and encouraging a voluntary program of marketing. The Board was to promote the formation of cooperatives and establish stabilization corporations where necessary, guaranteeing these organizations against loss by loans from a special revolving fund of $500,000,000. After two and a half years of activity the Board had stimulated the founding of COOPERATIVES nationally and had lent them $165,000,000. Having made heavy purchases in cotton and wheat through the new stabilization corporations it succeeded in raising the prices of these commodities above world prices. It proved an utter failure later when the corporations abandoned the market and prices dropped below their former figures. By 1932 the Board's agencies found themselves in possession of large surpluses purchased at prices far in excess of the current declining market prices resulting from the world DEPRESSION. When it was abolished in 1933 it had consumed the $500,000,000 appropriation without succeeding in stabilizing prices.

Agricultural Revolution. The term applied to the mechanization of AGRICULTURE after the Civil War. Farming methods had changed little since the colonial period. With the exceptions of the COTTON GIN, steel tipped plow, and reaper,

8

few improvements in agriculture machinery had been made. After the Civil War the United States assumed world leadership in the invention and manufacture of agricultural machines. In 1869, James Oliver produced the chilled-steel plow. Other INVENTIONS were the twine-binder (John F. Appelby, 1878), disk-plow, disk-harrow, straddle-row cultivator, seed-drill, hay-stacker, manur spreader, harvester, combine, automatic milker, and refrigerated car. The application of steam, electric, and gasoline power to these machines enormously increased the yield. Between 1855 and 1894 the average time required to produce one bushel of corn declined from four and one half hours to 41 minutes. The simultaneous improvement of scientific agriculture through educational and research work in such fields as pest control, land reclamation, and IRRIGATION tripled the agricultural yield between 1860 and 1900. Technology in farming produced the "factory in the field," making agriculture an industrialized economy. The TENANT FARMER, SHARE-CROPPER, and agricultural worker came into being as new forms of farm labor. This evolution in agriculture produced many serious problems for the FARMER, consumer, and government. See FARM PROBLEM.

Agriculture. The chief industry in the British colonies. Primitive subsistence farming was practiced on the abundant, rich soil. The geographical and climatic characteristics of the Atlantic seaboard determined the nature of agriculture in the three sections of the colonies. New England farming was thus the production of truck crops for a local market, determined by the mountainous terrain which cut the land into disparate valleys watered by local streams and rivers. The middle Atlantic states were the producers of bread crops. Here agriculture consisted of local market and large plantation production. The wide, level topography of the South permitted the development of plantation farming which emphasized the production of tobacco, sugar, rice, cotton, and indigo. These crops were produced for sale in northern and foreign markets. At the opening of the Revolution fully 90 percent of the American people were engaged in agricultural pursuits. The INDUSTRIAL REVOLUTION after the War of 1812 stimulated agricultural improvement because of the need for more raw materials and a larger food supply for the growing population. The great farming area of the Ohio territory was exploited as a result of the WESTWARD MOVEMENT after the war. Encouraged by CLAY's AMERICAN SYSTEM, internal improvements, agricultural inventions, and a seemingly inexhaustible supply of European labor this area rapidly became the nation's greatest source of farm products. The result was that the New England and mid-Atlantic sections turned to livestock production. Horses, cattle, hogs, sheep, and their dairy and meat products became the agricultural bulwark of these communities. Small farmsteads gave way to larger holdings for the grazing of flocks. In the era before the Civil War wheat farming moved from the Delaware, Susquehanna, and Genessee Valleys to Wisconsin, Minnesota, Iowa, and Illinois. The tremendous agricultural revolution after the Civil War developed this section as the "breadbasket" of the United States. At this time cattle raising moved from the northeast to the southwest. The stimulus of the HOMESTEAD ACT, increasing IMMIGRATION, and RAILROAD construction opened the far west to agriculture. Such machines as the reaper, thresher, harvester, tractor, combine, automatic milker, automatic seed-drill, and mechanical refrigeration helped link the agricultural west to the industrial east. The consequent problems of over-production, declining prices, and indebtedness brought about the demand for agrarian reform which took the form of the GRANGER LAWS and other types of public assistance and regulation. In 1963 the tremendous changes in agricultural production were manifested by the movement from the farm to the city, the increase in per capita production, and the relative improvement of farm conditions as compared to the pre-World War II era. Only 7 percent of the American people lived on farms, yet produced 4,081,791,000 bushels of corn, 1,137,-641,000 bushels of wheat, 18,548,000 bales of cotton, 2.271,942.000 pounds of tobacco, and 4,722,000,000 pounds of beet and cane sugar. In 1962 the value of horses, mules, sheep, swine, and cattle on the farms of the United States was about $16,000,000,000. See FARMS.

Agriculture, U.S. Department of. Established in 1889 as an EXECUTIVE DEPARTMENT. Its purposes were to aid the farmer by research, educational activities, publications, and supervision of the county agent system. Operates its own school system for departmental personnel, with accredited courses. Its published literature has wide circulation in agricultural, labor, and consumer fields. Among its more important publications are the Yearbook of Agriculture, Weekly News Letter, and the Farmer's Bulletin.

AGUINALDO, Emilio. 1869-1964. Filipino leader. b. Philippine Islands. Led a rebellion against Spain (1896); exiled to Hong Kong; returned to the Philippines to lead an insurrection against the U.S. army troops during the Spanish-American War (1899); established a republic at Malolos with himself as President (1899); captured (1901); ran for the presidency of the islands but was defeated (1935); accused of aiding the Japanese during World War II and imprisoned (1945); freed and forced to retire from public life.

AIKEN, Conrad Potter. 1889-1965. Poet, critic and writer of fiction. b. Georgia. Graduated Harvard University (1911). Author of Turns and Movies (1916); Selected Poems (1929) for which he was awarded the PULITZER PRIZE; And In the Human Heart (1940); novels, Blue Voyage (1927), Great Circle (1933), Conversation (1940); and volumes of short stories.

Air Brake. An improved method of slowing and halting railroad trains by the application of compressed air upon the brake shoes of the cars and locomotives. The system operates through a complex core of cylinders, rods, and levers, valves, a train pipe, and a storage reservoir. The automatic compressed air brake in use today was first invented by GEORGE WESTINGHOUSE in 1868.

Aircraft Industry. See Aviation.

Air Forces, United States. Air force operation was administered by the Signal Corps of the United States Army until 1918, when it was reorganized into the United States Air Service. In 1926 Congress established the United States Air Corps which retained that name until 1942 when it was changed to the United States Air Forces. Naval Air Forces were originally attached to the various fleets under the orders of fleet commanders. These included Marine Corps aviation. In 1947 Congress united all the air services into the United States Air Forces as a unit within the newly established DEPARTMENT OF DEFENSE. It was given equal status with the ground and sea forces.

Air Mail. The first experimental air mail line in the United States was established in 1918 between New York City and Washington, D.C. This joint effort of the War and post office departments came under the sole jurisdiction of the latter three months later. Subsequently short lines between New York and Cleveland, Cleveland and Chicago, and Chicago and Omaha, were discontinued because of inadequate revenue. A successful trans-continental service was established between New York and San Francisco. In 1927 the POST OFFICE DEPARTMENT transferred all air mail carriage to private contractors who rapidly added branch lines and north-south lines. By 1934 air mail service covered the United States, and joined with lines to Canada, Mexico, and Latin America. The following year regular mail service was established across the Pacific between San Francisco and Manila. In 1939 transatlantic service was established between New York and London. In 1963 the civilian air mail lines carried a volume of approximately 356,600,000 ton-miles.

AITKEN, Robert. 1734-1802. Printer. b. Scotland. Owner of a bookstore in Philadelphia (1771); published first complete English Bible printed in America (1782).

Akron. A city in Ohio that is the 39th ranking city in the United States. Its 1952 population of 275,000 occupies an area of 54.1 square miles. It is an important industrial center, its chief product being manufactured RUBBER. The Akron factories consume about two-fifths of the world's supply of crude rubber. Although the first rubber factory was established there by DR. B. F. GOODRICH in 1870 it was not until the development of the AUTOMOBILE INDUSTRY in the 20th century that rubber manufacturing became important. Akron's other products include aircraft, breakfast food, matches, and sewer pipe.

Alabama. The 29th state in size, with an area of 51,609 square miles. Organized as a territory in 1817 and admitted as the 22nd state on December 14, 1819. Seceded on January 11, 1861 and readmitted on July 13, 1868. Montgomery is the capital. In 1950 Alabama's population of 3,061,743 made it 17th in rank. Its largest cities are Birmingham, Mobile, and Montgomery. Alabama is the most important industrial state in the South, producing iron, steel, lumber products, and textiles. Other crops include nuts, corn, hay, sweet potatoes, and raw cotton. Muscle Shoals, the center of the TENNESSEE VALLEY AUTHORITY Development, lies on the Tennessee River. THE CONFEDERATE STATES OF AMERICA was established at Montgomery in February, 1861. The state was first discovered in 1540 by DE SOTO. Its nickname is the "Yellow-hammer State."

Alabama Claims. Claims upon England by the United States for shipping losses suffered during the Civil War as a result of British built ships sold to the Confederacy. American charges based on alleged violations of international law by Great Britain. Ultimate settlement in 1872 negotiated through ARBITRATION by United States, Great Britain, Italy, Switzerland, and Brazil at Geneva, resulting in payment of $15,500,000 to the United States.

Alamance, Battle of the. See Regulators, Uprising of the.

Alamo, The. The heavy walled mission building in San Antonio, Texas which was besieged from February 23 to March 6, 1836 by 7,000 Mexican troops under the command of SANTA ANNA. About 220 Texans, under the command of William B. Travis and JAMES BOWIE, resisted the Mexicans despite their repeated assaults upon the Alamo. On March 6th the Mexicans finally breached the walls of the buildings, engaging the remaining Texan defenders in hand-to-hand combat until, by the evening, the last Texans had fallen. Although thirty non-combatants were spared, all the defenders perished after having inflicted a loss of 1,500 casualties upon the Mexicans. Its effect upon the Texans was to stimulate morale under the cry "Remember the Alamo," ultimately resulting in the Texan victory at the BATTLE OF SAN JACINTO.

Alaska. A territory purchased by the United States from Russia in 1867 for $7,200,000. It has an area of 586,400 square miles and a population in 1952 of approximately 130,000. Its capital is Juneau. By Act of Congress in 1912, Alaska was established as an organized territory with an appointed governor and judiciary and a popularly elected bicameral legislature. At its acquisition the territory was referred to as the "Arctic Wasteland" and as "SEWARD'S ICEBOX." Nevertheless Alaska has produced great fortunes in mineral wealth, furs, precious metals, timber, and fisheries. In 1958, Alaska became the 49th state. It is two and one-fifth times the size of Texas and the estimated population in 1960, exclusive of military personnel, was 227,000.

Alaska Boundary Controversy. A diplomatic controversy between the United States and Great Britain over the Alaskan-Canadian boundary. The Treaty of 1867 by which the United States acquired ALASKA from Russia, confirmed the boundary agreed upon in an Anglo-Russian treaty of 1825. A question of interpretation whether the line between Alaska and British Columbia should be measured from the islands in the sea or from the shoreline raised no problem until the discovery of gold in the Canadian Klondike in 1896. The problems of jurisdiction thereafter raised were referred in 1903 to a mixed commission consisting of two Americans, two Canadi-

ans, and an Englishman. The final line was a compromise between the extreme claims of Canada and the United States but is generally conceded to have been an American victory.

Alaska Pipe Line. The Alaska Pipeline Service C., a consortium of eight oil companies, is the operator of the Alaska pipeline whose job it is to pump oil from the North Slope of Alaska down to the "lower states." Environmental controversies delayed construction of the pipeline for about four years and the costs for meeting environmental demands have been estimated as high as $2 billion. Operation began during the summer of 1977 and during the first month of flow, the $10 billion project was beset by five physical mishaps, three of which caused shutdowns which lasted 13 days during the initial 28 day period. It is anticipated that 2.0 million barrels of oil will flow through the pipeline each day when the project operates at maximum efficiency.

Albany Congress. A meeting in 1754 of delegates of seven of the colonies, called for the purpose of attaining some sort of colonial union in the face of imminent danger from the French and their Indian allies. At the Congress BENJAMIN FRANKLIN proposed the famous Albany Plan of Union providing for a federal congress with powers to create an army, deal with the Indians, control public lands, and assess general taxes. The Plan was rejected by the colonial legislatures loath to surrender their power. The Parliament similarly was cool to the idea fearing the potential increases of colonial strength. The meeting is nevertheless important as a precedent for the convening of the later CONTINENTAL CONGRESSES.

Albany Plan of Union. See Albany Congress

ALCOTT, Amos Bronson. 1799-1888. Educator and transcendentalist. b. Connecticut. Peddler in Virginia and the

Carolinas (1818-23); teacher in small towns of Conn. (1823-27); Boston (1828-30); Germantown, Pa. (1831-33). Opened school in Boston which failed; established co-operative community, Fruitlands, near Harvard in Massachusetts (1844) which also failed (1845). Interested in transcendental philosophy, and lectured occasionally (1853-59). Appointed superintendent of schools in Concord, Mass. (1859). Years of poverty for family finally ended with success of daughter, LOUISA's book, *Little Women* (1868). Opened Concord School of Philosophy and Literature (1879) which continued until his death. Author of *The Doctrine and Discipline of Human Culture* (1836).

ALCOTT, Louisa May. 1832-1888. Author, daughter of above. b. Germantown, Pa. Nurse in Union hospital at Georgetown during Civil War; her letters to her family were published under title *Hospital Sketches* (1863). Editor, *Merry's Museum,* a magazine for children (1867). *Little Men* (1871) and many other popular books for children.

ALDEN, John. 1599?-1687. MAYFLOWER PILGRIM, was governor's assistant in PLYMOUTH COLONY (1633-41); signer of the MAYFLOWER COMPACT; moved to Duxbury (1627); deputy from Duxbury (1641-49); treasurer (1656-58); Deputy Governor (1664-5, 1677). Hero, with friend MILES STANDISH, of fictional poem by LONGFELLOW.

ALDRICH, Nelson Wilmarth. 1841-1915. Financier and statesman. b. Rhode Island. Member, U.S. House of Representatives (1878-81); U.S. Senator(1881-1911). Leading Republican, completely in control of Rhode Island politics. Advocate of high tariff and sound currency legislation, especially ALDRICH-VREELAND CURRENCY ACT (1908) and PAYNE-ALDRICH TARIFF ACT (1909). Responsible for GOLD STANDARD ACT OF 1900. The FED-ERAL RESERVE ACT, passed during WILSON's administration, was based on the "Aldrich plan."

Aldrich-Vreeland Act. Enacted in 1908. Its objective was to supply the need for a more elastic CURRENCY by allowing banks to issue additional notes on depositing approved state or municipal bonds and by forming associations with joint responsibility to issue notes secured by COMMERCIAL PAPER. Was opposed by nation's banks. Senator ALDRICH became chairman of the monetary commission provided for by the statute.

Aleutian Islands, The. An archipelago in the Bering Sea with an area slightly over 10,000 square miles. They were discovered in 1741 by Vitus Bering on behalf of Russia. Their lucrative fur trade linked them closely with the mainland Russian province of ALASKA, their port of Unalaska becoming one of the three Russian settlements on that peninsula. They were transferred to the United States as part of the Alaskan purchase of 1867. Their only value today is as a military outpost in the Arctic area.

ALEXANDER, John White. 1856-1915. Painter. b. Pennsylvania. Best known for portraits of Rodin, CLEVELAND, CARNEGIE, HOWELLS, TWAIN, WHITMAN and many others. His works hang in the METROPOLITAN MUSEUM in New York and in the Boston Museum. President of the National Academy (1909-1915).

ALEXANDER, Stephen. 1806-1883. Astronomer. b. New York. Professor of astronomy, Princeton University (1840-77); noted for his work with solar eclipses. One of the original members of the National Academy of Sciences (1862).

ALEXANDER, William. Known as Lord Stirling. 1726-1783. Revolutionary general. b. New York City. Member, Council of New Jersey; suspended for opposition to the STAMP ACT, Brigadier General in CONTINENTAL ARMY; had part in exposing The CONWAY CABAL (1778); served at inquiry into fate of JOHN ANDRE. (1780) Fought at GERMANTOWN, BRANDYWINE and MONMOUTH.

Algeciras Conference. Jointly called by Great Britain, France, Germany, and Spain for the purpose of negotiating German claims upon Morocco. The meeting was held in 1906-1907 at Algeciras, Morocco. President THEODORE ROOSEVELT, pursuing his foreign policy of expanding American interests in world affairs, was represented at this conference.

ALGER, Horatio. 1834-1899. Author. b. Massachusetts. Graduated, Harvard University (1852); author of more than 100 books for boys based on the theme that virtue is always rewarding. His "rags to riches" theme influenced a generation of American youth.

ALGER, Russell Alexander. 1836-1907. Politician. b. Ohio. Served in the Civil War rising from the ranks to a colonelcy. Elected governor of Michigan (1884); received many votes at the Republican convention of 1888 for the presidency; Secretary of War in MCKINLEY's cabinet (1897); after criticism, resigned (1899). U.S. Senator (1902-07).

Algonquin Indians. The name of a linguistic group of Indians referring to many tribes. Originally in Canada, they spread through out the northeast, the Atlantic coast, and into the mid-west. They were the bitter enemies of the IROQUOIS. They engaged in AGRICULTURE and were expert hunters and fishermen. Their outstanding leaders include TECUMSEH, PONTIAC, SAMOSET, MASSASOIT, POWHATAN, and KING PHILIP.

Alien Property Custodian. An office established in 1917 to which enemy property was transferred during and for resale after World War I, to prevent its use by the enemy. Innumerable German patents and other property were disposed of by the Custodian under the terms of the TRADING WITH THE ENEMY ACT which established the office and of subsequent amending legislation including the Settlement of War Claims Act of 1928. Under the latter legislative provisions were made for agreements between the United States and the former enemy nations, Germany and Austria, in settlement of many claims. In 1945 it was transferred to the DEPARTMENT OF JUSTICE as the Office of Alien Property. During and after World War II the Alien Property Custodian acquired property totalling $335,000,000. Among these were MOTION PICTURE theaters, films, ART treasures, lingerie factories, DAIRY farms, and hormone laboratories. By 1934 the property seized in World War I had been sold, liquidated, or returned, and the agency became moribund. It was reactivated after the attack on PEARL HARBOR. Today its vesting program is limited to property in the United States which was owned by enemy governments and nationals prior to December 31, 1946. The agency's income from the sale or operation of properties goes to the United States Treasury and is used to pay the claims of Americans who were prisoners of war of the Japanese or the Germans. These latter can never get it back. By 1952 it had turned over to the War Claims Fund of the TREASURY DEPARTMENT $150,000,000. Of the 264 active businesses vested in the Office of Alien Property since 1941 only 55 remained by January, 1952. The largest property taken was the $120,000,000 General Aniline and Film Corporation, the second largest manufacturer of film in the United States.

Alien and Sedition Acts. Series of four laws passed in 1798 by FEDERALIST controlled Congress. Designed to combat pro-French activities of JEFFERSONIAN RE-

PUBLICANS. Laws provided for extension of residence as requirement of NATURALIZATION from 5 to 14 years, for deportation of aliens by the President, and for arrests of editors, writers, and speakers charged with attacking the government. Under its terms scores of Jeffersonian leaders and supporters were arrested and they were convicted. The Laws were repealed by the Jeffersonian controlled Congress in 1801, and those imprisoned released by JEFFERSON's pardon.

Alien Registration Act. See Smith Act.

Aliens. CITIZENS or subjects of other nations emigrating into the United States, generally seeking ultimate CITIZENSHIP. Certain rights, available to citizens as defined in the CONSTITUTION, are denied to them pending final NATURALIZATION, such as VOTING, holding public office, and attending certain types of public schools.

ALLEN, Ethan. 1738-1789. Revolutionary hero; leader of GREEN MOUNTAIN BOYS of Vermont, captured TICONDEROGA. b. Connecticut. Served during the French and Indian Wars (1757). Associated with early Vermont history (known then as New Hampshire grants) (from 1769). Colonel commanding Green Mountain Boys (1770-75). With aid of BENEDICT ARNOLD on May 10, 1775 in a surprise attack captured Fort Ticonderoga. While attempting a surprise attack at Montreal, captured and held prisoner (1775-78). Exchanged and returned to Vermont; major general of militia; to CONTINENTAL CONGRESS to present Vermont's claims to independence and recognition (1778). Negotiated with British (1780-83) in attempt to force recognition of Vermont's claims.

Alliance for Progress. The United States and 19 other American Republics pledged $20,000,000 for economic development in Latin America (1961). The United States agreed to provide the major part of the funds. Since December 1963, the United States had extended nearly $450,000,000 in assistance (1964).

Alliance with France. The first military alliance made by the United States. It was negotiated with France by the two treaties of 1778, two years after France had begun contributing arms and supplies to the CONTINENTAL CONGRESS. The treaties provided for a defensive alliance to aid France should England attack her, and declared that neither signatory would make peace with England until the independence of the United States was recognized. The two powers further guaranteed each other's American possessions, and provided that the United States should grant to France, if at war, more favorable treatment than would be accorded to France's enemy.

Allied Council for Japan. The governing body administering the interests of the ALLIED POWERS in Japan after World War II. By the terms of the surrender of August 14, 1945 Japan agreed to her occupation until an ultimate peace treaty would be negotiated. General DOUGLAS MACARTHUR was appointed Supreme Commander of the Allied Council which consisted of representatives of the United States, the Soviet Union, China, Australia, and the Philippine Islands. In 1951 General MacArthur was succeeded by General MATTHEW B. RIDGWAY. See Japan, occupation of.

Allied High Commission. The three man body consisting of high commissioners designated by the governments of the United States, Great Britain, and France, which exercises supreme authority in the German Federal Republic. The powers of the Commission are defined in the OCCUPATION STATUTE. It is authorized to veto laws of the Republic and to exercise plenary powers over foreign policy, reparations, decartelization, security of allied

15

occupation forces, disarmament, demilitarization, and control of the Ruhr. The Commission may also veto amendments of the Bonn Constitution. On April 28, 1949 it established the international Ruhr Authority to allocate the production of this industrial area. It has also approved federal statutes reorganizing the education system, agriculture, steel production, transportation and communication facilities, and trade. See Bonn Republic, occupation of Germany, and Occupation Statute.

Allied Powers. The term applied to the twenty-one Allied and Associated powers which defeated the CENTRAL POWERS in World War I. The leading nations included the "BIG FIVE," the United States, Great Britain, France, Italy, and Japan. The other sixteen allied powers were Belgium, Bolivia, Brazil, China, Cuba, Czechoslovakia, Ecuador, Greece, Guatemala, the Hejaz, Honduras, Liberia, Nicaragua, Panama, Peru, Poland, Portugal, Romania, Yugoslavia, Siam, and Uruguay. The name is also occasionally applied to the members of the UNITED NATIONS in World War II.

ALLISON, William Boyd. 1829-1908. Political leader. b. Ohio. Moved to Iowa (1855); important Republican leader, member, U.S. House of Representatives (1862-70); U.S. Senator (1872-1908); co-author of the BLAND-ALLISON ACT OF 1878. Chairman of the Committee of Appropriations, U.S. Senate (1881-1908).

ALLSTON, Washington. 1779-1843. Painter and author. b. South Carolina. Pupil of BENJAMIN WEST; friend of WASHINGTON IRVING; teacher of SAMUEL MORSE. Noted for *Moonlight Landscape* at Museum of Fine Arts, Boston, *The Deluge* at the Metropolitan Museum of Art, N.Y., and other paintings; author of *The Sylph of the Seasons* and *Other Poems* (1813).

Almanacs. Encyclopedic collections of data in the fields of astronomy, weather, farm production, and other general material. The first published almanac in North America was *An Almanac, Calculated for New England,* printed in 1639 in Cambridge, Massachusetts. An almanac appeared in Boston in 1676, in Philadelphia in 1686, and in New York in 1697. Beginning in 1700 the *New England Almanac* was published in Boston for eight years. Almanacs were the first and most popular books published in the British colonies, providing most of the reading material until the development of the NEWSPAPER industry.

"Alphabet Agencies". The derisive term applied by the political opponents of the NEW DEAL to the many administrative agencies it created in the early years of the GREAT DEPRESSION.

ALTGELD, John Peter. 1847-1902. Governor of Illinois. Famous for pardoning two anarchist leaders in the HAYMARKET AFFAIR of 1886, charging a miscarriage of justice. First Democratic governor of a state since the Civil War (1892-1896). In 1894, he protested President CLEVELAND's dispatch of Federal troops into Chicago without his permission. In 1896 he was defeated for re-election.

Aluminum Industry. The perfection, by CHARLES MARTIN HALL in 1825, of a process for reducing aluminum began this important industry. Aluminum's value is due to its light weight, good conductivity, reflective properties, and its resistance to corrosion. It is widely used in pure and alloy form in the manufacture of household utensils, but its fundamental industrial use is in the manufacture of automotive and aircraft parts, bridges, train bodies, vessels, and machine parts. The first important aluminum manufacturing company in the United States was the Pittsburgh Reduction Company, organized in 1888 by Hall and Alfred E. Hunt. In 1907 this firm was reorganized into the Aluminum Company of America which is today the greatest producer of the metal in this country. In 1963 the U.S. produced 2,285,000 short tons of aluminum. This country is the world's largest producer of the metal, manufacturing 2½ times as much aluminum as Russia, the world's second largest producer.

Amendments. Additions to the original Constitution of 1787. Provided for by Article V of the Constitution. Amendment proposals are submitted either by two-thirds vote of both houses of Congress or by a convention called upon the petition of two-thirds of the state legislatures. Ratification is obtained by either a vote of three-fourths of the state legislatures or by three-fourths of conventions in the states. Twenty-six amendments have been added to the Constitution.

America, Discovery of. Generally attributed to the discovery of CHRISTOPHER COLUMBUS, and his party, who landed on October 12, 1492 on the Indian Island of Guanahani, which he renamed San Salvador. There is considerable evidence to support the theory that Norsemen, known as the Vikings, voyaged to North America under Leif Ericsson, and reached America in 1000 A.D. Columbus made three subsequent voyages to America in 1495, 1499, and 1502, touching the coast of South and Central America. The discovery of North America is ascribed to the landing of JOHN CABOT on Cape Breton Island and Nova Scotia in 1497. The name "America" was applied to the continents by the German geographer, Martin Waldseemüller, in a book published in 1507. It was coined from the name of AMERICUS VESPUCIUS who wrote popular accounts of his own travels in the New World.

America First Committee. An organization created in 1940 for the express objective of preventing the entry of the United States into World War II. Consisting basically of isolationist and politically conservative elements it opposed the efforts of various organizations which had sprung up in the preceding year devoted to a program of aiding England and France. The organization conducted parades and picket lines, and carried on newspaper and radio propaganda to this end. They were frequently attacked as being anti-Semitic and pro-fascist. Following the attack on PEARL HARBOR the movement disintegrated, although it ran candidates in the 1944 election who polled 1751 votes.

American Antislavery Society. Organized in 1833 on a national scale. It demanded the immediate and uncompensated ABOLITION OF SLAVERY. It was formed by the consolidation of the New England Anti-slavery Society (1832), organized by WILLIAM LLOYD GARRISON, and other abolitionist groups. By 1840 the society contained 2000 local organizations with a total membership of more than 200,000. The stimulus to its creation was the British emancipation in the West Indies, the creation of the Pennsylvania Anti-slavery Society, and the vigorous activity of New York ABOLITIONISTS. The Society issued pamphlets and books, published periodicals, and deluged Congress with petitions. Among its leaders were Garrison, Arthur and Lewis Tappan, Theodore D. Weld, and the famous evangelist George G. Finney.

American Civil Liberties Union. An organization devoted to defending CIVIL RIGHTS guaranteed in state and federal constitutions. Its services are available to clients upon request, or are voluntarily donated by the legal staff of the Union. Outstanding leaders include Roger Baldwin, Osmond K. Fraenkel, and Arthur Garfield Hayes. It was founded in New York City in 1920, and became famous because of its defense of John T. Scopes in 1925.

American **Colonization Society.** An organization founded in 1816 by anti-slave supporters including HENRY CLAY and JOHN RANDOLPH for the purpose of returning Negroes to Africa. It was also supported by some slave owners in Virginia, Maryland and Kentucky who feared the continued existence in the United States of free Negroes. In 1827 the Society sought but failed to obtain a congressional appropriation towards colonizing Negroes in Liberia, a part of which it had previously purchased. By 1831 it had returned to Liberia only 1420 Negroes, in number only one-third of those born into SLAVERY in the United States annually. Nevertheless, Liberia has since grown as one of the few independent Negro states in the world.

American **Equal Rights Association.** See Women's Suffrage.

American **Expeditionary Forces.** American contingents to allied armies in World War I. Commanded by General JOHN J. PERSHING. Total forces by 1919 numbered 4,500,000 personnel of whom approximately one-half were overseas by that date. However, token troops in small numbers were already in France by 1917 to bolster allied morale.

American **Farm Bureau Federation.** A lobbying organization of wealthy western farmers. The Federation has consistently opposed federal programs designed to aid the small farmer. It is basically against excessive governmental expenditures, and has many times called for economy spending in non-agricultural areas. Many statutes of Congress have been prepared and drafted by leaders of the Federation in phases of farm policy to their advantage.

American **Federation of Labor.** Founded by SAMUEL GOMPERS and Adolph Strasser in 1886. Originally organized in 1881 under the name of Federation of Trades and Labor Unions. A confederation of autonomous trade unions based on craft or horizontal organization, with few exceptions such as the International Ladies Garment Workers Union. The A.F. of L. has traditionally opposed direct political activity (with the exception of the election of 1924), and has been based on British trade union orientation. Generally considered to be conservative and opportunistic. Samuel Gompers, the first president, was succeeded by William Green (1924-1952). George Meany headed the A. F. of L. until Dec. 1955 when he became president of the AFL-CIO merger (See AFL-CIO).

American **Fur Company.** A fur trading organization founded by JOHN JACOB ASTOR in New York State in 1808. By acquiring control over competing companies in the Great Lakes and Rocky Mountain area the AMERICAN FUR COMPANY became the largest business firm in the United States after the War of 1812. It operated subsidiary companies in the lead trade, GREAT LAKES fishing interests, and STEAMBOAT activities. It established strategically located posts which became the centers of great cities. Although Astor withdrew from the Company in 1834 it continued as a MONOPOLY organization in the far west, lasting as such until the 1840's. By 1847 it had dwindled in importance, and disappeared shortly thereafter.

American **Labor Party.** Organized as a left-wing group in New York State in 1936. Supported NEW DEAL policies of F. D. ROOSEVELT. Has generally opposed policies of TRUMAN administration since 1945. Supported PROGRESSIVE PARTY candidate HENRY A. WALLACE in election of 1948.

"American Lake." See Caribbean Policy.

American **League, The.** A professional BASEBALL organization which was originally organized as the Western League. It was established in 1900 under its present name by Ban Johnson, who became its first president. The refusal by the NATIONAL LEAGUE to recognize it as a "major" league led to a fierce rivalry between the two organizations until 1903 when they reconciled their differences and agreed to meet in a World Series. Thereafter the American League gave up its franchise jumping, long term contract schemes, and raiding of players from the old league. Since the inception of the World Series in 1903 the American League has won 37 world championships. From the beginning of the All Star series in 1933 it has won 17 games. In 1965 the ten member clubs of the American League were the Baltimore Orioles, Boston Red Sox, Chicago White Sox, Cleveland Indians, Detroit Tigers, Kansas City Athletics, Los Angeles Angels, Minnesota Twins, New York Yankees, and the Washington Senators. The League's president was Joseph E. Cronin.

American Legion. Veterans organization established after World War I and incorporated by an act of Congress in 1919. Consisted of veterans of that war in its inception. Veterans of other wars were subsequently admitted to membership. Has lobbied in national and state legislatures for benefits of veterans.

American Liberty League. An organization established in 1934 for the purpose of combatting radical movements. Its principal activities were aimed against the reform program of the NEW DEAL in the first two administrations of F. D. ROOSEVELT. It dissolved in 1940, having been assailed during its brief lifetime by liberal political elements for its allegedly reactionary policies.

American Museum of Natural History. Located in New York City. It was founded in 1869. In the group of buildings comprising the Museum are exhibited large displays picturing the habits of man and animal life from prehistoric times to the present. The exhibits include extensive reconstruction of primitive remains, dioramas of man and animals in their natural habitats, and collections of objects from the smallest insects to the skeleton of a prehistoric brontosaurus which, when alive, weighed over 25 tons. The great hall of birds maintains 750,-000 specimens of the world's birds. The animal life of the various sections of the United States is represented in special exhibits. There are also famous collections of minerals and gems, fossil fishes, marine life, woods, and trees. The Museum maintains the HAYDEN PLANETARIUM.

American Party. See Know-Nothing party.

American Philosophical Society. The first scholarly society in America. It was founded in 1743 in Philadelphia by BENJAMIN FRANKLIN who was its first president. Its first great scientific undertaking was in the field of astronomy when it conducted observations on the transit of Venus, the results of which were published in 1771 in *Transactions*, the publication of the Society. A roster of prominent men, including THOMAS JEFFERSON and the famous astronomer DAVID RITTENHOUSE, succeeded Franklin in the presidency of the Society.

"American Plan." See "Open Shoppism" and "Welfare Capitalism."

American Railway Express Company. Organized in 1918 as a merger of the United States Express Company and the American Express Company. In 1929 it was absorbed by the Railway Express Agency, a wholly owned subsidiary of American RAILROADS. See RAILWAY EXPRESS AGENCY.

American Red Cross. Its full name is American National Red Cross. It was first organized in 1881 as the American Association of the Red Cross by CLARA BARTON in accordance with the Treaty of Geneva. It was reincorporated under its present title by Congress in 1905. The President of the United States is honorary chairman. Its 1965 membership was 28,600,000 adults, with 18,100,000 children enrolled in the Junior Red Cross. Its primary functions are to furnish volunteer aid to armies in time of war, to serve as a medium of communication between the American civilian population and the armed forces, to provide relief in national and international calamities, and to carry on research and organizational programs designed to prevent such disasters. Its many health services include first aid instruction, water safety, accident prevention, home nursing, and nutrition. One of its notable contributions is its collection, processing, and distribution of blood and its derivatives for medical use without charge.

American Revolution. Also known as the War of Independence. The revolt of 13 British colonies in North America in the late 18th century. The causes of the Revolution are complex, including political, economic, social, cultural, and religious factors. Its origins may perhaps be traced back to the Seven Years War which ended in 1763. Following its conclusion the British government decided to abandon its policy of "salutary neglect" by enforcing the 17th century NAVIGATION ACTS, reviving old tax and tariff measures, and compelling the colonies to assume a share of the financial burden of that war. The British government attempted to accomplish the latter by instituting a program of new revenue measures, commencing with the Stamp Tax. Under the sponsorship of Lords North, Greenville, and Townshend, this was followed by such measures as the SUGAR ACT, the TOWNSHEND ACTS, the DECLARATORY ACTS, the TEA ACT, the QUARTERING ACT, the QUEBEC ACT, and the INTOLERABLE ACTS. The early colonial resistance did not consider the question of Revolution and ultimate independence, being content in the beginning with declarations of opposition to these revenue measures. The opposition took the form of the creation of organizations of resistance such as the STAMP ACT CONGRESS, the COMMITTEES OF CORRESPONDENCE, the SONS OF LIBERTY, and the two CONTINENTAL CONGRESSES. It has been recognized that the leadership of colonial resistance was basically divided into two groups, a radical leadership and a conservative business leadership. Among the former were included SAMUEL ADAMS, PATRICK HENRY, RICHARD HENRY LEE, THOMAS JEFFERSON, and THOMAS PAINE. The latter group included ALEXANDER HAMILTON, GEORGE WASHINGTON, JOHN JAY, ROBERT and GOUVERNEUR MORRIS, JOHN HANCOCK, and JAMES WILSON. The intransigence of the British government, overcoming the sympathetic understanding of such Parliamentary leaders as William Pitt and EDMUND BURKE, rapidly compelled a change of feeling in the colonies. By 1775, with the first bloodshed at LEXINGTON AND CONCORD, open war between the colonies and the mother country became inevitable. The following year the desire for independence, which had been growing in the minds of the radical leaders, took the form of the LEE RESOLUTION in the VIRGINIA HOUSE OF BURGESSES shortly followed by the DECLARATION OF INDEPENDENCE. The military struggle continued for six more years with French, Dutch, and Spanish financial and military aid to the colonists. By the TREATY OF PARIS IN 1783 the Revolution had achieved its success and provided for the independence of the 13 colonies. Now transformed into states, they included Connecticut, Delaware, Georgia, Maryland, Massachusetts, New Hampshire, New Jersey, New York, North Carolina, and Virginia. The difficulties of the struggle for independence involved conflicts between PATRIOTS and LOYALISTS, financial problems, inadequacies of men and military supplies, treasonable conduct within the continental military leadership, desertions from the army, speculation and profiteering behind the lines, and personal rivalries between political and military leaders.

American, Second Generation. The name applied to the offspring born in the United States of naturalized American parents. The birth of millions of these Americans in the last fifty years has presented serious sociological problems ai :;-ing out of conflicts at home, in the school, and in the community. These problems have developed out of the different languages, customs, traditions, and behavior patterns of parent and child. Much has been attempted by community organizations to reconcile these conflicts and assist the assimilation of the second generation American into useful community life.

Americans for Democratic Action. A political organization of liberal Democrats, seeking more progressive action within the Democratic party. Its principal appeal is to professional and intellectual groups although it has attracted some adherents from labor. Among its leaders are A. A. BERLE JR., F. D. Roosevelt Jr., and Francis Biddle.

"American System." As conceived by HENRY CLAY it referred to the nationalist policy of uniting the three economic sections of the nation in the period following the War of 1812. His objective was to render the United States economically independent and self sufficient. The plan provided for the adoption of a HIGH PRO-

TECTIVE TARIFF, a national bank, and for the construction of a network of ROADS and CANALS. The desired result was to provide the industrial East with the raw materials and food of the West and the South, and to furnish the latter areas with its manufactured goods. Under this program Congress established the second BANK OF THE UNITED STATES in 1816 and the high tariff of 1816. The "American system" was generally well received by all sections of the country in this period of expanding nationalism from 1816 to 1828.

American Telephone and Telegraph Company. The largest corporation in the United States, owning or controlling assets of more than $28,000,000,000. It was organized as a HOLDING COMPANY in 1885, with a capital of $100,000. By 1900 it had absorbed the American Bell Telephone Company and the facilities of the former Bell Telephone Company, the New England Bell Telephone Company, the National Bell Telephone Company, and others in the industry. At its inception the important figures connected with it were THOMAS A. WATSON and William H. Forbes. In 1956 the Company settled government suits charging "conspiracy to monopolize" by agreeing to the following: (1) A. T. & T. to license without fee all its existing 8600 patents; also make available all future patents at reasonable rates. (2) Western Electric, a manufacturing subsidiary, was to continue undivorced from the parent Company but must sell its subsidiary, Westrex. (3) Western Electric may continue to manufacture A. T. & T. equipment but at competitive prices.

American Veterans Committee. An organization of veterans of World War II. It was established in 1945 with a program of political and lobbying activities designed to obtain legislation favorable to veterans. Under the slogan "Citizens first, Americans second" it has emphasized the importance of general reform legislation to improve the conditions of the American people as a prerequisite to aiding the veteran. Its national headquarters are located in Washington, D.C.

AMES, Fisher. 1758-1808. Political leader. b. Massachusetts. Defeated SAMUEL ADAMS in election for representative from Boston district to the First Congress (1789-97); played important part in shaping FEDERALIST legislation. Supported HAMILTON's policies; opposed JEFFERSON's democratic ideas. Made great speech which turned the tide in favor of JAY'S TREATY. Was important influence in party even after retirement due to ill health.

AMES, Oakes. 1804-1873. Manufactuer, railroad promoter, and politician. b. Massachusetts. Fortune accumulated in manufacture of shovels; interested in UNION PACIFIC RAILROAD and became involved in CREDIT MOBILIER, after gaining control by ousting T. C. DURANT, the founder. Responsible for scandal and finally investigated publicly and rebuked by the United States House of Representatives. Member, U.S. House of Representatives (1863-73).

AMES, Oliver. 1831-1895. Governor and capitalist. b. Massachusetts. Inherited shovel factory founded by his grandfather and debts from the UNION PACIFIC RAILROAD inherited from his father. By capable management he paid off debts, including philanthropic bequests of his father amounting to $1,000,000; Massachusetts state senator (1880-82); lieutenant governor (1882-86); governor (1886-89).

AMHERST, Jeffrey. Baron Amherst. 1717-1797. British Army Officer and Governor in America. b. England. Commanded army against the French at Louisburg in America (1758); commander in chief in North America (1759); captured TICONDEROGA and Crown Point; captured Montreal (1760); governor general of British North America (1760-63).

Amnesty Act. Passed by Congress in 1872 at the end of the RECONSTRUCTION period for the purpose of easing some of the reconstruction problems. It provided for the restoration of political privileges to all but approximately 500 important Confederate political and military officers. The result was to return into southern political life a more conservative type of southern leadership.

Amtrak. On October 30, 1970 President Nixon signed the Rail Passenger Service Act creating a national corporation, AMTRAK, a word combining "American" and "track." Amtrak was formed to manage and operate the U.S. railroad network. Directed by the National Railroad Passenger Corporation, Amtrak aims to "get people back on trains" with efficient, modern, and profitable service.

"Anaconda Policy." The plan of squeezing the Confederate armies by Union armies converging on LEE in Northern Virginia. The plan was developed after the FALL OF VICKSBURG which permitted GRANT and SHERMAN to move eastward across Mississippi and Alabama, pushing the Confederate armies into Georgia. While this flanking movement was taking place in the west the ARMY OF THE POTOMAC was ordered to move down on Lee in northern Virginia, the objective thus being to destroy the Confederate Army in Virginia and Georgia. This vast movement in 1863 marked the beginning of the end of the Civil War.

Anaesthesia. The use of drugs in surgery to relieve or eliminate pain. In the United States DR. CRAWFORD W. LONG first used sulphuric ether in 1842 in a neck operation. Two years later Dr. Horace Wells, a Connecticut dentist, administered nitrous oxide, popularly known as "laughing gas", to himself in the extraction of a tooth. In 1846 DR. W. T. G. MORTON, a Boston dentist, again used sulphuric ether in a dental operation. Its use soon spread in Massachusetts, having been accepted by the Massachusetts General Hospital. Today many new and improved drugs are employed by different methods in anaesthesia. These include the inhalation of vinethene, ethyl chloride, and cyclopropane, and the injection of thiopental sodium. Spinal anaesthesia is also practiced by the injection of procaine and procaine derivatives.

Anarchism. The political philosophy that equality and justice may be obtained only through the abolition of the state and its organs. It opposes CAPITALISM and FREE ENTERPRISE. In the United States, anarchists exercised some influence in the trade union and radical political movement in the last third of the 19th century. Anarchists were accused of perpetrating the HAYMARKET AFFAIR in Chicago in 1886, leading to the arrest of seven anarchists and the ultimate execution of four of them. An anarchist assassinated President MC KINLEY in 1901. SACCO AND VANZETTI, two anarchists, were arrested in 1921 and executed in 1927. Today anarchism has lost all influence in American political thinking.

ANDERSON, Marian. 1908- . Contralto. b. Philadelphia, Pa. World renowned contralto who has appeared in concerts in Europe and America, considered to have one of the richest, most beautiful voices heard in the United States. Winner of the Spingarn medal which is awarded to an outstanding Negro in the United States (1939).

ANDERSON, Maxwell. 1888-1959. Playwright. b. Pennsylvania. Graduated, University of North Dakota (1911), Stanford (M.S. 1914); worked on newspapers on the west coast and in New York City. Writer of outstanding plays including *What Price Glory* (with Lawrence Stallings, 1924), *Saturday's Children* (1927), *Mary of Scotland* (1933), *Winterset* (1935), and *Key Largo* (1939).

ANDERSON, Robert. 1805-1871. General. b. Kentucky. Graduated U.S.M.A. West Point (1825); defended FORT SUMTER against Confederate attack in the first battle of the Civil War.

ANDERSON, Sherwood. 1876-1941. Author and editor. b. Ohio. Served in Cuba in the Spanish-American War; editor of weekly newspapers. Author of *Winesburg, Ohio* (1919), *Poor White* (1920), and *Memoirs* (1942) which exercised an important influence on the younger writers of the school of American realism.

ANDRE, John. 1751-1780. British spy who came to America in 1774 as a lieutenant in the Royal Fusileers. Made a major under command of SIR HENRY CLINTON, and entrusted with the task of carrying on secret negotiations with BENEDICT ARNOLD who had agreed to betray West Point to the British. Captured on return to New York with the secret papers in his boots. Hanged as a spy.

ANDREW, John Albion. 1818-1867. Governor of Massachusetts during the Civil War. b. Maine. His anti-slavery sympathies started him in politics, and he became one of the organizers of the FREE-SOIL PARTY. Elected to the legislature in 1857 and governor by a vast majority in 1860. At his urging the Massachusetts troops were the first to answer LINCOLN's call for aid, and were the first troops to reach the capitol at the outbreak of the Civil War.

ANDREWS, Christopher Columbus. 1826-1922. General, diplomat and author. b. Vermont. Major in Civil War; minister to Sweden and Norway (1869); consul general to Brazil (1882). Pioneer advocate of forest culture in the United States.

ANDREWS, Roy Chapman. 1884-1960. Naturalist, explorer, and author. b. Wisconsin. Headed expeditions for the American Museum of Natural History to Tibet, China, Burma, Mongolia, and Central Asia. Known for discoveries of the world's great fossil fields, geological strata, dinosaur eggs, remains of largest known land mammals. Director of the museum (1935-41.) Author of *Across Mongolian Plains* (1921), *On the Trail of Ancient Man* (1926), and *This Business of Exploring* (1935).

ANDROS, Sir Edmund. 1637-1714. British colonial governor in America. Arrived in New York in 1675, an appointee of the Duke of York to administer the colony. In 1686 he was appointed governor of the "DOMINION OF NEW ENGLAND", formed by uniting several of the New England colonies; interfered with rights and customs of the colonists and they revolted (1689). He was sent as a prisoner to England. Released and made governor of Virginia (1692-97).

Anglican Church. Also known as the Church of England. Its members established the first English settlement in JAMESTOWN in 1607. It became the established church of Virginia soon afterwards. Its influence spread, and it became the established church in Maryland in 1689 and in New York in 1702.

Annapolis. See United States Naval Academy.

Annapolis Convention. A meeting in 1786 at Annapolis, Maryland to discuss commercial questions and other important matters. It was convened by a call of the Virginia legislature at the suggestion of delegates who had met at the MOUNT VERNON CONFERENCE the previous year. Nine states appointed delegates to this convention, but representatives from only five appeared. The result was that little could be accomplished and the delegates adopted a report by ALEXAN-

DER HAMILTON calling for another convention to meet at Philadelphia in May, 1787 to consider problems arising out of the weaknesses of the ARTICLES OF CONFEDERATION.

Annexation of Texas. Accomplished by joint resolution of Congress in 1845, after failure to achieve senatorial ratification of a treaty in 1844. Texas entered as the 28th state. At the time of its ADMISSION TO THE UNION, Texas was in its ninth year of independence as a republic known as the LONE STAR STATE.

ANTHONY, Susan Brownell. 1820-1906. Woman suffrage leader. b. Massachusetts. Teacher; lecturer on temperance, abolition, and women's rights (1851-60); an organizer of Women's Loyal League in support of LINCOLN (1863) and emancipation; organized the National Woman Suffrage Association (1869); president, National American Woman Suffrage Association (1892-1900); with ELIZABETH STANTON and Matilda Gage she wrote Volumes I to III of the *History of Woman Suffrage* (1881-87); lectured all over the country for equal rights for women.

Anthracite Coal Strike. Called in 1902 by the UNITED MINE WORKERS OF AMERICA. In Pennsylvania 150,000 miners struck, after the Union's failure to negotiate arbitration of its grievances with the mine operators. The strike continued throughout the summer and fall of that year creating a potential hardship as the winter approached inasmuch as anthracite was virtually the only fuel used in the East. The refusal by the operators to accede to a request by President T. ROOSEVELT for investigation and ARBITRATION led to his creation of an investigating commission, the adoption of a plan for operating the mines under military protection and the attempt of Secretary of War, ELIHU ROOT, to seek J. P. MORGAN's influence on the operators to arbitrate. Work was resumed on October 23. After several months the arbitrators' award granted the miners a 10 percent wage increase, union recognition, and the establishment of a board of conciliation to negotiate future disputes.

"Anti-Chain Store Act." See Robinson-Patman Act.

Antietam, Battle of. A bloody battle fought in September, 1862 between Antietam Creek and the Potomac River in Maryland. The battle is noteworthy because it might have marked the end of the Civil War, but for the reluctance of MC CLELLAN to pursue LEE across the Potomac. The armies engaged numbered 50,000 Union troops and 40,000 Confederates, suffering casualties of 12,000 and 9,000 respectively.

Anti-Federalist Party. Created in 1787 by the Jeffersonians for the purpose of opposing RATIFICATION OF THE CONSTITUTION. The party represented the interests and had the support of FARMERS, city mechanics, frontiersmen, and debtors. Opposed the constitutional features providing for a strong national government. Disappeared from politics shortly after the ratification of the Constitution, but its leaders and followers formed the nucleus of the later DEMOCRATIC-REPUBLICAN party.

Anti-Inflation Act. See Economic Stabilization Act.

Anti-Inflation Act. See Emergency Price Control Act.

Anti-Lynch Bills. Federal bills which have attempted to provide the protection of the United States courts against attempts at illegal lynching. In over 99 percent of all lynching cases there have been no arrests, presentments, or court convictions. In 1922 the Dyer Anti-Lynch Bill was passed in the House, but was rejected by the Senate. Thereafter successive attempts to legislate against this evil failed. In 1937 alone 59 anti-lynch bills were introduced in Congress,

all unsuccessful. By 1955 no such legislation had secured the approval of both houses of Congress despite its advocacy by the last five administrations. These bills have consistently been opposed on STATES' RIGHTS grounds.

Anti-Masonic Party. A short lived minor party which came into existence in western New York in the early 1830's in opposition to the Masonic order, of which President JACKSON and many Democratic leaders were members. It held the first NATIONAL CONVENTION in 1831 in which WILLIAM WIRT was nominated for the presidency. Its anti-Jackson program attacked CATHOLICS, foreigners, and secret societies. The national convention method of nominating presidential and vice-presidential candidates was subsequently adopted by the major POLITICAL PARTIES and is today a permanent political institution.

Anti-Monopoly Party. A minor party organized in Chicago in 1884. Its program included demands for a graduated INCOME TAX, the establishment of a DEPARTMENT OF LABOR, the direct election of Senators, the payment of the NATIONAL DEBT, assistance to FARMERS, federal regulation of MONOPOLIES in INTERSTATE COMMERCE, and economy in governmental expenditures. It denounced tariff protectionism and the granting of lands to corporations. Subsequently it merged with the GREENBACK LABOR party under the name of The People's Party. Like that of many third parties, its program was later adopted in part or in whole by the major parties, and many of its planks were ultimately enacted.

Antioch College. A coeducational college located at Yellow Springs, Ohio. It was founded in 1853 by HORACE MANN, who became its first president. Mann's objectives were the stimulation and development of all aspects of the student's personality, character, and talent. Although

25

originally unsuccessful in this purpose, a reorganization under the presidency of Arthur E. Morgan in 1921 realized this program to a degree. The college's chief feature is the cooperative program in which students choose alternating periods of full time work and study. Its friendly relations with neighboring business organizations enable the college to successfully guide its students into avenues of their interest.

Anti-Saloon League. An organization opposed to the sale of alcoholic beverages. It was founded in 1893 in Ohio as the Ohio Anti-Saloon League, drawing its membership from church and temperance societies. To the time of the adoption of the 18TH AMENDMENT in 1919 it conducted vigorous LOBBYING activities in the national and state legislatures seeking prohibition legislation. Although still in existence its influence has declined markedly.

Anti-Trust Laws. A series of federal statutes attempting to control the activities of business combinations considered to be in restraint of interstate and foreign commerce. The first of these laws was the SHERMAN ANTI-TRUST LAW of 1890. This act was subsequently amended and supplemented by the CLAYTON ANTI-TRUST LAW of 1941, the FEDERAL TRADE COMMISSION ACT of 1914, the WEBB-POMERENE ACT of 1918, the CAPPER-VOLSTEAD ACT OF 1922, the NATIONAL RECOVERY ACT of 1933, 1936, the MILLER-TYDINGS ACT of 1937, and the REED-BULWINKLE ACT of 1948.

Anti-Yazoo Party. See Yazoo Land Frauds.

Anzio Landings. On January 22, 1944 the United States 6th Corps and the British 1st Division landed at Anzio below Cassino in Italy for the purpose of cutting German communications from Rome to Cassino and inducing General Kesselring to evacuate Cassino. The landings were unopposed. A general advance on January 30th met with only limited success. On February 8, 1945 the Germans counter-attacked and took Carroceto. They attacked again on February 16th and February 20th and inflicted heavy casualties upon the United States 3rd Division. Despite the great losses suffered by both armies, no material gains were achieved.

Apache Indians. A tribe of nomadic Indians who did not work the fields but survived by making raids on their more peaceful neighbors. They were famous as expert horsemen. They lived in the region of New Mexico and Arizona. Their most famous leader and chief was GERONIMO. They were at constant war with the PUEBLO INDIANS whose culture and religious beliefs they adopted in part. Most Apache Indians today are on reservations in Arizona.

APPLEGATE, Jesse. 1811-1888. Oregon pioneer. Elected captain of one of the two divisions of the large train of over 900 people in the emigration of 1843 to Oregon. Member of legislature committee which ruled that territory (1845-49); surveyor-general of Oregon, he made a number of explorations into southern part of the territory and opened a wagon route to California.

APPLETON, Nathan. 1779-1861. Manufacturer and congressman. b. New Hampshire. Invested in FRANCIS C. LOWELL'S new cotton mill at Waltham, where the first power loom in America was put into operation. Bought water rights at the falls of the Merrimac river and founded the manufacturing center of Lowell. Elected U.S. Representative for the Boston district (1830). Helped frame TARIFF OF 1832.

Appomattox, Surrender at. The surrender of the Confederate Army under General ROBERT E. LEE to General ULYSSES S. GRANT at Appomattox farmhouse on

April 9, 1865. The surrender occurred a week after the fall of Petersburg and RICHMOND. The terms laid down by General Grant provided that the Army of Northern Virginia was to lay down its arms, but the officers were to retain their horses and side arms, with the exception of cavalrymen and artillery men who were allowed to keep their animals. Lee surrendered a total of 26, 765 men.

Appropriations, Committee on. A standing committee of the two Houses of Congress which prepares all appropriations bills. Until 1865 all appropriations originated in the House Committee on WAYS AND MEANS. The Appropriations Committee established that year was supplemented by eight other appropriations committees subsequently created. By the BUDGET AND ACCOUNTING ACT of 1921 all appropriations were placed within the hands of a single committee on appropriations.

Arbitration, Industrial. Generally the last step in COLLECTIVE BARGAINING negotiations. The parties to a labor dispute agree upon a single arbitrator or board of arbitrators whose decision is accepted by employer and union. Arbitration awards are enforceable in the courts. Outstanding labor or legal figures in public life are customarily selected. Public agencies such as the FEDERAL MEDIATION and CONCILIATION SERVICE, state mediation boards, or the American Arbitration Association frequently select the personnel. In the United States arbitration is voluntary, although other nations, like France, have on occasion adopted a system of compulsory arbitration.

Arbitration, International. Performed by agreement between two or more nations which have failed to peaceably negotiate a conflict. Prior to 1899 the arbitrating nations were selected by the opposing parties, as in ALABAMA CLAIMS and VENEZUELA BOUNDARY DISPUTES. The creation of the Court of Arbitration by the Hague Convention (1899) provided an easier way for settling such disputes. Inasmuch as the HAGUE TRIBUNAL possessed no material means of enforcing its decisions its work was relatively unsuccessful. The United States has settled over 100 disputes with 25 nations through arbitration.

Archangel-Murmansk Campaign. An Allied invasion of Russia in 1917-1918 in which American troops participated. The campaign, under British command, was organized to assist the White Russians against the revolutionary Bolsheviks. By September, 1918 President WILSON had ordered a total of 5100 United States troops to the Arctic cities of Archangel and Murmansk to defend the harbor areas. By May, 1919 they had suffered 500 casualties. The last American troops were withdrawn in July, 1919.

Architecture. Colonial architecture was the outgrowth of European influence modified by native conditions. Wood was used widely in the South and stone in New England. The middle colonies duplicated European homes. In the 18th century the splendid colonial mansions were modified versions of English Georgian architecture. The rococo classical styles were seen on southern plantations and in New England towns. The most prominent of these were the Lee Mansion in Marblehead and the Jumel house in New York City. The small Cape Cod farmhouse, the Dutch colonial home, and the typical stone and brick Pennsylvania homestead have remained popular forms to this day. Early 19th century architecture retained the FRONTIER LOG CABIN, the urban colonial homestead, and the PLANTATION mansion. The homes of wealthy urbanites and the new public buildings fell under the influence of neoclassic European designs. Greek pillars and porticos and Roman domes and columns became the characteristics of the larger edifices. University buildings, post offices, and legislative halls were replicas of ancient Greek temples. The "Gothic Revival" followed the "Greek Revival" in the pre-Civil War era, importing forms that were equally alien to the American scene. By the 1880's the Gothic importations had degenerated into overdecorated buildings. Urban tenements and rows of attached brownstone buildings created depressing sights. With the return of European-trained architects like Henry Hobson Richardson and RICHARD MORRIS HUNT, architecture slowly improved. Romanesque and Renaissance styles replaced the Greek and Gothic in public buildings. The baroque was supplanted by simple designs which reached their climax in the CHICAGO EXPOSITION of 1893. The Chicago school of LOUIS SULLIVAN, DANIEL BURNHAM, and John W. Root experimented with skyscrapers of steel and concrete. After World War I American architecture developed native styles based on the theories of functionalism which had been so successfully developed by Sullivan and FRANK LLOYD WRIGHT.

ARGALL, Sir Samuel. 1572?-1626. British navigator and adventurer. Commanded first ship to sail the northern route directly to Virginia (1609); captured POCAHONTAS who later married JOHN ROLFE and sailed to England aboard Argall's ship; deputy governor, Virginia (1617-19).

Arizona. The sixth state in size, with an area of 113,909 square miles. Organized as a TERRITORY in 1863 and admitted as the 48th state on February 14, 1912. Phoenix is the capital. In 1950 Arizona's population of 749,587 made it 37th in rank. Its largest cities are Phoenix, Tucson, and Mesa. The mining of copper, gold, silver, and vanadium is Arizona's principal industry. Copper smelting and refining is important. Formerly useless land has been made arable by irrigation, and now produces important crops of cotton, corn, wheat, vegetables, and citrus fruits. Arizona has the second largest Indian population in the United States, the HOPI, NAVAJO, and the APACHE tribes being located on 14 federal reservations. The state is famous for its scenic wonders, among them being the Petrified Forest and the Grand Canyon. Phoenix is a popular health and recreation resort. It was discovered in 1539 by Marcos de Niza. Its nickname is the "Grand Canyon State."

Arkansas. The 27th state in size, with an area of 53,102 square miles. Organized as a territory in 1819 and admitted as the 25th state on June 15, 1836. Seceded on May 6, 1861 and readmitted on June 22, 1868. Little Rock is the capital. In 1950 Arkansas population of 1,909,511 made it 30th in rank. Its largest cities are Little Rock, Fort Smith, and North Little Rock. Arkansas is the source of about 90 per cent of the nation's bauxite, and contains the only known diamond mine in the United States. Important crops include cotton, corn, fruit, potatoes, oats, rice, and wheat. Petroleum and lumbering are large industries. Arkansas' 47 mineral springs draw large numbers of guests each year. The Hot Springs National Park is owned by the federal government. Arkansas was discovered in 1541 by DE SOTO. Its nickname is the "Wonder State."

Arlington National Cemetery. It is located at Fort Myer, Virginia on the south bank of the Potomac River, opposite Washington, D.C. It was established in 1864 on a tract of 200 acres, now increased to 440 acres, for the burial of military and naval leaders and members of the armed forces. By 1952, 73,166 persons, of whom 4720 were unidentified, had been buried in the Cemetery. The TOMB OF THE UNKNOWN SOLDIER of

World War I is situated in an amphitheater facing Washington, D.C. Among famous Americans buried there are General PHILIP SHERIDAN, WILLIAM HOWARD TAFT, General JOHN J. PERSHING, and WILLIAM JENNINGS BRYAN.

ARMISTEAD, George. 1780-1818. Army officer. b. Virginia. Commander of Ft. McHenry, near Baltimore, in September, 1814 when British attacked. Saved the city and inspired FRANCIS SCOTT KEY to write the *Star-Spangled Banner.*

Armistice. An agreement between belligerent armies for a cease-fire pending peace treaty negotiations. During World War I the German government requested President WILSON for an armistice on October 4, 1918, to be based on the FOURTEEN POINTS. Despite Wilson's insistence on certain demands, the request was accepted by Marshal Foch, and Germany was notified on November 8th. The agreement was signed on November 11th to take effect at 11 A.M. The one month armistice, renewed periodically until the TREATY OF VERSAILLES was negotiated, required Germany to evacuate all territory west of the Rhine, surrender quantities of munitions, trucks, and railway trains, withdraw her troops from Russia, Rumania, and Turkey, and renounce the treaties of Brest-Litovsk and Bucharest. The allied BLOCKADE was to remain in force until the peace.

Armistice Day. The day of acceptance in 1918 by Germany of the armistice terms of the ALLIED POWERS. This day, November 11th, is now celebrated as Veterans Day (since 1954).

ARMOUR, Philip. 1832-1901. Industrialist, one of the organizers of Armour & Co. meat packers. b. New York. Responsible for methods of utilizing waste products; introduced refrigeration and preparation of canned meats; founded Armour Institute of Technology (1893).

Arms Embargo. A clause in the NEU-TRALITY ACTS of 1935 and 1937 conferring upon the President the power to proclaim the existence of a state of war and invoke an embargo upon the export of arms, munitions, or implements of war to belligerent states or to neutral states for trans-shipment to belligerents. The President was empowered to enumerate such items. This provision was imposed in the Italo-Ethopian war of 1934, 1935, the Spanish Civil War of 1936-1939, and in the Japanese-Chinese War from 1937 to the adoption of the CASH AND CARRY program in 1939.

ARMSTRONG, John. 1758-1843. Army officer and diplomat. b. Pennsylvania. Aide-de-camp during the Revolution to GATES. Probably with his encouragement wrote the "NEWBURGH ADDRESSES" which were a series of anonymous letters stating the grievances of the army officers, and attempting to force Congress to pay money due them. U.S. Senator (1800-02; 03-4); Minister to France (1804-10); Secretary of War (1813-14) forced to resign because of failure of campaign against Montreal.

Army, Department of. Formerly an EXECUTIVE DEPARTMENT known as the Department of War. It was merged into the newly created DEPARTMENT OF DEFENSE by the NATIONAL SECURITY ACT of 1947. It supervises the organization, equipment, and training of the land forces of the United States. The Ordnance Department in the Department of the Army develops weapons. The Department administers the construction of certain public works such as flood control, river, and harbor installations. It supervises the PANAMA CANAL ZONE.

Army of the Potomac. Technically, the Division of the Potomac, created on July 25, 1861 as the eastern section of the Union army. Under the original command of General GEORGE B. MCCLELLAN its objective was to defend Washington,

29

D.C. by protecting the Potomac River entry to the city. It was called into being after the defeat of the Union forces in the first BATTLE OF BULL RUN. By the end of the year it numbered 138,000 troops; consisting of volunteers and regulars from all sections of the country and abroad. Despite political intrigue and bungling military leadership it became the best trained army of the United States up to that date. It participated in the PENINSULAR CAMPAIGN, the Seven Days' Battles, the battles at ANTIETAM and GETTYSBURG, and in the surrender of LEE at APPOMATTOX Courthouse. McClellan was replaced as its commander by General HALLECK in 1862 who was subsequently succeeded by Generals BURNSIDE, HOOKER, MEADE, and GRANT.

Army, United States. The standing land forces of the United States. It does not include draftees or the militia. In 1964 the U.S. Army contained approximately 1,000,000 men. Its table of organization is based on the conventional hierarchical form with the President of the United States as the commander-in-chief at the apex and the enlisted men at the base. Some of the outstanding branches of the army are the Infantry, Artillery, Ordnance, Quartermaster, Signal Corps, Medical Corps, and Military Intelligence. The highest rank is General of the Army, a five star rank. The lowest is that of private. JOHN J. PERSHING held the rank of six star General of the Armies, especially conferred upon him by Congress.

ARNOLD, Benedict. 1741-1801. Revolutionary general and traitor. b. Connecticut. With ETHAN ALLEN, captured FORT TICONDEROGA (1775); leader of the famous march through the Maine forests against Quebec. This campaign was unsuccessful and Arnold was wounded. Brigadier general (1776); although defeated by the British at LAKE CHAMPLAIN, his heroic action delayed the British sufficiently to prevent their invasion

that year. In February, 1777 despite WASHINGTON's protests and Arnold's brilliant record, Congress appointed five brigadier generals to major generalship over Arnold's head. This action embittered him and may have motivated his future treason. Major general (1777) after spectacular opposition to Tryon in his invasion of Connecticut. Aided in forcing BURGOYNE's surrender. In command at Philadelphia (1779); quarrelled with civil authorities; court-martialled and reprimanded. Began correspondence with CLINTON, the British commander. In command at West Point (1780), which he planned to surrender to the British. Plot was discovered by the capture of Major ANDRE (September 23, 1780) and Arnold was forced to flee to the British; led raids in Virginia (1780) and Connecticut (1781 where he burned the town of New London. The rest of his life was spent in poverty and disgrace in England and Canada.

ARNOLD, Henry Harley. 1886-1950. General. b. Pennsylvania. Graduated, U.S.M.A., West Point (1907); commanded U.S. Army Alaskan flight (1934); chief of U.S. Army Air Corps (1938); chief of U.S. Air Forces (June 1941); lieutenant general (1941); general (1943); general of the army (1944); famous during World War II as an outstanding leader and called by his nickname of "Hap" Arnold.

Aroostook War. An undeclared war "fought" in 1839 between Maine and Canada. Following the admission of Maine as a state, in 1820, its legislature granted land to settlers along the Aroostook River in the Aroostook Valley bordering the Canadian province of New Brunswick. In 1839 the dispute area, 10,-000 Maine militia moved into the valley, having obtained federal support in the form of an appropriation of $10,000,000 and a promise of 50,000 men in the

30

event of war. To avoid open fighting General WINFIELD SCOTT was sent by Congress to negotiate a truce with the Canadian government. The resulting agreement was incorporated into the WEBSTER-ASHBURTON TREATY of 1842.

"Arsenal of Democracy." See World War II.

Art. With the exceptions of ARCHITECTURE and cabinetmaking, artistic development in colonial America was seen chiefly in the products of the silversmiths and portrait painters. Primitive portraits were painted and widely accepted as the beginnings of "folk art" in America. Edward Hicks, a Quaker preacher, was outstanding in this style. The late colonial period produced three painters of merit, GILBERT STUART, BENJAMIN WEST, and JOHN SINGLETON COPLEY. From portrait painting in this period, the emphasis shifted to the painting of landscapes. The early 19th century saw the evolution of the "Hudson River School" and the work of such painters as JOHN TRUMBULL and GEORGE CALEB BINGHAM. The realistic school of portrait painting by THOMAS SULLY, and the paintings of birds by JOHN JAMES AUDUBON became well-known. The "GILDED AGE" saw a renascence in art. The younger artists broke away from the limitations of traditional paintings and developed new techniques. Among them were JOHN S. SARGENT, JAMES A. MCNEIL WHISTLER, and THOMAS EAKINS. The landscapes of GEORGE INNIS, seascapes of ALBERT B. RYDER, and watercolors of WINSLOW HOMER dominated this period. In the early 20th century, American painting remained under the influence of European leadership with a distinct tendency toward realism. The leaders of the realistic "Ash Can School" of painting were JOHN SLOAN, ROBERT HENRI, and GEORGE BELLOWS. The modern school of American art, which developed after the famous Armory Show in 1913, sponsored by many outstanding American artists and critics including ARTHUR B. DAVIES and Walter Pach, was influenced by Cezanne and the post-impressionists, include MAX WEBER, JOHN MARIN, MARSDEN HARTLEY, GEORGE GROSZ, EDWARD HOPPER, and Ben Shahn.

ARTHUR, Chester Alan. 1830-1886. 21st President of the United States. b. Fairfield, Vt. Graduated Union College, Schenectady, N. Y.; studied law, and before the Civil War practised in N.Y. City. Collector of the Port of New York (1871-78). At the Republican National Convention in 1880, GARFIELD was nominated for the presidency, and to placate the CONKLING "men" because GRANT had not received the nomination, Arthur was chosen for the vice-presidency. Vice-President of the United States. (Mar. 4-Sept. 18, 1881); on death of Garfield, he became President (1881-85). He had an efficient administration; supported a Civil Service Reform Bill which passed in 1883; and vetoed a Chinese Exclusion Bill which violated a treaty with China.

Articles of Confederation. Name applied to the constitution drawn up by the Second CONTINENTAL CONGRESS in 1781. Provided the basic charter of the thirteen states then in rebellion against Great Britain. The Articles established a loose union of the states with virtually no powers assigned to the central government. The states retained their sovereign powers until this charter was replaced in 1789 by the present Constitution of the United States. See Critical Period, the.

ASBURY, Francis. 1745-1816. First bishop of the Methodist Episcopal church to be consecrated in America. Born in England, he volunteered to go to America where there were about 400 METHODISTS. When asked to return to England before the Revolution, he refused. Became a citizen of Delaware (1778); led formation of Methodist Episcopal Church in the United States (1779-84); consecrated as superintendent at conference in Baltimore (1784); assumed title of Bishop (1785); established the Circuit Rider system, which was excellent for frontier conditions. He started churches from Maine to Georgia and into the West. His excellent organization ability is largely responsible for the way his church has become so strongly intrenched throughout the nation.

ASHE, John. 1720-1781. Revolutionary general. b. North Carolina. Speaker of North Carolina's colonial assembly (1762-65); led opposition to STAMP ACT, became a member of the COMMITTEE OF CORRESPONDENCE and was important in patriot cause. Made brigadier general of North Carolina troops in 1776, but unsuccessful as general. Defeated at Briar Creek enabling British to win Georgia and gain access to the Carolinas.

ASHLEY, James Mitchell. 1824-96. Legislator. b. Pennsylvania. Delegate to the first national Republican convention; served as U.S. Representative (1859-69); governor of Montana territory (1869-70). Ashley prepared and pushed through bill to abolish SLAVERY in DISTRICT OF COLUMBIA (1862); introduced bill to amend the Constitution so as to prohibit slavery and secured its passage 1865; initiated move to impeach President JOHNSON; was one of the radical reconstructionists.

ASHLEY, William Henry. 1778-1838. Fur trader, explorer, politician. b. Virginia. In 1820 he was elected lieutenant governor of Missouri. He sent many famous expeditions out to explore the West. In 1825 he accompanied his expedition, passing west up the Platte and across to Green river. There he held the first rendezvous in the mountains, an innovation in the fur trade. In 1826 he led an expedition to the vicinity of the Great Salt lake. Defeated for governor of Missouri, he was U.S. Representative (1831-37).

ASHMEAD, William Harris. 1855-1908.

Entomologist on the staff of the UNITED STATES DEPARTMENT OF AGRICULTURE in 1887. After 1895 he was assistant curator of insects in the National Museum. Did excellent taxonomical work with new species and wrote *The Monograph of North American Proctotrypidae* (1893).

ASHMUN, Jehudi. 1794-1828. U.S. agent to Liberia. b. New York. Interested in the LIBERIA enterprise of the AMERICAN COLONIZATION SOCIETY, he sailed in 1822 with reinforcements. He repulsed two native attacks and reorganized the colony successfully. He published a *History of the American Colony of Liberia, 1821 to 1823.* (1826).

"As Maine Goes, So Goes the Nation." See MAINE.

ASPINWALL, William Henry. 1807-1875. Merchant and railroad builder. b. New York City. After discovery of gold in California, he set about opening a western route. Obtained a charter, and with associates, built the railroad across Panama and organized the Pacific Mail Steamship Co. With the completion of connections between San Francisco and New York, he held a MONOPOLY on California trade until 1869. He was administration representative to England during the Civil War.

Assembly Line. A method of MANUFACTURING employing the use of long conveyor belts which move a product from the raw material stage to the finished item. As the belt moves along workers, specialized in performing specific functions, add their part to the product until it rolls off the end of the line. The assembly line was first introduced by HENRY FORD in the manufacture of automobiles, and has since spread to virtually every mass production industry in the United States. Its benefits include uniformity of product, specialization of labor, MASS PRODUCTION, low unit cost, and improved quality.

"Assistant President." See War Mobilization, Office of.

Associated Press. A news-gathering agency which supplies news and features to member NEWSPAPERS throughout the United States. Under the name of the New York Associated Press, a group of New York City newspapers coordinated their efforts in 1827 in seeking news from off-shore vessels before they docked. In the 1850's the agency utilized the TELEGRAPH system to bring news from Europe two days before the arrival of ships in New York. By the opening of the Civil War, the Associated Press had enlarged its facilities to cover the entire nation. Although attacked as a MONOPOLY, it grew in importance and power, gaining major control over news-gathering in the United States and Canada. After the defection of the Chicago Associated Press and the Western Associated Press in the last two decades of the 19th century, the agency was reorganized in 1900. Despite the entry into the field of the UNITED PRESS, International News Service, Newspapers Enterprise Association, and lesser press associations, the Associated Press has remained the largest news-gathering medium in the United States. new company, the Anglo-American Telegraph Company, employed the *Great Eastern* to lay a second cable. On July 23, 1865, after laying 1,000 miles of cable, the cable parted and the project was abandoned. The following year a new cable was successfully laid.

Assumption Act. See assumption of state debt.

Assumption of State Debt. The proposal by Secretary of the Treasury, ALEXANDER HAMILTON, that the Congress pay the state debts which had been contracted during the American Revolution. Those states like Virginia, Maryland, Georgia, New Hampshire, and North Carolina, which had paid off their debts in whole or in part by TAXATION and land grants, opposed this scheme. Massachusetts, Connecticut, South Carolina, New York, and New Jersey favored the plan. Ultimately a political agreement between JEFFERSON and Hamilton was reached by which the former consented to support the plan as a *quid pro quo* for the latter's support of a new national capital on the Potomac. By the Assumption Act of 1790, also known as the Funding Act, Congress appropriated $21,500,000 to pay off the entire amount of the outstanding debt.

ASTOR, John Jacob. 1763-1848. Fur trader and financier. b. Germany. Came to the United States (1784); entered fur trade; incorporated AMERICAN FUR COMPANY (1808). Organized Pacific Fur Company (1810) in order to establish a post at Astoria on the Columbia river; lost Astoria to British (1813). In 1813 he aided the United States TREASURY in securing a much needed loan. Invested heavily in New York City real estate and owned vast lands elsewhere. Retired from the American Fur Company in 1834, which had monopolized Mississippi Valley and upper Missouri fur trade. Had acquired the largest fortune in the United States when he retired. A small part of his fortune went into establishing the Astor Library in New York.

ATCHISON, David Rice. 1807-1886. Politician. b. Kentucky. Served in U.S. Senate (1843-55). Chairman of Committee on Indian Affairs after 1846, and was frequently PRESIDENT PRO TEMPORE of the Senate. Instrumental in defeat of BENTON for re-election to the Senate in 1850. Influential in framing of KANSAS-NEBRASKA BILL. Active pro-SLAVERY leader in struggle for control of Kansas. Supported Confederacy during the Civil War.

ATKINSON, Henry. 1782-1842. Army office. Colonel in War of 1812. Commanded Yellowstone expedition of 1824; in general command in the BLACK HAWK WAR; superintended removal of WINNE-

BAGO INDIANS from Wisconsin to Iowa. Founded Jefferson Barracks, Mo. and Fort Leavenworth, Kansas.

Atlantic Charter. A joint declaration of peace aims by President F. D. ROOSEVELT and Prime Minister Churchill. It was signed in August, 1941 and provided for the following: the signatory nations would seek no territory or other aggrandizement, no territorial changes not in accord with the wishes of the inhabitants concerned would be recognized, the right of self-determination of all peoples would be provided for, the restoration of self-government to those who had lost it would be granted, collaboration among the nations for improved labor standards, social security, and economic adjustment would be sought, a peace providing security and freedom from fear and want would follow the defeat of the enemy, FREEDOM OF THE SEAS would be established, and disarmament of potential aggressors established. In its purpose the Atlantic Charter closely resembled President WILSON'S FOURTEEN POINTS, but was couched in general terms. As World War II progressed other nations signified acceptance of the document as an expression of their war aims. Ultimately the 60 members of the UNITED NATIONS subscribed to its objectives.

Atlantic Cable. In 1845 John and Jacob Brett organized the General Oceanic Company to sponsor telegraphic COMMUNICATION between Europe and America. In 1856 they joined CYRUS FIELD in a syndicate organized as the Atlantic Telegraph Company. Construction was begun in February, 1857 between Trinity Bay, Newfoundland and Valentia Bay, Ireland, a distance of 1,640 nautical miles. The cable length was 2,500 nautical miles. The British vessel *Agamemnon* and the *U.S.S. Niagara* were selected for laying the cable. The first message was cabled across the ATLANTIC on August 17, 1858. It read, "Europe and

America are united by TELEGRAPH. Glory to God in the highest; on earth peace and good-will toward men." In 1865 Field's

Atlantic Ocean. The eastern boundary of the United States. It has an area of 31,-830,800 square miles and an average depth of 12,880 feet. Its greatest known depth of 30,246 feet is located off PUERTO RICO. The American area of the ocean is 2,298 square miles and its general coast line is 1,888 miles. The general tidal shore line is 6,370 miles which is increased to 28,377 miles including the shore lines of bays, sounds, and other bodies of water running into the Atlantic Ocean. COLUMBUS' first trip across the ocean took 70 days. In 1946 the *Queen Mary* made a crossing in three days, 15 hours, and 48 minutes.

Atomic Age. The era introduced by the successful development of the ATOMIC BOMB. It is hoped that further development of atomic energy will take place in industrial, transportation, and commercial fields. The latent power sources of atomic energy are virtually unlimited, and provide a potential for economic expansion to an extraordinary degree. It is believed that, if an international atomic energy control agreement is achieved, the peaceful development of mankind will be enormously enhanced by the application of atomic energy to non-military pursuits. The economic exploitation of under-developed areas of the world will be accelerated beyond present means, and the world standard of living increased accordingly.

Atomic Bomb. First constructed in the United States in 1945 after a three year development project which cost $2,000,-000,000. Its production was the result of the combined efforts of some of the world's outstanding physicists and chemists including the German, Lisa Meitner, the Dane, Nils Bohr, the Italian, Enrico Fermi, and many English and Canadian scientists. Famous Americans involved in

34

the original project were ALBERT EIN-STEIN, ROBERT J. OPPENHEIMER, HAROLD UREY, KARL T. COMPTON, ROBERT MILLI-KAN and ARTHUR H. COMPTON. The atomic bomb was first tested in New Mexico on July 16, 1945. Its first military use was the dropping of a bomb on HIROSHIMA, Japan on August 2, 1945. The city of Nagasaki was hit by an atomic bomb on August 9th. Later that year President TRUMAN suggested a world ban on the use of atomic bombs in war, and asked for federal control of atomic development in the United States. At a conference in Washington, D.C. in 1945, President Truman, Prime Minister Attlee, and Prime Minister McKenzie King of Canada agreed that the secret of the atom bomb would not be shared until the UNITED NATIONS had devised a firm control plan. By law the U.S. ATOMIC ENERGY COMMISSION now has complete control over all atomic energy installations in the United States. It has constructed the world's first full scale plant for atomic bombs at the Hanford Engineer Works in the state of Washington. To date the conflicting provisions of the BARUCH PLAN and the various Soviet plans have not been reconciled and there is as yet no international control over atomic bomb construction.

Atomic Energy Commission, U.S. A body of five members established in 1946 by the Act of the Development and Control of Atomic Energy. Also known as the McMahon Bill. The Commission is a civilian body with exclusive authority over fissionable material and the production of ATOMIC BOMBS, and over their production facilities. The Commission is forbidden to distribute fissionable material or information to any foreign government or person without congressional consent. It may not license the use of atomic energy until Congress has studied the proposed project for 90 days. The Commission has cooperated with universities and with INDUSTRY in research projects deal-ing with industrial and medical as well as military possibilities. It has already released certain radio-active substances for research and therapeutical services. There is a military liaison between the Commission and the armed forces although the Commission is itself civilian in composition. It employs 6,800 personnel and spent over $908,000,000 in the 1951 fiscal year. For fiscal year 1953 the executive budget has proposed an expenditure of $5,000,000,000 to $6,000,000,-000 for atomic energy installations and production to be spent over a period of three years. On April 22, 1952 the Commission announced that it was negotiating with the Dow Chemical Company and Detroit Edison Company to continue jointly financed research aimed at bringing atomic power into industrial use. For the fiscal year 1965 Congress authorized $2,637,000,000 for plant and capital equipment and operating expenses.

Attica Prison. In 1971 at the Attica Correctional Facility in New York State 1,200 inmates held 38 guards hostage. 43 Persons including 9 prison guards who had been held as hostage died and 80 others suffered gunshot wounds. The 4-day rebellion ended on September 13 when New York State troopers and police stormed the prison. Subsequent investigations showed that nearly all including the guards had been killed by troopers' bullets. Civil Rights groups strongly criticized the handling of the revolt by Governor Nelson Rockefeller and demanded prison reform.

Attorney General's List of Subversive Organizations. A list of organizations which the Attorney General of the United States designates as totalitarian, Fascist, Communist, or subversive after appropriate investigation and determination. The Attorney General was charged with preparing this list by an EXECUTIVE ORDER in 1947. Acting under this directive, he issued a list of proscribed organizations which, by 1952, totalled 115. The directive and the methods employed in preparing the list were attacked as unconstitutional. It has been charged that the list was compiled without any notice or hearing to the organizations concerned and with no disclosure by the Attorney General of the criteria employed or the evidence upon which the listing was based. On April 30, 1951 the Supreme Court ruled that three of the organizations listed had been denied the opportunity to prove themselves non-Communist.

Attorney-General, U.S. Office established by Congress in 1789. It was one of the first four executive heads of government. At that time the Attorney-General did not preside over an EXECUTIVE DEPARTMENT. In 1814 he was made a member of the cabinet. In 1870 he became the executive head of the newly established DEPARTMENT OF JUSTICE. He is the chief law officer of the federal government, representing it in legal matters, and giving advice and opinions to the President and to executive heads. He administers the work of United States attorneys and marshals in the judicial districts, and provides special counsel for the federal government when the nature of specific legal matters requires it. This office has been a stepping-stone to the Supreme Court bench as in the case of Tom Clark, Francis Biddle, and Frank Murphy.

ATWATER, Wilbur Olin. 1844-1907. Chemist, important for his work in agricultural chemistry. b. New York. Founded government research stations studying especially animal nutrition. First director of office of Experiment Stations, U.S. DEPARTMENT OF AGRICULTURE (1888). Co-inventor of Atwater-Rosa calorimeter, by which he demonstrated the law of the conservation of energy in human metabolism.

AUDUBON, John James. 1785-1851. Ornithologist and artist. Educated in France. Came to the United States (1804) to father's estate near Philadelphia, where he conducted first American bird-banding experiments. To Kentucky (1808) where he was unsuccessful in business, but began painting birds. Traveled down the Mississippi observing and painting birds; tutor and drawing teacher in New Orleans. *Birds of America* published (1827-38), the accompanying text called *Ornithological Biography* (5 vols.) (1831-39) was prepared in Edinburgh, in collaboration with William MacFillivray, who was responsible for its more scientific information. *Synopsis of the Birds of North America* (1839) made him famous. Settled on his estate, now Audubon Park, N. Y. City (1841-51) working on but not completing *The Viparous Quadripeds of North America* (with John Bachman).

AUSTIN, Moses. 1761-1821. Pioneer. b. Connecticut. Worked in Virginia developing lead mines; moved to Missouri; went to Texas where he received a grant of land to settle 300 families but died before he could carry out his plans. See Austin, Stephen.

AUSTIN, Stephen Fuller. 1793-1836. Colonizer and leader of Texas. b. Virginia. Grew up in Missouri; served in territorial legislature (1814-20); took over his father's (Moses) plans and founded the first American settlement in Texas (1822); he had settled over 1,000 families (by 1833); sent to Mexico City to petition for a separate government for the TERRITORY, but was imprisoned; released and returned; defeated for the presidency of Texas by SAM HOUSTON.

Australian Ballot. Introduced in 1888. Provides for secret voting. Strongly opposed in its earlier days by PARTY MACHINES but has been generally accepted in the last half century as a victorious step forward in democratic political reform. Originally developed in Australia in the 1880's.

Automobile Industry. Although the automobile industry did not become important until the development of the internal combustion engine, designs for steam-driven vehicles had been made as early as the 1780's. The Germans and French pioneered the gasoline-powered engine in the 1870's and 1880's. Gottfried Daimler built a gasoline-driven motor cycle in 1885. The following year Carl Benz built the first gasoline-powered automobile. In the United States Charles E. and Frank Duryea constructed and operated the first automobile in 1892. In that decade HENRY FORD (1893) and ELWOOD HAYNES (1894) built automobiles powered by internal combustion gasoline engines. The absence of good ROADS and the economy and efficiency of railroad TRANSPORTATION prevented a rapid extension of automobile construction until the turn of the 20th century. By the opening of World War I there were more than 70 automobile MANUFACTURING companies in the United States producing almost 200,000 vehicles annually. The automobile gained quick appeal. Local and national automobile clubs were organized throughout the nation, speed contests were held, and trade magazines appeared in large numbers. This interest stimulated a legislative program aimed at road improvement, and regulation of the new transportation medium. The companies, which were later to achieve international recognition as the industry's leaders, came into being in this period. The Packard Motor Car Company was organized in 1900 and was quickly followed by Ford and Cadillac (1903), Buick and Studebaker (1904), Willys-Overland (1908), and GENERAL MOTORS and Hudson (1809). The failures of rival companies were numerous because of inferior organization and improper

financing. PATENT conflicts and sharp competition involved the INDUSTRY in extended litigation up to the eve of World War I. The result was a decline in production and an increase in business failures until the demand for automobiles created by the War produced an upswing. The MASS PRODUCTION techniques of Henry Ford, based on the use of specialized labor, automatic machinery, interchangeable parts, standardized production, and the assembly line, made the industry the world's largest after the War. In 1920, 84 companies manufactured almost 2,000,000 vehicles valued at $1,900,000,000. The United States became the world's largest manufacturer and exporter of passenger and commercial automotive vehicles. Mass production made the automobile available to medium and low income groups. Improvements in roads combined with low prices to stimulate production. Despite the reduction in output during the GREAT DEPRESSION more than 5,000,000 vehicles, with a value of $3,000,000,000, were manufactured in 1937. In that year 30,-000,000 vehicles were registered in the United States, of which 25,500,000 were passenger cars. The federal, state, and municipal governments had merged their facilities in the construction and improvement of over 1,000,000 miles of automobile HIGHWAYS. The production of trucks and buses made deep inroads into railroad freight transportation. For the American people new RECREATION and business opportunities were opened up on a spectacular scale. The industry created new jobs and stimulated the development of auxiliary industries such as RUBBER, nickel, STEEL, fabrics, paint, oil and machinery. By 1965, the leadership of the industry had been concentrated in the hands of three major producers: General Motors, Ford, and Chrysler. In 1955 about 9,188,000 motor vehicles were built in the United States, or nearly 1,000,000 more units than were produced in the record year of 1950. In 1964 passenger car sales exceeded 8.1 million. Nearly 500,000 of these units were imported. Sales during the first quarter of 1965 exceeded those of the same period in 1964.

AVERELL, William Woods. 1832-1900. Union general in the Civil War. Graduated U.S.M.A. West Point (1855) and saw service against the Indians in the Southwest. Won brilliant engagements at Kelly's Ford (1863); commanded a cavalry division in SHERIDAN's famous operations in the valley, taking a major part in the battles of Winchester, Moorfield and Fisher's Hill, winning major general's rank in U.S. Army. Resigned (1865); consul general at Montreal (1865-68); financially independent through asphalt paving patents.

Aviation. In 1783 Jean Pilâtre de Rozier flew five and one half miles in 20 minutes in the first human balloon flight. In 1852 Henry Giffard flew a steam-powered dirigible in France. In 1860 Samuel Archer King and William Black made two photographs of Boston from a balloon. The first major experiments in airplane construction were undertaken by SAMUEL P. LANGLEY between 1887 and 1903 with the aid of a federal subsidy. In 1903 WILBUR and ORVILLE WRIGHT accomplished the first heavier-than-air flight at Kittyhawk, North Carolina. In 1909 the Wright Brothers sold the first plane to the federal government. The following year Glenn H. Curtis flew a plane from Albany to New York at an average speed of 49 miles per hour. In this period the emphasis in the United States was on the construction of seaplanes. For a long time patent conflicts between the Wrights and Curtis inhibited the growth of the industry, and most flights were privately undertaken as experimental or exhibition contests. In 1910 Eugene Ely flew a Curtis plane from the deck of the cruiser Birmingham to Norfolk, Virginia. In 1911 Galbraith P. Rogers flew from New York to California in 68 days with an elapsed flying time of 49 days. In 1923 an army plane flew non-stop from New York to San Diego in 26 hours and 50 minutes. By 1939 this trip had been reduced to seven and one-half hours. Altitude records were rapidly increased after 1912 when Lincoln Beachy attained 11,642 feet. By 1930 the record was 43,166 feet. On August 15, 1951 a United States army plane attained a record of 77,500 feet. In 1919 a navy seaplane was the first to cross the Atlantic. In 1924 two army planes circumnavigated the globe in an elapsed time of 15 days and 11 hours and a total time of 175 days. In 1933 WILEY POST made the first round-the-world solo flight in seven days and 18 hours. In 1938 Howard R. Hughes flew around the world in three days and 19 hours. In 1949 Captain James Gallagher flew a Boeing B-50A from Fort Worth, Texas in the first round-the-world non-stop flight. The time was 94 hours and one minute. He required four air refuelings. Military aviation received its first major test in World War I and became an integral part of offensive action by all the armies in World War II. On November 8, 1950 the first jet plane battle took place in Korea. The first air mail was carried in May, 1918 and, with federal GRANT-IN-AID, developed into an important branch of the postal service. In the 1950's the development of supersonic planes with speeds in excess of 600 miles per hour had revolutionized the INDUSTRY. In this period the industry developed radar-controlled planes, guided missiles, and planes operated by remote control. Jet planes were rapidly introduced into military service and more slowly into commercial transport. Experiments were being undertaken to furnish nuclear energy to power planes. Air transport became a serious rival to land and sea TRANSPORTATION services. The continuing high rate of aircraft accidents had created a serious problem of public welfare as huge airports moved ever closer to urban centers. The La Guardia and New York International (Idlewild) Airports in New York City were the largest in the world. The United States was the largest producer of military and commercial aircraft in the world. In 1944 it manufactured 96,-318 military airplanes, the single highest annual production iñ its history. The largest peace-time production was reached in 1946 when 36,644 military, personal, and transport planes were manufactured. Between 1940 and 1945 a total of 303,218 military planes were produced. In 1963 scheduled airlines amassed a total of nearly 50,000,000,000 passenger miles, an increase of 50 per cent over 1960.

Axis Powers. The alliance between Germany and Italy which began in the political collaboration between these two powers during the Italian invasion of Abyssinia in 1936 and continued during the Spanish Civil War from 1936 to 1939. The Axis became effective in December, 1937 after Italy's withdrawal from the LEAGUE OF NATIONS. After the attack on PEARL HARBOR Japan became a member of the Axis Powers.

B

BABBITT, Irving. 1865-1933. Scholar and educator. b. Ohio. Graduated Harvard (1889). Taught French at Harvard (1894-1933); professor of French literature (from 1912). Founded (with Paul Elmer More) modern humanistic movement. Author of *Literature and the American College* (1908), *The Masters of Modern French Criticism* (1912) and *Democracy and Leadership* (1924). He greatly influenced American literary criticism (1929-1931).

BABCOCK, Stephen Moulton. 1843-1931. Agricultural chemist. b. New York. Professor of agricultural chemistry, University of Wisconsin (1887-1913); chief chemist of the Wisconsin Agricultural Experiment Station. Known chiefly for the *Babcock test* for butter fat content of milk (1890), which is a basic development in the modern dairy industry.

BACHE, Alexander Dallas. 1806-1867. Physicist, educator, established first American magnetic observatory. b. Philadelphia, Pa. Professor University of Pennsylvania (1828-36). President, Girard College (1836-42). Developed a system of free education in the public schools of Philadelphia. Superintendent, U.S. Coast Survey (1843-67). A founder of the National Academy of Sciences, and its first president; president of the AMERICAN PHILOSOPHICAL SOCIETY.

BACHE, Richard. 1737-1811. Merchant. In Philadelphia he developed a mercantile business which had a large West India trade. Married Sarah, daughter of BENJAMIN FRANKLIN (1767). Favored patriotic viewpoint during the Revolution and served on many committees including the Board of War. Succeeded Franklin as Postmaster General (1776-82).

back country. See Piedmont region.

"back pay steal." See "salary grab" act.

BACON, Henry. 1866-1924. Architect. b. Illinois. Designer of the Lincoln Memorial, Washington, D.C. Designer of many important buildings. Presented in 1923, by President of the United States, with gold medal of the American Institute of Architects.

BACON, Nathaniel. 1647-1676. Colonial planter and leader of BACON'S REBELLION. Emigrated to America (1673); settled in Virginia at "Curles Neck" on the James River. Tried to force Governor BERKELEY to protect the colonists against the Indians; when he refused, Bacon and others took the field on their own and were declared rebels. While working out conciliatory policy, he died. See BACON'S REBELLION.

Bacon's Rebellion. An uprising of 300 volunteer farmers and frontiersmen under the leadership of NATHANIEL BACON in 1675. The refusal of Governor WILLIAM BERKELEY of Virginia to send troops

40

against the Susquehannock Indians, who were attacking the upper settlements of the colony, prompted Bacon's march against these Indians without any commission. Despite Bacon's victory he was branded a rebel by the governor who set a price on his head. The Civil War which followed resulted in the expulsion of the governor from his capital and in the burning of Jamestown by Bacon's forces. Bacon's death at that point resulted in the collapse of the movement. Berkeley's return led to the arrest and execution of Bacon's followers although the "old and rotten" assembly and the subsequent recall of the governor were two important results of the rebellion.

BAEKELAND, Leo Hendrick. 1863-1944. Chemist and inventor of *Bakelite*. Born in Belgium. Educated at the University of Ghent. Came to the United States (1889); research in the field of photography; developed very sensitive photographic papers which he manufactured; best known for his discovery of the synthetic resin *Bakelite*.

BAER, George Frederick. 1842-1914. Lawyer and industrialist. b. Pennsylvania. Lawyer for MORGAN interests; president of the Reading RR, and mining properties. Known for his part in opposing the UNITED MINE WORKERS OF AMERICA in the great ANTHRACITE COAL STRIKE of 1902. His statements helped win support for the miners.

BAILEY, Ann. 1742-1825. Frontier heroine. Came from England to the western border of Virginia (1761). After the death of her husband, she dressed as a man and acted as a border messenger; was involved in many remarkable exploits. When Indians were attacking Fort Lee, she escaped alone, rode 100 miles to Lewisburg, got fresh supply of gun powder and returned alone. She had saved the fort.

BAILEY, Gamaliel. 1807-59. Antislavery journalist. b. New Jersey. Founded (with JAMES BIRNEY) *Cincinnati Philanthropist*, first antislavery paper in the west (1836-46). Mobs constantly attacked their offices, and at one time it was completely destroyed. Edited *National Era*, a Washington, D.C., weekly journal, under the auspices of the AMERICAN ANTI-SLAVERY SOCIETY. He was an excellent editor, and his fair-minded opinions had far reaching influence.

BAILEY, Joseph Weldon. 1863-1929. Political leader. b. Mississippi. Elected to Congress (1890); minority leader (1896). FREE-SILVER advocate; important influence on BRYAN. After Spanish-American war he led Democratic opposition to imperialism. During administration of TAFT and ROOSEVELT, he was opposition leader in Congress. Opposed WILSON, becoming increasingly conservative.

BAILEY, Theodorus. 1805-77. Naval commander. Famous for command of Gulf blockade squadron (1862). Commanded the *Lexington* during the Mexican War; commanded *Colorado* during the Civil War and led the gunboat *Cayuga* thru Confederate forces. Promoted to rear-admiral (1866), but retired.

Bailey vs. Drexel Furniture Company. A decision of the United States Supreme Court in 1922 in which it held unconstitutional the SECOND CHILD LABOR LAW. The court's decision was based on the grounds that Congress was attempting "to regulate child labor through the use of the so-called tax as a penalty." The tax was held not to have been legally imposed for the purpose of raising revenue, but as a penal law directed against child labor, an area over which Congress had no direct constitutional control. Congress was therefore, in effect, invading the rights of the states, and thereby violating the tenth amendment of the Constitution as well as Article I, Section 8, Clause 1.

BAINBRIDGE, William. 1774-1833. Naval officer. b. New Jersey. His capture by Turkish potentate and the indignation of the United States caused by this episode, resulted in the WAR WITH TRIPOLI. Commanded the *Constitution* and 2 other vessels during War of 1812.

BAIRD, Henry Carey. 1825-1912. Publisher and economist. Believed in a nationalist economy based on a PROTECTIVE TARIFF and managed CURRENCY. Frequently testified before congressional committees; founder of the GREENBACK party; supporter of FREE SILVER movement. Author of *Political Economy* (1875); and *Money and Bank Credit* (1891).

BAIRD, Spencer Fullerton. 1823-1887. Zoologist. b. Pennsylvania. Assistant secretary of the SMITHSONIAN INSTITUTION (1850); secretary (1878). First U.S. Fish Commissioner (1871-1887). Author of 1,000 scientific writings, including *North American Reptiles* (1851); *Catalogue of North American Mammals* (1857). Started Baird system of accurate ornithological description.

BAKER, Edward Dickinson. 1811-61. Senator and soldier. b. England. Came to the United States (1815). Famous lawyer in Springfield, Illinois in LINCOLN's time. Served in both state house and state senate; defeated Lincoln (1844) for Republican nomination; elected to Congress. Resigned to lead a regiment in the Mexican War; commander at Cerro Gordo. In 1852 he went to California where he became prominent Republican leader. Moved to Oregon (1860), elected U.S. Senator; friendly to Lincoln, being his only supporter from the west; raised the first California Regiment during the Civil War and was made a colonel. Killed in action at Balls Bluff.

BAKER, George Fisher. 1840-1931. Financier. b. New York. One of the founders of the First National Bank, N. Y.; president (1877), board chairman (1909). He made First National Bank one of the strongest financial institutions in this country. Associated with MORGAN and HILL in many enterprises. He gave $6,000,000 to found and endow the Graduate School of Business Administration at Harvard University. Baker Field of Columbia University was also a gift from him.

BAKER, Newton Diehl. 1871-1937. Statesman. b. West Virginia. Graduated Johns Hopkins University (1892); LL.B. Washington and Lee (1894); practised in Cleveland, Ohio; city solicitor (1902-12) and mayor (1912-16). U.S. Secretary of War (1916-21). Strong advocate of LEAGUE OF NATIONS; member, PERMANENT COURT OF ARBITRATION at The Hague (1928). Appointed by HOOVER member of Law Enforcement Commission. Awarded medal by National Institute of Social Sciences (1933) "for services to humanity."

BAKER, R. Stannard. 1870-1946. Author. b. Michigan. Joined staff of *McClure's Magazine* (1897) and became famous contributor of the "muckraking" period, attacking railroad and financial abuses of the period, in the *American Magazine* (1906-15); director of press bureau for American Commission to Negotiate Peace, Paris (1919). Biographer of WOODROW WILSON. Author of *Woodrow Wilson and World Settlement, a History of the Peace Conference* (3 vols. 1922); and, under the name of David Grayson, *Adventures in Understanding* (1925), and *Adventures in Solitude* (1931).

balance of trade. Refers to the difference between exports and imports. Is called unfavorable balance of trade when there is a surplus of imports over exports and favorable balance when the exports exceed the imports. Up to the period immediately preceding World War I the U.S. experienced unfavorable trade balances (including "invisible" items) which were reversed in the post-war period.

After World War II the surplus of exports over imports ranged from $12,000,-000,000 to $15,000,000,000.

BALBOA, Vasco Nunez de. 1475-1517. Spanish explorer, discoverer of the Pacific Ocean. Sailed to America with Bastidas (1500); settled in Hispaniola. To Darien (1510) governor of settlement (1512). Discovered the Pacific Ocean (Sept. 25, 1513). Made other explorations of discovery; served under Pedarias, new governor of Panama. Fought with him and accused of sedition (probably unjustiied); condemned and executed.

ALDWIN, Abraham. 1754-1807. Statesman. b. Connecticut. Member from Georgia of the CONTINENTAL CONGRESS. Leading delegate to FEDERAL CONSTITUTIONAL CONVENTION. His change of vote resulted in a tie in his committee, causing the framing of the compromise system of representation, by states in the senate, and by population in the house. Elected to first U.S. House of Representatives (1790-99); U.S. Senate (1799-1807). Supported JEFFERSON's policies. A founder of the University of Georgia.

BALDWIN, James Mark. 1861-1934. Psychologist. b. South Carolina. Graduated Princeton University (1884) Ph.D (1889); taught philosophy, University of Toronto (1889-93); founding the first psychological laboratory in the British empire. Taught at Princeton (1893-1903) where he established a psychological laboratory. Taught at Johns Hopkins University (1903-09) and National University of Mexico (1903-13). Specialist in child and social psychology. A founder and editor of the *Psychological Review* (1894-1909). Editor of *Dictionary of Philosophy and Psychology* (1901-06).

BALDWIN, Simeon Eben. 1840-1927. Jurist. b. Connecticut. Professor, Yale Law School (1869-1919). He is chiefly responsible for its success. Associate Justice of the supreme court of Connecticut (1893-1907) chief justice (1907-10). One of the founders of the American Bar Association, and its president (1890). Governor of Connecticut (1910-14). Author of *Modern Political Institutions* (1898), *American Railroad Law* (1904), and *The American Judiciary* (1905).

Ball-Burton-Hatch-Hill Resolution. A bipartisan resolution submitted in 1943 calling for the establishment of a UNITED NATIONS agency for various purposes. These purposes included the furnishing of funds and materials for relief and rehabilitation, the establishment of machinery for the peaceful settlement of international disputes, and the creation of a United Nations military force for the suppression of aggression. The Resolution was defeated in the Senate as too strong an expression of internationalism, and was replaced by the CONNALLY RESOLUTION.

Ballinger-Pinchot Controversy. In August, 1909 GIFFORD PINCHOT, chief of the Division of Forestry, accused Secretary of the Interior RICHARD BALLINGER of collaboration with groups seeking to plunder the public domain, and attacked him for reopening for sale public lands which had been previously withdrawn by President T. ROOSEVELT. Ballinger was also charged with favoring the wealthy Cunningham syndicate in patents on valuable COAL lands in ALASKA, and with refusing to protect WATER POWER sites. After an investigation, President TAFT supported Ballinger and dismissed Pinchot for insubordination. Pinchot, an INSURGENT Republican and close personal and political intimate of Roosevelt, publicly condemned Ballinger and was supported by friends in Congress who influenced Taft to appoint an investigating committee. The committee exonerated Ballinger, but later investigations resulted in cancellation of the Cunningham claims. Although Ballinger subsequently resigned, the controversy contributed to the split between Taft and Roosevelt which culminated in the formation of the PROGRESSIVE PARTY in 1912.

BALLINGER, Richard Achilles. 1858-1922. Cabinet officer. b. Iowa. Mayor of Seattle (1904-06); U.S. Secretary of the Interior under TAFT (1909-11). Accused by L. R. Glavis and GIFFORD PINCHOT, of the Land Office, of impeding investigation of certain coal lands in ALASKA. Articles in *Collier's Weekly* by Glavis aroused public opinion. President Taft upheld Ballinger, and Glavis was dismissed. A joint committee of the two houses of Congress exonerated Ballinger. He resigned in 1911. This incident worked against Taft politically in 1912.

ballot. The instrument used in voting. Historically, miscellaneous material such as balls and grains of corn were employed, giving way later to written papers. The first use of the ballot in America was in the election of the pastor of the Salem Church in 1629. This and subsequent balloting *viva voce*, prevailed until the introduction in 1888 of the AUSTRALIAN or secret BALLOT into American states. In recent years the use of automatic voting machines has replaced the paper ballot in many states.

Baltimore and Ohio Railroad. An important eastern railroad in the United States. It was chartered in 1827 to run a line from Baltimore to the Ohio country. The line played an important role in opening the Ohio Valley by providing a rapid and efficient means of TRANSPORTATION for new settlers. In the 1880's it was extended westward to Chicago and, by agreements with other RAILROADS, eastward to Philadelphia and New York.

Baltimore Incident, The. A diplomatic dispute between the United States and Chile arising out of an attack in Valparaiso, Chile in 1891 upon American sailors from the cruiser *Baltimore*. Secretary of State BLAINE demanded an apology for the insult and an indemnity for the two dead and 18 wounded Americans. The

refusal of the Chilean government to discuss the matter resulted in an American ultimatum to Chile. The readying of a squadron of eight American cruisers threatened war for a time. The firm American attitude, however, caused the Chilean government to open negotiations which ended in an apology.

Balzac vs. Puerto Rico. See Insular Cases.

BANCROFT, Edward. 1744-1821. Scientist and secret agent. b. Massachusetts. Settled in Dutch Guiana; wrote *Natural History of Guiana* (1769). Settled in London; discovered important dyes used in the manufacture of textiles. Friend of BENJAMIN FRANKLIN and SILAS DEANE the American commissioners in Paris. Taken into their pay, entrusted with secretarial duties, and sent repeatedly to London to gather information for the United States (1776-78). Never suspected by Americans or French as being a British spy, simultaneously. It was revealed by Paul Ford in 1891.

BANCROFT, George. 1800-1891. Historian and statesman. b. Massachusetts. Graduated Harvard (1817) Ph.D. University of Gottingen (1820). Teacher (1822-31); published *History of the United States* (3 vols. 1834-40). Appointed collector of the port, Boston (1837). U.S. Secretary of the Navy in POLK's cabinet (1845-46); established U.S. Naval Academy, Annapolis. U.S. Minister to Great Britain (1846-49). Supported LINCOLN through Civil War. Wrote first annual message as President for ANDREW JOHNSON (1865). U.S. Minister to Germany (1867-74). Added volumes to history and revised into 6 volumes (1876). Additional works include *History of the Formation of the Constitution of the U.S.* (2 vols. 1882), *Martin Van Buren to the End of his Public Career.* (1889)

bank failures. The financial insolvency of banks resulting from over expansion, excessive speculation, business depressions, poor investment, or administrative malpractices. In the United States such failures have characterized the banking industry from its inception. From 1789 to the Civil War it has been estimated that the losses to the holders of CURRENCY averaged five percent annually. Federal regulation in the form of the NATIONAL BANKING SYSTEM, the FEDERAL RESERVE SYSTEM, the GLASS-STEAGALL ACT, and the BANKING ACT OF 1935 has served to reduce such failures, but not to eliminate them. By 1882, for example, 487 national banks had gone into either voluntary or involuntary bankruptcy. The DEPRESSION OF 1893 alone produced over 600 failures. After the establishment of the Federal Reserve System only the year 1918 saw no failures. From the end of World War I to the onset of the GREAT DEPRESSION the United States saw 11,000 bank failures, climaxed in 1930 by the largest collapse in American history, that of the Bank of United States. The greatest improvement in the record of bank failures has occurred since 1933 as a result of the NEW DEAL legislation in this field.

Bankhead Cotton Act. Passed by Congress in 1934 as a supplement to the AGRICULTURAL ADJUSTMENT ACT. It provided for a national quota of cotton production, and imposed a tax equal to 50 percent of the market price upon cotton produced in excess of the individual quota. No tax was to be less than five cents per pound. The Act was part of the early NEW DEAL program designed to accelerate agricultural recovery. Upon the Supreme Court's invalidation of the Agricultural Adjustment Act Congress repealed the Bankhead Act in 1936.

Bankhead-Jones Act. A law of Congress in 1937 which authorized the Soil Conservation Service to buy submarginal cutover lands which are no longer capable of maintaining satisfactory living standards for FARMERS. It provided further for the development of such lands in co-operation with state and local agencies. This aspect of the program has contributed greatly to the redevelopment of the Dust Bowl Area of the Great Plains and the Southwest. The Act also authorized the FEDERAL SECURITY ADMINISTRATION to lend funds at low interest rates to SHARE-CROPPERS and TENANT FARMERS.

"bank holiday." Refers to the closing of the nation's banks between March 6th and March 15, 1933. Over 5,100 banks with deposits of $3,250,000,000 had failed in 1930-32, in the early period of the "GREAT DEPRESSION." In the two weeks preceding the bank holiday, 21 states and the District of Columbia had declared banking moratoria or had imposed special regulations controlling banking operations.

banking. The first American bank was the Bank of North America at Philadelphia in 1781. The participation of the federal government in banking activities began with the establishment of the first BANK OF THE UNITED STATES in 1791 with its principal branch at Philadelphia. After 1800 the exploitation of the resources of the Mississippi Valley required greater credit facilities. These were met by the chartering of banks by the states. The second Bank of the United States competed with these institutions after 1816, but with the expiration of its charter in 1836 state banks once more furnished the principal credit and CURRENCY facilities of the nation. The rapid expansion of "WILD-CAT BANKS" and the rise of JACKSON'S "PET BANKS" created an overexpansion of credit and currency which led to the PANIC OF 1837. The National BANKING ACT OF 1863 once more brought the federal government into direct banking operations. In 1914 the FEDERAL RESERVE SYSTEM attempted to correct some of the defects of the national banking system. Farm banking has taken many forms, the first of these being the twelve federal farm banks established in 1916 under the FEDERAL FARM LOAN ACT. The AGRI-CULTURAL ACT of 1923 and other farm credit agencies were merged into the FARM CREDIT ADMINISTRATION in 1933. In 1932 the RECONSTRUCTION FINANCE CORPORATION was established to provide easy credit to depressed industries. The NEW DEAL administrations witnessed the greatest development of federal participation and regulation of banking activities. Important legislation included the BANK-ING ACTS OF 1933 AND 1935, SECURITIES ACT OF 1933, SECURITIES AND EXCHANGE ACT OF 1934, and important legislation establishing the EXPORT-IMPORT BANK and modifying the organization, functions, and powers of the Federal Reserve System. POSTAL SAVINGS BANKS were established in 1910. The largest private bank in the United States is the Bank of America National Trust and Savings Association operated by the Giannini family in California. In 1962 there were a total 13,422 commercial banks in the United States. The total assets of these banks were $252,493,000,000, their deposits $229,310,000,000.

Banking Act of 1933. See Glass-Steagall Act.

Banking Act of 1935. An Act which reorganized the Federal Reserve Board into a seven man Federal Reserve Board of Governors, eliminating the SECRETARY OF THE TREASURY and the COMPTROLLER from their ex-officio membership. It created a Federal Open Market Committee consisting of the seven members of the Board of Governors and five elected representatives of the twelve regional banks. This committee was authorized to control credit fluctuations by purchasing and selling government obligations in the open · market and where necessary, to limit speculation by doubling the required reserves percentage. The Act per-mitted national banks to make real estate loans, but prohibited them from engaging in the business of underwriting securities.

Bank for International Settlements. An international bank incorporated and chartered in Switzerland in 1930 as provided by the YOUNG PLAN of the previous year. Its initial authorized capital was $100,-000,000 of which $25,000,000 was immediately subscribed. Of its 39 member banks, 24 are located in Europe, 14 in Japan, the 15th being The First National Bank of New York. Its board of directors consists of the executive officers of the central banks of Belgium, England, France, Germany, Italy, Japan, a representative of the United States, and 16 other directors jointly chosen by the aforementioned officers and the member banks. The bank was founded to assist the transfer of international funds, to act as trustees for German REPARATIONS payments, and to foster the cooperation of central banks. It does not issue notes, make loans to governments, or accept bills of exchange.

banking reform. Various movements aimed at improving banking operations for the purposes of providing sound CUR-RENCY, stable credit activities, protection of savings, and financial stability. Such reforms have frequently involved the federal and state governments in direct banking operations as well as in regulatory activities. From the beginning of its history the United States, by chartering the first BANK OF THE UNITED STATES in 1791, participated actively in the nation's banking. Thereafter, it has continued its interest by providing for the National Banking System, the FEDERAL RESERVE SYSTEM, and wholly owned federal banking corporations such as the RECONSTRUCTION FINANCE CORPORATION and the EXPORT-IMPORT BANK. State banking regulation is exercised through the work of state banking commissions.

Bank of the United States. First charter

granted by Congress in 1791, expiring in 1811. Second Bank of the United States chartered in 1816 expiring in 1836. The Bank acted as a depository for federal funds. Twenty percent of its invested capital of $10,000,000 was subscribed by Congress. The first Bank was established as part of HAMILTON'S ECONOMIC PROGRAM, being strongly opposed by the JEFFERSONIAN REPUBLICANS. The second Bank, chartered during the "ERA OF GOOD FEELING," was supported by all political segments of the population, but was later bitterly attacked by JACKSON who accused it after the election of 1832, of having meddled in that election, and of having established a MONOPOLY over banking in the United States. Jackson succeeded in destroying the Second Bank of the United States.

BANKS, Nathaniel Prentiss. 1816-1894. Civil War general and Congressman. b. Massachusetts. Representative to Congress (1853-57), Speaker (1856); governor of Massachusetts (1858-61). Served as major general in Civil War capturing Port Hudson (1863). Again member of the U.S. House of Representatives (1865-73; 75-79; 89-91).

Baptists. The first Baptist Church in America was founded in 1638 in Providence, Rhode Island by ROGER WILLIAMS. In 1787, an offshoot known as the Free-Will Baptists was organized in New Hampshire by Benjamin Randall. In 1814 a General Missionary Convention was called to permit followers to declare their desires. In 1845 Southern Baptists withdrew from the General Missionary Convention over the question of SLAVERY and formed the Southern Baptist Convention. In 1880 the National Baptist Convention, U.S.A., Inc. was founded in Montgomery, Alabama as the parent body of Negro Baptists in the United States. In May, 1950 the American Baptist Convention succeeded the Northern Baptist Convention, which had been organized in 1907,

as the body coordinating the activities of northern and western Baptists. There are many other Baptist organizations in the United States which conduct missionary, evangelical, and publishing activities. Theological conflicts among them have prevented the merging of their work. In 1964 there were more than 22,000,000 Baptists in the United States.

Barbary Wars. See Tripoli, Wars with.

barbed wire. Introduced in the 1870's to keep live stock out of newly developed agricultural areas. It served as an invaluable instrument in the development of farm production at the end of the 19th century by fencing in such areas. For a time a bitter struggle raged between RANCHERS and FARMERS as a result of the use of barbed wire.

BARCLAY, Thomas. 1753-1830. Loyalist and British official. Served as captain and major in the British Army during Revolution. Settled with other LOYALISTS in Nova Scotia. Appointed commissioner for Great Britain to carry out terms of the JAY'S TREATY. Appointed consul general for Great Britain in New York City (1799-1830). His *Correspondence* (published 1894) gives a clear picture of Anglo-American relations in his time.

BARD, Samuel. 1742-1821. Physician to GEORGE WASHINGTON; after the Revolution he founded the first medical school in New York. Also founded the New York Hospital and the New York Dispensary.

BARKER, Albert Smith. 1843-1916. Naval commander. Served during the Civil War; took part in capture of NEW ORLEANS and Port Hudson; commanded the *Enterprise* (1882-86) and ran a line of deep-sea soundings around the globe. At opening of Spanish-American War he was made a member of the Board of Strategy of the Navy. Commanded the cruiser *Newark* in bombardment of SAN-

TIAGO; relieved ADMIRAL DEWEY as commander of the Asiatic fleet (1899); commander of North Atlantic fleet (1903); retired (1905). Raised to rank of rear admiral (1905).

BARKLEY, Alben William. 1877-1956. Political leader. b. Kentucky. Graduated, Marvin College (1897); studied law at Emory College and the University of Virginia (1897-1903); county prosecuting attorney (1905-09); judge, Kentucky (1909-13); member House of Representatives (1913-27); U.S. Senator (1927-49); leader in the Democratic party and supporter of NEW DEAL legislation; majority leader (1937-46); elected Vice-President of the United States (1949-53), elected to U. S. Senate (1954-1956).

BARLOW, Francis Channing. 1834-1896. Civil War general and New York state official. Made brigadier general of volunteers for gallantry at ANTIETAM; commanded a brigade at GETTYSBURG where he was believed dead and left on the field. Commanded a division under HANCOCK in the WILDERNESS campaign; made major general at end of war. Secretary of State in New York (1865); attorney-general (1871). Prosecuted TWEED RING.

BARLOW, Joel. 1754-1812. Poet and diplomat. b. Connecticut. Served in American Revolution. Appointed (1795) U. S. consul to Algeria; negotiated treaties with Algiers, Tunis and Tripoli. U. S. Minister to France (1811). Wrote the important Advice to the Privileged Orders urging that the state is responsible for the welfare of all the people. Was considered one of the "Connecticut Wits" for his writing of The Anarchiad and The Vision of Columbus (1787) which was revised into The Columbiad (1807).

BARNARD, Frederick Augustus Porter. 1809-1889. Educator, president of Columbia College (1864-89). b. Massachusetts. Graduated Yale (1828). Taught at the University of Alabama (1837-54);

University of Mississippi (1854-56) president (1856-58) chancellor (1858-61). After the Civil War he became president of Columbia University (1864-89). He greatly expanded the college and gave the sciences needed support. He advocated higher education for women and Barnard College, named in his honor, was opened a few months after his death.

BARNARD, George Grey. 1863-1938. Sculptor. b. Pennsylvania. Studied at the Art Institute of Chicago, and in Cavelier's atelier at the Ecole des Beaux-Arts, Paris (1884-87). Taught at the Art Students' League, New York (1900-04). His best known work, The Two Natures is in the Metropolitan Museum, N. Y. His other works include The Urn of Life, a group of nineteen figures (Carnegie Museum), God Pan (Columbia University), bust of LINCOLN (Metropolitan Museum, N. Y.). His collection of art Barnard's Cloister was purchased by John D. Rockefeller, Jr., and presented to the Metropolitan.

BARNARD, Henry. 1811-1900. Educator. b. Connecticut. Graduated, Yale (1830); admitted to the bar (1835). Member of Connecticut legislature (1837-39); sponsored an act to provide better supervision of the public schools (1838). Gave up successful law practice to go into education. Worked for Connecticut public school system until 1842 when his office was abolished. He went to Rhode Island and did similar work. In 1851 he returned to Connecticut as superintendent of schools. Chancellor of the University of Wisconsin (1858-60); president, St. John's College, Annapolis, Md. (1866-67). First U. S. Commissioner of Education (1867-70). Editor, American Journal of Education (1855-82); compiler of Library of Education (52 vols.).

BARNARD, John Gross. 1815-1882. Army engineer. Graduated, U. S. M. A., West Point (1833); served as superintending engineer in general reconstruc-

48

tion of port fortifications at Portland, New York, Memphis, San Francisco and at the mouth of the Mississippi. During the Mexican War he constructed fortifications at Tampico. At outbreak of Civil War he was in charge of the construction of the defenses of Washington, D. C. Appointed chief engineer of armies in the field by GRANT (1864); became major general; made number of reports on coast defense and his reports of his work during the Civil War are important to military history.

"barnburners." The name applied to the New York faction of the Democratic party in the late 1840's and early 1850's. They were the followers of MARTIN VAN BUREN who in 1848 was not nominated by their party and who attended the party convention in that year for the purpose of revenging themselves on LEWIS CASS who had "stolen" the nomination. For a time the "barnburners" supported the FREE-SOIL party of which their leader, Van Buren, was the candidate in the election of 1848, but they returned to the Democratic party fold in 1852. The name stems from the derisive declarations of their enemies that they were acting like the Dutch farmer who burned his barn to rid it of rats.

BARNEY, Joshua. 1759-1818. Naval officer. b. Maryland. Served through the American Revolution. Served on the *Wasp, Sachem, Virginia* and *Saratoga;* captured three times by British. Most famous engagement was when he captured British vessel *General Monk;* commodore in French navy (1796-1802); PRIVATEER during War of 1812; commanded flotilla in Chesapeake Bay to check British advance against Washington, D. C.; wounded and captured at the battle of Bladensburg.

BARNUM, Phineas Taylor. 1810-1891. Showman, founder of "The Greatest Show on Earth." b. Connecticut. First

show was the "American Museum" in New York (1842) which was extravagantly advertised and promoted. He presented the midget, Charles Stratton, who he called "General Tom Thumb"; traveled with him and the rest of the show to Europe for the first time (1841); successfully presented Jenny Lind to America (1850); opened famous circus (1871), which has become an American institution; merged with J. A. Bailey (1881) to form Barnum and Bailey Circus, which continued after his death. Author of *Life* (1855) his autobiography.

BARRON, Clarence Walker. 1855-1928. Editor and publicist. b. Boston. On staff of *Evening Transcript,* Boston (1875-84); founded Boston *News Bureau* (1887) serviced brokers and operators with financial and business news; founded Philadelphia *Financial Journal* (1896); purchased *Wall Street Journal* (1902); founded *Barron's, the National Financial Weekly* (1921) which he edited himself. Author of *The Federal Reserve Act* (1914), and *A World Remaking* (1920).

BARROWS, Samuel June. 1845-1909. Clergyman and reformer. b. New York. Newspaper reporter and private secretary to WILLIAM SEWARD he entered Harvard Divinity School; Unitarian pastor at Dorchester, Massachusetts; edited the *Christian Register* (1880-1896); member of Congress (1896-98) working for civil service and prison reform. Sponsored the passage of New York's first probation law and was influential in securing passage of a Federal parole law. Helped plan new prison at Sing Sing; president, International Prison Congress (1905).

BARRY, John. 1745-1803. Naval officer. b. Ireland. Settled in Philadelphia, Pa. (1760); entered naval service at outset of American Revolution; commanded the brig *Lexington;* captured the first British ship of the war, the English tender, *Ed-*

ward; commanded many other vessels, and next to JOHN PAUL JONES was perhaps the outstanding naval hero of the Revolution.

BARRY, William Farquhar. 1818-1879. Army officer. b. New York City. Graduated, U. S. M. A., West Point (1838); famous as artillery expert; chief of artillery on MCCLELLAN's staff; chief of artillery for SHERMAN (1864-65); brevetted major general; organized Artillery School, Fort Monroe, Va. (1867-77).

BARRY, William Taylor. 1785-1835. Political leader. b. Virginia. Graduated, William and Mary College; practiced law at Lexington, Ky.; served in Kentucky house of representatives, and was Democratic leader during the War of 1812. State senator (1817-21); lieutenant governor (1821-23); Postmaster General in JACKSON's cabinet, the first incumbent in that office to be a part of the presidential cabinet. Resigned (1835).

BARTLETT, John Russell. 1805-1886. Historian and bibliographer. Moved from Rhode Island to New York (1836) was book dealer (1836-50); secretary of state, R. I. (1855-72). Arranged and classified the public archives, edited the *Records of the Colony of Rhode Island* (10 vols.); prepared an elaborate *Biography of Rhode Island* (1864). Aided John Carter Brown in assembling a remarkable collection of books, which became a well-known library in Providence.

BARTLETT, Josiah. 1729-1795. Revolutionary patriot and physician. b. Massachusetts. Well-known physician, Kingston, N. H. (1750-95); delegate to the CONTINENTAL CONGRESS(1775-78); signer of the DECLARATION OF INDEPENDENCE; Associate justice of superior court of New Hampshire (1782-88); chief justice (1788-90). First Governor of New Hampshire (1790-94).

BARTON, Clara. 1821-1912. Founder of the AMERICAN RED CROSS. b. Massachusetts. Taught school (1836-54); clerk in patent office, Washington, D. C. (1854-61). When Civil War broke out she organized an agency for getting supplies to the soldiers. Appointed by LINCOLN (1865) to attend to correspondence of relatives of missing prisoners. Went to Geneva (1869) as member of International Red Cross. Campaigned (1877-82) to have the United States sign the Geneva agreement; succeeded (1882). In 1877 she organized the American National Committee, which three years later became the American Red Cross. First president (1882-1904) of the organization. Served in CUBA during Spanish-American war. Author of *History of the Red Cross* (1882).

BARTRAM, John. 1699-1777. Pioneer botanist. b. Pennsylvania. Self-taught; bought a farm near Philadelphia and planted first botanical garden in the United States. Established wide correspondence with many famous European botanists, by exchanging plants, bulbs, and seeds, he introduced many new plants into this country. World famous; all great people of his time visiting his gardens. Wrote *Observations* (1751).

BARTRAM, William. 1739-1823. Naturalist. Son of above. b. Pennsylvania. Traveled widely throughout the Carolinas, Florida, Georgia and the Indian country gathering seeds and new specimens (1773-77). Wrote *Travels* (1791) an extremely interesting work. Kept up work of his father and began an interest in birds. His listing of 215 native birds was the most complete one of its kind in his time.

BARUCH, Bernard Mannes. 1870-1965. Financier and statesman. Graduated, College of the City of New York (1889). In the brokerage business, New York City. Appointed by President WILSON as a member of the Advisory Commission of Council for National Defense (1916);

50

chairman, WAR INDUSTRIES BOARD (1918-19); member of the drafting committee on economics with the American Commission to Negotiate Peace, Paris (1919); member, President's conference for capital and labor (1919); appointed by President ROOSEVELT (1934) chairman of the committee to recommend legislation to take profits out of war; his recommendations for wartime industrial mobilization was presented to the Senate Military Affairs Committee (1937); chairman of the committee investigating the rubber situation (1942). Author of *Making of Economic and Reparation Section of Peace Treaty* (1920). Author of the BARUCH PLAN of atomic energy control. Held the position of "elder statesman" longer than anyone since THOMAS JEFFERSON.

Baruch Plan. A proposal for international atomic energy control submitted in 1946 to the UNITED NATIONS by Bernard Baruch, the chairman of a combined state department and atomic physicists committee. The plan recommended international ownership of all mines and plants producing atomic material, and a system of licensing the control and use of such material under international inspection. It provided that the United States would progressively destroy its atomic weapons and release its technical data to the world as the ownership and inspection features went into effect. It was later widened into the so-called LILIENTHAL PLAN which provided for the establishment of an International Atomic Development Agency which would own existing and future power stations and inventions employed in the production of fissionable material. The Lilienthal version of the Plan prohibited the use of the VETO POWER. The Baruch - Lilienthal plans were rejected by the Soviet Union as incompatible with its sovereignty and as a method of acquiring control of that nation's industrial machine.

baseball. Although tradition holds that ABNER DOUBLEDAY invented baseball at Cooperstown, N. Y. in 1839, it is now known that a game by that name was played in the United States and in England before then. The first team game was played at the Elysian Fields, Hoboken, N. J., on June 19, 1846 between the Knickerbockers and the New York Nine. The Civil War provided an impetus to the growth of the game when troops played it in camp for RECREATION. The first professional team was the Cincinnati Red Stockings which, in 1869, set an all-time record by winning 64 consecutive games. Professional leagues came into existence at the end of the 19th century and captured popular imagination. The "major" leagues began with the formation of the NATIONAL LEAGUE in 1876 and the AMERICAN LEAGUE in 1901. As a result of the Chicago White Sox Scandal in 1919 the professional baseball leagues established the office of Commissioner of Baseball in 1921 and appointed Judge KENESAW MOUNTAIN LANDIS as the first Commissioner. Baseball became the "national pastime." Although it is played widely in Latin America and Japan, baseball has failed to acquire popularity in Europe. The World Series, which began in 1903, became the end-of-the-season climax to the year's schedule. In 1951 more than 16,000,000 persons attended major league baseball games. In the era of World War I the outstanding stars of the game included Christy Mathewson, Walter Johnson, Rube Waddell, Ty Cobb, Tris Speaker, Babe Ruth, Honus Wagner, George Sisler, Roger Bresnahan, Eddie Collins, and Willie Keeler. The stars of the modern period included Lou Gehrig, Joe DiMaggio, Hank Greenberg, Rogers Hornsby, Mel Ott, Jimmy Foxx, Carl Hubbell, Ted Williams, Stan Musial, Dizzy Dean, Bob Feller, and Jackie Robinson.

Bases-Destroyers Agreement. An agreement between President F. D. ROOSEVELT and Prime Minister Churchill in September 1940 by which the United States exchanged fifty "overaged" World War I destroyers for 99-year leases on Naval and Air Bases in the western hemisphere. The areas included Newfoundland, Bermuda, the Bahamas, Jamaica, Trinidad, British Guiana, Antigua, and St. Lucia. The agreement met general approval although many opposed the method of its achievement by EXECUTIVE AGREEMENT rather than by treaty or congressional authority.

basketball. The most popular amateur sport in the United States. The game was invented by Dr. James Naismith in Springfield, Massachusetts in the winter of 1891-1892. Naismith created basketball as an inter-season sport for the students of Springfield College. United States troops introduced the game into Europe during World War I and it was quickly adopted by various nations. In the United States it is generally played indoors, but flourished as an outdoor sport in other countries. Basketball quickly became popular among the youth of the nation and was introduced into schools, colleges, and clubs. In modified form it was taken up by women as an amateur sport. Although it remained primarily amateur in standing, professional basketball has become increasingly popular in the United States. The National Basketball Association and the American League had become the two largest professional basketball leagues in the United States by the 1950's. The game's importance in intercollegiate athletic programs attracted criminal elements for gambling purposes. In 1951 five New York City basketball players and their briber were jailed for manipulating the results of games. The revelation of this scandal stimulated investigations throughout the nation and resulted in the arrests of players and gamblers in other cities. Outstanding stars have included Nat Holman, Howard Cann, Angelo Luisetti, Chester Jaworski, and George Mikan.

Bataan, Battle of. The struggle by the United States forces under General Wainwright to maintain their foothold on the peninsula of BATAAN located on the island of Luzon in the Philippines. In the first weeks of the War in the Pacific, the United States and Filipino armies under the command of General MACARTHUR retreated across Luzon, moving into the peninsula in January, 1942. For three months they suffered privations due to lack of food, medicines, and supplies until forced to surrender to the Japanese in April. Previously, General MacArthur had left for Australia, leaving the command in the hand of General Wainwright. Bataan was liberated by United States troops in February, 1945.

BATE, William Brimage. 1826-1905. Confederate general and U. S. Senator. b. Tennessee. Served in the Mexican War; studied law; attorney-general Nashville. Entered Civil War as a private in the Confederate army and after a spectacular career emerged a major general. Governor of Tennessee (1882-86); U. S. Senator (1886-1905).

BATES, Edward. 1793-1869. Statesman. b. Virginia. Studied law; began practice in Missouri; U. S. district attorney, state attorney-general and member of lower house of the Missouri legislature. Leader of the WHIG PARTY in the state. Attorney-General in LINCOLN's cabinet.

Battle Act. A law of Congress passed in 1951. It provided that any nation which shipped war-useful materials to Soviet-dominated countries would automatically lose United States aid unless the President determined that the cessation of such aid would hurt the nation's security.

52

Battle Hymn of the Republic. The patriotic hymn written in 1861 by Mrs. JULIA WARD HOWE. The text of the song was written by Mrs. Howe because she thought the words she had heard a regiment of troops sing to the music written by William Steffe in 1852, unsuitable to that tune. The song had been known as "John Brown's Body." It was originally printed in the February, 1862 issue of the *Atlantic Monthly,* and almost immediately became popular throughout the nation. It has subsequently been included among the liturgical hymns of many churches.

"Battle of the Maps." An amusing incident arising out of the negotiations leading to the WEBSTER-ASHBURTON TREATY in 1842, which finally settled the Maine-Canada boundary controversy. Secretary of State WEBSTER came into possession of a map believed to have been prepared by BENJAMIN FRANKLIN for the French Foreign Office. This map, discovered by an American historian in the French archives, supported the extreme English claims. Simultaneously, a map drafted by the British Peace Commissioners in 1783, was discovered in the British Museum. It supported the extreme American claims. In the United States Webster concealed the French map from the British, using it as a lever upon the President to accept most of the British offer. In Parliament the British map was used to convince the former's members of the validity of American claims. The ultimate compromise in the treaty gave to the United States most of what it had demanded.

BAUER, Louis Agricola. 1865-1932. Magnetician, chief of the division of terrestrial magnetism, U. S. Coast and Geodetic Survey (1899-1906); director of the department of terrestrial magnetism of the Carnegie Institution of Washington (which he organized).

BAYARD, James Asheton. 1767-1815. Statesman, a leader of the FEDERALIST PARTY. b. Philadelphia. U.S. Representative from Delaware (1797-1805); U. S. Senator (1805-13). Important in securing the election of JEFFERSON rather than BURR in 1800; appointed by MADISON with JOHN Q. ADAMS and ALBERT GALLATIN on the commission to negotiate the terms of the TREATY OF GHENT with Great Britain (1813-14).

BAYARD, James Asheton. 1799-1880. Senator. As a Jacksonian Democrat in the state of Delaware, he was constantly defeated in elections; as supporter of the WILMOT PROVISO, he was elected U. S. Senator (1851), served (1851-64, 67-69). Became a Republican for awhile, but his sympathies were with the South in the Reconstruction period, and he again became a Democrat.

BAYARD, Thomas Francis. 1828-1898. Statesman. b. Delaware. Elected U.S. Senator (1869-85) to succeed his father JAMES A. BAYARD. Secretary of State in the CLEVELAND administration (1885-89); appointed by Cleveland as the first U. S. Ambassador to Great Britain (1893-97).

BAYLEY, Richard. 1745-1801. Physician. Studied under William Hunter in England; practised in New York City. Famous for handling of the croup epidemic of 1774; after the Revolution his lectures in anatomy were broken up by destructive mobs. Professor of anatomy in the Columbia college medical faculty (1792) working with yellow fever epidemics. Author of *Account of the Epidemic Fever* (1795). Instrumental in formulating quarantine laws for the New York harbor.

BAYLOR, Robert Emmett Bledsoe. 1793-1873. Jurist and Baptist clergyman. b. Kentucky. Served in the War of 1812; moved to Alabama from Kentucky where he served in legislature and was elected U. S. Representative (1828-31). Moved to Texas (1839); appointed associate justice of the supreme court of Texas and was judge of 3d district (1841); prominent in state constitutional convention; U. S. district judge (1845-61). President of Baptist Education Society of Texas (1843); secured passage of charter for first Baptist college, known as Baylor University.

Bay of Pigs. During the Eisenhower administration relations between Cuba and the United States were greatly weakened and diplomatic relations were severed. Under Kennedy's administration tension was brought to a climax when close to 1,500 Cubans who had fled from the Castro regime attempted to liberate Cuba through an unsuccessful invasion at the Bay of Pigs in April 1961. Many of these Cuban exiles had been trained in Central America with the tacit assistance of the United States but they were no match for Castro's army and were repulsed. Many of the invaders were captured but were later released in return for private donations of medical supplies and food. Kennedy was sharply criticized by some for not giving the invaders enough support and by others for assisting them when he should have maintained a hands-off policy.

Bay Psalm Book. The first book published in America in the English language. It was published at Cambridge in the MASSACHUSETTS BAY COLONY in 1640.

BEALE, Edward Fitzgerald. 1822-1893. Frontiersman and naval officer. b. District of Columbia. With KIT CARSON, he crawled through the Mexican lines (1846) to get aid for KEARNY from Commodore STOCKTON. Messenger across the country six times (1847-49); brought first authentic news from California of the discovery of gold (1848); superintendent of Indian affairs for California and Nevada (1852-65); surveyor-general of California (1861-66); U. S. Minister to Austria-Hungary (1876-77).

BEARD, Charles A. 1874-1948. Historian, educator, and political scientist. b. Indiana. Graduated DePauw University (1898); Ph.D. Columbia University (1904); taught history and politics at Columbia until 1917; director of the Training School for Public Service (1917-22); author of *The Development of Modern Europe* (2 vols. 1907 with J. H. Robinson) important for emphasis on social and economic factors; *American City Government* (1912); *Economic Interpretation of the Constitution* (1913); *Economic Origins of Jeffersonian Democracy* (1915); and *The Rise of American Civilization* (1927, with wife, Mary).

BEARD, Daniel Carter. 1850-1941. Artist, naturalist, boy scout leader. b. Ohio. Studied at the Art Student's League, New York City; illustrated books and magazines; famous as the founder of the BOY SCOUTS OF AMERICA (1910); wrote books and articles on nature.

"Bear Flag Republic." The name applied to the former Mexican province of California seized by rebellious Americans in January, 1846. Although Congress did not declare war against Mexico until May 11, 1846, an army under Colonel STEPHEN W. KEARNY had been ordered to occupy the area of the Mexican republic from the Rio Grande to the Pacific. On his way he received news of the American revolt in the Sacramento valley and the proclamation of the Republic of California at Sonoma. It was referred to as the "Bear Flag Republic." The explorer, JOHN C. FREMONT and the frontier scout, KIT CARSON united their forces with the revolutionists. Fremont was made the rebel commander and their combined forces marched against Sacramento. By this time news had come that the United States and Mexico were at war and that Commodore SLOAT had captured Monterrey. By midsummer of

1847 San Francisco, Sutter's Fort, and Sonoma had been taken. By New Year's Day the conquest of California had been completed, and United States authorities took over in California.

BEAUMARCHAIS, Pierre Augustin Caron de. 1732-1799. French playwright and political figure. Wrote *Le Barbier de Seville* (*The Barber of Seville*) and *Le Mariage de Figaro* (*The Marriage of Figaro*), comedies which inspired the later operas by Rossini and Mozart respectively. Noted for friendship with BENJAMIN FRANKLIN and his purchase of supplies for American colonies during the Revolution. His witty MEMOIRES cleverly attack social and judicial injustice.

BEAUMONT, William. 1785-1853. Surgeon, famous for his contribution to the study of gastric digestion. b. Connecticut. By his study of the exposed and perforated stomach of a wounded soldier, he learned the processes of digestion. Author of *Experiments and Observations on the Gastric Juice and the Physiology of Digestion* (1833).

BEAUPRE, Arthur Matthias. 1853-1919. Diplomat. Consul general to Guatemala (1897) appointed by President MCKINLEY; served as mediator between Great Britain and Honduras in connection with the detention by Honduras of a British schooner; U. S. Minister to Colombia (1903) during difficult time of HAY-HERRIAN TREATY; U. S. Minister to the Argentine Republic (1904-08); U. S. Minister to the Netherlands (1908-11); U. S. Minister to Cuba (1911-13).

BEAUREGARD, Pierre Gustave Toutant. 1818-1893. Confederate general. b. Louisiana. Graduated U.S.M.A., West Point (1838); served in the Mexican War under General SCOTT; superintendent of West Point (1860) resigned to enter the Civil War on the Confederate side; brigadier general assigned to Charleston; fired upon FORT SUMTER opening the Civil War; served at BULL RUN, as a general at SHILOH and Corinth. Commissioner of public works, New Orleans (1888-1893). Author of *Principles and Maxims of the Art of War* (1863).

BECKER, George Ferdinand. 1847-1919. Geologist. b. New York City. Educated at Harvard, Heidelberg and Berlin. On the staff of Clarence King, whose work led to the establishment of the U. S. Geological Survey, with which Becker was later associated. Wrote *Geology of the Comstock Lode and Washoe District* (1880) which introduced a new scientific approach to the study of mineral deposits and brought fame to its author. Pioneer in the study of chemicophysical problems.

BEDFORD, Gunning. 1747-1812. Statesman. b. Philadelphia. Graduated Princeton. Settled in Delaware; attorney-general (1784-89); delegate to the CONTINENTAL CONGRESS (1785-86); delegate to the FEDERAL CONSTITUTIONAL CONVENTION (1787) where he championed the rights of small states. U. S. district judge for Delaware (1789-1812).

BEEBE, Charles William. 1877-1962. Naturalist, explorer, and author. b. Brooklyn, N. Y. Graduated Columbia University (1898); curator of ornithology at the New York Zoological Society, originating the great collection of living birds. Headed expeditions to Nova Scotia, South America, the Himalayas and other regions. Studied marine life in Bermuda waters. Author of *Jungle Days* (1925), *The Arcturus Adventure* (1935), *Beneath Tropic Seas* (1928), *Half Mile Down* (1934) and many other works.

BEECHER, Catherine Esther. 1800-1878. Educator and reformer, daughter of LYMAN BEECHER. b. Connecticut. Founded Western Female Institute (1832) and similar schools at Quincy, Ill., Milwaukee, Wis., and Burlington, Iowa. Wrote and lectured to promote liberal education for women.

BEECHER, Henry Ward. 1813-1887. Clergyman and lecturer. Son of LYMAN BEECHER. b. Connecticut. Pastor, Plymouth Congregational Church, Brooklyn, N. Y. (1847-87). He was an impressive speaker on all subjects of vital interest to his times, and his influence was nationwide. He spoke against SLAVERY and was an advocate of WOMEN SUFFRAGE. Accused of adultery but cleared of charges, his church remained loyal to him. Editor of the *Independent* (1861-63); *Christian Union* (1870-78). Author of many books of sermons and lectures and *Evolution and Religion* (1885). During the Kansas-Nebraska war he was responsible for sending into the territory large quantities of rifles known as "BEECHER'S BIBLES," for the use of the anti-slave forces.

BEECHER, Lyman. 1775-1863. Presbyterian clergyman. b. Connecticut. Graduated and studied divinity at Yale. Pastor of many churches leading to the important one at Litchfield, Conn. (1810); prominent in organization of the American Bible Society; helped found the *Connecticut Observer*. Pastor in Boston (1826); moved to Cincinnati where he became president of the Lane Theological Seminary (1832). His liberal views brought him into constant conflict with the more conservative elements in his church. Father of HENRY WARD, HARRIET B. STOWE, CATHERINE and 10 other children.

"Beecher's Bibles." The term applied to Sharps Rifles forwarded by the Reverend HENRY WARD BEECHER in 1856 to the anti- SLAVERY forces in the Kansas territory. Beecher pledged rifles to the existing groups and to settlers emigrating to Kansas, as a stronger force than the moral arguments of the Bible.

"beef trust." A monopoly in the meat PACKING INDUSTRY at the beginning of the 20th century. In 1902 the National Packing Company was organized by the three largest midwestern packing houses, Swift, Morris, and Armour. In a short time it had obtained control of the meat packing industry in Kansas City, Omaha, and St. Louis. The companies survived the federal government's prosecution in 1905 under the SHERMAN ANTI-TRUST ACT and continued as a monopoly until 1920.

BEER, George Louis. 1872-1920. Historian. b. Staten Island, N. Y. Retired as a successful tobacco merchant (1893-1903) to devote himself to historical research. After much study in the archives of London he wrote *British Colonial Policy, 1754-65* (1907); and *The English-Speaking Peoples* (1917). Requested by President WILSON to make a study of African colonial problems, he was the first to use the term "mandate" in its modern meaning. Member of American Peace Delegation and the Mandates Commission.

BELASCO, David. 1854-1931. Playwright and producer. b. San Francisco. Stage manager of the Madison Square Theatre, New York City (1880-87); owner and manager of Belasco Theater, New York City. Widely known for his novel and effective stage lighting and scenery, and his ability to discover and develop the talents of his actors. Author of *Lord Chumley* (1887), *The Girl of the Golden West* (1905), *The Return of Peter Grimm* (1911), and many others.

BELKNAP, William Worth. 1829-1890. Army officer and politician. b. New York. Studied law at Georgetown University, Washington, D. C. and began practice in Iowa. Brigadier general in Civil War (1864); commanded 4th Division under SHERMAN in Georgia campaigns and march across the Carolinas. Collector of internal revenue in Iowa; Secretary of War in GRANT'S CABINET (1869) brought up on charges by a House Committee for accepting a bribe, and before he could be impeached he resigned (1876).

BELL, Alexander Graham. 1847-1922. Scientist, inventor of the telephone. Born in Edinburgh; came to the United States (1871) to demonstrate a system of visible speech, invented by his father, to be taught to the deaf in Boston. His method, taught to teachers of the deaf all over the country, is still in use. Became a citizen (1882); by experimentation he conceived the notion that speech could be transmitted by electric waves. He received patents for his invention of the telephone (1876, 1877). The Bell Telephone Company was organized (July, 1877). Daniel Drawbaugh and Johann P. Reis, who filed claims to the invention of a telephone on the same day as Bell, brought suit, but the Supreme Court finally decided in favor of Bell. Established the Volta laboratory for research; invented cylindrical wax recorders for EDISON'S phonograph; and with LANGLEY and others solved the problem of stability of balance in a flying machine. Regent of the Smithsonian Institution (1898); president of the National Geographic Society (1896-1904).

BELL, John. 1797-1869. Lawyer and Statesman. b. Tennessee. Leading member of the Nashville bar; U. S. Representative (1827-41); Speaker of the House (1836); U. S. Secretary of War (1841); U. S. Senator (1847-59); leader of the conservative elements in the South which supported the Union, though they believed in SLAVERY. Supported CLAY'S COMPROMISE OF 1850; nominated for the presidency by the CONSTITUTIONAL UNION PARTY (1860); tried to keep Tennessee in the Union; when he failed, he took no part in the war.

BELL, Peter Hansborough. 1808-1898. Statesman. Served in War for Texan Independence; lieutenant colonel in the Mexican War; leader of many campaigns against the Indians. Governor of Texas (1849-53); founded a public school system; U. S. Representative (1851-57).

BELLAMY, Edward. 1850-1898. Author. b. Massachusetts. Famous for *Looking Backward* (1888) a Utopian romance picturing the world as it would appear in the year 2000 A. D. It was mildly socialistic in tone and selling over a million copies, had influence on the thinking of the time. Founded the *New Nation*, a Boston weekly (1891); wrote *Equality* (1897) a sequel to *Looking Backward* but it was unsuccessful.

Belleau Wood, Battle of. See Chateau-Thierry, Battle of.

BELLOWS, George Wesley. 1882-1925. Painter, illustrator and lithographer. b. Ohio. Pupil of ROBERT HENRI; leader of the American realists, his paintings are in the leading museums of the country. Painted *Emma and Her Children* (Boston Museum of Fine Arts), *Portrait of My Mother* (Chicago Art Institute), *Up The Hudson* (Metropolitan Museum, N. Y.), and other well-known works.

BELLOWS, Henry Whitney. 1814-1882. Unitarian clergyman. b. Boston. Graduated, Harvard Divinity School; pastor of First Unitarian Church (later All Souls), New York City (1839-82); founded the *Christian Inquirer* (1847); important influence in the founding of Antioch College, Ohio; president, U. S. Sanitary Commission during the Civil War; founded National Conference of Unitarian Churches; edited (1866-67) *Christian Examiner.*

BELMONT, August. 1816-1890. Banker. Came to the United States from the

Rhine (1837); established the banking house of August Belmont & Co., became a naturalized citizen; consul general for Austria in the United States. (1844-50). U. S. Minister to the Netherlands (1853-57). Union supporter during the Civil War. Art collector and sportsman.

BENET, Stephen Vincent. 1898-1943. Poet, novelist. Brother of WILLIAM ROSE BENET. b. Pennsylvania. Author of *Five Men and Pompey* (1915), *Young Adventure* (1918), *The Beginnings of Wisdom* (1921), *Tiger Joy* (1925), *John Brown's Body,* a book-length epic poem of the Civil War which won him the Pulitzer Prize for verse (1928) and wide acclaim. He also wrote *Ballads and Poems* (1931), *The Devil and Daniel Webster* (1937) and many other books and poems.

BENET, William R. 1886-1950. Poet, editor, and novelist. b. New York. Graduated Yale, Ph.B. (1907); editor, or assistant editor on the staff of *Century Magazine,* the *Nation's Business,* the New York *Evening Post Literary Review,* and the *Saturday Review of Literature.* Author of *Merchants from Cathay* (1913); *Man Possessed* (1927); and *The Dust Which Is God* (1941) for which he was awarded the Pulitzer Prize.

BENJAMIN, Judah Philip. 1811-1884. Confederate statesman, lawyer. b. British West Indies. Settled in South Carolina and then Louisiana; U. S. Senator from Louisiana (1853-61); Attorney General in JEFFERSON DAVIS' cabinet (1861); also Confederate Secretary of State and Secretary of War (1861-2-5); unpopular with people, but had the confidence of Davis. Hoped to get England's support for the Confederacy. Went to England after the fall of the Confederacy, and became a famous barrister and Queen's counsel (1872). Author of *Treatise on the Law of Sale of Personal Property* (1868) which is the standard work in its field.

BENNETT, Floyd. 1890-1928. Aviator. b. New York. Accompanied the MacMillan expedition to northwest Greenland (1925); awarded the CONGRESSIONAL MEDAL OF HONOR. Died of pneumonia, contracted while attempting to rescue the stranded *Bremen* flyers. Floyd Bennett Field, Brooklyn, N. Y., named in his honor.

BENNETT, James Gordon. 1795-1872. Newspaper owner and editor. Born in Scotland; came to the United States (1819); Washington correspondent on the staff of New York *Enquirer* (1826-28); editor of *Courier and Enquirer* (1829-32); started the New York *Herald* (May 6, 1835), a one-cent paper that ran four pages; in 15 months he had run the circulation up to 30,000. He created many new innovations in American journalism; established European correspondents (1838); first to use the telegraph as a means of getting news; retired (1867).

BENNETT, James Gordon. 1841-1918. Newspaper owner son of above. Took over the management of the *Herald* (1867) when his father retired. Retained high standards and large circulation for the paper; financed Stanley's expedition into Africa to find Livingstone (1869-71), a daring journalistic stunt; financed expedition of George DeLong to the Arctic (1879-81); established Paris edition of the *Herald* (1887); joined JOHN MACKAY in Commercial Cable Co. which laid transatlantic cables successful in breaking the GOULD monopoly. Established Gordon Bennett international trophies in yachting and other races.

Bennington, Battle of. A minor battle of the American Revolution in which 1,000 German mercenary troops, commanded by Colonel Baum under General BURGOYNE, attempted to seize the American-held town of Bennington, Vermont. Attacked in front and in rear by a force half their number they suffered 907 casualties, including 207 dead and 700 captured. The American loss was 14 killed and 42 wounded. The victory served to improve the morale of the American forces.

BENSON, Egbert. 1746-1833. Political leader and jurist. Member of the provincial congress (1776); state legislature (1777-80); delegate to the CONTINENTAL CONGRESS (1781-84); first attorney-general of New York state; important in securing the RATIFICATION OF THE FEDERAL CONSTITUTION by the state convention. Member of Congress (1789-93); supporter of HAMILTON justice of New York supreme court (1794-1801); founder and first president of the New York Historical Society.

BENSON, William Shepherd. 1855-1932. Naval officer. b. Georgia. Graduated U.S.N.A., Annapolis (1877); rear admiral (1915); chief of naval operations (1915-19); represented the United States on commission which prepared Armistice terms; naval adviser to American commission at Versailles. Member U. S. Shipping Board and Chairman (1920); admiral (1930).

BENT, William. 1809-1869. Frontiersman. Built trading post, Bent's Fort, Arkansas river (1832); first permanent white settler in Colorado, and one of the best known men of the West.

BENTON, Thomas Hart. 1889-1975. Painter. b. Missouri. Studied at Chicago Art Institute (1906-07) and in Paris (1908-11). Well-known for an individual realistic (1815); editor of Missouri Enquirer. Member, U. S. Senate (1821-51); supported JACKSON (1828) for the presidency and after his election became administration leader of the Senate. As floor leader, he played an important part in the war against the national bank; he stood for sound money and opposed paper issues, which gained him the name

"Old Bullion." Sponsored the SPECIE CIRCULAR; aided all legislation that supported the frontier settlers; suggested the homestead plan; opposed the CALHOUN RESOLUTION OF 1847; opposed SECESSION in the SLAVERY issue; member, U. S. House of Representatives (1853-55). Author of Thirty Years' View (1854-56) an autobiography.

BENTON, Thomas Hart. 1889-. Painter. b. Missouri. Studied at Chicago Art Institute (1906-07) and in Paris (1908-11). Well-known for an individual realistic technique in the portrayal of the American middle western people and their lives. Best known paintings are Cotton Pickers, Lonesome Road, Homestead, Susanna and the Elders, and July Hay. Gained recognition for his many murals and lithographs.

BERENSON, Bernard. 1865-1959. Art critic and author. b. Lithuania. Graduated Harvard University (1887). Has lived most of his life in or near Florence, Italy, famous for his knowledge of the Italian painters. Author of Venetian Painters of the Renaissance (1894), Florentine Painters of the Renaissance (1896), The Study and Criticism of Italian Art (1901, 1902, 1915), and Venetian Painting in America (1916).

BERGER, Victor Louis. 1860-1929. Socialist leader and Congressman. Came to the United States from Austria (1878); editor Milwaukee Daily Vorwaerts (1892-98); Social Democratic Herald (1900), Milwaukee Leader (strongest Socialist Daily Newspaper in the United States, from 1911). Opposed the policies of SAMUEL GOMPERS in the A.F. OF L. With DEBS he founded the SOCIAL DEMOCRATIC PARTY which in 1901 became the SOCIALIST PARTY; succeeded Debs as chairman of its national executive committee in 1927, was a leader of the party all his life. Member, U. S. House of Representatives (1911-13) being the first socialist elected to Congress. Elected again in 1918 and 1919; (excluded (1919) on grounds of disloyalty); elected and seated (1923-29). Sentenced to prison for 20 years on grounds of aiding the enemy (1918) but the U. S. Supreme Court reversed the decision (1921).

Bering Sea Controversy. A dispute between the United States and Great Britain over the seal fisheries in the Bering Sea. The United States contended that the Bering Sea was a *mare clausum* (closed sea) solely within the jurisdiction of the United States. The British claimed it to be part of the high seas (outside of the legal three mile limit). Under EXECUTIVE ORDERS American naval vessels seized eight British ships in 1889, thus precipitating a virtual threat of war. In 1890 the United States government agreed to submit the matter to an arbitral tribunal at Paris which in 1893 decided every disputed point against the United States. The Bering Sea was declared open and the United States paid damages of $473,000 to Great Britain.

BERKELEY, Sir William. 1606-1677. Colonial governor of Virginia. Appointed (1641) and except for brief interruption, was governor until 1677. The opening years of his administration were well administered. His dictatorial policies in later years led to BACON'S REBELLION (1676). Although the rebellion was suppressed, Berkeley was recalled.

BERLE, Adolph Augustus, Jr. 1895-. Lawyer and political leader. b. Boston, Mass. Graduated Harvard (1913), Harvard Law School (1916); entered law firm in Boston. Served with military intelligence in World War I, sent to peace conference in Paris as expert. Taught law at Harvard and Columbia law schools; leading member of ROOSEVELT'S "BRAIN TRUST"; prominent in LAGUARDIA administration in N. Y.; leader of LIBERAL PARTY, N. Y., and of AMERICANS FOR DEMOCRATIC ACTION.

Berlin Airlift. A concerted attempt by the United States Air Force to fly food and other supplies into Berlin in 1948 and 1949 in an effort to overcome the Soviet BLOCKADE of that city. On April 1, 1948 the Soviet military government in Berlin began a land blockade of the allied areas of that city by refusing to permit American and British supply trains to pass through their zone. By September 30, 1949, when the blockade was lifted, American and British air craft had flown 2,243,315 tons of food and coal into western Berlin.

Berlin and Milan Decrees. Two edicts issued by Napoleon, at Berlin in 1806 and at Milan in 1807, in reply to the British Orders-in-Council. The Berlin Decree declared a BLOCKADE of the British Isles, making all COMMERCE with England illegal, and announcing that Englishmen found in French-controlled TERRITORY would be seized as prisoners of war. The Milan Decree stated that all vessels carrying a British license or stopping at British ports would be subjected to capture. These laws interfered with the neutral trade of the United States during the Napoleonic Wars and led to Congress' enactment of three laws which had the effect of virtually destroying American commerce. Napoleon's cancellation of the decrees on American commerce in 1810 removed a source of diplomatic difficulty in Franco-American relations, and ultimately contributed to the onset of the War of 1812. The program inaugurated by these edicts is popularly known as the CONTINENTAL SYSTEM.

BERNARD, Sir Francis. 1712-1779. Colonial governor of Massachusetts. Governor of New Jersey (1758-60); governor of Massachusetts (1760-69). Although

60

an able administrator, he was unfortunately governor at the time the STAMP ACT and SUGAR ACT were passed. He attempted to enforce the unpopular laws including the QUARTERING ACT. Incurring hostility of colonists, he was recalled.

BERRIGAN, Philip. Reverend Philip Berrigan and six other militant anti-war activists were serving sentences for destroying draft records when they were accused of a plot to kidnap Henry Kissinger. During the trial their attorney produced evidence which revealed that a prisoner who had served as an informant against them had been paid for his testimony by the FBI. In April 1972 the case ended in a mistrial.

BEVERIDGE, Albert Jeremiah. 1862-1927. Political leader and historian. b. Ohio. Elected to U. S. Senate (1899-1911); prominent supporter of THEODORE ROOSEVELT. Opposed the PAYNE-ALDRICH TARIFF (1909) and other Republican policies and was not reelected. Became one of the organizers of the PROGRESSIVE PARTY; defeated for governor of Indiana (1912). Author of *Life of John Marshall* (4 vols. 1916-1919); uncompleted *Life of Abraham Lincoln* (2 vols. 1928).

BIBB, William Wyatt. 1781-1820. U. S. Senator and first Governor of Alabama. Graduated with medical degree from the University of Pennsylvania; practised in Georgia. Served in both houses of Georgia legislature; U. S. Representative (1805-13); U. S. Senator (1813-16). Appointed by President MONROE, governor of Alabama (1817).

bi-cameral legislature. A two chamber legislative assembly. It originated in 13th century England with the calling of two representatives from each shire and town to sit as a House of Commons. This supplemented the existing House of Lords. In America bi-cameralism was adapted to local conditions from British experience. With one exception all state legislatures today are bi-cameral. Since 1936 Nebraska's legislature has contained one chamber.

Bicentennial. On July 4, 1976 America celebrated its 200th year as a nation. Special events took place throughout the country including Operation Sail in New York City where some 6 million people gathered to watch hundreds of sailing boats, including a unique armada of 16 tall ships from all over the world. Queen Elizabeth II of England visited the United States on July 6th to honor the special observance.

BICKMORE, Albert Smith. 1838-1914. Naturalist, founder of the American Museum of Natural History in New York City. Graduated Dartmouth; studied with Agassiz at Harvard. Served in the Civil War; made many collections in many parts of the world. Aided by THEODORE ROOSEVELT in founding the museum, acted as superintendent (1869-84). Author of *Travels in the East Indian Archipelago* (1868).

BIDDLE, James. 1783-1848. Naval officer. b. Philadelphia, Pa. At the opening of WAR OF 1812, he was first lieutenant on the *Wasp,* which captured the *Frolic;* when re-captured by British ship, he was taken prisoner; exchanged; commanded the *Hornet* (1813-15) and captured the superior British vessel the *Penguin.* Sent with sloop *Ontario* (1817) to ·Columbia river to take possession of the Oregon territory; cruised South American waters to protect American SHIPPING. While commanding East Indian squadron, he negotiated first treaty between the United States and China (1846).

BIDDLE, Nicholas. 1786-1844. Financier and author. b. Philadelphia, Pa. With Paul Allen he edited the notes and journals of the LEWIS AND CLARK expedition into the official *History of the Expedition of Captains Lewis and Clark* (1814). U. S. Representative (1810-11); state senator (1814-18); appointed by President MONROE, one of the five government directors of the second BANK OF THE UNITED STATES; elected president of the bank (1822). Center of attack by JACKSON on the bank; new charter was refused and Biddle resigned (1839).

BIENVILLE, Sieur de Jean. 1680-1768. French provincial governor in America. b. France. Explorer of the lower Mississippi River (1699); governed the colony in Louisiana in the name of the King of France (1701-12, 1718-26, 1733-43).

BIERCE, Ambrose Gwinett. 1842-1914?. Journalist and author. b. Ohio. Famous for his short stories. Served through the Civil War; worked for periodicals in San Francisco; famous for biting wit as evidenced in such works as *The Fiend's Delight* (1872), *Cobwebs from an Empty Skull* (1874); contributed column of "Prattle" in San Francisco *Examiner* (1887). Became leading literary light of the west coast and wrote *Tales of Soldiers and Civilians* (1891) and, *Can Such Things Be?* Disappeared into Mexico (1913) and his fate is still unknown.

"big business." The popular term applied to the giant corporation in American industry. Organized as TRUSTS or HOLDING COMPANIES, and controlled by means of INTERLOCKING DIRECTORATES and TRADE ASSOCIATIONS, large corporate establishments have become effective MONOPOLIES within their industries. They have succeeded in controlling production, patents, sales, marketing, labor relations, inventions, and prices. See trust, POOL, MERGER, holding company, interlocking directories, trade association, BUSINESS CONSOLIDATION, and ABSENTEE OWNERSHIP.

BIGELOW, Jacob. 1786-1879. Physician and botanist. b. Massachusetts. Graduated Harvard University, medical degree University of Pennsylvania. Professor, Harvard Medical School (1815-1855); wrote *Discourses on Self-limited Diseases* (1835) which was a protest against bloodletting and had a reformed effect upon medical practices in this country. Author of *Florula Bostoniensis* (1814), *American Medical Botany* (3 vols. 1817, 1818, 1820) and other works in the field.

BIGELOW, John. 1817-1911. Editor and diplomat. b. New York. Graduated Union College, admitted to the bar (1838); co-editor and co-owner with WILLIAM CULLEN BRYANT of the New York *Evening Post* (1848-61); consul general at Paris (1861-65); U. S. Minister to France (1865-66) and considered one of our best diplomats. Author of *France and the Confederate Navy* (1888) *Life of Benjamin Franklin* (10 vols. 1874), *Retrospections of an Active Life* (5 vols. 1909-1913) an autobiography.

"Big Five." The name applied to President WILSON, Prime Minister Lloyd George, Premier Clemenceau, Premier Orlando, and Premier Saionjii at the *Versailles Conference*. The term also is applied to President F. D. ROOSEVELT, Prime Minister Churchill, PREMIER DE GAULLE, Premier Stalin and Generalissimo Chiang Kai-shek, during and after World War II. After World War II President TRUMAN and Prime Minister Attlee succeeded to executive leadership in the United States and Great Britain.

"Big Four." The name applied to President WILSON, Prime Minister Lloyd George, Premier Clemenceau, and Premier Orlando at the VERSAILLES CONFERENCE. The term is also applied to President ROOSEVELT, Prime Minister

Churchill, Premier Stalin and General-issimo Chiang Kai-shek during and after World War II. After World War II President TRUMAN and Prime Minister Attlee succeeded to executive leadership in the United States and Great Britain.

"big stick." The term applied to the advocacy by President T. ROOSEVELT of strong method in meeting foreign and domestic problems. Its origins lie in his expression "SPEAK SOFTLY AND CARRY A BIG STICK" in a request for a large naval appropriation. As it grew the policy developed into the "ROOSEVELT COROLLARY" which involved direct American intervention into several Latin American states.

"Big Three." The term applied to President WILSON, Prime Minister Lloyd George, and Premier Clemenceau at the VERSAILLES CONFERENCE. It is also applied to President ROOSEVELT, Prime Minister Churchill and Premier Stalin during World War II.

Biglow Papers. A series of humorous poems written by JAMES RUSSELL LOWELL in 1846, expressing the anti-slave opposition to the Mexican War then in progress. They were published in the Boston *Courier*.

BIGGS, Herman Michael. 1859-1923. Physician and public health administrator. Famous as a pioneer in preventative medicine. Professor of medicine at Bellevue Hospital Medical College (1886-1923); introduced diphtheria antitoxin into the United States (1894). Worked for the control of tuberculosis; State commissioner of health organizing division of infant and maternity welfare.

Bi-Metallic Standard. See gold standard.

Billeting Act. An Act of Parliament in 1765 which compelled the colonial legislatures to contribute to the support of an army in the colonies. It was strongly resisted in New York and South Carolina, and was one of the parliamentary acts aggravating Anglo-Colonial relationships in the period leading up to the American Revolution.

BILLINGS, John Shaw. 1838-1913. Surgeon and librarian. Served in medical service of the U. S. Army (1861-95); after Civil War he was placed in charge of the Surgeon General's Library in Washington; increased catalogue entries; prepared (with Dr. Robert Fletcher) *Index-Catalogue* (16 vols. 1880-95) and *Index Medicus* (1879-95), a monthly guide to medical literature. Became director of New York Public Library (1896-1913) and is considered the "creator" of the library.

bill of attainder. A legislative act declaring a deed illegal without judicial trial. It is generally directed against a given person or persons. Bills of attainder may not be passed by the Congress under the terms of Article I, Section 9 or by the states under Article I, Section 10 of the Constitution of the United States.

bill of rights. Refers to the first ten amendments to the Constitution which guarantee CIVIL LIBERTIES against infringement by Congress. Of the amendments, added to the Constitution in 1791, only the first prohibits congressional and state legislative action, the other nine applying only against congressional infringement. Among the more important of the rights therein assured are freedom of speech, press, and religion; trial by jury; grand jury indictment; and guarantees against cruel and unusual punishments, excessive bail, and unreasonable searches and seizures.

bills of credit. See fiat currency.

BILLY the KID. *Real name* William H.

Bonney. 1859-1881. Outlaw. b. New York City. Lived in the Southwest and became a notorious desperado with a legend growing up around his exploits.

bimetalism. The circulation of two currencies based on two forms of specie with an established relationship between them, as a gold and silver standard. Has existed in the United States at various times as between 1837-1873, 1878-1900, and between 1934 and the present. The relationships have varied depending upon congressional act, being generally 15-1 or 16-1.

BINGHAM, George Caleb. 1811-79. Painter and public official. b. Virginia. Moved to Missouri where he did most of his work; studied art at the Pennsylvania Academy of Fine Arts (1837) and in Europe (1856-59); elected to the Missouri Assembly (1849); state treasurer (1862-65); served in the Union army; appointed Missouri adjutant-general (1875); best known for his genre paintings of local scenes including *The Verdict of the People, Stump Speaking, The Jolly Flatboatman* and *Raftsmen Playing Cards*.

BINGHAM, Hiram. 1875-1956. Historian, archaeologist, aviator and U. S. Senator. Graduated Harvard (Ph.D.); professor of Latin American history at Yale (1907-24); traced Bolivar's footsteps and write *Journal of an Expedition across Venezuela and Colombia* (1909); followed an old Spanish trade route from Buenos Aires to Lima and wrote *Across South America* (1911); headed many expeditions to explore Inca ruins for Yale; in charge of all U. S. military flying schools(1917); served as chief of Air Personnel Division and commanded largest allied flying school, located at Issoudun, France. Lieutenant governor of Connecticut (1923-24); governor (1924-25); U. S. Senator (1925-33). Author of *Lost City of the Incas* (1948).

BINNEY, Horace. 1780-1875. Lawyer. b. Philadelphia, Pa. Graduated Harvard. Director of first BANK OF THE UNITED STATES (1808); published first of six volumes of *Binney's Reports* of Pennsylvania supreme court cases. Leading lawyer in Pennsylvania for decades and very prominent throughout country. Headed opposition party in Congress during JACKSON's administration. Wrote in support of LINCOLN on the right to suspend the writ of HABEAS CORPUS.

BIRNEY, James Gillespie. 1792-1857. Anti-slavery leader. b. Kentucky. Graduated Princeton; practiced law in Kentucky and Alabama, where he secured laws helping the slaves; agent of AMERICAN COLONIZATION SOCIETY (1832-34); formed Kentucky Anti-Slavery Society; published *Philanthropist,* anto-slavery paper; executive secretary of American Anti-Slavery Society (1837-57). In contrast with W. L. GARRISON, he proposed merely political action; formed LIBERAL PARTY (1840); nominated for President (1840-44), polled enough votes in 1844 to gain the presidency for POLK instead of CLAY.

Bismarck Sea, Battle of. A major air-sea battle of World War II. It was fought on March 2, 1943 against a Japanese fleet which was discovered approaching New Guinea. In the battle, which lasted four days, the Japanese lost 22 warships and transports. The American fleet was led by Admiral Halsey under the overall command of General MACARTHUR.

Bituminous Soft Coal Act. Also known as the Guffey-Snyder Coal Act. Passed by Congress in 1935, as part of the program of industrial recovery in the early NEW DEAL period. Its objective was the stabilization of conditions in the industry. The law provided for a bituminous coal code making authority to establish minimum and maximum prices. It also contained other provisions dealing with labor relations, wage regulation, working conditions and competitive practices. It is sometimes referred to as the "Little N.R.A." It was declared unconstitutional by the United States Supreme Court in 1936 in the case of CARTER VS. CARTER COAL COMPANY.

"black belt." See Plantation System.

Black Codes. Laws passed by southern governments established under the JOHNSON RECONSTRUCTION PROGRAM for the social, political, and economic control of FREEDMEN. These laws imposed severe restrictions upon Negroes such as prohibiting their right to vote, forbidding them to sit on juries, limiting their right to testify against white men, requiring them to have steady work, and subjecting them to special penalties for violations of labor contracts. They also included various harsh vagrancy and apprenticeship laws, draconic penal codes, and cruel and arbitrary punishments. Negroes were not allowed to bear arms, appears in public places, or take certain jobs. The results was the reduction of the freedom to a state of virtual peonage. Vestiges of the black codes still exist in some southern states.

Blackfeet Indians. Comprising a group of three Algonquin tribes, theirs was a typical Plains culture. They lived near the Yellowstone River and westward to the Rocky Mountains. They were at one time a large tribe, but less than half their number are alive today and are living on reservations in Montana and in Alberta, Canada.

"Black Friday." Refers to the attempt by two stock speculators, JAY GOULD and JAMES FISK, to corner the nation's gold market in 1869. With the passive assent of high placed persons in the White House and the Treasury their purchases of gold between September 20 and 24 drove its price up from 140 to 163½ on Friday September 24, 1869. This created a violent stock exchange panic and confronted scores of Wall Street brokers and legitimate businessment with ruin. When the government, at President GRANT's order, dumped $4,000,000 in gold on the market the corner collapsed. President Grant was accused of criminal incompetence in allowing himself to be involved in the affair. This is one of the many sordid scandals of the two Grant administrations.

BLACK, Hugo LaFayette. 1886-1971. Politician and Jurist. b. Alabama. Graduated, Alabama Law School (1906) and practiced in Birmingham; U.S. Senator (1927-37); appointed by F. D. ROOSEVELT, Associate Justice of the U. S. Supreme Court (1937) and his appointment was finally confirmed after much debate; his decisions have been liberal and without prejudice.

BLACK, Jeremiah Sullivan. 1810-1883. Jurist and Cabinet officer. b. Pennsylvania. President judge of district court in Pa. (1842); justice of state supreme court (1851); appointed by BUCHANAN, U. S. Attorney-General (1857-60); exposed California land title frauds; was Buchanan's political advisor and moved to protect all Federal property from the secessionists. U. S. Secretary of State (1860-61) just prior to Civil War.

BLACK HAWK. 1767-1838. *Indian name* Ma-ka-tae-mish-kia-kiak. b. Illinois. War chief of SAUK AND FOX INDIANS, leader in the BLACK HAWK WAR (1832), which ended in victory for U. S. army troops. He was trying to lead his starving people into different territories. His action was misinterpreted and they were fired on by frontier forces. Many women and children were killed, and the slaughter was unjustified. Black Hawk was captured and taken to Washington and presented to President JACKSON (1833). He wrote *Autobiography of Black Hawk* (1833) which is his presentation of his case and a classic in American literature.

Black Hawk War. An Indian war in 1830 caused by an attack against a village of the Sac tribe at the mouth of Rock River, the site of the present city of Rock Island, Illinois. After their women and children had been driven from the village and their land seized, the tribe under the leadership of BLACK HAWK attacked and recaptured the village. Following a brief period of peace the War was renewed in 1831 until BLACK HAWK was driven into Wisconsin and captured. Fighting lasted through 1832, involving the SAUK AND FOX tribes. The Black Hawk War was the final Indian conflict on the northwestern frontier until the gold hunters renewed the warfare in the 1860's.

Black Legion, the. A secret organization arising in Michigan in 1936. Its program involved anti-labor propaganda and occasionally terroristic activities in its attempts to destroy the growing trade union movement in that state. The widespread public indignation stemming from its assassination of Charles A. Poole in Detroit finally brought police action into play. There were many prosecutions, leading to its ultimate dissolution.

Blacklist. A list of the names and other identifying data of prominent union leaders, organizers, and members. Such a list was used before the 1930's by anti-union business firms in their attempts to prevent the employment of such persons. The enactment of the WAGNER ACT has rendered the blacklist unworkable.

"Black Republicans." A term of contempt applied by southerners during the Reconstruction period to Republicans who aided the FREEDMEN.

Black Warrior Affair. A dispute between the United States and Spain in 1854. The American vessel, the *Black Warrior,* was held in Havana, Cuba by the Spanish government which demanded a cargo manifest. Upon failure to produce the document the ship was seized, and subsequently released only upon payment of a six thousand dollar fine. The protests of Secretary of State WILLIAM L. MARCY and the American ambassador to Spain Pierre Soulé temporarily threatened war. The dispute was settled by the remission of the fine.

BLACKWELL, Elizabeth. 1821-1910. Physician, first woman to receive a medical degree. Born in England; educated in New York; established the New York Infirmary for Women and Children (1850); medical college for women added (1865). Returned to England (1869) to teach medicine to women. Blackwell's Island, in the East River in New York City, is named in her honor.

BLAINE, James Gillespie. 1830-1893. Statesman. b. Pennsylvania. Studied law; influential editor of the KENNEBEC JOURNAL, Augusta, Maine (1854-60); leader in the formation of Republican party in Maine, and a delegate to the first Republican national convention. Member, U.S. House of Representatives (1863-76); Speaker of the House (1869-75); U.S. Senator (1876-81); due to the scandal of the "MULLIGAN LETTERS" he was an unsuccessful candidate for the Republican nomination (1876, 1880); supported HAYES administration; successful in getting GARFIELD nominated for the presidency (1880) despite Conkling's opposition. Secretary of State under Garfield, but resigned at his death; retired and wrote TWENTY YEARS IN CONGRESS (2 vols. 1884-86) a widely read autobiography. Nominated for the presidency by the Republicans (1884) against CLEVE-

LAND. The campaign was bitter and many of his supporters made statements that lost votes for him. He was defeated by Cleveland. Supported HARRISON and was made Secretary of State (1889-92) one of the ablest ever to hold office. Fostered better relations with Latin-America and presided over the first PAN-AMERICAN CONFERENCE. His ideas have served as a model for action.

BLAIR, Francis Preston. 1791-1876. Politician and journalist. b. Virginia. Edited *Washington Globe* which was very influential as an organ of the Jacksonian wing of the Democratic party. Leading member of the "KITCHEN CABINET"; with J. C. Rives, started the *Congressional Globe* which recorded daily proceedings in Congress. His attitude to slavery led him to leave the Democratic party and become one of the founders of the Republican party; presided over first national convention; supported LINCOLN. Accused of influencing JOHNSON in his opposition to Congressional reconstruction. His dislike of the policies drove him back into Democratic party ranks.

BLAIR, Francis Preston. 1821-1875. Civil War general and politician. Son of above. Graduated Princeton University; studied law; established *Barnburner,* a free-soil paper; organized and led FREE-SOIL PARTY in Missouri (1848); member, U.S. House of Representatives (1856-58, 1860-62). Saved Missouri for the Union both as a speaker and organizer of troops; served at VICKSBURG; major general with SHERMAN in march to sea. Organized Democratic Party in state of Missouri; nominated as Vice-President with Seymour (1868) but lost election. Became liberal Republican and served as U.S. Senator (1871-75).

BLAIR, James. 1655-1743. Founder of William and Mary College, served as its first president (1693-1743). Acting governor of Virginia (1740-41).

BLAIR, Montgomery. 1813-188?. Statesman. b. Kentucky. Graduated, U.S.M.A., West Point; studied law; prominent in Missouri as Democratic leader. Free-soil views caused him to join Republican Party. As counsel for Scott in DRED SCOTT CASE, he gained a national reputation. Postmaster General in LINCOLN's cabinet (1861-64).

Bland-Allison Act. Passed in 1878 as a result of extreme pressure brought by FARMERS, westerners, DEBTORS, and silver miners. Provided for the monthly purchase by the treasury of $2,000,000 to $4,000,000 worth of silver as the standard for the circulation of silver certificates. The objective was to achieve a greater circulation of currency for the purpose of raising commodity prices. This act re-established a bi-metallic standard after a lapse of five years, and under it 378,166,000 silver dollars were coined. For many reasons the price of silver did not rise, and in 1890 Congress passed the SHERMAN SILVER PURCHASING ACT.

"Bland Dollar." The silver dollar consisting of 412½ grains of silver to be coined as a result of the BLAND-ALLISON ACT of 1878. It was named after Representative RICHARD P. BLAND of Missouri, co-author of the law.

BLAND, Richard. 1710-1776. Statesman. b. Virginia. Member Virginia HOUSE OF BURGESSES from 1745 until the Revolution; delegate to the CONTINENTAL CONGRESSES (1774-75); author of *Inquiry into the Rights of the British Colonies* (1766), earliest published defense of colonies' stand on taxation.

BLAND, Richard Parks. 1835-1899. Lawyer and legislator. b. Kentucky. Member, U.S. House of Representatives from Missouri (1873-95, 1897-99). Co-author of BLAND-ALLISON ACT (1878); leader of FREE SILVER bloc in Congress; defeated by BRYAN (1896) for nomination for the presidency. Known by nickname "Silver Dick."

"bleeding Kansas." The name applied to the five year border war in the Kansas Territory following the enactment of the KANSAS-NEBRASKA bill in 1854. From the North and the South came squatters, speculators, and adventurers, to supplement the influx of anti-slave and pro-slave immigrants. The slavery issue was thus complicated by claim jumping, lynching, pillaging, and other criminal activities. The warfare that followed included the plundering of Lawrence on May 21, 1856, JOHN BROWN's massacre of five pro-slavery men at Pottawatamie on May 24th, the anti-slave burning of Osawatomie, and the massacre of nine free-state men on May 19, 1858 at Marais des Cygne. Other battles included those at Black Jack, Franklin, Fort Saunders, Hickory Point, and Slough Creek, all free state victories. The major fighting stopped early in 1859 but disorders continued until the opening of the Civil War.

BLENNERHASSET, Harman. 1765-1831. Conspirator. b. England. Graduated, Trinity College, Dublin; studied law; came to the United States (1796); financially very successful; lent money to AARON BURR to back his western schemes (from 1805); took part in the conspiracy to invade Mexico; arrested in Natchez (1806-07) but when Burr was acquitted of treason, he was not tried; his mansion and island were destroyed by the militia; went to Montreal to practice law.

BLISS, Tasker Howard. 1853-1930. Army officer, statesman. Graduated, U.S.M.A., West Point (1875); fought in Puerto Rico and Cuban campaigns during the Spanish-American War (1898); brigadier general (1902); major general (1915); general, chief of staff (1917); appointed by President WILSON as member of Allied Conference, of the Allied Supreme War Council, and one of five delegates to Peace Conference. He opposed Foch in plan for allied invasion of Russia and won. Member of American Commission to Negotiate Peace (1918-19). Supported Wilson on LEAGUE OF NATIONS and was an advocate of DISARMAMENT after the war.

BLOCH, Ernest. 1880-1959. Composer, Born in Switzerland; came to the United States (1916); naturalized (1924); founder and director of Cleveland Institute of Music (1920-25); director (1925-30) of San Francisco Conservatory of Music. Best known for opera *Macbeth*, *Schelomo*, for cello and orchestra, epic for orchestral rhapsody *America*. Famous for compositions based on ancient Hebrew melodies.

blockade. During a war the shutting off of goods to the ports of a belligerent by the navy of its enemy. In American history blockades have been attempted and effected many times. The first of these was the blockade on Mexican ports in the Gulf of Mexico and the Pacific Ocean at the outbreak of the Mexican War. During the Civil War LINCOLN ordered a blockade on Confederate ports, the most effective in history. The navy blockaded Cuba and Puerto Rico during the Spanish-American War and German costal ports during World Wars I and II. United States interpretation of blockades under international law has always maintained that they must be effective in order to be considered valid. This principle was stated in 1784 in the Treaty Plan of the CONTINENTAL CONGRESS. On the basis of this reasoning it protested the British and French blockades during the Napoleonic War. The theory was embraced for the first time in the treaty with Colombia in 1824 which declared that a blockaded port could only be one so effectively attacked by an enemy as to prevent any neutral trade with it. The principle was reiterated in the United States Naval War Code in 1900.

blockade running. The violation of a blockade by the ships of a neutral power or of the blockaded nation. During the Civil War blockade runners frequently put in at the Bahamas and then smuggled goods to Confederate ports. The estimated number of blockade runners was 8250, and the risk of failure averaged only 16 percent. This, plus the Confederate law requiring all English vessels entering its ports to bring arms and supplies, made blockade running a profitable venture. It is believed that the total value of goods entering the Confederacy during the Union blockade was over $200,000,000 which included more than 600,000 small arms, munitions, manufactured goods, and other commodities. The Confederacy exported more than one and a quarter million bales of cotton in running the blockade, successfully escaping the vigilance of 600 Union vessels. Nevertheless the Union blockade was effective. Southern cotton exports, which had totalled $191,000,000 in 1860, declined to $4,000,000 in 1862.

blockhouse. A small structure erected as a temporary fortification for military defense. In colonial America such structures were erected as isolated forts at mountain passes and river fords. They were two story edifices built of timber or stone and used for the storage of munitions or supplies for community defense and for the garrisoning of troops. In the colonies these blockhouses were generally built on the frontier for protection against the Indians and the French. After the American Revolution they were seen in Kentucky, Tennessee, and the Ohio country, and used for the same purposes. Early government posts in the far west in the 19th century were built around blockhouses. They were used, with modifications of structure, in the Civil War and the Spanish-American War.

BLOOMER, Amelia Jenks. 1818-1894. Social reformer and pioneer in fight for women's rights. b. New York. Wrote and lectured on WOMAN'S SUFFRAGE, social reform and temperance. Famous for her wearing of a new costume for women which included trousers which were called "bloomers."

BLOUNT, William. 1749-1800. Political leader and legislator. b. North Carolina. Served with North Carolina troops in Revolution; member of state house of commons (1780-84); member, CONTINENTAL CONGRESS (1782-83, 86-87); state senator (1788-90); served as delegate to FEDERAL CONSTITUTIONAL CONVENTION (1787). Governor of territory south of Ohio River (1790); president of Tennessee constitutional convention (1796); elected one of Tennessee's first Senators (1796-97); expelled from the Senate for inciting CREEK and CHEROKEE INDIANS to cooperate with the British fleet in attack on Spanish Florida and Louisiana. Elected state senator and made speaker.

BLOW, Susan Elizabeth. 1843-1916. Educator, pioneer kindergartener in the United States. b. Missouri. Opened the first successful kindergarten at Carondelet, St. Louis (1873). Established a training school for kindergarten teachers (1874).

"Blue Eagle." The symbol of industrial recovery attempted by the passage of the NATIONAL RECOVERY ACT in 1933. It was a blue colored American eagle appearing in display posters and other publicity material relating to the codes of fair competition established under the law. Such posters reproduced the Blue Eagle accompanied by the slogan "Member N.R.A. We Do Our Part."

"blue laws." Name applied to the severe colonial laws passed by Church controlled legislatures demanding religious conformity, prohibiting recreational activities on the sabbath, limiting such activities at other times, setting aside periods of prayer, and emphasizing the value of work. Such laws to a limited degree exist today in many states.

BLUNT, James Gilpatrick. 1826-1881. Union General. b. Maine. Opposed slavery and aided JOHN BROWN in helping escaped slaves reach Canada; member Kansas Constitutional Convention (1859); lieutenant colonel Union Army; brigadier general (1862); defeated (1862); defeated Price in battle of "Price's Raid" (1864) which brought an end to Confederate action in the west.

Board of War Communications. An agency established by EXECUTIVE ORDER on September 24, 1940 for the purpose of coordinating plans for the most efficient use of the nation's RADIO, TELEGRAPH, TELEPHONE, and cable facilities during the national emergency. After the attack on PEARL HARBOR the Board was authorized to use, control, or close down any COMMUNICATIONS facility which was deemed necessary to the war effort, and to set up preferences or priorities in handling essential war communications. The Board was composed of the chairman of the FEDERAL COMMUNICATIONS COMMISSION who was named its chairman and of the Chief of the Army Signal Corps, Director of Naval Communications, Assistant Secretary of State in charge of the Division of International Communications, and Assistant Secretary of the Treasury in charge of Treasury Enforcement Activities.

BOAS, Franz. 1858-1942. Anthropologist and ethnologist. Born and educated in Germany; came to the United States; was one of first anthropologists to do field work; first professor of anthropology at Columbia University (from 1899); curator of anthropology, American Museum of Natural History (1901-05); pioneer in statistical analysis of physical measurements of man; opposed to theories of racial supremacy; author of THE MIND OF PRIMITIVE MAN (1911), AN-THROPOLOGY AND MODERN LIFE (1928), edited and contributed largely to HANDBOOK OF AMERICAN INDIAN LANGUAGES (2 vols. 1911-22).

BOGGS, Lillburn W. 1792-1860. Public official. b. Kentucky. State senator in Missouri (1826-32); lieutenant governor (1832-36); governor (1836-40); during his administration the first state bank was established; the first public school law of the state passed; severely criticized for expelling MORMONS from the state by use of the militia.

BOLTWOOD, Bertram Borden. 1870-1927. Chemist and physicist. b. Massachusetts. Graduated, Yale University (Ph.D. 1897); professor of radiochemistry, Yale (1910-1927); well-known for experiments in the field of radioactivity; discovered the element *ionium* which led to the discovery by others of *isotopes*.

bonded servant. See indentured servant.

BOND, George Phillips. 1825-1865. Astronomer. Graduated Harvard University (1845); director of Harvard College Observatory (1859-65); discovered new satellite Hyperion; writing on Donati comet most complete description in existence; called the father of photographic astronomy, his photographs of the moon taken in Europe in 1851 caused a sensation in the field: measured brightness of stars, double stars and planets.

BOND, Thomas. 1712-1784. Physician, founded the first hospital in the United States; established the first medical school; according to BENJAMIN RUSH, introduced the use of mercury into general practice in Philadelphia. With help of BENJAMIN FRANKLIN opened first hospital for the sick, injured and insane (1752); began delivery of the first clinical lectures at the hospital (1766); a founder of the AMERICAN PHILOSOPHICAL SOCIETY.

70

BOND, William Cranch. 1789-1859. Astronomer. Expert in making chronometers; supervised building of Harvard Observatory and was its director (1839-59); he developed the chronograph for recording the position of the stars; pioneer in use of chronometer and telegraph for determining longitude.

Bonds, U. S. Savings. Issued in three series, E. F and G by the TREASURY DEPARTMENT for various purposes. Among these have been the attempt to raise funds for financing World War I and II and as an anti-inflation measure to siphon off surplus purchasing power. Although aimed at the consumer population, many important institutional investors have purchased them in considerable quantities. Known as LIBERTY BONDS in World War I and DEFENSE AND WAR BONDS in the period of World War II. They pay varying rates of interest. In World War I $21,435,370,600 worth of bonds were subscribed as compared to approximately $185,000,000 in World War II.

Bonhomme Richard, The. The name by which an old French ship had been rechristened by its master JOHN PAUL JONES during the American Revolution. In this vessel Jones attacked the powerful British frigate, the *Serapis*, which was convoying a merchant fleet to the Baltic. In the great battle which followed, with the ships lashed to each other, the *Bonhomme Richard* compelled the *Serapis* to strike her colors. The battle occurred in 1779.

Bonn Republic. The German Federal Republic established on September 21, 1949 when the Allied Control Council turned over to it the administration of the United States, British, and French zones of occupation. This step marked the culmination of a series of political and economic moves designed to restore German sovereignty and modify the restrictions on German industry laid down in the Yalta and Potsdam Declarations. In January, 1947 the United States and England agreed to treat their zones as a single area for economic purposes. In February, 1948 these nations created an economic council to regulate economic affairs in their zones. In April, 1949 the three western powers adopted the Occupation Statute establishing the basis for a merger of the United States, British, and French Zones. In May, 1949 the Bonn constituent assembly approved a constitution for Western Germany which became effective on May 23. Parliamentary elections were held on August 14, a President elected on September 12, and on September 15, the lower house confirmed the appointment of Konrad Adenauer as Chancellor. Bonn was selected as the federal capital on November 3. On May 5, 1955, France and Great Britain announced ratification of the Paris Agreements which ended the 10 year occupation and established West Germany as a sovereign state. On May 9, 1955 the republic became a full member of NATO.

BONNEVILLE, Benjamin Louis Eulalie de. 1796-1878. Army officer. Born in Paris, France. Graduated U.S.M.A., West Point (1815); explored northwestern country (1832-35); served as major in Mexican War and in Civil War; retired (1861). Hero of WASHINGTON IRVING's *Adventures of Captain Bonneville* (1837).

Bonneville Dam. One of the dams in the Columbia River Reclamation Project. It is situated at the head of tide-water on the river in Oregon. The original work on the dam was undertaken in 1933 under the provisions of the NATIONAL RECOVERY ACT and was formalized by Congress in the Rivers and Harbors Act of 1935. Its main features include a dam, a power house, shiplocks and fishways.

Its total estimated cost with its ten power units is $87,565,000. Its works are operated and maintained by the Corps of Engineers, U.S. Army. The dam's installed capacity is 518,400 kilowatts. The transmission and sale of electric energy are under the supervision of the Secretary of Interior through the Bonneville Power Administration.

Bonney, William. See Billy the Kid.

Bonus Act of 1936. A law of Congress passed in January, 1936 providing for the immediate payment in cash to veterans of World War I of Adjusted Compensation Certificates. It was passed over President F. D. ROOSEVELT'S veto. The enactment of this law culminated 17 years of agitation by the veterans for the payment of a special bonus.

"Bonus Army." A group of unemployed veterans of World War I who marched to Washington, D.C. in May, 1932 from all sections of the United States. About 15,000 of these veterans petitioned Congress for immediate payment of the Adjusted Compensation Certificates. For more than a month the veterans lived under difficult conditions of housing and sanitation. When Congress defeated the Bonus Bill in June the veterans were ordered to leave Washington. When they refused to do so they were driven forcibly from their camps on July 28th, by troops under the command of General DOUGLAS MAC ARTHUR, upon the order of President HOOVER.

"Boondoggling." The term of derision applied by opponents of the NEW DEAL to the alleged useless public works programs of the early 1930's.

BOONE, Daniel. 1734-1820. Most famous American pioneer frontiersman. b. Pennsylvania. Moved to North Carolina (1750); first pioneer in the region which is now Kentucky (1767, 69-71); guided settlers into Kentucky (1775); at the site of what is now Boonesboro, he created a fort (1775); captured by Indians and taken to Detroit (1778); escaped back to Boonesboro in time to help resist Indian attack; despite his service to the frontier territory all his land titles were invalidated (after 1780); spent (1788-98) in western Kentucky; moved to what is now Missouri and secured grant of land (about 1799); confirmed by Congress (1814). Author of *Discovery, Settlement, and Present State of Kentucky* (1784).

BOOTH, Edwin Thomas. 1833-1893. Actor. b. Maryland. Famous as interpreter of Shakespeare; appeared on New York stage and toured the continent. Appeared with Lawrence Barrett and Mme. Modjeska; chief roles; Hamlet, and King Lear.

BOOTH, John Wilkes. 1838-1865. Actor and assassin of ABRAHAM LINCOLN. Appeared in Shakespearean plays with brother EDWIN; violent SECESSIONIST; joined militia which captured and executed JOHN BROWN (1859); conspired to kidnap Lincoln which failed; assassinated Lincoln at the Ford theatre in Washington and leaped to stage shouting "Sic semper tyrannis! The South is Avenged." (April 14, 1865); escaped, but was shot and killed two weeks later.

bootlegging. Illegal manufacture and sale of intoxicating liquors after the passage of the VOLSTEAD ACT of 1920. Resulted in growth of large-scale criminal activity in the big cities, with considerable political control exercised by the gangster elements over local machine politics.

BORAH, William Edgar. 1865-1940. Lawyer and statesman. b. Illinois. Admitted to the bar (1889); practiced in Boise, Idaho (from 1891); U. S. Senator from Idaho (1907-1940); chairman, Senate Foreign Relations Committee (from 1924). Supported THEODORE ROOSEVELT for Republican nomination (1912); played leading role in defeating entry of the United States into the LEAGUE OF NATIONS; opposed WORLD COURT; suggested the Washington Disarmament Conference (1920-21); urged recognition of Russia; opposed intervention in Latin America; opposed veteran's bonus; opposed MC-NARY-HAUGEN bill.

border states. The group of slave states in which considerable anti-slave sentiment existed on the eve of the Civil War. The prompt action of President LINCOLN in sending federal troops into Delaware, Kentucky, Maryland, and Missouri kept these states within the Union after South Carolina seceded in December, 1861. Although Virginia seceded, manufacturing and mining interests in the western portion "seceded" from Virginia and were recognized by Congress as the new state of West Virginia in 1861.

border war. See "bleeding Kansas."

BOREMAN, Arthur Ingram. 1823-1896. Senator and governor of West Virginia. Important in securing the separation of that state from Virginia. Admitted to the bar (1845); served in Va. house of delegates (1855-61); opposed SECESSION and joined WHEELING CONVENTION (June 11, 1861) elected president; elected first governor of West Virginia when it became a separate state (1863); re-elected (1864 and 1866); U. S. Senator (1869-75); chairman for a time on Committee on Territories.

BORGLUM, Gutzon. 1871-1941. Sculptor. b. Idaho. Well known for statue of SHERIDAN, head of LINCOLN and other works. But gained national fame for his carved figures of WASHINGTON, LINCOLN, JEFFERSON and T. ROOSEVELT on Mt. Rushmore in the Black Hills of South Dakota.

Boston. The tenth largest city in the United States. In 1952 its population was almost 900,000, inhabiting a land and water area of 65.9 square miles. It was incorporated in 1822 and is the capital of Massachusetts. Boston was first explored by JOHN SMITH in 1614 but was not heavily settled until the Puritan GREAT MIGRATION led by JOHN WINTHROP in 1630. It was the seat of the first free public school in America, which was opened in 1635. Today nine prominent colleges and universities are located in Boston and Cambridge, across the Charles River. Among these is Harvard University, the oldest institution of higher learning in North America. Historic sites in Boston include the Old Statehouse in front of which occurred the BOSTON MASSACRE and from whose balcony the DECLARATION OF INDEPENDENCE was proclaimed, the Old South Meeting House, erected in 1669, the Paul Revere House, and FANEUIL HALL, the "Cradle of Liberty," now used as a military museum. Boston is an important port, being the greatest fishing harbor in the United States. It is the largest shoe and leather market in the world and the largest wool market in the United States.

Boston Massacre. The name applied to the killing of five men and the wounding of others when British troops fired into a crowd of men and boys in Boston. The "massacre" occurred in 1770 as a result of the quartering of two regiments of troops in Boston, sent to protect British officials in executing the Customs Acts. JOHN ADAMS acted as counsel for the British in the trial that followed. The British officer in command was acquitted, though accused of giving the order to fire. Two British soldiers were given light sentences for manslaughter. It is one of a series of occurrences developing colonial resistance to Parliamentary policy on the eve of the American

Revolution.

Boston Police Strike. A strike of 75 percent of the Boston police force on September 9, 1919. The immediate cause was a refusal of the police commissioner to recognize the policemen's union. Governor COOLIDGE was requested to intercede after the outbreak of the strike but refused. Mayor Petes then brought in sections of the militia which broke the strike. Coolidge followed this act by commanding the police commissioner to assume charge, and called out the entire state guard, after order had already been established. His often quoted declaration that "there is no right to strike against the public safety by anybody, anywhere, anytime" projected him into the national limelight as a supporter of law and order. This resulted in his consideration by the Republican party as an outstanding candidate in the convention of 1920.

Boston Port Act. One of the series of parliamentary acts of 1774 known as the INTOLERABLE ACTS. These laws were enacted as a result of the BOSTON TEA PARTY of 1773. The Boston Port Act provided for the closing of the Port of Boston, moved the custom house to Salem, and stationed ships in the harbor to enforce the law. The ban was to be removed by the king when compensation was made for the tea destroyed and when he was satisfied that the duties would be paid in the future. The acts aroused instant resentment among the colonists because of what, in effect, was a BLOCKADE of Boston. Fear that this punishment might be imposed on the other colonies created a bond of sympathy among them. Neighboring towns kept Boston supplied with provisions. Supplies came from cities as far away as Charleston and Wilmington. A resolution of the Virginia HOUSE OF BURGESSES expressed that colony's sympathy. The ultimate result was the calling of the first CONTINENTAL CONGRESS in September 1774, a move leading directly to the American Revolution.

Boston Symphony Orchestra. One of the most famous symphonic organizations in the United States. It was founded in 1881 by Henry L. Higginson, and gave its first concert on October 22, 1881 under Sir George Henschel. The organization was incorporated in 1918 by nine trustees, who brought in Pierre Monteux as its conductor. In 1924 its most famous conductor, SERGE KOUSSEVITSKY, was appointed permanent conductor. A supplementary series of popular concerts is given each summer under the leadership of Arthur Fiedler. These are known as the Boston "Pops" concerts.

Boston Tea Party. An affair resulting from the attempt by Parliament to confer upon the East India Company a monopoly of the importation of tea into the colonies. In 1773 considerable cargoes of tea arrived in American ports. Customs officials in Boston insisted upon the unloading of the tea against the wishes of colonial leaders. Determined to prohibit the landing of the cargo a band of Boston citizens disguised as Indians boarded the ships on December 16, ripped open the 342 chests of tea valued at $90,000, and dumped their contents into the harbor. The result was the imposition of a series of harsh laws known as the INTOLERABLE ACTS, serving to inflame colonial public opinion against England. The colonial reply was the assembling of the FIRST CONTINENTAL CONGRESS in 1774 to consider united measures of resistance.

Boulder Canyon Project Act. See Colorado river Compact.

Boulder Dam. See Hoover Dam.

Boulder Dam Project. A project established by the Boulder Canyon Project Adjustment Act of 1940. Its purposes are flood control, irrigation, navigation improvement, power production, and the control of water for domestic, industrial, and municipal uses. The Project is administered by the Bureau of Reclamation within the DEPARTMENT OF THE INTERIOR. Its benefits will be distributed through the Colorado River territory.

bounties. SUBSIDIES or grants-in-aid by government to private business enterprises. Parliament paid bounties on the export of flax, hemp, indigo, and other commodities in an effort to encourage exports from the English colonies in America. These bounties stimulated the production of naval stores and rice in the Carolinas. Bounties were also paid by the colonial governments to the manufactures of brick, glass, iron, woolens, and other products to encourage increased production. The MCKINLEY TARIFF ACT provided a bounty of two cents a pound on sugar to supplement grants made by the state to the beet sugar industry in the 1890's. Land bounties were granted by the states and Congress to veterans of the Indian Wars and soldiers of the Mexican War. Bounties in cash and land were granted by Congress and the states to recruit troops in the colonial wars, the Revolution, and the War of 1812. These ranged from six dollars to $1,000 and from 100 acres to 320 acres. Bounty-jumping and re-enlistment became common practices. In the Civil War cash bounties, ranging from $25 to $100, were provided by Congress, the total aggregating well over $300,000,000. Bounties have also been provided by Congress to the' railroad, shipbuilding, and aircraft industries.

BOUTWELL, George Sewall. 1818-1905. Lawyer and political leader. Served in Massachusetts legislature; elected governor as a result of a coalition of Free-Soilers and Democrats (1851-52); Member, U. S. House of Representatives (1863-69); important in impeachment proceedings against ANDREW JOHNSON; appointed by GRANT as Secretary of the Treasury (1869-73); debt lessened during his administration; released government gold to defeat "BLACK FRIDAY"; U. S. Senator (1873-77); considered authority in field of international law.

BOWDITCH, Henry Ingersoll. 1808-1892. Physician. b. Massachusetts. Graduated Harvard Medical School (1832); Specialist in diseases of the chest; recommended out-door treatment for tuberculosis cases (1889); professor of clinical medicine, Harvard (1859-67); furthered public-health as member of state board, the first important state department of its kind in the country; ABOLITIONIST who aided runaway slaves; during Civil War acted as medical examiner; influenced Congress to establish ambulance unit; wrote *Public Hygiene in America* (1877).

BOWDITCH, Nathaniel. 1773 - 1838. Mathematician, navigator and astronomer. b. Massachusetts. Self-educated; mathematical genius; corrected errors in Moore's *Practical Navigator* and prepared it for publication (1799); expanded it and published as *The New American Practical Navigator* (1802); this is the standard work in the field and has gone through 60 editions. Translated, with commentaries and additions, first four volumes of Laplace's *Celestial Mechanics* (1828-39); president of various insurance companies.

BOWDOIN, James. 1726-1790. Merchant and Revolutionary statesman. b. Boston, Mass. Leading figure in council of 28 which governed the state constitutional convention (1779); governor, succeeding HANCOCK (1785-87); suppressed SHAY'S

REBELLION; urged Federal CONSTITUTIONAL CONVENTION and was an advocate of strong central government; helped found and was the first president of the American Academy of Arts and Sciences. Bowdoin College (chartered 1794) was named in his honor and received a large part of his estate.

BOWEN, Herbert Wolcott. 1856-1927. Diplomat. Graduated Yale University (1878); admitted to the bar (1881); U. S. Consul General, Spain (1895); Minister Resident, Persia (1899-1901); Minister, Venezuela (1901-04); had extremely difficult dealings with Castro, dictator of that country; went over head of ROOSEVELT and state department to HAGUE TRIBUNAL; reprimanded and recalled.

BOWIE, James. 1799-1836. Texas soldier and hero. b. Georgia. Settled in Texas; served as a colonel in the Texas army and fought against SANTA ANNA (1835-36); killed at the battle of the ALAMO. Either James or his brother Rezin invented the bowie knife.

BOWLES, Chester Bliss. 1901-. Political leader and diplomat. b. Massachusetts. Graduated, Yale University(1924); journalist and leading advertising executive; state OPA Director for Connecticut (1942-43); national director of the OFFICE OF PRICE ADMINISTRATION (1943-46); director, OFFICE OF ECONOMIC STABILIZATION (February-June, 1946); elected governor of Connecticut (1949-51); appointed U.S. Ambassador to India.

BOWLES, Samuel. 1826-1878. Newspaper editor. b. Connecticut. Son of Samuel Bowles (1797-1851) who published the Hartford *Times* (1819-22) and founded Springfield *Republican* (1824-44 as a weekly, from 1844 as a daily). Succeeded to control of paper (1851) and made it one of the most influential papers in the country. He supported LINCOLN; denounced radical elements during Reconstruction period; condemned political and financial corruption and was once sued for libel by JAMES FISK; leader of LIBERAL REPUBLICAN movement.

BOWMAN, Isaiah. 1878-1950. Geographer and educator. b. Ontario. Yale University (Ph.D. 1908); instructor and assistant professor Yale (1905-35); president, Johns Hopkins University (from 1935). Led many expeditions and served on many important councils and committees. Authority on physiography and political geography.

Boxer Rebellion. Uprising by Chinese nationalists in 1900. Aimed against reactionary Dowager Empress of China and intervening foreign nations which had established sphere of influence there. The United States sent marines to assist the military forces of 5 other nations in suppressing the uprising. Of the $300,-000,000 indemnity levied upon the Chinese government, the United States received approximately $25,000,000, of which some $18,000,000 was returned to China in subsequent years. These funds were earmarked for the use of Chinese students in American universities.

Boycott. In international trade the refusal of a nation to purchase goods from other nations. In the colonial period boycotts were voted and undertaken against British by the STAMP ACT CONGRESS and the CONTINENTAL CONGRESSES. In labor relations the boycott is an organized refusal by workers to purchase goods from an employer considered to practice unfair LABOR RELATIONS. The labor boycott also involves an attempt by the workers to influence the general public to abstain from such purchases. Its purpose is to obtain improved labor conditions. The methods in conducting a boycott include picketing and other publicity in the form of leaflets, petitions, and handbills. A secondary boycott by labor is an attempt to persuade workers or the public to refuse dealings with a second employer. Judicial interpretations have generally upheld the boycott in most states in the absence of violence or intimidation. Fourteen states prohibited the secondary boycott in 1952. One of the most famous Supreme Court decisions involving a boycott was the DANBURY HATTERS case. Despite the efforts of the CLAYTON ANTI-TRUST ACT to legalize boycotts the courts continued to penalize unions which undertook them. The TAFT-HARTLEY ACT declared the secondary boycott illegal.

BOYD, Belle. 1843-1900. Confederate spy in Civil War. Gathered information from Union troops and reported to STONEWALL JACKSON (1860-62). Imprisoned twice but released; escaped to England (1863); went on the stage. Wrote of her activities in *Belle Boyd in Camp and Prison* (1865).

BOYDEN, Roland William. 1863-1931. Lawyer and diplomat. b. Massachusetts. Graduated Harvard Law School; consul for the United States FOOD ADMINISTRATION during the war; member of U. S. delegation to Peace Conference (1919); appointed by HARDING to REPARATIONS COMMISSION; succeeded HUGHES as justice of the PERMANENT COURT OF INTERNATIONAL JUSTICE.

BOYDEN, Seth. 1788-1870. Inventor. Noted for work with leather. Improved his father's invention for leather-splitting; duplicated European process for lacquered leather; established first "patent" leather factory in the United States; solved problem of malleable cast-iron (granted patent 1831); worked with steam engines and locomotives and invented first automatic "cut-off" governor.

BOYLE, W.A. On April 11, 1974, Boyle,

the deposed United Mine Workers president, was convicted of murder in the slaying of union rival Joseph Yablonski, his wife, and daughter. He was given a life sentence. A new trial was ordered and in February 1978 the conviction was sustained.

BOYLSTON, Zabdiel. 1679-1766. Physician, first to innoculate against smallpox. During the smallpox epidemic (1721) he was persuaded by COTTON MATHER to innoculate, and achieved a better record than had been obtained in England. Public sentiment was against Boylston and Mather and violent action was used against them. Lectured in England (1724-26).

Boy Scouts of America. An organization of boys dedicated to the ideals of patriotism, honesty, good health, and sportsmanship. It was created in 1911 by the union of the Woodcraft Indians of Ernest Seton-Thompson and the Sons of Daniel Boone. Dan C. Beard was its founder. Its membership in 1956 was approximately 3,800,000.

BRACKENRIDGE, Henry Marie. 1786-1871. Lawyer and author. Author of *Views of Louisiana* (1814), historically significant for its description of the Missouri River; aided in framing judiciary system of Louisiana; urged policy similar to MONROE DOCTRINE; appointed secretary of a commission which went to South America to study political conditions there; wrote *Voyage to South America* (2 vols. 1819); urged extension of our judicial system into Florida territory; author of *Recollections of Persons and Places in the West* which is a good historical source book.

BRACKENRIDGE, Hugh Henry. 1748-1816. Lawyer and author. Graduated Princeton University (1781); practiced law in frontier town of Pittsburgh. Helped found first Pittsburgh newspaper, the *Gazette* (1786); leading supporter of Federal CONSTITUTION; prominent Republican; played role of peacemaker in *Whisky Rebellion* (1793-94); justice of Pennsylvania supreme court (1799-1816); wrote a satire on Western democracy *Modern Chivalry* (4 vols. 1792-97); also wrote plays and poetry.

BRADDOCK, Edward. Commander in chief of British forces in America. Major General in charge of expedition against Fort Duquesne (1755); defeated in surprise attack by a combined force of French and Indians and died of wounds suffered in the battle.

Braddock's Expedition. A major military effort of the British to destroy the French in the West in the early part of the French and Indian War. An army of 2200 British and colonial troops was sent against Fort Duquesne in 1775. On July 9th, 1200 men under General BRADDOCK approached the fort on the Monongahela River. A French force of 250 troops and 600 Indians met them and joined the battle. After three hours of intense fire Braddock retreated. He and several officers were killed. WASHINGTON, Braddock's aide-de-camp, had remained at Little Meadows, Maryland. He now sent aid for the wounded, and then retreated towards Philadelphia. The importance of the expedition lay in the experience gained in Indian fighting.

BRADFORD, Augustus Williamson. 1806-1881. Civil War governor of Maryland. As Maryland's delegate to the peace conference at Washington (early 1861) he strongly supported the Union. Elected governor (1862-66) gave support to Federal government which helped the Union cause considerably; called a constitutional convention at Annapolis (1864) which framed a new constitution abolishing slavery.

BRADFORD, John. 1749-1830. Pioneer printer. b. Virginia. Moved to Kentucky (1779). Published the first newspaper in Kentucky territory, the *Kentucky Gazette*

(1787); printed the *Kentucke Almanac,* the first pamphlet in the West (1788); published the first book in Kentucky (1792); helped found Transylvania University; chairman of the board (1799-1811).

BRADFORD, William. 1590-1657. Pilgrim leader and governor of the PLYMOUTH COLONY. Born in England, emigrated to Holland (1609); joined the emigrants aboard the MAYFLOWER (1620); signer of the MAYFLOWER COMPACT (1620); at death of JOHN CARVER became governor of Pilgrims of New England. He was a firm, determined man and an excellent leader; kept relations with the Indians on friendly terms; tolerant toward newcomers and new religions (unlike Puritan leaders at Boston); kept the colony independent of the MASSACHUSETTS BAY COLONY. Author of *History of Plimmoth Plantation* (published in full 1856) which is the chief source of information on the colony.

BRADFORD, William. 1663-1752. Pioneer printer. Born in London; came to the United States (1685); established first press, Philadelphia; established first paper mill in the colonies (1690); quarreled with authorities and moved press to New York City where he became king's official printer (1693-1742); printed first legislative proceedings to be published in America; first American Book of Common Prayer (1710); first drama written in the colonies (1714); first N.Y. paper money (1709); first history of N.Y. (1727); and the first N.Y. newspaper, the *New York Gazette* (1725). He was official printer to New Jersey (1703-33).

BRADFORD, William. 1722-1791. Revolutionary printer and patriot. Grandson of WILLIAM BRADFORD. Established his own shop in Philadelphia; founded and edited *Weekly Advertiser, or Pennsylvania Journal* (1742); supported colonial side and was called the "patriot printer"; opposed the STAMP ACT; signer of the NON-IMPORTATION RESOLUTIONS; leading member of Philadelphia SONS OF LIBERTY; advocated a continental congress; official printer to the first Congress; major in Revolutionary army.

BRADSTREET, Anne. 1612?-1672. Poet. Born in England; came to the United States (1630); first woman poet in America; she was well-known in the colonial period.

BRADSTREET, Simon. 1603-1697. Colonial governor. Came to the United States (1630); secretary, MASSACHUSETTS BAY COLONY (1630-36); assistant in colony (1630-79); helped form NEW ENGLAND CONFEDERATION (1643); representative from Mass. (1643-76); deputy governor of the colony (1673-79); governor (1679-86, 1689-92).

BRADY, Mathew B. 1823-1896. Pioneer photographer. Accompanied Union armies (1861-65); his photographs were used as basis for pictorial history of the Civil War; photographed famous personages of his time.

BRAGG, Braxton. 1817-1876. Confederate general. b. North Carolina. Graduated U.S.M.A., West Point (1837); served in the Seminole and Mexican wars; major general Confederate army (1862); general (April 1862); succeeded BEAUREGARD in command of the Army of Tennessee; won battle of CHICKAMAUGA; lost at CHATTANOOGA; relieved of field command (1863); military adviser to President DAVIS (1864-65).

Braintree Resolutions. A series of resolutions in the form of a petition drafted by SAMUEL ADAMS in 1764 in Braintree, Massachusetts. The Resolutions expressed the first colonial opposition to the STAMP ACT of that year. Having been presented to the SELECTMEN of the town, a meeting of the town's people was called to vote on them. The meeting unanimously adopted the resolutions which were subsequently approved by the people of Boston.

brain trust. Term applied to group of specialist advisers to President F. D. ROOSEVELT in the years following his first inauguration. These outstanding economists, scholars, and lawyers, played a significant role in developing the social and economic principles of the NEW DEAL. They included such authorities as Raymond Moley, A. A. BERLE, JR., Samuel Rosenman, Robert M. Lovett, and FRANCIS PERKINS.

BRANDEIS, Louis Dembitz. 1856-1941. Jurist. b. Kentucky. Graduated Harvard Law School (1877); practiced in Boston (1879-1916); known as "people's attorney" when he aided Boston citizens, without fees, in their fight to control price of gas; acted for policyholders in investigation of life insurance companies and drafted state legislation to control them; was special counsel for people in legal struggle involving constitutionality of Oregon and Illinois women's ten-hour wage laws and Ohio, California and Oregon's wage laws; counsel opposing railroad monopolies; associate justice, U.S. Supreme Court (1916-39); retired. Author of *Other People's Money* (1914), *Business, a Profession* (1914).

Brandywine, Battle of. A battle of the American Revolution which was fought on September 11, 1777. WASHINGTON, commanding an army of 11,000 men, moved on 18,000 British and Hessian troops commanded by Generals HOWE and CORNWALLIS who were stationed at Brandywine Creek in Pennsylvania. While the American center was engaged by General Knyphausen, Cornwallis made a flank attack upon the American right which was resisted by General SULLIVAN's division until the latter was compelled to retire. The American center fell back in orderly retreat under General GREENE as the right flank retreated under the assault of Generals Cornwallis and Knyphausen. In the evening Washington withdrew his army in good order to Chester, Pennsylvania with a loss of about 1,000 men. British casualties slightly exceeded this figure.

Brannan Plan. A program of aid to FARMERS sponsored by Secretary of Agriculture Charles F. Brannan in an appearance before the House Committee on Agriculture on April 11-12, 1949. The Plan advocated the maintenance of high farm prices to assist the farmer and low food prices to aid the consumer by expanding the agricultural price support program. It sought to support farm incomes by providing SUBSIDIES equal to the difference between market prices and incomes at the 1939-1948 level. Secretary Brannan defended the Plan as less costly than the existing PARITY payment program. Although supported by President TRUMAN and the administration, it was rejected by Congress.

BRANT, Joseph. 1742-1807. Indian name Tha-yen-da-ne-ge-a. War chief of the MOHAWK tribe. Educated in Connecticut; member of the ANGLICAN CHURCH; aided SIR WILLIAM JOHNSON in fight against the colonists in the Revolution; responsible for CHERRY VALLEY MASSACRE (1778); granted land in Canada by the British after the Revolution.

"bread colonies." The nickname of the middle colonies, New York, New Jersey, Pennsylvania, Maryland, and Delaware. They were called thus because of their specialized agriculture, growing almost exclusively wheat, oats, and barley.

BRECKENRIDGE, John. 1760 - 1806. Statesman. b. Virginia. Graduated, William and Mary; admitted to the bar (1785); attorney-general of Kentucky (1795-97); member of state legislature (1798-1801); U.S. Senator (1801-05); put KENTUCKY RESOLUTIONS thru state legislature; influential in LOUISIANA PUR-

CHASE; Attorney-General of the United States (1805-06) appointed by JEFFERSON.

BRECKENRIDGE, John Cabell. 1821-1875. Lawyer, statesman and confederate soldier. b. Kentucky. Graduated, Centre College, studied law at Transylvania University and began practice in Lexington, Ky. (1845); member, U.S. House of Representatives (1851-55); leader of Democratic party in Kentucky and southern running mate of BUCHANAN in presidential election; Vice-President of the United States (1857-61); for slavery, but against SECESSION, presidential candidate, southern faction of the Democratic party (1860); U.S. Senator (1861) trying hard to prevent civil war. However, he denounced Kentucky's action in remaining with the Union and escaped to the Confederate army; major general; Secretary of War, Confederacy (1865).

Breed's Hill, Battle of. See Bunker Hill, Battle of.

BRENT, Margaret. 1600-1671? Pioneer feminist. Born in England; settled in Maryland (1638); first woman to demand a vote and a seat in the colonial assembly, claiming she was a land owner and entitled to certain privileges. Refused; but she was allowed to address the assembly on various occasions.

Bretton Woods Conference. A meeting of 28 nations at Bretton Woods, New Hampshire in 1944, convened for the purpose of establishing the INTERNATIONAL BANK FOR RECONSTRUCTION AND DEVELOPMENT, also known as the World Bank.

BREWSTER, Wiliam. 1567-1644. Pioneer colonist. Born in England; emigrated to Holland (1608); printer in Leiden (1609-16); sailed aboard the *Mayflower* (1620) for America; only officer of PLYMOUTH colonists empowered to conduct religious services until 1629; influential in colonial affairs although he did not hold public office.

BRIGGS, LeBaron Russell. 1855-1934. Educator. b. Massachusetts. Graduated, Harvard University; professor of English, Harvard (1890); with Barrett Wendell, completely modernized the teaching of English; dean of the college (1891-1902); dean of the faculty (1902-25); served simultaneously as president of Radcliffe College (1903-23); important influence in education.

BRISTOW, Benjamin Helm. 1832-1896. Lawyer and statesman. b. Kentucky. Practiced law in Kentucky; served in Union army during CIVIL WAR; U.S. Solicitor General (1870-72); U.S. Secretary of Treasury (1874-76); conducted thorough investigation of his department; reorganized the department after obtaining evidence against and conviction of the WHISKY RING.

Broadway. The longest street in the world and probably the most famous in the United States. It extends 150 miles from Bowling Green at the southern tip of Manhattan Island in New York City to Albany, New York. In New York City it ends at 263rd Street at the Yonkers line. Broadway is the commercial, financial, business, and theatrical hub of New York City. In its course up Manhattan it is cut by many squares. The most famous of these include Union Square at 14th Street, Madison Square at 23rd Street, Herald Square at 34th Street, Times Square at 42nd Street, and Columbus Circle at 59th Street. Its important and interesting buildings are Trinity Church at Wall Street, St. Paul's Chapel (oldest church building in New York City), City Hall at the BROOKLYN BRIDGE entrance, Woolworth Building at Barclay Street, R. H. Macy's and Company at 34th Street, Columbia University at 116th Street, and Van Cortlandt Park at the Bronx-Yonkers line. The area of Times Square is popularly known as the "Great White Way" because of its millions of electric lights illuminating the scores of theatres and restaurants.

BRODERICK, David Colbreth. 1820-1859. Politician. Moved from New York City to California (1849); member, state constitutional convention (1849); state senator (1850-54); president of the California senate (1851); leader of the northern faction of the Democratic party of state; a bitter rivalry existed between Broderick and W. M. Gwin, a senator who led the southern faction; killed in a duel with Chief Justice Terry and mourned as a national hero of the Union cause.

BRODHEAD, Daniel. 1736-1809. Revolutionary soldier. Deputy surveyor-general of Pennsylvania; colonel of Pa. regiment during Revolution; stationed in Pittsburgh; commandant (1779); led army against IROQUOIS INDIANS and subdued them; held DELAWARE INDIANS in check; brigadier general after the war.

Bronx Zoo. See New York Zoological Park.

BROOKE, Edward. Brooke, a Republican from Massachusetts, was the first Black United States Senator in 85 years · His election took place on November 8, 1966.

BROOKE, John Mercer. 1826-1906. Scientist and naval officer. Graduated, U.S.N.A., Annapolis (1847); served in the coast survey and at the Naval Observatory in Washington (1849-53); invented deep-sea sounding device; joined North Pacific and Bering Straits Surveying and Exploring Expedition preparing maps and charts (1854-58); commander in Confederate navy; he planned conversion of the *Merrimac* to iron-clad *Virginia;* invented "Brooke" gun, a successful Confederate artillery weapon; professor of physics and astronomy at Virginia Military Institute (1866-1899).

81

Brook Farm. A communal organization set up in 1844 as a phalanx according to the FOURIER principles of collective living. It originated among the members of the Transcendental Club of Boston and included such famous figures as NATHANIEL HAWTHORNE, CHARLES A. DANA, GEORGE RIPLEY, and other notable leaders of the New England intellectuals. Originating as the Brook Farm Institute for Agriculture and Education it stated that its principal purpose was "to substitute a system of brotherly cooperation for one of selfish competition." The activities of Brook Farm included labor, farming, education, social, intellectual, and recreation programs. Its end in 1847 resulted from the destruction by fire of its phalanstery, lack of capital, poor business leadership, popular opposition, and the general decline of the Fourier phalanx movement. The experiment was one of the wide-sweeping humanitarian and utopian socialist movements of the Jacksonian period which included such other establishments as the ONEIDA COMMUNITY and NEW HARMONY in Indiana. All of these were expressions of the vast movement of reform known as JACKSONIAN DEMOCRACY.

Brooklyn Bridge. The first bridge built across the East River between Brooklyn and Manhattan. It was the longest suspension bridge in the world when it was opened on May 24, 1883. The construction corporation which built it was aided by a grant of $3,000,000 from Brooklyn and $1,500,000 from New York. The chief engineer, JOHN A. ROEBLING, was succeeded by his son Washington after his death in 1869. The construction took 13 years and cost $15,500,000.

BROOKS, John. 1752-1825. Revolutionary patriot, physician, governor. He led the Reading minute-men against the British at CONCORD, BUNKER HILL, and throughout the war; went with the group from Newburg to present complaints to Congress; after war served in various offices in Massachusetts; governor of the state for six terms.

BROOKS, Phillips. 1835-1893. Protestant Episcopal Bishop. b. Boston. Graduated, Harvard University (1855); rector of Church of Advent, Holy Trinity Church, Philadelphia (1859-69); Trinity Church, Boston (1869-91) where he became famous as a magnificent preacher and spiritual leader. Consecrated bishop of Massachusetts (1891); author of *Lectures on Preaching*, a collection of his BEECHER lectures at Yale (1877); and *The Light of the World* (1890). Famous for his Christmas hymn *O Little Town of Bethlehem*.

BROUGH, John. 1811-1865. Civil War governor of Ohio. Published Lancaster *Eagle* (1833) made it powerful Democratic paper; joint owner and editor, Cincinnati *Enquirer*, leading paper in the west (1844); reorganized state's financial system as auditor (1839-46); supported the Union during the Civil War; governor (1863-65).

BROWN, Aaron Venable. 1795-1859. Lawyer, legislator. b. Virginia. Tennessee lawyer; member, Tennessee state senate (1821-25); member, U.S. House of Representatives (1839-45); governor of Tennessee (1845-47); framed platform of Democratic party (1852) upon which PIERCE was elected; appointed by BUCHANAN U.S. Postmaster General (1857-59) establishing many overland mail routes.

BROWN, Benjamin Gratz. 1826-1885. Lawyer and senator. b. Kentucky. Leader of the FREE-SOIL movement in Missouri; helped in formation of Republican party in his state; U.S. Senator (1863-67); governor of Missouri (1871-73); prominent in LIBERAL REPUBLICAN PARTY and Vice-President on the GREELEY ticket.

BROWN, Henry Kirke. 1814-1886. Sculptor. b. Massachusetts. One of the first American sculptors to cast in bronze.

Works include *Washington*, in Union Square, N.Y., Gen. WINFIELD SCOTT and Gen. NATHANAEL GREENE (equestrian statues) in Washington, D. C. and many busts of famous people.

BROWN, Jacob Jennings. 1775-1828. General in War of 1812. b. Pennsylvania. Owned thousands of acres of land on Lake Ontario and founded village of Brownsville; defended base at Sacket's Harbor, Lake Ontario against British (1813); given command of Western New York at battle of Niagara (1814); General in Chief of the U.S. Army (1821-28).

BROWN, John. 1744-1780. Revolutionary soldier. b. Massachusetts. Graduated, Yale University; studied and practiced law in Mass.; member of town's COMMITTEE OF CORRESPONDENCE and provincial congress; mission to Canada to secure friendship in war against Britain; friend of ETHAN ALLEN, suggested his attack on TICONDEROGA; participated in many raids and attacks; after quarrel with BENEDICT ARNOLD, temporarily resigned; led regiment against BURGOYNE (1777) and captured Fort George; elected to Mass. lower house (1778); killed in the invasion of the Mohawk Valley.

BROWN, John. 1800-1859. Fanatic abolitionist. b. Connecticut. Kept station of UNDERGROUND RAILWAY at Richmond, Ohio; surveyor and militia captain of colony on Osawatomie, Kansas; killed five pro-slavery men at Pottawatamie river (1856) during the Kansas-Nebraska conflict, took strong stand to gain territory for emancipated slaves; aided by Mass. abolitionists; captured Harper's Ferry (1859); Gen. ROBERT E. LEE and marines took Brown prisoner; convicted of treason and hanged (Dec. 2, 1859); regarded by northern sympathizers as martyr; hero of marching song "John Brown's Body." Sometimes referred to as "Old Brown of Osawatomie."

BROWNING, Orville Hickman. 1806-1881. Senator and cabinet officer. b. Kentucky. Lawyer, Quincy, Ill.; member of Illinois state senate (1836-43); an organizer of Republican party in that state; drafted state platform (1856); helped secure nomination of LINCOLN at Chicago convention (1860); U.S. Senator (1861-63); disagreed with Lincoln on emancipation stand; supported JOHNSON'S reconstruction policy and was appointed Secretary of the Interior (1866-69); published *Diary*, which is an important source of information on the Lincoln and Johnson administrations.

Brownlow Committee. See executive reorganization.

BROWNLOW, William Gannaway. 1805-1877. Known as "the Fighting Parson", was Union governor of Tennessee during the Reconstruction period. b. Virginia. Itinerant Methodist preacher (1826-36); editor, *Jonesboro Whig and Independent* (1839-49); *Knoxville Whig* (1849-61) which he made most influential paper in state, paper was suppressed because of sympathy with Union cause; made prisoner and later sent into Federal lines; made successful lecture tour of North; wrote *Rise, Progress, and Decline of Secession* (1862); returned to Tennessee and organized a reconstruction government; elected governor by acclamation (1865-69); used state guards against KU KLUX KLAN; U.S. Senator (1869-75).

BROWNSON, Orestes Augustus. 1803-1876. Clergyman and writer. b. Vermont. Important influence on American thinking in his time. Universalis' minister (1826-29); free-lance preacher because of socialistic views; worked for short-lived WORKINGMAN'S PARTY; Unitarian minister (1832-44); founded a new "Church of the Future" (1838-42); leader of TRANSCENDENTALISM; interested in BROOK FARM experiment; converted to

83

Roman Catholicism (1844); Author of *The Convert* (1857).

Brown University. One of the oldest institutions of higher learning in America. It was established in 1760 at Warren, Rhode Island under the name of Rhode Island College, and moved to Providence in 1770, being renamed in honor of Nicholas Brown. It is a college for men, being affiliated with Pembroke College for women. It contains a notable collection of Americana in the John Hay Library and the John Carter Brown Library.

Bryan-Chamorro Treaty. A treaty between the United States and Nicaragua in 1914, granting to the United States in perpetuity the exclusive right to construct a canal in Nicaragua. It also provided for a 99 year lease to the United States of the Great and Little Corn Islands and rights to a naval base in the Gulf of Fonseca. Nicaragua was paid $3,000,000 for granting these rights. Costa Rica and El Salvador protested the Treaty, appealing it to the Central American court from which a verdict was received that Nicaragua had infringed upon these neighbors' rights. The Treaty, however, was not invalidated. The proposed naval base has not yet been established, and the Corn Islands remain to this date under Nicaraguan jurisdiction, although the Treaty continues in force.

BRYAN, William Jennings. 1860-1925. Lawyer and political leader. Often called "The Great Commoner." b. Illinois. Graduated, Illinois College (1881); studied law at Union College of Law, Chicago; moved to Lincoln, Nebraska (1887); member, U.S. House of Representatives (1891-96); became identified with silver forces in Congress and made famous "CROSS-OF-GOLD" SPEECH at the Democratic convention, Chicago, which won him the nomination for the presidency (1896); defeated by MC KINLEY; renominated (1900) and again defeated by McKinley-T. ROOSEVELT ticket; founded and edited the *Commoner*, a weekly newspaper which expressed his ideas; nominated a third time for the presidency (1908) and defeated by TAFT, who was strongly backed by T. Roosevelt. His backing secured the nomination of WOODROW WILSON (1912); named by Wilson as Secretary of State (1913-15) and advocated and negotiated non-aggression treaties with many nations; resigned after the sinking of the *Lusitania* because he did not agree with Wilson's policies; however, supported Wilson's renomination (1916); famous speaker on the CHAUTAUQUA circuit; interested in Fundamentalism; opposed the idea of evolution; prosecuting attorney for Tennessee in case of J. T. Scopes on teaching evolution in the public schools; cross-examined by CLARENCE DARROW, the defense attorney, and defeated. He had no knowledge of modern science. Died suddenly (July, 1925) shortly after the trial had ended.

BRYANT, William Cullen. 1794-1878. Poet and editor. b. Massachusetts. Practiced law, Mass. (1815-25); famous poem *Thanatopsis* (1811), *To a Waterfowl* published in *North American Review* (1817); assistant editor of New York *Evening Post* (1825); editor-in-chief (1829); joint owner with JOHN BIGELOW (1849); he held to a strong antislavery, pro-union policy for the paper; other poems include *Rispah, Monument Mountain, Autumn Woods, The Fountain, The Battlefield* etc. Most famous lines are "Truth, crushed to earth, shall rise again" from *The Battlefield*.

BRYCE, James Viscount. 1838-1922. British historian and diplomat. Born in Ireland. Graduated, Oxford University (1862); author of *Holy Roman Empire* (1864); regius professor of Civil Law, Oxford (1870-93); served in Parliament as member of Liberal Party; Undersecretary of Foreign Affairs (1886) under Gladstone; president of the Board of

Trade (1894); chief secretary for Ireland in Campbell-Bannerman's cabinet (1905-6); Ambassador to the United States (1907-13); signer of Anglo-American arbitration treaty (1911); member, Hague Tribunal (1913). Author of *The American Commonwealth* (1888), famous as a foreigner's viewpoint of American history and government, *Studies in Contemporary Biography* (1903), and *Modern Democracies* (2 vols., 1921).

BUCHANAN, Franklin. 1800-1874. Naval officer; b. Maryland. Commander (1841); chief adviser to Secretary of the Navy BANCROFT; planned U.S. NAVAL ACADEMY at Annapolis; first superintendent (1845-47); commanded the *Susquehanna*, flagship of PERRY's expedition to China and Japan (1853); commander of Chesapeake Bay unit for Confederate navy (1862); promoted to admiral and fought at Mobile Bay against FARRAGUT (1864); after war, president of Maryland Agricultural College.

BUCHANAN, James. 1791-1868. Fifteenth President of the United States. b. near Mercersburg, Pennsylvania. Graduated, Dickinson College (1809); admitted to the bar (1812); served in the War of 1812; member, U.S. House of Representatives (1821-31), chairman of the Judiciary Committee; joined the Democratic party; U.S. Minister to Russia (1832-34); U.S. Senator (1834-45) supported JACKSON, VAN BUREN and TYLER; Secretary of State during POLK's administration (1845-49) responsible for the treaty which followed the Mexican War; attempted to buy Cuba, failed; U.S. Minister to Great Britain (1853-56); helped to draw up the OSTEND MANIFESTO; elected President of the United States (1857-61); tried to maintain balance and peace between North and South; failed to take action on South Carolina's secession (1860); supported the Union during his retirement.

BUCHANAN, Joseph Ray. 1851-1924.

Labor leader. Founder and editor *Labor Enquirer*, Denver, Colo. (1882-87); member, executive board, KNIGHTS OF LABOR (1884); moved to New York (1888) became labor editor of American Press Association; labor editor, New York *Evening Journal* (1904-15); helped organize the POPULIST PARTY and served on the national committee (1892-1900).

BUCHANAN, William Insco. 1825-1909. Diplomat, U.S. Minister to the Argentine Republic (1894-1900); director, Pan-American Exposition (1901); first American Minister to Panama (1903-5); chairman of American delegation to third PAN-AMERICAN CONGRESS (1906); U.S. commissioner at second HAGUE PEACE CONFERENCE (1907); helped establish Permanent Court of Arbitration for Central America (1908); high commissioner to Venezuela (1908); valuable to State Department as authority on Latin-American relations.

BUCKNER, Simon Bolivar. 1823-1914. Confederate army officer. b. Kentucky. Graduated, U. S. M. A., West Point (1844); served through the Mexican War; brigadier general in the Confederate army (1861); surrendered to GRANT at Fort Donelson (1862); exchanged and made major general; lieutenant general (1864); returned to Kentucky after the war and became editor, Louisville *Courier* (1868); governor of Kentucky (1887-91); candidate for Vice-President on Democratic ticket (1896).

"Buckshot War." A bloodless political revolt in Pennsylvania in 1838. It arose when the results of the state election in 1838 were contested by the WHIGS and Democrats, each claiming a majority of the House of Representatives. A mob, assembled at the state capitol in Harrisburg, forced THADDEUS STEVENS, Thomas H. Burrowes, and Charles B. Penrose to flee for their lives from the capitol buildings. Upon the refusal of the President to dispatch federal troops the governor sent in the militia whose equipment included several rounds of buckshot. Ultimately some Whigs joined the Democrats in organizing the house and the "war" came to an end.

budget. A regular and periodic accounting of income and expenditures. In the federal government the executive budget was established by the BUDGET AND ACCOUNTING ACT OF 1921. It is an annual budget whose fiscal year runs from July 1st to June 30th. State budgets are also accountings whose fiscal years vary. The growth of the federal budget has been enormous since the 1930's as a result of depression, defense, and war expenditures. In 1933 the budget was $5,000,-000,000. The budget for fiscal year 1945 was $98,700,000,000. As a result of the Korean War and the consequent expenditures for defense and aid to the European allies of the United States the budget for the fiscal year 1953 had gone up to $85,400,000,000, the highest peacetime budget in American history and second only to that for 1945.

Budget and Accounting Act of 1921. A law of Congress which established the General Accounting Office, headed by the COMPTROLLER GENERAL, and the BUREAU OF THE BUDGET, headed by the Budget Director. It required the President to transmit the executive budget to Congress on the first day of every regular session and to recommend new taxes and expenditures. The Budget Bureau performs the actual work subject to the rules and regulations of the President. The Comptroller-General of the United States is independent of the President. The Act established a fiscal year for the United States government running from July 1st to June 30th. See Bureau of the Budget and Comptroller General.

BUELL, Don Carlos. 1818-1898. Union general. b. Ohio. Graduated, U. S. M. A., West Point (1841); served in Seminole and Mexican Wars; brigadier general of volunteers at outbreak of the Civil War; aided in organizing the ARMY OF THE POTOMAC; given command of the Army of the Ohio (1861); major general of volunteers (1862); relieved of command after battle at Perryville (1862) for allowing BRAGG's escape; resigned (1864).

Buenos Aires Conference. A Pan-American conference personally attended by PRESIDENT F. D. ROOSEVELT in 1936. Formally called the Inter-American Conference for the Maintenance of Peace, the meeting provided for the mutual consultation of the Latin American nations on all matters affecting hemispheric peace. The Conference adopted a neutrality convention obligating its members to take a common joint attitude as neutrals in the event of an outbreak of hostilities between any two of them.

building industry. Performed notable feat of providing essential housing for defense workers following the establishment of the national defense program in June 1940. During World War II the industry was unable to continue its residential construction program, but in the years following the war it expanded its facilities and produced almost 1¼ million housing units in 1950. Due to the war in Korea, federal restrictions in 1951 brought about a great curtailment of residential construction. In 1951 about 850,000 residential units were constructed. In the decade 1930-40 the industry constructed approximately 4,950,-000 units as compared with a need of 5,980,500 on the basis of a 50 year maximum life of residential building. The Federal Public Housing Authority estimated in 1946 that the nation's housing needs for the next 10 years would be 16,000,000 units based on the increase of population, establishment of new family units, and obsolescence of existing housing. This annual average of 1,600,000 units has never been attained, the highest having been 1,250,000 in 1950. For the seventh straight year (1955) over 1,000,000 units were produced.

86

BULFINCH, Charles. 1763-1844. Architect. b. Boston, Massachusetts. Graduated, Harvard (1781); chairman of the Boston Board of Selectmen (1799-1818) which is equivalent to mayor; often called the "first American architect" his works include: Massachusetts State House, Boston; Maine State Capitol, Augusta; succeeded LATROBE as architect of the National Capitol, Washington, D.C. (1817-30).

Bulge, Battle of the. A strong counter attack in the Ardennes by 15 German divisions under General Von Rundstedt, begun on December 16, 1944. Within five days the 1st United States Army had been driven out of Germany by the enemy push which succeeded in penetrating 60 miles into the American lines. Reinforced by General PATTON's 3rd Army on December 21st, the Americans stemmed the Nazi drive by Christmas. The counter offensive from that day succeeded in wiping out the bulge by January 31, 1945. Estimated United States losses were 40,000 as compared with the German casualties of 220,000 dead, wounded, and prisoners. This marked the last German offensive effort in World War II.

BULLARD, William Hannum Grubb. 1866-1927. Naval officer. Graduated U.S. N.A., Annapolis (1907); superintendent, Naval Radio Service (1912); director of naval communication (1919-21) acted to prevent sale of radio patents to other countries; commanded battleship *Arkansas* during World War I; commanded Yangtze patrol of American Asiatic fleet (1921-22); retired with rank of rear admiral (1922); leading founder of the Radio Corporation of America; chairman of U.S. Radio Commission.

BULLITT, William Christian. 1891-. Diplomat. b. Philadelphia, Pa. Graduated, Yale (1912); writer on the staff of the Philadelphia *Public Ledger* (1915-17); assistant in the DEPARTMENT OF STATE (1917-18); U.S. Ambassador to Russia (1933-36) and to France (1936-41); special assistant to the Secretary of the Navy (1942). Served in French Army as major (1944-45).

Bull Moose Convention. A nominating convention called on August 5, 1912 by the PROGRESSIVE PARTY. It adopted the Bull Moose as its emblem after nominating former president THEODORE ROOSEVELT and HIRAM JOHNSON as its presidential and vice-presidential candidates respectively. The term was first coined in 1900 when Roosevelt, the vice-presidential nominee of the Republican party, is reputed to have informed the Republican manager MARK HANNA, that "I'm as strong as a bull moose" and therefore was ready to be used to the limit in the campaign. See Progressive Party.

Bull Moose Party. see Progressive Party of 1912.

BULLOCK, William A. 1813-1867. Inventor who revolutionized the printing industry and journalism. b. New York. Expert mechanic who patented many small inventions; began working on printing press (1850) and placed on the market the Bullock press (1865) which was the first to feed automatically from a continuous roll of paper; printed both sides of the paper in one operation; cut the paper at designated intervals.

Bull Run, Battles of. Two important battles fought at the beginning of the Civil War. The first great battle of the war took place at Bull Run, Virginia, on July 21st, 1861 between a Union army of 29,000 troops, commanded by General MC DOWELL, and a Confederate army of 28,000, led by Generals JOHNSON and BEAUREGARD. The initial Union victory was stemmed by General "STONEWALL" JACKSON until the arrival of Confederate reinforcements who drove McDowell into retreat. The retreat became a panic which spread almost to Washington, D.C. The second battle of Bull Run, known as the battle of Manassas, was fought on August 29th and 30th, 1862. A Union army of 40,000 men, commanded by General Pope, attacked Jackson's 23,000 troops, who were awaiting reinforcements from LEE. The battle that ensued involved artillery and infantry fighting with both commanders awaiting reinforcements. On the evening of August 29th, LONGSTREET came to Jackson's assistance. The next day the Confederates made a brilliant charge, forcing Pope to retreat from the field. The Union army lost 500 killed, 1,000 wounded, and 1200 missing in the first battle, the Confederates suffering casualties of 400 killed, 1600 wounded, and 13 missing. In the second battle the Union losses totalled 14,462, and the Confederates suffered casualties of 9,112.

BUNCHE, Ralph Johnson. 1904-1971. Statesman. b. Detroit, Michigan. Graduated, University of California (1927) Harvard (M.S., 1928; Ph.D. 1936); studied at Northwestern University and the London School of Economics; taught at Howard University (1928); appointed chief research analyst in the OFFICE OF STRATEGIC SERVICES (1942-44); became the first Negro division head in the STATE DEPARTMENT (1945); director the Trusteeship Division of the UNITED NATIONS (1946); secretary, United Nations Palestine Commission (1947) and special mediator (1948); was able to restore peace in Palestine; received the Nobel Peace Prize (1950). Now serving as an Undersecretary of the United Nations (1956).

Bunker Hill, Battle of. The first major engagement of the American Revolution. Anticipating General Gage's intention to occupy the heights surrounding Boston, a patriot force of 1,200 under Colonel PRESCOTT was sent to seize Bunker Hill on the peninsula of Charlestown. Instead, the force occupied and fortified Breed's Hill, nearer Boston. On the morning of June 17, 1775, the British opened artillery fire on the American works. In the afternoon 3,000 British troops under Generals HOWE and Piggott charged up the hill, only to be met by a withering fire from above. They retreated. A second charge was similarly repulsed, with great British losses. Because of the lack of reinforcements and ammunition, the third British charge in the evening carried the Hill after a stubborn hand to hand struggle. The British lost 1,054 killed, more than one third of their total number, as compared to the American loss of 449, representing one quarter of their troops. The result of the battle was to inspire the patriots in the struggle to come.

BUNTLINE, Ned. pseudonym of Edward Zane Carroll Judson. 1823-1886. b. New York. Adventurer and pioneer writer of dime novels and adventure fiction. Led fabulous life of adventure in the Seminole wars and in the fur trade in the Northwest. Tried for murder in Nashville, Tenn. (1846), lynched by the mob, cut down in time; fled to New York City and established a newspaper; one of the organizers of the KNOW-NOTHING PARTY (failed 1856); met WILLIAM CODY, called him "Buffalo Bill," and wrote a series of dime novels on his life. Wrote over 400 dime novels and adventure stories.

BUNYAN, Paul. Legendary hero of the lumber camps; created a native mythology from Michigan westward; ruled his giant lumber camp from the winter of the blue snow until the spring came up from China; had a prize blue ox, named Babe; in southern lumber camps the hero's name is John Henry; also known as Tony Beaver.

BURBANK, Luther. 1849-1926. Horticulturist. b. Massachusetts. Experimented with thousands of varieties of plants and fruits; developed many new types; famous for Burbank potato; moved to California (1875); developed spineless cactus to feed cattle; developed many varieties of lilies, famous SHASTA DAISY, poppies and others. Author of *Harvest of the Years* (1927).

bureaucracy. Technically the working members of an establishment organized on the basis of a hierarchy. This highly centralized and autonomous system of administration is divided into bureaus, each headed by a chief. The complex structure of ever increasing supervisory posts renders such an establishment semi-independent of political control. The result is the development of rigid formulae not responsible to higher authorities.

Bureau of the Budget. Established by the BUDGET AND ACCOUNTING ACT OF 1921. Headed by a Director of the Budget, appointed by the President, its primary function is the preparation of the annual executive budget jointly with the President and the Secretary of the Treasury. Other important functions include supervision of the administrative management of executive agencies, approving agency forms, supervision and coordination of proposed departmental legislation, improvement of federal statistical services, and promotion of more economical and efficient governmental operation.

Bureau of Reclamation. An agency established in the DEPARTMENT OF THE INTERIOR by the RECLAMATION ACT of June 17, 1902. It was authorized to survey, examine, construct, and operate public works for the reclamation of arid and semi-arid lands in 17 western states. Later AMENDMENT: increased its jurisdiction to ALASKA and empowered it to develop water conservation, HYDRO-ELECTRIC POWER generation, domestic and industrial water supplies, flood control, IRRIGATION, and fish and wild life protection. By 1950 the Bureau of Reclamation had administered the construction of more than 100 dams with a storage capacity of 75,000,000 acre-feet as well as 30 power plants, 16,000 miles of CANALS, and 4,520 miles of hydro-electric power trans-

mission lines. It had supplied 5,000,000 acres of land with irrigation water and 9,000,000 people with power and water. The plants under its control had a generating capacity exceeding 3,500,000 kilowatts.

BURGESS, John William. 1844-1931. Educator, historian, and author. b. Tennessee. Served in the Union army during the Civil War; graduated Amherst College and taught political science at that college (1873-76); taught political science and constitutional law at Columbia University (1876-1912); first Roosevelt professor at the University of Berlin (1905-6). Author of *The Foundations of Political Science* (1933), *The Middle Period, 1817-58, Reconstruction and the Constitution* (1902) and other works in this field.

BURGOYNE, John. 1722-1792. British general and dramatist. Landed in Boston (May 1775) with troops to re-enforce Gage's command; commanded troops which came down from Canada and fought against the American colonies (1776); forced to surrender at SARATOGA (1777) which was a turning point in the Revolution; commander-in-chief in Ireland; participated in impeachment of Warren Hastings, who was acquitted. Author of plays, the best known being *The Heiress* (1786).

Burke Act. A federal law of 1906 which conferred citizenship on those Indians who had renounced tribal allegiance, as provided by the DAWES ACT of 1887, but only at the expiration of a probationary period of 25 years. This modification of the Dawes Act thus withheld citizenship until Indians had acquired full title to the land and then only when the President thought them worthy of it. It also forbade the sale of intoxicating liquors to Indians not citizens. Under its operations 8248 allotments in fee were made between 1906 and 1911.

BURKE, Edmund. 1729-1797. British statesman and orator. Member of Parliament (1765); author of *An Account of the European Settlements in America* (1757); advocated liberal treatment of colonies in a speech *American Taxation* (1774) and again *Conciliation with America* (1775); against the use of Indians in American wars (1778); opposed slave trade; secured Warren Hastings' impeachment (1788); retired from parliament on pension (1794); his letters and speeches published and acclaimed.

Burke-Wadsworth Act. See Selective Service and Training Act.

BURLESON, Edward. 1798-1851. Texas pioneer. b. North Carolina. Served as captain under ANDREW JACKSON in the Creek War in Alabama; moved to frontier settlement on Colorado River in Texas (1831); led settlers in holding back Indians, made lieutenant colonel of district; commanded regiment under HOUSTON against SANTA ANNA; took leading part in Cherokee War; senator of Texas (1836); Vice-President (1841); favored annexation of Texas by United States.

BURLINGAME, Anson. 1820-1870. Lawyer and diplomat. b. New York. Graduated, University of Michigan; studied law at Harvard; practiced in Boston. Member, U.S. House of Representatives (1855-1861); U.S. Minister to China (1861-67); came to the United States as representative of China to sign treaties of friendship; BURLINGAME TREATY signed establishing international relations between China and the United States, and establishing reciprocal rights of citizens of both countries (1868).

Burlingame Treaty. A treaty between China and the United States in which the latter nation guaranteed its non-intervention in Chinese domestic affairs, recognized the right of voluntary Chinese immigration, agreed to China's right to regulate its domestic commerce not affected by any treaty, and in which both governments pledged the privilege of residence and travel in their countries on the "most-favored-nation" basis. Both also promised to secure the exemption from persecution or disability of their respective nationals on account of religion. The treaty is unique because ANSON BURLINGAME, the Chinese representative, had been American ambassador to China in 1861 and had subsequently been retained by the Chinese government as its head of mission to European states. Burlingame had so affected the Chinese with his ability and tact as to lead to this appointment.

Burma Hump. The name applied to the eastern range of the Himalaya Mountains in Burma over which supplies were shipped into China from India during World War II. During the closing of the BURMA ROAD from February, 1942 to January, 1945, this was the only method of supplying the Chinese from the southwest. The Burma Hump was noted for the perils of the flight because of the distance and the unusual height over the mountains.

Burma Road. The ROAD constructed between 1936 and 1938 to enable Anglo-American supplies to reach China. It ran from the railroad at Lashio, Burma to Kumming, China. It was opened in January, 1939 as China's principal trade route until blocked by the Japanese capture of Rangoon in February, 1942. A new road was built by the United States in 1943-44, linking Assam, India with the Burma Road. The original Burma Road was reopened in January, 1945 following the successful Burma campaign under the British Admiral Louis Mountbatten. It was later renamed the Stilwell Road in honor of General JOSEPH J. STILWELL.

Byrnes Law. A law of Congress passed on June 29, 1938 barring the TRANSPORTATION of strikebreakers across state lines for the purpose of interfering with peaceful PICKETING.

BURNET, David Gouverneur. 1788-1870. Texas statesman. Lived adventurous early life; lived with COMANCHE INDIANS; settled on San Jacinto river in Texas (1831); drew up declaration of rights of Texas citizens in protest against SANTA ANNA (1835); provisional president of Texas (1836); quarreled with HOUSTON and resigned when Houston was elected first president under the new Constitution; vice-president under LAMAR (1838); U.S. Secretary of State (1846-47); opposed SECESSION.

BURNET, William. 1688-1729. Colonial governor. Appointed governor of New York and New Jersey (1720); governor of Massachusetts and New Hampshire (1728); able governor, tried to win friendship of Indians and extend Indian trade; built first English fort on Great Lakes at Oswego.

BURNET, William. 1730-1791. Revolutionary patriot and physician. Established military hospital at Newark, N.J., at outbreak of Revolutionary war; active in securing troops and ammunition in New Jersey; member of CONTINENTAL CONGRESS (1776-77, 1780-81); appointed (1777) Congress physician and surgeon-general of the army for the eastern district; founder of New Jersey Medical Society, the first state medical society in the country.

BURNHAM, Daniel Hudson. 1846-1912. Architect. b. New York. Associated with John Root in firm of Burnham & Root, architects (1873); formed firm of D.H. Burnham & Co. (1891) at Root's death; chief of construction for CHICAGO WORLD'S FAIR (1893), his buildings had a great influence on civic design; consultant in city planning for Cleveland, San Francisco and other cities; chairman, commission of experts planning development of Washington, D.C. (1901); submitted Chicago plan (1909); buildings include Flatiron Building, New York and Union Railroad Station, Washington, D.C.

BURNS, Otway. 1775?-1850. Privateer and shipbuilder. Converted a Baltimore clipper, the *Snap-Dragon*, into a PRIVATEER in the War of 1812; destroyed or captured many millions of dollars worth of enemy shipping; British put a price on his head; after the war he became a shipbuilder in the South; served in the state legislature (1821-35).

BURNSIDE, Ambrose Everett. 1824-1881. Union army commander. b. Indiana. Graduated, U.S.M.A., West Point (1847); served in the Mexican War; organized the first Rhode Island regiment at the outbreak of the Civil War; major general (1862); in command of the ARMY OF THE POTOMAC; failed at the battle of FREDERICKSBURG; given command of the Army of the Ohio; resigned commission (1865); Governor of Rhode Island (1866-69); U.S. Senator (1875-81); known for famous side whiskers, called "burnsides" in his honor.

BURR, Aaron. 1756-1836. Revolutionary officer and political leader. b. New Jersey. Son of Aaron Burr (1716-1757) who was second president of Princeton. Graduated with honors, Princeton (1772); served during the Revolution; went with BENEDICT ARNOLD to Quebec; served on WASHINGTON's staff; lieutenant colonel at the BATTLE OF MONMOUTH and VALLEY FORGE; practiced law, New York City (from 1783); state attorney-general (1789); U.S. Senator (1791-97); organized the Republicans in New York in 1800 election, making use of the TAMMANY SOCIETY for political purposes for the first time; tied with JEFFERSON in the election of 1800 for the presidency, each receiving 73 electoral votes; election thrown into the House which was led by HAMILTON and the FEDERALISTS; Jefferson elected President and Burr Vice-President of the United States

(1801-05); rivalry with Hamilton lost him the governorship of New York and resulted in the duel (July 11, 1804) at Weehawken, N.J. at which Burr mortally wounded his rival; this brought Burr's political career to an end. He started a colonization plan in the Southwest hoping to start a new political career; WILKINSON, commander in Louisiana, turned against Burr and sent in a report to Washington, D.C. condemning him; Burr was tried for treason and acquitted of conspiring to seize territory from Spanish-America, but popular opinion was against him; went to England (1808-12); returned to the United States and the practice of law in New York City.

Burr Conspiracy. An attempt by AARON BURR to establish a political empire under his control in the Mississippi Valley. After he had served his term as Vice-President, he left Washington, D.C. in 1805, negotiating with General JAMES WILKINSON who commanded the United States Army on the Mississippi. Burr outfitted an expedition of 60 men to colonize the Bastrop grant on the Washita River with funds obtained from Harman Blennerhassett. Wilkinson, now at Louisiana, betrayed Burr and accused him of treason. Burr, meanwhile, had unsuccessfully sought financial and political assistance from England, France, and Spain. As Burr's men moved down the lower Mississippi, Wilkinson ordered their arrest. Burr was taken, paroled, re-captured, and brought to Richmond, Virginia, for trial on a charge of treason. Chief Justice JOHN MARSHALL presided at the Burr trial in the United States Circuit Court. Burr was acquitted and ultimately went to England.

BURRITT, Elihu. 1810-1879. Linguist, world peace advocate; often called "the learned blacksmith." b. Connecticut. Apprenticed to a blacksmith; studied mathematics and ancient and modern languages; founded and edited the *Christian Citizen*, a weekly devoted to peace, antislavery and self-education (1844-51); organized League of Universal Brotherhood (1846); organized the Brussels Peace Conference (1848); lectured in the United States and Europe for international peace. Author of *Sparks from the Anvil* (1846).

BURROUGHS, John. 1837-1921. Naturalist and author. b. New York. Teacher (1854-63); clerk in Treasury Department, Washington, D.C. (1863-73); spent rest of his life on a farm near Esopus, N.Y. developing new kinds of fruits. Author of *Walt Whitman as Poet and Person* (1867) which was a study of his friend; *Wake-Robin* (1871) was his first nature book; *Winter Sunshine* (1875), *Birds and Poets* (1877), *Indoor Studies* (1889), *The Summit of the Years* (1913) and many other books on nature.

BURT, William Austin. 1792-1858. Surveyor and inventor. b. Massachusetts. Settled in the Michigan territory (1824); U.S. deputy surveyor (1833-55); surveyed entire northwestern region near Michigan; discovered iron ore; inventor of the solar compass (1836); invented the typographer (1829), first American writing machine, forerunner of the typewriter; invented the equatorial sextant.

BURTON, Theodore Elijah. 1851-1929. Lawyer and politician. b. Ohio. Graduated, Oberlin College; member, U.S. House of Representatives (1889-91, 1895-1909, 1921-29) chairman of Inland Waterways Commission (1907-8); member of National Monetary Commission; member, U.S. Senate (1909-15); president of American Peace Society; author of *Life of John Sherman* (1906) and *The Constitution* (1923).

BURTON, William Meriam. 1865-1954. Chemist and industrialist; introduced the process of cracking petroleum (1912); awarded medals for his work in the chemistry of petroleum.

business consolidation. The elimination of competing firms within an industry by MERGERS or the creation of HOLDING COMPANIES or other forms of MONOPOLY. The greatest era of such consolidation occurred after World War I. Although there were only 22 mergers in the PUBLIC UTILITIES in 1919, by 1926 3,744 public utility companies had disappeared. By 1930 it was estimated that one-half of the electric power generated by the larger power companies was controlled by the United Corporation, Electric Bond and Share Company, and the Insull System. It was believed that two-thirds of electric power was controlled by six groups, and over 90 percent by 15 groups. From 1919 to 1929 there were 1268 combinations in MANUFACTURING and MINING, involving the merging of 4,000 and the disappearance of 6,000 firms. In 1920 there were 30,139 banks which, by 1935, had been reduced in number to 16,053. In retail trade, CHAIN STORES replaced the independent shop keeper, and in finance, TRANSPORTATION, and COMMUNICATIONS combinations eliminated scores of thousands of formerly independent enterprises. In 1933 594 corporations, each capitalized at $50,-000,000 or more, controlled 53 percent of the nation's corporate wealth. The remaining 47 percent was owned by 387,970 corporations. In manufacturing one-tenth of one percent of the corporations owned 46 percent of the assets. Two-tenths of one percent of mining corporations owned 35 percent of the assets, and one and two-tenths percent of the utilities corporations owned 84 percent of the assets. The three largest AUTOMOBILE companies manufactured 90 percent of all automobiles, the four largest TOBACCO companies manufactured 90 percent of all CIGARETTES, and the four largest typewriter firms produced 95 percent of all typewriters. This concentration of capital extended to the field of NATURAL RESOURCES. By the 1920's four companies owned over 50 percent of the copper resources of the nation, UNITED STATES STEEL CORPORATION controlled over half of the nation's IRON ore, the Aluminum Company of America produced virtually all ALUMINUM in the United States, eight corporations owned three quarters of the anthracite COAL, and five companies one third of the nation's OIL. Whereas, in 1920 the 20 largest banks in the nation held 14 percent of all loans and investments, in 1935, 25 banks held almost 35 percent of all banking deposits. See pool, holding company, trust, merger, trade association, and absentee ownership.

business cycle. The periodic fluctuations of business activity. The economic history of the United States shows that over a period of 10 to 20 years the private economy has undergone cyclical changes through four general phases. These are prosperity, crisis, DEPRESSION, and recovery. Among those factors which have been advanced as causes of the business cycle are: sun spots, excess profits, overspeculation, overexpansion of credit and CURRENCY, overproduction, underconsumption, and inadequate financial controls.

BUTLER, Benjamin Franklin. 1818-1893. Lawyer, army officer and politician. b. New York. Practiced law in Massachusetts; well-known as a criminal lawyer; served in the Union army during Civil War; major general of volunteers and placed in command of Baltimore (1861); commanded land forces in capture of NEW ORLEANS (1862); military governor, New Orleans; removed from command and transferred to the Department of East Virginia; member, U.S. House of Representatives (1867-75, 1877-79); Governor of Massachusetts (1882-84); candidate for President of ANTI-MONOPOLY and GREENBACK parties (1884).

BUTLER, John. 1728-1796. Loyalist soldier during Revolutionary War. b. Connecticut. At the outbreak of the war he gathered a force of Indians and rangers known as "Butler's Rangers" (1777-78); invaded Wyoming Valley, Pa.; responsible for Wyoming Massacre by Indians, defeated near Elmira, N.Y. (1779); joined British in raids near Mohawk Valley (1780); British commissioner of Indian affairs at Niagara, Canada, after the war.

BUTLER, Matthew Calbraith. 1836-1909. Confederate general. Captain of cavalry at outbreak of Civil War; brigadier general (1863); major general (1864); played an important part in the Reconstruction politics of South Carolina; nominated WADE HAMPTON for governor and was elected U.S. Senator (1876-1894); served in the Spanish-American War.

BUTLER, Nicholas Murray. 1862-1947. Educator, president of Columbia University. b. New Jersey. Graduated, Columbia (Ph.D. 1884); professor of philosophy and education at that university (1890-1902); president of Columbia (1902-45); Barnard (1904-45); Bard (1928-45), New York Post-Graduate Medical School (1931-45); an organizer and first president of New York College for Training of Teachers (now Teacher's College, Columbia) (1886-91); president, CARNEGIE ENDOWMENT FOR INTERNATIONAL PEACE (from 1925); awarded with JANE ADDAMS, the Nobel peace prize (1931); received electoral vote for Republican candidate for Vice-Presidency (1912); author of books and articles on education and world peace.

BUTLER, William Orlando. 1791-1880. Lawyer, army officer, and politician. b. Kentucky. Served in War of 1812; wounded and captured; exchanged; served under JACKSON against Pensacola, Fla. and BATTLE OF NEW ORLEANS; elect-ed to Kentucky state legislature; member, U.S. House of Representatives (1839-43); served as major general under TAYLOR during Mexican War; nominated as Vice-President with LEWIS CASS on the Democratic ticket (1848).

BUTLER, Zebulon. 1731-1795. Colonial leader and army officer. b. Massachusetts. Served in French and Indian War; led Connecticut settlers to Wyoming Valley, Pa.; director of Susquehanna ·Company; defeated during the war by "Butler's Rangers," during raid on Wyoming Valley known as Wyoming Valley Massacre. See Butler, John.

BUTTERFIELD, John. 1801-1869. Stagecoach owner and expressman. Owned various stagecoach lines; consolidated them into American Express Company; owned telegraph lines and railroads; given difficult job of building Overland Mail route across the south (1858); used successfully until (1861); mayor of Utica (1865).

BYRD, Richard E. 1888-1957. Aviator and polar explorer. b. Virginia. Graduated, U.S.N.A., Annapolis (1912); commander, U.S. air forces in Canada (1918); director of aviation unit, Navy-MacMillan Polar Expedition (1925); flew over North Pole, with FLOYD BENNETT, (1926); flew from New York to France with three other aviators (1927); flew over South Pole (1929); made expeditions to antarctic (1928-30, 1933-35); rear admiral (1930); author of *Skyward* (1928), and *Little America* (1930).

BYRD, William. 1674-1744. Colonial planter. Elected to the Virginia House of Burgesses (1692); member, council of state (1683-1744); president of council (1703); had the largest library in the colonies.

94

C

CABELL, Joseph Carrington. 1778-1856. Virginia statesman. Graduated William and Mary College (1798); member, Virginia House of Delegates (1808-10); state senator (1810-29); again member, House of Delegates (1831-35); supported popular education; helped found the University of Virginia.

cabinet. Popular name for the heads of the nine executive departments. Not provided for as such in the Constitution, but it is generally included among those political traditions and customs known as the "UNWRITTEN CONSTITUTION." The title of each head is "secretary" with the exception of the heads of the DEPARTMENT OF JUSTICE whose title is ATTORNEY GENERAL and the Post Office Department whose title is Postmaster General. The members of the cabinet are appointed by the President and serve at his pleasure, being responsible to and removable by him without senatorial consent.

Cable Act. Enacted in 1922 and amended by the legislation of 1930, 1931, and 1934. It made nationality between the sexes equal and uniform in every respect. An alien woman now marrying a CITIZEN of the United States does not automatically acquire American CITIZENSHIP. She may however be naturalized on somewhat easier terms than in the usual case. Similarly an American woman marrying an alien retains her American citizenship unless she chooses to renounce it, even though her husband is ineligible for NATURALIZATION.

CABOT, George. 1752-1823. Merchant and statesman. b. Massachusetts. Principal leader of the FEDERALIST group, the ESSEX JUNTO; in shipping business (1768-95); U.S. Senator (1791-96) supported HAMILTON; director of United States Bank (1793); president of HARTFORD CONVENTION.

CABOT, John. (Ital. Giovanni Caboto) 1450-1498. Italian navigator and explorer. Born in Genoa, Italy; became a naturalized citizen of Venice (1476); moved to England (about 1484); Henry VII granted him a patent (1497) and he sailed from Bristol in the *Mathew;* reached coast of North America (generally thought to be Cape Breton Island): made a second voyage (1498) going down the coast to the 38th parallel. His discoveries were used later as a basis for the claims of the British to North America.

CADILLAC, Sieur Antoine de la Mothe. 1656?-1730. French colonial administrator in America. b. France. In command of the French forces at Mackinac in America (1683); was granted a large tract of land which is now Detroit, Michigan and settled a French colony there (1701); governor of Louisiana (1713-16).

CADWALADER, John. 1742-1786. Revolutionary general. b. Philadelphia, Pa. Brigadier general of Pennsylvania militia (April 1777); fought at battles of PRINCETON, BRANDYWINE and GERMANTOWN. When CONWAY started his attempt to oust WASHINGTON (see CONWAY CABAL), Cadwalader challenged him to a duel and succeeded in wounding Conway.

CAFFERY, Jefferson. 1886-1974. Diplomat. b. Louisiana. Graduated, Tulane University; studied law; served in Venezuela, Stockholm and Teheran; counselor of embassy at Madrid, Tokyo and Berlin. Was chairman of AMERICAN RED CROSS relief activities in Japan (1923); was envoy to Salvador (1926-28); Colombia (1928-33); Assistant Secretary of State; delegate to PAN AMERICAN CONFERENCE at Montevideo; Ambassador to Cuba (1933); U.S. Ambassador to France (1944).

CAHAN, Abraham. 1860-1951. Journalist, Socialist leader, author. b. Russia; came to the United States (1882); a founder and editor of *Jewish Daily Forward* (1897); a founder of the SOCIAL DEMOCRATIC PARTY (1897); leader of the SOCIALIST PARTY (from 1902). Author of *Yekl, a Tale of the New York Ghetto* (1898); *The Rise of David Levinsky* (1917), *Bletter von mein Leben* (5 vols.) his autobiography.

Cairo Conference. A meeting of President F. D. ROOSEVELT, Prime Minister Winston Churchill, and Premier Chiang Kai-Shek in November 1943. It was called for the purpose of formulating a Far Eastern program. The declaration issued stated that, following allied victory, Japan would lose all the islands in the Pacific seized since 1914, and that all the territories stolen from China (Manchuria, Formosa, and the Pescadores) would be restored to the Republic of China. Agreement was reached that Korea would become a free and independent state.

CALAMITY JANE. Nickname for Martha Jane Burke. 1852?-1903. Well-known frontier character. Noted for horsemanship and marksmanship. Lived most of her life in Deadwood, in the Black Hills of South Dakota. Wore masculine clothing, and is supposed to have been a scout for CUSTER.

CALDER, Alexander. 1870-1945. Sculptor. b. Philadelphia, Pa. Son of Alexander Stirling Calder, well-known sculptor (1870-1945). Calder is famous for his unusual bent wire and metal constructions known as *stabiles* ("static abstract sculptures") and *mobiles* ("plastic forms in motion").

CALHOUN, John Caldwell. 1782-1850. Lawyer and statesman. b. South Carolina. Graduated, Yale (1804); studied law in Connecticut; elected to South Carolina legislature (1808-1810); member, U.S. House of Representatives (1811-1817); worked with CLAY in advocating War of 1812; U.S. Secretary of War (1817-25) under MONROE; Vice-President of the United States (1825-32). Broke with JACKSON in 1832, after being an ardent supporter of his, during TARIFF and NULLIFICATION crisis in South Carolina. Resigned as Vice-President (1832), the only one in American history to do so. Calhoun was famous as a champion of STATES' rights. He upheld SLAVERY and presented the southern point of view in Senate debates on this issue. U.S. Senator (1832-43); as U.S. Secretary of State (1844-45) he sought the admission of Texas into the Union; he opposed the WILMOT PROVISO; approved the COMPROMISE OF 1850 despite objection to many of its provisions; again U.S. Senator (1845-50). His writings exerted great influence in his time.

California. The third state in size, with an area of 158,693 square miles. Admitted to the Union as the 31st state on September 9, 1850. Sacramento is the capital. In 1950 California's population of 10,586,223 made it second in rank. Its largest cities are Los Angeles, San Francisco, and Oakland. California is the largest food raising and fishing state in the Union. Its three other most important industries are petroleum, lumbering, and manufacturing. Industrial products include automobile and aircraft parts, gas, wood products, liquors, cement, sand, gravel, ships, furniture, and machinery. Its important crops include barley, cotton, grapes, hay, lettuce, citrus fruits, tomatoes, peaches, and potatoes. The state is a leader in industrial energy and irrigation. Its notable scenic wonders include Death Valley (280 feet below sea level), Mount Whitney (14,495 feet high, highest point in the United States), and Sequoia National Park (estimated to be 3500 years old). HOLLYWOOD, the nation's motion picture center, is situated outside Los Angeles. California was discovered in 1542 by Juan Rodriguez Cabrillo. Its nickname is the "Golden State."

CALL, Richard Keith. 1791-1862. Governor of Florida. b. Virginia; moved to Kentucky; fought with JACKSON in Florida; studied law and practised in Florida; sent to Congress as a delegate from that territory (1823); expert on legal status of Florida and became governor of that territory (1836-39); fought in wars against SEMINOLES; reappointed governor of the territory by HARRISON (1841-44). Strong opponent of SECESSION.

CALVERT, Charles. 3d Lord Baltimore. 1637-1715. Governor of Maryland (1661-75); suppressed rebellion in Maryland similar to BACON'S REBELLION; argued with WILLIAM PENN over northern boundary of his grant; became proprietor of Maryland (1675-1715) at death of his father Cecilius.

CALVERT, George. 1st Lord Baltimore.

1580?-1632. English colonizer in America. Graduated Oxford (1597); M.P. (from 1609); clerk of knighted privy council (1617); after announcing his conversion to Roman Catholicism he resigned secretaryship of state; created Baron of Baltimore in Ireland (1625). Granted (1623) peninsula in Newfoundland for a colony; unsuccessful; granted (1632) territory north of Potomac river which became territory of Maryland. He died before the charter was issued and it was issued to his son Cecilius who founded the colony.

CAMERON, Andrew Carr. 1834-1890. Labor leader. b. England, but emigrated to Illinois. Editor of weekly *Workingman's Advocate* (1864) official organ of NATIONAL LABOR UNION which he helped organize; active in various trade and labor organizations, he believed that labor should use its influence politically; owner and editor of *Artist Printer* (1888).

CAMERON, Simon. 1799-1889. Financier, politician, senator. b. Pennsylvania. U.S. Senator (1845-49, 1857-61, 1867-77); established the Republican party machine in Pennsylvania which he controlled all his life; backed LINCOLN as *quid pro quo* for cabinet post (1860); U.S. Secretary of War (1861-62); embarrassed Lincoln by his corrupt methods of awarding army contracts; U.S. Minister to Russia (1862).

CAMPBELL, John. 1653-1728. Journalist. b. in Scotland; emigrated to Massachusetts in about 1695; postmaster of the city of Boston (from 1702); printed a weekly half sheet the *Boston News-Letter* (1704-22), which was the first newspaper printed regularly in the United States.

CAMPBELL, John Archibald. 1811-1889. Jurist. b. Georgia. Associate Justice of the Supreme Court of the U.S. (1853-61); Assistant Secretary of War in Confederate cabinet (1862-5), although as a jurist he was strongly opposed to SECES-

97

SION. He took part in the SLAUGHTER HOUSE CASES which tested the 14TH AMENDMENT.

CAMPBELL, William. 1745-1781. Revolutionary hero. b. Virginia. Married PATRICK HENRY's sister; justice of county; captain of militia; fought CHEROKEES; led company in fight to oust LORD DUNMORE, royal governor (1776); fought against British under LAFAYETTE; joined in assault on King's Mountain.

Canadian Boundary Dispute. See Rush-Bagot Treaty, Webster-Ashburton Treaty, and Aroostook War.

canals. The greatest era of canal building was the 30 year period after the War of 1812. Stimulated by the success of the ERIE CANAL, many states sought to enhance their commerce by building canals. Between 1826 and 1834 Philadelphia developed a system of canals from the Delaware to the Ohio. The Pennsylvania Canal retained for Philadelphia its share in the western trade. In 1828 Maryland and Virginia joined in the construction of the Chesapeake and Ohio Canal. The Morris Canal was built by New Jersey between Jersey City and Phillipsburg on the Delaware River, to transport coal from Pennsylvania to New York City. New Jersey also constructed the Delaware and Raritan Canal from Bordentown to New Brunswick as an inland water route from New York to Philadelphia. In the Old Northwest the Ohio and Erie Canal joined Cleveland to Portsmouth, and the Miami and Erie Canal connected Cincinnati with Toledo. In Indiana the Wabash and Erie Canal ran from the Miami and Erie to Evansville on the Ohio River. Illinois built the Illinois and Michigan Canal between Lake Michigan and the Mississippi. By 1837 3,000 miles of canals had been constructed with state aid to private capital. In that year 12 states had contracted an aggregate debt of $60,000,000. The competition of the railroad and the unprofita-

bility of the canals brought about defaults on these debts. Foreign investors, who had purchased state bonds, lost' heavily. In later years many of these canals were supported by federal land grants and physical improvements. In the 50 years after the Erie Canal was opened, Congress granted almost 4,500,-000 acres of land to the states for canal building.

Canal Zone. See Panama Canal Zone

CANBY, Edward Richard Sprigg. 1817-1873. Union General in Civil War. b. Kentucky. Graduated, U.S.M.A., West Point (1839); lieutenant in SEMINOLE War; captain in Mexican War; colonel at outbreak of Civil War stationed in New Mexico; prevented SIBLEY from capturing that territory or California for the Confederacy; promoted to brigadier general and called to Washington, D.C. as assistant adjutant general; sent as major general to Mississippi (1864); killed by Indians on way to conference (April 1873).

canning industry. The United States has the largest canning industry in the world. Commercial canning was begun in New York City and Boston in the 1820's when meats, fruits, and vegetables were sealed in airtight glass containers after immersion in boiling water. The tin can was introduced by Peter Durand in 1818 and rapidly replaced glass. Canning quickly became important in Maine, Maryland, and New York. The greatest stimulus to canning in the 19th century was the demand for prepared food by the armies during the Civil War. The INDUSTRY moved to the west coast when canning was introduced in California in 1862. The canning of condensed milk was begun by Gail Borden in the 1870's. Improved machinery, such as the closed steam pressure kettle (1875), automatic pea podder (1885), and the automatic corn husker (1892), stimulated a great expansion in the industry. Improvements in food packaging, to eliminate spoilage and retain nutrients, were important advances in the 20th century. Planting of crops specifically for canning purposes became popular.

CANNON, Annie Jump. 1863-1941. Astronomer. b. Delaware. Graduated, Wellesley College (1884); assistant curator of astronomical photographs at the Harvard Observatory (1896-1911); curator (1911-38); discovered 300 variable stars, five new stars, one spectroscopic binary etc; compiled bibliography of 200,000 variable stars.

CANNON, Joseph Gurney. 1836-1926. Known as "Uncle Joe." Politician. b. North Carolina. Admitted to the bar (1858); moved to Danville, Illinois, where he practised law; member U.S. House of Representatives (1873-91; 1893-1913; 1915-23); leader of the "Old Guard" Republicans; as Speaker of the House, he carried to extreme the power to appoint legislative COMMITTEES, and by suppressing the minority was a virtual dictator; called "Czar" by political opponents; resolution offered by GEORGE NORRIS (March 1910) placed the power to appoint committees in the hands of the House; resolution passed by a combination of Democrats and INSURGENT Republicans stripped the Speaker of much of his power in the "Revolution of 1910."

capitalism. The economic system based on the investment of capital funds for private profit. Under this system the means of production are privately owned. Production of goods and services is done for the market. Characteristics of capitalism are FREE ENTERPRISE, individualism, a market economy and, LAISSEZ-FAIRE. In America capitalism has evolved from the colonial and early American commercial capitalism through the industrial capitalism of the nineteenth century to the finance capitalism of the twentieth century.

Capital Punishment. The Supreme Court ruled in the Furman decision in 1972 that Capital Punishment was a violation of the eighth amendment of the Constitution which prohibited "cruel and unusual punishments." Those who argued against this decision stated that the death penalty would be a deterrent to crime. More recently consideration has been given to reinstating Capital Punishment for crimes such as kidnapping, assassination, hijacking, and killing a prison guard.

capitation tax. See poll tax

Capitol, The. The building in Washington, D.C. which houses the United States Congress. It is 751 feet long and 350 feet wide, and contains 431 rooms. The two wings, constructed of marble, house the Senate and the House of Representatives. The grounds on which it is located cover 131.1 acres. The building was originally planned and constructed in 1793, but has been increased and transformed many times since then. Its floor area covers 14 acres and its rooms are devoted to office, committee, and storage purposes. Inaugurations of Presidents take place over the great steps on the east front. The building was partially burned by the British during the War of 1812.

Capper-Volstead Act. A law of Congress passed in 1922 which exempted agricultural cooperatives from the ANTI-TRUST LAWS. It provided that such associations, created to process, handle, and market their products, could form combinations without prosecution under this legislation if voting power of members was restricted to one vote per person, and if membership dividends were limited to eight percent per year. Agricultural cooperatives were also prohibited from handling products of non-members in an amount greater than that processed for members.

CARDOZO, Benjamin Nathan. 1870-1938. Jurist. b. New York City. Gradu-

99

ated Columbia University (1889); admitted to the bar (1891); practised law in New York City; justice, supreme court of New York (1914-28); appointed by President HOOVER Associate Justice, U.S. Supreme Court (1932-38). Author of *The Nature of the Judicial Process* (1921), *The Growth of the Law* (1924), and *The Paradoxes of Legal Science* (1928). He is remembered as a philosopher and a jurist in the liberal tradition. Frequently voted with Associate Justices BRANDEIS, HOLMES and STONE in dissents from court's invalidation of NEW DEAL legislation.

Carey Land Act. Passed by Congress in 1894. It provided for the granting of 1,000,000 acres of public lands in the mid-western arid regions which were to be transferred to private companies for improvement by IRRIGATION. Because of the lack of necessary capital for dams, CANALS, and reservoirs, the work lagged. In the early T. ROOSEVELT administrations it became evident that supplementary legislation was required to carry forward the work initiated by this act. This was done by the passage of the amending statute, the RECLAMATION ACT OF 1902.

CAREY, Joseph Maull. 1845-1924. Legislator. b. Delaware. Graduated, University of Pennsylvania (LL.B.); appointed U.S. Attorney, Wyoming (1869); associate justice of supreme court of that new territory (1871-1876); mayor, Cheyenne (1881-85); territorial delegate, House of Representatives (1885-90); one of the first U.S. Senators from that state (1890-95); chairman, Public Lands Committee; author CAREY LAND ACT; governor of Wyoming (1910); supported IRRIGATION projects in his state.

CAREY, Mathew. 1760-1839. Publisher. b. Dublin, Ireland. Editor, *Freeman's Journal*, Dublin (1780-83); founded, *Volunteer's Journal* (1783-84) which was very pro-Irish; he was forced to escape to America (1784) after publishing articles attacking the British government; founded the *Pennsylvania Herald* (1785) with a gift from LAFAYETTE; editor and publisher of the *Columbian Magazine* (1787-1792), leading magazine of the time; well-known publisher of Philadelphia; author of influential political pamphlet of War of 1812, *The Olive Branch.*

Caribbean Policy. The term expressing the interest of the United States and its program of political control in the islands and mainland of the Caribbean Sea. Although this interest was demonstrated before the Spanish-American War in such forms as the CLAYTON-BULWER TREATY and the OSTEND MANIFESTO, it was not until the acquisition of PUERTO RICO and control over CUBA after the war that a well-defined policy was developed. Political disorders and the inability of the Caribbean republics to pay their debts led to the enunciation of the ROOSEVELT COROLLARY in 1905. Subsequently, the United States intervened in Cuba, HAITI, SANTO DOMINGO, and NICARAGUA for the double purpose of excluding European intercession and the protection of American persons and property. In the WILSON, HARDING, COOLIDGE, and HOOVER administrations repeated interventions were conducted in these nations and in Mexico. It was not until the adoption of the "GOOD-NEIGHBOR" POLICY of President F. D. ROOSEVELT that the last American military forces were withdrawn. The Caribbean Policy led to denunciation of the United States as the "COLOSSUS OF THE NORTH." The Latin-Americans accused the United States of being guilty of "YANKEE IMPERIALISM", and referred to the Caribbean as the "American Lake."

CARLISLE, John Griffin. 1835-1910. Lawyer and statesman. b. Kentucky. Served in both houses of the state legislature; lieutenant governor of Kentucky (1871-75); member, U.S. House of Representatives (1877-90); Speaker of the House (1883-89); interested in TARIFF reform; supported the Mills Bill (1888); U.S. Senator (1890-93); served as U.S. Secretary of the Treasury (1893-97) during the PANIC OF 1893.

CARNEGIE, Andrew. 1835-1919. Industrialist and humanitarian. b. Dunfermline, Scotland. Came to the United States (1848); settled in Allegheny, Pennsylvania. Worked in cotton textile factory, telegraph company, and Pennsylvania Railroad; served with the WAR DEPARTMENT in TRANSPORTATION department during the Civil War; became interested in STEEL (1873) gaining control of eight steel companies; consolidated them into Carnegie Steel Company (1899); sold out to UNITED STATES STEEL (1901) for $250,000,000. Wrote *"The Gospel of Wealth"* which appeared in the *North American Review* (June, 1889) and expressed his opinion that wealth should be used for the benefit of all humanity. He established PUBLIC LIBRARIES, contributed to public education; established CARNEGIE ENDOWMENT FOR INTERNATIONAL PEACE; left a fund of $125,000,-000 to continue his "aid to mankind" after his death.

Carnegie Endowment for International Peace. Established in 1910 with the aim of hastening "the abolition of international war." From its principal office in New York City it supervises research and educational activities through the media of publications, lectures, and conferences with the objective of renouncing war as an instrument of national policy. The Endowment works with individuals and groups in the United States and abroad in its efforts to encourage and promote methods for the peaceful settlement of international controversies. It offers its aid to international organizations through the UNITED NATIONS.

Caroline Affair. A dispute between the United States and Great Britain, arising in 1837 out of a rebellion in Canada. The rebellious forces of William L. McKenzie were suppressed by the Canadian government and they fled to Navy Island in the Niagara River where they were supplied with food, arms, and recruits by American sympathizers. The steamer *Caroline* was employed in this service and was seized by Canadian troops with the resulting death of an American. The *Caroline* was destroyed by the Canadians, and President VAN BUREN made a vigorous protest which was ignored by Great Britain. Strong feeling for a number of years prevented a settlement of the dispute until the negotiation of the WEBSTER-ASHBURTON TREATY in 1842 which was accompanied by an expression of regret and apology on the part of England.

CARPENTER, John Alden. 1876-1951. Composer. b. Chicago, Ill. Graduated, Harvard University (1897); studied under Paine, Elgar, and Ziehn; composer of *Adventures in a Perambulator*, an orchestral suite, *Skyscrapers*, a ballet.

carpetbaggers. A name applied to Northern politicians who migrated to the South during the Reconstruction period after the Civil War. The name derived from the fact that they packed their few belongings into the then popular luggage called "carpetbags." They and southern politicians known as "SCALAWAGS" came into control of many southern state and municipal governments for purely personal gain. The end result of their political activities during the Reconstruction period was the aggravation of the already existing political chaos.

CARRINGTON, Henry Beebee. 1824-1912. Army officer and historian. b. Connecticut. Graduated, Yale (1845) and studied at Yale Law School; served through the Civil War; won recognition for recruiting of soldiers; commissioned brigadier general of volunteers (1862); author of *Battles of the American Revolution* (1876), and *Washington, the Soldier* (1898).

CARROLL, Charles. 1737-1832. Revolutionary leader. b. Annapolis, Maryland. Educated in Paris and London; leader of Maryland Catholics; member, COMMITTEE OF CORRESPONDENCE and COMMITTEE OF SAFETY (1775); appointed by the CONTINENTAL CONGRESS on a mission with FRANKLIN and CHASE to Canada to secure aid for the Revolution; elected to Continental Congress (1776-78); signer of the DECLARATION OF INDEPENDENCE; elected one of the first U.S. Senators from Maryland (1789-92); director of Baltimore and Ohio R.R.

CARROLL, Daniel. 1730-1796. Revolutionary patriot. b. Maryland. Delegate, CONTINENTAL CONGRESS (1780-84); delegate, CONSTITUTIONAL CONVENTION (1787); Maryland representative, U.S. House of Representatives (1789-91).

CARROLL, John. 1735-1815. Roman Catholic prelate. b. Maryland. Educated in France as a Jesuit priest; returned to America (1774); first Roman Catholic bishop (1790); first archbishop of Baltimore (1808) and founder of Roman Catholic hierarchy in the United States; supported the Revolution; accompanied BENJAMIN FRANKLIN on a mission to Quebec (1776); founded Georgetown University (1791); important figure in the history of Roman Catholic Church in the United States.

CARSON, Christopher. 1809 - 1868. Known as Kit Carson. Frontiersman, scout, Indian agent. b. Kentucky. Ran away from home in Missouri to join an expedition to Sante Fe (1826); joined Young's expedition across the Mohave desert to the San Joaquin valley in California (1829-31); led trapping expeditions (1831-42); served on three FREMONT expeditions as guide (1842-43 and

45); served during the Mexican War in California with Fremont and with KEARNY at the Battle of San Pascual (1846); famous for the exploit of crawling through enemy lines to get aid from San Diego; appointed Indian agent (1853-61); appointed colonel of New Mexican volunteers during the Civil War and led groups against the Indians in the Southwest; made a brigadier general (1865); resigned (1867).

CARTER, James Earl, Jr. 1924-   Born in Archery, Georgia the son of a farmer. He attended the Naval Academy and after his graduation from Annapolis married Rosalynn Smith in 1947. He studied nuclear engineering and then went to work for Adm. Hyman G. Rickover, the guiding force of the Navy's nuclear submarine program. In 1953 he returned to Georgia to take over his father's agribusiness. He became a deacon in the Plains Baptist Church and was known as a "born-again" Baptist. After a contested election, he won a seat in the Georgia Senate in 1962. In 1970 he was elected governor of Georgia. He was elected President of the United States in 1976 defeating the incumbent Republican, Gerald Ford. Frederick Walter Mondale became Vice-President.

CARTER, Samuel Powhatan. 1819-1891. Army and naval officer. b. Tennessee. Studied at Princeton and U.S.N.A., Annapolis; sent by the War department to organize regiments in Tennessee at the outbreak of the Civil War; known for his defeat of MORGAN, SMITH and other Confederate cavalry leaders; after war returned to navy. He was the only American to be both a major general and a rear admiral.

CARTERET, Philip. 1639-1682. First colonial governor of New Jersey. b. Channel Island. Appointed by Sir George Carteret, a distant cousin, and Lord John Berkeley, proprietors of the colony as governor in 1664; opened session of the first legislature of N.J. in 1668; in 1676 the province was divided and he became governor of East New Jersey only (1676-82); fought with SIR EDMUND ANDROS, governor of New York, over the collection of customs duties at N.J. ports; captured by Andros and kept in prison until 1681 when New Jersey was declared independent of New York and Carteret was returned.

Carter vs. Carter Coal Company. A decision of the United States Supreme Court in 1936 which invalidated the GUFFEY-SNYDER COAL ACT of 1935 on the grounds that it was not a proper exercise of Congress' interstate commerce power.

CARTIER, Jacques. 1491-1557. French sailor, first explorer of the Gulf of the St. Lawrence river. At the command of the King of France (1534, 1535-6), he made two voyages to Canada exploring the St. Lawrence river. Attempted to establish a colony (1541-42), but failed. On this last trip he reached Montreal, Quebec and established the French claims to this TERRITORY.

CARVER, George Washington. 1864-1943. Botanist. b. of slave parents in Missouri. He and his mother were stolen and taken into Arkansas, but they were bought back by their former master who realized George's potentialities and helped him. Graduated B.A. (1894), M.S. in Agriculture (1896) Iowa State University, where he was in charge of their greenhouses; taught at TUSKEGEE INSTITUTE (from 1896) where he was director of agricultural research; worked with the Bureau of Plant Industry, U.S. DEPT. OF AGRICULTURE doing research in the division of mycology and plant disease (from 1935). Famous for his work with the peanut, and his discovery of its many industrial uses.

CARVER, John. 1576?-1621. First governor of the Plymouth Colony. b. England. Emigrated to Holland (1609); joined the PILGRIMS at Leiden; as a wealthy merchant he was able to contribute liberally to the cause of the Pilgrims and he was responsible for securing the charter and arranging for the expedition to the New World (1616-20). With the aid of merchants in London, he chartered the *Mayflower,* gathered the Pilgrims together and sailed from London (May 15, 1620); helped select site at Plymouth; elected governor under the MAYFLOWER COMPACT (Nov. 11, 1620).

CARVER, Jonathan. 1710-1780. Explorer. Noted for the exploration of Lake Superior and Minnesota. Served in the French and Indian War; hired by Major ROBERT ROGERS to travel to western tribes in the interest of the fur trade; traveled by Fox-Wisconsin route to Mississippi and up into Minnesota; wintered with the SIOUX on the Minnesota River; in 1767 he went on trip to Lake Superior. Went to London (1769) and published his *Travels in Interior Parts of America* (1778) which was very popular and eased his bad financial situation. He also published a treatise on tobacco (1779).

Casablanca Conference. A meeting between President ROOSEVELT and Prime Minister Churchill and their principal military and political leaders at Casablanca, Morocco in January, 1943. The meeting was convened for the purpose of planning the succeeding stages of military strategy following the North African invasion of November, 1942. From this conference came the demand for UNCONDITIONAL SURRENDER of the Axis powers in World War II.

"cash-and-carry." See Neutrality Acts.

CASS, Lewis. 1782-1866. Lawyer and statesman. b. New Hampshire. Lawyer in Zanesville, Ohio (1800); U.S. marshal for Ohio (1807-12); resigned to serve during War of 1812; major general of volunteers with HARRISON in successful battle of the Thames against the British; left in command at Detroit he became civil governor of Michigan (1813-31); negotiated many Indian treaties while visiting the various Indian tribes in Lake Superior region during a 5000 mile canoe trip; built roads, and forts and generally was responsible for establishing the territory. U.S. Secretary of War (1831-36) appointed by JACKSON; U.S. Minister to France (1836-42); U.S. Senator (1845-48) urging the annexation of Texas; Democratic candidate for President (1848) defeated by TAYLOR; again U.S. Senator (1849-57); appointed by BUCHANAN U.S. Secretary of State (1857-60). Author of the doctrine of POPULAR SOVEREIGNTY later adopted by STEPHEN A. DOUGLAS.

CASSATT, Mary. 1845-1926. Artist. b. Pennsylvania. Studied in Europe (1868-74); lived in Paris most of her life and was closely associated with the Impressionist school of painters. She is best known for her studies of mothers and children. Her painting *Mother and Child* is in the METROPOLITAN MUSEUM OF ART, N.Y.

CATHER, Willa Sibert. 1876-1947. Novelist. b. Virginia. Graduated, University of Nebraska (1895); staff writer for Pittsburgh *Daily Leader* (1898-1901); associate editor of *McClure's Magazine* (1906-12). Well-known author of *My Antonia* (1918), *One of Ours* (1922) which was awarded the Pulitzer Prize, *A Lost Lady* (1923), *Death Comes for the Archbishop* (1927), *Shadows on the Rock* (1931) and other works.

Catholics. The first Catholics migrated to the Maryland colony in the 17th century to escape religious persecution in Europe. Religious prejudice within the colonies caused political and social conflicts of a serious nature, particularly where, as in New England and the Middle Col-

onies, the Protestants outnumbered the Catholics. This friction was temporarily ended by the passage in 1649 of the TOLERATION ACT which granted toleration to both the Catholics and Protestant Dissenters in Maryland. Maryland remained a refuge for persecuted Catholics under the leadership of GEORGE CALVERT and his son Cecilius. The first organized Catholic Church was established in 1784, and six years later Father John Carroll was appointed Bishop of Baltimore as the spiritual leader of the 40,000 Catholics in the United States at that time. In the early 19th century dioceses were established in Boston, Philadelphia, and New York, and the number of Catholic communicants increased greatly thereafter. The peak of this growth occurred in the 1840's as a result of increased IMMIGRATION, principally from Ireland. In this period the Catholics became the object of attack by anti-foreign, anti-Catholic movements of which the most important was the KNOW-NOTHING PARTY. At the end of the 19th century the large immigration from Italy, Austria-Hungary, and other Catholic countries increased the number of Catholics in the United States. The continuance of religious prejudice merged with nationalist fervor after World War I to create the most striking anti-Catholic sentiment that the nation had seen up to that time. The revival of the KU KLUX KLAN in the post-war years was directed against NEGRO, Catholic, Jew, and aliens. The Catholic Church has frequently been the focus of political conflict as in the elections of 1884 and 1928. These and many social, theological, and cultural problems have involved the Church in persistent controversy. The Church has engaged in wide-spread educational, missionary, charitable, and publishing activities. The National Catholic Welfare Conference was organized in 1919 to promote the welfare of Catholics in the United States. It conducts educational, legal, youth, and social welfare activities under the direction of bishops of the Church. In 1964 there were almost 45,000,000 Catholics in the United States.

CATLIN, George. 1796-1872. Artist, traveler, author. b. Pennsylvania. Well-known for his studies of Indians. Author of *Manners, Customs, and Condition of the North American Indians* (2 vols. 300 engravings 1841); a series of Indian portraits (1829-38) are in the National Museum, Washington, D.C.; his sketches of Indian life are in the AMERICAN MUSEUM OF NATURAL HISTORY, N.Y.

CATT, Carrie Chapman nee Lane. 1859-1947. Woman-suffrage and peace advocate. b. Wisconsin. Graduated, Iowa State College; superintendent of schools, Mason City, Iowa (1883-84); married Lee Chapman (1884;d.1886); married George Catt (1890;d.1905); State organizer, Iowa Woman Suffrage Association (1890-92); worked with National American Woman Suffrage Association (from 1892), president of the organization (1900-04, and from 1915); organized the LEAGUE OF WOMEN VOTERS (1920); delegate to Berlin International Council of Women; president, International Woman Suffrage Alliance (1904-23); worked for world peace.

"cattle baron." The nickname of the wealthy ranchers who dominated the CATTLE INDUSTRY during the era of the "CATTLE KINGDOM."

cattle industry. Cattle became important in the Spanish American colonies in the early 17th century. The breeding of cattle spread northward in the 19th century into the present states of Arizona, New Mexico, and Texas. Although cattle were raised on the seaboard it was not until the western movement had opened the Ohio and Mississippi valleys to settlement that the industry developed. Local grain crops were important as feed. By the opening of the Civil War, Arkansas,

Iowa, Kansas, and Missouri were the most important cattle states in the country. After its independence Texas rapidly assumed the leadership in cattle raising, having more than 3,500,000 head by 1860. At the close of the Civil War the

"cattle kingdom." Came into its own with the tremendous increase of cattle in the southwest. The "LONG DRIVE" to railway points in Kansas, Nebraska, and Illinois became one of the dramatic features of Western life. By 1890 more than 6,500,-000 head had been driven from Texas to the slaughterhouses in these areas. Important packing plants and stockyards were established in St. Louis, Kansas City, St. Joseph, and Chicago. Federal and state assistance in breeding, feed, storage, and packing were furnished through the United States and state departments of agriculture. By the 20th century the cattle industry had declined in importance. The huge ranches of the 19th century had been broken up into smaller livestock farms which bred cattle scientifically. In 1964 there were 106,-488,000 cattle of all kinds on United States farms. These were valued at $15,-708,000,000 with an average value of $150 per head.

"Cattle Kingdom, The." The nickname applied during the 1870's and 1880's to the "old West", including the present states of Arizona, Colorado, Nevada, New Mexico, Oklahoma, Texas, Utah, and Wyoming. It arose out of the rapid development of cattle ranching in this region following the decline of the "*Mining Kingdom.*" The rich grass-covered plains of the area offered excellent grazing fields for cattle breeding. The most famous were the Texas longhorn cattle. Huge ranches dotted the area, tended by the *cowboy.* Cattle men realized huge profits until the migration of farmers upon the open range, attracted by the agricultural possibilities and the liberal provisions of the *Homestead Act*. Other outstanding features of the "Cattle Kingdom" were the *"cattle baron"*, the development of the mid-western packing houses and stockyards, the invention of the refrigerated car, the development of a strong cattle export industry, the acceleration of railroad construction in the Far West, and the *"long drive."*

caucus. A method of nominating presidential candidates. Congressional leaders of political parties met, originally in secret, later openly, to nominate candidates. The system was undemocratic and was opposed by the supporters of JACKSON. After 1824 the cacus was replaced by the national NOMINATING CONVENTION.

census. Provided for in Article I, Section 2 of the Constitution. Must be taken by Congress every ten years. Necessary for purposes of determining representation of each state in the House of Representatives and for direct taxation.

Centennial Exposition. A great World's Fair at Philadelphia, Pa., in 1876 celebrating the centennial of American independence. Three million visitors came to the Exposition grounds to view the wonderful achievements in science and invention. The Fair was a symbol of the recovery of the United States from the political, industrial, and financial difficulties of the Civil War. The Exposition was notable for the gathering of the most famous artists and architects in the U.S., including FREDERICK L. OLMSTEAD, who landscaped the grounds, STANFORD WHITE, DANIEL BURNHAM, AUGUST SAINT-GAUDENS, and DANIEL CHESTER FRENCH.

Central Intelligence Agency. See C.I.A.

Central Powers. The name of the coalition of nations which opposed the Allied Powers in World War I. Led by Germany, these nations included the Austro-Hungarian Empire, Turkey, and Bulgaria.

Chaco War. A series of wars between Bolivia and Paraguay over possession of the Gran Chaco region. On December 6, 1928 military skirmishes broke out and diplomatic relations between these nations were severed. An ARBITRATION TREATY of the PAN-AMERICAN CONFERENCE was prepared on August 31, 1929 but rejected by both governments. A temporary truce was negotiated on April 4, 1930 after a year's continued battles. Major fighting was resumed in 1932 despite the efforts of the LEAGUE OF NATIONS and the PAN-AMERICAN UNION to mediate the dispute. Paraguay succeeded in capturing the greater part of the Chaco but failed in attempts to occupy Bolivia proper. On June 14, 1935 Bolivia and Paraguay concluded a truce at the insistence of the United States and five South American Republics. A final peace treaty was negotiated on July 21, 1938 on the basis of an arbitration award handed down by the United States and the Latin American governments. By its terms· 30,000 square miles of the Gran Chaco region were given to Bolivia and 70,000 square miles to Paraguay, but Bolivia was furnished with an outlet to the sea through the Paraguay River.

CHADWICK, French Ensor. 1844-1919. Naval officer, historian. b. Virginia (territory now West Virginia). Graduated, U.S.N.A., Annapolis (1864); naval attaché American legation, London (1882); comander, cruiser, *Yorktown* (1889-92); chief, Office of Naval Intelligence; head of Naval Equipment Bureau; commander of cruiser *New York* (1897) flagship of North Atlantic squadron; chief of staff under Admiral WILLIAM T. SAMPSON during Spanish American War; served at the BATTLE OF SANTIAGO, Cuba (July 3, 1898); rear admiral (1903); commander in chief of South Atlantic squadron (1905); retired (1906). Author of *Causes of the Civil War* (1906) and *Re-*

lations of the United States and Spain (3 vols. 1909-11).

chain stores. As defined by the DEPART-MENT OF COMMERCE, any business organization with four or more stores which operate through central purchasing and storage facilities. CHAIN STORES have become important retail outlets in the United States in the 20th century. The Atlantic and Pacific Tea Company, begun as a single store in 1859, is the largest chain in the country. The F. W. Woolworth Company, begun in 1879, is the nation's largest variety chain. After World War I chains became one of the most important retail enterprises, making great inroads upon independent retailers. This competition has compelled the independent retailer to seek relief in legislation. In 1929 Indiana passed a tax law discriminating against c hains, the rates of which were graduated in relation to aggregate gross sales. Although sustained by the courts, similar legislation in Kentucky was subsequently nullified. The ROBINSON-PATMAN ACT attempted discriminatory taxation against chains on a national basis. In 1955 chain stores had a total volume of about $32,000,-000,000 in sales, representing about 19% of all retail sales for that year.

CHAMBERLAIN, George Earle. 1854-1928. Lawyer and Senator; b. Mississippi. Admitted to the bar in Oregon (1878); member, state legislature (1880-82); U.S. Attorney (1884-86); attorney-general of Oregon (1891-94); Governor of Oregon (1902-09); U.S. Senator (1909-21); chairman, Public Lands Committee; chairman, Military Affairs Committee (from 1913-21) responsible for such legislation as selective draft, food controls and war financing. Appointed to U.S. Shipping Board (1920).

CHAMBERLAIN, Joshua Lawrence. 1828-1914. Army officer and educator. b. Maine. Professor, at Bowdoin College (1855-62); lieutenant colonel in the Civil War; awarded CONGRESSIONAL MEDAL OF HONOR for his defense of Little Round Top at the BATTLE OF GETTYSBURG; major general of volunteers (1865); chosen to receive the formal surrender of the Confederate army. Elected governor of Maine (1866-70); president, Bowdoin College (1871-83). Author of *The Passing of the Armies* (1915) which deals with the Civil War.

CHAMBERLAIN, Thomas Chrowder. 1843-1928. Geologist. b. Illinois. Graduated, Beloit College (1866); professor, Beloit (1873-82); worked with U.S. Geological Survey (1892-1908); investigator for Carnegie Institution (1902-09); president, University of Wisconsin (1887-92); professor of geology, head of Walker Museum, University of Chicago (1892-1928); founded and editor in chief of the *Journal of Geology* (1893-1922); well-known for study of glacial deposits and with F. R. Moulton, formulated the planetesimal hypothesis accounting for the earth's origin. Author of *The Geology of Wisconsin* (4 vols. 1873-82), *The Origin of the Earth* (1916) and other books in the field of geology.

CHAMPLAIN, Samuel de. 1567?-1635. French explorer in America. b. France. Commanded a Spanish vessel that visited West Indies, Mexico and Panama (1599-1601); accompanied Pontgrave on a fur-trading expedition along the St. Lawrence River (1603); went with a group of settlers to Port Royal; explored the coast from Nova Scotia down to Vineyard Haven (1604-07); as lieutenant governor, he arrived in Quebec with settlers and succeeded in founding the city (1608), the first permanent French settlement in America. While traveling with the Indian tribe of HURONS in a war against the IROQUOIS, he discovered the lake which bears his name. He built a trading post in Montreal (1611); explored northern New York, Ottawa River (1613), GREAT LAKES (1615); governor of the Quebec colony (1633-35) when Quebec was captured by the British (1629), Champlain was captured and held prisoner in England for four years. Author of *The Savages* (1603) and *Travels and Discoveries in New France* (1619).

CHANDLER, Charles Frederick. 1836-1925. Chemist. b. Massachusetts. Professor of chemistry, and dean (1864-97) Columbia University School of Mines, which he helped found. Resigned as dean but taught as Mitchell professor of chemistry (1897-1911); planned Havemeyer Hall, best chemistry laboratory in the country at that time; professor of chemistry, College of Physicians and Surgeons of Columbia University. Leader in founding of the American Chemical Society; one of countries first and leading industrial chemists; president, New York City Board of Health (1873-1883); responsible for milk control, tenement house health regulations, helped establish State Board of Health and served as chairman of its Sanitary Committee. He was an authority on water supply, sanitation, and oil refining.

CHANDLER, Zachariah. 1813-1879. Politician and statesman. b. New Hampshire. Moved to Michigan (1833); elected to succeed LEWIS CASS as Senator (1857-75); appointed U.S. SECRETARY OF THE INTERIOR (1875-77) by U. S. GRANT.

CHANNING, William Ellery. 1780-1842. Clergyman and author. b. Rhode Island. Often referred to as the "Apostle of Unitarianism." Graduated, Harvard University (1798); pastor, Federal Street Church, Boston (1803-42); became leader of Unitarian group (from 1819); organized the American Unitarian Association (1825); met Coleridge, Wordsworth and others while in Europe (1822-23);

important influence on the thinking of his time. Although not an ABOLITIONIST, his opinions and writings on SLAVERY helped the cause. Author of *Works* (6 vols., 1841-43), *Negro Slavery* (1835), and *Self Culture* (1838).

CHANUTE, Octave. 1832-1910. Civil engineer and glider pioneer. b. Paris, France. Came to the United States (1838); worked in railway and bridge construction (1853-83); helped the WRIGHT BROTHERS who acknowledged their indebtedness to his experiments in their own work. Author of *Aerial Navigation* (1891), *Progress in Flying Machines* (1894).

CHAPLIN, Charles Spencer. 1889-1977. Motion-picture actor. b. London, England. Considered the world's greatest pantomimist. Came to the United States as part of a vaudeville act (1910); made his first motion picture (1914); became known as a great comedian; formed his own company (1918); best known for *The Kid, The Gold Rush, City Lights, Modern Times, The Great Dictator,* and many other fine films.

CHAPMAN, John. Known as Johnny Appleseed. 1775?-1847. Frontiersman. b. in New England. He had a large nursery near Pittsburgh Landing in Pennsylvania. He sold or gave apple saplings and seeds to settlers going west; because of the shortage of fruit trees in the Ohio River Valley, he took bags of apple seeds and planted them there; for years he planted and pruned and cared for these trees. There are many legends and stories about him.

Chapultepec, Act of. An agreement negotiated in February, 1945 at Chapultepec, Mexico between the United States and all Latin American states except Argentina. It provided for close military and naval collaboration to prevent aggression on the American continent. Subsequent conferences were held for the purpose of coordinating the training and equipment of the signatory powers. Argentina was not invited to the conference because it was presumed to be in sympathy with the AXIS POWERS. Canada, although not a party to the agreement, concluded separate negotiations with the United States for their common defense.

Charleston. The largest city in South Carolina, and one of the oldest in America. It was founded in 1670 on the Ashley River, and named in honor of King Charles II. By the opening of the American Revolution, it was the wealthiest and largest city south of Philadelphia, remaining the state capital until 1790. Charleston was unsuccessfully attacked by the British in 1776, and was the scene of the first fighting of the Civil War, which occurred in the attack on FORT SUMTER in its harbor. The city was the hub of the nullification controversy of 1828 and 1832-33, and of the secession agitation of 1860.

chartered company. A joint stock company chartered by a European government to carry on foreign trade and exploit the economic resources of its colonies. Colonization was undertaken by these companies in the effort to attract settlers. The first English company that colonized the new world was the Virginia Company, chartered in 1606. Other important chartered companies that contributed to settlement were the New-foundland Company (1619), MASSACHU-SETTS BAY COMPANY (1629), and Providence Island Company (1630).

CHASE, Salmon Portland. 1808-1873. Lawyer and statesman. b. New Hampshire. Graduated Dartmouth College (1826); practiced law in Cincinnati, gaining fame as defense lawyer for fugitive slaves; leader of LIBERTY PARTY and FREE-SOIL movement (1848); U.S. Senator from Ohio (1849-55; 1860); elected

Republican governor cf Ohio (1855-59); resigned Senate seat to be U.S. SECRETARY OF THE TREASURY, appointed by LINCOLN (1861-64); had problems of nation's fiscal policy during Civil War; greatest accomplishment was formulating a national banking system (1863); resigned after disagreement with Lincoln on appointment of assistant treasurer at N.Y. (1864); appointed, Chief Justice, U.S. Supreme Court, by the President to succeed R. TANEY; presided at trial of JEFFERSON DAVIS; presided over Senate in impeachment proceedings against JOHNSON; gave dissenting opinion in SLAUGHTERHOUSE CASES.

CHASE, Samuel. 1741-1811. Revolutionary leader and Justice of U.S. Supreme Court. b. Maryland. Leader of SONS OF LIBERTY; member, Maryland COMMITTEE OF CORRESPONDENCE (1774); delegate to CONTINENTAL CONGRESS (1774-78, 1784, 1785); signer of DECLARATION OF INDEPENDENCE; helped in writing the ARTICLES OF CONFEDERATION; was opposed to the adoption of the Constitution; appointed by WASHINGTON an Associate Justice, U.S. Supreme Court (1796-1811); because of his anti-JEFFERSON position, he was impeached (1804) but acquitted (1805).

CHASE, William Merritt. 1849-1916. Painter. b. Indiana. Studied in New York and Europe. Famous as teacher at Art Student's League, N. Y.; member, National Academy of Design; president Society of American Artists; won many honors. His works are shown in many museums.

Chateau-Thierry, Battle of. An important engagement in World War I in which the United States 2nd and 3rd Divisions, assisted by French forces, broke the German advance on June 4, 1918. In this battle 85,000 American troops prevented the Germans from crossing the MARNE and continuing their march on Paris. On June 5th the MARINES of the 2nd Division opened a six day battle against enemy forces entrenched in nearby Belleau Wood. By June 11th the Germans had been ejected. Mopping up the surrounding area in the next two weeks, the United States Army had succeeded in clearing the area by June 25th. American casualties totalled 9,500.

Chattanooga Campaign. A drawn out series of battles fought during October and November 1863. These included the battles at CHATTANOOGA, Brown's Ferry, Knoxville, LOOKOUT MOUNTAIN, MISSIONARY RIDGE, and Ringgold Gap. Under the command of GRANT, the Union armies, released by their capture of VICKSBURG, moved estward against General BRAGG who was defeated in front of Chattanooga and at Brown's Ferry. Bragg retreated and the Union army captured Lookout Mountain on his left. This was followed by the Union capture of Missionary Ridge, and an advance that was halted only by a brilliant rear guard stand at Ringgold Gap. Grant returned to Chattanooga while the Confederate Troops went into winter quarters at Dalton, Georgia.

CHAUNCEY, Isaac. 1772-1840. Naval officer. b. Connecticut. Lieutenant in the U.S. Navy (1799); served in the attack on Tripoli (1802-05); promoted to captain (1806); commanded New York navy yard (1807-1812); command of naval forces on Lakes Erie and Ontario during the War of 1812; commanded the Mediterranean squadron (1816-1818); member, Board of Navy Commissioners, Washington (1821-24; 1832-40) president of the board (1838).

Chautauquas. Organized ADULT EDUCATION centers which originated in the 1870's for Bible study and recreation. The name stems from the first meeting at Chautauqua, New York, on August 4, 1874, when John H. Vincent organized an assembly for Bible study. Two years later the summer session was extended and new study materials introduced. By 1878, 7,000 adults were attending these sessions. At the end of the century the Chautauqua program included lay subjects such as mathematics, science, music, arts, hygiene, and languages. In 1912 it cooperated with the agricultural college of Cornell University in farm studies. New buildings, including theatres, libraries, lecture halls, and gymnasiums, were constructed. By 1930 more than 45,000 students attended annually. Hundreds of local Chautauquas appeared throughout the United States and Canada, most of them engaged in secular studies. After 1900 itinerant Chautauquas carried the lecture movement to the small towns of the United States, sponsoring weekly forums and concerts.

Checkoff. A method of collecting dues from union members. The employer, by agreement with the union, withholds the amount of dues from employees' wages and pays it to the union. The checkoff was made legal under the TAFT-HARTLEY ACT only after approval by a majority of the union members as determined by an election conducted by the NATIONAL LABOR RELATIONS BOARD.

checks and balances. As described in Federalist Paper No. LI on February 8, 1788 it is a system of "contriving the interior structure of the government (so) that its several constituent parts may, by their mutual relations, be the means of keeping each other in their proper places." Popularly attributed to the French political philosopher Montesquieu this device is designed to provide a check by each branch of a government upon the others, the result being a balance of powers. It is assumed to develop out of SEPARATION OF POWERS theory which Montesquieu propounded.

chemical industry. Chemical enterprises in early America involved the production of potash, glass, salt, sugar, paints, iron, and fertilizers. Rudimentary developments in these fields were made, but the chemical industry did not keep pace with the general industrial development of the United States in the early 19th century. By 1900 inorganic chemistry had become firmly established, but it was in the 20th century that the production of industrial chemicals saw its greatest progress. Synthetic organic chemical production is today one of the most important industries in the nation. In 1900 the contact process for sulfuric acid was developed. The development of chlorine in 1901 led to a termendous expansion in the use of chlorinated products in sanitation. Bakelite was synthesized in 1907. Carbon black was introduced in 1915, rubber latex in 1921, and rayon cord in 1937. In the 1920's synthetic sodium nitrate was introduced as an important fertilizer. The production of butanol and acetone contributed to the paint industry in the 1920's. Solid carbon dioxide was an important improvement in refrigeration in 1925. Safety glass in 1927, the hydrogenation of petroleum in 1929, and high octane gasolines in 1934 were other significant advances in chemistry. In that period progress was made in the production of dichlorodifluoro methane as a non inflammable refrigerant, the synthesization of camphor from turpentine, vitamin B1 and hormone synthesization, and in the production of fertilizers. The production of nylon in 1938 followed by other synthetic fabrics such as ninon, velon, and orlon virtually revolutionized the textile industry. In agriculture the remarkable developments in fertilizers, insecticides and fungicides, food processing, refrigeration, and hormone stimulants have increased manyfold the quality and quantity of crops. The inventions of new disinfectants and germicides as well as improvements in medical chemistry have contributed to the betterment of public health. In 1964, the chemical industry chalked up its sixth consecutive year of gains in output, sales, and profits. Industry sales were estimated at more than $36,000,000,000. By 1965, five individual companies had sales exceeding one billion dollars.

Cherokee Indians. The largest and most important single tribe in the southeastern part of the United States. They often fought the IROQUOIS tribes of New York. They were important British allies against the French. The Cherokees cooperated with the United States during the War of 1812 and fought the CREEKS who were causing the government trouble. They set up a government of their own and formed the Cherokee Nation in 1827. Gold was discovered on their land, and through pressure by the whites they were forced, despite a decision of the United States Supreme Court that upheld their autonomy, to abandon their lands and move into the West. Their leader on the long trek to Tahlequah, where they settled, was JOHN ROSS. The Cherokees became a part of the Five Civilized Tribes. They were divided in their allegiance during the Civil War., but many of them freed Negro slaves and admitted them into their tribes. They became U.S. citizens and gave up their tribal allegiance in 1906, having sold their land, known as the "Cherokee Strip", in 1892. The majority of the Cherokees, now of pure or mixed blood, live west of the Mississippi River, and only a small proportion of their original number live on a reservation in North Carolina.

Cherry Valley Massacre. An attack on November 11, 1778 on an American settlement in Cherry Valley, in central New York, by a band of Tories and Seneca Indians commanded by JOSEPH BRANT. Thirty persons were slain and 71 taken prisoner, most of whom were released the next day. The entire community was burned to the ground and all live stock carried off. Sixteen defending troops were killed although the fort defending the town held out against the marauders.

Chesapeake-Leopard Incident. A dispute between the United States and Great Britain in 1807 arising out of the overhauling of the American frigate. *Chesapeake* by the British ship *Leopard* in Hampton Roads, Virginia. The British commander demanded the surrender of four seamen claimed to be British deserters. When the American commander refused to give up these men the *Leopard* opened fire upon the unprepared American vessel. The *Chesapeake* was struck with 14 shots, and lost or suffered damage to her main-mast, mizzenmast, and riging, sustaining casualties of three men killed and 20 wounded. She surrendered. After she was boarded, one deserter and three Americans were removed by force, an act which was vigorously protested by President JEFFERSON. Following prolonged negotiations, Great Britain disavowed the act in 1811 and returned two of the Americans, the third having died in the meantime. The incident was used as a propaganda weapon by the "WARHAWKS" and other prowar elements in the United States in assisting the onset of the War of 1812.

CHEVES, Langdon. 1776-1857. Banker and legislator. b. South Carolina. Member, state legislature (1802-09); member, U.S. House of Representatives (1810-15); Speaker of the House (1814-15), succeeding HENRY CLAY; refused the office of Secretary of the Treasury offered by MADISON; justice of South Carolina court of appeals (1816-1819); president, SECOND UNITED STATES BANK (1819-22) which he saved from bad financial management and placed on a sound credit basis; often called "the Hercules of the United States Bank."

Cheyenne Indians. A member of the Algonquin linguistic family, they were a plains tribe. They originally lived in the territory that is now the state of Minnesota, but are now divided and spread throughout the West as far as Oklahoma. They were a warlike tribe but usually friendly with the whites. In 1864, in Colorado, their women and children were indiscriminately massacred by government troops and they sought revenge. One of the bitterest Indian wars followed and was finally stopped by troops led by General CUSTER. The Cheyenne Indians who lived in the far north had not taken part in this war. There is still communication and a friendly relationship existing between the various Cheyenne tribes distributed throughout the West.

Chicago. The third largest city in the United States. Its population of almost 3,550,000 persons in 1960 inhabits a combined land and water area of 211.3 square miles. Its site was first explored by the French Jesuit missionaries, MARQUETTE and JOLIET, in 1673. The present city, laid out in 1830, was preceded by a combined BLOCKHOUSE and stockade built in 1804 under the name of Fort Dearborn. Chicago is the greatest slaughtering and meat packing center in the world, and one of its major grain trading centers. It houses the Merchandise Mart, the second largest office building in the world, covering an area of two square blocks. Its factories produce important quantities of agricultural implements, rail-way cars, and electrical machinery. It is the largest railroad terminal in the United States. The Chicago Natural History Museum is one of the world's foremost museums of anthropology, zoology, geology, and botany, containing the world's largest collection of meteorites. Chicago is almost invariably chosen by

112

the two major political parties as the seat of their quadriennial national conventions. It has been the location of many world fairs, including the WORLD'S COLUMBIAN EXPOSITION of 1893 and the Century of Progress Exposition of 1933.

"Chicago Seven". During the Chicago Democratic convention in 1968 seven activists were charged with conspiracy to incite a riot, but they were cleared of this conspiracy charge in December 1970. Five were convicted of crossing a state line to incite to riot; however, in November 1972 an Appeals Court overturned the conviction, stating that they found that the remarks of the previous trial judge had prejudiced the jury.

Chicago World's Fair. See World's Columbian Exposition.

Chickamauga, Battle of. A sanguinary battle fought at Chickamauga, Georgia on September 19th and 20th, 1863. Of the 57,000 Union troops, commanded by General ROSECRANS, 11,135 men were lost. The Confederate Army, commanded by General BRAGG, lost 15,801 men of their army of 71,000. Rosecrans was driving on CHATTANOOGA against the retreating Confederate army when sudden reinforcements for Bragg brought an end to the retreat. As the result of a misinterpreted order the Confederate army launched an attack upon a weak point in the Union line, and Rosecrans fled to Chattanooga in great disorder. Bragg's failure to follow up this victory prevented the distruction of the Union Army.

Chickasaw Indians. One of the Five Civilized Tribes of the Muskhogen group. They lived in the area around the northern part of the Mississippi River. They were independent and hostile. However, they were interested in educating their youth and many of them were sent to eastern schools. In 1832 they signed a contract with the United States, the Treaty of Pontotoc. They migrated to the West and lived on territory shared with the Choctaw tribes, whose culture was similar to theirs although they had been enemies before. They shared with the Choctaws a common government and school system. They now live principally in Oklahoma.

chief executive. See presidency.

child labor. Signifies employment of persons under certain specified ages, usually 16 years. Presented a serious social problem in early days of INDUSTRIAL REVOLUTION. Some states have enacted legislation designed to restrict child labor under certain ages and/or in certain occupations. Two early federal attempts in 1916 and 1918 at eliminating such labor were invalidated by the U.S. SUPREME COURT. Since 1938 Congress has exercised this power only in INTERSTATE COMMERCE under the FAIR LABOR STANDARDS ACT, although some restrictions were included in the WALSH-HEALEY ACT of 1936 pertaining to government contracts.

Child Labor Amendment. Although passed by the necessary two-thirds vote of each house of Congress in 1924, and thereafter submitted to the states for ratification it has not yet received the necessary 36 ratifying votes. By 1952, 28 states had ratified this Amendment. The Amendment proposal was initially submitted to Congress as a result of the Supreme Court's decision in the case of BAILEY VS. DREXEL FURNITURE COMPANY in 1922. This decision declared the SECOND CHILD LABOR LAW of 1919 unconstitutional. Today the Congress has the power to regulate the labor of children under 16 years of age who are employed in activities affecting INTERSTATE COMMERCE.

child labor laws. See Keating-Owen Act and Second Child Labor Law.

Children's Bureau. An agency in the United States DEPARTMENT OF LABOR which investigates and reports on problems of CHILD WELFARE. It administers all national laws concerning child and maternal welfare. It has been active in studying juvenile delinquency, the employment of children in industrial plants and mines, child hygiene and related problems. The Bureau has published and distributed valuable literature including millions of copies of a booklet dealing with the care of small children. After 1935 it was authorized to supervise the child health, child welfare, and crippled children's program of the SOCIAL SECURITY ACT. Under this program the agency was empowered to spend $1,-500,000 annually in aiding state public welfare agencies to develop adequate methods of community child welfare organization. These funds provide expert child welfare and child psychology services to those children needing attention. The Bureau is also charged with promoting the health of mothers and children and with diagnosing and treating crippled children. About $4,000,000 annually is distributed on a matching basis to the states and territories for these services. Each year 150,000 crippled children are cared for. The Children's Bureau is now part of the Social Security Administration.

children's courts. Special courts established to solve the unusual legal and judicial problems of juvenile delinquency. Although a considerable body of protective legislation for the administration of juvenile crime was enacted in the Jacksonian period, it was not until the late 19th century that special children's tribunals were founded to handle such cases. In 1877 Massachusetts and New York provided for separate judicial terms for children's cases. In 1899 special children's courts were set up for the first time in Illinois and Colorado. It had now come to be accepted that juvenile lawbreakers were to be considered apart from adult criminals, and subject to the special guardianship and administration of children's courts. The juvenile court in Denver, Colorado, presided over by Judge BEN LINDSEY, achieved national fame after 1901. In 1906 a children's court was established in Washington, D.C. by Congress. Thereafter, such courts were set up in most of the states of the Union. A system of jurisprudence developed which emphasized informal procedures, separate hearings, psychiatric care, and probation and parole provisions. The medical and psychological SCIENCES have contributed much to the concepts of prevention, therapy, and penology.

child welfare. Generally applies to public assistance to widowed mothers of dependent children. Under former ELIZABETHAN POOR LAW concepts such aid was granted by local welfare agencies. With the onset of the DEPRESSION in the 1930's the problems grew beyond the powers of the municipalities to meet, resulting in the supplementation of state and local funds by federal grants-in-aid. Such aid is now extensive as a separate categorical form under the SOCIAL SECURITY ACT of 1935, amended in 1939, 1950, and 1954.

China Trade. A flourishing trade with China after 1785, which developed as a replacement for the loss of the West Indian trade following the American Revolution. The commercial possibilities of this trade were revealed by the profitable voyage of the *Empress of China* which returned to New York in 1785. The merchants of New York, Philadelphia, Boston, Baltimore, and other Atlantic ports quickly grasped the new possibilities. The early routes went around the Cape of Good Hope, across the Indian Ocean, and by way of the Dutch East Indies to China. The cargoes comprised silver bullion, fur, machinery, and certain farm crops for which the Americans received tea, china, silks, teakwood, handicrafts, enameled ware, carpeting, and spices. Despite the lengthy voyages and hazards the profits were unusually high. In 1819, it has been estimated, the combined import-export trade reached $19,000,000. The original and sole port of Canton was supplemented after the Opium War of 1842 by four additional ports which were confirmed by the Treaty of Wanghia of 1844.

China White Paper. A document issued by the STATE DEPARTMENT on August 5, 1949 absolving the United States from responsibility for the success of the Chinese COMMUNISTS against the nationalist regime of Chiang Kai-Shek. In November, 1945 President TRUMAN had appointed General GEORGE MARSHALL as his special envoy to China for the purpose of investigating the possibility of creating a strong, united, and democratic China. The President declared that the United States government favored the termination of one-party government and the establishment of a coalition government of the two major political forces in China. This hope was repeated by the foreign ministers of the United States, Great Britain, and the Soviet Union on December 27, 1945. In February, 1946 General Marshall's headquarters in China declared that an agreement had been reached. The opposition of the nationalist regime to admit Communists into a coalition government prevented the agreement from being carried out. In the summer of 1946 Marshall returned to China in the attempt to develop new conditions of agreement, but announced in August that a settlement was impossible. In January, 1947 he returned to the United States and issued a statement in which he denounced the "dominant group of reactionaries" in the national government who had prohibited the formation of a genuine coalition govern-

ment. He attacked the propaganda of the Chinese Communist party as harmful. Subsequently the United States dissolved its special agencies and withdrew all American troops from China. The White Paper was the justification of United States policies in this conflict.

Chinese Exclusion Acts. A series of laws, the first of which was passed in 1882. The law of 1882 prohibited Chinese laborers from entering the United States for a period of 10 years. It followed President ARTHUR's veto of a 20 year exclusion act in 1880 on the grounds that the 20 year term meant "prohibition" rather than "suspension" of Chinese immigration. The 1882 law nevertheless produced the same effect inasmuch as it was extended for an additional 10 year period in 1892 by the GEARY ACT, and extended indefinitely in 1902. The original Exclusion Act developed out of the anti-Chinese sentiment on the west coast which in San Francisco had resulted in violence. The laws were repealed in 1943 at which time Chinese immigrants were admitted into the United States under the quota system established under the NATIONAL ORIGINS PLAN of 1929.

CHIPMAN, Nathaniel. 1752-1843. Jurist. b. Connecticut. Graduated, Yale University (1777); served in the Revolutionary Army; practiced law at Rutland, Vermont (1779); chief justice, supreme court of Vt. (1789); important in securing RATIFICATION OF THE CONSTITUTION by the state convention; sent to Washington, D.C. to secure admission of Vermont into the Union; judge, U.S. district court, Vt. (1791-1793); chief justice, state supreme court (1796-98; 1813-15); U.S. Senator (1798-1804).

Chippewa Indians. See Ojibway and Chippewa Indians.

Chisholm Trail, the. A cattle trail from

northern Texas to Abilene, Kansas. From San Antonio, Texas it ran northeast to the Red River near Ringgold, Texas, across Oklahoma northward to Caldwell, Kansas, then north by east past Wichita to its terminus at Abilene. The establishment of a cattle depot and stockyards in Abilene in 1867 brought the Chisholm Trail into prominence as one of the routes of the "LONG DRIVE" of Texas longhorns. After 1871 this route declined in importance with the rise of Dodge City, as a shipping point, farther to the west. After 1880 the construction of RAILROADS southward into Texas provided cheaper and a more efficient transportation to the cattle markets. It is believed that the Chisholm Trail was named after Jesse Chisholm, a CHEROKEE Indian who freighted supplies and guided troops over it after the Civil War.

CHOATE, Joseph Hodges. 1832-1917. Lawyer and diplomat. b. Massachusetts. Graduated, Harvard Law School (1854); famous for handling of such cases as the TWEED RING prosecution, and the Standard Oil antitrust cases. Appointed U.S. Ambassador to Great Britain by MCKINLEY (1899-1905); aided in establishing an open-door policy in China; head of the United States delegation to second International PEACE CONFERENCE AT THE HAGUE (1907).

CHOATE, Rufus. 1799-1859. Lawyer. b. Massachusetts. Graduated, Dartmouth College (1819); admitted to the bar (1822); practiced law in Salem and Boston, Mass. (from 1834); famous as a trial lawyer and orator; member, U.S. House of Representatives (1831-34); U.S. Senator (1841-45) completing WEBSTER's term.

Choctaw Indians. See Chickasaw Indians.

CHOUTEAU, Jean Pierre. 1758-1849. Frontiersman and fur trader. b. New Orleans, La. Traded among OSAGE INDIANS where his family held a MONOPOLY (1794-1802); appointed by JEFFERSON. U.S. Indian agent for the tribe; famous for establishing the first permanent white settlement in Oklahoma.

Christian Churches. A Congregationalist movement which stemmed from the revivalist period at the end of the 18th century. They were strongly influenced by the theological doctrines of John Wesley. In 1931 they were merged with the Congregationalist Church under the name of the Congregational Christian Church. See Congregationalists.

C.I.A. The Central Intelligence Agency was established by Congress under the National Security Act of 1947. The Agency evaluates intelligence reports and coordinates the intelligence activities of the various government departments in the interest of national security. In recent years the C.I.A. came under a good deal of attack for its actions in the "Watergate Affair" and for alleged furtherance of death plots against Fidel Castro and Patrice Lumumba.

cigarette industry. An important consumer's goods industry based on tobacco crop. In 1964 this industry produced under 500,000,000,000 cigarettes in about 1,000 plants employing nearly 100,000 workers. The center of the industry is located in North Carolina. Among the largest manufacturers of cigarettes are R. J. Reynolds Tobacco Company, P. Lorillard Company, American Tobacco Company, Liggett, Myers Company, and Philip Morris Company, Ltd.

Cincinnati, Society of the. An aristocratic organization of officers of the Continental army, formed, after the American Revolution, for the purpose of creating an hereditary officer group. Although it did not last long, it achieved a degree of success in influencing the adoption of the Constitution.

citizens. Prior to 1868 those who were declared to be citizens under state law. Following adoption of the 14TH AMENDMENT in that year, citizens have been those falling within the definition framed in section 1 of the amendment. Citizens enjoy certain rights, privileges, and immunities not enjoyed by the alien population. These vary among the states but generally include attendance at public schools and universities, holding of public office, and voting.

citizenship. Defined in section 1 of the 14TH AMENDMENT. Prior to the date of adoption of this amendment in 1868, citizenship status was conferred by the state legislatures. As a result of the decision of the U.S. Supreme Court in the case of DRED SCOTT VS. SANDFORD in 1857, it was generally assumed that federal citizenship derived from state citizenship. Under the 14th amendment federal citizenship is primary and state citizenship secondary, thus reversing the Dred Scott doctrine.

city government. Established by state legislatures. These governments are entirely subordinate to the states, exercising no sovereign powers of their own. Within the last half century the development of the home rule principle has provided a degree of autonomy. The home rule charters thus granted are, however, subject to revision and/or revocation by the state constitutions. The three prevailing forms of city government are the MAYOR-COUNCIL form, the COMMISSION form, and the CITY-MANAGER form.

city-manager plan. A plan of municipal government in which an appointive manager exercises almost complete discretion in the administration of the city government. Selected by the city council for an indefinite term, this official enforces city ordinances and supervises the administration of municipal finances, public works, EDUCATION, RECREATION, health, policing, and other services. He may be chosen from outside the city and thus be free from local political control. He is generally appointed because he is an expert in municipal administration, being responsible to the council for his performance. He appoints the commissioners of departments and agencies, and they are responsible to him. The city-manager system was introduced as a reform measure in Staunton, Virginia in 1908, and subsequently spread swiftly, about 600 cities operating under it in 1952. It is generally conceded that the city-manager plan is the most superior of all forms of municipal government. In recent years it has spread to county governments in the United States.

city planning. A movement designed to plan the growth and development of cities in the United States for the purpose of creating well-defined and systematic areas of residence, business, COMMERCE, RECREATION, and TRANSPORTATION. Although its origins go back to WILLIAM PENN's plan in 1692 for his new city of Philadelphia, the greatest growth of the movement occurred in the first half of the 20th century. In the last decade of the 18th century Major L'Enfant was brought from Paris to plan the new national capital on the Potomac River. Although most major cities in the United States developed aimlessly, attempts have been made from time to time to organize their later growth. The upper portion of New York City was planned by a special commission in 1807. The pedestrian plan of rectangular bisecting streets and avenues was copied by other cities. In recent times public authorities have become concerned with more than the mere organization of streets. The direction and character of the growth of virtually all large American cities today are being planned by City Planning Commissions with these views in mind. The recent growth of suburban communities and the development of metropolitan areas have added new problems of zoning, education, and transportation to the traditional problems.

Civil Aeronautics Act. Also known as the Lea-McCarran Act. Passed by Congress in 1938. It established a Civil Aeronautics Authority of five members to administer a program of regulation over mail, passenger, and freight air lines. All the functions formerly exercised by the Bureau of Commercial Aviation, the POST OFFICE DEPARTMENT, and the INTERSTATE COMMERCE COMMISSION in air traffic were transferred to this agency. The C.A.A., as the agency is popularly known, was originally empowered to regulate air line rates and schedules, control agreements between companies, designate new airways, and administer the financial matters of airline companies. The Act also established an Air Safety Board of five members for the investigation of accidents and the establishment of safety rules. By an amendment and presidential EXECUTIVE ORDERS in 1940 the C.A.A. was reorganized and placed within the DEPARTMENT OF COMMERCE. At present the Civil Aeronautics Authority consists of an Administrator of Civil Aeronautics and the Civil Aeronautics Board, known as the C.A.B. The Air Safety Board was abolished. The functions of the Administrator include the construction and maintenance of the Federal airways system and airports, the development and testing of aircraft radio equipment, the examination and licensing of airmen and aircraft, and the enforcement of safety rules. The C.A.B. exercises rule making and administrative duties, promulgates safety regulations, authorizes air routes and air service by issuing certificates of public convenience and necessity, issues regulations on passenger and express rates, and controls the suspension or revocation of pilot and aircraft certificates.

Civil Defense Act. A law of Congress passed on January 2, 1951 for the purpose of providing a program of civil defense against atomic attack. It established a three year program for the construction of ATOMIC BOMB shelters and the stockpiling of medical supplies. The Administrator of the program was authorized to coordinate the defense activities of state and local governments by distributing defense data, establishing COMMUNICATIONS systems, seizing property, and requisitioning the facilities and services of other federal agencies.

Civilian Conservation Corps. Popularly known as the CCC. It was established by Congress in March 1933 as the first move in a series designed to solve the unemployment problem of the early DEPRESSION. The functions of this agency involved a program of public works projects in connection specifically with reforestation, flood and fire control, IRRIGATION, and similar projects. Young men from families on public welfare rolls were accepted for such work, a portion of their earnings being allotted to their families. By 1943 when the agency was absorbed into the FEDERAL WORKS AGENCY, some 300,000 men had received this kind of work. The agency's work was administered by the United States War Department.

Civilian Defense, Office of. An agency established by EXECUTIVE ORDER in May, 1941. It was authorized to coordinate civilian defense efforts with military plans, prevent unnecessary dislocation of local community life by defense efforts, and promote civilian morale. The agency conducted analyses of similar activities in England, and drafted a program for the establishment of local civilian defense units in air-raid precautions, first aid, and fire protection. Mayor FIORELLO H. LA GUARDIA of New York City was appointed its director. In 1945 the President abolished the OCD.

Civilian Production Administration. An administrative agency established by EXECUTIVE ORDER on November 3, 1945. It succeeded to the work of the WAR PRODUCTION BOARD and was authorized to further a swift and orderly transition from wartime industrial production to a maximum peacetime production free from wartime government controls. The CPA was empowered to bring about the expanded production of materials in short supply, limit the manufacture of products whose materials and facilities were scarce, and control inventory accumulation to avoid speculative hoarding and unbalanced distribution. It was granted power to break bottlenecks in reconversion, facilitate the federal government's relief and export programs, and allocate scarce materials necessary to the success of the government's economic stabilization program. The agency followed a policy of assistance to business, with few controls or detailed planning and directing, in order to permit industry to reach peacetime production goals. It worked by conference, meetings, and committees, its formal functions generally being limited to the regulation of the use and distribution of specific materials and areas such as veterans' HOUSING, the production of low cost clothing, and aid to small business. It was transferred to the Office of Temporary Controls in December, 1947.

Civil Law. The codified law derived from Roman Law. It is written law classified as to subject matter, with doctrines applicable to all types of disputes or questions. Although distinguished from the English COMMON LAW which is based principally on precedents and judge-made decisions, Roman civil law also makes use of precedents based on custom and legislation. The civil law derives from the Roman codes, particularly the Corpus Juris

Civilies, and has been transmitted chiefly through French law. Civil law is also distinguished from criminal law and is that branch which concerns suits between one person and another. Such suits may relate to a contract, damages, torts, real estate transactions, domestic relations, and many other issues. The rules of procedure in civil law provide for a "judgment" in a case at law or a "decree" in an equity case.

civil rights. Theory of rights developed in the political philosophy of John Locke, English political scientist. In the United States, as evolved by THOMAS JEFFERSON, JOHN ADAMS, and THOMAS PAINE, these rights included the right to life, liberty, property, and the pursuit of happiness. Assertions of these rights first appeared in the Virginia Declaration of Independence and in the DECLARATION OF INDEPENDENCE. They are included among the rights guaranteed in Article I Sections 9 and 10 of the federal Constitution, and in the first 10 amendments, and include freedom of speech, press, and religion, guarantees against cruel and unusual punishment, excessive fines and bail, assurance of grand jury indictment and jury trial, and protection against loss of life, liberty, and property without due process of law.

Civil Rights Act, the. A law of Congress in 1866 designed to protect the rights of freedmen. It attempted to nullify the BLACK CODES by defining CITIZENSHIP and safeguarding CIVIL RIGHTS, providing for its terms to be enforced in the federal courts. Although vetoed by President JOHNSON on March 27, it was enacted over his veto on April 9th. Ultimately its provisions were embodied in the FOURTEENTH AMENDMENT.

Civil Rights Act of 1875. A law of Congress passed on March 1, 1875. It was designed to protect all CITIZENS in their civil and legal rights irrespective of "nativity, race, color, or persuasion, religious or political." The law guaranteed the full and equal enjoyment, to all persons within the jurisdiction of the United States, of the accommodations, advantages, facilities, and privileges of inns, public conveyances on land or water, theatres, and other places of public amusement. It imposed a fine for violation of not less than $500 nor more than $1000 or imprisonment for 30 days to one year. The district and circuit courts of the United States were given exclusive jurisdiction in trial of violations. The Act was tested in the United States Supreme Court in 1883. See Civil Rights Cases.

Civil Rights Act of 1964. The most potent legislation in this area since the end of the Civil War. Provides equal rights for all citizens in voting, education, public accommodations and in federally assisted programs. The Act provides for strict enforcement through the Department of Justice and other federal agencies.

Civil Rights Act of 1968. Six days after the assassination of Martin Luther King in April 1968 Congress adopted the Civil Rights Act of 1968 which opened four-fifths of the nation's housing units to buyers or renters without discrimination by authorizing any person denied housing because of race to file a complaint with the Department of Housing and Urban Development.

Civil Rights Cases. A series of five cases tried by the United States Supreme Court in 1883 as tests of the constitutionality of the CIVIL RIGHTS ACT OF 1875. In each case a Negro had been denied some accommodation or privilege in violation of the Act. The Court held that the rights which the law attempted to protect were social rather than CIVIL RIGHTS, and that the Congress therefore had no jurisdiction over these matters. The Court's decisions virtually terminated Congress' efforts to enforce the civil liberties guarantees of the 14TH AMENDMENT.

civil service. Refers to the entire corps of personnel of governments, excluding military and top administrative and judicial officers. Also known as the public service. This is not to be confused with the term "MERIT SYSTEM" which refers specifically to the method of appointing civil servants through competitive examination. The federal civil service is the largest body of employees under a single employment head in the United States today. During World War II there were approximately 3,800,000 personnel employed by the United States government.

Civil Service Commission. See Pendleton Act.

civil service reform. Attempts to introduce a MERIT SYSTEM into the public service. The first public demands for civil service reform were made in the 1830's as a reaction to the SPOILS SYSTEM of the Jacksonian period. In 1853 a system of examinations was established by Congress, but was generally unsuccessful. In 1871 the President was authorized to set down a general system of personnel appointment on the basis of merit and fitness. Its failure led to the first comprehensive national program of merit system examinations in the passage of the PENDLETON ACT in 1883. This was supplemented in 1903 by the Civil Service Rules and Orders drawn up by President T. ROOSEVELT. Thereafter, legislative amendments and executive orders extended the scope of the Pendleton Act by increasing the number of classified occupations and eliminating PATRONAGE appointments. In the states civil service reform was inaugurated by the enactment in 1883 in New York of the Civil Service Act. Massachusetts (1884), Wisconsin and Illinois (1905), Colorado (1907), New Jersey (1908), Ohio (1912), and California and Connecticut (1913), had established civil service regulations before World War I, either by legislation or constitutional provisions. Subsequently, six other states put such programs into effect. In this period approximately 500 cities established similar merit system programs.

Civil War. Also known as the War Between the States. Although the fundamental causes of the Civil War are complex, it may be stated that they include the following: the political conflict between the North and South over the doctrines of NULLIFICATION and SECESSION, the strong growth of the ABOLITIONIST movement in the 1850's, the increasing political strength of the North in Congress in that period, the rapid industrialization of the North, the conservatism of southern politics, the search of northern business for new markets and areas of investment in the South and West, the need of northern industry for a greater supply of labor which would be provided by emancipation, the backwardness of southern economic development as contrasted with the northern, southern agrarianism versus northern industrialism, and the clash of the conservative southern culture with progressive northern thinking. The secession movement beginning in December, 1861 culminated a historic sectionalism that had manifested itself for 40 years in struggles over the issues of STATES RIGHTS, nullification, agrarian expansionism, and the TARIFF. At the outbreak of War the Union consisted of 23 states with 22,000,000 people, and the Confederacy of 11 states and 9,000,000 people, including 3,500,000 slaves. Its bold leadership, morale, and military training enabled the Confederacy to resist for four years the overwhelming superiority in numbers, equipment, and economic strength of the Union. On both sides the War involved internal conflicts over the issues of SLAVERY and secession, often leading to bitter political struggles. It was not until 1862 that LINCOLN's hand was forced on the issue of emancipation, although the struggle continued between him and the RADICAL REPUBLICANS led by STEVENS, SUMNER, WADE, and CHASE. The Union's early military defeats were turned into victories after 1863 with the appointment of General GRANT to command its armies. Despite the gallantry and heroism of the Confederate army, commanded by LEE, JACKSON, BEAUREGARD et al, the overwhelming superiority of Union forces brought victory at APPOMATTOX COURTHOUSE in April, 1865. The results of the Civil War included the final destruction of the theories of secession and nullification, and established the supremacy of the federal government. The War elevated the veteran into an important political influence in the form of the GAR, brought about the abolition of slavery, destroyed for generations the political influence of the South, opened that area to industrialization and the economic penetration of northern capital, destroyed the PLANTATION SYSTEM and laid the groundwork for redistribution of small land holdings. It also established the foundation for the racial supremacy doctrines that have manifested themselves in anti-Negro social and legal measures. It marked the ascendency of the Republican Party to power in national politics, the inauguration of a high tariff policy, and the establishment of the "SOLID SOUTH" in national politics. It has been felt by many that the Civil War opened wounds that have not yet healed, these being exhibited in the sectional hatred and various states rights movements which have sprung up from time to time since the end of the Civil War.

Claiborne Rebellion. An attempt in 1631 by WILLIAM CLAIBORNE to acquire possession of Kent Island in the upper Chesapeake Bay. His settlement of a plantation on this territory was recognized by Virginia which accepted its representation in the Assembly. Lord Baltimore claimed title under the Maryland Charter of 1632, and six years later seized Kent Island as his legal possession, denying the validity of Claiborne's occupation.

CLAIBORNE, William. 1587? - 1677. Virginia colonist. b. England. Settled in Virginia (1621); became surveyor for the colony; secretary of state for the colony (1626-37; 1652-60); traded with Indians at Kent Island in Chesapeake bay (later claimed as part of Maryland grant); opposed Lord Baltimore's claim to territory; treasurer of Va. (1642); invaded Maryland and drove out CALVERT; controlled Maryland (1652-57) as member of its governing commission.

CLAIBORNE, William Charles Coles. 1775-1817. Lawyer and governor. b. Virginia. Practiced law in Tennessee; judge of superior court Tennessee (1796); member, U.S. House of Representatives (1797-1801); governor of Mississippi territory (1801-03); governor of Territory of Orleans (1804-12); governor of Louisiana (1812-16); U.S. Senator (1817).

CLARK, Abraham. 1726-1794. Patriot and political leader. Often referred to as "Congress Abraham." b. New Jersey. Secretary of New Jersey COMMITTEE OF CORRESPONDENCE; member CONTINENTAL CONGRESS (1776-78; 1779-83); signer of the DECLARATION OF INDEPENDENCE; member, U.S. House of Representatives (1790-94).

CLARK, Champ (James Beauchamp Clark). 1850-1921. Political leader. b. Kentucky. Graduated Cincinnati Law School (1875); moved to Missouri to begin practice (1876); prosecuting attorney of Pike County (1885-89); member, U.S. House of Representatives (1893-95, 1897-1921); Speaker of the House (1911-19); served on Foreign Affairs, and WAYS AND MEANS COMMITTEES; Democratic leader of the House (from 1907); was candidate for Democratic nomination for the presidency (1912) but lost when W. J. BRYAN switched his support to WOODROW WILSON.

CLARK, Charles Edgar. 1843-1922. Naval officer. b. Vermont. Served under FARRAGUT at Mobile Bay; commanded battleship *Oregon* during Spanish-American War; when ordered to join the Atlantic fleet, he left San Francisco (March 19, 1898) and made a famous 14,000 mile trip around Cape Horn in time to join SAMPSON's fleet in the blockade of SANTIAGO, Cuba (July 3, 1898); his ship played an important part in routing the Spanish fleet; commander of Philadelphia naval yard (1899); rear admiral (1902); retired (1905).

CLARK, George Rogers. 1752-1818. Revolutionary frontier hero. b. Virginia. Surveyor of lands in West Virginia (1772-74); captain in LORD DUNMORE's War against the Ohio Indians (1776); with the approval of PATRICK HENRY, governor of Virginia, he led expedition into the Illinois country (called the Northwest); despite floods and other difficulties he captured important points of Kaskaskia and Vincennes (1778); stopped British from capturing St. Louis (1780); wanted to fight on to Detroit, but Kentucky treasury was depleted; fought against the British and the Indians to hold the Illinois and Kentucky territory for the colonies (1779-83).

CLARK, John Bates. 1847-1938. Economist. b. Rhode Island. Graduated Amherst College (Ph, D. 1890); studied at Heidelberg; professor, Carleton College (1877-81); Smith College (1882-93). Amherst (1892-95); Columbia University (1895-1923). Editor, *Political Science Quarterly* (1895-1911). Author of *Philosophy of Wealth* (1885), *The Distribution of Wealth* (1899) considered his most important book, *Essentials of Economic Theory* (1907). He was an important influence on the economic thinking of his time.

Clark Memorandum. A statement of foreign policy prepared in 1928 and released in 1930 by Undersecretary of State J. Reuben Clark. The Memorandum denied the validity of the ROOSEVELT COROLLARY to the MONROE DOCTRINE and held that the United States did not have the right to intervene in the affairs of Latin-America. The Clark Memorandum was translated into an international treaty by the agreement of the Latin American states and the United States in the Declaration of the MONTEVIDEO CONFERENCE in 1933. In June 1934, the United State Senate's ratification of this treaty signalled the formal repudiation of the Roosevelt Corollary.

CLARK, Walter. 1846-1924. Chief Justice of North Carolina. Served with Confederate army at ANTIETAM and FREDERICKSBURG. Judge of superior court of North Carolina (1885-89); judge of supreme court (1889-1924); progressive independent thinker who gained a national reputation for his forward looking decisions. Edited 16 volumes of *North Carolina Records* and translated Constant's *Memoirs of Napoleon*.

CLARK, William. 1770-1838. Explorer. Leader of LEWIS AND CLARK EXPEDITION. Brother of GEORGE ROGERS CLARK. b. Virginia. Lieutenant, U. S. Army (1792); served against the Indians (1791-96); joined Captain MERIWETHER LEWIS in expedition to find route to Pacific Ocean; started from St. Louis (1804); crossed the country reaching the mouth of the Columbia River (November, 1805); returned to St. Louis (1806); superintendent of Indian Affairs at St. Louis (1807); governor of Missouri Territory(1813-21); with LEWIS CASS negotiated Indian treaty of Prairie de Chien (1825).

CLARK, William Andrews. 1839-1925. Industrialist and Senator. b. Pennsylvania. Copper magnate in Montana; president, Montana state constitutional conventions (1884,1889); fought with MARCUS DALY to control Democratic party in Montana

(1888-1900); U.S. Senator (1899-1900), but he was refused a seat because of doubt that he was "duly and legally elected"; U.S. Senator (1901-07). His art collection is in the Corcoran Gallery in Washington, D.C.

CLARKE, John. 1609-1676. Pastor, physician and a founder of Rhode Island. b. England. Came to America (1637); aided ANNE HUTCHINSON, and joined exiles in founding Rhode Island (1638); went to England (1651-64) with ROGER WILLIAMS to further the interests of the colonies by joining the Rhode Island and Providence settlements; helped Williams in maintaining a liberal colony with religious toleration an important factor; served in general assembly (1664-69); elected deputy governor of the colony three times.

CLARKE, John Hessin. 1857-1945. Jurist. b. Ohio. Graduated Western Reserve (1877); admitted to the bar in Ohio (1878); practiced law in Lisbon, Youngstown and Cleveland, Ohio (1878-1914); opposed MARK HANNA; appointed by President WILSON as U. S. District Judge (1914) and to the U. S. Supreme Court (1916 and 1922). Resigned to further the cause of the LEAGUE OF NATIONS. Author of *America and the World Peace.*

Clarke-McNary Act. See national forests.

CLAY, Clement Claiborne. 1816-1882. Confederate Senator. Served in state legislature; U.S. Senator (1853-1859); sent by JEFFERSON DAVIS (1864) on mission to Canada hoping to negotiate peace with LINCOLN; imprisoned as conspirator in Lincoln's assassination and held for one year without trial.

CLAY, Henry. 1777-1852. Lawyer and statesman. b. Virginia. Self-educated, reading law under Robert Brooke, attorney-general of Virginia; practised in Lexington, Kentucky (from 1797); elected to the state legislature (1803-06); U.

S. Senator (1806-07; 1810-11); member, U.S. House of Representatives (1811-14, 1815-21, 1823-25); immediately elected Speaker and served every year except 1821; as one of the "WAR HAWKS," he urged the War of 1812; refused appointments as Minister to Great Britain and Secretary of War, preferring the Democratic leadership in Congress; backed the TARIFF of 1824, the MISSOURI COMPROMISE (1820), recognition of South American republics (1817); by supporting JOHN Q. ADAMS for the presidency (1824) he acquired the name of "President Maker." U.S. Secretary of State (1825-29) appointed by Adams. U.S. Senator (1831-42); presented the COMPROMISE OF 1833 in nullification crisis preventing conflict; became the WHIG candidate for the presidency (1832, 1844) but was defeated; most famous for his COMPROMISE OF 1850 which was an attempt to prevent civil war. Became known as "The Great Compromiser" and "The Great Pacificator."

Clayton Anti-Trust Act. Enacted by Congress in 1914 as a supplement to the SHERMAN ANTI-TRUST ACT of 1890. It was called "LABOR'S MAGNA CARTA" because it attempted to exclude organized labor from the restrictive provisions of the Sherman Act. It prohibited INTERLOCKING DIRETORATES in the same INDUSTRY and forbade CORPORATIONS from purchasing the securities of other corporations for the purpose of eliminating competition. It provided that corporation officers be held personally liable for violating the ANTI-TRUST LAWS. In December, 1950, Congress amended the Act prohibiting purchases by one company of the assets of another company if the transaction tended toward MONOPOLY. The Act, like its predecessor, has not effectively curbed the growth of monopolies. See Business consolidation and merger.

Clayton-Bulwer Treaty. A treaty between the United States and Great Britain in 1850 which provided that the signatories would jointly guarantee the NEUTRALITY of any CANAL subsequently to be built across the isthmus of Panama. Each further agreed not to seek exclusive control over the canal, never to erect fortifications upon it, nor to acquire any Central American colonies. In addition both nations promised to extend their protection to any company undertaking the construction of such a canal and to use their influence with the Central American governments to grant their aid to the project. The treaty was a result of American interest in Latin-America stimulated by the GOLD RUSH of 1848 and 1849. It was abrogated in 1901 by the HAY-PAUNCEFORTE TREATY.

CLAYTON, Henry De Lamar. 1857-1929. Legislator and Jurist. b. Alabama. Practiced law in Alabama (1880-1914); U.S. district attorney (1893-1896); member, U.S. House of Representatives (1897-1915); chairman, judiciary committee (1911-15); known for CLAYTON ANTI-TRUST ACT (1914); U.S. district judge (1914-29).

CLAYTON, John Middleton. 1796-1856. Jurist and statsman. b. Delaware. Graduated, Yale (1815); Litchfield Law School; state legislature (1824); secretary of state for Delaware (1826-28); U.S. Senator from Delaware (1829-36) opposing the BANK OF THE UNITED STATES;; supported JACKSON's nullification policy; helped CLAY pass the COMPROMISE OF 1833; chief justice of Delaware (1837-39); U.S. Senator (1845-49); U.S. Secretary of State (1849-50) appointed by TAYLOR; negotiated the CLAYTON-BULWER TREATY checking the expansion of Great Britain into Central America and providing for a neutral canal across the American isthmus (1850); U.S. Senator (1853-56).

CLEAVELAND, Moses. 1754-1806. Pioneer. b. Connecticut. Went to the Western Reserve to survey and settle land bought by the Connecticut Land Company of which he was an official; known as the founder of Cleveland, Ohio, which was first called Cleaveland in his honor.

CLEAVER, Eldridge. After spending seven years in exile former Black Panther leader Eldridge Cleaver returned to the U.S. on November 17, 1975. He was immediately arrested on a federal warrant for flight to avoid imprisonment. Cleaver had fled to Cuba, violating bail, in order to avoid murder charges in connection with a 1968 shootout between the Black Panthers and the police. On November 19, 1975 Cleaver was placed in a Federal Correctional Facility in San Diego, California. He is the author of a book *Soul on Ice* as well as numerous magazine articles.

CLEBURNE, Patrick Ronayne. 1828-1864. Confederate army officer. b. Ireland. After serving in the British army (1846-49), came to America (1849); served in Confederate army commanding a brigade at the BATTLE OF SHILOH; major general (1863) commanding a division at Murfreesboro, CHICKAMAUGA, MISSIONARY RIDGE earning the name "STONEWALL JACKSON of the West"; persistently used Negro troops; founded the Order of the Southern Cross; killed in action.

CLEMENS, Samuel Langhorne. See TWAIN, Mark.

CLEVELAND, Stephen Grover. 1837-1908. Twenty-second and twenty-fourth President of the United States. b. Caldwell, New Jersey. Practised law, Buffalo, N. Y. (from 1859); elected mayor of Buffalo (1881-82) and succeeded in reforming the city administration; governor of New York (1883-85); cooperated with T. ROOSEVELT in securing legislation to reform municipal government in New York City; Democratic President of the United States (1885-89); supported lower TARIFF and CIVIL SERVICE REFORM; vetoed the undeserved Civil War pension bills; defeated by B. HARRISON for the presidency (1888) but was again elected President (1893-97); after the PANIC OF 1893 he opposed currency INFLATION and caused the repeal of the SHERMAN SILVER PURCHASE ACT OF 1890; favored lower tariff rates; sent United States troops into Chicago during the PULLMAN STRIKE when the strikers interfered with the movement of United States mail; opposed the use of troops by the British in VENEZUELA BOUNDARY DISPUTE; refused to recognize HAWAII after the revolution there; lost the nomination for the presidency to BRYAN. Author of *Presidential Problems* (1904). Retired to private life in Princeton, New Jersey (1897-1908).

CLIFFORD, Nathan. 1803-1881. Jurist. b. New Hampshire. Practised law in Maine. Member, U.S. House of Representatives (1839-43); appointed U.S. Attorney General (1846-48) by POLK; Associate Justice, U.S. Supreme Court (1858-81). Believed that TILDEN was elected when presiding over Hayes-Tilden Electoral Commission (1877).

CLINTON, De Witt. 1769-1828. Lawyer and political leader. b. New York. Graduated, Columbia (1786); secretary to Governor GEORGE CLINTON, his uncle, (1790-95); member, New York Assembly (1798); member, state senate (1798-1802; 1806-1811); U.S. Senator (1802-03) introduced 12TH CONSTITUTIONAL AMENDMENT; mayor, New York City (1803-07; 1810, 1811, 1813, 1814-15); candidate for the presidency (1812) defeated by MADISON; governor of New York (1817-21; 1825-28) sponsoring the Erie and Champlain-Hudson canals; promoted public education and legal reform.

CLINTON, George. 1739-1812. Lawyer and statesman. b. New York. Studied law; revolutionary party leader; member, CONTINENTAL CONGRESS (1775-76); sent to command troops at Hudson Highlands which prevented him from being a signer of the DECLARATION OF INDEPENDENCE; brigadier general (1777); elected the first governor of New York state (1777-95; 1801-04); signed peace treaties with Indians; opposed Federal Constitution; Vice-President of the United States (1805-12) and as presiding officer of the Senate his deciding vote killed the bill to recharter the BANK OF THE UNITED STATES (1811).

CLINTON, Sir Henry. 1738?-1795. Commander in chief of the British forces during the American Revolution, son of GEORGE CLINTON, royal governor of New York. Served in French and Indian war; major general (1772); fought in battles OF BUNKER HILL and LONG ISLAND; succeeded HOWE as commander in chief in North America (1778); c a p t u r e d CHARLESTON (1780); after CORNWALLIS disobeyed his orders they quarreled; resigned (1781); returned to England. Author of *Narrative* (1792) record of his campaigns. Died while governor of Gibraltar.

CLINTON, James. 1733-1812. Revolutionary officer. b. New York. Brother of GEORGE and father of DE WITT CLINTON. Captain of militia in Bradstreet's expedition against Fort Frontenac in French and Indian War; brigadier general, CONTINENTAL ARMY (1776); with Gen. JOHN SULLIVAN, he led successful campaigns against the British LOYALISTS and the Indians in western New York and Pennsylvania; fought in final YORKTOWN campaign.

clipper ships. Fast wooden vessels important in American foreign trade after 1845. They were designed for speed, being built on sharp lines and carrying a large amount of canvas. It is believed that they were derived from a type of Chinese coasting vessel known as the "Singapore fast boat." With favorable winds clipper ships could outrun steamships, and it was common for a clipper to sail over three hundred miles a day. Between 1851 and 1853 records were made of 86 days from Singapore to New York, 84 from Canton to New York, and 96 from Manila to Salem. The first clipper ship, the *Rainbow*, was designed by John W. Griffiths and constructed in New York City. The record was held by the *Flying Fish*, built in Boston in 1851, with an average of 100¾ days in four passages. Until 1868 the Clipper ship era held its sway over the steamship. During that period a flourishing tea, spices, and luxury trade sprang up with China. The discovery of gold in California in 1848 and in Australia in 1851 further stimulated the building of clipper ships. It is believed that the origin of the word "clipper" derived from the verb "clip," meaning to run fast.

closure. Also spelled cloture. The cessation of debate preparatory to holding a vote on an issue. In the Senate it is used to halt filibustering. Closure is adopted by two-thirds vote on a petition containing at least 16 signatures. Speeches thereafter are limited to one hour.

clothing industry. In colonial America clothing was manufactured in the household. The housewife spun and wove wool, flax, or cotton for clothes. Leather for shoes, gloves, and work clothes was produced and processed on the farm. This production was generally for home use or for a limited local market. The growth of the TEXTILE INDUSTRY in the 19th century stimulated the industrial manufacturing of clothes in New England and the middle states. By 1860 there were 1909 establishments MANUFACTURING woolen goods, with a capital investment of $35,520,527, consuming 90,000,000 pounds of wool. Increasing amounts of flax, cotton, and silk rapidly made the clothing industry one of the most important in the nation. In 1860 there were 42 silk mills in the Northeast producing an output valued at more than $6,500,000. The ready-made clothing industry developed with the invention of the sewing machine. Hosiery and knit-goods mills, which numbered 197 in 1860, increased to 1,821 by 1937. Tariff protection brought about an enormous increase in the manufacture of silk clothing, its value rising from $6,608,000 in 1860 to $404,734,000 in 1937. The United States silk output is greater than that of any other nation. The production of rayon and other synthetic fabrics was greater in the 1950's than that of silk. Modern clothing factories, utilizing automatic machinery and specialized labor, developed the ready-made clothing industry into one of the most important in the nation. New York City became the greatest clothing center in the world. Chicago, Philadelphia, Rochester, Baltimore, and Los Angeles became other leaders. In 1963 the production of all types of hosiery was 179,000,000 dozen pairs of which 76,000,000 dozen pairs were women's hosiery. In 1949 there were 31,000 firms in the apparel and related products industries. These employed 1,009,000 workers who added a value of $4,245,000,000 to the product by manufacturing. There were 115,707 retail clothing establishments that year. The American people spent $37,000,000,000 for clothing in 1963.

CLYMER, George. 1739-1813. Patriot and political leader. b. Philadelphia. Successful merchant who aided colonial cause; member, Pennsylvania COUNCIL OF SAFETY; delegate, CONTINENTAL CONGRESS (1776-78; 1780-83); signer of DECLARATION OF INDEPENDENCE; founder and president of Bank of Philadelphia; member first U.S. Congress (1788); Jef-fersonian Democrat in his thinking; negotiated treaty with CREEK and CHEROKEE INDIANS (1796).

coal industry. Bituminous coal is the greatest source of power in the United States. Although it is mined in 29 states about 90 percent of the production is found in 13 Eastern states. Pennsylvania and West Virginia produce half of the nation's bituminous output. Pennsylvania produces virtually the entire national output of anthracite coal which was the mainstay of colonial power and heat. Although used domestically anthracite became an important industrial fuel after the Revolution. By 1837 the nation was mining more than 1,000,000 tons of anthracite coal, a figure that was increased to 10,000,000 tons by the Civil War. By the opening of the 20th century anthracite had been far outstripped by bituminous production. At the end of World War I 580,000,000 tons of bituminous coal were mined as compared with 99,600,000 tons of anthracite. By the 1950's anthracite was being used principally as a domestic fuel, 85 percent of it for heating purposes. By the opening of World War II its production had declined to approximately 50,000,000 tons annually. The increase of bituminous mining arose from the tremendous industrialization and railroad construction program after the Civil War. The competition of natural gas, petroleum, and electric power have challenged the coal industry as the prime source of energy. Coal areas occupy 13 percent of the land mass of the United States and contain more than half of the world's supply. In 1963 the nation produced approximately 395,600,000 tons valued at about $2,500,000,000.

Coal Strike of 1902. See Anthracite Coal Strike.

Coast Guard Academy, U.S. Established in 1876 under the name of "School of Instruction" of the Revenue Cutter Service. It took its present name in 1914 when the Revenue Cutter Service was merged with the Life-Saving Service. Since 1932 the Academy has been situated at New London, Connecticut. Candidates serve four years in the study of marine engineering, seamanship, navigation, naval architecture, physics, mathematics, and general academic subjects. Upon graduation they receive a degree of Bachelor of Science and are commissioned as ensigns in the U.S. Coast Guard.

Coast Guard, U.S. This revenue-military service dates its antecedents back to 1790 in the creation of the Revenue Cutter Service by act of Congress. In 1915 Congress merged this service and the Life-Saving Service into the U.S. Coast Guard. In 1939 the Lighthouse Service of the DEPARTMENT OF COMMERCE was transferred to the Coast Guard. Before the creation of the NAVY DEPARTMENT in 1798 it was the only armed force afloat. Today it operates within the TREASURY DEPARTMENT in time of peace and in the Navy Department in war time. Among its functions are the prevention of SMUGGLING, the clearance of debris in harbors, the maintenance of an ice patrol in northern waters, flood service, and service as one of the military units in time of war. In 1956 the Coast Guard had 25,-000 men and officers who maintained approximately 40,000 aids to navigation in the form of lighthouses, lightships, buoys, daymarks, fog signals, and radio beacons. Its women's affiliate is known as SPARS of whom 10,000 served in World War II.

COBB, Howell. 1815-1868. Lawyer and statesman. b. Georgia. Graduated, University of Georgia (1834); member, U.S. House of Representatives (1843-51; 1855-57); Speaker of the House (1849-51); governor of Georgia (1851-53); U.S. Secretary of the Treasury (1857-60) appointed by BUCHANAN; after LINCOLN's election, he advocated the immediate secession of Georgia; brigadier general, Confederate army (1862); major general (1863).

COCKRAN, William Bourke. 1854-1923. Lawyer and political leader. b. Ireland. Came to New York (1871); member, U.S. House of Representatives (1887-89; 1891-95; 1904-09; 1921-23); supported organized labor and immigration reforms. Well-known as defense attorney in the THOMAS J. MOONEY case (1918).

COCKRELL, Francis Marion. 1834-1915. Confederate general. b. Missouri. Graduated, Chapel Hill College; studied law and began practice (1855); brigadier general leader of well-known "Cockrell's Brigade"; elected to U.S. Senate (1874-1905); appointed by T. ROOSEVELT, although a well-known Democrat, to INTERSTATE COMMERCE COMMISSION (1905-1910).

CODDINGTON, William. 1601-1678. Colonial governor and founder of Rhode Island. b. England. Came to Massachusetts as an officer of the Massachusetts Bay Company (about 1630); treasurer of the company (1634-36); protested prosecution of ANNE HUTCHINSON (1637); with JOHN CLARKE moved to Rhode Island (1638); founded colony at Newport (1639); when Newport and Portsmouth were combined (1640) he was elected governor; refused to combine with ROGER WILLIAMS settlement at Providence and Clarke went to England to protest; Coddington patent revoked (1652); colonies combined into one government of Rhode Island and Providence Plantations; served as governor (1674, 1675, 1678).

codes of fair competition. Industry-wide agreements established under the National Recovery Act of 1933. These rules were administered under the supervision of the NATIONAL RECOVERY ADMINISTRA-

TOR who prosecuted violations of them as misdemeanors. Among the codes' more important provisions were: the right of employees to organize and bargain collectively through representatives of their own choosing, a 40 hour work week, the banning of the labor of children under 16 years of age, minimum wages of $12-$15 per week, control of production, PRICE CONTROL, and detailed rules concerning fair trade practices of the various industries. By 1935 when the act was invalidated by the United States Supreme Court, more than 400 codes had been put into effect covering about 20,000,000 workers.

Coercive Acts. See Intolerable Acts.

Coinage Act of 1792. The first CURRENCY act of the United States. Accepting HAMILTON's recommendations Congress established a bi-metallic standard, providing that the new American dollar be fixed at 24.75 grains of gold and the new silver dollar contain 371.25 grains of pure silver, smaller coins to be of proportionate weight. The newly-established ratio between silver and gold was thus 15 to 1. The act also permitted the free and unlimited coinage of both metals which were made full legal tender.

Coinage Act of 1873. See Demonetization of Silver Act.

COKE, Richard. 1829-1897. Governor of Texas. b. Virginia. Graduated, William and Mary College; admitted to the bar and moved to Texas to practice;. served through Civil War; associate justice of state supreme court (1866-67); led Democrats to victory as governor (1873-76); reorganized state affairs, established public school system; U.S. Senator (1876-94).

COLBY, Bainbridge. 1869-1950. Lawyer. b. Missouri. Graduated, Williams College (1890); LL.B. New York Law School

(1892); counsel for Equitable Life Insurance Company; important in election of T. ROOSEVELT as president (1912); founder of PROGRESSIVE PARTY (1912); Commissioner of U.S. Shipping Board during World War I; U.S. Secretary of State (1920-21) appointed by WILSON; established law partnership with Wilson (1921-23). Author of *The Close of Woodrow Wilson's Administration and the Final Years.*

COLDEN, Cadwallader. 1688-1776. Colonial administrator and scholar. b. Ireland. Graduated, University of Edinburgh (1705); studied medicine in London; to Philadelphia (1710); practised medicine; asked by Governor HUNTER to come to New York (1720) and made surveyor-general; important aid to Governor CLINTON; LOYALIST lieutenant governor of New York (1761-76); well-known scholar, botanist, and writer on Newton's theories. Author of *The History of the Five Indian Nations* (1727).

"cold war." The popular name applied to the deterioration of American-Soviet relations after 1946. In the absence of outright warfare a series of diplomatic controversies developed to a point of open political hostility, fed by the mutual propaganda attacks of these nations' governments and publicity media. The more outstanding controversies included the TRUMAN DOCTRINE, MARSHALL PLAN, NORTH ATLANTIC TREATY, MUTUAL SECURITY PROGRAM, BERLIN BLOCKADE, BERLIN AIRLIFT, JAPANESE PEACE TREATY, KOREAN WAR, extension of Soviet power in central and eastern Europe, assumption of power by the Chinese Communists, and the division and OCCUPATION OF GERMANY.

COLE, Thomas. 1801-1848. Landscape painter. b. England. Came to America (1819); famous as the founder of the Hudson River school. His large landscapes hang in various museums in the country.

129

collective bargaining. The determination of the terms and relationships of employment, jointly arranged by an employer and the freely chosen representatives of his employees. Although inhibited by the application of the common law doctrine of conspiracy to labor organizations, COLLECTIVE BARGAINING was a typical instrument of union negotiation as far back as 1794 when the local unions of printers and cordwainers in New York and Philadelphia practised it. Today labor organizations bargain collectively on an industry-wide basis. The NATIONAL LABOR RELATIONS ACT protects most industrial employees in the exercise of this right. Other federal and similar state legislation guarantee collective bargaining for additional categories of workers.

collective security. A plan among the nations to take concerted action against military aggression in order to defend international peace and security. From time to time such plans have been embodied in international agreements and in the work of world organizations such as the LEAGUE OF NATIONS, the UNITED NATIONS, and the HAGUE TRIBUNAL. Among the international agreements providing for collective security have been the arbitration treaties drafted at the Hague Tribunal, the KELLOGG-BRIAND PEACE PACT, and the NORTH ATLANTIC TREATY.

colonial assemblies. The legislative bodies of the English colonies in North America. The first of these was the VIRGINIA HOUSE OF BURGESSES, established in 1619. A representative assembly was set up in the PLYMOUTH COLONY, followed by one in the MASSACHUSETTS BAY COLONY in 1632. The FUNDAMENTAL ORDERS OF CONNECTICUT of 1639 established the most democratic assembly up to that time. Subsequently representative bodies were provided for either in the charters or the laws of Maryland, Rhode Island, New York, and the other colonies. These as-semblies are of great importance because of the legislative experience provided to the colonial and early American leaders of a later era. Among the powers they exercised were: control of the finances, limitations on the powers of the governor, the determination of the charter of local government, tax powers, and authority to determine military affairs. Towards the end of the colonial period the leaders in these assemblies assumed the direction of the struggle against Parliament, and from their ranks sprang some of the outstanding Revolutionary leaders.

colonial bounties. See bounties.

colonial boycott. See boycott.

colonial commerce. Trade among the British colonies or between any of them and the mother country or other European nations and/or their colonies. Boston and Philadelphia were the centers of colonial commerce. Other important trade areas were New York, Charleston, and Newport. Trade was carried on principally in colonial-built ships on a barter, cash, or credit basis. The legislation inspired by mercantilist thinking imposed occasional restrictions, but colonial trade remained nevertheless the single most lucrative economic activity. The export of farm crops to Europe was exchanged for imported manufactured goods, slaves, sugar, and certain foods. See triangular trade.

colonial currency. The various materials and metals established as legal tender by the colonial governments. In early years wampum and beaver skins were utilized until over-production of the latter rendered them useless as a medium of exchange. From that time forward the various legislatures experimented with different commodities. In 1619 Virginia declared tobacco to be legal tender. In 1631 Massachusetts set a price on beaver skins and corn, and on grain nine years later. South Carolina accepted rice in payment of taxes in 1719. In 1690 Massachusetts printed paper currency, shortly followed by other legislatures. The absence of sound banking and of a metal basis for this currency quickly brought about its depreciation in the 18th century. Simultaneously foreign coins of various denominations circulated throughout the colonies, although in short quantities. The shortage of precious metals inhibited colonial coinage for a long time, although Massachusetts embarked on a coinage program in 1652.

colonial manufacturing. Industry in the British colonies was primitive. It was basically household manufacturing of clothing, meat products, beer, lumber products, and foods. Production was for domestic consumption or for sale in a local market. The "putting out" system, in which the businessman distributed raw materials to individual workers in their homes and later collected and sold the finished product, was widely prevalent. Saw mills dotted the river communities. Despite available resources, labor, and British capital, the greater profits of trade and agriculture inhibited the growth of manufacturing. Bounties were paid by the British on the manufacture of specified products such as iron and wool simultaneously with the prohibition by Parliament of the erection of rolling mills, steel furnaces, and other industries. Other English laws prohibited preferential treatment to colonial manufactured products. Despite the restrictions, important manufactures included leather, soap, candles, cotton and woolen goods, linens, hemp, foundry ware, iron tools, and utensils, and furniture.

Colonies. Those areas owned and administered by nations with more advanced political, economic, and social cultures. In modern times European governments sent out exploration expeditions to discover and settle these undeveloped territories for various reasons. After the Crusades the migrations of Asiatic peoples into Eastern and Central Europe furnished the stimulus of novel ideas and products for Europeans. Additional inducements included the INVENTION or rediscovery of the compass, astrolabe, and cross-staff, the religious stimulation of the Reformation, the economic drives of mercantilist ideology, the expanding TRADE of newly-risen cities, improved geographical knowledge, the demand in Europe for spices, silks, and new commodities, and the striving of the emerging middle class for political power. To the settlements came the common people who sought relief from religious persecution, greater economic opportunity, and escape from Europe's incessant wars. Although the Portuguese were the first explorers, they were quickly followed by Spain, Sweden, France, Holland, and England. By the opening of the 18th century the Swedes and Dutch had been eliminated from North America. France was in possession of Canada, the Ohio and Mississippi valleys, and islands in the Atlantic. Spain had conquered all of South and Central America, with the exception of Brazil, and England had, by settlement or conquest, come into the possession of the 13 colonies along the Atlantic coast from Canada to Florida. The quest for liberty and commercial supremacy was soon to involve her in war with France for possession of the North American continent.

colonies, types of. The different kinds of colonial organization established by Great Britain during the seventeenth and eighteenth centuries. Basically these were ROYAL COLONIES, COMMERCIAL COLONIES, and PROPRIETARY COLONIES.

colonization. The process of a major nation seeking and acquiring overseas areas which are economically, politically, and culturally undeveloped. From the fifteenth century on, spurred by the principles of MERCANTILISM, the European nations acquired vast colonial realms in North and South America, in Asia, and in the islands of the seas. The imperialist expansion developing out of the second INDUSTRIAL REVOLUTION after 1870 resulted in the acquisition of huge colonial areas in Africa, Australia, and the remaining areas of Asia not previously colonized. The United States participated in the colonization movement on a broad scale after the Spanish American War of 1898.

Colorado. The eighth state in size, with an area of 104,247 square miles. Organized as a territory in 1861 and admitted as the 38th state on August 1, 1876. Denver is the capital. In 1950 Colorado's population of 1,325,089 made it 34th in rank. Its largest cities are Denver. Pueblo, and Colorado Springs. Colorado has the highest mountain ranges in the United States. Fifty peaks rise over 14,000 feet and more than 1,000 are over 10,000 feet high. The state is the nation's largest producer of uranium and vanadium. Other important minerals include gold, silver, cooper, zinc, lead, and molybdenum. AGRICULTURE is the most important industry, the crops including beans, barley, corn, hay, potatoes, sugar beets, wheat, and vegetables. IRRIGATION is extremely important. Important manufactured goods are iron, steel, brick, and tile. Colorado Springs is the most popular tourist resort in the Rocky Mountains. Summit Lake, 12,740 feet high, is the highest lake in the United States. Mount Evans Highway is the highest automobile road in the world. The highest suspension bridge in the world is located 1,053 feet over the Arkansas River. Colorado was explored in 1540 by Coronado. Its nickname is the "Centennial State."

Colorado River Compact. An interstate compact negotiated in 1922 between Arizona, California, Colorado, Nevada, New Mexico, Utah, and Wyoming. The purpose of the Compact was the development of the water resources of the lower and upper basins of the Colorado River. It was the first such compact to develop interstate waters and, when approved by Congress in the BOULDER CANYON PROJECT ACT in 1928, represented the 47th interstate compact in American history. Arizona refused to ratify the compact at first and it went into effect for the other six states. The terms of the compact and the federal statute authorized the construction of BOULDER (HOOVER) DAM, the All-American Canal, and other projects which have included the Parker Dam, the Colorado River Aqueduct, the Imperial Dam, the Parker-Gila Dam, the Bartlett Dam, and the Trans-Mountain Diversion in Colorado. In 1930 agreement was reached settling water controversies in Arizona which has since adhered to the Compact. The total estimated cost of all projects is $275,-000,000. The Colorado River Compact, like the COLUMBIA RIVER COMPACT, THE T.V.A., and other proposed river valley programs, is an illustration of the growing interest in the importance of regional development projects to provide cheap power, erosion control facilities, flood control, etc.

"Colossus of the North." See Caribbean Policy.

COLT, Samuel. 1814-1862. Inventor. b. Connecticut. Inventor of revolving breech pistol (U.S. patent issued 1836); on an order of 1,000 revolvers from the United States government (1847) he established a manufacturing business; invented submarine battery used in harbor defense and submarine telegraph cable.

COLTER, John. 1775?-1813. Trapper and explorer. b. Virginia (?). Joined LEWIS

AND CLARK EXPEDITION; discovered Yellowstone Lake and Hot Springs; first white man to see Wind River and Teton ranges; made dramatic escape after capture by BLACKFEET INDIANS (1808).

Columbian Exposition. See World's Columbian Exposition.

Columbian Order. See Tammany Societies.

Columbia River. One of the longest rivers in the United States. It flows 1,214 miles from its source in Columbia Lake, British Columbia, to the Pacific Ocean. It was first explored in 1775 by the Spaniard, Captain Bruno Hezeta. In 1792 the American, Captain ROBERT GRAY reached the river and named it after his ship the *Columbia.* Gray's discovery of the river for the United States was one of the bases for its claims on the Oregon Territory in subsequent years. The most thorough going early explorations of the River were made by the LEWIS AND CLARK EXPEDITION in 1804-1806. JOHN JACOB ASTOR'S fur depot, Astoria, was established there in 1811. The Columbia River is a great aid to inland traffic, tapping a rich area much of which has been improved by the BONNEVILLE and GRAND COULEE DAMS.

Columbia River Project. A project created by Congress on September 9, 1933 for the purpose of constructing a power, navigation, and flood control dam on the Columbia River with a potential electric power production of 518,400 horsepower. The Bonneville Administration was established to administer the power production and other facilities of the BONNEVILLE DAM on the Columbia River and link its transmission lines to the GRAND COULEE DAM up the river. A Columbia River Authority was established to coordinate the activities of the two dams. Although more limited in its power than the TENNESSEE VALLEY AUTHORITY, its

possibilities for developing the area were recognized in 1949 when President TRUMAN recommended legislation to enlarge its work. Eventually the Grand Coulee and Bonnesville Projects will irrigate about 1,200,000 acres of land and expand its electric power reserves enormously. Additional projects in flood control, navigation, and irrigation have been planned, including carrying Columbia River water from the Grand Coulee Dam to 400,000 acres of wasteland in Washington. When the program of expansion is completed the Columbia River Project will be the largest power system in the world. It will supply an area of 12,000 to 14,000 farm units with new SCHOOLS, HIGHWAYS, shopping centers, and recreational facilities. A 12 day fete was announced on May 22, 1952 to celebrate the first water released from Lake ROOSEVELT behind Grand Coulee Dam. The governors of the seven states in the project were invited to attend the celebration on May 28th.

Columbia University. One of the largest and oldest institutions of higher learning in the United States. It is situated in upper New York City. Among its famous colleges are Teachers' College, the School of Law, the College of Dentistry, and the Columbia-Presbyterian College of Medicine. Originally founded as King's College in 1754.

COLUMBUS, Christopher. (Italian, Cristtoforo Colombo). 1446?-1506. Known as the discoverer of America. b. Genoa, Italy. Spent his early years as a weaver and at sea; moved to Lisbon, Portugal (1477); influenced by Portuguese navigators and his brother, Bartholomew, who was a chart maker; believing that the earth was round, he wanted to sail west in order to reach Asia; had no success in setting up an expedition until he went to Spain (about 1485) and convinced Ferdinand and Isabella to support his plans (April 17, 1492); sailed from Spain (August 3, 1492) with three small ships, the *Santa Maria, Nina,* and *Pinta;* sighted land (October 12, 1492); landed at San Salvador of the Bahamas Islands; sailed along the north coast of CUBA and HAITI and then returned home; accorded a royal welcome and made governor of all the land he had discovered; on his second voyage, he landed at the Leeward Islands, St. Christopher, PUERTO RICO, and Jamaica; his third voyage landed him at Trinidad and at the mouth of the Orinoco River (August 1, 1498) which was his first discovery of the mainland of South America; sent back to Spain in chains; released, but lost his honors, and the lands he had been given; on his fourth voyage he discovered Honduras and Panama (1502); he died in poverty and neglect, still believing he had discovered the coast of Asia. His discoveries changed the course of world history.

Columbus Day. Observed on October 12th. It is a legal holiday in 36 states and in the territory of PUERTO RICO. It is celebrated as Fraternal Day in Alabama, Discovery Day in Indiana and North Dakota, and Landing Day in Wisconsin. It commemorates the discovery of America by CHRISTOPHER COLUMBUS in 1492. It is probable that the first celebration of Columbus Day was organized in 1792 by the Society of St. Tammany, more widely known as TAMMANY HALL.

Comanche Indians. They are known as the finest horsemen of the American Indian tribes. They lived on the Plains and were generally a warlike people. They drove the APACHE INDIANS out of the southern part of the Plains territory and caused the early settlers in Texas a considerable amount of trouble. In 1875 the Comanches became cattle ranchers, and settled on a reservation in western Oklahoma.

Combined Food Board. A joint Anglo-American-Canadian agency established in 1942 for the purpose of coordinating the production and distribution of food during World War II.

Combined Production and Resources Board. A joint American-British-Canadian Agency established in 1942 for the purpose of integrating the war production plans of the member nations.

Combined Raw Materials Board. A joint Anglo-American agency established in 1942 for the purpose of allocating, distributing, and conserving raw materials necessary to the war programs of the member governments.

Combined Shipping Adjustment Board. A joint Anglo-American agency established in 1942 for the purpose of unifying the work of the WAR SHIPPING ADMINISTRATION of the United States and the Ministry of War Transportation of the British government.

Commerce. The revival of commerce in 15th and 16th century Europe was the direct cause of EXPLORATION and colonial settlement in America. Trading companies, chartered by the English, French, Dutch, Swedish, Spanish, and Portuguese governments, discovered and settled colonies in the New World. In the colonial period trade was the most important industry, particularly in New England. Despite the restrictions of the NAVIGATION ACTS, the tonnage of American vessels engaged in foreign trade rose to 325,000 by the end of the Revolution. The bulk of trade by the end of the 18th century was carried on with England and the WEST INDIES. At that time two-thirds of all imports came from England and half the exports were shipped to that country. New England and New York were the chief commercial areas. Trade problems arose out of the "RIGHT OF DEPOSIT" at New Orleans and with England during the Napoleonic Wars because of the "RULE OF 1756." Diplomatic controversies with England stemmed from American neutral commerce in these wars and led directly to the War of 1812. After the war a flourishing CLIPPER trade developed with the Far East, the West Coast becoming the center of this commerce. During the Civil War commercial difficulties arose with England and France over their attempts to run the Union BLOCKADE. The post-war era witnessed the rise of Latin-American trade which was to remain the single most important era of United States commerce. During World War I American export trade increased tremendously. Munitions exports rose from $5,000,000 in 1913 to $803,-000,000 in 1917. WHEAT exports increased from $39,000,000 to $300,000,-000 in the same period. Whereas the trade balance in 1914 was $435,800,000, it had increased in 1917 to $3,567,800,-000. The United States was to emerge from the War as a creditor nation with a well established favorable trade balance. The defense and war period of the 1940's marked the greatest increase in American foreign trade in history. By the end of World War II the United States was exporting goods at the rate of $20,-000,000,000 annually as compared with imports of $8,000,000,000. Roughly half of this export trade was financed by the federal government. In the post-war era United States commerce was keyed to aid to Europe and the Far East under the ECONOMIC COOPERATION, POINT FOUR, and MUTUAL SECURITY programs. In 1950 the United States exported goods valued at $10,275,000,000, a decline of 15 percent from 1949 exports. Imports in that year totaled $8,842,000,000, an increase of 33 percent over the previous year. The change in trade balance was attributable to European currency devaluation, economic recovery, increased dollar earnings of European nations, and a decline of trade with the Soviet Union and other Communist powers.

Commerce, Department of. An executive department established by Congress in 1913. The Department was created in a reorganization of the Department of Commerce and Labor which had been established in 1903. Its secretary is a cabinet member. Among its important functions are the conduct of the decennial census, the supervision of the work of the Civil Aeronautics Administration, the administration of patent rights, the operation of the federal weather services, and the establishment of standards of weights and measures. The Department also collects, analyzes, and distributes commercial statistics, promotes foreign and domestic commerce, and assists in the development of inland waterway transportation. In it are housed the following important agencies: National Production Authority, Coast and Geodetic Survey, Inland Waterways Corporation, WEATHER BUREAU, Census Bureau, U.S. Patent Office, and the National Bureau of Statistics.

Commerce and Labor, Department of. An executive department established by Congress in 1903. Its functions were those which are exercised today by the DEPARTMENT OF COMMERCE and the DEPARTMENT OF LABOR, which were created in 1913 to supplant the earlier agency.

commercial colony. Also known as corporate colony. A type of British colony in America. A commercial colony was organized on the basis of a charter granted to a JOINT STOCK TRADING COMPANY. The charter generally conferred upon the company complete powers to establish the government and exploit the resources of the colony. Members of the company were CITIZENS of the colony, sharing in the election of the governor and the legislative body. The MASSACHUSETTS COMPANY founded the MASSACHUSETTS BAY COMPANY in 1628 as the first commercial colony.

Commission on the Health Needs of the Nation. An agency established by EXECUTIVE ORDER in December, 1951 to make a critical study of the health requirements of the American people and to recommend courses of action to meet these needs. The specific fields of investigation assigned to its jurisdiction were: the supply of physicians, dentists and nurses, the adequacy of local public health units, the number of available hospital beds where needed, medical research, the needs of the chronically ill and aged, and the requirement of diagnostic, rehabilitative, and other medical services to all income groups regardless of financial ability. The 15-member Commission consists of representatives of the medical profession, the American Medical Association, EDUCATION and research institutions, and farm, labor, and consumer organizations.

commission plan. A system of municipal government first introduced in Galveston, Texas in 1901 to cope with the severe problems of the flood of that year. In this plan all executive, administrative, and legislative powers are merged in a five or six man commission. Each member of the commission is head of a department, exercising his functions under the supervision of the entire body. Although superseded in later years by the CITY-MANAGER PLAN it has been adopted by many cities including Newark, New Jersey, New Orleans, Louisiana, and Portland, Oregon. In 1952 about 250 cities had adopted this plan, a decline from 500 in 1917 when the movement reached its peak.

Commission on Reorganization of the Executive Branch of the Federal Government. See Hoover Commission.

Committee on Administrative Management. See executive reorganization.

Committee on Public Information. An agency established by Congress in April, 1917 for the purpose of mobilizing public opinion in support of the American war effort. GEORGE CREEL was appointed chairman. His undertakings included the enlistment of artists, advertisers, poets, historians, educators, and actors in the campaign to flood the country with propaganda pamphlets, posters, magazines, and newspapers. Over 100,000,-000 pieces of literature were distributed. Some 75,000 "four minute men" participated in meetings and demonstrations at movie houses and public gatherings with the objective of engendering patriotic support of the war effort and hatred of the enemy. Materials were published in foreign languages. The Committee published a daily *Official Bulletin* which was strongly criticised as an organ of propaganda. The criticism against Creel and the Committee's efforts were widespread throughout the nation, the principal charge being that they were attempting to force the American people to accept as final truth such war news and interpretations as the government chose to reveal. This propaganda program was also known as POLITICAL WARFARE.

committee system. The organization of the work of both houses of Congress into various types of committees. Although not provided for in the Constitution, this system has evolved into a complex network of standing committees, special committees, and joint committees. The most important are the standing committees, among which are Appropriations, Agriculture, Armed Services, Banking and Currency, Post-Office and Civil Service, Interstate and Foreign Commerce, and Rules. By the Legislative Reorganization Act of 1946 the total number of Congressional standing committees was reduced from 81 to 34. Today there are 19 committees in the House of Representatives and 15 in the Senate as compared with the former number of 48 and 33 respectively.

Committees of Correspondence. Organization created in 1772 for the purpose of exchanging views and information among the colonies. The first committee was established by a resolution of a Boston town meeting at the urging of SAMUEL ADAMS, and others rapidly came into existence in the following year in other Massachusetts towns and in Virginia, Rhode Island, Connecticut, New Hampshire, and South Carolina. In Virginia, PATRICK HENRY and THOMAS JEFFERSON led the movement for their establishment. The committees served as powerful agencies for molding public opinion and obtaining joint action in the developing colonial struggle against Great Britain.

Committees of Safety. Committees organized in the colonies in 1775 to supplement the work of the COMMITTEES OF CORRESPONDENCE. The first was a committee of 11 men established in Massachusetts in February, 1775 to encourage resistance against the Acts of Parliament. It was authorized to mobilize the MILITIA and take possession of military stores. In April the Committee corresponded with various Massachusetts towns and with patriots in New Hampshire and Connecticut, requesting that similar organizations be established. The result was the creation of Committees of Safety in the other colonies, generally appointed by popular conventions. On July 18, 1775 the second CONTINENTAL CONGRESS issued its official support for the establishment of such committees to exercise the functions of government. In that year, and until the formation of the new state constitutions in 1776, the Committees

supplied the Continental army with troops and equipment, maintained order, policed the rear, arrested LOYALISTS, and performed other necessary duties in the first year of the Revolution. After the adoption of state constitutions the committees largely disappeared, being replaced by the new state governments. In New Hampshire and Connecticut, however, the Committees of Safety continued their efforts until after the war.

Commodity Credit Corporation. A congressionally chartered corporation located within the DEPARTMENT OF AGRICULTURE. It was created by the RECONSTRUCTION FINANCE CORPORATION in 1933 for the purpose of authorizing loans on agricultural commodities and for purchasing such commodities with the objective of stabilizing the farm market. Its functions are supervised by the Production and Marketing Administration, also within the Department of Agriculture. The Corporation capital of $100,000,000 is supplemented by bond issuances which it may offer up to a maximum of $14,500,000,000. In the fiscal year 1964, it spent approximately $3,420,000,000 in its activities.

common law. In its origins the law common to all the people of England as it arose out of the decisions of the king's judges. Since it was not statute law it went through many historical changes, being broadened by local custom and judicial interpretation. As transferred to the colonies the doctrines of the common law came to mean a fundamental law protecting the people against the oppressive acts of government. The federal nature of the United States government after 1789 implied that the principles of the common law were reserved to the states since Congress could exercise only DELEGATED POWERS which were enumerated in the federal Constitution. In the growth of American constitutional law these principles have been modified by legislative revision and judicial decision. Among the better known aspects of the common law are the rights set forth in the DECLARATION OF INDEPENDENCE, the civil liberties guaranteed by the BILL OF RIGHTS, and other inherent doctrines protecting life, liberty, and property.

Common Sense. A pamphlet by THOMAS PAINE, which was published in Philadelphia in January, 1776. In this work Paine powerfully challenged royal authority, calling upon mankind to oppose hereditary tyranny. In the plain language of the people he reflected their needs, making the first open plea for independence in that time.

Commonwealth Fund. Established in 1918 by Mrs. Stephen V. Harkness and enlarged by additional gifts from Edward S. Harkness. The Fund offers fellowships to graduate students and civil servants from the British Commonwealth for medical education and research, and experimental services. Additional appropriations are granted for advanced training in medicine and its associated fields to assist teaching and research in the United States. Its principal office is in New York City.

Commonwealth vs. Hunt. A decision of the Massachusetts Supreme Court in 1842 declaring the common law doctrine of conspiracy inapplicable to labor unions. The importance of the doctrine herein laid down lies in the recognition of the legality of labor unions. Thereafter the courts of the other states rapidly handed down similar decisions, making it possible for unions to engage in legal economic and political activites.

communications. In colonial America communications were related directly to transportation facilities. Economic and social life developed around river and harbor communities or on pioneer paths which became the roads to the west. After the Revolution the huge turnpike and canal programs of the federal and state governments facilitated cheaper and more efficient communications among the sections of the country. The invention of the telegraph in 1844 opened a new era in long distance communication, supplemented before the Civil War by the postal service. After the war the tremendous railroad expansion brought the sections of the nation closer than ever before. Urban and inter-urban electric street railways, the telephone, and wireless telegraphy were significant communications advances in the 20th century. In recent years the remarkable developments in cable, radio, motion picture, and television communications have provided relatively inexpensive and rapid communications within the United States and between it and the rest of the world.

Communications Act of 1927. See Federal Radio Commission.

Communications Act of 1934. See Federal Communications Commission.

Communist Party. A radical party organized in 1919 as consolidation of the Communist and Communist Labor Parties. It claims to represent the interests of workers, farmers, and the lower middle class. Its program has varied from time to time, having evolved from open revolutionary objectives to so-called "popular front" purposes. Its largest vote was in the presidential election of 1932 when it polled 102,991 votes. Originally affiliated with the Communist International it severed this relationship in 1940 following the passage of the VOORHIS ACT in that year. Among its leaders have been Elizabeth Gurley Flynn, Eugene Dennis, William Z. Foster, and Earl Browder.

compact theory. The political theory first expressed by JEFFERSON and MADISON in the VIRGINIA AND KENTUCKY RESOLUTIONS. It declared that the states had founded the national government by making the compact whose provisions were established in the Constitution and that it was therefore the states who could decide when the compact was broken. This theory spelled out, in part, the doctrine of STATES' RIGHTS later to be repeated in varying forms in the resolutions of the HARTFORD CONVENTION, EXPOSITION AND PROTEST, WEBSTER-HAYNE DEBATES, and ORDINANCE OF NULLIFICATION.

company union. A labor organization dominated by an employer. As interpreted by the courts such domination may include financial aid, the use of the employer's materials or services for union work, or any open or concealed control exercised by the employer. Company unions have been declared illegal under the NATIONAL LABOR RELATIONS ACT and the various state labor relations laws.

Compromise of 1850. See Omnibus Bill of 1850.

Compromise Tariff. Sponsored by HENRY CLAY in 1833 to reconcile opposing elements within the Democratic party. It provided that the rates of the TARIFF OF 1832 be progressively reduced until 1842 when they would be approximately equal to the TARIFF OF 1816, namely a maximum of 20 per cent. The Act succeeded in bringing about a repeal by South Carolina of the ORDINANCE OF NULLIFICATION which had been passed by its legislature the previous year. However, the question of state sovereignty as opposed to federal authority remained unsettled. JACKSON's struggle against CALHOUN continued, as exemplified by the simultaneous passing of the FORCE BILL.

COMPTON, Arthur H. 1892-1962. Physicist. b. Ohio. Brother of KARL T. COMPTON. Graduated, Wooster (B.S., 1913) Princeton (Ph.D., 1916), studied at Cambridge, England (1919-20); professor and head of physics, Washington University (1920-23); professor at Chicago University (from 1923). Awarded the Nobel prize for physics (with C. T. R. Wilson, 1927) for the discovery of the change in the wave length of scattered X rays, known as the *Compton effect;* discovered the total reflection of X rays; investigated cosmic rays discovering their electrical nature.

COMPTON, Karl Taylor. 1887-1954. Physicist. b. Ohio. Ph.B. Wooster (1908); Ph.D., Princeton University (1912); assistant professor of physics (1915-19); professor (1919-30); president Massachusetts Institute of Technology (1930-48); awarded Rumford Medal of American Academy of Arts and Science for research on contact difference of potential and Peltier effect, and the structure of crystals by X-ray photography. Contributed to the ATOM BOMB project. Chairman of the research and development board of the National Military Establishment (1948-49). Notable for research in photo-electricity, atomic energy, radar, electric arcs.

Comsat. Abbreviation for Communications Satellite Corp. Represents the first commercial venture in space. Sale of ten million shares of stock provided $200,000,000 capital to develop a series of satellites to provide telephone, television, and other communication systems on a global basis. One-half of the stock was allocated to major companies in the communications industry and the remainder to the general public.

compulsory medical insurance. See medical insurance.

COMSTOCK, Henry Tompkins Paige. 1820-1870. Prospector and discoverer of the COMSTOCK SILVER LODE. b. Canada. Served in BLACK HAWK and Mexican wars; trapped for AMERICAN FUR COMPANY; to Nevada (1856-62); discovered lode (1859) but not realizing its value sold his claim for very little money.

Comstock Lode. A famous silver deposit in Nevada which yielded $306,000,000 worth of the metal in the 20 years following its discovery in 1859. This, one of the richest silver veins in the world, was located on the eastern slopes of the Sierra Nevada, near Lake Tahoe in the territory of Nevada. The growth of the territory in the first decade of its existence was largely dependent on the yield of the Comstock Lode. Most of this enormous wealth left Nevada, the bulk going to California mining companies or to gamblers and speculators in the East. The Lode is also the foundation of the Sutro Tunnel one of the greatest engineering enterprises of the 19th century. This tunnel built by Adolph Sutro over a period of eight years in the heart of the mountain, runs to a depth of three miles and made possible the continuous mining of the lode.

concentration of capital. See business consolidation.

conciliation. In international relations, the attempt by a third party to resolve a dispute between nations by examining the issues and making a recommendation for solution. In labor relations the efforts of an impartial body to settle a dispute between employer and employee. In the United States the impartial body is often provided by the Federal Mediation and Conciliation Service, the state mediation boards, or the American Arbitration Association. Unlike arbitration conciliation is not compulsory, and is unenforceable.

Conciliatory Act. Passed by Parliament in 1777 following the defeat of the British at the BATTLE OF SARATOGA. Sponsored by Lord North the Act repealed the Tea Tax and the INTOLERABLE ACTS, declaring that in the future no "duty, tax, or assessment whatever" would be laid upon the colonies without their consent. The purpose of the legislation was to establish a peace offer to the colonists, providing thereby the authorization of a British commission to sail to America to discuss the terms on which the patriots would conclude the Revolution. The possibilities of peace aroused French fears upon which BENJAMIN FRANKLIN skillfully played, hinting at possible acceptance of the terms by the colonists. The result was that the French government recognized the United States of America as an independent power, and on February 6, 1778 signed treaties of alliance and commerce with the United States.

Concorde. On October 17, 1977 France and Great Britain were permitted by the U.S. Supreme Court to conduct Concorde supersonic jet airliner flights to New York City and Washington, D.C. There were many demonstrations by Concorde opponents who argued that the planes were too noisy and posed the danger of increasing incidence of a non-fatal form of skin cancer. The U.S. Government earlier had decided against approving the manufacture in the U.S. of a similar supersonic passenger plane as an impractical venture.

concurrent powers. Powers exercised both by the Congress and the state legislatures. Although Congress' powers are specifically enumerated in the Constitution and the states' powers are reserved to them in an apparently unlimited number, their authority overlaps at many points. Examples of concurrent powers are found in the fields of TAXATION, LABOR RELATIONS, PUBLIC WELFARE, AGRICULTURE, EDUCATION, highway construction, public works, and RECREATION.

concurrent resolution of Congress. A resolution which, upon passage of both houses of Congress, has the effect of law.

Unlike the JOINT RESOLUTION it requires the President's signature, and its subject matter is generally not legislative in nature. Concurrent resolutions will normally deal with expressions of sympathy over a deceased member of Congress, private bills, monetary awards to satisfy claims against the United States, and similar matters.

Confederacy. See Confederate States of America.

Confederate Army. The nucleus was the regular army established on March 6, 1861 by the Confederate Provisional Congress. On May 8, 1861 the Confederate Congress empowered President JEFFERSON DAVIS to call for volunteers. The establishment of a Department of War aided in the task of obtaining enlistments and keeping those already in the service. These rudimentary forces were at first armed with the equipment in the United States arsenals located in the seceded states. Many states armed their own volunteers, their arms being paid for by the Confederate government. Emissaries were sent to Europe to purchase arms which arrived in large quantities by the end of 1861. Domestic production of arms was shortly undertaken, most of it limited to small pieces. The Confederate Army remained short of heavy artillery for the entire war. The difficulty of keeping the 12 month recruits in the army brought conscription into being on April 16, 1862, making all able bodied white men from 18 to 35 years of age liable to military service. Amendments increased the age range from 17 to 50 years by the end of the war. The estimate of the number of enlistments in the Confederate Army has ranged from 600,000 to 1,500,000. It is probable that the most accurate figure was between 800,000 and 900,000. The Confederate MILITIA, serving short terms, totalled approximately 100,000. Losses during the war so crippled the Confederate army that only 174,223 were left in the surrender at APPOMATTOX COURTHOUSE. Although no official records of the Army's casualties remain, it is estimated that 133,785 died in battle, or of wounds and disease.

Confederate debt. The obligations of the CONFEDERATE STATES OF AMERICA incurred during the Civil War. It began with a $500,000 loan by Alabama and grew rapidly as a result of loans from other states and from French and English bankers. It is estimated that the Confederate debt was approximately $2,000,000,000 at the end of the Civil War. All member states of the Confederacy were required to repudiate the debt by the 14TH AMENDMENT.

Confederate States of America. Organized in February, 1861 as government in rebellion against the United States. Consisted of seven states at time of founding to which four additional states adhered shortly thereafter. These states were Alabama, Arkansas, Florida, Georgia, Louisiana, Mississippi, North Carolina, South Carolina, Tennessee, Texas, and Virginia. The government of the Confederacy was based on STATES RIGHTS doctrines, the principles of which were incorporated into its constitution.

Confederation of New England. See New England Confederation.

Conference of the Governors. A meeting called at the WHITE HOUSE in 1908 to discuss cooperation between the federal government and the states in preserving the forests, the mineral lands, and the waterways of the country. Attending the proceedings were the governors of 34 states and five territories, the members of the Supreme Court and the Cabinet, several members of Congress, delegates from 68 national societies interested in CONSERVATION, and a number of special guests invited by President T. ROOSEVELT. As a result of the three day conference the president appointed a National Conservation Committee with GIFFORD PINCHOT, as chairman. Forty state conservation commissions were appointed by the governors.

Confiscation Acts. Enacted by Congress in 1861 for the purpose of depriving the Confederacy of the military and economic help of the slaves. This series of laws provided that all Negroes employed as workers on forts or trenches or in the transportation of stores or munitions should be liberated. It further declared that all slaves in Confederate areas conquered by Union armies would be freed. On the basis of these statutes the Union generals FREMONT in Missouri and HUNTER in South Carolina issued military proclamations emancipating all the slaves in the districts held by them. Although President LINCOLN signed the Confiscation Acts he immediately annulled the military proclamations, considering them to be unstrategic in terms of the existing military and political situation. However, he shortly followed this disavowal with the issuance of the EMANCIPATION PROCLAMATION.

Congregationalists. Congregationalism was brought to America by the Pilgrim Fathers in 1620. Following the great immigration to Massachusetts after 1630, the Congregationalists rapidly increased their numbers. They became the ESTABLISHED CHURCH in New Hampshire, Massachusetts, and Connecticut where they maintained their hold for a generation after the Revolution. Their numbers began to decline in the early 19th century, and an attempt was made to win converts by sending out missionaries and resident pastors to the backwoods communities of the FRONTIERS during the JACKSONIAN period. By the end of the century the Congregationalists had become a lesser church organization in the United States. In 1961 the Congregationalist Church merged with the Evangelical and Reformed Church. The membership in 1964 was over 2,000,000.

Congress of the United States. Provided for in Article I of the Constitution. It theoretically enjoys exclusive legislative powers under the SEPARATION OF POWERS system established in the first three articles of the basic document. Consists of two houses, the House of Representatives and the Senate. Exercises DELEGATED POWERS, also known as enumerated powers and expressed powers, provided for in Article I, Section 8 of the Constitution. May also increase its powers by use of the "ELASTIC CLAUSE", the popular name applied to the 18th clause of Article I, Section 8. Powers which are denied to Congress are found in Article I, Section 9, the first ten amendments, the FIFTEENTH AMENDMENT, and the NINETEENTH AMENDMENT.

Congressional Medal of Honor. The highest military award conferred by the United States upon its own troops and officers. It was established by Congress in 1862, and is granted for courage in action at the risk of life beyond the call of duty. It is bronze, five-pointed star superimposed upon a green laurel wreath. Recipients of the Medal enjoy certain benefits and privileges.

Congressional Reapportionment Act. A law of Congress in 1929 which provided for the reapportionment of seats in the House of Representatives and placed a maximum on the number of representatives. Although Article I, Section 2 of the federal Constitution requires reapportionment according to the decennial CENSUS the present number of 435 representatives, established in 1910, was not altered after the 1920 census because of the reluctance of slow-growing states to lose representation. In 1929 the Act fixed 435 as the maximum membership of the House by reducing the number of seats of slow-growing states and increasing the number for others. It provided for automatic reapportionment thereafter by having the Census Bureau submit census figures every decade showing population changes. Each state would be entitled to that proportion of 435 that its population bore to the national population. If Congress failed to act the apportionment would be according to the system last used. In 1932 the President, acting under the authority of the law, issued a report providing for the present apportionment of the House because of Congress' inaction. By the 1960 census the average state quota of representatives was one for 410,481 persons. Nevada, with only 226,167 is furthest from having a quota.

Congressional Record. Published by Congress as a verbatim record of all speeches and statements either made on the floor of Congress or prepared for such delivery, but for some reason not delivered. It has been published daily since its establishment in 1873, when it replaced the *Congressional Globe*, a private publication.

Congress of Industrial Organizations. Originally conceived in 1935 as Committee for Industrial Organization. This committee of AMERICAN FEDERATION OF LABOR leaders included JOHN L. LEWIS, Sidney Hillman, Emil Rieve, David Dubinsky, et al. Assumed present name in 1938. General plan of organization of CIO is based in vertical or INDUSTRIAL UNIONISM, with the objectives of organizing the MASS PRODUCTION industries of the nation. In December, 1955, the CIO merged with the AFL. Walter Reuther, president of the CIO, became vice president of the new AFL-CIO. (See AFL-CIO.)

Congress' Reconstruction Plan. A plan arising out of the deep opposition of the RADICAL REPUBLICAN Congress to the prior programs of Presidents LINCOLN and JOHNSON. The philosophy of Congress' plan grew out of strong antagonism to the seceded states based on the feeling that, since these states had actually departed from the Union, they were subject to Congress' constitutional power concerning the terms of their readmission. The notable measures of Congress' plan included the WADE-DAVIS Bill of 1864, the CIVIL RIGHTS BILL and the FREEDMEN'S BUREAU BILL of 1866, the FOURTEENTH AMENDMENT adopted in 1868, and a series of laws known as the RECONSTRUCTION ACTS OF 1867. The two latter were drawn up by the famous JOINT COMMITTEE OF FIFTEEN in 1867. Subsequent reconstruction legislation included the TENURE OF OFFICE ACT of 1867, the FIFTEENTH AMENDMENT of 1870, the ENFORCEMENT ACTS of 1870 and 1871, the KU-KLUX KLAN ACT of 1871, and the CIVIL RIGHTS ACT of 1875.

CONKLING, Roscoe. 1829-1888. Lawyer and political leader. b. Albany, New York. Member, U.S. House of Representatives (1859-63; 1865-67); U.S. Senator (1867-81); leader of Republican party in N.Y.; fought with BLAINE for Republican nomination for the presidency (1876) but HAYES was finally nominated; opposed Hayes who started an investigation of Conkling's activities; opposed GARFIELD and resigned his Senate seat in protest (1881); failed to be reelected and retired from public office to a successful law practice.

Connally Resolution. A resolution sponsored by Senator Tom Connally of Texas in November, 1943. It provided that the United States should join with other nations in creating an international organization dedicated to the prevention of aggression and the preservation of international peace. The Resolution specified that the United States government must undertake this matter only through normal constitutional procedures, and must preserve its sovereign power. The Resolution was adopted by the Senate in lieu of the BALL-BURTON-HATCH-HILL RESOLUTION.

Connecticut. The 48th state in size, with an area of 5,009 square miles. Entered the union as the fifth state on January 9, 1788. Hartford is the capital. In 1950 Connecticut's population of 2,007,280 made it 28th in rank. Its largest cities are Hartford, New Haven, and Bridgeport. Connecticut is famous for the production of machinery and light consumers' goods. These include sewing machines, typewriters, hardware, tools, hats, cutlery, clocks, and locks. It also has an important arms and airplane parts industry. Its dairy industry produces quantities of milk, butter, eggs, cheese, and cream. Connecticut shade grown tobacco is the costliest in the United States. The Hartford *Courant,* established in 1764, is the oldest newspaper in the United States. The FUNDAMENTAL ORDERS were the first written constitution in the new world. Connecticut was discovered in 1614 by Adrian Block. Its nicknames are the "Nutmeg State," "Constitution State," and "Land of Steady Habits."

Connecticut Compromise. Submitted by the Connecticut delegation to the CONSTITUTIONAL CONVENTION of 1787. The plan reconciled the conflicting plans of the Virginia and New Jersey delegations by proposing a BI-CAMERAL federal legislature consisting of a House of Representatives (lower chamber) whose members were to be elected on the basis of the states' population and a Senate (upper chamber) consisting of two representatives from each state.

Connecticut Western Reserve. See Western Reserve.

CONNELLY, Henry. 1800-1866. Territorial governor of New Mexico. b. Kentucky. Graduated, Transylvania University (M.D.); traded over SANTA FE TRAIL; important in settling territorial difficulties in that area and elected governor of newly organized state (1850); appointed territorial governor by LINCOLN (1861).

Conquistadores, the. Spanish for "conquerors." The name applied to the leaders of the Spanish conquest of the Americas in the 16th and 17th centuries. The name stems from their cruel and ruthless oppression of the natives of these lands and their exploitation of their natural resources. The most notable of the *Conquistadores* were CORTEZ, the conqueror of Mexico, DE LEON who discovered Florida, Espejo who discovered Arizona, Pizarro, the conqueror of Peru, DE SOTO, the discoverer of the Mississippi, and Oñate who established settlements in New Mexico. Their contributions include detailed diaries and maps setting out the geography and the resources of the areas they discovered. They introduced into the new world the Spanish language and culture, including its architecture, music, folklore, and religion.

conscientious objectors. Name applied to those who refuse to take up arms in defense of the United States because of religious, moral, or pacifist scruples. Includes individuals and organizations, among the latter being the AMERICAN FRIENDS SOCIETY and the Fellowship of Reconciliat•ɔn. The disposition of such cases generally takes the form of assignment to non combatant duty such as work in labor camps and hospitals. There have been instances of arrests and imprisonment of conscientious objectors. In virtually all cases presidential pardons have furnished ultimate freedom.

conscription. Compulsory military service. First introduced into the United States during the Civil War as a result of the failure of President LINCOLN's call for volunteers. Subsequently employed during World War I and World War II. The first peace-time military conscription law passed by Congress was the BURKE-WADSWORTH ACT of 1940. Conscription was continued following the conclusion of World War II. With the exceptions noted above the United States has always raised its military forces by volunteer enlistments.

conservation. The preservation, defense, and organized use of the nation's NATURAL RESOURCES including the mineral lands, the forests, and water power. The conservation movement has made great strides since the work initiated by President T. ROOSEVELT at the beginning of the twentieth century. The development of the NATIONAL PARKS, RURAL ELECTRIFICATION, soil erosion control, flood control, the construction and operation of river projects, dam and reservoir construction, and reforestation programs have become major objectives of federal and state conservation planning. Among the federal agencies participating have been the DEPARTMENTS OF THE INTERIOR, AGRICULTURE, COMMERCE, DEFENSE, and the TREASURY, the TENNESSEE VALLEY AUTHORITY, and the RECONSTRUCTION FINANCE CORPORATION.

conspiracy laws. State legislation in the first half of the 19th century which held illegal combinations of persons whose activities were considered conspiracies against the public interest. These acts were applied to the activities of labor organizations which were considered such combinations. The attempts of workers to organize and use such unions in enhancing their economic status were thus considered illegal. Following the decision of the Massachusetts Supreme Court in 1842 in the case of COMMONWEALTH VS. HUNT the conspiracy laws were rendered inapplicable to LABOR UNIONS.

Constitution, The. The American frigate which, with sister vessels, destroyed six British warships during the War of 1812. It, and the *United States* and the *President*, had been designed to outfight and outrun other ships of the line, being so heavily timbered and planked as to earn the name "Old Ironsides." These frigates were manned by volunteer officers and crews, veterans of the naval war against France and the war against the Barbary pirates. Its most famous victory was the defeat of the *Guerriere* in two and one half hours on August 19, 1812. In 1807, the *Constitution* had been the subject of the IMPRESSMENT controversy with Great Britain. At that time it was acknowledged that of the crew of 419, 149 were avowed British subjects.

Constitution, the federal. The document which lays down the basic law of the United States. It was produced by the CONSTITUTIONAL CONVENTION at Philadelphia in 1787, having been signed by 39 of the 55 delegates who attended the four month meetings. The original document consisted of seven articles to which have been added 22 AMENDMENTS. The fundamental principles of the American Constitution include FEDERALISM, SEPARATION OF POWERS, DEMOCRACY, CIVIL LIBERTIES, and POPULAR SOVEREIGNTY. The first three articles of the document deal respectively with the legislative, executive, and judicial branches of the government. Article Four, sometimes called the "INTERSTATE COMITY CLAUSE," established interstate relationships. The fifth article provides the amendment procedure. Article Six, referred to as the supremacy clause, established the superiority of the Constitution, and federal laws and treaties, over state constitutions and laws. The last article merely declared the method of ratification and establishment of the new government and is thus of historical significance only. The first ten amendments of 1791 provide certain civil liberties, and are known as the BILL OF RIGHTS. The ELEVENTH AMENDMENT of 1798 withdraws from the jurisdiction of the FEDERAL COURTS suits against a state by the CITIZENS of another state. The TWELFTH AMENDMENT of 1804 provides for separate balloting by the ELECTORAL COLLEGE for the President and Vice-President. The THIRTEENTH AMENDMENT of 1865 abolished SLAVERY. The FOURTEENTH AMENDMENT of 1867 defined CITIZENSHIP, and provides for the protection of certain civil liberties against infringement by the states. The FIFTEENTH AMENDMENT of 1870 prohibits the United States or any state from denying or abridging the suffrage on account of race, color, or previous condition of servitude. The SIXTEENTH AMENDMENT of 1913 provides for the INCOME TAX. The SEVENTEENTH AMENDMENT of 1913 provided for popular election of United States Senators. The EIGHTEENTH AMENDMENT of 1919 provided for PROHIBITION and was repealed by the TWENTY-FIRST AMENDMENT of 1933. The NINETEENTH AMENDMENT of 1920 prohibits the United States or any state from denying or abridging the suffrage on account of sex. The TWENTIETH AMENDMENT of 1933, known as the "lame duck" amendment, adjusted the inaugural date of the President and congressional sessions. The TWENTY SECOND AMENDMENT of 1950 established a two term tenure for the President. The Twenty-third Amendment of 1961 allows the citizens of the District of Columbia to vote in presidential elections. The Twenty-fourth Amendment of 1964 outlaws the poll tax as a requisite for voting.

constitutional amendments. See amendments.

Constitutional Convention. Originally called by the delegates who had met at the ANNAPOLIS CONVENTION in 1786. The Congress supplemented this call by an official declaration that such a convention would meet in Philadelphia in May, 1787 for the purpose of revising the ARTICLES OF CONFEDERATION. Of the 55 delegates who convened only 39 remained by September to sign the Constitution which had been produced. GEORGE WASHINGTON was the president of the convention. The official minutes of the secret meetings were kept by JAMES MADISON. As a result of the impossibility of successfully amending the Articles of Confederation, agreement was ultimately reached for the creation of a new basic document. The present Constitution of the United States was the result of the proceedings.

constitutional law. The aggregate rules, doctrines, and principles which determine the nature of governmental power. In the United States they include the provisions of the federal Constitution and its interpretation by the judiciary as well as the legislative acts applying to constitutional matters.

Constitutional Union Party. Also known as the National Constitutional Union, a new political party organized in the presidential campaign of 1860. It nominated Senator James Bell of Tennessee as its presidential candidate, and established a platform which declared "no politica! principle other than the Constitution of the country, the union of the states, and the enforcement of the laws." The Party was composed largely of WHIG remnants, or as LINCOLN referred to them, "the nice, exclusive sort" of Whigs. It ignored SLAVERY, the one vital issue of the campaign. Its strength lay in the BORDER STATES, Bell polling a popular vote of 588,879 and 39 electoral votes.

consular service. A part of the foreign service of the United States. It is located within the DEPARTMENT OF STATE. Consuls are public officials established in the important industrial and commercial cities of foreign nations. Their functions are the enhancement of the economic interests of the United States and its CITIZENS, and the protection of the welfare of American citizens travelling or living within their jurisdiction. Consuls of the United States are established in various grades, such as consuls-general, consuls, vice-consuls, and consular agents. The official resident of a foreign consul is known as the Consulate.

Continental Army. Also known as the Patriot Army. The regular troops of the Colonial army during the American Revolution. These troops did not include the militia and guerilla army. The name was first used in June, 1775 when Congress appropriated 6,000 dollars for the support of a "Continental Army," and appointed WASHINGTON as commander-in-chief. Beset by difficulties including desertions, inadequate supplies and equipment, treasonable conduct among the officers, and lack of finances, the Army nevertheless successfully fought the war against Great Britain. It is estimated that Washington never had more than 25,000 troops under his command at any one time.

Continental Congresses. The first Continental Congress met at Philadelphia in 1774 to discuss the problems raised by Britain's passage of the INTOLERABLE ACTS. The second Continental Congress met in 1775 shortly after the outbreak of fighting at the Battles of LEXINGTON and CONCORD. The latter immediately constituted itself a provisional government with the objective of organizing an army and carrying on the war with Great Britain. It remained a revolutionary government without a constitutional foundation until the enactment of the ARTICLES OF CONFEDERATION in 1781. Subsequently the second Continental Congress was popularly known as the "Congress."

continental currency. FIAT CURRENCY issued as bills of credit by the Second CONTINENTAL CONGRESS. The first issue was made on June 25, 1775 in the sum of $2,000,000. By the end of 1779 the

Congress had issued a total of $241,-552,780 in continental currency. Its value quickly declined as a result of its overabundance, colonial military defeats, lack of faith in the Congress, and the absence of a metal standard. In relation to specie this currency depreciated to one cent on the dollar by 1781, giving birth to the phrase "not worth a continental." Ultimately Congress provided, by the FUNDING ACT OF 1790, that these notes be accepted for United States bonds in the ratio of 100 to 1.

"Continental System." See Berlin and Milan Decrees.

contract labor. Foreign workers brought into the United States under contract to replenish the short supply of labor in the United States during and immediately after the Civil War. As a result of the influx of hundreds of thousands of alien workers, threatening to flood the nation with cheap labor, Congress enacted a law in 1868 making alien labor contracts unenforceable in the courts.

Contract Labor Law. An Act of Congress in 1885 which prohibited aid to immigrants coming to the United States under alien labor contracts. The law applied only to laborers, exempting professional, skilled, and house workers. It was enacted as a result of the influx of large numbers of workers, during and after the Civil War, to replenish the short supply of labor.

Convention of Saratoga. See Saratoga, Battle of.

Conway Cabal. One of the military-political conspiracies during the American Revolution. This plot reflected the desire of the New England members of the CONTINENTAL CONGRESS to recapture the control of the revolutionary movement which had passed from its hands with the appointment of WASHINGTON as commander-in-chief. The role of Brigadier

General THOMAS CONWAY was minor in the conspiracy, the leadership having been exercised by Generals GATES, LEE, WILKINSON, and MIFFLIN. Washington's loss of the Battles of BRANDYWINE and GERMANTOWN had evoked criticism of his ability, and he was accused of incompetence. Conway was promoted to Major General and Inspector General in 1777, but after the inadvertent revelation of the plot, Congress accepted his resignation in 1778. Gates, Conway, and the others, wrote letters of apology and self-justification to Washington and the conspiracy collapsed.

CONWAY, Thomas. 1735?-1800. Revolutionary general. b. Ireland. Brigadier general in CONTINENTAL ARMY (1777); made major general despite WASHINGTON's protest; involved in conspiracy to supplant Washington with GATES known as CONWAY CABAL; on discovery of plot, he resigned his commission.

COOK, Frederick Albert. 1865-1940. Physician and arctic explorer. b. New York. Graduated New York University (M.D., 1890); surgeon, Peary Arctic Expedition (1891-92); led expedition that climbed Mt. McKinley (1903-06); claimed he had reached the North Pole (1908) but was rejected for lack of evidence. Author of *Through the First Antarctic Night* (1900), *To the Top of the Continent* (1908), *My Attainment of the Pole* (1909).

COOLIDGE, John Calvin. 1872-1933. Thirtieth President of the United States. b. Plymouth, Vermont. Graduated, Amherst College (1895); studied law and practiced in Northhampton, Massachusetts; mayor of Northhampton (1910-11); elected to Massachusetts state senate (1912-15); president (1914); lieutenant governor of Massachusetts (1916-18); governor (1919-20); gained national reputation through his handling of the BOSTON POLICE STRIKE; elected Vice-President of the United States (March 4,

1921-August 2, 1923); succeeded to the presidency on the death of HARDING and took the oath of office (August 3, 1923); elected (1924) President of the United States and served until 1928. His years in office were uneventful, but he was popular because of the nation's prosperity. He backed Hoover for President in 1928, not caring to run for office again.

COOPER, James Fenimore. 1789-1851. Novelist. b. New Jersey. Went to Yale University at 13 years of age (1803-05); failed and went to sea (1806); midshipman, U. S. Navy (1808); resigned (1811); settled in Westchester, New York; first novel, *Precaution* (1820) a failure, but second, *The Spy* (1821) a success; also author of *The Pioneers* (1823), *The Pilot* (1823), *The Last of the Mohicans* (1826), *The Pathfinder* (1840), *The Deerslayer* (1841), *History of the Navy of the U. S.* (1839), and many other books.

COOPER, Peter. 1791-1883. Inventor, manufacturer and philanthropist. b. New York City. One of the owners of Canton Iron Works, Baltimore (from 1828); designed and built the *Tom Thumb*, the first American railway locomotive; with the locomotive he saved the Baltimore and Ohio Railroad from bankruptcy; promoted and financed the laying of the ATLANTIC CABLE; most important man in the IRON INDUSTRY; outstanding leader in civic affairs, New York City; founded Cooper Union, New York City, which gave free courses in SCIENCE and ART (1857-59).

COOPER, Thomas. 1759-1839. Scientist, educator, political philosopher. b. London, England. Educated at Oxford; came to the United States (1794); supported the Jeffersonian group; taught at Dickinson College and the University of Pennsylvania; was president of College of South Carolina (1820-1834). Author of *Political Essays* (1799); *Political Econ-*

omy (1826); and *The Statutes at Large of South Carolina* (5 vols. 1836-39).

Cooperative Marketing Act of 1929. See Agricultural Marketing Act.

cooperative movement. The organization of consumers' and workers' societies for the management of enterprises in their interest. Members of cooperative associations purchase stock in the organization on which they receive dividends in the form of price reductions or cash REBATES at specified intervals. Each member has one vote. The earliest known consumers' cooperative in the United States was established in Boston in 1844. Within three years the Workingmen's Protective Union comprised twelve divisions. After the Civil War the GRANGE MOVEMENT, FARMERS' ALLIANCES, NATIONAL LABOR UNION, and the KNIGHTS OF LABOR organized producers' and consumers' cooperatives as part of their general program. The Northern States Cooperative League contained over 80 societies and 50,000 members in 1952. In that year the Eastern Cooperative League contained almost 30 societies and 15,000 members. The total number of consumers' cooperatives in the United States is well over 2,000. Among the various enterprises they conduct are groceries, oil and gasoline stations, building construction, farming, marketing, BANKING, restaurants, and miscellaneous agricultural, industrial and household businesses.

Coordinator of Railroads. Also known as the Coordinator of Transportation. An office established by the EMERGENCY RAILROAD TRANSPORTATION ACT OF 1933 to perform the following functions: conduct studies and make reports to the President for the purposes of eliminating duplication and waste, encourage railroad consolidations, reorganize railroad financing, promote means of improving TRANSPORTATION conditions, survey traffic carloadings, LABOR RELATIONS, and the condition of railroad facilities, and to undertake investigations concerning railroad services and their charges. Although established for one year the life of the office was extended by EXECUTIVE ORDERS to June 16, 1936. JOSEPH B. EASTMAN held the office during this period.

Coordinator of Transportation. See Coordinator of Railroads.

Copeland Act. See Pure Food and Drug Acts.

COPLAND, Aaron. 1900-. Composer. b. Brooklyn, New York. Pupil of Rubin Goldmark; music introduced in the United States with a *Symphony for Organ and Orchestra* (1925); wrote for radio, motion pictures, and the theater; ballets include *Billy the Kid* (1938), *Rodeo* (1942), and *Appalachian Spring* (1944); popular orchestral works include *El Salón México* (1936) and *A Lincoln Portrait* (1942); organized the American Festivals of Contemporary Music at Saratoga Springs (1932). Author of *What to Listen for in Music* (1939) and *Our New Music* (1941).

COPLEY, John Singleton. 1738-1815. Portrait painter. b. Boston, Mass. Settled in England (1775). Best known works are his portraits of *John Hancock, Samuel Adams* and *The Copley Family* in the Boston Art Museum, and *Lord Cornwallis*, London. His work is typical of the ART of that period.

"Copperheads." Also known as Peace Democrats. The name applied to Northern Democrats who opposed the Union war policy. It was first used in the July 20, 1861 issue of the New York *Tribune*. The "Copperheads'" program supported a negotiated peace in the pursuit of which they published and spoke against the Union war effort. In suppressing their activities President LINCOLN assumed strong EXECUTIVE POWERS, including arrests, censorship, suppression of the press, and the SUSPENSION OF HABEAS CORPUS. The "Copperheads" created various organizations of anti-war Northerners during the Civil War, among them the Knights of the Golden Circle (1862), Order of American Knights (1863), and Sons of Liberty (1864). Their greatest strength lay in the northwest states of Illinois, Indiana, and Ohio. Among their leaders were Representative Clement L. Vallandigham who was arrested, Alexander Long, and Fernando Wood.

Coral Sea, Battle of. An unusual naval-air battle of World War II in which the waterborne air fleets of the United States and Japan attacked each other's navies. The battle was fought in May, 1942, and was the first engagement fought entirely by naval planes from ships that had neither sight nor range of each other. American casualties were 66 planes and 543 men. The Japanese were estimated to have lost 80 planes and 900 men.

CORBIN, Henry Clark. 1842-1909. Army officer. b. Ohio. Served as brigadier general in the Civil War; fought in various Indian campaigns; virtual dictator of the Army, as adjutant general, during the Spanish-American War; made commander of Eastern Department of the army by T. ROOSEVELT (1903); served in the PHILIPPINES (1904); lieutenant general (1906).

CORNELL, Alonzo B. 1832-1904. Businessman and governor, son of EZRA CORNELL. b. New York. Director and vice-president, WESTERN UNION Telegraph Company; surveyor of customs at the Port of New York (1868) appointed by GRANT; elected governor of New York (1879-83); improved the state's financial situation. Author of *True and Firm* (1884) a biography of his father; *Public Papers* (1880-82).

CORNELL, Ezra. 1807-1874. Financier and philanthropist. b. New York. Associated with MORSE in sending the first test messages over the TELEGRAPH line between Baltimore and Washington; devised method of carrying telegraph wires on poles; director and largest stockholder in WESTERN UNION Telegraph Company; founded, with ANDREW G. WHITE, and heavily endowed Cornell University.

CORNWALLIS, Charles, 1st Marquis. 1738-1805. British general in the American Revolution. Educated at Cambridge; M.P. (1760); major general in American War of Independence (1761-62); largely responsible for HOWE's success at New York and New Jersey (1776); won at BRANDYWINE (1777); lieutenant general (1778); second in command to SIR HENRY CLINTON; defeated GATES at Camden; defeated GREENE at Guilford Court House (1781); surrounded at YORKTOWN by WASHINGTON and LAFAYETTE and forced to surrender (1781); governor general of India.

corporate colony. See commercial colony.

corporation. Form of business organization which came into prominence in the post-Civil War period, although the corporate form had been known prior to the war. Corporations are generally chartered by state legislatures, although occasionally by Congress. This form of business organization is in great favor because of the advantages of limited liability, continuous life, the right to sue and be sued, and the extensive opportunity of acquiring additional investment capital by the issuance of corporate securities.

Corregidor Island. An island in the PHILIPPINES off the southern tip of the peninsula of BATAAN on Luzon. It was the scene of the last defense of the combined American-Filipino army in the opening months of the War in the Pacific. After surrendering Bataan on April 9, 1942, the army under the command of General WAINWRIGHT established its position on Corregidor, holding out until compelled to surrender on May 6th. Corregidor was recaptured from the Japanese in February, 1945.

"corrupt bargain." The phrase used by JACKSON and his followers after the election of 1824 in charging that CLAY and J. Q. ADAMS had conspired to deprive him of the presidency. Although Jackson obtained a plurality of the ELECTORAL and POPULAR VOTES in that election, the Constitution required that the presidential choice be made by the House of Representatives. During the balloting in the House Clay threw his support to Adams, insuring his election. Immediately after inauguration Adams appointed Clay his Secretary of State. Jackson attacked this as a "corrupt bargain," and immediately began a four year campaign for the presidency, culminating in his election in 1828.

corrupt practices acts. A series of state and federal laws enacted after 1890 for the purpose of eliminating political practices deemed undesirable. These laws attempted to eliminate bribery, illegal registration, and padded voting, and placed limitations upon contributions to and expenditures by POLITICAL PARTIES. The first state law was passed in New York in 1890, and was shortly followed by similar legislation in California, Colorado, Kansas, Massachusetts, and Michigan. By 1952 all the states had such legislation. These laws vary in content, some applying merely to PRIMARY or other nominating activities, while others apply to elections and/or nominations. Because of their ambiguous phraseology and the lack of enforcement measures, these acts have never been fully successful. Evasions by individuals and lobbying organizations, coupled with machine control of municipal and state politics, have rendered them ineffective. Their general provisions include clauses requiring publicity on campaign finances, identification of donors, and penal provisions concerning violations.

CORTELYOU, George Bruce. 1862-1940. Lawyer, businessman and public official. b. New York City. Graduated, Georgetown University (LL.B., 1895); Secretary to President MC KINLEY (1900-01) and to President T. ROOSEVELT (1901-03); appointed first Secretary of the U.S. DEPARTMENT OF COMMERCE AND LABOR (1903-04); appointed by T. Roosevelt U.S. POSTMASTER GENERAL (1905-07); U.S. Secretary of the Treasury (1907-09); retired to private business and became president of Consolidated Gas Company of N.Y. (1909-35).

CORTES, Hernando. 1485-1547. Spanish conqueror of Mexico; discoverer of Lower California. b. Estremadura. Entered Mexico City (1519); captured city after death of Montezuma (1521); attempted to make settlement in Lower California (1536); died forgotten in Seville.

cotton belt. The nickname of the COTTON-producing section of the United States. Originally centered in the South, it spread southwestward as far as Texas. In the 20th century Arizona, New Mexico, and California became important cotton producing states, and by 1952, 70 percent of the nation's cotton was produced west of the Mississippi.

Cotton Crop Control Act. See Bankhead Cotton Act.

cotton gin. See Whitney, Eli.

cotton industry. One of the most important agricultural industries in the United States. The production in 1963 was 15,300,000 bales weighing 500 pounds each. Cotton income in that year was

$2,846,000,000. The largest cotton area in the United States is the South and Southwest, Texas being the largest producer. However, the world's largest cotton plantation, 35,000 acres in area, is located at Scott, Mississippi. The U.S. produces approximately one third of the world's cotton. In 1964 there were 19,-355,000 spindles manufacturing cotton TEXTILES in this country.

COTTON, John. 1584-1652. Clergyman and author known as "The Patriarch of New England". b. England. Graduated, Cambridge (1603); Emmanuel College (B.D. 1613); emigrated to Boston, Massachusetts (1633); teacher, First Church, Boston (1633-52) becoming the spiritual and intellectual leader of the colony; participated in dispute which caused ANNE HUTCHINSON's banishment from the colony; had quarrels with ROGER WILLIAMS; although a non-conformist in his youth he became increasingly undemocratic and dogmatic in his beliefs. Author of *The Keyes of the Kingdom of Heaven* (1644), and *The Way of the Churches of Christ in New England* (1645).

Cotton Stabilization Corporation. An agency established in 1929 by the FEDERAL FARM BOARD under the authority of the AGRICULTURAL MARKETING ACT of that year. It was empowered to go into the market and purchase cotton or "cotton futures" for the purpose of raising prices. With the GRAIN STABILIZATION CORPORATION, it spent almost $500,000,-000, and succeeded for a short time in maintaining prices at a level slightly higher than the world market average.

Council of Economic Advisors. See Employment Act of 1946.

Council of Foreign Ministers. A council of the foreign ministers of the United States, Great Britain, the Soviet Union, France, and China which was established by agreement at the POTSDAM CONFER-ENCE. The Council was created for the purpose of drafting the peace settlements with the defeated AXIS POWERS. It held its first session in London on September 11, 1945, but adjourned on October 2nd without success. The second meeting was held in December, 1945 in Moscow, but again ended in disagreement over the procedure on TREATY drafting. In April, 1946 the Council of Foreign Ministers convened in Paris to draw up peace treaties for all the Axis Powers, except Germany and Japan, and adjourned after issuing a call for a peace conference to meet in Paris in July. The next meeting was held in November-December in New York City and produced peace treaties for Finland, Italy, Hungary, Roumania, and Bulgaria. A seven-week conference in Moscow in March, 1947 failed in an attempt to prepare peace terms for Germany and Austria. A second meeting in London on November 25th for the purpose of preparing peace treaties for Germany and Austria again failed because of basic differences between the United States and the Soviet Union. In May and June, 1949 a meeting of the Council of Foreign Ministers in Paris failed to agree on terms of German unification, the result leading to a conference in New York on September 19, 1950 of the foreign ministers of the United States, Great Britain, and France in which agreement was reached to end the state of war with Germany. On March 5, 1951 a conference of the deputy ministers of these nations and the Soviet Union was called for the discussion of international tensions with emphasis on treaties for Germany and Austria, reduction of armed forces, demilitarization of Germany, and re-establishment of German unity. The conference was adjourned on June 21st without success.

Council of National Defense. Established by Congress in 1916 as part of the defense preparations prior to the entry of the United States into World War I. It consisted of the Secretaries of War, Navy, Interior, Commerce, and Labor who were assisted by an advisory council of seven experts and by subordinate committees. These committees dealt specifically with the problems of SHIPPING, aircraft production, munitions, coal production and inland waterways. Its principal function was the "mobilization of industries necessary for military preparedness." Among outstanding members of the Council were Daniel Willard, president of the BALTIMORE AND OHIO RAILROAD, SAMUEL GOMPERS, president of the AMERICAN FEDERATION OF LABOR, and Julius Rosenwald of the Sears-Roebuck Company.

Council of National Defense, World War II. An agency established by President F. D. ROOSEVELT in May, 1940. Composed of the Secretaries of War, Navy, Interior, Agriculture, Commerce, and Labor, it was provided with a National Defense Advisory Commission consisting of experts to supervise production, solve LABOR PROBLEMS, encourage increased farm production, stabilize prices, and obtain raw materials during this national defense period. The lack of coordination among its fields of administration prevented rapid and efficient work, and on January 7, 1941 it gave way to the OFFICE OF PRODUCTION MANAGEMENT.

Council of New England. The Plymouth Branch of the VIRGINIA COMPANY chartered in 1620. It was given the power to colonize and govern the area that generally comprises the present state of Massachusetts. Its 40 members were landed aristocrats whose fundamental desire was the exploitation of the land by dividing its most valuable portions into manors to be distributed to themselves. The autocratically run council was dominated by its president, Sir Ferdinando Gorges, whose son Robert was appointed the first governor-general. Attempts to execute the Council's plan in New Eng-

land failed despite many reorganizations. Success came from other directions however, with the settlement by the PILGRIMS in 1620 and the grant of a PATENT to the MASSACHUSETTS BAY COMPANY in 1628. With the conferring of royal charters upon these two colonies the Council was eliminated as a power in New England.

Council of Ten. Also known as the Supreme Council. It was a committee at the VERSAILLES PEACE CONFERENCE in 1919 consisting of two delegates from each of the BIG FIVE, the United States, Great Britain, France, Italy, and Japan. This group was the core of the Conference, which decided the basic issues of the Treaty.

county executive. The chief executive of a county government. Historically, counties in the United States have been governed by a board of supervisors or a board of trustees exercising combined LEGISLATIVE and EXECUTIVE POWERS. To overcome the duplication, waste, and inefficiency provided by this form of county government state legislatures in the last generation have established the office of the county executive. He is the apex of the county governmental organization. A few states have conferred upon him the usual powers of a chief executive.

county-manager plan. See city-manager plan.

Court of Claims. A special or legislative court established by Congress under the powers delegated to it in Article I, Section 8 of the Constitution. Claims against the United States are adjudicated in these courts. Awards, if granted by Court of Claims judges, are paid only if the funds are appropriated by the Congress for that purpose. Certain claims against the United States are tried in the federal district courts and executive agencies as provided for by law. See particularly

FEDERAL TORT CLAIMS ACT, Title IV of LEGISLATIVE REORGANIZATION ACT of 1946.

"court packing" plan. The term was applied to the plan of President F. D. ROOSEVELT in 1937 for reorganizing the United States Supreme Court. The plan requested Congress to enact authorization for the President to appoint a justice of the Court for each incumbent 70 years of age or over. The opponents of the plan attacked it as an attempt of the President to control the Court and seek its validation of NEW DEAL legislation. Although defeated in Congress a law was enacted providing for pensions in the full amount of existing salaries for all justices 60 years of age and over who resigned their offices.

courts, federal. The courts established or provided for by Article III of the federal Constitution, and established by Congress under its DELEGATED POWERS. As defined by the United States Supreme Court these include the constitutional courts, such as the United States Supreme Court, the Courts of Appeal, and the District Courts as well as the special or legislative courts customarily established by Congress by virtue of its powers under Article I, Section 8 of the Constitution.

courts, state. The various judicial systems in the 50 states. Authorized under the Tenth Amendment of the federal Constitution they are established by the state constitutions or state legislation. Three features are common to the organization of all state court systems. Each state has a high court of appeals (usually a Supreme Court), a level of courts of original and general jurisdiction commonly called district or county courts, and at the bottom a tier of justice of the peace courts, including a miscellany of municipal, police, and magistrate courts for the trial of minor civil and criminal cases. Some states have an additional group of intermediate courts of appeal. All states have varying specialized courts for the administration of estates, wills, domestic relations and children's problems, juvenile delinquency, and small claims.

Covenant on Human Rights. See human rights.

cowboys. Those who herd beef CATTLE on western ranches. Although they patterned their dress and work after the Mexican *vaquero,* American cowboys nevertheless developed local customs and traditions unique to the United States. Cowboy folk MUSIC and POETRY as well as the provincial institutions of the campfire, roundup, rodeo, speech, and work activities developed into specific American forms. Cowboys on the open range in Texas date back to the early 1820's but did not become important until after the Civil War. During the era of the "CATTLE KINGDOM" the Texas and northern cowboy tended cattle and conducted the "LONG DRIVE" to the stockyards and railroad terminal, developing unusual skills in horsemanship and the use of arms. With the advent of the sheep grazing and farming the open range was fenced in, and by the disappearance of the FRONTIER in 1890 the cowboy virtually vanished from the American scene. Today he occupies a relatively insignificant place in western RANCHING as a result of industrial mechanization and improved methods of TRANSPORTATION. He has survived principally in pulp fiction and the MOTION PICTURES.

COX, Archibald. 1912-   .; A graduate of St. Paul's, Harvard, and Harvard Law School, Cox first served as law clerk to Judge Learned Hand on the U.S. Circuit Court of Appeals in New York. In 1941 he moved into government, the National Defense Mediation Board, and then the Solicitor General's office at the Justice Department, and later the Department of Labor. After World War II, he held a full professorship at the Harvard Law School. In 1961, President Kennedy named him Solicitor General. In 1967, he served as special mediator in the New York City school strike and then as chairman of the commission that investigated the 1968 riots at Columbia University. In 1973, Cox was selected to conduct a full-scale investigation of Watergate and was given authority to prosecute and punish all legal offenders in the scandal. During the investigation, it was learned that President Nixon had taped conversations with key numbers of the "conspiracy" and when the President refused to yield the tapes, Special Prosecutor Cox stated that he would ask the courts to cite the President for contempt. Nixon ordered his immediate dismissal. Attorney General Elliot Richardson resigned his office and was replaced by Robert Bork as acting Attorney General. Bork then fired Cox and his entire staff. See Saturday Night Massacre.

Coxey's Army. A group of 500 unemployed led by Jacob Coxey in 1894 on a march from Massillon, Ohio to Washington, D.C. for the purpose of demanding that Congress issue $500,000,000 in FIAT CURRENCY to finance a public works program for the idle. The march occurred during the depth of the DEPRESSION of 1893 and ended in a fiasco on May 1, 1894. As the men marched across the lawn of the WHITE HOUSE they were arrested for "walking on the grass" and were soon dispersed. "General" Coxey succeeded to the extent that several bills were enacted by Congress designed to inflate the CURRENCY, bring down interest rates, inaugurate public improvement, and provide work for the unemployed. In 1914 Coxey led another "army" to Washington.

COX, Jacob Dolson. 1828-1900. Lawyer, army officer and statesman. b. Canada. Graduated, Oberlin College and started

practice of law (1853); served with Union army with ARMY OF THE POTOMAC, at South Mountain and ANTIETAM; major general of campaign in Atlanta; governor of Ohio (1866-68); appointed by GRANT U.S. Secretary of the Interior (1869-70); urged CIVIL SERVICE REFORM; member, U.S. House of Representatives (1877-79); Dean, Cincinnati Law School (1881-97); president, University of Cincinnati (1885-89).

COX, Samuel Sullivan. 1824-1889. Lawyer and congressman. Often referred to as "Sunset Cox". b. Ohio. Graduated Brown University (184b); studied law and began practice in Cincinnati; editor, *Ohio Statesman;* member, U.S. House of Representatives (1857-65); moved to New York and elected to Congress (1869-73; 1873-85; 1886-89); proposed TARIFF and CIVIL SERVICE REFORMS; instigated HAMPTON ROADS CONFERENCE (1865); author of *A Buckeye Abroad* (1852); and *Three Decades of Federal Legislation* (1885).

"Cradle of Liberty." See Faneuil Hall.

CRANE, Winthrop Murray. 1853-1920. Manufacturer and Senator. b. Massachusetts. Manufacturer, paper mills; supplied government with paper on which United States bank notes and treasury certificates were printed; prominent Republican; lieutenant governor of Mass. (1897-99); governor (1900-02); important influence on T. ROOSEVELT although declined cabinet posts offered; U.S. Senator (1904-13); interested in LEAGUE OF NATIONS.

CRAWFORD, William Harris. 1772-1834. Lawyer and statesman. b. Virginia. U.S. Senator from Georgia (1807-13), president *pro tempore* (1812-13); U.S. Minister to France (1813-15); appointed U.S. Secretary of War (1815-16) by President MADISON; served as U.S. Secretary of the Treasury (1816-25) during both MONROE administrations; unsuccessful candidate for the Presidency (1824); judge of Northern circuit in Georgia (1827-30) retiring from politics due to poor health.

CRAZY HORSE. Indian name, Tashunca-Uitco. 1849?-1877. Indian chief of the Oglala tribe of the SIOUX. Involved in wars against United States troops; took part in the battle of Little Big Horn in which CUSTER was killed; attacked by Gen. Miles he was forced to surrender in Nebraska (1877); killed while resisting arrest.

Credit Mobilier of America. Construction company organized to build the UNION PACIFIC RAILROAD in the years following the Civil War. Involved in one of the greatest post war scandals of the GRANT administrations. The company bribed congressmen by selling to them its shares of stock at one-half their market value in return for favorable legislation regarding PUBLIC LAND grants and right of way. The revelation of the scandal of 1873 showed that Congressman OAKES AMES had distributed such stock to the Speaker of the House, SCHUYLER COLFAX (later Vice-President), Senator HENRY WILSON (later Vice-President), and Congressman JAMES A. GARFIELD (later President).

Creek Indians. A tribe of handsome Indians living in Georgia, Alabama, and Florida. They had fought against the Spaniards who had mistreated them, and allied themselves with the British. Their outstanding leader was TECUMSEH who caused them to rebel and massacre the white settlers in that region in 1813. ANDREW JACKSON was sent to stop the uprising. After their defeat by Jackson's troops, they relinquished their lands in the South and were moved to INDIAN TERRITORY. They were divided during the Civil War. In 1906 the Creeks became American CITIZENS and gave up the autonomy of their tribe. They are largely self-supporting, and are occupied in various professions today in the West.

CREEL, George. 1876-1953. Journalist and publicist. b. Missouri. Editor, Kansas City *Independent* (1899-1909); Denver *Post* (1909-1910); *Rocky Mountain News* (1911-1913); chairman, COMMITTEE ON PUBLIC INFORMATION (1917-19); chairman, national advisory board, WORKS PROGRESS ADMINISTRATION (1935). Author of *Wilson and the Issues* (1916), and *Tom Paine-Liberty Bell* (1931).

Creole Affair. A diplomatic incident between the United States and Great Britain. It arose out of the uprising of 17 slaves on November 7, 1841 against the officers of the brig *Creole* which was transporting these slaves from Norfolk, Virginia to New Orleans. The slaves brought the ship to the British island of Nassau where all were liberated except those charged with the murder of one of the vessel's owners. The demand of the United States government for the surrender of the slaves was refused, an act which aggravated the existing Anglo-American controversy arising out of the Maine-Canada conflict and other matters. These controversies were finally settled in the WEBSTER-ASHBURTON TREATY of the following year.

CRESWELL, John Angel James. 1828-1891. Postmaster General. b. Maryland. Graduated, Dickinson College and admitted to the bar. U.S. Postmaster General (1869-74). Many new reforms and new types of postal service including one-cent post cards were introduced during his administration. He suggested the POSTAL SAVINGS SYSTEM and the postal TELEGRAPH which were adopted for use later.

crime. Crimes of violence and sex predominated in the colonial period. Court records show relatively few cases of homicide, theft, and vagrancy. Cruel punishments were common, including whipping, branding, mutilation, the stocks, ducking, and imprisonment. Capital punishment was rare, Massachusetts listing only ten crimes so punishable. In the 19th century theft and crimes of violence were predominant, including HIGHWAY robbery, horse stealing, and cattle thefts. Local family feuds, whose causes had long since been forgotten, characterized a large part of Southern crime after the Civil War. The URBANIZATION of the country produced new types of crime against property. These included forgery, embezzlement, and bankruptcy. Crimes resulting from violations of regulatory statutes became common after 1900. These included crimes arising out of ANTI-TRUST, LABOR RELATIONS, PURE FOOD AND DRUGS, and similar legislation. A report of the FEDERAL BUREAU OF INVESTIGATION in April, 1964 disclosed that in 1963 there had been 2,250,000 serious offenses, an increase of more than 10 per cent over the previous year. The report indicated a rise of homicide, burglary, robbery, larceny, rape, automobile theft, and assault. A notable feature of crime in 1963, labeled by the F.B.I. as a "tragedy of our times", was the increase in youthful offenders.

"Crime of 1873." A reference to the Coinage Act of 1873 which omitted silver from the list of coins to be minted. The phrase was applied because of the feeling of western silver miners and FARMERS that "WALL STREET" had conspired with Congress to limit CURRENCY circulation to gold and thus establish a hard currency system detrimental to their interests. Simultaneously with its passage discoveries of large deposits of silver in Nevada threw the metal on the market although the Treasury could not purchase it for coinage under the law. The miners and farmers, incensed by the alleged plot, demanded the remonetization of silver and the reestablishment of a bimetallic standard.

Crimes Against Humanity. See war crimes.

Crisis papers. A series of political pamphlets written by THOMAS PAINE during the Revolution. The first appeared in the *Pennsylvania Journal* on December 19, 1776. Paine wrote a total of 16 papers, all designed to stimulate patriotic morale and furnish an awareness of the purposes of the war.

"Critical Period, The." The name applied to the period from 1781 to 1789 during which the nation was governed under the ARTICLES OF CONFEDERATION. Borrowed from the title of a historical work written by John Fiske in the 1890's this phrase describes the chaotic conditions in the United States after the American Revolution. The flaws and weaknesses of the government ran through all political, economic, and social aspects of American life. The Articles themselves could be amended only by an unanimous vote of the 13 states and required the approval of nine states to enact ordinary legislation. They did not provide for a federal judiciary, leaving the interpretation of federal and state laws to the conflicting decisions of the STATE COURTS. The office of the President was supernumerary, he exercising virtually none of the typical administrative, executive, legislative or other powers of the contemporary President. Actually he was merely a chairman at the meetings of Congress. The Congress itself was severely limited in power, being unable to impose taxes directly upon the people. Its requests for levies from the states could be constitutionally refused by them. It could not regulate COMMERCE among the states or with foreign nations, the result being the imposition of interstate TARIFFS and other trade restrictions. Unable to coin money or regulate its value, the Congress was confronted with a financial situation characterized by the circulation of continental and state CURRENCY as well as foreign coins. Although Congress was able to negotiate TREATIES with foreign nations it lacked the power to enforce them. Its military powers were restricted to its requests upon the states to furnish troops in time of need. The consequences of this were a "CRITICAL PERIOD" in which INFLATION angered the creditor, England violated the Treaty of 1783, the currency lacked stable backing, the states imposed TARIFF restrictions against each other, and finally the SHAYS' REBELLION shocked the nation into a realization of the government's inadequacies.

Crittenden Compromise. Offered by Senator JOHN CRITTENDEN of Kentucky as a method of solving the SECESSION problem following the election of ABRAHAM LINCOLN in November 1860. The plan proposed to extend the MISSOURI COMPROMISE line to the Pacific Coast. The compromise was not acceptable either to the seceded states or to the federal government.

CRITTENDEN, John Jordan. 1787-1863. Lawyer and statesman. b. Kentucky. Member Kentucky legislature (1811-16); served in WAR OF 1812; U.S. Senator (1817-19; 1835-41; 1842-48; 1855-61); appointed U.S. Attorney General (1841; 1850-53) by HARRISON and FILLMORE; introduced "CRITTENDEN COMPROMISE" (sometimes called Crittenden Resolutions) (1860) but measure was killed in committee.

CROCKETT, David. 1786-1836. FRONTIERSMAN. b. Tennessee. Served under JACKSON in the Creek Wars (1813-14); magistrate, member of state legislature, Tennessee (1821); member, U.S. House of Representatives (1827-31; 1833-35); he was a well-known humorist and his clever backwoods comments on life in his times made him a popular figure in Washington. He joined the Texas forces (1836) in their fight for independence and was killed in the battle of the ALAMO.

CROKER, Richard. 1841-1922. Politician. Called "Boss Croker". b. Ireland. TAMMANY HALL leader in New York City (1886-1902); opposed to BOSS TWEED; finally lost control of city politics at election of SETH LOW as mayor. Spent last years in England and Ireland living as a country squire.

Crosser-Dill Act. Also known as the Railway Labor Act of 1934 and Railroad Disputes Act. Passed by Congress in 1934 as an amendment to the WATSON-PARKER ACT. It established a smaller board of mediation and provided for a National Railway Adjustment Board with members jointly chosen by railroad management and unions. The statute also provided for regional or railroad system boards. Valid labor organizations were safeguarded by clauses which rendered it difficult for COMPANY UNIONS to exist. An ARBITRATION provision required arbitration under certain conditions. The Act made it unlawful for carriers to interfere with the organization of employees or to coerce employees into joining or not joining a union. It outlawed the "YELLOW-DOG" CONTRACT. The National Mediation Board of three members was authorized to certify the majority representative of railroad workers, mediate disputes arising out of new contracts and changes in wages, hours, and working conditions, and persuade parties to arbitrate. In the event of failure in arbitration the Board was authorized to refer disputes to the President, who could appoint a fact-finding board for a 30 day investigation during which no change could occur in the conditions of labor except by agreement of the parties. The National Railway Adjustment Board was to consist of 36 members empowered to handle individual grievances on interpretations of contracts.

"Cross of Gold" Speech. The famous speech made by WILLIAM JENNINGS BRYAN on July 8, 1896 at the Democratic NATIONAL CONVENTION at Chicago. Bryan, a Nebraska delegate to the convention, made the concluding speech in the debate on the adoption of the platform. It is generally conceded to have been the most notable of his career and one of the most distinguished in American political oratory. It focused convention attention upon Bryan and made his nomination virtually inevitable. The speech ended with the phrase "Having behind us the producing masses of this nation and the world, supported by the commercial interests, the laboring interests and the toilers everywhere, we will answer their demand for a GOLD STANDARD by saying to them: You shall not press down upon the brow of labor this crown of thorns, you shall not crucify mankind upon a cross of gold."

CROWDER, Enoch Herbert. 1859-1932. Army officer and first American Ambassador to CUBA. b. Missouri. Graduated, U.S.M.A., West Point (1881); Missouri (L.L.M., 1886); served as judge advocate with rank of major (1895); judge advocate of expeditionary forces and the Department of the Pacific in the Spanish-American War; associate justice of supreme court, PHILIPPINE ISLANDS (1899-1901); judge-advocate general of the U.S. Army with rank of brigadier general (1911); provost-marshal-general in World War I in charge of administering the SELECTIVE SERVICE ACT; appointed first U.S. Ambassador to Cuba (1923-27).

Crow Indians. A friendly people living near the Big Horn River in Wyoming and in Montana. They were excellent hunters and guides. They were enemies of the SIOUX and acted as scouts for the United States troops in their wars against that tribe.

Cuba. An island republic in the Caribbean Sea. It is the largest of the WEST INDIES, its 1952 population of 5,500,000 inhabiting an area of 44,217 square miles. Havana is the capital, largest city, and chief port and industrial center. The principal POPULATION elements are 75 percent white and mulatto, 24 percent NEGRO, and one percent Mongolian. The prevailing religion is Roman Catholic, and Spanish is the language. Cuba was discovered by COLUMBUS in 1492 and remained a Spanish colony until 1898. Various native rebellions against Spanish control from 1867 to 1878 and from 1895 to 1898 finally resulted in independence after the defeat of Spain by the United States in the latter year. Under the PLATT AMENDMENT Cuba remained under the military, political, and economic control of the United States until 1934. From the end of the Spanish-American War until 1902 American troops occupied Cuba, and they again intervened in Cuba during native insurrections in 1906, 1912, and 1917. The most important Cuban crop is sugar which accounts for nine-tenths of its exports. Other important products are tobacco, coffee, corn, pineapples, henequen, fruits and vegetables. In recent years relations between Cuba and the United States have deteriorated. The rise of Fidel Castro led to a break in diplomatic relations. In 1961, 1000 anti-Castro Cubans, with the tacit support of the United States, launched an unsuccessful invasion attempt (Bay of Pigs). A Cuban blockade was effected by the United States after Russia sent to that country long range bombers and nuclear missiles. The strong stand taken by President Kennedy persuaded Premier Khrushchev to reverse himself and to remove all offensive weapons from Cuba (1962).
Travel ban lifted. Effective March 18, 1977 President Carter lifted the ban on travel by U.S. citizens to Cuba, Vietnam, North Korea, and Cambodia. On March 26 the ban was lifted on spending dollars by U.S. travelers in Cuba.

CULLOM, Shelby Moore. 1829-1914.

Statesman. b. Kentucky. Elected city attorney in Springfield, Ill. soon after admission to the bar (1855); member U.S. House of Representatives (1865-71); state legislature (1873-74); governor of Illinois (1876-83); U.S. Senator (1883-1913); chairman of committee that drew up the bill establishing the INTERSTATE COMMERCE COMMISSION (1887); leading Republican and chairman of Committee on Foreign Affairs.

Cumberland Compact. A series of constitutional articles drafted in 1780 for the purpose of establishing a governmental organization for settlers moving into the Cumberland Settlements. These agreements between the Transylvania Company and the settlers provided for the distribution of the lands to be acquired by them from the company. The Settlements had been obtained from the CHEROKEE INDIANS by treaty in 1775.

Cumberland Road. See National Road.

CUMMINS, Albert Baird. 1850-1926. Lawyer and statesman. b. Pennsylvania. Practiced law in Des Moines, Iowa; gained recognition as attorney for Farmers' Protective Association in fight against the BARBED WIRE TRUST; governor, Iowa (1902-08); U.S. Senator (1908-26); as chairman, Committee of INTERSTATE COMMERCE prepared and helped pass ESCH-CUMMINS TRANSPORTATION ACT (1920); president *pro tempore* of the Senate.

currency. After the Revolution the money of the United States depreciated as a result of the oversupply of CONTINENTAL CURRENCY. Despite HAMILTON's desire to provide a stable circulating currency through the establishment of the BANK OF THE UNITED STATES, a national medium did not come into existence. The nation's unfavorable balance of TRADE and the lack of gold prevented the establishment of gold notes. Coins were generally limited in number and of varying denominations, and competed with foreign coins. In 1834 Congress established a ratio of approximately 16-1 between silver and gold. In 1857 copper and nickel coins were minted, supplanting Spanish coins which Congress had been declaring legal tender since the Revolution. State bank notes competed with the notes of the Bank of the United States in business loans and speculation. Ineffective regulation plus overexpansion of investments in western lands, CANALS, and RAILROADS produced financial chaos which was not relieved until the Civil War. The GREENBACKS issued by the Union government during the War were the second attempt by Congress to finance its operations through bills of credit. They were redeemable after 1879 but remained in circulation until today. Meanwhile, the agrarian program of bi-metallism brought silver certificates and treasury certificates into circulation under the BLAND-ALLISON and SHERMAN SILVER PURCHASE Acts respectively. These notes vied with the national bank notes provided under the Act of 1863. By the end of the century the United States witnessed in circulation gold notes, depreciated silver certificates, greenbacks, national bank notes, and a variety of coins, each possessing a special legal tender position. In 1913 Federal Reserve Notes were added to the circulating medium. In 1933 Congress authorized the issue of Federal Reserve Bank Notes. The financial problems of the GREAT DEPRESSION produced a complete reorganization of United States currency. Although silver certificates were again authorized by legislation in 1934, gold certificates, Federal Reserve Bank Notes, and national bank notes were withdrawn from circulation. The ABOLITION of the gold standard completely altered the bullion status of this currency. In 1965 there was approximately $38,-000,000,000 of currency in circulation.

CURRIER and IVES. Famous American lithographers and print publishers. Na-

160

thaniel Currier was born in Massachusetts; started business in New York City, and published his first lithograph (1835); took J. Merritt Ives into partnership (1857) and from that time on they printed lithographs signed Currier and Ives depicting scenes in the lives of Americans.

CURTIN, Andrew Gregg. 1817-1894. Civil War governor of Pennsylvania. Important supporter of LINCOLN during the war; appointed Minister to Russia by GRANT, serving three years; supported GREELEY for President (1872); elected to Congress on Democratic ticket (1881-87).

CURTIS, Charles. 1860-1936. Thirty-first Vice-President of the United States. b. Kansas. His mother was a Kaw Indian. Admitted to the bar and practiced in Topeka, Kansas (1881); member, U.S. House of Representatives (1893-1907); U.S. Senator (1907-13; 1915-29); elected Vice-President of the United States (1929-33), serving with HOOVER.

CURTIS, Cyrus Hermann Kotzschmar. 1850-1933. Publisher. b. Maine. Worked on Philadelphia *Press;* started a periodical the *Tribune and Farmer* which became a part of *Ladies Home Journal;* founded Curtis Publishing Co. (1890); bought *Saturday Evening Post* (1897); also owned and published *The Country Gentleman,* Philadelphia *Public Ledger* (1913), New York *Evening Post* (1923), Philadelphia *Inquirer* (1930). Endowed the Curtis Institute of Music, Philadelphia, and other schools and colleges.

CURTIS, George William. 1824-1892. Essayist and editor. b. Rhode Island. Member of BROOK FARM community (1842-43); editorial writer *Harper's Magazine;* editor *Harper's Weekly* (from 1863); influenced by thinking of EMERSON and in turn influenced the thinking of his time. Author of *Nile Notes* (1851),

Pure and I (1857) etc. His *Orations and Addresses* (edited by Charles Eliot Norton; 3 vols., 1893-94).

CURTISS, Glenn Hammond. 1878-1930. Inventor and aviator. b. New York. Owned motorcycle factory and won motorcycle speed races; held world record (1905-07); designed dirigibles (1907-09); won many prizes for flights and races in airplanes with motors of his own design; demonstrated hydroplane (1911) and flying boat (1912); owned aviation schools and factories; first Atlantic crossing by a seaplane made by a "Wasp" Navy Curtiss (NC).

CUSHING, Caleb. 1800-1879. Lawyer and statesman. b. Massachusetts. Graduated, Harvard University (1817); WHIG member, U.S. House of Representatives (1835-43); special envoy to China to negotiate treaties and open Chinese ports to American TRADE (1843-45); responsible for nomination of FRANKLIN PIERCE for President at Democratic convention (1852); appointed U.S. Attorney General (1853-57) by Pierce; supported LINCOLN and became a Republican; nominated to Supreme Court, but not confirmed; chairman, committee to codify United States statutes (1866-70); U.S. Minister to Spain (1874-77).

CUSHMAN, Pauline. 1835-1893. Union spy in Civil War. b. New Orleans. Came to New York City to become an actress; served behind the Confederate lines supplying valuable information to the Union generals; captured with papers and court-martialed at General BRAGG's headquarters and sentenced to be hanged; saved from execution when the Confederates had to abandon Shelbyville, and she was left behind.

CUSTER, George Armstrong. 1839-1876. Army officer. b. Ohio. Graduated U.S.M.A., West Point (1861); served at battle of BULL RUN; served with MC CLEL-

LAN and made brigadier general of volunteers; celebrated for service with SHERIDAN; made major general (1865); lieutenant colonel of 7th Cavalry unit (1866); served in fights against Indians (1867-76); killed in battle of Little Big Horn.

Custer's Last Stand. The culminating event in the INDIAN WARS in the post-Civil War period. The struggle was climaxed by the massacre of General GEORGE A. CUSTER and his force of 264 men by the SIOUX INDIANS under the leadership of SITTING BULL. The slaughter was an ambush at the Little Big Horn River in Montana. The subsequent defeat of the Sioux Confederacy by the army concluded the Indian Wars and opened up the Far West to migration.

CUTLER, Manasseh. 1742-1823. Clergyman, botanist, and colonizer. b. Connecticut. Graduated, Yale (1765); practiced law; became a pastor in the Congregational Church in Massachusetts (1771-1823); studied MEDICINE and botany; published his account of the flora of New England; an organizer of the OHIO COMPANY which was granted land along the Ohio River for settlement purposes (1786); helped to draft the ORDINANCE OF 1787 for the NORTHWEST TERRITORY; helped establish the colony at what is now Marietta, Ohio (1788); member, U.S. House of Representatives (1800-1804).

D

DAHLGREN, John Adolphus Bernard. 1809-1870. Naval officer and inventor. b. Philadelphia. Entered U.S. Navy(1826); on ordnance duty, Washington, D.C. (1847-63); built first ordnance laboratory in the Navy; designed 9-inch and 11-inch guns called *Dahlgrens*(1851); chief of Bureau of Ordnance and commandant of ordnance yard (1862); rear admiral, Union navy (1862); cooperated with SHERMAN in taking Savannah (1864); commanded the South Pacific Squadron (1866-68).

dairy industry. The greatest and most lucrative section of the farm industry in the United States. Until the technological advancement of the late nineteenth century the production and marketing of dairy products, particularly milk, were severely limited by the lack of adequate TRANSPORTATION, sanitation, and refrigeration facilities. The development of the centrifugal separator, automatic milking machinery, artificial refrigeration, the glass bottle, the can, the paper container, and pasteurization vastly improved the distribution of dairy products. Among the more important consumers' dairy products are milk and skimmed milk, ice-cream, buttermilk, casein, cheese, butter, and oleomargarine. American consumers spend an annual total of nearly five billion dollars for dairy products which are produced by more than 25 million on the farm, in the factory, and in the distributive media.

Dakota Indians. See Sioux Indians.

DALE, Sir Thomas. d. 1619. Colonial administrator. Acting governor of Virginia (1611; 1614-16); placing colonists under strict martial law; published *Dale's Code* which he carefully enforced, making the lives of the colonists miserable during his administration; returned to England (1616).

DALLAS, Alexander James. 1759-1817. Statesman. b. Jamaica, West Indies. Settled in Philadelphia, Pennsylvania (1783); became a naturalized citizen; admitted to the bar (1785); secretary of state for Pennsylvania (1791-1801); appointed by JEFFERSON U.S. district attorney for the eastern district of Pennsylvania; appointed U.S. Secretary of the Treasury by MADISON(1814-16); restored public credit; urged a national banking institution(passed 1816); advocated PROTECTIVE TARIFF; served as acting Secretary of War (1815).

DALLAS, George Mifflin. 1792-1864. Statesman. b. Philadelphia, Pa.; son of ALEXANDER J. DALLAS. Graduated, Princeton University; secretary to ALBERT GALLATON; counsel for THE BANK OF THE UNITED STATES; U.S. Senator (1831-33); appointed U.S. Minister to Russia (1837-

39) by VAN BUREN; elected Vice-President of the U.S. (1845-49), serving with POLK; appointed U.S. Minister to Great Britain (1856-61); persuaded Great Britain to discontinue the right of search, which had caused long disagreement between the two nations.

DALY, John Augustin. 1838-1899. Playwright and theatrical manager. b. North Carolina. Drama critic, New York City NEWSPAPERS (1859-69); successful adaptations of French and German plays; wrote original melodramas that were successful, including *Under the Gaslight* (1867), and *The Red Scarf* (1869). Organized his own company and leased the Fifth Avenue Theater (1869-77); presented such favorites as *Divorce* (1871), and *Roughing It* (1873); company included John Drew, Ada Rehan, and Otis Skinner. Produced Shakespearean comedies, Tennyson's *The Foresters* (1891) and many others; bought old Broadway Theater and made it Daly's Theater (1879). Important influence on American THEATRE.

DALY, Marcus. 1841-1900. Wealthy mine owner and politician. b. Ireland. Came to the United States (1856) and settled in California; important for development of Anaconda Copper mines in Butte, Montana; organized Amalgamated Copper Company; because of rivalry with WILLIAM A. CLARK he built up a powerful political machine in the state; published *Anaconda Standard,* an influential newspaper.

Damon Runyon Fund. Established in 1947 for the conduct of research in the field of cancer. The Fund does not maintain or support any clinical facilities or operate its own laboratories. It is primarily a collection and disbursement erganization which by 1952 had collected almost six million dollars of which approximately five million dollars had been distributed in 191 grants to 137 institutions in forty-five states, the District of Columbia, and eleven foreign nations. By that time it had also subsidized 147 student fellowships. Its office is located in New York City.

DAMROSCH, Leopold. 1832-1885. Conductor. b. Poland. Breslau Philharmonic Orchestra; came to the United States as guest conductor; organized New York Oratorio Society (1873) and NEW YORK SYMPHONY SOCIETY (1878); conducted Wagnerian operas at Metropolitan Opera House, N. Y. City (1884-85); known chiefly for introducing Wagner to American audiences.

DAMROSCH, Walter Johannes. 1862-1951. b. Germany. Came to the United States (1871); assistant director (1885) of German opera at Metropolitan Opera House; presented Wagner's *Parsifal* for the first time in the U.S. (1896); founder of Damrosch Opera Company (1894); director, NEW YORK SYMPHONY ORCHESTRA (1903-27); at request of PERSHING he organized U.S. bands (1918); musical advisor for National Broadcasting Company, introducing music appreciation programs for children; composer of the operas *Cyrano* (1913) and *The Man Without a Country* (1937) and other music.

DANA, Charles Anderson. 1819-1897. Newspaper editor. b. New Hampshire. Studied at Harvard University; member and managing trustee of BROOK FARM community (1841-46); first on staff and then managing editor, New York *Tribune* (1847-62); Assistant Secretary of War (1863-64); editor and owner of New York *Sun* (1868-97), making it a prominent and influential paper. Author of *Recollections of the Civil War* (1898), *The Art of Newspaper Making* (1900); with GEORGE RIPLEY he edited the *American Cyclopaedia* (1857-63).

DANA, Francis. 1743-1811. Jurist and Diplomat. Went to England (1774-75) to settle differences between the colonies and Great Britain; member, Massachusetts council (1776-80); member, CONTINENTAL CONGRESS (1776-78); signer, ARTICLES OF CONFEDERATION (1778); secretary to JOHN ADAMS at negotiations of peace treaties in France (1780); sent to Russia by Congress (1780-83) as representative to the court of Catherine the Great to sign treaties of peace and commerce, but never officially recognized by Russia; associate justice Massachusetts Supreme Court (1785-91); chief justice (1791-1806).

DANA, James Dwight. 1813-1895. Geologist. b. New York. Graduated, Yale University (1833). Assistant to Professor SILLIMAN at Yale; wrote *System of Minerology* (1837), a standard work in the field; appointed geologist and minerologist on United States government expedition to the northwest coast and the South Pacific led by CHARLES WILKES (1838-42); his reports of the expedition were published under titles *Zoophytes* (1846), *Geology* (1849) and *Crustacea* (1852-54); editor *American Journal of Science* (from 1840); professor at Yale (1849-90). Author of *Manual of Geology* (1862) and *Characteristics of Volcanos* (1890).

DANA, Richard Henry. 1815-1882. Sailor, Lawyer and author. b. Massachusetts. Studied at Harvard University; shipped to California via Cape Horn (1834-36); wrote *Two Years Before the Mast* (1840), the story of his experiences and a classic book about the sea; admitted to the bar (1840); specialized in admiralty law and wrote *The Seaman's Friend* (1841), a standard manual in the field; a founder of the FREE-SOIL PARTY.

Danbury Hatters' Case. A decision of the United States Supreme Court in 1908 sustaining a district court award of $250,-000 against the United Hatters of North America. The judgment of the district court resulted from a strike and BOYCOTT of the union against the hat making firm of Dietrich Loewe in Danbury, Connecticut. The award was held payable by members of the union, the homes of 140 of them ordered sold by the district court in 1917 to satisfy the judgment. Also known as Loewe vs. Lawlor.

Dancing Rabbit, Treaty of. An agreement between the United States and the CHOCTAW INDIAN nation on September 27, 1830 providing for the removal of the tribe from Mississippi to INDIAN TERRITORY west of the Mississippi River. The Treaty culminated a long struggle, ending the tribe's claims to the eastern lands, and providing a total of 7,800,000 acres of land in the new territory.

DANIELS, Josephus. 1862-1941. Journalist and statesman. b. North Carolina. Editor of Raleigh, N.C. *State Chronicle* (1885-94); editor, Raleigh *News and Observer* (1894-1933); in charge of publicity for BRYAN (1908) and WILSON (1912) in their campaigns for the PRESIDENCY; appointed U.S. Secretary of the Navy by Wilson (1913-21); appointed U.S. Ambassador to Mexico (1933-42) by F. D. ROOSEVELT. Author of *The Wilson Era* (1944), *Tar Heel Editor* (1939) and *Shirt Sleeve Diplomat* (1947).

"dark horse." Person at a NATIONAL CONVENTION who is not an avowed candidate or "FAVORITE SON." At the onset of the convention, seldom, if ever, has any state delegation's support, and if mentioned denies all ambition. A dark horse is selected as the nominee when there is a deadlock between two or more strong candidates. Among such in American history have been JAMES K. POLK, who in the 1844 Democratic party convention received no votes whatever until the eighth BALLOT and yet was nominated on the ninth. In the 1852 Democratic party convention FRANKLIN PIERCE secured no votes until the 35th ballot, yet was nominated on the 49th ballot. The most recent illustrations of the nomination of a "dark horse" were the choice of WARREN G. HARDING by the Republican convention of 1920 and that of Wendell Willkie in 1940.

DARROW, Clarence Seward. 1857-1938. Lawyer. b. Ohio. Admitted to the bar (1878); practiced first in Ohio then in Chicago (from 1888); corporation counsel for Chicago and Northwestern Railroad, but resigned in sympathy with Pullman strikers; gained national recognition for defense of EUGENE V. DEBS in the Railroad Union conspiracy case (1894); counsel for miners in anthracite coal disputes (1903); defense counsel for Leopold and Loeb in murder case (1924); defended SCOPES in evolution case (1925); defense counsel for the Negroes in the SCOTTSBORO CASE (1932). Author of *Crime, its Cause and Treatment* (1925), and *The Story of My Life* (1932).

Dartmouth College vs. Woodward. A decision of the United States Supreme Court in 1819 in which the court laid down the doctrine that the charters of business corporations are contracts, the obligations of which may not be impaired by the states. The court held that the state of New Hampshire had violated Article I, Section 10 of the federal CONSTITUTION by passing a law granting a new charter for Dartmouth College in 1809 in violation of the charter conferred upon the college by the English Crown in 1769. The case is important as an expression of nationalist sentiment in the United States after the War of 1812.

"date which will live in infamy, a." The quotation from the address to Congress by President F. D. ROOSEVELT on December 8, 1941. Coming a day after the Japanese attack on PEARL HARBOR the President denounced the "unprovoked and dastardly attack" and referred to December 7, 1941 as "a day which will live in infamy." He called upon Congress to declare war on Japan.

Daughters of the American Revolution. An organization of women who claim descent from those who fought in the American Revolution. They are a conservative, patriotic group whose program is dedicated to the preservation of the ideals of Americanism. Their headquarters are in Washington, D. C., where they have a library of more than 38,000 volumes and pamphlets plus many thousands of manuscripts available to researchers.

DAVENPORT, John. 1597-1670. Puritan clergyman; founder of the colony of New Haven. b. England. Clergyman for the Church of England, London (1619-33); helped to obtain charter for the MASSACHUSETTS BAY COLONY (1629); to Boston (1637); with T. EATON he founded the colony at New Haven, Conn. (1638); opposed the merger of the colonies of New Haven with the Connecticut colonies; preached at First Church in Boston (1668); founded the Third or "Old South" church.

DAVIDSON, George. 1825-1911. Geographer and astronomer. b. England. With U.S. Coast Survey (1845-95); compiled the *Directory for the Pacific Coast of the U.S.* (1858); surveyed the Alaskan coast; published his *Coast Pilot of Alaska* (1869) built and operated the first observatory on the Pacific coast at San Francisco (1879); headed American expedition to Japan to study the Transit of Venus (1874); to New Mexico for the same reason (1882); published catalogs of star positions; studied meteors; important in building of the Lick Observatory.

DAVIE, William Richardson. 1756-1820. Revolutionary officer and statesman. b. England. Graduated, Princeton University; studied law in North Carolina; served at Camden and in North Carolina as colonel during Revolutionary War; served in North Carolina legislature (1786-98); important in getting Tennessee into the Union; helped establish the

University of North Carolina; elected governor of North Carolina (1798-99); negotiated with France at Convention of 1800.

DAVIES, Arthur Bowen. 1862-1928. Painter. b. New York. Well-known as a painter of the Romantic School; helped arrange the Armory Show, an important international exhibition in New York (1913), introducing the "modern" artists for the first time to the American public. His works are in many museums.

DAVIS, Charles Henry. 1807 - 1877. Naval officer. b. Boston. Served during the Civil War as commander of a gunboat (1862); defeated the Confederate's *Memphis* (1862); served with FARRAGUT at VICKSBURG; chief, Bureau of Navigation (1862); rear admiral (1863); commanded Norfolk navy yard (1870-73); superintendent Naval Observatory (1865-67; 1873-77).

DAVIS, George Breckenridge. 1847-1914. Army officer and lawyer. b. Massachusetts. Graduated, U.S.M.A., West Point (1871); wrote *Outlines of International Law* (1883); graduated, Columbia Law School (1895); judge advocate general, U.S. Army(1901); professor of Law (1895-1901) West Point; major general (1911). Author of *A Treatise in the Military Law of the United States* (1898).

DAVIS, George Whitefield. 1839-1918. Army officer. b. Connecticut. Captain, Connecticut troops throughout Civil War; brigadier general throughout Spanish-American War; military governor of PUERTO RICO(1899-1900); commander in PHILIPPINES (1901-03); major general (1903) retired; appointed by T. ROOSEVELT member of Isthmian Canal Commission; first governor of CANAL ZONE (1904-05); chairman, board of engineers designing canal; diplomatic agent, Guatemala (1913).

DAVIS, Henry Gassaway. 1823-1916. Business man and Senator. b. Maryland. Controlled lumber, coal, and railroad corporations; member, West Virginia legislature (1865); U.S. Senator (1871-83); delegate to PAN-AMERICAN CONFERENCES; chairman Pan-American Railway Committee; nominated Vice-President of the U. S. (1904) with ALTON B. PARKER as Presidential candidate; defeated.

DAVIS, Henry Winter. 1817-1865. Lawyer and political leader. b. Maryland. Graduated, Kenyon College; studied law at University of Virginia; practiced law in Alexandria, Virginia and Baltimore; member, from Maryland of U.S. House of Representatives (1855-61; 1863-65); leader of anti-secession forces in Maryland and was largely responsible for keeping Maryland in the Union; opposed LINCOLN'S RECONSTRUCTION PROGRAM; radical reconstruction program of his own, in the WADE-DAVIS BILL, was killed by Lincoln's POCKET VETO (1864); attacked the President in the Wade-Davis Manifesto (Aug. 1864); leader of his party; opposed JOHNSON and again advanced his own congressional plan of reconstruction.

DAVIS, Jefferson. 1808-1889. President of the CONFEDERATE STATES OF AMERICA. b. Kentucky. Graduated U.S.M.A.; West Point (1828); served in various frontier army posts (1828-35); resigned from the army (1835); lived as a planter in Mississippi (1835-45); member, U.S. House of Representatives (1845-46); resigned to serve in the Mexican War; served under TAYLOR at BUENA VISTA; U.S. Senator from Mississippi (1847-51); appointed by PIERCE, U.S. Secretary of War (1853-57); again U.S. Senator (1857-61); left the Senate when Mississippi seceded; chosen President of the provisional government at Montgomery (1861); elected for six years (1862-68); when the Confederacy failed to gain foreign aid or recognition, there was serious criticism of Davis; he was determined to gain independence for the Confederacy at the HAMPTON ROADS CONFERENCE not realizing its poor military condition (Feb. 3, 1865); fled from Richmond (April 3, 1865); he was captured and imprisoned at Fortress Monroe, Virginia (1865-67); never was brought to trial; released on bail (May, 1867); a *nolle prosequi* was entered by the government (December, 1868); spent the last years of his life in retirement in Biloxi, Mississippi. Author of *The Rise and Fall of the Confederacy* (1878-81).

DAVIS, John W. 1873-1955. Lawyer and political leader. b. West Virginia. Practiced law in Clarksburg; elected to U.S. House of Representatives (1911-13); U.S. Solicitor General (1913-18); Ambassador to Great Britain by WILSON (1918-21); Democratic candidate for President of the U.S. (1924) and defeated by COOLIDGE. Author of *Party Government in the United States* (1929).

DAVIS, Katherine Bement. 1860-1935. Sociologist, penologist. She was the first superintendent of the New York State Reformatory for Women (1904-14); first woman to be appointed Commissioner of Corrections for New York City (1914); chairman, Parole Commission (1915-17).

DAVIS, Norman Hezekiah. 1878-1944. Financier and diplomat. b. Tennessee. Organizer of The Trust Company of Cuba (1905-17); U.S. Treasury representative in England and France (1918); chairman, finance section, Supreme Economic Council; appointed by WILSON as Assistant Secretary of the U.S. Treasury (1919-20); Undersecretary of State (1920-21); appointed by COOLIDGE as delegate to International Economic Conference at Geneva (1927); appointed by HOOVER as delegate to GENEVA DISARMAMENT CONFERENCE (1932); appointed by F. D. ROOSEVELT head of American delegation to International Sugar Conference (1937).

DAVIS, Richard Harding. 1864-1916. War correspondent, journalist, novelist. b. Philadelphia, Pa. First big assignment covering the JOHNSTON FLOOD obtained for him a staff job with the New York *Sun* (1889); became managing editor, *Harper's Weekly* (1890); started as war correspondent during the Spanish-American War and served through six wars; author of *Gallegher and Other Stories* (1891) *Van Bibber and Others* (1892), *Ranson's Folly* (1904), *The Dictator* (1904), and other works.

Dawes Act. A law of Congress in 1887 which attempted to secure for the Indians ownership of land in severalty. It conferred CITIZENSHIP and ownership of a tract of land upon those Indians who renounced their tribal allegiance. Family heads received one hundred acres, single adults and orphans 80 acres, and each dependent child 40 acres. These allotments were to be made as the President might designate, to be held in TRUST for 25 years, at the end of which time the holder was to acquire full title with the right to sell. Upon receipt of an allotment Indians were given full personal, property, and political rights. The lands were given in trust to prevent wasteful sale. The remainder of Indian lands was to be held in trust by the federal government for the Indians with the power to open them to settlement upon satisfactory payment of them. The Act discouraged many Indians because of the long waiting period. Their RIGHT TO VOTE was oftentimes abused by political leaders. These inadequacies resulted in amending legislation in 1906 (BURKE ACT) and 1934 (WHEELER-HOWARD ACT).

DAWES, Charles Gates. 1865-1951. Lawyer, financier, and statesman. b. Ohio. Practiced law in Nebraska and Chicago; leading Republican, active in MCKINLEY movement (1896); appointed, U.S. Comptroller of the Currency (1897-1901); organized the Central Union

Trust Company, Chicago (1902), and was president (1902-21) and chairman of the board (1921-25); active in utilities in Chicago; chairman of the board of the City National Bank and Trust Company (from 1932); appointed to PERSHING's administrative staff and served as brigadier general with A.E.F. in France (1917-19); became the first director of the U.S. BUREAU OF THE BUDGET (1921); appointed by Reparations Commission to investigate German finances and their ability to meet REPARATIONS payments (1923); proposed the DAWES PLAN which was put into effect (1924); elected Vice President of the U.S. under COOLIDGE (1925-29); appointed U.S. Ambassador to Great Britain by HOOVER (1929-1932); president, RECONSTRUCTION FINANCE CORP. (1932); awarded the Nobel Peace Prize (1925); author of *A Journal of the Great War* (1921), and *A Journal of Reparations* (1939).

DAWES, Henry Laurens. 1816-1903. Political leader. b. Massachusetts. Graduated, Yale University; served in both houses of the state legislature; U.S. district attorney for western Massachusetts (1853-57); member, U.S. House of Representatives (1857-75); U.S. Senator (1875-93); known for the DAWES ACT which gave the rights of citizenship to Indians.

Dawes Plan. A plan of REPARATIONS payments recommended in 1924 by a committee headed by Charles G. Dawes. Although the committee did not establish a total payment it provided that, in 1924-25, Germany begin payment of 1,-000,000,000 gold marks to rise, in 1928-29, to 2,500,000,000. An index of industrial production was to be established as a criterion for determining the possibility of an increase in these payments. The Plan also involved arrangements for an Allied loan to stabilize German currency, and recommended the immediate evacuation of the Ruhr. With the aid of exten-sive borrowing from the United States, Germany met these reparation payments until the Plan was replaced in 1929 by the YOUNG PLAN.

DAWSON, Thomas Cleland. 1865-1912. Diplomat. b. Wisconsin. Secretary, U.S. legation at Brazil (1897-1904); minister, DOMINICAN REPUBLIC (1905-07); envoy extraordinary and minister plenipotentiary to Colombia (1907-09); head of Latin-American affairs, State Department (1909-10); negotiated the Dawson agreement with NICARAGUA.

DAY, William Rufus. 1849-1923. Jurist and statesman. b. Ohio. U.S. Secretary of State (1898); chairman, U.S. commission which negotiated peace terms with Spain (1898-99); opposed acquisition of PHILIPPINES, advocating purchase of the islands instead; judge of U.S. Court of Appeals for Ohio; appointed associate justice, U.S. Supreme Court (1903-22) by T. ROOSEVELT.

DAYE, Stephen. 1594?-1668. Printer. b. England. Settled in Massachusetts. (1638); first printer in English colonies in America; printed a broadside called *The Freeman's Oath* which was the first piece of printing in the colonies; published the *Bay Psalm Book* (1640) which was the first book printed in English in America.

D-Day. Name applied to the UNITED NATIONS invasion of German-occupied France on June 6, 1944. This marked the beginning of the last stage of World War II which was to culminate in the complete military defeat of Germany within the following year.

DEADY, Matthew Paul. 1824 - 1893. Jurist. b. Maryland. President of Oregon constitutional convention (1857); U.S. district judge (1859); important in the development of the laws of the Northwest; codified the laws of the state (1864; 1872); wrote editorials for the *Oregonian;* important influence in that part of the country.

DEAN, Bashford. 1867-1928. Zoologist. b. New York. Graduated, College of the City of New York; Ph.D. Columbia; professor of zoology (1904-27), Columbia; curator, reptiles and fishes, American Museum of Natural History (1903-10); curator, arms and armor, Metropolitan Musem of Art (1906-27). Author of BIBLIOGRAPHY OF FISHES (3 vols. 1916-23).

DEANE, Silas. 1737-1789. Lawyer and diplomat. b. Connecticut. Graduated, Yale University; active in revolutionary activities in Connecticut; member, CONTINENTAL CONGRESS (1774-76); appointed as agent to France for purpose of securing supplies and aid (1776); persuaded DEKALB, LAFAYETTE, STEUBEN, and PULASKI to help the American forces (1776-77); with B. FRANKLIN and ARTHUR LEE he negotiated treaty of alliance and commercial treaty with France (1778); called back because of accusations against him by Lee; urged reconciliation with England (1781); accused as traitor; vindicated by Congress and money paid to heirs (1842).

DEARBORN, Henry. 1751-1829. Political leader. b. New Hampshire. Studied and practiced MEDICINE; captain of militia at LEXINGTON, CONCORD, BUNKER HILL; with ARNOLD to Quebec; major general of militia (1783); U.S. marshal for Maine; member, U.S. House of Representatives (1793-97); appointed by JEFFERSON U.S. Secretary of War (1801-09); served in War of 1812 and made major general; commanded forces on Canadian border; commander at New York (1813-15); resigned commission (1815); appointed U.S. Minister to Portugal (1822-24); Ft. Dearborn, Chicago, named after him.

death penalty. The Supreme Court, on July 2, 1976 in a 7-2 decision, ruled that the death penalty in itself is not a form of cruel and unusual punishment and in certain cases it is a constitutionally acceptable form of punishment. This overturned a decision that the Court had reached in 1972 when it decided that capital punishment violated the 8th amendment ban on cruel and unusual punishment.

DEBS, Eugene Victor. 1855-1926. Socialist leader. b. Indiana. Railroad fireman (1870-74); worked in grocery store (1874-79); active in union activities and made national secretary and treasurer, Brotherhood of Locomotive Firemen (1880); editor, *Locomotive Firemen's Magazine;* as a leader in the PULLMAN STRIKE, Chicago (1894) he was arrested and sentenced for contempt of court to six months in prison; organizer of SOCIAL DEMOCRATIC PARTY (1897); nominated for the presidency of the United States by the Socialists (1900, 1904, 1908, 1912, 1920); arrested for violation of ESPIONAGE ACT (1918) and sentenced to ten years in prison; ordered released by President HARDING (Dec. 25, 1921).

Debt Funding Commission. See War Debt Commission.

debt, national. The money owed by the United States government as a result of the sale of bonds. At the beginning of the nation's history the national debt included a foreign debt and a domestic debt inherited from the government of the ARTICLES OF CONFEDERATION. These were ultimately funded on the recommendation of HAMILTON. As a result of the War of 1812, the national debt increased from $45,000,000 to $127,334,-933 in 1816. With the increasing prosperity of the post-war years, the debt fell to $37,513 in 1835. It reached its peak in 1866 when the debt stood at $2,332,-331,208, representing the costs of the Civil War. The largest increase in the national debt, up to that time, resulted from World War I when, by 1919, it had reached a total of $25,234,496,274. The prosperity period of the 1920's enabled a reduction of the debt, so that by 1930 it had declined to $15,770,000,000. The extensive government expenditures arising out of the needs of the GREAT DE-PRESSION increased the national debt to $37,000,000,000 in 1938. As a result of the costs of World War II it had attained the figure of $269,400,000,000 in 1946 from which three BUDGET surpluses in the late 1940's reduced the amount to the 1952 debt of $260,200,000,000. The estimated debt at the end of fiscal year 1963 is $309,350,000,000.

debtors. Those classes or groups in American history who consistently owed considerable sum on obligations contracted for important economic purposes. The farmers have been debtors through most of the 19th and 20th centuries. Out of this situation have arisen sharp political conflicts which have occasionally erupted into armed violence. See Shays' Rebellion and Whiskey Rebellion.

DECATUR, Stephen. 1779-1820. Naval Officer. b. Maryland. Commander of the schooner *Enterprise* (1803); famous for capture and burning of the frigate *Philadelphia* during War with Tripoli (1804); commanded *United States* and the *President* in victorious battles during War of 1812; commanded squadron which sailed to Algeria and forced terms of peace (1815); on Board of Navy Commissioners (1815-20); killed in duel by James Barron (Mar. 22, 1820).

Declaration of Independence. On June 7, 1776 RICHARD HENRY LEE of Virginia introduced in Congress three resolutions declaring that the 13 colonies were and ought to be free and independent, that Congress should engage in foreign alliances, and that a general plan of union should be adopted. Congress appointed a committee consisting of JOHN ADAMS, FRANKLIN, JEFFERSON, ROBERT R. LIVINGSTON, and ROGER SHERMAN to draft a dec-

laration of independence. On July 2 Congress voted to discuss the question of independence and two days later formally adopted the document. By August 2 the delegates of all the colonies in Congress had signed the declaration. The famous document drew freely on the work of Locke and was divided basically into three sections. The first set forth principles which were regarded as self-evident, namely that all men are endowed by nature with certain inalienable rights, that governments are established to preserve these rights, that governments derive their power from the consent of the governed, and that the governed may alter or abolish their government if it proves destructive of the ends for which it was established. The second section enumerated and denounced the acts of the English King which were deemed violations of his "compact" with the colonies. The concluding section declared that "these united colonies are, and of right ought to be, free and independent states." The final draft of the document was written by Jefferson.

Declaratory Act. An act of Parliament of 1766 reiterating the supremacy of the crown and Parliament over the colonies. It stated Parliament's power to make laws of sufficient force to bind the American colonies, and declared void all votes and resolutions of the colonies which denied the authority of Parliament and the King. The Act was passed as an accompaniment to another which repealed the STAMP ACT, and was designed to clarify the constitutional relationships of the colonies and the mother country. Instead of mollifying the colonies it only served as an additional grievance and threat to colonial autonomy.

Decoration Day. See Memorial Day.

Deerfield Massacre. An attack on February 29, 1704 on the inhabitants of Deerfield, Massachusetts by a combined force of 50 French troops and 200 Indian allies from Canada. Of the 300 inhabitants of the town 50 were killed, 137 escaped, and 111 were captured. The prisoners were taken to Canada, 17 of them dying en route from exposure or at the hands of their Indian captors.

DEERING, William. 1826-1913. Manufacturer. b. Maine. Owner of large harvesting MANUFACTURING company in Illinois; merged with International Harvester Company, Chicago (1902).

Defense Plant Corporation. An affiliated agency of the RECONSTRUCTION FINANCE CORPORATION which was established in 1942 for the purpose of making government funds available for construction and conversion of war industries. By October, 1943 the agency had lent more than $9,000,000,000 for these purposes. Sixty synthetic rubber plants and six long distance oil pipe lines were constructed. Farm implement manufacturers were converted to the production of tanks and ordnance; automobile plants were converted to the manufacture of aircraft, jeeps, and trucks, and other civilian goods industries underwent similar changes.

Defense Production Act. Also known as the Economic Controls Law. A law of Congress passed in September, 1950 which authorized the President to curb prices, wages, and consumer credit, and to increase defense production. The Act was amended on June 30, 1951 with its provisions extended to June 30, 1952. It barred price rollbacks below those existing during the January 25-February 24, 1951 level. Although President TRUMAN signed the amendment he criticized it as a measure that would stimulate increased prices and threaten the national economy. The sections he denounced were those permitting a 20 percent increase over 1947 rent levels, the easing of federal restrictions on private home financing, the extension of the credit period for instalment purchases of automobiles and household furnishings, and price increases in certain farm commodities. On June 30, 1952 Congress extended the Act until April 30, 1953. Under the provisions of the amendment federal price and wage control was continued until such time "that condition of supply, existence of below-ceiling prices, historical volatility of prices, wage pressures and wage relationships or relative importance in relation to business costs or living costs will permit, and to the extent that such action will be consistent with the avoidance of a cumulative and dangerous unstabilizing effect." Certain commodities and services such as processed fruits, vegetables, and fluid milk were exempted from price control. Professional engineers, architects, accountants, and certain other categories were exempted from wage and salary controls. Alterations were made in the authority of the WAGE STABILIZATION BOARD. See Wage Stabilization Board and Price Stabilization, Office of.

Defense Transportation, Office of. An agency established by EXECUTIVE ORDER in 1941 to "assure maximum utilization of the domestic transportation facilities of the Nation." It was authorized to grant certificates of necessity and convenience to persons seeking the use of railroad, motor, inland waterway, pipeline, air transport, and coastal and intercostal SHIPPING lines. It could discontinue TRANSPORTATION services where the traffic did not justify the use of facilities. The agency was abolished on July 1, 1949.

deficit. The net deficiency resulting from an excess of expenditures over revenues. In federal budgeting there have been approximately 60 annual deficits. Generally, federal deficits have been met by bond issues. Each annual deficit is applied to the existing NATIONAL DEBT and is ultimately financed when budget surpluses may be used to reduce the debt. Wars, depressions, and defense armaments programs have been the principal causes of deficit financing. The War of 1812 resulted in a deficit of $68,000,000. The Mexican War caused a $53,000,000 deficit. The Civil War produced a deficit of $2,619,000,000. The Spanish-American War caused a deficit of $127,000,000. World War I resulted in a deficit of $24,900,000,000. After 1931 the GREAT DEPRESSION produced an average annual deficit of approximately $3,000,000,000. World War II caused a deficit of $185,000,000,000.

DeFOREST, Lee.1873-1961. Inventor. b. Iowa. Pioneer in wireless telegraphy, sound pictures, RADIO, telephone, and TELEVISION. Patented hundreds of inventions; added third electrode to electron tube; designed and installed first high-power radio stations for the U.S. Navy; broadcast the first news by radio (1916); his sound-on-film motion pictures were shown at the Rivoli Theater, New York City (1923).

DeKOVEN, Reginald. Name in full Henry Louis Reginald. 1859-1920. Composer. b. Connecticut. Studied in Europe; organizer and conductor of the Washington Philharmonic Orchestra (1902-05); known for light operas including *Robin Hood* (1890), *The Highwayman* (1897), *Student King* (1906) and for grand operas *The Canterbury Pilgrims* (1917), *Rip Van Winkle* (1920) and many songs including *O Promise Me.*

DELANY, Martin Robinson. 1812-85. Negro leader. b. West Virginia. Studied MEDICINE at Harvard Medical School (1849); wrote important study of the problems of his people *The Condition and Elevation, Emigration and Destiny of the Colored People of the United States* (1852); became army physician with rank of major, the first Negro to hold that rank in the U.S. Army; leader of the Negroes during the Reconstruction period; he was a candidate for lieutenant-governor of South Carolina (1874).

Delaware. The 49th state in size, with an area of 2,057 square miles. Entered the Union as the first state on December 7, 1787. Dover is the capital. In 1950 Delaware's POPULATION of 318,085 made it 46th in rank. Its largest cities are Wilmington, Newark, and Dover. Delaware's important industries include CANNING, FISHING, MANUFACTURING, and AGRICULTURE. Finished products are chemicals, leather, textiles, paper, machinery, metal products, and TRANSPORTATION equipment. Crops include peaches, strawberries, apples, corn, wheat, and hay. Delaware is the greatest source of chickens in the East. Although a slave state it remained within the Union at the outbreak of the Civil War. It was discovered in 1609 by HENRY HUDSON. Its nicknames are the "Diamond State" and "Blue Hen State."

Delaware Indians. A group of three closely related tribes who lived in New Jersey, Pennsylvania, and Delaware. They originally lived in the Northwest and migrated to the East. They were friendly to the whites and successfully traded with the Dutch. They were the Indians who made the famous pact of peace with WILLIAM PENN. They were defeated by the IROQUOIS tribe and the Six Nations in a war in 1720 and were forced to move into Ohio. They sided with the French during the French and Indian Wars. When finally removed to INDIAN TERRITORY they were joined by the CHEROKEE tribe.

De La WARR, Thomas West, Baron. 1577-1618. First governor of the Virginia colony. b. England. Member of the council, VIRGINIA COMPANY OF LONDON (1609); governor and captain general,

Virginia colony (1610); arrived in Jamestown just in time to prevent the settlers from leaving the colony (1610); went to England for further aid for the colonies (1611); died on return voyage. Worked hard for the success of the colony.

delegated powers. Also known as enumerated and expressed powers. The specific powers conferred upon Congress in Article I, Section 8 of the federal Constitution. In the evolution of American CONSTITUTIONAL LAW the federal nature of the government has developed the understanding that Congress may exercise only these powers and those which are specifically delegated elsewhere in the Constitution, all others being reserved to the states by the TENTH AMENDMENT. There are 18 such powers, the last being the famous "ELASTIC CLAUSE." Among the more important of Congress' delegated powers are the following: lay and collect taxes, coin and regulate the value of money, regulate COMMERCE among the states, with foreign nations, and with the Indian tribes, declare war, establish post offices and post roads, grant PATENTS and copyrights, and dispose of the territory of the United States.

delegation of power. The legislative conferral upon a chief executive of power normally within the jurisdiction of the legislature itself. In American CONSTITUTIONAL LAW the principle has signified the requirement of adequate legislative standards and safeguards beyond which the executive may not proceed. Among the many United States Supreme Court decisions involving the doctrine of delegation of power probably the most notable is that of the SHECHTER POULTRY CORPORATION VS. UNITED STATES in which a law of Congress was invalidated because it delegated power to the President without such safeguards, and thus was a violation · of the SEPARATION OF POWERS principle.

DE LEON, Daniel. 1852-1914. Socialist leader. b. Curacao. Settled in New York City (1874); studied law at Columbia University (1876); prize lecturer at Columbia on Latin-American diplomacy (1883-89); joined KNIGHTS OF LABOR (1888); SOCIALIST LABOR PARTY (1890); candidate for governor of N.Y. (1891); edited paper the *People;* helped found the I.W.W. (1905); published many pamphlets.

De Lima vs. Bidwell. See Insular Cases.

de Lôme letter. A letter written by the Spanish minister to the United States to a friend in Cuba which referred to President MCKINLEY as "weak and a bidder for the admiration of the crowd, besides being a would-be politician who tries to leave a door open behind himself while keeping on good terms with the jingoes of his party." The letter was stolen and published on February 9, 1898. Its repercussions were instantaneous and widespread. De Lôme resigned but a strong impression was left and resentment against Spain, the incident serving as a propaganda weapon against that country leading up to the Spanish-American War.

democracy. From two Greek words, demos meaning "people" and kraetos meaning "rule". In the United States this has come to mean the right of the people to vote and to hold public office. Although not completely provided for in the original Constitution these rights have become more firmly established by amendments to that document and by the political growth of the nation. Today members of the House of Representatives, the Senate, and the ELECTORAL COLLEGE are elected by UNIVERSAL MANHOOD SUFFRAGE.

Democratic Party. The origins of the Democratic party go back to the ANTIFEDERALIST and DEMOCRATIC-REPUBLI-

CAN parties in the last two decades of the 18th century. Its support came from the farmer, city mechanic, small businessmen, and certain groups of the professional classes. The present name was adopted during the administrations of JACKSON as an abbreviation of the original Democratic-Republican party. With the exceptions of the elections of 1824, 1840, and 1848 the party was victorious from JEFFERSON's election in 1800 through the election of BUCHANAN in 1856. The party's policies in this period included opposition to central BANKING, PROTECTIVE TARIFFS, and INTERNAL IMPROVEMENTS. Its control by the southern planter group brought the adoption of a policy of expansionism which culminated in the war with Mexico. The post-Civil War era witnessed a decline in the party's power until the election of F. D. ROOSEVELT in 1932. With the exceptions of the elections of CLEVELAND in 1884 and 1892 and of WILSON in 1912 and 1916 the Democratic party lost every national election. By 1952 the party had held national power for 20 years with the exception of the loss of Congress to the REPUBLICAN PARTY in 1946. Modern support of the party has come from the farmer, labor, and the middle class. Among its outstanding leaders have been Jefferson, MADISON, MONROE, JACKSON, Cleveland, Wilson, and F. D. Roosevelt.

Democratic-Republican party. An offshoot of the former ANTI-FEDERALIST PARTY. Organized during the administration of JOHN ADAMS in opposition to the policies of the FEDERALIST PARTY. The program of the Democratic-Republican party, better known as the Republicans, expressed opposition to a strong central government, the economic policies of HAMILTON, and to the support of England during the wars of the French Revolution. The party advocated an AGRARIAN DEMOCRACY, a STRICT CONSTRUCTION OF THE CONSTITUTION, and other reforms tending to eliminate aristocratic control of government. Among its leaders were JEFFERSON, MADISON, MONROE, and FRENEAU. Also known as Jeffersonian Republicans.

Demonetization of Silver Act. The popular name for the Coinage Act of 1873 which omitted silver from the list of coins to be minted. Its omission remained for twenty years a powerful political issue in national politics, leading to the cry by silver miners and farmers of the "Crime of 1873." In the years preceding its enactment very little silver had been brought to the treasury for coinage, and there is no evidence that a conspiracy had been entered into between Congress and the hard-money East. All told barely $8,000,000 worth of silver had been brought to the treasury, and it appeared natural for Congress to demonetize the metal. For a generation to follow the miner and the easy-money farmer were to carry on the free silver campaign.

DENISON, William. 1815-1882. Civil War governor of Ohio; b. Ohio. Graduated, Miami University; admitted to the bar (1840); state senator (1848); governor of Ohio (1860-62); appointed by LINCOLN U.S. Postmaster General (1864-66).

DENVER, James William. 1817-1892. Territorial governor. b. Virginia. Graduated, Cincinnati Law School (1844); state senator of California (1852); secretary of state, California (1853); member, U.S. House of Representatives (1855-57); Commissioner of Indian Affairs (1857); appointed by BUCHANAN territorial governor of Kansas (1858); established strong and efficient government in that TERRITORY; suggested separation of territory and calling part of it COLORADO; the city of Denver is named for him; served as brigadier general of volunteers during the Civil War.

department store. As defined by the Bureau of Census it is a retail establishment with yearly sales in excess of $100,-000. Today the department store has assumed a very large proportion of retail sales through the merchandising of its commodities in departmentalized operations. Department stores first appeared in the United States in the late 1860's, the first one having been A. T. Stewart of New York, the forerunner of John Wanamaker & Company. Other large department stores are J. C. Penney Company, Allied Stores Corporation, Marshall Field & Company, Gimbel Brothers, Inc., and R. H. Macy & Company, Inc. Of these J. C. Penney Company is the largest department store chain in the nation with total sales of nearly $2 billion in 1964.
The Federated Department Stores had sales totaling about $1 billion.

DEPEW, Chauncey Mitchell. 1834-1928. Lawyer. b. New York. Graduated, Yale University (1856); member of state legislature (1862-63); secretary of state for N. Y. (1863-65); attorney for VANDERBILT RAILROADS (from 1866); attorney for NEW YORK CENTRAL RAILROAD (1875); president, of N.Y.C.R. (1885-99); U.S. Senator (1899-1911); famous as an after-dinner speaker.

desegregation. In the Brown vs. Board of Education of Topeka case, Chief Justice Warren of the Supreme Court read the unanimous opinion of the Court (1954) which declared that segregation of children in public schools solely on the basis of race, even though physical facilities and other "tangible" factors are equal, deprives such children of equal educational opportunities. Later, in 1955, the Court decreed that the implementation of this decision was to be assumed by the lower federal courts which were to supervise and enforce desegregation within a reasonable time. In Bolling vs.

Sharpe (1954) the Court also ruled, unanimously, that segregation deprives children of due process of law under the Fifth Amendment.

Desert Land Act. Passed by Congress in 1877. The Act was the first of many laws in Congress' program of stimulating the reclamation of arid lands through IRRIGATION. It provided that the federal government should sell up to a section of land (640 acres) at the prevailing price of $1.25 per acre to any person who would reclaim the land within a three year period. After the 1880's the Act was successful in inducing irrigation companies to avail themselves of its provisions. By 1890 well over three and one half million acres were being irrigated by almost 55,000 persons.

DE SOTO, Hernando. 1500?-1542. Spanish explorer in America, discoverer of the Mississippi River. b. Spain. Sent by landed in Florida (May 30, 1539); explored country discovering and crossing the Mississippi River (1541); died and buried on the banks of the river.

destroyers-for-bases deal. An agreement in September, 1940 between President F. D. ROOSEVELT and Prime Minister Churchill by which the United States gave to England fifty "overage" destroyers in exchange for niney-nine year leases on sites for eight sea and air bases in Newfoundland, British Guiana, Bermuda, the Bahamas, Jamaica, Antigua, Trinidad, and St. Lucia. England promised not to scuttle her fleet under any circumstances, as a condition of this transaction.

Detroit. Located in Michigan, it is the fifth largest city in the United States. Its 1960 POPULATION of approximately 1,-671,000 inhabits a combined land and water area of 142 square miles. It is the oldest important city west of the coastal states, having been founded by the

French in 1701. The Detroit River on which the city is located forms part of the international boundry and is the only point where Canada lies south of American TERRITORY. Detroit has been owned by the French, the British, and the Americans. It is the largest automobile manufacturing center in the world and ranks fourth in the United States as an exporting port, servicing hundreds of ships on the Great Lakes. Its other important manufactures include television equipment, aircraft parts, office machinery, and pharmaceuticals.

devaluation of the dollar. See Gold Reserve Act.

De Vinne, Theodore Low. 1828-1914. Printer. b. Connecticut. Worked in Hart's printing shop in New York City (1850-58); became a partner (1858-77) and sole owner when Hart died (1877); changed the business to De Vinne Press (1908); responsible for many great improvements in American typography. Author of *The Invention of Printing* (1876).

DEWEY, George. 1837-1917. Naval officer. b. Vermont. Graduated U.S.N.A., Annapolis (1858); served under FARRAGUT during the Civil War; commanding officer of Asiatic fleet (1898); was in Hongkong when he received news of war with Spain; sailed for Manila in the PHILIPPINES and destroyed the Spanish squadron in the BATTLE OF MANILA BAY (Aug. 13, 1898); admiral (from 1899); president, general board, U.S. Navy Dept., in Washington, D.C. (1900-17).

DEWEY, John. 1859-1952. b. Vermont. Taught at University of Minnesota (1885-89), University of Michigan (1889-94), Chicago University (1894-1904), and Columbia University (from 1904); He is a follower of WILLIAM JAMES and his influence in philosophy, psychology, and EDUCATION in the United States has been of very great importance. Author of

School and Society (1899), *Democracy and Education* (1916), *Art as Experience* (1934), *Liberalism and Social Action* (1935) and many other important books.

DEWEY, Melvil. 1851-1931. Librarian. b. New York. Chief librarian Columbia University (1889-1906); founder and director of the first school for training librarians in the United States, the New York State Library School (1889-1906); a founder of the American Library Association; founder and editor, Library Journal (1876-81); originator of the Dewey Decimal classification system for LIBRARIES; author of *Decimal Classification and Relative Index* (1876-1929).

DEWEY, Thomas Edmund. 1902-1971. Lawyer and political leader. b. Michigan. Graduated, Michigan University (1923), Columbia University LL.B., (1925); U.S. attorney, southern district of New York (1933); district attorney of New York county (1937-38); well-known for prosecution of organized CRIME in New York city; Republican candidate for governor of New York (1938); elected governor (1942); candidate for President of the United States (1944 and 1948); defeated by ROOSEVELT and TRUMAN; re-elected governor of New York (1946 and 1950).

DICKINSON, Daniel Stevens. 1800-1866. Lawyer and political leader. b. New York. State senator (1837-41); lieutenant governor (1842-44); elected U.S. Senator (1844); leading Democratic attorney-general of New York state (1861-65); U.S. attorney for southern district (1865-66).

DICKINSON, Emily Elizabeth. 1830-1886. Poet. b. Massachusetts. Lived strict, secluded Puritanical life; started writing POETRY (1861); not published during her lifetime; many volumes of poems appeared after her death. Important influence on American poetry.

177

DICKINSON, Jacob McGavock. 1851-1928. Lawyer. b. Mississippi. Graduated University of Tennessee (1871); studied law in Europe; important lawyer in Tenn.; Assistant Attorney-General of the United States (1895-97); attorney for Illinois Central Railroad(1899-1909); appointed by TAFT, U.S. Secretary of War (1909-1911).

DICKINSON, John. 1732-1808. Statesman. b. Maryland. Admitted to the bar (1757); prominent lawyer in Philadelphia; member, CONTINENTAL CONGRESS (1774-76); opposed BENJAMIN FRANKLIN and voted against the DECLARATION OF INDEPENDENCE; member Continental Congress (1776-7; 1779-80); delegate from Delaware to CONSTITUTIONAL CONVENTION (1787); helped secure adoption of the Constitution by publishing a series of letters signed "Fabius" which set forth its merits.

DICKINSON, Philemon. 1739 - 1809. Revolutionary soldier. Younger brother of JOHN DICKINSON. b. Maryland. Brigadier general of New Jersey militia (1775); major general and commander in chief (1777); stopped British retreat toward New York before BATTLE OF MONMOUTH (1778); member. of the CONTINENTAL CONGRESS (1782-83).

DICKMAN, Joseph Theodore. 1857-1927. Army officer. b. Ohio. Graduated, U.S.M.A., West Point (1881); served in Spanish-American War; during BOXER REBELLION in China; in World War I commander of the Third Division in France (to 1918); also commanded the Fourth Corps and the First Corps, taking part in the battles of ST. MIHIEL and MEUSE-ARGONNE; organized and commanded the Third Army of occupation, Germany, (1918-19); retired (1921).

Dies Committee. See Un-American Activities Committee.

DILLON, John Forrest. 1831-1914. Jurist. b. New York; professor, Columbia University Law School (1879-1882); famous as great railroad lawyer and for his treatise *Municipal Corporations* which is a standard work in the field.

Dingley Tariff Act. A high PROTECTIVE TARIFF named for Nelson Dingley of Maine, chairman of the HOUSE WAYS AND MEANS COMMITTEE. It was passed in 1897 as a result of the pressure of big business interests which had contributed millions of dollars to the Republican campaign of 1896. The Act virtually restored the high schedules of the MCKINLEY TARIFF ACT of 1890. Although somewhat lower than the latter bill it was more protective than the WILSON-GORMAN ACT of 1894 which it replaced. Wool and hides were removed from the free list but there was a total of 2,024 items in the Act. The Dingley bill remained unchanged for a dozen years until modified by the PAINE-ALDRICH ACT of 1909. The average rate was 46.49 percent.

Diplomatic Service. Located within the DEPARTMENT OF STATE it consists of the whole body of foreign deplomatic agents residing at home and in foreign capitals.

Dixon-Yates Power Project. The project took its name from Edgar H. Dixon, pres., Middle South Utilities, and Eugene A. Yates, ch., Southern Co., who were to organize the Mississippi Valley Generating Co. to produce 600,000 kw. of electrical energy for T. V. A. President Eisenhower's order (June 17, 1954) that a contract be negotiated stirred up a year-long controversey over private vs. public power. Democratic opposition to the project was intensified after the Democrats won control of the 84th Congress. Cancellation of the contract was ordered by the President after receiving assurances from Mayor Frank Tobev that Memphis was ready to build its own plant (July 11, 1955).

disarmament. The U. S. has participated in various international conferences designed to reduce the burden of armaments. The first major attempt was the WASHINGTON NAVAL CONFERENCE of 1921-22. Although the United States was never a member of the LEAGUE OF NATIONS it participated in the GENEVA CONVENTION of 1927. The United States also took part in the discussions at the LONDON CONFERENCES in 1930 and 1936. The United States was one of the major powers engaged in the disarmament discussions called by the UNITED NATIONS in Geneva, 1962.

disestablishment. See separation of church and state.

displaced persons. Persons uprooted from their homes during World War II. By the Displaced Persons Act of June 25, 1948 Congress permitted the admission of 205,000 European displaced persons, including 3,000 orphans, into the United States. On June 16, 1950 the Act was amended to allow 415,744 displaced persons to enter the United States, and eliminated certain discriminatory provisions of the earlier measure. The Displaced Persons Commission reported on January 2, 1952 that it had resettled 300,000 persons in the United States, and that 36,000 more would be admitted within two months. This number is about 30 percent of all displaced persons resettled, and is the largest taken by any nation. The total cost for resettling these people was $100,-601,000. In March, 1952 President TRUMAN called for emergency legislation to provide for the admission of 300,000 more displaced persons in addition to the 339,494 Europeans who had migrated to the United States by December 31, 1951. By the summer of 1952 the only congressional action on this proposal was a pending omnibus bill providing for the merger of the Immigration Acts of 1917 and 1924 and 200 additional laws, treaties, EXECUTIVE ORDERS, proclamations,

rules, and regulations dealing with immigration.

Distinguished Service Cross. A bronze medal in the form of a cross granted to soldiers for extraordinary heroism in war. It was instituted by Congress in 1918. The cross bears the American eagle, oak leaves, stars, and the motto "E Pluribus Unum" on a scroll. The reverse side has words "For Valor."

Distinguished · Service Medal. A bronze medal awarded by Congress since 1917 to members of the armed services for exceptionally meritorious services in war. The Army medal bears the coat of arms of the United States surrounded by a blue enamel circle carrying the epigram "For Distinguished Service." The Navy medal bears the figure of an American eagle within a band on which is written the motto "United States of America and Navy."

District of Columbia. The federal district, seat of the government of the United States. Established by grants of land to Congress by the States of Maryland and Virginia. The government thereof is established by Congress under the authority delegated by Article I, Section VIII, clause 17. Since the ratification of the twenty-third amendment (1961) the District of Columbia is entitled to choose three presidential electors.

district government. A unit of municipal government established by a state legislature for the purpose of carrying out a specific task. Many district governments are short-lived, ceasing their operations when they have completed their work. An example of this would be a sanitary district established to construct a sewage system. Typical district governments are created to administer the state's program in EDUCATION, sanitation, public roads, parks, RECREATION, and water supply. The district government consists generally of a Board of Supervisors or Trustees with limited powers over finances and personnel. There are approximately 160,-000 district governments in the United States.

division of powers. See federalism.

DIX, Dorothea Lynde. 1802-1887. Reformer and philanthropist. b. Maine. Important pioneer in the reform of prisons, almshouses, and insane asylums; superintendent of women nurses during the Civil War.

DIX, John Adams. 1798-1879. Army officer and political leader. b. New Hampshire. Served through War of 1812; secretary of state, New York (1833-39); U.S. Senator (1845-49); appointed U.S. Secretary of the Treasury by BUCHANAN (1861); commissioned major general (1863) and served during the Civil War; U.S. Minister to France (1866-69); president, Erie Railroad (1872); governor of New York (1873-75).

"Dixiecrats." See States Rights party.

"Dixie Highway." See Wilderness Road, the.

DIXON, Joseph. 1799-1869. Inventor of uses for graphite. He discovered that graphite can be used in pencils and he designed most of the machinery used in the process, developing the largest pencil MANUFACTURING plant in the world in New Jersey (1847); had a virtual MONOPOLY in making lead crucibles; invented a frictionless bearing metal and the colored-ink process by which bank notes are marked for detecting counterfeits.

DOBBS, Arthur. 1689-1765. Colonial governor of North Carolina. b. Ireland.

Owned a 400,000-acre estate in North Carolina when he became governor (1754); unpopular because of his slightly dictatorial management.

DODD, Samuel Calvin Tate. 1836-1907. Lawyer. b. Pennsylvania. Graduated, Washington and Jefferson College; studied law; important lawyer for ROCKERFELLER oil interests; started the business TRUST; planned and organized the STANDARD OIL COMPANY of New Jersey the first large HOLDING COMPANY; defended the company against anti-trust charges.

DODGE, Grenville Mellen. 1831-1916. Army officer and civil engineer. b. Massachusetts. Major general of volunteers (1864). serving at the battle of Atlanta and through the Civil War; chief engineer, UNION PACIFIC RAILROAD (1866-70); chief engineer, Texas & Pacific R.R. (1870-90) building over 9,000 miles of road throughout the Southwest; built railroad in Cuba (1899-1903). Author of *How We Built the Union Pacific Railroad.*

DODGE, Henry. 1782-1867. Frontiersman and political leader. b. Indiana. Major general in Missouri militia and served in War of 1812; served in BLACK HAWK campaigns; governor of Territory of Wisconsin (1836-41); delegate from that territory to U.S. House of Representatives (1841-45); governor (1845-48); U.S. Senator from Wisconsin (1848-57).

"Does the Constitution follow the flag?" The question raised after the Spanish-American War in an attempt to determine the constitutional status of the overseas TERRITORY acquired from Spain. The Supreme Court, in a series of test cases, was called upon to determine which constitutional rights were enjoyed by the natives of these areas. In the INSULAR CASES the court answered with a modified "yes." See Insular Cases.

DOLE, Sanford Ballard. 1844 - 1926.

Lawyer and leader in the HAWAIIAN IS-LANDS. b. Massachusetts. Graduated, Harvard University; admitted to the bar (1868); practiced, Honolulu; associate justice Hawaii supreme court (1887-93); led revolution in Hawaii for a more democratic constitution and became President of new provisional government (1893); President, Republic of Hawaii (1894-98); first governor, TERRITORY of Hawaii (1900-03); judge, U.S. district court Hawaii (1904-15); Owned vast pineapple and sugar plantations in Hawaii.

"dollar diplomacy." The name applied to the policy of employing the military and diplomatic power of the national government to protect the commercial and financial interests of American CITIZENS in overseas areas. The phase is particularly applied to the American policy in the Caribbean and Central American area during the administration of President TAFT, and was specifically supported by the President in a message to Congress on December 3, 1912. In this message Taft stated that American diplomacy "is an effort frankly directed to the increase of American trade." "Dollar diplomacy" fell into disrepute during the "good neighbor" period after 1934.

Dollar Devaluation. In December 1971 President Nixon devaluated the dollar by 8.57%. This action was preceded by the previous move in August of the same year of denying foreign central banks the right to convert dollars into gold. A second dollar evaluation was reported to the International Monetary Fund in February 1973. Dollar devaluation by the United States has as its aim the improvement of the overall United States balance of payments by making our exports cheaper and our imports more expensive.

domestic system of manufacturing. The system of MANUFACTURING in the colonies and in the United States before the INDUSTRIAL REVOLUTION. Manufacturing was conducted by a single entrepreneur in his home, utilizing his labor services and those of his family and an occasional hired workman. In the absence of machinery, small tools and lathes were employed in the production of goods for local markets. Work of this sort was generally of a handicrafts nature and frequently performed on commission.

Dominican Republic. Formerly known as Santo Domingo. An island of 19,327 square miles in the West Indies. Its 1950 POPULATION of 2,121,083 was 70 percent mulatto, 15 percent white, and 15 percent Negro. Ciudad Trujillo is the capital and principal city. AGRICULTURE is the country's leading industry. The crops are sugar, coffee, tobacco, bananas, rice, corn and sweet potatoes. CATTLE and hog raising has become important in recent years. The republic occupies the eastern two thirds of the island now called Hispaniola. It was discovered by COLUMBUS in 1492. It became independent in 1865 after having been ruled by Spain, France, and HAITI. In 1916 United States Marines occupied it to protect American lives and property. They withdrew in 1924 after the adoption of a new constitution. American economic interests have remained strong in the Dominican Republic since then.

Dominican Republic (U.S. Invasion). In April, 1965 a civil war broke out in the Dominican Republic and President Johnson, feeling that American lives might be in danger, ordered U.S. Marines to invade the country. The United Nations arranged a truce on May 21 and American troops began to withdraw on June 28, 1965. Despite statements made by Johnson in Mexico City, the use of force caused much anxiety among the Latin American countries.

181

Dominion of New England. The name applied to a consolidation in 1686 of the colonies and regions of Connecticut, County of Cornwall, King's Province, Maine, Massachusetts, New Hampshire, Plymouth, and Rhode Island. New York and New Jersey were added in 1688. The purpose of the union was to improve the defense and trade of the New England area by centralizing colonial administration into one body. Ruling power was placed into the hands of a governor and council appointed by the king. The autocratic rule of the first governor, Sir EDMUND ANDROS, was met with resistance of the colonists who sought the establishment of a representative assembly and an allievation of the tax burden. In 1689 the Puritan leaders within the Dominion forced his removal, and the effective life of the Dominion came to an end.

DONELSON, Andrew Jackson. 1799-1871. Army officer and diplomat. b. Tennessee. Nephew of ANDREW JACKSON. Aide-de-camp to Jackson during the SEMINOLE WAR; admitted to the bar (1823); secretary to Jackson (1829-37); sent to Republic of Texas to negotiate the treaty of annexation (1844-45); U.S. Minister to Prussia (1846-49); editor, *Washington Union* (1851-52); candidate for the Vice-Presidency of the United States (1856), defeated.

DONGAN, Thomas. 1634-1715. Colonial governor of New York. b. Ireland. Very able governor of New York (1682-88). Important for keeping the IROQUOIS on friendly terms with the colony.

DONIPHAN, Alexander William. 1808-1887. Lawyer and soldier. b. Kentucky. Practiced law in Missouri; member, state legislature (1836) proposed bill to segregate MORMONS; brigadier general of state militia ordered by governor to execute JOSEPH SMITH and other Mormon leaders, refused; fought in Mexican War; opposed SECESSION; was offered high command but did not fight in Civil War.

DONNELLY, Ignatius. 1831-1901. Politician and author. b. Philadelphia, Pa. Studied law; moved to Minnesota (1857); member, U.S. House of Representatives (1863-69); joined LIBERAL-REPUBLICAN PARTY; editor, *Anti-Monopolist* (1874-79), an independent weekly journal; state senator (1874-78); state house (1887-88); tried to pass many important reform bills. Author of *Atlantis* (1882), *The Age of Fire And Gravel* (1883) *The Great Cryptogram* (1888) in which he tried to prove that Francis Bacon had written the plays attributed to Shakespeare.

"Don't Give Up the Ship." The famous motto on the pennant of Commodore OLIVER H. PERRY's flagship, the *Lawrence*. During the BATTLE OF LAKE ERIE on September 10, 1813 the *Lawrence* bore the brunt of the principal British attack. After two hours of bombardment, the vessel had begun to list, compelling Perry to transfer to the *Niagara*. Here he hoisted the penant, flaunting the slogan at the enemy as an inspiration to American morale.

DORR, Rheta Childe. 1866-1948. War correspondent, author and feminist. b. Nebraska. Leader in fight for WOMEN'S SUFFRAGE; war correspondent for New York *Evening Mail* (1917-18); foreign correspondent (1920-23). Author of *What Eight Million Women Want* (1910), *Biography of Susan B. Anthony* (1928), *A Woman of Fifty* (1924) autobiography.

DORR, Thomas Wilson. 1805-1854. Lawyer and leader of DORR'S REBELLION. b. Rhode Island. Graduated, Harvard University (1823); studied and practiced law in R.I.; organizer and leader of People's Party which framed a democratic and more liberal constitution for the state that won the approval of the people; the state authorities declared it illegal and submitted their own constitution; Dorr elected governor by People's Party and there were then two governments in the state; Dorr arrested, convicted and sentenced to life imprisonment (1844); released a year later.

Dorr vs. United States. See Insular Cases.

DORSEY, George Amos. 1868-1931. Anthropologist. b. Ohio. Graduated, Ph.D. Harvard University; curator of anthropology, Field Museum of Natural History, Chicago (1898-1915); professor of anthropology, Chicago University (1905-15); specialized in the study of the American Indian; lectured at New School for Social Research, N.Y. City (from 1925). Author of *Why We Behave Like Human Beings* (1925), *The Nature of Man* (1927), and other books.

DOS PASSOS, John Roderigo. 1896-. Author. b. Chicago, Ill. Graduated, Harvard (1916); served through World War I. Well-known author of *The 42d Parallel* (1930), *Nineteen Nineteen* (1931), *The Big Money* (1936), *Number One* (1943), *Year of Decision* (1943) and other books which are realistic presentations of American life.

DOUBLEDAY, Abner. 1819-1893. Union general in Civil War. b. New York. Graduated, U.S.M.A., West Point; served under TAYLOR in Mexican War; aimed first shot fired at Confederates in the Civil War at Fort Sumter. Famous for creating and naming the game of BASEBALL at Cooperstown, N.Y. in 1839, although question has been raised of Doubleday's invention of the game.

DOUGLAS, Stephen Arnold. 1813-1861. Political leader. b. Vermont. Admitted to Illinois bar (1834); judge, Illinois supreme court (1841); member, U.S. House of Representatives (1843-47); U.S. Senator (1847-61); responsible for KANSAS-NEBRASKA BILL (1854); advocate of the doctrine of POPULAR SOVEREIGNTY; unsuccessful candidate for democratic nomination for presidency (1858); took part in a series of platform debates on the question of slavery with LINCOLN (1858); nominated for President on northern Democratic ticket (1860); defeated by Lincoln; supported Lincoln's administration.

DOUGLAS, William. 1898-. Jurist. b. Maine. Professor of Law, Yale University (1931-39); worked with the U.S. DEPARTMENT OF COMMERCE in studies of bankruptcy (1929-32); member (1934-36) and chairman (1936-39), SECURITIES AND EXCHANGE COMMISSION; appointed to United States Supreme Court by President Franklyn Delano Roosevelt (1939). He retired from the Supreme Court on November 13, 1975 because of failing health, having served longer on the nation's highest court than any other man in history.

DOUGLASS, Frederick. 1817-1895. Actual name Frederick Augustus Washington Bailey. Lecturer and writer. b. Maryland. His mother was a slave and his father a white man; escaped from SLAVERY (1838); worked in New Bedford, Massachusetts under the name of Frederick Douglass; successfully addressed a meeting of Mass. Anti-Slavery Society and was employed as a lecturer by the society (1841); wrote his autobiography *Narrative of the Life of Frederick Douglass* (1845); to escape capture as a fugitive slave he went to England and Ireland (1845-47); made enough money to buy his freedom; founded and edited (1847-60) the *North Star*, an abolitionist paper which favored legal and political methods of obtaining freedom for the slaves; recruited Negro regiments during the Civil War; invited to confer with LINCOLN; U.S. marshal for District of Columbia (1877-81); recorder of deeds, D.C. (1881-86); U.S. Minister to HAITI (1889-91).

DOW, Herbert Henry. 1866-1930. Chemist and manufacturer. b. Canada. Graduated, Case School of Applied Science as a chemical engineeer (1888); professor of chemistry and toxicology (1888); president of the Dow Chemical Company, Michigan; patented many new chemical processes and products.

DOW, Neal. 1804-1897. Temperance reformer. b. Maine. Organized Maine Temperance Union (1838); mayor of Portland (1851); drafted the "Maine Law" a PROHIBITION law, and it was passed; gained a wide reputation for administering the law in Portland; candidate for President of the United States on PROHIBITION PARTY ticket (1880) defeated.

DOWNES, John. 1784-1854. Naval officer. Served through War with Tripoli and in command of the *Epiervier* during the War of 1812; served in Sumatra.

Downes vs. Bidwell. See Insular Cases.

draft. See Selective Service Act and Selective Service and Training Acts.

draft riots. The first DRAFT riots occurred in New York City in the summer of 1863. The riots could not be put down by the local authorities, resulting in the dispatch of federal troops by President LINCOLN. The riots expressed the anger of the draftees who could not avail themselves of those provisions in the draft act which allowed persons to escape conscription by the payment of money or by obtaining substitutes to serve for them.

Drago Doctrine. Formulated by Luis Drago, foreign minister of Argentina, in 1902. The doctrine expressed the opposition of the Latin-American nations to the intervention of European nations into their internal affairs by stating that force should not be used by a nation to collect debts owed its nationals by other nations or their nationals. This new principle of international law was adopted by the HAGUE CONFERENCE in 1907.

DRAKE, Edwin Laurentine. 1819-1880. First to drill oil well. b. New York. The first man in the world to tap petroleum at its source by drilling; struck oil at 69 feet (Aug. 27, 1859) in western Pennsylvania.

"Drake's Folly." The term of ridicule applied to the drilling of the first commercial oil well in the United States. On August 28, 1859 E. L. Drake completed the work on this 69½ foot well on his farm at Titusville, Venango County, Pennsylvania. Scorned by his contemporaries because of the presumed worthlessness of the mineral, Drake nevertheless went on from the early daily production of 25 barrels to accomplish an output of more than 2,000 barrels by the end of the year. "Drake's Folly" is generally acknowledged as the beginning of the PETROLEUM INDUSTRY in the United States.

DRAPER, John William. 1811 - 1882. Scientist, philosopher and author. b. England. Came to the United States (1831) to study at the University of Pennsylvania and graduated with his M.D. (1836); helped organize New York University Medical School; president (1850-73); important for his work in the research in radiant energy, photochemistry, photography and electric TELEGRAPH. Author of *Human Physiology, Statical and Dynamical* (1856), *History of the Intellectual Development of Europe* (1863), *History of the American Civil War* (3 vols. 1867-1870), *History of the Conflict Between Religion and Science* (1874), and *Scientific Memoirs* (1873).

DRAPER, Lyman Copeland. 1815-1891. Historical researcher and collector. b. New York. Secretary and librarian of the Wisconsin Historical Society (1854-86) where he established a well-known historical library; edited first ten volumes of *Wisconsin Historical Collections;* author of *King's Mountain and Its Heroes* (1881); known for his collection of the papers of G. R. CLARK and D. BOONE.

DRAYTON, William Henry. 1742-1779. Revolutionary leader. b. South Carolina. Educated in England and in early years pro-British; member, Governor's council South Carolina (1772-75); joined colonial cause; president, provincial congress (1775); president of the COUNCIL OF SAFETY; chief justice of S.C. (1776); delegate to CONTINENTAL CONGRESS (1778-79). *Memoirs of the American Revolution* is based on his papers and edited by his son (1821).

Dred Scott vs. Sandford. Decision by the United States Supreme Court in 1857 invalidating the MISSOURI COMPROMISE ACT of 1820. This decision was the result of an obiter dictum since the fundamental issue in the case involved the CITIZENSHIP of Dred Scott, a slave who had been taken by his master into free territory from the slave state of Missouri. The case also established the principle of CITIZENSHIP that prevailed until the adoption of the 14TH AMENDMENT in 1868.

DREISER, Theodore. 1871-1945. Editor and author. b. Indiana. Editor, *Smith's Magazine* (1905-06), *Broadway Magazine* (1906-07); editor in chief for Butterick publications (1907-10); edited *American Spectator* (to 1934). Author of well-known novels *Sister Carrie* (1900), *The Financier* (1912), *The Titan* (1914), *An American Tragedy* (1925) and others which are important as the first attempts at writing books with realism and social significance in America.

DREW, Daniel. 1797-1879. Financier. b. New York. CATTLE and horse trader (1815-34); steamboat business along the Hudson River; Wall Street broker (from 1844); director, Erie Railroad (1857) and allied himself with GOULD and FISK and by clever stock manipulation in the so-called "Erie War" with VANDERBILT he was victorious; his gifts founded the Drew Theological Seminary, Madison, N.J.; after PANIC OF 1873 he was bankrupt.

DREXEL, Anthony Joseph. 1826-1893. Banker and philanthropist. b. Philadelphia, Pa. Admitted to his father's BANKING firm of Drexel & Company (1847); developed the company becoming senior partner (1885); co-owner George Childs of Philadelphia *Public Ledger* (from 1864); was very generous and gave a great deal of money to many causes; founded the Drexel Institute of Philadelphia with a gift of three million dollars.

drug abuse. Even though there has been a good deal of publicity given to the entire problem of drugs and narcotic addiction, this problem is still one of the major ones in the country. Penalties for drug dealing vary throughout the country and there has been the suggestion made that marijuana be legalized. Many of the state penalities allow a judge ample discretion in sentencing. A tangential issue is that organized crime is certainly involved in the trafficking of drugs. It is estimated that the number of opiate addicts in the country in 1970 was probably close to 200,000.

dual sovereignty. See federalism.

DUANE, James. 1733-1797. Revolutionary jurist. b. New York City. Admitted to the bar and practiced (1754); attorney-general of New York (1767); member, COMMITTEE OF CORRESPONDENCE (1774); member, CONTINENTAL CONGRESS (1774-84); helped draft the ARTICLES OF CONFEDERATION; mayor of New York City (1784-89); member, state convention that ratified the Federal Constitution; U.S. district judge (1789-94).

DUANE, James Chatham. 1824-1897.

Military engineer. b. New York. Graduated, U.S.M.A., West Point (1848); chief engineer in charge of organization for the ARMY OF THE POTOMAC under MC CLELLAN (1863); made brigadier general; served on various naval boards; chief of engineers (1886-88).

DUANE, William. 1760-1835. Journalist. b. New York. Edited Philadelphia *Aurora* with BACHE and was owner and editor after Bache's death (1798); the paper was the leading Jeffersonian paper; arrested and tried under both ALIEN and SEDITION ACTS (1799) and for inciting mobs to violence; acquitted and charged again and finally had charge dismissed when JEFFERSON became President; political power lessened when government moved to Washington; served as adjutant general during War of 1812; sold the *Aurora* (1822).

DUANE, William John. 1780-1865. Lawyer. b. Ireland. Brought to the United States by his father WILLIAM DUANE (1796); on staff of *Aurora,* Philadelphia (1798-1806); admitted to the bar (1815); important in politics of Pennsylvania; appointed U.S. Secretary of the Treasury by JACKSON (1833); because of disagreement with JACKSON over the deposit of government funds in the BANK OF THE UNITED STATES he was dismissed.

DUBINSKY, David. 1892-   . Labor leader. b. Poland. Engaged in labor organizing in Lodz and was arrested and imprisoned. Came to the United States (1911); became cutter in ladies garment INDUSTRY and member of International Ladies Garment Workers Union (1911); became leader in union locals and then Secretary-Treasurer of the union (1929-32); president of ILGWU (1932); vice-president of A.F. OF L. (1934) but left A.F. of L. to help organize the CIO (1936); was one of the founders of the AMERICAN LABOR PARTY (1936); left CIO (1938) and his union was independent until it rejoined the A.F. of L. (1945); strong supporter of President F. D. ROOSEVELT and the NEW DEAL program; bitter opponent of COMMUNISM; and, as a result, left the ALP (1944) and helped found the anti-Communist Liberal Party; one of the organizers of the AMERICANS FOR DEMOCRATIC ACTION (1947); conducted policy of "business unionism", working amicably with the ladies garment industry.

DUDLEY, Joseph. 1647-1720. Colonial governor of Massachusetts. Graduated, Harvard College (1665); fought in King Philip's war and assisted in the negotiation of the peace treaty; commissioner of UNITED COLONIES OF NEW ENGLAND (1677-81); president of the council and governor of Mass., New Hampshire and mainland of Rhode Island west of Narragansett Bay until relieved of authority by ANDROS (Dec. 1686); member of Andros's council and chief justice of superior court (1686-89); when Andros was overthrown he was tried in England and acquitted; made chief of the council of New York (1691-92); he was again made governor of Massachusetts (1702-15) and was very unpopular with the colony.

DUDLEY, Plimmon Henry. 1843-1924. Civil and metallurgical engineer. b. Ohio. Inventor of dynamometer (1874); track indicator(1880); stremmatograph(1884) etc. His designs of heavier rails and other inventions made for speedier and safer railroad TRANSPORTATION.

due process clause. The provision of the Fifth and FOURTEENTH AMENDMENTS of the federal Constitution which, respectively, prohibit the United States and the states from depriving any person of his life, liberty, or property without due process of law. Although the due process clause of the Fourteenth Amendment originated as a measure to protect the

CIVIL LIBERTIES of the freedman it has subsequently been interpreted by the United States Supreme Court as a device for the protection of the property rights of corporations. The eminent American historian CHARLES A. BEARD declared that the due process clause wrote the theory of LAISSEZ-FAIRE into the federal constitution.

DUER, William. 1747-1799. Revolutionary leader and financier. b. England. Settled in New York province (1768); delegate, provincial congress (1775); New York Constitutional Convention (1776); member COMMITTEE OF PUBLIC SAFETY; delegate, CONTINENTAL CONGRESS (1777-78); signer ARTICLES OF CONFEDERATION; appointed Assistant Secretary of the Treasury under HAMILTON (1789); helped secure Ohio land grant; very influential financier; due to speculation with his holdings and accused by the government of manipulation of funds, he was arrested for debt and imprisoned; his failure caused a financial panic (1792). He died in prison.

DUER, William Alexander. 1780-1858. Jurist and educator. b. New York. Studied law and practiced in New York City with EDWARD LIVINGSTON; went to New Orleans with LIVINGSTON; member, New York legislature (1814-20); judge, state supreme court (1822-29); president, Columbia College (1829-42).

DULANY, Daniel. 1685-1753. Lawyer and colonial leader. b. Ireland. Settled in Maryland (1703); admitted to the bar; member, Maryland legislature (1722-42); held many important posts in the colony and upheld colonial cause in a pamphlet he wrote *The Rights of the Inhabitants of Maryland to the Benefits of English Laws* (1728).

DULLES, John Foster, 1888-1959. Statesman. b. Wash. D. C. Graduated, Princeton (1908), George Washington Univ. Law School (1911). Participant in Paris Peace Conference (1919) and U. N. organizing conference, San Francisco (1945). Drafted Japanese Peace Treaty and Pacific Treaties. U. S. Ambassador-at-large (1951). Appointed Secretary of State 1953; afflicted with cancer and forced to resign in April, 1959. Died in May, 1959.

Dumbarton Oaks Conference. A meeting in 1944 at Dumbarton Oaks, a mansion near Washington, D.C., which laid down the foundations of the UNITED NATIONS. The attending nations included the United States, the Soviet Union, Great Britain, and China. The proposals therein adopted provided for the creation of an organization of nations for the maintenance of world peace. These proposals led to the calling of the United Nations organizational conference at San Francisco in April, 1945.

DUMMER, Jeremiah. 1680?-1739. Collonial agent. b. Boston. Graduated, Harvard College; practiced law 'in England; appointed colonial agent for Massachusetts(1710) and for Connecticut(1712); helped Elihu Yale in establishing a college; donated over 1,000 books to the Yale library; dismissed as agent by both colonies. Author of *Defence of the New England Charters* (1721).

DUNBAR, Paul Lawrence. 1872-1906. Poet. b. Ohio. Son of slaves. Worked as an elevator boy in Dayton, Ohio (1891-95); praised by HOWELLS for poems *Majors and Minors* (1895); gained wide recognition with *Lyrics of Lowly Life* (1896). His other works include: *Poems of Cabin and Field* (1899), *Lyrics of Love and Laughter* (1903), and the novels *The Uncalled* (1896), *The Fanatics* (1901).

DUNBAR, William. 1749-1810. Frontiersman and scientist. b. Scotland. Settled in territory that is now Mississippi; traded with Indians; built up a cotton plantation and did scientific research; sent on expedition by JEFFERSON to explore Washita and Red River country and discovered and wrote a scientific explanation of the Hot Springs of Arkansas; set up astronomical observatory with instruments from Europe; took first systematic meteorological observations in the Southwest; studied the Mississippi River and wrote on the plants, animals and Indians of that region.

DUNMORE, John Murray. Earl of. 1732-1809. Colonial governor. b. Scotland. Governor of New York (1770); governor of Virginia (1771-75); led the colonists in Indian campaign known as Lord Dunmore's War in which he defeated them and signed a TREATY with them; when the news of the fighting in New England reached Dunmore he removed the powder-stores to a British warship; the colonists threatened his life and he was forced to go aboard the ship; he ordered out the troops and declared martial law, but was defeated and forced to return to England.

DUNNE, Finley Peter. 1867-1936. Humorist. b. Chicago, Illinois. On the editorial staff of the Chicago *Evening Post* and *Times-Herald* (1892-97); editor, Chicago *Journal* (1897-1900); famous as the creator of *Mr. Dooley.* Author of *Mr. Dooley in Peace and War* (1898), *Mr. Dooley's Philosophy* and many others.

DUNNING, William Archibald. 1857-1922. Historian. b. New Jersey. Graduated, Columbia University (Ph.D. 1885); taught at Columbia (1886-1922); well-known for work in the Reconstruction period in American History; editor, *Political Science Quarterly* (1894-1903). Author of *Essays on the Civil War and Reconstruction* (1898), and *A History of Political Theories: Ancient and Mediaeval* (1902).

Du PONCEAU, Pierre Etienne. In America called Peter Stephen. 1760-1844. Lawyer, ethnologist, and author. b. France. Came to America as secretary and interpreter for Baron STEUBEN (1777); aide-de-camp to Steuben (1777-79); became an American CITIZEN (1781); secretary to ROBERT R. LIVINGSTON; admitted to the bar and practiced in Philadelphia (1785); prominent in international law; well-known for writings in history, law, and philology particularly for his studies of North American Indian languages.

DU PONT, Eleuthere Irenee. 1771-1834. Industrialist. b. Paris. Worked in powder works; took charge of his father's large publishing plant, Paris (1791-97) closed by French radicals (1799); to Wilmington, Delaware (1802-04); organized the E. I. Du Pont de Nemours & Company for the purpose of MANUFACTURING gunpowder; sold large quantities to the government in the War of 1812; sold to South American Companies, the AMERICAN FUR COMPANY and others. The Du Pont Company today is famous the world over for the manufacture of numerous products including chemicals, munitions, plastics, and synthetics such as nylon.

DU PONT, Samuel Francis. 1803-1865. Naval officer. b. New Jersey. Midshipman, U.S. Navy (1815); served through the Mexican War; member of the board organizing the Naval Academy (1850); commanded the frigate *Minnesota* on diplomatic voyage to China (1857-59); served through the Civil War; rear admiral (1862); although victorious in many battles he was defeated at Charleston, after following orders with which he did not agree, and he asked to be relieved of command.

DURANT, Thomas Clark. 1820 - 1885. Important in construction of the UNION

PACIFIC RAILROAD. b. Massachusetts. Interested in road building and secured the charter of the CREDIT MOBILIER (1863-67); became president and largest stockholder; long fight over control of line but he remained director until completion of the road (1869); finally ousted from directorate by OAKES and OLIVER AMES.

DURFEE, William Franklin. 1833-1899. Engineer. b. Massachusetts. Studied at Harvard University; at a plant in Michigan he produced the first Bessemer steel made in America; built the first laboratory for the study of steel-making processes in the United States; constructed the first successful furnaces to refine copper by use of gaseous fuel.

DURKEE, John. 1728-1782. Revolutionary soldier. b. Connecticut. Leading member of Connecticut SONS OF LIBERTY; opposed STAMP ACT and led group of men who forced stamp agent to resign; led a train load of Connecticut settlers to Wyoming Valley, Pa. (1769); established stockade called Ft. Durkee and named the city Wilkes-Barre; led settlers in land fights known as First Pennamite War; fought at BUNKER HILL during the Revolution; commanded a Connecticut regiment under WASHINGTON; wounded at MONMOUTH.

dust bowl. The term applied in the 1930's to the plains area of the Southwest and Mississippi valley. As early as the 19th century severe dust storms and droughts had been recorded. Extensive farming, "land butchery," deforestation, and soil erosion led to ever more disastrous droughts which drove the FARMER from the soil. Dust storms, five miles high, buried the land so as to destroy its fertility. Through river developments, resettlement programs, rural ELECTRIFICATION, soil erosion control, IRRIGATION programs, reforestation, and scientific pest control operations, the federal and state governments undertook to solve the problems of the dust bowl in the 1930's.

Dutch Reformed Church. See Reformed Church in America.

Dutch West India Company. A joint stock trading company chartered in 1621 with political and commercial powers to explore and settle Africa, the West Indies, Australia, and America. In 1624 the company founded a colony at Fort Orange which was merged the following year with the Manhattan settlement to form the NEW NETHERLAND colony. An appointive director and council governed the colony under the rigid instructions of the company whose principal interest was the exploitation of the colony's FUR TRADE.

DUVAL, William Pope. 1784-1854. Frontiersman, territorial governor of Florida. b. Virginia. Studied and practiced law, Kentucky; served as commander of company of volunteers in War of 1812; member, U.S. House of Representatives (1813-15); U.S. Judge of East Florida district (1821-22); appointed territorial governor of Florida (1822-34); created a good government in that territory.

DYER, Eliphalet. 1721-1807. Jurist. b. Connecticut. Graduated, Yale College; member, Governor's council (1762-84); judge, Connecticut Superior Court (1766-93); chief justice (1789-93); delegate, CONTINENTAL CONGRESS (1774-79, 1780-83); member, COMMITTEE OF SAFETY (1775); one of the organizers of the Susquehanna Company that settled the Wyoming Valley.

189

E

EADS, James Buchanan. 1820 - 1887. Engineer and inventor. b. Indiana. Inventor of the diving bell (1841); with a partner he established a salvage business, using his diving bell; by salvaging wrecks in the Mississippi River he made a great deal of money (1848-57); after a consultation with LINCOLN he agreed to supply the government with a fleet of armorplated GUNBOATS: in sixty-five days (1861), and did; designed and supervised the building of the first bridge across the Mississippi River at St. Louis (1867-74); best known for his construction of a system of jetties at the mouth of the Mississippi which kept the channel at the right depth for navigation, and free of sediment (1879); this project opened up New Orleans as a port.

EAGLETON, Thomas. Eagleton was born in St. Louis, Mo., September 4, 1929. He attended St. Louis Country Day School and then went on to Amherst College, graduating from Harvard Law School in 1950. He was elected attorney general in Missouri in 1960 and senator in 1968. He was a member of the anti-war block and sought a cease-fire in the Viet Nam conflict. He was McGovern's vice-presidential candidate in 1972 but when it was revealed that Eagleton had earlier been hospitalized for nervous exhaustion and had received electric shock treatment he resigned and was replaced by Sargent Shriver.

EAKINS, Thomas. 1844-1916. Painter. b. Philadelphia, Pa. Professor of painting at the Pennsylvania Academy of Fine Arts, Philadelphia; best known for portraits and *The Surgical Clinic of Professor Gross* which hangs at the Jefferson Medical College, Philadelphia; his other well known works which hang in various museums include *The Clinic of Professor Agnew, The Cello Player, The Chess Players,* and *Max Schmitt in a Single Scull.*

EARHART, Amelia. 1898-1937. Aviatrix. b. Kansas. First woman to fly across the ATLANTIC OCEAN in an airplane; she flew from Newfoundland to Wales (June 17, 1928); flew across the PACIFIC OCEAN alone from Honolulu to California (1935); lost (July 1937) on a flight across the Pacific; author of *20 Hrs. 40 Min.,* (1928) *Last Flight,* edited by husband G. P. Putnam (1938).

EARLY, Jubal Anderson. 1816 - 1894. Confederate general. b. Virginia. Graduated, U.S.M.A., West Point (1837); studied law and practiced in Virginia; member, Virginia convention voting against SECESSION, but later joining the Confederate army; brigadier general after BATTLE OF BULL RUN (1861); major general (1863); lieutenant general in Shenandoah Valley charge (1864); defeated by SHERIDEN; relieved of command and fled to Mexico and then to Canada (1866); returned to Virginia to practice law; never took oath of allegiance to United States after the Civil War and was a rebel to the end.

Eastern Cooperative League. See cooperative movement.

EASTMAN, George. 1854-1932. Inventor and industrialist. Invented dry-plate process for photography (1880) and established a company to manufacture them; patented flexible film (1884) and invented the Kodak camera (1888); became treasurer and general manager of Eastman Kodak Co., Rochester, N. Y.; president and then chairman of the board until his death; gave a great deal of money to various schools and welfare organizations including the University of Rochester, Eastman School of Music, M. I. T., and Tuskegee Institute.

EASTMAN, Joseph Bartlett. 1882-1944. Federal Coordinator of Railroads. b. New York. Graduated, Amherst College; member, Massachusetts Public Service Commission (1915-19); appointed by President WILSON to INTERSTATE COMMERCE COMMISSION; (from 1919) appointed by F. D. ROOSEVELT Federal COORDINATOR OF RAILROADS (1933-36); director, OFFICE OF DEFENSE TRANSPORTATION (1941-44).

EATON, Dorman Bridgman. 1823-1899. Lawyer and Civil Service Reformer. Practiced law in New York City (1850-70); interested in municipal reform; drafted Metropolitan Health Law which created a health department for the city (1866); organized the New York city fire department and the city dock department and reorganized the police department; chairman, national CIVIL SERVICE COMMISSION (1873-75); drafted the PENDLETON ACT (1883); head of Civil Service Commission (1883-86); donated funds to establish a professorship of science of government, Harvard University and municipal

government at Columbia University. Author of *The Government of Municipalities* (1899).

EATON, John Henry. 1790-1856. Lawyer and politician. Graduated, University of North Carolina; studied law; friend and supporter of A. JACKSON; married Jackson's ward; U.S. Senator (1818-29); appointed by Jackson U.S. Secretary of War (1829-31); after his marriage to PEGGY O'NEILL, an innkeeper's daughter, a social problem arose when the CABINET members' wives refused to accept Eaton's wife and he was forced to resign his cabinet post (1831) although Jackson tried to intervene in his behalf; appointed governor of Florida (1834-36); U.S. Minister to Spain (1836-40).

EATON, Theophilus. 1590-1658. Colonial administrator and founder of NEW HAVEN COLONY. b. England. One of the first patentees of the MASSACHUSETTS BAY COMPANY; with group of colonists he emigrated to Massachusetts (1637); decided to move on into Connecticut and founded the colony at New Haven (April 1638); governor until his death; with the help of JOHN DAVENPORT he established a code of laws for the colony.

EATON, William. 1764-1811. Army officer. Captain, U. S. Army (1792); U. S. consul at Tunis (1798); had extraordinary adventure in attempting to return Hamet, the exiled pasha, to throne of Tripoli; captured Derna, an important seaport and had success within his grasp when the United States concluded an unfortunate peace with Tripoli; resigned from service.

EBERLE, Edward Walter. 1864-1929. Naval officer. Graduated, U.S. Naval Academy, Annapolis (1885); lieutenant on the *Oregon* when it sailed around the Horn to battle at SANTIAGO in the Spanish-American War; chief of staff in the PHILIPPINES; commander, Atlantic Torpedo Fleet (1912); superintendent, U.S. Naval Academy (1915-19); rear admiral (1919); chief of naval operations (1923-27).

ecology. During the past decade because of the unlimited use of cars, innumerable electrical conveniences and mass production of consumer goods, the problem of environmental pollution has become more pronounced. As a result many measures to promote ecological reform requiring the expenditure of vast amounts of money to reduce the pollution of air and waterways, to improve sewage treatment and to dispose of industrial waste have been proposed. The public sees that ecological problems are more than just local. On April 22, 1970 Earth Day demonstrated to all the people of the nation the need to study man's relationship with his environment.

Economic Controls Law. See Defense Production Act.

Economic Interpretation of the Constitution. The title of a work by CHARLES A. BEARD. Upon its publication in 1913 it gained international renown for its novel concept of the economic factors which motivated the founding fathers in drawing up the United States Constitution. Beard's thesis was predicated on the argument that the businessmen and land owners, overwhelmingly represented at the CONSTITUTIONAL CONVENTION, shaped a document in terms of their economic interests. In defense of his interpretation, he pointed to the provisions protecting property rights and giving Congress the power to tax, regulate COMMERCE, coin money, and establish post offices. Beard's thesis had a profound effect upon scholarly thinking in the decades that followed and stimulated a vast amount of research in the constitutional history of the United States.

Economic Opportunities Act of 1964. Authorized yearly $1 billion for fiscal 1965. The federal government, working with state and local authorities, hopes to eliminate the causes of poverty through training programs and by direct assistance to those handicapped by substandard living conditions.

Economic Stabilization Act. Also known as the Anti-Inflation Act. A law of Congress passed in October, 1942 for the purpose of preventing INFLATION by regulating prices, wages, rents, and rationing. The President was authorized to stabilize the cost of living. Pursuant to the power conferred upon him, President F. D. ROOSEVELT issued executive orders stabilizing wages and farm prices, exending rent ceilings to the entire nation, and temporarily freezing salaries of more than $5,000 a year. He appointed former Supreme Court Justice JAMES F. BYRNES as Director of the newly established OFFICE OF ECONOMIC STABILIZATION. The powers of the OFFICE OF PRICE ADMINISTRATION were increased. It was authorized to stabilize prices, prevent speculative and unwarranted increases in prices and rents, eliminate profiteering, hoarding, and other disruptive practices resulting from scarcities of the war, assist in obtaining satisfactory production of commodities and facilities, and prevent a post war collapse of prices. The Act provided a statutory basis for the OPA's control over the rationing program which it had taken from the WAR PRODUCTION BOARD after the enactment of the EMERGENCY PRICE CONTROL ACT. It also conferred upon the NATIONAL WAR LABOR BOARD full regulatory power over wages up to $5,000 per year. See Office of Price Administration, National War Labor Board, and Emergency Price Control Act.

Economic Stabilization Administration. An agency established by EXECUTIVE ORDER under the authority of the DEFENSE PRODUCTION ACT of 1950. On January 26, 1951 the agency ordered a wage-price freeze. It established ceiling prices for all commodities and services, with specified exemptions, on the basis of prices in effect from December 19, 1950 to January 25, 1951 inclusive. WAGE STABILIZATION was defined by the Administrator as forbidding compensation beyond the rate paid on January 25th or lower than that paid from May 24 to June 24, 1950. Because of the dissatisfaction with the stabilization program, modifications were announced in April 21, 1951. A new PRICE CONTROL program based on industrial earnings was set up.

Economic Stabilization, Office of. An agency established by EXECUTIVE ORDER in 1942 to formulate an over-all policy concerning salaries, wages, prices, rents, profits, and other matters relating to economic stabilization. Its purpose was the evolution of a program designed to prevent an increase in the cost of living, the maintenance of economic stabilization, and the reduction of the cost of war. The agency did not participate directly in the economic stabilization program, leaving the daily specific stabilization tasks to the OFFICE OF PRICE ADMINISTRATION and NATIONAL WAR LABOR BOARD. It acted as an over-all policy-making administrative body governing the programs of these two agencies. In 1945 the OES was assimilated into the OFFICE OF WAR MOBILIZATION AND RECONVERSION.

economic warfare. The conduct of an economic program designed to limit the economic capacity of an active or potential enemy. Economic warfare is undertaken through the media of export embargoes, government trading, freezing of foreign assets, exchange controls and operations, international allocation of SHIPPING, control of critical materials, and re-export controls. During and after World War II the United States conducted an economic warfare program by means of LEND-LEASE, TRUMAN DOCTRINE, EUROPEAN RECOVERY PROGRAM, NORTH

ATLANTIC TREATY, and POINT FOUR PROGRAM. As part of this policy, the federal government undertook to control domestic buying and selling, develop special exchange procedures and financial operations, regulate its TRADE with neutral countries, and exercise foreign asset control.

Economic Warfare, Board of. A defense agency established by EXECUTIVE ORDER in July, 1941. Chaired by Vice-President WALLACE its membership included the Secretaries of States, War, Navy, Treasury, Commerce, and Agriculture, and the Attorney-General. The Board was authorized to plan the international aspects of the defense and, later, war programs, and the postwar economy. It advised the President on economic matters related to the national defense programs, coordinated the work of the other agencies concerned with defense, and planned transactions in foreign exchange, international investments, international SHIPPING and COMMUNICATIONS, and the acquisitions of materials from foreign countries. In 1943 it was merged with other agencies into the Foreign Economic Administration.

EDDY, Mary Baker. 1821-1910. Founder of the Christian Science Church. b. New Hampshire. As an invalid she turned to healing by faith upon which Christian Science is based; chartered the first Church of Christ, Scientist (1879); founded *The Christian Science Journal* (1883), *The Christian Science Quarterly* and *The Christian Science Monitor* (1908).

EDDY, Thomas. 1758-1827. Reformer and philanthropist. Wealthy broker and insurance man who built insane asylums and free schools. Important for his work in prison reform.

EDGERTON, Sidney. 1818-1900. First territorial governor of Montana. b. New York. Studied, Cincinnati Law School; member, U.S. House of Representatives

(1859-63); appointed by LINCOLN, first chief justice of Idaho TERRITORY (1863); successfully appealed to the government to separate the territory and form Montana (1864), becoming its first governor; resigned when JOHNSON became President, and returned to Ohio to practice law.

EDISON, Thomas Alva. 1847-1931. Inventor. b. Ohio. Worked as newsboy and TELEGRAPH operator in Port Huron, Michigan and other cities; first INVENTIONS in the field of telegraphy enabled him to make enough money to set up his own shop in Newark and later Menlo Park, N.J.; invented the carbon telephone transmitter, a vote recorder, quadruplex telegraph, electric pen, mimeograph, microphone, PHONOGRAPH, Ediphone, incandescent electric lamp, kinetoscope, Edison storage battery, and others; produced his first talking pictures (1913); worked on dynamos, a magnetic method of concentrating iron ores, and synthetic rubber; he worked on chemicals for the government during the first World War; the most prolific American inventor, he was able to patent over 1,200 inventions.

Edmunds Act. Passed by Congress in 1882. It provided for the regulation and restriction of Mormon polygamy in Utah. Under the law MORMONS, to a great degree, were excluded from local offices, and many were indicted and punished for polygamous practices.

EDMUNDS, George Franklin. 1828-1919. Lawyer and Senator; admitted to the Vermont bar (1849); U.S. Senator (1866-91); helped pass federal Electoral Commission Act (1877); wrote most of the SHERMAN ANTITRUST ACT (1890); president pro tempore of the Senate when ARTHUR became President; reform wing of the party backed him against BLAINE for presidential nomination (1884) but he was defeated. Well-known authority on CONSTITUTIONAL LAW.

Education. Private tutoring and parochial SCHOOLS were the principal sources of education in the middle colonies and the South. The clergy played a major role in colonial education throughout the colonies, particularly in the establishment of colleges. In 1642 the Massachusetts General Court directed parents to require that their children be taught to read. Every town with 50 householders or more was required to appoint a teacher of reading and writing whose wages were to be paid by the parents or town inhabitants. This was the first attempt in the English-speaking world to require communities to establish and maintain schools. Compulsory education in the rudiments was adopted in all New England colonies except Rhode Island. Except for the three R's, education for girls was virtually non-existent. Illiteracy was widespread. Clerical influence led to the founding of Harvard (1636), Yale (1701), Princeton(1746), Brown(1764), Rutgers(1766), Dartmouth(1769), William and Mary(1693), King's College (Columbia, 1754), and Pennsylvania (1749). By the opening of the 19th century elementary education had declined as a result of the breaking up of old communities and the movement of the people to the West. Public education remained chiefly in New England and, only slowly, moved westward. In these schools the semesters were brief, discipline severe, materials unsatisfactory, and the teachers untrained. Mass education was unknown. The wealthy hired private tutors or sent their children to academies or seminaries. By 1800 there were 24 colleges in the United States, small in size and limited in curriculum. Languages, theology, and mathematics constituted the principal course materials. Education for the ministry was still the fundamental objective. Harvard, however, had established a medical school in 1783, and slowly other colleges were adopting non-theological courses. Supported by con-

194

gressional sponsorship in the various land acts, townships set aside portions of the public domains in the Ohio territory for tax-supported schools. The educational ideas of JEFFERSON and others pointed the way for the American education of the future in the incorporation into the curriculum SCIENCE, history, law, politics, economics, and modern languages. In the period leading up to the Civil War the colleges introduced the study of MEDICINE, law, and science on a fairly wide basis. The Jacksonian period provided the greatest spur to universal public education that the United States had yet seen. The development of urban life, the increase in VOTING, and the rise of CRIME stimulated public expenditures for mass schooling. Although opposed by the wealthy taxpayer, private schools, and certain churches, the movement increased in scope. In New England HORACE MANN and James G. Carter spread information about this need by lectures and publications. Normal schools for the training of teachers rapidly came into being. In Connecticut and Rhode Island HENRY BARNARD aroused public interest as Mann had in Massachusetts. Educational periodicals were established in which the need was expressed by Thomas H. Gallaudet, Calvin E. Stowe, and Caleb Mills. By 1850 there were 6,000 private seminaries and academies in the United school systems at that time. In 1860 there were 252 colleges in the country, 17 of them state institutions. The MORRILL ACT of 1862 encouraged the establishment of 69 state agricultural and mechanical arts colleges. The LYCEUM became the nucleus of ADULT EDUCATION. Co-education revolved principally around the development of seminaries such as those of Emma Willard at Troy (1821) and MARY LYON at South Hadley, Massachusetts (1836). In 1834 OBERLIN became the first co-educational college, and was followed by ANTIOCH in 1853. By the end of the 19th century, women's colleges had spread in number, many being added to the great universities. The nation's educational system was still characterized by low salaries for teachers, inadequately trained teachers, and lack of facilities. Curriculum and methods improved with the return of European-trained administrators. Scholarships, especially in science, became increasingly important through the work of such institutions as the Rennsaelaer Polytechnic Institute and the Massachusetts Institute of Technology. The contributions of G. STANLEY HALL, JOHN DEWEY, WILLIAM JAMES, E. L. Thorndike, and others, in the philosophy and psychology of education in the early 20th century, brought about great strides. Education to meet contemporary needs began to include vocational training, guidance, testing, and progressive methods to meet individual requirements. The physical facilities of the schools were improved as was the training of teachers. In 1900 there were 15,500,000 pupils in the public schools. Between the Spanish-American War and the end of World War I high school attendance increased from 500,000 to 3,500,000. College attendance increased more than five times in this period. In the 20th century, the right of every child to a high school education was recognized by the American people. In the 1920's virtually half of all children of high school age were attending public and private high schools. The new concepts included the use of laboratories, gymnasiums, auditoriums, theaters, swimming pools, playgrounds, and LIBRARIES. College enrollment had risen to more than 1,000,000 by 1935 at which time it was considered that American youth had the right to college education. State universities and city colleges throughout the nation provided tax-supported higher education for those of the nation's youth who could benefit by it. Private foundations sponsored by GEORGE EASTMAN, James B. Duke, JOHN D. ROCKEFELLER, and ANDREW CARNEGIE, furthered the study of specialized subjects. In the 1930's the NATIONAL YOUTH ADMINISTRATION and WORKS PROGRESS ADMINISTRATION assisted high school and college students, as well as teachers, in public support of educational projects. By 1965 nearly 5 million students were attending institutions for higher education. High school graduates have doubled during the past fifteen years. In 1964, the federal government expended nearly three billion dollars in loans and grants to educational institutions.

Educational land grants. Originally provided for in the MORRILL LAND GRANT ACT of 1862 and supplemented by the SMITH-LEVER ACT of 1914. The original statute proposed the grant of federal lands to the states, the proceeds of which are ear-marked for agricultural and mechanical arts colleges. The work in scientific agronomy of these institutions has contributed a great deal to the improvement of AGRICULTURE.

Education, United States Office of. Established by Congress as an independent department in 1867 for the purpose of conducting research, experimentation, and publication of educational materials to be distributed to state and municipal educational institutions. The agency does not itself administer any school systems, but under the SUBSIDIES policies of Congress provides GRANTS-IN-AID to local systems. The first commissioner of the Office of Education was HENRY BARNARD. This agency is administered through the Department of Health, Education and Welfare.

EDWARDS, Jonathan. 1703-1758. Theologian, metaphysician and philosopher. b. Connecticut. Graduated Yale College (1720) when 17 years of age; well-known as preacher; led a revival (1734-35) that had far-reaching effect, known as the "Great Awakening"; became missionary to the Indians (1751) after he was dismissed by his congregation for disputing the terms of admission to membership in the church; president, College of New Jersey (now Princeton) (1757); important influence on thought of his time. Author of many theological works.

EGAN, Maurice Francis. 1852 - 1924. Writer and Diplomat. b. Philadelphia, Pa. Journalist in New York and Philadelphia; professor of English, Notre Dame University (1888-96); Catholic University Washington, D.C. (1896-1907); appointed by T. ROOSEVELT, minister to Denmark (1907); served in the same post during the TAFT and WILSON administrations; helped negotiate the purchase of the Danish West Indies (now the VIRGIN ISLANDS) (1916). Author of *Recollections of a Happy Life* (1924) and a series of Sexton Maginnis stories (1902-09).

Eighteenth Amendment. See prohibition.

eight-hour law. Is in existence throughout most of American INDUSTRY today. Struggles for the establishment of the eight-hour day continued through the last half of the nineteenth century, being highlighted by STRIKES, demonstrations, and meetings of various organizations.

EINSTEIN, Albert. 1879-1955. Physicist. b. Germany. Made the first statement on his famous theory of relativity in Switzerland (1905); came to the United States to become the head of the school of mathematics at the Institute of Advanced Study, Princeton (1933-45); naturalized American; won Nobel prize in physics (1921); developed the law of photoelectricity effect to explain the transformation of light quanta. Author *The Meaning of Relativity* (1923), *Builders of the Universe* (1932), *On the Method of Theoretical Physics* (1933) and many other works.

EISENHOWER, Dwight David. 1890-1969. Army officer. b. Texas. Graduated,

U.S.M.A., West Point (1915); member, American military mission to the PHILIPPINE ISLANDS (1935-39); brigadier general (1941); chief of war plans division, U.S.; general staff (1942); lieutenant general (1942); commander of allied forces in the NORTH AFRICA INVASION (Nov. 1942); general, supreme allied commander in North Africa (Feb. 1943) command in western Mediterranean in charge of the INVASION OF SICILY (Jul 1943) and Italy; commander-in-chief of allied forces in western Europe (from Dec. 1943); in charge of the invasion of Normandy (June 1944) and western Germany; 5 star general of the army (Dec. 1944); U.S. member of Allied Control Commission for Germany; chief of staff of U.S. Army (Nov. 1945); resigned (1948); appointed president of Columbia University (1948); appointed chief of NATO (1950); elected President of the United States (1952) defeating Adlai Stevenson. Was reelected in 1956 by a large margin over Stevenson. During his administration he urged free market system vs. wage and price controls; built up U.S. defense; promoted Polaris and other missile programs; continued foreign aid; hastened termination of Korean war; supported defense treaties with Taiwan and S.E. Asia. In retirement served as elder statesman advising the next 3 presidents. Died March 28, 1969 after 4th heart attack.

Eisenhower (Middle East Doctrine). A joint resolution of the House and Senate (1957) which authorizes the President to use armed forces to assist any nation or group of nations requesting assistance against armed aggression from any country controlled by international communism.

"elastic clause." Article I, Section 8, Clause 18 of the federal Constitution. It provides that Congress shall have all powers necessary and proper to carry into execution all other powers conferred upon it in the document. It is also known as the "implied powers clause" since Congress may assume more powers by applying it liberally to its DELEGATED POWERS. In the early history of the United States its use was strongly advocated by the FEDERALIST PARTY under Hamilton's leadership. The decisions of the United States Supreme Court under Chief Justice JOHN MARSHALL assisted in widely increasing Congress' powers by a liberal application of the "elastic clause."

Election Day. As established by Congress in 1845 it is the day when VOTING for federal officers is done in all states except Maine. It is the first Tuesday after the first Monday in November. It is recognize as a legal HOLIDAY in 35 states. State and municipal elections are also generally held on this day.

electoral college. Established in Article II of the Constitution. It consists of 531 members at the present time. Each state is entitled to a number of electors equal to its total representation in the House of Representatives and the Senate. The voters choose these electors who, on the first Monday after the second Wednesday in December following ELECTION DAY, meet at their respective state capitals and cast their BALLOTS for President and Vice-President. The American voters have never directly elected these two executive officers. The device of the electoral college has frequently produced MINORITY PRESIDENTS because of the requirement that a majority of ELECTORAL VOTES be necessary for such election. This occurred in the elections of 1824, 1860, 1876, 1888, 1912, and 1948.

Electoral Commission. Established in 1876 for the purpose of determining the validity of the challenged ELECTORAL VOTES submitted by Oregon, Florida, Louisiana, and South Carolina. These states had sent in double sets of returns, and in the absence of any constitutional or legislative provision to decide on the proper set Congress created the Commission. It consisted of five Representatives, five Senators, and five justices of the United States Supreme Court. The bipartisan Commission contained seven Democrats and seven Republicans, the fifth justice, presumably independent, to be selected by his colleagues. As it turned out this figure was a Republican, and the vote was strictly partisan, eight Republicans against seven Democrats. The result was the election of the Republican candidate RUTHERFORD B. HAYES, even though his Democratic opponent SAMUEL J. TILDEN had a majority of the popular vote. The vote of the Commission gave the twenty disputed electoral votes to Hayes making his total 185 to Tilden's 184.

electoral vote. The casting of BALLOTS by the members of the ELECTORAL COLLEGE. As provided for in Article II, Section 1 of the federal Constitution and the TWELFTH and TWENTIETH AMENDMENTS, the President and Vice-President of the United States are elected by a majority of the electoral vote.

electricity. The form of power most widely used in American INDUSTRY, comprising 80 percent of existing factory power equipment. Developed out of the experimentations of European and American scientists. This form of power is produced by the use of various fuels including gas, coal, and water. Hydro-electric power has become the single most important development in electricity in the first half of the 20th century providing two-thirds of all MANUFACTURING power. The federal government has participated widely in the development of this form of power through the establishment of important regional authorities such as the TENNESSEE VALLEY AUTHORITY, the COLUMBIAN RIVER PROJECT, and the COLORADO VALLEY PROJECT. The proposed MISSOURI VALLEY and ST. LAWRENCE RIVER PROJECTS, if enacted, will further this program.

Eleventh Amendment. Adopted in 1798. It removed from the jurisdiction of the FEDERAL COURTS any suit in law or equity against a state by CITIZENS of another state or by citizens or subjects of a foreign state.

Elgin-Marcy Treaty. See reciprocity.

ELIOT, Charles William. 1834 - 1926. Educator. b. Boston, Mass. Graduated, Harvard (1853); professor, mathematics and chemistry, Harvard (1858-63); professor of chemistry, Massachusetts Institute of Technology (1865-69); president Harvard University (1869-1909); developed the undergraduate "elective system;" organized graduate school of arts and science (1890); established the school of business administration (1908); edited the *Harvard Classics;* important for many educational reforms and is largely responsible for the growth and prominence of Harvard University.

ELIOT, John. 1604-1690. "Apostle to the Indians." b. England. Settled in Boston (1631); teacher at the church in Roxbury for 60 years; spent a great deal of time with the Indians learning their language and teaching them; his work was almost destroyed by King Philip's War. Wrote an Indian translation of the Bible which was the first Bible printed in North America (1654).

Elizabethan Poor Laws. See home relief.

Elkins Act. An amendment of 1903 to the INTERSTATE COMMERCE ACT of 1887. It increased the Commission's power by authorizing it to outlaw REBATES. It declared that the published freight rates of the RAILROADS constituted a standard of lawfulness, and substituted civil for criminal penalties for violation of former statutes. Under the provisions of this act the Attorney-General instituted proceedings against the Chicago and Alton Railroad, the Burlington Railroad, and the packing combine of Swift, Armour, Cudahy, and Morris. The Act was weak and was later supplemented by the HEPBURN ACT, MANN-ELKINS ACT, ESCH-CUMMINS ACT, and EMERGENCY RAILROAD ACT of 1933.

ELKINS, Stephen Benton. 1841-1911. Lawyer, industrialist and statesman. Graduated, Missouri State University (1860); served in Union army in Civil War; admitted to the bar and practiced in New Mexico (1864); served as attorney-general of the territory and as U.S. District Attorney; member, U.S. House of Representatives (1872-77); moved to Elkins, West Virginia, which he founded (1890); appointed U.S. Secretary of War by HARRISON (1891-93); U.S. Senator (from W. Va., 1895-1911); author of ELKINS ACT and co-author of MANN-ELKINS ACT.

ELLERY, William. 1727-1820. Revolutionary political leader. b. Rhode Island. Member, CONTINENTAL CONGRESS (1776-81, 1783-85); signer of the DECLARATION OF INDEPENDENCE; chief justice, Rhode Island (1785).

ELLIS, George Washington. 1875-1919. Lawyer and sociologist. Prominent Negro; appointed secretary of the legation at LIBERIA by T. ROOSEVELT (1902-10); assistant corporation counsel, Chicago (1917). Author of *Negro Culture in West Africa* (1914) and *Negro Achievements in Social Progress* (1915).

ELLSBERG, Daniel. Daniel Ellsberg was a defense department employee who helped to compile a report on Viet Nam policy. He supplied parts of this report to the newspapers in the hope that the publication of this material would bring about a speedy conclusion of the Viet Nam War. When in June 1971 he was indicted on charges of violating the Espionage Act Ellsberg and his co-defendant, Daniel Russo, Jr., claimed that the documents supplied to the press were of historical interest only and did not present any threat to national security. The case against them was dismissed in May 1973 before the ac-

tual conclusion of the trial. It was shown that the CIA had supplied agents who burglarized the office of Ellsberg's psychologist in the hope that they would be able to find evidence which could be used against him.

ELLSWORTH, Henry Leavitt. 1791-1858. Agriculturist. b. Connecticut. Graduated, Yale (1810); first United States commissioner of patents (1835-45); called the "father of the DEPARTMENT OF AGRICULTURE" because he was influential in securing the first government appropriation for such a department.

ELLSWORTH, Lincoln. 1880-1951. Polar explorer. b. Chicago, Illinois. Led geological expedition to Andes Mountains (1924); went with Amundsen from Spitsbergen to Alaska in seaplane (1925); transarctic submarine expedition with Wilkins (1931); 2300-mile airplane flight across Antarctic (Nov. 1935) claiming the new land for the United States. Author of *Beyond Horizons* (1938) and with Amundsen wrote *First Crossing of the Polar Sea* (1927).

ELLSWORTH, Oliver. 1745-1807. Jurist and statesman. b. Connecticut. Graduated, Princeton; delegate, CONTINENTAL CONGRESS (1777-84); member, Connecticut delegation to CONSTITUTIONAL CONVENTION (1787); important role in CONNECTICUT COMPROMISE; first to use term "United States" in reference to the new government; U.S. Senator (1789-96); chairman, committee responsible for federal judiciary organization bill; chief justice of the United States (1796-99); a commissioner to France to negotiate with Napoleon on American SHIPPING rights (1800).

ELY, Richard Theodore. 1854 - 1943. Economist. First head of the political economy department at Johns Hopkins University (1881-92); professor, University of Wisconsin (1892-1925); Northwestern University (1925-33); very important and influential teacher of such men as WOODROW WILSON, NEWTON D. BAKER and others; influenced the LA-FOLLETTE progressive movement; leader and secretary of the American Economic Association (1885); author of many books on economics.

Emancipation Proclamation. Issued by President LINCOLN on September 23, 1862 as a war measure designed to gain world public support of the Union cause. It provided that all slaves would be declared free in those states still in rebellion against the United States on January 1, 1863. Under these provisions slaves were freed only in those states which, after that date, came under the military control of Union armies. The Proclamation did not apply to the BOR-DER STATES of Delaware, Kentucky, Maryland, and Missouri, nor to that part of the Confederacy already occupied by Northern troops such as Tennessee and parts of Virginia and Louisiana. Several states availed themselves of the opportunity to adopt ABOLITION measures in 1864 and 1865. It should be clear from the above that the document did not abolish SLAVERY as is commonly believed. Abolition did not occur until the adoption of the 13TH AMENDMENT in 1865.

Embargo Act. Passed by Congress in 1807 because of the failure of the NON-INTERCOURSE ACT. It prohibited American vessels from sailing to foreign ports and allowed coastal trade only upon the posting of bonds by ship owners equal to twice the value of the cargo and contingent upon that cargo being shipped to the TERRITORY of the United States. The Embargo Act failed of its purpose in bringing England to terms. Instead it succeeded in virtually destroying American COMMERCE. Exports dropped from $108,343,000 in 1807 to $22,431,000 in 1808 while imports declined from $138,-500,000 to $56,990,000 in that same period. New England docks were closed down and her seamen and SHIPPING workers unemployed. Port areas were deserted. It has been estimated that during the embargo 55,000 sailors and 100,000 laborers were thrown out of work, and $12,500,000 in net earnings lost to the shippers. Customs revenues fell from $16,000,000 to virtually nothing. Because of its failure the Act was repealed in 1809 and replaced by the NON-IMPORTATION ACT.

Emergency Banking Act. Passed by Congress in 1933. The Act was prepared for the purpose of reopening the nation's banks which had been closed on March 5th in the "BANK HOLIDAY." The Act conferred upon the President emergency powers to regulate transactions in credit, CURRENCY, and foreign exchange. The Secretary of the Treasury was authorized to call in all gold and gold certificates and the Comptroller to appoint conservators for national banks in difficulty or needing reorganization. The FEDERAL RESERVE SYSTEM was empowered to license the reopening of banks and to strengthen their position by authorizing the RECONSTRUCTION FINANCE CORPORATION to purchase or receive as collateral for loans the banks' preferred stock. Under these regulations the "bank holiday" came to an end on March 13th after an eight day period.

Emergency Detention Act. See McCarren-Wood Act.

Emergency Fleet Corporation. See Ship Purchase Act.

Emergency Management, Office of. A defense agency set up in the Executive Office on May 25, 1940 to have general oversight over the national defense program. The President's special assistant in national defense matters was attached to the agency to advise him on developments. Into the Office of Emergency Management were placed the NATIONAL WAR LABOR BOARD, OFFICE OF PRICE ADMINISTRATION, WAR PRODUCTION BOARD, and other defense and war agencies.

Emergency Price Control Act. A law of Congress passed in January, 1942 for the purpose of combatting INFLATION in the war period. It reorganized the OFFICE OF PRICE ADMINISTRATION, making it an independent agency under the supervision of a single administrator, and set up an emergency court of appeals to pass on challenged decisions. It strengthened the responsibility of the OPA by extending its price-fixing control over rents, general commodity prices, and farm products. The Act stipulated that price regulations should be issued only after consultation with the industries affected, and that a statement be made explaining the basis of the ceilings to be applied. The Act said nothing about rationing, a control which was not legislatively vested in the OPA until the ANTI-INFLATION ACT OF 1942. See Office of Price Administration and Economic Stabilization Act.

Emergency Quota Act. See Quota Act of 1921.

Emergency Railroad Transportation Act of 1933. See Coordinator of Railroads.

EMERSON, Ralph Waldo. 1803-1882. Essayist and poet. b. Boston, Massachusetts. Graduated, Harvard (1821); studied at Divinity School, Cambridge, and was licensed to preach (1826); minister, Second Church of Boston, Unitarian (1829-32); resigned; went to Europe and met Wordsworth, Coleridge and Carlyle; lived in Concord, Massachusetts (from 1834); formed a circle of friends including THOREAU, HAWTHORNE and others; first published piece of writing was *Nature* (1836) which gave the essence of TRANSCENDENTAL philosophy and the importance of the freedom of the individual; gave famous address at Harvard graduation, *The American Scholar* (1837); two volumes of essays (1841, 1844) made him famous; lectured widely in United States and in England (1847); made anti-slavery speeches. Author of *Poems* (1847), *English Traits* (1856), *Society and Solitude* (1870) and many other works. Well-known and an important influence on American thought and writing.

eminent domain. The power of a government to take private property for public purposes. This power is considered an attribute of sovereignty and is deemed justifiable when necessary for the proper performance of governmental functions. The power may be properly delegated to the subdivisions of the government, to public utilities, and even to businesses not affected with a public interest when the seizure is considered essential for public use. The only limitations on eminent domain are that the property must be taken for a public use and that a fair compensation must be paid for it. The FIFTH and FOURTEENTH AMENDMENTS of the United States Constitution establish the right and the limitations of eminent domain.

Empire State Building. The tallest structure in the world. It is located on Fifth Avenue between 33rd and 34th Streets in New York City. Its original height of 1250 feet was augmented in 1950 by the addition of a 222 foot television tower. It was completed on May 1, 1931 from plans drawn by Shreve, Lamb and Harmon. It is located on the site of the original Waldorf-Astoria Hotel. There are 102 stories, 69 elevators, and two basements. Its capacity is 25,000 tenants. Its famous observation stations are located on the 86th and 102nd floors. The building is administered by a corporation whose first president was ALFRED E. SMITH, former governor of New York. Among its directors have been Pierre S. DuPont, August Heckscher, John J. Raskob, and Louis G. Kaufmann. The original structure contained a mooring mast for dirigibles that was never used.

Employers Liability Laws. See Workmen's Compensation Laws.

Employment Act of 1946. Also known as Full Employment Act. A federal law designed to investigate employment conditions in the United States with the view of utilizing the resources of the national government in coping with a major economic DEPRESSION resulting in mass unemployment. The act created a three man Council of Economic Advisors within the Executive Office of the President and a Joint Committee on the Economic Report within Congress. The Council is required to investigate and report annually through the President on employment conditions in the nation. The Joint Committee analyzes the data contained therein and initiates legislation on the basis of the President's recommendations. The first report was made on December 18, 1946 and contained a summary of the philosophy behind the act, a discussion of the importance of full employment, and the perspective in the nation for continued production and jobs.

employment bureau. Private and public agencies established for the purpose of seeking employment for applicants. The private agencies have been created under the authority of the SOCIAL SECURITY ACT of 1935. They are known as state employment services which, as a condition for receiving federal grants under the statute, must furnish free employment service to the unemployed.

energy crisis. In the 1970's, the United States, with only 6% of the world's population, had been consuming more than 40% of the world's energy output. Oil and natural gas produced over 75% of the energy consumed in the U.S. in 1972. Estimates predicted that, unless changes were made, there would be a critical energy shortage in the U.S. by 1980. By then consumption of energy would have been increased by 55% over 1972. Statistics showed that the use of energy in the U.S. was doubling every 16 years. The energy crisis made energy conservation programs essential and accelerated research for alternate sources of energy.

Energy, Department of. The first new department of the Federal Government since the Department of Transportation was created in 1966, was proposed by President James Carter and was approved by the Congress in August, 1977. The Department of Energy assumed some of the authority and personnel of the Department of the Interior, the Department of Housing and Urban Development, and other agencies. It combined existing units into one department with about 20,000 employees and a budget of over 10 billion dollars for the year that started October 1, 1977. The new department replaced the Federal Energy Administration and the Energy Research and Development Administration. The Federal Power Commission was replaced by another new body, the Federal Energy Regulatory Commission. The former CIA Director and Secretary of Defense, James Schlesinger, was appointed the first Secretary of the Department of Energy.

"enumerated articles." See Navigation Acts.

entail. A principle of law originating in medieval England which provided that, upon the death of the owner of an estate, the entire estate was bequeathed to his heir, and subsequently to an established line of legatees. The system was imported into the British colonies where it was met with great resistance because of its undemocratic features. Virginia took the lead in abolishing entail in 1776, and was followed by other states. By the Jeffersonian period entail had disappeared from the United States.

E Pluribus Unum. A Latin motto appearing on the Great Seal of the United States and on much of its CURRENCY. It means "one from many." It was first suggested by BENJAMIN FRANKLIN, JOHN ADAMS, and THOMAS JEFFERSON on August 10, 1776 after their appointment by the CONTINENTAL CONGRESS as a committee to choose a design. Its first appearance was on a coin in New Jersey in 1786. The motto occurs in a Latin poem, *Moretum,* attributed to Virgil.

EPSTEIN, Jacob. 1880-1959. Sculptor. b. New York City. Went to London (1905) and has done most of his work there; well-known for his symbolic figures that decorate the British Medical Association Building, London (1907-08); tomb of Oscar Wilde (1909); life-size bronze Christ (about 1920); *American Soldier* at the Metropolitan Museum, N. Y.; and his bronze portraits of famous people.

Equal Employment Opportunity Commission. In 1972 the EEOC was created by an act of Congress. The function of the commission is to enforce remedies in cases where women and minorities are discriminated against in employment practices.

Equal Rights Amendment. (E.R.A.) As early as 1923 the National Women's Party first proposed this amendment to the U.S. Constitution which gained congressional approval in 1972. The text of the amendment is: Section 1: Equality of rights under the law shall not be denied or abridged by the United States or by any State on ac-

count of sex. Section 2: The Congress shall have the power to enforce, by appropriate legislation, the provisions of this article. Section 3: This amendment shall take effect two years after the date of ratification by at least thirty-eight states. The deadline for ratification being March 22, 1979. By November 1977 thirty-five states had ratified, three of which recinded later.

Equal Rights party. A minor POLITICAL PARTY organized in 1884 for the purpose of securing WOMEN'S SUFFRAGE. Its program also included demands for the repression of the liquor traffic, CIVIL SERVICE REFORM, an anti-war policy, and uniform legislation concerning marriage, divorce, and property. Until its dissolution in 1888 its presidential candidate was Belva A. Lockwood, a leader in the suffragette, peace, and TEMPERANCE MOVEMENTS of the time. Its maximum vote at any time, was 2,000. It is also another name for the LOCOFOCOS.

"Era of Good Feeling." Name given to the period from the end of the War of 1812 to the mid-1820's. The name indicates the absence of political conflict, manifested by the disappearance of the FEDERALIST PARTY and the supremacy of the DEMOCRATIC-REPUBLICAN PARTY. This period reflects the development of NATIONALISM as demonstrated by the virtually unanimous election of President MONROE in 1816, and by the chartering of the second BANK OF THE UNITED STATES, the passage of the first PROTECTIVE TARIFF in 1816, the development of HENRY CLAY'S AMERICAN SYSTEM, the growth of a native American LITERATURE, and the beginnings of the INDUSTRIAL REVOLUTION. The phrase came from a paragraph in the July 12, 1817 issue of the *Columbian Centinel.*

Erdman Act. A law of Congress passed in 1898 to provide machinery for the mediation and ARBITRATION of labor disputes on RAILROADS. It declared the "YEL-

LOW DOG CONTRACT" illegal, and forbade discriminatory discharges. It was unsuccessful in accomplishing its purpose and was supplemented by additional legislation in the form of the NEWLANDS ACT, ESCH-CUMMINS ACT, WATSON-PARKER ACT, and CROSSER-DILL ACT.

ERICSON, Leif. 999?-? Norse discoverer of land in America. Born probably in Iceland; on trip to Greenland where he lived he was blown off his course and discovered new lands which he called Vinland. There has been much speculation as to the locality of Vinland. Some scholars believing it to be Newfoundland, others Nova Scotia, and others the coast of New England.

ERICSSON, John. 1803-1889. Engineer and Inventor. b. Sweden. Came to the United States (1839); built the *U.S.S. Princeton* (1844) which was the first warship with a screw propeller; designer and builder of the ironclad *Monitor* (launched 1862); responsible for many innovations in naval engineering; worked on the designs for heavy guns and mountings and steam machinery; interested in solar physics.

Erie Canal. Completed and opened to traffic in 1825 by Governor DEWITT CLINTON of New York State after seven years of construction and an expenditure of $8,000,000. It provided an all-water passage from Europe to the Mid-West by linking the Mississippi River with the ATLANTIC OCEAN through the tributaries of the former, the GREAT LAKES, and the Hudson River. The canal was part of the wide-spread program of CANAL and TURNPIKE construction in the period following the War of 1812, all designed to reduce passage time and expense in the shipment of goods from the industrial East to the western markets. The canal ran 363 miles from Albany to Buffalo.

"escalator clause." See London Naval Conference of 1930.

Esch-Cummins Act. See Railroad Transportation Act.

Espionage Act. Passed by Congress in 1917. It prescribed a $10,000 fine and 20 years' imprisonment for interfering with the recruiting of troops or the disclosure of information dealing with national defense. Additional penalties were included for the refusal to perform military duty, the advocacy to TREASON, or the resistance to laws. The Act was attacked as unconstitutional, but its enforcement nevertheless resulted in many arrests and imprisonments. Notable among these were the arrests of EUGENE V. DEBS, former SOCIALIST PARTY candidate for the presidency who was sentenced to a ten-year jail term and Socialist Congressman VICTOR BERGER who was sentenced to 20 years. The latter's paper, the *Milwaukee Leader*, was denied the use of the mails. Some 450 conscientious objectors were sentenced to military prisons.

Essex Case. A diplomatic incident between the United States and Great Britain developing out of the British capture of the American merchant ship, the *Essex*. Taken as a prize, the British High Court of Admiralty ruled in 1804 that the *Essex* had engaged in a continuous voyage between a French colony and France, at that time an enemy of Britain. As such she had come under the prohibition of the RULE OF WAR OF 1756 which forbade neutrals from engaging in the COLONIAL TRADE in war time if such prohibition existed in peace time. In this instance the American vessel had attempted to carry on TRADE and evade the British rule by interrupting the voyage at an American port prior to continuing to France. The ruling increased Anglo-American tension and contributed to the diplomatic ill-feeling between the two nations that led to the War of 1812.

Essex Junto. A conspiracy of Federalist

politicians of Massachusetts who in 1802 and 1803 planned to detach New England from the Union and to establish a New England Confederacy "exempt from the corrupt and corrupting influence and oppression of the aristocratic democrats of the South." These conservative-minded politicians, including high churchmen, sought to enlist the political support of ALEXANDER HAMILTON in their intrigue but were rejected. The leaders of the conspiracy were TIMOTHY PICKERING and AARON BURR. As late as 1814 the plotters, led by Pickering, planned the detachment of the New England states and called the HARTFORD CONVENTION in December of that year for that purpose. The victory of the JEFFERSONIAN REPUBLICANS politically and their military success in the War of 1812 brought an end to the intrigues.

established church. A church which is officially declared to be the state church, being politically affiliated with a state and enjoying certain privileges and exemptions not possessed by other churches. Normally the established church is financially supported by the state, pays no taxes, has its expenses defrayed by the state, and exercises political influence in government. In the American colonies only four had no established church. The Congregational Church was the state church of Connecticut, Massachusetts, and New Hampshire, while the Anglican church was established in Georgia, Maryland, certain areas of New York, North Carolina, South Carolina, and Virginia. DISESTABLISHMENT of state churches occurred during and after the American Revolution and was virtually completed by the end of the Jacksonian period. Also known as State church.

European Defense Community. A six nation army established by a TREATY signed on May 27, 1952 by the GERMAN FEDERAL REPUBLIC, France, Italy, Belgium, the Netherlands and Luxembourg. It provided for the establishment of a European Army consisting of 300,000 troops of the signatories, under a unified command. The treaty consisted of 131 clauses and 9 protocols in which the member nations pledged a peace-time army for 50 years wearing a single style uniform, receiving the same pay, and commanded by a mixed general staff. It also set up a ruling council, an advisory chamber, a court of ARBITRATION, and an operative commission. France was pledged to contribute 14 divisions, Germany and Italy 12 divisions each, and the other three powers a joint total of 5 divisions. Accompanying the treaty was a declaration by the United States and Great Britain to defend the six nations and the Allied-held sectors of Berlin against attack "from any quarter" and to guarantee the integrity and unity of the new army. The pledge was designed specifically to assure France against a German withdrawal. Three of the protocols set out the close relationship of the European Army with the NORTH ATLANTIC TREATY Organization and included a mutual aid pact with England and a formula for financing the army. The link with NATO established the first alliance in history to include the United States, Britain, France, and Germany. The treaty was subject to the ratifications of the member nations.

European Recovery Program. See Marshall Plan.

EUSTIS, William. 1753-1825. Politician. b. Massachusetts. Army surgeon during the Revolutionary War; practicing surgeon in Boston; served in state legislature as an ANTI-FEDERALIST(1788); appointed by JEFFERSON, U.S. Secretary of War (1809-13); resigned after criticism of his department during MADISON's administration; Madison appointed him U.S. Minister to Holland (1814-18) member, U.S. House of Representatives (1820-23); governor of Massachusetts (1823-25).

EVANS, George Henry. 1805-1856. Editor and agrarian reformer. b. England.

Came to the United States (1820); editor, *Workingman's Advocate* (1829-37, 1844-47) which was the first important labor paper in the country; important in the development of labor and social reform.

EVANS, Oliver. 1755-1819. Inventor. b. Delaware. Invented many important machines used in milling and constructed the first high-pressure steam engine in the United States (before 1802); built the first steam river dredge to be used in this country. Often called the "Watt of America."

EVARTS, William Maxwell. 1818-1901. Lawyer and statesman. b. Boston, Mass. Partner of Charles E. Butler in law practice handling many famous cases (1843); secretary of Union defense committee during the Civil War; sent on diplomatic missions to England (1863-64); chief counsel for President JOHNSON in IMPEACHMENT proceedings and it was through his efforts that Johnson was acquitted (1868); appointed by Johnson U.S. Attorney-General (1868-69); counsel for the United States at the Geneva court of arbitration (1871-72); appointed U.S. Secretary of State by HAYES (1877-81); president of New York Bar Association which led fight against "TWEED RING"; U.S. Senator (1885-91) from New York.

EVERETT, Edward. 1794-1865. Unitarian clergyman, orator and statesman. b. Massachusetts. Graduated, Harvard and Boston Divinity School; Ph. D. in Europe (1817); member, U.S. House of Representatives (1825-35); governor of Massachusetts (1836-40); appointed U.S. Minister to Great Britain by TYLER (1841-45); president, Harvard University (1846-49); resigned; appointed by FILLMORE U.S. Secretary of State (1852-53) during which four month period he aided in explaining the MONROE DOCTRINE in a letter about Cuba; U.S. Senator (1853-54); made many famous speeches in Union cause the best known at Gettysburg the same day as LINCOLN's.

"ever normal granary." The term applied to the program designed to assist the FARMER in marketing his crops at satisfactory prices and in adjusting his production demand. The plan was originally embodied in the AGRICULTURAL ADJUSTMENT ACT OF 1938 and modified by AMENDMENTS in 1941, 1944, 1948, and 1950. As finally constituted, it provided for the establishment of national acreage allotments for staple commodities such as cotton, corn, rice, tobacco, and WHEAT based on prior computations of probable consumer demands. When supplies of these commodities are excessive marketing quotas are established by two-thirds REFERENDUM votes of the farmers. The COMMODITY CREDIT CORPORATION purchases excess production which would otherwise cause a price decline, in order to prevent farm prices from falling below established minima. By 1965 the DEPARTMENT OF AGRICULTURE was required by law to support the prices of most major agricultural commodities.

EWELL, Benjamin Stoddert. 1810-1894. Educator. b. District of Columbia. Graduated, U.S.M.A., West Point and taught there; president of William and Mary College (1854); served in the Confederate army; after the war he re-opened William and Mary College and worked hard to re-establish the institution; he personally maintained the college until the state took over the expense, and he became president emeritus (1888).

EWELL, Richard Stoddert. 1817-1872. Confederate general. b. District of Columbia. Graduated U.S.M.A., West Point (1840); joined the Confederate army (1861); brigadier general (June, 1861); major general (1863); took part in major campaigns including Gettysburg, and the defense of Richmond.

excess profits tax. A graduated tax on the profits of business in excess of a fixed percentage of capital investment or of average profits over a given period. It was first levied by Congress in 1916 to siphon off high war profits and to produce greater revenues for the defense preparation of the time. This law was repealed in 1921 but revived in 1933 and has since remained in force, with AMENDMENTS. The importance of this tax is demonstrated by the increasing revenues it has produced. The first excess profits tax produced an annual yield of approximately $2,000,000,000. In 1934 the yield had dropped to $2,600,000, rising in 1938 to $37,000,000. At the outbreak of World War II the yield was once more $2,000,000,000, rising to over $16,000,-000,000 by 1945. The law of 1951 yielded nearly $1,000,000,000.

excise taxes. Taxes on goods sold within the nation. These are enacted by Congress as one of its DELEGATED POWERS authorized in Article I Section 8 of the Constitution. All excises must be uniform throughout the United States. These taxes are part of the general revenue program of the Congress, but in time of war are widely expanded to include new items and the rates are simultaneously increased. Some common items taxed are furs, jewelry, automobiles, photographic materials, and cosmetics.

executive agreement. An agreement between the President of the United States and his opposite number in other governments. Such an agreement is undertaken under his authority as commander-in-chief of the armed forces or by virtue of his executive power under the Constitution. Occasionally Congress confers specific power upon the President to make such agreements. An executive agreement does not require Senate ratification as does a treaty and, therefore, is frequently negotiated to avoid a probable defeat in that body. The diplomatic and political areas in which an executive agreement is concluded are generally of lesser importance than those which would require a treaty. Examples of executive agreements have been the NAVAL-BASES-FOR-DESTROYERS TRADE of 1939, the ATLANTIC CHARTER, and the World War II agreements negotiated at TEHERAN, YALTA, and POTSDAM.

Executive departments. Provided for in Article II of the Constitution. The heads of these departments are known collectively as the CABINET, a name which does not itself appear in the Constitution. The first Congress of 1789 established four such executive departments: the DEPARTMENTS OF STATE, TREASURY, WAR, and the office of the ATTORNEY GENERAL. In 1956 there were ten such departments including the Department of Defense which merged the War and Navy departments in 1947 and the Department of Health, Education, and Welfare created in 1953.

executive order. A rule issued by the President or an administrative agency under his jurisdiction to interpret or carry out a provision of a law or TREATY. His power to issue executive orders lies in his constitutional mandate to see to it that the laws of the United States be faithfully executed. Congress frequently delegates this power to him by specific legislative provision.

executive powers. The powers of the President of the United States derived from the constitutional requirement that he take care that the laws be faithfully executed. Among these powers are the enforcement of the laws. the commissioning of officers of the United States, the filling of vacancies in the Senate, and the command of the armed forces of the United States. The President also exercises an enormous range of legislative, judicial, diplomatic, ceremonial, political, and administrative powers.

executive privilege. Since the Constitution of the United States provides for a separation of powers, the President is independent of the other branches of government. There have been occasions when the President as Chief Executive of the nation has exercised the doctrine of executive privilege which holds that the internal, advisory communications of the executive branch are protected from public disclosure. The aim of this is to preserve the President's recommendations and opinions. The whole matter of executive privilege was discussed widely during the Watergate affair when President Nixon became the first chief executive to be served with subpoenas by Congress. However, the term itself was first used by President Eisenhower.

executive reorganization. Various programs designed to reorganize the executive branch of government in the interests of greater economy and efficiency. In the 1930's and 1940's congressional plans for executive reorganization resulted principally from the recommendations of the three-man Committee on Administrative Management (Brownlow Committee) and the Commission on Reorganization of the Executive Branch of the Federal Government (HOOVER COMMISSION). Established in 1936, the Brownlow Committee issued its report in 1939 recommending increased staff assistance, the creation of an Executive Office, reorganization of the BUREAU OF THE BUDGET, and coordination of public works, welfare, lending, and social security activities. By the Reorganization Act of 1939 Congress conferred power upon the President to establish the offices of six executive assistants, the Executive Office, the FEDERAL SECURITY AGENCY, FEDERAL WORKS AGENCY, and FEDERAL LOAN AGENCY. He was forbidden to reorganize the INTERSTATE COMMERCE COMMISSION, FEDERAL TRADE COMMISSION, FEDERAL COMMUNICATIONS COMMISSION, and 12 other independent agencies as well as the EXECUTIVE DEPARTMENTS. The President effected these reorganizations and also shifted bureaus and independent establishments allowed by the law. See Hoover Commission.

expatriation. Refers to the voluntary surrender of CITIZENSHIP by natural-born or naturalized citizens. This right was explicitly recognized by congressional enactments in 1868, 1907, and 1940. Under this legislation citizens lose their citizenship by being naturalized in, or taking an oath of allegiance to, any foreign state. Congress' power to legislate in this field is set forth in Article I, Section VIII of the Constitution.

explorations. The search for colonies by European nations in the 16th-18th centuries. Stimulated by the mercantile theory with its emphasis on the possession of gold, Portugal began colonial explorations in 1450 under the sponsorship of Prince Henry the Navigator. By the end of the 15th century Spain, England, France, Sweden, and Holland had sent out hundreds of exploring expeditions to search for new lands. Although the basic motivation was economic, explorations were also carried on to provide relief for surplus population, seek raw materials, find markets for the sale of goods, elevate the prestige of the mother country, enable the religious conversion of non-Christian populations, and establish military and naval bases. The results of these explorations included the discovery and settlement of North and South America, the increased wealth of the European nations, and a series of colonial wars that lasted until 1815.

Export Import Bank. A government corporation chartered by Congress in 1934. It was established by EXECUTIVE ORDER in that year but was provided a statutory basis and additional powers by Congress in 1945. Its functions are to make loans directly or guarantee private loans in periods when private credit resources are scarce. The purpose of such loans is to finance COMMERCE between the United States and its possessions as well as with foreign nations. Its authorized capital is $1,000,000,000. Whether in the form of guarantees or loans its obligations may equal three and one half times its capitalization. In the fiscal year 1962 its expenditures were $101,086,544.

Exposition and Protest. Also called the South Carolina Exposition. A document drafted by JOHN C. CALHOUN and approved by the legislature of South Carolina in 1828. Expressing the opposition of the South to the high TARIFF OF 1828 it developed a new theory of STATES RIGHTS doctrine, embodying, with modifications, the principles of NULLIFICATION which had previously been expressed in the VIRGINIA AND KENTUCKY RESOLUTIONS and in the Resolutions of the HARTFORD CONVENTION. Calhoun departed from these states rights theories by holding that a state convention was the immediate organ of state sovereignty and possessed the full power to determine the constitutionality of an act of Congress. Since the Union was a compact of sovereign states, these states were indivisible and indestructible entities which had the authority to nullify a congressional law considered unconstitutional and detrimental to their sovereign interests. Calhoun held that the Constitution and the nation had been created by these states and that each of them could take its own sovereign action. Only by an AMENDMENT to the Constitution, adopted in the usual manner, could an individual state action be limited. This doctrine of nullification was further developed by Calhoun in the ORDINANCE OF NULLIFICATION in 1832 and was seized upon by the pro-slave and other states rights groups in the era leading up to the Civil War.

ex post facto law. A law declaring an act illegal which was legal when committed. Article I, Section 9 of the Constitution of the United States forbids Congress to enact *ex post facto* laws.

Article I, Section 10 of the Constitution places the same prohibition upon the state legislatures.

extradition, international. The exchange of escaped prisoners or persons on bail from one nation to another. These exchanges are accomplished by treaties between the nations. The United States has negotiated many such treaties with other nations. As is typical under international law the governments of these nations interpret the treaties, thus frequently refusing demand for extradition. An outstanding recent illustration of extradition TREATY interpretation was the refusal of Great Britain to return Gerhart Eisler, who had jumped bail in 1949 and fled the jurisdiction of the United States.

extradition, interstate. Also known as rendition. It refers to the exchange of escaped prisoners from one state to another. As provided for in Article IV of the Constitution, known as the "INTERSTATE COMITY" clause, the governor of a state "shall" return such prisoners to the state whence they have fled, upon the demand of the governor of such state. The Supreme Court has defined the term "shall" to mean "ought" rather than "must," thus justifying the many refusals for rendition which have taken place.

extraterritoriality. Special rights conferred by a government upon the CITIZENS and subjects of other nations who are resident within the conferring nation. Such rights have in the past included exemption from laws of the conferring nation and/or privileges pertaining to railroad concessions, harbor rights, and TAXATION. These rights are frequently embodied in TREATY agreements such as the Treaty of 1830 by which Turkey exempted resident American citizens from Moslem law. Thereafter the United States participated in many extraterritorial agreements in-

209

cluding treaties with China in 1844, Japan in 1858, Britain and China in 1863 in establishing the Foreign Settlement in Shanghai, and other treaties with Siam, Egypt, and Persia. The United States has oftentimes assumed the lead in abrogating extraterritorial treaties, recognizing the undemocratic nature of the system. Thus extraterritoriality was abolished by treaty in Japan in 1894 and in China in 1943.

EZEKIEL, Mordecai Joseph Brill. 1899-. Agricultural Economist. b. Virginia. Expert in statistical analysis for the DEPARTMENT OF AGRICULTURE (1922-30); assistant chief economist to FEDERAL FARM BOARD (1930-33); economic adviser to the Secretary of Agriculture (1933); largely responsible for the plan of the FARM CREDIT ADMINISTRATION and other agricultural legislation during F. D. ROOSEVELT's administration.

F

factory system. The system of MANUFAC-TURING introduced by the INDUSTRIAL REVOLUTION after the War of 1812. The new method of manufacturing transferred production from the home to a plant which housed large and complicated machinery which could be operated only by skilled and semi-skilled workers. Although the first factory was established by Samuel Slater in Pawtucket, Rhode Island in 1791, factories were not built in large numbers until the industrialization program after the war.

FAIRBANKS, Charles Warren. 1852-1918. Lawyer and political leader. b. Ohio. Graduated, Ohio Wesleyan University; studied law and practiced in Indianapolis; successful railroad lawyer; controlled Republican organization of his state and was elected U.S. Senator from Indiana (1897-1905); Vice-President of the United States (1905-09) serving with President T. ROOSEVELT.

FAIRBANKS, Erastus. 1792-1864. Manufacturer and political leader. b. Massachusetts. Established in Vermont (1815) with his brother, Thaddeus, a large manufacturing plant for stoves, plows, scales and other implements; governor of Vermont (1852-53, 1860-61); considered an able war governor.

FAIRBANKS, Thaddeus. 1796-1886. Inventor. b. Massachusetts. Famous for his invention of the platform scale which he patented (1831); with brother ERASTUS FAIRBANKS he developed a large MANU-FACTURING plant in Vermont.

Fair Deal. The nickname applied to the administration of President HARRY S. TRUMAN after his election in 1948. The phrase was coined by the President in a speech during his campaign for election that year. It is presumed to represent an extension of the NEW DEAL program, and embodies principles seeking the enactment of legislation on CIVIL RIGHTS, HOUSING, fair employment practices, opposition to LYNCHING, opposition to POLL TAX requirements for the suffrage, EDU-CATION appropriations, and improvement in existing public welfare laws. By 1952 the bulk of these principles had not been enacted.

Fair Employment Practices Committee. Sometimes called the Committee on Fair Employment Practice. Popularly known as the FEPC. An agency established by EXECUTIVE ORDER in 1942 which required that all federal agencies include in their contracts with private employers a provision obligating such employers not to discriminate against persons of any race, color, creed, or nationality in matters of employment. The Committee was empowered to accept and investigate all complaints of discrimination, take appropriate steps to eliminate such discrimination, and make recommendations to

211

the President concerning discrimination in war industry.

FAIRFAX, Thomas Fairfax, Baron. 1693-1781. Colonial proprietor. Owned Northern Neck of Virginia; famous as patron of GEORGE WASHINGTON who surveyed his lands and managed his estate; went unharmed during the Revolution but his property was confiscated.

FAIRFIELD, John. 1797-1847. Political leader. b. Maine. Practiced law; member, U.S. House of Representatives (1835-9); governor of Maine (1839-1844); his actions were responsible for the AROOSTOOK WAR and the WEBSTER-ASHBURTON TREATY; U.S. Senator (1844-47) supported POLK and a policy of expansion.

Fair Labor Standards Act. Also known as the Wages and Hours Law. An Act of Congress passed on June 25, 1938 for the purpose of eliminating "labor conditions detrimental to the maintenance of the minimum standards of living necessary for health, efficiency and well-being of workers." It established maximum working hours of 44 a week for the first year, 42 for the second, and 40 thereafter. Minimum wages of 25 cents an hour were established for the first year, 30 cents for the second, and 40 cents over a period of the next six years. The Act covered all workers engaged in INTERSTATE COMMERCE or the production of goods for interstate commerce. It established the Wages and Hour Division in the DEPARTMENT OF LABOR. Committees were to be appointed by the Administrator of the Division to determine proper rates between 30 and 40 cents for given industries. Premium pay for time and one half was required for labor in excess of the specified maximum hours. The Act also included provision which prohibited child labor in all industries engaged in producing goods in interstate commerce and placed a limitation on the labor of boys and girls between 16 and 18 years of age in hazardous occupations. On October 26, 1949 the Act was amended to increase minimum wages from 40 to 75 cents an hour. In later amendments the minimum was increased to $1.25 (1964).

Fair Oaks, Battle of. Fought on May 31, 1862, GENERAL MC CLELLAN's advance on Richmond was held up by a CONFEDERATE ARMY commanded by General JOHNSTON. The wounding of Johnston led to the transfer of the command to LEE who launched a major attack upon McClellan's forces compelling the latter to retreat. The result was that the Union armies did not succeed in capturing Richmond until the last weeks of the war in April, 1865.

fair trade laws. State laws passed under the authorization of the MILLER-TYDINGS ACT for the purpose of allowing manufacturers of branded products to establish minimum resale prices. The laws required all retailers to sell at the established price when the manufacturer contracted with one of them to do so. By 1952, 45 states had passed fair trade laws over the opposition of consumer groups who charged that they increased the cost of living and tended toward MONOPOLY control. Congress never passed a federal resale maintenance law despite efforts since 1914 to accomplish this. The first such law was passed in California in 1931. In May, 1951 the United States Supreme Court ruled that the Miller-Tydings Act did not give manufacturers the right to enforce retail price maintenance on non-contracting retailers in products moving in INTERSTATE COMMERCE. By eliminating this "non-signer clause" fair trade laws were left toothless. Immediately afterwards four bills were introduced in the House of Representatives as amendments to the Miller-Tydings Act for the purpose of restoring this type of state legislation in interstate commerce. On July 14, 1952 Congress passed the McGuire Fair Trade Bill, restoring the right of manufacturers and wholesalers to set the price of brandname products at retail, even though the goods are shipped across state lines. The act restored the "non-signer" clause in state fair-trade laws, which provide that a manufacturer must sign with only one retailer in a state to fix the price for the entire state. All states except Vermont, Missouri, and Texas, and the District of Columbia had fair trade laws in 1952.

FALL, Albert Bacon. 1861-1944. Lawyer and politician. b. Kentucky. Rancher and lawyer in New Mexico (from 1889); U.S. Senator from New Mexico (1912-21); appointed by HARDING U.S. Secretary of the Interior (1921-23); resigned because of involvement in the TEAPOT DOME scandal; convicted of charges and imprisoned (1931-32).

Fallen Timbers, Battle of. A struggle in the NORTHWEST TERRITORY between an Indian confederacy and American troops under General ANTHONY WAYNE in August, 1794. Between 1500 and 2000 Indians were defeated by the American infantry in a 40 minute battle ending in the destruction of their villages and fields by General Wayne. The battlefield was located near Toledo, Ohio. The battle ended a 20 year period of warfare during which the Indians had taken the initiative.

fall line. The line joining the coastal waters of the colonies with the foothill region of the western PIEDMONT. The name is derived from the waterfalls in the rivers flowing eastward from the hills. The fall line is generally considered the first FRONTIER, and exercised considerable influence upon the colonial WESTWARD MOVEMENT. The first migration westward to the foothills of the Piedmont area occurred in the early 18th century as a result of the influx of European immigrants to the coastal TIDEWATER REGION. The changes in the American character, personality, and modes of life

customarily attributed to frontier existence were first manifested in the movement along the fall line. Important cities that grew up along it were Columbia, Fredericksburg, Petersburg, and Richmond.

Faneuil Hall. Called the "Cradle of Liberty" because of the radical speeches made there by patriot leaders during the American Revolution. It was built in 1740 as a market house and a place of public meeting, and donated as a gift to the city of Boston by Peter Faneuil, a merchant. The Hall was used as a theater during the British occupation in 1775.

FANNIN, James Walker. 1804?-1836. Texas Colonel. b. Georgia. Famous agitator for Texas independence; led force against SANTA ANNA; captured and shot with all his men.

FANNING, Edmund. 1769-1841. Trader and explorer. b. Connecticut. Traded in seal skins (1797-98); discovered Fanning Island in the South Pacific which led to later EXPLORATIONS into this region. Author of *Voyages around the World* (1833).

Far Eastern Commission. See Japan, Occupation of.

FARGO, William George. 1818-1881. Express owner. b. New York. Messenger and part owner of Wells & Co., first express company west of Buffalo (1844); later merged with other company to form the AMERICAN EXPRESS COMPANY (1850). Wells was president and Fargo secretary of the new company; became president of the company after a still larger merger (1868-81). WELLS, FARGO & CO. which handled express business between New York and California (1852) was also organized by Fargo.

FARLEY, James Aloysius. 1888-1976. Politician. b. New York. In the building supply business; president, General Building Supply Company (1929-33); chairman,

213

N.Y. State Athletic Commission (1925-33); chairman, Democratic National Committee (1932-40); managed ROOSEVELT's campaign for presidential nomination (1932); appointed by Roosevelt U.S. Postmaster General (1933-40); famous for his memory of names and faces. Author of *Behind the Ballots* (1938), and *Jim Farley's Story* (1948), autobiographies.

"farm bloc." A group of Senators and Representatives, who, in the 1920's sponsored bills to aid AGRICULTURE to relieve farm distress in the mid-West. The most important bill the farm bloc supported was the MC NARY-HAUGEN BILL.

Farm Credit Administration. An agency established by EXECUTIVE ORDER and given statutory basis by the Farm Credit Act of March 27, 1933. It was established as a division of the DEPARTMENT OF AGRICULTURE to supervise the work of the FEDERAL LAND BANKS, INTERMEDIATE CREDIT BANKS, Production Credit Corporations, and Regional Banks for Cooperatives. The nation was divided into twelve districts under the supervision of the officers of these constituent agencies. The governor of the FARM CREDIT ADMINISTRATION was authorized to aid loan operations, charter and administer cooperative lending associations, provide production credit, refinance farm mortgages, and repurchase property that had been foreclosed.

Farm Loan Act. A law of Congress passed on July 17, 1916 for the purpose of improving farm credit facilities. The act established a FEDERAL FARM LOAN BOARD to supervise 12 central farm land banks authorized to furnish funds for the support of mortgage loans made by FARM LOAN ASSOCIATIONS. Farm loan associations were defined as cooperative organizations of 10 or more owners or prospective owners of farm land. The law permitted these associations to as-

sume stock memberships in a land bank and make mortgage loans to their members not in excess of 50 percent of land value and 20 percent of the value of improvements. Mortgages were endorsed to the land bank as collateral for funds furnished by it. The bank raised its funds by selling bonds to the public. By the beginning of the NEW DEAL administration more than $1,128,500,000 in loans had been made. The Federal Farm Loan Board was abolished in 1933 and its activities assumed by the FARM CREDIT ADMINISTRATION.

Farm Loan Associations. See Federal Farm Loan Act.

Farm Mortgage Foreclosure Act. A law of Congress passed in 1934 for the purpose of providing mortgage relief for FARMERS. The law extended the authority of the Land Bank Commissioner by permitting him to grant loans to farmers to assist them to redeem farm properties which they had owned prior to foreclosure.

FARMER, Moses Gerrish. 1820-1893. Inventor. b. New Hampshire. Installed in Boston the first electric fire-alarm service which he had worked out with W. F. CHANNING (1851); invented new method of using duplex and quadruplex telegraphy (1855); patented self-exciting dynamo (1866); developed incandescent electric light and produced electric lamps (1858); worked with U.S. Torpedo Station in working out improvements in torpedo warfare (1872-81).

Farmer-Labor Party. A THIRD PARTY MOVEMENT with a semi-Socialist program. It was organized during World War I and polled over 260,000 votes for Arthur Christensen for President in 1920. In 1924 it did not run independent candidates, supporting the LA FOLLETTE PROGRESSIVE PARTY.

farmers. At the beginning of the nation's

history farmers comprised the bulk of the POPULATION, representing approximately 90 percent of the people. As a result of the increasing URBANIZATION of the United States the proportion of farmers to the total population had fallen in 1952 to approximately 20 percent.

Farmers' Alliances. Organizations of FARMERS for the purpose of advancing their interests. The first Farmers' Alliance was founded in New York in 1873, but developed its greatest strength in the Northwest where the Northwestern Farmers' Alliance was founded in 1880 by Milton George. Many local organizations were established in the Dakotas, Kansas, Michigan, Minnesota, Nebraska, Ohio, and Wisconsin. Their fundamental objective was the elimination of RAILROAD ABUSES, but they simultaneously embarked upon a program calling for INFLATION of the CURRENCY through GREENBACKS, regulation of PUBLIC UTILITIES, extended educational opportunities, consumers' cooperatives, direct election of United States Senators, government relief for mortgage indebtedness, and anti-trust legislation. In the 1870's the order spread into Texas in the form of the National Farmers' Alliance and Industrial Union, slowly absorbing local farmers' organizations in that state and in Arkansas and Louisiana. By 1890 this organization had spread widely into the other southern states and was in turn absorbed into the Southern Farmers' Alliance whose principal method was political activity. Attempts to unite the Northwestern and Southern Alliances were unsuccessful and by 1892 both organizations had declined in importance, their membership gravitating to the POPULIST PARTY and the Democratic party. At their height the Farmers' Alliances are estimated to have had a total membership well over 700,000.

farmers' organizations. Associations of FARMERS developing in the mid-West

after the Civil War. They came into being to lobby for state legislation aimed at curbing RAILROAD ABUSES, and to seek debt relief through an INFLATION of the CURRENCY. Other aspects of their program included the creation of cooperatives, educational activities, direct election of Senators, and other social programs. Among these organizations were the National Grange, the FARMER'S ALLIANCES, and various political parties such as the GREENBACK PARTY, GREENBACK-LABOR PARTY, and POPULIST PARTY. In the 20th century FARM organizations have adopted similar but more extensive demands and have operated through national LOBBIES like the AMERICAN FARM BUREAU FEDERATION and the NATIONAL FARMERS UNION.

Farm Mortgage Refinancing Act. A law of Congress passed on January 31, 1934 to aid FARMERS in refinancing their debts by guaranteeing, as to principal and interest, federal bonds exchanged for farm loan bonds. The law established the Federal Farm Mortgage Corporation to administer this program under the direction of the FARM CREDIT ADMINISTRATION. The Corporation was authorized to issue up to $2,000,000,000 worth of bonds guaranteed by the federal government. These could be either invested directly in mortgage loans or exchanged for the bonds of the land banks. The agency succeeded in bringing about a reduction in farm debt and interest rates. The total mortgage debt on farm lands was reduced, in the period from April 1, 1930 to January 1, 1935, from $9,214,000,000 to $7,645,000,000. The Federal Farm Mortgage Corporation was transferred to the DEPARTMENT OF AGRICULTURE in 1939.

farm problem. The collective term describing the economic problems of the FARMER in the late 19th and in the 20th centuries. RAILROAD ABUSES compelled the American farmer to seek regulatory legislation. Overproduction, as a result of the introduction of FARM machinery, brought a decline of prices of crops. Between 1885 and 1890 the value of the corn crop shrank over $70,000,000, and the farmer was burning it for fuel. Wheat fell from one dollar per bushel in 1865 to 50 cents in 1900. Mortgage indebtedness increased rapidly. In 1900 40 percent of all farms were mortgaged. Between 1930 and 1937, 25 percent of the nation's farms were lost on foreclosure. Whereas in 1880 farmers owned 62 percent of the equity in the country's farms they owned only 39 percent by 1935. Banks and INSURANCE COMPANIES came into possession of formerly independent farms and merged them into giant "factories in the field." In the 1930's one insurance company had merged 7,000 farms and was employing 350 agricultural experts to supervise them. The problem of national income for the farmers of the United States became pressing during the GREAT DEPRESSION. The net income of agricultural workers was $200 a year, and of sharecroppers $122 per year. In 1936 only eight percent of the nation's farmers had an annual income over $2,500. Farm income, which had been $16,000,000,000 in 1919, fell to $5,000,-000,000 in 1932. An upswing resulting from the prosperity of the World War II period increased this figure to $23,000,-000,000 in 1945. Meanwhile the dispossession of the farmers produced a new class of tenant farmers, sharecroppers, and migratory agricultural workers. Whereas 25 percent of the nation's farmers were tenants in 1880, this figure had risen to 42 percent by 1930. In 1948 the number had declined to 30 percent. Other problems which beset the farmer included soil exhaustion, erosion, floods, insect pests, high priced manufactured goods, dust storms, droughts, and depressed living conditions. The 1940's witnessed an upswing in farm income as a result of federal and state aid and the general prosperity accompanying the war and defense periods.

farms. In 1964, about 13,000,000 people lived on less than 4,000,000 farms in the United States. This represented a decrease of nearly 2,500,000 people since 1960. Gross farm income, including government subsidies, amounted to nearly $42,000,000,000. Farm expenses totaled $29.3 million.

Farm Relief and Inflation Act. See Agricultural Adjustment Act of 1933.

Farm Security Administration. An agency established in the DEPARTMENT OF AGRICULTURE in 1937 to take over the functions of the RESETTLEMENT ADMINISTRATION. It was authorized to provide funds for the rehabilitation of FARMERS, acquaint them with approved principles of farm management and budgeting, purchase sub-marginal lands to employ needy tenant farmers and farm laborers on reforestation and road building projects, and extend loans to farmers for the purchase of FARMS. The agency maintains 2,000 county offices which are supervised by district, state, and regional offices. It also operates camps for migratory farm laborers, most of them in the Pacific Coast region. By 1944 it had lent almost $250,000,000 to more than 35,000 farm families for the purchase of farms. An additional 1,000,000 low-income farm familes have been aided by loans to purchase farm and home supplies.

FARNHAM, Russell. 1784-1832. Furtrader. b. Massachusetts. Member JOHN J. ASTOR's expedition to the Columbia River valley to set up FUR TRADE in that area (1811); sailed around Cape Horn in the *Tonquin* described by W. IRVING in his *Astoria*; carried money from Asia across Europe to the United States crossing Siberia and Russia on foot (1814-16);

his life was exciting and dangerous; worked with AMERICAN FUR COMPANY in upper Mississippi Valley.

FARRAGUT, David Glasgow. 1801-1870. Admiral. b. Tennessee. Commanded sloop *Saratoga* during MEXICAN WAR; ordered to take New Orleans and put in command of West Gulf Blockading Squadron (1861); bombarded Fort Jackson (April, 1862); captured New Orleans and spent rest of year in Gulf Coast on BLOCKADE duty; hero of Mobile Bay by dispersing the Confederate fleet and capturing Forts Gaines and Morgan (1864); vice-admiral (December, 1864) admiral (July, 1866) being the first to hold those ranks created especially for him by Congress; there are many statues of Farragut by famous sculptors and he is a member of the HALL OF FAME.

FARRAGUT, George. 1755-1817. Naval and army officer. b. Minorca. Father of DAVID G. FARRAGUT. Offered services and a cargo of arms and ammunitions to Charleston, South Carolina (1776); served in defense of Savannah and the siege of Charleston; served as captain of cavalry under MARION; major of MILITIA against the CHEROKEES in the southwest territory; appointed by JEFFERSON commander of GUNBOAT and served at battle of New Orleans (1807).

FARRAND, Livingston. 1867-1939. Educator. b. New Jersey. Graduated Princeton (1888), College of Physicians and Surgeon N.Y. (1891); M.D.; teacher of psychology, Columbia University (1893-1903); professor of anthropology, Columbia (1903-14); wrote on Indians of the Northwest after expeditions to that area; executive secretary of the National Association for the Study and Prevention of Tuberculosis (1905-14); president, University of Colorado (1914-19); president, Cornell University (1921-37).

FASSETT, Jacob Sloan. 1853-1924. Lawyer and political leader. Editor, Elmira *Advertiser* (1879-96); state senator (1883-1891); chairman, committee investigated

New York city government (1889); member, U.S. House of Representatives (1904-11); prominent Republican known as a fighter for reform causes.

"father of the Constitution." See Madison, James.

FAULKNER, Charles James. 1806-1884. Statesman. b. West Virginia. Practiced law; member, U.S. House of Representatives (1851-59, 1875-77); U.S. Minister to France (1859-61); served with "STONEWALL" JACKSON as assistant adjutant general during CIVIL WAR; influential in West Virginia CONSTITUTIONAL CONVENTION (1872.)

FAULKNER, William (also spelled Falkner). 1897-1962. Novelist. b. Mississippi. Studied at the University of Mississippi (1919-21); served with British Royal Air Force (1918); well-known for novels of the South; winner of the NOBEL PRIZE for literature (1950). Author of *The Marble Faun* (1924), *As I Lay Dying* (1930), *Sanctuary* (1936), *The Wild Palms* (1939), *Requiem for a Nun* (1951), and many others.

FAUQUIER, Francis. 1704?-1768. Colonial administrator. Lieutenant governor of the Virginia colony (1758); told Pitt of trend toward independence in colonies; dissolved House when it passed its resolution against the STAMP ACT.

"favorite son." The term applied to an outstanding political leader of a state party organization who is submitted for the presidential nomination by his party's delegates at the NATIONAL CONVENTION. These politicians have won local, and occasionally national, prominence as governors of their states, or United States Senators, or as federal CABINET members. Their support at the convention is generally limited to their states. As "presidential possibilities" their principal hope is to swing their support behind a national favorite for later PATRONAGE appointments.

Federal Alcohol Control Board. An agency created by Congress in 1933 for the purpose of regulating the branding and grading of alcoholic beverages and for dealing generally with the new problems of interstate liquor traffic raised by the 21ST AMENDMENT. It was authorized to establish proper business standards for the liquor industry and foster fair trade methods in the interests of producers and consumers. The agency was later reorganized into the Federal Alcohol Administration.

Federal Barge Lines. See Inland Waterways Corporation.

Federal Bureau of Investigation. A bureau within the DEPARTMENT OF JUSTICE, established by Attorney General Charles J. Bonaparte in 1908. Since 1924 its director has been J. EDGAR HOOVER. The function of the Bureau is the investigation of violations of federal law, although it assists the police and other criminal investigating agencies of state and municipal governments upon request. The Bureau has achieved considerable fame as a result of its work in interstate kidnaping and narcotics cases. It is noted for its accumulated files of photographs, fingerprints, and other materials relating to convicted or suspected criminals. In 1962 its fingerprints file contained almost 163,-000,000 cards.

Federal Communications Commission. A seven man administrative agency established by the Communications Act of 1934. It replaced the old FEDERAL RADIO COMMISSION and was given extensive jurisdiction over the RADIO, cable, TELEPHONE, and TELEGRAPH INDUSTRIES. The last three were withdrawn from the jurisdiction of the INTERSTATE COMMERCE COMMISSION by the law. By subsequent amendment the Commission's power was extended to include the TELEVISION INDUSTRY. With considerations of the public welfare in mind, the Commission was authorized to grant or withhold permits or licenses for broadcasts, to allocate existing and future wave lengths, to prescribe uniform accounting systems, to determine rate schedules, and otherwise to exercise discretion in the regulation of COMMUNICATIONS in interstate and foreign commerce. It is a quasi-judicial agency exercising plenary administrative powers including the issuance of rules and regulations, the holding of hearings, and the determination of final orders.

Federal Corrupt Practices Act. See Hatch Act of 1939.

Federal Council of the Churches of Christ in America. A federation of 23 Protestant religious bodies representing approximately 30,000,000 members. It was established in 1908, and conducts its affairs through biennial meetings of 300 delegates elected by the constituent bodies. The organization's program has included educational, social, and cultural reform planks. It has steadfastly upheld the principle of SEPARATION OF CHURCH AND STATE, and has opposed congressional and state legislation furnishing financial or other assistance to religious denominations. Merged with several other groups in 1950. See NATIONAL COUNCIL OF CHURCHES OF CHRIST IN THE U.S.A.

Federal Crop Insurance Corporation. An agency established by the Federal Crop Insurance Act of 1938 to insure FARMERS against losses from flood, drought, hail, insects, and winterkilling. Crops were insured up to 75 percent of the normal yield. Farmers were to pay premiums in cash or a WHEAT equivalent, the latter to be stored as part of the nation's "EVER NORMAL GRANARY." The annual premium was established on the basis of the annual average loss of the individual farmer. When a loss occurred, he could draw compensation from the accumulated reserves of the Corporation.

Federal Deposit Insurance Corporation. A congressionally chartered CORPORATION created by the GLASS-STEAGALL ACT in 1933. Its function is to insure deposits in member banks of the FEDERAL RESERVE

SYSTEM and in those STATE BANKS desiring to participate. The maximum amount of original insurance was $5,000 per account, increased by amendment in 1951 to $10,000 per account. The insurance fund is established by the payment by member banks of annual premiums of one-twelfth of one percent of their average daily deposits. These sums supplement the original congressional appropriation of $150,000,000 stock for the financing of the system. It is managed by a bi-partisan board of two directors plus the Comptroller of the Currency. The Corporation is empowered to act as receiver of closed banks, adopt measures to avoid improper banking practices, and buy a bank's assets in order to facilitate the MERGER of such a bank with another.

Federal Emergency Administration of Public Works. See Public Works Administration.

Federal Emergency Relief Act. Passed by Congress in May, 1933 as the first step in the program of relief to the needy at the beginning of the NEW DEAL administration. It created the FEDERAL EMERGENCY RELIEF ADMINISTRATION which was allotted an initial fund of $500,-000,000 by the RECONSTRUCTION FINANCE CORPORATION for emergency relief. These funds, supplemented by congressional appropriations, were granted as outright SUBSIDIES to states and local communities over the next two years until eventually an aggregate of $3,000,-000,000 was disbursed by the agency. Wtih the passage of the SOCIAL SECURITY ACT of 1935 the work of the agency was concluded.

Federal Emergency Relief Administration. An agency created in May, 1933 by the FEDERAL EMERGENCY RELIEF ACT for the purpose of meeting the immediate economic needs of those suffering from the effects of the GREAT DEPRESSION. Until it was abolished in 1935 it dispensed a total of $3,000,000,000 to the states and TERRITORIES for their distribution to municipal HOME RELIEF bureaus and departments of welfare for poor relief. With the easing of the depression by 1935 and the reabsorption of great numbers of the 17,-000,000 unemployed, the agency's life came to an end. Its work was subsequently taken up by the Social Security Board. The director of the F.E.R.A. was Harry Hopkins.

Federal Farm Banks. See Rural Credits Act.

Federal Farm Board. See Agricultural Marketing Act.

Federal Farm Loan Act. A law of Congress passed on July 17, 1916 for the purpose of providing a more flexible system of bank credits for FARMERS. Under its provisions the nation was divided into 12 districts in each of which a farm loan bank was established. These central banks were to be supervised by a seven-man FEDERAL FARM LOAN BOARD in furnishing funds to support mortgage loans made by farm loan associations. As provided by the plan, farm loan associations acquired stock memberships in the district land bank and extended mortgage loans to their members up to 50 percent of the value of land and 20 percent of the value of improvements. The 12 banks were not authorized to conduct general BANKING business but were empowered to receive deposits of federal money and funds from the loan associations. These funds were to be applied toward farm loan bonds to be issued by the banks. Loans were to be negotiated under conditions described in the statute. Bonds issued by the banks were secured by farm mortgages, the credit of the 12 farm loan banks, and the assets of the farm loan associations. Under the statute, loans at low rates had exceeded $1,128,-500,000 by 1932.

Federal Farm Loan Board. See Federal Land Banks.

Federal Farm Mortgage Corporation. An agency established in 1934 for the purpose of extending loans to FARMERS. These loans were to be secured by first or second mortgages on land or crops. The original interest rate of 4.5 percent was later reduced to 3.5 percent. The Corporation was administered by a board consisting of the governor of the FARM CREDIT ADMINISTRATION, the Land Bank Commissioner, and a representative of the TREASURY DEPARTMENT. Its capital of $200,000,000 was subscribed by the Treasury Department. The agency was authorized to issue bonds up to $2,000,-000,000, with its principal and interest guaranteed by the federal government. Within a dozen years its obligations had reached the figure of $1,143,085,000.

Federal Food Administration Grain Corporation. See Lever Act.

Federal Home Loan Bank Board. See Home Loan Bank Act.

Federal Housing Administration. An agency established by EXECUTIVE ORDER under the provisions of the NATIONAL HOUSING ACTS of 1934 and 1938. An administrator was authorized to extend loans to approved banks for re-lending to individuals for the construction or repair of homes. He was also empowered to insure lending institutions against financial loss. Mortgage insurance aggregated $953,824,128 for the period 1938-1939 of which two-thirds was for small homes. Half of the borrowers with insured mortgages earned incomes of $1,500 to $2,-500. The results included an increase of HOUSING construction, a reduction of interest rate, a decline of the risk assumed by banks, and an extension of amortization periods up to 25 years. The construction standards set down by the agency brought about architectural, planning, and neighborhood improvement. By 1939 a total of 275,000 small homes had been constructed as a result of the stimulus provided by the agency.

Federal Intermediate Credit Banks. Twelve FARM loan banks established by acts of Congress in 1916 and 1923. They were located in the same cities as the FEDERAL LAND BANKS and were administered by their boards of directors. Each Intermediate Credit Bank was authorized a subscribed capital stock of $5,000,000. Its principal purpose was to buy or discount intermediate-term commercial paper from banks, agricultural credit associations, livestock associations, and farm cooperatives. The Banks were empowered to make direct loans to any cooperative association created for the purpose of producing or marketing farm products or livestock. They could also obtain capital by the sale of bonds on the open market.

Federal Kidnapping Law. See Lindbergh Law.

Federal Land Banks. Twelve cooperative banks established on July 17, 1916 to make loans to FARM loan associations. Their capital stock was subscribed by the farm loan association, although at first advanced by the United States Treasury. The banks granted loans to FARMERS, to run from five to 40 years, and secured by farm mortgages and promissory notes. They obtained the largest share of their capital from the sale of bonds based on the mortgages and notes which they held. In 1943 the amount of their outstanding issues was $1,489,450,000. The Federal Land Banks were administered by a FEDERAL FARM LOAN BOARD of seven members, consisting of the Secretary of the Treasury and six members appointed by the President.

Federal Loan Agency. An agency established by EXECUTIVE ORDER in 1939. It represented a MERGER of 15 non-FARM federal credit agencies and was headed by an administrator. The absence from it of the COMMODITY CREDIT CORPORATION, Farm Mortgage Corporation, and other credit agencies rendered its work ineffectual. It became a shadow agency when, on February 24, 1942, executive orders caused the withdrawal from it of five HOUSING credit agencies and 11 others concerned with general and war financing.

Federal Maritime Board. A three-man agency established on May 24, 1950 by President TRUMAN's Reorganization Plan Number 21. Its chairman was made the *ex-officio* Administrator of the MARITIME ADMINISTRATION. The Federal Maritime Board was given the regulatory powers of the former MARITIME COMMISSION and also its power to determine SUBSIDIES. The Board was authorized to administer controls for the construction of new ships and to manage the differential subsidies granted to ship builders and ship operators. It was also empowered to direct the building of vessels for its own account or for sale to private operators, including those under construction by the Maritime Commission when it was abolished. The Board was made responsible for maintaining the National Defense Reserve Fleet which numbered almost 2100 vessels in 1951. It was also given the responsibility of mobilizing and directing merchant SHIPPING in war time and administering the charter and sales program.

Federal Open Market Committee. See Banking Act of 1935.

Federal Power Commission. See Federal Water Power Act.

Federal Public Housing Authority. An agency established by EXECUTIVE ORDER on February 24, 1942 within the NATIONAL HOUSING AGENCY. It succeeded the UNITED STATES HOUSING AUTHORITY and was given the responsibility for carrying on the SLUM clearance and low cost public HOUSING program of that ag-

ency. As an emergency agency its principal activities were concerned with facilitating the construction of war housing. It built a total of 840,000 units at a cost of $2,300,000,000.

Federal Radio Commission. A five man INDEPENDENT REGULATORY COMMISSION established by the Communications Act of 1927. All regulatory powers vested in the DEPARTMENT OF COMMERCE by the laws of 1912 were transferred to the Commission. Its authority was extended to the granting of licenses of broadcasting stations and to the approval of their location and equipment. The Commission was also empowered to prescribe wavelengths and hours of operation, promulgate rules to prevent interference, and regulate chain broadcasting. It was forbidden to censor programs except for "obscene, indecent, or profane language." In 1934 the Federal Radio Commission was abolished and its functions transferred to the new FEDERAL COMMUNICATIONS COMMISSION established by the Federal Communications Act of that year.

Federal Railroad Administration. See United States Railroad Administration.

Federal Register. A daily publication of the United States government. It was established by Congress in 1935 to provide a complete official publication of executive and administrative orders, presidential proclamations, and other presidential documents.

Federal Reserve Act. See Glass-Owen Act.

Federal Reserve System. See Glass-Owen Act.

Federal Securities Act. See Securities Act.

Federal Security Agency. An administrative agency established by EXECUTIVE ORDER in 1939. Into it were brought various federal agencies concerned with welfare and relief activities. It was authorized to administer all federal welfare laws through a Social Security Board, OFFICE OF EDUCATION, PUBLIC HEALTH SERVICE, NATIONAL YOUTH ADMINISTRATION, and CIVILIAN CONSERVATION CORPS. The Federal Security Agency acts as an overall supervisory policy-making body in controlling the functions of its constituent bodies.

Federal Surplus Commodities Corporation. A federal CORPORATION established by EXECUTIVE ORDER in 1935 for the purpose of purchasing surplus farm products for distribution among the needy. It replaced the Federal Surplus Relief Corporation which had been established in October, 1933. The agency purchased goods and distributed them to state welfare departments which in turn allocated these goods to relief recipients and certain needy non-relief families. The latter group included such persons as work relief employees and old age pensioners. These commodities were distributed as supplements to established relief allowances. In the year ending June 30, 1940 the agency purchased and allotted nearly 3,000,000,000 pounds of food stuffs to an average of about 3,000,000 families per month. Among the commodities distributed were corn, dairy products, flour, fruits, poultry, and vegetables.

Federal Surplus Relief Corporation. See Federal Surplus Commodities Corporation.

Federal Tort Claims Act. Title IV of the LEGISLATIVE REORGANIZATION ACT of 1946. Under its provisions the federal District Courts were authorized to render judgments on claims against the United States because of property damages or personal injury or death caused by the negligence of a government employee. Administrative agencies were empowered to make cut-of-court settlements on

claims under $1000. The heads of federal agencies were required to submit annual reports to Congress of all claims made under the law. The United States government was made liable in respect of claims tried in the District Courts, including costs. Employees of the government were exempted from any action by claimants in the event of District Court action. The decisions of the District Courts were made reviewable on appeal in the Courts of Appeal or in the Court of Claims of the United States. The ATTORNEY GENERAL was authorized to arbitrate, compromise, or settle any claim, after its institution, with the consent of the court. A one-year statute of limitations was laid down on claims not exceeding $1,000. The law contained many exemptions. These included claims arising out of loss or miscarriage of postal matter, assessment or collection of taxes or customs, damages inflicted by a quarantine, false arrest, imprisonment, slander, libel, misrepresentation, deceit, or interference with contract, and those arising in a foreign country or out of the activities of the military forces in time of war, or of the TENNESSEE VALLEY AUTHORITY.

Federal Trade Commission Act. Passed by Congress in 1914. It abolished the Bureau of Corporations which had been established in 1903, and replaced it with a Federal Trade Commission of five members to be appointed by the President. The Commission was authorized to prevent persons, partnerships or corporations from using UNFAIR METHODS OF COMPETITION, to gather information concerning corporations, to require corporations to file with it annual or special reports concerning their organization, business, and practices, to investigate TRADE conditions in and with foreign countries, and to readjust and reorganize businesses charged with violating the ANTI-TRUST LAWS. Exempted from its jurisdiction were RAILROADS, banks and other businesses for which legislative provision was made elsewhere. The Commission was clothed with quasi-judicial powers to conduct investigations, issue subpoenas, hold hearings, promulgate rules and regulations, accept testimony, and issue cease and desist orders. It was empowered to invoke the aid of the courts in enforcing these orders. On occasion the Commission has undertaken special investigations of violations of the anti-trust laws upon the request of the President or Congress. It conducted such an investigation of the PUBLIC UTILITIES in the 1930's. It employs more than 1100 lawyers, economists, statisticians, analysts, and clerks in its activities.

Federal Transportation Board. An agency whose establishment was sought by railroad executives in 1919 during the controversy over the disposition of the nation's RAILROADS. The railroad management recommended the establishment of a Federal Transportation Board with the power to recommend rates to the INTERSTATE COMMERCE COMMISSION sufficient to ensure fair profits for the roads. Such a board would also be authorized to prohibit STRIKES and lockouts. The Board was not established because of the opposition of railway labor and government officials.

Federal Water Power Act. Passed by Congress in 1920. It created the Federal Power Commission of five members. The Commission was authorized to license CITIZENS who use navigable streams for power, such licenses being limited to 50 years. The licenses authorized the construction of HYDRO-ELECTRIC POWER works and were granted to organizations to improve navigation at federally-owned power works and on navigable waters. The Commission also sets rates for electric power which is generated and transmitted in INTERSTATE COMMERCE and for natural gas which is carried and sold in interstate commerce. It controls the issuance of securities by companies performing such activity and supplements state regulation of power utilities.

Federal Works Agency. An administrative agency established by EXECUTIVE ORDER in 1939 to supervise the maintenance of public buildings, administer federal HIGHWAY funds, and coordinate all federal HOUSING activities. Into it were placed the WORKS PROJECTS ADMINISTRATION, PUBLIC WORKS ADMINISTRATION, Bureau of Public Roads, UNITED STATES HOUSING AUTHORITY, and other agencies. The Federal Works Agency acts as an overall supervisory policy-making body in controlling the functions of its constituent bodies.

federalism. The system of government in which there are two sovereign entities, a central government with complete sovereign powers and constituent governments with subordinate powers. The federal nature of the United States government is provided for in Article I, Section 8 and in the Tenth Amendment of the Constitution. Federalism is also known as dual sovereignty and the system which provides for a division of powers.

Federalist Papers. A series of 85 political essays written by ALEXANDER HAMILTON, JAMES MADISON and JOHN JAY during 1787 and 1788. The objective of these was to influence the delegates at the state conventions to ratify the Constitution of 1787. These papers have since been acknowledged to represent the most lucid and profound political thinking of the founding fathers. Their influence was considerable in bringing about ratification in New York and Virginia.

Federalist party. Organized in the autumn of 1787 for the purpose of bringing about the RATIFICATION OF THE CONSTITUTION. Among its outstanding leaders were GEORGE WASHINGTON, ALEXANDER HAMILTON, JOHN ADAMS and JOHN JAY. The party generally was acknowledged to represent the interests of the PLANT-ERS, merchants, bankers, and manufac-turers. Its political philosophy was con-servative, being expressed in a program of sound money, government BANKING, and strong federal powers. It was strong-ly opposed to the STATES RIGHTS agrarian philosophy of the Jeffersonians.

FEKE, Robert. 1705?-1750?. Portrait painter. b. Long Island, N. Y. Known for his early American portraits; his works are in various museums and his-torical societies.

FELTON, Rebecca Latimer. 1835-1930. First woman Senator. b. Georgia. Mar-ried DR. WILLIAM H. FELTON (1853); wrote influential articles in *Atlanta Jour-nal;* supported her husband in fight for progressive legislation; worked for prison reform and WOMAN SUFFRAGE; appointed by Governor Hardwick, U.S. Senator (Oct. 3, 1922-Nov. 22, 1922).

FELTON, William Harrell. 1823-1909. Political leader. Physician and clergy-man. Strongly opposed Democratic party machine in Georgia and worked for pro-gressive legislation; member, U. S. House of Representatives (1875-81).

feminism. The movement to insure the political, social, and economic equality of women with men. As early as the mid-17th century a demand was made for equal VOTING rights for women in Mary-land. ABIGAIL ADAMS in 1776 sought the support of her husband, JOHN ADAMS, for more liberal legislation for women. The Jacksonian period produced the greatest wave of feminism up to that time. In the 1840's LUCY STONE, Lucretia Mott, and ELIZABETH CADY STANTON merged the demand for general reforms with an anti-slavery program and feminism. At the first women's rights convention, held at SENECA FALL in July, 1848, demands were made for equal educational and vo-cational opportunities. The convention proposed equal political rights for wom-en, more equitable divorce laws, legal rights concerning property ownership, and rights of women to their wages. The emphasis upon WOMAN'S SUFFRAGE be-came paramount after the Civil War, and led to the adoption by western states of legislative and constitutional provisions granting women the RIGHT TO VOTE. In the 1930's feminism sought the adoption of an "equal rights amendment" to the federal Constitution to eliminate the ves-tiges of legal discrimination still existing in the various states.

FENNO, John. 1751-1798. Editor. b. Boston, Massachusetts. Publisher of the *Gazette of the United States* (New York, 1789-90); moved to Philadelphia and published there (from 1799); the *Ga-zette* was an influential FEDERALIST or-gan supported by and a supporter of ALEXANDER HAMILTON.

FENTON, Reuben Eaton. 1819-1885. Politician. b. New York. Member, New York assembly (1849-52); member, U. S. House of Representatives (1852, 1856-64); a founder of the Republican party in New York; governor (1865-68); ac-cused of corruption in connection with the Erie Railroad but exonerated; U. S. Senator (1869-75); chairman, U. S. dele-gation to the International Monetary Conference, Paris (1878).

FERREL, William. 1817-1891. Meteor-ologist. With U.S. Coast and Geodetic Survey (1867-1882) and Signal Service (1882-86); formulated FERREL'S LAW re-garding deflection of moving bodies on the earth's surface.

FERRIS, Woodbridge Nathan. 1853-1928. Educator and political leader. b. New York. Founder of Ferris Institute, Big Rapids, Mich. (from 1884); governor of Michigan (1913-16); first Democratic Senator from Michigan to be elected since 1863 (1923-28).

FESSENDEN, William Pitt. 1806-1869. Political leader. b. New Hampshire.

Graduated, Bowdoin College; studied and practiced law in Maine; served in state legislature; member, U.S. House of Representatives (1841-43); U.S. Senator (1854-64); strong opponent of the KANSAS-NEBRASKA ACT; member, Senate Finance Committee (1857-64); opposed BUCHANAN and supported LINCOLN; served short time as Secretary of the Treasury; again a U.S. Senator (1865-69); did not vote to impeach JOHNSON; opposed TENURE OF OFFICE ACT.

Fetterman Massacre. Refers to a slaughter by the SIOUX INDIANS in Wyoming in 1866 of a military force of 80 men under Colonel Fetterman. He allowed himself to be led off the trail by the Sioux chieftain Red Cloud, against orders from his superiors. In the ambush which followed every man was killed.

FEW, William. 1748-1828. Statesman. Childhood spent in North Carolina; in Georgia during the Revolution he was a soldier, surveyor-general, and commissioner to the Indians; member, colonial assembly; delegate to CONTINENTAL CONGRESS (1780-82 and 1785-88); delegate to federal CONSTITUTIONAL CONVENTION (1787); one of Georgia's first Senators.

fiat currency. CURRENCY issued without metal backing. Also referred to as bills of credit. In American history fiat currency has included CONTINENTAL CURRENCY and GREENBACKS.

FIELD, Charles William. 1828-1892. Confederate general. b. Kentucky. Served as colonel of Virginia cavalry; brigadier general (1852); major general (1864); served in almost every important engagement on Virginia front.

FIELD, Cyrus West. 1819-1892. Financier. b. Massachusetts. Accumulated his wealth in the paper business (1841-53); responsible for organizing and promoting the first submarine TELEGRAPH cable between America and Europe (1854-58); first cable messages exchanged between

Queen Victoria and President BUCHANAN (Aug. 16, 1858); a new and much improved cable was laid (1866) which was very successful; became interested in the building of an elevated railway in New York City (from 1877).

FIELD, David Dudley. 1805-1894. Lawyer. b. Connecticut. Admitted to the bar and practiced in New York City; argued many important cases before the U.S. Supreme Court; chief counsel for "Boss" Tweed; counsel for TILDEN in election of 1877; important in codification of the law and law reforms.

FIELD, Marshall. 1834-1906, Merchant and philanthropist. b. Massachusetts. Moved to Chicago (1856); worked as clerk in dry-goods store and worked his way up into partnership finally taking over the company and changing its name to Marshall Field & Co. (1881); head of business which became the largest retail dry-goods business in the world (1881-1906); denoted funds to Columbian Museum at CHICAGO WORLD'S FAIR (1893) which later became the Field Museum of Natural History; gave the land for the University of Chicago.

FIELD, Stephen Johnson. 1816-1899. Jurist. b. Connecticut. Chief justice, California supreme court (1859); associate justice, U.S. Supreme Court (1863-97); important for his decisions that aided in the development of CONSTITUTIONAL LAW.

Fifteenth Amendment. An amendment to the federal Constitution which declared that the right of citizens to vote shall not be denied or abridged by the United States or by any state on account of race, color or previous condition of servitude.

"54-40 or fight." The slogan raised by the Democrats in the political campaign of 1844. This slogan was based on the conflict between the United States and Great Britain over the boundary of the Oregon territory, and expressed the demand of these forces for a military invasion and occupation of the territory up to the parallel 54 degrees 40 minutes.

filibuster. In the United States Senate this refers to unlimited debate. It is authorized under the constitutional provision allowing each house of Congress to make its own rules of procedure. The filibuster is designed to prevent a vote on a pending measure. It may be stopped by the adoption of a CLOSURE petition.

filibustering. In American history an armed attack by Americans against a country at peace with the United States. It is erroneously used to define the arming of rebels in such a country. Early illustrations of the expeditions of soldiers-of-fortune are associated with political ambitions. The abortive ESSEX-JUNTO and BURR CONSPIRACY are examples. At the middle and end of the nineteenth century filibustering expeditions were frequently undertaken by expansionist elements of the south into Mexican and Latin-American territories. Of these the most noteworthy were the expeditions against CUBA in 1850 and 1851 by Lopez, and by William Walker in 1853 in lower California. In 1855 Walker led native revolutionary bands against the government of NICARAGUA. In all such instances the United States government dissociated itself, and in at least one took specific action in opposition. All filibustering expeditions ultimately failed.

FILLMORE, Millard. 1800-1874. Thirteenth President of the United States. b. Locke, New York. Admitted to the bar, Erie County, N.Y. (1823); practiced in Buffalo (1830-33); member, U.S. House of Representatives (1833-35, 1837-43); WHIG leader in the house; Chairman, WAYS AND MEANS COMMITTEE; nominated Vice-President on ticket with ZACHARY TAYLOR and elected (1849-50); succeeded to the presidency on the death of Taylor (July 9, 1850); signed COMPROMISE BILL OF 1850; signed FUGITIVE SLAVE LAW; defeated for presidential nomination (1852) as a WHIG candidate; defeated (1856) for the presidency as a candidate of the KNOW-NOTHING party.

FINDLEY, William. 1741-1821. Congressman. b. Ireland. Emigrated to Pennsylvania (1763); served in Revolution as captain; member, U. S. House of Representatives (1791-1817); except for four years in state senate; important Anti-Federalist; opposed HAMILTON; suggested the COMMITTEE ON WAYS AND MEANS, first STANDING COMMITTEE in Congress; advisor to WASHINGTON.

FINK, Mike. 1770? - 1822. Legendary border hero, although an actual person by that name existed. Born near FRONTIER post at Pittsburgh; became keelboatman on the flatboats of the Ohio and Mississippi rivers; went on expedition into Missouri; famous teller of tales, marksman, and fighter. Many stories about his exploits are similar to the PAUL BUNYAN stories in flavor.

"Fire-eaters." A name applied to south ern politicians who were most extreme in their advocacy of SECESSION and in their hostility to ABOLITIONIST and free-soil agitation. Their extremism reacted against their leaders after the formation of the Confederacy, and they were not given important posts in that government. Among their leaders were Thomas Ruffin, William L. Yancey, and R. B. Rhett.

First Child Labor Law. See Keating-Owen Act.

First Lady. Either the wife of the President of the United States or the woman whom he designates as the WHITE HOUSE hostess. The date of its origin is obscure but it was used in the mid-nineteenth century. As a description of the President's wife it probably was first applied to Lucy W. Hayes by Mary Clemmer, who described President HAYES' inauguration in 1877. It received wide acceptance following the production in 1911-

1912 of the play "The First Lady of the Land."

First War Powers Act. See war powers of the President.

Fisheries controversy. See fishing.

FISH, Hamilton. 1808-1893. Statesman. b. New York City. Graduated, Columbia University; admitted to the bar and practiced in New York City (1830); member, U. S. House of Representatives (1843-45); governor of New York (1849-50); U. S. Senator (1851-57); appointed by GRANT as U.S. Secretary of State (1867-77); settled the "ALABAMA CLAIMS" northwestern boundary disputes with Great Britain; settled dispute with Spain over the seizing of the ship *Virginius* and the execution of the crew; retired to law practice in New York City, but remained influential in civic affairs.

Fishing. As early as 1500, fishermen from Brittany in France were working the Newfoundland coast. The small profits from these fisheries turned the early French settlers to the FUR TRADE. In the 18th century fishermen from the American colonies had access to the fishing grounds of Labrador, Newfoundland, and the St. Lawrence Gulf. Canadian protests resulted in a conflict that was settled by the TREATY OF PARIS OF 1783. New England became the center of the fishing INDUSTRY in North America. From the ports of Falmouth, Maine, Portsmouth, New Hampshire, Salem and Boston, Massachusetts, Providence, Rhode Island, and Bridgeport, Connecticut, hundreds of fishing boats set forth for cod, mackerel, lobster, and whales. The fisheries dispute with Great Britain continued until the War of 1812, when the rights granted in the 1783 agreement were denied the United States. A bilateral commission agreed in 1818 that American fishermen forever have the right to fish on the western and northern shores of Newfoundland and the Magda-

len Islands. In 1847 fishing was allowed the United States in all British colonies except Newfoundland. The 1818 conditions were revived in 1866 by an agreement which was terminated by the Treaty of Washington in 1871 which permitted United States fishermen to take fish of all kinds, except shell fish, in Canadian waters. After the Revolution the inland RIVERS yielded huge quantities of salmon, herring, shad, sturgeon, and trout. The industry benefited in this period by congressional bounties on dried codfish which were granted to fishing villages. These bounties were continued through JEFFERSON's administrations. During the 19th century fishing moved southward to the Gulf of Mexico and westward to the Pacific coast. By 1900 San Francisco had become one of the greatest fishing centers in the world. The diplomatic controversy with Great Britain over fishing rights continued after the Treaty of Washington. With the termination of the fisheries clause in 1885, disputes arose as to the jurisdiction of Great Britain in waters not covered by the treaty. In 1909 the HAGUE TRIBUNAL arbitrated the dispute, handing down an award on September 7, 1910 which defined the limits of the TERRITORY at issue. In 1950 the value of the products of United States fisheries totaled $149,000,-000.

FISK, Clinton Bowen. 1828-1890. Civil War general and philanthropist. Served with Missouri volunteers (1861); brigadier general (1862); breveted major general (1865); assistant commissioner in the FREEDMAN'S BUREAU (1865); founded Fisk University for NEGROES (chartered 1867); president, Board of Indian Commissioners (1874); unsuccessful candidate for the presidency of the United States (1888) as the PROHIBITION PARTY candidate.

FISK, James. 1834-1872. Financier. b. Vermont. Established brokerage house, aided by DANIEL DREW, in New York (1866); succeeded in making a fortune by defeating VANDERBILT and wrecking the Erie R.R.; with Drew and JAY GOULD raised the price of gold (1868) causing panic and making millions; responsible for BLACK FRIDAY (September 1869) when they attempted to corner the gold market but were defeated when GRANT released the government gold; operated ferry boats on the Hudson and had many other interests; shot in fight over a woman.

FISKE, Bradley Allen. 1854-1942. Naval officer and inventor. b. New York. Graduated U.S.N.A., Annapolis (1874); served heroically at MANILA BAY (1898); rear admiral (1911); retired (1916); invented system of electric COMMUNICATIONS aboard ship, an electric range finder, telescope sight, method for detecting submarines and the torpedoplane.

FITCH, John. 1743-1798. Inventor. b. Connecticut. Served in the Revolutionary War; bought land in Ohio River Valley (1780); captured by Indians (1782); held by British in Canada (1782-83); unsuccessful in developing land in Northwest (1783); interested in invention of STEAMBOAT; successfully launched first vessel (Aug. 22, 1787) on Delaware River; received United States PATENT (1791); when his fourth large ship was destroyed by storm and he couldn't commercialize his invention, he lost his financial backers.

FITCH, Thomas. 1699-1774. Colonial governor of Connecticut. Graduated, Yale (1721); studied law; assistant to governor (1734-35, 40-50); governor, (1750-53); supported British in FRENCH AND INDIAN WARS; again governor (1754-66); served as lawyer in land disputes with Mohicans and Massachusetts.

FITZ, Reginald Heber. 1843-1913. Physician. b. Massachusetts. Graduated, Harvard Medical School (1868); important for his work in appendicitis and for proposing surgery for the cure of this disease. His paper *Perforating Inflammation of the Vermiform Appendix* (1886) explained his discoveries.

FITZGERALD, F. Scott. In full Francis Scott Key. 1895-1940. Novelist. b. Minnesota. Princeton (1913-17); served in World War I; well-known author of *This Side of Paradise* (1920), *The Great Gatsby* (1925), and *Tender is the Night* (1934). His work is important as a picture of the life of youth during the "roaring twenties" and their feeling of instability and desire to find themselves.

FITZPATRICK, Benjamin. 1802 - 1869. Political leader. Large PLANTER in Alabama; elected governor (1841-5); U.S. Senator (1848-60); president pro tempore (1857-60); opposed SECESSION but supported the Confederacy.

FITZPATRICK, Thomas. 1799? - 1854. Fur trader and guide. b. Ireland. Guided first emigrant train to Pacific through northwestern Montana (1841); guided FREMONT's second expedition (1843-44); lead KEARNY's expeditions (1845 and 1846); appointed Indian agent for TERRITORY that is now Colorado (1846-50; 1851-54); considered important FRONTIERSMAN.

Five Power Treaty. A treaty negotiated by the United States, Great Britain, Japan, France, and Italy at the WASHINGTON NAVAL CONFERENCE. By its terms the powers agreed to the scrapping of a number of battleships which were either afloat or in the process of construction. In the building of capital ships they agreed to a "naval holiday" until 1931 and established the following ratio for capital ship tonnage: 5:5:3 for the United States, Great Britain, and Japan, and 1.75 each for France and Italy. It limited fortifications in the PACIFIC OCEAN generally to those maintained by the signatory powers at the time. Also known as Washington Naval Treaty. See Washington Naval Conference, Four Power Treaty, and Nine Power Pact.

Flag Day. Celebrated on June 14th. It is the day commemorating the adoption by the Second CONTINENTAL CONGRESS in 1777 of the Stars and Stripes as the official United States flag. Although it is a legal HOLIDAY only in Pennsylvania, President TRUMAN signed a bill on August 3rd, 1949 requesting the President to call for its observance each year by proclamation.

Flag of the United States. The first official American flag was called the Continental or Grand Union flag and was displayed on Prospect Hill on January 1, 1776 in the American lines besieging Boston. On June 14, 1777 the CONTINENTAL CONGRESS adopted a new flag design by BETSY ROSS with the red cross of St. George and the white cross of St. Andrew replaced on the blue field by thirteen stars, one for each state. The stars were customarily arranged in a circle. Its first official announcement is believed to have been on September 3, 1777. Of the many stories about Betsy Ross her own is that she was asked by a committee of GEORGE WASHINGTON, ROBERT MORRIS, and George Ross in Philadelphia in June 1776 to design a new flag. By 1818 there were twenty states in the Union and Congress realized that the flag was becoming unwieldly because of the addition of stars as new states entered the Union. On April 18th, Congress voted to return to the original 12 stripes and to indicate the admission of a new state simply by the addition of a star the following July 4th. The 49th and 50th stars were added on July 4, 1959 and 1960 for Alaska and Hawaii.

FLETCHER, Thomas Clement. 1827-1899. Political leader. Commanded Missouri Regiment during Civil War; governor of Missouri (1865-69) establishing an efficient administration during a difficult period.

Fletcher vs. Peck. A decision of the United States Supreme Court in 1810 declaring an act of Georgia unconstitutional. The case before the court arose out of the YAZOO LAND FRAUD, when the Georgia legislature passed a law repealing an earlier law providing land grants to the Yazoo Companies under fraudulent circumstances. The Court held that the second legislative act was unconstitutional because it impaired the obligations of contract in violation of Article I Section 10 of the federal Constitution, and because it divested persons of rights granted in the prior law. The constitutional doctrine set down in this decision was the power of the United States Supreme Court to hold laws of the states unconstitutional.

Flood Control Act. See Missouri River Basin Project.

Florida. The 22nd state in size, with an area of 58,666 square miles. Organized as a TERRITORY in 1822 and admitted as the 27th state on March 3, 1845. Seceded on January 10, 1861 and readmitted on June 25, 1868. Tallahassee is the capital. In 1950 Florida's POPULATION of 2,771,305 made it 20th in rank. Its largest cities are Miami, Jacksonville, and Tampa. Florida's most important INDUSTRY is AGRICULTURE, the crops including citrus fruits, corn, celery, tomatoes, peanuts, and potatoes. The state's coast line, longest in the nation, provides scores of seashore communities which attract a large tourist business. FISHING and truck gardening are other leading industries. In recent years CATTLE raising has become a significant enterprise. Its manufactured goods include cigars, ship lumber, and naval stores. St. Augustine, founded in 1565, is the nation's oldest city. Key West is the southernmost city. Florida has more than 30,000 small lakes. It was discovered in 1513 by Ponce de Leon. Its nickname is the Sunshine State."

Florida, Annexation of. After the War of

1812 Florida was a center of SMUGGLING, haven of escaped slaves, and origin of attacks on Georgia and Alabama by Englishmen and Indians. Spain's inability to control her TERRITORY led to the occupation of Amelia Island in 1817, followed by the Seminole War in 1817-1818. During the action General JACKSON occupied the Spanish fort at St. Marks in April, 1818 and seized Pensacola in May, 1818. Despite the protests of Spain Secretary of State JOHN ADAMS pursued a vigorous course, declaring that the Spanish commandant had made himself "a partner and accomplice of the hostile Indians." Negotiations finally led to the signing of the treaty on February 22, 1819 by which Spain ceded east and west Florida to the United States. The treaty defined the western boundary of Louisiana at the 42nd parallel and declared that line as the northern extension of Spanish territory. The United States agreed to surrender its claims against Spain and take over those of its CITIZENS for damages up to the date of the treaty, in an amount not exceeding $5,000,000.

FLOWER, Benjamin Orange. 1858-1918. Editor. b. Illinois. Founder of *American Spectator*, Boston (1886); *Arena* (1889) and editor of both (1886-96, 1904-09) after their MERGER; founded and edited *Twentieth Century* Magazine, Boston (1909-11); edited *Menace* an anti-Catholic paper. Author of *Civilization's Inferno* (1893), *Persons, Places and Ideas* (1896) etc.

FLOYD, John Buchanan. 1807-1863. Politician. b. Virginia. Practiced law; governor of Virginia (1849-52); appointed by BUCHANAN U.S. Secretary of War (1857-60) and asked by him to resign; served as brigadier of volunteers in CONFEDERATE ARMY.

FLOYD, William. 1734-1821. Revolutionary leader. b. New York. Member, CONTINENTAL CONGRESS (1774-77, 1778-83); a signer of the DECLARATION OF INDEPENDENCE; member, U.S. House of Representatives (1789-91).

FOGG, George Gilman. 1813-1881. Journalist and statesman. Studied at Dartmouth and Harvard Law School; founded the *Independent Democrat*, Concord, N.H. (1846); interested in FREE-SOIL PARTY and helped establish the Republican party; appointed minister to Switzerland during the Civil War and U.S. delegate to GENEVA CONVENTION (1864).

FOLGER, Charles James. 1818-1884. Jurist and politician. b. Massachusetts. Admitted to bar; state senator, New York (1861-69); chief justice of state court of appeals (1870-80); U. S. Secretary of the Treasury (1881-84) inaugurating civil service in the TREASURY DEPARTMENT.

FOLK, Joseph Wingate. 1869-1923. Lawyer and politician. b. Tennessee. Circuit attorney, St. Louis, Missouri (1900-04) exposed corruption in city administration; governor of Missouri (1905-09); appointed by WILSON solicitor, U.S. DEPARTMENT OF STATE (1913-14); counsel, INTERSTATE COMMERCE COMMISSION (1914-18).

FOLKS, Homer. 1867-1963. Social Worker Important for work in state charities and in securing progressive legislation in public health, prison reform child welfare etc.; chairman, New York State Probation Committee (1907-17); completely reformed the department of charities of New York City; did important work with International Red Cross.

FOLSOM, Nathaniel. 1726-1790. Revolutionary leader. b. New Hampshire. Member, CONTINENTAL CONGRESS (1774, 75, 77-80); major general, in command of N.H. State MILITIA (1775); executive councilor (1778); president, New Hampshire CONSTITUTIONAL CONVENTION (1783).

FOLWELL, William Watts. 1833-1929. Educator and historian. Served in ARMY OF THE POTOMAC as lieutenant colonel;

taught at Kenyon College; first president of the University of Minnesota (1869); librarian and professor of political science (1884-1907); helped found and was president of Minneapolis Academy of Fine Arts; president, Minnesota Historical Society (1924-27). Author of *History of Minnesota* (1921-30).

Food and Fuel Control Act. Passed by Congress in August, 1917, after the entry of the United States into World War I. It established the United States Food Administration and the United States Fuel Administration with wide powers over the production and conservation of food and fuel. The Act forbade the hoarding or willful destruction of food, and prohibited discrimination in the sale and distribution of food and fuel. The President was authorized to purchase, store, and sell certain food and fuel items, and to regulate their prices. Under the stimulus of the Act the production of food was increased, although domestic consumption of WHEAT and beef was cut by 30 percent through the operation of wheatless and meatless days. A program of fuel CONSERVATION and price control was promulgated by the Fuel Administration.

Football. To be distinguished from the European game of soccer, which dates back to thirteenth century England. Although known earlier, football's importance dates from the 1870's when it became a significant part of inter-collegiate sports programs. Princeton and Rutgers are recorded as having engaged in the first inter-collegiate football game. The rules were adopted in 1876 by the "Ivy League" colleges but were modified by the newly-established Intercollegiate Football Association in 1880. Since then inter-collegiate football has assumed paramount importance in the United States. Large universities have been heavily subsidized by alumni in the attempt to gain national recognition for their football teams. As a consequence the hiring of outstanding high school and preparatory school players has become an open scandal, with little attention paid to the customary scholastic standards. Emphasis on the game has developed rivalries not considered proper to the accepted objectives of higher EDUCATION, and bribery and corruption have played conspicuous roles. Various reform movements have failed to remedy this condition. Outstanding football teams have been developed by Notre Dame University, University of Southern California, Army, Michigan, and many state colleges. Within the last generation professional football leagues have gained public favor.

FOOT, Solomon. 1802-1866. Senator. b. Vermont. Practiced law; served in state legislature; member, U.S. House of Representatives (1842-47) opposing MEXICAN WAR; anti-slavery sympathies made him join the Republican party; U.S. Senator (1850-1866); president pro tempore and master of parliamentary law; responsible for much of present Senate's procedure.

FOOTE, Henry Stuart. 1804-1880. b. Virginia. Practiced law in Mississippi; U.S. Senator (1847-51); supported MISSOURI COMPROMISE; defeated JEFFERSON DAVIS for governor (1852-54); member, Confederate Congress; opposed Davis' administration and was imprisoned; went to England; after war practiced law in Washington, D.C.; superintendent, U.S. mint at New Orleans (1878-80).

FOOTE, Lucius Harwood. 1826-1913. Diplomat. b. New York. Admitted to bar in California; adjutant general of state; consul, Chile (1879); minister to Korea to exchange first diplomatic relations for the United States with that country (1882).

FOOTE, Samuel Augustus. 1780-1846. Politician. Served in Connecticut legislature; U. S. House of Representatives

(1819-21); U.S. Senator (1828-34); proposed FOOTE RESOLUTION on public land sales (1829) which led to WEBSTER-HAYNE DEBATES; governor of Connecticut (1834).

Foote's Resolution. A proposal on December 29th, 1829 by Senator Samuel A. Foote of Connecticut requesting the Committee on Public Lands to investigate the expediency of restricting the sale of PUBLIC LANDS for a stated period. The Resolution proposed to limit sales to that acreage which had already been offered for public sale. The suggestion was at once opposed by the Western Senators who claimed that this was an attempt to check the drain of eastern POPULATION to the West. Senator BENTON of Missouri charged New England with consistently intriguing against the West's development, and led the Senate's opposition to Foote's proposal. The Resolution provided an opportunity for Senator HAYNE of South Carolina to defend the South in the sectional conflict then developing. His brilliant speech of January 19, 1830 launched the series of speeches since known as the WEBSTER-HAYNE DEBATES.

Foraker Act. Enacted in 1900 to provide civil government for the TERRITORY of PUERTO RICO, acquired from Spain by the TREATY OF PARIS, 1898. The Act established a legislature whose lower house was popularly elected. A territorial governor had the power of VETO over legislative acts. The upper house, known as the executive council, consisted of 11 members (six of them Americans) appointed by the President.

FORAKER, Joseph Benson. 1846-1917. Political leader. b. Ohio. Served in Civil War; Graduated, Cornell University; admitted to bar and practiced law in Cincinnati, Ohio; judge of superior court; governor of Ohio (1885-89); U.S. Senator (1897-1909); supported MC KINLEY; opposed ROOSEVELT and became leader of "Old Guard" of Republican party.

Force Bill. Passed by Congress in 1833 at the request of President Jackson. It accompanied the enactment of the COMPROMISE TARIFF Act of that year and empowered the President to use the army and navy to enforce the execution of federal laws in South Carolina. Specifically the objective was the collection of the customs provided for by the TARIFF Acts of 1832 and 1833. The Bill was symptomatic of the deep cleavage within the Democratic party arising over the tariff issue.

FORCE, Peter. 1790-1868. Historian. b. New Jersey. Served in War of 1812; printer, Washington, D.C. (1815); published *National Journal* (1823) which supported J. Q. ADAMS and was an influential daily; chief historical effort *American Archives* (9 vols. pub. 1837-53; covering years 1774-76) it presented original source material; his LIBRARY of Americana was bought by the government for the LIBRARY OF CONGRESS.

Ford Foundation. Organized in Michigan as a non-profit organization in 1936. It receives and administers the expenditure of funds for scientific, educational, and charitable purposes in the public interest. The Foundation's funds are spent to support research studies and other activities on social human needs rather than the physical. Its assets in 1964 were almost $2,500,000,000. It operates offices in Detroit, New York, and Pasadena.

FORD, Gerald R. 1913- Born Omaha, Neb. as Leslie King. After parents' divorce his mother married Gerald R. Ford who formally adopted him at age 2 and gave him his name. Educated at U. of Michigan and Yale Law School. After brief law practice served in Navy during World War II. Left service in 1946 as lieutenant commander. Resumed law practice, and in 1948 entered politics becoming U.S. Congressman representing Michigan. Served 25 years in House of Representatives. After V.P.

Agnew resigned while under investigation for fraud, Ford, then House Minority Leader, was nominated by Nixon to be vice president. When Nixon resigned Aug. 9, 1974 Ford became president. On September 8, 1974 he pardoned Nixon for any federal crimes he might have committed while president. He vetoed many welfare and other bills as too costly. The Democratic Congress overrode 8 vetoes. He lost the 1976 presidential election by a close margin to Jimmy (James Earl) Carter.

FORD, Henry. 1863-1947. Automobile manufacturer. b. Michigan. Worked as machinist; chief engineer, Edison Illuminating Co. Detroit (1887-89); organized and became president of the Ford Motor Co. (1903), one of the largest manufacturers of automobiles in the world; sold over 15,000,000 of his famous Model T Fords, a light inexpensive car; put profit sharing plan into effect in his company (1914); headed a peace delegation to Europe at his own expense in an attempt to end World War I but was unsuccessful (1915-16); donated $7,500,000 to build the Henry Ford Hospital in Detroit; and considered one of the wealthiest men in the country. Inaugurated the ASSEMBLY LINE system of production. ISOLATIONIST before World War II, but supported the war effort by converting his plants to war production (1941-42); retired in 1945.

Fordney-McCumber Tariff Act. Passed by Congress in 1922. This Act established higher rates than ever before in American TARIFF history. Duties on chinaware, pig iron, textiles, sugar, and rails were restored to the level of the PAYNE-ALDRICH TARIFF ACT of 1909. Increases ranging from 60 to 400 percent were established on dyes, chemicals, lace, toys, and hardware. To provide a degree of elasticity it authorized the President, on recommendation of a new TARIFF COMMISSION, to raise or lower rates up to 50 percent. The Act was passed because of the fear of a deluge of cheap European goods, a desire to protect new war industries, and a wish to conciliate the FARM community. The Act was bitterly denounced by the Democrats and other low tariff groups who claimed that it would add billions of dollars to the cost of living and would impair trade and political relations with European nations whose only method of repaying their WAR DEBT was by sending their goods to the United States. The economic consequences of the Fordney-McCumber Tariff were the fostering of MONOPOLY growth in the United States, the prevention of repayment of European obligations in the form of goods, and tariff reprisals from these foreign nations. The average rate was 38.24 percent.

Ford's Peace Ship. A ship, the OSCAR II, outfitted by HENRY FORD and sent to Europe during World War I in an attempt to arouse public feeling against continuance of the war. A group of pacifists, headed by Rosika Schwimmer, journeyed to the Scandinavian nations on board this vessel in an attempt to influence their governments to mediate the war and submit an acceptable ARMISTICE to the belligerents. The vessel sailed from Hoboken, New Jersey on December 4, 1915. The movement was scoffed at in the United States and Europe and met with failure.

Foreign affairs. The relationships of the United States with other sovereign nations. Governed by the principles of international law and by TREATY agreements it has conducted its foreign affairs through the DEPARTMENT OF STATE under the overall supervision of the President.

Foreign Economic Administration. An agency established by EXECUTIVE ORDER in 1943 to unify and consolidate federal programs concerned with the economic aspects of the war effort. To it were transferred the Lend-Lease Administration, BOARD OF ECONOMIC WARFARE, EXPORT-IMPORT BANK, and the foreign activities of the WAR FOOD ADMINISTRATION COMMIDITIES CREDIT CORPORATION, and Rubber Development Corporation. The program of the agency attained huge proportions in its efforts to obtain foreign economic resources. It was abolished in 1945 and its facilities transferred to other agencies.

Foreign Policy. The objectives and methods of the foreign policy of the United States are the result of custom, TREATIES, and national interests as determined by historical events. Inconsistencies have resulted from the occasional departures from the early principles of foreign policy as established after the Revolution. These principles included avoidance of European politics, FREEDOM OF THE SEAS, a demand for neutral commercial rights during foreign wars, the doctrines of the MONROE DOCTRINE, RECIPROCAL TARIFF agreements, pan-Americanism, expansion to the Pacific, and, in the period of World War II, COLLECTIVE SECURITY. After the Revolution trade and diplomatic conflicts involved the United States in war with Great Britain, although armed struggle was avoided with Spain and France by the negotiation of treaties for the "RIGHT OF DEPOSIT" at New Orleans and for the purchase of the LOUISIANA TERRITORY. Before the Civil War the policy of expansionism, as expressed in the slogan "MANIFEST DESTINY", brought the United States into war with Mexico and led to the acquisition of Texas, California, Oregon, the GADSDEN Territory, and the MEXICAN CESSION. The Spanish-American War opened the era of IMPERIALISM and ownership or control by the United States of numerous overseas areas. The ROOSEVELT COROLLARY developed a CARIBBEAN POLICY of intervention into the affairs of Latin American states. In the Far East the rise of Japanese power clashed with American interests in the Pacific and contributed to the promulgation of the "OPEN DOOR" POLICY. The United States was a major factor in world politics at the opening of World War I. It emerged out of the war as a creditor nation and, although one of the three or four great powers, retreated once more into a policy of ISOLATIONISM. This policy was negated by the nation's frequent participation in international conferences on DISARMAMENT, peace, and TRADE. The "GOOD-NEIGHBOR" POLICY of the NEW DEAL administrations restored sounder relations between Latin America and the United States. The nation's interests in the Far East and the continued aggressions of the AXIS POWERS once more turned this country to a policy of collective action to resist aggression. Unlike its refusal to join the LEAGUE OF NATIONS after World War I, the United States participated actively in the organization of the UNITED NATIONS after World War II. In the postwar world it assumed the leadership in international reconstruction and rehabilitation. Through the media of the TRUMAN DOCTRINE, MARSHALL PLAN, NORTH ATLANTIC TREATY, and MUTUAL SECURITY Program the United States showed clearly that it had turned its back to isolationism.

Forest resources. The total forest land of the United States in 1952 was 459,-541,000 acres, consisting of old growth, second-growth, saw timber, pole timber, and seedling and sapling area. There are more than 800 different kinds of trees in the forests of the United States. In the past 300 years commercial forest land has been reduced by half. The condition of the remaining half of the timber land has deteriorated badly, although widespread conservation and rehabilitation programs have been instituted in the last half century.

Formosa. An island province of China located in the western Pacific ninety miles off the China coast. Its POPULATION of 7,500,000 occupies an area of 13,836 square miles. Its principal agricultural products are sugar cane, rice, bananas, pineapples, and tea. Other industries include CANNING, chemicals, wood pulp, and sugar refining. Ceded to Japan in 1895, Formosa was restored to China in 1945 in conformance with the Cairo Declaration. Although the regime of Chiang Kai Shek was overthrown on the Chinese mainland in 1949, Formosa remained in his hands. At the outbreak of the Korean War in June, 1950 President TRUMAN ordered the United States Seventh Fleet to defend the island against any attempted invasion by the Chinese Communists. The latter government has consistently refused to renounce its sovereign rights over Formosa, this issue remaining a fundamental cause of the exclusion from the UNITED NATIONS of that government, and of the deterioration of relations between it and the United States.

FORREST, Nathan Bedford. 1821-1877. Confederate general. b. Tennessee. Head of famous cavalry unit in the CONFEDERATE ARMY; brigadier general (1862); important commands and successful general against great odds; lieutenant general (1865).

FORSYTH, John. 1780-1841. Political leader and statesman. b. Virginia. Graduated, Princeton (1799); admitted to bar (1802); attorney general of Georgia; member, U.S. House of Representatives (1813-18); U.S. Senator (1818-19); resigned to become U.S. Minister to Spain and secured Florida for the United States by the TREATY of 1819 (1819-23); member, U.S. House of Representatives (1823-27); governor of Georgia (1827-29); U.S. Senator (1829-34); appointed U.S. Secretary of State by JACKSON and VAN BUREN (1834-41).

FORTAS, Abe. born in Memphis, Tennessee, June 19, 1910, the youngest son of a cabinet maker who had emmigrated from Great Britain. He attended South West College and received his B.A. in 1930. He then received his law degree from Yale. He served as unofficial advisor to President Johnson who appointed him to the Supreme Course in 1965. He became the first justice in the history of the Supreme Court to resign under fire. Even though he stressed that he was not guilty of wrongdoing, he was embarrassed when disclosures were made of his financial arrangements with a former client who was later sent to prison for selling unregistered stocks.

Fort Knox Gold Depository. Also known as the Gold Bullion Depository. The vaults, located in Kentucky, hold the major portion of the total gold assets of the United States. In 1964 these gold assets amounted to $15,600,000,-000. The Fort Knox vaults were built in 1935 to provide a safe depository as United States gold holdings mounted and could not be maintained in the regular federal mints. The Depository is located in the middle of a large military reservation and is designed for a maximum of $19,000,000,000 in gold.

Fort Sumter, firing on. The opening engagement of the Civil War. Located in Charleston Harbor, the fort was held by Major Anderson, commanding 129 Union soldiers. Earlier in command of Forts Sumter, Moultrie, Johnson, and Castle Pinckney, Anderson secretly moved his forces to Sumter on December 26, 1860 to avoid a surprise attack by South Carolina. Moultrie, Castle Pinckney, the Arsenal, the Custom House, and the Post Office were seized by Governor PICKENS who immediately demanded Anderson's surrender. On April 8, 1861 LINCOLN notified Pickens and his commanding officer, BEAUREGARD, of his intention to supply Anderson with provisions. Fol-

235

lowing another unsuccessful demand for Anderson's surrender on April 12th, Beauregard commenced firing on the fort. The bombardment lasted two days until Anderson's capitulation on April 14th. This act revealed the impossibility of compromise, and was followed the next day by Lincoln's call for volunteers.

"Forty-niners." Name given to those who migrated to California in 1848 and 1849 following the discovery of gold in that state. Their importance derives from the rapid settlement of California leading to the political struggle over its ADMISSION INTO THE UNION the following year.

FOSTER, Charles. 1828-1904. Political leader. b. Ohio. Successful banker; member, U.S. House of Representatives (1871-79); governor of Ohio (1880-84); appointed by HARRISON as U.S. Secretary of the Treasury (1891-93).

FOSTER, John Watson. 1836 - 1917. Statesman. b. Indiana. Graduated, Indiana (1855); admitted to bar (1857); served through Civil War; U.S. Minister to Mexico (1873-80), Russia (1880-81), Spain (1883-85); appointed by HARRISON U.S. Secretary of State at resignation of BLAINE (1892-93); United States agent in Alaska-Canadian boundary settlement (1903).

FOSTER, Stephen Collins. 1826-1864. Song writer. b. Pennsylvania. Wrote many very popular songs such as *My Old Kentucky Home, Old Folks at Home, O Susanna,* and *Old Black Joe.*

"Founding fathers." The nickname applied to the fifty-five members of the CONSTITUTIONAL CONVENTION who drafted the present Constitution of the United States. Among the more prominent "founding fathers" were ALEXANDER HAMILTON, JAMES MADISON, LUTHER MARTIN, GEORGE MASON, EDMUND RANDOLPH, GEORGE WASHINGTON, and JAMES WILSON.

Four Freedoms, The. An address by President F. D. ROOSEVELT to Congress on January 6, 1941, in which he stated the domestic objectives of his third administration. The four freedoms include freedom of speech and expression, freedom of worship everywhere in the world, freedom from want by securing to every nation a healthy, peaceful life for its inhabitants, and freedom from fear by the world wide reduction of armaments.

FOURIER, Francois Marie Charles. 1772-1837. Social scientist, reformer and Utopian. b. France. BRISBANE and GREELAY sponsored his ideas of communal and Utopian living in the United States; BROOK FARM was for awhile Fourierist; best known colony of Fourierists was at Red Bank, N.J. Important influence on thinking of the time.

"Four Minute Men." See Committee on Public Information.

Four Power Treaty. One of seven treaties emerging from the WASHINGTON NAVAL CONFERENCE in 1921. The TREATY abolished the Anglo-Japanese Alliance of 1902. It further provided that the signatory nations respect each other's possessions in the PACIFIC OCEAN, that they confer for the adjustment of controversies arising in the Far West, and that they agree on joint measures in the event of aggression in the Pacific by non-signatory power. It recognized the legality of the mandated territories in the Pacific and, by a supplementary treaty in 1922, included among these the Pescadores, FORMOSA, and southern Sakhalin. The Treaty was to run for ten years and thereafter until denounced by any signatory on one year's notice.

"Fourteen points." A program for an ARMISTICE with the CENTRAL POWERS announced by President WILSON in a speech to Congress in January, 1918. This program proposed such principles as FREE-

DOM OF THE SEAS, OPEN CONVENANTS OPENLY ARRIVED AT, destruction of trade barriers, equal adjustment of colonial claims, certain territorial adjustments, and a LEAGUE OF NATIONS. The fourteen points were accepted by Germany as the basis for the armistice of November, 1918.

Fourteenth Amendment. Adopted in 1868. Framed by the JOINT COMMITTEE OF FIFTEEN in 1867. The AMENDMENT was designed to grant CITIZENSHIP to and protect the CIVIL LIBERTIES of the FREEDMAN. This was to be accomplished by prohibiting the states from denying or abridging the privileges or immunities of CITIZENS of the United States, depriving any person of his life, liberty, or property without due process of law, or denying to any person within their jurisdiction the equal protection of the laws. The first section defines citizenship in such a way as to make it impossible for any state to withhold this status from freedmen. A section is included requiring the former Confederate states to repudiate their debts upon readmission to the Union. The DUE PROCESS CLAUSE has been interpreted by the Supreme Court to protect the PROPERTY RIGHTS of CORPORATIONS against state infringement, and has been referred to by CHARLES A. BEARD, the eminent historian, as having written the theory of LAISSEZ-FAIRE into the Constitution.

FOX, Gustavus Vasa. 1821-1883. Naval Officer. b. Massachusetts. Graduated, U.S.N.A., Annapolis (1841); served as Assistant Secretary of the Navy during the Civil War and rendered very valuable service; helped secure the use of the *Monitor* by the Union.

Fox Indians. See Sauk and Fox Indians.

France, Liberation of. The last major campaign on the western front in World War II began after the successful INVASION OF NORMANDY in June, 1944. On July 9th Allied forces entered Brittany, after taking St. Lo, and pursued the fleeing Germans toward Paris. On August 15th an amphibious operation landed troops on the French Mediterranean coast between Marseilles and Nice. Supported by the uprising of the French Forces of the Interior the Allies captured Paris on August 25th. On September 2nd Brussels was taken and by early December the Germans had been driven almost completely from France and Belgium. The Allied lines stretched along the German frontier from Holland to Switzerland. The last German counter-offensive took place in Belgium and Luxembourg in Mid-December in the famous BATTLE OF THE BULGE. By January, 1945 the Germans had been repulsed and the Allies were prepared to invade Germany.

FRANCIS, David Rowland. 1850-1927. Political leader. b. Kentucky. Prominent grain merchant, St. Louis, Missouri; reform mayor (1885-89); governor of Missouri (1889-93); appointed by CLEVELAND, U.S. Secretary of the Interior (1896-97); U.S. Ambassador to Russia (1916-18).

FRANCIS, Edward. 1872-1957. Bacteriologist. b. Ohio. Graduated Ohio State (1894); University of Cincinnati (M.D. 1897); worked for the U.S. PUBLIC HEALTH SERVICE (from 1900); surgeon (1913-30); medical director (from 1930); important for his discovery of tularemia in rabbits and in men.

FRANKFURTER, Felix. 1882-1965. Jurist. b. Austria; to United States (1894). Graduated, College of the City of New York (1902), LL.B., Harvard (1906); famous professor, Harvard Law School (1914-39); Assistant Secretary of Labor (1918); appointed associate justice U.S.

Supreme Court by F. D. ROOSEVELT (from 1939-1962).

FRANKLIN, Benjamin. 1706 - 1790. Statesman, scientist, and philosopher. b. Boston, Massachusetts. Apprenticed as a printer (1718-23); printer in Philadelphia; published the *Pennsylvania Gazette* (1730-48); successful with *Poor Richard's Almanack* (1732-57); established the first circulating LIBRARY in America (1731); organized the AMERICAN PHILOSOPHICAL SOCIETY; improved city lighting and police department; deputy postmaster (1737-53); deputy Postmaster General for the colonies (1753-74); invented an improved heating stove; tried famous kite experiment with ELECTRICITY (1752); delegate to ALBANY CONGRESS (1754); represented Pennsylvania in England on estates taxes (1757-62) and appeared before the House of Commons to explain the colonial resentment against the STAMP ACT; returned as war seemed inevitable (1775); member, second CONTINENTAL CONGRESS (1775); on committee that drafted the DECLARATION OF INDEPENDENCE and was one of the signers; one of the committee sent to France to get assistance for the colonies (1776); signed a TREATY of defense alliance and a treaty of commerce; with JAY and ADAMS negotiated peace with Great Britain (1781); member, CONSTITUTIONAL CONVENTION (1787); asked Congress to abolish SLAVERY (1790). Published his *Autobiography*. One of the outstanding men of American history.

FRANKLIN, William. 1730?-1813. Colonial administrator. b. Philadelphia, Pa. Son of BENJAMIN FRANKLIN. His father appointed him comptroller of the general post office (1754-56); to England with his father (1757); admitted to bar, London; appointed governor of New Jersey (1763); opposed STAMP ACT CONGRESS; remained a royalist and became estranged from his democratic father; arrested and imprisoned in Connecticut;

went to England (1782) and stayed there the remainder of his life.

FRANKLIN, William Buel. 1823-1903. Army officer. b. Pennsylvania. Graduated, West Point (1843); served through Mexican War and Civil War; brigadier general of volunteers, (1861); major general (1862); served under BURNSIDE at FREDERICKSBURG and accused by him of being responsible for the defeat; Franklin proved he did not disobey orders but was relieved of his command; served in Louisiana (1863); resigned from army (1866).

Frazier-Lemke Bankruptcy Act. A law of Congress, passed in 1934, which authorized the FEDERAL COURTS to extend five year moratoria to FARMERS under certain conditions. Its efforts to aid the farmer by halting foreclosures were only moderately successful because of its invalidation by the United States Supreme Court in 1935. In that year Congress enacted new legislation attempting to remove the constitutional disabilities, and this act was upheld by the Court in 1937.

Fredericksburg, Battle of. One of the most important battles of the Civil War. It was fought in Virginia on December 13, 1862. The Union army of 125,000, commanded by General BURNSIDE, occupied the heights north of Fredericksburg in a march designed to capture Richmond. The Confederate army of 80,000, led by LEE, lay entrenched behind the city on the south side of the Rappahanock River. Attacks across the river by the wings of the Union army under Sumner and HOOKER were repulsed with great slaughter, and two days later Burnside withdrew from the city. The Union loss in the battle was 12,653 while the Confederate army lost 5,115 men.

Freedman. A slave who had been emancipated. It was the generic term applied to all ex-slaves after the adoption of the THIRTEENTH AMENDMENT. The total number of four million freedmen posed a serious problem in this period because of the resentment by the South against their political importance in some of the states and the aggressive Reconstruction policy of the RADICAL REPUBLICANS in Congress.

Freedman's Bureau. Established by Congress in the War Department on March 3, 1865. Its duty was to protect the interests of the former slaves, obtaining for them labor contracts, settling their disputes, assisting them in finding homes, and obtaining employment for them. It was created for a period of one year after the close of the war. It distributed hundreds of its agents throughout the South charged with the responsibility of administering the above program and additional work in educational facilities, relief, and the administration of justice. During its brief existence it established over 100 hospitals, rendered medical aid to 500,000 patients, distributed over 20,000,000 rations to NEGROES and white persons, settled thousands of FREEDMEN on abandoned or confiscated lands, and established over 4,000 schools for Negro children. The Bureau spent $17,000,000 in this program.

Freedman's Bureau Act. A bill which was vetoed by President Johnson in February, 1856. The second Freedman's Bureau bill was passed by Congress over his VETO on July 16, 1866. It established the FREEDMAN'S BUREAU to carry out certain functions relating to the employment, relief, and welfare of the ex-slave.

Freedom of the seas. In American foreign policy this refers to the frequent attempts to open the seas to all nations on an equal basis. The colonial opposition to the NAVAGATION ACTS was the earliest

expression of this principle. In the beginning of its national history the United States fought the wars against the Barbary pirates for the freedom of the seas. Its demands for the rights of neutral trade brought it into conflict with England and France during the Napoleonic Wars. The United States has occasionally deviated from this doctrine as in the establishment of a BLOCKADE against the Confederacy during the Civil War. In the opening years of World War I its insistence on the freedom of the seas involved the United States in diplomatic controversy with Great Britain when that nation stopped American ships on the high seas. The principle was enunciated as one of President WILSON'S FOURTEEN POINTS in 1918 but was not repeated in the Covenant of the LEAGUE OF NATIONS.

Free enterprise. The economic system which is characterized by the private ownership of the means of production and the investment of capital for profit purposes. As developed by the English economists Adam Smith and David Ricardo, free enterprise postulated an absence of government interference with business. In the United States its proponents have opposed government regulation of private business, and have advocated competition and the dependence upon "natural economic laws." See laissez-faire.

Free port. A port in the United States in which foreign vessels may unload cargoes for inspection, grading, and repackaging prior to trans-shipment to their ultimate destinations, without paying customs duties. In 1952 the only free port in the United States was located in Staten Island, New York.

Freeport Doctrine. The name applied to the answer of Senator STEPHEN A. DOUGLAS on August 27, 1858 to a question asked of him by ABRAHAM LINCOLN in the second of a series of debates, held at Freeport, Illinois. Lincoln had asked whether a TERRITORY could lawfully exclude SLAVERY from its constitution upon admission into the Union. Douglas declared that it could not but that slavery could be excluded, in effect, by unfriendly local legislation. Douglas' reply was aimed at retaining southern and northern Democratic support for his nomination for the presidency in 1860, but resulted in the loss of both. Lincoln sarcastically commented that Douglas believed that a thing could be lawfully driven out of a place where it had a lawful right to be. The result of the debate was to project Lincoln into the political limelight as the outstanding leader of the Republican Party. Although Douglas was reelected as Senator, Lincoln received his party's presidential nomination in 1860 and was elected.

FREER, Charles Lang. 1856-1919. Art collector. b. New York. Wealthy railroad and car manufacturer (1873-99); a founder of American Car and Foundry Co. (1899); collector of Whistler and oriental art; presented collection and funds for the building of the Freer Gallery of Art at Washington, D.C. to the SMITHSONIAN INSTITUTION (1906).

free silver. Expresses the demand of FARMERS, westerners, DEBTORS, and silver miners in the last third of the 19th century that Congress purchase and coin silver in unlimited quantities. Prior to 1873 Congress had done so under the Coinage Act of 1834, thus providing for a bi-metallic standard with an established relationship of 16 to 1 between silver and gold. With the DEMONETIZATION ACT OF 1873 silver was removed from the coinage list, leading to the demand for free silver. As a result of the pressure of the above mentioned groups Congress enacted the BLAND-ALLISON ACT of 1878 and the SHERMAN SILVER PURCHASE ACT of 1890. The SILVER PURCHASE

ACT OF 1934 has provided for the coinage of this metal through the present date.

Free Soil party. A minor party organized in the 1840's to combat the extension of SLAVERY into the newly acquired TERRITORIES of the United States. It was not an ABOLITIONIST party, being principally concerned with the status of slavery in the territory obtained from Mexico. Its presidential candidate in the election of 1848, MARTIN VAN BUREN, drew sufficient votes from LEWIS CASS, the Democratic candidate, to assure the election of the WHIG candidate, ZACHARY TAYLOR. Thereafter, the expanding strength of the southern Democrats brought about a reduction in the party's power, and its following was absorbed into the Republican party after 1854.

Free trade. The system of free and unlimited international exchange of goods without the payment of TARIFFS. Up to 1816 the U.S. practiced a variation of free trade, having imposed a REVENUE TARIFF in 1789. Since 1816 the United States has had a policy of high PROTECTIONISM with the exception of the period since 1934 when the reciprocal tariff policy was one of the FOURTEEN POINTS of President WILSON in 1918.

FRELINGHUYSEN, Frederick. 1753-1804. Revolutionary leader. b. New Jersey. Graduated College of New Jersey (later Princeton), (1770); studied law; fought in the Revolution as aide-de-camp to General DICKINSON; member, CONTINENTAL CONGRESS (1778, 1779, 1782, 1783); U.S. Senator (1793-96); helped suppress the WHISKEY REBELLION as major-general of the militia.

FRELINGHUYSEN, Frederick Theodore. 1817-1885. Statesman.. b. New Jersey. Graduated, Rutgers (1836); practiced law in Newark; attorney general of New Jersey (1861-66); U.S. Senator (1866-69, 1871-77); appointed U.S. Sec-

240

retary of State by ARTHUR (1881-85); negotiated with NICARAGUA and signed treaty which allowed the United States to build a canal.

FRELINGHUYSEN, Theodore. 1787-1862. Lawyer, educator and political leader. b. New Jersey. Graduated Princeton (1804); admitted to bar (1808); practiced law in Newark, N.J.; proposed moving CHEROKEES and other Indians west of the Mississippi; mayor of Newark (1836-39); chancellor, New York University (1839-50); president, Rutgers College (1850-62); WHIG candidate for Vice-President on ticket with HENRY CLAY (1844), defeated by a narrow margin.

FREMONT, John Charles. 1813-1890. Often referred to as "the pathfinder." Explorer and army officer. b. Georgia. Lieutenant, U.S. Army; member, Nicollet's expedition exploring the Mississippi and Missouri river areas (1838-39); led three expeditions into Oregon territory and succeeded in mapping the OREGON TRAIL; third expedition reached California (December, 1945); served in California during Mexican War; involved in STOCKTON-KEARNY quarrel and by refusing to obey orders was arrested; courtmartialed and convicted (1848); released by order of President POLK; gold discovered on his estate in California; one of first two U.S. Senators from California (1850-51); nominated presidential candidate on Republican ticket (1856); defeated by BUCHANAN; major general, CIVIL WAR; lost fortune in railroad venture; appointed governor of Arizona TERRITORY (1878-83).

French Alliance. See Alliance with France.

FRENCH, Daniel Chester. 1850-1931. Sculptor. b. New Hampshire. Best known works are The Minute Man of Concord at Concord, the bronze doors of the Boston Public Library, and many fine statues and portrait busts.

French and Indian War. The American phase of the Seven Years' War. It was fought in North America between 1754 and 1763 between England and France and their Indian allies. The struggle was one of a series of dynastic and colonial wars which had begun in 1689 and was not to end until the defeat of Napoleon in 1815. In North America its immediate cause was the rival claims of England and France on the region between the Alleghenies and the Mississippi. The first battle was fought for Fort Duquesne, the present site of Pittsburgh. The two year British expedition under General Braddock proved unsuccessful by 1755. With the transfer of the French command to Marquis de Montcalm and the accession of William Pitt as Prime Minister of England, the war took a more intense character. Following the British capture of Louisbourg, Fort Frontenac, and Fort Duquesne in 1758, Pitt planned the conquest of Canada. In 1759 victories at Ticonderoga, Crown Point, and Niagara brought the British to the doors of Quebec. The famous battle on the Plains of Abraham which led to the deaths of Montcalm and Wolfe, resulted in the fall of Quebec. Montreal fell the next year and the conquest of Canada was concluded. By the terms of the TREATY OF PARIS OF 1763, the French empire in North America came to an end.

FRENEAU, Philip Morin. 1752-1832. Poet. Referred to as the "poet of the American Revolution." b. New York City. Graduated, Princeton University (1771); as a privateer captured by British in West Indies (1776-79); worked in Philadelphia post office (1781-84); wrote poems for Freeman's Journal; appointed by JEFFERSON clerk in U.S. DEPARTMENT OF STATE (1791); founded and edited National Gazette, a democratic paper in opposition to FENNO's Gazette (1791-93). Author of many books of poetry including Poems Written and Published During *the American Revolutionary War* (2 vols. 1809).

FRICK, Henry Clay. 1849-1919. Industrialist. b. Pennsylvania. Controlled the building and operation of coke ovens in Connellsville coal district of Pennsylvania, (1889); chairman, Carnegie Steel Co. (1889-1900) in large part responsible for merger and formation of U. S. STEEL CORP. (1901); donated and endowed his home and ART treasures which became the Frick Museum in New York City.

FRIES, John. 1750?-1818. Leader of Fries' Rebellion. b. Pennsylvania. Served in American Revolution; opposed federal property tax (1798); collected army of Pennsylvania Germans to fight assessors (1799); arrested by Federal troops sent by President ADAMS, tried and sentenced to death; pardoned by the president (1800).

Frontier. In American history, the westernmost line of TERRITORY inhabited and cultivated by concentrated groups of people. The frontier line was generally known by the existence of villages, or other organized communities, and fairly well established TRADE relationships. It was an irregular north-south line starting at the Atlantic coast in the early days of settlement in the 17th century and running constantly westward till its disappearance at the Pacific coast according to the census of 1890. The EFFECTS OF THE FRONTIER on American civilization have been thoroughly analyzed in the works of FREDERICK JACKSON TURNER and Frederick L. Paxson.

Frontier, effects of. As interpreted by FREDERICK JACKSON TURNER in his volume, *The Frontier in American History*, the FRONTIER has exercised a profound effect upon American culture. It was Turner's thesis that the frontier produced the spirit of DEMOCRACY, individualism, and the desire for liberty. The conditions of frontier life were claimed to have molded the character of the settlers and strongly influenced the political and social institutions of the American people. The frontier fostered the development of self reliance, independence, FREE ENTERPRISE, faith in material progress, and a belief in the future. It witnessed greater social and economic equality and was the inspirational source and home of much of the reform political legislation of the 19th and 20th centuries. These have included the spread of VOTING, WOMAN SUFFRAGE, the PRIMARY, SHORT BALLOT, REFERENDUM, RECALL, and the INITIATIVE.

Frontiersman. See pioneers.

FROST, Robert L. 1874-1963. Poet. b. San Francisco, California. Studied at Dartmouth (1892); Harvard (1897-99); professor of English, Amherst (1916-20; 1923-25; 1926-38); professor of POETRY, Harvard (1936); winner of Pulitzer prize for 1923, 1930, 1936, 1942. Author *A Boy's Will* (1913), *Mountain Interval* (1916), *From Snow to Snow* (1936) etc.

FRYE, William Pierce. 1831-1911. Political leader. b. Maine. Graduated, Bowdoin College (1850); studied law, member, U. S. House of Representatives (1871-81); U.S. Senator (1881-1911); conservative Republican; opposed STRONG CENTRAL GOVERNMENT; expansionist; president pro tempore of the Senate (1896).

Fugitive slave laws. Two laws passed by Congress in 1793 and 1850 for the purpose of achieving the return of escaped SLAVES. The most notable of these laws was the fugitive slave provision of the OMNIBUS ACT of 1850. Like most of its predecessors its enforcement was vitiated by the enactment of PERSONAL LIBERTY LAWS by the northern state legislatures. With the help of the UNDERGROUND RAILROAD this northern legislation successfully accomplished the transfer of thousands of slaves to freedom in the North and in Canada.

Fulbright Act. A law of Congress passed in June, 1946 for the purpose of providing the financial means for student exchanges between the United States and foreign countries. It was estimated that a total of 100,000 American students would ultimately go abroad to study and teach at government expense and 50,000 foreign students would be admitted to the United States. The program contemplated a limit of $1,000,000 per year for each country. The law provided that a nation, buying surplus American war equipment, could pay for it, in part, by sponsoring the EDUCATION of American students there. In 1949 grants were made under the Fulbright Act to 831 Americans and 1,002 Europeans. The Americans included 61 professors, 100 researchers, 123 teachers, and 547 students. In 1950-51 it was estimated that 1,000 Americans would go abroad for graduate study, research, and teaching. In that period 28,000 foreign students were located in American colleges and universities and 15,000 Americans were abroad, many of them under Fulbright grants. In the United States 1190 colleges and universities participated in the preliminary selection of persons for Fulbright awards. The Fulbright Act was considered an important contribution to international peace and understanding. Its significance is seen by the knowledge that, before World War II, only 9353 ALIENS came to study in the United States between 1935 and 1939.

Fulbright Resolution. A resolution submitted to the House of Representatives by Fulbright of Arkansas on September 21, 1943 which declared that the House favored the participation of the United States in "appropriate international machinery with power to establish and maintain a just and lasting peace." Although the resolution was adopted by a vote of 360 to 29 it was discarded by the Senate on November 5th in favor of another which adopted the declaration of the MOSCOW CONFERENCE.

"Full Dinner Pail." The slogan of the Republican party in the election campaign of 1900 which was designed to attract the votes of industrial labor by stressing the economic prosperity of the period of MC KINLEY'S administration.

Full Employment Act. See Employment Act of 1946.

FULLER, Margaret. Marchioness Ossoli. 1810-1850. Critic and social reformer. b. Massachusetts. Held literary and cultural group meetings for women (1839-44); friend of EMERSON; an editor, *Dial,* journal of TRANSCENDENTALISTS (1840-42); literary critic, New York *Tribune* (1844-46); one of the best literary critics in America.

FULLER, Melville Weston. 1833-1910. Jurist. b. Maine. Graduated, Bowdoin (1853); Harvard Law School; admitted to bar (1855); prominent lawyer, Chicago; appointed chief justice, U.S. Supreme Court (1888-1910) by CLEVELAND; member, PERMANENT COURT OF ARBITRATION, The Hague (1900-10).

FULTON, Robert. 1765-1815. Engineer, artist and inventor. b. Pennsylvania. Portrait painter, Philadelphia (1782-86); studied with WEST in England (1786-93); became interested in engineering and patented machine for sawing marble; machine for twisting hemp into rope, etc.; invented submarine, Paris (1797-1806); ROBERT R. LIVINGSTON, the American Minister to France commissioned him to build a STEAMBOAT (1802); his boat the *Clermont* sailed up the Hudson to Albany and back (Aug. 17-22, 1807); his was not the first steamboat but the first commercially successful one; also designed other steamboats, a torpedo boat, a ferry and built a steam frigate at request of the government (launched 1815). Author of *A Treatise on the Improvement of Canal Navigation* (1796).

Fundamental Constitution of Carolina. A series of constitutional articles drawn up in 1667 by John Locke for the proprietors of the Carolina colony. Their complex and involved governmental machinery were wholly unsuited to the needs of a FRONTIER community and thus they never went into practical operation. Interesting among their provisions were the guarantees of certain CIVIL LIBERTIES, although property qualifications and aristocratic control were maintained.

Fundamental Orders of Connecticut. Adopted in 1639 by the residents of the Connecticut towns of Hartford, Windsor, and Wetherfield. This series of laws has the distinction of being the first written constitution in North America. They are also notable for their democratic provision, making church membership unnecessary for suffrage purposes. Suffrage was also extended to all persons accepted by a majority of the township in which they resided. The document provided for the election of a governor, six assistants, and a legislative assembly. It is generally acknowledged that it was a product of the inspiration of THOMAS HOOKER. Although superficially more liberal than the government of Massachusetts, the Puritan leadership of Connecticut was not less exclusive and intolerant so that the provisions were frequently ignored.

Funding Act. See assumption of state debts.

FUNSTON, Frederick. 1865-1917. Army officer. b. Ohio. Served in CUBA with the insurrectionists (1896-98); served in PHILIPPINES (1898); helped to suppress rebellion against AGUINALDO; famous for his capture of Aguinaldo (1901); brigadier general and awarded MEDAL OF HONOR; in command at San Francisco when earthquake occurred (1906); major general (1914).

Fur trading. One of the most important INDUSTRIES in the colonial period. It was probably the single greatest lure to European settlers before the Revolution. Early settlements were established in New England, the St. Lawrence valley, GREAT LAKES area, and the Ohio and Mississippi valleys in the search for fur. As the WESTWARD MOVEMENT opened the trans-Mississippi region to settlement, fur trading moved to the ROCKY MOUNTAIN and Pacific coast areas. Although it later became subordinate to more lucrative industries, fur trading served the extremely useful purpose of opening the West and attracting immigrants. It involved the colonies, and later the United States, in diplomatic and military conflicts with the Indians, Spain, Russia, England, Holland, and France.

Furuseth Act. See LaFollette Seamen's Act.

G

GADSDEN, Christopher. 1724-1805. Revolutionary leader. b. South Carolina. Leader of South Carolina opposition to STAMP ACT; delegate to CONTINENTAL CONGRESS (1774-76); brigadier general, Continental army (1776); voted for ratification of Constitution at the convention (1788).

GADSDEN, James. 1788-1858. Army officer and diplomat. b. South Carolina. Grandson of CHRISTOPHER GADSDEN. Graduated, Yale University; served in War of 1812; in Florida against the SEMINOLES (1821-39); U.S. commissioner in charge of moving Indians to Florida reservations (1823); wanted to build railroad across the south to California; appointed by PIERCE as U.S. Minister to Mexico (1853-54); responsible for GADSDEN PURCHASE which acquired from Mexico the TERRITORY that is now New Mexico and Arizona.

Gadsden Purchase. Refers to the purchase in 1853 from Mexico of a small strip of land measuring 45,535 square miles in area, south of the Gila River in what is today southern Arizona. The land was purchased because it offered the best route for a railroad across the southern Rockies to the Pacific Coast. The large sum of $10,000,000 paid by the United States has often been referred to by critics of the Mexican War as "conscience money" paid to Mexico

for the provinces obtained by the United States in the TREATY OF GUADALUPE-HIDALGO. The negotiator of this treaty was JAMES GADSDEN, the U.S. Minister to Mexico at the time.

gag rule. A rule adopted by Congress in 1836 on the motion of JOHN C. CALHOUN. It provided that all anti-slavery petitions thenceforth to be submitted to Congress be laid on the table without action. The measure was taken by the pro-slave Congressmen to stem the flood of anti-slavery petitions to Congress which followed the establishment of the AMERICAN ANTISLAVERY SOCIETY in 1833. Although originally supported by northern Democrats, the struggle against the rule, led by JOHN QUINCY ADAMS, forced its repeal in 1844. The rule was attacked during this eight year period as an unconstitutional deprivation of the right of petition.

GAINES, Edmund Pendleton. 1777-1849. Army officer. b. Virginia. Studied law and practiced in Mississippi TERRITORY; as colonel defended Fort Erie in War of 1812; served in Seminole War, Black Hawk War, Florida War, and Mexican War; commanded eastern department.

GAINES, George Strother. 1784?-1873. Pioneer in Alabama. b. North Carolina. His ability to deal with Choctaw tribe gained the Alabama TERRITORY for the

United States; gained help of the tribe against the CREEK: (1812); later became wealthy merchant in Mobile, Ala.

GALLATIN, Albert. Full name Abraham Alfonse Albert. 1761-1849. Financier and statesman. b. Switzerland. To United States (1780); served in Pennsylvania legislature (1790-92); U.S. Senator (1793) but unseated because he had less than nine years of CITIZENSHIP; member, U.S. House of Representatives (1795-1801); leader of Republican minority in the House; appointed U.S. Secretary of the Treasury by JEFFERSON (1801-1814); after War of 1812 negotiated peace TREATY with Great Britain (1814); U.S. Minister to France (1816-23); Minister to Great Britain (1826-27); president of National Bank, New York (1831-39).

GALLAUDET, Edward Miner. 1837-1917. Educator. Studied at Trinity College; Head of the Columbia Institution for the Deaf and Dumb, Washington D.C. Made important progress with the handicapped started by his father, Thomas, who was the first to teach the deaf in America.

GALLINGER, Jacob Harold. 1837-1918. Physician and politician. b. Ontario, Canada. M.D. New York Homeopathic Medical College (1868) Practiced Concord, New Hampshire; U.S. Senator (1891-1918); prominent Republican but backed WILSON's war policies; supported strong MERCHANT MARINE.

GALLOWAY, Joseph. 1729?-1803. Lawyer and Loyalist. Prominent lawyer in Philadelphia; member, Pennsylvania colonial legislature (1756-64; 1765-75); delegate, CONTINENTAL CONGRESS (1774-75); opposed independence of colonies; made administrator of Philadelphia by HOWE; escaped, after its capture, to England.

GAMBLE, Hamilton Rowan. 1798-1864. Political leader. b. Virginia. Practiced law in Missouri; justice, state supreme

court (1851-54); opposed SECESSION and was made territorial governor; tried for emancipation of the slaves (1863) in the TERRITORY but was defeated.

GARFIELD, Harry Augustus. 1863-1942. Scholar and educator. b. Ohio. Son of President JAMES A. GARFIELD. Graduated, Williams College (1885); studied law, Columbia University; practised law, Cleveland (1888-1903); taught law at Western Reserve University; taught politics at Princeton University (1903-08); President, Williams College (1908-34); U. S. FUEL ADMINISTRATOR (1917-19).

GARFIELD, James Abram. 1831-1881. b. Cuyahoga County, Ohio. Graduated Williams College (1856); teacher and head of Hiram College. Ohio (1857-61); Colonel, Ohio volunteer infantry regiment (1861); brigadier general (1862) major general (1863); member, U.S. House of Representatives (1863-80); chairman, BANKING committee (1869-71); conservative Republican leader (from 1876); elected President (1880); had difficulty with appointments; shot by Charles Guiteau (July 2, 1881; died Sept. 19, 1881) and succeeded by CHESTER A. ARTHUR.

GARLAND, Augustus Hill. 1832-1899. Lawyer and politician. Prominent Arkansas lawyer; member, Confederate provisional congress, lower house (1861-64); senate (1864-65); elected U.S. Senator from Arkansas but was refused seat (1867); Governor of Arkansas (1874-76); U. S. Senator (1877-85); worked for CIVIL SERVICE REFORM; appointed by CLEVELAND U.S. Attorney General (1885-89).

GARNER, John Nance. 1868-. Politician. b. Texas. Admitted to bar (1890); member, U.S. House of Representatives (1903-33); minority leader and member of WAYS AND MEANS COMMITTEE; Speaker of the House (1931-33); elected Vice-President of the United States and served with F. D. ROOSEVELT (1933-41).

GARRETSON, James Edmund. 1828-1895. Oral Surgeon. Graduated Philadelphia College of Dentistry (1856); University of Pennsylvania medical school (1859); practiced and taught in Philadelphia; often referred to as the "father of modern oral surgery"; author of standard work in the field of *A System of Oral Surgery* (1869).

GARRETT, Thomas. 1789-1871. ABOLITIONIST. b. Pennsylvania. Member of Pennsylvania Abolition Society; Quaker; operated a station on the UNDERGROUND RAILROAD and is said to have helped over 2,000 slaves.

GARRISON, William Lloyd. 1805-1879. ABOLITIONIST. b. Massachusetts. Famous as the founder of the *Liberator* (1831), an anti-slavery journal; leader of radical abolitionists; a founder of the AMERICAN ANTI-SLAVERY SOCIETY (1833); president (1843-65); attacked by mob in Boston (1835); with a prominent NEGRO FREDERICK DOUGLASS he gave lectures (1847); opposed COMPROMISE OF 1850; after Civil War he campaigned in behalf of the Indians and for WOMAN SUFFRAGE.

GARVEY, Marcus. 1887-1940. NEGRO leader and agitator. b. Jamaica, British West Indies. Edited the *Negro World* in New York City (1917); called himself the "Leader of the Negro Peoples of the World"; started "Back to Africa" campaign and collected a great deal of money which he later could not account for; convicted of fraud and deported.

GARY, Elbert Henry. 1846-1927. Lawyer and industrialist. b. Illinois. Practiced as corporation lawyer, Chicago; with the help of MORGAN he organized the Federal Steel Co. (1898); an organizer of the UNITED STATES STEEL CORPORATION, then the largest in the country (1901-03); chairman, board of directors, U.S.

Steel Corp. (1903-27); believed in OPEN SHOP and opposed LABOR UNIONS.

GARY, James Albert. 1833-1920. Industrialist and politician. b. Connecticut. Head of large textile business in Maryland; banker in Baltimore and director of many companies; Republican leader of the state; appointed U.S. Postmaster General by MC KINLEY (1897-98); urged establishment of POSTAL SAVINGS bank system.

Gas Industry. Gas springs were discovered before the Revolution adjacent to what is today Charleston, West Virginia. In the first decade of the 19th century similar springs were located in upper New York State along the Lake Erie shore. In 1806 gas was first used for lighting a home in Newport, Rhode Island. In 1816 Baltimore, Maryland became the first city in the United States to be lighted by gas. Before this, OIL had replaced candles as a means of public street lighting in the larger cities. With the opening of new sources of gas supply, street lighting by gas was adopted by Boston in 1822, New York in 1823, and Philadelphia in 1837. In 1847 gas lighting was adopted by Congress for the CAPITOL building and grounds. The first commercial use of gas was probably by a lighthouse on Lake Erie in 1826. In the 1840's gas was used in salt MINING in Pennsylvania and West Virginia and, after its discovery in Erie, Pennsylvania, as a fuel in nearby factories. The first CORPORATION to dispense gas was organized in Fredonia, New York in 1865. Thereafter its use in commercial production spread rapidly to the pottery INDUSTRY in Ohio and IRON and STEEL INDUSTRY in Ohio and Pittsburgh. The development of the gas industry provided a stimulus to the growth of factory cities in Ohio, Michigan, and Indiana by the end of the 19th century. At this time gas was also being used to heat homes. In the early 20th century new wells were opened in California, Kansas, Louisiana, Oklahoma, and Texas. Gas and its by-products were widely developed for many industrial and residential uses in the first half of the 20th century. It dominated the fuel field for residential usage. According to the Gas Appliance Manufacturers Association more than 30,000,000 American homes used gas for cooking in 1952. In the decade up to that year the use of gas for house heating has risen by more than 400 percent. Over 2,400 different types of industrial gas equipment, involving 25,000 adaptations, were employed in American industry for heat-treating and other processes. In 1950 an estimated 627,978,-581,000 cubic feet of gas were employed in the production of electric energy in the United States. Although natural gas was little used before 1870, except for lighting purposes, it has in recent years been more widely accepted for heat and power. Its production more than doubled between 1922 and the 1940's at which time approximately 20 percent was used for household light and heat and the remainder in industry. The total production of natural gas in 1950 was 6,124,302,000,000 cubic feet, valued at $404,204,000. Proven recoverable reserves of natural gas were estimated at nearly 200,000,000,000,000 cubic feet. The nation's pipeline system, including field and gathering lines, exceeded 400,-000 miles. The production of manufactured gas was 2,660,000,000 therms, including all manufactured gas products produced and purchased by gas utilities. The importance of the industry and the growth of MONOPOLY control in it led to federal regulation in 1938. The Natural Gas Act of that year placed all persons owning or operating any gas TRANSPORTATION facilities in INTERSTATE COMMERCE under the regulation of the FEDERAL POWER COMMISSION. Gas pipe lines were required to file reports and rates and maintain uniform accounting systems. The Commission was authorized to investigate the cost of transporting and producing natural gas upon its own motion or at the request of any state public utility or public service commission. The interstate nature of natural gas transportation had developed difficulty in regulation by these commissions, a problem which the Act sought to solve by leading to more effective regulation of local gas utilities by the state agencies. The Act dealt only with natural gas operations and applied to the transportation of gas in interstate commerce and to its sale for "ultimate public consumption." It specifically excluded the production of natural gas and the local distribution of gas. The Commission's fact-finding powers were broader than its regulatory authority, consisting of the power to investigate the cost of production and transportation. No attempt was made to regulate manufactured gas which is almost completely intrastate in nature and therefore subject to the jurisdiction of the state agencies. It has been estimated that about one-third of the nation's natural gas production moves in interstate commerce and is therefore subject to the regulatory power of the Commission. The state governments by and large have provided for the regulation of the rates and services of natural gas retailers. In 1950 President TRUMAN vetoed the Kerr Natural Gas Bill which would have removed from the jurisdiction of the FPC control on prices of natural gas distributed by interstate pipelines. Although no trend toward municipal ownership and operation of gas has been noted, by 1940 34 cities over 5,000 population distributed gas to their communities. An additional 44 cities manufactured and distributed gas. These 78 communities represented 3.9 percent of the total gas plants in existence at that time. In July, 1952 the American Gas Association announced that the gas distribution and pipeline industry will have spent a record high of $5,600,000,000 in the five year period through 1956 for new construction and plant expansion. Of this sum the natural gas branch of the industry expected to spend over $5,-000,000,000.

Gaspée Affair. Refers to the forceable boarding by a group of Rhode Islanders of the British revenue vessel *Gaspée* on June 9th, 1772. The colonists burned the vessel to the water's edge. The incident was the result of the friction between British customs officials and colonial importers. A special royal commission, sent from England to investigate the affair, collected no evidence and thus no convictions were made. Nevertheless it served to further aggravate the unfriendly feeling between the colonies and the mother country.

GATES, Frederick Taylor. 1853-1929. Baptist clergyman. b. New York. Secretary, Baptist Education Society; helped to found the University of Chicago; became business associate of J. D. ROCKEFELLER (1893); organized and chairman of general education board (1903) and the Rockefeller Institute for Medical Research; responsible for spending of Rockefeller bequests and in large part for the establishment of the ROCKEFELLER FOUNDATION.

GATES, Horatio. 1728?-1806. Revolutionary general. b. England. Joined Braddock's army in Virginia (1755); at suggestion of WASHINGTON he bought land in Virginia (1772); brigadier general on colonial side at outbreak of Revolution (1776-77); major general (1776); in command of FORT TICONDEROGA (1776-77); credited with repulsing BURGOYNE's army, although SCHUYLER and ARNOLD were in large part responsible for the success of the campaign; participated in the CONWAY CABAL which tried to replace Washington with Gates; failed; lost Battle of Camden (1780) and relieved of command; served with Washington at

headquarters throughout the remainder of the war.

GATES, Sir Thomas. 1585?-1621. Colonial administrator. Part of Drake expedition to Virginia (1585-86); one of grantees in original charter to Virginia and Plymouth companies (1606); lost in hurricane on vessel *Sea Venture* and stranded on a Bermuda island (1609); to Jamestown (1611-14) as governor of colony.

GATLING, Richard Jordan. 1818-1903. Inventor. b. North Carolina. Invented a rice planter, wheat drill and hempbreaker; best known for invention of a rapid-fire revolving machine gun known at the "Gatling Gun" (patented Nov. 4, 1862).

GAYNOR, William Jay. 1849-1913. Jurist and politician. Practiced law Brooklyn, N.Y.; justice of supreme court of New York City (1893-1909); mayor (1909-13).

Geary Act. See Chinese Exclusion Acts.

GEARY, John White. 1819-1873. Political leader. b. Pennsylvania. Served in Mexican War; mayor of San Francisco (1850); territorial governor of Kansas (1856); established a strong and peaceful government in the territories, but when neither PIERCE nor BUCHANAN supported his policies he resigned (1857); brigadier general of volunteers in Civil War (1862); brevetted major general (1865); governor of Pennsylvania (1867-1873).

General Accounting Office. Established by Congress in the BUDGET AND ACCOUNTING ACT of 1929. It is administered by the COMPTROLLER GENERAL of the United States, and has the power to install and supervise accounting procedures in most EXECUTIVE DEPARTMENTS and agencies of the federal government. Its other functions include the examination of claims against and payments by the

United States, the auditing of federal expenditures, and the checking of receipts.

General Court, Colonial. This typically New England institution originated with the Massachusetts Bay Colony. It consisted of the governor, eighteen assistants and the freeman of the company. The charter gave this body full powers to govern, correct, punish and rule. Other colonies adopted this practice and thus there developed the notion that all reserve powers of government resided in the General Court.

General Electric Company. The largest manufacturer of electrical appliances and equipment in the United States. It was organized in 1892 as a merger of the Thomson-Houston Electric Company and the Edison General Electric Company. All INVENTIONS, PATENTS, legal rights, and goodwill in the manufacturing and developing of electric motors and generators, dynamos, recording equipment, and public address systems were assumed by the new organization. Its first president was Charles A. Coffin. Through subsidiary corporations the company operates similar plants in foreign nations.

General Motors Corporation. The largest manufacturer of automotive vehicles in the world. It is also the largest manufacturing establishment. It was founded in 1908 in Michigan when William C. Durant brought together the formerly independent Buick, Oakland, and Oldsmobile companies. In 1955 its principal production was of automobiles which included the Chevrolet, largest selling in the world, Pontiac, Oldsmobile, Buick, and Cadillac. In 1964 the Company had a net income of $1,592,000,000 on sales of $17,000,000,000.

Genêt Affair. An incident in 1793 arising out of the demand of France for American assistance in the former's war against England at that time. Citizen Edmont Genêt was sent as the first minister of the French Republic to the United States to argue that his country was entitled to assistance under the Treaty of Alliance of 1778 which he alleged to be still in existence. Received enthusiastically by the American people Genêt set about raising troops and commissioning PRIVATEERS. The JEFFERSONIANS generally supported his efforts which were roundly attacked by the FEDERALISTS. WASHINGTON'S PROCLAMATION OF NEUTRALITY on April 22, exactly two weeks after Genêt's arrival, angered him and induced him to appeal openly to the American people for aid. Outraged by this Washington convened his CABINET which demanded that France recall its minister. A governmental change in that country brought about an order for Genêt's arrest. Washington's generosity in refusing his extradition preserved Genêt's safety in the United States.

Geneva Convention. An international conference of 13 nations held in Geneva, Switzerland in 1864. The participating nations concluded a agreement which established rules for the care of the sick and wounded in war. The agreement provided for the neutrality of ambulance and military hospitals, the non-belligerent status of persons who aid the wounded, and sick soldiers of any nationality, the return of prisoners to their country if they are incapable of serving, and the adoption of a white flag with a red cross for use on hospitals, ambulances, and evacuation centers whose neutrality would be recognized by this symbol. Ultimately, practically every civilized nation adhered to the Geneva Convention. As a result of the persistence of CLARA BARTON the United States adhered to the agreement in 1884 by the "American Amendment" which simultaneously extended the scope of the AMERICAN RED CROSS to peacetime humanitarian work in connection with floods, earthquakes, and other public disasters.

Geneva Disarmament Conference. See World Disarmament Conference.

Geneva Naval Conference. A conference which met at Geneva, Switzerland from June 20, to August 24, 1927. It was called at the proposal of President COOLIDGE to discuss the extension to smaller types of vessels of the naval DISARMAMENTS treaties of the WASHINGTON NAVAL CONFERENCE. Japan and Great Britain attended the Conference. France and Italy declined the invitation. The United States delegation proposed to extend the 5:5:3 ratio to other types of vessels and to limit the tonnage in each class as well as the size of guns and torpedo tubes. England attempted to retain freedom in the construction of 7,500 ton cruisers. The United States opposed England's demand, requesting in turn a small number of 10,000 ton cruisers. The failure to reconcile the Anglo-American proposals brought the Conference to an unsuccessful conclusion.

Geneva Summit Conference (1955). The Big Four (President Eisenhower, Prime Minister Anthony Eden, Premier Edgar Faure, and Premier Bulganin) met in Geneva for six days beginning July 18, 1955. Russia opposed unification of Germany. President Eisenhower advanced a new proposal on disarmament which provided exchange with Russia of military blue prints showing location and strength of each country's armed forces; and allowed aerial reconnaissance of each other's military installations. The West urged the lifting of the Iron Curtain and the interchange of personal travel, ideas, and information between East and West. To explore further the topics discussed at the Summit Conference, a subsequent meeting of the Foreign Ministers was arranged to take place on Oct. 27, 1955, in Geneva. The Eisenhower proposals on armaments were turned over to a 5 power subcommittee of the U. N. Disarmament Commission.

GEORGE, Henry. 1839-1897. Economist. b. Philadelphia, Pennsylvania. Learned PRINTING business and worked as typesetter, San Francisco (1856-59); started working on single-tax theory (1868-69); wrote a pamphlet explaining his theories entitled *Our Land and Land Policy* (1871); he believed that the entire tax burden should be placed on land, granting more equal opportunity and relieving INDUSTRY from taxes, and destroying the possibility of advantage by MONOPOLY; his most famous work was *Progress and Poverty* (1877-79); lectured and traveled abroad; ran for mayor of New York City but was defeated (1886); died while campaigning again for mayor (1897). Other works include *Social Problems* (1883), *Protection or Free Trade* (1886).

Georgia. The 21st state in size, with an area of 58,876 square miles. Entered the Union as the fourth state on January 2, 1788. Seceded on January 19, 1861 and readmitted on July 15, 1870. In 1950 Georgia's POPULATION of 3-444,-578, made it 13th in rank. Atlanta is the capital. Its largest cities are Atlanta, Savannah, and Columbus. Georgia is one of the most important producers of peaches, COTTON, tobacco, peanuts, and pecans in the United States. It is the nation's largest producer of resin and turpentine. CATTLE raising has come into recent prominence. Manufactured goods include automobile parts, processed food, marble, clay products, TEXTILES, and LUMBER products. The celebrated infantile paralysis foundation, where President F. D. ROOSEVELT died, is located at Warm Springs. Georgia was discovered in 1540 by DE SOTO. Its nicknames are the "Cracker State" and "Empire State of the South."

GERARD, James Watson. 1867-1952. Lawyer and diplomat. Graduated Columbia University; practiced law in New York City (from 1892); associate justice of New York Supreme court (1908-13);

Ambassador to Germany in opening years of World War I handling many difficult situations with great skill (1913-17). Author of *My Four Years in Germany* (1917), *Face to Face with Kaiserism* (1918).

German Federal Republic. See Bonn Republic.

German Peace Contract. A series of 15 "contractual agreements" signed on May 26, 1952 by the United States, Great Britain, France, and the GERMAN FEDERAL REPUBLIC. The agreements technically ended the OCCUPATION OF GERMANY by the three Allied Powers, but provided for the stay in West Germany of the 500,000 allied troops there at the time of signing. Other provisions included a financial agreement whereby West Germany was to split her defense BUDGET between the maintenance of Allied forces and 12 German divisions for the new EUROPEAN ARMY, an ARBITRATION agreement to cover future disputes, a protocol pledging the Allies to remain in the western sector of Berlin, and a troop agreement pertaining to the relations between West Germany and the Allied troops. The Western Powers retained the right to maintain defense forces as long as the international situation makes it necessary, to intervene to restore order in West Germany in the event of attack from the outside, and to negotiate with the Soviet Union over Berlin and German unification. Allied forces were thereafter to be subject to German law and to continue the use of special "occupational currency." Other provisions included clauses dealing with the settlement of matters arising out of the war and the occupation, decartelization, the continuance of property restitution to Nazi victims, and compensation for injuries suffered in concentration camps. The contract repealed the occupation statute, abolished the AL-LIED HIGH COMMISSION, and placed relations between the German Federal Republic and the Allied Powers on a government-to-government basis with the exchange of ambassadors. The document was subject to the ratification of the signatory powers.

Germantown, Battle of. A battle of the Revolution which was fought on October 4, 1777. After WASHINGTON's defeat at BRANDYWINE on September 11th, he learned that HOWE had sent a detachment to seize Forts Mercer and Mifflin. In the morning of October 4th he divided his army into two columns under Generals SULLIVAN and GREENE who advanced upon the village of Germantown, just outside Philadelphia. Sullivan's wing drove Howe's forces back as Greene attacked the British outposts opposite Sullivan. Misled by a heavy fog, General Stephen mistook the American left-center for the enemy and charged upon them. This error, plus the lack of ammunition, caused a panic, which brought on a general retreat. CORNWALLIS, bringing his reserves from Philadelphia, aided Howe in driving back the patriot army. Although the battle was lost, the American army retreated in good order, carrying with it its own guns and some captured from the enemy. American casualties totaled 1,071. The British lost 535.

Germany, Battle of. After the defeat of the Germans at the BATTLE OF THE BULGE the Western Allies coordinated their defenses with the Russians moving in from Poland. At the end of January, 1945 a combined Anglo-American-Canadian Army, of which two-thirds were Americans, massed for the final campaign. The British Twenty-First Army Group was commanded by Field Marshal Montgomery in the north. In the center the American Twelfth Army Group was commanded by General BRADLEY. In the south General Devers commanded the American Sixth Army

Group which included French troops. On February 7th the United States Third Army crossed the German frontier in 10 places. The next day British and Canadian troops moved forward from Holland. By March 5th American troops had crossed the Saar River and advanced into the Ruhr, having captured a total of 954,377 prisoners since D-Day. With the breach in the German "West Wall" defense, Trier and Cologne fell in March. On March 8th the Rhine River was crossed and by the end of the month all the Allied armies were beyond the Rhine. On April 18th the Third Army under General PATTON reached Czechoslovakia. On April 11th the United States Ninth Army reached the Elbe River. By April 29th German resistance in northern Italy was broken and German troops surrendered unconditionally on May 2nd. On that day Russian troops entered Berlin from the East, and on May 7th Admiral Donitz, who had been proclaimed head of the German government after Hitler's alleged suicide on April 29th, surrendered unconditionally. On May 8th President TRUMAN and Prime Minister Churchill proclaimed V-E DAY, the end of the war in Europe.

GERONIMO. 1829-1909. Apache Indian leader. b. Arizona. Chief of the Chiricahna group of the APACHE tribe; fought constantly against the white settlers on Apache land and although defeated and forced to surrender to the army (1885) he escaped; later imprisoned in Florida; moved to Alabama and then to INDIAN TERRITORY in Oklahoma. He was an outstanding leader and many legends have grown around his name.

GERRY, Elbridge. 1744 - 1814. Statesman. b. Massachusetts. Graduated Harvard University (1762); member, Massachusetts Provincial Congress (1774-75); CONTINENTAL CONGRESS (1776-81, 1782-85); a signer of the DECLARATION OF INDEPENDENCE and ARTICLES OF CONFEDERATION; delegate, CONSTITUTION CONVENTION (1787); opposed DRAFT of Constitution; member, U.S. House of Representatives (1789-93); member of mission to France in famous XYZ AFFAIR (1797-98); after trying to negotiate separate terms with Talleyrand he was recalled (1798); governor of Massachusetts (1810, 1811); his plan for redistricting of Massachusetts to give Republicans control was known as "GERRYMANDERING"; elected Vice-President of United States with MADISON as President (1813-14).

Gerrymander. Refers to the redistricting of a state for the election of congressional or state legislature representatives. The purpose of such redistricting is to establish a greater number of districts which will return members of the majority party of the state legislature to itself or to the House of Representatives of the Congress. The move is always taken by the majority party of the state legislature and has been attacked as a violation of the principles of equal and compact districting and homogeneity of popular interests. The origin of the term goes back to the drawing of a sprawling district created in Massachusetts in 1812. The drawing, with its wings, teeth, and claws, so strongly resembled a salamander that it was called such. A NEWSPAPER editor changed the name to gerrymander after Governor ELBRIDGE GERRY of Massachusetts who had been responsible for so many redistrictings of this type.

GERSHWIN, George. 1898-1937. Composer. b. Brooklyn, New York. Famous composer of popular songs, musical comedies, and orchestral works. Best known works *Rhapsody in Blue* (1923), *Piano Concerto in F* (1925), *Porgy and Bess* (1935), *An American in Paris,* and other works.

Gettysburg Address. The famous commemorative address, delivered by President LINCOLN on November 19, 1863, at the dedication of a military cemetery on the battlefield at Gettysburg, Pennsylvania. The speech contains the notable

253

phrase that the United States is a "government of the people, by the people, and for the people."

Gettysburg, Battle of. The turning point of the Civil War. It marked the defeat of LEE's attempt to invade Pennsylvania and reach Washington. It was fought between July 1st and 3rd, 1863, resulting in casualties of 23,003 to the Union army and 20,451 to the Confederate army, including many generals. The Confederate army of 70,000 was repulsed on the third day by the Union army of 93,000, commanded by General MEADE. Having replaced HOOKER, Meade concentrated his troops at Pike Creek, fifteen miles from Gettysburg. His plans were frustrated when Lee attacked REYNOLDS' division at Gettysburg on July 1st. Reinforced by the arrival of troops under General HOWARD and HANCOCK, the Union army held on July 2nd, the bloodiest day of the battle. The following day the battle swung in favor of the Union army when Meade attacked, driving EWELL from Rock Creek. PICKETT's disastrous charge upon Cemetery Ridge failed, with a loss of 4,600 Confederates. Lee was compelled to retreat, and the Union army had stemmed Lee's march to the North. The South's simultaneous loss of VICKSBURG turned the tide in the favor of the North.

Ghent, Treaty of. Negotiated in 1814 between the United States and Great Britain. Ended the War of 1812. It provided that Great Britain would give up IMPRESSMENT of American seamen, surrender British held forts on the northwest frontier, and extend FISHING rights to the U.S. in Canadian waters. Boundry commissions were established to determine the line between Canada and the United States. Other provisions concerned commercial relations, the question of naval forces on the GREAT LAKES, and an agreement to postpone the OREGON BOUNDARY question to a later time.

GIBBONS, James Cardinal. 1834-1921. Roman Catholic archbishop of Baltimore. b. Maryland. Graduated St. Charles College (1858); ordained priest (1861); chaplain, Fort McHenry (1861-65); bishop of Adramyttium (1868); head of vicariate apostolic of North Carolina; bishop of Richmond, Va. (1872); bishop of Baltimore (1877); played important part in establishing Catholic University, Washington, D.C.; created cardinal (1886); close personal friend of many Presidents and prominent people.

Gibbons vs. Ogden. A decision of the U.S. Supreme Court in 1824 in which it interpreted the INTERSTATE COMMERCE power of the Congress. The decision of the Court, written by Chief Justice JOHN MARSHALL, held that Congress was supreme in all aspects of interstate commerce and could not be limited by STATE POWERS in this area. The Court went on to define COMMERCE as including the articles of commerce, the means of TRANSPORTATION, and the routes. It also interpreted the phrase "to regulate" to mean that Congress could foster, inhibit, or protect interstate commerce. This doctrine has gone far in establishing Congress's comprehensive powers over interstate commerce which, although temporarily abandoned during the period of ROGER TANEY's chief justiceship, was revived in the post-Civil War era. This is the established constitutional principle today.

GIBBS, Josiah Willard. 1839-1903. Physicist. b. Connecticut. Graduated Yale University (1858); Ph.D. (1863); professor of mathematical physics at Yale (1871-1903). Important for his work in the field of thermodynamics and establishing the basic theory for physical chemistry. Author of books and papers.

G.I. Bill of Rights. A law passed in 1944 and subsequently amended, providing EDUCATION and training for veterans at the expense of the federal government.

Veterans in any type of training, except correspondence school courses, may be eligible to receive additional subsistence allowances. They must start their courses within four years after discharge. The program is scheduled to end on July 25, 1956, with the exception that those veterans who enlisted or reenlisted between October 6, 1945 and October 5, 1946 have nine years from the end of that time in which to complete their training. Under this program approximately 7,600,-000 veterans, or nearly one half of those who served during World War II, had received education or training by 1952. In the fiscal year 1949 $3,058,758,230 was allocated for veteran tuition, equipment, supplies and materials, subsistence allowances, building, equipment, and other facilities. Its statutory title is "Servicemen's Readjustment Act." On July 16, 1952 Congress passed a law extending most of the World War II benefits to veterans of the Korean War. The act provided these veterans with free schooling, government-guaranteed home and business loans, mustering-out pay, and other benefits. Honorably discharged service men since June 27, 1950 with at least 90 days service were declared eligible. It was estimated that from 600,000 to 700,000 veterans a year would go to school under the new program. In order to eliminate illegal acquisition of the funds, government payments for schooling were to be made directly to the veterans instead of the SCHOOLS. The law provided free schooling, monthly payments ranging from $110 to $160 for veterans in full-time training, on-the-job and farm training with monthly benefits ranging from $95 to $130, exclusion of avocational courses, loan guarantees on homes, farms, and business operations, unemployment compensation of $26 a week for 26 weeks, and mustering-out pay ranging from $100 for less than 60 days service to $300 for more than 60 days service including overseas or in Alaska.

GIBSON, John. 1740-1822. Revolutionary officer and frontiersman. b. Pennsylvania. Indian fur trader; part of the expedition that captured Fort Duquesne (later Fort Pitt) (1758); fur trader (1758-74); served as colonel in WASHINGTON'S Continental army (1777); in command, Fort Pitt (1781-82); appointed by JEFFERSON secretary of INDIANA TERRITORY (1800-16).

GIBSON, Randall Lee. 1832-1892. Confederate general and legislator. Prominent lawyer, New Orleans; brigadier general in Confederate army during Civil War; member, U.S. House of Representatives (1875-83); U.S. Senator (1883-92); helped Paul Tulane found Tulane University becoming first president of the board of administrators.

GIDDINGS, Franklin Henry. 1855-1931. Sociologist. b. Connecticut. First professor of sociology at Columbia University (from 1894); well-known teacher and author of many books including *The Elements of Sociology* (1898) and *The Scientific Study of Human Society* (1924).

GIDDINGS, Joshua Reed. 1795-1864. ABOLITIONIST and legislator. b. Pennsylvania. Practiced law in Ohio; member, U.S. House of Representatives (1838-1842); radical abolitionist; resigned from house on criticism of his anti-slavery policy but was re-elected (1842-59); opposed Mexican War and COMPROMISE OF 1850; U.S. consul general to Canada (1861-64).

Gilbert Islands, Battle of the. Several of the Gilbert Islands were taken by Japan at the opening of World War II. In November, 1943 the MARINES, supported by off-shore naval and air bombardment, recaptured them in one of the bloodiest battles of the Pacific war.

"Gilded Age," the. The term applied to

the intellectual and aesthetic revival in the United States between 1865 and 1890. The name derives from the title of a novel written by MARK TWAIN and Charles D. Warner in 1873. The period was marked by rapid industrialization, economic expansion, and political control by wealthy eastern INDUSTRY. American culture assumed new, and occasionally eccentric, forms. The mixed ARCHITECTURE of Graeco-Roman, Gothic, and "modernistic" forms which merged the best and worst of classic design characterized some of the more extraordinary cultural aspects of the "Gilded Age." Nevertheless, the contributions to American scholarship and art of such figures as Josiah Royce, THORSTEIN VEBLEN, WILLIAM and HENRY JAMES, Charles S. Pierce, JOHN DEWEY, HENRY GEORGE, WINSLOW HOMER, JOHN LAFARGE, and THOMAS EAKINS were internationally famous. Among architects were Richard Upjohn, James Renwick, and JOHN ROEBLING. New literary MAGAZINES like *Harper's Weekly* and *Scribner's* appeared. The THEATRE produced prominent figures like Charles Frohman, James A. Herne, and DAVID BELASCO. A renaissance in MUSIC was characterized by the growth of the NEW YORK SYMPHONY SOCIETY, BOSTON SYMPHONY, and METROPOLITAN OPERA. The economy of the nation witnessed a great business boom, PROTECTIONISM in TARIFF policy, a tremendous technological advance, and expansion of the CURRENCY.

GILES, William Branch. 1762 - 1830. Legislator. Practiced law in Virginia; member, U.S. House of Representatives (1790-98); supported JEFFERSON and opposed HAMILTON; U.S. Senator (1804-15); opposed GALLATIN and MONROE and led opposition to administration policies in War of 1812; governor of Virginia (1827-30).

GILLESPIE, Mabel. 1867-1923. Labor organizer. Studied, Radcliffe College, secretary, Boston Associated Charities; secretary, Women's Trade Union League, Boston (from 1909); organized women workers; secured social legislation; member first minimum wage commission in the U.S.; vice president state branch of AMERICAN FEDERATION OF LABOR.

GILLMORE, Quincy Adams. 1825-1888. Military engineer. b. Ohio. Graduated, U.S.M.A., West Point (1849); brigadier general of volunteers during Civil War (1862); major general (1863); in command, Department of the South (1865) in charge of fortifications and harbor improvements along Atlantic coast south of New York City; president, Mississippi River Commission 1879).

GILMAN, Daniel Colt. 1831-1908. Educator. b. Connecticut. Graduated, Yale University (1852); helped to found Sheffield Scientific School at Yale (1856) librarian, secretary and librarian there (1861-72); president, University of California (1872-1875); first president of Johns Hopkins University (1875-1901); retired; became president of new Carnegie Institution, Washington, D.C. (1901-04) organizing its research activities; president, National Civil Service Reform League (1901-07).

GIRARD, Stephen. 1750-1831. Businessman, banker and philanthropist. b. France. Settled in Philadelphia (from 1777); successful export business; founded Bank of Stephen Girard (1812) to take over business of BANK OF THE UNITED STATES; helped government with funds during War of 1812; helped to establish the Second Bank of the United States (1816); gave huge sums to charities and founded institution for EDUCATION in Philadelphia.

GIST, Christopher. 1706?-1759. FRONTIERSMAN. b. Maryland. Explored West for OHIO COMPANY; accompanied WASHINGTON and saved his life on trip to Fort Duquesne (1753-54); guide in BRADDOCK'S EXPEDITION (1755).

GLASS, Carter. 1858-1946. Statesman. b. Virginia. An owner of the Lynchburg *Daily News* and *Daily Advance;* state senator (1899-1903); member, U. S. House of Representatives (1902-19); chairman, House Banking and Currency Committee and largely responsible for the FEDERAL RESERVE ACT (1914); appointed U.S. Secretary of the Treasury by WILSON(1918-20); U.S. Senator(1920-1946).

Glass Industry. According to Captain JOHN SMITH'S HISTORY OF VIRGINIA the first glass factory was built in Jamestown in 1615 and a second in 1622. The principal product was glass bottles. In 1754 a factory was erected in Brooklyn whose products included window glass. Factories were established in Temple, New Hampshire in 1779 and in Pittsburgh in 1795. These factories had begun to produce excellent glassware for home use as well as commercial products at the end of the 18th century. By the War of 1812 Pittsburgh had become the center of the industry, operating five factories valued at $160,000. After the Civil War there were over 200 glass factories in the United States with a total capitalization of more than $14,000,000. Considerable supplies of potash, sand, lime, and soda furnished the raw materials for the industry. At the end of the 19th century the use of NATURAL GAS as fuel stimulated the industry's growth. The introduction of lamps, electric light fixtures, and new industrial products provided a tremendous impetus to glass production. With the allied stone and clay industries, the glass industry employed approximately 390,000 workers in 12,000 firms in 1950. The value added to their products by MANUFACTURING in 1949 was $2,451,000,000.

Glass-Owen Act. Also known as the Federal Reserve Act. A law of Congress passed on December 23, 1914 for the purpose of regulating the CURRENCY and credit operations of banks in the United States. It was enacted in part as a result of the findings of the PUJO COMMITTEE, created by Congress in 1912 to investigate charges of "MONEY TRUST" manipulations in financial markets. The law aimed at rectifying the lack of cooperation among the nation's banks, the inelasticity of currency, and the concentration of financial control. It divided the United States into 12 districts with a Federal Reserve Bank in each. These banks became depositories for the cash reserves for all national banks and of those state banks and trust companies which became members of the system. The subtreasury system was abolished and the Federal Reserve Banks became the depositories of government funds. These banks were authorized to accept and discount member banks' commercial paper in exchange for federal reserve notes. A Federal Reserve Board, of seven men, appointed by the President for terms of 14 years, was authorized to supervise the conduct of the banks in the system. See Federal Reserve System.

Glass-Steagall Act. Passed by Congress on June 16, 1933. It is also known as the Banking Act of 1933. The provisions of the Act included a requirement that parent banks of the FEDERAL RESERVE SYSTEM separate themselves from security affiliates, the establishment of the FEDERAL DEPOSIT INSURANCE CORPORATION, the restriction on the use of Federal Reserve Bank credit for speculative purposes, the restraint on such banks from dealing in foreign securities, and the prohibition on private banks from acting simultaneously as banks of deposit and as securities underwriters. It also permitted national banks to establish branch banks in those states permitting branch banking. The objective of the Act was to stabilize the BANKING system of the United States following the reopening of the nation's banks by the EMERGENCY BANKING ACT OF MARCH 9,1933.

GLENN, Colonel John H. In February 1962 Colonel Glenn became the first United States astronaut to orbit the globe. He was later elected to the Senate of the United States and suggested as a possible presidential candidate in the 1976 Democratic Convention.

GLIDDEN, Joseph Farwell. 1813-1906. FARMER who invented the form of twisted "BARBED WIRE" now in use (patented 1873).

GLYNN, Martin Henry. 1871-1924. Publisher and politician. Graduated, Fordham University; managing editor and later editor and publisher of Albany *Times-Union;* member, U.S. House of Representatives (1899-1901); lieutenant governor of New York (1912); governor (1913) during his administration he established a state EMPLOYMENT BUREAU; WORKMAN'S COMPENSATION LAW; acted as mediator in settlement of Irish Free State (1921).

"Gobbledygook." The derisive term for the involved language employed by federal office holders in preparing official documents. The nickname was generally applied to the NEW DEAL by its enemies.

GODKIN, Edwin Lawrence. 1831-1902. Editor. b. Ireland. Emigrated to United States (1856); founder and editor, N.Y. *Evening Post* merging the *Nation* into that paper (1881); editor in chief, N.Y. *Evening Post* (1883-1900); a liberal and independent writer. Author of *Problems of Modern Democracy* (1896).

GOETHALS, George Washington. 1858-1928. Army engineer. b. Brooklyn, New York. Graduated, U.S.M.A., West Point (1880); appointed by President T. ROOSEVELT, chief engineer, Panama Canal Commission (1907); succeeded in completing the construction of the canal (1914); major general(1915); governor of CANAL ZONE (1914-16); head of Bureau of Purchase and Supplies during World War I; head of own firm of consulting engineers (1923-28).

GOLDBERGER, Joseph. 1874-1929. Physician. b. Austria. Came to the United States when very young; worked on the staff of the Hygienic Laboratory, Washington, D.C.; famous as the discoverer of the nature and the cure of the disease pellagra (1913-25).

Gold Bullion Depository. See Fort Knox Gold Depository.

Gold Bullion Standard. As established in the GOLD RESERVE ACT of 1934 it refers to a monetary standard in which the currency of the United States is based on gold but is not freely convertible. Gold may not circulate, and its possession in sums above $100 is illegal. It may be acquired on license only for the payment of TRADE balances and by jewelers for their trade. As provided by the Act the gold content of the dollar was to be fixed at 50-60 percent of the former gold dollar. The President subsequently devalued the gold dollar by 59.06 percent, fixing the new value at 13.71 grains of pure gold. The new rate raised the price of gold from $20.67 to $35 per ounce.

Gold Democrats. Those members of the Democratic party who, in the convention of 1896, repudiated the FREE SILVER PLATFORM of WILLIAM JENNINGS BRYAN, and bolted the convention. On September 2, they organized the National Democratic party at Indianapolis, and nominated J. M. Palmer and S. B. Buckner as their candidates. Their conservative gold platform attracted those anti-Bryan Democrats who balked at supporting MCKINLEY. Palmer's vote totalled only 134,-645. By the election of 1900 it had disappeared from politics.

"Gold, glory, and gospel." The phrase describing the objectives of colonial IMPERIALISM between the 16th and 18th centuries. The search for gold was an aim of MERCANTILE thinking, while prestige was considered to lie in acquisition of new colonies. The conversion of so-called "heathens" to Christianity through extensive missionary work was the "gospel" of the term.

Gold Repeal Joint Resolution. See gold standard.

Gold Reserve Act. Passed by Congress in 1934. It authorized the President to purchase all the gold on deposit in the Federal Reserve Banks and to impound it in the Treasury. The gold was to be established as a permanent reserve for the paper CURRENCY in circulation. Most of this gold, valued in 1964 at $15,600,-000,000, has been stored in the GOLD BULLION DEPOSITORY at Fort Knox, Kentucky. The President was further empowered to fix the value of the dollar at 50 to 60 cents in terms of its former gold content and to manage it within these limits, to assure to the federal government whatever profit might accrue from this DEVALUATION, and to place $2,-000,000,000 of this profit into an Exchange Stabilization Fund to stabilize the dollar by permitting the Treasury to use it for the purchase and sale of gold, foreign exchange, and limited states securities. The fundamental objective of the Act was to produce a price increase in the nation's economy during the GREAT DEPRESSION. Under its authority President F. D ROOSEVELT fixed the value of the dollar at 59.06 cents in terms of its former PARITY. This plus other currency measures subsequently adopted brought about a slow rise in prices. Another consequence of the Act was to prevent the hoarding or shipment abroad of gold.

Gold rushes. Refers to the large migrations of miners into California, Colorado, Nevada, Utah, and Arizona in the 1850's, 1860's, and 1870's following the discovery of gold in these areas. Their contributions to the growth of the United States lay in the settlement of the territories, their MINING of the precious metal which simultaneously added to the wealth of the nation and contributed to the CURRENCY struggle in this period, and to their advertising of the economic at-

tractions of the TERRITORY. Collectively this movement has been referred to as the "MINING KINGDOM."

Gold standard. A currency system based on gold. The Currency Act of 1792 established a bimetallic standard in which the United States dollar was valued at 24.75 grains of gold in a relationship of 15 to 1 to the silver dollar, which contained 371.25 grains of pure silver. In 1834 this relationship was changed to 15.98 to 1 and the gold dollar reduced in value to 23.22 grains of pure gold. Whereas silver had been overvalued under the original currency act, gold was now overvalued, and disappeared from circulation. Under both laws the two metals were declared to be legal tender. During the Civil War, and until January 1, 1879, the nation's currency was based on a depreciated paper money standard which resulted from 'the authorization of FIAT CURRENCY (GREENBACKS) on December 30, 1861 and the DEMONETIZATION OF SILVER on February 12, 1873. Under the latter act only gold remained legal tender and the unit of value for the circulating currency. With the resumption of specie payment on January 1, 1879 all currency was tied to gold. The enactment of the BLAND-ALLISON ACT in 1878 and SHERMAN SILVER PURCHASE ACT in 1890 restored the currency to a bi-metallic standard. Under these laws the silver dollar contained 412.5 grains of silver. By the GOLD STANDARD ACT of 1900 the currency was restored to the gold standard. The EXECUTIVE ORDER of April 19, 1933, forbidding the export of gold, took the nation off the gold standard. The Gold Repeal Joint Resolution of June 5, 1933 cancelled the gold clauses in public and private debts, requiring that debts be paid in legal tender. Previously, on March 10, 1933 gold exports had been halted except when licensed by the Treasury, and on April 5, 1933 the hoarding of gold and gold certificates had been prohibited. Finally, under authority of the GOLD RE-

SERVE ACT of January 30, 1934, the President fixed the value of the dollar at 59.06 cents, placing the nation on the so-called managed GOLD BULLION STANDARD. The SILVER PURCHASE ACT of June 19, 1934 provided for silver purchases, until the nation's holdings would be in the proportion of 25 percent silver and 75 percent gold.

Gold Standard Act. A law of Congress, passed on March 14, 1900, declaring all forms of money redeemable in gold on demand, and enlarging the redemption fund to $150,000,000. The gold dollar was fixed at 25.8 grains, nine-tenths fine. The price of gold was established at $20.67 an ounce, and gold was declared to be the monetary standard of value, "and all forms of money issued or coined by the United States shall be maintained at a parity" with it. The law made the government's gold reserve a separate fund, not to be drawn upon to meet current revenue deficiencies. It provided that, when paper notes were submitted for redemption, they should not be reissued except for gold.

Goldwater, Barry Morris. 1909- . Politician, b. Arizona. Republican nominee for president in 1964. Senator from Arizona, 1953-1964.

GOMPERS, Samuel. 1850-1924. Labor leader. b. England. To United States (1863); cigar maker; helped to reorganize Cigarmaker's Union (1877); chairman, committee on constitution, Federation of Organized Trades and Labor Unions (1881) which later became the AMERICAN FEDERATION OF LABOR(1886); president, of A. F. of L. (1886-1894; 1896-1924); successful in fight against KNIGHTS OF LABOR, he is largely responsible for the success of his organization; member, COUNCIL OF NATIONAL DEFENSE during World War I, appointed by WILSON; member, Commission on International Labor Legislation at VERSAILLES

PEACE CONFERENCE(1919). Author of his autobiography, *Seventy Years of Life and Labor* (2 vols. 1925).

"Good neighbor policy." The popular phrase applied to the Latin American policy of the early administrations of F. D. ROOSEVELT. It signified the reversal of the earlier "BIG STICK" and "DOLLAR DIPLOMACY" foreign policies of the THEODORE ROOSEVELT and TAFT administrations. The good neighbor policy was manifested by the withdrawal of the remaining American MARINES from HAITI, SANTO DOMINGO, CUBA, and NICARAGUA, the amicable settlement of the railroad and land disputes with Mexico in 1936 and 1938, and the abrogation of the PLATT AMENDMENT. The statement of this policy was declared at the Seventh PAN AMERICAN CONFERENCE at MONTEVIDEO in 1933. Since then, relations between the United States and Latin-America have been sound.

GOODYEAR, Charles. 1800-1860. Inventor. b. Connecticut. After experimenting for years, he accidently dropped some rubber treated with sulphur on a hot stove and thus originated the process of vulcanized rubber; patented (1844), forming the basis of the RUBBER INDUSTRY.

GORDON, John Brown. 1832 - 1904. Confederate general. b. Georgia. Served in Confederate army through the Civil War; brigadier general (1862); major general (1864); lieutenant general (1865); served under LEE and led charge at APPOMATTOX; leader in Reconstruction politics; U.S. Senator from Georgia (1873-80; 1891-97); governor (1886-90).

GORGAS, William Crawford. 1854-1920. Surgeon-general of United States army and sanitarian. b. Alabama. Graduated, Bellevue Medical College (1879); officer, medical corps., U.S. army (1880); chief sanitary officer, Havana, CUBA (1898-1902) in charge of yellow-fever camp; successfully rid Havana of yellow fever following the discoveries of the WALTER REED board that mosquitoes are the carriers of the disease; chief, sanitary officer, Panama Canal Commission (1904-13); largely responsible for ridding the area of yellow fever, making the construction of the canal possible; surgeon general, with rank of brigadier general, U.S. army (1914); retired (1918).

GORMAN, Arthur Pue. 1839-1906. Political leader. b. Maryland. Served in Maryland house of representatives and state senate; U.S. Senator (1881-99; 1903-06); chairman, Democratic National Executive Committee (1884) directed CLEVELAND's campaign for the presidency; co-author of WILSON-GORMAN ACT (1894) which raised TARIFFS.

GORTON, Samuel. 1592?-1677. Colonist and religious leader. b. England. To MASSACHUSETTS COLONY(1637); banished for religious belief (1637-8); aided by Earl of Warwick, settled town of Warwick in Rhode Island (1648); represented Warwick in Rhode Island legislature (1649-66); led "Gortonianites" who denied the Trinity, did not believe in heaven or hell and that each man makes his own faith with God.

GOULD, Benjamin Apthorp. 1824-1896. Astronomer. b. Boston, Massachusetts. Graduated Harvard University (1844); founded *Astronomical Journal*(1849)and acted as editor (1849-61; 1886-96); director, longitude department, U.S. Coast Survey (1852-67); director, Dudley Observatory, Albany, N.Y.(1855-59); organized and established observatories in Argentina (1870); important for work in southern celestial hemisphere and preparation of zone catalogues of the southern stars.

GOULD, Jay. Real first name Jason. 1836-1892. Financier. b. New York. Clerk, surveyor and leather merchant (1859-60); known for railroad stock manipulation (from 1860); with aid of FISK and DREW he gained control of the Erie Railroad after fight with VANDERBILT (1867-68); attempt to corner gold market, with Fisk and Drew, caused panic of BLACK FRIDAY (Sept. 24, 1869); gained control of many RAILROADS; owned New York *World* (1879-83); controlled WESTERN UNION Telegraph Company.

"Government by injunction." The slogan by which the LABOR MOVEMENT expressed its opposition to the widespread use of the INJUNCTION procedure of the SHERMAN ANTI-TRUST ACT in labor disputes.

"Government by judiciary." The slogan raised by those who opposed the decisions of the United States Supreme Court which invalidated progressive social and labor legislation.

Government ownership. The system in which the state owns and operates business enterprises. In the United States the federal, state, and muncipal governments own many enterprises, particularly in the field of PUBLIC UTILITIES. Federally chartered corporations operate RAILROADS, hotels, restaurants, barge lines, HYDROELECTRIC POWER plants, armories, shipyards, merchant SHIPPING lines, and BANKING facilities. Among the prominent corporations are the PANAMA CANAL COMPANY, the Inland Waterways Corporation, the TENNESSEE VALLEY AUTHORITY, and the RECONSTRUCTION FINANCE CORPORATION.

Government regulation of business. The regulation of private enterprises by agencies of the federal, state, or municipal governments. Derived from the English common law, PUBLIC UTILITY DOCTRINE it was early recognized that regulation of rates, competition, securities issuances, LABOR RELATIONS, and other business practices were proper to protect the public interest. With the increasingly complex technology of modern industrial production the earlier controls by municipal and state governments have been supplemented by federal regulation.

Although such regulation with respect to TARIFFS and foreign COMMERCE are known as early as 1790, textensive state regulation did not develop until after the Civil War with the enactment of state laws, among which the most famous were the GRANGER LAWS. Beginning with the INTERSTATE COMMERCE ACT the Congress inaugurated a program of government regulation of business on a large scale. In the years that followed, established EXECUTIVE DEPARTMENTS and agencies were supplemented in this work by newly created INDEPENDENT REGULATORY BODIES. These include the FEDERAL TRADE COMMISSION, PURE FOOD AND DRUGS ADMINISTRATION, NATIONAL LABOR RELATIONS BOARD, SECURITIES AND EXCHANGE COMMISSION, FEDERAL COMMUNICATIONS COMMISSION, and CIVIL AERONAUTICS ADMINISTRATION. In time of war or economic DEPRESSION areas of business operation, not generally subject to regulation, are also brought under public control. Such areas have been prices, wages, manpower, and raw materials allocation.

Governor. This is the title of the CHIEF EXECUTIVE of the STATE GOVERNMENTS in the United States. The office derives from the colonial office established by Parliament. The duties of the American governor closely resemble those of the President of the United States. They consist of executive, legislative, judicial, military, administrative, and protocol functions. The governor also exercises the power of SELECTIVE VETO, a power prohibited to the President. The governorship is often the stepping stone to the WHITE HOUSE, as in the cases of the two ROOSEVELTS, COOLIDGE, HARDING, and WILSON.

GRAHAM, William Alexander. 1804-1875. Political leader. b. North Carolina. Graduated, North Carolina State University (1824); member, North Carolina legislature (1833-40); U.S. Senator (1840-43); governor (1845-49); appointed U.S. Secretary of the Navy, by FILLMORE (1850-52); unsuccessful WHIG candidate for Vice-Presidency (1852); opposed SECESSION; member, Confederate Senate (1864).

Grain Futures Act. An act of Congress passed in 1922 for the purpose of regulating dealers in WHEAT, corn, and certain other grains. "Contract markets" were designated by the Secretary of Agriculture to be conducted by boards of trade acting under definite regulations. They were to keep records for federal inspection and take measures to prevent price manipulation. A dealer who failed to comply with these regulations could be deprived of the right to transact interstate business. The Secretary of Agriculture was authorized to close an entire market when its board of trade acted unlawfully.

Grain Stabilization Corporation. An agency established in 1929 by the FEDERAL FARM BOARD under the authority of the AGRICULTURAL MARKETING ACT of that year. It was empowered to go into the market and purchase grain or grain "futures" for the purpose of raising prices. With the COTTON STABILIZATION CORPORATION, it spent almost $500,000,-000, succeeding for a brief period in maintaining grain prices at levels slightly higher than the world market averages.

Grain Standards Act. A federal law of 1916 which authorized the establishment of national standards for the various grains, requiring the use of these standards for all grains moving in INTERSTATE COMMERCE. The law was administered by the Bureau of Agricultural Economics of the DEPARTMENT OF AGRICULTURE and enforced by licensed inspectors. Its purpose was to protect FARMERS who customarily suffered losses resulting from dishonest grading.

Gran Chaco Region. See Chaco War.

Grand Army of the Republic. Popularly known as the GAR. It is the first important veterans' organization, having been organized in 1865-66 in Springfield, Illinois. Its principal leader was Dr. B.F. Stephenson, former surgeon of the Fourteenth Illinois Infantry. The first post of Civil War Veterans was established in 1866 in Decatur, Illinois. Its membership consists of all men who served in the United States army, navy, or MARINE CORPS between April 12, 1861 and April 9, 1865, who were honorably discharged. Grand army posts have been established in nearly all cities of the North and West. The GAR held its 83rd and final encampment in August, 1949 in Indianapolis, Indiana. The organization will continue to exist until the last member is deceased. Its peak membership of 408,489 was reached in 1890.

Grand Coulee Dam. Built in 1942 on the Columbia River in the state of Washington for power and IRRIGATION. It is the largest concrete dam in the world and contains the world's most powerful hydro-electric plant with the capacity of producing a continuous output of 2,340,-000 kilowatts. It is part of the Columbia River Reclamation Project and will ultimately irrigate 1,200,000 acres of land, and regulate the flow of the river. The height of the dam is 550 feet, and its length 4,173 feet. Its volume is 10,585,-000 cubic yards. It is operated by the Bureau of Reclamation within the DEPARTMENT OF THE INTERIOR. Its power serves the industries of the Pacific Northwest and is distributed over the transmission system of the BONNEVILLE POWER ADMINISTRATION. The irrigated area will provide sustenance for more than 250,-000 persons. Large scale irrigation began in 1952 for 87,000 acres. The development rate annually will be 70,000 acres.

"Grandfather Clauses." Provisions in southern state constitutions after the Civil War which attempted to disfranchise NEGROES despite the FIFTEENTH AMENDMENT. They were generally alike, pro-

viding the RIGHT TO VOTE to those who had voted on January 1, 1867 or to the descendants of those who had had the right to vote on that date. All persons in the above category were exempted from state laws requiring tax payment, property ownership, or educational training as a condition of the suffrage. Since, by and large, Negroes could not meet these three requirements, and did not have the right to vote on the specified date, they were effectivly barred from VOTING. Such laws were enacted in Alabama, Georgia, Louisiana, North Carolina, Oklahoma, South Carolina, and Virginia between 1895 and 1910. In 1915 the United States Supreme Court declared these clauses unconstitutional.

Grand Old Party. Better known by its abbreviation GOP. The nickname of the Republican party.

Granger Cases. A series of decisions by the United States Supreme Court sustaining the constitutionality of the GRANGER LAWS. The first of these was the case of MUNN VS. ILLINOIS in 1876 upholding the Illinois law regulating grain elevators. In the same year the court's decision in the case of Peik vs. Chicago and Northwestern Railway Company upheld Wisconsin's law regulating RAILROADS. In 1886, the Court reversed its former decisions in the case of WABASH, ST. LOUIS, AND PACIFIC RAILWAY VS. ILLINOIS.

GRANGER, Francis. 1792-1868. Political leader. b. Connecticut. Graduated, Yale University and practiced law; leader of WHIG party in New York (1834); appointed U.S. Postmaster General by HARRISON; important minority leader.

Granger Laws. A series of state laws enacted by the legislatures of Illinois, Minnesota, Iowa, and Wisconsin between 1869 and 1875. These laws sought the regulation of RAILROADS, grain elevators, and storage warehouses in the interests of the midwestern FARMER. Among other provisions they established maximum rate schedules, attempted to prohibit greater charges for a short haul than for a long one, forbade free passes for public officials, and tried to maintain competition by prohibiting the consolidation of parallel lines. This legislation was vigorously opposed by the railroad companies who immediately sought to have them nullified in the courts. Although originally sustained in the famous GRANGER CASES, they were declared unconstitutional in 1886.

Granger movement. Named after the activities of the granges and FARMERS' ORGANIZATIONS formed in the mid-West after the Civil War. Although the granges, organized into the NATIONAL GRANGE, concerned themselves with educational and social activities their principal objective was the furtherance of state legislation designed to protect themselves against the economic abuses of RAILROADS, storage warehouses, and grain elevators. They succeeded in obtaining favorable legislation in the 1870's and 1880's in such states as Illinois, Indiana, and Wisconsin. It is this political aspect of the grangers' activity that constitutes the granger movement. The word granger itself refers to any individual farmer member of a grange.

Grants-in-aid. See subsidies.

GRANT, Ulysses Simpson. 1822--1885. Eighteenth President of the United States. b. Point Pleasant, Ohio. Graduated U. S. M. A., West Point (1843); served through the Mexican War; resigned from the army (1854); unsuccessful in business (1854-61); colonel, Illinois volunteer regiment at the outbreak of the Civil War; brigadier general (1861); led the capture of Fort Henry, Fort Donelson, and the force under BUCKNER (1862); major general (1862); captured VICKSBURG and gained control of the Mississippi River (1863); impor-

tant because it then divided Confederacy in two; promoted to lieutenant general after success at CHATTANOOGA, Lookout Mountain, and Missionary Ridge (1863); became commander of all the armies of the United States under LINCOLN; headquarters with the Army of the Potomac; received LEE'S surrender at APPOMATTOX COURT HOUSE (April 9, 1865); general (1866); elected President of the United States (1868); re-elected (1872); although honest and well-meaning his administration was corrupt and badly administered. Author of *Personal Memoirs*.

GRAY, Elisha. 1835-1901. Inventor. b. Ohio. Invented many TELEGRAPH and telephone appliances; had same invention for telephone as BELL, but his PATENT was a few hours too late; patent fight with Bell for years was decided in Bell's favor by the U.S. Supreme Court; patented telautograph (1888-91).

GRAY, George. 1840-1925. Jurist. b. Delaware. Graduated Princeton University; studied at Harvard Law School; attorney general of Delaware (1879-85); U.S. Senator (1885-99); U.S. Circuit Court judge (1899-1914); appointed by MCKINLEY; member, joint high commission which settled differences between United States and Canada (1898); negotiated peace with Spain as member of U.S. commission (1898); member, PERMANENT COURT OF ARBITRATION, The Hague (1900-1920); chairman, commission to arbitrate ANTHRACITE COAL STRIKE (1902) appointed by T. ROOSEVELT.

GRAY, Horace. 1828-1902. Jurist. b. Boston, Massachusetts. Graduated, Harvard University and Harvard Law School; associate justice, Massachusetts supreme judicial court (1864-73); chief justice (1873-81); appointed associate justice, U.S. Supreme Court (1882-1902) by President CHESTER ARTHUR.

GRAY, Robert. 1755 - 1806. Navigator and explorer. b. Rhode Island. Served in the navy during the American Revolution; first American to sail around the world leaving Boston in the sloop, *Lady Washington* (Sept. 1787); he transferred to the *Columbia* and arrived back at Boston (Aug. 10, 1790); discovered the Columbia River (1792) (named after his ship); this discovery became one of the bases of the American claims to the Oregon territory in the 1840's.

Great American Desert. Sometimes called the Great Salt Lake Desert. It runs 80 miles west of the GREAT SALT LAKES to the Nevada-Utah line. It is approximately 50 miles wide and has an elevation of 4500 feet. Its conspicuous features include a high salt content with numerous salt flats which have been the setting of many famous international automobile races. Many world speed records have been set here.

Great Depression. The extreme economic crisis which, with minor upswings, beset the United States from 1929 to 1940. It began with the STOCK MARKET CRASH of 1929 and led to an economic decline that witnessed no recovery until the spring of 1933. In every field of business endeavor huge losses were suffered, with the consequent rise of unemployment and social upheavals. Exports declined from $5,241,000,000 in 1929 to $1,611,-000,000 in 1933. In that period imports fell from $4,399,000,000 to $1,323,000,-000. Unemployment rose from 3,000,000 to an estimated 17,000,000. Wholesale prices declined from an average index of 95.3 to 65.9. Commercial failures increased from 24,000 in 1928 to 32,000 in 1932, and more than 5,000 banks failed in the first three years of the Great Depression. Factory payrolls fell below half the 1929 level, and total paid wages declined from $55,000,000,000 to $33,000,-000,000 in 1931. Except for public construction, building virtually ceased, and the national income declined from $85,-000,000,000 on the eve of the DEPRESSION to $37,000,000,000 in 1932. Similar hard-

ships befell the farmer, aggravating economic dislocations which had been his lot since the end of World War I. Despite minor and temporary upswings, full recovery was not achieved until the defense and war programs after 1940. See Panic of 1929.

Great Lakes. The name applied to the five lakes located in northeast and north central United States, acting as a boundary between it and Canada at those points. The largest is Lake Michigan with a total of 22,178 square miles of water area. The other four lakes are Lake Superior, Lake Huron, Lake Ontario, Lake Erie. The total water area of the Great Lakes is 60,306 square miles. They form the largest body of fresh water in the world and, with their connecting waterways, rank as the world's largest inland transportation unit. Among the most important commodities transported are American and Canadian WHEAT, and American steel and iron.

Great Plains. The vast, treeless, semi-arid area comprising about two-thirds of the LOUISIANA TERRITORY. It ranges in elevation from 1,000 feet at the eastern border to 6,000 feet at the base of the ROCKY MOUNTAINS. Although the Great Plains had possessed quantities of water, fertile land, and timber in earlier times, these had vanished by the 19th century. The area was first explored by adventurers, hunters, traders, and trappers at the end of the 18th century at which time countless herds of bison, antelope, and elk roamed the prairies. The region is sometimes considered to be divided into two geographic provinces, the southern and northern Plains. Coronado is believed to have first explored the Great Plains in 1541, followed by many Spaniards and, later, Frenchmen under LaSalle after 1682. American EXPLORATIONS in the 19th century included the LEWIS AND CLARK EXPEDITION, and those of ZEBULON PIKE (1806-1807), STEPHEN

265

H. LONG (1820), JOHN C. FREMONT (1842-1844), the Mormons (1846-1947), and the "FORTY-NINERS." Other prominent explorers included traders and scouts John Colter, Jim Bridger, N. J. Wyeth, Jedediah Smith, and the Sublette brothers and missionaries MARCUS WHITMAN, Jason Lee, and Father De Smeet. From the Great Plains have come the nation's wealth of fur, agricultural commodities, bison, cattle, and minerals.

"Great power veto." See rule of unanimity.

Great Salt Lake. A famous lake in northwest Utah whose salt density ranges from 15 to 28 percent, about six times that of the ocean. It is 35 by 75 miles in size, ranging in depth from 25 to 30 feet. Its altitude is 4,218 feet. It has no known outlet. Early reports by explorers and Indians in the 17th and 18th centuries about its existence and properties are unsubstantiated. In December, 1824 the famous fur trapper and scout James Bridger discovered it, mistaking it for an extension of the Pacific because of its salt content. Later surveys and tests were made by JOHN C. FREMONT in 1843 and by Howard Stansbury in 1850.

Great Society. President Lyndon B. Johnson, in a campaign speech (October 31, 1964) declared that his goal would be to end squalor, poverty and ignorance; and that the abundance of our economy shall be made available—not just to the privileged few, but to everyone.

"Great White Way." See Broadway.

GREELEY, Horace. 1811-1872. Editor and political leader. b. New Hampshire. Founded and edited the *New Yorker*, a weekly journal (1834-41); edited and wrote for other political papers; founded

New York *Tribune* (1841) a successful and influential paper; advocated the organization of labor; opposed the Mexican War, the COMPROMISE OF 1850, and SLAVERY; one of the first Republican editors; supported LINCOLN; signed bail to release JEFFERSON DAVIS from prison; nominated for the presidency by LIBERAL REPUBLICANS, and endorsed by Democrats, but beaten by GRANT in the election (1872). Author of *The American Conflict* (2 vols. 1864-5), a history of the Civil War.

Greenback Labor Party. A minor party organized in Toledo, Ohio in 1878 as a consolidation of members of the GREENBACK PARTY and urban labor groups. In the year of its organization it polled over 1,000,000 votes, with the center of its strength in California, Georgia, Maine, New York, Ohio, Pennsylvania and the mid-western states. Fourteen Greenback Labor candidates were elected as congressmen. Its platform of financial and labor demands included: the suppression of national banknotes, payment of government bonds in legal tender, an adequate supply of money, the coinage of silver on a par with gold, the taxing of government bonds, and the institution of an INCOME TAX. By 1880 the labor elements of the party had practically disappeared, and its candidate General JAMES B. WEAVER polled only 308,500 votes. In 1888 the party gave up its independent status, merging its forces with the newly created UNION LABOR PARTY.

Greenback Party. Also known as the National Greenback Party. A minor party organized in 1875 with PETER COOPER as its presidential candidate. Its principal support derived from western FARMERS and DEBTORS whose objective was to induce Congress to issue additional GREENBACKS for the purpose of stimulating a general price increase. In the election of 1878 the party obtained over 1,000,000 votes and elected numerous state officials as well as 15 representatives to Congress. The party began to decline after the election of 1880 in which its standard bearer, General James B. Weaver, polled only 308,000 votes. In 1884 it merged with the ANTI-MONOPOLY ARTY. Though the party lost its struggle for CURRENCY IN-FLATION by means of a large volume of greenbacks, it finally succeeded in 1878 in preventing further contraction of this currency. Its other demands were: the EIGHT-HOUR DAY for labor, a graduated INCOME TAX, an INTERSTATE COMMERCE law, and opposition to RAILROAD LAND GRANTS.

Greenbacks. The popular name given to the FIAT CURRENCY printed by Congress under the LEGAL TENDER ACT of 1862 and subsequent AMENDMENTS. The official name of this CURRENCY is United States notes. Approximately $450,000,000 worth of greenbacks were issued by Congress as credit instruments. Prior to and following the enactment of the RESUMP-TION OF SPECIE PAYMENT ACT in 1875, effective on January 1, 1879, about $100,000,000 worth of this was redeemed for gold. Congress decided in 1878 to maintain in circulation $346,681,016 worth of greenbacks. They form part of the circulating currency today. As a political issue the printing and withdrawal of greenbacks played an exceedingly important role in the struggle between the East and the West in the post-Civil War era. Two THIRD-PARTY MOVEMENTS, organized in this period for the purpose of inducing Congress to issue more greenbacks, were the GREENBACK PARTY of 1875 and the GREENBACK-LABOR PARTY of 1878.

GREEN, Duff. 1791-1875. Journalist and politician. b. Kentucky. Served in War of 1812; settled in Missouri (1816); admitted to bar; member, CONSTITUTIONAL CONVENTION and state legislature; edited St. Louis *Inquirer*, supported JACKSON; bought *United States Telegraph*, Washington, D.C. (1825); opposed ADAMS; member, Jackson's KITCHEN CABINET; supported CLAY for presidency after breaking with Jackson (1832); supported HARRISON and TYLER (1840); sent by Tyler as unofficial representative of the United States to England and France (1840-44); sent to Mexico to purchase Texas, New Mexico, and California for the United States; failed; supported Confederacy during Civil War.

GREENE, Nathaniel. Revolutionary general. b. Rhode Island. Member state legislature; commissioned brigadier general in Continental army (June 22, 1775); major general (1776); led successful attack at TRENTON (1776); quartermaster general of the army (1778); resigned after criticism by Congress (1780); appointed by WASHINGTON to succeed GATES, after his defeat at Camden, in command of Army of the South (1780); famed for his well-planned retreat and final defeat of the British in Georgia and the Carolinas (1782); retired to Georgia.

"Green Mountain Boys." The popular name for an irregular body of MILITIA formed by Vermont settlers in 1771. It was organized for the purpose of defending their land titles under New Hampshire grants against the claims and conflicting grants of New York. ETHAN ALLEN was their self-appointed leader, supported by Remember Baker and SETH WARNER as his lieutenants. Their defense against the threats of New York helped establish Vermont as an independent region throughout the Revolution and for a time afterwards. In May, 1775 Allen used this organization in his dramatic capture of the British forts at TICONDER-GOA and at Crown Point.

Greenville, Treaty of. A TREATY signed in 1795 between the United States and an Indian confederacy of the OTTAWA, Chippewa, Shawnee, and Pottawatomi tribes. The Treaty followed the defeat of

WAYNE at the BATTLE OF FALLEN TIMBERS, marking the victorious conclusion of a twenty year war with the Indians in the OLD NORTHWEST. By its terms the Indians ceded the southeastern corner of the NORTHWEST TERRITORY comprising all of the present state of Ohio except the northwestern tip. They also ceded sixteen enclaves including Vincennes, Detroit, and the site of Chicago in return for annuities of approximately $10,-000. This treaty ended a period of warfare in which the Indians had on the whole been the aggressors and began one in which the Americans took the offensive.

GREEN, William. 1873-1952. Labor leader. b. Ohio. Sec.-Treas. of the UNITED MINE WORKERS (1912-24); president, AMERICAN FEDERATION OF LABOR (from 1924); largely responsible for the growth of the A.F. of L. until today its membership reaches approximately 8,000,000; in opposition to JOHN L. LEWIS on the organization of mass production industries and split with him (1935-1936). See AFL-CIO for recent merger of the two great unions with George Meany as president (1955).

GREGG, William. 1800-1867. Manufacturer. b. West Virginia. Famous as the "father of southern cotton manufacture"; established first southern mill town at Graniteville in South Carolina; introduction factory welfare legislation and was generally speaking progressive.

GRESHAM, Walter Quintin. 1832-1895. Lawyer, army general and statesman. b. Indiana. Served through Civil War; brevetted major general (1865); appointed U.S district judge (1869-83) by GRANT; appointed U.S. Postmaster General (1883-84) by ARTHUR; served as U.S. Secretary of the Treasury in Arthur's CABINET (1884); appointed U.S. Secretary of State by CLEVELAND (1893-95) having joined the Democrats in opposition to high PROTECTIVE TARIFFS.

GRIDLEY, Richard. 1711-1796. Colonial military engineer. b. Boston, Massachusetts. Served with British at capture of Quebec (1759); joined colonial army at outbreak of Revolution and served as chief engineer with rank of major general (1775); directed the building of breastworks on BREED'S HILL; fortified Dorchester heights (1776); chief engineer of Continental Army (1775-76) and engineer general, eastern department (1777-80).

GRIER, Robert Cooper. 1794-1870. Jurist. b. Pennsylvania. Graduated, Dickinson College (1812); admitted to bar (1817); presiding judge Alleghany district court (1833-46); appointed associate justice, U.S. Supreme Court (1846-70) by POLK; held progressive and independent views during Civil War period.

GRINNELL, Josiah Bushnell. 1821-1891. Clergyman and statesman. b. Vermont. After preaching at church in Washington, D.C. (1851), he followed advice of GREELEY who said "Go west, young man, go west," and settled in Iowa (1854); with others founded town of Grinnell and planned Grinnell College; trustee of the college for thirty years; a founder of Republican party in state, and a leading ABOLITIONIST; member, U.S. House of Representatives (1863-67); gave support to LINCOLN; lost leadership when he supported Greeley (1872); leader in CATTLE breeding and president, American Agricultural Association (1885).

GRISWOLD, Matthew. 1714-1799. Jurist. Admitted to bar (1743); member, Connecticut general assembly (1751-69); deputy governor of Connecticut (1769-84) and ex officio presiding judge of highest court in the state; governor (1784-86); presided at convention which ratified the federal Constitution.

GROSZ, George. 1893-1959. Artist. German-American painter of the modern school; famous satirist of World War I, post-

268

war conditions in Germany, and the Nazi regime; to New York (1932) to teach and paint; his works show an unusual understanding of his fellow men.

Group insurance. See compulsory medical insurance.

GRUNDY, Felix. 1777-1840. Political leader. b. Virginia. Well-known lawyer in Kentucky (from 1780); member, U.S. House of Representatives (1811-14); supported War of 1812; member, state legislature (1819-25); U.S. Senator (1829-38); supported JACKSON; appointed U.S. Attorney General (1838-39) by VAN BUREN; U.S. Senator (1839-40).

Guadalcanal, Battle of. The first military offensive of the United States in World War II. Following the defeat of the Japanese fleet at the Battles of the CORAL SEA and MIDWAY the United States came to the decision to assume the offensive in the Pacific. On August 7, 1942 the battle began with a combined air and sea attack on Guadalcanal in the SOLOMON ISLANDS. MARINES landed and established a beachhead on Guadalcanal and the island of Tulagi, capturing them after months of severe fighting. Under Admiral WILLIAM F. HALSEY JR. the American fleet soundly defeated the Japanese in the naval battle off Guadalcanal between November 13 and 15 in what has been referred to as the greatest naval battle since Jutland. By February, 1943 the last Japanese troops had been driven off the island, and the first success in the stepping stone strategy to the Japanese mainland had been achieved.

Guadalupe-Hildalgo, Treaty of. Negotiated in 1848 between Mexico and the United States, concluding the Mexican War. It provided for the session of the territories of New Mexico and Utah for which the United States paid $15,000,-000, and the annexation of California. Mexico simultaneously agreed to recognize the prior annexation of Texas by the United States and the establishment of the Rio Grande River as the definitive boundary line between the two nations.

Guam. The largest of the Mariana Islands in the Pacific Ocean. It is 206 square miles in area and had a POPULATION in 1950 of 59,498. Its chief products are copra, coconut oil, bananas, pineapples, and corn. Guam came into the possession of the United States as a result of the TREATY OF PARIS OF 1898 after the Spanish-American War. From then until August 1, 1950 it was administered by the Department of the Navy. On December 11, 1941 the island was captured by Japan. It was retaken on July 27, 1944. Prior to 1950 Guamanians were considered nationals of the United States, their political and CIVIL RIGHTS subject to the control of the naval officer in command of the island. In that year the Organic Act of Guam transferred administration to the DEPARTMENT OF THE INTERIOR and established a UNICAMERAL LEGISLATURE elected biennially by the permanent residents. Guamanians were made CITIZENS of the United States.

Guerriere, the. See Constitution, the.

Guffey-Snyder Coal Act. See Bituminous Soft Coal Act.

Guggenheim M e m o r i a l Foundation. Named after John Simon Guggenheim. It was founded in 1925 and grants fellowships to CITIZENS and permanent residents of the United States for the conduct of research in all fields of knowledge, and for creative work in the fine arts. The normal stipend of $3,000 per year is granted to those who have exhibited exceptional capacity for creative scholarship or unusual competence in the fine arts. A limited number of fellowships is offered to citizens of the PHILIPPINE Republic for work carried on in the United States or Canada. Its principal office is located in New York City.

269

gun control. President Johnson proposed an anticrime bill in February, 1967 which included gun control by regulating interstate shipment of guns. There was strong opposition to this bill by the National Rifle Association and Congress did not act on this measure. After the assassination of Senator Robert F. Kennedy in June 1968, Congress passed the gun control bill which included control the President had long recommended. It forbid interstate mail-order sales of guns and ammunition; required a license check before guns could be sold to residents of other states; and forbid the sale of guns to people under eighteen, felons, and mental defectives. A proposed amendment to require registration of all firearms was defeated.

Gunboats. Small armed vessels first used during JEFFERSON's administration. In 1803 Congress appropriated $50,000 at his suggestion, to build gunboats for use in the BARBARY WARS. Three years later $60,000 more were appropriated for 240 gunboats for harbor defense. The FEDERALISTS opposed these appropriations because of their demand for a large land force. Although gunboats were used to some extent during the War of 1812, Congress' final appropriation for such vessels was in 1813. Steam gunboats were used in river operations in the Civil War and in the Spanish-American War, and were later employed for patrolling purposes in the Far East. One of these, the *Panay,* was sunk by the Japanese on December 12th, 1937.

GWINNETT, Button. 1735?-1777. Revolutionary patriot and leader. b. England. Settled in Savannah, Georgia (about 1765); member, CONTINENTAL CONGRESS (1776, 1777); a signer of the DECLARATION OF INDEPENDENCE; acting governor of Georgia (1777).

H

Habeas Corpus. An equity writ derived from the COMMON LAW experience of England referring to the right of an arrested person to demand his freedom unless the arresting party can demonstrate sufficient evidence to warrant holding him for trial. This right is guaranteed against infringement in Article I, Section 9 of the Constitution. The document is general in its wording, not specifying whether it is Congress or the President who may not suspend *habeas corpus* (except in time of invasion or rebellion). The result is that its suspension by President LINCOLN during the Civil War was attacked as unconstitutional. The phrase is of Latin origin, meaning literally "have the body."

Habeas Corpus, Suspension of. Although Article I, Section 9 of the federal Constitution forbids Congress to suspend the writ of *habeas corpus*, except when in cases of rebellion or invasion the public safety may require it, President LINCOLN, on July 2, 1861, authorized General SCOTT to suspend the writ without Congressional authorization. It was not until March 3, 1863 that Congress granted this power to the President for the period of the war. Under this power Lincoln ordered the arrests of those Maryland legislators in favor of SECESSION and held them prisoners without benefit of HABEAS CORPUS. Other arrests were made of those who opposed the Union's military policies, some in areas outside the actual war zones. Although several cases were raised before the United States Supreme Court, Lincoln's power was never successfully challenged. The most important of these cases were *Ex parte* Merryman (1861) and *Ex parte* Milligan (1866). It is estimated that, during this period, 13,500 persons were arrested without benefit of habeas corpus proceedings and 400 newspapers suspended.

HABERSHAM, James. 1712-1775. Colonial royalist and leader. b. England. Imported slaves into Georgia and had successful rice plantation (1749); important leader of royal colony of Georgia and acting governor (1771-73); dissolved assembly for radical views and remained strong LOYALIST.

HABERSHAM, Joseph. 1751-1815. Revolutionary leader. b. Georgia. Member, COMMITTEE OF SAFETY; served as colonel in army under WASHINGTON; member, CONTINENTAL CONGRESS (1785-86); delegate to state convention that ratified federal Constitution; U.S. Postmaster General (1795-1801); president, Georgia branch of the BANK OF THE UNITED STATES (1802-15).

HADLEY, Arthur Twining. 1856-1930. Economist and educator. b. Connecticut. Graduated, Yale University (1876); professor, Yale (from 1886); president, Yale University (1899-1921); popular teacher and expert in railroad economics. Author of *Railroad Transportation* (1885), and *Economics* (1896).

HADLEY, Herbert Spencer. 1872-1927. Lawyer and political leader. b. Missouri. Admitted to bar and practiced in Kansas City, Mo.; Attorney General (1905-09); well-known for prosecution of STANDARD OIL COMPANY in anti-trust case; governor of Missouri (1909-13).

Hague Conferences. Two international conferences at The Hague in Netherland. called for the purpose of dealing with the problems of war, DISARMAMENT, and international disputes. The first conference met in 1899 and was attended by an American delegation headed by Andrew D. White, American Ambassador to Germany. The conference adopted rules for the mitigation of the cruelties of war, under the sponsorship of the American delegation, established the PERMANENT COURT OF ARBITRATION. The United States was the first great nation to submit a case for ARBITRATION to this tribunal (1902). The second conference was called in 1907 with delegates from 44 nations meeting in the Peace Palace built by ANDREW CARNEGIE. The conference adopted the DRAGO DOCTRINE and a series of resolutions looking toward the more humane conduct of war, the protection of the rights of neutrals, the use of the SUBMARINE, and the bombing of ports. The attempts of the American delegation under the leadership of JOSEPH H. CHOATE to persuade the Conference to adopt a plan for the limitation of naval armaments and to create a permanent international court of justice failed.

Hague Tribunal. See Permanent Court of Arbitration.

Hail, Columbia. The first national hymn of the United States. It was a result of the political struggles in the 1790's be-

tween the FEDERALISTS and the Republicans. The latter, sympathetic to the French Revolution, adopted the *Marseillaise* as their song. In 1798 Judge Joseph Hopkinson, a prominent Federalist politician, wrote the text to the tune of the *President's March,* the music of which had been written in the early 1790's by Philip Roth, and revised in 1798 by one Pfyles, the orchestra leader at the John Street Theater in New York City.

HAILMANN, William Nicholas. 1836-1920. Educator. b. Switzerland. To Louisville, Kentucky (1852); important for establishment of the kindergarten movement in the United States.

Haiti. A Republic in the Carribbean Sea. Its 1963 population of 4,500,000 occupies an area of 10,748 square miles, comprising the western third of the island of Hispaniola. Since 1843, the eastern two-thirds have constituted the DOMINICAN REPUBLIC. The island is thus the only one in the world containing two sovereign nations. Haiti established its independence in 1804, following its revolt against France three years earlier. The United States intervened in 1915 to protect American economic interests in the National Bank and National Railroad and to forestall European intervention during the revolution which had broken out in 1911. Americans thereafter served as officials of the Haitian government, exercising control over its public works, sanitation, finances, and police activities. In 1922 the President of the United States appointed John H. Russell as American high commissioner in Haiti to supervise improvements in HIGHWAYS, IRRIGATION, and sanitation. A loan of $16,000,000 granted by American banks in that year contributed to the financing of these ventures. By TREATIES of 1916 and 1924 with Haiti, American MARINES remained until 1934 at which time they were removed in conformance with the

"GOOD NEIGHBOR" policy of the first F. D. ROOSEVELT administration. The occupation of Haiti was part of the program known as "DOLLAR DIPLOMACY", and was attacked by Latin-America as "YANKEE IMPERIALISM."

HALE, Edward Everett. 1822-1909. Unitarian minister and author. b. Boston, Massachusetts. Graduated, Harvard University (1839); pastor of churches in Worcester and Boston, Massachusetts (1846-1901); chaplain, U. S. Senate (1903-09); most famous for his story *Man Without A Country* which appeared in *The Atlantic Monthly* (ec. 1863).

HALE, Eugene. 1836 - 1918. Political leader. b. Maine. Lawyer; member, U.S. House of Representatives (1869-79); supported BLAINE and became Republican leader; U.S. Senator (1881-1911).

HALE, Nathan. 1755-1776. Revolutionary hero. b. Connecticut. Graduated, Yale College (1773); lieutenant in Continental Army (1775); captain (1776); caught as spy behind British lines on Long Island and hanged (Sept. 21, 1776); famous for his last words, "I only regret that I have but one life to lose for my country."

HALE, William Bayard. 1869 - 1924. Journalist. b. Indiana. Episcopal clergyman (1893-1900)); editor, *Cosmopolitan Magazine* (1900); on staff of New York *World*(1902); managing editor, Philadelphia *Public Ledger* (1903-07); WILSON'S confidential agent in Mexico (1913); exposed as German propagandist prior to World War I.

"Half-Breeds." A term of contempt applied by former RADICAL REPUBLICANS to President HAYES, his CABINET, and LIBERAL REPUBLICANS who favored a conciliatory policy to the South after 1877. Such leaders as SIMON CAMERON and ZACH CHANDLER, the political descendants of THADDEUS STEVENS and BENJAMIN BUTLER, attacked this moderate policy as a betrayal of Republican Reconstruction promises. The "half-breeds" advocated CIVIL SERVICE REFORM, opposed the SPOILS SYSTEM, fought against the corruption within the Republican party, and favored friendly Latin-American relations. Among their leaders were JAMES G. BLAINE, JOHN SHERMAN, and JAMES GARFIELD.

HALL, Charles Martin. 1863 - 1914. Chemist, inventor and manufacturer. Invented process for making aluminum inexpensively (1889); became vice-president of Aluminum Company of America (1890) which manufactured his product.

HALL, Granville Stanley. 1846-1924. Psychologist and educator. b. Massachusetts. Professor, psychology and pedagogics, Johns Hopkins (1883-88); President, Clark University (1889 - 1919); founder and editor of the *American Journal of Psychology* (1887); first president, American Psychological Association (1891). Author of many books on psychology. Famous for founding the school of gestalt psychology.

HALL, Lyman. 1724-1790. Revolutionary leader. b. Connecticut. Graduated, Yale College (1747); practiced MEDICINE in Georgia (1758); member, CONTINENTAL CONGRESS (1775-80); signer of DECLARATION OF INDEPENDENCE; governor of Georgia (1783); largely responsible for establishment of state university.

HALLECK, Henry Wager. 1815-1872. Union general. Graduated U.S.M.A., West Point (1839); expert on fortifications; appointed by LINCOLN to command Missouri Department during Civil War (1861-62); commissioned major general; military adviser and general-in-chief at Washington, D. C. (1862-63); when GRANT became supreme commander he became chief of staff; commanded various divisions after the war.

Hall of Fame, The. Its full name is The Hall of Fame for Great Americans. It was established in 1900 on the Bronx campus of New York University as an open air colonnade containing busts of 78 of the 83 persons so far honored for national achievements. Additional names are determined every five years by the vote of a committee of 100 men and women from the 48 states. To be chosen, an individual must have been deceased more than 25 years, must have been an American CITIZEN, and must receive three-fifths of the committee vote. Nominations may be made by any citizen. The last election was held in 1950.

HALSEY, William Frederick. 1882-1959. Admiral. b. New Jersey. Graduated, U.S.N.A., Annapolis (1904); commander of destroyer squadrons in World War I; interested in naval aviation; assigned to carrier units (after 1935); during World War II responsible for raids on the MARSHALL AND GILBERT ISLANDS (January, 1942) and commanded attack on the Solomon Islands (August, 1942); appointed commander of the South Pacific theatre; commander of United States 3rd fleet (1944-45); led action against the PHILIPPINES (1945) and Japan (1945); became admiral of the fleet (November, 1945); retired because of ill health (1947).

HALSTED, William Stewart. 1852-1922. Surgeon. b. New York City. Important for his discovery of "local ANESTHESIA" which he accomplished by injecting cocaine into certain nerves and anesthetizing certain regions of the body (1885); professor of surgery, Johns Hopkins University (from 1890).

HAMBIDGE, Jay. 1867 - 1924. Full name Edward John. Artist. b. Ontario, Canada. Came to the United States (1882); originated the principle of dynamic symmetry found in the study of Greek ART; taught the theory and wrote many books on the subject.

HAMILTON, Alexander. 1757? - 1804. Statesman. b. Leeward Islands. Student at King's College (Columbia University); served through the Revolution as a secretary and aide-de-camp to Washington; through study of army administration he worked out the defects in the ARTICLES OF CONFEDERATION and suggested a plan for a stronger central government (1780); member, CONTINENTAL CONGRESS (1782, 83, 87, 88); studied law in Albany; practised in New York City (from 1783); New York delegate to the ANNAPOLIS CONVENTION (1786); with MADISON he urged the CONSTITUTIONAL CONVENTION but was out-voted on a STRONG CENTRAL GOVERNMENT plan; was conservative statesman, and opposed democratic controls of government; distrusted capacity of people to rule; advocated appointive President and opposed CIVIL LIBERTIES guarantees at the Constitutional Convention; contributed to the *Federalist papers*; important in the RATIFICATION OF THE CONSTITUTION by New York; appointed by Washington the first U.S. Secretary of the Treasury (1789-95); responsible for the planning and establishment of a national fiscal system; fought for strong powers for central government, establishment of a sound basis for public credit, and the development of NATURAL RESOURCES; opposition to his policies by JEFFERSON created different POLITICAL PARTIES; retired to his law practice; appointed major general (1798-1800) at the suggestion of WASHINGTON; opposed ADAMS; supported Jefferson against BURR and helped defeat Burr in his fight for the presidency (1800-1810); again defeated him when he ran for governor of New York (1804); in a duel with Burr he was wounded (July 11, 1804) and died the next day. He was one of America's greatest political thinkers.

HAMILTON, Andrew. d. 1703. Colonial governor. b. Scotland. Deputy governor of East Jersey (1687); governor of East and West Jersey (1692-97); strong administrator; deputy governor of Pennsylvania (1701-03) appointed by PENN; deputy postmaster general for the colonies (1692-1703) and founder of colonial postoffice system establishing uniform postal rates and setting up the first system of postriders in America.

HAMILTON, Andrew. d. 1741. Lawyer. Important for his defense of JOHN PETER ZENGER, publisher of *New York Weekly Journal* against charges of seditious libel; the decision established the principle of freedom of the press in the colonies.

HAMILTON, Andrew Jackson. 1815-1875. Political leader. b. Alabama. To Texas (1847); member, state legislature (1851-53); member, U.S. House of Representatives (1859-61) strong anti-secessionist; appointed by LINCOLN, a brigadier-general and provisional governor of Texas; re-appointed by JOHNSON and was responsible for establishing a strong reconstruction administration; appointed to supreme court of Texas.

HAMILTON, James. 1786-1857. Political leader. Practiced law, South Carolina; served in War of 1812; member, U.S. House of Representatives (1822 - 29) leader of Jacksonian Democrats; opposed ADAMS; strong supporter of STATES RIGHTS; elected governor of South Carolina (1830-32); strong advocate of NULLIFICATION policy, presiding at convention that passed ORDINANCE OF NULLIFICATION (1832); brigadier general and commander of state MILITIA; became interested in Texas and attempted settlement with Mexico on Texas independence; rejected by SAM HOUSTON.

Hamilton's Economic Program. A financial and business program submitted by Secretary of Treasury ALEXANDER HAMILTON in the form of four reports to Congress. The first was submitted on January 14, 1790 and provided that Congress refund the continental debt of $56,124,463, consisting of the foreign debt amounting to $11,710,378, the domestic debt of $42,414,085, and a floating debt of $2,000,000. The second report of December 13, 1790 recommended a program of excise taxes on distilled liquors. The third report, submitted on the same day, recommended a national bank. The fourth report was submitted on December 5th and argued the need of a high TARIFF to protect manufacturers. Despite the great opposition of the Jeffersonians to Hamilton's program all but the last recommendation were adopted by the Congress. In 1790 Congress established a sinking fund for the redemption of the debt. In 1791 Congress established the first BANK OF THE UNITED STATES. In that same year the Whiskey Tax was enacted. In addition, Hamilton's plan for assuming the states' debt of $21,500,000 was enacted in 1790, and a mint was established.

HAMLIN, Hannibal. 1809-1891. Political leader. b. Maine. Practiced law, Bangor; member, Maine legislature (1836-41); member U.S. House of Representatives (1843-47); U.S. Senator (1848-57); supported PIERCE; joined Republican party (1856); elected governor (1857); resigned to return to Senate (1857-61); strong ABOLITIONIST; elected Vice-President of the United States (1861-65) with LINCOLN as President; returned to Senate (1869-91) supported strong Reconstruction policies; appointed by ARTHUR, U.S. Minister to Spain (1881-82).

HAMMERSTEIN, Oscar. 1847? - 1919. Theatrical manager and producer. b. Germany. Came to United States (about 1863); invented cigar-MANUFACTURING machine which was very successful; founded and edited *United States Tobacco Journal*; built Harlem Opera House (1888); Republic Theater (1900); Manhattan Opera House (1906) where he produced Pelleas et Mélisande, Louise, Elektra, etc.; sold out to METROPOLITAN OPERA (1910) built Lexington Opera House (1913); important for his contribution to development of the opera in this country.

HAMMOND, James Henry. 1807-1864. Political leader. b. South Carolina. Strong advocate of SECESSION; fought for STATES' RIGHTS; member, U.S. House of Representatives (1835-36) elected governor of South Carolina (1842-44); U.S. Senator (1857-60)where he made a speech using well-known phrase "Cotton is king."

HAMMOND, John Hays. 1855 - 1936. Mining engineer. b. South Carolina. Staff member, U.S. Geological Survey, working in gold mines of California (1880); known for his association with Cecil Rhodes in development of gold mines in South Africa (1895-96); involved in Jameson Raid during Transvaal reform movement; arrested and sentenced to death; finally freed after payment of $125,000 fine; became interested in other *mining* projects in the United States and Mexico; became special envoy of President TAFT at coronation of King George V (1911).

Hampton Roads, Battle of. The famous naval battle between the IRONCLADS, the Confederate *Merrimac* and the Union *Monitor*. The *Monitor*, known as the "cheesebox on a raft" was built at Brooklyn by JOHN ERICSON. On the morning of March 9th, 1862 it engaged the *Merrimac* in a four hour close range duel. Although the battle ended in a draw, the Union vessel compelled the *Merrimac* to steam back to the Virginia shore, thus saving the Union's wooden vessels in Hampton Roads, after having lost two of them to the *Merrimac* the preceding day. The affair is noteworthy because it signaled the end of wooden naval vessels.

Hampton Roads Peace Conference. A meeting on February 3, 1865 aboard a steamship in Hampton Roads, Virginia, between President LINCOLN and Secretary of State SEWARD of the United States and ALEXANDER H. STEPHENS heading a three man committee of the Confederate States of America. It was called for the purpose of discussing the possibility of restoring peace. The Conference failed because Lincoln and Seward refused to consider any plan which permitted the continuance of SLAVERY.

HAMPTON, Wade. 1818-1902. Confederate general and political leader. b. South Carolina. Served during Civil War at BULL RUN and in Peninsular Campaign; brigadier general (1862); important cavalry commander serving with J. E. B. STUART; served at GETTYSBURG and in the Wilderness; led raids in upper Shenandoah Valley; major general(1863); commanded cavalry units (after 1864); lieutenant general(1865); elected governor of South Carolina (1876-79); U.S. Senator (1879-91).

HANCOCK, John. 1737-1793. Revolutionary statesman. b. Massachusetts. Graduated, Harvard College (1754); inherited large mercantile business (1764) the profits of which were increased by smuggling (1764); led merchants in protesting STAMP ACT; worked with SAMUEL ADAMS in pre-Revolutionary activities; elected to Massachusetts legislature (1766-72); member, CONTINENTAL CONGRESS (1775-80, 85, 86); president of the Congress (1775-77); his imposing signature is well-known, and he was the first signer of the DECLARATION OF INDEPENDENCE; elected the first governor of Massachusetts (1780-85; 1787-93); presided over state convention which ratified the federal Constitution which he favored.

HANCOCK, Winfield Scott. 1824-1886. Union general and political leader. b. Pennsylvania. Served in Mexican war; brigadier general of volunteers (1861) commanded division at ANTIETAM; major general (1862); served brilliantly at Gettysburg; because of his lenient and humane policy in Texas and Louisiana he was transfered to command of Department of Dakota (1870); Democratic candidate for the Presidency of the United States (1880); defeated by GARFIELD.

HANNA, Marcus Alonzo. Known as

Mark. 1837-1904. Businessman and politician. b. Ohio. Worked with his father in a grocery and commission business (1853-62); partner in the company (from 1862); served with Union army during the Civil War (1864); became interested in politics and by 1880's he was Republican leader of Ohio; sponsored JOHN SHERMAN (1888); supported MCKINLEY and largely responsible for his being elected to governor of Ohio (1891 and 1893); contributed large sums to McKinley for presidency (1896 and 1900); important as advisor to the President; elected to U.S. Senate (1897-1904).

HANSON, John. 1715-1783. Revolutionary political leader. b. Maryland. Member, Maryland House of delegates (1757-81); member, CONTINENTAL CONGRESS (1780-82); elected first president of the Congress after ratification of the ARTICLES OF CONFEDERATION (Mar. 1, 1781); although he is often said to have been first President of the United States, he was merely a presiding officer of the Congress and not a President as set forth in the present Constitution.

HAPGOOD, Norman. 1868-1937. Editor and author. b. Chicago, Illinois. Editor, *Collier's Weekly* (1903-12) fought for pure food and drug reforms, conservation, etc; *Harper's Weekly* (1913-16); *Hearst's International Magazine* (1923-25); appointed by WILSON U.S. Minister to Denmark (1919). Author of *Daniel Webster* (1899), *Abraham Lincoln* (1899), and *Industry and Progress* (1911).

Harbors. The great importance of harbors has always been their attraction to settlers who have built up great cities on their sites. Around the colonial harbors of Boston, New York, Philadelphia, Baltimore, and Charleston grew up the largest urban communities. For a long time Boston was the leading port, but was replaced in the 19th century by New York with its deeper water and superior inland channels. Along the Atlantic coast great harbors sprang up at Portland, Norfolk, and Savannah. On the Gulf of Mexico, New Orleans and Galveston took the lead. By the mid-nineteenth century San Francisco and Seattle had become serious rivals of the eastern ports for world TRADE. Simultaneously, important harbors developed in inland waters such as the Mississippi and its tributaries and on the GREAT LAKES. On the latter the great cities of Buffalo, Cleveland, Chicago, and Milwaukee came into being. Privately owned and operated, the harbor installations developed efficient TRANSPORTATION facilities. Under its constitutional authority Congress later delegated to the Army Corps of Engineers the responsibility of assisting these areas. The first congressional appropriation was made in 1802 for the construction of public wharves in Philadelphia. Subsequently, funds were appropriated in 1822, 1826, and later years for additional work.

HARDEE, William Joseph. 1815-1873. Confederate general. b. Georgia. Graduated, U.S.M.A., West Point (1838); served in war with Mexico and promoted to lieutenant colonel; served with Confederate army; set up "Hardee's Brigade" in Arkansas which served with him in Army of Tennessee; major general (1861); lieutenant general (1862); best known for strong defense against SHERMAN in his march to the sea; strong general defeated because of inadequate troops and supplies.

HARDING, Warren Gamaliel. 1865-1923. Twenty-ninth President of the United States. b. Ohio. Owner and editor of Marion *Star* in Ohio (from 1884); served in state senate and was lieutenant governor of state; elected U.S. Senator (1915-21); prominent Republican who favored PROTECTIVE TARIFF and opposed the League of Nations; elected President (1921-23); although he had many able men in his administration he also appointed corrupt officials; died while on speaking tour at San Francisco (Aug. 12, 1923) before exposure of his Secretary of the Interior A. FALL and Attorney-General Daugherty on charges of corruption and fraud.

Hare-Hawes-Cutting Act. See Hawes-Cutting Act.

HARKNESS, William. 1837-1903. Astronomer. b. Scotland. Graduated, University of Rochester; aid, U.S. Naval Observatory (1862); discovered coronal line K 1474 while observing total solar eclipse (Aug. 1869); an original member, Transit of Venus Commission (1871); official observer of transits (1874, 1882); inventor of the spherometer caliper and other astronomical instruments; astronomical director, U. S. NAVAL OBSERVATORY (1894-99). Author of *The Solar Parallax and Its Related Constants.*

HARLAN, James. 1820-1899. Political leader. b. Illinois. President, Iowa Wesleyan University (1853); leader, Free-soil movement; U.S. Senator (1855-57; 57-65; 67-73); interested in EDUCATION and HOMESTEAD LAWS; appointed by LINCOLN U.S. Secretary of the Interior (1865-66) resigned in protest against JOHNSON'S policies.

HARLAN, John Marshall. 1833 - 1911. Jurist. b. Kentucky. Served as colonel in Union Army (1861-63); attorney general of Kentucky (1863-67); supported HAYES and appointed by him to the U.S. Supreme Court (1877-1911) as associate justice; known for his independent views and as a constant "dissenter"; served on Bering Sea Tribunal at Paris.

HARMON, Judson. 1846-1927. Political leader. b. Ohio. Graduated Cincinnati Law School (1869); appointed by Cleveland U.S. Attorney General (1895-97); reform Democratic governor of Ohio (1909-13) being responsible for many

progressive measures including a WORKMEN'S COMPENSATION ACT etc.

HARMON, Millard Fillmore. 1888-1945. Air Force General. b. California. Graduated U.S.M.A., West Point (1912); major general in command of 2d air force (1941-42); chief of air staff of U.S. Army (Jan. 1942); in command of AIR FORCES in South Pacific (June, 1942).

HARNETT, Cornelius. 1723?-1781. Revolutionary leader. Successful planter in North Carolina; member, COLONIAL ASSEMBLY (1754-75); leader in protest against the STAMP ACT; delegate to CONTINENTAL CONGRESSES; captured by British at Wilmington, North Carolina (1781) and died a prisoner.

HARNETT, William Michael. 1848-1892. Painter. b. Ireland. Studied and painted in the United States, Munich, Paris and New York. Known for his very realistic still-life studies. Best known work, *After the Hunt.*

HARNEY, William Selby. 1800 - 1889. Army officer. Fought in Florida against the Indians and gained rank of colonel; cavalry leader under SCOTT during Mexican War; relieved of command for personal reasons by Scott but reinstated by superiors at Washington; hero at Cerro Gordo; successful in fights against the SIOUX; commanded Department of the West, St. Louis before Civil War; southern sympathizer but did not serve during war.

HARPER, Robert Goodloe. 1765-1825. Politician. b. Virginia. Member, U.S. House of Representatives (1795-1801); served in War of 1812; major general of Maryland forces; U.S. Senator (1816); an original organizer of AMERICAN COLONIZATION SOCIETY and responsible for the names *Liberia* and *Monrovia* for the colony and its capital in Africa.

Harper's Ferry. See Brown, John.

Harper's Weekly. A periodical founded by Harper and Brothers in 1857. The political cartoons of Thomas Nast made the MAGAZINE internationally famous after the Civil War and were instrumental in the destruction of the TWEED RING in 1872. In 1916 it was merged with the *Independent*.

HARPER, William Rainey. 1856-1906. Educator. First president of University of Chicago (1891-1906) and largely responsible for its development into one of the largest universities in the country. Author of *The Trend in Higher Education* (1905).

HARRIMAN, Edward Henry. 1848-1909. Railroad magnate. b. New York. Worked as office boy in WALL STREET (1862-69); bought a seat on the stock exchange (1869); won recognition for successful handling of finances for Illinois Central Railroad and became a director (1883); vice-president (1887); director and president UNION PACIFIC; lost fight with HILL over control of Northern Pacific Railroad which resulted in stockmarket panic (May 9, 1901); public anger aroused against Harriman when his lines were investigated by the INTERSTATE COMMERCE COMMISSION (1906-07) and method of operation condemned.

HARRIMAN, William Averell. 1891-. Statesman. b. New York City. Son of EDWARD HENRY HARRIMAN. Graduated, Yale University (1913); chairman of the board of UNION PACIFIC RAILROAD (1934); appointed by F. D. ROOSEVELT, administrative officer of the NATIONAL RECOVERY ADMINISTRATION (1934-35) and to the Department of Commerce (1937-40); chief administrator of the LEND-LEASE program in Europe (1941); U.S. Ambassador to the Soviet Union (1943-46) and to England (1946); Secretary of Commerce (1946-48); ambassador-at-large in command of the EUROPEAN RECOVERY PROGRAM (1948); head of the mutual assistance program (1952); a candidate for presidency (1952 and 1956); elected governor of New York (1954).

HARRIS, Joel Chandler. 1848 - 1908. Author. b. Georgia. Writer on the staff of the Atlanta *Constitution* (1876-1900); famous for his Uncle Remus stories. Author of *Uncle Remus, His Songs and His Sayings* (1880), *The Tar Baby* (1904), and *Uncle Remus and Brer Rabbit* (1906).

Harrisburg Convention. A meeting called at Harrisburg, Pennsylvania in 1827 by the protectionist congressmen for the purpose of drawing up resolutions to be presented to the people in their effort to seek a higher TARIFF measure. Spurred by the woolen interests who had failed to put through the "Woolens Bill" in 1827 the convention prepared a memorial to Congress setting forth the particular need for such a tariff. The result was the passage of the high TARIFF ACT OF 1828. Led by HENRY CLAY, 100 delegates from 13 New England, middle Atlantic, and mid-western states attended the Convention.

HARRIS, Elisha. 1824-1884. Physician and sanitation expert. Planned quarantine regulations for the ports; one of founders of U.S. Sanitary Commission; designed hospital cars used in war service; led sanitary survey of New York City (1864); established first vaccination service for the general public; a founder and secretary, American Public Health Association; commissioner, N. Y. State Board of Health.

"Harris-Forbes-Chase National" combination. A powerful PUBLIC UTILITY HOLDING COMPANY combination in the early 20th century. Through subsidiary, investment, and management companies it operated a huge aggregation of public utilities, furnishing management, finance, research, and coordination services.

HARRIS, Isham Green. 1818-1897. Lawyer and politician. State senator Tennessee; member; U.S. House of Representatives (1849-53); governor of Tennessee (1857-63); influenced the joining of Tennessee with the Confederate cause; served during war; practiced law in Memphis after the war; U.S. Senator (1877-1897).

HARRIS, Thaddeus William. 1795-1856. Entomologist and librarian. Librarian at Harvard (1831-56); called the "father of economic entomology." Author of important work in the field, *A Treatise on Insects of New England Injurious to Vegetation* (1842).

Harrison Act. See Land Act of 1800.

HARRISON, Benjamin. 1726? - 1791. Revolutionary leader. b. Charles City County, Virginia. Member, Virginia House of Burgesses (1749-75); opposed the STAMP ACT; member, CONTINENTAL CONGRESS (1774-78); a signer of the DECLARATION OF INDEPENDENCE; governor of Virginia (1782-84); member, Virginia legislature (1784-91).

HARRISON, Benjamin. 1833 - 1901. Twenty-third President of United States. b. North Bend, Ohio. Grandson of President WILLIAM HENRY HARRISON. Graduated, Miami University (1852); studied law in Cincinnati; moved to Indianapolis (1854); served during Civil Was as colonel of Indiana regiment; brevetted brigadier general (1865); leading CORPORATION attorney; served as prominent Republican U.S. Senator (1881-87) voting for CIVIL SERVICE REFORM and a big navy; ran for President on Republican ticket against CLEVELAND, and although he obtained fewer popular votes than his opponent, he received a majority of the ELECTORAL VOTES and was made President of the United States (1889-93); first PAN-AMERICAN CONFERENCE held during his administration (1889); defeated by CLEVELAND in presidential election (1892).

HARRISON, William Henry. 1773-1841.

Ninth president of the United States; son of BENJAMIN HARRISON (1726?-1791). b. Charles City County, Virginia. Served in Indian campaigns in the NORTHWEST TERRITORY (1791-98); secretary of Northwest Territory (1798); governor, Territory of Indiana (1801-13); fought against TECUMSEH (1811); commanded army of the Northwest during War of 1812 and given rank of brigadier general; major general (1813); resigned form the army (1814); member, U.S. House of Representatives (1816-1819) from Ohio; U.S. Senator (1825-28) supported CLAY; U.S. Minister to Colombia (1828-29); WHIG candidate for President (1836) defeated; elected President by a large majority as a result of an ANTI-JACKSON movement (1840); died of pneumonia after having served just one month as President (Mar. 4-Apr. 4, 1841). Inaugurated at the age of 67 he was the oldest President of the United States.

HARTE, Francis Brett. Known as Bret. 1836-1902. Writer. b. New York. Worked as journalist in California; editor, *Overland Monthly* (1868-70); writer in New York City (1871-78); U.S. consul in Prussia and Scotland (1879-85). Author of *The Luck of Roaring Camp* (1868), *The Outcasts of Poker Flat* (1869), and *The Heathen Chinee* (1870).

Hartford Convention, The. A secret meeting on December 15, 1814 of representatives of Massachusetts, Rhode Island, and Connecticut. It was called for purpose of expressing the opposition of the New England FEDERALISTS to the War of 1812. Its report of January 5th, 1815 severly attacked President MADISON's administration and the War. For the second time in American history an expression of STATES' RIGHTS doctrine was made in the principle of NULLIFICATION when the New England states were invited to nullify the conscription bill then before Congress. No overt declaration of SECESSION was made although the idea was discussed at the Convention. The Federalist party suffered its last blow by this meeting, the stigma of unpatriotism being attached to it. The party never recovered.

HART, Hastings Hornell. 1851 - 1932. Social service worker and penologist. b. Ohio. Graduated, Cleveland Military Institute, Oberlin College and Andover Theological Seminary; served in social service work; superintendent Illinois Children's Home and Aid Society (1898-1909); helped frame first JUVENILE COURT laws in United States; director children's aid department of RUSSELL SAGE FOUNDATION (1909-24); consultant in delinquency and penology (from 1924) for the Foundation.

HART, John. 1711?-1779. Revolutionary leader. b. Connecticut. Successful FARMER and miller, Hopewell, New Jersey; member, N.J. provincial assembly (1761-71); member, CONTINENTAL CONGRESS (1776); signer of DECLARATION OF INDEPENDENCE; served on state COMMITTEE OF CORRESPONDENCE; chairman, N. H. COMMITTEE OF SAFETY (1777-78); speaker, first assembly of New Jersey.

Harvard University. The oldest institution of higher learning in America. It was founded in 1636 in New Towne (now Cambridge), Massachusetts by a grant of the MASSACHUSETTS BAY COLONY. In 1639 it was named Harvard College because of an endowment by Reverend John Harvard. It was chartered in 1657 since which time control has been jointly vested in a board of overseers and in the officers of the corporation which was created in 1650. In 1851 it separated itself from the church and in 1855 from the state. The election of the overseers was transferred from the legislature to the alumni in the latter year. From its founding the institution has played an important part in American cultural life. One of its early presidents was INCREASE

MATHER. Famous faculty members have been LONGFELLOW, HOLMES, SANTAYANA, Whitehead, and WILLIAM JAMES.

HARVEY, George Brinton McClellan. 1864-1928. Journalist and diplomat. b. Vermont. Owner and editor, *North American Review* (1899-1926); president and holder of controlling interest, Harper & Bros. (1900-15) and *Harper's Weekly* (1901-13), *Harvey's Weekly* (1918-21) editor of the weeklies; supported WILSON for governor of New Jersey (1910); supported Wilson for presidency (1912); opposed Wilson and LEAGUE OF NATIONS; HARDING for presidency (1920); appointed by Harding U.S. Ambassador to Great Britain (1921-23).

HASTINGS, Serranus Clinton. 1814-1893. Jurist. b. New York. Admitted to bar, Indiana (1836); moved to Iowa and served in first legislature in that TERRITORY; first member, U.S. House of Representatives from Iowa (1846); chief justice, supreme court of California.

Hat Act of 1732. One of a series of restrictive British laws applying to the North American colonies. The statute declared that no American-made hats could be exported from one colony to another or to Europe.

Hatch Act. Passed by Congress in 1887. It was one of the earliest federal statutes to provide agricultural assistance. The act was a recognition of the joint responsibility of the federal and state governments for agricultural development and of the inability of the DEPARTMENT OF AGRICULTURE to solve the problems peculiar to state boundaries. It appropriated $15,000 annually to each state and TERRITORY for agricultural experiment stations, and specified means for making their findings available to the public. Under its operations state work was coordinated, supervised, and enlarged, although farmers did not fully accept the stations before 1910. The Act gave new impetus to agricultural research throughout the country, and experts soon formed an Association of Economic Entomologists for the development and correlation of their scientific work.

Hatch Act of 1939. A law of Congress enacted "to prevent pernicious political activities." Designed to eliminate corrupt political practices, it forbade anyone to intimidate, threaten, or coerce any person in order to influence his vote for a federal office. It further prohibited promise of employment or other advantage for political support, and made illegal the soliciting of political contributions by relief workers and federal executive or administrative employees. The latter were also prohibited from engaging in political management or in political campaigns. Exempted from its provisions were certain policy-determining officials, principally department heads, assistant heads, and the thousands of officers appointed by the President and Senate who determine foreign policy or are engaged in the "Nationwide administration of Federal laws." The amendment of 1940 attempted to regulate campaign contributions and expenditures by limiting to $5,000 per annum the contribution of any one person, committee, or corporation in the nomination or election of any candidate for federal office. No political committee may receive contributions or make expenditures in any calendar year in excess of $3,000,000. No firm under contract with a federal agency for supplies or materials may be solicited or may contribute to any POLITICAL PARTY, committee, or candidate. No CORPORATION or union may contribute to political parties or campaigns. The Act and its amendment of 1940 have proved unsuccessful in eliminating these practices. Expenditures and contributions by individual committees and persons have raised the amounts far beyond those laid down in the law. The law is also known as the

Federal Corrupt Practices Act and the Political Activities Act of 1939.

Havana Conference. A PAN-AMERICAN CONFERENCE held at Havana, CUBA in July, 1940. It proposed a TREATY setting up an Inter-American Commission of Territorial Administration to assume control of and supervise all Latin-American territories concerning which there might be a "transfer or intent to transfer sovereignty." Although never established the mere proposal to set up such an agency was sufficient to forestall any attempted Axis invasion of the western hemisphere. Also the Sixth International Conference of American States meeting from January 16th to February 20, 1928. At this Conference progress was made in providing for conciliation in Latin-American disputes and for international cooperation in cultural matters.

Hawaii vs. Mankichi. See Insular Cases.

Hawaii. Formerly known as the Sandwich Islands. A group of 20 islands, 6,407 square miles in area, with a POPULATION in 1959 of over 575,000. They are located in the north PACIFIC and were, until made the 50th state in 1959, a TERRITORY of the United States administered by a presidentially appointed governor and a popularly elected bicameral legislature. They were formally annexed on August 12, 1898 by a JOINT RESOLUTION OF CONGRESS, bringing to an end their independent status as a republic. The capital, Honolulu, is the largest city in the islands. Hawaii grows 90 per cent of the world's pineapples. Other important products are cane SUGAR, coffee, RICE, COTTON, bananas, nuts, and potatoes. There is some CATTLE grazing. The tourist business is Hawaii's third largest source of income. To this date 86 percent of the Islands' population is native. This heterogeneous population consists of native Hawaiians intermixed with Japanese, Koreans, Chinese, Spaniards, Americans, and Portuguese.

Hawes-Cutting Act. Also known as the Hare-Hawes-Cutting Act and the Philippine Independence Act of 1933. A law of Congress enacted over President HOOVER'S VETO in January, 1933 providing for the complete independence of the PHILIPPINE ISLANDS after a ten year period of political and economic tutelage. The Act was not to become effective unless its terms were approved by the Philippine legislature within one year. It immediately produced political conflict within the Islands between an element favoring its acceptance and a group which demanded immediate and complete independence. It was ultimately turned down by the Island legislature. In 1934 Congress renewed the offer of independence in the MC DUFFY-TYDINGS ACT.

Hawley-Smoot Tariff Act. One of the highest TARIFFS in American history. It was enacted in 1930 and raised the high duties of the FORDNEY-MC CUMBER TARIFF. The average of all schedules was increased. One-third of the items were changed, 890 being raised, including 50 transfers from the free to the tax list. Two hundred and thirty-five items were reduced, including 75 transfers from the dutiable to the free list. Cement, boots, shoes, and hides were made dutiable. The average rate upon agricultural RAW MATERIALS was increased from 38.10 to 48.92 percent, while other commodities were increased from 31.02 to 34.30 percent. Heavy increases were made on minerals, chemicals, dyestuffs, and textiles. It was estimated that the average for all dutiable articles was 41.57 percent as compared to the Fordney-McCumber average of 38.24. The act hastened the decline in world TRADE and aroused deep resentment abroad. In the United States FARMERS and manufacturers with export surpluses and bankers with foreign investments opposed the law. Although 1028 prominent economists petitioned President HOOVER not to sign the bill he did so. The Act produced immediate foreign retaliation. Within two years 25 nations established high tariffs. This resulted in a further slump in American foreign trade.

HAWTHORNE, Nathaniel. 1804-1864. Author. b. Massachusetts. Graduated, Bowdoin College (1825); *Twice-Told Tales* and *Mosses from an Old Manse* (1846) were his first successes; worked in Boston customhouse (1839-41); lived at BROOK FARM for a year; lived in Concord (1842-45); friendly with EMERSON, THOREAU, ALCOTT and others; surveyor of port of Salem (1845-49); U.S. consul, Liverpool, England (1853-58); lived in Italy and London (1858-60). Author of *The House of Seven Gables* (1851), *The Scarlet Letter* (1850), *The Marble Faun* (1860), and other works.

Hay-Bunau-Varilla Treaty. A treaty negotiated in 1903 by the United States Secretary of State JOHN HAY and the Panamanian minister to the United States. By its terms the newly established Republic of Panama leased to the United States in perpetuity a 10 miles zone across the Isthmus of Panama for which the United States agreed to pay $10,000,000 down and $250,000 a year after nine years. Following the treaty's ratification the United States began the construction of the PANAMA CANAL which was opened to traffic in 1914.

Hayden Planetarium. A section of the American Museum of Natural History, located in New York City. It is a theatre of the heavens where the stars and other celestial bodies are projected in rays of light by an astronomical calculating mechanism on a 75 foot dome, producing an illusion of the night sky. About 9,000 stars, including some of the sixth magnitude, may be seen. From time to time the Planetarium prepares special exhibits such as a Trip to the Moon, End of the World, Riddles in the Sky, and Conquest of Space. Each December, a special Christmas show is given in which the many theories concerning the identity of the Star of Bethlehem are examined with the aid of the Planetarium projector. The Planetarium also maintains, in its corridors interesting scientific exhibits of meteorites, photographs, and weather cycles. It encourages interest in astronomy by making its facilities available to the public in telescope making. There are many interesting children's programs given as part of the educational service of the Planetarium.

HAYES, Patrick Joseph. 1867-1938. Roman Catholic cardinal. b. New York City. Graduated, Manhattan College (1888), Catholic University (S.T.D. 1894), Rome (D.D. 1904); chancellor of archdiocese of New York (1903); archbishop (1919), cardinal (1924); interested in social and industrial reforms.

HAYES, Rutherford Birchard. 1822-1893. Nineteenth President of the United States. b. Delaware, Ohio. Graduated, Harvard Law School and admitted to bar (1845); practiced law in Cincinnati (from 1850); served as major in Civil War; brigadier general (1864), brevetted major general (1865); Republican member, U. S. House of Representatives (1865-67); governor of Ohio (1868-72; 1876-77); nominated for presidency (1876); very close Hayes-TILDEN contest which finally resulted in Hayes being declared the winner by one ELECTORAL VOTE, although Tilden received a majority of the POPULAR VOTE; had strong, able administration; vetoed BLAND-ALLISON ACT.

Hay-Herran Treaty. A treaty negotiated in 1903 between United States Secretary of State JOHN HAY and the Colombian foreign minister Herran by which Colombia offered to lease to the United States in perpetuity a 10 miles zone across the Isthmus of Panama for a $10,000,000 down payment plus an annual payment of $250,000 after nine years. The Colombian senate refused to ratify the agreement, demanding $10,000,000 of the $40,000,000 appropriated to pay France for her canal rights in the Isthmus plus an additional $5,000,000 from the United States. This refusal to ratify resulted in the PANAMANIAN REVOLUTION of that year followed by the HAY-BUNAU-VARILLA TREATY.

HAY, John Milton. 1838-1905. Statesman. b. Indiana. Graduated, Brown University (1858); studied law, Springfield, Ill. where he met LINCOLN and became his secretary (1860-65); worked in various legations in Europe and as a journalist in New York City; U.S. Assistant Secretary of State (1878); wrote many popular ballads, poems and novels (1870-90) and an excellent history of ABRAHAM LINCOLN (with John Nicolay, 10 volumes 1890); appointed by MC KINLEY U. S. Ambassador to Great Britain (1897); U.S. Secretary of State under MC KINLEY and ROOSEVELT (1898-1905); responsible for OPEN DOOR POLICY in China (1899); provided for construction of PANAMA CANAL by negotiating TREATIES with Colombia, England, and Panama.

Haymarket Affair. An incident arising out of the EIGHT HOUR movement in the 1880's. A meeting was called by anarchist labor leaders and newspaper editors, to be held on May 4, 1886 in Haymarket Square, Chicago, in protest against the shooting of several strikers in a recent labor dispute. Mayor Harrison, police Captain Bonfield, and 180 police attended the meeting. Following the Mayor's departure, and against his advice, the crowd was ordered to leave. A bomb, thrown by an unknown person, exploded and resulted in the deaths of seven persons and injuries to many others. Eight anarchists were arrested and convicted for conspiracy. In 1887 four were hanged. One later committed suicide, and in 1893 Governor ALTGELD of Illinois pardoned the remaining two. It has never been determined who threw the bomb, and labor and radical elements have always claimed the Haymarket Affair to have been an anti-labor conspiracy. The movement for the eight hour day collapsed for a generation, as a result.

HAYNE, Issac. 1745-1781. Revolutionary soldier. b. South Carolina. Served as colonel of South Carolina troops in Revolution; captured by British and hanged as a spy without trial, causing a furore and protest by the Americans.

HAYNE, Paul Hamilton. 1830 - 1886. Poet. Known as "poet laureate of the South." b. South Carolina. Known for *Poems* (1855), *Sonnets and Other Poems* (1857), and *The Mountain of Lovers* (1875).

HAYNE, Robert Young. 1791-1839. Politician. b. South Carolina. Admitted to bar (1812); U. S. Senator (1823-32); known for famous debates with WEBSTER on STATES RIGHTS against federal government control as stated in the Constitution (1830); governor of South Carolina (1832-34), leaving the Senate to make way for CLAY whom he supported.

HAYNES, Elwood. 1857-1925. Inventor. Graduated, Worcester Polytechnic Institute (1881); designed and built the first successful "horseless carriage" or gasoline automobile (1893-4); which is now at the SMITHSONIAN INSTITUTION, Washington, D.C.; discoverer of a tungsten chrome steel (1881), alloy of chromium and nickel (1897), alloy of cobalt and chromium used in manufacture of cutting instruments (1900), and other alloys; patented stainless steel (1919).

HAYNES, John. 1594?-1654. Colonial administrator. b. England. To Massachusetts (1633); as governor of Massachusetts (1635) he banished ROGER WILLIAMS from the colony; first governor of Connecticut under the FUNDAMENTAL ORDERS (1639 and alternate years thereafter until 1654); urged the NEW ENGLAND CONFEDERATION.

Hay-Pauncefote Treaty. A treaty negotiated in 1901 between United States Secretary of State JOHN HAY and the British emissary Sir Julian Pauncefote. By its terms Great Britain agreed to abrogate the CLAYTON-BULWER TREATY and allow the United States to build a canal across the Isthmus of Panama, having "the exclusive management and policing" of it. The next step in the construction of a PANAMA CANAL was the purchase of the rights of the French Panama Company. See Spooner Act.

HAYWOOD, William Dudley. 1869-1928. Labor leader. b. Salt Lake City, Utah. Worked as a miner; joined SOCIALIST PARTY (1901); member executive board, Western Federation of Miners; a founder of INDUSTRIAL WORKERS OF THE WORLD (1905); charged with having a part in the murder of the governor of Idaho (1907) but acquitted; led textile workers' strike; advocated violence; arrested on charge of sabotage and sedition and convicted (1918); forfeited bail and fled to Russia.

HAZLEWOOD, John. 1726?-1800. Revolutionary naval commander. Prepared defense of Delaware River; commodore, Pennsylvania navy and commander of vessels, fire-boats, etc., which were constructed at his direction; defeated British above Philadelphia on the Delaware; his system of naval defense helped the American cause.

H-bomb. See hydrogen bomb.

Head Tax. See poll tax.

285

HEARN, Lafcadio. 1850-1904. Writer. b. Ionian Islands. Came to the United States (1869); worked on various NEWSPAPERS and wrote for MAGAZINES; went to Japan (1890); taught English in Japanese schools; became Japanese citizen; author of *Two Years in the French Indies* (1890), *Japan, An Attempt at Interpretation* (1904) etc.

HEARST, William Randolph. 1863-1951. Newspaper publisher. b. California. Studied at Harvard (1882-85); owner of large newspapers such as the San Francisco *Examiner*, Chicago *American*, New York *Journal-American*, and *Daily Mirror* and others; owner of MAGAZINES including Hearst's *International-Cosmopolitan, Good Housekeeping;* the newspaper syndicate *King Features;* and *International News Service;* member, U.S. House of Representatives (1903-07); defeated for mayor (1905 and 1909) and for governor of New York (1906); violently opposed the LEAGUE OF NATIONS; supported "yellow-peril" campaign; known for sensational journalism and extreme nationalistic campaigns; unsuccessfully supported General DOUGLAS MACARTHUR for presidential nomination(1948); ART collector; opposed by liberals for his "YELLOW JOURNALISM" and conservative politics.

HECKER, Isaac Thomas. 1819-1888. Roman Catholic priest, founder of Paulist Fathers. b. New York City. Converted to Catholicism (1844); joined Redemptorists (1845); missionary priest (1851-57); with consent of the Pope he founded, with four associates, the Congregation of the Missionary Priests of St. Paul the Apostle, known as Paulist Fathers; he was first superior (1858-88); purpose of organization was to work for the conversion of Americans; founded the *Catholic World* (1865), the *Young Catholic* (1870), and the Catholic Publication Society (1866).

"He Kept Us Out of War." The political slogan devised by the leaders of the Democratic party for President WILSON in the campaign of 1916. Its two-fold purpose was the solicitation of Democratic votes from the "BRYAN country" (the border states, South, and Far West) in the effort to win Republican and independent votes for the party. In campaign speeches, Bryan used the slogan to excellent advantage.

HEMINGWAY, Ernest. 1898-1961. Writer. b. Illinois. Served as European war correspondent. Author of well-known books including *The Sun Also Rises* (1926), *A Farewell To Arms* (1929), *Death in the Afternoon* (1932), *For Whom the Bell Tolls* (1940), etc. Leader of school of hard-hitting realistic writers.

HENDERSON, Richard. 1735-1785. Colonizer. b. Virginia. Sent DANIEL BOONE to investigate Kentucky country (1764); retired, judge of superior court, North Carolina (1773); organizer of Transylvania Company (1775) which settled in Boonesboro, Kentucky; failed because of opposition from Virginia and North Carolina, and the outbreak of the Revolution; successfully promoted COLONIZATION of French Lick, now Nashville, Tennessee.

HENDRICKS, Thomas Andrews. 1815-1885. Political leader. Admitted to bar (1843); practiced in Indiana; member, U.S. House of Representatives (1851-55); Democratic U.S. Senator (1863-69); governor of Indiana (1873-77); unsuccessful candidate for vice-presidency with TILDEN (1876); elected Vice-President of the United States with CLEVELAND as President (1885).

HENRI, Robert. 1865-1929. Painter. b. Ohio. Studied in Philadelphia and Europe; well-known instructor at Art Student's League, New York City. Best known works are *The Equestrian, Spanish Gypsy, Young Woman in Black*, etc. His works are part of museum collections throughout the country.

HENRY, Joseph. 1797-1878. Physicist.

b. New York. Professor at Princeton (College of New Jersey 1832-46); made many discoveries in field of electromagnetism; discovered method of producing induced current and the name of the unit of induction is called in his honor, *henry;* discovered principle underlying electromagnetic TELEGRAPH. First secretary and director, SMITHSONIAN INSTITUTION, Washington, D.C. (1846).

HENRY, O. Pseudonym of William Sydney Porter. 1862-1910. Short-story writer. b. North Carolina. Worked as clerk, bookkeeper, bank teller, and draftsman in Texas (1885-94); columnist, Houston *Daily Post* (1895-06); served three years on conviction for embezzlement (1898); worked for the *World* in New York City (1903). Author of well-known collections of short stories including *Cabbages and Kings* (1904), *The Four Million* (1906), and *The Voice of the City* (1908).

HENRY, Patrick. 1736-1799. Revolutionary statesman and orator. b. Virginia. After unsuccessful attempt at working as a storekeeper (1751-60) he studied law and was admitted to the bar (1760); served in Virginia legislature (1765); leader of Virginia radicals; organized the Virginia COMMITTEE OF CORRESPONDENCE (1773) with the help of THOMAS JEFFERSON and RICHARD LEE; member, CONTINENTAL CONGRESS (1774-76); in speech urging strong colonial defense he used famous phrase, "Give me liberty, or give me death"; elected governor of Virginia (1776-79; 1784-86); member, convention which ratified the Federal Constitution(1788) although he opposed ratification, and proposed first ten AMENDMENTS to United States Constitution, which are known as the BILL OF RIGHTS.

HENSON, Josiah. 1789-1883. NEGRO leader. b. Maryland. Foreman and Methodist preacher to slaves on PLANTATION; escaped with family to Canada (1830); leader of cause of the Negro in America; went to England to lecture; thought to be the original Uncle Tom used by HARRIET STOWE in her famous book *Uncle Tom's Cabin.* Author of autobiography *Truth Stranger than Fiction* (1858).

Hepburn Act. Enacted in 1906 as an AMENDMENT to the INTERSTATE COMMERCE ACT of 1887. It enlarged the INTERSTATE COMMERCE COMMISSION from five to seven members and empowered it to determine just and reasonable rates upon complaint of a shipper. The Commission's jurisdiction was extended to cover express and sleeping car companies, pipelines, switches, spurs, tracks, and terminal facilities. The Act also forbade free passes and made it illegal for RAILROADS to haul commodities that they had themselves produced. The Commission was empowered to prescribe bookkeeping methods that the railroads must adopt. Rates changes must be published thirty days before they went into effect. The Act obviated many of the flaws of the original statute and its 1903 amendment, constituting for the first time basic railroad regulatory practice.

HEPBURN, Alonzo Barton. 1846-1922. Banker and legislator. b. New York. Member, New York legislature (1875-80); chairman investigating committee on railway rate discrimination; his report resulted in the "HEPBURN Act" to correct abuses (1879); state superintendent of banking, N.Y. (1880-83); U.S. bank examiner, New York City (1889-92); U.S. comptroller of the CURRENCY (1892-93); president, Chase National Bank (1904-11) and chairman of the board (1911-19).

Hepburn vs. Griswold. See Legal Tender Cases.

HERBERT, Victor. 1859-1924. Conductor and composer. b. Ireland. Came to New York (1886); cello soloist METROPOLITAN OPERA HOUSE; organized and conducted his own orchestra(from 1904); famous for light operas *The Fortune Tell-*

er (1898), *Babes in Toyland* (1903), *Mlle. Modiste* (1905) *The Red Mill* (1906), and *Naughty Marietta* (1910).

HERKIMER, Nicholas. 1728-1777. Revolutionary general. b. New York. Lieutenant of MILITIA in French and Indian War (1758); strong agitator in colonial cause before the Revolutionary War; brigadier general (1775); led force to defend Fort Schuyler, killed in losing battle.

Hermitage, The. The PLANTATION estate near Nashville, Tennessee purchased by ANDREW JACKSON in 1795. Of the original 28,000 acres Jackson sold 22,000 when he moved into the Hermitage in 1804. After his death the estate was occupied by his son until 1888 with the permission of the state of Tennessee which had acquired it in 1856. Today the Hermitage is preserved by the state as a shrine.

HERNDON, William Henry 1818-1891. Lawyer. b. Kentucky. Junior law partner of ABRAHAM LINCOLN (from 1844); strong anti-slavery advocate and influenced Lincoln into taking strong action; wrote biography (with J. W. Weik, 3 vols. 1889) entitled *Lincoln, the True Story of a Great Life.*

HERTER, Christian A. 1895-1966. b. Paris, France. Graduated Harvard (1915). Attaché Am. Embassy, Berlin, 1916-1917, special assistant, U.S. Dept. of State, 1917-1918. Governor of Mass., 1953-1955. Under Secretary, Department of State, 1956-1959. Succeeded John Foster Dulles as Secretary of State in 1959.

HEWES, Joseph. 1730-1779. Revolutionary leader. b. New Jersey. Merchant, North Carolina; member of COLONIAL ASSEMBLY (1766-75); served on COMMITTEE OF CORRESPONDENCE; member, CONTINENTAL CONGRESS (1774-77; 1779); signer of DECLARATION OF INDEPENDENCE.

HEWITT, Abram Stevens. 1822-1903. Industrialist and political leader. Admitted to bar (1845); owner, with Edward Cooper, of successful iron manufacturing business; introduced first open-hearth furnace in America (1862); made first American-made steel (1870); took part in the establishment of Cooper Union college; member, U.S. House of Representatives (1875-79; 1881-86); chairman, Democratic National Committee and directed TILDEN's campaign; mayor of New York City (1887-88) with strong reform administration that did not cooperate with TAMMANY and was not reelected.

HEWITT, Peter Cooper. 1861-1921. Electrical engineer and inventor. Invented a mercury-vapor electric lamp and a mercury-vapor rectifier (1903); discovered the fundamental principle of the vacuum-tube amplifier important in RADIO; experimented with hydro-airplanes; built first successful helicopter (with F. B. Crocker, 1919); designed aerial torpedo for navy.

HEYWARD, Thomas. 1746-1809. Political leader. b. South Carolina. Member, provincial congresses (1775-6); served on COMMITTEE OF SAFETY (1775, 1776); member, CONTINENTAL CONGRESS (1776-78); signer of DECLARATION OF INDEPENDENCE; circuit court judge (1779-80); served in Revolutionary War and was taken prisoner at defense of Charleston.

HIBBEN, Paxton Pattison. 1880-1928. Diplomat and writer. b. Indiana. Served in U.S. DIPLOMATIC SERVICE (1905-12); war correspondent in Germany (1914-15) and Greece (1915-16); worked for war relief in Russia and Near East; author of biography *Henry Ward Beecher* (1927).

HICKOK, James Butler. Known as Wild Bill Hickok. 1837-1876. Frontier marshal. b. Illinois. Stage driver on SANTA FE TRAIL and OREGON TRAIL; served as

288

Union scout during Civil War; served as U.S. marshal in the West and became famous for his exploits against rustlers and outlaws; on tour with BUFFALO BILL CODY (1872-73); murdered (Aug. 2, 1876) in Deadwood, Dakota Territory by Jack McCall.

HICKS, Elias. 1748-1830. Quaker preached. b. New York. Worked as a FARMER and carpenter on Long Island; became well-known as a preacher for the QUAKERS all over the country; responsible for a division in the ranks of the SOCIETY OF FRIENDS, the liberal element following Hicks and becoming known as "Hicksites" (1827).

HICKS, Thomas Holliday. 1798-1865. Political leader. b. Maryland. Governor of Maryland (1858-62); although a southerner he opposed SECESSION and delayed calling legislature into session (1860-61), preventing the radical pro-southern group from voting Maryland into the Confederacy; U.S. Senator (1862-65).

Highways. See roads.

HILL, Ambrose Powell. 1825-1865. Confederate general. Graduated, U.S.M.A., West Point (1847); served in Mexican and Seminole Wars; colonel in Confederate army (1861); brigadier general (1862), major general (1862); lieutenant general (1863); served at ANTIETAM. FREDERICKSBURG; directed first day's fighting at GETTYSBURG; killed in defense of Petersburg against U. S. GRANT.

HILL, Benjamin Harvey. 1823-1882. Political leader. b. Georgia. Prominent Georgia lawyer; favored COMPROMISE OF 1850; member KNOW-NOTHING PARTY; opposed SECESSION but signed the ordinance of secession and supported Confederacy; senator, Confederate Provisional Congress (1861-65); member, U.S. House of Representatives (1875-77); U.S. Senator (1877-82).

HILL, Daniel Harvey. 1821-1889. Con-

federate general and educator. b. South Carolina. Graduated, U.S.M.A., West Point (1842); taught mathematics at Washington and Davidson colleges; entered Confederate service; brigadier general (1861); major general (1862); lieutenant general (1863); served in defense of RICHMOND and in important battles; published MAGAZINES in South; president, University of Arkansas (1877-84) and of Georgia Military College (1885-89).

HILL, David Bennett. 1843-1910. Politician. b. New York. Admitted to bar (1864); practiced, Elmira, New York; became Democratic "boss" of upstate New York; aided TILDEN in exposing TWEED RING (1871); elected lieutenant governor on ticket with GROVER CLEVELAND (1882); governor of New York (1885-91); U.S. Senator (1892-97) sided with conservative Republicans against his own party.

HILL, David Jayne. 1850-1932. Diplomat and historian. b. New Jersey. Graduated, Bucknell; studied in Europe; president of Bucknell (1879-88); and University of Rochester (1888-96); assistant Secretary of State (1898-1903); U.S. Minister to Switzerland (1903-05); the Netherlands (1905-08); and Germany (1908-11). U.S. delegate to Second HAGUE CONFERENCE (1907). Author of *A History of Diplomacy in the International Development of Europe* (3 vols. 1905-14) and many other books on political science and diplomacy.

HILL, James Jerome. 1838-1916. Railroad magnate. b. Canada. Settled in St. Paul, Minnesota (about 1856) and worked with STEAMBOAT companies (1856-65); with others he bought St. Paul and Pacific Railroad (1878) extending run to Canadian boundary; organized the Great Northern Railway Company, merging various interests, and became president of the road (1882-1907); chairman of board (1907-12); with J. P. MORGAN he fought HARRIMAN for control of Northern Pacific Railroad, causing panic of 1901; established HOLD-ING COMPANY but was forced to dissolve it by U. S. Supreme Court decision (1904); owned Canadian RAILROADS, steamship lines, mines, and banks. Is often referred to as an "Empire Builder."

HILLIARD, Henry Washington. 1808-1892. Statesman. Served in Alabama legislature; opposed SECESSION; member, U.S. House of Representatives (1845-51); served in Confederate Army as commander of "Hilliard's Legion" under BRAGG; U.S. Minister to Brazil (1877-81).

HILLMAN, Sidney. 1887-1946. Labor leader. b. Lithuania. Came to the United States (1907); worked in the clothing industry and led a successful strike; became president of the Amalgamated Clothing Workers (1915); fostered cooperation of union with management; sponsored LABOR activities such as cooperative HOUSING and BANKING, and social security programs within the union; helped to found the CIO (1935) and was one of its vice-presidents; headed labor section, OFFICE OF PRODUCTION MANAGEMENT; vice-chairman, WAR PRODUCTION BOARD (1940-42); established the POLITICAL ACTION COMMITTEE of the CIO supporting F. D. ROOSEVELT (1943-46); helped to found the AMERICAN LABOR PARTY (1936) acting chairman (1944-45); CIO delegate to the conference which established the World Federation of Trade Unions (1945).

HILLQUIT, Morris. 1869-1933. Lawyer and Socialist leader. b. Latvia. Came to the United States (1886); joined SOCIAL-IST PARTY (1888); guided the policies of the party; candidate for mayor of New York City on the Socialist ticket (1917) defeated; backed LA FOLLETTE'S PRO-GRESSIVE PARTY (1924). Author of *History of Socialism in the United States* (1903).

HINES, John Leonard. 1868-1968. General of the Army. b. West Virginia. Graduated, U.S.M.A., West Point (1891); served in Spanish-American War and in the PHILIPPINES (1898-1912); assistant adjutant general of A.E.F. (1917); brigadier general (1918); major general (1921); succeeded PERSHING as chief of staff, U.S. Army (1924); commander of Philippine department (1930-32); retired.

HINES, Walker Downer. 1870-1934. Lawyer and Railroad Administrator. U.S. director-general of railroads (1919-20) succeeding MC ADOO; successful lawyer in New York City (from 1921). Author of the authoritative *The War History of the American Railroads* (1929).

Hiroshima, bombing of. The first military use of the ATOMIC BOMB. It was dropped on August 6, 1945 on Hiroshima, Japan, a military and naval center with a population of 250,000. Several square miles of buildings, representing three-fifths of the city, were demolished, and 135,000 casualties inflicted. These included 66,000 dead and 69,000 wounded.

HIRSCH, Emil Gustav. 1851-1923. Rabbi. b. Luxembourg. To United States (1866). Graduated University of Pennsylvania and studied in Europe; rabbi in Baltimore, Maryland, Louisville, Kentucky, and Chicago, Illinois (from 1880); first rabbi to have a Sunday service in place of Saturday sabbath; advocated modern liberal ideas in religion; professor of rabbinic LITERATURE and philosophy, University of Chicago (from 1892); editor Reform Advocate (1891-1923); president, Chicago Public Library Board (1885-97); important influence in Reformed Judaism.

Hispanic Society of America, The. A cultural organization established in 1904 in New York City. Its objective was the fostering of the Spanish and Portuguese language and culture. Membership is honorary, and is limited to 100 specialists of any nationality in these fields. The Society has a LIBRARY, a museum of reference, and ART materials, including a notable gallery of paintings by El Greco, Goya, Murillo, and Velasquez. Its collection of SCULPTURE and handicraft objects includes rare pottery, ivories, and other treasures.

Historical Writing. See literature.

HITCHCOCK, Ethan Allen. 1835-1909. Political leader. b. Alabama. U.S. Minister to Russia (1897-98); appointed by MC KINLEY; first U.S. Ambassador to Russia (1898); U.S. Secretary of the Interior (1898-1907) in T. ROOSEVELT'S CABINET; exposed fraudulent administration of PUBLIC LANDS and corrected the situation; sponsored a strong CONSERVATION program; instituted the Reclamation Service; reorganized the Bureau of Indian Affairs.

HITCHCOCK, Frank Harris. 1869-1935. Lawyer and politician. Practiced law in Washington, D.C.; chief of division of foreign markets, U.S. DEPARTMENT OF AGRICULTURE (1897-1903); first assistant Postmaster General (1905-8); appointed U.S. Postmaster General (1909-13) by TAFT; established POSTAL SAVINGS BANK and PARCEL POST and started the first air-mail service.

HITCHCOCK, Gilbert Monell. 1859-1934. Lawyer, publisher and political leader. b. Nebraska. Practiced law in Omaha (1881-85); founded Omaha *Evening World* (1885) and the Omaha *Morning Herald* and combined the two papers (1889) into the *World-Herald*; supporter of W. J. BRYAN; broke with Bryan which resulted in a political feud (1910); member, U.S. House of Representatives (1903-5; 1907-11); U.S. Senator (1911-23) where he was strong supporter of WILSON's policies.

HOAR, Ebenezer Rockwood. 1816-1895. Lawyer and political leader. b. Massa-

chusetts. Graduated, Harvard Law School; judge of court of common pleas (1849-55); associate justice of Massachusetts court (1859-69); U.S. Attorney-General (1869-70); member of *Alabama* claims commission (1871); member of U.S. House of Representatives (1873-5).

HOAR, George Frisbie. 1826-1904. Legislator. b. Massachusetts. Graduated, Harvard Law School and practiced in Worcester (from 1849); Republican member, U.S. House of Representatives (1869-77); U.S. Senator (1877-1904) interested in CIVIL SERVICE REFORM. Author of history of post-Civil War period in American history, *Autobiography of Seventy Years* (2 vols., 1903).

HOE, Richard Marsh. 1812-1886. Manufacturer and inventor. b. New York City. Worked in his father's printing press MANUFACTURING business and succeeded to the management of the company (1830); invented the rotary press (1847), the web press (about 1847), and made other improvements which resulted in the present modern NEWSPAPER press.

HOFFA, James R. On July 30, 1975 the ex-president of the Teamsters Union disappeared mysteriously. The FBI was called in and officially entered the search on August 3rd of the same year. He was never located.

HOFFMAN, Malvina. 1887-1966. Sculptor. b. New York City. Studied with Rodin; well-known for bronzes of 101 different racial types, exhibited at Field Museum, Chicago; prize winner, Paris (1911); work appears in various museums. Author of *Heads and Tales* (1930) an autobiography and *Sculpture Inside and Out* (1939).

HOLC. See Home Owners Loan Act.

Holding Company. A form of MONOPOLY organization in which a CORPORATION is organized to hold a sufficient share of the stock of other companies to afford it control over the operations of these companies. By so doing the board of directors of the holding company dominates the policies of its subsidiaries, and eliminates competition by determining their prices, marketing policies, LABOR RELATIONS, and production. Led by the STANDARD OIL COMPANY in the 1890's, holding companies were established in steel, RAILROADS, PUBLIC UTILITIES, and other important INDUSTRIES. See Business Consolidation.

Holidays. There are no national holidays in the United States. The President and Congress designate holidays only for the District of Columbia and for federal employees throughout the nation. Each state has jurisdiction over the holidays it will observe. These are designated either by legislative enactment or executive proclamation. The sole instance where Congress has purported to declare a "national holiday throughout the United States" seems to have been the Act of March 2nd, 1889 which employed this expression with reference to April 30, 1889 the centennial of the inauguration of the first President of the United States.

HOLLINS, George Nichols. 1799-1878. Naval officer. Served under DECATUR during War of 1812; bombarded Greytown, NICARAGUA because of damages to American lives and property (1854); served with the Confederate Navy (1861); defeated Union BLOCKADE off Mississippi and placed in command of Confederate naval forces on upper Mississippi (1862).

Hollywood. A suburb of Los Angeles, California. It is generally considered the center of the MOTION PICTURE INDUSTRY in the United States, but is actually only one of the communities in metropolitan Los Angeles which house the major studios. The RKO studio is located in Hollywood and the Republic studio in North Hollywood. Three others, however, are situated in Burbank, three in Culver City, two in Los Angeles proper, and one in Universal City. This suburban region produces more than two-thirds of the motion pictures in the United States. In 1950 this area had a capital investment in motion pictures of $2,922,600,000 and employed 210,000 workers. In that year the gross income from domestic and international sales was $2,220,500,000.

HOLMES, Oliver Wendell. 1809-1894. Physician and author. b. Massachusetts. Graduated, Harvard College (1829); studied at Harvard Medical School and in Paris (1833-35); received degree from Harvard (M.D. 1836); professor of anatomy, Dartmouth (1838-40) and Harvard Medical School (1847-82). Member, HALL OF FAME. Best known works are *Autocrat of the Breakfast-Table* (1858), a biography of *Ralph Waldo Emerson* (1885), and poems *Old Ironsides, The Wonderful One-Hoss Shay,* and many books of POETRY, novels, etc.

HOLMES, Oliver Wendell. 1841-1935. Jurist. Son of OLIVER WENDELL HOLMES (1809-1894). b. Boston, Massachusetts. Graduated, Harvard University (1861); served at ANTIETAM, Fredericksburg etc. in Civil War; graduated, Harvard Law School (1866); practiced in Boston; professor of law, Harvard Law School (1882) associate justice (1882-99) and chief justice (1899-1902) Massachusetts supreme court; associate justice, U.S. Supreme Court (1902-32); famous for his liberal dissents from majority decisions which invalidated progressive social and labor legislation. Author of *The Common Law* (1881).

HOLMES, William Henry. 1846-1933. Anthropologist and archaeologist. Geologist. U.S. Geological Survey (1879); archaeologist, Bureau of American Ethnology (1889-98); chief of bureau (1902-9); head curator of anthropology, U.S.

National Museum (1910-20); curator and director of National Gallery of Art (1910-20); Author of *Handbook of Aboriginal American Antiquities* (1919).

HOLT, Joseph. 1807-1894. Political leader. b. Kentucky. Admitted to bar and practiced in Kentucky; leader in Democratic party; appointed by BUCHANAN, U.S. Commissioner of PATENTS (1857); U.S. Postmaster General (1859-61); U.S. Secretary of War (1861); appointed by LINCOLN judge advocate general U.S. Army (1862-75); prosecuted conspirators in the assassination of Lincoln.

Home Loan Bank Act. Passed by Congress on July 22, 1932. It established the federal home loan bank system administered by a Federal Home Loan Bank Board to provide credit facilities for urban real estate financing. The members of the system consist of banks and savings and loan institutions whose principal investments are in real estate mortgages. The system was similar to the FEDERAL RESERVE SYSTEM in that the 12 Federal Home Loan Banks were authorized to extend credit facilities to member banks and loan associations for the purpose of rendering financial assistance to the banks for real estate development. In 1933 the act was supplemented by passage of the HOME OWNERS LOAN ACT.

Home Owners Loan Act. Passed in 1933 as a supplement to the HOME LOAN BANK ACT of the previous year. Under its provisions the Federal Home Loan Bank Board created a new government corporation known as the Home Owners Loan Corporation. This agency was given a capital of $200,000,000 from the Treasury and the power to issue bonds up to $3,000,000,000 to refinance first mortgages on homes valued up to $20,000. The HOLC carried on a three year program of mortgage refinancing at lower interest rates, bringing relief to DEBTORS

and creditors, and saving the homes of hundreds of thousands of people. The average loan was $3,272. The Act also provided for the establishment of federal savings and loan associations which would join the Federal Home Loan Bank System and enjoy government aid through the investment of federal funds in their securities. Since 1936 the HOLC has been administering its portfolio of mortgages, operating within the overall jurisdiction of the NATIONAL HOME AND HOUSING FINANCE AGENCY. By June, 1936 when its operation ceased, the agency had refinanced more than 1,000,000 mortgages for a total of $3,100,000,000. By 1946 the HOLC had liquidated three-fourths of its portfolio, having reduced its original investment from $3,500,000,-000 to $853,951,000.

HOMER, Winslow. 1836-1910. Painter. b. Boston, Massachusetts. Apprenticed to lithographer (1855-57); studied in New York; contributing artist to *Harper's Weekly* (1859-67). Best known for water-colors and marines; examples of his work hang in most of the largest museums in the country.

Home Relief. Public assistance granted to families in their homes. Under the Elizabethan Poor Law concept relief was granted to individuals in established institutions rather than in the home. The consequent social indignities and disruption of family life were long fought by social workers who sought legislation empowering state and municipal agencies to furnish cash and commodity aid in the home. Although home relief was instituted in many states prior to 1930, it was not until the GREAT DEPRESSION that the principle was accepted on a wide scale. The FEDERAL EMERGENCY RELIEF ACT OF 1933 was the first broad national program of home relief assistance to the states and municipalities.

Homestead Act. Legislated by Congress

in 1862 for the purpose of inducing settlers to migrate to the TRANS-MISSISSIPPI WEST. The Act provided that a head of a family could acquire a quarter section of land consisting of 160 acres, settle it, and cultivate it for five years, at the expiration of which time he acquired title to the land. Such family head either had to be a CITIZEN or have declared his intention to acquire CITIZENSHIP. This Act was of the most extreme importance in stimulating the post-Civil War WESTWARD MOVEMENT. By 1890 all available federal land had been settled under the provisions of the legislation. The Act is current, although the available land is restricted to ALASKA and other TERRITORIES.

Homestead Steel Strike. Occurred in 1892 as a result of the inability of the Carnegie Steel Company and the Amalgamated Association of Iron and Steel Workers to negotiate a wage increase. The strike is notable for the bloodshed which resulted when 300 STRIKE-BREAKERS were brought into the plant. The Pinkerton Detective Agency supplied these professional strike breakers. The pitched battle that followed resulted in the deaths of 10 persons. The strike was effectively broken after six months.

HOOD, John Bell. 1831-1879. Confederate general. b. Kentucky. Graduated, U.S.M.A., West Point (1853); joined Confederate Army (1861); brigadier general in command of "Texas Brigade" (1862); major general (1862); served at GETTYSBURG; lost right leg at CHICKAMAUGA; lieutenant general (1864); led defense of Atlanta against SHERMAN; after Civil War was a commission merchant in New Orleans.

HOOKER, Joseph. 1814-1879. Union general. b. Massachusetts. Graduated, U.S.M.A., West Point (1837); brigadier general of volunteers in Civil War(1861); called "Fighting Joe"; wounded at AN-TIETAM; brigadier general, U.S. Army (1862); became commander of Army of the Potomac succeeding BURNSIDE (1863); defeated by LEE at Chancellorsville (1863) and asked to be relieved of command; succeeded by MEADE; served with THOMAS and SHERMAN; major general (1868) retired.

HOOKER, Thomas. 1586?-1647. Clergyman and colonial leader. b. England. Puritan sympathies caused him to flee to Holland before trial before Court of High Commission (1639); came to America with JOHN COTTON (1633); pastor, Newtown (Cambridge, Massachusetts, 1633-36); disagreement with thinking in colony forced him to migrate with his congregation to Hartford, Connecticut (1636); strong advocate of NEW ENGLAND CONFEDERATION; took leading part in drawing up constitution for Connecticut, the "FUNDAMENTAL ORDERS"; organized the "United Colonies of New England" for defense (1643).

HOOPER, William. 1742-1790. Revolutionary leader. b. Boston. Graduated, Harvard College (1760); important in North Carolina activities leading to the Revolution; member, COMMITTEE OF CORRESPONDENCE; member, CONTINENTAL CONGRESS (1774-77); signer of the DECLARATION OF INDEPENDENCE.

Hoover Commission. Established by Congress in June, 1947 as the Commission on Reorganization of the Executive Branch of the Federal Government. It consisted of twelve Senators, Representatives, executive officers, and private CITIZENS. The Commission employed 300 "task force" members. In its report in 1949 the Commission recommended the appointment of a staff secretary to keep the President informed of current developments in executive agencies, an Office of Personnel within the Executive Office to advise the President on civil service matters, the replacement of the COUNCIL OF ECONOMIC ADVISERS by an Office of the Economic Adviser, and the transfer to the TREASURY DEPARTMENT of the RECONSTRUCTION FINANCE CORPORATION, FEDERAL DEPOSIT INSURANCE CORPORATION, and EXPORT-IMPORT BANK. The report also advised MERIT SYSTEM appointments for the Postmaster General and career postmasters and transfer to the DEPARTMENT OF LABOR of the Selective Service System and compensation and employment security units of the FEDERAL SECURITY AGENCY. Other recommendations included reorganization of the DEPARTMENTS OF THE INTERIOR, AGRICULTURE, and COMMERCE, and regrouping of units of the UNITED STATES MARITIME COMMISSION, INTERSTATE COMMERCE COMMISSION, COAST GUARD, and the Army and Navy. The Commission found the EXECUTIVE BRANCH to be split up into an unworkable number of agencies with divided responsibilities. It declared that the line of command from the President down was weak and that administrators lacked the tools with which to organize adequate programs and policies. It charged that administrative controls were unnecessarily rigid and detail, budgetary and accounting processes inadequate, and purchasing badly coordinated. Its program, therefore, was to create a more orderly grouping of functions into major departments and agencies, organize clear lines of control, establish strong staff services, develop superior administrators, encourage initiative and enterprise by making administrators accountable to the executive, and allow more freedom to the operating agencies in the conduct of routine business. By 1951 the Congress had provided for reorganization equal to 55 percent of the Hoover Commission recommendations. These were done either by special laws or presidential reorganization plans, among which the most important was the Reorganization Act of 1949. The outstanding reforms were in the field of budgeting, PUBLIC WELFARE, and social security. The "task force" investigations were financed by a congressional appropriation of $2,000,000. In the summer of 1952 important Hoover Commission proposals before Congress included reorganization of the Post Office, personnel, AGRICULTURE, veterans, NATURAL RESOURCES, and health. It was estimated that these reorganizations would gain an annual saving of $6,000,000,000.

Hoover Dam. Formerly called Boulder Dam. It is located in Black Canyon of the Colorado River in Arizona-Nevada and is the greatest water barrier in the world. It is 726 feet high, 660 feet at the base, and 1,244 feet long at top, creating the 115 mile long artificial Lake Mead, the largest in the world. It was completed in 1936 with a volume of 4,400,-000 cubic yards. By 1950 its power plant had an installed capacity of 1,034,800 kilowatts with an additional 215,000 kilowatts under contract. By 1952 it had generated well over 50,000,000,000 kilowatts of energy and had paid over $60,-000,000 in net revenues into the U.S. Treasury. The dam is operated by the Bureau of Reclamation under the provisions of the Boulder Canyon Project Adjustment Act of 1940. Its power plant has been leased to the city of Los Angeles and the Southern California-Edison Company as agents of the United States, and supplies about half the power required in Southern California.

HOOVER. Herbert C.1874-1964. Thirty-first President of the United States. b. West Branch, Iowa. Graduated Stanford University as a MINING engineer (1895); worked in the West and as a mining expert in Australia and other parts of the world; and as a gold-mining engineer in various places (1895-1913); chairman, American Relief Commission in London (1914-15); chairman, Commission for

Relief in Belgium (1915-19); U.S. Food Administrator (1917-19); member, War Trade Council; chairman, U.S. Grain Corporation, Interallied Food Council; in charge of relief in countries of eastern Europe (1921); appointed by HARDING, U.S. Secretary of Commerce (1921-28); reappointed by COOLIDGE; elected President of the United States (1929-33); STOCK MARKET CRASH and the DEPRESSION resulted in difficult administration problems; Farm Relief Act, and FEDERAL FARM BOARD secured through his efforts; created the RECONSTRUCTION FINANCE CORPORATION; ordered troops to evict Bonus Expeditionary Force from the capital (1932); denounced by liberal groups for his conservative domestic politics and his ISOLATIONIST foreign policy; coordinator of food supply to 38 nations (1946); headed HOOVER COMMISSION of 12 men to study the reorganization of the executive branch of the government and recommended these reorganization plans to Congress; in opposition to TRUMAN's foreign policy. Author of *The Basis for Lasting Peace* (1945), and his autobiography in several volumes (1951 and 1952).

HOOVER, John Edgar. 1895-1972. Lawyer and criminologist. b. Washington, D.C. Graduated, George Washington University (LL.B., 1916); on staff of the DEPARTMENT OF JUSTICE (1917); gained nationwide recognition as Director of the FEDERAL BUREAU OF INVESTIGATION, Department of Justice (from 1924) which is active in counter-espionage activities.

Hoover Moratorium. Name applied to the decision adopted by President HOOVER in 1931 providing for the suspension of DEBT payments by European nations to the United States and REPARATIONS payments to the former ALLIED POWERS by Germany. This decision arose out of the international economic DEPRESSION of the time and the consequent inability of the European nations to pay off their international obligations. The moratorium was to run for one year, but the continuing depression prevented any subsequent payments.

Hopi Indians. A Pueblo Indian tribe living in Arizona. They are noted for their beautiful pottery. The Hopis perform the famous snake dance and have many elaborate ceremonial customs. They are good FARMERS and today are moving to farm areas. They were generally a very peaceful people. However, they fought the APACHES and NAVAJOS when attacked in 1700.

HOPKINS, Edward. 1600-1657. Colonial governor. b. England. Emigrated to Hartford, Conn. (1637); wealthy and capable governor of the Connecticut colony (1640, 44, 46, 50, 52, 54); delegate to NEW ENGLAND CONFEDERATION (1643) and elected one of the commissioners.

HOPKINS, Esek. 1718-1802. Revolutionary naval commander. b. Rhode Island. Sea captain; commanded a privateer during French and Indian War; commanded Rhode Island militia at outbreak of Revolution and built up defenses of the colony; commander in chief of the Continental navy (1775); succeeded in destroying important British supplies in the Bahamas; could not man his ships properly and fleet was blockaded in Narragansett Bay (1776); suspended form command (1777) and dismissed (1778); served in assembly, Rhode Island (1777-86).

HOPKINS, Harry Lloyd. 1890-1946. Administrator and political leader. b. Iowa. Graduated, Grinnell College (1912); worked in social welfare agencies in New York; appointed Federal Administrator of Emergency Relief (1933); WORKS

PROGRESS ADMINISTRATOR (1935-38); U.S. Secretary of Commerce (1938-40); in charge of LEND-LEASE administration (1941); served as personal envoy for President ROOSEVELT to Russia and Britain (1941) to maintain cooperation during World War II; member of WAR PRODUCTION BOARD (1942); member, Pacific War Council (1942); special assistant to President Roosevelt (1942-45); sent by TRUMAN to the Soviet Union to try and settle Polish boundary disputes; retired from public life (1945).

HOPKINS, Johns. 1795-1873. Financier and philanthropist. b. Maryland. Important in development of the BALTIMORE & OHIO RAILROAD; gave $7,000,000 to found the Johns Hopkins University and the Johns Hopkins Hospital in Baltimore.

HOPKINS, Samuel. 1721-1803. Congregational theologian. b. Connecticut. Friend and disciple of JONATHAN EDWARDS; founded doctrine of systematic theology known as Hopkinsianism; opposed SLAVERY and the slave trade. Author of System of Doctrines Contained in Divine Revelation, Explained and Defended (2 vols. 1793).

HOPKINS, Stephen. 1707-1785. Colonial governor and Revolutionary leader. b. Rhode Island. Served in COLONIAL ASSEMBLY; chief justice of superior court (1751-54); governor of Rhode Island (1755, 56, 58-61, 63, 64, 67); delegate to ALBANY CONGRESS (1754); member, CONTINENTAL CONGRESS (1774-80); on committee that drafted ARTICLES OF CONFEDERATION; signer of DECLARATION OF INDEPENDENCE; helped found first public LIBRARY in Providence, Rhode Island; first chancellor of Rhode Island College.

HOPKINSON, Francis. 1737-1791. Political leader and poet. b. Philadelphia, Pa. Admitted to bar (1761); practiced in Philadelphia and Bordentown, N.J.; wrote political satires in pre-Revolutionary agitation (1774); member CONTINENTAL CONGRESS (1776); signer of DECLARATION OF INDEPENDENCE; a designer of the American FLAG (1777); U.S. district judge, eastern district of Pa. (1789-91) appointed by WASHINGTON. Author of The Battle of the Kegs (1778), A Letter from a Gentleman in America on Whitewashing (1785), etc. His Seven Songs (1788) was the first book of music published by an American composer.

HOPKINSON, Joseph. 1770-1842. Jurist. b. Philadelphia, Pa. Son of FRANCES HOPKINSON. Practiced law in Philadelphia; gained success as defense counsel in impeachment of Justice SAMUEL CHASE; member, U.S. House of Representatives (1815-19); judge, U.S. district court, eastern district of Pennsylvania (1828-42); chairman, state CONSTITUTIONAL CONVENTION (1837). Author of well-known song, Hail, Columbia (1798).

HOPPER, Edward. 1882-1967. Painter. b. New York. Known for realistic paintings that create a mood, usually of loneliness in the "big city." His works are exhibited at the Museum of Modern Art, New York City and elsewhere throughout the country.

HOPPER, Isaac Tatem. 1771-1852. Abolitionist. Member, SOCIETY OF FRIENDS, and Pennsylvania Abolition Society; helped with UNDERGROUND RAILROAD; defended NEGRO slaves in courts; worked for prison reform in Philadelphia; disowned by QUAKERS for anti-slavery activities (1841).

Horizontal Union. A labor organization established on a craft or trade basis. Generally it contains only skilled workers. The unions of the AMERICAN FEDERATION OF LABOR are usually horizontally organized, such as the International Brotherhood of Electrical Workers, the International Brotherhood of Teamsters, and the International Jewelry Workers Union.

Horseshoe Bend, Battle of. The battle on the Tallapoosa River in Alabama, on March 29, 1814, in which ANDREW JACKSON destroyed the power of the CREEK INDIANS. The battle culminated a six months campaign and involved an attack by 2,000 United States troops against 800 Indians entrenched at Horseshoe Bend on the River. After seven hours of hand-to-hand fighting the Indian fortifications were breached and all but 50 were killed. The American troops lost 49 dead and 157 wounded.

HOUGH, Benjamin Franklin. 1822-1885. Physician, historian and pioneer in forestry. Practiced medicine in New York; superintendent of Federal census (1870); wrote many books on local history; edited *American Constitutions* and other historical documents; his efforts led to the establishment of the division of forestry.

HOUGH, George Washington. 1836-1909. Astronomer. Director, Dearborn Observatory, Chicago and Evanston, Illinois (1879-1909); measured a number of double stars and discovered new ones; studied planet Jupiter (1879-1909) and invented many important and ingenious astronomical instruments.

HOUSE, Edward Mendell. 1858-1938. Diplomat. b. Texas. Studied at Cornell University (1878-79); became important in Democratic politics in his state and became known as "Colonel House" because he was a colonel on Governor Culberson's staff; helped get WILSON the Democratic nomination for the presidency (1912); personal representative of the President in Europe (1914-16); American delegate to negotiate the ARMISTICE (1918); member of commission to frame the covenant of the LEAGUE OF NATIONS.

House Foreign Affairs Committee. An important STANDING COMMITTEE of the House of Representatives. Its functions are to prepare legislation dealing with FOREIGN AFFAIRS. It consists of members of both major POLITICAL PARTIES in numbers proportional to their respective memberships in the House. Its chairman is always a member of the majority party.

House of Representatives. The lower house of Congress. It is provided for in Article I of the United States Constitution. Members must be 25 years of age, CITIZENS of the United States, and residents of the state which they represent. It was the only popularly elected body provided for in the original Constitution. Although it shares with the Senate general legislative functions, it exercises several specific powers exclusively. Among these are the powers to initiate revenue bills, impeach federal officers, and elect the President in the event of a tie or lack of majority in the ELECTORAL COLLEGE. Membership is based on the population of each state, and in 1965 numbered 435 on the basis of the Reapportionment Act of 1929.

Housing. See building industry.

Housing Act of 1950. A law of Congress passed in April, 1950. It authorized a new program of mortgage insurance for low-priced new rural HOUSING, a program of technical aid, and a program of mortgage insurance for cooperative housing projects. It also enlarged and liberalized the loan guarantee privileges of World War II veterans by administering a direct loan program for these veterans unable to obtain private home financing. The law established a program of financial aid for student and faculty housing in colleges and universities.

Housing Problems. The URBANIZATION of the United States in the late 19th and

20th centuries produced HOUSING problems of a serious nature. These included crowding, inadequate light and ventilation, rodent and insect infestation, racial discrimination, high rentals, inadequate toilet and water facilities, unsatisfactory recreational outlets, fire hazards, poor planning, and fire and safety hazards. Although New York City established a building code in 1849 other state and municipal governments were slow to enact remedial legislation. At the opening of the 20th century the ever-increasing problem of SLUM dwellings stimulated the movement for reform. See slums and tenement laws.

HOUSTON, David Franklin. 1866-1940. Educator and political leader. Studied at Carolina College and Harvard; president, Texas A. and M. (1902-05) and the University of Texas (1905-08); chancellor, Washington University, St. Louis, Mo. (1908-16); appointed by WILSON U.S. Secretary of Agriculture (1913-20); and U.S. Secretary of the Treasury (1920-21); chairman, Federal Reserve Board and FARM LOAN BOARD. Author of *A Critical Study of Nullification in South Carolina* (1890), *Eight Years with Wilson's Cabinet* (2 vols. 1926).

HOUSTON, Samuel. Known as Sam. 1793-1863. Frontier hero and political leader. b. Virginia. Lived with CHEROKEE INDIANS as a boy; served in CREEK campaign with JACKSON and known for bravery at BATTLE OF HORSESHOE BEND; studied law and admitted to bar; practiced in Tennessee; member, U.S. House of Representatives (1823-27); elected governor of Tennessee (1827-29); moved with the Cherokee to Oklahoma (1829) and went to Texas (1833); commander in chief of forces of Texas provisional government at start of War with Mexico; defeated SANTA ANNA at SAN JACINTO (1836); first president of the Republic of Texas (1836-38; 1841-44); when Texas

was admitted to the Union he became one of the first U.S. Senators (1846-59); strong supporter of Union and when again governor (1859-61) he was deposed for refusing to join the Confederacy and retired to his farm.

HOWARD, Bronson Crocker. 1842-1908. Playwright. Known for play *Saratoga* (1870), *Young Mrs. Winthrop* (1882) which was one of the first plays stressing social criticism in the United States, *The Henrietta* (1887), and *Shenandoah* (1888), which made him a fortune.

HOWARD, Oliver Otis. 1830-1909. Union General. b. Maine. Graduated, U.S. M.A. West Point (1854); served through Civil War; brigadier general (1861) and major general (1862); served at BULL RUN, Chancellorsville, GETTYSBURG; led right wing in SHERMAN's march on Atlanta and to the sea; commissioner, Bureau of Refugees, Freemen, and Abandoned Lands (1865-74), also known as FREEDMEN'S BUREAU; founder and president of Howard University (1869-74); commissioner to APACHE INDIANS (1872).

HOWE, Elias. 1819-1867. Inventor. b. Massachusetts. Served as apprentice to an instrument and watch maker in Boston (1837); worked on design for a SEWING MACHINE (from 1843); received PATENT (1846); unable to secure financial backing in the United States he marketed the first machine in England; returned to the United States to fight patent infringement suits and won royalty rights (1849-54); member HALL OF FAME.

HOWE, Julia Ward. 1819-1910. Writer and social reformer. b. New York City. With husband, SAMUEL GRIDLEY HOWE, edited *The Commonwealth*, vigorous anti-slavery paper; leader in WOMAN SUFFRAGE movement; best known as composer of *The Battle Hymn of the Re-*

public (1862). Leader of the ABOLITION-IST movement.

HOWE, Samuel Gridley. 1801-1876. Educator and Philanthropist. b. Boston, Massachusetts. Graduated, Harvard Medical School (1824); served as soldier and surgeon in Greek war of independence from Turkey (1824-30); chairman, Massachusetts Board of State Charities (1865-74); worked with schools for the blind, deaf and insane; edited, with his wife JULIA WARD HOWE, *The Commonwealth* which was an anti-slavery publication.

HOWE, William 5th Viscount. 1729-1814. British General. Commanded regiment in defense of Quebec (1759-60); led British troops at battle of BUNKER HILL (1775); commander in chief of British forces in America during the Revolution; defeated Americans on LONG ISLAND (1776); captured New York City, White Plains, and won at BATTLE OF BRANDYWINE (1776); resigned command (1778); made a general (1793).

HOWELL, Clark. 1863-1936. Newspaper Editor. Graduated, University of Georgia (1883); on staff of Atlanta *Constitution* (from 1884); managing editor (1889) and editor in chief (from 1897); won PULITZER PRIZE for JOURNALISM for his paper (1929); served in state legislature (1886-91) and state senate (1900-1906); member, Democratic National Committee; director of ASSOCIATED PRESS from start of the organization (1900).

HOWELL, James Adams. 1840-1918. Naval officer and inventor. Graduated, U.S.N.A., Annapolis (1858); served as lieutenant in the navy throughout the Civil War; head of department of astronomy and navigation at Annapolis; commander of Mediterranean squadron during Spanish-American War; rear admiral (1898); retired (1902); invented a gyroscopic steering torpedo, high-explosive shells; disappearing gun carriage and torpedo-launching apparatus. Author of *The Mathematical Theory of the Deviations of the Compass* (1879) first scientific work by an American on this subject.

HOWELLS, William Dean. 1837-1920. Novelist, editor and critic. b. Ohio. Editor *Ohio State Journal* (1858); contributed poems to *Atlantic Monthly*; U.S. consul, Venice, Italy (1861-65); assistant editor and then editor of *Atlantic Monthly* (1866-81); on editorial staff of *Harper's Magazine* (1886-91) and *Cosmopolitan Magazine* (1891-92). Prolific author of *Venetian Life* (1866), *The Rise of Silas Lapham* (1885), *The Quality of Mercy* (1892), *The Leatherwood God* (1916) and many other novels, dramas, farce comedies, travel sketches, literary criticism, memoirs, and POETRY. He was an important influence on the young American writers.

HUDSON, Henry. d. 1611. English navigator. Unsuccessful in attempt to find northeast passage to the Far East on expeditions for the English Muscovy Company (1607-08); on a third voyage for the Dutch East India Company in the *Half Moon*, he discovered the Hudson River and sailed up the river to a point that is now Albany (1609); reached Hudson Bay in the *Discovery* (1610-11); seized by mutineers and set adrift in a small boat with eight other men (June 23, 1611); fate unknown.

HUDSON, Manley Ottmer. 1886-1960. Jurist. b. Missouri. Graduated, Harvard Law School (1910); professor of international law at Harvard (from 1923); member, American Commission at Paris Peace Conference (1919); judge, PERMANENT COURT OF INTERNATIONAL JUSTICE (from 1936). Author of books on the World Court, international law, and international affairs.

Hudson River. It runs 306 miles from Henderson Lake in Essex County New York State to Upper New York Bay between New York and New Jersey. It was discovered by VERRAZANO in 1524, and visited by Spanish and French traders in the next 20 years. The present site of Albany was established as a trading post by the French in 1540. It was not until 1609, when HENRY HUDSON ascended the River as far as Albany, that it became an important commercial artery. Around it grew up the first Dutch settlements, Albany being re-established in 1614. Until the railroad era after the War of 1812, the Hudson River provided the principal COMMUNICATION and TRANSPORTATION medium between lower and upper New York and between the latter and the GREAT LAKES via the Erie Canal. The first successful STEAMBOAT, the *Clermont*, was tested there in 1807. The railroad bridge at Poughkeepsie, built in 1889, was the first such structure over the river. In 1925 a second bridge was constructed at Bear Mountain, and the George Washington Bridge, completed in 1932, was the last to span the River. The Lincoln and Holland Tunnels provide automotive connection between New York and New Jersey which are also serviced by the Pennsylvania and Hudson and Manhattan Railroads, operating through their own tunnels under the Hudson River.

HUGHES, Charles Evans. 1862-1948. Jurist. b. New York. Graduated, Brown University (1881); Columbia (LL.B. 1884); admitted to bar and practiced in New York City; counsel for N.Y. State legislative commission investigating INSURANCE COMPANIES (1905-6); Republican governor of New York (1907-10); associate justice, U.S. Supreme Court (1910-16); defeated by WILSON for the presidency of the United States (1916); appointed by HARDING and COOLIDGE U.S. Secretary of State (1921-25); member, HAGUE TRIBUNAL (1926-30) and judge, PERMANENT COURT OF INTERNATIONAL JUSTICE (World Court) (1928-30); appointed by HOOVER chief justice, U.S. Supreme Court (1930); retired (1941). Generally included among the conservative justices in the NEW DEAL period.

HUGHES, Howard Robard. 1905-1976. Businessman. b. Houston, Texas. Was aircraft designer and record-breaking flier, also a Hollywood film producer. He pyramided the family business, Hughes Tool Co., into a billion dollar operation with aircraft manufacture, Nevada real estate, and casinos. He withdrew from public appearance living as an eccentric recluse for many years. Died in a plane above south Texas enroute to a hospital. Left a multi-million dollar estate for which many people claimed inheritance rights.

HUGHES, John Joseph. 1797-1864. Roman Catholic prelate. b. Ireland. To United States (1816); ordained a priest in Roman Catholic church (1826); coadjutor bishop of New York (1838); consecrated bishop of New York (1842); first archbishop of New York (1850); laid the cornerstone of St. Patrick's Cathedral, New York City (1858).

Huguenots. Calvinists who fled from France to the English colonies in the 17th century as a result of the revocation of the Edict of Nantes in 1642 by the French chief minister, Richelieu Many of the Huguenots had been successful business and professional men and, as a result, contributed considerably to the intellectual and economic development of the colonies. One of the important cities they founded in the east was New Rochelle.

HULL, Cordell. 1871-1955. Statesman. b. Tenn. Graduated, Cumberland University (1891); admitted to the bar (1891); judge, 5th judicial circuit of Tennessee (1903-07); member, U.S. House of Representatives (1907-21; 1923-31); U.S.

Senator (1931-33); author of federal IN-COME TAX law (1913) and its revision (1916), and the federal estate and inheritance tax law (1916); appointed by ROOSEVELT U.S. Secretary of State (1933-44); negotiated RECIPROCAL TRADE AGREEMENTS with Latin-American countries; awarded NOBEL PEACE PRIZE (1945). Author of autobiography *The Memoirs of Cordell Hull* (1948).

HULL, Isaac. 1773-1843. Naval officer. b. Connecticut. Served in WAR WITH TRIPOLI (1803-4); commanded the *Constitution* (called "OLD IRONSIDES") and defeated the British frigate *Guerriere* (1812); commodore (1823); in command of the Pacific squadron (1824-27).

Hull-Litvinoff Agreement. See Recognition of the U.S.S.R.

HULL, William. 1753-1825. Army officer. b. Connecticut. Governor, Michigan Territory (1805-12); brigadier general (1812); led attack into Canada from Detroit (July 1812); defeated by British and forced to surrender (Aug. 1812); court-martialed and convicted of cowardice and neglect of duty; sentenced to be shot, but not executed because of excellent record during the Revolution.

Humanitarian Revolt. The movement of reform during the Jacksonian era against the cruelty of 18th century civilization. Great progress was made in the fields of charity, alcoholism, economic DEPRESSION, penology, imprisonment for debt, institutional care of the mentally ill, juvenile delinquency, the mentally defective, and pauperism. In 1817 the Society for the Prevention of Pauperism was organized in New York City to combat human poverty based on drink, UN-EMPLOYMENT, and other causes. JOSIAH QUINCY and Joseph Tuckerman expanded these efforts in New England in the 1820's and 1830's. Branding, whipping, and mutilation slowly gave way to fines and imprisonment. Kentucky in 1821 and

New York in 1831 abolished imprisonment for debt, the movement spreading to the other states, until by 1860 the entire system had vanished. Conditions within prisons were improved by separating the sexes, juveniles from adult offenders, and the mentally ill from normal prisoners. As a result of the untiring efforts of DOROTHEA L. DIX, the plight of mental patients was improved in state asylums. The TEMPERANCE MOVEMENT spread after the founding of the American Society for the Promotion of Temperance in Boston in 1826. In 1851 Maine became the first state to enact a PROHIBITION law, quickly followed by 13 other states in the North.

Human Rights. Those rights defining the basic freedoms and liberties of human beings. As discussed by the members of the United Nations Human Rights Commission in 1952, human rights include freedom of religion, freedom of expression, the right to work, a decent living for all families, the right to social security, the right to HOUSING, and the right of everyone to continuous improvement of living conditions. Some delegates argued that human rights legislation should include bars against racial and religious discrimination, ABOLITION of segregation, the RIGHTS OF LABOR to STRIKE and picket, the outlawing of discrimination in employment because of political affiliation, and cultural freedom to pursue basic research and EDUCATION in the SCIENCES. On April 12, 1952 the United Nations Human Rights Commission convened in an attempt to conclude a six year old effort to define those basic freedoms which should be included in international pacts on human rights. Considerable conflict arose between small states and large states over a clause dealing with the autonomy rights of colonial dependencies. In the United States opposition was expressed by the American Bar Association and other groups to the Covenant on Human Rights because of the clauses dealing with labor, employment, and housing.

HUMPHREY, Hubert Horatio. 1911-1978. Political leader. b. Wallace, S.D. Educated at U. of Minn. and Louisiana State U. Was pharmacist, college teacher, mayor of Minneapolis. Elected to U.S. Senate 1948. Acquired great influence in Senate. Elected majority whip in 1961. Responsible for ratification of Limited Nuclear Ban Treaty in 1963 and the Civil Rights Act of 1964. Became vice president in 1964 with President Lyndon B. Johnson. When Johnson withdrew from 1968 campaign Humphrey became Democratic nominee for presidency. Lost to Nixon in very close race. Temporarily resumed college teaching. Reelected to Senate in 1971. Carried on public life with great dignity and cheerfulness while he made public his condition of terminal cancer. Died Jan. 13, 1978. His body was lying in state at the Capitol Rotunda for a memorial service, V.P. Mondale's eulogy stated, "He taught us all how to hope and how to love, how to win and how to lose. He taught us how to live and, finally, he taught us how to die."

HUMPHREYS, David. 1752-1818. Revolutionary officer and diplomat. b. Connecticut. Graduated, Yale College; lieutenant colonel and aide-de-camp to WASHINGTON (1780); U.S. commissioner in Algeria (1793); U.S. Minister to Spain (1796-1801); interested in woolen manufacture and imported first Merino sheep into the United States (1801); associated with the "Hartford Wits" and author of *A Poem on the Happiness of America* (1786).

Humphrey's Executor vs. United States. Also known as Rathbun vs. United States. A decision of the United States Supreme Court in 1935 which established the doctrine that the President's removal power was limited to purely executive officers. The Court held that William Humphrey, a FEDERAL TRADE COMMISSIONER, was an administrative officer with quasi-judical and quasi-legislative powers, and was thus removable only for cause as provided for by Congress in the statute establishing the position.

HUMPHREYS, Joshua. 1751-1838. Ship designer. Commissioned by CONTINENTAL CONGRESS to outfit the ships under ESEK HOPKINS (1776); appointed first U.S. naval constructor (1794-1801); designed and supervised the building of the frigates *Constitution, President, United States, Chesapeake,* etc. which were the most important ships in the U.S. navy during the War of 1812.

"Hunkers." The name applied to the conservative urban Democrats who opposed VAN BUREN'S INDEPENDENT TREASURY Bill of 1837. Many of these had profited illegally by the connection between state chartered banks and federal deposits. Their opposition to the Independent Treasury Bill prevented it from becoming law until 1840. Their exodus from the Democratic party in New York State was one of the factors leading to the victory of the WHIG party in the presidential election of that year.

HUNT, Richard Morris. 1827-1895. Architect. Brother of WILLIAM MORRIS HUNT. Best known examples of his work: Administration Building, CHICAGO WORLD'S FAIR (1893), main section of Metropolitan Museum of Art, N.Y., Lenox Library, N.Y., National Observatory, Washington, D.C. Fogg Museum, Harvard, and Tribune Building, New York, one of the first elevator buildings.

HUNTER, David. 1802-1886. Union general. Graduated, U.S.M.A., West Point (1822); served in Mexican War; served through the Civil War; brigadier general (1861); commanded the Department of the South (1862); freed the slaves in his department (May 1862) annulled by

LINCOLN; served on court-martial duty and was president of the military commission that tried conspirators for assassination of Lincoln.

HUNTER, Robert. d. 1734. British colonial administrator. b. Scotland. Successful governor of New York and New Jersey (1710-19); governor of Jamaica (1727-24).

Hunting. With fishing, hunting was one of the principal economic activities in colonial America. The FRONTIERSMAN was primarily a hunter. His importance lay ultimately in his pioneering the wilderness and attracting the FARMER, tradesman, and businessman who settled and exploited the resources of the original FRONTIER communities. Military forts oftentimes employed hunters to keep the armies supplied with beef. The Great Plains area became the source of supply of antelope, buffalo, deer, and elk in the post-Civil War area. Many hunters became famous military and historic figures. These included DANIEL BOONE, DAVID CROCKETT, "BUFFALO BILL", and "KIT" CARSON.

HUNTINGTON, Samuel. 1731-1796. Revolutionary leader. b. Boston, Massachusetts. Representative from Connecticut to CONTINENTAL CONGRESS (1775-84); signer of DECLARATION OF INDEPENDENCE; president of the Congress (1779-81); governor of Connecticut (1786-96).

HURLEY, Patrick Jay. 1883-1963. Lawyer and diplomat. b. Oklahoma. Practised law in Tulsa, Oklahoma (from 1908); lieutenant colonel in World War I; appointed by HOOVER U.S. Secretary of War (1929-33); appointed by ROOSEVELT his personal representative in Near and Middle East (1943); went on missions to Afghanistan and China (1944); temporary major general (Feb. 1944); U.S. Ambassador to China (1944-1945); protested administration's China policy and

resigned: awarded Medal for Merit for services in China (1946).

Huron Indians. First seen by Champlain in 1615 in Canada. They lived in bark wigwams. They were bitter enemies of the IROQUOIS who wiped them out, along with the Tobacco nation, their neighbors. The few survivors found their way to Michigan and Ohio. Changing their name to Wyandots, they fought with the British against the Americans in both the Revolution and the War of 1812. The few survivors are on a reservation in Oklahoma.

HUTCHINS, Robert Maynard. 1899-1977. Educator. b. Brooklyn, New York. Graduated, Yale University (A.B. 1921; LL.B. 1925); secretary of Yale (1923-27); dean of Yale Law School (1928-29); president of University of Chicago (from 1929). Well-known authority on education problems. Reorganized curriculum and established "Chicago Plan," a four-year junior college and a liberal arts curriculum separated from professional schools. Made chancellor in 1945. Strong advocate of ADULT EDUCATION. In 1946 began program to foster great books. Wrote *The Higher Learning in America* (1936) and *Education for Freedom* (1943).

HUTCHINSON, Anne. née Marbury. 1581-1643. Colonial religious leader. b. England. Married William Hutchinson. To Boston (1634); led discussion groups in her home and preached individual salvation through love and not obedience to laws of the church; tried, convicted (1637), and banished from MASSACHUSETTS BAY COLONY; emigrated to Aquidneck, Rhode Island and later to New York (1642) where she and her family were massacred by Indians (1643).

HUTCHINSON, Thomas. 1711 - 1780. Colonial administrator. b. Boston, Massachusetts. Graduated, Harvard College (1727); successful merchant; member,

304

an area of 56,400 square miles. Organized as a TERRITORY in 1809 and admitted as the 21st state on December 3, 1818. Springfield is the capital. In 1950 Illinois' POPULATION of 8,712,176 made it fourth in rank. Its largest cities are Chicago, Peoria, and Rockford. Illinois manufactures large quantities of railroad cars, automobile parts, aircraft parts, farm equipment, liquor, watches, clothing, and furniture. The largest public arsenal in the world is located on a small island in the Mississippi off Rock Island. The state is the largest soy bean producer in the nation and one of its most important producers of corn, oats, hogs, WHEAT, rye, barley, potatoes, and truck vegetables. Chicago is the nation's largest railroad center and one of its largest iron and steel and MEAT PACKING areas. The famous wheat pit is located there. Illinois was discovered in 1673 by Marquette and Joliet. Its nickname is the "Prairie State."

Immigration. The movement of people from one nation to another. In American history immigration has played an unusually significant role in aiding the development of the United States. Three great periods of immigration are noted: the colonial period up to the Revolution, the period after the War of 1812, and the period from the Civil War to the end of World War I. These are loose categories, reflecting the height of immigrant movement into the country, inasmuch as immigrants have come to the United States throughout its history. Until 1890 the masses of immigrants, numbering approximately 85 percent of the total, came from northern and western Europe, including England, France, Germany, Ireland, the Lowlands, Scandinavia, and Scotland. These are popularly known as "the old immigrants." Following 1890 "the new immigrants" came from central, southern and eastern Europe, including the Austro-Hungarian Empire, the Balkan nations, Greece, It-

aly, Poland, Russia, the Slavic nations, and Spain. By 1910 these numbered 80 percent of the total. The causes of immigration have always been much alike, stemming from religious persecution, the desire for economic improvement, political inequality, and occasionally sheer adventurism. At the outbreak of the Revolution the bulk of the American population of 2,500,000 was English. It has been estimated that 250,000 persons migrated to the United States between then and the end of the War of 1812. The importance of immigration is readily understood by the knowledge that of the 76,000,000 people in the United States in 1900, 10,500,000 had been born abroad and an additional 26,000,-000 had been born in the United States of foreign parentage. In the 1850's approximately 2,600,000 came to the United States, which increased in the 1870's to more than 5,000,000. Between 1820 and 1898 a total of 17,000,000 immigrants came to the United States. The greatest volume of immigration in American history occurred in the first two decades of the 20th century when the number totaled 8,795,386 for the first decade and 5,735,811 for the second. Until 1921 no general limitation of immigration was attempted by Congress. In that year, and in 1924 and 1929, Congress enacted the first general restrictive legislation in its history. In 1952 Congress codified all immigration statutes in the MC CARRAN-WALTER ACT.

Impeachment. Provided for in Article 1 of the Constitution. This is the method for removing political and judicial officers before the expiration of their term. In the federal government it is accomplished by the passage of an impeachment resolution by a majority vote of the House of Representatives. Trial of impeachment proceedings is conducted by the Senate in which a two-thirds vote is necessary for conviction. Conviction of impeachment charges leads only to removal from office following which established judicial procedures may be instituted if a CRIME has been committed. In the states and municipalities legislative impeachment may be supplemented by popular RECALL. In American history there have been impeachments of one Senator, seven District Court judges, one Supreme Court Justice, one President, one Secretary of War, and one Commerce Court judge. Of these, three District Court judges and the Commerce Court judge were removed.

Impeachment of Andrew Johnson. The only IMPEACHMENT and trial of a President of the United States. Among the causes of the conflict between Johnson and the RADICAL REPUBLICAN Congress were his many VETOES, his adoption of LINCOLN'S RECONSTRUCTION PLAN in opposition to Congress, his rejection of the aggressive CONGRESSIONAL RECONSTRUCTION PROGRAM, and the Republican fear that the Democratic party would return to political power under his leadership. The culminating act was his defiance of Congress by removing Secretary of War STANTON in February, 1868 in violation of the TENURE OF OFFICE ACT passed by Congress in March, 1867. The day after Stanton's removal the House, by a vote of 126 to 47, voted his impeachment for this act. The Senate trial began on March 13th. Johnson's defense was based on his alleged power to remove appointive officers. He charged that the Tenure of Office Act was unconstitutional. On May 16, 1868 the Senate voted, acquitting Johnson by a vote of 35 against and 19 for his conviction. The acquittal lay in the Senate's inability to obtain a two-thirds majority for conviction as required by the Constitution. Conviction thus failed by one vote.

Imperialism. The system of expansionism involving either direct acquisition of, or control over, colonial areas. In the 19th and 20th centuries imperialism has had economic, military, religious, and prestige objectives. Basically the mother country has sought areas for the investment of surplus capital, sources of RAW MATERIALS, and export markets. The demand for strategic naval and military bases as well as the religious zeal of missionaries have also contributed to imperialist expansion. Although first used as a political term of attack on the Republican party during the MC KINLEY-BRYAN election campaign of 1900, the word has often been applied to the agrarian expansionism which resulted in the acquisition of Louisiana, Florida, Oregon, Texas, the MEXICAN CESSION, the GADSDEN PURCHASE, and ALASKA. The broad-scale overseas expansion after the Spanish-American War had its preliminaries in the attempts of SEWARD and GRANT to obtain the DANISH WEST INDIES and the DOMINICAN REPUBLIC. Similar post-Civil War policies were evidenced with respect to CUBA in the OSTEND MANIFESTO, NICARAGUA, SAMOA, and HAWAII. The Spanish-American War finally projected the United States into a major imperialist program. The open acquisition of PUERTO RICO, GUAM, the PHILIPPINES, and the VIRGIN ISLANDS was accompanied by indirect but firm control over Cuba, HAITI, SANTO DOMINGO, Nicaragua, and other areas in Latin America and China. The economic basis of imperialism is revealed in the statistical data on American TRADE and financial investments abroad in the last quarter of the 19th century. In the 1890's two-thirds of all the land in Hawaii was owned by Americans and Europeans and three-quarters of all SUGAR lands owned by Americans. Whereas only 18,000,000 pounds of sugar were imported from Hawaii in 1875, 260,000,000 pounds were imported in 1890. At the outbreak of the Spanish-American War the annual trade with Cuba totalled $100,000,000 and American investments there were $50,000,-

000. By 1928 these investments had increased to $1,200,000,000. Total American investment abroad in 1898 were $500,000,000.

Implied Powers. Those powers of Congress which are derived from the application of the "ELASTIC CLAUSE" to the powers delegated to it by the Constitution. These powers are not specifically expressed in the Constitution but are assumed by a LOOSE CONSTRUCTION of the "elastic clause."

Impressment. Refers to the drafting of men into the navy. In England it was a royal prerogative deriving from medieval practice. In the period from 1804 to 1812 Great Britain exercised this power by impressing 10,000 seamen from American ships into the British navy. It has been estimated that 90 percent of these were Americans. The resort to impressment was made to keep her ships at fighting strength as an antidote to the frequent desertions from her navy. The British government never claimed the right to impress native born Americans, but, as the years went on, her naval officers paid no attention to nationality. Under the theory "once an Englishman always an Englishman" the British government did not recognize the right of expatriation. The continued impressment up to the eve of the War of 1812 was one of its principal causes.

Income Tax. The first federal income tax was imposed by law of Congress on August 5, 1861. It placed a tax of 3 percent on all incomes over $800. AMENDMENTS in 1862 and 1865 increased the rate to 5 percent on incomes between $600 and $5,000 and 10 percent on those above $5,000. By the Internal Revenue and Tariff Act of July 14, 1870 Congress provided for termination of the income tax. In 1894 a second income tax was established by a clause in the WILSON-GORMAN TARIFF ACT which imposed a rate of two percent on incomes over $4,000. This was declared unconstitutional the following year in the case of POLLOCK VS. FARMERS' LOAN AND TRUST COMPANY. The adoption of the 16TH AMENDMENT in 1913 enabled Congress to enact a third income tax law. Since then income tax receipts have steadily increased in importance. Whereas the law of 1861 yielded about $347,000,000, the 1951 law produced receipts totalling $40,000,000,000, representing approximately 78 percent of the gross federal revenue for that year. The rates for that year ranged from 20.4 percent on incomes over $2,000 to 91 percent on incomes over $200,000 in a complex system of rates. Beginning with the Wisconsin income tax law of 1911, a total of 32 states and the District of Columbia had enacted personal and corporate income tax legislation by 1940. Two others were taxing corporate income only.

Indentured Servant. Sometimes called bonded servant. The most important source of labor in the colonies in the 17th century and for a large part of the 18th century. Voluntary servants, known as redemptioners, were those who, of their own volition, sold their labor for a period of four to seven years in exchange for passage to America. The contract entitled the indentured servant to food, clothing, shelter, and medical attention. At the end of his term of service he was provided with 50 acres of land, funds, and a rifle. Involuntary servants included children and adults who were kidnapped in Europe and sold to ship masters who in turn bonded them to PLANTATION owners and farmers, usually for a period of seven years. Other involuntary servants included convicts. These groups were resented by the colonists and were referred to as "His Majesty's Seven Year Passengers." and paupers. The treatment of servants varied among the colonies, most of which regulated their care. Generally their lot was difficult, many dying before their redemption. Estimates of the number of indentured servants in the pre-Revolutionary period are impossible to determine, but it is known that to Virginia alone there came over 125,000 between 1635 and 1705.

Independence Day. A holiday in all the states and TERRITORIES commemorating the Fourth of July, the effective date of the adoption of the DECLARATION OF INDEPENDENCE in 1776.

Independence Hall. The familiar name of the State House located on the corner of Sixth and Chestnut Streets on Independence Square in Philadelphia, Pa. The building was begun in 1732 and completed in 1759. The Pennsylvania Assembly, original possessor of the structure, relinquished it to the second CONTINENTAL CONGRESS in 1775. It was the seat of the Congress in 1776 when the DECLARATION OF INDEPENDENCE was adopted and of the conferences of the CONSTITUTIONAL CONVENTION of 1787. From 1790 to 1800 one of the buildings of this group, known as Congress Hall, and erected in 1787, was the seat of government of the United States. The Courthouse, known as the City Hall and completed in 1790, was the first seat of the United States Supreme Court. All the buildings in the group were made a national shrine in 1943 by an agreement between the city of Philadelphia and Congress. Many famous and historic portraits of GEORGE WASHINGTON and early American public figures are located in the National Portrait Gallery in Independence Hall. It was formally opened as a National Museum on July 4, 1876, the centennial of the adoption of the Declaration of Independence. It also contains famous collections of furniture, manuscripts, musical instruments, watercolors, maps, books, utensils, wearing apparel, weapons, metals, and prints.

Independent Regulatory Commissions. The name applied to the various federal and state commissions, boards, authorities, and other agencies established for the purpose of regulating the activities of business. These commissions exercise quasi-judicial powers within their jurisdiction. Among these powers are the right to make rules and regulations, hold hearings, accept evidence, hear witnesses, and issue subpoenas, cease and desist orders, final orders, and awards. They may seek judicial enforcement of their decisions. Although their members are appointed by the President of the United States or the state governors, they are generally independent with respect to the powers enumerated. The most important of the federal agencies are the INTERSTATE COMMERCE COMMISSION, the FEDERAL TRADE COMMISSION, the FEDERAL COMMUNICATIONS COMMISSION, the NATIONAL LABOR RELATIONS BOARD, the Federal Power Commission, and the SECURITIES AND EXCHANGE COMMISSION. In the states they are known as PUBLIC SERVICE COMMISSIONS or Public Utilities Commissions.

Independent Republicans. See "mugwumps."

Independents. See Separatists.

Independent Treasury System. Established in 1840 under the pressure of the VAN BUREN Democrats. It provided a depository for federal funds which up to then had been held either in the first and second BANK OF THE UNITED STATES or, following their withdrawal in 1833 by the Secretary of the Treasury, from the Second Bank of the U.S., in JACKSON's "PET BANKS." The system was abolished in 1841, reestablished in 1846, and finally abolished in 1920.

Independent Union. A labor organization unaffiliated with the AMERICAN FEDERATION OF LABOR or CONGRESS OF INDUSTRIAL ORGANIZATIONS. It is estimated that, in 1952, there were 2,500,000 workers in 69 independent unions, many of them limited to company or plant membership. Some of these unions were members of the Confederated Unions of America. The most prominent independent unions in the United States are the RAILROAD BROTHERHOODS, Foreman's Association of America, and UNITED MINE WORKERS OF AMERICA.

Indiana. The 38th state in size with an area of 36,291 square miles. Organized as a TERRITORY in 1800 and admitted as the 19th state on December 11, 1816. Indianapolis is the capital. In 1950 Indiana's POPULATION of 3,934,224 made it 12th in rank. Its largest cities are Indianapolis, Gary, and Fort Wayne. The manufacture of iron, steel and oil products is Indiana's most important industry. Additional industrial products include automobiles, farm equipment, aviation and railroad equipment, and SEWING MACHINES. Its important agricultural crops are soy beans, corn, tobacco, onions, wheat, oats, rye, and tomatoes. Indiana produces most of the peppermint and spearmint oil in the United States. Well known mineral springs are located at West Baden and French Lick. Indiana was discovered in 1671 by La Salle. Its nickname is the "Hoosier State."

Indian Affairs, Bureau of. In 1849 this agency was transferred from the WAR DEPARTMENT to the DEPARTMENT OF THE INTERIOR. Its administrative chief is the Commissioner of Indian Affairs. The Bureau supervises TRADE and finance within the Indian tribes. It administers the reclamation of Indian lands and the development of their NATURAL RESOURCES. Its measures seek the improvement of the physical conditions of the Indians and of their inter-tribal relations. EDUCATION in general, and agricultural education in particular, are some of the most important programs of the Bureau. Only Indians in the United States proper are involved in these programs, the Alaskan Indians being excluded.

Indian militancy. Just as many blacks insisted on developing cultural identity so, too, American Indians began to demand a new place in American society. In 1972, 600 Indians occupied Washington offices of the Bureau of Indian Affairs for a week protesting not only the treatment given to their forebears but also the government's neglect of the contemporary Indian. In 1973, 200 members of the militant American Indian Movement occupied the town of Wounded Knee, South Dakota.

Indian Territory. In American history it occasionally refers to all Indian lands in general. More specifically it is applied as the official name of the Territory set aside for the Five Civilized Tribes, the CHEROKEE, CREEK, SEMINOLE, CHOCTAW, and CHICKASAW, by TREATY between them and the United States in 1834. Other tribes were later introduced. With the subsequent settlement of the western portions, the eastern part was organized as Oklahoma Territory into which other tribes were settled. In 1889 these remaining unoccupied portions, were opened to settlement, and in 1893 the Dawes Commission was appointed to transfer Indian titles to lands in the Territory from tribal to individual allotments. Oklahoma was admitted to the Union as a state in 1907.

Indian Wars. The fifteen year period of intermittent warfare from 1865 to 1880 culminating in the ultimate defeat of various Indian confederacies of the CROW, BLACKFEET, SIOUX, APACHE, and Nez Percés tribes. Altogether the Indian Wars cost the government hundreds of millions of dollars and the lives of thousands of men. These wars have been defended on the grounds of necessity, westward expansion, economic penetration, and the removal of a military menace. They have been attacked because of the methods employed, involving murder, deceit, and uncompensated seizure of Indian lands.

311

Industrial Development, Office of. See Atomic Energy Commission, U.S.

Industrial Management. See Scientific Management.

Industrial union. Also known as vertical union. Refers to a type of labor organization in which membership is open to all classifications of workers from nonskilled to skilled and including office and professional as well as industrial workers. The first important national industrial union was the KNIGHTS OF LABOR. The most important such organization in American history has been the CONGRESS OF INDUSTRIAL ORGANIZATIONS with a claimed membership of 6,000,000 in 1952. Other industrial unions have been the INDUSTRIAL WORKERS OF THE WORLD and the MOLLY MAGUIRES. In the last 20 years the C.I.O. has organized its industrial unions in the MASS PRODUCTION industries such as steel, coal, rubber, automobiles, aircraft, SHIPBUILDING, nonferrous metals, etc.

Industrial Workers of the World. Also known as the "wobblies." A radical national organization of LABOR UNIONS organized on an industrial basis. It was established in 1905 in Chicago by delegates of 43 unions, under the leadership of WILLIAM HAYWOOD, EUGENE V. DEBS, and DANIEL DE LEON. Its program was anarchist-syndicalist-socialist in nature, demanding the revolutionary overthrow of capitalism through political and economic means. Its methods included "DIRECT ACTION" such as STRIKES and sabotage, the militant nature of which resulted in severe repression under the syndicalist laws of many states. From its origin to World War I it was particularly strong in western LUMBER and MINING camps, and among textile and migratory farm workers. Its opposition to the entry of the United States into World War I resulted in the arrest and imprisonment of many of its leaders and members. At its peak the Industrial Workers of the World had more than 100,000 members, declining to 10,000 after the war. Of its 150 strikes the chief ones included the gold strike at Lena, Nevada in 1906-07, the Lawrence, Massachusetts textile strike in 1912, the Paterson, New Jersey silk strike in 1913, and the Seattle, Washington general strike in 1919. Although virtually non-existent today the contributions of the I.W.W. have been important in its organization of skilled and unskilled labor and of migrant workers, and in the improvement of labor conditions in the areas where it was strong.

Industry. See manufacturing.

"Infant Industries." See manufacturing.

Inflation. A situation of rapidly rising prices. Inflation may be caused by any or all of the following factors: short supply of commodities, increased demand for goods, large supply of money, or printing of FIAT CURRENCY. Those who benefit from inflation include DEBTORS and speculators. The evils of inflation generally fall heavily on creditors, unorganized labor, bond holders, salaried employees, and those who live on fixed incomes. The over-supply and variety of COLONIAL CURRENCY caused inflation frequently before the Revolution. The issue of excessive amounts of CONTINENTAL CURRENCY produced an inflation for a decade after the Revolution. A mild inflation resulted from the oversupply of banknotes during and after the War of 1812. The financing of the Civil War by the issuance of GREENBACKS created inflation until 1865. Between 1919 and 1921 inflation brought the price index to 244 percent of the 1909-1913 level. Up to World War II the greatest inflation occurred as a result of securities speculation between 1924 and 1929. During World War II and until 1946 federal price control and other anti-inflation legislation kept prices to within relatively small increases. With the removal of price controls in that year prices began to move forward steadily, stimulated greatly by the outbreak of the Korean War in June, 1950. In May, 1952 the Bureau of Labor Statistics announced that the purchasing power of the dollar had fallen to 54.6 percent of the 1935-1939 value. Its index rose in mid-April to 188.7 percent of the 1935-1939 average. The all-time high of 189.1 was reached in January, 1952.

INGALLS, John James. 1833-1900. Orator and political leader. b. Massachusetts. Graduated, Williams College (1855); admitted to bar (1857); practiced law in Kansas (from 1860); prominent Republican U.S. Senator from Kansas (1873-91).

INGERSOLL, Charles Jared. 1782-1862. Lawyer and politician. Republican member of U.S. House of Representatives (1813-15, 1841-49); U.S. district attorney for Pennsylvania (1815-29). Author of *History of War of 1812* (4 vols. 1845-52) and autobiography, *Recollections* (2 vols. 1861).

INGERSOLL, Jared. 1749-1822. Jurist. Member, CONTINENTAL CONGRESS (1780, 81); delegate to CONSTITUTIONAL CONVENTION (1787); attorney general of Pennsylvania (1790-99, 1811-17); FEDERALIST candidate for Vice-President of the United States (1812).

INGERSOLL, Robert Green. 1833-1899. Lawyer and orator. Known as "the great agnostic." Admitted to bar, Illinois (1854) served in Union army during Civil War; colonel (1861); attorney general of Illinois (1867-69); nominated BLAINE for presidency in famous "plumed knight" speech (1876); became well-known agnostic lecturer and great influence on American thinking in his time. Author of *The Gods, and Other Lectures* (1876),

Some Mistakes of Moses (1879), etc.

Initiative. A method by which the voters are able to legislate. A proposal for a statute or a state constitutional AMENDMENT is submitted to the legislature, containing the signatures of interested individuals. In the constitutional initiative the number of signatures varies from eight to fifteen percent of the voters, depending upon the state. If the signatures are bonafide the proposal is then referred to the whole body of voters for approval or rejection. In the statutory initiative the required number of signatures varies from three to ten percent or from 10 to 50,000. The initiative was introduced in 1898 in South Dakota. By 1918 it had been adopted by a total of 13 states. No state has provided for the initiative since 1918. This procedure is available to the electorate only in state and municipal governments.

Injunction. An equity writ ordering a person to perform or refrain from performing an act which would irreparably injure another person or his property. An injunction may be either mandatory or preventive and may be issued by a court of competent jurisdiction in either a preliminary or a permanent form. Violation of an injunction is contempt of court and may be punished by either fine or imprisonment, or both.

Inland Waterways Corporation. A federal CORPORATION created by Congress in 1924 for the purpose of operating a barge line on the Mississippi and Warrior Rivers. The agency assumed jurisdiction of the line from the War Department. Although it had been Congress' plan to dispose of the line to private operation at a later date, public management of the line has continued. By subsequent amending legislation the Inland Waterways Corporation's jurisdiction was extended to the coastal canal from New Orleans to Mobile and Port Burmingham, Lake Pont-chartrain, and the Tombigbee River. In 1952 it also operated a service from New Orleans to Minneapolis, Chicago to St. Louis, and Kansas City to St. Louis. In 1939 it was transferred to the DEPART-MENT OF COMMERCE. The Secretary of Commerce, who is the agency's governor and director, declared in 1942 that the Federal Barge Lines, as the Corporation is now known, had saved shippers $33,-000,000 in the period 1924-1939. In 1940 its fleet consisted of 27 towboats and 277 barges. The agency's operation has often been attacked because of its competition with private SHIPPING and other TRANSPORTATION facilities.

INNES, James, 1754-1798. Soldier and lawyer. b. Virginia. Graduated, William and Mary (1771); commander of Virginia regiment during Revolution; president, board of war, Virginia (1779); largely responsible for RATIFICATION OF CONSTITUTION in Virginia legislature; U.S. Attorney General of Virginia (1786).

INNESS, George. 1825-1894. Painter. b. New York. Well-known landscape painter; member Hudson River School. Best known works include *Millpond, Rainbow after a Storm*, and *Spring Blossoms*.

Insular Cases. A series of United States Supreme Court decisions from 1901 to 1922 in which the court laid down the constitutional status of the outlying pos-sessions of the United States. The doc-trines established held that American dependencies are to be considered in-corporated or unincorporated, Congress' control over the latter being deemed complete, limited only by certain funda-mental provisions of the Constitution. Its control over incorporated territories is bound by all constitutional provisions. In Hawaii vs. Mankichi (1903) and Rasmussen vs. United States (1905) the court held HAWAII and ALASKA to be in-corporated territories. In Balzac vs. PUER-TO RICO (1922) and Dorr vs. United States (1904) it was held that Puerto Rico and the PHILIPPINE ISLANDS were unincorporated. In attempting to define the limitations of Congress' power the court held in Downes vs. Bidwell (1901) and De Lima vs. Bidwell (1901) that fundamental guarantees did not include equality in TAXATION, trial by jury, grand jury indictment, or any of the formal pro-cedural or remedial guarantees of the Constitution. The DUE PROCESS CLAUSE is, however, considered a fundamental guar-antee.

Insurance Companies. The earliest in-surance companies appeared in Philadel-phia and Boston to underwrite marine risks and life policies. Such organizations appeared in Philadelphia in 1721 and in Boston in 1724. Mutual societies were founded after the Revolution, principal-ly to insure against fire loss, although such companies had appeared for brief periods before the Revolution. The de-velopment of business and COMMERCE by the end of the 18th century had brought more than 30 insurance com-panies into existence to write policies on all risks. Much of the insurance writing was however, still done by foreign com-panies. Fire insurance companies became extremely important in the 20 years be-fore the Civil War as the risk of fire be-came serious in the growing urban centers of the United States. Commercial life in-surance companies were formed in the same period, some occasionally selling other forms of policies. This era is charac-terized by the bankruptcies of many poorly-financed and administered organi-zations, particularly in the FRONTIER com-munities of the Mississippi region. The result was the passage of state laws, be-gun in 1849 in New York, which attempt-ed the regulation of certain insurance practices by charter. After the Civil War these charters were extended in scope to permit companies to insure against virtu-ally all forms of loss or damage including water, collision, war, riot, STRIKES, and the elements. Through the 19th and early 20th centuries the companies increased their capital holdings and became among the most important financial institutions in the United States. Group policies and industrial insurance became popular as did accident and disability insurance. Many companies became carriers of municipal and state compensation and insurance programs. In 1861 Massachusetts became the first state to impose fairly complete regulations upon the practices of insurance companies. State insurance commissions were subsequently established throughout the United States, principally as a result of the investigations of LOUIS D. BRANDEIS in Massachusetts before World War I. Leading companies today include the Metropolitan Life Insurance Company, Equitable Life Assurance Company, Aetna, John Hancock, Mutual, Commercial Travellers, Empire State and Prudential. In 1963 the assets of all life insurance companies in the United States were $145,000,000,000. The total life insurance in force that year was $765,000,000,000.

"Insurgents." Those progressive Republicans who opposed the conservative policies of the TAFT administration. In the western states they supported the DIRECT PRIMARY, tax reform, and railroad control. At the national capital the insurgents joined the Democrats in the House of Representatives to destroy the arbitrary power which custom had given to the Speaker of the House. They opposed the PAYNE-ALDRICH TARIFF and supported GIFFORD PINCHOT in the BALLINGER-PINCHOT CONTROVERSY in 1910. They advocated anti-trust regulation, TARIFF reciprocity, CONSERVATION, and liberalization of labor and welfare laws. Among their leaders were THEODORE ROOSEVELT, CHARLES EVANS HUGHES, and HENRY L. STIMSON. In 1912 they bolted the Republican party and nominated Roosevelt as the candidate of the PROGRESSIVE PARTY.

Intercolonial relations. The various attempts of the British colonies in the 17th and 18th centuries to cooperate in the furtherance of trade, COMMERCE, culture, and mutual defense against the French and Indians. Such efforts took the form of the NEW ENGLAND CONFEDERATION, the ALBANY PLAN OF UNION, the STAMP ACT CONGRESS, the COMMITTEES OF CORRESPONDENCE, and the two CONTINENTAL CONGRESSES.

Interior, Department of the. Created by Congress in 1849 as an EXECUTIVE DEPARTMENT known as the Home Department. The Secretary of the Interior is a member of the President's CABINET. The primary task of the department is the development and CONSERVATION of the NATURAL RESOURCES of the United States and its territories. The various divisions such as the General Land Office, the Bureau of Reclamation, the Geological Survey, the BUREAU OF INDIAN AFFAIRS, the National Park Service, the Bureau of Mines, and the Division of Territories and Island Possessions, carry on various functions under the supervision of a commissioner or director subject to the overall administration of the Secretary. Such functions include the disposition of the PUBLIC LANDS (surveys, claims, homestead applications, etc.), Indian affairs, IRRIGATION, construction of reservoirs, drains, and CANALS, distribution of water over reclaimed lands, health and safety regulation of the nation's mines, oversight of NATIONAL PARKS and national monuments, and supervision of affairs in ALASKA and HAWAII. The Department also exercises general control over the building and grounds of the CAPITOL at Washington, D.C., and in the District of Columbia of St. Elizabeth's Hospital, The Freedman's Hospital, Howard University, and the Columbia Institution for the Deaf and Dumb.

Interlocking directorate. A method of MONOPOLY control by which a member of the board of directors of a CORPORATION is simultaneously a member of one or more boards of other corporations in the same industry or in different industries related in business operations. The CLAYTON ANTI-TRUST ACT attempted to limit interlocking directorates in competing corporations within the same industry and in banks. Its lack of success is evidenced by the increased number of interlocking directorates that have come into existence since its enactment. In 1930 the directors of the NEW YORK CENTRAL RAILROAD held 306 directorships in other corporations. Those of the PENNSYLVANIA RAILROAD 241, of the Radio Corporation of America 232, of the GENERAL ELECTRIC COMPANY 218, of UNITED STATES STEEL 174, and of the AMERICAN TELEPHONE AND TELEGRAPH COMPANY 226. The Senate Committee on Banking and Currency estimated that, through interlocking directorates, the J. P. MORGAN banking house directly or indirectly controlled about $74,000,000,000 of corporate wealth, a sum equal to 25 per cent of the corporate assets of the United States. This situation arose because of loopholes in the law and because of interpretations by the courts.

Internal Improvements. In the first third of the nineteenth century the program of ROAD, TURNPIKE, bridge, CANAL, and railway construction. This program became a serious political issue around the question whether such construction should be undertaken at federal expense. A constitutional question was raised because of the lack of specific provision in the document for internal improvements. Although Congress steadily appropriated funds from 1789 on for lighthouses, buoys, and public piers, construction wholly within federal jurisdiction, its first appropriation for interstate internal improvements was the sum provided in 1806 for the construction of the CUMBERLAND ROAD. In 1824, $30,000 was appropriated for a survey of roads and canals, and $300,000 was donated to the construction of the Chesapeake and Delaware Canal. In 1822 President Monroe vetoed the Cumberland Road Bill because of its alleged unconstitutionality. For the same reason Jackson vetoed the Maysville Road Bill in 1830. The result was to throw internal improvements into the hands of the states despite the vigorous opposition of CLAY, WEBSTER, and the WHIG PARTY in general.

Internal Revenue. The revenue receipts of the United States other than customs. These include individual and corporate INCOME TAXES, estate and gift taxes, alcohol taxes, tobacco taxes, stamp taxes, manufacturers excise taxes, and miscellaneous taxes on admissions, TRANSPORTATION, and telephone service. The overwhelming bulk of internal revenue is derived from the combined individual and corporation income tax. Of the total of $112,260,257,000 internal revenue collections during the fiscal year of 1964, $95,892,000,000 was yielded by these taxes.

Internal Security Act. See McCarran-Wood Act.

International Bank for Reconstruction and Development. Established December 27, 1945 when 28 nations signed Articles of Agreement drawn up at the BRETTON WOODS CONFERENCE of 1944. In 1964 there were 102 members. United States participation was authorized on July 31, 1945 and the Bank began operations on June 26, 1946. Of the subscribed capital of $8,438,500,000 the United States share totalled $3,175,000,000 or 37.63 percent of the total capital subscription. The Bank's purpose is to lend money for reconstruction in war torn areas and in underdeveloped countries and to guarantee government loans and loans from private agencies for such purposes.

It also aims to promote long range balanced growth of international trade so that labor productivity and living standards may be improved. By 1964 the Bank had made 392 loans to 72 member countries totaling $8,204,000,000. Loans in 1950 and 1952 were granted to member nations for the purchase of airplanes and the development of ELECTRIC POWER, railways, and ports. The largest loan was the sum of $250,000,000 to France in 1947, but only four have been greater than $40,000,000. Twenty-eight loans have been for $10,000,000 or less.

International Broadcasting Service. See Voice of America.

International Labor Organization. An affiliated agency of the LEAGUE OF NATIONS. It was established in 1919 by the VERSAILLES PEACE CONFERENCE for the purpose of engaging in research in international labor and welfare matters, in the attempt to promote economic and social stability and improve labor conditions and living standards. It became a specialized agency of the UNITED NATIONS in 1945. Because of United States opposition to the League of Nations it did not join the ILO until 1934 although Americans had previously been appointed to its various commissions.

International Monetary Fund. Established by 44 nations at the BRETTON WOODS CONFERENCE in July, 1944 and effective on December 27, 1945. By 1952, 49 nations had become members. The objectives of the fund were to promote international trade by insuring the stability of exchange rates, encourage international monetary cooperation, avoid competitive exchange DEVALUATION, establish a system of multi-lateral payments in current transactions by eliminating restrictions, eliminate discriminatory CURRENCY arrangements, and to permit members to draw upon the resources of the Fund.

The Fund's resources are provided by the payment of quotas by members in gold, United States dollars, or its own currency. In 1964 total quotas amounted to $15,850,000,000 of which the United States' subscription was $5,304,000,000 The United States exercises 30 percent of the voting control of the Fund. By 1964 it had extended loans totalling $7,800,000,000 to 52 countries. See International Bank for Reconstruction and Development.

International News Service. A press association founded by WILLIAM RANDOLPH HEARST in 1909 as a service to his morning NEWSPAPERS. Subsequently the agency sold its news service to other papers and, by 1948, was serving 2400 papers and RADIO stations throughout the world. These included 420 newspapers in the United States. The INS was the third largest news service in the United States in 1952.

"Interstate Comity Clause." The popular name of Article IV of the Constitution of the United States. This clause deals with the relationships of the states to each other, and provides that each state shall give full faith and credit to the public acts, records, and judicial proceedings of every other state. The CITIZENS of each state are declared to be entitled to all the privileges and immunities of the citizens of all the states.

Interstate Commerce. Trade among the states. Under the federal constitution, Congress was given the power to regulate interstate commerce. As defined in the case of GIBBONS VS. OGDEN in 1824 the United States Supreme Court interpreted this power to include control over traffic, TRANSPORTATION, intercourse, and all methods appertaining thereto. Subsequent decisions of the court have conferred upon Congress the power to regulate those intrastate activities which substantially affect interstate commerce.

317

Interstate Commerce Act. A law of Congress passed on February 4, 1887. It established a five man INTERSTATE COMMERCE COMMISSION to administer its provisions. The law declared that all railroad charges should be just and reasonable, and forbade discriminations in the form of REBATES, or otherwise, among persons and discrimination among localities, freight classifications, or connecting lines. It also prohibited a greater charge for a short haul than for a long haul, forbade POOLING and traffic agreements, and ordered the public posting of all rates prior to change. Rate changes could not be made except after 10 days notice. RAILROADS were required to submit to the Interstate Commerce Commission annual reports concerning their financial condition and rates. The Commission was authorized to accept and hear complaints and issue orders to the carriers. Enforcement of these orders was vested in the federal courts upon petition of the Commission. The Act was weak because of the absence of enforcement powers of the Commission, poor definitions, and interpretations by the courts. Opposition of the railroads led to constant and widespread violation. The result was the enactment of amending legislation in later years.

Interstate Commerce Commission. Created by Congress in the INTERSTATE COMMERCE ACT of 1887. Consisted originally of five commissioners whose number was subsequently increased to 11 by amending legislation. Under the original statute plus the amendments (ELKINS ACT of 1903, HEPBURN ACT of 1906, MANN-ELKINS ACT of 1910, ESCH-CUMMINS ACT of 1920, EMERGENCY RAILWAY TRANSPORTATION ACT of 1933, and the MOTOR CARRIER ACT of 1935), the powers of the Commission have been steadily enhanced. By 1952 the jurisdiction of the Commission had been extended to RAILROADS, pipelines, ferries, bridges, internal waterways, coastal SHIPPING, intercoastal

shipping, trucking, and bus transportation. Until 1934 the Commission also exercised jurisdiction over the TELEPHONE, TELEGRAPH, and cable industries, losing these to the newly established FEDERAL COMMUNICATIONS COMMISSION of that year. The industries described are regulable by the Interstate Commerce Commission only insofar as they are engaged in or substantially affect INTERSTATE COMMERCE. In intrastate industries the regulatory power is conferred upon the state PUBLIC SERVICE COMMISSIONS or state public utilities commissions. By the REED-BULWINKLE ACT of 1948 the railroads were exempted from federal ANTITRUST LEGISLATION, such regulation being handed over to the Commission. The powers of the Commission today extend to the setting of minimum and maximum rates, railroad consolidations, abandonment of lines, securities issues, and virtually all other railroad practices except LABOR RELATIONS. The importance of the establishment of the Commission lies in its pioneer work in the field of regulatory practice, the Commission having been the first of the many INDEPENDENT REGULATORY BODIES. Like the others which followed, the I.C.C. exercises the customary quasi-judicial powers.

Intolerable Acts. Also known as Restraining Acts and Coercive Acts. A series of five parliamentary acts in 1774 passed for the purpose of punishing the colonists for the BOSTON TEA PARTY. The laws provided that British officers in America, accused by colonists, could be tried in England, that the old QUARTERING ACTS be extended so as to compel colonists to open their homes to British troops where existing barracks were inadequate, that the government of Massachusetts be reorganized so that its charter was revoked, bringing the colonial government directly under royal control, and that the port of Boston be closed. The Quebec Act was a fifth law not directly associated with the Intolerable Acts except in colonial

318

thinking. The effect of the laws was to arouse deep colonial resentment in the inevitable move towards war with Britain. See Boston Port Act and Quebec Act.

Inventions. Prior to the Civil War American inventions were few in number and generally applicable to agricultural rather than industrial production. These are best represented by the flour mill of Oliver Evans in 1780, the Cotton Gin of ELI WHITNEY in 1793, and the reaper of CYRUS H. MC CORMICK in 1834. Industrial inventions included the work of JOHN FITCH, ROBERT LIVINGSTON, and ROBERT FULTON on the STEAMBOAT, the TELEGRAPH of SAMUEL MORSE in 1844, and the rotary press of RICHARD HOE in 1847. With the advent of the INDUSTRIAL REVOLUTION in the generation before the Civil War great progress was made in the invention of the SEWING MACHINE of ELIAS HOWE in 1844, the typewriter of WILLIAM BURT in 1829, and the linotype of OTTMAR MERGENTHALER in 1884. The tremendous industrial development in the last third of the 19th and the beginning of the 20th centuries furnished the greatest stimulus to American inventiveness. This period saw the production of the telephone of ALEXANDER G. BELL (1876), the PHONOGRAPH of THOMAS A. EDISON (1877), the WESTINGHOUSE AIR BRAKE (1872), the aircraft of the WRIGHT BROTHERS (1903), and vast improvements and refinements in the fields of photography, printing machinery, office machinery, the MOTION PICTURE, electric and electronic equipment, metallurgy, the automobile, and farm machinery.

Investment Trust Act. A law of Congress passed on August 22, 1940 as an amendment to the SECURITIES AND EXCHANGE ACT. Under its terms, investment advisers were required to register with the Securities and Exchange Commission and were prohibited from making false claims concerning securities. Investment trusts were required to reg-

ister with the Commission and were prohibited from buying securities for their own portfolios unless in the interest of stockholders. Such companies were forbidden the use of improper accounting systems. If affiliated with BANKING, brokerage, or investment advisory companies, the number of directors was restricted. The Act was designed to protect the stockholders of investment companies. Also known as the Wagner-Lea Act.

Iowa. The 25th state in size, with an area of 56,280 square miles. Organized as a TERRITORY in 1838 and admitted as the 29th state on December 28, 1846. Des Moines is the capital. In 1950 Iowa's POPULATION of 2,621,073 made it 22nd in rank. Its largest cities are Des Moines, Sioux City, and Davenport. Iowa is the nation's largest producer of corn and hogs, this production frequently netting it the greatest agricultural income in the nation. Ninety percent of its area is devoted to AGRICULTURE which produces important crops of oats, soy beans, hemp, hay, popcorn, fruit, nuts and vegetables. Des Moines publishes more farm papers and MAGAZINES than any other city in the United States. MEAT PACKING is the most important industrial enterprise but Iowa also manufactures farm implements, washing machines, and railroad and automotive equipment. The state has the lowest illiteracy rate in the nation. It was discovered in 1673 by MARQUETTE and JOLIET. Its nickname is the "Hawkeye State."

Iron Act of 1750. One of a series of British laws attempting to restrict colonial MANUFACTURING and trade. It imposed large fines for the establishment of colonial rolling mills and steel furnaces, and favored Great Britain by allowing bar iron and pig iron to be admitted to England without the payment of customs.

Ironclad. See Hampton Roads, Battle of, *Merrimac,* the, and *Monitor,* the.

Iron Industry. The first blast furnace was constructed in Virginia in the second decade of the 17th century, although it never went into production. At the beginning of the 18th century, furnaces were reopened in Virginia and then in Massachusetts, Connecticut, and New Jersey. By the opening of the Revolution, the iron industry was well-established in every colony except Georgia, production exceeding that of Great Britain. By 1800 Pennsylvania and New Jersey had become the center of a well-established industry that produced almost 20 percent of the world's iron. The original fuel used was wood, obtained from the PLANTATIONS where iron works were established. Subsequently charcoal, and then anthracite were substituted as fuels. The industry moved westward into the Lehigh, Delaware, and Susquehanna valleys. After 1850 bituminous coal became a widely used fuel, displaced by coke in the 1870's. In 1964 the United States was the leading producer of iron and ferro-alloys. The production in 1963 of pig-iron was approximately 72,000,000 tons, and of iron ore over 74,000,000 tons.

Iroquois Indians. An important Indian tribe in New York. The Iroquois Confederacy consisted of five including the Seneca, Cayuga, Onondaga, Oneida, and MOHAWK Indians. They lived in "long houses" of bark and were expert basket-weavers. They also did some farming and had a high degree of culture. Women were generally respected more in these tribes than in other Indian tribes. They used Wampum. The Iroquois Indians were very warlike and would attack tribes as far west as Illinois. They fought with the British against the French although many French Jesuit priests were welcomed by the tribe. Supplied by the Dutch with guns they destroyed the HURON Indian tribe. During the Revolution they again sided with the British, being involved in the CHERRY VALLEY and Wyoming Valley massacres. They were finally defeated by an expedition led by General JOHN SULLIVAN in 1779. Those that were on the British side moved to Ontario, Canada, the remaining Iroquois, under the leadership of chief RED JACKET, made peace with the United States, and remained in New York. Later the Confederacy split up and moved into various parts of the West.

Irrigation. The supply of water to arid areas for agricultural use. Irrigation was used sparsely during the colonial period, but was highly developed in the dry regions of Utah by the MORMONS, after 1840. By 1860 their cooperative methods of reclaiming the desert area had increased its value to almost $1,500,-000. Irrigation developed rapidly in California after its ADMISSION INTO THE UNION in 1850. Within 30 years there were 890 ditches providing water for more than 250,000 acres. Subsequently the federal government enacted legislation to provide for the reclamation and irrigation of hitherto useless land. Such laws included the DESERT LAND ACT of 1877, the CAREY ACT of 1894, the NEW-LANDS ACT of 1902, and the various laws establishing regional authorities and compacts in the Tennessee Valley, the Colorado Valley, and the Columbia Valley. By 1950 the various dams and power plants providing water for the arid areas of the United States had a total storage capacity of 75,000,000 acre-feet, furnishing 5,000,000 acres of land and 9,000,000 people with water by means of 16,000 miles of irrigation canals. The crops produced in these areas were in excess of $500,000,000 per annum. It has been estimated that the cumulative value of irrigated crops since the opening of the century has exceeded $7,000,000,000, a figure which is three and one-half times the federal expenditure of $2,000,000,-000 for such purposes.

IRVINE, William. 1741-1804. Revolutionary general. b. Ireland. Served as colonel in Pennsylvania regiment at outbreak of Revolution; brigadier general (1779); in command of Fort Pitt and western FRONTIER (1782-83); member of Congress under the Confederation (1786-88) and under the Constitution (1793-95); served during WHISKY REBELLION (1794) and against France (1798).

IRVING, Clifford. In 1972 multi-millionaire Howard Hughes became the subject of a fraudulent biography by the writer, Clifford Irving, who claimed that he had in his possession letters and affidavits of meetings with Hughes. McGraw Hill and Look Magazine became interested in the publication of this material and began to negotiate with Irving for the publication of a biography of Hughes and advanced Irving $750,000. Irving later admitted that all of his material was based on a hoax and he pleaded guilty in Federal Court of conspiracy to defraud McGraw Hill. Partial restitution of the money advanced to him was made but he was declared guilty and after serving time in prison was released.

IRVING, Washington. 1783-1859. Author and diplomat. b. New York City. Studied law and admitted to the bar; worked in England with brothers (1815); largest contributor to *Salmagundi Papers* (1807-08) essays similar to Addison's *Spectator;* wrote under name of Geoffrey Crayon in England; traveled in Germany and France (1822-25); on staff of U.S. embassy in Madrid (1826-29); secretary of U.S. legation, London (1829-32); U.S. Minister to Spain (1842-46). Author of *The Sketch Book* (1820), *Oliver Goldsmith* (1849), *Life of Washington* (5 vols. 1855-59); best known for short stories *The Legend of Sleepy Hollow,* which introduced the character Ichabod Crane, and *Rip Van Winkle.*

"Island-Hopping Campaign." The offensive effort of the United States Navy in World War II in the Pacific theater. It began with the invasion and capture of the SOLOMON ISLANDS in August, 1942 and was concluded with the invasion of the Japanese homeland after the atomic BOMBING OF HIROSHIMA and Nagasaki in 1945.

Isolationism. The name applied to that foreign policy which, historically advocated America's estrangement from European affairs. The origins of isolationism are found in WASHINGTON'S PROCLAMATION OF NEUTRALITY of 1793. The FAREWELL ADDRESS of Washington, which contained the famous "NON-ENTANGLING ALLIANCES" clause, and the MONROE DOCTRINE of 1823 are customarily considered as additional factors in having established this as the foreign policy of the United States. The foreign policy of the administrations of HARDING and COOLIDGE represented the acme of isolationist feeling. The advent of World War II brought about a reversal of thinking, and through the bi-partisan efforts of Republican and Democratic leaders the traditional isolationism of the Republican party was abandoned. Senator ARTHUR H. VANDENBERG of Michigan was principally responsible for the new Republican policy in the war and immediate post-war period.

Item Veto. See selective veto.

ITT Controversey. The Republican Convention of 1972 was originally slated for San Diego. A memorandum from a lobbyist for the International Telephone and Telegraph Company linked a contribution to the convention to a favorable settlement of a government antitrust suit against ITT. There was a Senate investigation on the nomination of Richard Kleindienst as Attorney General which concluded that he had no part in the transaction and recommended his confirmation.

IVES, Frederick Eugene. 1856-1937. Inventor. b. Connecticut. Credited with the invention of half-tone photoengraving process (1886); pioneer in color photography; developed a process for making MOTION PICTURES in natural color (1914); invented half-tone process printing plates (1881); invented the short-tube single-objective binocular microscope, the parallax stereogram and the photochromoscope.

Iwo Jima, Battle of. One of the famous battles in the "stepping stone" process leading to the end of the Pacific campaign in World War II. It was begun by an invasion of a United States expeditionary force on February 19, 1945 with land action by U.S. Marines. The invasion used 495 ships including 17 aircraft carriers and 1170 planes. The total number of American troops engaged was 111,308, of whom 75,144 participated in the assault landings. The island was conquered by March 16th with the loss of 4,590 American troops. The Japanese deaths were estimated at over 20,000.

IZARD, Ralph. 1742-1804. Revolutionary leader. b. South Carolina. Wealthy planter; went from London, where he was living, to Paris at outbreak of Revolution; appointed by CONTINENTAL CONGRESS commissioner to Tuscany but not recognized; disagreed with FRANKLIN in Paris and recalled (1799); member, Continental Congress (1782, 1783); U.S. Senator (1789-95).

J

JACKSON, Andrew. 1767-1845. Seventh President of the United States. b. Waxhaw, South Carolina. Served during the Revolution, and was captured and imprisoned by the British at Camden; admitted to the bar, Salisbury, North Carolina (1787); moved to a town, now Nashville, in Tennessee territory (1788); member, U.S. House of Representatives (1796-97); and U.S. Senator (1797-98); judge, Tennessee Supreme Court (1798-1804); major general of Tennessee militia (1820); became major general in the regular army after defeating the CREEK INDIANS at HORSESHOE BEND (1814); his defense of NEW ORLEANS against the British made him a hero in the War of 1812; successful in campaigns against the SEMINOLE INDIANS (1818) involving the federal government when he followed the Indians into Spanish territory of Florida; appointed by MONROE, first governor of Florida; U.S. Senator (1823-25); defeated for the presidency (1824) because of CLAY's support of ADAMS; elected President of the United States (1828 and 1832); involved in the scandal over PEGGY O'NEILL; his veto of the charter and withdrawal of funds from the BANK OF THE UNITED STATES resulted in its collapse; strong administrator; known as "Old Hickory"; advocated rotation in office.

JACKSON, Charles Samuel. 1860-1924. Newspaper publisher. To Oregon from Virginia (1880); published *East Oregonian;* owner of *Oregon Daily Journal,* Portland; strong advocate of liberal and efficient government; largely responsible for political innovations known as the "Oregon System"; supported INCOME TAX and other tax reforms; supported WOMAN SUFFRAGE.

JACKSON, Charles Thomas. 1805-1880. Physician and scientist. Graduated, Harvard Medical School; studied in Europe; practised in Boston (1832-36); worked in chemistry, geology and minerology; claimed to have suggested to SAMUEL MORSE the basic principles of electric telegraph; also claimed to have suggested the use of ether in anesthesia to MORTON; acclaimed as the discoverer of surgical anesthesia; claimed to be first to discover guncotton.

JACKSON, Clairborne Fox. 1806-1862. Civil war governor. Speaker of the Mississippi legislature (1844-46); overthrew power of Senator T. H. BENTON and became governor of the state (1860); wanted to secede and opposed LINCOLN's call for volunteers; deposed by legislature and retired.

JACKSON, James. 1757-1806. Political leader. b. England. To Georgia (1772); officer of Georgia forces in Revolution; represented Georgia in first Congress

(1789-91) and U.S. Senator (1793-95, 1801-06); opposed YAZOO FRAUDS; leader in drawing up state constitution (1798); governor of Georgia (1798-1801).

Jacksonian Democracy. The name given to the great period of reform instituted by the election of JACKSON in 1828 and continuing for a generation thereafter. This movement of reform involved virtually every area of American life, including specifically the fields of EDUCATION, PENOLOGY, LABOR RELATIONS, POLITICS, FEMINISM, and humanitarian endeavors. Among the leaders of the reform movement of this era were HORACE MANN, HENRY BARNARD, DOROTHEA DIX, SUSAN B. ANTHONY, AMELIA BLOOMER, et al.

JACKSON, Robert H. 1892-1954. Jurist. b. Pennsylvannia. Admitted to the bar (1913); practised in Jamestown, New York; general counsel Bureau of Internal Revenue (1934); assistant Attorney General in charge of the anti-trust division (1936-38); strong advocate of NEW DEAL policies; solicitor general of the United States (1938-39); Attorney General of the United States (1940-41); appointed by F. D. ROOSEVELT, Associate Justice of the United States Supreme Court (from 1941); on leave from the Court to serve as United States Chief Counsel at the Nuremberg WAR CRIMES trial (1945-46). Author of *The Struggle for Judicial Supremacy* (1940), and *The Case Against the Nazi War Criminals* (1945).

JACKSON, Sheldon. 1834-1909. Missionary, educator, and Alaskan industrialist. Served on Presbyterian Home Mission Board in Wisconsin and Minnesota; established first churches of his denomination in the West; superintendent of missions in ALASKA (1883); educated the Eskimos; founded reindeer industry; established mail routes and played an important part in Alaskan affairs.

JACKSON, Thomas Jonathan. Known as "Stonewall" Jackson. 1824-1863. Confederate general. b. West Virginia. Graduated, U.S.M.A., West Point (1846); served in the MEXICAN WAR; resigned from the army (1852) but entered the Confederate service at the outbreak of Civil War; brigadier general (1861); known for outstanding leadership at BULL RUN; major general (1861); led Confederate troops in Shenandoah Valley campaign (1862); routed right wing of the Union forces at Chancellorsville and wounded in battle by fire from his own troops (May 2, 1863); died on May 10, 1863.

JACOBI, Mary Putnam. 1842-1906. Physician. b. England. Pioneer woman physician; graduated, Woman's Medical College, Pennsylvania (1864); clinical professor of children's diseases, New York. Postgraduate Medical School; first woman member of many medical societies; furthered the cause of women in medicine.

JACOBS, Joseph. 1854-1916. Scholar and writer. b. Australia. Edited *Jewish Encyclopaedia* in the United States; taught at the Jewish Theological Seminary in New York City; wrote many books on Jewish history.

JADWIN, Edgar. 1865-1931. Army engineer. b. Pennsylvania. Graduated, U.S. M.A., West Point (1890); as assistant to General GOETHALS in the building of the PANAMA CANAL (1907-11); served overseas in World War I (1917-19); major general and chief of engineers, U.S. army (1926); planned Mississippi River flood control (1928); retired with rank of lieutenant general (1929).

JAMES, Henry. 1843 - 1916. Son of Henry James (1811-1882); brother of WILLIAM JAMES. Novelist. b. New York City. Studied at Harvard Law School (1862); wrote for the *Nation* and the *Atlantic* (1865-69); lived in London (from 1876); became a British citizen (1915). Author of well-known works including

The American (1877), *The Portrait of a Lady* (1881), *Washington Square* (1881), *The Bostonian* (1886), *The Ambassadors* (1903), *The Turn of the Screw* (1898), biographies, autobiographical works, essays, and criticism.

JAMES, Jesse Woodson. 1847-1882. Outlaw and desperado. b. Missouri. Leader of a band of outlaws who robbed trains and banks in the West; murdered by one of his own men.

Jamestown, settlement of. The first English settlement in North America. On May 13, 1607, 105 colonists under Christopher Newport landed at the mouth of the James River. Problems with the Indians were solved through the efforts of Captain JOHN SMITH, although on March 22, 1622 an Indian raid resulted in the massacre of several hundred colonists. The principal economic activity was the cultivation of tobacco. Jamestown was the seat of the VIRGINIA HOUSE OF BURGESSES, established in 1619 as the first colonial assembly.

JAMES, William. 1842-1910. Brother of HENRY JAMES. Psychologist and philosopher. b. New York City. Graduated, Harvard Medical School (1869); taught anatomy, physiology, and hygiene at Harvard (from 1872); professor of philosophy and psychology (from 1881); known as founder of philosophical schools of "pragmatism" and "radical empiricism" important contributions to psychology; important influence on American thought. Author of *The Principles of Psychology* (1890), *Pragmatism* (1907), *The Meaning of Truth* (1909), *Essays in Radical Empiricism* (1912) and many other important works.

JANEWAY, Edward Gamaliel. 1841-1911. Physician. b. New Jersey. Graduated, Columbia (M.D.); practiced in New York City; leading consultant and diagnostician; recognized condition known as leukemia; established the first hospital for contagious diseases in New York City; Commissioner of Health, N.Y. (1875-81).

Japan, Occupation of. The POTSDAM DECLARATION of July 26, 1945 set down the terms of the Japanese surrender. Among other provisions it declared that Japan would be occupied by Allied forces until the objectives of DISARMAMENT, REPARATIONS, territorial transfer, and punishment of war criminals would be achieved. The surrender terms established on September 2, 1945 provided that Japan must accept the provisions of the Potsdam Declaration and that "the authority of the Emperor and the Japanese Government to rule the state shall be subject to the Supreme Commander for the Allied Powers." On August 14, 1945 General MACARTHUR was appointed Supreme Commander as head of Allied Occupation forces in Japan. A Far Eastern Commission, consisting of representatives of Australia, Burma, Canada, China, Great Britain, France, India, Holland, New Zealand, Pakistan, the PHILIPPINES, the Soviet Union, and the United States, was established. The Commission was authorized to form the policies, principles, and standards by which Japan's obligations under the surrender terms would be fulfilled. It was authorized to review directives issued to SCAP and all actions taken 'by the latter within the Commission's jurisdiction. The Allied Council for Japan was established to advise and consult with SCAP in carrying out the surrender terms and the policies approved by the Commission. The Council consisted of the United States' member of SCAP, a member from China and from the Soviet Union, and a member representing jointly the United Kingdom, New Zealand, and India. In 1946 General MacArthur ordered the Japanese CABINET to carry out a series of political purges. In July 1947 the United States suggested a conference of the 11 members of the Far Eastern Commission to consider a peace settlement for Japan. All member nations, except the Soviet Union, accepted the proposal. The latter insisted that the treaty be prepared by the four-power Council of Foreign Ministers. On April 11, 1951 General MacArthur was replaced by General Ridgeway as the Supreme Commander for the Allied Powers. During the occupation political, economic, and social reforms were undertaken. The Japanese government was democratized, with sovereignty transferred from the Emperor to the popularly elected House of Representatives. The school curriculum was simplified and purged of militarist and chauvinist influences. Repatriation of war prisoners was almost completed. The dissolution of the business and financial MONOPOLIES was effected, with VOTING rights taken over by a government commission which seized securities of the *Zaibatsu* families, for resale to the public. Between 1946 and 1949 reparations in the form of industrial products were delivered until, in the latter year, the United States declared its opposition to further reparations. On May 1, 1951 General Ridgeway announced the relaxation of occupation directives. On September 8, 1951 a treaty of peace with Japan was signed at San Francisco by the United States and 40 other nations.

Japanese Peace Treaty. A treaty signed at San Francisco on September 8, 1951 between Japan and 49 nations including the United States. The representatives of the Soviet Union, Poland, and Czechoslovakia attended the peace conference, but refused to sign. The provisions of the treaty ended the state of war among the signatories, recognized the full sovereignty of Japan and its right to apply for UNITED NATIONS membership, and established Japanese renunciation of all rights to Formosa, the Pescadores, the Kuriles, Sakhalin, and all the islands formerly mandated to Japan by the LEAGUE OF NATIONS. It further provided for Japanese agreement to U.N. TRUSTEESHIP over the Ryukyu Islands, the Bonins, and several other islands. It required Japan to agree to peaceful settlement of international disputes, and provided for the continued occupation of Japan until 90 days after the treaty had been ratified by a majority of the signatories. The Treaty also provided for FISHERIES, TARIFF, and maritime relations among the signatories, and for the payment by Japan of REPARATIONS through manufactured goods. Japan agreed to recognize the industrial, literary, and artistic PROPERTY RIGHTS of the signatory nations in Japan and to indemnify war prisoners with claims against the Japanese government. The United States Senate ratified the Treaty on March 20, 1952.

JARVIS, Thomas Jordan. 1836 - 1915. Political leader. Member, state legislature, North Carolina; leader in overthrow of carpetbag regime; lieutenant governor (1876-79); governor of N.C. (1879); U.S. Minister to Brazil (1885-89).

JAWORSKI, Leon. On November 1, 1973, Jaworski a conservative Democrat from Texas, was named by the Nixon administration to succeed Archibald Cox as special prosecutor. His prime responsibility was the investigation of administrative wrongdoings.

JAY, John. 1745-1829. Jurist and statesman. b. New York City. Graduated, Columbia (1764); member, CONTINENTAL CONGRESS (1774-77, 1778, 1779); president (1778-79); Minister to Spain (1779); appointed one of commissioners to negotiate peace and joined FRANKLIN in Paris; U.S. Secretary of Foreign Affairs (1784-89); with HAMILTON and MADISON wrote the *Federalist* which explained and advocated the new Constitution (1787-88); first Chief Justice, U.S. Supreme Court (1789-95); negotiated JAY TREATY with Great Britain (1794-95); governor of New York (1795-1801).

Jay Treaty. Negotiated between the

United States and Great Britain in 1794 by Chief Justice JOHN JAY. The Treaty arose out of the dissatisfaction of the United States over England's persistent violations of the terms of the TREATY OF PARIS of 1783. The provisions of the Jay Treaty included merely a set of promises by England to observe the terms of the earlier convention by establishing mixed commissions to examine the following problems: England's surrender of the northwest trading posts, the Maine boundary, debts owed to British subjects, and trade between the United States and her West Indian colonies. The Treaty was unpopular with the JEFFERSONIAN REPUBLICANS and Jay was burned in effigy throughout the country upon his return to the United States.

Jazz. A form of popular MUSIC which came into prominence during World War I. It is either vocal or instrumental music in an animated style. Accompanying dance modes are lively and carefree. The term was first used in Chicago in 1916 in the announcement by a club of the appearance of Bert Kelly's "Jazz Band." Jazz music and dancing attained the height of its popularity in the 1920's. The origin of the word may be from the African "jazz," the native name for the Barbary Coast.

Jazz Age, the. The derogatory term applied to the culture of the United States in the 1920's. It draws its name from the syncopated dance music of the era, popularly known as JAZZ. The characteristics of the jazz age were the defiance of authority and convention, the wearing of bizarre clothes, sexual license, eccentric forms of address, the glorification of youth, and grotesque development in MUSIC, ART, and LITERATURE. It is generally acknowledged that the post war neurosis, war weariness, economic prosperity, and PROHIBITION were the fundamental causes of these phenomena.

Jeffersonian Democracy. The term applied to the movement of reform in- augurated by the election of JEFFERSON in 1800 and continuing through the succeeding generation. Among the great reforms by which Jefferson and his followers attempted to establish his long-hoped-for "AGRARIAN DEMOCRACY" were the final abolition of ENTAIL and PRIMOGENITURE in all the STATES, the enactment of more liberal land legislation, the purchase of the LOUISIANA TERRITORY, the repeal of the WHISKEY EXCISE, the pardon of the imprisoned Whiskey rebels, the repeal of the ALIEN AND SEDITION LAWS and the pardon of those imprisoned under these acts, and other reforms in humanitarian, social, and political affairs.

Jeffersonian Republicans. See Democratic-Republican party.

JEFFERSON, Thomas. 1743-1826. Third President of the United States. b. Goochland, now Albemarle County, Virginia. Graduated, William and Mary (1762); admitted to the bar (1767); member, Virginia HOUSE OF BURGESSES (1769-74); with R. H. LEE and PATRICK HENRY, he created the Virginia COMMITTEE OF CORRESPONDENCE (1773); member, CONTINENTAL CONGRESS (1775, 76); chairman of committee that prepared the DECLARATION OF INDEPENDENCE, having written and presented the first draft of the declaration to Congress (July 2, 1776); signer of the Declaration; governor of Virginia (1779-81); member, Continental Congress (1783-85); U.S. Minister to France (1785-89); U.S. Secretary of State (1790-93); disagreed radically with HAMILTON, then Secretary of Treasury; elected Vice-President of the United States (1797-1801); President of the United States (1801-09) winning the 1800 election by the vote of the House of Representatives after a tie with BURR in the electoral vote; responsible for the purchase of LOUISIANA; westward expansion; prohibition of importation of slaves, drafted the KENTUCKY RESOLUTIONS in protest against the ALIEN AND SEDITION ACT:; helped organize the LEWIS AND CIARK EXPEDITION; helped to found the University of Virginia (1819); retired to his plantation "MONTICELLO," near Charlottesville, Virginia. One of the most learned men in the country and undoubtedly one of the greatest Americans of all times.

Jehovah's Witnesses. A religious sect founded in 1872 in Pennsylvania by Charles Taze Russell. It has also been known as the Russellites, Dawnites, and the Watchtower People. It has spread to Europe. The Jehovah's Witnesses are a semi-secret society who call themselves "the Lord's Organization." They consider established religious bodies as part of "Satan's Organization." They base their theology on the Bible as interpreted by their leaders, and disseminate their views largely through the publication of pamphlets and their periodicals, *The Watchtower, Announcing Jehovah's Witnesses,* and *Consolation.* These materials are sold from door to door and on the streets in the belief that this is the biblical way of disseminating truth. Their adherents recognize the authority of Jehovah only and believe that "millions now living will never die." The Jehovah's Witnesses have often been in conflict with municipal and STATE GOVERNMENTS because of the public method of spreading their religion through door knocking, demonstrations, meetings, parades, and the street sale of their literature. These activities plus their refusal to salute the flag or enlist in military service have produced many Supreme Court cases based on CIVIL RIGHTS principles.

JEMISON, Mary. 1743-1833. Known as "The White Woman of the Genesee" captured by the Indians at the age of 15 and lived with them all her life. Helped white settlers in the Genesee, Pa. area.

JENKINS, Charles Jones. 1805 - 1883. Politician. Wrote compromise resolutions known as the "Georgia Platform" (1850); judge, Georgia state supreme court (1860-65); important in drafting of the state constitution (1865); governor of Georgia (1865-70); president of state constitutional convention (1877); important leader of Southern WHIGS.

JENKINS, John. 1728 - 1785. Pioneer leader of Susquehanna Company. b. Connecticut. Explored Wyoming Valley region and founded Susquehanna Company (1753); settled the territory (1762); driven out by Indians (1763); organized settlement at Kingston and Jenkins' Fort, near Pittston; stayed until Wyoming massacre (1777).

JENNY, William Le Baron. 1832-1907. Architect and engineer. Designed and built the Home Insurance Company building, Chicago (1884) using for the first time anywhere in the world a type of skeleton construction with a framework of metal. He is known as "the father of the modern skyscrapers."

JEROME, William Travers. 1859-1934. Lawyer. Graduated, Columbia Law School; practiced in New York City; known for political reform activities, and as an opponent of TAMMANY HALL; managed campaign of reform mayor Strong (1895)); justice court of special sessions (1895-1901); district attorney New York county (1901-09); prosecutor in trials of Harry Thaw.

JERVIS, John Bloomfield. 1795-1885. Civil engineer and railroad builder. Helped in building of Erie and Delaware and Hudson canals; designed the *Experiment* (1832) fastest locomotive built up to that time; chief engineer of the Croton Aqueduct supplying water to New York City (1836); inventor of the railroad truck.

Jesuits. A reform group within the Catholic Church which originated in the early 16th century under the leadership of a

Spanish soldier-monk, Ignatius Loyola. They were organized on a quasi-military basis for the purpose of conducting missionary and educational programs designed to recapture areas of the church during the early Reformation. The first Jesuits in colonial America established a short-lived mission in 1566-1571 in Florida. In 1611 French Jesuits founded the Mission of New France in Canada. Subsequently, French Jesuit missions were established in the GREAT LAKES, Ohio, and Mississippi regions. The earliest white settlement in Michigan grew up around an Algonquin mission established at Sault Ste. Marie in 1668 by Father JACQUES MARQUETTE. The French Jesuits carried on extensive missionary and educational work among the SIOUX, Algonquin, HURON, Ontario, MOHAWK, Yazoo, CHOCTAW, and FOX Indians. As a result of their work a wealth of geographic, ethnological, economic, and social data was accumulated. They established SCHOOLS and universities during the colonial period and after the Revolution. Among the more notable universities are Fordham, Georgetown, Holy Cross, Boston College, and St. Louis. In 1965 there were 28 Jesuit institutions of higher learning and 52 secondary schools. In that year Jesuits in the world were organized into eleven administrative sections with a total membership of approximately 36,000. The term "Jesuits" is the popular name of the Society of Jesus.

JESUP, Morris Ketchum. 1830 - 1908. Merchant, banker and philanthropist. Chiefly known as the founder of the American Museum of Natural History (1869) giving $2,000,000 to the museum; he aided many scientific expeditions and gave to Negro schools in the south.

Jet Planes. The principle of jet propulsion was understood and a model design made by the famous Hellenistic scientist Hero in the second century B.C. In contemporary times the idea was first developed by Sir Frank Whittle in 1928. He obtained his first patent in 1930, and in 1936 Power Jets, a corporation, was organized to build jet engines to Whittle's specifications. In May, 1941 the first jet-propelled plane was flown in England. Simultaneously, the United States began secret development of the jet engine. There is belief that the Germans flew a Heinkel He-178 plane powered by a Heinkel S3B turbojet engine on August 27, 1939. The first American jet plane flight was undertaken by Robert Stanley who flew a Bell XP-59 Airocomet at Muroc Army Base, California on October 1, 1942. The first jet plane battle occurred on November 8, 1950 when four UNITED NATIONS jets were attacked by a dozen North Korean jets near Sinuiju, Korea. In July, 1951 the Eastern Airlines announced a two year $100,000,000 program of 90 jet-propelled transports. In August, 1951 the British Overseas Airways Corporation announced a plan for round the world jet service. That same month a British twin-jet plane flew from Belfast to New Foundland in four hours, 19 minutes. The United States Navy announced that on June 11, 1951 an experimental jet plane had surpassed all altitude and speed records, indicating that it had reached a speed of about 1,000 miles per hour and an altitude above 73,000 feet. On May 2, 1952 a British jet commercial transport flew a scheduled journey from London to Capetown in less than 24 hours, inaugurating the first jet commercial transportation schedule in history. During 1964, the 4-engine jet (600 miles per hour) became the major craft used by airlines for long distance service. In the same year the medium range Boeing 727 was introduced by American carriers. This plane mounts three jet engines in the rear of the fuselage.

Jews. Few Jews settled in the New World. Most of these emanated from Holland and migrated to Virginia, New Amsterdam, and Maryland. By the end of the 17th century, several thousand Jews were living in Massachusetts, Rhode Island, and the Carolinas. Since the Jews were generally limited in their political and economic opportunities many of them entered business and the professions. The mid-nineteenth century saw a large influx of Jewish immigration, and by the close of the Civil War there were 200,000 Jews in the United States. The persecutions of the Russian, Polish, Romanian, and Austro-Hungarian government at the turn of the 20th century produced the greatest migration of Jews in American history. In the 40 years before World War I 2,000,000 Jews came to the United States. The greatest number settled in the large Eastern cities. In 1917 the American Jewish community established the National Jewish Welfare Board as its spokesman for meeting the needs of Jewish troops. This agency served the same purpose in World War II by which time it had become the recognized representative of many Jewish organizations. In 1963 there were more than 5,500,000 Jews in the United States.

"Jim Crow" Laws. Refers to anti-Negro legislation in many of the STATES of the Union. These laws discriminate against NEGROES with respect to attendance in the public schools, and the use of such public facilities as RAILROADS, restaurants, theaters, hotels, motion pictures houses, and public bathing places. Many of these states also prohibit marriage between Negro and white persons.

"Jingoism." The term applied to the extreme nationalism which seeks to im-

pose a nation's will upon other nations. In the United States it has customarily been applied to the "JINGO PRESS" which incited public opinion against Spain in the period leading up to the Spanish American War. Led by the *New York Journal* and the *New York World* these newspapers demanded American intervention in the Cuban Revolution between 1895 and 1898, and engaged in competition to expand their circulation by sensationalism, lurid headlines, and scandal reports.

"Jingo Press." Sometime called the "yellow press." The term applied to newspapers which, at the end of the 19th century, embarked upon competitive efforts to expand their circulation. Led by the *New York Journal* and the *New York World,* published respectively by WILLIAM RANDOLPH HEARST and JOSEPH PULITZER, these papers resorted to extreme sensationalism such as scare headlines, scandal reporting, lurid details of the private lives of public figures, the distortion of news, and the use of cartoons and photographs to emphasize their reports.

JOHNSON, Allen. 1870 - 1931. Editor and historian. Graduated, Columbia University, (Ph.D. 1899); taught at Grinnell College, Bowdoin, and Yale University (1910-1926); edited *The Chronicles of America* (50 vols., 1918-21); editor in chief, *Dictionary of American Biography* (from 1926).

JOHNSON, Andrew. 1808-1875. Seventeenth President of the United States. b. Raleigh, North Carolina. Apprenticed to a tailor at the age of 10; settled in Greenville, Tennessee (1826); self-educated man of character and perseverance; mayor of Greenville; member of the Tennessee legislature; member, U.S. House of Representatives (1853-55); U.S. Senator (1857-62); appointed military governor of Tennessee by LINCOLN; when Tennessee seceded, he remained loyal to the Union during the Civil War, and succeeded in establishing a loyal government in his state; brigadier general (1862); elected Vice-President of the United States on the Union-Republican ticket and succeeded to the presidency on the death of Lincoln (1865-69); because of his moderate Reconstruction policies he disagreed with Congress, this led to the IMPEACHMENT proceedings against him (1868); he believed that Reconstruction was an executive not a legislative function; he was acquitted and served out his term as President; U.S. Senator (1875).

Johnson-Clarendon Convention. An agreement between the United States and England negotiated in January, 1869. It provided for a commission to choose an arbitrator who would reconcile the conflicting claims of the two nations arising out of alleged British violations of neutrality during the Civil War. In April, 1869, the Senate defeated the treaty by a vote of 54 to 1. Senator SUMNER bitterly attacked the agreement, contending that the United States was entitled to $15,000,000 for direct injuries and an additional $2,110,000,000 for indirect damages resulting from the decline of the American MERCHANT MARINE. Sumner's extreme demands temporarily prevented a settlement, but the TREATY OF WASHINGTON two years later finally settled all outstanding claims.

Johnson Debt Default Act. Passed by Congress in 1934. It prohibited foreign governments in default on their debts to the United States from floating public bond issues in this country. The law was part of a series designed to maintain United States neutrality in European wars, and reflected the ISOLATIONIST sentiment of the Republican membership in Congress. As a result, the passage of the LEND-LEASE ACT in 1941 required that assistance to the enemies of Germany be granted directly by the United States government.

JOHNSON, Eastman. 1824-1906. Portrait and genre painter. Studied in Europe; known for portraits of presidents and famous personalities and his genre paintings in the style of the Dutch masters.

JOHNSON, Guy. 1740?-1788. British colonial official. b. Ireland. Superintendent of Indian affairs (1774-82); tried to organize Indians to fight against the colonial armies at the outbreak of the Revolution (1775); with headquarters at Niagara, he led Indian raids against the nearby colonies (1779-81); considered responsible for the Wyoming massacre; to England (from 1783).

JOHNSON, Herschel Vespasian. 1812-1880. Jurist and political leader. Practiced law in Georgia; opposed secession; judge, Georgia superior court (1849-53); governor (1853-57); nominated for vice president of the U. S. on ticket with STEPHEN DOUGLAS (1860); opposed suspension of writ of HABEAS CORPUS and conscription; strong advocate of states rights; judge of superior court (from 1873).

JOHNSON, Hiram Warren. 1866-1945. Politician. b. California. Admitted to the bar (1888); practiced in Sacramento (1888-1902); practiced in San Francisco (from 1902); assisted in prosecution of political grafters and bosses in San Francisco (1908) and gained wide popularity; governor of California (1911-17); close friend of T. ROOSEVELT with whom he founded the PROGRESSIVE PARTY (1912); ran for vice-president on the national ticket; U.S. Senator (from 1917); leading Republican ISOLATIONIST; opposed ratification of the TREATY OF VERSAILLES (1919, 1920); sponsored JOHNSON DEBT ACT (1934); voted against the UNITED NATIONS Charter (1945).

JOHNSON, Hugh Samuel. 1882-1942.

Lawyer and army officer. b. Kansas. Graduated, U.S.M.A., West Point (1903); judge advocate with PERSHING into Mexico (1916); deputy provost marshal general in Washington (1917); originated plan for DRAFT and assisted in the writing of the SELECTIVE SERVICE ACT; administered Act (1917-18); brigadier general (1918); N.R.A. administrator (1933-34); W.P.A. administrator in New York City (1935); writer, publicist for Scripps-Howard newspapers (from 1934).

JOHNSON, James Weldon. 1871-1938. Author. b. Florida. Graduated, Atlanta University (1894); admitted to Florida bar (1897); practiced in Jacksonville (1897-1901); U.S. consul, Puerto Cabello, Venezuela (1906), NICARAGUA (1909-1912); founder and secretary, NATIONAL ASSOCIATION FOR ADVANCEMENT OF COLORED PEOPLE (1916-30); awarded Spingarn medal for services to NEGROES (1925); professor of creative literature Fisk University (from 1930). Author of *The Autobiography of an Ex-Colored Man* (1912) and *The Book of American Negro Poetry.*

JOHNSON, Lyndon Baines. 1908-1973. President of the United States. 1963-1969, b. Texas. Succeeded to the presidency, November 22, 1963, after the assassination of President Kennedy. In 1964 as the Democratic candidate, President Johnson won an overwhelming victory at the polls. The electoral vote was 486 to 52. He was U.S. Senator from Texas (1948-1960), and Vice-President of the U.S. (1960-1963).

Johnson-Reed Act. An act limiting IMMIGRATION. It was also known as the Quota Act of 1924 when it was passed by Congress. It established a quota of two percent of the nationals of any country, residing in the United States in 1890. Exempted from its provisions were Canada, Mexico, and the independent nations of Latin America. By abrogating the "GENTLEMEN'S AGREEMENT" of 1907

it thereafter prohibited all immigration from Japan. The law further provided that the two percent quota should remain in force until 1927 when a "NATIONAL ORIGINS" quota should be substituted. The law was passed as a result of congressional thinking that the immigration permitted under the QUOTA ACT OF 1921 contained too many "NEW IMMIGRANTS" from southern and eastern European nations. Its objective was to encourage a greater number of "old immigrants" from the northern and western European nations such as England, Scotland, Germany, France, and the Scandinavian nations.

JOHNSON, Reverdy. 1796-1876. Jurist and Diplomat. Practiced law in Baltimore; served in state legislature (1821-29); well-known constitutional lawyer; U.S. Senator (1845-49); U.S. Attorney General (1849-50); counsel for defense in DRED SCOTT CASE; important influence in keeping Maryland in the Union during the Civil War; U.S. Senator (1863-68); supported JOHNSON'S RECONSTRUCTION PROGRAM; appointed U.S. Minister to Great Britain (1868-69) by Johnson.

JOHNSON, Richard Mentor. 1780-1850. Political leader. b. Kentucky. Admitted to the bar (1802); member, U.S. House of Representatives (1807-19; 1829-37); U.S. Senator (1819-29); supported JACKSON and was nominated on ticket with VAN BUREN as Vice-President of the United States; no candidate received a majority in the electoral college and it was thrown into the Senate; he was the only Vice-President ever to be elected that way (1837-41).

JOHNSON, Robert Underwood. 1853-1937. Poet and editor. With *Century Magazine* (1873-1913); important influence in American letters; secretary, American Copyright League securing important copyright legislation. Author of *The Winter Hour and Other Poems* (1891), and *Songs of Liberty* (1897).

JOHNSON, Samuel. 1696-1772. Clergyman and philosopher. b. Connecticut. Studied at Yale; entered Congregational ministry; changed to the Church of England (1722); started first ANGLICAN church in Connecticut at Stratford; leader of Anglican church in New England; first president, King's College (now Columbia University) (1754-1763).

Johnson's Reconstruction Plan. President JOHNSON accepted LINCOLN'S RECONSTRUCTION PLAN as the basis of his own. Following Lincoln's death he issued an amnesty to all formerly in rebellion against the United States with the exception of certain prominent former Confederate officers, statesmen, and owners of large properties. Military governors were appointed in the Carolinas, Texas, Florida, Alabama, Mississippi, and Georgia. Conventions were ordered held in these states for the framing of new constitutions, the repeal of the secession ordinances, the support of existing federal legislation, and the election of new officers. Upon the ratification of the 13TH AMENDMENT and the acceptance by Congress of these states' new senators and representatives they were to be ADMITTED INTO THE UNION. The RADICAL REPUBLICAN Congress refused to admit these southern legislators. The reasons for the bitter conflict between Johnson and Congress arose out of Johnson's alleged leniency to the South, his veto of the WADE-DAVIS, FREEDMEN'S BUREAU, and CIVIL RIGHTS ACTS, and Congress' fear that political power would be transferred to the Democratic Party, inasmuch as Johnson was a Democrat.

JOHNSON, Thomas. 1732-1819. Revolutionary leader. Lawyer, Annapolis, Maryland; member, CONTINENTAL CONGRESS; (1774-77); at the suggestion of ADAMS, he nominated WASHINGTON commander-in-chief, Continental army (1775); first governor of Maryland (1777-79); supported federal CONSTITU-TION; appointed by Washington one of the first Associate Justices of the U.S. Supreme Court (1791-93).

JOHNSON, Tom Loftin. 1854 - 1911. Politician. b. Kentucky. Owned streetrailway lines in several cities and acquired a fortune; member, U.S. House of Representatives (1891-95); mayor of Cleveland (1899-1909); follower of HENRY GEORGE; known for efficient administration and municipal reforms.

JOHNSON, Sir William. 1715-1774. British colonial administrator. b. Ireland. Settled in Mohawk Valley (about 1738); known for successful dealings with the Six Nations, Indian tribes; kept IROQUOIS loyal to English; superintendent of Indian affairs (1755-74).

JOHNSON, William Samuel. 1727-1819. Jurist and educator. Son of SAMUEL JOHNSON. Graduated, Yale (1744), Harvard (1747); practised law in Connecticut; delegate, STAMP ACT CONGRESS; judge, Connecticut supreme court (1772-74); member, CONTINENTAL CONGRESS (1784-87); U.S. Senator (1789-91); president of Columbia College (1787-1800).

JOHNSTON, Albert Sidney. 1803-1862. Confederate general. b. Kentucky. Graduated, U.S.M.A., West Point (1826); brigadier general in Texan army (1837); secretary of war, Texas (1838); resigned (1840); re-entered army, served against the MORMONS (1857); general in Confederate army (1861); defeated GRANT at SHILOH Church in surprise attack, but was killed in action (Apr. 6, 1862); considered a great loss to the Confederate cause, as he was one of the most able of their generals.

JOHNSTON, Joseph Eggleston. 1807-1891. Confederate general. b. Virginia. Graduated, U.S.M.A., West Point (1829); served through the MEXICAN WAR; brigadier general, Confederate army (1861); general (July 1861); lost to GRANT at

VICKSBURG; outmaneuvered by SHERMAN and relieved of command (1864); returned to the Army of Tennessee, but lost and had to surrender to Sherman (1865); member, U.S. House of Representatives (1879-81); appointed by CLEVELAND, U.S. Commissioner of Railroads (1887-91).

JOHNSTON, Samuel. 1733-1816. Political leader. b. Scotland. To North Carolina (1736); admitted to the bar; member, colonial assembly (1759-75); delegate to CONTINENTAL CONGRESS (1781-82); governor of North Carolina (1787-89); one of first U.S. Senators from N.C. (1789-93); judge, North Carolina superior court (1800-1803).

Johnstown Flood, The. A disastrous flood in May 1889 in Johnstown, Pennsylvania, resulting from the collapse of the Conemaugh Reservoir. As a result of heavy rains the reservoir rapidly filled, smashing its walls, and thrusting into the Conemaugh Valley just above Johnstown. The accompanying destruction from water and fire reduced Johnstown and its suburbs to a shambles. Property losses totaled $10,000,000, and identified human losses were 2,142 persons, although estimates place the human casualties at 5,000.

Joint Committee of Fifteen. The popular name of the Joint Congressional Committee on Reconstruction appointed on December 13, 1865 under the chairmanship of Senator FESSENDEN. Dominated by RADICAL REPUBLICANS it worked out a punitive reconstruction program designed to humiliate the South. By 1867 it had drafted and reported to the Congress the FOURTEENTH AMENDMENT and the RECONSTRUCTION ACTS which became the basis of CONGRESS' RECONSTRUCTION PROGRAM.

Joint Committee on the Economic Report. See Employment Act of 1946.

Joint Occupation, Treaty of. The convention of October 20, 1818 by which the United States and England agreed to jointly occupy the Oregon country. The Treaty stipulated that the nationals of the signatories could settle and trade in the area for a ten year period. In 1827 the treaty was renewed indefinitely, subject to termination on one year's notice by either party.

Joint Resolution of Congress. A resolution passed by both houses of Congress which, when signed by or passed over the President's VETO, has the full force of an act. In contrast with a CONCURRENT RESOLUTION its subject matter is legislative in nature, although generally it is concerned only with a single event. The ANNEXATIONS OF TEXAS and HAWAII were accomplished by joint resolutions.

Joint Stock Company. A non-corporate form of business organization whose capital stock is owned by private holders. From the 16th to the 18th centuries such companies were organized and chartered by European governments for the purpose of carrying on the discovery and exploration of new colonies. They were customarily granted MONOPOLY rights in these colonies with respect to political rule and economic exploitation. Among the most famous joint stock companies of the colonial era were the LONDON COMPANY, DUTCH WEST INDIA COMPANY, and British East Indies Company.

Joint Stock Land Banks. Privately owned and privately financed banks formed under the authorization of the FEDERAL FARM LOAN ACT OF 1916. Their capital stock was subscribed wholly by private individuals. These banks were authorized to obtain capital by issuing bonds secured by the mortgages held against farm land. They made loans on the collateral of such land. See Federal Land Banks.

JOLIET, Louis. French explorer and discoverer of the Mississippi River. b. Canada. On expedition to find copper in Lake Superior region he met MARQUETTE at Sault Ste. Marie; sent on an expedition by Canadian authorities to find great river mentioned by Indians; he sighted the Mississippi (June 17, 1673); made other explorations in the Gulf of St. Lawrence and Hudson Bay region.

Jones Act. Passed by Congress in 1916. The law provided a civil government for the PHILIPPINE ISLANDS. It conferred Philippine CITIZENSHIP upon all inhabitants in the Islands on April 11, 1899 and their descendents, and granted the franchise to all literate male citizens over 21 years of age. It established an elective BICAMERAL LEGISLATURE consisting of a Senate and House of Representatives to replace the Philippine Commission. The justices of the insular Supreme Court were to be appointed by the President of the United States.

Jones Act. Also known as The Organic Act of PUERTO RICO. Passed by Congress in 1917. It conferred American CITIZENSHIP upon Puerto Ricans and established an elective upper house called the Senate. To the President of the United States was reserved the power to VETO bills of the legislature and to appoint the governor, the auditor, island judges, the attorney-general, and the commissioner of education. The other six administrative chiefs were to be appointed by the governor with the advice and consent of the upper house. This law did not satisfy the aspirations of Puerto Rican nationalists who continued to agitate for a greater measure of autonomy. The result was the passage in 1947 of another Organic Act dealing with the governmental organization of the island. See Foraker Act and Organic Act of Puerto Rico.

Jones Act. Also known as the Merchant Marine Act of 1920. Passed by Congress as the first of a series of laws designed to liquidate the government-owned merchant fleet constructed during World War I. It provided heavy mail subsidies to private shipping companies, authorized the UNITED STATES SHIPPING BOARD to dispose of its merchant fleet to such companies, permitted preferential TARIFFS on goods transported in American ships, and limited trade with American colonies to American ships. The terms by which the Board disposed of its holdings were unusually liberal, in some instances the ships being purchased by private operators at one-tenth their value.

Jones-Connally Act. Passed by Congress in 1934. It was an amendment to the AGRICULTURAL ADJUSTMENT ACT of 1933, and provided for benefit payments under that Act to cattle ranchers and to the growers of peanuts, rye, barley, and flax.

Jones-Costigan Act. An amendment to the AGRICULTURAL ADJUSTMENT ACT of 1933. It was enacted in 1934, and provided for benefit payments, under the terms of the original statute, to growers of sugar cane and sugar beets.

Jones, George Wallace. 1804 - 1896. Statesman. Lived in Michigan territory; delegate to Congress from the territory; secured organization of Wisconsin Territory (1836); one of first U.S. Senators from Iowa (1848-1858); U.S. Minister to Colombia (1859-61); opposed the Civil War.

JONES, James Kimbrough. 1839-1908. Politician. b. Mississippi. Served in Arkansas state senate (1873-79); member, U.S. House of Representatives (1881-85); U.S. Senator (1885-1903); prominent in TARIFF reform legislation; chairman, Democratic National Committee (1896-1900).

JONES, Jesse Holman. 1874-1956. Political leader. b. Tennessee. Moved to Texas; extremely successful business man and political leader in Texas; appointed by HOOVER, Chairman of the Board, RECONSTRUCTION FINANCE CORPORATION, and retained by F. D. ROOSEVELT (after 1933); administrator, FEDERAL LOAN AGENCY (1939); at one time he was head of 12 federal agencies including Secretary of Commerce, RFC, EXPORT-IMPORT BANK and the RUBBER RESERVE CORPORATION; left government service (1945) and broke with TRUMAN.

JONES, John Paul. 1747 - 1792. Naval officer. b. Scotland. Settled in Fredericksburg, Va. (about 1773); entered American navy at outbreak of the Revolution; lieutenant (1775); captain (1776); commanded *Ranger* in waters around British Isles (1778); commanded flagship *Bonhomme Richard* which defeated the superior British ship *Serapis* (Sept. 1779); was an admiral in the Russian navy (1788-1790); famous for words "I'VE NOT YET BEGUN TO FIGHT"; buried in crypt of U.S. Naval Academy chapel, Annapolis, Md. (1913).

JONES, Samuel Milton. 1846-1904. Industrialist and political reformer. b. Wales. Worked in oil fields of Pennsylvania and Ohio; owned MANUFACTURING plant, Toledo, Ohio; known for modern treatment of employees using a system based on the Golden Rule; mayor of Toledo (1897-1904); noted for program of municipal reform and called "Golden Rule Jones."

JONES, Wesley Livsey. 1863-1932. Lawyer and political leader. b. Illinois; practiced law in Washington; member, U.S. House of Representatives (1899-1909); U.S. Senator (1909-32); supported strong merchant marine; Republican whip in the Senate during HOOVER administration; author and sponsor of JONES ACT which provided for severe penalties for violators of VOLSTEAD ACT.

Jones-White Act. Also known as the Merchant Marine Act of 1928. One of a series of laws passed by Congress to liquidate the merchant fleet built during World War I. It authorized the sale of government-owned vessels not yet disposed of under the JONES ACT OF 1920, increased mail subsidies, and appropriated $250,000,000 for loans for construction purposes. As a result of the law private companies secured vessels in perfect condition at about ten percent of their original cost, and were enabled to build 68 new vessels. The reduction of international trade arising out of the world depression shortly thereafter rendered it difficult to determine whether Congress' liberal terms would have stimulated the growth of the American merchant marine, as designed by the statute.

JORDAN, David Starr. 1851-1931. Biologist and educator. b. New York. Graduated, Cornell (M.S. 1872); Indiana Medical College (1875); head of department of natural science, Indiana University; president of Indiana University (1885-91); president (1891-1913) and chancellor (1913-16) of Stanford University, largely responsible for making it one of the outstanding universities in the country. Author of many books on ichthyology and science.

Journalism. See newspapers.

"Journey for Peace". In February 1972 President Nixon visited mainland China and met with Chairman Mao Tse-tung and Premier Chou En-lai. The main topic under consideration was the normalization of relations between the two major powers. In May of the same year President Nixon journied to Moscow to confer with Communist party general secretary Leoneid Brezhnev. President Nixon described these trips as a "Journey for Peace."

Judicial Powers. The powers of the courts to interpret the laws and constitutions, define the powers of the branches

336

of government, distinguish between the powers of the national government and those of the states, maintain private rights against illegal public encroachment, and void legislative acts. These powers arise either out of constitutional grant or judicial interpretation in the hearing of cases and controversies and in the rendering of decisions.

Judicial Review. Term popularly applied to the power of the Supreme Court to review the CONSTITUTIONALITY of the acts of Congress and the states. The power to review federal legislation is not specifically conferred upon the court but was assumed by it in the case of MARBURY VS. MADISON, 1803. The brilliant exposition of Chief Justice JOHN MARSHALL of the Court, in this decision, has laid the groundwork for what has since been wholly accepted in American political and judicial thinking as a proper power of the court.

Judiciary. See Courts, Federal and Courts, State.

Judiciary Act. Passed by Congress in 1789. It created the office of Attorney-General, established the Supreme Court as provided in Article III of the federal Constitution, and created a series of federal circuit and district courts. The Supreme Court was to be staffed by a chief justice and five associate justices. The Act gave to the federal courts the power of the JUDICIAL REVIEW over the decisions of state courts with respect to the constitutionality of state or federal legislation. Although not specifically conferred upon the Supreme Court the power of judicial review over acts of Congress was assumed by it in 1803 in the case of MARBURY VS. MADISON on the basis of Section 13 of the law.

Judiciary, Federal. See courts, federal.

JULIAN, George Washington. 1817-1899. Political leader. Prominent WHIG in Indiana legislature (1845-49); member, U.S. House of Representatives (1849-52, 1861-71); prominent Republican; chairman of committee on public lands; became Democrat and was appointed by CLEVELAND surveyor-general of public lands, New Mexico (1885-89).

Justice, Department of. An executive department established by Congress in 1870. The Attorney-General is the head of the department although that office was created by Congress in 1789 and became a cabinet position in 1814. The FEDERAL BUREAU OF INVESTIGATION and the Bureau of Prisons are located within the Department. See Attorney-General, U.S.

K

KAHN, Julius. 1861-1924. Legislator. b. Germany. To California when a child; practised law in San Francisco (from 1894); member, U.S. House of Representatives (1899-1903; 1905-24) known as strong supporter of military and naval preparedness.

KAHN, Otto Hermann. 1867-1934. Banker and patron of the arts. b. Germany of naturalized American parents; came to the United States (1893); member, banking firm of Kuhn, Loeb & Co., New York (from 1897); associated with HARRIMAN in reorganization of the Union Pacific and other RAILROADS; president and chairman of the board, Metropolitan Opera Company, New York (to 1931); helped support the Theatre Guild and Civic Repertory organizations.

KAISER HENRY J. 1882-1967. Industrialist b. New York. Worked in highway construction in British Columbia, Washington, and California (1914-29); chairman of executive committee of companies building the BOULDER and Parker dams (1933); president of companies contracting for piers for Oakland-San Francisco Bay Bridge (1933), BONNEVILLE DAM (1934), GRAND COULEE DAM (1939); interested in shipbuilding, and produced Liberty ships for the navy in record time during World War II; awarded contract to construct giant cargo planes for the government (1942); an owner of an automobile company in Willow Run, Michigan.

KALB, Johann, Known as Baron de Kalb. 1721-1780. Revolutionary general. b. Germany. French observer on secret mission to America (1768); persuaded by SILAS DEANE to enter the services of the Continental army he was commissioned a major general (1777); took part in Philadelphia campaign, served with WASHINGTON at VALLEY FORGE; mortally wounded at Camden (Aug. 16, 1780).

Kanagawa, Treaty of. An agreement between the United States and Japan. It was negotiated in 1854 as a result of the successful accomplishment of Commodore MATTHEW C. PERRY's mission to Japan in 1853. The Treaty provided for the establishment by the United States of a consulate in Japan. It further permitted American vessels to visit specified Japanese ports for supplies and trade. It is this Treaty which is frequently referred to as the "opening of Japan."

Kansas. The 14th state in size, with an area of 82,276 square miles. Organized as a territory in 1854 and admitted as the 34th state on January 29, 1861. Topeka is the capital. In 1950 Kansas' population of 1,905,299 made it 31st in rank. Its largest cities are Wichita, Kansas City, and Topeka. Kansas' most important economic enterprises are wheat growing and flour milling. Slaughtering and meat packing are also notable activities. Agricultural crops include corn, oats, potatoes,

338

barley, and soy beans. Important minerals are oil, zinc, salt, lead, and coal. Kansas is the geographical center of the United States and the geodetic center of North America. It is the area from which official longitudes and latitudes are measured. Important manufactured goods include aircraft, cement, and natural gas. The state was discovered in 1541 by Coronado. Its nicknames are the "Sunflower State" and "Jayhawker State."

Kansas-Nebraska Act. Enacted in 1854 following its introduction and vigorous support by Senator STEPHEN A. DOUGLAS of Illinois. The statute provided that Kansas and Nebraska be organized as territories on the basis of POPULAR SOVEREIGNTY. The result was to open Kansas to organized migrations of pro-slave and anti-slave groups which within the next five years were to wrack the territories in a bloody civil war, each group seeking to prepare a territorial constitution based on its slave or anti-slave philosophy. The territory became known as "BLEEDING KANSAS" in this period.

KEARNEY, Dennis. 1847-1907. Labor and political leader. b. Ireland. Lived in San Francisco (from about 1868); became a naturalized citizen (1876); led workers in protest against UNEMPLOYMENT, unjust taxes and bitterly fought the employment of Chinese labor; organized the WORKINGMAN'S PARTY of California (also called the sand-lot party because he addressed meetings in the sand-lots of San Francisco).

KEARNY, Stephen Watts. 1794-1848. Army officer. Served in War of 1812; brigadier general in Mexican War; conquered New Mexico; defeated at San Pascual; with STOCKTON captured Los Angeles; arrested FREMONT, after quarrel with Stockton; military governor of California territory; governor in Mexico (1848); brevetted major general.

Keating-Owen Act. Also known as the First Child Labor Law. Passed by Congress in 1916 as its initial attempt to regulate child labor. It forbade the shipment in INTERSTATE COMMERCE of the products of factories, shops, or canneries employing children under 14 years of age, of mines employing children under 16 years of age, and the products of any of these employing children under 16 years who worked at night or more than eight hours a day. The law was declared unconstitutional two years later in the case of HAMMER VS. DAGENHART.

KEEN, William Williams. 1837-1932. Surgeon. b. Philadelphia, Pa. Graduated, Brown (1859), Jefferson Medical College (M.D. 1862); served during the Civil War as a surgeon in the U.S. Army, and wrote standard work on nerve injuries; first American president of the International Congress of Surgery, receiving many honors; successfully removed a cancer from President CLEVELAND'S mouth (1893).

Kefauver Investigation. An inquiry into organized crime in INTERSTATE COMMERCE by the Senate Crime Committee. The five man committee was established on May 10, 1950 under the chairmanship of Senator Estes Kefauver to investigate illegal operations, the influence of crime on political leaders, the use of criminal funds for business investments, and the bribery of police by criminal elements. Former assistant district attorney of New York, Rudolph Halley, was named chairman of counsel. The first part of the Committee's work was ended April 30, 1951, at which time Senator Kefauver was replaced by Senator Herbert R. O'Conor of Maryland. By February 28, 1951 the committee had interviewed 500 witnesses in New York, Chicago, Kansas City, Philadelphia, Los Angeles, and other large cities. These witnesses included public officers, political leaders, racketeers, and gamblers. In its first report the Committee declared that gambling involved over $20,000,-

000,000 annually. It recommended the establishment of a national crime commission, a federal ban on interstate transmission of bets and gambling information, a strengthening of federal law enforcement, and an improvement in federal tax laws to reach concealed profits from illegal deals. The Committee highlighted the work of national crime syndicates whose control over state and local politics rendered them immune from prosecution. It charged that crime had infiltrated into such legal businesses as real estate, restaurants, laundries, hotels, and nightclubs. In its final report on August 31, 1951 the Committee declared that conditions in the smaller cities were similar to those in large cities, and recommended attacking crime at the local level. It suggested a congressional appropriation of $100,000 to the private National Crime Coordinating Council to aid its work. It also recommended the continuance of crime investigation by other Senate committees and a widespread program of education, increased appropriations for inquiries, stricter enforcement of existing legislation, coordination of the work of private and public crime agencies, and the prohibition of political contributions by racketeers.

KELLER, Helen Adams. 1880-1962. Author and lecturer. Blind and deaf from childhood she learned to speak; became well-known author and lecturer on aid to the blind.

KELLEY, Florence. 1859-1932. Social worker. One of the first women students at Cornell University; studied law at Northwestern University; first woman chief factory inspector of Illinois (1893-97); executive secretary of National Consumer's League for 32 years; responsible for much labor legislation benefiting women and children; worked at Hull House, Chicago (1891-99) and Henry Street Settlement, New York (1899-1924).

KELLEY, Hall Jackson. 1790-1874. Publicist. b. New Hampshire. Teacher in Boston public schools; published many works on the subject of the importance of the colonization of the Oregon territory and was largely responsible for the successful settlement of that area.

KELLEY, Oliver Hudson. 1826-1913 Grange organizer. b. Boston, Mass. Farmer in Minnesota (1849-1864); worked in U.S. Bureau of Agriculture; one of original organizers of the National Grange of the PATRONS OF HUSBANDRY (1867) which was the basis of the GRANGER MOVEMENT.

KELLEY, William Darrah. 1814-1890. Legislator. b. Philadelphia, Pennsylvania. Practised law; prominent Republican member, U.S. House of Representatives; served on House WAYS AND MEANS COMMITTEE for 20 years and is responsible for a great deal of the high PROTECTIVE TARIFF legislation of that period.

Kellogg-Briand Pact. Also known as Pact of Paris and Pact of Peace. A series of treaties reciprocally negotiated by 15 states in 1928 in which the signatory nations agreed to renounce war as an instrument of national policy. Its significance lies in its pioneer effort to secure an international affirmation of the renunciation of war despite its material failures in preventing subsequent outbreaks of hostilities. The idea of the pact was first broached to Secretary of State FRANK B. KELLOGG by the French foreign minister Aristide Briand as a bi-lateral agreement. Upon the suggestion of Kellogg the treaty was expanded to include the other 13 nations. Subsequently, most of the nations of the world adhered to the Pact, some with reservations.

KELLOGG, Frank Billings. 1856-1937. Statesman. b. New York. Moved to Minnesota (1865); studied law and was admitted to the bar (1877); became prominent lawyer acting as special counsel for the government in the paper and STAND-

ARD OIL trust cases; U.S. Senator (1917-23); appointed U.S. Ambassador to Great Britain (1924-25) by COOLIDGE; U.S. Secretary of State (1925-29); with Briand he negotiated the KELLOGG-BRIAND pact outlawing war (1928); winner of the Nobel Peace Prize (1929); judge, PERMANENT COURT OF INTERNATIONAL JUSTICE, (WORLD COURT) (from 1930).

KELLY, John. 1822-1886. Politician. b. New York City. Member, U.S. House of Representatives (1855-58); sheriff, city and county of New York (1859-62; 1865-67); leader of TAMMANY HALL; comptroller of New York (1876-79).

KELLY, William. 1811-1888. Inventor. b. Pittsburgh, Pa. Inventor of the basic principle of the converter for the making of steel (Bessemer process) using an air blast on molten iron and the natural carbon content of molten cast iron to get greater heat; patent issued (1857).

KENDALL, Amos. 1789-1869. Politician. b. Massachusetts. Practised law in Kentucky; supporter and friend of JACKSON; important member of the "KITCHEN CABINET" and Jackson's chief adviser in the Bank of the United States controversy; U.S. Postmaster General (1835-40).

KENDALL, George Wilkins. 1809-1867. Journalist. b. New Hampshire. Founder and editor, New Orleans *Picayune* (1837); covered the Mexican War for his paper, and is considered the first of the modern war correspondents.

Kennebec Expedition. A military move during the American Revolution aimed at the invasion of Canada. In 1775 WASHINGTON dispatched 1100 men under the command of BENEDICT ARNOLD to assist General MONTGOMERY in this invasion. Arnold proceeded along the Kennebec River toward Quebec, whose garrison refused to surrender at his demand. He withdrew, and sent BURR to join Montgomery after the latter's capture of

Montreal. Montgomery then joined Arnold at Quebec, their joint forces laying siege to the city for three months until its defenders were relieved by reinforcements under BURGOYNE.

KENNEDY, John Fitzgerald. 1917-1963. President of the United States, 1961-1963, b. Massachusetts. U.S. Senator from Massachusetts (1953-1961). U.S. Representative from Massachusetts (1947-1953). Served in USN (1941-1945). Author of WHILE ENGLAND SLEPT (1940); PROFILES IN COURAGE (1956); STRATEGY OF PEACE (1960); and TO TURN THE TIDE (1961). Assassinated in Dallas, Texas (November 22, 1963).

KENNEDY, Robert F. (Assassination). Senator Robert F. Kennedy was a potential presidential candidate in 1968. He strongly opposed President Johnson's Viet Nam policy. In June 1968 Kennedy defeated McCarthy in the California primary and at a victory celebration he was assassinated. Sirhan Sirhan, an Arab nationalist, was accused of his murder and imprisoned after a trial. Following the assassination Congress passed the Gun Control Bill which limited the sale of arms.

KENNER, Duncan Farrar. 1813-1887. Politican and Confederate agent. b. New Orleans. Member, Confederate House of Representatives; sent by JUDAH BENJAMIN and President DAVIS on mission to England and France to offer emancipation of the slaves in exchange for recognition of the Confederacy, but cause was hopeless; appointed by ARTHUR U.S. Tariff Commissioner.

KENT, James. 1763-1847. Jurist. b. New York. Graduated, Yale (1781); admitted to the bar (1785); professor of law at Columbia (1793-98; 1823-26); judge, New York supreme court (from 1798); chancellor, New York court of chancery (from 1814); retired (1823). Author of *Commentaries on American Law* (4 vols. 1826-30).

KENTON, Simon. 1755-1836. Frontiersman and Indian fighter. b. Virginia. Associated with DANIEL BOONE at Boonesborough settlement and during an Indian attack saved his life; brigadier general of militia (1805); served through War of 1812.

Kent State. On May 4, 1970, National Guardsman attempting to quiet a protest against the U.S. moving into Cambodia shot and killed four students at Kent State College (Ohio). Students throughout the nation protested and this protest resulted in the first general student strike forcing over 400 colleges to suspend classes. A commission appointed by President Nixon and headed by William Scranton found that the shootings at Kent State were unwarranted.

Kentucky. The 37th state in size, with an area of 40,395 square miles. Entered the Union June 1, 1792 as the 15th state. Frankfort is the capital. In 1950 Kentucky's population of 2,944,806 made it 19th in rank. Its largest cities are Louisville, Covington, and Lexington. Kentucky's manufactured products include furniture, household wares, lumber, machinery, textiles, iron, and steel. Minerals include coal, oil, quarry products, and natural gas. Tobacco and liquor are the state's two most important market commodities. Louisville is the home of the Kentucky Derby and a large producer of cigarettes. Mammoth Cave, with many miles of underground passages, is a famous tourist attraction. Although the state remained in the Union at the outbreak of the Civil War, a secessionist group in the southwestern part set up a government that was subsequently suppressed by the loyal government. Kentucky was discovered in 1673 by MARQUETTE and JOLIET. Its nickname is the "Blue Grass State."

KERN, John Worth. 1849-1917. Lawyer and politician. Graduated, University of Michigan Law School (1869); served in state legislature (1893-97); Democratic floor leader of the U.S. Senate (1914); strong supporter of WILSON.

Kerr Natural Gas Bill. See Gas Industry.

KEY, Francis Scott. 1779-1843. Lawyer, wrote the *Star-Spangled Banner.* b. Maryland. Practiced law; U.S. Attorney for the DISTRICT OF COLUMBIA (1833-41); on a ship watching the bombardment of Fort McHenry by the British he sighted the American flag still flying over the fort and wrote the poem *The Star-Spangled Banner* on the back of an envelope; he went back to his law practice and wrote no other poetry of note.

Kickapoo Indians. Originally settled in Wisconsin but driven into what is now Illinois and Indiana by the advance of the white man. They fought with TECUMSEH against the Americans and sided with the British in the War of 1812. They gave their lands to the United States in the Treaty of Edwardsville in 1819. Some of the tribe settled in Missouri and Kansas, the rest moving down into Mexico. They were responsible for many raids in Texas. The Kickapoos never were anxious to be friendly with the encroaching whites and finally, after much difficulty, settled in INDIAN TERRITORY.

King Committee. See tax frauds.

King Cotton. The nickname applied to the COTTON INDUSTRY of the South which became the nation's most important export after the War of 1812. The steady growth of SLAVERY and the acquisition of new territories developed the cotton interests of the South by 1850 to the point of complete dominance of the southern economy. In that year the cotton crop was valued at more than $100,-000,000 annually and represented almost 50 percent of the exports of the United

States as compared with nine percent in manufactured goods and seven percent in beef, pork, and flour.

King George's War. The American name for the War of the Austrian Succession. It was fought in North America between 1744 and 1748 as part of the Anglo-French colonial and dynastic rivalry frequently referred to as the Second hundred years' war. In America the immediate cause were the conflict over the boundary of Acadia and Northern New England, and the struggle over the Ohio Valley. Seven of the English colonies mobilized troops to assist England after the British conquest of Louisburg in 1745. Two French fleets, dispatched to reconquer Louisburg, were destroyed in 1746 and 1747. On the frontier bloody attacks by the colonists and their respective Indian allies characterized the fighting. The Treaty of Aix-la-Chapelle, in October, 1748, ended the war without

KING, Martin Luther, Jr. (1929-1968). He was a clergyman born in Georgia and received a good deal of notice for his work for Civil Rights for Negroes by non-violent means. In 1964 he was awarded the Nobel Prize for Peace. King led the boycott in 1955-1956 which forced desegration of Montgomery, Alabama city bus lines. On April 4, 1968 during a visit to Memphis, Tennessee where he had come to lead a march on behalf of striking sanitation workers King was shot and killed. His death touched off a period of rioting and looting in many cities but also affected the conscience of both the white and black communities of America. A period of national mourning was declared.

King Philip's War. An Indian war in New England in 1675-1676. The organization of an Indian confederacy under Philip, MASSASOIT's son, brought the WAMPANOAG, Nipmuck, NARRAGANSETT, and other tribes into the struggle against the colonists who had been moving inward

from the coast. The struggle spread to Connecticut and Rhode Island, marked by bloody fighting and large casualties on both sides. In May, 1676, 120 Indians were killed on the Connecticut River, after Canonchet, the Narragansett king, had been slain. On August 12, 1676 Philip himself was killed by Colonel Church. His death marked the end of the war, although fighting continued in New Hampshire and Maine where the Abnakis were reinforced with French arms. Articles of Peace were signed at Casco on April 12, 1678, providing for the reciprocal exchange of captives and property. In the two years' fighting twenty towns in Massachusetts and Rhode Island had been destroyed and hundreds of Indians and white men slain.

KING, Rufus. 1755-1827. Political leader and diplomat. b. Maine. Practised law in Massachusetts; member, CONTINENTAL CONGRESS (1784-87); delegate to federal CONSTITUTIONAL CONVENTION (1787); helped win RATIFICATION OF CONSTITUTION at Massachusetts convention (1788); moved to New York City (1788) and chosen one of the state's first U.S. Senators (1789-96; 1813-25); appointed by WASHINGTON U.S. Minister to Great Britain (1796-1803); defeated candidate for Vice-President of the United States (1804 and 1808) and for President (1816); appointed by ADAMS U.S. Minister to Great Britain (1825-26). King was one of the ablest diplomats of his time.

King's College. See Columbia University.

King, William Rufus De Vane. 1786-1853. Politician. b. North Carolina. Graduated, University of North Carolina (1803); admitted to the bar (1806); moved to Alabama (1818); U.S. Senator (1819-44; 1848-53); appointed by TYLER U.S. Minister to France (1844-46); Vice-President of the United States (1853).

King William's War. A dynastic and co-

343

lonial war between England and France which set off more than a century of conflict known as the second hundred years' war. In America it broke out in 1689, after the French incited an Indian attack on an English post in retaliation for an attack instigated by the English. In 1690 Governor Frontenac of Canada sent three Indian expeditions against Schenectady, Salmo Falls, and Fort Loyal. In reply to these border battles, Sir William Phipps was sent with a fleet and 1,800 men against Acadia and Port Royal, both of which he captured in 1691. In 1696 Frontenac took Newfoundland. With the lack of support of the colonies by their respective mother countries the bloody warfare finally came to an end by the Treaty of Ryswick in 1697. The peace did not, however, resolve any of the colonial problems.

Kiowa Indians. Great Plains Indians who had started in Minnesota and worked their way south. They were skillful horsemen and great warriors. They were, however, driven out of the Black Hills by the SIOUX. They had trouble with the Texans in the panhandle when they moved farther south. In 1854 the Kiowas joined the COMANCHE, APACHE, and CHEYENNE tribes in the INDIAN TERRITORY. They were troublesome during the Revolution and continued giving trouble to the American troops in Texas in 1874-75.

KIRKWOOD, Samuel Jordan. 1813-1894. Lawyer and politician. b. Maryland. Moved to Ohio (1835) and was a member of Ohio constitutional convention (1850); moved to Iowa (1855); governor of Iowa (1860-64; 1876-77); U.S. Senator (1866-67; 1877-81); appointed by GARFIELD, U.S. Secretary of the Interior (1881-82).

KISSINGER, Henry Alfred. born May 27, 1923- Henry A. Kissinger—he changed his first name to Henry after coming to the U.S.—was born in the Bavarian City of Furth. His family migrated to the United States in 1938 after suffering severe discrimination when Hitler came to power. In 1943 Kissinger was drafted into the Army of the United States and became a naturalized American citizen. In September 1946 he entered Harvard College under a New York State scholarship and earned a B.A. degree in 1950. He achieved his M.A. degree from Harvard in 1952 and his Ph.D. in 1954. He taught at Harvard and also served as director of Harvard's Defense Studies Program. He was a consultant to the State Department from 1965-1969. In 1969, he assumed the post of Assistant to the President for National Security Affairs under the Nixon Administration and served as Secretary of State under both President Nixon and President Ford. He is the author of many books and numerous articles for popular as well as scholarly publications.

"Kitchen Cabinet." Refers to the coterie of advisers to President ANDREW JACKSON who met with him unofficially in the kitchen of the WHITE HOUSE for the discussion of public affairs. They were not members of the official cabinet and were criticized for their extra-legal counsel to the President. Most of them were newspaper editors referred to in derision by Jackson's enemies as the "TYPOGRAPHICAL CROWD." Included among these men were Major William B. Lewis, who lived with Jackson in the White House, AMOS KENDALL, and FRANCIS B. BLAIR, the editor of the Washington *Globe*.

Kitty Hawk Riot. In 1972 there erupted rioting between blacks and whites aboard the U.S. aircraft carrier Kitty Hawk while the carrier's plane was attacking North Viet Namese targets. There was a Congressional inquiry to determine the cause of the tension between whites and blacks. The navy contended that young black men were not assigned to skilled duties because their education was inferior but black sailors claimed that there was definite prejudice against them because of their race.

Klamath Indians. This Indian tribe lives on the lake and the upper headwaters of the Klamath River in southern Oregon. They are an agricultural, fishing, and hunting people who have been generally friendly and unwarlike.

Klondike Gold Rush. The migration of more than 100,000 persons in 1897-99 to the Klondike River in ALASKA, following the discovery of gold there on August 16, 1896. News of this discovery reached the United States in January 1897, and in July two steamships arrived in San Francisco with a total of $1,550,000 in gold from the Klondike. This information electrified the country and the Rush began. It had extraordinary economic consequences for Alaska, bringing in settlers who ultimately spread out into other pursuits such as lumbering, farming, hunting, and MANUFACTURING.

KNAPP, Seaman Asahel. 1833-1911 Agricultural leader. b. New York. President, Iowa State College; organized farm experimentation in Louisiana; developed the RICE INDUSTRY; known for scientific methods for fighting the boll weevil.

Knights of the Golden Circle. A secret political organization established in 1855 to support the pro-slavery and expansionist policies of the South. One of its principal objectives was the conquest of Mexico, quickly giving way during the Civil War to a program of opposition to LINCOLN'S war policy. Its members included Peace Democrats and "COPPERHEADS" who committed minor acts of violence. It was reorganized in 1863 as the ORDER OF AMERICAN KNIGHTS, and in 1864 became known as the SONS OF LIBERTY.

Knights of Labor. The second and, up to that time, the most important national

LABOR ORGANIZATION. Organized in 1869 by Uriah S. Stephens, it consisted of local unions and trade assemblies in most industries. Organized as a vertical or INDUSTRIAL UNION it contained in its membership unskilled as well as skilled workers, FARMERS, housewives, and small businessmen. The Knights specifically excluded from membership such occupations as lawyers, bankers, saloon-keepers, gamblers, and stock brokers. The organization adopted a program of education, cooperatives, and economic activities such as striking and picketing. At its height in the early 1880's it attained a membership of over 700,000, but quickly declined thereafter. Among the reasons for its ultimate disintegration were the failures of two railroad strikes, the conflicting objectives of its mixed membership, and the public feeling aroused by the HAYMARKET AFFAIR which was attributed, unjustly, to the Knights. Its greatest leader was TERENCE V. POWDERLY.

Know-Nothing Party. Organized as the American Party in the 1850's. It constituted one of the earliest THIRD PARTY MOVEMENTS in American politics. The name derives from the fact that upon questioning as to their motives, purpose, and program, the members would reply "I know nothing." The organization was fanatically patriotic in its program, being particularly opposed to Roman CATHOLICS. For a time, following the large migration of the Irish into the United States in the 1850's, the animus of the movement was directed against Irish-Americans. Its candidate in the election of 1856 was MILLARD FILLMORE who carried only the state of Maryland. It quickly disintegrated after this election. They were also referred to as "Native Americans."

KNOX, Henry. 1750-1806. Revolutionary general. b. Boston, Massachusetts. Served at BUNKER HILL; friend and adviser to WASHINGTON; in charge of artillery for the army; brigadier general (1776); served in many big battles; major general (1781); commanded at West Point (1782-84); founded the SOCIETY OF THE CINCINNATI (1783); U.S. Secretary of War (1785-94).

KNOX, Philander Chase. 1853-1921. Political leader. b. Pennsylvania. Successful corporation lawyer, Pittsburgh (from 1875); appointed by MCKINLEY and ROOSEVELT, U.S. Attorney General(1901-04); responsible for legislation creating the U.S. DEPARTMENT OF COMMERCE AND LABOR (1903); U.S. Senator (1904-09); U.S. Secretary of State appointed by TAFT (1909-13); protecting financial interests abroad he initiated what is often referred to as "DOLLAR DIPLOMACY," U.S. Senator (1917-21) strong opponent of TREATY OF VERSAILLES and the LEAGUE OF NATIONS.

Knox vs. Lee. See Legal Tender Cases.

KNUDSEN, William. 1879-1948. Industrialist. b. Denmark. Came to the United States (1899); rose from mechanic to president of the General Motors Corporation (1937); member, National Defense Commission (1940); co-director (with Sidney Hillman), OFFICE OF PRODUCTION MANAGEMENT (1941); director of production for the WAR DEPARTMENT with rank of lieutenant general (1942-45); retired.

KOHLER, Kaufmann. 1843-1926. Rabbi and educator. b. Germany. Came to the United States (1869); Rabbi, New York City (1879-1903); president Hebrew Union College, Cincinnati (1903-21); one of the editors of the *Jewish Encyclopedia;* prominent leader of reformed Judaism in America.

Korean influence peddling. On July 20, 1977 Leon A. Jaworski was placed in charge of the Congressional committee which had been investigating the alleged implication of at least 115 Congressmen in the acceptance of South Korean favors from Korean businessman Park Tong Sun who acted as KCIA agent to obtain more military aid for Korea in exchange for his becoming exclusive agent for sale of U.S. rice in Korea. On August 23, 1977 Park Tong Sun was indicted by a federal grand jury. Former Representative Mark Hanna of California was named as an unindicted co-conspirator. South Korea eventually agreed in early 1978 that Park Tong Sun could appear before a special Congressional hearing to answer questions but with immunity to prosecution.

Korean War. At the Cairo Conference ROOSEVELT, Churchill, and Chiang Kai Shek declared that Korea should be "free and independent." At the POTSDAM CONFERENCE the 38th parallel was designated as the dividing line between the Soviet and American occupations of Korea. In August, 1945 Soviet and United States troops entered Korea. In December, 1945 Secretary of State JAMES F. BYRNES, Foreign Minister Ernest Bevan, and Foreign Minister V. M. Molotov agreed to a five year TRUSTEESHIP over Korea to be administered by the three powers. On May 10, 1948 the Republic of Korea was established below the 38th parallel nine days after the organization in North Korea of the People's Democratic Republic of Korea. The inability of the major powers to reconcile their political conflicts, the "COLD WAR," the division of Korea, and the internal political struggle within Korea formed the background of the war which began when the North Korean Army crossed the 38th parallel on June 25, 1950. The same day President TRUMAN ordered General MAC ARTHUR to come to the aid of South Korea and the SECURITY COUNCIL ordered resistance to the invasion. On July 7 President Truman named MacArthur as the UNITED NATIONS commander-in-chief. The United States 7th Fleet was ordered to FORMOSA to prevent an attack on or from it. The first three months of the fighting witnessed a steady UN retreat into South Korea until its forces held, in September, behind the Naktong River. The diversionary action which resulted in the capture of Inchon on September 14-15 led to a counter-offensive which brought the UN Army within sight of the Manchurian border at the Yalu River. On November 24th General MacArthur opened a major offensive with 100,000 troops. On November 26th a Chinese force, estimated at 200,000, crossed the Yalu River. By January 1, 1951 the combined Chinese-North Korean Army had reached the 38th parallel once more. Here, fighting within 70 miles north and south of the parallel continued at a stalemate for the next six months. Attempts at negotiating an end to the war began in January, 1951 with the demand by the Chinese Communists for a seat in the United Nations. In the ensuing months charges and counter-charges were made by the belligerents and on February 1, 1951 the General Assembly voted Communist China an aggressor. The months of bickering, accusations, and interruptions finally ·culminated in the opening of ARM-ISTICE negotiations on July 10th in which Admiral Charles T. Joy was named the UN negotiator and General Nam Il the North Korean negotiator. For the next year limited ground and air action went on as the negotiations proceeded with bitter accusations made by the negotiators against each other. An Armistice was finally signed in July, 1953. United States casualties totalled 137,051 while those of Korea were estimated as high as 1,312,836. Of these totals the U. S. dead and missing were reported to be 33,559 and Korea, 875,000.

KOSCIUSKO, Thaddeus. 1746-1817. Polish hero. b. Lithuania. Graduated, Royal College, Warsaw (1769); studied engineering and military tactics in France;

served with American army during the Revolution; appointed colonel of engineers (1776); supervised the construction of West Point fortifications (1778-80); brigadier general (1783) one of founders of SOCIETY OF THE CINCINNATI; led rebellion and became dictator of Poland; visited America again (1797-98).

KOUSSEVITZKY, Sergei Alexandrovitch. 1874-1950. Orchestra conductor. b. Russia. Conductor of BOSTON SYMPHONY ORCHESTRA (from 1924); organized the Berkshire Music Center and the symphonic festivals held there every summer since 1934; important influence on American musical interpretation and composers.

Ku Klux Klan. Also know by its abbreviation, K.K.K. A terrorist organization of southerners, organized during the Reconstruction period after the Civil War for the purpose of preventing the enjoyment of the CIVIL RIGHTS guaranteed to the ex-slaves in federal legislation and the Constitution. Typical terrorist practices consisted of LYNCHING, arson, and assaults upon NEGROES. Federal legislation provided protection in the early 1870's and the movement declined. It was revived after World War I as an anti-Catholic and anti-Semitic as well as anti-Negro organization. The movement was characterized by the donning of white cloaks and masks, secret meetings, the unusual titles of its officers (Grand Kleagle, etc.) and the burning of crosses.

Ku Klux Klan Act. Passed by Congress in 1871. The Act was part of a series of laws, including the FORCE ACTS OF 1870, designed to protect the rights of FREEDMEN during the Reconstruction period. It authorized the President to suppress disturbances by military force and to suspend the right of HABEAS CORPUS. It was hoped that the President's military powers would result in the suppression of the KU KLUX KLAN, and in its execution in the autumn of 1871 he put nine counties of South Carolina under martial law. Some 7373 indictments were handed down under these Acts but, because of southern opposition, there were few convictions. The net result was to exascerbate the hatred between North and South at this time.

L

Labor. Generally refers to industrial workers who became an important economic and social segment of the population after the INDUSTRIAL REVOLUTION. By and large industrial labor is organized into TRADE UNIONS although some agricultural and professional workers are similarly organized today. In 1964 the total labor population of the United States was about 76,000,000. In the last half century organized labor has become a potent political force, operating through trade union LOBBIES or its own POLITICAL PARTIES.

Labor Day. Observed on the first Monday in September in all states and territories. It was first celebrated in New York State in 1882 under the sponsorship of the Central Labor Union, pursuant to the suggestion of Peter J. McGuire of the KNIGHTS OF LABOR that the day be set aside in honor of LABOR.

Labor, Department of. Established in 1913 as an EXECUTIVE DEPARTMENT headed by a secretary of labor who is a member of the President's CABINET. The functions of this agency formerly were performed by a bureau of labor within the DEPARTMENT OF COMMERCE. The department has various notable divisions such as the Children's Division, Women's Division, the Wages and Hours and Public Contracts Division, and the Bureau of Labor Statistics. These units have the objective of investigating, conducting research, and publishing significant materials concerning LABOR RELATIONS and LABOR PROBLEMS.

Labor Disputes Joint Resolution. See National Labor Board.

Labor-Management Relations Act. See Taft-Hartley Act.

Labor Movement. The program of industrial workers who organized themselves into LABOR UNIONS for the purpose of improving their conditions of work. The open FRONTIER, cheap and abundant land, and a frontier culture long inhibited the development of a labor movement in the United States. American workers were motivated by individualist and FREE ENTERPRISE principles and therefore remained relatively free of class conscious doctrines. Although labor unions existed on a minor and local scale as early as the Revolution, they did not assume importance until the 1840's. In the late 1820's labor organized various POLITICAL PARTIES which sought improvement in the conditions of child and woman labor and elimination of SWEAT SHOP conditions in the factory. These parties advocated the ten hour day, increased wages, and other ameliorative legislation. The WESTWARD MOVEMENT and the continuing flow of IMMIGRATION acted as deterrents against the growth of unions. The organization of the NATIONAL LABOR UNION in 1866 and the KNIGHTS

OF LABOR in 1869 heralded the formation of unions on a national scale. The rapid industrialization of the United States after the Civil War stimulated the growth of unions on a local, state, and national basis. See labor, labor union, industrial union, trade union, affiliated union, independent union, labor problems, and labor relations.

Labor Problems. In the development of the complex technological structure of modern industry important problems have arisen pertaining to workers' health and well being. These include CHILD LABOR, woman labor, unhealthful conditions of work, slum dwellings, work at unguarded, dangerous machinery, disability, UNEMPLOYMENT, old age, and illness. These problems were originally left to private care under the prevailing doctrines of LAISSEZ-FAIRE and rugged individualism. By the opening of the twentieth century state legislation attempted to bring public aid to their solution. In the 1930's federal laws tried to cope with them on a national scale. Among the most important or these have been the SOCIAL SECURITY ACT, the WALSH-HEALEY ACT, the FAIR LABOR STANDARDS ACT, the WAGNER-STEAGALL ACT, and others in the fields of compensation, housing, and child labor.

Labor Relations. The relations of employer and employee affecting the conditions of LABOR. As defined in federal and state labor relations acts, and interpreted by the courts, labor relations include matters dealing with wages, hours, tenure, security, hiring, discharge, union organization and activities, representation, and promotion.

"Labor's Magna Carta." The term applied by SAMUEL GOMPERS to those clauses of the CLAYTON ANTI-TRUST ACT which exempted LABOR UNIONS and agricultural organizations from the operation of the ANTI-TRUST LAWS, and which held peaceful STRIKES and BOYCOTTS legal and forbade the courts to grant INJUNCTIONS in labor disputes. The high hopes of Gompers and the labor movement were premature since SECONDARY BOYCOTTS, a strong weapon of labor, were not legalized, nor injunctions prohibited in disputes which might result in irreparable injury to property. In the years following dozens of injunctions were issued in labor disputes, one of these in 1921 being the most widesweeping in labor history.

Labor's Nonpartisan League. An organization of leaders of the C.I.O. and A.F. OF L. created in 1936 as a political agency to seek the reelection of President F. D. ROOSEVELT. It subsequently established the AMERICAN LABOR PARTY in New York State. This party's vote was important in the 1936 and 1940 elections in swinging that state behind Roosevelt.

Labor Unions. Organizations of workers formed for the purpose of negotiating with employers in the fields of wages, hours, conditions of work, tenure, seniority rights, and general grievances concerning the employment relationship. Unions on a national scale did not develop until after the Civil War when the NATIONAL LABOR UNION was organized in 1866. The first labor union in North America was a union of cordwainers established in Philadelphia in 1776. Subsequently local union and local state trade assemblies developed. In 1850 the printers organized the first national union in the United States, of which there were 25 by 1860. The legality of unions was not recognized in the United States until the decision of the Massachusetts supreme court in the case of COMMONWEALTH VS. HUNT, 1842. Thereafter unions grew through the exercise of their economic, and after the Civil War, political power. The first federation of Unions in the United States was the National Labor Union, established in 1866. Outstanding labor organizations have been the KNIGHTS OF LABOR, the AMERICAN FEDERATION OF LABOR, the MOLLY MAGUIRES, the INDUSTRIAL WORKERS OF THE WORLD, and the CONGRESS OF INDUSTRIAL ORGANIZATIONS There were 18,-000,000 members of labor unions in 1956.

LADD, Edwin Fremont. 1859-1925. Chemist and senator. Professor of chemistry and dean of School of Chemistry and Pharmacy, North Dakota (1890); president (1916-21); food commissioner North Dakota (1920-21); edited NORTH DAKOTA FARMERS; supported FARMERS against speculators and packers; pushed for pure food laws; elected by the NONPARTISAN LEAGUE to U.S. Senate (1920); supported LAFOLLETTE.

LADD, George Trumbull. 1842-1921. Philosopher and psychologist. Professor of philosophy at Bowdoin College; professor, Yale University (1881-1905); founder of psychology laboratory at Yale, and the first to introduce experimental psychology into the United States. Author of *Philosophy of Mind* (1895), *Philosophy of Knowledge* (1897), and *The Secret of Personality* (1918).

LADD, William. 1778-1841. Promoter of international peace. b. New Hampshire. Founded the American Peace Society (1828); planned and proposed a congress of nations and an international court, these ideas were later adopted and incorporated into the LEAGUE OF NATIONS and the WORLD COURT.

LADD - FRANKLIN, Christine. 1847-1930. Psychologist and logician. b. Connecticut. Graduated, Vassar (1869); first woman student at Johns Hopkins University (1874); published, in the field of logic, an original method for reducing all syllogisms to a single formula; best known for her studies in the theory of color vision and man's color sense.

LaFARGE, John. 1835-1910. Artist. b. New York City. Known chiefly for his excellent work with stained glass, his landscape paintings, and his murals.

LAFAYETTE, Marquis de. Marie Joseph Paul Yves Roch Gilbert du Motier. 1757-1834. French general and statesman. Served in the American Revolution; major general in Continental army (1777); friend and associate of WASHINGTON; went to France to aid the American cause (1778-80); served at YORKTOWN and in Virginia (1781); returned to France to take an active part in the French Revolution; liberal member of French National assembly (1789); revisited the United States (1794; 1824-25); during Napoleon's reign he took no part in politics.

LaFollette Civil Liberties Committee. A subcommittee of the Senate Committee on Education and Labor which was established in 1936 for the purpose of investigating "violations of the right of free speech and assembly and undue interference with the right of labor to organize and bargain collectively." Under the chairmanship of Senator ROBERT M. LAFOLLETTE of Wisconsin the Committee conducted public hearings, thoroughly investigated the field, and ultimately submitted voluminous reports. These revealed that CIVIL LIBERTIES and the RIGHTS OF LABOR were being systematically infringed by the malpractices of public officials and private persons. Among the practices decried by the Committee were the denial of free speech, hiring of professional STRIKEBREAKERS, use by employers of private detectives and gangsters, physical assaults upon union personnel, and denial to labor of many of the procedural guarantees of the courts. The Committee particularly attacked the "force employed by the police (as) far in excess of that which the occasion required" in the Memorial Day shootings of the steel strikers in Chicago in 1937. Although the Committee recommended a program of legislation designed to eliminate infringements of civil liberties, Congress did not subsequently enact such a program.

La Follette-Monroney Act. See Legislative Reorganization Act.

LaFOLLETTE, Robert Marion. 1855-1925. Political leader. b. Wisconsin. Graduated, University of Wisconsin; admitted to the bar (1880); member, U.S. House of Representatives (1885-91); reform governor of Wisconsin (1900-06); U.S. Senator (1906-25); leader of progressives and liberals; opposed United States entry into World War I; opposed the LEAGUE OF NATIONS and the WORLD COURT; sponsored investigation into TEAPOT DOME scandal; defeated for presidency of the United States (1924); organizer of National Progressive Republican League (1911).

La Follette Seamen's Act. A federal law of 1915 which radically altered labor conditions on ocean going, river, and lake vessels. It enforced regulation of wage rates, determined wage payments, and controlled conditions of employment on such vessels. The law also set down minimum standards for the feeding and housing of crews on board ship, and prohibited strikes at sea.

LAGUARDIA, Fiorello Henry. 1882-1947. Lawyer and political leader. b. New York City. Graduated N.Y.U. Law School (1910); admitted to the bar and practised in New York City; member, U.S. House of Representatives (1917-21; 1923-33); major, commander of U.S. air forces on Italian-Austrian front during World War I; president, Board of Aldermen, New York City (1920-21); elected reform mayor of New York City on a Fusion ticket (1933-1945); chief, U.S. OFFICE OF CIVILIAN DEFENSE (1941-42); director of UNRRA (1946). Author of *Making of an Insurgent: An Autobiography* (edited by M. L. Werner, 1948). Responsible for a

new city charter (1938), slum clearance projects, improved health conditions and many other reforms in New York City. He was a popular and honest mayor.

LAIDLER, Harry Wellington. 1884-1970. Socialist leader. b. Brooklyn, New York. Graduated, Columbia University (Ph.D.); lawyer. Founder (1905) and secretary (1910-21), Intercollegiate Socialist Society; director, National Bureau of Economic Research (from 1920) president (1930-32); executive director, League for Industrial Democracy; unsuccessful Socialist candidate for governor of New York (1936); candidate for the U.S. Senate (1938); elected to the New York City Council (1940-41). Author of *A Program for Modern America* (1936), *Social-Economic Movements* (1944) and many other books on social and economic problems.

Laissez-Faire. A French phrase originating among the Physiocrats in the 18th century. Literally translated it means "let do," and has been applied to the principle of the FREE ENTERPRISE SYSTEM, having come to mean a hands-off policy by government with respect to business operation. The doctrine presupposes the existence of natural economic laws of the market place which control the buying and selling of commodities, and assumes the existence of unfettered competition.

Lake Champlain, Battle of. Also known as the naval Battle of Plattsburg. One of the two important naval victories of United States forces in the War of 1812. It was fought in September, 1814 on Lake Champlain off Cumberland Head. Prevented from pushing home a frontal land attack because of American forts at Plattsburg, the British fleet was engaged by the American fleet under Commodore THOMAS MC DONOUGH, and defeated. The British army under General Prevost retreated to Canada. McDonough's victory at Plattsburg improved the American position in the war and led to the British agreement to negotiate a peace on the basis of the *status quo ante bellum*.

Lake Erie, Battle of. The most important naval battle of the War of 1812. In command of his flagship, the *Lawrence*, Commodore OLIVER H. PERRY led an American fleet of eight small vessels against a British squadron of six ships under Commodore Barclay. The battle was fought on September 10, 1813. After two hours of bombardment, Perry transferred from the *Lawrence* to the *Niagara*. He broke through the British line, and within ten minutes the enemy flagship and three other vessels had surrendered. The remaining two were pursued and captured. American casualties were 27 killed and 96 wounded. The British lost 200 killed and 600 prisoners. Sent famous message "We have met the enemy, and they are ours."

LAKE, Simon. 1866-1945. Mechanical engineer and naval architect. b. New Jersey. Inventor of even-keel type of submarine; built *Argonaut* (1897), first submarine to operate successfully in the open sea; invented submarine apparatus for locating and recovering sunken vessels; invented a heavy-oil internal combustion engine for marine use.

LAMAR, Lucius Quentus Cincinnatus. 1825-1893. Jurist, politician and lawyer; settled in Mississippi (1855); member, U.S. House of Representatives (1857-60); although opposed to secession he served with Confederate army during the Civil War; supported DAVIS and was Confederate commissioner in Europe (1862-63); member, U.S. House of Representatives (1873-77); U.S. Senator (1877-85); appointed U.S. Secretary of the Interior by CLEVELAND (1885-88); associate justice, U.S. Supreme Court (1888-93).

LAMAR, Mirabeau Buonaparte. 1798-1859. President of Republic of Texas. b. Georgia. Settled in Texas (1835); served with SAM HOUSTON at BATTLE OF SAN JACINTO; attorney-general, vice-president of Texas (1836); president (1838-41); advocated ANNEXATION OF TEXAS to the United States (after 1844); served in Mexican War; U.S. Minister to NICARAGUA and Costa Rica (1858-59).

LAMB, John. 1735-1800. Revolutionary soldier and patriot. Prominent leader of SONS OF LIBERTY, New York; served in Quebec campaign and throughout the Revolution; collector of customs, New York.

"Lame Duck" Amendment. The 20th Amendment to the Constitution of the United States. It was adopted in 1933. Sponsored by Senator FRANK NORRIS, it abolished the so-called "lame duck" session of Congress. This short session, opening in December of even numbered years, contained members of Congress who had failed of re-election a month earlier, but continued to legislate until the end of its life on March 4th of the following odd numbered year. These "lame duck" congressmen were those "ducks whose wings had been clipped." The Amendment moved all congressional sessions forward to January 3rd, required Congress to convene annually on that date, advanced the date of the President's inauguration to January 20th, and provided for the inauguration of the Vice-President-elect in the event of the death of the President-elect prior to January 3rd.

LAMONT, Thomas William. 1870-1948. b. New York. Graduated, Harvard; Vice-president, Bankers Trust Company, N.Y. (1905-09); First National Bank, N.Y. (1909-11); member of firm, J. P. Morgan & Co. (from 1911); overseer of Harvard (1912-25); trustee, Metropolitan Museum of Art, N. Y. City.

Land Act of 1796. The first important land act of the federal government. It adopted the basic features of the ORDINANCE OF 1785, providing for the survey of townships, six miles square, to be sub-divided into sections of 640 acres. The smallest purchasable unit was one section of land, to be sold at public auction at or above the minimum price of two dollars per acre. One year was allowed for payment, with a discount of ten percent for full advance payment. The statute was fundamentally undemocratic because of the auction feature which permitted land speculators to acquire the choicest parcels, and because of the high price and minimum parcel of land that could be purchased. Subsequent amending legislation in 1800, 1820, 1830, 1841, and 1862 corrected these basic flaws.

Land Act of 1800. A land reform measure designed to increase the number of small farmsteads. The law provided for the reduction of the amount of land that could be purchased from half a section (320 acres) to a quarter section (160 acres) to be sold at two dollars an acre. The Act did not achieve its purpose because the typical FRONTIERSMAN was too poor to afford 160 acres at that price and the credit system had promoted speculation and overexpansion. Also known as the HARRISON ACT.

Land Act of 1820. Part of the vast movement of economic reform of the Jeffersonian era. The Act attempted to overcome some of the defects of the HARRISON ACT of 1800 by reducing the amount of land that could be purchased from 160 to 80 acres, and lowering the price from two dollars an acre to $1.25. It also abolished the system of purchasing PUBLIC LANDS on credit. This system had, under the earlier statute, encouraged speculation and overexpansion.

Land Bounties. See bounties.

"Land Butchery." The extensive farming of soil in colonial America. The rich virgin soil, with an inexhaustible supply to the West, provided no incentive to scientific farming. Colonial farmers scarcely appreciated the value of manure and rarely practiced crop rotation. He ploughed up the fresh land, exhausted it, and moved on to new land in the same manner. "Land butchery" was practiced principally in the middle and southern states because of the virtually unlimited supply of land.

LANDER, Frederick West. 1821-1862. Civil engineer and soldier. Chief engineer, Northern Pacific Railroad; superintendent, great overland wagon route to California; served on MC CLELLAN'S staff during the Civil War; brilliant war record; died after leading charge at Blooming Gap.

Land Grant Railroads. The railroads which in the 1850's-1870's received vast grants of the PUBLIC LANDS from Congress. The first of these was the Illinois Central Railroad which, in 1850, acquired 3840 acres for each mile of railroad it constructed. From the STATES it received more than 2,600,000 acres of land. The success of the railroad in attracting immigrants to areas previously barred from settlement by the lack of transportation facilities encouraged a tremendous demand by railroad groups for additional land grants. Until 1871, when Congress discontinued such grants, a total of 158,293,377 acres of public land was granted to the railroads or to the states for the purpose of subsidizing railroad construction. The Northern Pacific Railroad received 44,000,000 of these acres, the Sante Fe System 17,000,000 acres, and the Central and Southern Pacific Railroads more than 24,000,000 acres. It has been estimated that the total value of the land, including its mineral, timber, grazing, and agricultural resources, was equal to the cost of construction of the nation's railroads. It is known, for example, that the Northern Pacific reported receipts from land sales in 1917 of more than $136,000,000 as compared with the $70,000,000 cost of the road. The Union and Central Pacific Railroads produced more income from land sales and land exploitation than the cost of their construction. The same is true of the Illinois Central Railroad and others. The roads in the post-Civil War period disposed of much of their agricultural and grazing lands at approximately five dollars an acre in contrast with the legal price of $1.25. They retained the most valuable mineral and timber land, and land suitable for urban development. Although the Federal government was given the right of free transportation of troops and supplies and rate concessions on mail service, much of this has been withheld or modified by the railroads. From time to time land grants have, as a result, been declared forfeit by Congress. A total of 42,000,000 acres has been recovered.

LANDIS, Kenesaw Mountain. 1866-1944. Jurist. b. Ohio. Practised law, Chicago, Ill. (1891-1905); U.S. district judge, Northern District of Illinois (1905-22); presided at anti-trust trial of STANDARD OIL of Indiana (1917) imposing fine of over $29,000,000; baseball commissioner for American and National Leagues of Professional Baseball Clubs (from 1920).

Land Ordinance of 1784. The first of the three famous laws dealing with the survey and sale of the public domain, and with the establishment of a plan for the admission of new states into the Union. It was drafted by THOMAS JEFFERSON as chairman of the committee appointed by Congress to provide for the government of the western areas ceded to the Congress by the states. The ordinance divided the western regions, from the mountains to the Mississippi, into 18 parts. Each of these was to enter the Union when its population equalled that of the smallest of the original 13 states. Prior to statehood these territories were to have certain rights of self-government under the supervision of Congress. The

law did not have any fundamental effect upon the area because of its inadequate population and slow growth at that time. In 1787 it was superseded by the more famous ORDINANCE OF 1787.

Land Ordinance of 1785. A statute of the Congress of the ARTICLES OF CONFEDERATION establishing a basic plan for the survey and sale of the public domain. It provided for the surveying of a "base line" running east and west, north and south of which meridians were marked off at six miles intervals. Lines parallel to the base lines, six miles apart, broke up the surveyed area into blocks 36 square miles each, known as townships. Each tier of townships between meridians was called a range. Each subdivision of a township, containing 640 acres, was called a section. Land sales would be made in sections at prices established by Congress from time to time. The law required that one square mile be reserved in each township for educational purposes.

LANE, James Henry. 1814-1866. Army officer and political leader. Moved to Kansas from Indiana (1855); leader of Free State movement in Kansas; major-general of militia campaigning and raiding pro-slavery districts (1856); often called "Liberator of Kansas;" U.S. Senator (1861-66); supported LINCOLN; advocated emancipation and arming of the Negroes.

LANE, Joseph. 1801-1881. Pioneer, soldier and territorial governor. b. North Carolina. Governor of Oregon Territory (1849-50); delegate to U.S. House of Representatives (1851-59) from that territory; U.S. Senator (1859-61); unsuccessful candidate for Vice-Presidency of the United States (1860).

LANGDELL, Christopher Columbus. 1826-1906. Lawyer and educator. b. New Hampshire. Graduated, Harvard Law School (1853); admitted to the bar and practised in New York City (1854); professor of law, Harvard Law School (1870-1900) and dean (1870-95); known primarily as the originator of the "case system" of teaching law.

LANGDON, John. 1741-1819. Revolutionary leader. b. New Hampshire. Leader in pre-Revolutionary activities; member, CONTINENTAL CONGRESS (1775, 1776); speaker, New Hampshire house of representatives (1776-82); organized, financed and served in Stark's expedition which fought against BURGOYNE; served at BENNINGTON and SARATOGA; president of New Hampshire (1785-86; 1788-89); governor of New Hampshire (1805-09, 1810-11); U.S. Senator (1789-1811); first PRESIDENT PRO TEMPORE of the U.S. Senate (1789).

LANGLEY, Samuel Pierpont. 1834-1906. Astronomer and pioneer in aviation. b. Massachusetts. High school education and largely self-taught in science; professor of physics and astronomy, Western University of Pa. (now University of Pittsburgh) and director of Allegheny Observatory (1867-87); popularized astronomy by his writings; invented the bolometer which records variations in heat radiation from the sun; secretary, Smithsonian Institution, Washington, D.C. (1887-1906); well-known for studies of solar eclipses; designed and built models of planes called heavier-than-air machines. His experiments with them were not altogether successful and he lacked the necessary funds for further trials. He is now recognized as the pioneer in the design and building of the airplane.

LANGMUIR, Irving. 1881-1957. Chemist. b. New York. Graduated, Columbia 1903); Göttingen (Ph.D. 1906); associate director of research laboratories, General Electric Company (1919); developed electron-discharge apparatus and a process of welding making use of atomic hydrogen; made important contributions to the field of radio with his work on the vacu-

um tube; with G. N. Lewis evolved the Lewis-Langmuir atomic theory; awarded the 1932 Nobel prize for chemistry.

LANIER, Sidney. 1842-1881. Poet and musician. b. Georgia. Served with Confederate army during the Civil War; practised law; flutist with Peabody Symphony orchestra, Baltimore (1874); lectured, John Hopkins University on English literature (1879). Author of *Tiger-Lilies* (1867), *Poems* (1877), his best-known poems include, *The Revenge of Hamish*, *The Marshes of Glynn*, *Ballad of Trees and the Master*, and *Corn*.

Lansing-Ishii Agreement. An agreement between the United States and Japan which was negotiated on November 2, 1917 for the purpose of adjusting the antagonistic claims of these parties in the Far East. The agreement affirmed the OPEN-DOOR POLICY and the territorial integrity of China. The United States recognized Japan's special interests in China but refused to agree that this acknowledgement applied to MANCHURIA. Japan subsequently insisted that the United States had extended this recognition, and the latter country was denounced by the Chinese for its alleged renunciation of the open-door policy. As a result of the negotiations at the WASHINGTON NAVAL CONFERENCE, a subsequent exchange of notes on March 30, 1923 provided for the mutual understanding of both nations that the Lansing-Ishii Agreement was abrogated.

LANSING, John. 1754-1829. Jurist and statesman. Delegate from New York, CONTINENTAL CONGRESS (1784-85); member, CONSTITUTIONAL CONVENTION (1787); presented the NEW JERSEY PLAN preserving the sovereignty of the states; delegate to N.Y. state convention and opposed RATIFICATION OF THE CONSTITUTION; justice of N.Y. supreme court (1790), chief justice (1798); chancellor of N.Y. (1801-14).

LANSING, Robert. 1864-1928. Lawyer and statesman. b. New York. Founder and editor, *American Journal of International Law* (1907-1928); U.S. associate counsel, Bering Sea arbitration (1892); U.S. solicitor, Alaskan Boundary Tribunal (1903); agent for the U.S., American and British Claims Arbitration (1812-14); counselor, U.S. DEPARTMENT OF STATE (1914-15); appointed U. S. Secretary of State by WILSON (1915-20); practiced law in Washington, D.C. (from 1920).

LARKIN, Thomas Oliver. 1802-1858. Merchant and consul. b. Massachusetts. Successful merchant in Monterey (from 1832); U.S. consul in California (1844-48); largely responsible for influencing the United States government in the acquisition of California.

LaSALLE, René Robert Cavelier, Sieur de. 1643-1687. French explorer in America. Traveled through Canada; spent time with IROQUOIS and OTTAWA INDIANS; settled near Montreal (1666); on expedition to the region of Lake Ontario he claimed to have discovered the Ohio River (1669); descended the Mississippi River to the Gulf of Mexico (1682) claiming the whole territory for France; named viceroy of North America; sailing from France (1684) he landed in Texas, he was on his way to the mouth of the Mississippi River to start a colony there, when he was murdered by his men (1687).

LATHROP, Julia Clifford. 1858-1932. Social worker. b. Illinois. Worked at Hull House, Chicago (from 1899); member Illinois State Board of Charities (1893-1901, 1905-09) chief, Children's Bureau, U.S. DEPARTMENT OF LABOR (1912-1921), assessor-member of advisory committee on child welfare, LEAGUE OF NATIONS (1925-32).

LATROBE, Benjamin Henry. 1764-1820. Architect and engineer. b. England. Came to the United States (1796); designed Bank of Pennsylvania building, Philadelphia (1798); proposed, designed and built the city water-supply system in Philadelphia, the first of its kind in America (1799); designed many famous buildings in this country and was one of the outstanding architects of his time; rebuilt the CAPITOL after it was destroyed in 1814 by the British (1815-17).

Latter-Day Saints. See Mormons.

LAUGHLIN, James Lawrence. 1850-1933. Political economist. b. Ohio. Graduated, Harvard (Ph.D. 1876); professor of political economy at Harvard (1878-88), Cornell (1890-92) and Chicago (1892-1916); promoted the passage of the FEDERAL RESERVE ACT; editor of *Journal of Political Economy* (1892-1933); author of many books on this subject.

LAURANCE, John. 1750-1810. Soldier and politician. b. England. To New York City (1767); studied law; admitted to the bar; joined the Continental army during the Revolution and served as aide-de-camp to MAC DOUGALL; judge-advocate-general of the army (1777-82); presided at trial of ANDRE; delegate, CONTINENTAL CONGRESS (1785-87); New York City's first member, U.S. House of Representatives (1789-94); judge, U.S. district court of N.Y. (1794-6); U.S. Senator (1796-1800).

LAURENS, Henry. Revolutionary statesman. b. South Carolina. Successful merchant and planter in Charleston; president, first provincial congress South Carolina and of the South Carolina COUNCIL OF SAFETY (1775); member, CONTINENTAL CONGRESS (1777-79); captured by the British and held in the Tower of London; exchanged for Lord CORNWALLIS (1782); served on a special mission to France and England (1782-84).

LAURENS, John. 1754-1782. Revolutionary general. b. South Carolina. Son of HENRY LAURENS. Served as an officer on WASHINGTON's staff (from 1777) and

357

saw action in all the battles from BRAN-
DYWINE on; sent as envoy extraordinary
to France (1780); served at YORKTOWN
and negotiated terms of surrender with
CORNWALLIS; killed in action while serving with Gen. GREENE in the South.

Lausanne Agreement. A treaty between
the former ALLIED POWERS of World War
I and Germany, negotiated in 1932 as
final settlement of the REPARATIONS problem. With the failure of the DAWES PLAN
of 1924 and the YOUNG PLAN of 1929 to
solve the reparations and FOREIGN DEBT
problems the HOOVER MORATORIUM of
1931 had provided for suspension of all
such payments for one year. In 1932 the
continuing world DEPRESSION made impossible the resumption of such payments and the Lausanne Agreement provided for one final payment in full of
$714,000,000 by Germany. The United
States did not recognize the validity of
the Agreement which did not include
provisions for debt payments to it.

LAWRENCE, Ernest O. 1901-1958.
Physicist. b. South Dakota. Graduated,
University of South Dakota (1922); Yale
(Ph.D. 1925); member of the faculty of
the University of California (from 1928);
director of the University's radiation laboratory (1936); invented the cyclotron
(1931) investigated the structure of the
atom and produced artificial radioactivity; awarded the Nobel prize for physics
(1939).

LAWRENCE, James. 1781-1813. Naval
officer and hero. b. New Jersey. Served
in Tripolitan war as first lieutenant; commander, *Enterprise,* under DECATUR;
comanded the *Hornet* (1812-13); defeated British brig *Peacock* (1813); commanded *Chesapeake*; defeated and mortally wounded in engagement with the
British frigate *Shannon* (June 1, 1813);
famous for words "DON'T GIVE UP THE
SHIP."

LAWRENCE, William Beach. 1800-

1881. Jurist. b. New York City. Graduated, Columbia University Law School
and practised in New York; chargé d'-
affaires, legation in Great Britain (1827);
lieutenant governor of Rhode Island
(1851); acting governor (1852). Author of many articles and books on
international law, political economy and
banking.

League of Nations. The first major world
organization dedicated to the prevention
of war. First formally announced as the
last of WILSON'S FOURTEEN POINTS in
1918, and included as a clause in the
TREATY OF VERSAILLES, 1919. The covenant of the League of Nations established the organization which lasted formally through 1946 when it surrendered
its property and records to the UNITED
NATIONS. The League's organization and
powers were such as to prevent the accomplishment of its purpose of maintaining international peace. The absence
from its membership of the United States
and, until later in its history, of Germany
and the Soviet Union, contributed much
to its ultimate decline. In disputes between small nations and in its research
and refugee work the League achieved
moderate success. The results of its attempts to prevent agression, and ultimately World War II, where major powers were involved, were a failure. Although the United States never joined
the League it participated in many of its
activities including among others the
work of the International Labor Organization and various DISARMAMENT conferences. President Wilson is credited
with the founding of the organization.

League of Women Voters. Founded in
1920 at the suggestion of CARRIE CHAP-
MAN CATT as an outgrowth of the National Woman's Suffrage Association. Its
first president was Mrs. Maude Wood
Park. The purpose of this non-partisan,
non-political organization is to foster
good CITIZENSHIP and more participation
in politics and government by the wom-

en voters of the country. In 1964 membership totaled more than ❞32,000.

Lea-McCarran Act. See Civil Aeronautics Act.

Lecompton Constitution. Drawn by a convention of pro-slavery Kansans between September and November, 1857. The Constitution provided for the protection of existing slave property in Kansas and required a vote only on the question whether it should be adopted with SLAVERY or without slavery. The latter phrase merely signified that no additional slaves would be admitted to the territory. This wording was denounced as a fraud by the Kansan Free-Soilers who demanded that the balloting should be a simple "yes" or "no" on the entire Constitution. They absented themselves from the polls and the ultimate vote approved the slavery clause on December 31, by 6226 to 569. At a new election on January 4th, the entire Constitution was voted upon and rejected by a vote of 10,226 to 162. The Lecompton Constitution was protested by STEPHEN DOUGLAS as a violation of the principle of POPULAR SOVEREIGNTY. When BUCHANAN, in spite of the overwhelming vote against the Constitution, recommended it for adoption by Congress, Douglas broke with him and the Democratic administration, personally rebuking Buchanan.

LEDYARD, William. 1738-1781. Revolutionary soldier. b. Connecticut. Known for heroic defense of Fort Griswold during British invasion of Connecticut (1781); surrendered his sword to Major Bronfield, who killed Ledyard immediately with his own sword.

LEE, Arthur. 1740-1792. Diplomat. b. Virginia. Studied law and admitted to the English bar; London agent for Massachusetts (1770-75); appointed by CONTINENTAL CONGRESS, with FRANKLIN and

DEANE, commissioner to negotiate treaty with France; involved in controversy with Deane; recalled (1779); member, CONTINENTAL CONGRESS (1781-85); member, treasury board (1784-89).

LEE, Charles. 1731-1782. Revolutionary general. b. England. Came to the United States (1773); settled in Virginia; second ranking major general at outbreak of the Revolution; joined WASHINGTON (1776); captured by British and submitted secret plan to General HOWE for defeating the Americans; exchanged (1778) and put in command of attack at MONMOUTH; retreated instead and only by arrival of Washington, GREENE STEUBEN and their forces was the situation saved; courtmartialed, found guilty and relieved of command; dismissed from the army for continual abuse of Washington (1780); now considered a traitor by historians.

LEE, Fitzhugh. 1835-1905. Confederate army officer. b. Virginia. Graduated, U.S.-M.A., West Point (1856); entered Confederate service (1861); famous as a cavalry commander; governor of Virginia (1886-90); consul general, Havana (1896-98); major general of volunteers in Spanis-American War; military governor of Havana (1899). Author of General LEE, and a biography of his uncle, ROBERT E. LEE.

LEE, Francis Lightfoot. 1734 - 1797. Revolutionary statesman. b. Virginia. Member, VIRGINIA HOUSE OF BURGESSES (1758-68, 1769-76); strong supporter of the Revolution; delegate, CONTINENTAL CONGRESS (1775-79); signer of the DECLARATION OF INDEPENDENCE.

LEE, Henry. Known as "Light-horse Harry." 1756-1818. Revolutionary general and statesman. b. Virginia. Famous as a cavalry commander during the Revolution and renowned especially for his success in covering GREENE's retreat across North Carolina to Virginia (1781);

member, CONTINENTAL CONGRESS (1785-88); governor of Virginia (1792-95); in command of the troops that put down the WHISKY REBELLION in Pennsylvania (1794); member, U.S. House of Representatives (1799-1801). It was in reference to WASHINGTON that he used the famous words, "First in war, first in peace, and first in the hearts of his countrymen."

LEE, John Doyle. 1812-1877. Religious fanatic responsible for the Mountain Meadows massacre by a band of MORMONS and the Indians under his leadership(1857). Tried and executed(1876).

LEE, Richard Henry. 1732-1794. Revolutionary statesman. b. Virginia. Educated in England; member, Virginia HOUSE OF BURGESSES (1758); protested against British taxation; worked with PATRICK HENRY and THOMAS JEFFERSON in pre-Revolutionary activities and in initiating the intercolonial COMMITTEES OF CORRESPONDENCE (1773); delegate, CONTINENTAL CONGRESS (1774-79; 1784-89); signer of DECLARATION OF INDEPENDENCE and ARTICLES OF CONFEDERATION; opposed the Constitution; U.S. Senator (1789-92).

LEE, Robert Edward. 1807-1870. Confederate general. b. Virginia. Graduated, U.S.M.A., West Point (1829); served in Mexican War; superintendent, West Point (1852); commanded troops that put down the uprising at HARPER's FERRY at the time of JOHN BROWN's raid (1859); resigned from army to become commander of Virginia forces at outbreak of the Civil War; military adviser to JEFFERSON DAVIS (1861-62); in command of Confederate forces at ANTIETAM, FREDERICKSBURG, Chancellorsville, GETTYSBURG; fought brilliantly against GRANT with a vastly inferior army; general in chief of Confederate army (1865); surrendered to Grant at APPOMATTOX COURT HOUSE (April 9, 1865); president, Washington College (1865-70) which later changed its name to Washington and Lee University.

LEE, William. 1739-1795. Merchant and diplomat. b. Virginia. Merchant in London, England (from 1768); elected sheriff of London (1773) and alderman (1775) the only American ever to hold this office; appointed (1777) by Congress to act as commercial agent in France; involved in LEE-DEANE controversy; commissioner to Berlin and Vienna (1777); negotiated commercial treaty with Holland (1778) not ratified; recalled (1779).

LEE, William Henry Fitzhugh. 1837-1891. Known as Rooney Lee. Son of ROBERT E. LEE. Confederate cavalry officer. b. Virginia. Cavalry commander during the Civil War; served with JEB STUART in many major battles (1862-64); major general (1864); member, U.S. House of Representatives (1887-1891).

Legal Tender Acts. A series of laws passed by Congress in 1862, 1863, and 1864 for the purpose of aiding in the financing of the Civil War. The First Act authorized the issuance of $150,000,000 in FIAT CURRENCY, called treasury notes, making them legal tender in payment of all taxes and debts. The amending legislation provided for the issuance of an additional $300,000,000 in such currency. These notes, popularly called GREENBACKS, fluctuated in value during and after the War. The question of the laws' constitutionality was decided in 1871 when the Supreme Court declared them a valid exercise of Congress' powers.

Legal Tender Cases. Three decisions of the United States Supreme Court in which it first invalidated and then sustained the LEGAL TENDER ACT of 1862. In the case of HEPBURN VS. GRISWOLD, 1870, the Court held that Congress had no power to enact the legal tender provisions of the law. The vote of 5-3 was reversed in the cases of Knox vs. Lee and

Parker vs. Davis, 1871, following the appointment by President GRANT of two new members of the Court to fill vacancies at the time.

LEGARE, Hugh Swinton. 1797?-1843. Lawyer and statesman. b. South Carolina. Attorney-general for South Carolina (1830-32); a founder and editor of the SOUTHERN REVIEW (1828-32); chargé d'affaires, Brussels (1832-36); appointed U.S. Attorney General by TYLER (1841-43); AD INTERIM Secretary of State (1843).

LEGGETT, William. 1801-1839. Editor. Part owner and assistant editor of the New York *Evening Post,* under WILLIAM CULLEN BRYANT (1829); strong Jacksonian Democrat; founded the *Plaindealer* which advocated the ABOLITION of SLAVERY (1837).

Legislative Power. The power to make law. Generally the power to make policy. In the federal Constitution this power is delegated to Congress in Article I. Under the SEPARATION OF POWERS principle legislative powers are theoretically exercised only by the legislature. In fact the President exercises considerable legislative powers, and the Supreme Court's power of JUDICIAL REVIEW may be considered a legislative power as well.

Legislative Reorganization Act. Also known as the La Follette-Monroney Act. Passed by Congress in 1946. It consists of six Titles dealing with problems of internal congressional organization and procedure, and of collateral problems in the fields of LOBBYING, court claims, legislative reference, and others. The Act reduced the number of standing committees in the House of Representatives from 48 to 19 and in the Senate from 33 to 15. It increased the salaries of members of Congress from $10,000 per annum to $12,500 plus a tax exempt expense allowance of $2500. Its other provisions included a retirement system for members of Congress, the establishment of four staff officers to assist committees, the improvement of the work of the Legislative Reference Service, the establishment of a legislative budget, a prohibition, with minor exceptions, against representatives sitting on more than one committee and senators on more than two, a restriction on the submission of private bills, a regulation of lobbying clause, and a reorganization of the federal procedures dealing with suits and claims against the United States.

LEHMAN, Herbert H. 1878-1963. Banker and political leader. b. New York City. Graduated, Williams College (1899); partner in Lehman Bros., bankers, N.Y. (from 1908); director of purchase and traffic of the U.S. Army during World War I; colonel (1919); lieutenant governor of New York (1928-32); governor (1932-42); director of foreign relief and rehabilitation (1942); U.S. Senator (1949-1957). He reformed the state administration, reduced income taxes and accumulated a budget surplus of $92,000,-000. He was responsible for much liberal social and welfare legislation passed during his term of office as governor of New York.

LEIB, Michael. 1760-1822. Politician. b. Philadelphia, Pa. Graduated, University of Pennsylvania (M.D.); served as a surgeon during the Revolution; member, U.S. House of Representatives (1799-1805); strong JEFFERSONIAN; U.S. Senator (1809-14); opposed MADISON's administration.

LEIDY, Joseph. 1823-1891. Naturalist. b. Philadelphia, Pa. Graduated, University of Pennsylvania medical school; professor of anatomy (1853-91); director of biology department (1884-91) at the University of Pennsylvania; known for his work in comparative anatomy and for his research in American vertebrate paleontology. Author of many books in his fields.

Leisler's Revolt. A popular uprising in the colony of New York in May, 1689. The insurrection was a reaction by the Protestant population of the colony against the appointments by James II of Catholics to colonial offices and his threat to introduce Catholicism into the colonies. The popular discontent was also a result of the absence of a truly representative assembly and of economic grievances. Jacob Leisler led the revolt which flared up into violent demonstrations after a rumor had circulated that Governor ANDROS' deputy, Francis Nicholson, had threatened to burn the town. Leisler called a convention of delegates from the counties and was appointed their commander-in-chief with considerable political powers. He ruled until 1691 when he turned over the government to the appointee of the new Protestant rulers of England, William and Mary. Leisler and his son-in-law were hanged, ostensibly for treason, but in reality as retaliation by the landed aristocrats and merchants for their economic losses during Leisler's control.

Lend Lease Act. Passed by Congress in March, 1941. It conferred upon the President the power to lend or lease any equipment to any nation whose defense he considered necessary to the defense of the United States. Under the Act and its renewals over $50,000,000,000 was extended to the allies of the United States in World War II by the end of 1945. Of this amount more than 60 percent went to Great Britain and about 22 percent to the Soviet Union. Approximately half of lend lease was in munitions and petroleum products, about one fifth in industrial commodities, and the rest in food and services. As provided in the law "reverse lend lease" accounted for much needed raw materials, food, and quarters for American troops abroad, the total valued at $17,000,000,000. Although nominally in the form of loans and/or rentals, this aid has in effect become, and probably was understood to be, open subsidies to those nations assisting the United States prior to and during World War II.

LEUPP, Francis Ellington. 1849-1918. Journalist. b. New York City. Graduated, Williams and Columbia Law School; Washington correspondent for New York *Evening Post* and the *Nation;* excellent journalist; authority on the Indians; appointed by T. ROOSEVELT, Commissioner of Indian Affairs (1903-09).

Lever Act. Passed by Congress in 1917. It authorized the President to requisition food, fuel, and other supplies necessary to the support of the army, or for any other public use connected with national defense. The law further authorized him to fix prices and regulate the distribution, purchase, storage, and sale of fuel, grain, and vegetables. Producers were compelled to sell commodities to government agencies designated by the President. Grain was withheld from the liquor market during the period of the war. The administration of the Act was entrusted to a FEDERAL FOOD ADMINISTRATION GRAIN CORPORATION to which was granted a monopoly of the purchase of wheat. The nation's wheat price was fixed at $2.20 a bushel.

LEVERETT, John. 1616-1679. Colonial governor. b. England. Came to America (1633); colonial agent in England and friend of Cromwell (1655-62); member, Massachusetts General Court (1663-65); member, council (1665-70); lieutenant governor (1671-73); governor (1673-

79) successfully directing the colony during KING PHILIP'S WAR.

LEWIS, Andrew. 1720-1781. Soldier and patriot. b. Ireland. Came to America (about 1732); settled in Virginia; served under WASHINGTON in Ohio valley (1754) defeated Indians at Point Pleasant (1774); brigadier general in Continental army (1776-77).

Lewis and Clark Expedition. The commissioning by President JEFFERSON of Captain MERIWEATHER LEWIS and WILLIAM CLARK to head a scientific exploring expedition to the northwest part of the Louisiana territory. The expedition started out in 1803 with a company of 35 men, ascended the Missouri River to its source, crossed the Rocky Mountains, and descended the Columbia River to the Pacific Coast in the summer of 1805. In 1806 they retraced virtually the same route, reaching St. Louis in September 1806. Their two and one half year study produced a considerable body of data concerning the topographical features of the country, its natural resources, the flora and fauna, and the habits of the native Indian tribes. One of the most important consequences of this journey was that it formed an important basis of the United States claim on the Oregon territory in the 1840's.

LEWIS, Francis. 1713-1803. Merchant and patriot. b. Wales. Came to America (1738); delegate to STAMP ACT CONGRESS (1765); New York delegate to CONTINENTAL CONGRESS (1774-79); signer of the DECLARATION OF INDEPENDENCE.

LEWIS, Issac Newton. 1858-1931. Inventor and army officer. Graduated, U.S.M.A., West Point (1884); invented first successful artillery range finder (pat. 1891), the Lewis Machine gun (1911), a system of signals for artillery fire control, a gas-propelled torpedo, and a quick-firing field gun and mount.

LEWIS, John Llewellyn. 1880-1969. Labor leader. b. Iowa. Coal miner. Joined the United Mine Workers' Union, A.F. OF L.; vice-president (1917); president (from 1920); A.F. of L. organizer (1911-17); helped elect GREEN president at GOMPERS death; organized COMMITTEE FOR INDUSTRIAL ORGANIZATION (C.I.O.) (1935); reorganized as CIO (1938); strong opponent of F. D. ROOSEVELT after election for third term.

LEWIS, Meriwether. 1774-1809. Explorer. b. Virginia. Captain in the WHISKY REBELLION and Northwest campaigns; private secretary to President JEFFERSON (1801-03); appointed by Jefferson to lead, with WILLIAM CLARK, an expedition to explore the LOUISIANA PURCHASE; governor of Louisiana Territory (1807-09).

LEWIS, Morgan. 1754-1844. General and statesman. b. New York. Chief of staff for General GATES at TICONDEROGA and Saratoga; chief justice of New York Supreme Court (1801-04); governor of New York(1804-07) sponsoring the public school system; major general in War of 1812.

LEWIS, Sinclair. 1885-1951. Novelist. b. Minnesota. Graduated, Yale (1907); newspaper reporter and editor (1907-16). Author of many well-known books including *Main Street* (1920), *Babbitt* (1922), *Arrowsmith* (1925), *Elmer Gantry* (1927), and *Dodsworth* (1929). First American winner of the Nobel prize for literature (1930). His books are primarily the life of the "average American."

Lexington and Concord, Battle of. The first battle of the American Revolution. It was fought on April 18th and 19th, 1775. General Gage sent a thousand troops to seize the arsenal at Concord and Acton and to arrest JOHN HANCOCK and SAMUEL ADAMS. Having heard of this mission, William Dawes and PAUL REVERE were sent to arouse the patriots,

70 of whom met the British troops on the village green at Lexington. In the skirmish that ensued eight patriots were killed while the British column marched on to Concord. At the Concord bridge the British were turned back on their long retreat to Boston, harassed by a continuing guerilla attack from behind walls and trees. By the time they had reached the British lines at Charlestown they had lost 273 troops, three times as many as the colonists. The militia pursued the British, closing in around the city in the commencement of a siege that was to result 11 months later in the evacuation of the city. Thus when the second CONTINENTAL CONGRESS met in May, 1775, war had already broken out and it constituted itself a revolutionary government to prosecute this war.

Leyte Gulf, Battle of. The greatest naval battle of history. It was fought between the United States and Japanese navies in three engagements October 22-27, 1944, and resulted in the destruction of Japanese naval power. In the three battles in Surigao Strait, off Samar, and off Cape Engano, the United States employed 166 ships and 1280 planes against 65 Japanese ships and 716 planes. American losses during these battles and the subsequent Philippine campaign were 27 ships and 967 planes. The Japanese, during this period, suffered casualties of five carriers, four battleships, 14 cruisers, and 43 other vessels, and an estimated 7,000 planes.

Liberalism. The political philosophy which advocates tolerance of diverse opinions, seeks improvement in political, economic, and social conditions, and advocates CIVIL LIBERTIES. Liberalism was frowned upon in colonial America and did not assume a major stature until the establishment of the new government in 1789. The impact of the thinking of THOMAS JEFFERSON, BENJAMIN FRANKLIN, and JAMES MADISON upon liberal thought in early American history was profound in shaping the doctrines of American ideology. The constitutional provisions protecting freedom of speech, religion, assembly, and the press, and defending the rights to HABEAS CORPUS, jury trial, property, life, and liberty are notable expressions of liberal thought. Although there never has been a strong national liberal party in the United States, local and state political movements have been organized around liberal principles. Such movements generally were supported by labor, professional, intellectual, and FARMER groups.

Liberal Republican Party. Organized in the late 1860's by Republican leaders who opposed the conservative policies and the scandals of the first GRANT administration. Its program included leniency to the South, Civil service reform and a lower tariff. Among leaders were CARL SCHURZ, CHARLES FRANCIS ADAMS and HORACE GREELEY, the latter of whom was the party's candidate in the election of 1872. A political compromise was made with the Democratic party in this election whereby Greeley was named its candidate as well. The reform movement within the Republican Party failed with the re-election of Grant and the continued leadership of such figures as BLAINE, Grant, and COLAX.

Liberator, The. The abolitionist newspaper founded by WILLIAM LLOYD GARRISON in 1831. The paper pursued a vigorous anti-slave policy under Garrison's editorship and was instrumental in rousing public sentiment against the institution of SLAVERY.

Liberia. One of the only two wholly sovereign states in Africa. It is a Negro republic whose population of 1,600,000 occupies an area of 43,000 square miles. It was first settled in 1822, six years after Congress conferred a charter upon the AMERICAN COLONIZATION SOCIETY, authorizing it to transport emancipated slaves to the west African coast. Its independence was officially proclaimed in 1847. In 1942 and 1944 treaties between Liberia and the United States permitted the latter to establish troops, airports, and military and naval bases in Liberia. The nation's major enterprise is the million acre rubber concession granted to the Firestone Plantations Company in 1925. An iron ore concession has been developed by the Republic Steel Corporation. Its principal crops are coffee, rice, and sugar cane. The city of Monrovia is the capital and chief port.

Liberty Bell. A new bell cast by Thomas Lister of London to celebrate the sesquecentennial of the Commonwealth of Pennsylvania. It cracked during its testing in Philadelphia in 1752 and was twice recast by two Philadelphia workmen, Pass and Snow. It was placed in the State House in Philadelphia in June 1753. Early in September it was cracked during another testing. The bell was then recast and hung permanently in a steeple where it remained until 1846. The cracked relic now known to the public resulted from its tolling at the funeral procession of Chief Justice JOHN MARSHALL in 1835. It gets its name from the inscription from Leviticus XXV, 10: "Proclaim liberty throughout all the land unto all the inhabitants thereof."

Liberty Loans. A series of five bond issues floated by the United States TREASURY DEPARTMENT between May, 1917 and April, 1919 for the purpose of financing the conduct of World War I. Including the fifth, or "Victory Loan", the total amount subscribed to was $21,435,-370,600. The Liberty Loans were bonds bearing interest rates of 3½ to 4½ percent. The "Victory Loan" comprised two series of short term notes bearing interest of 3¾ percent and 4¾ percent. The loans were oversubscribed as a result of the energetic canvassing of the American population by means of mass meetings and pleas in public places such as theaters, motion picture halls, restaurants, hotels, and churches. Liberty Bonds have been either paid or refunded as they have matured.

Liberty Party. A minor party movement organized in April 1840 at Albany, New York by delegates from six states. With an ABOLITIONIST platform it polled only 7,000 votes in that year's election, but in the ensuing years was to succeed in splitting the WHIG PARTY and thus contribute to the creation of the anti-slave Republican party in 1854. Its candidate JAMES G. BIRNEY, with a total of 62,300 votes in the election of 1844, drew enough votes from CLAY, the Whig candidate, to throw New York State into the Democratic column thus electing its candidate JAMES K. POLK. The party merged into the FREE-SOIL MOVEMENT in 1848. Among its leaders were SALMON P. CHASE, Myron Holley, and Charles Torrey.

Liberty Poles. Trees or poles before which the SONS OF LIBERTY convened and pledged their efforts in the cause of liberty. The best known Liberty Pole was constructed in New York City in 1766 to celebrate the repeal of the STAMP ACT. It rapidly became the scene of street fights between the Sons of Liberty and British troops. The first Liberty Pole was an elm tree at Washington and Essex Streets in Boston.

Libraries, Public. The first public library collection in America was formed by the donation by John Harvard of 300 volumes to the Harvard College Library in 1636. South Carolina enacted the first library law in 1700. The Library Company of Philadelphia, established in 1732, was the first subscription library. In 1752 the Redwood Library erected the first library building in Newport, Rhode Island. By the mid-19th century tax-supported libraries had been established in the larger eastern cities. The largest of these was the Boston Public Library, established by an act of the Massachusetts legislature in 1848. The New York Public Library, formed by a merger of three foundations in 1895, became the largest public library in the United States with the exception of the Library of Congress. With the grants of philanthropists like Astor and Carnegie the library movement expanded rapidly in the 20th century. Many of these became affiliated with secondary schools and collegiate institutions. In 1956 there were approximately 7500 public libraries in the United States. In cities of more than 100,000 population these libraries contained almost 50,000,000 volumes.

Library Association. The first private circulating library in North America. It was organized by BENJAMIN FRANKLIN in Philadelphia in 1731 to meet the reading needs of the colonists. As a result of its work the circulating library became common in the colonies in the following years.

Library of Congress. Located in the CAPITAL, in WASHINGTON, D. C. It occupies the world's two largest buildings devoted exclusively to library work. In 1952 it contained an estimated total of more than 20,000,000 pieces plus approximately 2,500,000 unbound newspaper and serial materials awaiting binding. Included are over 9,250,000 volumes and pamphlets, 12,000,000 manuscripts, 2,-000,000 maps, and miscellaneous bound newspaper volumes, micro-cards, micro-print cards, micro-films, motion picture reels, volumes of music, phonograph records, photographic materials, fine prints, photostats, and posters. The Library was established in 1800 and was burned by the British on August 24, 1814. It was later reestablished. It administers the Legislative Reference Service for answering inquiries from members of Congress. It registers copyrights, distributes materials to the blind, and maintains a huge bibliography. There are important permanent exhibits of such documents as the DECLARATION OF INDEPENDENCE, the Constitution of the United States, the BILL OF RIGHTS, the ARTICLES OF CONFEDERATION, and letters and manuscripts by and concerning WASHINGTON, JEFFERSON, and LINCOLN. From time to time the Library displays special exhibits.

LIEBER, Francis. 1800-1872. Publicist, educator and political philosopher. b. Germany. Came to the United States (1827); planned and edited *Encyclopaedia Americana* (13 vols. 1829-33); professor of history and political economy, Columbia University (1857-65), Columbia Law School (1865-72). Author of *Manual of Political Ethics* (2 vols. 1838-39), and *On Civil Liberty and Self-government* (2 vols. 1853) which were the first published expression of a philosophy of the state in America. He wrote many other books on political science.

LIGGETT, Hunter. 1857-1935. Army officer. b. Pennsylvania. Graduated, U.S. M.A., West Point (1879); commanded the 1st army of the A.E.F. (1918-19) in the battles of the MARNE, ST. MIHIEL and MEUSE-ARGONNE; retired as major general (1921).

Lilienthal Plan. See Baruch Plan.

LILIUOKALANI, Lydia. 1838-1917. Queen of the Hawaiian Islands. Not in sympathy with reforms, her people revolted, instigated by many American residents on the islands, and deposed her (1893); sued the United States government for damages. Wrote well-known song ALOHA OE.

Lima, Declaration of. The statement of the Eighth PAN-AMERICAN CONFERENCE which met in Lima, Peru in 1938. At the meeting the United States specifically repudiated the ROOSEVELT COROLLARY to the MONROE DOCTRINE. The Declaration further adopted resolutions proclaiming the members' will for peace, their sentiment of humanity and tolerance, their adherence to the principles of international law, their belief in the equal sovereignty of states, and their belief in individual liberty without religious or racial basis. The sentiments expressed in these resolutions were strengthened by subsequent reciprocal trade agreements and the exchange of cultural and educational facilities.

LINCOLN, Abraham. 1809-1865. Sixteenth President of the United States. b. in a log cabin in Kentucky. Had little formal schooling; clerked in a store, managed a mill, split rails, and studied law in Illinois (1831-37); elected to Illinois legislature (1834-41); practiced law in Springfield, Illinois (from 1837); married Mary Todd (1842); member, U.S. House of Representatives (1847-49); joined the Republican party (1856); after his speech "A house divided against itself cannot stand" he was nominated for the U.S. Senate (1858); debated against DOUGLAS, defeated for the Senate, but was elected President of the United States (1861); slave states started to secede and Lincoln issued a call for volunteers; proclaimed a BLOCKADE on southern ports; issued the EMANCIPATION PROCLAMATION (January 1, 1863); made immortal GETTYSBURG ADDRESS, after LEE'S defeat, in a dedication of the national cemetery there (November 19, 1863); re-elected President (1864); advocated FREE SOIL DOCTRINE before the Civil War but was not an ABOLITIONIST until his later years; opposed the Mexican War and voted against it in the House. Opposed the Radical Republican Reconstruction policy and was violently attacked by them for his moderate views; assassinated by JOHN WILKES BOOTH at the Ford Theater, Washington, D. C., dying the next day (April 15, 1865). Unquestionably one of the most beloved and outstanding of American Presidents.

LINCOLN, Benjamin. 1733-1810. Revolutionary general. b. Massachusetts. Farmer; served in colonial legislature and provincial congress; commanded Massachusetts militia (1776); major general under GATES at SARATOGA; commanded army of the South (1778); served at YORKTOWN (1781); elected secretary of war under Confederation congress (1781-83); in command of forces that put down SHAYS' REBELLION (1787); lieutenant governor of Massachusetts (1788); delegate to state convention that ratified the Constitution; collector of the port, Boston (from 1789).

LINCOLN, Levi. 1749-1820. Lawyer and political leader. b. Massachusetts. Graduated, Harvard; delegate to state constitutional convention; U.S. Attorney General (1801-04); lieutenant governor of Massachusetts (1807-8); governor (1808); served on governor's council (1810-12).

LINCOLN, Levi. 1782-1868. Lawyer and political leader. b. Massachusetts. Graduated, Harvard; practiced law; Republican member of state legislature (1812-22); lieutenant governor of Massachusetts (1823); associate justice of state supreme court (1824); governor 1825-34); member, U.S. House of Representatives (1834-41).

LINCOLN, Robert Todd. 1843-1926. Lawyer. Son of ABRAHAM LINCOLN. b. Illinois. Graduated, Harvard (1864); served on GRANT'S staff during the last few months of the Civil War; studied law in Chicago and practiced there; capable corporation lawyer working particularly with RAILROADS; appointed by GARFIELD U.S. Secretary of War (1881-85); appointed by HARRISON U.S. Minister to Great Britain (1889-93); president, Pullman Company (1897-1911).

Lincoln's Birthday. Observed on February 12th; it commemorates the birth of ABRAHAM LINCOLN. It is a legal holiday in 32 states and in the territories of

ALASKA, HAWAII, and the VIRGIN ISLANDS. This day was first formally observed in WASHINGTON, D. C. in 1866 when both houses of Congress gathered for a memorial address in honor of the dead President.

Lincoln's Reconstruction Plan. This plan was based on LINCOLN's theory that the southern states had not seceded from the Union because they could not constitutionally do so. He considered that he was treating rebellious individuals in his capacity as commander-in-chief of the armed forces, not political entities. The result was his proclamation of December 1863 in which he declared that as soon as ten percent of the voters of 1860 in any seceded state would form a government, accept congressional and presidential decisions on the subject of SLAVERY, and take oaths of allegiance to the Constitution, they would be re-admitted to the Union. By the end of the war Arkansas and Louisiana had established such governments, but their representatives and senators were refused admittance by the RADICAL REPUBLICAN chambers. Grounds for the conflict between Lincoln and the Congress arose out of Lincoln's sentiment of leniency, the Radical Republicans' demand for vengeance against the South, and the absence from his plan of any provision of electoral and CIVIL RIGHTS for the FREEDMEN.

LINDBERGH, Charles Augustus. 1902-. Aviator. b. Michigan. Served as air-mail pilot on the Chicago to St. Louis run (1926); made first solo nonstop transatlantic flight from New York to Paris (1927); helped promote aviation through the Guggenheim Foundation fund; made various "good will" tours; worked with Dr. Alexis Carrel on various experiments; awarded CONGRESSIONAL MEDAL OF HONOR; associated with various air line companies; a leading "ISOLATIONIST" prior to World War II.

Lindbergh Law. Also known as the Federal Kidnapping Law. A law of Congress passed in 1932 as a result of the abduction of CHARLES A. LINDBERGH's infant son on March 1, 1932. The statute forbade the TRANSPORTATION of kidnapped persons across state borders and permitted the death penalty if a jury so recommended. In February, 1952 the DEPARTMENT OF JUSTICE indicted a group of Ku-Klux-Klansmen under this law for having flogged a man and woman in North Carolina and having taken them across the South Carolina state line. On May 13, 1952 a United States District Court in North Carolina found 10 of the 11 members of the Klan guilty of kidnapping and conspiracy in the first case invoked against the Klan under the Lindbergh Law.

LINDSEY, Benjamin Barr. 1869-1943. Jurist. b. Tennessee. Judge, juvenile court, Denver, Colorado (1900-27) which he helped to establish and was one of the first of its kind in the United States; authority on juvenile delinquency and laws; judge, Superior Court of California (from 1934). Author of many books on the problems of juvenile delinquency.

LIPPMAN, Walter. 1889-1974. Editor and columnist. b. New York City. Graduated, Harvard; associate editor, *New Republic;* on editorial staff, New York *World;* writer of a column on political and economic affairs in the New York *Herald-Tribune* (from 1931).

Liquidation Commission. An ad hoc agency established by the WAR DEPARTMENT after World War I for the purpose of disposing of its surplus war goods in Europe. It transferred to France all permament American structures and improvements for a sum of $400,000,000. Materials and supplies abroad were sold for $850,000,000, roughly half their value.

Lisbon Conference. A conference of the

12 member nations of the NORTH ATLAN-
TIC TREATY ORGANIZATION at Lisbon,
Portugal in February, 1952. At this meeting the participants pledged to SHAPE
that they would increase NATO's military strength in Europe to 25 field divisions, 25 reserve divisions, and 4,000
operational aircraft. Political agreement
was reached on the problems of defense,
trade, and other relationships among
themselves and *vis-à-vis* the Soviet Union.

Literacy Test. A test established as a
criterion for NATURALIZATION, VOTING, or
admission of aliens to the United States.
Many state literacy tests have been employed to limit the suffrage of minorities.
Prominent among these have been such
tests in southern states whose purpose
was the restriction of Negro voting. In
1923 New York State was the first in the
North to enact a literacy test. In 1913
President TAFT vetoed the first federal
literacy test bill which was passed by
Congress to restrict alien IMMIGRATION.
In 1915 President WILSON vetoed a second bill which became law over his VETO
in 1917.

Literature. Colonial literature emphasized theology, history, and political philosophy. Educated men read Greek and
Latin classics in the original and in trans-
lations. Poetry frequently dealt with religious themes, and Wigglesworth's *Day
of Doom* was referred to as the "epic of
fire and damnation." The colonies produced little fiction. Historical writings included those of WILLIAM BYRD II and
BENJAMIN FRANKLIN. The first generation
after the Revolution was an era of political writing in which the work of JEFFER-
SON, MADISON, HAMILTON, WILSON, JAY,
and RANDOLPH played a conspicuous role.
After 1800 a new American school appeared in which the names of Tyler,
Brackenridge, and Brown were foremost.
Royall Tyler satirized American life in
The Contrast. Hugh H. Brackenridge

wrote of the back country in his *Modern
Chivalry.* Charles Brockden Brown advocated social reforms and rationalism as a
cure for the ills of the times. PHILIP FRE-
NEAU wrote the most beautiful poetry of
his day as well as outstanding political
defenses of Jeffersonian Republicanism.
The Golden Age of American literature
occurred in the first half of the 19th century. The nationalism of the period after
the War of 1812 produced a feeling of
certainty in the destiny o the United
States that was revealed in the self-con-
fidence of writers of essays, fiction, history, biography, and poetry. In the early
decades New York became the center of
literary activity and was the home of the
first completely American school of literature. WASHINGTON IRVING interpreted
the history and culture of the Hudson
Valley in his *History of New York, by
Diedrich Knickerbocker* (1809). JAMES
FENIMORE COOPER in *The Spy* (1821)
and *The Pioneers* (1823) pictured the
simple life of the American frontier. WIL-
LIAM CULLEN BRYANT began American
poetry with his *Thanatopsis* (1817). ED-
GAR ALLAN POE, the greatest American
poet of that era, created the short story
form. HERMAN MELVILLE's novels gained
a wide audience. By the 1830's the focal
point of American literary genius had
moved to New England. Here WILLIAM
ELLERY CHANNING, RALPH WALDO EMER-
SON, HENRY DAVID THOREAU, and NA-
THANIEL HAWTHORNE wrote voluminous-
ly as champions of reform, free thought,
and rationalism. Poetry reached new
heights in the glorification of the com-
monplace in the writings of HENRY WADS-
WORTH LONGFELLOW, OLIVER WENDELL
HOLMES, JAMES RUSSELL LOWELL, and
JOHN GREENLEAF WHITTIER. Historical
writing attained a peak in the work of
GEORGE BANCROFT, WILLIAM H. PRES-
COTT, John L. Motley, and FRANCIS PARK-
MAN. One of the greatest of American
poets, WALT WHITMAN, published his
Leaves of Grass in 1855. It was the first

example of free verse, and was recognized by Emerson as a work of genius. The writers of this era were substantially akin in their detestation of tyranny. Their work expressed and interpreted the reforms of Jacksonian democracy, and partook of the political struggles of the age. Whittier, Longfellow, and Lowell were anti-SLAVERY as were many of the lesser figures in the literary milieu of New England. At the end of the 19th century the social and economic problems of the Gilded Age evoked some of the greatest literary expression in American history. MARK TWAIN satirized American life in *The Gilded Age* (1873). Henry Adams denounced party patronage and political abuses in his *Democracy* (1880) and *The Education of Henry Adams* (1907). WILLIAM DEAN HOWELLS, JOHN HAY, and Hamlin Garland wrote important novels depicting the facets of American social life. The "local-color school of fiction" included Edward Eggleston, GEORGE W. CABLE, LAFCADIO HEARN, BRET HARTE, Mark Twain, JOEL CHANDLER HARRIS, and Sarah O. Jewett. In their writings the life of growing America on the Mississippi, in the mining camps, in the cattle country, and on the farms of the South was warmly and, occasionally, oversentimentally recorded. The poetry of the 1880's and 1890's included the works of Whitman, SIDNEY LANIER, Will Carlton, JAMES WHITCOMB RILEY, and Eugene Field. This is the era which produced the tasteless romances of Bertha M. Clay and Laura Jean Libby and the dime-novel pulp fiction of HORATIO ALGER JR. and Burt L. Standish. The early 20th century witnessed a revival of interest in American history in the publication of *The Chronicles of America* (1918-1921), *The Pageant of America* (1926-1929), and *The Dictionary of American Biography* (1928-1936). MUCKRAKING literature found its expression in the writings of Frank Norris, JACK LONDON, UPTON SINCLAIR, IDA TARBELL, David Graham Phillips, Thomas Howard Lawson, and S. S. McClure. The era of World War I produced a literature that returned to realism in the work of THEODORE DREISER, SINCLAIR LEWIS, and Upton Sinclair. After the war a reaction against the futility and evils of contemporary civilization was expressed in the fiction and poetry of a new school of distinguished writers which included F. SCOTT FITZGERALD, ERNEST HEMINGWAY, JOHN DOS PASSOS, SHERWOOD ANDERSON, and WILLIAM FAULKNER. The literary criticism of H. L. Mencken and George Jean Nathan reflected and encouraged this pessimism. A renaissance in poetry developed in the harsh realism and new free verse forms of CARL SANDBURG, EDGAR LEE MASTERS, ROBERT FROST, Edward Arlington Robinson, AMY LOWELL, Vachel Lindsay, and EDNA ST. VINCENT MILLAY. Scholarly writing appeared in the works of THORSTEIN VEBLEN (economics and sociology), CHARLES A. BEARD and James Harvey Robinson (history), WOODROW WILSON and Roscoe Pound (politics and law), and WILLIAM JAMES, JOSIAH ROYCE, and Charles Pierce (psychology and philosophy). During the GREAT DEPRESSION literature became, in part, a public obligation in the grants for writing projects offered by the WPA. New young talents were subsidized to write local history, fiction, and poetry. Disillusionment after World War II turned many writers against war and militarism. Expressions of this sentiment appeared in the work of Norman Mailer, Irwin Shaw, and James Jones. Novels of social protest in the pre-war era were written by JOHN STEINBECK whose *Grapes of Wrath* made a profound impression in the 1930's. Howard Fast wrote distinguished historical fiction. Fine poetry was written by Archibald MacLeish, Mark Van Doren, WILLIAM ROSE BENET, STEPHEN VINCENT BENET, and W. H. Auden. Important biographies came from the pens of Douglas Southall Freeman (Robert E. Lee),

Ralph Barton Perry (William James), Samuel Flagg Bemis (John Quincy Adams), Nathan Schachner and Dumas Malone (Thomas Jefferson), and Mary Earhart Dillon (Wendell Willkie). Scholarly writing pioneered new fields in labor relations in the works of John R. Commons, Selig Pearlman, E. E. Witte, Emanuel Stein, Paul F. Bressenden, and Lois McDonald. Historical writing drew on the past in the works of Merle Curti, Arthur M. Schlesinger Jr., Roy F. Nichols, and Van Wyck Brooks.

"Little Assembly." See Security Council.

"Little Group of Willful Men." A phrase of President WILSON in March, 1917 in which he attacked a five day FILIBUSTER by the Senate designed to defeat a bill to arm merchant ships. The bill had already passed in the House of Representatives. The President denounced the group of five Democrats and six Republican Senators as "a little group of willful men, representing no opinion but their own, who have rendered the great Government of the United States helpless and contemptible."

"Little N.R.A." See Bituminous Soft Coal Act.

"Little Steel Formula." Refers to the rule adopted by the NATIONAL WAR LABOR BOARD in 1942 by which it permitted general wage increases to groups of employees. As the name suggests the plan grew out of a wage dispute in the STEEL INDUSTRY which was resolved by the board in permitting an increase of 15 per cent over the average straight time hourly earnings of the group on January 15, 1941.

LIVINGSTON, E d w a r d. 1764-1836. Statesman. b. New York. Graduated, Princeton (1781); admitted to the bar (1785) and practiced in New York City; member, U.S. House of Representatives

(1795-1801); appointed by JEFFERSON, U.S. district attorney for N.Y. (1801); mayor of New York City (1801-03); moved to New Orleans (1804); served on JACKSON's staff during War of 1812 and at the BATTLE OF NEW ORLEANS (1815); prepared legal code and criminal procedure for state of Louisiana (1821); member, U.S. House of Representatives (1823-29); U.S. Senator (1829-31); appointed by Jackson, U.S. Secretary of State (1831-33); resigned to become U.S. Minister to France (1833-35).

LIVINGSTON, Henry Brockholst. 1757-1823. Jurist. b. New York City. Graduated, Princeton (1774); practiced law in New York City; strong Jeffersonian Republican; appointed by JEFFERSON, Associate Justice of the U.S. Supreme Court (1806-23).

LIVINGSTON, Peter Van Brugh. 1710-1792. Merchant and political leader. Graduated, Yale (1731); wealthy merchant in New York City; vigorously opposed the STAMP ACT and other British methods of TAXATION; leader of the committee of one hundred that governed the colony at that time.

LIVINGSTON, Philip, 1716-1778. Wealthy merchant and political leader. Graduated, Yale (1737); importer; member, provincial assembly (1758-68); member, COMMITTEE OF CORRESPONDENCE for N.Y.; delegate, CONTINENTAL CONGRESS (1774-78); signer of DECLARATION OF INDEPENDENCE; advocated founding of King's College, now Columbia University.

LIVINGSTON, Robert. 1654-1728. Colonial leader. b. Scotland. Came to America (1673); settled in Albany, N.Y. becoming a wealthy fur trader, and establishing Livingston Manor which included about 160,000 acres of land; secretary of Indians affairs (from 1695) having a great deal of influence over the colony in their relations with the Indians; member, New

York provincial assembly (1709-11; 1716-25).

LIVINGSTON, Robert R. 1746-1813. Statesman. b. New York City. Graduated Columbia (1765); admitted to the bar; law partner of JOHN JAY; member, CONTINENTAL CONGRESS (1775-77; 1779-81); one of the committee of five who drew up the DECLARATION OF INDEPENDENCE; first U.S. Secretary of Foreign Affairs (1781-83); chancellor of New York State (1777-1801); one of the outstanding lawyers of his time; appointed by JEFFERSON, U.S. Minister to France (1801-04); financed ROBERT FULTON in his experiments and the building of the *Clermont* and together they controlled the navigation of the Hudson for many years.

LIVINGSTON, William. 1723-1790. Political leader. b. New York. Graduated, Yale (1741); admitted to the bar and practiced in New York City; moved to New Jersey (1772); member, CONTINENTAL CONGRESS (1774-76); governor of New Jersey (1776-90); delegate to CONSTITUTIONAL CONVENTION, and a signer of the Constitution (1787).

LLOYD, Henry Demarest. 1847-1903. Writer. b. New York City. Writer for the Chicago *Tribune* (1872-85); wrote *Story of a Great Monopoly* (1881) which appeared in the *Atlantic Monthly* magazine and was an expose of the STANDARD OIL COMPANY and the RAILROADS; gained recognition as the first of the "MUCKRAKERS."

Lobbies. Private organizations of special interest groups which seek to interest legislatures in enacting or defeating proposed legislation. The name derives from the habit of the spokesmen of these organizations meeting representatives in the lobbies of legislative halls for the purpose of invoking their aid. The typical methods of lobbying activity have been promises of financial aid, drafting of bills, campaign assistance, and threats of retaliation for failure to support desired legislation. It is well known that bribery and other corrupt practices have also been employed. In the United States important lobbies have included the NATIONAL ASSOCIATION OF MANUFACTURERS, Chambers of Commerce, TRADE ASSOCIATIONS, AMERICAN FARM BUREAU FEDERATION, NATIONAL FARMERS UNION, Associated Farmers of California, AMERICAN LEGION, AMERICAN VETERANS COMMITTEE, POLITICAL ACTION COMMITTEE, LABOR'S NON-PARTISAN LEAGUE, LEAGUE OF WOMEN VOTERS, and other groups advocating measures for the consumer, youth, women, and welfare reform.

Local Self Government. The administration of municipal affairs under general state laws or charters conferred by the states upon their cities, counties, towns, townships, villages, districts, and parishes. The powers of local governments vary widely, depending upon state law or the local charter. Where home rule has been granted wide powers exist in the fields of municipal TAXATION, highways, traffic, policing, EDUCATION, health, and other matters of local concern. Local self government was established in the British colonies in North America as the heritage of a principle which had long since developed in Great Britain.

Lockout. The refusal of an employer to keep his workers employed by excluding them from his plant. The purpose is to prevent or destroy their union organization, or to hinder their union activities. Lockouts are regulated, although not prohibited, by the TAFT-HARTLEY ACT.

LOCKWOOD, Belva Ann. 1830-1917. Lawyer and political leader. b. New York. Admitted to the bar (1873); practiced in Washington, D.C., and was the first woman to practice before the U.S. Supreme Court (1879); active as a leader in the women's rights movement and for WOMAN SUFFRAGE; nominated by the National Equal Rights party for the presidency of the United States (1884-1888).

Locofocos. The name given to a group of urban Democrats whose main support lay in the remnants of the old WORKINGMEN'S PARTY of 1829. The group included many idealists and reformers who supported the INDEPENDENT TREASURY BILL of 1837 and who opposed paper money and the credit system as being responsible for the PANIC OF 1837. They represented the radical wing of the Democratic Party in New York State. They were so-called as a result of having provided themselves at a party CAUCUS with candles and the new loco-foco matches to replace the gas illumination which was turned out by the conservatives. The Locofocos are not to be confused with the rural supporters of President VAN BUREN known as the "BARNBURNERS."

LODGE, Henry Cabot. 1850-1924. b. Boston, Massachusetts. Graduated, Harvard Law School and received a Ph.D. in political science; member, U.S. House of Representatives (1887-1893); U.S. Senator (1893-1924); chairman of Foreign Affairs Committee; leader of the opposition to the Covenant of the LEAGUE OF NATIONS (1919); leading conservative Republican. Author of books on historical subjects and biographies of famous Americans.

Lodge Reservations. A series of 15 resolutions introduced by Senator HENRY CABOT LODGE on November 6, 1919. Their purpose was to reconcile President WILSON's demand for Senate ratification of the TREATY OF VERSAILLES with the Republican Senators' objections to the Treaty. Supported by the ISOLATIONIST Senators BORAH and JOHNSON the Resolutions provided the following: the United States to be the judge of its obligations to the LEAGUE OF NATIONS and of the issues falling within its domestic jurisdiction, the MONROE DOCTRINE to be exempted from foreign interference, Congress to determine financial contributions to the League and the United States military obliga-

tions under Article X, no American to represent the United States in League activities unless approved by an act of Congress, the United States to decide unilaterally on action to be taken in Sino-Japanese conflicts, the United States to determine its armaments if threatened with invasion or engaged in war despite any agreements covering armaments limitation, and the United States to assume no responsibility for the control of German colonies. Although modified in the Senate debates that followed the Lodge Reservations were unacceptable to Wilson. Ultimately the Senate turned down the Treaty and the League Covenant.

LOEB, James. 1867-1933. Banker. b. New York City. Graduated, Harvard (1888); member of the banking firm of Kuhn, Loeb & Co.; founder of the Loeb Classical Library; founded Institute of Musical Art, N.Y. City now a part of Juilliard Musical Foundation.

Loewe vs. Lawlor. See Danbury Hatters' Case.

LOGAN, Benjamin. 1743?-1802. Pioneer. Built Fort Logan in Kentucky against Indian attack (1775); led many important expeditions into the west and led fights against the Indians; served in Virginia assembly as representative from Kentucky, and in the state constitutional convention.

LOGAN, George. 1753-1821. Physician, agriculturist and statesman. b. Pennsylvania. Member of the SOCIETY OF FRIENDS; member, Pennsylvania legislature; at own expense and initiative he visited France to prevent a war; he succeeded and reported to President ADAMS (1798-99); his actions resented by FEDERALISTS who passed the Logan Act (1799) forbidding a private citizen to undertake diplomatic negotiations with a foreign power without official authority; U.S. Senator(1801-07).

LOGAN, James. 1674-1751. Colonial

statesman. b. Ireland. Came to Philadelphia (1699) as secretary to WILLIAM PENN; member, provincial council (1703-47); mayor of Philadelphia (1722); acting governor of province(1736-38); chief justice, Pennsylvania supreme court (1731-39); bequeathed valuable library to the city of Philadelphia.

LOGAN, James or John. Indian name Tah-gah-jute. 1725?-1780. Indian chief of the Mingo tribes. Friendly with white settlers until his family was massacred (1774) then seeking vengeance, he attacked the settlers, during the Revolution served with the British.

LOGAN, John Alexander. 1826-1886. Union general and legislator. b. Illinois. Practised law; member, U.S. House of Representatives (1859-62); organized Illinois regiment and served as colonel at Fort Henry; in command of the Army of the Tennessee; brigadier general and major general (1862); campaigned for LINCOLN; member, U.S. House of Representatives(1867-71); U.S. Senator(1871-77; 1879-86); unsuccessful candidate for vice-presidency on the BLAINE ticket (1884).

LOGAN, Stephen Trigg. 1800-1880. Jurist and politician. b. Kentucky. Leader of Illinois bar and law partner of LINCOLN in Springfield (1841-44); member of Republican convention that nominated Lincoln for the presidency.

Log Cabin. Conventionally a one story one or two room house built of logs. Occasionally wealthier FARMERS or town dwellers constructed two story log cabins of several rooms. Such buildings were used in Europe before the discovery of America, and were introduced into the Swedish colony of Delaware in 1638. The log cabin became the most popular form of rural and frontier construction in the 17th and 18th centuries. The exteriors of the logs were flattened and their chinks filled with stones, wood chips, and clay, except when used for tobacco curing in which case the chinks were left unfilled for the wind to blow through and dry the leaves. Although the pioneer-built log cabin was raised single-handedly, those in settlements were frequently constructed cooperatively, the process becoming the nucleus of important social functions.

"Log Cabin and Cider Campaign." The WHIG campaign of 1840. The term was used by a Democratic newspaper which ridiculed the Whigs for selecting a military man of unassuming manners for the presidency. The Whigs were advised that General HARRISON be given a log cabin and a barrel of hard cider and he would remain happily in Ohio. The phrase was successfully exploited by the Whigs in popularizing their candidate. Political demonstrations were organized in which barrels of cider figured prominently while log cabins were erected in great numbers in the cities.

Log-Rolling. A practice of legislators exchanging votes to insure the enactment of bills providing for local pet projects. The term applies particularly to appropriations measures of only local interest such as the construction of a post office, road, bridge, or the improvement of a local waterway. The practice often results in extravagant legislation which, but for the reciprocal voting, would not ordinarily be passed.

London Company. Chartered as the Virginia Company of London. A joint stock trading company chartered in 1606 by King James I. Shares of stock sold at 12 pounds 10 shillings, each stockholder having a vote in choosing the board of directors. Its Council was appointed by the stockholders in quarterly meetings called the General Court after 1612, having originally been appointed by the King. The Company was given the right to explore Southern Virginia, an area from Maryland to the Carolinas. Under the leadership of Sir Thomas Smith, Sir Edwin Sandys, and Nicholas Ferrar the Company established its first colony, the "Old Dominion" of Virginia, on the Thames. Three ships under Captain Christopher Newport landed 104 men, 16 having died during the long and tedious voyage. This settlement at JAMESTOWN was eventually abandoned because of poor government, flimsy housing, illness, and inability to support itself. Relief was sent in 1608 and 1609 under Sir Thomas Gates whose flagship was wrecked. Difficulties between the colonies and the Company arising out of the latter's indentured servant policy and alleged misrule led in 1623 to an investigation by the Privy Council. By a judgment of this body the Company was dissolved the following year.

London Economic Conference. Technically called the World Monetary and Economic Conference. A Conference in London in June and July, 1933 convened for the purpose of halting the world DE-PRESSION through international financial and economic agreement. Commodity agreements were negotiated by silver and wheat producing nations, but attempts at bringing about currency stabilization and tariff reduction failed. Belgium, France, Holland, and Switzerland, still on the GOLD STANDARD, refused to discuss TARIFF reduction until agreement could be reached on CURRENCY stabilization. Governed by strong nationalist sentiment the United States refused to discuss the issue of war debts or to cooperate in international currency stabilization. While the Conference was still in session, President F. D ROOSEVELT requested the recall of the American delegation, basing his decision on the thinking that the United States could extricate itself from the world depression by itself. The Conference failed to solve these fundamental problems.

LONDON, Jack. 1876-1916. Author. b.

San Francisco, California. Sailor and adventurer (1891-94); sought gold in the Klondike (1897-98). Author of well known adventure stories and books including *The Call of the Wild* (1903), *The Sea Wolf* (1904), *Martin Eden* (1909), *The Cruise of the Snark* (1911). Was interested in socialist theories, and wrote attacks on capitalism, including *The Iron Heel* and *War of the Classes.*

London Naval Conference of 1930. A conference of the United States, Great Britain, Japan, France, and Italy for the purpose of limiting the size and number of naval vessels not restricted by the WASHINGTON NAVAL CONFERENCE. France and Italy withdrew from the Conference because of the refusal of the other parties to grant a greater ratio of naval power to these two nations. Britain refused to extend guarantees to France without American support. The three power treaty finally gave Japan equality in submarines and a 10:10:7 ratio in small cruisers and destroyers as compared with England and France. The 5:5:3 ratio for large cruisers of the Washington Naval Treaty was retained. Excluding capital ships and carriers the tonnage limitation under the Treaty was 541,700 tons for Britain, 526,-200 tons for the United States, and 367,-050 tons for Japan. An "ESCALATOR CLAUSE" permitted the signatory nations to increase the treaty ratio if they felt imperilled by new ship construction by a non-signatory power. The naval holiday on capital ships was extended to 1936.

London Naval Conference of 1936. A conference of the United States, Great Britain, and Japan from December, 1935 to March, 1936. It was convened to discuss the problems raised by the Japanese denunciation in December, 1934 of the WASHINGTON NAVAL TREATY. Upon the refusal of the United States and Great Britain to recognize Japan's claim to parity the latter withdrew from the conference. In the two power pact of March

375

25, 1936 England and the United States agreed to exchange data on their naval construction program. They also agreed to limit certain types of warships but to set aside these limits in the event of war or if they were exceeded by a non-signatory power. No provisions were contained for a quantitative limitation. As a result of inability to secure information from Japan about its naval construction program the two signatories agreed in 1938 to remove the limit of 35,000 tons for capital ships.

Lone Star State. See Annexation of Texas.

LONG, Crawford Williamson. 1815-1878. Surgeon. b. Georgia. Considered the first surgeon to use ether as an anesthetic. He published an account of 8 operations performed between 1842 and 1846 (Dec. 1849). Dr. MORTON gave a public demonstration of the use of ether in 1846 and claimed priority in the discovery.

"Long Drive." The drive northward of cattle from Texas to the stockyards and slaughter houses in cities at or near a railroad terminus. In the era of the "CATTLE KINGDOM" the most famous of these cities were Abilene and Dodge City in Kansas, Ogallala in Nebraska, and Myles City and Glendive. Following the beef round-up in July or August cattle were gathered in and the fatted animals were segregated from the herd for the "long drive" to the stockyards. The cattle traveled from 10 to 15 miles a day, the total march taking many weeks. The drives were noteworthy for the monotony and danger that beset both cattle and cowboys, frequently characterized by stampedes, rustling, and Indian attacks. In 1871 more than 600,000 cattle crossed the Red River on such drives.

LONGFELLOW, Henry Wadsworth. 1807-1882. Poet. b. Maine. Graduated, Bowdoin (1825); professor of modern languages, Bowdoin (1829-35); studied in Europe; Smith professor of modern languages, Harvard (1835-54). Known for his many poems including The Wreck of the Hesperus, The Skeleton in Armor and The Village Blacksmith which appeared in Ballads and Other Poems (1841), Evangeline (1847), The Song of Hiawatha (1855), The Courtship of Miles Standish (1858), and Tales of a Wayside Inn (1863).

LONG, Huey Pierce. 1893-1935. Lawyer and politician. b. Louisiana. Admitted to the bar (1915); member of Railroad Commission (1918-21) and the Public Service Commission (1921-28); governor of Louisiana (1928-31); U.S. Senator (1931-35); national reputation for dictatorial control of Louisiana through his strong political machine; assassinated (1935).

Long Island, Battle of. A crucial battle in the first year of the Revolution whose success enabled WASHINGTON to preserve the Continental army. Washington was encamped on Brooklyn Heights with 9,000 men on August 27, 1776 when General HOWE decided to dislodge him. He landed 20,000 men at Gravesend, Brooklyn. Generals Sterling and Sullivan, with 1,000 men were captured, permitting the British to appear before the American line. Instead of attacking, Howe laid siege to the American forces. Realizing his predicament Washington simulated a reinforcement move and conveyed his troops across the East River under cover of night, on August 29. Although Long Island and New York fell to the British the Continental army remained intact.

LONG, John Davis. 1838-1915. Lawyer and politician. b. Maine. Graduated, Harvard; practiced law in Boston (from 1862); governor of Massachusetts (1880-82); member, U.S. House of Representatives (1883-89); appointed by MCKINLEY, U.S. Secretary of the Navy (1897-1902) serving during the Spanish-American War.

LONG, Stephen Harriman. 1784-1864. Army officer, explorer and engineer b. New Hampshire. Graduated, Dartmouth; led expedition exploring the upper Mississippi region (1817), the Rocky Mountain region (1820); discovered the Long Peaks, Colorado; worked as railroad engineer.

LONGSTREET, James. 1821-1904. Confederate general. b. South Carolina. Graduated, U.S.M.A., West Point (1842); entered Confederate service after resigning from the army (1861); brigadier general, later major general (1861); lieutenant general (1862); commanded at BULL RUN(1862), the right wing of LEE's army at ANTIETAM (1862); served at GETTYSBURG (1863) where his delay in carrying out orders is often considered responsible for the Confederate defeat there; surrendered with Lee at APPOMATTOX COURT HOUSE (1865); settled in New Orleans; appointed by GRANT, U.S. Minister to Turkey (1880-81); U.S. marshall (1881-84); U.S. Railroad Commissioner (1898-1904).

LONGWORTH, Nicholas. 1869-1931. Lawyer and legislator. b. Ohio. Graduated, Harvard Law School; practised law in Cincinnati; member, U.S. House of Representatives (1903-13; 1915-31); Speaker of the House (1925-31); married Alice, daughter of THEODORE ROOSEVELT.

Lookout Mountain, Battle of. A battle of the Civil War which was fought on November 4, 1863. It was the opening move of GRANT to raise the siege of CHATTANOOGA, and began with an attack by General HOOKER, commanding the right wing of Grant's army. General LONGSTREET's troops were cleared from Lookout Mountain and retreated across Chattanooga Creek to join the Confederate forces at MISSIONARY RIDGE. The battle marked the beginning of the North's victory in the Chattanooga campaign.

LOOMIS, Francis Butler. 1861-1948.

Diplomat. U.S. Minister to Venezuela (1897-1901), Portugal (1901-02); Assistant Secretary of State (1902) and Secretary of State *ad interim* (1905); responsible for the final negotiations which led to the acquisition of the PANAMA CANAL ZONE by the United States.

Loose Construction of the Constitution. An interpretation of the Constitution which advocates a liberal use of the "ELASTIC CLAUSE" in order to increase the powers of the central government. This interpretation was supported by the FEDERALIST party under HAMILTON in opposition to the strict construction policy of JEFFERSON.

Los Alamos. An ATOMIC BOMB laboratory at Los Alamos, New Mexico where specialized research was undertaken in creating the first atomic bomb. Under the direction of J. ROBERT OPPENHEIMER the laboratory succeeded in its work in 1945. It was later renamed the Los Alamos Scientific Laboratory and was one of many atomic research centers which included Oak Ridge National Laboratory in Tenessee, Argonne National Laboratory in Chicago, Brookhaven National Laboratory in Long Island, and Knolls Atomic Power Laboratory in Schenectady, New York.

Louisiana. The 31st state in size, with an area of 48,523 square miles. Organized as a territory in 1804 and admitted as the 18th state on April 8, 1812. Seceded on January 26, 1861 and readmitted on May 29, 1865. Baton Rouge is the capital. In 1950 Louisiana's population of 2,-683,516 made it 21st in rank. Its largest cities are New Orleans, Shreveport, and Baton Rouge. Louisiana is the nation's leading fur state, producing mink, muskrat, opossum, and racoon pelts. It is a leader in sugar cane, sweet potatoes, and rice production. Other important products are cotton, lumber, fish, oil, sulphur, and salt. The world's largest complex of drainage pumps prevents flooding of New Orleans. The state is famous for its old world flavor, New Orleans frequently being referred to as the "Little Paris" of the New World. It is the home of the greatest abundance of game birds in the United States. Between 1945 and 1952 Louisiana was one of the three states involved in litigation with the federal government over the disposition of off-shore oil lands. The area was discovered in 1540 by de Soto. Its nicknames are the "Pelican State," "Creole State," and "Sugar State."

Louisiana Purchase. The purchase from France in 1803 of the area between the Mississippi Valley and the Rocky Mountains and between Canada and the Gulf of Mexico. President JEFFERSON, upon learning in 1802 that this territory had been ceded to France by Spain, feared the prospect of having the control of the Mississippi River transferred to the powerful leadership of Napoleon. At that time roughly three eighths of American commerce passed through the Mississippi Valley. His fears were realized in the autumn of 1802 when the Spanish Intendant closed the mouth of the Mississippi at New Orleans and withdrew the right of deposit secured by the PINCKNEY TREATY OF 1795. Jefferson obtained a $2,000,000 appropriation from Congress for the purpose of buying New Orleans and West Florida from France, sending JAMES MONROE to Paris to aid ROBERT LIVINGSTON in the negotiation. At this point Napoleon decided to sell the entire territory, needing money for his wars against England, and the ultimate price agreed upon was $15,000,000. The purchased doubled the area of the United States and brought within it those lands that ultimately were to produce the immense wealth of the mineral resources the agricultural produce, the hydro-electric power, and the meat products. Despite the constitutional objections to the President's purchase, it was sanctioned by popular support and justified by Jefferson on the grounds of military need.

Louisiana Territory. An area of 529,911,-680 acres purchased from France in 1803. This territory represented the first accession of land to the United States. It extended from Canada to the Gulf of Mexico and included the areas now occupied by Louisana, Arkansas, Oklahoma, Kansas, Missouri, Nebraska, Iowa, the Dakotas, Montana, most of Minnesota, and portions of Colorado and Wyoming. Upon taking formal possession of the territory on March 10, 1804 Congress divided it into the Territory of Orleans and the Territory of Louisiana. The original price of approximately $15,000,000 was raised by interest accruals to a final total cost of $27,267,622 representing a cost of 4 cents per acre. See Lousiana Purchase.

LOVE, Alfred Henry. 1830-1913. Pacifist. Prominent Quaker who led fight for peace and the outlawing of war from the Civil War until the end of his life.

LOVEJOY, Elijah Parish. 1802-1837. Abolitionist. Editor, St. Louis *Observer* condemning SLAVERY. Shot and killed by a mob (Nov. 7, 1837). His death caused great resentment in the North.

LOVEJOY, Owen. 1811-1864. Abolitionist. Leader of ABOLITIONIST movement in Illinois; Republican leader; urged LINCOLN to lead Republican party; member, U.S. House of Representatives (1856-64).

LOW, Seth. 1850-1916. Merchant, politician and educator. b. Brooklyn, N.Y. Graduated, Columbia College (1870); worked in his father's importing company (1870-87); mayor of Brooklyn (1882-86); president, Columbia University (1890-1901); reform mayor of New York City (1901-03).

LOW, Will Hicok. 1853-1932. Illustrator and painter. b. New York. One of the original members of the Society of American Artists (1878) and National Academy

(1890); known for murals and stained glass windows.

LOWELL, Abbott Lawrence. 1856-1943. Political scientist and educator. b. Boston, Massachusetts. Graduated, Harvard (1877); practised law in Boston (1881-97); professor of political science, Harvard (1900-09); president of Harvard (1909-33). Author of books on political science.

LOWELL, Amy. 1874-1925. Poet and critic. b. Massachusetts. Known as a poet of the Imagist School. Known for many volumes of verse and a biography of Keats.

LOWELL, Francis Cabot. 1775-1817. Industrialist. b. Massachusetts. Graduated, Harvard; successful merchant in Boston (1793-1810); in association with Paul Moody, he built the first complete cotton spinning and weaving mill in the United States at Waltham, Mass. (1812-14).

LOWELL, James Russell. 1819-1891. Poet, essayist, editor and diplomat. b. Massachusetts. G r a d u a t e d, Harvard (1838), Harvard Law School (1840); succeeded to LONGFELLOW's chair at Harvard (1855-86); editor, *Atlantic Monthly* (1857-61); associate editor, *North American Review*; appointed by HAYES, U.S. Minister to Spain (1877-80); Great Britain (1880-85); elected to American HALL OF FAME (1905). Author of *Poems* (1844), *The Biglow Papers* and the *Vision of Sir Launfal* (1848); *Commemoration Ode* (1865), *Fireside Travels* (1864), *Democracy and Other Addresses* (1887). In his *Biglow Papers* he opposed the Mexican War.

LOWELL, John. 1743-1802. Jurist and legislator. b. Massachusetts. Graduated, Harvard; practised law in Boston; member, state constitutional convention (1777); member, CONTINENTAL CONGRESS (1782-83); U.S. judge, district of Massachusetts (1789-1801) chief judge, first circuit (1801-02).

LOWELL, Josephine Shaw. 1843-1905. Social worker and philanthropist. Member, New York State Board of Charities (1876-89); introduced reforms in hospitals, asylums and prisons; founder *Charity Organization Society;* first president and founder of Consumer's League and the Women's Municipal League.

LOWELL, Percival. 1855-1916. Astronomer. b. Massachusetts. Graduated, Harvard; traveled in the Orient particularly Japan (1877-93); author of many books on the Far East; built astronomical observatory in Arizona (1893-94); known for his studies of the planet Mars. Author of many books on astronomy.

LOWNDES, William Jones. 1782-1822. Statesman. Member, U.S. House of Representatives (1810-22); chairman of the WAYS AND MEANS COMMITTEE; advocated the TARIFF OF 1816; helped work out the MISSOURI COMPROMISE; considered one of the most brilliant men in the legislature.

Loyalists. Also known as tories. Refers to British colonists in America who supported the mother country during the American Revolution. Such support took the form of open military aid to the British armies, financial and material assistance to Great Britain, and espionage on its behalf. JOHN ADAMS believed that one-third of the colonists were loyalists, and it has been estimated that about 30,000 loyalists served in the British army during the Revolutionary War, representing a number approximately equal to the greatest number of troops WASHINGTON had under his command at any one time. The treatment of captured loyalists by the patriot troops was extremely harsh. Basically the loyalists consisted of large landed proprietors, royalists, officials, professionals, and conservatives from all classes. They were strongest in New York, New Jersey, and Pennsylvania.

Loyalty Program. A program requiring the pledging of loyalty to the United States by members of the federal CIVIL SERVICE. It was inaugurated by EXECUTIVE ORDER in 1947, and provided that charges of disloyalty based on F. B. I. reports would be heard before a loyalty board. Upon a finding of disloyalty and affirmation by the Loyalty Review Board the employee would be discharged. In making its decision the loyalty board was to consider "membership in, affiliation with, or sympathetic association with" any organization which the Attorney-General designates as "totalitarian, Fascist, Communist, or subversive." The program has been attacked as unconstitutional and many of those discharged have appealed to the federal courts. On April 30, 1951 the Supreme Court upheld its validity in sustaining the dismissal of Dorothy Bailey, the first government employee dismissed under the program.

LUCE, Henry Robinson. 1898-1967. Editor and publisher. b. China of American parentage. Founder of important magazines *Time*, (1923), *Fortune* (1930), and *Life* (1936), also serving as editor and publisher. Important influence on public opinion in the United States.

Ludlow Amendment. Also known as the Ludlow Resolution. A proposal for a constitutional amendment submitted to the House of Representatives in 1938 providing for a popular REFERENDUM before American troops could be used in foreign wars. The resolution did not apply in the event of attack or threat of attack on the United States or its possessions. Both President ROOSEVELT and Secretary of State HULL opposed this diminution of executive power, and it was only through patronage arrangements by

Postmaster FARLEY that the members of the House rejected it reluctantly by a vote of 209 to 188. The resolution reflected the widespread ISOLATIONIST feeling and fear of being involved in Europe's wars in 1938.

LUKS, George Benjamin. 1867-1933. Painter. Staff artist on Philadelphia *Press* and *Bulletin*; many of his works hang in museums throughout the country. He painted *The Wrestlers, Woman and Black Cat, The Breaker Boys,* and *The Old Duchess.*

Lumber Industry. The first commercial saw mill was set up in Maine in 1631, but the lumber industry remained a local business until the beginning of the 19th century. By the opening of the Civil War, Bangor, Maine was one of the largest saw mill cities in the world. The original searches for white pine in New England and the middle Atlantic states spread to the forest lands of Michigan after the Civil War. Until 1885 that state was dominant in the industry. After exploiting Michigan and Wisconsin, lumbering migrated to the South and to the Northwest, the latter having developed as the center of the industry since World War I. The original use of oxen and horses for moving logs was replaced by donkey engines and locomotives which in turn have given way to the tractor and truck. Steam power was long used in saw mills. Today electric power is primarily employed to operate the automatic machinery in these mills. Some plants cut more than 1,000,000 board feet of lumber in a day. The world's largest lumber mill is located at Lewiston, Idaho. Among the important woods cultivated in the United States are pine, fir, spruce, larch, hemlock, cedar, maple, and oak. The largest timber producing state is Oregon, closely followed by Washington. Other important lumber states are California, Nevada, Alabama, Georgia, and North Carolina. In 1952 approximately 27,000 establishments, employing over 600,000 workers, produced approximately 35,-000,000,000 board feet of lumber valued at about $2,250,000,000.

LUNDY, Benjamin. 1789-1839. Abolitionist. Organized The Union Humane Society in Ohio (1815), one of the first anti-SLAVERY organizations, published anti-slavery weekly, *National Enquirer*, edited by WHITTIER (1836); one of the pioneer ABOLITIONIST journalists and organizers.

LURTON, Horace Harmon. 1844-1914. Jurist. b. Kentucky. Served in the Confederate army during the Civil War; chief justice, Tennessee supreme court (1893); professor of law, Vanderbilt University (1898-1910); appointed by TAFT, Associate Justice of the U.S. Supreme Court (1910-14).

Lusitania, The. The name of the British-owned liner which was sunk by a German submarine on May 7, 1915. Loaded with 5,000 cases of ammunition for the ALLIED POWERS, and carrying Canadian troops, the submarine, the U-20, sank it with one torpedo off the coast of Ireland, with the loss of 1,198 crew and passenger members including 124 American men, women and children. The incident caused a great feeling of revulsion in the United States and was successfully exploited by pro-British propagandists in creating anti-German sentiment.

Lusk Laws. A series of laws passed by the New York state legislature in 1919. They were enacted as a result of an exhaustive report of 4,450 pages of the Lusk Committee headed by New York state senator Clayton R. Lusk. The laws are an extreme example of the attempts in the period following World War I to suppress alleged unpatriotic and subversive activities. All schools or organizations giving instruction in any subject were required to obtain a state license and all teachers who advocated by word of mouth or in writing any form of government different from that of the United States or of the state were to be denied licenses. Although VETOED by Governor SMITH they were signed by his successor Governor Miller. These laws are an expression of the general anti-radical feeling that swept the United States in this period as shown by the passage of similar laws in other states and by the deportation of radical aliens.

Lyceums. Societies organized for adult EDUCATION. The first lyceum was established at Millbury, Massachusetts in November, 1826 by Josiah Holbrook. Within the year a dozen lyceums had been founded in Massachusetts and Connecticut, receiving the support of such prominent New Englanders as DANIEL WEBSTER. In 1831 state lyceums were created in Maine, Massachusetts, and New York. In that year the New York State Lyceum convened a meeting in New York City for the organization of a national lyceum. By 1835 more than 3,000 village and town lyceums had been established throughout the nation. Their work was conducted on the basis of lectures, discussions, and readings in all fields of culture except religion and politics. By World War I it is estimated that there were 12,000 lyceums in the United States.

LYMAN, Theodore. 1833-1897. Naturalist. Graduated, Harvard; worked with AGASSIZ at Lawrence Scientific School; served as aide to General MEADE during the Civil War; Massachusetts commissioner of inland fisheries (1866-83); responsible for the research and development in the preservation of food fish; member, U.S. House of Representatives (1883-85) interested in CIVIL SERVICE REFORM.

LYNCH, Charles. 1736-1796. Justice of the Peace. b. Virginia. Served with General GREENE during the Revolution; presided over extralegal court to punish lawlessness and the LOYALISTS; *Lynch law* or *Lynch's law* is named for him.

Lynching. The illegal execution of an accused person by a mob. The term is believed to have derived from a Revolutionary leader, LYNCH, who executed LOYALISTS without judicial sanction. In the South lynching has been practiced principally against Negroes, usually on the alleged charge of rape, attempted rape, or homicide. Between 1882 and 1950 a total of 4,729 lynchings was reported of which 3,436 were Negro. The year with the highest total was 1901 when 130 lynchings occurred of which 105 were Negro.

LYNCH, Thomas. 1727-1776. Planter and statesman. Served in South Carolina provincial assembly; delegate to STAMP ACT CONGRESS (1765); delegate to First and Second CONTINENTAL CONGRESSES.

LYNCH, Thomas. 1749-1779. Legislator. Served in first and second provincial congresses; delegate to first general assembly; member, Second CONTINENTAL CONGRESS (1776-77); signer of the DECLARATION OF INDEPENDENCE; lost at sea while on his way to France (1779).

LYON, Mary. 1797-1849. Educator. b. Massachusetts. Important pioneer in higher education for women; opened Mount Holyoke Seminary, Mass. (1837) which later became Mount Holyoke College; president (1837-49); elected to AMERICAN HALL OF FAME (1905).

LYON, Matthew. 1750-1822. Journalist and politician. b. Ireland. Came to America (1765); ANTI-FEDERALIST member of the Congress representing Vermont (1797-1801); member, House of Representatives from Kentucky (1803-11); elected first delegate to Congress from Arkansas territory (1820); expert on frontier America.

LYON, Nathaniel. 1818-1861. Union general. b. Connecticut. Graduated, U.S.-M.A., West Point (1841); served through the Mexican War; brigadier general in charge of Union forces at St. Louis during the Civil War (1861); killed in battle.

M

McADOO, William. 1853-1930. Lawyer and city magistrate. b. Ireland. Practised law in New Jersey; member, U.S. House of Representatives (1883-91); appointed by CLEVELAND, U.S. Assistant Secretary of the Navy; practised law in New York City; police commissioner (1905-06); chief city magistrate (1910-30); largely responsible for a complete reorganization and reform in the municipal court system.

McADOO, William Gibbs. 1863-1941. Lawyer and political leader. b. Georgia. Practised law in Tennessee (1885-92), New York City (from 1892); president, Hudson & Manhattan Railroad which built the first tunnel under the Hudson River; appointed by WILSON, U.S. Secretary of the Treasury (-1913-18); U.S. Director-General of Railways (1917-19); chairman, FEDERAL RESERVE BOARD, FEDERAL FARM LOAN BOARD and the WAR FINANCE CORPORATION; unsuccessful candidate for nomination on the Democratic ticket for President of the United States; U.S. Senator from California (1933-39).

McANENY, George. 1869-1953. Civic administrator. b. New Jersey. President of Borough of Manhattan (1910-13); president of the board of aldermen, and acting mayor of New York (1914-16); chairman, transit commission of the Board of Estimate, largely responsible for planning the city subway system for New York City; executive manager, N. Y. Times (1916-21); interested in CITY PLANNING, and CIVIL-SERVICE REFORM.

McCALL, Samuel Walker. 1851-1923. Legislator. Graduated, Dartmouth College; practised law in Boston; served in state legislature; member, U.S. House of Representatives (1893-1913); Republican leader largely responsible for the Lincoln Memorial in Washington, D.C.; governor of Massachusetts (1916-18).

McCarran-Walter Act. A law of Congress passed over President TRUMAN'S VETO on June 27, 1952. It codified all existing IMMIGRATION legislation and added new features over the President's objections that it would "repudiate our basic religious concepts of the brotherhood of man" and would submit all CITIZENS returning from abroad to "serious risk of unreasonable invasions of privacy." The law eliminated discriminations against the immigration of Asians but was attacked as having developed more rigid restrictions in entry quotas considered discriminatory against Asia and Eastern and Southeastern Europe. It stiffened the existing law relating to the admission, exclusion, and deportation of dangerous aliens. This feature was denounced as being subject to arbitrary administration and as potentially harmful to the NATURALIZATION of persons committing minor offenses. It limited the entry of Asians to the quotas of the Pacific areas of their ancestry or half-ancestry. It coordinated all immigration, naturalization, and nationality laws into permanent statutes, separate from emergency and temporary legislation, a feature attacked by its opponents on the grounds that it would result in an anti-alien, anti-immigration, and anti-American program. The law also provided for a system of selective immigration through preference of skilled aliens, broadened the grounds for exclusion and deportation, and provided for JUDICIAL REVIEW of official decisions concerning aliens. The President's veto approved "some improvements in the structure of immigration laws" but denounced the "many undesirable" new features, including particularly the sections continuing the national origins quota system, those making naturalization more difficult, those limiting the rights of first generation Americans, and those subjecting returning American citizens to intensive investigation.

McCarran-Wood Act. Also known as the Internal Security Act. A law of Congress passed on September 23, 1950 and amended in March, 1951. Part I, the Subversive Activities Control Act, requires registration with the Attorney-General of Communist organizations, their affiliates, and their officers. Identifying data relating to finances and publications must be filed. The other sections of this Part declared it unlawful to conspire to establish a totalitarian dictatorship, to conceal Communist membership when seeking government employment, to contribute to such an organization if government employee, to work in a defense facility, or use a United States passport if a Communist. Aliens dangerous to the public safety may be excluded or deported. Naturalization was prohibited to all members of such organizations and naturalized citizens who are members could be denaturalized within five years of their NATURALIZATION unless they could prove they were dupes. With certain exceptions the Act excluded from the United States all those who had been members of a totalitarian organization. Part II, the Emergency Detention Act, authorized the President to proclaim an internal security emergency in the event of an invasion of the United States or its possessions, declaration of war, or insurrection in aid of a foreign enemy. Persons suspected of conspiracy for espionage or sabotage may be detained, subject to a hearing and access to the courts.

McCARTHY, Charles. 1873-1921. Political scientist. b. Massachusetts. Graduated, University of Wisconsin (Ph.D. 1901); in charge of legislative library, Madison, Wis.; important influence in progressive legislation in Wisconsin under the LA FOLLETTE regime; first director of the U.S. Commission on Industrial Relations (1914-15).

"McCarthyism." The term applied to the attacks by Senator Joseph McCarthy of Wisconsin against the TRUMAN administration in 1951-52. These attacks were based upon the allegation that President Truman was harboring Communists in various federal agencies. The STATE DEPARTMENT was the particular object of Senator McCarthy's investigations. Among those charged with Communist and pro-Soviet bias were General GEORGE MARSHALL, Owen D. Lattimore, Philip Jessup, and DEAN ACHESON. "McCarthyism" has been denounced as having employed undemocratic tactics such as falsehoods, unsupported allegations, senatorial immunity, and lack of opportunity for reply by those attacked. Charges against Senator McCarthy by the Department of the Army were aired in public by the Senate Subcommittee on Permanent Investigations on Government Operations. Senator Karl Mundt replaced McCarthy as chairman of the Subcommittee during the hearing. Extensive television, radio, and newspaper coverage reached millions of citizens during the 36 days from April 22 to June 17, 1954. After receiving the report from the Select Committee to Study Censure Charges against Senator McCarthy, the Senate on Dec. 2, 1954 approved, by a vote of 67-22, a resolution condemning certain acts by McCarthy which "tended to bring the Senate into dishonor and disrepute, to obstruct the constitutional processes of the Senate." Senator McCarthy died in 1957 at the age of 48.

McCLANE, Louis. 1786-1857. Lawyer and statesman. b. Delaware. Studied law and admitted to the bar (1807); member. U.S. House of Representatives (1817-27); U.S. Senator (1827-29); U.S. minister to England; negotiated agreement to open the British West Indies trade to United States; appointed by JACKSON, U.S. Secretary of the Treasury (1831-33); U.S. Secretary of State (1833-34); U.S. Minister to England (1845-46) while discussions about Oregon were in progress; delegate to Maryland constitutional convention (1850).

McCLELLAN, George Brinton. Union general. b. Philadelphia, Pennsylvania Graduated, U.S.M.A., West Point (1846); served through the Mexican War; commissioned major general at outbreak of the Civil War; commanded the Department of the Ohio; played important part in keeping Kentucky in the Union; commanded division of the Potomac (1861); commissioned general in chief (1861); commanded at ANTIETAM (1862); replaced for not following LEE across the Potomac; Democratic candidate for President of the United States (1864); defeated; chief engineer, N.Y.City Department of Docks (1870-72); governor of New Jersey (1878-81).

McCLERNAND, John Alexander. 1812-1900. Lawyer and soldier. b. Kentucky. Admitted to the bar and practised in Illinois; member, U.S. House of Representatives (1843-51; 1859-61); served in Civil War; major general (1862); circuit judge, Illinois (1870-73); presided over Democratic National Convention (1876).

McCLURE, Alexander Kelley. 1828-1909. Journalist and politician. b. Pennsylvania. Leader of the LIBERAL REPUBLI-

CAN movement; founder and editor of the Philadelphia *Times* (1875-1901).

McCOOK, Alexander McDowell. 1831-1903. Union general. b. Ohio. Graduated, U.S.M.A., West Point (1852); major general in the Civil War; served on western frontier; aide-de-camp to SHERMAN (1875-81).

McCORMICK, Cyrus Hall. 1809-1884. Invented the reaper. Invented a successful reaping machine which was demonstrated (1831; patented 1834); built a factory for the manufacture of the reapers in Chicago, Illinois (1847); introduced the reaper into Europe at the International Exhibition in London (1851); formed the McCormick Harvesting Machine Company with his brother Leander which later became the International Harvester Corp.

McCOY, Frank Ross. 1874-1954. Army officer. b. Pennsylvania. Graduated U.S.M.A., West Point (1897); served in CUBA; in the PHILIPPINES; served as aide to T. ROOSEVELT (1906-08); served in Mexico (1915-16); with the A.E.F. in France (1917-19); assistant to the governor of the Philippines (1921-25); director of RED CROSS work in Japan (1923); appointed by COOLIDGE to supervise the election in NICARAGUA (1928); chairman, commission of mediation between Bolivia and Paraguay (1929); member, LEAGUE OF NATIONS Lytton Commission investigating Japanese invasion of MANCHURIA (1932); major general (1929); retired (1938); member, Far Eastern Commission (until 1949).

McCULLOCH, Ben. 1811-1862. Scout and Indian fighter. b. Tennessee. Leader in battle of SAN JACINTO (1836); member, Texan congress (1839); fought Indians (1840-41); leader of spy and scout service during Mexican War; U.S. marshal for coast district of Texas (1853-60); brigadier general in Confederate army (1861); killed in battle of Pea Ridge (1862).

385

McCULLOCH, Hugh. 1808-1895. Lawyer and financier. b. Maine. Studied law in Boston; practised in Indiana (1833); banker (1835-63) U.S. Comptroller of the Currency (1863-65); appointed by LINCOLN, U.S. Secretary of the Treasury (1865-69); went to London; again U.S. Secretary of the Treasury appointed by ARTHUR (1884-85).

McCulloch vs. Maryland. A decision of the United States Supreme Court in 1819 upholding the constitutionality of the SECOND BANK OF THE UNITED STATES. The case is important because it gave the highest judicial sanction to the LOOSE CONSTRUCTION doctrine, the Court holding that the Congress could not be limited in its exercise of power under the ELASTIC CLAUSE if it could be established that the end was legitimate within the scope of the Constitution, and the means taken were appropriate. It is generally conceded that Chief Justice JOHN MARSHALL'S opinion in this case was his most brilliant. The decision was significant as an expression of growing nationalist sentiment after the War of 1812.

McDOUGALL, Alexander. 1731?-1786. Revolutionary general. b. Scotland. Came to America (1738); commanded British PRIVATEERS during the French and Indian War; leader of the SONS OF LIBERTY; imprisoned for Revolutionary pamphlet (1770-71); served in the Revolution becoming a major general (1777); commanded at West Point after ARNOLD'S treason; member, CONTINENTAL CONGRESS (1781-82, 1784-85).

McDOUGALL, Alexander. 1845-1923. Shipbuilder. b. Scotland. To Canada (1854); settled in Duluth, Minnesota; important for his design and construction of the "whaleback" freighter (1888) which was used for shipping on the GREAT LAKES; established first yards for building steel ships in the Pacific Northwest at Everett, Washington.

McDOWELL, Ephraim. 1771-1830. Surgeon. Practised in Kentucky; pioneer in abdominal surgery; famous for having performed the first ovarian surgery recorded in the United States.

McDOWELL, Irvin. 1818-1885. Union general. b. Ohio. Graduated, U.S.M.A., West Point (1838); served at Buena Vista in the Mexican War; brigadier general in charge of troops south of the Potomac (1861); lost at BULL RUN and replaced by MC CLELLAN; commanded Army of the Rappahannock; lost again at the second Battle of Bull Run (1862) and relieved of command; major general (1872); retired (1882).

McDOWELL, James. 1795-1851. Statesman. b. Virginia. Governor of Virginia (1843-45); member, U.S. House of Representatives (1845-51); made important speech in favor of admitting California to the Union as a free state.

McDUFFIE, George. 1790?-1851. Lawyer and legislator. b. Georgia. Member South Carolina state legislature (1818); member, U.S. House of Representatives (1821-34); governor of South Carolina (1834-36); leader of South Carolina group throughout the NULLIFICATION crisis; U.S. Senator (1842-46).

McDuffie-Tydings Act. Passed by Congress in 1934. Also known as the Philippine Independence Act. It provided that the PHILIPPINE ISLANDS would obtain independence under a commonwealth government in 1946. Pending ultimate independence the law established an island government under a constitution to be drafted. This document was drawn in 1935 and accepted by the United States President. Under it the government was inaugurated in November of that year. During the commonwealth period a United States High Commissioner resided in the Philippines with the power of veto over certain acts of the Philippine legislature. The commonwealth government, headed by an elected president, was autonomous for most internal matters. The statute also provided that the United States retain power over foreign loans and foreign relations, that American imports be admitted free into the Philippines, that Philippine exports to the United States be placed on quotas and be subject to progressively increasing export taxes. On July 4th, 1946 the Islands received their independence under the provisions of this law.

McGILLIVRAY, Alexander. 1759?-1793. CREEK INDIAN chief. Educated in Charleston and Savannah; LOYALIST during the Revolution because Americans confiscated his property; incited attacks on American settlements (1785-87); played the Spanish against the Americans in hope of obtaining best deal for his people; received with ceremony in New York and made brigadier general in U.S. Army, but opposed Americans until his death.

McGOVERN, George Stanley. 1922- . Political leader. b. Avon, S.D. Educated at Dakota Wesleyan U. and Northwestern U. Was executive secretary S.D. Democratic party 1953-55. Elected to U.S. House of Representatives 1956; reelected 1960. Special assistant to President Kennedy 1961; director of Food for Peace program. Elected to U.S. Senate 1961; reelected 1968. Democratic nominee for presidency 1972; charged Nixon administration as "the most morally corrupt in American history" with big-business favoritism and political sabotage in the wake of the Watergate break-in of Democratic Party headquarters.

McGUFFEY, William Holmes. 1800-1873. Educator. b. Pennsylvania. Graduated, Washington and Jefferson College (1826); professor, University of Virginia (1845-73). Famous for his Eclectic Readers which sold more than 120,000,000 copies in original and revised editions.

McHENRY, James. 1753-1816. Revolutionary patriot and statesman. b. Ireland. Came to America (1771); studied medicine under Dr. BENJAMIN RUSH; surgeon of Continental Army (1775-78); secretary to General WASHINGTON (1778-80); served with LAFAYETTE (1780-81); member, CONTINENTAL CONGRESS (1783-86); Maryland delegate to CONSTITUTIONAL CONVENTION (1787); signed the CONSTITUTION; appointed by Washington, U.S. Secretary of War (1796-1800); supported HAMILTON.

McINTIRE, Samuel. 1757-1811. Architect and woodcarver. b. Massachusetts. Famous for his designs and beautifully carved cornices and mantelpieces in the homes, churches, and public buildings of Salem, Mass.

McINTOSH, Lachlan. 1725-1806. Revolutionary officer. b. Scotland. Came to America (1736); brigadier general in the Continental army (1776); killed BUTTON GWINNETT in duel (1777); served with WASHINGTON at VALLEY FORGE; captured by British at Charleston, South Carolina (1780) brevetted; major general (1783).

McINTOSH, William. 1775?-1825. Creek Indian Chief. b. Georgia. Led CREEKS against British in the War of 1812; brigadier general in U.S. Army serving with JACKSON against SEMINOLES (1817-18); signed treaty ceding lands to the Americans; killed by the Indians.

McKEAN, Thomas. 1734-1817. Statesman. b. Pennsylvania. Admitted to the bar in Delaware (1755); member, Delaware assembly (1762-75); member, CONTINENTAL CONGRESS (1774-83); signer of the DECLARATION OF INDEPENDENCE; chief justice of Pennsylvania (1777-99); helped draft and signed the ARTICLES OF CONFEDERATION (1778); governor of Pennsylvania (1799-1808).

McKIM, Charles Follen. 1847-1909. Architect. b. Pennsylvania. A founder of McKim, Mead and White one of the largest and most important architectural firms. Important in designing and planning the Boston Public Libary; a group of Columbia University buildings on Morningside Heights, N.Y.; restoration of the WHITE HOUSE, Washington, D.C., etc.

McKinley Tariff Act. A PROTECTIVE TARIFF passed in 1890. It placed agricultural products on the dutiable list and increased rates on iron, steel, glass, tinplate, woolens, cottons, linens, and clothing. Although duties were removed from sugar, a bounty of two cents per pound was granted to domestic producers. The President was authorized to raise the duties on certain commodities in retaliation for discriminatory duties against American goods. The average rate was 48.39 percent.

McKINLEY, William. 1843-1901. Twenty-fifth President of the United States. b. Niles, Ohio. Served throughout the Civil War; studied law and practised in Ohio; member, U.S. House of Representatives (1877-83; 1885-91); chairman of the WAYS AND MEANS COMMITTEE (1889-91); largely responsible for the MC KINLEY TARIFF ACT (1890); supported by MARK HANNA, he was elected governor of Ohio (1892-96); elected Republican President of the United States (1896-1900); approved annexation of HAWAII; signed CURRENCY ACT putting the country on the GOLD STANDARD; shot by an assassin (Sept. 6, 1901) and died (Sept. 14).

McLEAN, John. 1785-1861. Jurist and legislator. b. New Jersey. Admitted to the bar and practiced in Ohio (1807); member, U.S. House of Representatives (1813-16); associate judge Ohio supreme court (1816-22); appointed by MONROE, U.S. Postmaster General (1823-29); Associate Justice, U.S. Supreme Court (1829-61); known for dissenting opinion in DRED SCOTT CASE; candidate for presidential nomination at FREE-SOIL convention (1848) and Republican convention (1856); defeated.

McMahon Bill. See Atomic Energy Commission.

McNary-Haugen Bill. A bill designed to raise the prices artificially of farm products. The bill was defeated in the House of Representatives in 1924 and in both chambers in 1926. It was passed in 1927 and 1928 but was VETOED both times by President COOLIDGE because of its alleged socialist aspects. It provided for the establishment of a federal farm corporation to purchase and store surplus grain, cotton, livestock, and tobacco until their prices rose or to sell them abroad at any prices. The corporation would pay FARMERS a price equal to the world price plus the TARIFF. Farmers were to pay an equalization fee to the corporation to reimburse it for the losses sustained in paying more for surpluses than the world price. This device was aimed at the maintenance of high consumer prices and the simultaneous insurance to the farmer of a good profit. The failure of its passage prevented any farm legislation until 1929.

McNUTT, Paul V. 1891-1955. Lawyer educator and politician. b. Indiana. Graduated, Harvard (LL.B. 1916); served as a major in World War I; professor of law, Indiana University (1919-33), dean (1925-33); national commander AMERICAN LEGION (1928-29); governor of Indiana (1933-37); U.S. High Commissioner to the PHILIPPINES (1937-9); administrator of FEDERAL SECURITY AGENCY (1939-45); director, Defense, Health and Welfare Services (1941-43); chairman, WAR MAN-POWER COMMISSION (1942-45); again U.S. High Commissioner to the Philippines (1945-46); member, WAR PRODUCTION BOARD and ECONOMIC STABILIZATION BOARD; member, Board of Directors, U.S. Life Insurance Company (since 1948).

McPHERSON, James Birdseye. 1828-1864. Union general. b. Ohio. Graduated, U.S.M.A., West Point (1853); chief engineer on GRANT's staff (1862); major general (1862); served at VICKSBURG in important capacity and named brigadier general (1863); succeeded SHERMAN in command of the Army of Tennessee (1864) and served with him in march South; killed near Atlanta, Georgia (July 22, 1864).

McREYNOLDS, James Clark. 1862-1946. Jurist. b. Kentucky. Graduated, University of Virginia law school (1884); practiced law in Tennessee; appointed by T. ROOSEVELT, assistant U.S. Attorney General (1903-07); appointed by WILSON, U.S. Attorney General (1913-14); known for prosecution of anti-trust cases; Associate Justice, U.S. Supreme Court (1914-41).

MacARTHUR, Arthur. 1845-1912. Army officer. b. Massachusetts. Served with Union army during the Civil War winning the CONGRESSIONAL MEDAL OF HONOR for his services at MISSIONARY RIDGE (1863); as major general served in both CUBA and the PHILIPPINES during the Spanish-American War; military governor of the Philippines (1900-01); lieutenant general and assistant chief of staff (1906); retired (1909).

MacARTHUR, Douglas. 1880-1964. Army officer. b. Arkansas. Graduated, U.S.M.A., West Point (1903); member of general staff in France during World War I; commanded 42nd division (called the Rainbow division) (1918-19); brigadier general (1920); superintendent at West Point (1919-22); major general (1925); commanded Philippine Department (1928); general and chief of staff, U.S. Army (1930-35); director of organization of national defense for the Philippine government (1935-37) retired; recalled to service (1941) as lieutenant general and placed in command of the U.S. forces in the Far East; general (1941) supreme commander of Allied forces in the Southwest Pacific (1942); 5 star general (1944); launched Philippine campaign from Australia (October,

1944-July, 1945); accepted Japanese surrender in Tokyo (September, 1945); appointed Supreme Commander for Allied Powers in Japan (1945-1951); named commander of UN forces resisting North Korea (June, 1950); dismissed from Korean and Japanese posts (1951) because of differences with President TRUMAN; on inactive list (1951); named keynoter of Republican NOMINATING CONVENTION (July, 1952); unsuccessful "DARK HORSE" candidate for Republican presidential nomination (1952).

MacDONOUGH, Thomas. 1783-1825. Naval officer. Served with DECATUR during WAR WITH TRIPOLI; commanded American fleet on Lake Champlain (1812-14); defeated a superior British squadron at Plattsburg sending them back into Canada (1814).

MacDOWELL, Edward Alexander. 1861-1908. Composer. b. New York City. Studied at Paris and in Germany; professor of music, Columbia University (1896-1904). Composer of symphonic poems, piano sonatas, orchestral suites, concertos for piano and orchestra, and many songs; best known for song *To a Wild Rose* and the shorter pieces in the *Woodland Sketches*.

"Machine Age." The popular term applied to the factory system which developed out of the INDUSTRIAL REVOLUTION. It signifies the INVENTION, improvement, and use of machines for industrial production as a replacement of hand tools.

MACKAY, John William. 1831-1902. Miner and financier. b. Ireland. Came to United States (1840); worked as miner in California (1851); struck rich ore in COMSTOCK LODE and became very wealthy (1873); with J. G. BENNETT, founded Commercial Cable Company and in order to break GOULD MONOPOLY they laid two submarine cables to Europe (1884); organized the Postal Telegraph Company in order to compete with WESTERN UNION (1886).

MacKAYE, James Morrison Steele. Known as Steele MacKaye. 1842-1894. Actor, playwright and producer. b. New York. Manager of Madison Square Theater, N.Y. (1879) which he designed; important for contribution of overhead lighting on state (1874), the first moving and double stage (1879); introduced folding theater seats and many other improvements. Author of many plays.

MACMILLAN, Donald Baxter. 1874-1970. Arctic explorer. b. Massachusetts. Graduated, Bowdoin and studied at Harvard; with PEARY on north-polar expedition (1908-09); led expeditions to arctic (1913-37). Author of books about the arctic.

MACON, Nathaniel. 1758-1837. Statesman. b. North Carolina. Attended College of New Jersey (Princeton); served in the Revolution; member, U.S. House of Representatives (1791-1815); Speaker of the House (1801-07); U.S. Senator (1815-28); strong supporter of STATES' RIGHTS, opposed ALIEN AND SEDITION ACTS, opposed the BANK OF THE UNITED STATES.

Macon's Bill No. 2. Passed by Congress in 1810. It had the purpose of compelling Great Britain and France to give up the illegal seizures of American merchant ships. Following the repeal of the NON-INTERCOURSE ACT OF 1809, it prohibited English and French armed vessels from entering American waters except when in distress. The measure once more opened American commerce to the world by repealing all trade restrictions with these two nations, provided however that if either of the two belligerents ceased its illegal activities against American neutral shipping, and the other refused to do so within a period of three months, the President was empowered to reopen trade with the first nation. Na-

poleon, profiting by the choice, promised to do so, the ultimate result being the involvement of the United States in war with Great Britain.

MADISON, James. 1751-1836. Fourth President of the United States. b. Port Conway, Virginia. Graduated, Princeton (1771); studied constitutional law; helped draft state constitution of Virginia (1776); member, CONTINENTAL CONGRESS (1780-83); delegate, CONSTITUTIONAL CONVENTION (1787) playing the leading role and probably more than anyone else can claim the title "father of the Constitution"; wrote a series of papers, with HAMILTON and JAY, in support of the Constitution, called the FEDERALIST; member, U.S. House of Representatives (1789-97); leader of the DEMOCRATIC-REPUBLICAN PARTY; opposed Hamilton; drafted the VIRGINIA RESOLUTIONS (1798) which opposed the ALIEN AND SEDITION LAWS; U.S. Secretary of State (1801-09); elected President of the United States (1809-17); leader during the War of 1812; rector, University of Virginia (1827-36).

Mafia Incident. A diplomatic incident between the United States and Italy which arose out of several lawless outbreaks in New Orleans in 1891. Police Chief Hennessy, active in hunting down members of the Mafia, a well known Italian terrorist organization, was brutally murdered. Nine Italians were brought to trial and six ultimately acquitted, the jury disagreeing on the others. Public opinion was outraged in the belief that the courts and jury had been bribed, leaving the lives and property of respectable citizens at the mercy of criminals. On March 15, 1891 a vast crowd, attending a meeting of protest, was roused to anger. It marched to the prison, sought out the Italian prisoners, and shot 11 of them. No demonstration was made against the jury and attorneys. It was clear that the city's population approved of the LYNCH-

ING, and ncne of the participants was arrested. The Italian people were outraged and the Italian government demanded the punishment of the lynchers and the payment of an indemnity. Secretary of State BLAINE discussed the situation with the Italian minister in Washington while urging the Governor of Louisiana to arrest the leaders. Italy withdrew her minister but ultimately Congress voted $25,000 for the families of the three of the victims who were shown to be NATURALIZED Americans. In 1892 Italy expressed her satisfaction with this decision and cordial relations were resumed.

Magazines. The first magazines in America were the *American Magazine, or Monthly View* and BENJAMIN FRANKLIN'S *General Magazine, and Historical Chronicle.* Both were published in 1741, but disappeared within the year. In 1743 an *American Magazine and Historical Chronicle* was published in Boston. In 1752 the *Independent Reflector* appeared in New York City. Other important magazines in the latter part of the 18th century were the *Pennsylvania Magazine* of 1775, the *American Museum* of 1787, the *Massachusetts Magazine* of 1789, and the *New York Magazine* of 1790. None of these lasted beyond 1797, this form of reading being supplied by British imports. The improvements in the printing industry and the spread of education encouraged the appearance of domestic magazines in the early 19th century. Of these the most important were the Philadelphia *Portfolio* in 1801 and the *Monthly Anthology* of Boston in 1803. The first literary review periodical was the *North American Review,* founded in Boston in 1815. It was followed by the *Knickerbocker* in 1832. Magazines of general interest included *Godey's Lady's Book,* the *New York Ledger,* the *Atlantic,* and *Harpers* in the 1850's. Magazines like *Century, Scribner's,* and *Forum* appeared after the Civil War. In 1952 magazines were published in various classifications. These included literary and critical periodicals such as the *Saturday Review of Literature* and the *Partisan Review,* digest magazines like *Reader's Digest* and *Reader's Scope,* scholarly periodicals such as the *American Political Science Review* and *Scientific American,* and "slicks" like the *Saturday Evening Post, Collier's, Cosmopolitan,* and *Red Book.* Comic magazines like the Marvel Comic Group and National Comics Group, and "pulps" like *Argosy* and *True Confession* have appeared in profusion since the 1920's. In addition there are many trade and LABOR UNION magazines. The role of advertising in magazine publication has become increasingly important. In 1963 magazine advertising cost $1,036,000,000, representing nine percent of the cost of advertising in all media. The magazine with the greatest circulation in the United States is READER'S DIGEST with a circulation of 14,500,000 in the United States and its possessions. TV GUIDE'S circulation was nearly 9 million and MC CALL'S over 8 million.

MAHAN, Alfred Thayer. 1840-1914. Naval officer and historian. b. New York. Graduated, U.S.N.A., Annapolis (1859); served in the Civil War; appointed commander (1872), captain (1885); president, Newport Naval War College, R.I. (1886-89; 1892-93); U.S. delegate to first HAGUE PEACE CONFERENCE (1899). Author of *The Influence of Sea Power upon History 1660-1783* (1890), *The Influence of Sea Power upon the French Revolution and Empire 1793-1812* (2 vols. 1892) and other books on naval strategy and history, and biographies of FARRAGUT and Nelson.

Maine. The 39th state in size, with an area of 33,215 square miles. Entered the Union on March 15, 1820 as the 23rd state. Augusta is the capital. In 1950

Maine's population of 913,774 made it 35th in rank. Its largest cities are Portland, Lewiston, and Bangor. Maine is the largest potato producer in the United States and has the greatest forests in the East. Pulp and paper are two important products. Agricultural crops include hay, oats, buckwheat, and apples. Manufactured goods are textiles and shoes. Canning of fruit is an important economic activity. A lucrative source of income is derived from tourists who visit the state's 2,465 lakes and hundreds of streams for FISHING and the hunting of deer, bear, and other game. York was the first chartered city (1642) in North America. Eastport is the easternmost city in the United States. Maine is presumed to be the nation's political barometer because it conducts its presidential election in September. The phrase "As Maine goes, so goes the nation" is, however, inaccurate since Maine is invariably Republican. Maine was discovered in 1604 by SAMUEL DE CHAMPLAIN. Its nickname is the "Pine Tree State."

Maine, U.S.S., Sinking Of. On February 15th, 1898 the second class battleship MAINE, on a visit in the harbor of Havana, was sunk by a huge explosion. Two hundred and sixty-four men and two officers were killed in the destruction of the ship. Although it has never been determined exactly who was responsible for its destruction the incident was exploded by the American press in whipping up public anger against Spain. The Spanish government immediately accepted the resignation of its ambassador to the United States and expressed its regret over the accident. Nevertheless, in the United States, the "YELLOW PRESS" carried on the campaign against Spain, and stimulated the appearance of buttons and flags with the slogan "Remember the *Maine*." Public opinion accepted this version of the accident and, therefore, by and large were prepared for the declaration of war two months later.

"Malefactors of Great Wealth." A quotation from a speech by President T. ROOSEVELT delivered at Provincetown, Massachusetts on August 20, 1907. In this address Roosevelt attacked those in the business world who he considered had been responsible for the PANIC OF 1907 in an attempt to defeat his anti-trust program.

MALLORY, Stephen Russell. 1813?-1873. Confederate leader. b. Trinidad, West Indies. Customs official in Florida; U.S. Senator (1851-61); chairman, committee on naval affairs; Secretary of the Navy, Confederate States of America (1861-65); fled with DAVIS; captured and imprisoned; released and resumed the practice of law in Florida (1866).

Manchukuo. See Manchuria.

Manchuria. The former Manchu state in eastern Asia which is bounded on the east by Siberia and Korea, on the south by China, and on the west by China, Siberia, and Mongolia. Manchuria was invaded by Japan in 1931 and wrested from China. It was proclaimed an independent nation on February 18, 1932 and renamed Manchukuo by the Japanese on March 1, 1932. The interest of the United States in this territory was first manifested in Secretary of State HAY's "OPEN DOOR" notes in September-November, 1899. The TREATY OF PORTSMOUTH in 1905, ROOT-TAKAHIRA AGREEMENT in 1908, Taft-Knox proposal of 1909-1910, LANSING-ISHII NOTES of 1917, and NINE POWER TREATY of 1922 were subsequent expressions of continuing interest of this country in the sovereignty and independence of China. After the creation of Manchukuo Secretary of State STIMSON proclaimed the doctrine of nonrecognition on January 7, 1932. Up to World War II the United States abided by the STIMSON DOCTRINE. At the close of the war Manchuria was returned to China under its original name.

Manhattan Island, Purchase Of. In 1626 PETER MINUIT, representing the DUTCH WEST INDIA COMPANY, bought Manhattan Island from the Canarsie Indians for $24 worth of trinkets. The Island had been discovered by VERRAZANO in 1524 and visited by HENRY HUDSON in 1609. Its name stems from the Indian tribe known as Manahata or Manhatoes. After the purchase, the latter tribe, with more valid claim to the Island, demanded additional payments from the Dutch, and these were made.

Manhattan Project. An ATOMIC BOMB project created on August 13, 1942 as the Manhattan District in the Corps of Engineers for carrying on special work in the atomic bomb program. In May, 1943 the Project took over all atomic energy research from the OFFICE OF SCIENTIFIC RESEARCH AND DEVELOPMENT which had administered the program since December 6, 1941. General Leslie G. Groves was placed in charge as coordinator of all work in atomic bomb research. The Project supervised research carried on at Columbia University, Princeton University, and the University of California. Under its sponsorship the first chain reaction in nuclear fission was accomplished at the University of Chicago on December 2, 1942 under the direction of ARTHUR H. COMPTON and Enrico Fermi.

Manifest Destiny. The doctrine in the 1830's and 40's that held that it was the clear and inevitable lot of the United States to absorb all of North America. Under the southern leadership of the Democratic party it became a purely sectional slogan aimed at the acquisition of additional lands suitable for SLAVERY. The agrarian expansionism thus exhibited ultimately ended in the acquisition of Texas, Oregon, California, and the Mexican Cession.

Manila Bay, Battle Of. The naval victory of Commodore GEORGE DEWEY over the Spanish fleet at Manila commanded by Admiral Montojo. Upon the declaration of war on April 25, 1898 Dewey, stationed at Hongkong, was ordered to attack the Spanish fleet at Manila. He moved his four cruisers and two gunboats to Manila on April 30 and attacked the ten small Spanish vessels the following morning. Within seven hours the shore batteries were silenced and every enemy ship sunk, burned, or deserted. The Spaniards suffered 381 casualties and the Americans only nine wounded. After a three and one half month blockade of Manila the city surrendered on August 13th.

Mann Act. Passed by Congress in 1910. It prescribes a heavy fine and imprisonment for any person who transports a woman or girl in foreign or INTERSTATE COMMERCE for an immoral purpose. Congress did not, by this law, attempt to prohibit prostitution, inasmuch as it has no constitutional authority to do so. The law is based on Congress' regulatory power over interstate commerce. The prohibition of prostitution within the states is an exercise of the states' POLICE POWERS reserved to them in the 10th amendment of the federal Constitution.

Mann-Elkins Act. Enacted in 1910 as an amendment to the INTERSTATE COMMERCE ACT. It extended the jurisdiction of the INTERSTATE COMMERCE COMMISSION to TELEPHONE, TELEGRAPH, and cable lines and increased the power of the commission by vesting in it the authority to fix maximum rates on its own motion. It also prohibited RAILROADS from charging more for a short haul than for a long haul over the same route. This statute failed to achieve the desired effect of eliminating all the RAILROAD ABUSES which had grown up after the Civil War thus leading to later railroad legislation.

MANN, Horace. 1796-1859. Educator. b. Massachusetts. Graduated, Brown(1819);

studied law and admitted to the bar in Massachusetts (1823); practiced in Boston (1823-37); first secretary, Massachusetts Board of Education (1837-48); reorganized entire public school system and methods of teaching; helped establish first normal school in the United States (1839); anti-SLAVERY WHIG member, U.S. House of Representatives (1848-53); founder and president, Antioch College (1852-59); elected to HALL OF FAME (1900); sometimes called "Father of American Public School System."

MANNING, Daniel. 1831-1877. Journalist and financier. Editor and owner of the Albany ARGUS; secretary and later chairman, N.Y. state Democratic committee (1879-85); important supporter of CLEVELAND for governor (1882) and President (1884); appointed by Cleveland, U.S. Secretary of the Treasury (1885-87).

Man Power Act. Passed by Congress in the summer of 1918 as a supplement to the SELECTIVE SERVICE ACT of 1917. The law provided for the induction into the armed services of all men between the ages of 18 and 45. On the date of registration, September 12th, 13,000,000 men registered for such service of whom less than one percent were ultimately inducted because of the armistice signed less than one month later.

Manufacturing. Colonial manufacturing revolved around the household production of clothing, tools, and implements. Hand power was supplemented by primitive water and animal-powered mills in the manufacture of paper, gun powder, flour, and lumber. Factory-produced goods were of little economic importance until the War of 1812. After the establishment of Samuel Slater's textile factory at Pawtucket, Rhode Island in 1791 English machinery was imported and a TEXTILE INDUSTRY begun. By the opening of the War of 1812 there were 200 cotton mills in New England and the middle states. Steam had already been introduced as the motive power. The war itself was the greatest stimulus to manufacturing up to the Civil War. Capital, made idle by the EMBARGO ACT, was invested in industry. The demand for manufactured goods was spurred by military needs. After the war the TARIFF OF 1816 protected these "infant industries." Stable financing was provided by the chartering of the SECOND BANK OF THE UNITED STATES that year. A widespread program of internal improvements linked the sections of the nation together. THE COINAGE ACT OF 1837 furnished a sound CURRENCY system. Increasing IMMIGRATION and an upswing in the birthrate furnished the necessary labor power and a consumer POPULATION. Markets and raw material sources lay in the West. The spirit of nationalism engendered by the war produced an ERA OF GOOD FEELING in which the sections joined, for more than a decade, in the manufacturing development of the country. New England took the leadership in this INDUSTRIALIZATION program, its native capital supplemented in considerable quantities by the investments of European businessmen. INVENTIONS, made or improved in the United States, changed the old industries and introduced new ones. Wood, metal, furniture, arms, and vehicles were produced. By the Civil War agricultural and TRANSPORTATION equipment was being manufactured in large quantities. Clothing, glass, and novelties became important manufactures. In the first half of the 19th century cotton spindles increased in number to 5,000,000. Pig iron production was raised from 60,000 to 1,000,000 tons. The use of automatic machinery and interchangeable standardized parts had already become hallmarks of American industrial production. The Civil War gave rise to the "second INDUSTRIAL REVOLUTION." By the use of specialized labor, automatic machinery, standardized parts, and the assembly line, MASS PRODUCTION methods became the distinguishing feature of American industry. New sources of raw materials in the Far West were made available. These included such novel resources as aluminum, tungsten, and petroleum. By the 20th century new industries such as RUBBER, CHEMICALS, PLASTICS, ALUMINUM, and synthetic fabrics had become important additions to manufacturing. Continuing immigration provided the necessary labor power. Government aid in the form of TARIFF protection, loans, grants spurred the industrialization of the country. Manufacturing moved westward to Chicago, St. Louis, Cleveland, and Detroit. By 1914 the number of workers had tripled as of 1865. The value of manufactured products rose in this period from $3,400,000,000 to $24,-200,000,000, and was greater than the value of farm products. Industrial combinations became a characteristic of manufacturing organization, and financial institutions began to acquire control of these integrated organizations. Private laboratory research became important supplements to the investigations of public and university laboratories. By 1900 the United States had become the greatest industrial producer in the world. In some industries, as OIL and STEEL, it was outproducing the rest of the world. By the opening of World War II the United States was leading the world in the production of steel, rubber, automotive equipment, textiles, transportation, AIRCRAFT, and food products. In 1963 there were 313,000 manufacturing establishments in the United States employing 17,000,000 workers. The value added by manufacturing to the goods produced that year was $179,289,000,000.

Marbury vs. Madison. The decision of the U.S. Supreme Court in 1803 in which the doctrine of JUDICIAL REVIEW was enunciated. This was the first important opinion of Chief Justice JOHN MARSHALL, who had been appointed to the court two years previously. See judicial review.

MARCY, William Learned. 1786-1857. Statesman. b. Massachusetts. Graduated, Brown (1808); admitted to the bar and practiced, Troy, N.Y. (1811-23); served in the War of 1812; member of a powerful political group called the "Albany Regency"; comptroller, N.Y. State (1823-29); associate justice, N.Y. supreme court (1829-31); U.S. Senator (1831-32); made speech referring to the "SPOILS SYSTEM" in which "to the victor belongs the spoils" (1832) made that phrase famous; governor of New York (1833-39); appointed by POLK, U.S. Secretary of War (1845-49); appointed by PIERCE, U.S. Secretary of State (1853-57).

MARIN, John. 1870-1953. Landscape painter. b. New Jersey. Studied at Stevens Institute of Technology, Pennsylvania Academy of the Fine Arts, and abroad after 1905. Exhibited at the STIEGLITZ gallery (1909); famous for his water colors of seascapes and landscapes of Maine and Jersey scenes; he is a leader of the "modern school" of artists; his work has been exhibited throughout the world and appears in leading museums in the United States.

Marine Corps. A specially trained military organization located as an autonomous body within the DEPARTMENT OF THE NAVY. It was established by the Second CONTINENTAL CONGRESS in 1776 and made permanent by Congress in 1798. Its training is designed to make it particularly efficient for amphibious military service. It has been dispatched to foreign countries by American Presidents in many instances to protect American lives and property during peace time. Such missions have included intervention in China during the BOXER REBELLION, in NICARAGUA, HAITI, and SANTO DOMINGO.

MARION, Francis. 1732?-1795. Revolutionary commander. b. South Carolina. Played an important role in the Revolutionary War; commanded militia troops in South Carolina which made raids on the British forces and then escaped to the swamps; he was given the name "the Swamp Fox"; made commandant of Fort Johnson in recognition of his services (1784); served in state senate (up to 1790).

Maritime Act of 1936. See Maritime Commission.

Maritime Administration. An agency established in the DEPARTMENT OF COMMERCE on May 24, 1950 by President TRUMAN'S Reorganization Plan Number 21. It was given the administrative functions of the former MARITIME COMMISSION. The agency is headed by an Administrator who is also the chairman of the FEDERAL MARITIME BOARD.

Maritime Commission, U. S. An independent regulatory agency established on June 29, 1936 by the Ship Subsidy Act. It replaced the UNITED STATES SHIPPING BOARD and was given the powers, property, and functions of that agency. Among these were the development of a merchant fleet by means of direct subsidy grants, the encouragement of American merchants to utilize American SHIPPING, and the collaboration with shipping companies in developing modern efficient vessels. Its regulatory powers included the establishment of maximum and minimum rates in INTERSTATE COMMERCE except on the GREAT LAKES, the prohibition of discriminatory rates, classifications, and practices, the grant of SUBSIDIES to assist weak lines, and the determination of foreign and American shipping costs. Through the Maritime Labor Board, created by the Act, it supervised LABOR RELATIONS and the labor provisions of federal maritime legislation in contracts between unions and operators receiving national subsidies. Under certain conditions it was authorized to build or recondition vessels and to charter them to private operators. The Maritime Commission was abolished on May 24, 1950 by President Truman's Reorganization Plan Number 21. It was replaced by the FEDERAL MARITIME BOARD which exercised the Commission's former regulatory powers and by the MARITIME ADMINISTRATION which exercised the Commission's former administrative functions.

Maritime Labor Board. See Maritime Commission, United States.

Marne, Second Battle of the. A part of the final German offensive which was met by a victorious allied counteroffensive on the Marne River in France in July, 1918. Two hundred and seventy-five thousand American troops supported the French in stemming the German advance, achieving brilliant successes.

MARQUETTE, Jacques. 1637-1675. Jesuit missionary and explorer. b. France. Sent to New France (1666); missionary to OTTAWA INDIANS (1668); accompanied JOILET on trip down the Wisconsin and Mississippi rivers to the mouth of the Arkansas River and back (1673); wrote a journal of his voyage published in (1681).

MARSH, George Perkins. 1801-1882. Diplomat and lawyer. b. Vermont. Graduated, Dartmouth College (1820); admitted to the bar and practiced in Vermont (1825); WHIG member, U.S. House of Representatives (1843-49); U.S. Minister to Turkey (1849-54); appointed by LINCOLN, first American Minister to Italy (1861-82). Also a well-known philologist and author *The Origin and History of the English Language* (1862) and many other books on that subject.

MARSH, Othniel Charles. 1831-1899. Paleontologist. b. New York. Graduated, Yale; first professor of paleontology at that university (1866-99); led expeditions into the West in search of fossils; his discoveries have had a considerable influence on the theories and teaching of evolution; presented large collection of fossils to Yale; author of many books on his subject.

MARSHALL, George Catlett. 1880-1959 General and statesman. b. Pennsylvania. Graduated, Virginia Military Institute (1901); served with A.E.F. in France during World War I (1917-19) in major battles; aide-de-camp to General PERSHING (1919-24) served in China (1924-27); chief of staff, U.S. Army (1939-45) with rank of general; retired; recalled to service as general of the army (1944); became five star general; U.S. ambassador to China (Nov. 1945); U.S. Secretary of State (1947-49); sponsored the EUROPEAN RECOVERY PROGRAM, know as the Marshall Plan for integrating the economy of European nations for recovery; appointed Secretary of Defense (1950-51).

MARSHALL, John. 1755-1835. Jurist. b. Virginia. Served in Continental army through the Revolution through many major battles; admitted to the bar (1780); member, Virginia executive council (1782-95); member, HOUSE OF BURGESSES (1782-88); FEDERALIST leader; member, U.S. House of Representatives (1799-1800); appointed by ADAMS U.S. Secretary of State (1800-01) and Chief Justice, U.S. Supreme Court (1801-35); his decisions established the fundamental doctrines of American constitutional laws as evidenced in MARBURY VS MADISON, MCCULLOCH VS MARYLAND, and GIBBONS VS OGDEN; generally considered the greatest Chief Justice in the history of the Supreme Court.

Marshall Plan. Also known as the European Recovery Program. A plan for the economic recovery of Europe after World War II. It was born in the announcement of Secretary of State GEORGE C. MARSHALL on June 5, 1947 to a Harvard University commencement audience that the United States would help European governments "willing to assist in the task of recovery." After a 10 week conference in Paris, 16 West European nations agreed on September 22 on a four year recovery plan. On April 3, 1948 President TRUMAN signed the first appropriation bill authorizing $5,300,000,000 for the first year of the European Recovery Program. The law established the Economic Cooperation Administration to head the program with Paul G. Hoffman as Administrator. On May 5, 1951 the ECA reported that industrial production of Western Europe had risen 30 percent above pre-war levels. On July 25 the ECA declared that a new plan to develop defenses, improve TRADE, and raise living standards in Marshall Plan countries would be put into effect. Its purpose was to create an expanding economy by having foreign plants "adopted by United States firms." Independent boards would be established to cooperate with the ECA in working out programs of technological improvements, fund distribution, and labor and business practices. In that month the agency reported that Marshall Plan countries had raised their industrial output 40 percent above the 1938 level. The program expired on December 31, 1951 after having spent almost $12,500,000,-000. It was succeeded by the MUTUAL SECURITY ADMINISTRATION.

MARSHALL, Thurgood. On October 2, 1967, Thurgood Marshall was sworn in as the first black U.S. Supreme Court Justice.

MARTIN, Luther. 1748?-1826. Lawyer and Revolutionary leader. b. New Jersey. Admitted to the bar, Virginia (1771); practised in Maryland; member, ANNAPO-

LIS CONVENTION (1774); member, CON-
TINENTAL CONGRESS (1785); delegate,
CONSTITUTIONAL CONVENTION (1787); first
attorney-general of state of Maryland
(1778-1805; 1818-22); joined the FED-
ERALISTS; defense attorney for CHASE in
impeachment trial (1804) and BURR in
treason trial (1807).

Martin vs. Hunter's Lessee. A decision of
the United States Supreme Court in 1816
in which it sustained the provision of the
JUDICIARY ACT OF 1789 providing for appeals from STATE COURTS in cases involving federal law. By asserting its authority
in face of the denial of the highest Virginia court to this right, the Supreme
Court, in effect, laid down the doctrine
of its power of JUDICIAL REVIEW over the
decisions of the highest state courts.
This is one of the notable decisions of
Chief Justice JOHN MARSHALL which was
part of the nationalist movement in the
period following the War of 1812.

Maryland. The 42nd state in size, with an
area of 10,577 square miles. Entered the
Union on April 28, 1788 as the seventh
state. Annapolis is the capital. Maryland's
1950 population of 2,343,001 made it
24th in rank. Its largest cities are Baltimore, Cumberland, and Hagerstown. As
a result of the jutting of Chesapeake Bay
into the heart of the state, Maryland has
the largest river frontage of any state in
the Union. The principal industries are
vegetable canning, chicken raising, and
crabbing. Crops include wheat, hay, barley, corn, and potatoes. Its leading minerals are coal, sand, gravel, stone, and
cement. Important manufactured products are airplanes, chemicals, steel, and
clothing. Annapolis is the site of the
United States Naval Academy. Maryland
was first settled in 1634 two years after
the charter was granted to Lord Baltimore. Its nicknames are the "Free State"
and "Old Line State."

Maryland Toleration Act. An act of the
Maryland colony granting limited religious toleration to all Christians. Severe
penalties were provided for violators and
for those who employed opprobrious
names such as heretic, idolator, PURITAN,
or JESUIT. The Puritan-controlled assembly which enacted the legislation also
inserted a clause providing the death
penalty for those who denied the divinity
of Christ. The Act did not grant full RE-
LIGIOUS TOLERATION and was not a true
measure of the sentiments of Lord Baltimore, the founder of the colony. Nevertheless, it was a significant contribution
towards religious toleration in early
America.

Mason and Dixon Line. A line surveyed
by two Englishmen, Charles Mason and
Jeremiah Dixon, in 1763 and 1767, to
settle boundary differences between the
PENN family of Pennsylvania and the
CALVERT family of Maryland. The line
runs along the parallel 39 degrees, 42
minutes, 23.6 seconds. It was originally
marked by milestones, every fifth one
bearing the coats of arms of the Penn and
Calvert families. With relation to contemporary geography, it is the southern
boundary line of Pennsylvania and the
northern boundry line of Delaware, Maryland, and West Virginia. Its historic importance lies in the customary understanding that it was the dividing line
between slave and free soil in the pre-
Civil War period. Today it is still accepted as the symbolic border between North
and South, both politically and socially.

MASON, George. 1725-1792. Statesman.
b. Virginia. Wealthy Virginia planter;
strong leader in opposition to the TOWN-
SHEND ACTS the STAMP ACT and the BOS-
TON PORT ACT; member, Virginia constitutional convention (1776); prepared
Declaration of Rights and most of the
constitution of Virginia; delegate, CON-
STITUTION CONVENTIQN (1787); did not
sign the Constitution and opposed its ratification; chosen first U.S. Senator from

Virginia, but declined to serve.

MASON, James Murray. 1798-1871. Lawyer and Confederate diplomat. b. District of Columbia. GRANDSON OF GEORGE MASON. Practised law in Virginia (from 1820); member, U.S. House of Representatives (1837-39); U.S. Senator (1847-61); drafted the FUGITIVE SLAVE LAW (1850); member of Confederate Congress (1861); sent as Confederate representative, with JOHN SLIDELL, to France (1861-65); seized by the British on the British mail steamer *Trent*, almost starting a war between the United States and Britain (called the TRENT AFFAIR) and creating sympathy for the Confederate side in the Civil War; released (1862).

MASON, Jeremiah. 1768-1848. Lawyer and legislator. Graduated, Yale (1788); practiced law in New Hampshire; attorney-general of New Hampshire (1802-05); FEDERALIST U.S. Senator(1813-17); president, New Hampshire branch of the Bank of the United States; prominent lawyer and opponent of DANIEL WEBSTER.

MASON, John. 1586-1635. English colonist in America. b. England. Governor of Newfoundland (1615-21); procured patent grant to Maine territory with Gorges (1622); patent from the COUNCIL FOR NEW ENGLAND for territory he named New Hampshire (1629); settled colony on Piscataqua River; is considered the founder of New Hampshire.

Massachusetts. The 45th state in size, with an area of 8,257 square miles. Entered the Union on February 6, 1788 as the sixth state. Boston is the capital. In 1950 Massachusetts' population of 4,-690,514 made it ninth in rank. Its largest cities are Boston, Worcester, and Springfield. Massachusetts is the greatest textile producing state in the nation. Boston has remained to date the biggest United States wool market. Important MANUFAC-TURING products include shoes, watches, machinery, small arms, electrical goods, soap, and candy. Boston and Gloucester are two of the most important fishing ports in the nation. Massachusetts produces important crops of tobacco, potatoes, wheat, corn, and apples. Massachusetts was first settled by the PILGRIMS in 1620, although it is believed the Norsemen under Eric the Red discovered it in 1000. Its nicknames are the "Bay State" and "Old Colony State."

Massachusetts Bay Colony. Established in 1630 by the Massachusetts Bay Company. In its beginnings it was the largest and most important of the British colonies in North America. Founded by PURITANS, the colony attempted to purify the "idolatrous remnants of popery" in the ANGLICAN CHURCH. Non-Puritans were forbidden participation in the government although they were permitted to reside in the colony as they did not resist authority, disturb the ministers, or bring discredit upon the Puritan religion or government. Among its leaders were JOHN ENDICOTT, JOHN COTTON, and JOHN WINTHROP who was its governor for many years. With its charter, making its stockholders "freemen," it was virtually independent of England. Its government of "freemen" was representative, although the franchise was restricted to church members. The most important economic activities of the colony were AGRICULTURE, FISHING, SHIPPING and SHIPBUILDING, the production of NAVAL STORES, LUMBER, and FUR TRADING.

Massachusetts Bay Company. A JOINT STOCK COMPANY chartered by the King of England in 1628 to JOHN ENDICOTT and five associates. Organized for the purpose of FISHING and FUR TRADING, it was given a patent to the land from a point three miles north of the Merrimac River to a point three miles south of the Charles River. The following year, enlarged to

26 members, the Company obtained a charter from Charles the First, delegating to it all political powers to administer the colony. The Puritan members of the Company emigrated to America in 1630 bringing 2,000 colonists to Boston harbor, thereby inaugurating the Massachusetts Bay Colony, the largest and most important British settlement in America. Prior to its reorganization in 1628 the Company was known as the New England Company.

Massachusetts Government Act. The second of the INTOLERABLE ACTS passed by Parliament in May, 1774 for the purpose of suppressing the disturbances created by the BOSTON TEA PARTY. It was also known as the Regulating Act. The law revoked the Massachusetts charter, and provided that the council members be appointed by the governor and their salaries paid by the Crown. Colonial judges and sheriffs were to be appointed by the governor. It abolished the TOWN MEETING. The Law aroused the instant public opposition, and focused inter-colonial attention upon the need for immediate action against Great Britain.

MASSASOIT. d. 1661. Wampanoag Indian Chief. Lived in Massachusetts between Cape Cod and Narragansett Bay; powerful chief in the New England area; signed a peace treaty with the PILGRIMS (1621)and remained friendly with them, he befriended ROGER WILLIAMS; father of KING PHILIP.

Mass Production. The volume production of industrial commodities by the application of machinery. This development in American industry was made possible by the simultaneous expansion of facilities in TRANSPORTATION, COMMUNICATION, and STEEL based upon the use of steam and electric power. At the end of the 19th and in the 20th centuries the mass production of goods increased enormously as a result of the use of automatic machinery, specialized labor, and standardized parts. Whereas in 1859 the value of manufactured products in the United States was $1,886,000,000, it had increased by 1929 to $70,435,000,000 and by 1963 to more than $179,000,000,000. Industry was organized on departmental and assembly line bases which standardized production processes. The pooling of PATENTS and merging of research facilities, resulting from BUSINESS CONSOLIDATION in such industries as AUTOMOBILES, ELECTRICITY, PETROLEUM, RUBBER, steel, COAL, CLOTHING, and communications, steadily increased the output of industrial products.

MATHER, Cotton. 1663-1728. Congregational clergyman and writer. b. Boston, Mass. Son of INCREASE MATHER. Graduated, Harvard (1678); M.A. (1681); ordained (1685); assisted his father, Second Church pastorate, Boston (1685-1723); succeeded him (1723-28); led revolt against royal governor ANDROS; supported Phipps, but lost control of state and people (1692); scholar interested in science; countenanced WITCHCRAFT TRIALS, but later denounced them (1692-93); controversial figure but one of great influence on the thinking of his time and considered the outstanding writer of the colonial period.

MATHER, Increase. 1639-1723. Congregational clergyman. b. Massachusetts. Graduated, Harvard (1656); Trinity College, Dublin (M.A.); preached in England (1658-61); returned after the Restoration in England and became pastor at the Second Church, Boston (1664-1723); secured new charter and a new governor for Massachusetts in England (1688-92); president of Harvard College (1685-1701); prominent leader and author of various books on religion and the colonial period.

MATTHEWS, Brander. Full name James Brander Matthews. 1852-1929. Educator and author. b. New Orleans, Louisiana. Graduated, Columbia (1871); professor LITERATURE (1892-1900) and dramatic literature (1900-24), Columbia; leading figure in the literary and theater world. Author of plays, works of criticism and books on the THEATER.

MAURY, Matthew Fontaine. 1806-1873. Naval officer and oceanographer. b. Virginia. Saw active service in the navy; superintendent, Depot of Charts and Instruments, Naval Observatory (1842-61); did research work on ocean winds and currents; wrote first textbook on modern oceanography, *The Physical Geography of the Sea* (1855); entered Confederate service (1861); agent in England for the CONFEDERACY (1862-65); professor meteorology, Virginia Military Institute (1868-73). Elected to HALL OF FAME. Author of many books.

Maximilian Affair. A diplomatic incident between the United States and France arising out of the attempt of Napoleon III to establish a French empire in Mexico. Supported by French armies, the Archduke Maximilian of Austria was established as the Emperor of Mexico in 1864. The demands of Secretary of State SEWARD that the French evacuate Mexico went unheeded during the Civil War, but in the fall of 1865 General SHERIDAN was sent to Texas with orders to mobilize a powerful force along the Rio Grande. Reverting to the MONROE DOCTRINE Secretary Seward informed the French government that the United States would not tolerate an alien army in Mexico. Seward refused Napoleon's offer to withdraw his army upon United States' recognition of Maximilian's regime. Instead he sent General SHERMAN on a mission to Benito Juarez, the Mexican Revolutionary leader. Understanding this as a tacit recognition of the latter, Napoleon withdrew his troops by May, 1866. Left without military aid, Maximilian was overthrown, captured, and executed by the Mexicans. The affair was an important diplomatic victory for the United States and the Monroe Doctrine.

"Mayday Tribe". In 1970 and 1971 there were many rallies and vigils held to protest the war in Viet Nam. Most were peaceful and orderly but the radical Mayday Tribe attempted to disrupt all government activities by blocking roads and bridges and over 12,000 protestors were arrested and jailed despite protests by civil libertarians.

MAY, Samuel Joseph. 1797-1871. Reformer. b. Boston, Massachusetts. Graduated, Harvard (1817); Unitarian minister, Connecticut (1822-36); ABOLITIONIST, friend of GARRISON; worked for UNDERGROUND RAILROAD; worked for EDUCATION reforms; leader in TEMPERANCE MOVEMENT and worked for equal rights for women.

Mayflower, The. The name of the 180 ton ship chartered in London to bring the PILGRIMS to America. With the *Speedwell*, the *Mayflower* sailed from Southampton on August 15, 1620, but returned to Dartmouth Harbor eight days later because of a leak the *Speedwell* had sprung. After embarking on September 2, they returned once to Plymouth Harbor where the *Speedwell* was abandoned. The *Mayflower* sailed alone with 102 passengers and crew on September 16, and came into sight of Cape Cod on November 19th. She arrived at what is now the port of Provincetown on November 21st, took on food and water, and arrived at the site of Plymouth on December 21st, 1620. She returned to England on April 5th 1621, remaining there until 1624 after which her history is uncertain.

"Mayflower Compact", The. An agreement signed by the PILGRIM passengers of the *Mayflower* acknowledging their loyalty to the King and pledging their obedience to such just and equal laws as would be necessary to the general good of the colony to be established after landing. This document is the first illustration of self-determination in American history. It is also considered as the first example of a written constitution in North America.

Mayo Clinic. Established in 1919 in Rochester, Minnesota by the Mayo Foundation for Medical Education and Research. It is a part of the graduate school of the University of Minnesota and is the first and largest organization of its kind to offer training in the clinical branches of medicine. Approximately 300 fellows students are generally in service for periods of three to four years in diagnosis, clincal assistance, and laboratory research. The members of the Clinic staff are members of the graduate faculty of the University and in part members of the faculty of its medical school. The Foundation was established by the donation of more than $2,500,000 by Doctors Charles H. and William James Mayo. It has become world famous for its advancement of medical education and research in human disease, and for its research into the problems of hygiene, health, and public welfare. It also carries on a broad program of assisting medical, surgical, and scientific investigation.

Mayor-Council Government. A plan of municipal government (usually city) in which there is an elective mayor as chief executive and a council as the legislative body. The council is customarily a UNICAMERAL body. In the strong-mayor form that officer exercises the usual EXECUTIVE POWERS including appointments, budgeting, legislative recommendations to the council, and VETO. In the weak-mayor plan the mayor is generally a ceremonial figure, and is oftentimes merely a council member designated by that body as the mayor. The mayor-council plan is the oldest and most prevalent form of city government in the United States. In 1952 more than 1,000 out of 1,800 cities with populations over 5,000 still used this system.

Maysville Veto. A VETO by President JACKSON in 1830 of a bill authorizing federal expenditures for the construction of the Maysville, Washington, Paris, and Lexington Turnpike. Jackson's veto was based on the intra-state character of the project. He declared that it was not eligible for federal aid under Congress' INTERSTATE COMMERCE power. The veto is important as having put an end to a decade of struggle over the political and constitutional issue of federal aid to internal improvements. In effect it turned over to the STATES the cost of such improvements.

MEADE, George Gordon. 1815-1872. Union general. b. Spain of American parents. Graduated, U.S.M.A., West Point (1835); brigadier general of volunteers; aided in defense of Washington, D.C. (1861); served in major battles of the Civil War; major general (1862); commanded ARMY OF THE POTOMAC (1863); served with GRANT.

Meat Inspection Act. Passed by Congress in 1906. It is one of the laws enacted as a result of the public outcry against conditions in the food industry revealed by the works of the "MUCKRACKERS." The Act authorized the Secretary of Agriculture to inspect all meat shipped in INTERSTATE COMMERCE to determine that it had come from healthy animals and had been packed under sanitary conditions. He was empowered to condem such products as were "unsound, unhealthful, unwholesome, or otherwise unfit for human food."

Meat Packing Industry. Local meat packing, based on pickling, smoking, and salting, grew up in the colonial period. Even before the growth of the RAILROADS slaughterhouses, to which cattle were driven, had come into existence. These grew up in Cincinnati which, by the opening of the Civil War, was the meat packing center of the United States. Its nickname "Porkopolis" derived from the thriving trade in swine. Shortly afterwards, Chicago grew in importance for beef slaughtering. The greatest era of meat packing evolved out of the "CATTLE KINGDOM" and "LONG DRIVE" after the Civil War. In Chicago the meat packing firms of PHILIP D. ARMOUR, John Cudahy, and Gustavus F. Swift were established. The accumulation of capital, the refrigerated car, and the development of the railroad made Chicago the meat packing center of the United States. Farther west important centers came into being in Kansas City, Omaha, and St. Louis. As a result of unhealthful slaughtering conditions federal and state legislation was enacted to protect the public interest. The growth of the industry is evidenced by the figures: in 1869 there were 768 meat packing houses, increasing to more than 1,200 in 1920. In Chicago alone in 1950 receipts were recorded of 1,779,945 cattle, 3,670,270 hogs, and 653,649 sheep. The largest stockyard and slaughtering plants in the world were located in this city.

Mecklenburg Declaration of Independence. A series of resolutions adopted on May 20, 1775 at Charlotte, North Carolina by the citizens of Mecklenburg County. The resolutions purported to declare the country a free and independent sovereign government. There is considerable controversy over the authenticity of the document, JEFFERSON himself denouncing it as spurious. In 1847 a copy of a Charleston newspaper of June 16, 1775 was found containing a set of resolutions adopted on May 31 which indicated that at a meeting (whether on May 20th or May 31st) no Declaration of Independence had actually been drafted.

Medical Insurance. The sharing of the costs of medical care by the payments of benefits from a fund established by the contributions of members of such a plan. In the United States medical insurance plans have generally been voluntary and private. As such they have covered only approximately 40 percent of the American people. This, plus the high premium costs and the alleged inadequacy of benefit payments, has promoted a drive in recent years for a national compulsory medical insurance system. In 1952 a bill pending in Congress, representing the essentials of President TRUMAN's proposals, embodied many features of a compulsory program. This bill provided for the coverage of all persons now under the SOCIAL SECURITY ACTS. It would require wage earners and employers to pay one and one-half percent each of salary and pay rolls, up to $3,600 annually per member, into a health insurance fund out of which would be paid medical and hospital costs. Dental and home-nursing service would be a federal subsidy. Covered employees would choose their own doctor from a previously established panel. Doctors could elect not to participate in the program, and those on panels could accept or reject a patient. Payments to doctors would be on a fee basis or a "capitation fee," the latter defined as a fixed annual sum per patient. Doctors also could be paid on a salary basis. Local medical associations would negotiate the range of fees and methods of payments. The Social Security Administrator estimated in 1952 that the insurance program would cost about $5,-300,000,000 a year for the first few years and increase to approximately $7,200,-000,000 in 10 years. The bill also provided for federal GRANTS-IN-AID for medical EDUCATION and clinic work. Its supporters argued that such a program would bring about a wider national distribution of medical care, reduce medical costs, ensure medical care where needed, stimulate increased medical training, and provide medical care for those at present unable to obtain it. Led by the American Medical Association, its opponents charged that the plan would introduce socialized medicine in the United States, destroy the doctor-patient relationship, increase medical costs, violate STATES RIGHTS, and infringe upon the freedoms guaranteed in the federal Constitution. The proponents of compulsory medical insurance pointed out that in 1951 private insurance plans covered only 55 percent of the American people for hospital insurance, 18 percent for medical care, 25 percent against loss of income, and 42 percent for surgical expense.

Medicare. On July 30, 1965 President Johnson signed into law a program of health insurance. This was added to the Social Security Act and provided health coverage for persons over 65 years of age. The insurance is financed by increases in social security payroll tax. The Medicare Bill offered basic hospital care for 60 days as well as supplementary benefits in terms of physician's fees. The supplementary plan for those paying a small additional amount also included fees for surgery.

Medicine. Colonial medicine had not advanced much beyond medieval medicine, depending greatly upon supernatural and mystical mythology, prayer, and the use of conventional herbs and drugs. The only medical publication in the colonies, a single sheet poster, was *A Brief Rule to guide the Common People of New England how to order themselves and theirs in the Small Pocks, or Measles.* This paper was published in Boston by Thomas Thatcher in 1677. The first scientific medical work was propounded by BEN-

JAMIN FRANKLIN in 1775. In the 19th century surgery, utilizing the methods of ANAESTHESIA and asepsis, developed widely with the work of EPHRAHAM McDOWELL (ovariotomy, 1809), JOHN COLLINS WARREN (operation under ether, 1846), REGINALD HEBER FITZ (appendectomy, 1886), and WILLIAM STEWART HALSTED (cocaine injection into nerves, 1885). In 1900 WALTER REED conquered yellow fever. THEOBALD SMITH developed Texas cattle serum in 1906. HIDEYO NOGUCHI isolated the syphilis spirochete in 1910. JOSEPH GOLDBERGER conquered pellagra in 1914. In 1921 EDWARD FRANCIS discovered tularemia. Thereafter rapid improvement in surgery developed through the work of Nicholas Senn in bone surgery, John B. Murphy in abdominal surgery, George Crile in surgical shock, and Harvey Cushing in brain surgery. Nobel Awards for outstanding developments in medicine have been awarded to Alexis Carrel (1912), Carl Landsteiner (1930), Thomas H. Morgan (1933), and George H. Whipple, William P. Murphy, and George R. Minot (1934). In 1964, the award was shared by Professor Conrad E. Block of Harvard University and Professor Feodor Lynen of the University of Munich.

MELLON, Andrew William. 1855-1937. Financier. b. Pittsburgh, Pennsylvania. Studied at the University of Pittsburgh; inherited fortune from his father and greatly increased his wealth by investing in coke, coal and iron enterprises; president, Mellon National Bank, Pittsburgh; appointed by HARDING, U.S. Secretary of the Treasury (1921-32); U.S. Ambassador to Great Britain (1932-33); his income was investigated by the Federal government (1935).

"Melting Pot." The descriptive phrase signifying the amalgamation of many ethnic and cultural groups. As applied to the United States it is derived from a drama of that name by Israel Zangwill.

404

MELVILLE, Herman. 1819-1891. Novelist. b. New York City. Served on whaler (1841-42); lived with cannibals after deserting ship; customs inspector, New York City (1866-85). Famous for books about the sea including *Typee* (1846), and *Moby Dick* (1851).

Memorial Day. Also known as Decoration Day. Observed on May 30th. It is a legal holiday in all the Northern states and in the territories, and is also observed by the armed forces. The holiday was originally devoted to honoring the memory of those who fell in the Civil War, but it is now also dedicated to the memory of the dead of all wars.

Mennonites. Originating in Switzerland in 1525, Mennonites first migrated to Pennsylvania in 1683. After the Revolution they moved westward into the Ohio country. Theological disputes produced many splits in the 19th century, some based on national rivalries of the members. After the World War large numbers of Mennonites moved to Canada. In 1963 there were approximately 75,000 Mennonites in the United States.

Mercantilism. An economic theory of the 16th-18th century whose principal doctrine was the belief that the wealth of nations was based on the possession of gold. In order to obtain gold stocks European governments attempted to secure favorable trade balances by imposing quotas on imports, levying TARIFFS, and paying export subsidies. They also chartered joint stock companies upon whom were conferred MONOPOLY rights in the discovery, settlement, and economic exploitation of colonies. Although restricting free trade and competition, the mercantile theory encouraged the colonial exploration of that period, and thus contributed to the settlement of the western hemisphere.

Merchant Marine. The existence of good harbors and luxurious forests contributed to the development of a large merchant marine in colonial America. By the opening of the Civil War the United States merchant marine comprised almost 5,500,000 tons. The Black Ball Line, established in New York in 1818, attempted the first scheduled trans-Atlantic merchant service. The sailing vessel received its last stimulus in the CLIPPER SHIP era during the two decades preceding the Civil War. United States shipbuilding superiority was lost to England after 1870 as a consequence of increased importance of steel ships, steam power, and her interest in westward expansion. This superiority was not regained until World War I. As a result of the war American foreign trade carried in American vessels increased from 10 percent before the war to 33 percent after the war while its proportion of world shipping increased from 12 to 24 percent. The bulk of this expansion resulted from the federal programs authorized in the SHIPPING ACT OF 1916 and the EMERGENCY SHIPPING ACT OF 1917. This trend of federal aid was a development from the original grant of a mail subsidy in 1838 succeeded by further SUBSIDIES in 1845, 1852, 1865, 1877, and 1891. Under these various Acts Congress liberally subsidized the shipping industry in the ocean carriage of mail. The trend continued after World War I in an effort to counteract the decline of American shipping during the international depression of the 1930's. By the Merchant Marine Act of 1936 new policies were put into effect of merging the needs of defense, COMMERCE, mail TRANSPORTATION, and economic revival. The effect of these policies was to raise the United States merchant marine to third position, behind England and Norway at the opening of World War II. As a result of the huge shipbuilding program during the war the United States ranked first in world fleets at the war's end. In May, 1952 the active merchant

405

fleet numbered 1,890 vessels of which 1,272 were privately owned. The remainder was government-owned and included 591 dry cargo ships, 24 combination passenger and cargo vessels, and three tankers. The total weight of the merchant fleet was well over 37,000,000 deadweight tons.

Merchant Marine Academy, U.S. An organization established in 1938 at King's Point, New York for the purpose of training cadet-midshipmen for the merchant marine. The Academy has a student body of 1,000 from every state and certain territories of the United States. Appointments are based on a state and territory quota system, and are made through competitive examinations. The four year course includes studies in marine engineering, ship construction, naval science, navigation, and general business and academic subjects. Upon graduation cadets are licensed, after examination, as deck or engineer officers in the United States Merchant Marine. Some may be commissioned as officers in the U.S. Maritime Service or the U.S. Naval Reserve. They receive degrees of Bachelor of Science. The Academy has graduated more than 10,000 officers since its establishment.

Merchant Marine Act of 1916. See Ship Purchase Act.

Merchant Marine Act of 1920. See Jones Act.

Merchant Marine Act of 1928. See Jones-White Act.

Merchant Ship Sails Act. A law of Congress passed in 1946. It was designed to maintain the Liberty ships as a reserve fleet and to sell to private companies all other vessels suitable for peacetime TRADE.

MERGENTHALER, Ottmar. 1854-1899. Inventor. b. Germany. Came to the United States (1872); became a natural-ized citizen (1878); famous for invention of the first Linotype typesetting machine (1884).

Merger. A form of business consolidation accomplished by a corporation's purchase of the securities or assets of competing corporations in the same industry. The greatest wave of mergers occurred after World War I. In 1926 alone there were over 1,000 mergers in the PUBLIC UTILITY industry. Between 1919 and 1927 more than 3700 utility companies disappeared. By 1930, it was estimated that one half of the electric power, generated by the major corporations, was controlled by ix groups and over 90 percent by 15 groups. Mergers spread rapidly in this decade in AUTOMOBILES, ALUMINUM, CHEMICALS, MOTION PICTURES, and COMMUNICATIONS. In November, 1951 the FEDERAL TRADE COMMISSION declared that "a great wave of mergers" had reached the highest level in 20 years. At the end of 1947 there were approximately 500 mergers annually. The Commission estimated that the current rate was 750 a year. In more than half of the mergers the acquiring company had assets of more than $10,000,000, and a quarter of them had assets of more than $50,000,000. It was stated that the clauses of the CLAYTON ANTI-TRUST ACT, prohibiting the purchase by one company of the stock and assets of another which tended toward monopoly, had been evaded. The Federal Trade Commission staff was directed to see that the law was more vigorously enforced.

Merit System. The method of appointing members of the Civil Service by open competitive examination. Although temporarily instituted by President GRANT in 1876 the permanent merit system was not established until the passage of the PENDLETON ACT in 1873. In 1789, at the beginning of the nation's history, the entire civil service was politically appointed. After the passage of the Pendleton Act, 13 percent were appointed on a merit basis. By 1932 the figure had risen to 80 percent. In 1952 President Truman declared that 93 percent of the Federal service was on a merit basis. Individual merit systems have been put into effect by some of the independent bodies. These include the FEDERAL BUREAU OF INVESTIGATION and the TENNESSEE VALLEY AUTHORITY. A merit examination may be written, or as in recent developments, it may take the form of a performance, oral, or interview examination. The merit system has spread widely to state and municipal governments, and has been adopted in part by private industry.

Merrimac, The. A 40 gun frigate which had been sunk at the Norfolk Navy Yard at the outset of the Civil War. She was raised by the Confederate government, renamed the *Virginia*, and converted into the first "ironclad" in history by having her sides covered with a sloping roof of iron rails and attaching a powerful iron ram to her bows. On March 8, 1862 she steamed into Hampton Roads in Virginia and easily destroyed two of the Union vessels of the wooden navy stationed there. See Hampton Roads, Battle of.

Methodists. A Pro .tant group which originated in England in 1739. It was organized in 1766 in Maryland by Robert Strawbridge and in New York by Philip Embury. Missionary work, emanating from England, brought about an increase in church membership by the opening of the Revolution. Religious conflicts caused their persecution in Maryland and Virginia. After the Revolution the formal organization of the church occurred in 1784 under the name Methodist Episcopal Church. It adopted a prayer book, developed a liturgy, and ordained preachers. The democratic aspects of Methodist theology, with its emphasis on individual choice, attracted thousands of frontier adherents. Internal theological conflicts caused many schisms, with the consequent organization of dissident groups such as the Methodist Protestant Church in 1830 and anti-slave Negro churches. After 1831 the Methodists embarked on a national educational program and by the opening of the Civil War they had established 34 colleges. They founded national publications including a press, periodicals, and books. In April, 1939 a comprehensive unification plan was evolved and the various branches of the Methodist Church were brought together in the Uniting Conference. In 1964 there were more than 12,800,000 Methodists in the United States.

Metropolitan Museum of Art. Located on Fifth Avenue in New York City. It was founded in 1870. It has the most extensive collection of works of art in the western hemisphere, covering 5,000 years of the world's cultures. The art of the peoples of the ancient world, the Near East, the Far East, Europe, Africa, and America are represented. Among its distinguished collections are the Egyptian Room, Costume Institute, Musical Instruments, Arms and Armor, Decorative Arts, Primitive Art, Sculpture of all Ages, American Indian Art, Oriental Art, Prints, the American Rooms, and Modern Art. The Museum maintains a branch at Fort Tryon Park, New York City, known as the Cloisters.

Metropolitan Opera Company. The oldest repertory opera company in the United States. The name describes the various organizations which have staged performances at the Metropolitan Opera House in New York City. The theater was built in 1883 and closed that year's season with a deficit of approximately $500,000. Its first performance was a production of FAUST on October 22. In the decades before World War I its most distinguished director was LEOPOLD DAM-ROSCH, who used the New York Symphony orchestra as the musical aggregation. The greatest European singers performed at the Metropolitan Opera House. These included Emma Eames, Lillian Nordica, Amelita Galli-Curci, Enrico Caruso, Feodore Chaliapin, Nelly Melba, Emma Calvé, Edouard de Reszke, Antonio Scotti, and Marcella Sembrich. In the period of World War I, with Giulio Gatti-Casazza as director (1908) and ARTURO TOSCANINI as conductor (1908), the Company achieved its greatest distinction. In later years the Company sponsored American singers and artists, among them Louise Homer, Lawrence Tibbett, John Charles Thomas, Leonard Warren, Jan Pearce, Richard Tucker, Robert Merrill, and Rise Stevens. On April 14, 1956 the Company completed its 71st season comprising 146 performances.

Meuse-Argonne, Battle of the. An American offensive between September 26th and November 11, 1918. It was the last general push, designed by Marshal Foch to destroy the German army and end the war. Commanded by General PERS.IING, the attack was launched in the Argonne along the Meuse River in France. It was aimed at Sedan, 35 miles Northwest. Nine United States divisions, supported by artillery, tanks, and aircraft, attacked, driving the Germans from Montfaucon on September 27th. A renewed attack on October 14th resulted in the capture of Romagne, followed by the destruction of the German center on November 2nd and the capture of Buzancy. With the negotiation of the armistice on November 11th, the American pursuit had reached Sedan, cutting all German communications. This offensive was the greatest battle involving American troops in World War I. Assisted on the flanks by British and French advances, more than 1,000,000 troops, operating over the seven week period, defeated 47 German di-

visions. They captured 26,000 enemy troops and 4,000 pieces of artillery and machine guns. American casualties aggregated 117,000 dead and wounded.

Mexican Cession. The TERRITORY acquired from Mexico by the TREATY OF GUADALUPE-HIDALGO on February 2, 1848. The territory comprised an area of 524,000 square miles and included New Mexico and upper California. Ultimately this region was divided by Congress into the states of Arizona, Nevada, New Mexico, Utah, and parts of Colorado and Wyoming.

Mexican War, The. A war between the United States and Mexico, fought between April, 1846 and September, 1847. The fundamental causes stemmed from the agrarian expansionism of the South seeking new land for cotton culture. Buttressed by the philosophy of "MANIFEST DESTINY" the southern planters, strong in Congress, advocated the forcible ANNEXATION OF TEXAS, California, and the New Mexico and Utah territory. American-Mexican diplomatic relations deteriorated after the annexation of Texas in December, 1845 and the failure of JOHN SLIDELL's mission in October of that year. On April 25, 1846, after many diplomatic disputes and negotiations, the Mexicans entered the disputed territory between the Nueces and Rio Grande Rivers into which General TAYLOR had moved his troops in July, 1845. Calling this an invasion of American territory, POLK requested a declaration of war which Congress made on May 12, 1846. Taylor struck at Mexico while General KEARNEY invaded New Mexico, conquering that entire territory, and proceding thenceforth to California. With the aid of FREMONT, who directed a native American rebellion, that area was rapidly taken. General SCOTT assumed command of the army in Mexico while Taylor remained in command in the North. The Mexicans were defeated at the first great battle of the war at Palo Alto on May 8, 1846. Successive Mexican defeats followed at the battles of Resaca de la Palma, Buena Vista, Pueblo, Molino del Rey, Chapultepec, and Mexico City, which was captured on September 14th. The Mexican commander-in-chief and president, Santa Anna, resigned the latter office shortly thereafter while the special American emissary NCHOLAS TR ST *sought to negotiate a treaty of peace*. On *February* B, 1848 the TREATY OF GUADALUPE-HIDALGO was concluded, terminating hostilities. The important results of the War were the revival of the SLAVERY controversy, the expansion of American territory, the reinforced control of the South in national politics, the extension of the frontier to the Pacific Ocean, and the genesis of the interocean canal problem of the future. The War was attacked then and since as an imperialist war of aggression for the purpose of seeking new slave states. Within Congress considerable opposition by FREE-SOIL and ABOLITIONIST elements was raised, and a large vote, including that of ABRAHAM LINCOLN, was cast against the declaration of war. United States casualties totalled 13,283 dead, including 1,733 battle deaths, and 8,304 wounded.

Miami Indians. A member of the ALGONQUIN family. They are frequently known as the Twightwees. They were originally organized in six tribes and settled in the Ohio and upper Mississippi regions after having been expelled from Wisconsin by more warlike tribes. By many treaties with the United States before the Civil War they ceded their lands and were transported to the trans-Mississippi region. Their most famous leader was Little Turtle who negotiated the TREATY OF GREENVILLE.

MIAs and POWs. The problem of the soldier who is missing in action (MIA) or was a prisoner of war (POW) was an important issue in the agreement which ended the Viet Nam war. Henry Kissinger, the Secretary of State, who was the principal American negotiator had the responsibility of providing for the release of the POWs and making efforts to locate those members of the military who were missing in action.

MICHELSON, Albert Abraham. 1852-1931. Physicist. b. Germany. Came to the United States (1854); graduated, U.S.-N.A., Annapolis (1873); professor and head of department of physics, University of Chicago (1892-1929); known for his having determined with a high degree of accuracy the speed of light; his other experimental work was later a basis for the development of the theory of relativity; first American scientist to receive the Nobel Prize in physics (1907).

Michigan. The 23rd state in size, with an area of 58,216 square miles. Organized as a territory in 1805 and admitted as the 26th state on January 29, 1837. Lansing is the capital. In 1950 Michigan's population of 6,371,776 made it seventh in rank. Its largest cities are Detroit, Grand Rapids, and Flint. Michigan manufactures 90 percent of the nation's automobiles. Other important manufactures are airplanes, furniture, boilers, pumps, refrigerators, and diesel engines. Grand Rapids is the furniture center of the United States. Farm crops include beans, potatoes, sugar beets, grapes, and peaches. Michigan is the only state completely divided into two parts. The northern part is an important MINING and LUMBER area. The southern is devoted to AGRICULTURE and MANUFACTURING. The Sault Ste. Marie Canal, connecting Lakes Huron and Superior, is the busiest CANAL in the world. A large tourist trade is attracted by Michigan's 6,000 inland lakes and 2,300 miles of GREAT LAKES shoreline. The state has the most valuable inland fisheries in the world. It was discovered by JACQUES CARTIER in 1535. Its nickname is the "Wolverine State." See Detroit.

"Midnight Judges." Those federal judicial officers appointed by President J. ADAMS under the authority of the Judiciary Act of 1801. Having been defeated in the election of 1800, the FEDERALIST PARTY sought to entrench itself in the federal judiciary by establishing hundreds of new judicial posts by means of this legislation. The name is derived from the fact that President Adams is presumed to have remained up until midnight of the day before he left office, signing the commissions of the appointees.

Midway Islands. Islands in the Pacific 1,200 miles northwest of Hawaii. They were discovered by Captain Brooks in 1859 in the name of the United States. Congress declared them a formal possession in 1867, and in 1903 they were made a naval reservation by President T. ROOSEVELT. They have since remained an important base under the administration of the Navy Department. In 1935 the Midways were established as a stopover point for transpacific flights. The area of the total group is 28 square miles. See Midway, Battle of.

Midway Islands, Battle of. On December 7, 1941 the Japanese attacked the MIDWAY ISLANDS. In a three day battle between June 3-6, 1942 United States land and carrier-based planes decisively repulsed a heavy Japanese naval and air assault. Japanese casualties included loss of four large carriers, two heavy cruisers, and three destroyers and damage to three battleships, four cruisers, and four transports. The Japanese lost 275 planes. American losses included one carrier, one destroyer, and 150 planes. The United States fleet was commanded by Admirals Spruance and Fletcher.

MIFFLIN, Thomas. 1744-1800. Revolutionary general and statesman. b. Philadelphia, Pennsylvania. Graduated, University of Pa.(1760); successful merchant; member, CONTINENTAL CONGRESS (1774-76, 1782-84); aide-de-camp to WASHINGTON (1775); quartermaster-general, Continental army (1775-77); brigadier general (1776), major general (1777); involved in CONWAY CABAL but later was again friendly with Washington; member, CONSTITUTIONAL CONVENTION (1787); first governor of Pennsylvania(1790-99) led in suppression of the WHISKY REBELLION.

Migratory Farm Workers. FARMERS who had been foreclosed off their land during the GREAT DEPRESSION. The introduction of farm machinery, DUST BOWL conditions, declining prices, and other aspects of the FARM PROBLEMS set former independent farmers adrift in large areas of Arkansas, Kansas, Oklahoma, and Texas. By 1940, more than 150,000 families had made their way to the West Coast, seeking farm employment. See "Okies."

MILES, Nelson Appleton. 1839-1925. Army officer. b. Massachusetts. Served through the Civil War; received the CONGRESSIONAL MEDAL OF HONOR; colonel, U.S. Army (1866); major general (1890); led army against Indians; served in CUBA and PUERTO RICO (1898); lieutenant general (1901); retired (1903).

Military Bounties. See bounties.

Military Government. The government established by the armed forces of a victorious state over the TERRITORY of the defeated enemy. After World War II the major powers of the UNITED NATIONS established military governments in Germany and Japan. See Germany, Occupation of and Japan, Occupation of.

Militia. The armed forces of the STATES in the United States. More popularly known as the National Guard, it theoretically consists of all able bodied male citizens over 18 years of age. It is actually formed of enlistments. The governors of the states are the commanders-in-chief of these military forces except in time of war when they are incorporated into the Army of the United States.

MILLAY, Edna St. Vincent. 1892-1950. Poet. b. Maine. Graduated, Vassar (1917); won Pulitzer Prize for poetry (1922). Best known for books of poetry including *Renascence* (1917), *The Harp-Weaver and Other Poems* (1923); *Conversation at Midnight* (1937), and the libretto for DEEMS TAYLOR's opera *The King's Henchman.*

Miller, William Edward. 1914- . Politician, b. New York. Republican nominee for vice-president in 1964. Representative in Congress, 1951-1964.

Miller-Tydings Act. Passed by Congress in 1937. It permitted manufacturers of trade marked articles to enter into contracts with retailers for the maintenance of resale prices. The law exempted from the operation of existing anti-trust legislation all such agreements by parties engaged in INTERSTATE COMMERCE, whenever such agreements were valid under the laws of the states where the goods were sold. Designed to curb competition it aided the setting of minimum prices through state-wide "FAIR TRADE LAWS" to the detriment of the consumer. In 1951 the United States Supreme Court declared unconstitutional all state fair trade laws affecting interstate commerce.

MILLIKAN, Robert. 1868-1953. Physicist-educator. b. Illinois. Studied at Oberlin, Columbia University and in Germany; taught physics at the University of Chicago (1896-1921); director, Norman Bridge Laboratory of Physics, California Institute of Technology (from 1921); outstanding American physicist; winner of the NOBEL PRIZE (1923) for having isolated the electron and measured its charge; chairman, executive council of California Institute of Technology (1921-45) and professor emeritus (from 1948). Author of *Cosmic Rays* (1939).

Milling Industry. Hand mills for the grinding of grain were used in the American colonies through the 17th century, although there is reason to believe that a windmill was put into use in New England in the 1630's. Water-powered mills came into wide use in the 18th century. Commercial mills were established to process grain for a fee in rural areas adjacent to the larger cities. These became particularly important with the development of the grain export trade from the middle Atlantic states prior to the Revolution. With the inventions of the grain elevator and the conveyor by OLIVER EVANS, in the 1790's milling in the United States was recognized as an important INDUSTRY. In this period Baltimore and Rochester became the centers of the industry, the latter producing over 5,000 barrels of flour a day by 1835. With the development of TRANSPORTATION facilities in the generation prior to the Civil War the industry moved westward to Missouri, Illinois, and Wisconsin. After the war the superior shipping facilities of the GREAT LAKES and their tributaries brought milling to Minnesota, Michigan, and the Dakotas. Minneapolis and St. Paul became the most important milling centers in the United States. The inventions of the purifier (1871) and the roller mill (1878) increased the productivity of the industry. In the 20th century cheap power, the use of Canadian WHEAT, and proximity to the transportation and financial facilities of the east coast transferred the industry to upper New York. By the 1950's Buffalo had become the milling center of the nation.

"Millions For Defense But Not A Cent For Tribute." An expression erroneously attributed to CHARLES COTESWORTH PINCKNEY in reply to the demand of the special French envoys, in 1797, who demanded a loan from the United States in the XYZ AFFAIR. The phrase was actually part of a toast offered by Representative Robert G. Harper of South Carolina at a dinner given by Congress in honor of JOHN MARSHALL on June 18, 1798. It reflected the opposition of the federal government to the French demands for a bribe or loan and contributed to the decision of Congress to build a navy in defense against French attacks.

Mills Bill. An attempted tariff reform measure introduced in the House in 1888 as a fulfillment of the Democratic party's pledge to bring about TARIFF reduction. The bill sought to reduce duties on pig-iron, cotton goods, and woolen goods, and place flax, hemp, lumber, tinplate, wool, and salt on the free list. Simultaneously the Republican-controlled Senate wrote a high-tariff bill which was immediately buried by the House WAYS AND MEANS COMMITTEE. The impossibility of reconciling the divergent House and Senate measures brought to an end this effort at TARIFF REFORM.

MILLS, Darius Ogden. 1825-1910. Financier and philanthropist. b. New York. Prominent banker and merchant in California; first president of the Bank of California (1864-73); moved to New York and established hotels for the very poor (1878); contributed to the METROPOLITAN MUSEUM OF ART, N.Y.

Minimum Wage Legislation. Laws passed by various state legislatures within the past 50 years establishing floors under wages. Such laws, enacted in the states of New York and Oregon, were originally declared unconstitutional by the U.S. Supreme Court. In 1937 the Court reversed its previous decisions, upholding such legislation in the case of West Coast Hotel Company vs. Parrish. Permanent minimum wage legislation was enacted on a national scale, for the first time, in the form of the FAIR LABOR STANDARDS ACT IN 1938.

Mining. The mining of precious metals was one of the greatest attractions to colonial settlers. Although gold and silver were not mined in quantity until the 19th century, COAL and IRON mining became one of the most important INDUSTRIES in the late 18th century. Connecticut, New Jersey, New York, and Pennsylvania ranked foremost in this activity. One of the earliest iron mines developed in the colonies was that of JOHN WINTHROP in Connecticut in 1651. In the early 19th century the search for precious metals pushed mining into the Mississippi area. Here again gold and silver gave way to lead and copper mining in the rich deposits in Missouri, Illinois, and the states of the Ohio Valley. By 1873 iron ore production was exceeding 1,000,000 tons a year. The discovery of gold in California in 1848 provided the first genuine opportunity for the mining of precious metals. Meanwhile anthracite and bituminous coal production had become important in Pennsylvania, Ohio, and West Virginia. At the close of the Civil War, the mining of gold in Colorado and silver in Nevada led to the "MINING KINGDOM" which was producing over $20,000,000 worth of silver annually and had already sent to the United States mints more than $26,000,000 worth of gold by the end of the war. Production of lead, copper, iron, and coal aided in the development of Idaho, Montana, and South Dakota. After 1900 mining in the United States was producing more minerals than ever before. Oil "mining" developed into a major industry by 1900 when the United States was outproducing the rest of the world. In 1951 the mining industry employed over 900,000 workers in 34,400 firms of all sizes and classes. The total value of mining, including the production of metals, coal, petroleum, and natural gas in 1950, was

$5,038,000,000. In that year the nation's mines produced 1,814,000,000 pounds of copper, 433,000 short tons of lead, more than 600,000 short tons of zinc, and 64,-586,907 tons of pig iron. See coal industry, iron industry, petroleum industry, and steel industry.

"Mining Kingdom, the." The nickname applied during the 1850's and 1860's to the area extending from the western boundary of Minnesota to the Gulf of Mexico and from the Mississippi Valley to the Rocky Mountains. It arose out of the rapid exploitation of precious metals and non-ferrous ores in this region. In 1858 gold was discovered near Pike's Peak in Colorado, and in the next year rich veins of silver were found in Nevada. By the end of the Civil War miners were prospecting unusually rich deposits of copper, gold, lead, and silver in the present states of Arizona, Colorado, Montana, Nevada, Utah, and Wyoming. By this time Colorado had mined over $10,000,-000 worth of gold, supplementing the $16,000,000 in gold taken from Montana. Nevada was yielding more than $20,-000,000 worth of silver annually, and similar production of other metals was aiding the enrichment of the nation. The contribution of the "Mining Kingdom" include the following: the opening of the trans-Mississippi West, the settlement and entry of new states into the Union, the increased wealth of the United States, the attraction of RAILROADS to the territory, the publicizing of the cattle and farming opportunities of the area, and the inception of the subsequent CURRENCY struggle between East and West.

"Mink Coat Scandals." See Reconstruction Finance Corporation Scandals.

Minnesota. The 12th state in size, with an area of 80,009 square miles. Organized as a TERRITORY in 1849 and admitted as the 32nd state on May 11, 1858. St. Paul is the capital. In 1950 Minnesota's POPULATION of 2,982,483 made it 18th in rank. Its largest cities are Minneapolis, St. Paul, and Duluth. The Mesabi, Cuyuna, and Vermilion Ranges in northern Minnesota produce 70 per cent of the iron ore in the United States. Important farm crops include oats, corn, wheat, potatoes, and dairy products. Manufactures are furniture, machinery, and foundry products. St. Paul is the nation's largest publisher of law books, and calendars. Minnesota's 11,000 lakes and hunting and trapping areas attract a large tourist trade. It was discovered in 1655 by two French traders Radisson and Groseilliers. Its nicknames are the "North Star State" and "Gopher State."

Minority Presidents. Candidates who have been elected President of the United States even though they have polled a minority of the POPULAR VOTE. This has been made possible by the constitutional requirement that a candidate be named President only if he has received a majority of the ELECTORAL VOTE. In those elections where three or more strong candidates have campaigned, none of them has normally received a popular majority. Thirteen minority Presidents have been elected in American history. These, and their percentage of the popular vote, were:

President	Year	% of popular vote
John Quincy Adams	1824	29.8
James K. Polk	1844	49.3
Zachary Taylor	1848	47.3
James A. Buchanan	1856	45.3
Abraham Lincoln	1860	39.9
Rutherford B. Hayes	1876	47.9
James A. Garfield	1880	48.3
Grover Cleveland	1884	48.8
Benjamin Harrison	1888	47.8
Grover Cleveland	1892	46.0
Woodrow Wilson	1912	41.8
Woodrow Wilson	1916	49.3
Harry S. Truman	1948	49.5

Mint, Bureau of the. Established by the

COINAGE ACT OF 1873 which consolidated all mint and assay activities under the newly organized Bureau of the Mint. It has since been located within the DE-PARTMENT OF THE TREASURY. The first U.S. Mint was established in Philadelphia on April 2, 1792. The Act creating it provided for gold, silver, and copper coinage. In 1899 the Mint was taken from the supervision of the Secretary of State and made an independent agency responsible to the President. The Bureau of the Mint manufactures all domestic coins, refines gold and silver, manufactures medals for the armed forces, conducts special assays of bullion and ores, protects federal stores or monetary metals, supervises the issuance of licenses for the acquisition, possession, and use of gold for commercial purposes, and coins money for foreign governments. It administers the federal gold holdings of $15,600,000,000, in the GOLD BULLION DEPOSITORY at Fort Knox, Kentucky and the silver holdings at West Point, New York. The branch offices of the mint are located in Philadelphia, San Francisco, and Denver. The Assay Offices are located in New York City and Seattle.

MINUIT, Peter. 1580-1638. Colonial administrator. b. Duchy of Cleves. Director-general of the Dutch colony of New Netherland (1626-31); known for having purchased Manhattan Island from the Indians for $24 worth of trinkets; established forts and trade with the PLYMOUTH COLONY; recalled (1631); later helped establish the Swedish Colony on Delaware Bay; lost at sea (1638).

Minutemen. Term applied to the colonists rallied to the patriot cause at the outbreak of the Revolution. The name was first given to the volunteer farmers who defended LEXINGTON AND CONCORD in April, 1775.

Miranda Decision. In 1966 the Supreme Court ruled that a suspect has certain rights. He has the right to remain silent, the right to counsel and the right to be told that anything said can be used against him. As part of this decision in case of a confession, the prosecution must prove that the suspect knowingly waived his rights to silence. Police officials argued that these decisions would render most confessions inadmissable as evidence.

Missionary Ridge, Battle of. See Chicamauga Campaign.

Mississippi. The 32nd state in size, with an area of 47,716 square miles. Organized as a TERRITORY in 1798 and admitted as the 20th state on December 10, 1817. Seceded on January 9, 1861 and readmitted on February 23, 1870. Jackson is the capital. In 1950 Mississippi's POPULATION of 2,178,914 made it 26th in rank. Its largest cities are Jackson, Meridian, Biloxi. Mississippi is one of the nation's largest producers of COTTON. The world's largest cotton plantation (35,000 acres) is located at Scott. Other crops are corn, peanuts, oats, pecans, and sugar cane. Growing industrialization has led to the production of TEXTILE, iron, LUMBER, newsprint, and fiber board. Mississippi is one of the two states that has retained prohibition. It has the second largest Negro population in the nation. The state was discovered in 1540 by de Soto. Its nickname is the "Magnolia State."

"Mississippi Bubble." The term applied to the failure of John Law's scheme to exploit the territory of Louisiana. In 1717 a French speculator, Antoine Crozat, transferred his 25 year MONOPOLY of commercial privileges in the area to Law, who organized the Mississippi Company for its exploitation. In 1719 he reorganized the Company to include the development of the French holdings in Africa, China, and the Indies, and was given the right of revenue collection. The Company assumed the state debt, becoming controller of French colonial trade. Public confidence in Law reached a peak of wild speculation in the company's shares. The resulting over-expansion of its activities, and its undercapitalization caused a reaction. The speculators tried to unload their shares and, despite drastic governmental decrees, the Mississippi Scheme collapsed. In 1720 the Company failed and the stockholders lost their entire investment. The French government abolished Law's system.

Mississippi River, The. First discovered by the Spanish explorer HERNANDO DE-SOTO in 1541. The most intensive subsequent explorations of it were conducted by the two French Jesuit Missionaries Fathers LOUIS JOLIET and JACQUES MARQUETTE. It formed the western boundary of the United States by the TREATY OF PARIS OF 1783 which ended the American Revolution. With its tributaries the Mississippi River system is the most extensive inland waterway network in the United States, linking the GREAT LAKES with the Gulf of Mexico. On this system the Corps of Engineers has constructed the nation's greatest system of navigation locks and dams to improve the deep water channels. From time to time the River has overflowed into disastrous floods, such as those in 1912, 1927, and 1936. Flood control has become one of the principal problems of the Mississippi in recent years. From its source in Lake Itasca, Minnesota, the Mississippi flows approximately 2,450 miles to its mouth in the Gulf of Mexico. The Mississippi-Missouri-Red Rock integral water system has a length of 3,872 miles.

Mississippi Scheme. See "Mississippi Bubble."

Missouri. The 19th state in size, with an area of 69,674 square miles. Organized as a TERRITORY in 1812 and admitted as the 24th state on August 10, 1821. Jefferson City is the capital. In 1950 Missouri's POPULATION of 3,954,653 made it 11th in rank. Its largest cities are St. Louis, Kansas City, and St. Joseph. Missouri leads the nation in lead mining and mule breeding. Farm crops include corn, WHEAT, barley, potatoes, tobacco, and COTTEN. Manufactures are AUTOMOBILES, shoes, drugs, CHEMICALS, street cars, and beer. Eads Bridge at St. Louis carries more freight cars than any other bridge in the world. Although Missouri remained within the Union at the outbreak of the Civil War a strong minority in the legislature adopted a secessionist resolution. LINCOLN'S aggressive military tactics kept the state within the Union, Missouri was explored in 1682 by La Salle. Its nickname is the "Show-me State."

Missouri Compromise. Act of Congress in 1820 submitted and sponsored by HENRY CLAY as the first of his three great compromises. The legislation arouse out of the application of the territory of Missouri for ADMISSION TO THE UNION as a slave state. Such admission would have weighted the Senate in favor of the slave states and was therefore opposed by the North. This moment of sectional hatred during the "ERA OF GOOD FEELING" was compromised by Clay with the admission of Missouri as a slave state, the admission of Maine (formed out of the territory of Massachusetts with the latter's and Congress' consent) as a free state, and an agreement that all territory north of the line 36 degrees 30 minutes within the LOUISIANA PURCHASE would thenceforth be admitted as free states and all territory south of that line as slave states.

Missouri-Mississippi floods. On July 11, 1951 eastern Kansas was struck by the most terrible flood in its history. By presidential proclamation Kansas, Missouri, and Oklahoma, were declared disaster areas. The Federal Housing Administrator was appointed to supervise a $25,-000,000 congressional appropriation to aid the flood stricken victims. On July 22nd the Mississippi River rose to a high mark of 40.28 feet, only 1.11 feet below the all time crest reached in 1844. Total flood losses surpassed $1,000,000,000 involving damage to 15 highways, 12 railroad lines, 17 bridges, and large meat packing plants. Unusual crop losses were suffered. Deaths totaled 41. In April, 1952 the Missouri River again overflowed its banks and flooded large areas in Illinois, Iowa, Kansas, Minnesota, Missouri, Montana, Nebraska, North Dakota, South Dakota, and Wisconsin. In some parts of Omaha the river was 15 miles wide and reached a crest of 30.24 feet, more than five feet above the 1881 peak. The two week flood caused estimated damages in excess of $200,000,000 and drove 100,-000 persons from their homes. Spring crops on hundreds of thousands of acres of rich midwestern farmland were destroyed. The cost of fighting the flood was approximately $2,000,000. On President TRUMAN's recommendation Congress unanimously voted an appropriation of $25,-000,000 for flood relief.

Missouri River. The second longest river in the United States. From its source at the junction of the Jefferson, Madison, and Gallatin Rivers in Montana it flows 2,475 miles to the Mississippi River near St. Louis. It was discovered by the French Jesuit missionary Father Jacques MARQUETTE in 1673. It drains a watershed of 600,000 square miles in the most fertile valley in the world. The river was first explored from its source to its mouth by the LEWIS AND CLARK EXPEDITION in 1804-1806. At various times it has been owned or claimed by the French, the Spanish, and the British, having come into the possession of the United States as part of the LOUISIANA PURCHASE in 1803. The first steamboat to ascend the river was the *Independence* in 1819, following which an established steamboat traffic led to the construction of many cities along the river's edge. Because of the great fluctuations of its flow its navigability is frequently altered and floods strike the area which it drains.

Missouri River Basin Project. Authorized by the FLOOD CONTROL ACT of 1944 and amending legislation the objectives of the project will be the construction of dams, diversions, pumping plants, and other works for the CONSERVATION, control, and use of the water resources of the Missouri River drainage basin. This is the first project to develop the water resources of a major river basin. The Missouri River basin occupies an area equal to one sixth of the continental United States. The plans are designed to provide hydro-electric power plants with an aggregate installed capacity of 2,500,000 kilowatts with future additions of 700,000 kilowatts of electric power. Under the supervision of the BUREAU OF RECLAMATION in the DEPARTMENT OF THE INTERIOR this power will be delivered for construction purposes, IRRIGATION, and the industrial needs of utilities in the municipal and rural areas of the basin. The arable area to be supplied by irrigation waters will exceed 6,000,000 acres of land. The project includes additional comprehensive developements such as flood control, domestic water supply, silt control, stream pollution abatement, and expansion of recreational facilities. It is planned to construct 100 major dams under the supervision of the Bureau of Reclamation and the Corps of Engineers. The overall administration agency controlling the program is the Missouri Basin Inter-agency Committee consisting of representatives of the federal Department of the Interior, Army, Commerce, and Agriculture, the FEDERAL POWER COMMISSION and the FEDERAL SECURITY AGENCY. Representatives of the ten Missouri Basin states are also on this agency.

Missouri Valley Authority. A proposed federal agency designed to coordinate the work of hydro-electric power, erosion control, flood control, and CONSERVATION agencies in the Missouri Valley. In January, 1952 the Missouri River States Committee, consisting of the delegates of the ten Missouri River Valley states, began work on the draft of an interstate compact for the unified management of the water, soil, and related resources of the basin in opposition to the proposal for the establishment of a valley authority modeled after the TENNESSEE VALLEY AUTHORITY. In 1951 President TRUMAN created the Missouri Basin Survey Commission to study the valley and its problems for the purpose of implementing the PICK-SLOAN PLAN authorized by Congress in 1944.

MITCHELL, John. 1870-1919. Labor leader. b. Illinois. Coal miner; member KNIGHTS OF LABOR (1885-90); joined UNITED MINE WORKERS of America (from 1890) president (1898-1908); condition for the miners greatly improved during his leadership; organized and directed ANTHRACITE COAL MINERS' STRIKE (1902); chairman, N.Y. State Industrial Commission (1915-19). Author of *Organized Labor* (1903) and *The Wage Earner and His Problems* (1913).

MITCHELL, Marie. 1818-1889. Astronomer. b. Massachusetts. Taught school; discovered comets (1847) and made a special study of sun spots; first professor of astronomy, Vassar College (from 1865); first woman elected to American Academy of Arts and Sciences; elected to HALL OF FAME (1922).

MITCHILL, Samuel Latham. 1764-1831. Physician and legislator. b. New York. Practised medicine in New York; professor of chemistry Columbia (1792-1801); founder and editor of *Medical Repository* (1797-1820) a scientific journal; member, U.S. House of Representatives(1801-04; 1810-1813); U.S. Senator(1804-09); professor, College of Physicians and Surgeons, N.Y. (1807-26); organizer and vice-president, Rutgers Medical College (1826-30).

Mohawk Indians. The easternmost tribe of the Five Nations of the IROQUOIS. They allied themselves with the English during the French and Indian Wars. In the 17th century they numbered approximately 5,000. They settled the Mohawk Valley in New York. During the Revolution the tribe, under Brant, supported the English against the colonists. In 1784 the Mohawks retired to upper Canada, although a few hundred tribesmen remained in New York state.

Molasses Act. Passed by Parliament in 1733. It put prohibitive duties on molasses imported from non-English islands in the Caribbean. The Act, if enforced, would have destroyed the New England rum industry. The result was that SMUGGLING developed as an important activity to evade the payment of the molasses duty. Under the policy of "salutary neglect" Parliament made little effort to enforce the laws until the period following the Seven Years' War. The passage of the post-war legislation under the sponsorship of Lords North, Grenville, and Townshend, attempting to enforce the Acts, was unsuccessful.

Molly Maguires. Name of a secret labor organization of miners in the West Virginia and Pennsylvania anthracite coal fields. Flourished in the 1870's. The union was industrially organized and conducted its activities in secret. This plus the fact that it believed in direct action such as arson and physical assaults upon company personnel led to public resentment and opposition. Its limited union program and small membership resulted in its ultimate decline.

MONDALE, Walter, Frederick. 1928- Born the son of a Methodist minister in Ceylon, Minn., he attended Macalester College, served two years in the army during the Korean war and got his law degree from the University of Minnesota. After

417

only four years in private law practice, he was appointed Attorney General to fill an unexpired term, and then was elected and re-elected to the post. After Mr. Humphrey became Vice-President in 1965 Mr. Mondale was appointed to his Senate seat and was later elected and re-elected. In 1955, he married Joan Adams. They have three children. In 1976 he was elected Vice-President of the United States, running on the Democratic ticket as Carter's running mate.

"Money Trust." Applied to banking combinations headed by the MORGAN and ROCKEFELLER institutions at the beginning of the 20th century. Accusations were made against these financial "chains" of eliminating competition in finance, controlling industry, contracting or expanding the bank reserves, and thus establishing control over the nation's economy. By order of Congress, the PUJO COMMITTEE investigated the "money trust," rendering a report to Congress in 1912, confirming the existence of such a combination.

Monitor, The. An ironclad naval vessel built at the Brooklyn Navy Yard by the Union in the first year of the Civil War. It was constructed from designs by John Ericsson and commanded by Lt. John L. Worden. The vessel was shaped like a torpedo boat, her decks flush with the water, and containing amidships a revolving gun turret rising only a few feet from the surface. She was aptly nicknamed "a cheesebox on a raft." On March 9, 1862 she met the Confederate ironclad the *Virginia,* formerly known as the *Merrimac,* in Hampton Roads, Va. See Hampton Roads, Battle of.

Monmouth, Battle of. An attack by the patriot army, under the command of General CHARLES LEE, on the British troops under CLINTON who had been ordered to evacuate Philadelphia, Pennsylvania. On his way to New York he was stopped at Monmouth, New Jersey on June 28, 1778.

In the midst of battle, while Clinton was retreating, Lee removed his troops. Summoned by LAFAYETTE, WASHINGTON arrived in time to stem the American retreat and rally the Continental troops. Clinton succeeded in escaping to the coast. Lee was cashiered from the army for this treasonable conduct.

Monopoly. A system of BUSINESS CONSOLIDATION in which one company controls the production and distribution of commodities within an industry. Technically monopolies do not exist within the United States since in most so-called monopoly industries there are two or more large producers. This system is more accurately referred to as an oligopoly. Nevertheless for practical economic purposes in terms of production, LABOR RELATIONS, marketing, prices, advertising, and distribution monopolistic conditions are considered to exist. Important industries where monopoly conditions obtain include AUTOMOBILES, ALUMINUM, CIGARETTES, MOTION PICTURES, electronics, TELEPHONE and TELEGRAPH, and PETROLEUM. The various forms of monopoly organizations have been the POOL, TRUST, HOLDING COMPANY, INTERLOCKING DIRECTORATE, and MERGER.

Monroe Doctrine. A statement of foreign policy made in the form of a message by President MONROE to Congress in 1823. The principles therein outlined have been customarily accepted as the basis of America's traditional foreign policy of ISOLATIONISM. In this message, written by JOHN Q. ADAMS, the President's Secretary of State, it was declared to be the fundamental policy of the United States not to tolerate further foreign colonial expansion in the western hemisphere. The United States would, for its part, not interfere with existing colonial holdings in this hemisphere. The historic events which provoked this statement of policy were twofold: the successful revolutions of the Latin American colonies of Spain in the first two decades of the 19th century, leading to declarations by the European Holy Alliance of intentions to reconquer these areas on behalf of Spain, and the extension of Russian settlements southward from ALASKA, accompanied by claims upon land to the 51st parallel. The Monroe Doctrine has been applied in its original form in many international situations such as the MAXIMILIAN AFFAIR in 1867 and the VENEZUELA BOUNDARY DISPUTE of 1895. The doctrine is a statement of policy not a congressional statute or a constitutional provision. Under the leadership of T. ROOSEVELT at the beginning of this century it was modified drastically in the direction of involving the United States directly in Latin American domestic affairs. This included the dispatch of American military forces and control of local finances. Instances of such participation have been our activities in HAITI (1915-34), SANTO DOMINGO (1916-24) and NICARAGUA (1912-33). This modification has been known as the ROOSEVELT COROLLARY to the Monroe Doctrine.

MONROE, James. 1758-1831. Fifth President of the United States. b. Westmoreland County, Virginia. Served in the American Revolution; studied law with JEFFERSON (1780-83); member, CONTINENTAL CONGRESS (1783-86); practised law, Virginia; U.S. Senator (1790-94) opposed the FEDERALISTS and attacked HAMILTON; U.S. Minister to France (1794-96); governor of Virginia (1799-1802); played important part in the LOUISIANA PURCHASE (1803); U.S. Minister to England (1803-07); appointed by MADISON, U.S. Secretary of State (1811-17) and was also U.S. Secretary of War (1814-15); elected President of the United States (1817-25); because of the lack of serious quarrels the period of his administration is known as the "ERA OF GOOD FEELING"; Florida was acquired (1819), MISSOURI COMPROMISE adopted (1820); ADAMS as U.S. Secretary of State was responsible for the MONROE DOCTRINE (1823) for which Monroe is chiefly remembered.

Montana. The fourth state in size, with an area of 147,138 square miles. Organized as a TERRITORY in 1864 and admitted as the 41st state on November 8, 1889. Helena is the capital. In 1950 Montana's POPULATION of 591,024 made it 42nd in rank. Its largest cities are Great Falls, Butte, and Billings. MINING is the state's most important industry. Minerals include lead, zinc, silver, coal, and oil. Other important economic activities are sheep raising, wool MANUFACTURING, LUMBER, and dude RANCHING. Glacier National Park is a popular tourist resort, offering beautiful scenery, HUNTING areas, and ranching. Montana was discovered in 1742 by the Verendryes. Its nickname is the "Treasure State."

Montevideo Conference. The seventh Pan-American Conference at Montevideo, Uruguay on December 3, 1933. Specifying the "GOOD NEIGHBOR" POLICY President F. D. ROOSEVELT declared that the United States was opposed to armed intervention in inter-American affairs. In June, 1934 the United States Senate ratified the Montevideo convention which declared that "no state had the right to interfere in the external or internal affairs of another."

MONTGOMERY, Richard. 1738-1775. Revolutionary general. b. Ireland. Came to America (1772); brigadier general in Continental army; served with SCHUYLER in expedition against Montreal and took command when Schuyler was ill; captured Montreal; killed in attack at Quebec.

Monticello. The home of THOMAS JEFFERSON, located on a knoll near Charlottesville, Virginia. The property was inherited by Jefferson from his father and on it Jefferson planned and built what was universally acknowledged to be the most beautiful of all colonial mansions. It was constructed in Italian style on the model of Palladio, but was later altered by Jefferson on the basis of his five year study of European architecture. The final result was a Italian villa with a Greek portico, a Roman dome, and various colonial features. After his death, the estate passed from his heirs to other hands being ultimately willed to the people of the United States. When the will was overridden by the courts, the estate came under the control of the Thomas Jefferson Memorial Foundation.

MOODY, William Henry. 1853-1917. Jurist and statesman. b. Massachusetts. Graduated, Harvard (1876); practised law in Massachusetts, member, U.S. House of Representatives (1895-1902); appointed by T. ROOSEVELT, U. S. Secretary of the Navy (1902-04); U.S. Attorney General(1904-06); Associate Justice, U.S. Supreme Court (1906-10).

Mooney-Billings Case. An internationally famous incident arising out of the arrest and conviction of Thomas J. Mooney and Warren K. Billings. During the Preparedness Day parade in San Francisco on July 22, 1916 a bomb exploded, killing 10 persons and wounding 40 others. Mooney and Billings were arrested, the former being sentenced to death and the latter receiving a sentence of life imprisonment. The evidence at the trial did not substantiate the charges, and nationwide protests led President WILSON in 1918 to request Governor Stephens of California to postpone the execution. Ultimately Mooney's sentence was commuted to life imprisonment. Organized labor and liberal organizations continued the struggle for the release of the two prisoners during the next two decades, convinced that the men's innocence and charging that

the case had been contrived to weaken the west coast LABOR MOVEMENT. Finally, on January 7, 1939, Governor Olson pardoned Mooney and, on October 16, released Billings by commuting his sentence.

moon landings. On July 20, 1969, Neil Armstrong, Commander of a three-man Apollo 11 crew, landed on lunar soil. This was a historic event for it represented the first time that a man was placed on the moon. Other moonshots followed and resulted in increasing scientific discoveries. The surface of the moon was explored in special vehicles which returned with quantities of rock and surface materials. The government ended the moon program after the Apollo 17 flight in December of 1972.

MOREY, Samuel. 1762-1843. Inventor. b. Connecticut. Experimented with STEAM BOATS (1790-97); presented his plans to FULTON who claimed not to be interested; Fulton later profited by Morey's ideas; obtained a patent (1826) for one of the first internal-combustion engines in the United States.

MORGAN, Arthur Ernest. 1878-1976. Civil engineer and educator. b. Ohio. President, Antioch College(1920-36); chairman, TENNESSEE VALLEY AUTHORITY (1933-38). Author of *The Small Community*(1942), *Nowhere Was Somewhere* (1946) and *Edward Bellamy* (1949).

MORGAN, Edwin Denison. 1811-1883. Politician. b. Massachusetts. Successful businessman in New York City; leading Republican; governor of New York (1859-63); U.S. Senator (1863-69); contributed a great deal of money to educational institutions, hospitals and charity.

Morgan "gold deal." A financial arrangement between President CLEVELAND and J. PIERPONT MORGAN in 1895. Under its terms, Morgan organized a syndicate for the purchase abroad of $60,000,000 in gold to be sold to the government to replenish the gold reserves, which were rapidly declining as a result of the redemption of treasury certificates. The bonds granted to cover the loan were 30 year four percents, then selling at 111. They were sold to the Morgan syndicate at 104½. In the country at large the transaction aroused great criticism, because of the premium profit to the syndicate. Eventually the agreement netted the bankers a profit of about 13 points, totalling approximately $7,-200,000.

MORGAN, John Hunt. 1825-1864. Confederate general. b. Alabama. Served in Mexican War; entered the cavalry unit in the Confederate army at the outbreak of the Civil War; famous for cavalry raids in Kentucky and Tennessee; killed in action.

MORGAN, John Pierpont. 1837-1913. Financier. b. Connecticut. Educated in Europe; served apprenticeship with representatives of his father's firm in London and New York (1856-60); member, Dabney, Morgan & Co. (1864-71) and Drexel, Morgan & Co. (1871-93) which became J. P. Morgan & Co. (1895); well-known for his government financing and his reorganization and purchase of large RAILROAD holdings; formed, organized the United States Steel Corporation (1901); collector of rare books and art; president, Metropolitan Museum of Art, N.Y.; endowed libraries; aided institutions and gave generously to charities.

MORGAN, Lewis Henry. 1818-1881. Ethnologist and anthropologist. b. New York. Graduated Union College; practised law as a railroad counsel; important for his studies of the American Indian; admitted into the Seneca tribe. Author of *League of the Ho-de-n-sau-nee or Iroquois* (1851), *Systems of Consanquinity and Affinity of the Human Fami-*

ly (1871), *Houses and House-Life of the American Aborigines* (1881) and many others.

MORGENTHAU, Henry. 1856-1946. Diplomat. b. Germany. Came to the United States (1865); Graduated, Columbia Law School and practised in New York City (1879-99); accumulated a fortune in banking and real estate; appointed by WILSON, U.S. Ambassador to Turkey (1913-16); represented the allied countries in Constantinople at the outbreak of World War I,; U.S. Ambassador to Mexico (1920); chairman, Greek Refugee Settlement Commission for the LEAGUE OF NATIONS (1923); known for many philanthropic activities.

MORGENTHAU, Henry Jr. 1891-1967. Agriculturist and public official. b. New York City. Studied architecture and agriculture at Cornell University; publisher of *American Agriculturist* (1922-33); chairman, New York Agricultural advisory committee in charge of farm relief programs for the state; governor, FARM CREDIT ADMINISTRATION (1933); U.S. Secretary of the Treasury (1934-45); raised more revenues than ever before in history, and sold $200,000,000,000 in government bonds to finance defense and war; advocated international monetary stabilization; advocated strong,punitive policy against Germany in his *Germany is Our Problem* (1945) believing that Germany's military potential should be destroyed, and that she should be made an agricultural nation; important in Jewish philanthropic work.

MORLEY, Edward Willams. 1838-1923. Chemist and physicist. b. New Jersey. Graduated, Williams College (1860); professor, Western Reserve (1869-1906); known for his research into the variations in the oxygen content of the atmosphere, the ether drift, thermal expansion of gases, and the density of oxygen and hydrogen.

Mormons. A group which organized the Church of Jesus Christ of Latter-Day Saints in 1830 at Fayette, New York. The six member organizing committee was headed by JOSEPH SMITH who became the church's first president. Its polygamous practices soon aroused public resentment, causing the group to flee to Ohio, then Missouri, and finally to Nauvoo, Illinois in 1839. Smith and his brother Hyrum were lynched in the Carthage jail in Illinois in 1844 following which BRIGHAM YOUNG led the church's followers in their escape from mob violence, entering Utah in 1847. The mormons displayed conspicuous leadership in missionary, religious, and IMMIGRATION work, making new converts not only in the United States but in Europe as well. Their organizing genius enabled tnese converts to reach Utah by a "Perpetual Emigration Fund" that paid their expenses. They established in Utah a theocratic state in which church and government were closely united and in which the political, social, and economic life was minutely controlled by the church. Membership in 1952 was 1,111,-314, located principally in Utah, Idaho, Arizona, and California. The practice of polygamy prevented the admission of Utah into the Union until 1896. Six years previously the Mormon church had abolished this practice. Their great contributions to the opening of the West were the wide-spread IRRIGATION, land reclamation, and immigration programs. The Mormons theology regards the Bible, the Book of Mormon, the Doctrine and Covenents, and the Pearl of Great Price as the word of God. It seeks a primitive church organization and the same gifts of tongues, revelation, healings, visions, prophesy, and interpretation of tongues.

Mormon Trail. See Salt Lake Trail.

MORRILL, Justin Smith. 1810-1898. Economist and political leader. b. Vermont. Organizer of Republican party in Vermont; member, U.S. House of Representatives (1855-67); known for MORRILL TARIFF BILL (1861); MORRILL LAND-GRANT ACT (1862); U.S. Senator (1867-98).

Morrill Land Grant Act. Passed by Congress in 1862. It provided for a grant to every state of 30,000 acres of public land for each of its senators and representatives in Congress. The income from the sale of this land was to be earmarked for the support of agricultural and mechanical arts colleges. Under its provisions 69 land grant colleges have been established in the United States either as separate institutions or as adjuncts to state universities. The federal government has disposed of 13,000,000 acres of the public domain in what is generally acknowledged as the single most important piece of education legislation ever enacted in the United States.

Morrill Tariff Act. Passed by Congress in 1861. This Act inaugurated the policy of protectionism which, with the exception of the UNDERWOOD-SIMMONS TARIFF ACT of 1913, was to last until 1934. The Act raised TARIFF rates to an average of 18.8 percent which was roughly equal to the rates of the Act of 1846. By its amendments in 1862 and 1864 this average was raised to 40.3 percent, the wool and iron schedules being consistently in the lead. Although its revenues were important in helping finance the Civil War, the Act's passage was the fulfillment of the Republican Party's platform pledge of 1860. This pledge had been designed to attract the support of eastern businessmen, and succeeded in doing so in the elections of the Civil War and post-War eras.

MORRIS, Gouverneur. 1752-1816. Statesman and diplomat. b. New York. Grandson of LEWIS MORRIS. Graduated, Columbia, studied law and practiced in New York City (from 1771); member, N Y. provincial congress(1775-77); signer of the ARTICLES OF CONFEDERATION (1775); member, CONTINENTAL CONGRESS (1777-78); assistant minister of finance (1781-85); member, CONSTITUTIONAL CONVENTION (1787); U.S. commissioner to England (1790-91); U.S. Minister to France (1792-94); U.S. Senator (1800-1803); chairman, Erie Canal Commission (1810-13).

MORRIS, Lewis. 1671-1746. Jurist. b. New York. Judge of court of common right, East New Jersey and member of the governor's council (1692); member of governor's council, and member of assembly when New Jersey became a royal colony (1707); chief justice, N.Y. supreme court (1715); governor of New Jersey (1738).

MORRIS, Robert. 1734-1806. Financier and statesman. b. England. To America (1747?); successful in business in Philadelphia; member CONSTITUTIONAL CONGRESS (1776-78); signer of the DECLARATION OF INDEPENDENCE; famous as "financier of the American Revolution" having purchased supplies for WASHINGTON'S army (1776-78); superintendent of finance (1781-84); founder of the Bank of North America (1782); delegate, CONSTITUTIONAL CONVENTION (1787); U.S. Senator from Pennsylvania (1789-95); speculated in western lands and lost his fortune.

MORROW, Dwight Whitney. 1873-1931. Lawyer, banker and diplomat. b. West Virginia. Graduated, Amherst College (1895); Columbia University Law School (1899); practised in New York City; partner in J. P. Morgan & Co. (1914-27); appointed by COOLIDGE, U.S. Ambassador to Mexico (1927-30); U.S. delegate to LONDON NAVAL CONFERENCE (1930).

MORROW, Prince Albert. 1846-1913. Physician. Known for important work in social hygiene; educated the public on venereal and genito-urinary diseases; pioneer in sex hygiene.

MORSE, Samuel Finley Breese. 1791-1872. Inventor and artist. b. Massachusetts. Graduated, Yale (1810); well-known portrait painter; founder and first president of National Academy of Design (1826-42); invented the TELEGRAPH and is known for the Morse code or alphabet used in sending messages; a founder of Vassar College; introduced (with DRAPER) the daguerrotype to this country.

MORTON, Julius Sterling. 1832-1902. Agriculturist. b. New York. Settled in Nebraska (1855); edited the state's first newspaper, the Nebraska City News; secretary of the Nebraska Territory (1858-61); U.S. Secretary of Agriculture (1893-97); originated Arbor Day.

MORTON, Oliver Perry. 1823-1877. Statesman. b. Indiana. Graduated, Miami University (1845); admitted to the bar (1847); Republican lieutenant governor of Indiana (1860); governor (1861-67); supported the Union cause and considered one of the greatest Civil War governors; U.S. Senator (1867-77).

MORTON, Rosalie Slaughter. 1876-. Surgeon and inventor. Graduated, Women's Medical College of Pa. (1897); studied in Europe; first woman member of the faculty of the College of Physicians and Surgeons, Columbia, as professor of gynecology (1916).

MORTON, William Thomas Green. 1819-1868. Dentist and physician. Studied dentistry at Baltimore College and medicine at Harvard; practiced dentistry in Boston; known for experiments with ether as a general anaesthetic; calling it letheon he gave first public demonstration (1846) and with CHARLES JACKSON he received a patent for its use; died in poverty unable to profit from his discovery; elected to HALL OF FAME (1920).

MOSBY, John Singleton. 1833-1916. Lawyer and Confederate commander. b. Virginia. Practiced law in Virginia (from

1855); served in the Confederate army in the Peninsula Campaign, at ANTIETAM (1862); commanded independent cavalry unit known as Mosby's Rangers; captured General STOUGHTON (1863) behind Federal lines; U.S. consul, Hong Kong (1878-85); Assistant Attorney, U.S. DEPARTMENT OF JUSTICE (1904-10).

Moscow Conference. A meeting in 1943 of the foreign ministers of the United States, Great Britain, and the Soviet Union. The Declaration of the conference contained a recognition of the need of a post-war world organization for the maintenance of international peace and security. It also recognized Austria as a defeated nation which, after the war, would be treated like all the victims of German aggression.

Motion Pictures. The modern motion picture developed out of the kinetoscope patented by Coleman Sellers in 1861. This primitive instrument was improved by THOMAS A. EDISON who exhibited a strip of photographic film in 1894. The Edison kinetoscope gained wide popular acceptance in penny arcade theatres as a coin-operated machine. This early peep-show apparatus was modified by Thomas Armat in 1896 into a projection machine which he called the vitascope. Theater production for group audiences now became possible, and the motion picture became an integral part of vaudeville shows. In 1905 the first movie theater opened in Pittsburgh, showing THE GREAT TRAIN ROBBERY, which was the first full length film produced around a scenario. Immediately, professional motion picture theaters sprang up throughout the nation. The typical admission of five cents enabled an audience to witness two to four reels of feature pictures and news reels. Professional companies were formed, including Biograph, Essanay, and Vitagraph. New York City and Los Angeles became the centers of the new industry. By the beginning of World War

I the latter had outstripped New York. The contributions of David W. Griffith, in the creation of new camera techniques such as the close-up, fade-out, and dissolve, launched the industry as a major entertainment factor. In 1912 Adolph Zukor founded the Famous Players Film Company which pioneered the full length feature film. Griffith's THE BIRTH OF A NATION in 1914 became the greatest revenue producer in motion picture history and a pioneer in new film techniques. The stimulus of this film attracted eminent personalities from the legitimate stage to the West Coast. National interest was manifested by the rise of the "star" system, national advertising and exploitation of films, huge investments in film companies, the publication of a press devoted exclusively to the industry, and the construction of thousands of motion picture theaters throughout the country. Comedy became popular through the contributions of CHARLES S. CHAPLIN, Mack Sennett, Ben Turpin, Fatty Arbuckle, and Harold Lloyd. The industry was widely utilized by the federal government to stimulate morale during the War. Liberty Bonds were sold in movie theaters and the stars participated in the drives and performed for the troops. Perhaps the greatest technological advance in the industry was the invention of the talking picture. With the showing of *The Jazz Singer* in 1927 the motion picture assumed greater importance as an entertainment medium. By 1930 practically every theater in the United States was showing sound pictures. Simultaneously the development of the color film added to the lure of the motion picture. In this era great stars captured the public imagination. These included Pola Negri, Rudolph Valentino, Gloria Swanson, Francis X. Bushman, Wallace Reid, Maurice Costello, John Gilbert, Douglas Fairbanks, Greta Garbo, Mary Pickford, Clara Bow, Constance Bennett, Norma Talmadge, and Lillian and Dorothy Gish. Among the distinguished directors and producers were Griffith, Cecil B. De-Mille, Clarence Brown, and Irving Thalberg. Modern stars include the Barrymores, Fredric March, Ronald Colman, Ingrid Bergman, Joan Crawford, Clark Gable, Bette Davis, Katharine Hepburn, Al Jolson, Norma Shearer, Walter Brennan, Walter Huston, Bing Crosby, Bob Hope, Charles Coburn, James Stewart, Margaret Sullavan, and Spencer Tracy. The development of television after World War II created a serious 'problem for the motion picture industry. In the 1950's producers were seriously considering the production of feature films for exclusive television viewing. Experimental short length films had revealed the popular interest in such entertainment fare. In 1951 there were 19,796 motion picture theaters in the United States with a seating capacity of 12,384,150. The capital investment in the film industry that year was $2,922,600,000. The industry employed 210,000 people who earned salaries of $487,870,000. More than 2,-000,000,000 feet of film were used in picture making in 1950. The income from the sale of films that year exceeded $874,000,000.

Motor Carrier Act. Passed by Congress in 1935. The law placed motor vehicles engaged in INTERSTATE COMMERCE under the jurisdiction of the INTERSTATE COMMERCE COMMISSION. The Commission was authorized to establish reasonable rates, prescribe uniform accounting methods, and coordinate the activities of motor carriers with those of other carriers. Motor carriers were forbidden to grant rebates or to discriminate between rates, persons, and localities.

Motor Transportation. The commercial TRANSPORTATION of goods by motor truck. The first commercial delivery by such a vehicle occurred in 1899, and within three years 75 rudimentary motor trucks had been built in the United States. By the opening of World War I

retail establishments had replaced the horse in great part by automotive transportation. In 1915 it is estimated that there were 136,000 trucks in use. Shortly thereafter trucking companies came into being to coordinate and expand this service. Although limited in the beginning to local service the improvement of HIGHWAYS expanded the radius of transportation to inter-city and inter-state distances. By the 1930's this development had become significant enough to warrant federal regulatory action, leading to the enactment of the MOTOR CARRIER ACT of 1935. Important technological improvements have brought into being the huge tractor-trailer, refrigerated equipment, and Diesel engines. In 1963 the AUTOMOTIVE INDUSTRY produced 1,462,708 motor trucks valued at $3,076,184,000.

Mount Vernon. The home of GEORGE WASHINGTON. It is located 16 miles below Washington, D.C. on the south bank of the Potomac River. It came into possession of the Washington family in 1690, and on it began the construction of the famous mansion in 1743. After the death of George Washington's half-brother, Lawrence, he acquired the property. Following his marriage in 1759 Washington set up his household at Mt. Vernon where he lived until the beginning of the Revolution. He returned there after the war and renewed the construction of the gardens and grounds. The main house and 13 minor buildings have survived to date as fine illustrations of Southern Colonial architecture. Upon his retirement from the presidency in 1797 Washington returned to Mt. Vernon where he died and was buried two years later. Today the property is maintained by the Mt. Vernon Ladies' Association.

Mount Vernon Conference. A conference of delegates of Maryland and Virginia, called at the suggestion of MADISON in March, 1785 for the purpose of negotiating an agreement for the trade and commerce of the Potomac River.

425

The commissioners met at Alexandria and then Mount Vernon, Virginia. After reaching an agreement the Maryland Legislature suggested the calling of a new conference on commercial questions, in which Pennsylvania and Delaware should be asked to participate. The Virginia Legislature agreed, but Madison recommended that delegates from all the states attend a general trade convention at Annapolis the next year.

MOYNIHAN, Daniel Patrick. 1927- Born in Tulsa, Okla. Attended City College of New York and received his B.A. in 1943. Received his M.A. from Tufts U. and his Ph.D. from Fletcher School of Law and Diplomacy. He was active in government work holding such positions as ass't. secretary to the governor of the State of New York 1955-58; member of the New York State Tenure Commission 1959-60; Director of the New York State Government Research Project at Syracuse University 1959-61; assistant secretary of labor 1963-65. In addition, he taught at Harvard and served as counsellor to the President from 1969 to 1973. He was the ambassador to India 1973-75 and the United States representative to the U.N. 1975-76. In 1976, he was elected Senator from New York. He is the author of numerous articles and books including *On Understanding Poverty, Maximum Feasible Understanding, The Politics of a Guaranteed Income, Coping: On the Practice of Government.* He serves on the editorial board of "The American Scholar."

"Muckrakers." Name applied by Theodore Roosevelt in 1906 to a group of writers and newspaper men who in their work attacked the political, economic, and social evils within the country. These "muckrakers" were part of the movement of reform from 1890 to the end of World War I commonly known as the Progressive Era. Among the better known writers were IDA TARBELL, UPTON SINCLAIR, RAY STANNARD BAKER, Henry Demarest Lloyd, and Frank Norris. Their influence was important enough to stimulate the passage by Congress of many laws. The most significant of these were the PURE FOOD AND DRUGS ACT, 1906, the MEAT INSPECTION ACT, 1906, and the FEDERAL RESERVE ACT, 1914.

"Mugwumps." Also known as the Independent Republicans. The word is derived from an Indian word meaning "big chief," and was first used by CHARLES A. DANA in the New York *Sun* The "mugwumps" were reform Republicans who bolted the Republican party after the nomination of JAMES G. BLAINE in 1884. This independent element refused to be bound by strict party discipline, and it insisted upon high standards of party morality. Its members dissented from the dominant group in respect to such issues as the party's attitude to the South, and its advocacy of a high PROTECTIVE TARIFF. At a conference they denounced the convention's action and invited the Democrats to nominate an honest, independent candidate for whom public spirited citizens could vote. After CLEVELAND's nomination by the Democratic party, the mugwumps endorsed him as the prototype of "political courage and honesty and of administrative reform" while simultaneously denouncing Blaine as a "representative of men, methods, and conduct which the public conscience condemns." Their support of Cleveland in the 1884 election was credited with being a strong factor in Blaine's defeat. The attempts of the "mugwumps" to purge the Republican party of machine politics and of the elements which had been responsible for the scandals of the GRANT administration bore fruit ultimately. "Mugwump" leaders included THEODORE ROOSEVELT, GEORGE CURTIS, HENRY CABOT LODGE, HENRY WARD BEECHER, CARL SCHURZ, and Presidents WHITE of Cornell, and ELIOT of Harvard.

MUIR, John. 1838-1914. Naturalist. b. Scotland. Came to the United States (1849); studied at the University of Wisconsin (1859-63); made many trips collecting botanical specimens; concentrated his studies at Yosemite Valley (1868-74); important influence in creating YOSEMITE NATIONAL PARK; interested T. ROOSEVELT in forest CONSERVATION; discovered an Alaskan glacier. Author of many books on his discoveries.

"Mulligan Letters, The." A group of letters written to James Mulligan by JAMES G. BLAINE from 1869 on. In these letters Blaine, then Speaker of the House of Representatives, discussed with Mulligan, a former clerk of a Boston business firm, the former's unexplained sale to the UNION PACIFIC RAILROAD of certain securities at prices higher than their value. In 1876, Blaine, a candidate for the Republican nomination, was summoned before a House committee to explain these letters. Having obtained the letters from Mulligan through a trick, Blaine appeared before the committee and made a brilliant speech in which he read the letters to an accompaniment of his own self-justifying comment. Although his address was received with applause he did not receive the nomination in 1876 or 1880. After his nomination in 1884 the Democrats revived the public exhibit of the Mulligan Letters, and on September 15, 1884 the press contained additional letters not hitherto made public. This revelation contributed heavily to Blaine's defeat

"Municipal Banker." See subsidies.

Municipal Home Rule. A plan whereby a greater measure of political autonomy is allowed a city within the terms of a charter granted by the state legislature. In 1952 more than 16 states had embodied home rule provisions in their constitutions. The home rule charter is forbidden to contain provisions contrary to the Constitution, statutes, or TREATIES of the United States, or to the constitution or laws of the state. The general clauses of a home rule charter provide for the incorporation of the city, describe its framework of government, and determine its officers, elections, tenure, and similar details. They also prescribe the city's power over contracts, finances, and other purely municipal functions which are left within its jurisdiction.

Municipal Reform. The attempts to increase popular controls over municipal government for the purpose of weakening or eliminating political machines. Some of the developments in this direction include the use of MUNICIPAL HOME RULE for larger cities, PROPORTIONAL REPRESENTATION, the SHORT BALLOT, the COUNTY EXECUTIVE PLAN, and the COUNTY MANAGER and CITY MANAGER SYSTEM.

Municipality. A local area of government in the United States. At various times it has taken the forms of parish, borough, town, township, village, county, and city government. In the constitutional system of the United States the municipality is a non-sovereign entity, its powers depending wholly upon state grant. Municipalities may be incorporated or unincorporated. In the former a state charter provides a degree of autonomy with respect to purely local functions. In the latter control is generally exercised by the state legislature operating by means of a local government. The governments of municipalities vary, but consist generally of a legislative body in the form of a council, board of trustees or supervisors, or board of SELECTMEN. If there is an executive it is usually a mayor although this office is customarily absent from the county. Other municipal offices include court, police, sheriffs, clerks, and legal officers.

Munitions Board. An agency established

by the NATIONAL SECURITY ACT of 1947. It has the responsibility of supervising and coordinating the manufacture of weapons. It analyzes the facilities of American industry recommending new plants where necessary. The Board compiles an inventory of existing tools and machinery as a basis for its recommendations.

Munitions Investigation. An investigation of the munitions industry by a special Senate committee appointed on April 19, 1934 under the chairmanship of Senator Gerald P. Nye. The Committee held public hearings at which testimony was given about the sale of munitions in World War I. The testimony disclosed that the munitions manufacturers had made huge profits, that munitions firms fostered "wars and rumors of wars," and that t hey sold munitions to all belligerents. The Committee also investigated the work of the MORGAN BANKING system as the financial agent of England and France during the war in an attempt to discover the link between war loans to the ALLIED POWERS and the entry of the United States into the war. The Committee's disclosures were one of the contributing factors to the passage of the NEUTRALITY ACT in 1935.

Munn vs. Illinois. The first of the GRANGER CASES. In 1876 the United States Supreme Court upheld the constitutionality of the Illinois law of 1871 which declared grain elevators to be public warehouses, and thereby provided for the establishment of maximum rates. The court threw out Munn's arguments that warehousing was not a public calling and that he was being deprived of his property without DUE PROCESS of law. It held that the English common law principle of protecting the PUBLIC WELFARE had been properly invoked under the police powers reserved to the states by the Tenth Amendment. It further held that rate making was a legislative not a judi-cial function. This decision was reversed 10 years later in the case of Wabash, St. Louis, and Pacific Railway vs. Illinois.

Murfreesboro, Battle of. In December, 1862 General ROSECRANS led the Union Army of the Cumberland from Nashville, confronting the Confederate Army under BRAGG at Murfreesboro, Tennessee. On December 31st, Bragg led his 38,000 troops against the 43,000 Union soldiers, sweeping away JOHNSON's division. He was stopped by SHERIDAN until Rosecrans could organize his artillery. Prevented by storms from resuming the battle on January 1st Bragg attacked again on January 2nd. His 10,000 men were routed by concentrated artillery fire, and on the 3rd Bragg retreated toward Chattanooga.

MURRAY, Philip. 1886-1952. Labor leader. b. Scotland. Came to the United States (1902); became a naturalized citizen (1911); elected vice-president, UNITED MINE WORKERS of America (1920-42); succeeded JOHN L. LEWIS as president of the CIO (1940); leader, CIO-PAC.

Muscle Shoals Act. Under the sponsorship of Senator GEORGE NORRIS of Nebraska. Congress passed a bill in 1928 providing for government operation of the station at Muscle Shoals in Alabama. It was vetoed by President COOLIDGE. A second bill, passed in 1931, providing for the construction of a second dam on the Tennessee River and for government manufacture and sale of fertilizer and power, was vetoed by President HOOVER. In 1933 the MUSCLE SHOALS ACT created the TENNESSEE VALLEY AUTHORITY with a widely extended power far beyond that conceived in the original bills. See Tennessee Valley Authority.

Museum of Modern Art. Organized in 1929 in New York City to encourage and develop the study of modern ART. It also aims at the application of such art to industrial activities, and provides instruc-

428

tion to this end. The collections of the Museum include exhibits of painting, sculpture, architecture, industrial and manual art, photography, theater arts, motion pictures, and the graphic arts. As part of its educational program it sends on tour many exhibits which have been seen in hundreds of localities in the United States and its possessions. Its motion picture collection is particularly notable, surpassing in quantity and quality any other collection in the world. It contains the outstanding films of past American, German, Russian, French, and Italian production.

Museums. The earliest museums were private collections of botanical and geological specimens during the colonial period. The oldest public museum was established by the Charles Town Library Society at Charlestown, South Carolina in 1773. A natural history museum was founded in Philadelphia in 1785 by CHARLES W. and Rembrandt PEALE. The present Peabody Museum at Salem, Massachusetts was established in 1799. In 1831 the Boston Society of Natural History emerged from a consolidation of the Academy of Natural Science (1812) and the Linnean Society of Boston (1814).

The internationally famous SMITHSONIAN INSTITUTION was organized in 1846, being renamed the United States National Museum in 1876. The AMERICAN MUSEUM OF NATURAL HISTORY, possessing probably the greatest collection of exhibits of its kind in the world, was established in New York City in 1869. Art museums followed slowly after science museums, the first having been established in Philadelphia in 1805. The Boston Atheneum was founded in 1807 and became the Museum of Fine Arts in 1870. The METROPOLITAN MUSEUM OF ART was opened in 1870 as the largest in the United States. Similar art museums were founded thereafter in Chicago, Cincinnati, Pittsburgh, and other large cities. Historical museums such as the Museum

of the American Indian and the New York Historical Society have also played a prominent role in American cultural life.

Music. With the exception of liturgical music, music was frowned upon in the PURITAN controlled colonies up to the Revolution. Professional music performance was prohibited by law. Secular music was allowed greater freedom in the middle and southern colonies, and by the mid-1720's professional musicians were permitted to play there. The Germans and Dutch in Pennsylvania and New York were more liberal in their approach to music. The first public concert in the British colonies occurred in Boston in 1731. The first native American composer was FRANCIS HOPKINSON. In the early 19th century the influence of European music stimulated the growth of important American musical organizations. Among these were the Handel and Haydn Society of Boston (1815), the NEW YORK PHILHARMONIC SOCIETY (1842), and the Musical Fund Society of Philadelphia (1820). The Boston Music Hall was erected in 1852 and the New York Academie of Music in 1854. Beginning in New Orleans in 1808, opera spread to New York in 1825. By 1850 music faculties had been established at the University of Virginia, Yale College, and Oberlin College. Important composers of this era include James Hewett, Benjamin Carr, and Victor Pelissier. After the Civil War, the METROPOLITAN OPERA COMPANY was established in 1883, the BOSTON SYMPHONY ORCHESTRA in 1881, and the PHILADELPHIA ORCHESTRA in 1900. Other operatic and symphonic organizations were established elsewhere in the nation. EDWARD MC DOWELL gained international recognition at this time. The famous "New England School" included such outstanding composers as George W. Chadwick, Horatio Parker, and Henry K. Hadley. In the field of folk music STEPHEN FOSTER was the most popular. In the 20th century the modernist schools have produced such famous personalities as AARON COPLAND, Howard Hanson, Roy Harris, DEEMS TAYLOR, and Virgil Thomson. With the development of the radio and recording industries music has been made available to an ever-growing American audience.

Mutiny Act. See Quartering Acts.

Mutual Security Act. Passed by Congress in October, 1951 as a replacement for the expiring ECONOMIC COOPERATION ACT. The law authorized $7,483,000,000 for foreign aid in the form of military and economic supplies. Ninety percent was to be used in building up European defenses, the balance to be allocated for economic purposes. On October 31st Congress appropriated $7,328,903,976 for the first year's operation of the agency, to begin on January 1, 1952. In March, 1952 President TRUMAN requested an additional appropriation of $7,-900,000,000, 90 percent of which was to be applied to military expenditures. The Act is administered by a Mutual Security Administration.

Myers vs. United States. A decision of the United States Supreme Court in 1926 in which the Court held that the President could remove executive officers from office, without consent of the Senate, even though their appointment required the Senate's approval. In so doing it held invalid an 1876 Act of Congress which restricted the President's power of removal by requiring the Senate's consent for the removal of postmasters. In this decision the Court found Frank S. Myers, the Portland, Oregon Postmaster, to be an executive officer necessarily subject to the power of the President in "taking care that the laws be faithfully executed" as mandated in Article II of the federal Constitution.

My Lai Massacre. William Calley was an army lieutenant who went on trial in November 1970 before a military court. He was charged with being in command of a platoon that massacred over 100 Viet Namese civilians in the village of My Lai on March 16, 1968. His trial was a highly emotional one with some debating whether or not he should be punished for carrying out orders. The public was shocked by the stories of American brutality and atrocities and Calley was found guilty in March 1971 and sentenced to life imprisonment. His sentence was later commuted to twenty years.

N

NADER, Ralph. 1934-   As a social reformer, Ralph Nader has been a leader in consumer protection throughout the 1960s and 1970s with a reputation for honesty and frank criticism. His attacks on the automobile industry's emphasis on style and power and neglect of safety resulted in The National Traffic and Motor Vehicles Act of 1966. He organized study groups in 1969 in his Center for the Study of Responsive Law. The Center included 5 lawyers full time and 100 students working for the summer. Known as Nader's Raiders, they made investigations of several governmental organizations and a division of the Agriculture Department. His Congress Project in 1971-72 prepared records of over 475 members of Congress giving voting records, campaign financing, and their personal conduct.

Napoleonic Wars. A series of wars between England and France between 1804 and 1815. The issuance of the English ORDERS IN COUNCIL and the French BERLIN AND MILAN DECREES in 1806, imposing a BLOCKADE upon neutral shipping, so interfered with American COMMERCE as to involve the United States in diplomatic difficulties with both nations. The consequent passage by Congress of the NON-INTERCOURSE ACT of 1806, the EMBARGO ACT of 1807, and the NON-IMPORTATION ACT of 1809 virtually ruined American SHIPPING. The ultimate result was to involve the United States in the War of 1812 with Great Britain.

Narragansett Indians. A leading tribe of New England that lived in the TERRITORY that is now Rhode Island. ROGER WILLIAMS originally bought the land from the Narragansetts in 1636 and established friendly relations with them. They sided with the colonists in the Pequot Wars. In the "Swamp Fight," led by Josiah Winslow against the tribe in 1675, they were almost wiped out. Their culture was primitive. They lived in wigwams made of mats, bark or skins. The Narragansetts were excellent fishermen and were expert at canoeing and swimming.

Nashville Convention. Called in two sessions in June and November, 1850, for the purpose of adopting a program designed to protect the slave rights of the southern states. The call for the Convention was issued by a Mississippi state convention in 1849 at the suggestion of JOHN C. CALHOUN "to devise and adopt some mode of resistance to northern aggressions." WHIG and Democratic delegates from nine states came to Nashville, Tennessee to adopt 28 resolutions maintaining that SLAVERY was guaranteed by the Constitution, that the TERRITORIES belonged to the people of the state, that the people could freely migrate to the territories, and that Congress was obligated to secure their rights. At the second session, following the enactment of the COMPROMISE ACT OF 1850, the Convention called for SECESSION. This Resolution proved an utter failure because of the general support of the Compromise Act.

Natchez Indians. In 1700 there were approximately 1,000 Natchez warriors living in nine villages on the east side of the Mississippi River. They were a Muskhogean tribe with a high degree of civilization. They earned their livelihood primarily by farming and were especially skilled in the arts. They were sun worshippers who on occasion even resorted to human sacrifice. The Natchez were friendly with the French, until attacked without reason. They were almost completely wiped out by Bienville in 1723, and were forced to abandon their villages in 1730 when attacked by a combination of French troops and CHOCTAW warriors. They fled in various directions, some of them being captured in Louisiana and sold into SLAVERY in the WEST INDIES. Some joined the CHICKASAWS, and the rest fled to South Carolina.

National Aeronautics and Space Administration. For fiscal 1965, this agency was to receive over $5 billion. Projects receiving substantial portions of this appropriation included Apollo ($2.6 billion) and Gemini ($308.4 million).

National Association for the Advancement of Colored People. Popularly known as the NAACP. Organized in 1910 as a private interracial group for the purpose of seeking the political and civil equality of the Negro people. Its several hundred branches engage in educational programs, lobbying activities, and political support of those concurring with its aims.

National Association of Manufacturers, the. Popularly known as the NAM. A lobbying organization, created in 1895,

to further the interests of domestic and foreign trade. It has become one of the most influential general business associations in the United States. Since 1902 the Association, through its subsidiary the League for Industrial Rights, has promoted a LABOR RELATIONS program through legislative and political activities. Its affiliated organization, the National Industrial Conference Board, is acknowledged to operate one of the most comprehensive labor and social research programs in the United States. In 1952 the NAM consisted of approximately 16,000 member firms with a capacity of 85 percent of the manufactured goods of the United States. Its annual BUDGET was $3,000,000.

National Banking Act. A law of Congress passed on February 25, 1863 and amended on June 3, 1864. It was designed to charter banks under national authority with the privilege of issuing CURRENCY supported by national bonds. STATE BANKS could become members of the National Banking System by purchasing, and depositing with the Treasury, national bonds equal to one-third of their paid-in capital. The office of the Comptroller of the Currency was established. He was empowered to administer the system by paying out national bank notes to member banks in amounts equal to 90 percent of the market value of the bonds. These notes were to be legal tender for all dues to the United States except imports. The capital stock of national banks must be $50,000 or more and such banks must maintain cash reserves equal to 15 percent of their circulation. Shareholders were made responsible for the debts of the banks to an amount equal to the par value of their stock. In March, 1865 an AMENDMENT placed a 10 percent tax on the currency issues of state banks, driving the note issuing function of these banks out of existence. In 1900 national banks were authorized to increase their bank note circulation to 100 percent of the value of the bonds purchased. In 1908 national banks were permitted to deposit certain other securities, besides United States bonds, as collateral for their currency. In 1913 all national banks were incorporated into the Federal Reserve System. The hopes of the framers of the Act that it would effectively control the credit and currency operations of the nation's economy were not fulfilled. The result was the passage of the FEDERAL RESERVE ACT in 1913 and the various NEW DEAL BANKING laws of the 1930's. In 1934 national bank notes were withdrawn from circulation.

National Capital. See Washington, D.C.

National Conservation Commission. Appointed by President T. ROOSEVELT in 1908 as an outcome of the Conference of the Governors of that year. It was chaired by GIFFORD PINCHOT. Opposition in Congress hampered the work of the Commission by the refusal to appropriate funds for its activities. Its functions nevertheless were carried out by the President's persuasion of the staffs of various EXECUTIVE DEPARTMENTS to volunteer their servies. President Roosevelt disregarded a CIVIL SERVICE bill AMENDMENT forbidding federal personnel to do outside work in such instances, declaring that "it is for the people to decide whether they believe in the CONSERVATION movement." His behavior won popular approval, and the Supreme Court upheld the constitutionality of his conservation policy.

National Convention. The quadriennial meeting of the POLITICAL PARTIES, called for the purpose of nominating candidates for the presidency and vice-presidency. Until 1832 the parties selected such candidates by congressional CAUCUSES of their leaders. In that year the ANTI-MASONIC PARTY inaugurated a national convention. This method of nomination has always been considered a democratic

move inasmuch as it took the choice of candidates out of the hands of party leaders and theoretically conferred this choice upon the delegates at these conventions. These delegates, chosen either by the state conventions of the parties or in PRIMARY elections depending upon the primary laws of the states, may be pledged to certain candidates.

National Council of Churches of Christ. An organization established on November 29, 1950 by the merger of eight Protestant inter-church agencies, the most prominent of which was the Federal Council of Churches. The organization was created for the purpose of achieving social action objectives through the co-operative and joint activities of the members. Funds have been allocated to carry on a program of foreign missions, home missions, Christian EDUCATION, RADIO and films, Christian life and work, and women's activities. In 1965 there were 31 Protestant denominations including Eastern Orthodox bodies in the organization, comprising almost 40,000,000 church members.

National Crime Coordinating Council. See Kefauver Investigation.

National Defense Act. Passed by Congress in 1916. It was part of a series of laws enacted as defense measures in the period preceding the entry of the United States into World War I. It authorized the increase of the regular army to reach a strength of 223,000 men in five years, federalized the NATIONAL GUARD of 425,-000 men, established civilian training camps, provided for military SCHOOLS in the nation's colleges and universities, and appropriated $20,000,000 for the erection of a nitrate and munitions plant. The Act reflected the national philosophy of dependence on volunteer CITIZEN effort employing local energies and avoiding the undesirable alternative of a huge standing army.

National Defense Advisory Commission. See Council of National Defense, World War II.

National Defense Mediation Board. An agency established by EXECUTIVE ORDER in 1940 for the purpose of resolving labor disputes in defense industries. It was composed of 11 members and 30 alternates, representing the general public, employers, and employees. With no legal authority to enforce its decision it was reduced to general conciliation and mediation efforts, employing its good offices in compromising the claims of labor and management in such disputes. Its inability to satisfactorily settle the Allis-Chalmers, North American Aviation, and captive coal mine strikes in 1940 and 1941, plus labor's opposition, rendered its work devoid of public confidence. During its life more than 25,000,000 man-days of labor were lost because of STRIKES involving over 2,000,000 workers. In January, 1942 it was succeeded by the NATIONAL WAR LABOR BOARD.

National Democratic Party. See Gold Democrats.

National Farmers Union. A national lobbying organization of small and medium FARMERS. It has advocated government programs designed to aid the low income farmer. Its specific objectives have been congressional and state legislation to furnish relief for needy farmers, for aid to SHARECROPPERS, TENANT FARMERS, and migratory laborers, and for assistance to farm cooperative organizations. In cooperation with organized labor it has pursued a strong anti-MONOPOLY policy.

National Forests. The United States government, under the administration of the Forest Service of the DEPARTMENT OF AGRICULTURE, maintains a total area of approximately 230,000,000 acres of national forests in 42 states and two TERRITORIES. Within the national forests are situated National Game Refuges estab-

lished by the Clarke-McNary Act of 1924. The bulk of this area is located in the western states. Additional federally owned forest land, exceeding 4,500,000 acres, is located in the NATIONAL PARKS AND MONUMENTS and more than 8,000,000 acres in Indian Reservations. The Forest Service carries on research work dealing with the problems of forest fires, tree diseases and pests, lumber products, and land drainage.

National Foundation for Infantile Paralysis. Established in 1938 by President FRANKLIN D. ROOSEVELT to conduct the struggle against infantile paralysis. Its source of funds is the voluntary contributions of the people of the United States during the annual "March of Dimes" campaign conducted in the final two weeks of January. Half of the funds so raised goes to the National Foundation for use in its national program of research, EDUCATION, and emergency aid in epidemics. The balance is retained by the local chapters for the care and treatment of indigent poliomyelitis patients. The work is conducted through recognized health and welfare agencies. The Foundation does not operate its own research facilities but makes grants to institutions throughout the country for work in the cause, prevention, and cure of the disease. In 1954 it paid $7,500,000 for test injections of the Salk vaccine for 422,000 children in 44 states (See Salk Polio Vaccine for subsequent activities in this field).

National Geographic Society. An organization established in 1888 to increase and spread geographic knowledge. The Society publishes a monthly periodical of popular geography, and has in the past distributed over 100 large supplementary maps covering major world areas. It frequently cooperates with scientific, educational, and government organizations in carrying on its work. It maintains free information service for NEWSPAPERS, press association, and radio and television commentators. The Society has sponsored or assisted EXPLORATION expeditions all over the world, including the Peary expedition to the North Pole in 1909 and the under-water investigations of William Beebe in 1934. Its projects have included scientific inquiries into the aurora borealis, cosmic ray, and astronomy.

Natonal Grange. Also known as the Patrons of Husbandry. A fraternal farmers' association founded by OLIVER H. KELLEY in Washington, D.C. on December 4, 1867 In its origins it was a secret order created for the purpose of fostering a pleasanter social life among FARMERS. Its non-political character changed after the PANIC OF 1873 in the attempt of the Grangers to curb the abuses of the railroad companies. By this time there were some 3,000 Granges in existence, which by 1875 had increased to 19,000 with a total membership of 1,500,000. The Granges sought state relief and succeeded in obtaining passage of the "GRANGER LAWS." Other aspects of the Granger program included social and educational reforms, cooperatives, publications, and lobbying. By the end of the 19th century the membership of the Grange had declined to 125,000, but by the 1930's had risen to 800,000. Its strength today lies in New England, the North Central States, and the Northwest.

National Guard. See militia.

National Housing Act. Also known as the Wagner-Steagall Act and the United States Housing Act. Passed by Congress in 1937 and amended in 1938. The Act established the United States Housing Authority to administer loans to state and local communities for SLUM clearance and low cost HOUSING projects. By its terms the Authority was empowered to sell bonds and make loans up to $500,000,000 over a three year period to state and municipal housing authorities. Up to 90 percent of

the funds spent by such local agencies could be loaned by the Authority at low interest rates, the remainder being furnished locally. Under these laws the federal government does not directly engage in housing construction and slum clearance. This responsibility has been thrust upon the state and municipal "public housing authorities" created under the terms of the legislation. By 1941 the agency had assisted in the construction of more than 120,000 family dwelling units designed for low income groups. In its origins the United States Housing Authority was located within the DEPARTMENT OF THE INTERIOR. In 1942 it was reorganized by EXECUTIVE ORDER into the Federal Public Housing Authority and relocated within the newly established NATIONAL HOUSING AGENCY. To date 38 states have provided for the requisite housing authorities as a precondition for receiving federal aid.

National Housing Act of 1934. See Federal Housing Administration.

National Housing Act of 1949. A law of Congress passed on July 15, 1949 for the purpose of providing public HOUSING and SLUM clearance projects. It coordinated the work of various existing public housing agencies by incorporating them into the newly created National Housing and Home Finance Agency. The program supported by federal funds, provided for a $1,500,000,000 slum clearance program and a $262,500,000 farm housing program. The law contemplated the construction of 810,000 housing units in six years and an extended 40 year program of public housing by state and local housing authorities, to be subsidized by government loans up to $308,000,000 annually.

National Housing Agency. Established by EXECUTIVE ORDER in 1942. Into it were placed 16 federal housing agencies with previously overlapping and conflicting functions. At its head was a National Housing Administrator. The three principal constituent units were the Federal Housing Authority, the FEDERAL HOUSING ADMINISTRATION, and the Federal Home Loan Bank Administration. At the time of its creation its principal objective was to supply HOUSING for war workers. It encouraged private construction by granting priority rating for materials, and supplemented this by public projects. Later its program was extended to the construction of SCHOOLS, water-supply systems, hospitals, and other public works. Ten regional offices were established to maintain this program. In 1949 it was abolished, its function being transfered to the NATIONAL HOUSING AND HOME FINANCE AGENCY.

National Housing and Home Financing Agency. An agency established by Reorganization Plan No. 3 on July 27, 1947 to coordinate all public HOUSING programs. It consisted of the HOME LOAN BANK BOARD, FEDERAL HOUSING ADMINISTRATION, and PUBLIC HOUSING ADMINISTRATION under the over-all supervision of an Administrator. The Agency was authorized to determine mortgage policy and to dispose of federally-owned war and veterans' housing. It was empowered to administer a program of technical research to foster standardization of parts and the production of building materials.

National Industrial Recovery Act. Also called National Recovery Act. Popularly known by its initials NIRA or NRA. Enacted by Congress in 1933 for the purpose of bringing about industrial recovery at the beginning of the NEW DEAL program. The statute provided that CODES OF FAIR COMPETITION be drawn up on an industry-wide basis. These codes were to include provisions barring CHILD LABOR, recognizing the COLLECTIVE BARGAINING RIGHTS OF LABOR, containing fair marketing features, fixing minimum

wages, and establishing price arrangements. The President was delegated the power to draw up "blanket codes" for those industries which did not voluntarily prepare their own. To avoid anti-trust prosecution arising out of collaboration for the accomplishment of the above stated aims, the Act provided for the suspension of the ANTI-TRUST LAWS. The Act was administered by a National Recovery Administration whose chief was General HUGH S. JOHNSON. The Supreme Court declared the Act unconstitutional in 1935 in the case of SCHECHTER POULTRY CORPORATION VS. UNITED STATES.

National Jewish Welfare Board. See Jews.

National Labor Board. An agency established by congressional act on August 5, 1933 to administer Section 7a of the NATIONAL RECOVERY ACT. It was ineffective and was replaced on July 9, 1934 by the NATIONAL LABOR RELATIONS BOARD. This three man board was made independent of the National Recovery Administration and worked in conjunction with the DEPARTMENT OF LABOR in coordinating the functions set down in the Labor Disputes Joint Resolution of June 16, 1934. The Board was authorized to investigate disputes between workers and employers arising out of the NRA, conduct elections among workers to determine representation for COLLECTIVE BARGAINING purposes, and prescribe rules and regulations it considered necessary to carry on its work. It was given the power to act as an appellate court over the decisions of the special labor boards such as the National Steel Labor Relations Board and National Longshoreman's Board.

National Labor Reform Party. See Greenback-Labor Party.

National Labor Relations Act. Also known as the Wagner Act. An act of Congress in 1935 which established a three man NATIONAL LABOR RELATIONS BOARD empowered to administer the regulation of LABOR RELATIONS in industries engaged in or affecting INTERSTATE COMMERCE. It was incorporated as Title I of the Taft - Hartley Act of 1947. The law established the rights of workers to organize or join LABOR UNIONS and to bargain collectively with their employers through representatives of their own choosing. It defines certain activities which, when committed by employers, are considered UNFAIR LABOR PRACTICES. Under the law unions grew rapidly, protected by the elimination from labor relations of the BLACKLIST, YELLOW DOG CONTRACT, COMPANY UNION, and other coercive measures formerly utilized by employers. See National Labor Relations Board, Unfair Labor Practices, and Taft-Hartley Act.

National Labor Relations Board. A three man administrative agency created by the NATIONAL LABOR RELATIONS ACT. In 1947 its size was increased to five members by the TAFT-HARTLEY ACT. The board is empowered to administer the two laws by the exercise of quasi-judicial powers. These include the right to make rules and regulations, hold hearings, issue subpoenas for witnesses and evidence, make decisions, and issue final orders. It is authorized to seek enforcement of its final orders by the United States Court of Appeals. The Board's functions fall into two basic categories: the prevention and remedy of UNFAIR LABOR PRACTICES and the holding of representation hearings for the purpose of determining employees' representatives in COLLECTIVE BARGAINING. See National Labor Relations Act, Unfair Labor Practices, and Taft-Hartley Act.

National Labor Relations Board vs Jones and Laughlin Steel Corporation. A decision of the United States Supreme Court on April 12, 1937 which sustained the constitutionality of the WAGNER ACT. In addition to upholding Congress' power to regulate LABOR RELATIONS in INTERSTATE COMMERCE and protecting the RIGHTS OF LABOR, the decision was significant as a reinterpretation of the power of Congress to legislate under the commerce clause of the Constitution. The Court held that "although activities may be intrastate in character when separately considered, if they have such a close and substantial relation to interstate commerce that their control is essential or appropriate to protect that COMMERCE from burdens and obstructions, Congress cannot be denied the power to exercise that control."

National Labor Union. The first important national labor organization in the United States. It was founded in 1866 by William H. Sylvis. Its organization was based on a coalition of local unions and city trade assemblies. The National Labor Union held seven annual conventions, and by 1871, when it disintegrated, it had a membership of 600,000. Its program included the establishment of consumers' cooperatives, opposition to Chinese IMMIGRATION, the establishment of a federal bureau of labor, the advocacy of the EIGHT-HOUR DAY, and political action. The rise of the KNIGHTS OF LABOR drew many members from this group. These losses were aggravated by the PANIC OF 1873 which brought its existence to an end.

National League, The. A professional BASEBALL organization, established in 1876 to replace the defunct National Association of Baseball Players. Its full name is The National League of Professional Baseball Clubs. M. G. Bulkeley, then president of the Hartford Baseball Club, was elected the League's first president. For a time it was the only "Major" league, but in 1882 the American Association was organized and in 1884 the Union League was established. Several smaller professional leagues were subsequently created as a rival to the National League. It was not until 1900, with the establishment of the present-day AMERICAN LEAGUE, that a permanent and powerful rival came into being. In 1965 the ten member clubs were the Chicago Cubs, Cincinnati Redlegs, Milwaukee Braves, New York Mets, Philadelphia Phillies, Pittsburgh Pirates, St. Louis Cardinals, Houston Colts, Los Angeles Dodgers, and the San Francisco Giants. Since the establishment of the World Series in 1903 the National League has won 24 world championships. Since the establishment of the All-Star series in 1933 it has won 17 games.

National Mediation Board. See Crosser-Dill Act.

National Mediation Board. See Railway Labor Act of 1926.

National Monuments. These consist of prominent buildings, statues, homes, homesteads, caves, trees, bridges, castles, lands, battle-fields, canyons, beaches, craters, bluffs, and similar natural or man made sites of historic, political, scenic, or ceremonial importance. They are administered by the Office of National Parks, Buildings, and Reservations within the DEPARTMENT OF THE INTERIOR. Although NATIONAL PARKS may be established only by Congress, the President has the authority to designate national monuments. Among the outstanding national monuments are Glacier Bay, Alaska, the Lewis and Clark Cavern, Montana, APPOMATTOX COURTHOUSE, Virginia Statue of Liberty, New York, Petrified Forest, Arizona, Fort Sumter, North Carolina, Death Valley, California-Nevada.

National Origins Act. A clause of the JOHNSON-REED ACT of 1924. It is not a separate congressional statute. Under the clause, a new method of determining annual immigration quotas was provided by ascertaining the real origin of the American people in 1920. Upon these findings IMMIGRATION was to be apportioned among the various national groups on the basis of the ratio of each country's nationals in the United States in 1920 to the total American POPULATION of that year. A maximum of 150,000 immigrants per year was established. Although scheduled to come into operation in 1927, the difficulty of determining the national origins of the American population postponed its commencement until 1929. The quota accomplished its purpose since only 48,500 immigrants were admitted in the fiscal year 1931 as compared to 805,-000 in 1921. Inasmuch as northern and western Europe sent 42.2 percent and southern and eastern Europe only 20.8 percent of these immigrants it was evident that the discouragement of "new immigrants" had been accomplished.

National Park System. It is administered by the National Park Service of the DEPARTMENT OF THE INTERIOR. The System contains a total of approximately 21,720-000 acres of federally owned park lands located in 175 areas. The first national park was the YELLOWSTONE NATIONAL PARK, established in 1872. Since then the System has spread to include extraordinary scenic wonders, not only in continental United States, but in ALASKA and HAWAII. Included is a large number of sites famous for their historic or scientific interest. Among the outstanding national parks are the Carlsbad Caverns, New Mexico, the Grand Canyon, Arizona, the Everglades, Florida, Mount Rainier, Washington, and YOSEMITE, California.

National Prohibition Act. See Volstead Act.

National Prohibition Party. See Prohibition party.

438

National Production Authority. An agency established by EXECUTIVE ORDER in the DEPARTMENT OF COMMERCE on September 11, 1950. It was authorized to exercise power over those priorities and allocations not reserved to the Secretaries of Agriculture and the Interior or to the INTERSTATE COMMERCE COMMISSION. It was headed by an Administrator who was to see that the rearmament requirements of the United States Defense program, as set down in the DEFENSE PRODUCTION ACT, were met on schedule. The agency was to administer the production of available materials and facilities to insure the equal distribution of those remaining for non-defense use after military needs had been provided for. It was to develop and promote measures for the expansion of productive capacity and of the production and supply of materials and facilities for the national defense. It was given the administrative authority to require producers to grant priority to defense contracts and to allocate materials and requisition facilities for defense production. The National Production Authority immediately issued regulations limiting inventories of materials in short supply and establishing a broad system of priorities.

National Railway Adjustment Board. See Crosser-Dill Act.

National Recovery Act. See National Industrial Recovery Act.

National Recovery Administration. See National Industrial Recovery Act.

National Republican Party. An opposition party to the JACKSON forces in the DEMOCRATIC REPUBLICAN PARTY. It came into existence as a result of the spilt in that party when CLAY threw his support to JOHN QUINCY ADAMS in the election of the President in 1824 by the House of Representatives. The Clay-Adams forces called themselves National Republicans and attracted former FEDERALIST elements. Their chief leaders included Clay, Adams, and WEBSTER.Their program advocated INTERNAL IMPROVEMENTS at federal expense, and sound CURRENCY, a PROTECTIVE TARIFF, and a BANK OF THE UNITED STATES. In 1834 the party was absorbed by the WHIG PARTY.

National Resources Committee. An agency established by EXECUTIVE ORDER in 1934 for the purpose of studying problems in planning and conserving the NATURAL RESOURCES of the United States. It replaced the National Planning Board which had been created in 1933 and was made an independent agency charged with encouraging the creation of state planning boards to carry on the field work. It recruited experts from the nation's universities and research institutions who undertook special studies under an eight-man committee, a full time director, and a permanent staff. The Committee consisted of the Secretaries of Agriculture, Commerce, Labor, War, and Interior plus three non-CABINET officers (HARRY HOPKINS, Frederic A. Delano, and Charles E. Merriam). The Committee stimulated, financed, and supervised the work of the state planning boards and the regional, county, and local planning agencies which were established under its sponsorship. In 1939 the National Resources Committee was reorganized by being merged with the Federal Employment Stabilization Office into the NATIONAL RESOURCES PLANNING BOARD. The latter was transferred to the executive office of the President. These changes took place under Reorganization Plan I, effective on July 1, 1939.

National Resources Planning Board. An agency created by EXECUTIVE ORDER in September, 1939, and abolished in July, 1943. It succeeded the National Resources Committee in developing planned programs for the exploitation, development, and use of the nation's resources. Its functions included the investigation of national resources, the preparation of statistical and descriptive material relating to their development, and the submission of reports of recommendation to the President and Congress for legislation.

National Road. The popular name of the Cumberland Road. It was the first and longest interstate HIGHWAY constructed with federal funds. It was begun in 1811 as a macadam-surfaced road from Cumberland, Maryland to Wheeling, Virginia. For many years its extension beyond Virginia was held up because of the serious constitutional issue of federal appropriations for INTERNAL IMPROVEMENTS. In 1825 Congress continued to build the road west of Wheeling, extending it to Zanesville, Ohio. By 1833 the road had reached Columbus, and by Congress' last appropriation in 1838 the road reached its terminus at Vandalia, Illinois. The total amount of congressional appropriations was $6,821,246. As it was completed each section was relinquished to the state in which it lay. By 1850 the competition of CANALS, RAILROADS, and TELEGRAPH lines had reduced its importance. Today it is U.S. Route 40, a motor highway.

National Roster of Scientific and Professional Personnel. See Scientific Research and Development, Office of.

National Science Foundation. A federal agency established on May 10, 1950 for the purpose of coordinating scientific research. As described in its first annual report in May, 1951, the agency concerns itself with "basic research" rather than with "applied research." The Foundation supports scientific investigation in astronomy, physics, and chemistry. It attempts to maintain the leadership of the United States in SCIENCE by granting fellowships to train research scientists. Much of its work is devoted to research in military service. During the fiscal year 1964 allocations for basic and applied research in physical, social, and life sciences totaled about $353,200,000. Grants for research in the biological, medical, and agricultural sciences were included.

National Securities Resources Board. An agency established by the NATIONAL SECURITY ACT of 1947 for the purpose of developing and coordinating the strategic needs of the United States. It analyzes the nation's industrial potential and relates it to military needs. The agency conducts studies of the raw materials and MANUFACTURING facilities of the nation, and draws plans and reports to the President, keeping him abreast of these facilities and their limitations, if any.

National Security Act. Passed by Congress in 1947. It reorganized the armed forces of the United States by consolidating the Department of War and the Department of the Navy into the newly created National Military Establishment under a Secretary of Defense. The name was changed in 1949 to DEPARTMENT OF DEFENSE. The U.S. AIR FORCE was created as an autonomous entity within the new department to be administered by a Secretary of the Air Force. Also within the Department of Defense, and subordinate to the Secretary of Defense, are the Chief of Staff of the U.S. Army, the Chief of Naval Operations, and the Chief of Staff, U.S. Air Force. The Department administers the work of the Munitions Board, the Research and Development Board, and the Military Liaison Committee to the Atomic Energy Commission.

National Security Council. A five man body established by the NATIONAL SECURITY ACT of 1947. These members are the President, Vice-President, Chief of the National Security Resources Board, and Secretaries of State and Defense. This "supercabinet" administers the planning, developing, and coordinating of all functions concerned with the defense of the

United States as provided in the Act. It has the responsibility of evaluating the aims and commitments of the United States in light of existing or potential war. It advises the President on foreign policy decisions, determines security problems, conducts studies, and defines long term American purposes.

National Security Training Commission. See Universal Military Training.

National Union Party. The name used by the Republican party in the campaign of 1864. Also the name of President JOHNSON's supporters who conducted an independent convention in August, 1866 in Philadelphia for the purpose of uniting the Republican opponents of the RADICAL REPUBLICAN leadership of the party. The Johnson group advocated a moderate RECONSTRUCTION policy, equality of the states, and an integration of Northern and Southern policies. It called for the election of conservatives in Congress. The success of the Radical Republicans in that year, ended this dissident movement.

National Union for Social Justice. A conservative organization founded in 1935 in Detroit, Michigan by the Reverend Charles E. Coughlin. Although its dedeclared program was the protection of the people against exploitation by "powerful vested interests", it was attacked by liberal groups as anti-Semitic, anti-Negro, and anti-labor. It consistently opposed NEW DEAL policies. Coughlin carried on a powerful campaign by radio and NEWSPAPERS. His magazine, *Social Justice*, had a wide circulation. Ultimately the widespread public opposition to his policies resulted in his removal from the air and the barring of his MAGAZINE from the mails.

National War Labor Board, World War I. A tripartite agency established in April, 1918 for the purpose of mediating industrial disputes. The Board offered its services as a voluntary mediator and arbitrator in the effort to prevent STRIKES from interfering with the war program. It announced plans recognizing COLLECTIVE BARGAINING, maintaining full production, and calling upon labor and management to join in peaceful adjustment of disputes.

National War Labor Board, World War II. An agency established within the OFFICE FOR EMERGENCY MANAGEMENT by EXECUTIVE ORDER in January, 1942 for the purpose of resolving labor disputes in industries affecting the war effort. It was a tripartite board composed of 12 members, four each representing the general public, labor, and management. To it were assigned the staff, facilities, records, and funds of the NATIONAL DEFENSE MEDIATION BOARD which it replaced. Although originally created for the purpose of mediating and arbitrating labor disputes it was given the additional task, in October, 1942, of stabilizing wages as part of the overall effort at preserving economic stability. Lacking the legal power to enforce its decisions the Board depended upon its good offices in conciliation, mediation, and voluntary ARBITRATION. Failing this it resorted to the President's EXECUTIVE POWER over raw materials allocations and tax allowances, and his military power to assume the operation of affected industries. It carried on its work through panels of experts, an established staff, and individual arbitrators. In September, 1945 it was transferred to the DEPARTMENT OF LABOR, and abolished the following year.

National Youth Administration. An agency created by EXECUTIVE ORDER in 1935 to furnish part time work for students in high schools and colleges. The purpose of the law were to relieve UNEMPLOYMENT distress, raise wages by reducing the number of unemployed, assist families on PUBLIC WELFARE rolls, and maintain educational standards by furnishing financial assistance to needy students. The agency was absorbed into the FEDERAL WORKS AGENCY in 1943.

Nationalism. The sentiment of patriotism directed towards a national state. In the colonial period national feeling was weak, individual patriotism being absorbed with local and colonial affairs. Although a strong nationalist group emerged at the CONSTITUTIONAL CONVENTION under the leadership of HAMILTON, WILSON, WASHINGTON, and JAY, powerful STATES RIGHTS feelings dominated in the first decades of the nation's history. The War of 1812 was the strongest stimulant to nationalism up to that time. States rights sentiment, as manifested by the defunct FEDERALIST PARTY in the resolutions of the HARTFORD CONVENTION, was swallowed up by the resurgent nationalist feeling reflected in the "ERA OF GOOD FEELING." Between 1816 and the rise of the WHIGS in the late 1830's virtually all aspects of American growth expressed the nationalist trend. Manifestations of this included the first PROTECTIVE TARIFF of 1816, the renewal of the charter of the BANK OF THE UNITED STATES, INTERNAL IMPROVEMENTS, CLAY'S "AMERICAN SYSTEM," JOHN MARSHALL'S decision, and the development of a school of native literary figures dealing with purely domestic themes. Among these were JAMES FENIMORE COOPER, WASHINGTON IRVING, HENRY W. LONGFELLOW, and NATHANIEL HAWTHORNE.

Nationality Act. Passed by Congress in 1940. It revised and consolidated all existing NATURALIZATION and IMMIGRATION laws into a comprehensive system. The many provisions of the Act deal with naturalization procedure, individual and group naturalization, the naturalization of persons marrying American CITIZENS, and immigration matters. Among the latter is much detail providing for the exclusion from the United States of opponents of organized government, persons advocating overthrow of the government of the United States, and persons supporting violence and sabotage. The statute is administered by the Immigration and Naturalization Service within the DEPARTMENT OF JUSTICE.

"Native Americans". See Know-Nothing Party.

NATO. See North Atlantic Treaty.

Nat Turner's Rebellion. A rebellion of 60 slaves led by the Negro preacher Nat Turner in Southampton, Virginia in August, 1831. Fifty-five white people were killed on the PLANTATIONS he attacked. The outbreak followed the disclosures of slave plots in many southern states and served to crystallize southern public opinion behind the FUGITIVE SLAVE ACTS and in opposition to the ABOLITIONIST movement then becoming strong. Turner was captured, convicted, tried, and hanged on Nov. 11, 1831. Sometimes referred to as Nat Turner's Insurrection.

Natural Gas. See gas industry.

Natural Gas Act of 1938. See gas industry.

Naturalization. Refers to the process of granting CITIZENSHIP to alien residents of the United States or its TERRITORIES. This power is delegated to Congress in Article I, Section 8 of the federal Constitution. The naturalization process may be either individual or group. The latter is illustrated by the congressional acts of 1900, 1916, and 1927 conferring citizenship status upon the entire populations of HAWAII, PUERTO RICO, and the VIRGIN ISLANDS. Individual naturalization requires a minimum total of nine years residence in the U.S. The procedure requires the filing of a petition known as the declaration of intention after two years of residence. This is popularly

442

known as the "first papers" and is filed with a national court or state court of record. Between two and seven years thereafter the applicant files his second papers accompanied by affidavits of two CITIZENS testifying to his moral character and the truth of his statements. Normally no investigation is made unless there is reason to question the validity of the application. Upon the establishment of the truth of all statements and the payment of all fees, an oath is administered by the presiding judge, and final papers are granted. The naturalization of one or both parents automatically confers citizenship upon children under 18 years of age. The Nationality Act of 1940 codified all previous naturalization laws. The administering agency is the Immigration and Naturalization Service in the DEPARTMENT OF JUSTICE.

Natural Resources. The United States is self-sustaining in almost all food products and the raw materials essential to industrial production. With the exception of RUBBER, tin, manganese, tungsten, coffee, and a few minor minerals, this country produces everything necessary for its own consumption as well as a considerable surplus for export. Whether native to America or imported from Europe, the United States has always produced sufficient quantities of the basic food crops such as WHEAT, barley, rye, oats, vegetables, and fruit. TOBACCO, potato, corn, and COTTEN found American soil and climate well-suited for their production and at the beginning of its history the United States was already growing a richer variety of crops than Europe. The products of American forests, the almost inexhaustible supply of game animals, and the fish in American waters furnished a source of great wealth. As the nation moved westward in the 19th century the land yielded huge resources of OIL, IRON, copper, zinc, lead, COAL, antimony, ALUMINUM, and other minerals necessary to

an industrial culture. Between the World Wars the United States produced 70 percent of the world's oil, half of its copper, 38 percent of its lead, 42 percent of the zinc, 42 percent of the coal, 46 percent of the iron, 54 percent of the cotton, and 62 percent of the corn. It was utilizing 36 percent of the world's HYDRO-ELECTRIC POWER, although it comprised only 6 percent of the land area and POPULATION of the world.

Natural Rights. Those rights believed to be intrinsic to the individual before the creation of the state. They were developed in the political philosophy of John Milton, John Locke, and Jean Jacques Rousseau, and modified in America by JEFFERSON, SAMUEL ADAMS, and PAINE. In the early Revolutionary period these rights were conceived of as part of the heritage of British constitutionalism, although Paine considered natural rights as independent of political CONSTITUTIONS. As developed in America, natural rights included POPULAR SOVEREIGNTY, the right of revolution against tyranny, DEMOCRACY, liberty, the pursuit of happiness, and property rights. Varying emphases on the importance of natural rights have played significant roles in American history. HAMILTON, for example, emphasized property rights. Jefferson and Paine emphasized personal and CIVIL RIGHTS. In the 19th century CALHOUN repudiated the entire doctrine of natural rights as unsound.

Nautilus. On January 21, 1954, the Nautilus, the first atomic powered submarine, was launched at Groton, Connecticut.

Navajo Indians. They became one of the most important tribes in the United States because they were able to adapt themselves to American occupation with more ease than most. They lived in Arizona and New Mexico at the outbreak of the Mexican War. Two attempts to sign treaties of peace with the Navajos failed until troops, under the command of KIT CARSON, destroyed their resistance in an invasion of the Canyon de Chelly. They were held prisoners until 1867 when they were returned to their own TERRITORY and given new flocks and herds. They signed a peace TREATY, and have become the most prosperous of the remaining Indian tribes in this country. The Navajos number over 30,000 today, and are most famous for their beautiful blankets, rugs, and silver jewelry.

"Naval Holiday." See Five Power Treaty.

Naval Observatory, The U.S. A branch of the Bureau of Navigation within the Department of the Navy. Its antecedent agency was the Depot of Charts and Instruments, created in 1830. The functions of the Naval Observatory are the development, maintenance, and inspection of navigational and aeronautical instruments for the navy, the preparation of the correct time by radio signals, the maintenance of regular observation of astral bodies for position and time, and the publication of the *American Ephemeris and Nautical Almanac.*

Naval War with France. An undeclared war between 1798-1800. It arose out of the diplomatic conflicts stemming from the European wars of the French Revolution, manifested in Franco-American relations by the GENET AFFAIR and the XYZ AFFAIR. The immediate cause was the seizure of American merchant vessels and IMPRESSMENT of American seamen. In the spring of 1798 Congress authorized the MERCHANT MARINE to repel assaults by force, and commission PRIVATEERS to assist the navy in seizing French vessels marauding the eastern coast. The establishment of the Navy Department provided a coordinating body which rapidly took the offensive on the high seas. The fleet was increased in size

from three to 55 ships, which were organized into squadrons designed to defend American shipping areas in the East and WEST INDIES. The French, at war in Europe, dispatched no vessels to American waters, and small engagements with privateers constituted the major fighting in this war. Three battles were fought between ships of the line and the French, all American victories. Although the United States Navy did not attempt to capture French possessions in the western hemisphere the *Patapsco* dispersed French forces from the Dutch island of Curaco. All told several hundred merchant vessels and one naval vessel were seized by France as compared with the American capture of 85 French ships. The war ended with the negotiation of the Treaty of September 30, 1800.

Navigation Acts. Also known as Acts of Trade. A series of laws passed by Parliament in the 17th century under the stimulus of mercantile philosophy. The Act of 1651 provided that all goods imported into England from Asia, Africa, and America, be carried in English ships manned by English crews, and that all goods imported into England from Europe must be carried in similar ships or in those of the nations producing these goods. The Act of 1660 provided that goods transported to and from England must be shipped on vessels built in England or her colonies and owned and manned by Englishmen. It also provided that "enumerated articles" including tobacco, dyes, indigo, wool, ginger, SUGAR, and COTTON, could be exported to the colonies only from English ports. Unenumerated articles, chief of which were fish, grain, and rum, could be exported anywhere. By the Act of 1663 Parliament placed heavy duties upon all European goods entering the colonies unless they were trans-shipped through England in British or colonial-built and staffed vessels. The Act of 1696 required royal approval for the acts of colonial governors, and also authorized the establishment of customs houses and admiralty courts directed from England. The purposes of the Navigation Acts were the strengthening of the English MERCHANT MARINE, the maintenance in English business hands of the profits of the carrying trade, the monopolization of the handling of imports into the colonies, the removal of colonial competition against English MANUFACTURING and the prevention of England's colonies from furnishing products to her European rivals.

Navy, Department of the. Established by Congress in 1798. Before then naval affairs had been placed under the War Department. In 1947 the NATIONAL SECURITY ACT created the National Military Establishment whose name was changed to the DEPARTMENT OF DEFENSE in 1949. The Navy Department is now located within this department and the Secretary of the Navy is subordinate to the Secretary of Defense, no longer having cabinet rank. The Secretary of the Navy is the overall civilian chief of the department, and the Chief of Naval Operations, an office created in 1915, administers its military affairs. The United States Marine Corps is located in the Navy Department. The United States Coast Guard s incorporated into the Navy in time of war. The Navy maintains the hydrographic office and the NAVAL OBSERVATORY. It also supervises the governments of certain Pacific Island possessions.

Navy, U.S. The first navy consisted of five schooners and a sloop which WASHINGTON used in September and October, 1775 to attack British supply ships. In December, 1775 the Second CONTINENTAL CONGRESS appropriated funds for the construction of naval craft and the creation of a naval committee. In 1794 Congress enacted legislation providing for additional vessels and naval manpower. In 1798 the Department of the Navy was established as the administrative head of the navy. In 1952 the navy's vessels included 12 carriers, 15 light carriers, 3 battleships, 15 cruisers, 250 destroyers and destroyer-escorts, 88 submarines, and 684 amphibious craft, patrol ships, and auxiliaries. This number does not include the "mothball fleet" and other vessels which had been decommissioned at the completion of World War II. In that year the Navy's manpower numbered 750,000 officers and men.

Nebraska. The 15th state in size, with an area of 77,237 square miles. Organized as a TERRITORY in 1854 and admitted as the 37th state on March 1, 1867. Lincoln is the capital. In 1950 Nebraska's POPULATION of 1,325,510 made it 33rd in rank. Its largest cities are Omaha, Lincoln, and Grand Island. Nebraska's most important economic activity is the production of bread crops. Rye, corn, and WHEAT are especially valuable, but the state also produces large crops of oats, clover, hay, and sugar beets. Omaha is a great STOCKYARD and MEAT PACKING center, servicing the state's important CATTLE and hog industry. Manufactures include flour, freight cars, farm equipment, precision instruments, brick, and tile. Lincoln is the site of one of the world's largest creameries. In 1937 Nebraska established a UNICAMERAL LEGISLATURE, the only one in the nation. The state was explored in 1541 by Coronado. Its nickname is the "Cornhusker State."

Negroes. An ethnic group numbering 15,000,000 Americans and comprising 10 percent of the population of the United States. The bulk of these are descendants of the slaves imported into the United States from 1619. Although their CITIZENSHIP STATUS and guarantees of CIVIL LIBERTIES were established in the 14th Amendment, Negroes have experienced racial prejudice and discrimination since the Civil War. Their status is particularly difficult in the southern states and the many legislative attempts to rectify this condition by means of anti-poll tax, anti-lynching, and FAIR EMPLOYMENT PRACTICES laws have failed. Despite the continuance of these onerous conditions the Negro people have succeeded in producing outstanding leaders in the ARTS, letters, SCIENCE, statesmanship, and athletics. Among these figures have been BOOKER T. WASHINGTON, RALPH BUNCHE, MARIAN ANDERSON, Richard Wright, GEORGE WASHINGTON CARVER, FREDERICK DOUGLASS, Dorothy Maynor, Paul Robeson, Jackie Robinson, Roy Campenella, Jesse Owens, Roland Hayes, Joe Louis, Angelo Herndon, William E. DuBois, and Walter White. The opportunities for political, educational, and economic improvement have greatly increased in the last decade as a result of widespread democratic reforms through state and federal legislation. Many Negro organizations such as the National Urban League and the N.A.A.C.P. have collaborated with non-Negro organizations in the mutual effort to enhance the position of the Negro.

Negro Suffrage. See universal suffrage.

NELSON, Knute. 1843-1923. Lawyer and legislator. b. Norway. To United States as a child; lived in Wisconsin (1850-71) and Minnesota (from 1871); member, U.S. House of Representatives (1883-89); governor of Minnesota (1893-95); U.S. Senator (1895-1923); best known for influencing the establishment of the DEPT. OF COMMERCE AND LABOR.

NELSON, Thomas. 1738-1789. Statesman. b. Virginia. Graduated, Trinity College, Cambridge, England (1761); member, VIRGINIA HOUSE OF BURGESSES; member CONTINENTAL CONGRESS (1775-77); signer of the DECLARATION OF INDEPEND-

ENCE; commanded Virginia MILITIA during the Revolution; governor of Virginia (1781).

Neutrality. Under international law the status of governments which take no part in an existing war. Such governments refrain from granting direct aid to the belligerents. Neutral nations are enjoined to deal with the belligerents impartially in the furnishing of indirect aid. The PROCLAMATION OF NEUTRALITY by President WASHINGTON in 1793 was the first official declaration of American policy in a foreign war, although well-formed opinions of neutrality predate the American Revolution. Washington's Proclamation was followed by the Neutrality Act of June, 1794 which attempted to regulate private trade with the belligerents in the wars of the French Revolution. Subsequent difficulties arose out of the continuing wars in Europe, leading to the evolution of American policy in the forms of the JAY TREATY of 1794, the NAVAL WAR WITH FRANCE, 1798, the NON-INTERCOURSE ACT of 1806, the EMBARGO ACT of 1807, and the NON-IMPORTATION ACT of 1808. In the period following the defeat of Napoleon in Europe, the United States attempted to crystalize the principles of neutral rights by forbidding paper blockades, establishing the doctrine of free ships-free goods, prohibiting profiteering, and assuring the safety of non-contraband neutral goods on enemy ships. The problems of neutrality during the Civil War arose out of the Union BLOCKADE of and Britain's assistance to the South. American concepts of neutrality were not accepted at the two HAGUE CONFERENCES in 1899 and 1907 or in the Declaration of London in 1909. Violations of neutral rights were a prime cause of the entry of the United States into World War I. Between the two World Wars problems arose out of the Japanese invasions of MANCHURIA and China (1931, 1937) and in the Italo-Ethiopian War in 1934-35.

Neutrality Acts. A series of laws passed in 1935, 1936, 1937, and 1939 for the purpose of maintaining the NEUTRALITY of the United States in various European and Far Eastern Wars. The Act of 1935 authorized the President to embargo the sale of arms, munitions, and war materials to belligerents upon his finding that a state of war existed. The Act of 1936 added loans to the forbidden list. The Act of 1937 conferred discretionary power on the President to prohibit the export on American ships of non-military materials, and included the so-called "CASH-AND-CARRY" provisions, to expire on May 1, 1939. It also provided for government licensing and control of the munitions industry in war and peace, and prohibited the arming of American ships trading with belligerent nations. The Act of 1939 was passed after the outbreak of World War II, and codified and revised all previous neutrality legislation, whose effect was to prevent Great Britain and France from purchasing arms and munitions in the United States. The Act was thus a departure from strict neutrality, performing actually as a diplomatic instrument to aid these two nations and their allies. It provided that the President could put it into effect by proclamation and omit the embargo features of the earlier statutes, although it forbade American ships to carry arms, ammunition, or implements of war. It forbade the arming of American merchant ships and their trade with belligerent ports in Europe and North Africa. The President was empowered to proclaim combat zones and forbid American ships to enter them. Goods could be shipped to European belligerent ports only on foreign ships and upon payment in the United States. This is the famous "cash-and-carry" clause. Such goods could be carried on American ships to all other places.

Neutrality, Proclamation of. Issued by President WASHINGTON on April 22, 1793 during the wars of the French Revolution. In this document Washington declared the foreign policy of the United States to be one of NEUTRALITY in these wars. The document has generally been considered as the fountainhead of the traditional American foreign policy of ISOLATIONISM.

Nevada. The seventh state in size, with an area of 110,540 square miles. Organized as a TERRITORY in 1861 and admitted as the 36th state on October 31, 1864. Carson City is the capital. In 1950 Nevada's POPULATION of 160,083 made it the smallest in the Union. Its largest cities are Reno, Las Vegas, and Sparks. MINING is Nevada's principal industry. Minerals include large quantities of gold, silver, zinc, copper, lead, quicksilver, and tungsten. Nevada's density of population is only one and one-half person per square mile. The state is famous for its easy divorce laws, Reno having acquired an international reputation as the "divorce capital of the world." Gambling is legalized. The HOOVER DAM on the Colorado River near Las Vegas is the highest in the world. The farm crops include WHEAT, barley, and potatoes. Carson City is the smallest state capital in population in the United States. Nevada was the first government in the world to use gas for capital punishment. The state was discovered in 1775 by Francisco Garcés. Its nicknames are the "Sagebrush State" and "Silver State."

NEVIN, Ethelbert Woodbridge. 1862-1901. Composer. b. Pennsylvania. Excellent pianist; best known for songs included in *Sketch Book* (1888), *Water Scenes* (1891), etc. Best known compositions are *Narcissus* and *The Rosary*.

New Amsterdam. A Dutch colony reorganized in 1625 from the former colony of New Netherland. In 1626 PETER MINUIT was appointed the first director-general, purchasing the island of MANHATTAN from the Indians to legalize the existing occupation. Control of the colony was in the hands of a few wealthy proprietors known as PATROONS, each of whom was granted a domain extending for either 16 miles on one bank or eight miles on both banks of the Hudson River for each group of 50 or more settlers he brought to the colony. The powers conferred upon the patroons were absolute, comparable to those of a feudal lord. Although RELIGIOUS TOLERATION was granted, the Dutch Reform Church was the ESTABLISHED CHURCH in the colony. Colonial resentment resulted in 1653 in a petition, the "Remonstrance and Petition" complaining of the favoritism to the patroons, and assailing their unusual power, the uncertainty of laws made by the director and his council, and the inadequacy of the defense against the Indians. The colonial convention which drew up this petition was dispersed by PETER STUYVESANT, who had become director-general in 1647. For ten years, until 1664, the colony fought three major INDIAN WARS. In 1664 rivalry with English traders over COMMERCE, TARIFFS, trade disputes, and boundaries finally resulted in the British conquest by the Duke of York.

Newberry vs. United States. A decision of the United States Supreme Court in 1921 which established the rule that PRIMARIES are not an essential part of an election. In the primary of 1920 Truman H. Newberry spent over $100,000, allegedly violating the federal CORRUPT PRACTICES LAWS of 1910 and 1911. Newberry argued that he had neither spent the money himself nor been aware that it had been spent. As a result of the Court's decision he was admitted to his Senate seat, but the unpopularity of the decision redounded to the Republican party's disadvantage and Newberry was persuaded to resign. In 1925, 1939, and 1940 Congress passed FEDERAL CORRUPT PRACTICE ACTS to prevent such political incidents.

Newburgh Sedition. Also known as New-

burgh Addresses. A meeting of unpaid Revolutionary officers at Newburgh, New York in March, 1783 to petition Congress for a redress of their grievances. The address, formulated at this meeting urged direct action and implied coercion upon Congress. After WASHINGTON's intervention a second address appeared, more moderate in tone. At a subsequent meeting with Washington, the agitation of the officers was calmed, and a set of resolutions was adopted approving Washington's advice of moderation. In 1823 Major JOHN ARMSTRONG JR., of General GATES' staff, admitted his authorship of the two addresses in an article in the *United States Magazine.*

NEWCOMB, Simon. 1835-1909. Astronomer. b. Nova Scotia. To United States (1853); graduated, Lawrence Scientific School, Harvard University (1858); computer, Nautical Almanac Office (1857-77); superintendent, *American Ephemeris and Nautical Almanac* (1877-97); professor of mathematics, U.S. Navy (1861-97); professor of mathematics and astronomy, Johns Hopkins University (1884-94; 1898-1900); his tables of the planetary system adopted by observatories of the world; author of many books on astronomy and economics.

New Deal. The name applied to the program of President F. D. ROOSEVELT following his inauguration in 1933. This program was based on the slogan "Relief, Recovery, Reform." Confronted with the serious problems of the DEPRESSION, the New Deal sought and enacted legislation in the fields of PUBLIC WELFARE, work relief, AGRICULTURE, PUBLIC UTILITIES, finance, labor, INDUSTRY, securities regulation, TRANSPORTATION, and HOUSING. Basically, the New Deal program was supported by the labor, farm, and small business elements of the population but was opposed by a large segment of "BIG BUSINESS." Familiar characteristics of the New Deal were the "ALPHABET

448

AGENCIES" and the "BRAIN TRUST." The phrase was first publicly used by President Roosevelt on July 2, 1932 in his speech accepting the Presidential nomination. This address declared, "I pledge you . . . I pledge myself . . . to a new deal for the American people. This is more than a political campaign; it is a call to arms."

NEWELL, Frederick Haynes. 1862-1932. Civil Engineer. b. Pennsylvania. Graduated, M.I.T. (1885); chief engineer, U.S. Reclamation Service (1902-14); head, civil engineering department, University of Illinois (1915-20); made important contributions in IRRIGATION engineering and water supply systems.

New England Confederation. Formed in 1643 by the colonies of Massachusetts, Plymouth, Connecticut and New Haven, principally as a defense organization against the Indians and the Dutch. The Confederation was theoretically a league of four equal states, its governing council consisting of two members from each colony. It proved weak, however, because the opposition of Massachusetts kept the liberal Rhode Island colony out of the Confederation and on the issue of a war declaration in 1653 against the Dutch colony of NEW NETHERLAND the two Massachusetts councillors vetoed the unanimous vote of the other six. The official name was the United Colonies of New England. Some of its successes included the settlement of boundary controversies between its members and one with the Dutch. Provision was made for the return of runaway servants and contributions were taken up for Harvard College and for the conversion of the Indians. Although the Confederation was short-lived it succeeded in holding together long enough to direct military operations during King Philip's War in 1675-76. Politically its principal contribution in North America was the fact that it showed the possibility of federal union among the colonies. It was the first such union in American history.

New Freedom. The name applied to the reform program of the Democratic administrations of President Wilson from 1913 to 1921. Having achieved political success for the first time since 1892 the Democratic party inaugurated a progressive program of political, economic, and social legislation. Among these laws were the FEDERAL RESERVE ACT, the FEDERAL TRADE COMMISSION ACT, the LA FOLLETTE SEAMEN'S ACT, the CLAYTON ANTI-TRUST ACT, the UNDERWOOD-SIMMONS TARIFF ACT, the INCOME TAX amendment, the ADAMSON ACT, the FEDERAL FARM LOAN ACT, and the ESCH-CUMMINS ACT. Also referred to as "Wilsonian Democracy."

New Hampshire. The 44th state in size, with an area of 9,304 square miles. Entered the Union on June 21, 1788 as the ninth state. Concord is the capital. In 1950 New Hampshire's POPULATION of 533,242 made it 44th in rank. Its largest cities are Manchester, Nashua, and Concord. Important farm products include fruit, truck vegetables, corn, oats, hay, and potatoes. Its chief manufactured products are TEXTILES, leather goods, pulp, and PAPER products. New Hampshire is the only state at which a TREATY was signed concluding a foreign war (Treaty of Portsmouth in 1905). It was the first state to declare its independence of Great Britain, and to adopt a constitution. Mt. Washington has recorded the world's strongest wind velocities, the highest having been 231 miles per hour. New Hampshire has the largest state legislative body in the United States, numbering up to 400 members. Its 1,300 lakes and fine climate attract winter and summer sports enthusiasts. The state was discovered in 1603 by Martin Pring. Its nickname is the "Granite State."

New Harmony. One of the cooperative communities established in the Jacksonian era as a result of the spread of UTO-PIAN socialist philosophy. It was founded in Posey County, Indiana in 1825 by ROBERT OWEN, the English philanthropist and retired TEXTILE manufacturer. On February 5, 1826 the organization established a charter of "The New Harmony Community of Equality," attempting to work out the principles of socialism and reform advocated by the Utopians. The document provided for equal ownership of property, freedom of speech, and equal opportunity for labor. The government of the community was chaotic because of the lack of strong central authority. Several attempts at improvement failed, and on May 26, 1827 Owen conceded the failure of his experiment.

"New Immigration." See immigration.

New Jersey. The 46th state in size, with an area of 7,836 square miles. Entered the Union on December 18, 1787 as the third state. Trenton is the capital. In 1950 New Jersey's POPULATION of 4,-835-329 made it eighth in rank. Its largest cities are Newark, Jersey City, and Paterson. New Jersey is one of the most highly industrialized areas of the world in proportion to its size. Its northern section, the "American Ruhr," produces huge quantities of TEXTILES, dye goods, warships, chemicals, electrical machinery, elevators, and silk products. Farm crops include corn, peppers, asparagus, lima beans, eggplant, potatoes, and fruit. Dairying is important, the state's milch cows commanding the highest prices in the United States. Minerals abound, including zinc, iron ore, quartz, sand, and talc. The oldest HIGHWAY in the United States was built in 1650 in Warren County. The Sandy Hook lighthouse (1764) is the oldest in the nation. Its extended seaboard of 120 miles has 40 popular beach resort areas. New Jersey was discovered in 1524 by Varrazano. Its nickname is the "Garden State."

New Jersey Plan. See Paterson Plan.

Newlands Act. Passed by Congress in 1913. It established a Board of Mediation and Conciliation to persuade parties in railroad labor disputes to engage in ARBITRATION. By 1916 this agency had succeeded in adjusting over 60 labor controversies and in averting STRIKES on 42 eastern railroads.

Newlands Act of 1902. See Newlands Reclamation Act.

Newlands Reclamation Act. Passed by Congress in 1902. It provided for the earmarking of the revenue from the sale of arid lands in 16 specified western states, the proceeds of which were to be placed in a fund for IRRIGATION work. The irrigated lands were to be sold to settlers at moderate prices on a 10 year installment plan. The revenues from these sales were to constantly replenish the fund. Under the profitable operation of this law formerly worthless land, suitable only for CATTLE grazing, has already been increased in value from a few cents to several hundred dollars per acre. Outstanding areas which have been reclaimed include the Elephant Butte Dam, New Mexico, the Shoshone Dam, Wyoming, the Lake Truckee Reservoir, Nevada, and the Gunnison Tunnel, Colorado. The law is administered by the Reclamation Service of the Department of the Interior.

New Mexico. The fifth state in size, with an area of 121,666 square miles. Organized as a TERRITORY in 1850 and admitted as the 47th state on January 6, 1912. Santa Fe is the capital. In 1950 New Mexico's POPULATION of 681,187 made it 39th in rank. Its largest cities are Albuquerque, Santa Fe, and Roswell. New Mexico is the only bilingual state in the Union, English and Spanish being accepted as official languages. MINING and CATTLE raising are its two leading economic activities. Important farm crops are COTTON, WHEAT, corn, and beans. There are large sources of fir, pine, and spruce LUMBER. The largest Indian reservation in the United States (16,000,000 acres), inhabited by the NAVAJO tribe, is located in New Mexico. Other reservations are inhabited by the APACHES and UTES. Carlsbad Caverns, the world's largest, draw thousands of tourists annually. The highest golf course in the world, 9,000 feet above sea level, is near Alamogordo. The state's dry climate is famous for the care of tubercular and asthmatic patients. Santa Fe is the oldest seat of government in the United States, having been founded by the Spaniards in 1609. New Mexico was discovered in 1528 by Cabeza de Vaca. Its nicknames are the "Land of Enchantment" and "Sunshine State."

New Nationalism. The slogan applied to the political philosophy and program of THEODORE ROOSEVELT's administrations. Referring to the belief that the nation was the most efficient unit for promoting progress and DEMOCRACY Roosevelt's program emphasized the need for political, social, and economic reforms. During his tenure such reforms were put into effect in the areas of MONOPLY control, extended suffrage, labor and social improvement, HOUSING, EDUCATION, railroad regulation, food and drug control, and CONSERVATION. Among the important laws enacted were: PURE FOOD AND DRUGS ACT, MEAT INSPECTION ACT, ELKINS ACT, HEPBURN ACT, and NEWLANDS ACT.

New Netherland. A Dutch colony in the Hudson Valley extending roughly from the present sites of New York City to Albany. The first settlement of 1624 was made by a group of 30 families sent over by the DUTCH WEST INDIA COMPANY under the leadership of Willem Verhulst, who also established a fort on what is toady Governor's Island. The following year the settlement was transferred to MANHATTAN and renamed New Amsterdam. See New Amsterdam.

New Orleans, Battle of. The last battle and only major military victory of the United States in the War of 1812. It was unique in that it was fought in January, 1815, two weeks after the TREATY OF GHENT had been signed, concluding the war. The appearance of a British fleet of 50 vessels, bearing 7,500 troops, off New Orleans in October, 1814, activated measures for the defense of the city under Governor CLAIBORNE. On December 1, General ANDREW JACKSON reached New Orleans with 7,000 troops to prepare its defense. After a number of unimportant squirmishes in late December the decisive battle was fought on January 8, 1815. The American defense against the British attack at Chalmette Plantation resulted in a complete repulse involving British losses of 2,000 troops, 289 were killed, including General Packenham and other major officers. Jackson lost only 17 men of whom 13 were killed. Although the American victory had no effect upon either the war or the peace TREATY, it was a significant contribution to the development of Jackson's political career.

New Plymouth Colony. See Plymouth Colony.

New South. The phrase applied to the changing economic and political character of the South after the Civil War. Although a few factories had been built in the South before the War, industrialization had been slow because of the domination of the PLANTATION SYSTEM. Even until the 1880's the South remained basically agricultural, producing the staple crops of TOBACCO and COTTON. The lack of capital resulted in the destruction of the plantation system by the end of the century and the rise, in its stead, of small farms. Between 1865 and 1900 southern farms increased in number by 2,500,000, a large number of which were operated by TENANT FARMERS, SHARECROPPERS, and MIGRATORY FARM WORKERS. The break up of the plantation system and the ABOLITION OF SLAVERY had a strong influence on the political and cultural life of the South. The resulting deconcentration of power led to a wider distribution of political control, particularly at local governmental levels. Negro and poor white suffrage increased despite the attempts of Southern leaders to overcome the effects of the 14th and 15th AMENDMENTS by the use of "GRANDFATHER CLAUSES," LITERACY TESTS, "BLACK CODES," and terrorism. By the end of the 19th century the trend toward URBANIZATION and industrialization was marked. RAILROAD mileage increased from 8,000 to approximately 16,000 by 1900. This stimulated a broad factory construction program based on the manufacture of textiles, furniture, lumber products, STEEL, and tobacco products. Durham, North Carolina became the center of the nation's tobacco MANUFACTURING industry while the rest of the state developed rapidly as one of the most important textile centers in the United States. Whereas, in 1880, there were fewer than 500,-000 spindles in Georgia, North Carolina, and South Carolina as compared to more than 8,500,000 in New England, by the opening of World War I more than half of the nation's raw cotton was being manufactured in the South. A flourishing IRON and steel industry, based on the natural deposits of COAL, iron, and limestone, grew up in Alabama, Tennessee, and Virginia. Alabama, which had produced 347,000 tons of iron in 1880, was producing 2,710,000 tons by 1930. Birmingham became the "PITTSBURGH OF THE SOUTH." The development of HYDROELECTRIC POWER stimulated the settlement and development of new urban centers. In 1951 the South had more than 2,500 industrial plants valued each at $1,000,000 or more. A survey listed 552 multi-million dollar plants in the TEXTILE INDUSTRY, 498 in chemicals, PETROLEUM, and fertilizer, 335 in foods and beverages, 264 in LUMBER and furniture, 252 in metals, 212 in machinery, 1661 in clay, coal, and other MINERALS, and 140 in PULP and paper.

New Spain. The name applied to the Spanish colonies in America. Its capital was located in Mexico City.

Newspapers. The first newspaper published in colonial America was the Boston *News Letter* which appeared on April 24, 1704. This two page weekly was suspended in 1776. By the opening of the Revolution more than 100 similar newspapers had appeared in the colonies. By 1800 approximately 500 new papers were begun in the United States. This had increased to well over 1,000 by 1830. The Pittsburgh *Gazette* was established in 1786 as the first newspaper west of the Alleghanies. In 1793 the *Centinel of the North-Western Territory* was established in Cincinnati as the first paper in the Ohio Territory. The prominent figures in news publishing in the first generation after the Revolution included John Scull of Philadelphia, JOHN BRADFORD and William Maxwell of Kentucky, and John P. Sheldon who founded the Detroit *Gazette* in 1817. By 1820 there were 250 newspapers in the West. The typical paper consisted of four sheets about 12 by 18 inches in size. It generally contained local advertising, letters from abroad, foreign news, local news, and letters. Political partisanship engendered editorial comment in the 1820's as a conventional aspect of the newspapers of that period. The primary income from these papers came from sales and advertising. Most of this press consisted of weekly and semiweekly papers. One of the earliest dailies was the Pennsylvania *Evening Post* and *Daily Advertiser*, published by Benjamin Towne in Philadelphia in 1783. The first Sunday newspaper was the *Weekly Museum*, published in Baltimore in 1797. The greatest stimulus to American newspaper publishing was the advent of the PENNY PRESS in the 1830's. Inventions in PRINTING machinery, such as the steam powered press (1822), cylinder press (1824), rotary press (1846), and curved stereotyping (1861), spurred the INDUSTRY's growth. The introduction of wood pulp PAPER permitted the reduction of newspaper prices. Syndicated material appeared in the nation's press in the 1870's. Photo-engraving was first used in 1873 by the New York *Daily Graphic*. The Mergenthaler linotype was introduced by the New York *Tribune* in 1886 and soon replaced the cumbersome and expensive setting of type by hand. In the 20th century the "YELLOW PRESS" and the tabloid newspapers became famous for their sensationalism in news reporting. Newspapers became internationally famous for their columns, book review sections, special articles, MAGAZINES, comics, cultural reviews, sports sections, and business and finance departments. In this period TRADE UNIONS, educational institutions, and business organizations published their own press. In 1951 there were 10,694 newspapers in the United States of which 1772 were dailies. Distinguished names in the field of American journalism have included HORACE GREELEY, CHARLES HENRY DANA, ADOLPH S. OCHS, WILLIAM RANDOLPH HEARST, JOSEPH PULITZER, EDWARD E. SCRIPPS, and Roy S. Howard.

New Sweden. See Swedish settlements.

New Year's Day. Observed on January 1st. It is a legal HOLIDAY in all states, the territories, and the District of Columbia. New Year's Day has its origin in Roman times, when sacrifices were offered to the two-faced god Janus who looked back on the past and forward to the future.

New York. The 30th state in size, with an area of 49,576 square miles. Entered the Union on July 26, 1788 as the 11th state. Albany is the capital. In 1950 New York's POPULATION of 14,830,192 made it the largest in the nation. Its greatest cities are New York, Buffalo, and Roches-

ter. New York leads the nation in population, MANUFACTURING, foreign trade, commercial and financial transactions, book and MAGAZINE publishing, and theatrical production. It has more collegiate institutions (115) than any other state in the Union, and leads the world as a tourist attraction. Important manufactured goods include CLOTHING, airplane and automobile parts, chemicals, furs, shoes, machinery, drugs, paints, paper, TEXTILES, building construction products, typewriters, washing machines, flour, photographic and optical equipment, and ships. Important agricultural products are potatoes, onions, cabbage, ducks, and apples Dairying and wine making are notable economic activities. New York is a key state in national elections, its governors and Senators frequently being chosen as President. The state was discovered in 1609 by HENRY HUDSON. Its nickname is the "Empire State." See New York City.

New York Central Railroad. The largest railroad in the eastern United States. By an act of the New York State Legislature on April 2, 1853 the New York Central Railroad Company was established as a consolidation of the Mohawk and Hudson Railroad and other small roads linking Albany, Schenectady, Utica, Buffalo, and New York City. In 1867 Commodore CORNELIUS VANDERBILT became its president, merging into one large transportation entity the New York and Harlem Railroad, Hudson River Railroad, and the New York Central. In the 1870's Vanderbilt secured interest in the Lake Shore and Michigan Southern and the Michigan Central Lines, joining New York with the Midwest via Erie, Cleveland, and Toledo. In 1885 Vanderbilt assumed control over the West Shore Railroad, and subsequently penetrated Pennsylvania by acquiring control over the Pittsburgh and Lake Erie road. Having acquired control over the Boston and Albany line in 1900, a unified system was established in 1914 by the consolidation of all these lines. By that time The New York Central System controlled more than 22,500 miles of railroad from New York City to Chicago.

New York City. The largest city in the United States, with a POPULATION of almost 8,000,000. Its area is 229 square miles. It is the center of finance, COMMERCE, and culture. New York possesses the largest port area in the United States and conducts the greatest volume of foreign TRADE in the world. More than 5,000 ships clear the port annually, carrying almost half of the trade of the United States. "WALL STREET" is the nucleus of financial activity, being the home of the largest banks in the United States. Such notable cultural institutions as the METROPOLITAN MUSEUM OF ART, the METROPOLITAN OPERA HOUSE, the AMERICAN MUSEUM OF NATURAL HISTORY, Carnegie Hall, the HAYDEN PLANETARIUM, the NEW YORK ZOOLOGICAL SOCIETY, the New York and Brooklyn Botanical Gardens, and the NEW YORK PUBLIC LIBRARY are located in New York City. The EMPIRE STATE BUILDING, tallest in the world, New York University, largest institution of higher learning in the country, and the STATUE OF LIBERTY are well-known features of the city. New York City is the permanent home of the UNITED NATIONS. The highest point on the Atlantic coast, Todt Hill in Staten Island (409.8 feet), is within New York City. The city was first discovered by HENRY HUDSON in 1609, and settled in 1614 by the Dutch. In 1664 it passed into the hands of the British, its former name of NEW AMSTERDAM being changed to New York.

New York Philharmonic-Symphony Orchestra. Probably the most famous symphonic organization in the United States. It was founded by Ureli C. Hill in April, 1842 as the Philharmonic Society of New York. It is the oldest symphonic orchestra in the United States and the third oldest in the world. The orchestra's first concert was given on December 7, 1842. In the years that followed the organization absorbed other orchestras. World famous musicians who have been its conductors include LEOPOLD DAMROSCH, VICTOR HERBERT, Felix Weingartner, Richard Strauss, Gustav Mahler, and Willem Mengelberg. From 1926-36 its conductor was the world-renowned ARTURO TOSCANINI. In 1918 the orchestra began an annual series of summer concerts at Lewisohn Stadium. In 1952 the Philharmonic performed its 5,000th concert.

New York Public Library. Its present organization is a result of the consolidation in 1895 of the Astor and Lenox libraries and the Tilden Trust. These constitute the Reference Department which is supported from private funds. The Circulation Department is maintained by New York City and operates 83 branches throughout the city. Its collections make it one of the three largest libraries in the United States, along with the LIBRARY OF CONGRESS and the Harvard University Library. The Reference Department contains over 4,265,667 volumes read by more than 3,000,000 people annually. A typical annual circulation is over 13,000,000 books. From time to time the Library conducts special exhibits of work of famous printers and illustrators, as well as of lithographs, historic valentines, United States postage stamps, paintings, portraits, historical prints, and recordings.

New York Symphony Society. See New York Philharmonic Symphony Orchestra.

New York University. A non-sectarian, co-educational privately endowed institution of higher learning chartered in New York State in 1831. It occupies six centers of learning in New York City in which are located 14 undergraduate and graduate colleges and SCHOOLS in the fields of liberal arts and sciences, law, dentistry, MEDICINE, engineering, business administration, public service, retailing, EDUCATION, and ADULT EDUCATION. The

University conducts numerous extension and seminar courses as well as specific institutes catering to the needs of the lay and professional public. It is the largest university in the United States, having a student body in 1952 of approximately 64,000 and a teaching faculty of about 3,800. The HALL OF FAME is located on its campus at University Heights.

New York Zoological Society. Familiarly known as the Bronx Zoo. It is located in the borough of the Bronx in New York City, and has one of the largest collections of living specimens in the world. In the 1940's the zoo inaugurated a unique program of modernizing its exhibits by removing bars, walls, and cages, turning its animals loose in open pits. Surrounded by moats, the zoo's specimens of lions, tigers, elephants, gorillas, and other animals now live, during a large part of the year, in their simulated natural environment. Other features of the zoo include a children's zoo, children's animal rides, a children's farm, a tourist train, and restaurants that serve 2,500,000 visitors a year.

Niagara Falls. Located on the Niagara River between Lake Erie and Lake Ontario. The Falls are 164 feet to the River. Historically, its strategic importance was recognized as the area for the control of the upper GREAT LAKES and it became the site of Fort Niagara in colonial times. The Niagara Falls has always been recognized as a source of power and the Hydraulic Canal project in 1847 was the beginning of a development leading to the formation of the Niagara Falls Power Company in 1886. The great cataract, consisting of the American Falls and the Canadian Falls, has achieved international fame as one of the scenic splendors of the world.

Nicaragua. A Central American republic whose 1952 POPULATION of 1,500,000 occupies an area of 57,143 square miles.

Managua is the capital and principal city. Farming is the leading industry, although it utilizes only 10 percent of the land area. The principal crops are coffee, sugar cane, beans, rice, cocoa, tobacco, corn, bananas, and COTTEN. Gold, silver, and LUMBER are other important products and exports. Nicaragua was discovered by the Spaniards in 1522, and achieved its independence by revolution in 1838. In 1909 an American naval force intervened, following the execution of two American CITIZENS. United States Marines remained in the country from 1912 to 1925. Disorder accompanying and following the 1924 elections led to a second intervention of Marines in 1926, to protect American lives and property. Under their protection the United States supervised the Nicaraguan election of 1928. Sporadic fighting continued thereafter between a combination of government and rebel troops under Augusto Sandino and the Marines, leading again to American supervision of the 1932 elections. These forces were gradually withdrawn in 1932 and 1933. During this period order was restored, arrangements were concluded with American bankers for the stabilization of Nicaraguan finances, and the BRYAN-CHAMORRO TREATY of 1916 was negotiated.

NICOLLS, Richard. 1624-1672. Colonial administrator. b. England. When NEW NETHERLAND was taken from the Dutch by the English, Nicolls was appointed governor of New York (1664-68) by the Duke of York; issued legal code known as the *Duke's Laws*; capable and liberal governor.

NILES, Hezekiah. 1777-1839. Journalist. b. Pennsylvania. Editor, Baltimore *Evening Post* (1805-11); founded *Niles' Weekly Register* (1811-36); important influence during his time; strong opponent of JACKSON and an advocate of a PROTECTIVE TARIFF.

Nine-Power Pact. One of the treaties

produced by the WASHINGTON NAVAL CONFERENCE of 1921-22.

Ninteenth Amendment. See women's suffrage.

NIXON, Richard Milhous, 1913- Politician. b. California. Graduated, Whittier College (1934); law degree, Duke Univ. (1937); member U. S. House of Representatives (1947-1951); member, U. S. Senate (1951-1952); elected Vice-President (1952, 1956). Republican candidate for president in 1960; lost by narrow margin to John F. Kennedy. Elected President in 1968 defeating Hubert H. Humphrey in close race. Was first U.S. President to visit China and U.S.S.R. while in office. Re-elected in 1972 by large majority over George McGovern. Ended U.S. military involvement in Vietnam. Watergate investigation of attempts to burglarize Democratic Party headquarters resulted in his resignation on August 9, 1974 avoiding almost certain impeachment. He was succeeded by Gerald Ford who declared Nixon to be pardoned for all federal crimes that he "committed or may have committed" while president. Nixon withdrew to the privacy of his home at San Clemente, California.

Nobel Prizes. A series of awards, first granted in 1901, under the provisions of the will of Alfred B. Nobel, Swedish chemist and engineer who died in 1896. The interest income of the Nobel Fund is divided every year among the outstanding contributors in the fields of physics, chemistry, physiology, MEDICINE, LITERATURE, or in work of an idealist or peace character. The physics and chemistry prizes are awarded by the Swedish Academy of Science in Stockholm, the the physiology and medicine prizes by the Caroline Medical Institute in Stockholm, those in literature by the Academy, and the peace prizes by a committee of five chosen by the Norwegian legislature. Only two prizes were awarded to American CITIZENS during the first decade of the awards, and only four in the next 10 years. Since then many Americans have received Nobel prizes. The 1906 peace prize, awarded to President THEODORE ROOSEVELT for his efforts in negotiating the Treaty of Portsmouth of 1905, was the first made to an American. Other Americans who have received Nobel Prizes include ELIHU ROOT(peace, 1912), WOODROW WILSON(peace, 1919); CHARLES G. DAWES (peace, 1925), FRANK B. KELLOGG (peace, 1929), SINCLAIR LEWIS (literature, 1930), JANE ADDAMS and NICHOLAS MURRAY BUTLER(peace, 1931), EUGENE O'NEILL (literature, 1936), Pearl S. Buck(literature, 1938), CORDELL HULL (peace, 1945), Emily G. Balch and John R. Mott (peace, 1946), WILLIAM FAULKNER (literature, 1949), RALPH J. BUNCHE (peace, 1950), GEN. GEORGE C. MARSHALL (peace, 1953), and ERNEST HEMINGWAY (literature, 1954).

NOBLE, John Willock. 1831-1912. Statesman. b. Ohio. Practiced law in St. Louis, Missouri (from 1865); brevetted brigadier general during the Civil War (1865); U.S. district attorney (1867-70); appointed by HARRISON, U.S. Secretary of the Interior (1889-93); important for creation of forest reserves and the organization of the Oklahoma Territory.

NOGUCHI, Hideyo. 1876-1928. Bacteriologist. b. Japan. Came to the United States (1899); worked in the laboratory of pathology at the University of Pennsylvania; joined the staff of the Rockefeller Institute (1904); famous for his important studies in etiology of syphilis and paresis; isolated the syphilis spirochete (1910) and devised a new method, called the Noguchi test, for the diagnosis of syphilis; also investigated the etiology of yellow fever.

Nominating Convention. A method by which the major POLITICAL PARTIES nominate their candidates for the presidency and vice-presidency of the United States. The method was first introduced in 1831 by the ANTI-MASON PARTY as a replacement for the Congressional CAUCUS. Conventions meet quadriennially in June or July. Their delegates range in number from 1,100 to 1,800. These delegates are selected either by state PRIMARY elections, state committees of the parties, or state conventions. In both major parties candidates are nominated by simple majority vote, although prior to 1936 the Democratic party nominated its candidates by a two-thirds vote.

"Non-entangling Alliances." The paraphrase from WASHINGTON'S "FAREWELL ADDRESS" in which, for a second time, he laid down a foreign policy principle designed to establish the political self-sufficiency of the United States. Washington held that, in extending the nation's commercial relations, it had with Europe "as little political connection as possible." Europe, he declared, has a set of PRIMARY interests which bear a very remote relation to the United States. A great rule of conduct in the foreign relations of this country would be to avoid implicating itself by artifical ties in "the ordinary vicissitudes" of European politics or the combinations or collisions of Europe's friendships or enmities. He strongly argued that the United States should avoid "interweaving" its destiny with that of any part of Europe or entangle its "peace and prosperity in the toils of European ambition, rivalship, interest, humor, or caprice." It is generally acknowledged that this doctrine is the foundation of the historic ISOLATIONIST policy of the United States that endured until World War II.

Non-Intercourse Act. Passed by Congress in 1809 to replace the repealed EMBARGO ACT. It prohibited TRADE with Great Britian and France until such time as either or both of these nations agreed to relinquish the measures, such as IMPRESSMENT, seizures, and trade restrictions, which had brought this and the Acts of 1806 and 1807 into existence. The trade with other nations which had

been embargoed by the Act of 1807 was reopened. In 1810 Napoleon, shrewdly recognizing the political force of the move, rescinded the BERLIN AND MILAN DECREES insofar as they applied to American trade. The result was as he expected, the continuing embargo on the trade with the British being one of the causes of the War of 1812.

Non-Importation Act. Passed by Congress in 1806 at the request of President JEFFERSON in his attempt to bring about the cessation of English seizures of American ships during the NAPOLEONIC WARS. The Act provided that certain goods could not be imported from Great Britain after November, 1806. The President supplemented the act by sending a diplomatic mission to England for negotiations on IMPRESSMENTS and seizures. The failure of this mission and of the Act to achieve their objective resulted in the passage of the EMBARGO ACT in the following year.

Nonpartisan League, the National. A FARMERS' movements in the Northwest from 1915-1924. In its origins it reflected the resentment of the spring WHEAT farmers against the abuses of the grain trade in North Dakota and Minnesota. Charges were made that the Minneapolis Chamber of Commerce exercised MONOPOLY control over the wheat trade. Led by the SOCIALIST PARTY organizer A. C. Townley of North Dakota, the Equity Cooperative Exchange, Socialist leaders, and farmers created the Nonpartisan League. Its programs included the demand for hail insurance, state rural credits, TAXATION reform, and state owned elevators, mills, and packing houses. Its political success in capturing North Dakota led to the adoption of its program by the legislature in 1919. Its influence spread into other midwestern and far western states with programs modified to meet local conditions, although the demand for state ownership of marketing facilities was prominent in all. For a time the movement was broadened to include labor elements. Its strength waned after 1920 as a result of the DEPRESSION of the post-war period. By 1924 the organization had disappeared, its elements surviving in the Farmer-Labor Party in North Dakota.

Normandy, Invasion of. The last successful major offensive campaign of the UNITED NATIONS in the European theatre of operations in World War II. Planned by the S.H.A.E.F. as a result of the agreements reached at the TEHERAN CONFERENCE in 1943, the United States and England opened "the western front" that the Soviet Union had been demanding for two years. On June 6, 1944, 10,000 planes safeguarded 4,000 ships across the English Channel under cover of an intense bombardment by 800 guns on 80 warships. Within 24 hours 250,000 troops had been landed on the Cherbourg Peninsula. The initial landings occurred between St. Marcouf and the Orne River on the Normandy coast, the invading troops occupying a strip 60 miles long. Artificial harbors were constructed by sinking concrete piers and pontoons to serve as docks. Within 100 days after D-Day the Allied forces had landed 2,200,000 troops, 450,000 vehicles, and 4,000,000 tons of equipment. Cherbourg was captured in late June. In July the invading troops stormed through the German lines at St. Lo into Brittany to begin the LIBERATION OF FRANCE.

NORRIS, George William. 1861-1944. Statesman. b. Ohio. Admitted to Indiana bar (1883); practiced in Nebraska (from 1885); member, U.S. House of Representatives (1903-13); U.S. Senator from Nebraska (1913-43); opposed entry into World War I; led the fight for T.V.A.; known as "father of the TWENTIETH AMENDMENT" also called the "Lame Duck Act" (1933).

Norris-La Guardia Anti-Injunction Act. An act of Congress in 1932 which declared the "YELLOW DOG CONTRACT" unenforceable in FEDERAL COURTS. It also forbade these courts to issue INJUNCTIONS against labor for striking, urging others to join a STRIKE, employing union funds to aid a strike, advertising a strike, or speaking, picketing, and meeting in furthering a strike. An employer may obtain injunctions by showing that he has made reasonable efforts to settle an existing strike, or that unlawful acts have been threatened or committed against him, or that the strike will cause him substantial and irreparable injury, if not enjoined. He must post a bond to compensate the strikers for damages if the preliminary injunction is wrongfully issued. In the event of contempt action against the strikers they are given the right to a trial by jury before a judge other than the one who issued the injunction. Labor is required to refrain from violence and fraud in publicising the facts of a dispute. This law was supplemented in the states in following years by "Little Norris-La Guardia Acts" dealing with labor disputes in intrastate commerce.

North African Invasion. The first United States offensive in the European theatre of operations in World War II. Commanded by General EISENHOWER, a combined army of 150,000 American and 140,000 British troops landed on the French North African coast on November 7-8, 1942. After a brief French resistance at Oran, Algiers, and Casablanca, the French under Admiral Darlan capitulated. The landing was made from a huge fleet of 500 transports guarded by 350 American and British warships. The landing points were Algiers, Casablanca, Fedhala, Oran, and Port Lyautey. The greatest casualties occurred at Casablanca and Oran. At Darlan's urging, French West Africa went over to the

458

Allies. The Anglo-American army, assisted by Fighting French troops, continued the fight eastward toward Tunisia. Meanwhile, the British Eighth Army, under General Sir Bernard L. Montgomery, was pursuing the Italian and German forces westward from El Alamein. The victory occurred on May 12, 1943 when General Von Arnim surrendered his 250,000 troops. Axis casualties totalled 340,000 including 267,000 prisoners. The Germans and Italians lost 41 warships, 1696 planes, and 500,000 tons of shipping. The Allied Powers lost 657 planes.

North Atlantic Treaty. A mutual assistance pact negotiated in 1949 by Belgium, Canada, Denmark, France, Great Britain, Iceland, Italy, Luxembourg, the Netherlands, Norway, Portugal and the United States. The TREATY provided that a military attack against any of the signatories would be considered an attack against all of them, requiring assistance to attacked nation or nations by the others. A mutual defense organization, The North Atlantic Treaty Organization, was subsequently created to implement the provisions of the pact. The treaty was a basic element in the "stop communism" foreign policy of the United States inaugurated by the TRUMAN DOCTRINE in 1947.

North Carolina. The 28th state in size, with an area of 52,712 square miles. Entered the Union on November 21, 1789 as the 12th state. Seceded on May 20, 1861. Readmitted on July 20, 1868. Raleigh is the capital. In 1950 North Carolina's POPULATION of 4,061,929 made it 10th in rank. Its largest cities are Charlotte, Winston-Salem, and Greensboro. North Carolina is the largest producer of manufactured TEXTILES and tobacco in the United States. It leads the southeastern states in population and in industrial and agricultural production. Leading manufactures include PAPER, LUMBER products, furniture, and tobacco. Farm crops are corn, COTTON, hay, peanuts, tobacco, and truck vegetables. North Carolina leads the South in social reforms. It operates the largest school bus system in the world. Its important recreational areas include 79 state and NATIONAL PARKS. Mt. Mitchell on the Blue Ridge Parkway near Asheville is the highest mountain in eastern United States. The largest military reservation (Fort Bragg) and the largest marine amphibious training base in the United States (Camp Le Jeune) are situated in North Carolina. Roanoke was the site of the first English colony in America. The state was discovered by Vasquez de Allyon in 1520. Its nicknames are the "Tar Heel State" and "Old North State."

North Carolina, University of. Chartered in 1789 as a coeducational institution of higher learning with the aid of state SUBSIDIES. It became the first state university in the United States in 1795. It is located at Chapel Hill and consists of undergraduate and graduate schools in liberal arts and sciences, COMMERCE, MEDICINE, law, EDUCATION, engineering, AGRICULTURE, public health, and social work. The buildings of the university house a planetarium, an ART collection, and university press. The university also operates the Woman's College at Greensboro and the State College of Agriculture and Engineering at Raleigh.

North Dakota. The 17th state in size, with an area of 70,655 square miles. Organized as a TERRITORY in 1861 and admitted as the 39th state on November 2, 1889. Bismark is the capital. In 1950 North Dakota's POPULATION of 619,636 made it 41st in rank. Its largest cities are Fargo, Grand Forks, and Minot. AGRICULTURE is North Dakota's leading economic activity, 87 per cent of its acreage being devoted to the production of barley, oats, rye, and WHEAT. Its most important mineral is lignite, the state containing two-thirds of the nation's supply. Dairying is important. North Dakota has the only state-owned bank, flour mill, and grain elevator in the United States. Pierce County is the geographic center of North America. North Dakota was discovered in 1738 by Verendrye, a French fur trader. Its nickname is the "Flickertail State."

Northern States Cooperative League. See cooperative movement.

Northwestern Farmers' Alliance. See Farmers' Alliances.

Northwest Ordinance. Also known as the Ordinance of 1787. Enacted by the Congress of the ARTICLES OF CONFEDERATION in 1787. The law set the precedent for admitting new states into the Union which has since been followed by the government of the United States. Specifically, it provided that a minimum of three and a maximum of five states should be created out of the NORTHWEST TERRITORY, to be admitted to the union upon petition of these territories after having attained a POPULATION of 60,000. It further provided for the ABOLITION of SLAVERY in these territories and guarantees of CIVIL LIBERTIES, and set aside land areas for public EDUCATION. The law was the work of THOMAS JEFFERSON.

Northwest Territory. The land area between the Mississippi River, the GREAT LAKES, and the Ohio River ceded to the United States after the American Revolution by various states claiming the territory under colonial charters. The territory was organized under three statutes of the government of the ARTICLES OF CONFEDERATION, the ORDINANCES OF 1784, 1785, and 1787. Ultimately five states, Ohio, Illinois, Indiana, Michigan, and Wisconsin were created out of this TERRITORY and ADMITTED TO THE UNION.

NOTT, Eliphalet. 1773-1866. Educator, clergyman and inventor. b. Connecticut.

Clergyman in Albany, N.Y.; aided in reform of public school system; president, Union College (1804-66); invented the first anthracite coal base-burning stove.

Nuclear Test Ban Treaty. The United States, the United Kingdom, and USSR signed the agreement in Moscow on August 5, 1963. Over 100 other nations have signed the treaty. To date, France and Communist China have refrained from signing. The treaty provides that each of the parties "undertakes to prohibit, to prevent, and not to carry out any nuclear weapon test explosion, or any other nuclear explosion at any place under its jurisdiction and control . . ."

Nullification Theory. The political doctrine upholding the right of a state to suspend or otherwise refuse to enforce an act of Congress when the state deems such an act narmful to its interests. The theory underwent many modifications from its first enunciation in the VIRGINIA AND KENTUCKY RESOLUTIONS to the resolutions of SECESSION in 1860-1861. Based upon the doctrine that the Union was a compact of sovereign states and the Constitution a document written by them for the guidance of the central government, the theory maintained that the states alone were the proper judge of the validity of congressional acts. In its evolution the nullification theory was altered by the many political crises which arose in the first half of the 19th century. The issues of CIVIL RIGHTS, support of the War of 1812, the TARIFF, and SLAVERY served to modify it. Among the important documents and events expressing the nullification theory were the EXPOSITION AND PROTEST, ORDINANCE OF NULLIFICATION, WEBSTER-HAYNE DEBATES, and ORDINANCES OF SECESSION.

Nuremberg Trials. See War Crimes.

Nye Investigating Committee. See munitions investigation.

O

Oberlin College. Established in 1834 as the first coeducational institution of higher learning in the United States. Its founding was part of the educational and humanitarian revolt of the Jacksonian period and reflected the strong women's rights movement of that time. For a period after its establishment it was the seat of strong anti-slave sentiment.

Occupation of Germany. First announced in the Declaration of the YALTA CONFERENCE, the United States, Great Britain, and the Soviet Union agreed that a central Allied Control Council, consisting of the supreme commanders of the three powers with headquarters in Berlin, be established to govern a defeated Germany. The three powers were each to occupy a separate zone of Germany, their work to be coordinated by the Control Council. France was to be invited to take over a zone of occupation and to participate as a fourth member of the Control Council. In 1945 Germany was divided into four national occupation zones, each headed by a military governor, assisted by supervisory and operating staffs. To the United States was given the TERRITORY bounded on the east by the Russian zone and Czechoslovakia, on the north by the British zone, on the west by the French zone, and on the south by Austria. The area of Greater Berlin was established, to be adminis-

tered by the Inter-Allied governing bodies, with representatives of the four powers. This area is located within but is not part of the Soviet zone. Problems of government have consistently troubled the Control Council's work, culminating in 1948 in the virtual partition of Germany into two zones under rival political and economic control. After repeated vetoes the Soviet delegation left the Control Council on March 20, 1948, and on May 31 the United States, Britain, France, and the Benelux nations agreed to establish a German state comprising the three Western zones. Simultaneously the western powers introduced a new German CURRENCY. The immediate Soviet response was the declaration of a BLOCKADE on all ground COMMUNICATIONS between the Western zones and Berlin. After a year of the blockade and allied AIR-LIFT an agreement was reached by which the Soviet government agreed to remove the blockade. On September 21, 1949 the German Federal Republic came into existence when the Control Council turned over to it the administration of the United States, British, and French zones of occupation. The United States and other Western nations ended the state of war in 1951, but the U.S.S.R. did not do so until early 1955 after the allied powers had forwarded plans to grant complete sovereignty to West Germany, which was done in May, 1955. (See Bonn Republic.)

461

Occupation Statute. The document drafted by the Allied High Commission in Germany on April 8, 1949 defining the terms for the MERGER of the United States, British, and French zones of occupation in Germany. Following the creation of the Bonn Republic in May the powers of the Commission were set down in the Occupation Statute which took effect on September 21, 1949. It was amended on March 6, 1951 by agreement among the three Western Powers, and provided for the creation of a German FOREIGN AFFAIRS ministry and the progressive relaxation of allied control of Germany. See Allied High Commission, Bonn Republic, and Occupation of Germany.

OCHS, Adolph Simon. 1858-1935. Newspaper publisher. b. Ohio. Owner and publisher, Chattanooga, Tennessee. *Times* (1878-1935); publisher, New York *Times* (1896-1935); owner of Philadelphia *Times* (1902-12) and Philadelphia *Public Ledger* (1902-12); important independent political influence.

O'CONOR, Charles. 1804-1884. Lawyer, b. New York City. Admitted to the bar and practiced in N.Y. City (from 1824); U.S. district attorney (1853-54); prosecuted the TWEED RING, causing its defeat (1871-75); unsuccessful candidate for public office; counsel for TILDEN in disputed election (1876); considered one of the ablest and best-known lawyers in the United States.

Office of Alien Property. See Alien Property Custodian.

Ogdensburg Agreement. A United States-Canadian TREATY negotiated in 1940. By its terms the two nations agreed to establish a permanent joint defense board to deal with mutual problems of defense.

OGLESBY, Richard James. 1824-1899. Union general and legislator. b. Kentucky. Practiced law in Illinois (from 1845); served in Mexican War and as major general (1863) in Union Army during the Civil War; governor of Illinois (1865-69; 1873); U.S. Senator (1873-79); elected governor for the third time (1885-89).

OGLETHORPE, James Edward, 1696-1785. English philanthropist and founder of the colony of Georgia. b. London. Received charter for colony of Georgia (1732); landed with group of emigrants (1733); founded the city of Savannah; successful governor; friendly with CREEK Indians; fought off Spaniards in attack on Georgia (1742); forced to return charter for Georgia to British government (1752).

Ohio. The 35th state in size, with an area of 41,222 square miles. Entered Union on February 19, 1803 as the 17th state. Columbus is the capital. In 1950 Ohio's POPULATION of 7,946,627 made it fifth in rank. Its largest cities are Cleveland, Cincinnati, and Columbus. Ohio is one of the nation's most important industrial states, capitalizing on its huge resources of COAL and OIL and its proximity to the IRON ore and TRANSPORTATION facilities of the GREAT LAKES. Its manufactures include nails, bolts, wire, nuts, machinery, PAPER, electronic equipment, refrigerators, and motors. Toledo is the nation's largest shipper of coal. Akron, the "RUBBER capital of the world," makes most of the AUTOMOBILE tires used in the United States. The state's other important industries are MINING and AGRICULTURE. Coal, oil, sand, clay, and gravel are the leading minerals. Crops include WHEAT, grapes, TOBACCO, soy beans, and corn. DAIRYING is an important economic pursuit. Ohio, the "Mother of Presidents", has sent eight men to the WHITE HOUSE. The state was explored in 1749 by a French officer, Céleron. Its nickname is the "Buckeye State."

Ohio Compact. An agreement by the federal government in 1806 to set aside five percent of the income from the sale of PUBLIC LANDS in Ohio as a special fund for the construction of TURNPIKES in that state. This decision was the result of JEFFERSON's desire to bring federal aid to the states west of the Alleghanies and of Secretary of the Treasury GALLATIN's concurrence. Its purposes were to open Ohio to settlement and to connect the Ohio River with those which flowed into the Atlantic. In 1806 Congress appropriated $30,000 for the construction of the famous NATIONAL ROAD to run from Cumberland, Maryland to Wheeling, West Virginia.

Ohio Company. A group of Virginians to whom was given a 500,000 acre tract of land west of the Appalachians and south of the Ohio River. The grant was made by George II in 1749. Thomas Lee was the original organizer of the company which was later led by Lawrence Washington. The terms of the grant required that 100 families be established upon it, a fort erected, and a garrison maintained. The company built many storehouses and sent out exploring expeditions between 1749 and 1754. The onset of the French and Indian War two years later caused the withdrawal of the settlers. After the war its plans for further land development were balked by the PROCLAMATION OF 1763. The Company's life came to an end in 1770 but it was important as a sign of Britain's program of colonial expansion into the Ohio Valley. Also a land company formed in 1786 by Rufus Putnam in Massachusetts for the purchase of federal land between the Ohio River and Lake Erie. Congress granted certain lots gratis, and sold a huge tract at nine cents per acre. COLONIZATION began immediately. SLAVERY was prohibited. The Company exerted great influence in attracting settlers and in shaping the NORTHWEST ORDINANCE of 1787.

"Ohio Gang." The name applied to the group of intimate friends who followed President HARDING to Washington after his inauguration in 1921. They included those politicians who, during and after Harding's death in 1923, were discovered to have been involved in the corruption and scandals of that time. The group included Veterans Bureau director Charles R. Forbes, Secretary of the Navy Denby, Secretary of the Interior FALL, and ATTORNEY GENERAL Daugherty.

"Ohio Idea." A proposal made in 1867 by the Cincinnati *Enquirer* to redeem the Civil War bonds in GREENBACKS instead of gold. Sponsored as an inflationary measure by western delegates to both major party conventions in 1868, the Ohio idea attempted to subordinate the questions of RECONSTRUCTION to financial issues. Although it was incorporated into the Democratic platform that year, the nomination of former governor Horatio Seymour of New York. for the presidency, ensured its ultimate rejection by that party. The Republican party endorsed it in the Midwest but did not adopt an inflationary platform.

Ohio River. It rises at the junction of the Alleghany and Monongahela Rivers in Pittsburgh, Pennsylvania, and flows 981 miles into the Mississippi River. The Ohio-Alleghany system is 1306 miles long. From time to time the River overflows its banks and causes disastrous floods. In 1913 such a flood took 730 lives. The historical records indicate that it was first discovered by the French explorer LA SALLE in the mid-17th century. The territory of the Ohio basin remained the possession of France until the Seven Years' War when it was transferred to England only to be lost to the United States after the American Revolution.

Oil Industry. Although the existence of petroleum in America has been known for over three centuries, the commercial exploitation of oil fields dates back to the 1870's. Petroleum is first mentioned in a letter in 1627 by a missionary. Although produced in small quantities as an incident to salt drilling, the mineral was considered worthless, being used generally by the Indians and early settlers for lighting and medical purposes. The first recorded refining of oil was done by Samuel M. Kier in 1849, the product being used as a lighting fuel. In 1854 the Pennsylvania Rock Oil Company was organized for the specific objective of MINING oil, after the results were made public of a chemical and geological analysis by Benjamin Silliman, Jr. in 1854-1855. The date from which profitable commercial exploitation of oil may be measured is August 28, 1859 when E. L. DRAKE sank a well 69½ feet deep which produced 25 barrels per day. Although ridiculed as "DRAKE'S FOLLY" because of its apparent worthlessness, petroleum production increased rapidly from then on. Oil boom towns sprang up throughout Pennsylvania, many of them disappearing as the INDUSTRY moved westward. The principal modes of transporting oil in this period were barges and teams. The first pipe line was built in 1865 from Pithole, Pennsylvania to the nearest railroad, five miles away. The Allegheny Transportation Company was the first pipe line company in the United States. In the 1870's petroleum was discovered and produced in California, Kentucky, New York, Ohio, Tennessee, and West Virginia. Wyoming became a leader in 1894, and by the end of the century huge deposits had been discovered in Kansas, Illinois, Louisiana, Oklahoma, and Texas. After World War I Michigan and New Mexico became important oil producing centers. The growth of the industry in the United States has been enormous. By 1900 this nation was producing more petroleum than the rest of the world combined. In 1951 the industry's output was 2,188,428,000 barrels of petroleum valued at $5,454,647,-000. This was over 55 percent of the world's production. The largest oil producing state is Texas with a 1950 output of 829,231,000 barrels of crude petroleum. The uses of petroleum are virtually inexhaustible, almost 400 products and thousands of finished commodities being manufactured from it. Among these are gasoline, lubricating oil, kerosene, and benzine. The outstanding producers are the STANDARD OIL COMPANY, organized in 1870, American Oil Company, Texas Oil Company, Sinclair Oil Company, Sun Oil Company, and Gulf Oil Company. In July, 1952 it was announced that the industry had spent nearly $20,000,000,-000 since the close of World War II to expand and develop its facilities to meet the increasing demand for petroleum products. The increase in demand was estimated at nearly 50 percent more than at the end of the war. In 1956 alone, oil companies were scheduled to invest $5,300,000,000 in new operations.

Ojibway or Chippewa Indians. A tribe of Indians belonging to the ALGONQUIN group that lived around Sault Ste. Marie in Michigan and on the shores of Lakes Superior and Huron. They were an important tribe and were able to hold their own against the IROQUOIS and the SIOUX. They had originally come from the west coast to join the OTTAWA and Potawatami tribes. The Ojibways lived mostly on fish, wild RICE, maple SUGAR, maize, squash, and corn. They lived in birchbark wigwams and used birch-bark canoes. They sided with the French in the French and Indian Wars. Part of the tribe joined PONTIAC in the rebellion of 1763. Subsequently they were won over by the British and fought with them in the War of 1812. They made a TREATY of peace in 1816 and relinquished all their lands in Ohio, and by 1851, after ceding all their TERRITORY bit by bit, they were moved west of the Mississippi into INDIAN TERRITORY.

"Okies." Migratory agricultural laborers set adrift in the 1930's by the introduc-

464

tion of tractors, foreclosures of mortgages, insect pest destruction of crops, and the exhaustion of the land by erosion. Emanating from large sections of Oklahoma, Texas, and Kansas they wandered over the Far West, following the crops. By 1937 it is estimated that more than 150,000 families found their way to the west coast. Most of these sought work in the fruit orchards and lettuce fields of California and the LUMBER camps of Washington and Oregon. The deplorable conditions of their feeding and temporary habitation in roadside camps aroused strong feeling throughout the nation. State laws frequently prohibited their entry and they were often physically attacked. They were treated with great brutality, paid starvation wages, and deprived of their CIVIL RIGHTS. Their desperate plight was poignantly described by JOHN STEINBECK in his novel *The Grapes of Wrath.* The word derives from the great number of these workers who came from Oklahoma.

Okinawa, Battle of. One of the famous battles in the "stepping stone" process leading to the end of the Pacific campaign in World War II. Okinawa was the principal Japanese base in the Ryukyu Islands. The invasion on April 1, 1945 required 1,300 ships including aircraft carriers. Total American troops engaged up to June 30th, after 83 days of battle, included 176,491 soldiers, 88,500 marines, and 18,000 seamen. American casualties were 49,151 of which 12,250 were dead or missing. The United States lost 763 airplanes and 36 ships. Japanese losses were estimated at 110,071 with 7,400 taken prisoner. The Japanese lost 783 aircraft of which 102 were destroyed on the ground. They lost 16 naval vessels including the 45,000 ton *Yamato.*

Okinawa return to Japan. In June 1971 in a treaty signed between the United States and Japan the island of Okinawa was re-turned to Japan but provision was given to the United States to retain a naval base there. The island had been a major staging area for air strikes against Korea and North Viet Nam.

Oklahoma. The 18th state in size, with an area of 69,919 square miles. Organized as a TERRITORY in 1890 and admitted as the 46th state on November 16, 1907. Oklahoma City is the capital. In 1950 Oklahoma's POPULATION of 2,233,351 made it 25th in rank. Its largest cities are Oklahoma City, Tulsa, and Muskogee. Oklahoma's leading product is PETROLEUM. Tulsa, as a result, is one of the world's wealthiest cities per capita. Its other industries are zinc smelting, oil refining, flour milling, and MEAT PACKING. Farm crops include corn, COTTON, oats, potatoes, sorghums, and WHEAT. The state has the largest Indian population in the nation. Many of these have become wealthy because of the discovery of oil on their land. With Mississippi, Oklahoma is one of the remaining two states with PROHIBITION. The state was discovered by Coronado in 1541. Its nickname is the "Sooner State."

Old Age Pension Laws. State and federal legislation providing lump sum payments and annuities to superannuated workers, generally at age 65. The rapid industrialization of the United States and improved medical practice have combined to increase longevity at a time when UNEMPLOYMENT became a chronic aspect of American economic life. In 1870 only three percent of the POPULATION was over 65 years of age. In 1952 this had increased to seven percent, and it is estimated that by 1975 persons over 65 years of age will comprise 13 percent of the population. In 1914 a law of Arizona, attempting to grant aid to the aged, was declared unconstitutional. The first successful state law in this field was passed in Montana in 1923 and by 1952 more than 30 states had enacted such legislation. The SOCIAL SECURITY ACT of 1935, as amended, established a coordinated national program of old age pension designed to strengthen state and local legislation by improving standards and providing federal GRANTS-IN-AID. In 1952 about 2,750,000 persons, representing 25 percent of all those 65 years of age or over, were receiving old age assistance. In 1964 the annual cost of such assistance to the states was $15,830,394,000. By January, 1965, about 20,000,000 persons were receiving monthly benefits.

OLDHAM, John. 1600?-1636. Colonist. b. England. To America (1623); banished from PLYMOUTH COLONY (1624); settled in MASSACHUSETTS BAY COLONY; representative to first General Court (1632); his murder by Indians became the direct cause of the Pequot War.

"Old Immigration." See Immigration.

"Old Ironsides." See Constitution, The.

"Old Man Eloquent." The nickname for JOHN QUINCY ADAMS. It was applied during his latter years as a member of the House of Representatives. The reference is to a line in John Milton's sonnet to the Lady Margaret Ley, in which Milton thus refers to Isocrates.

Old Northwest. The area between the Ohio, the Mississippi, and the GREAT LAKES, comprising 248,000 square miles. The territory was transferred to the United States by Great Britain under the terms of the TREATY OF PARIS OF 1783. It was subsequently organized as the NORTHWEST TERRITORY by the ORDINANCES OF 1784, 1785, and 1787.

"Old South." See plantation system and slavery.

Olympia, The U.S.S. The name of the cruiser which was Admiral DEWEY's flagship at the BATTLE OF MANILA BAY on May 1st, 1898.

Olympic Games. A series of athletic activities in which the nations of the world participate every four years. Orginally conducted in ancient Greece, they were revived in Athens in 1896 with the informal participation of the United States and eight other nations. Since then more than 29,000 athletes from 58 nations have competed. They were resumed in London in 1948 after a wartime interuption. As proclaimed by Baron Pierre de Coubertin, a French educator, their purpose is to promote interest in EDUCATION and culture, and to foster improved international relationships. In the United States, the United States Olympic Association supervises the choice of athletes and the administration of their participation in these games. Outstanding among American Olympic champions have been the famous Indian athlete Jim Thorpe, track stars Jesse Owens, Charles Paddock, Eddie Tolan, Harrison Dillard, Cornelius Johnson, Robert Mathias, Mildred "Babe" Didrickson, and swimmers Johnny Weissmuller, Clarence "Buster" Crabbe, William Smith, Helene Madison, and Eleanor Holm.

Omaha Indians. A wandering tribe of Dakota or SIOUX Indians who settled mostly in the Dakotas, Omaha, and Nebraska TERRITORY. They fought with the Sioux. They ceded their lands to the United States, but by an Act of 1882 they can own land individually, and do so in many parts of northeastern Nebraska. Their homes are made of earth, bark, and mats or they live in skin tents.

OLNEY, Richard. 1835-1917. Statesman. b. Massachusetts. Graduated, Brown College and Harvard Law School; practised in Boston; U.S. Attorney General (1893-95); secured sweeping injunction against the American Railway Union in Pullman Strike, which broke the strike

(1895); U.S. Secretary of State (1895-97) appointed by Cleveland; set precedent for American foreign policy by his settlement of the Venezuela Boundary Dispute with Great Britain (1895).

Omnibus Bill of 1850. Also known as the Compromise Act of 1850. Submitted by HENRY CLAY as the last of his three great compromises. The Act resulted from the conflict arising out of the petition of California for ADMISSION TO THE UNION as a free state. As ultimately adopted the Act provided for California's admission as a free state, the division of the MEXICAN CESSION into the territories of New Mexico and Utah based on the principle of POPULAR SOVEREIGNTY, the ABOLITION of the SLAVE TRADE in the District of Columbia, a stricter FUGITIVE SLAVE LAW, and a reduction in the size of the state of Texas. In addition a payment of $10,-000,000 was made to Texas by Congress, theoretically as compensation for the Texas war debt accrued prior to 1845. The law was bitterly contested in the Senate, being opposed by CALHOUN and supported by WEBSTER. Webster's famous "SEVENTH OF MARCH SPEECH" is generally acknowledged as one of the highlights of his career.

Omnibus Crime Control Act. A group of anti-crime bills were incorporated into one crime control act in 1970 which permitted the FBI to investigate campus bombings and which also widened federal authority over the illegal transportation of explosive materials. This Act also made it a federal crime to kill, assault or kidnap a member of Congress. The Act stated that persons using or unlawfully carrying guns during commission of a federal crime could receive stiff penalties.

Oneida Community. One of the experiments in cooperative community living established in the Jacksonian era as a result of the widespread UTOPIAN SOCIAL-IST philosophy. John Humphrey Noyes founded the colony in 1848 in northern New York. A branch colony was subsequently established in Wallingford, Connecticut. The principles on which the Oneida Community was based revolved around communal ownership of property, polygamous marriage, eugenics, cooperative economic functions, and other radical modifications of social relationships. The colony was a self-sustaining community of 600 acres which housed machine shops, smithies, tailoring establishments, and TEXTILE mills. It raised its own food. Its assets of well over $500,000 were profitably employed in communal life that emphasized women's rights, economic training, and a more equitable distribution of income. Public pressure compelled many changes in 1879, and the group adopted more conventional rules of marriage and property ownership. The Oneida Community today is a JOINT STOCK CORPORATION engaged in the commercial production of cutlery and housewares.

O'NEILL, Eugene Gladstone. 1888-1953. Playwright. b. New York City. Studied at Princeton (1906-07) and Harvard (1914-15); associated with Provincetown players (1918); won PULITZER PRIZE for drama (1920, 22, 28); NOBEL PRIZE for literature (1936). Famous for his plays including *Beyond the Horizon* (1920), *Emperor Jones* (1921), *Anna Christie* (1922), *The Hairy Ape* (1922), *Desire Under the Elms* (1924), *Strange Interlude* (1927), *Mourning Becomes Electra* (1931), and *Ah, Wilderness!* (1932). Considered America's outstanding playwright.

O'NEILL, Margaret. 1796?-1879. Known as "Peggy." Wife of U.S. Secretary of war in JACKSON'S CABINET, Major JOHN EATON. She caused a great social and political disturbance in Washington when Jackson tried in vain to get the wives of

467

the other cabinet members to accept her socially despite her humble birth.

"One-third of a nation ill-housed, ill-clad, ill-nourished." The famous quotation from the second inaugural speech of President F. D. ROOSEVELT, delivered on January 20, 1937. In it the President forcefully focused the attention of the American people on the inequitable distribution of the national income. Summarizing the need for an expanding social and labor legislative program he pointed out the existence in the United States of millions of families living on meager incomes, being denied EDUCATION, RECREATION, and the opportunity to improve their lot, and lacking the means to buy "the products of farm and factory and by their poverty denying work and productiveness to many other millions."

"Open covenants openly arrived at." The first of President WILSON'S FOURTEEN POINTS. It refers to the proposal by the President that henceforth the TREATIES among nations should be open to the world. Wilson did not imply, by this phrase, opposition to secret negotiations but rather to secret treaties. The principle was embodied in Article 18 of the Covenant of the LEAGUE OF NATIONS which contemplated the registration and publication of treaties.

Open-Door Policy: Refers to the policy originally enunciated by Secretary of State, JOHN HAY, in 1899. It was applied to the conditions in China in that period during which England, France, Russia, Japan, and lesser nations had marked out for themselves SPHERES OF INFLUENCE and EXTRATERRITORIAL rights in that country. The policy declared the desire of the United States that equal commercial, TARIFF, and railroad rights be granted to all nations. It was not then openly accepted by the great powers, but in the NINE-POWER PACT drawn at the WASH-INGTON NAVAL CONFERENCE in 1921-22 the signatories recognized the open-door policy. In 1943, during World War II, the United States renounced its extraterritorial rights in China.

open enrollment. In order to remedy what was considered unfair treatment of minority groups in the educational field and to achieve greater integration of schools some school districts provided for the voluntary transfer of minorities to predominantly white schools through busing. This changed the concept of the neighborhood school. There has been a good deal of controversy over forced busing as in the case in Pontiac, Michigan when a violent struggle erupted in 1971 in response to a Federal Court busing order desegregating the schools.

Open Shop. A company which employs either union or non-union workers. In practice this has meant the hiring of non-union labor exclusively.

"Open Shoppism." The term applied to the policy of large CORPORATIONS after World War I when it attempted to weaken the LABOR MOVEMENT by adopting various instruments of attack against labor, emphasizing the OPEN SHOP. Corporations curtailed their welfare operations, employed the labor spy and *agent provocateur,* and utilized the services of the state MILITIA in breaking STRIKES. Alleging that the open shop was the "American Plan", employers asserted that organized labor was responsible for the high cost of living and attempted to invoke popular feeling against labor. COMPANY UNIONS were fostered and employers endeavored to promote employee loyalty by stock subscription plans, PENSION plans, GROUP INSURANCE projects, free vacations and trips, community centers, and profit sharing. Corporations successfully utilized the decisions of the courts in breaking strikes and weakening unions as in the "outlaw" shopmen's strike of

1922. The "YELLOW DOG CONTRACT", BLACKLIST, and INJUNCTION were freely used. By 1927 company unions numbered over 1,400,000 members. The result of this program was a sharp decline in union membership. The AMERICAN FEDERATION OF LABOR dropped from its membership of 4,078,740 in 1920 to 2,-803,966 in 1926. Union organization virtually ceased, particularly in the MASS PRODUCTION industries.

OPPENHEIMER, Robert J. 1904-1967. Atomic scientist. b. New York City. Graduated, Harvard University (1925); University of Gottingen (Ph.D., 1927); taught at the University of California and California Institute of Technology; director of atomic energy research project at Los Alamos, New Mexico (1942-45); appointed director of the Institute for Advanced Study at Princeton, New Jersey (1947); made important contributions to the development of the ATOMIC BOMB; supported civilian control of atomic energy after World War II; chairman of the general advisory committee of the United States ATOMIC ENERGY COMMISSION and consultant to the American delegate to the UNITED NATIONS Atomic Energy Committee.

Order of American Knights. See Knights of the Golden Circle.

Orders-in-Council. A series of measures of the British government in 1806 which forbade neutral ships to visit ports from which the British were excluded, unless they had first put in at British ports to take on a consignment of British goods. The Orders-in-Council were Britain's reply to Napoleon's BERLIN AND MILAN DECREES in the ECONOMIC WARFARE between France and England. They resulted in serious interference with the neutral trade of the United States whose ships were seized on the high seas and whose seamen impressed into British service. The resulting aggravation of Anglo-American relations was a contributing cause of the War of 1812.

Ordinance of 1784. See Land Ordinance of 1784.

Ordinance of 1785. See Land Ordinance of 1785.

Ordinance of 1787. See Northwest Ordinance.

Ordinance of Nullification. A resolution passed on November 22, 1832 by a state convention of South Carolina summoned for the purpose of resisting the customs collections under the TARIFF OF 1832. Acting in the name of the sovereign people of South Carolina the Ordinance declared that the Tariff Act was "unauthorized by the Constitution of the United States, null, void, and no law, nor binding upon this State, its officers or citizens." It forbade federal officials to collect customs duties within the state after February 1, 1833, and threatened immediate SECESSION if any attempt were made to collect them by blockade or other force. The threat contained in the Ordinance was met by the vigorous action of President JACKSON who instantly called upon Congress for authority to send an army into Charleston to forcibly collect the revenues. On March 2, 1833 Congress enacted the FORCE BILL clothing Jackson with this power.

Ordinance of Secession. The resolution of the special convention called by the legislature of South Carolina for the purpose of seceding from the Union. The Convention met at Charleston on December 20, 1860 and by the unanimous vote of its 169 members passed the Ordinance of Secession, declaring that the act of May 23, 1788 which ratified the Constitution of the United States, "is hereby repealed and the Union now sub-

469

sisting between South Carolina and the other states, under the name of the United States of America, is hereby dissolved."

Oregon. The tenth state in size, with an area of 96,981 square miles. Organized as a TERRITORY in 1848 and admitted as the 33rd state on February 14, 1859. Salem is the capital. In 1950 Oregon's POPULATION of 1,521,341 made it 32nd in rank. Its largest cities are Portland, Salem, and Eugene. Oregon's single greatest source of income is from timber. It has the largest reserve of standing timber in the United States. Its salmon FISHING INDUSTRY is one of the world's most important. Farm crops include hops, in which Oregon leads the nation, and nuts, WHEAT, hay, oats, and potatoes. The MINING of antimony, chromite, and mercury is important. Manufactures include LUMBER products, food products, machinery, and flour. Its most important source of ELECTRIC POWER is the BONNEVILLE DAM. Oregon was discovered by the Spaniards in 1543. Its nickname is the "Beaver State."

Oregon boundary dispute. A long term diplomatic conflict between the United States and Great Britain over the ownership of Oregon and the boundary between it and Canada. At various times claims by Russia and Spain complicated the controversy. The initial Anglo-Spanish conflict was settled in Britain's favor by a TREATY in 1790. The conflicting claims of the United States and Spain were settled by a treaty in 1819, by which Spain relinquished to the United States all claims north of 42 degrees. By treaties with the United States in 1824 and Great Britain in 1825 Russia waived all claims south of 54 degrees, 40 minutes. The Anglo-American convention of 1818 drew the Canadian boundary to the ROCKIES, determined the boundary of Oregon, and provided for the JOINT OCCUPATION of Oregon by the signatories.

Thereafter, considerable diplomatic negotiation was undertaken between the two governments. British claims were based upon the discoveries of Sir Francis Drake, Captain James Cooke, Captain George Vancouver, and the treaties with Spain and Russia. The claims of the United States were based upon the discovery of the Columbia River by Captain ROBERT GRAY, the EXPLORATIONS of LEWIS AND CLARK, the establishment of Astoria, the treaties with Spain and Russia, and the settlement in the TERRITORY by Americans. Despite the aggressive slogan "FIFTY-FOUR FORTY OR FIGHT" of the 1844 election, the boundary question was finally settled by treaty on June 18, 1846. By its terms the 49th parallel was extended to the Pacific Coast.

Oregon Trail, The. The route from the Missouri River to the Columbia River originally traversed by fur traders. After 1842 it became the highway of the PIONEERS moving westward into the Oregon Territory. The LEWIS AND CLARK EXPEDITION had covered a portion of this HIGHWAY in 1805. In the 1830's and 1840's it became a well defined, heavily travelled road for missionaries and emigrants moving into the TERRITORY under the leadership of the Rev. MARCUS WHITMAN. Its origin was Independence, Missouri from which travellers followed a portion of the old SANTE FE TRAIL to Fort Laramie. The next stop was Fort Bridger whence travellers used South Pass through the Rockies. On the Pacific side of the ROCKY MOUNTAINS, Fort Hall led through the Grande Ronde Valley in the Blue Mountains. From the mountains, the Umatilla River flowed into the Columbia to Fort Vancouver, the terminus of the Oregon Trail. The entire journey was 2,000 miles long.

Organic Act of Puerto Rico. The legislative name for the Jones Act of 1917 and for the Act of 1947 providing for the governmental reorganization of PUERTO

470

RICO. The latter Act gave Puerto Rican CITIZENS the right to elect their governor, thus providing a relatively complete popular elective government. A bill passed by Congress in 1950 permitted Puertő Rico to establish its own constitution. Such a document was voted by Puerto Ricans in a special election conducted on June 4th, 1951 and overwhelmingly ratified on March 3, 1952. Under its terms the United States Congress may no longer repeal insular laws and the President no longer appoint auditors and Supreme Court justices. He may, however, still send troops to the island in case of invasion or rebellion. The preamble contains a provision for a future vote on making Puerto Rico a state if it so desires. See Foraker Act and Jones Act.

ORR, James Lawrence. 1822-1873. Statesman. b. South Carolina. Graduated, University of Virginia (1842); admitted to the bar; member, U.S. House of Representatives (1849-59); fought for SECESSION; served with a rifle regiment in the Confederate army; served as Confederate Senator; governor of South Carolina (1866); appointed by GRANT, U.S. Minister to Russia (1872-3).

Osage Indians. They migrated from the Ohio Valley to Missouri and Arkansas. They were friendly with the French, having met MARQUETTE in 1673 and fought with them against the British. The Osages were finally forced to cede lands to the United States and were moved to northern Oklahoma. OIL was discovered on their lands and they are today one of the wealthiest tribes in the United States. They have a typical Plains culture.

OSBORN, Henry Fairfield. 1857-1935. Paleontologist. b. Connecticut. Graduated, Princeton; professor of comparative anatomy, Princeton (1883-90); professor, Columbia University (from 1890); curator of vertebrate paleontology, American Museum of Natural History (from 1891). Author of many books on evolution.

OSBORN, Thomas Mott. 1859-1926. Penologist. b. New York. Graduated, Harvard University; chairman, N.Y. State Commission on Prison Reform (1913); instituted many modern prison reforms.

Ostend Manifesto. An unofficial declaration made at Ostend, Belgium in 1854 by the American Ministers to Spain, France, and England. The Manifesto declared that the possession of CUBA was necessary to the peace of the United States. If Spain should refuse to sell Cuba, then the United States was "justified by every law, human and divine" in seizing the island by force. The imperialist declaration was promptly disavowed by Secretary of State, WILLIAM L. MARCY, but it was nevertheless an indication of growing American interest in overseas expansion long before the Spanish-American War.

OTIS, Elisha Graves. 1811-1861. Inventor. b. Vermont. Important for invention of automatic safety device for elevators (1854); installed first passenger elevator in N.Y. City (1857); patented a steam elevator (1861); founded Otis elevator business.

OTIS, Harrison Gray. 1765-1848. Statesman. b. Boston, Massachusetts. Graduated, Harvard (1783); admitted to bar and practiced in Boston (from 1786); FEDERALIST member, U.S. House of Representatives (1797-1801); delegate to the HARTFORD CONVENTION (1814-15); U.S. Senator (1817-22); mayor of Boston (1829-32).

OTIS, James. 1725-1783. Revolutionary statesman. b. Massachusetts. Graduated, Harvard (1743); practiced law in Boston (from 1750); king's advocate general when royal customs collectors attempted to get WRITS OF ASSISTANCE to search for violations of the SUGAR ACT

(1733); resigned and appeared as defense counsel for the Boston merchants who resisted the issuance of the writs; upheld NATURAL RIGHTS of colonists in brilliant speech (1761); author of *The Rights of the British Colonies Asserted and Proved* (1763) based on the principles of natural law; led Massachusetts COMMITTEE OF CORRESPONDENCE (1764); patriotic leader of the colonial cause.

Ottawa Indians. A tribe of Indians belonging to the ALGONQUIN group who sided with the French and the HURONS against the British. They fought against the IROQUOIS, but supported the British during the Revolution. They joined in the INDIAN WARS, as PONTIAC was partly an Ottawan. They live in INDIAN TERRITORY or on a reservation in Michigan, having ceded their lands to the United States.

Overland Trail, The. A variation of the OREGON TRAIL. It was the short route from the Platte River fork to Fort Bridger, Wyoming. It received its name in 1862 from Ben Holliday's Overland Stage Line which was moved to it from the old road along the North Platte River. The Overland Trail was superior to the old route because of its shorter distance and relative absence of danger from the Indians. In later years the Lincoln Highway and the UNION PACIFIC RAILROAD followed the general route of the Overland Trail through western Wyoming.

Overman Act. Passed by Congress in May, 1918. This Act was the climax of the vast powers delegated to the President by Congress during World War I.

It gave him the power to establish new administrative agencies and alter existing ones without regard to current law. He was authorized to redistribute the personnel, powers, and funds of these agencies according to his own judgment. The Act made the President a political "dictator" for the remainder of the war.

OWEN, Robert. 1771-1858. Utopian socialist. b. Wales. In mills which he owned in Manchester, he instituted many social reforms; founder of several UTOPIAN communities of "Owenites" on a cooperative basis in Great Britain and the United States; unsuccessful. Author of *A New View of Society* (1813) contending that a man's character is determined by his environment, *Revolution in Mind and Practice* (1849).

OWEN, Robert Dale. 1801-1877. Legislator and social reformer. b. Scotland. Son of ROBERT OWEN. To United States with his father (1825); taught school and edited NEW HARMONY, Ind. *Gazette;* edited *Free Enquirer* in New York (1829); member, U.S. House of Representatives, from Indiana (1843-47); supported the annexation of Texas; U.S. Minister to Italy (1855-58); supported extension of property rights for women and emancipation of the slaves. Author of books on the ABOLITION of SLAVERY.

OWEN, Ruth Bryan. 1885-1954. Diplomat. Daughter of WILLIAM J. BRYAN. b. Illinois. Member, from Florida, U.S. House of Representatives (1929-33); U.S. Minister to Denmark (1933-36) first U.S. woman diplomat.

P

PACA, William 1740-1799. Revolutionary leader. b. Maryland. Admitted to the bar in London; practiced law in Maryland; member, CONTINENTAL CONGRESS (1774-79); signer, DECLARATION OF INDEPENDENCE; governor of Maryland (1782-85); U.S. district judge (1789-99).

Pacific Ocean. The largest expanse of water in the world. It measures 7,000 miles from North to South, with a maximum breadth of 10,000 miles. It lies between America on the East and Asia and Australia on the West, and extends from the Bering Sea southward to 40 degrees south latitude. Its area is 55,-624,000 square miles, constituting 40 percent of the total water surface of the earth. The mean depth is 2.9 miles. The Pacific was discovered by de Balboa in 1513 and first navigated by Magellan in 1520. The development of the FUR TRADE on the northwest coast after the Revolution, followed by the growing trade with China in the early 19th century, marked the first attention of the United States to the Pacific. Through the 19th century other factors contributed to the growing interest in this area. Among these were the settlement of Oregon and California, the acquisition of the MEXICAN CESSION, the WHALING industry, Commodore PERRY's expedition to Japan, the annexation of HAWAII, and the desire for an interoceanic CANAL. The purchase and development of ALASKA and the acquisition of the PHILIPPINES, GUAM, SAMOA, WAKE, and Midway Islands were additional factors in the 19th and 20th centuries in maintaining the sharp interest of the United States in the Pacific region. The rise of Japan as a major power led to various attempts at the reconciliation of claims between her and the United States. By the end of World War II the United States had become one of the strongest powers in the Pacific.

Packers and Stockyards Act. An act of Congress passed in 1921. It forbade packers to establish MONOPOLIES, to discriminate between persons and localities, or to manipulate prices. STOCKYARDS were forbidden to furnish discriminatory services, charge unreasonable rates, or to conceal their schedules of charges. The administration of the Act was vested in the Secretary of Agriculture upon whom were conferred strong quasi-judicial powers to hold hearings, and to issue rules, regulations, and cease and desist orders.

Pack Trains. A line of 10 to 20 horses commanded by a master driver and two or three assistants to transport western products across the Alleghany mountains to eastern markets. The principal crops thus carried were ginseng, whisky, feed, flax, and potash. These pack trains were generally organized by the neighboring FARMERS of a FRONTIER community during the colonial and early American period. They usually followed the old Indian trails to principal eastern cities.

PAGE, Thomas Jefferson. 1808-1899. Naval officer and explorer. Served with navy in Paraguay; signed TREATY with Paraguay and made EXPLORATIONS up the Paraguay River (1859-60); served in Confederate Navy throughout the Civil War.

PAGE, Walter Hines. 1855-1918. Journalist and diplomat. b. North Carolina. Studied at Randolph-Macon and Johns Hopkins University; on the staff of the *Forum*, N.Y. (1887-95), *Atlantic Monthly* (1895-98); partner in Doubleday, Page & Co., publishers (from 1899); founded and edited *The World's Work* (1900-13); U.S. Ambassador to Great Britain (1913-18).

PAINE, Robert Treat. 1731-1814. Jurist. b. Boston, Massachusetts. Graduated, Harvard (1749); admitted to the bar (1759); member, CONTINENTAL CONGRESS (1774-78); signer, DECLARATION OF INDEPENDENCE; attorney general of Massachusetts (1777-90); judge, Massachusetts supreme court (1790-1804).

PAINE, Thomas. 1737-1809. Political philosopher and writer. b. England. Quaker; to America (1774); published *Common Sense* (1776) which urged an immediate DECLARATION OF INDEPENDENCE from England; served in Continental army (1776); published the *Crisis* papers which had wide acceptance and lifted the morale of the patriots (1776-83); secretary, Congress's committee on foreign affairs (1777-79); inspired by the French Revolution, he wrote *The Rights of Man* (1791, 92) which advocated the overthrow of the British monarchy and the establishment of a republic; fled to Paris; convicted of TREASON and outlawed from England (1792); released from prison in France, where he had been imprisoned as an English subject,

at the request of MONROE, American Minister to France (1794); wrote *The Age of Reason* (Part I 1794, Part II 1796) a philosophical explanation of the Deist belief; among his political programs were a plan for a world peace organization, and social security plans for indigent, unemployed, and aged persons; returned to America (1802); died in obscurity and poverty.

PALMER, John McCauley. 1817-1900. Lawyer and political leader. b. Kentucky. Admitted to the bar, Illinois (1839); Republican leader; served through Civil War gaining rank of major general (1862); elected governor of Illinois (1869-73); switched party affiliation and became Democratic U.S. Senator (1891-97); unsuccessful presidential candidate of GOLD DEMOCRATS (1896).

Palmer Raids. A series of raids upon private homes and labor headquarters by Attorney-General A. Mitchell Palmer in 1919-20. Employing private spies and *agents-provocateurs,* Palmer arrested and imprisoned thousands of aliens. Held without trial for long periods and ultimately given mock trials without legal safeguards, hundreds were deported. In December, 1919 the transport *Buford* alone carried 249 aliens from New York to Russia. Palmer was criticized by prominent CITIZENS for his over-zealous application of existing espionage and sedition legislation as violations of the Constitution. He was accused of political maneuvering to obtain the 1920 presidential nomination of the Democratic party.

Panama Canal. The canal across the Isthmus of Panama whose construction was begun in 1904 and opened to traffic in 1914. It was officially declared open in 1920. The original cost of $400,-000,000 was subsequently increased by expenditures for improvements and additions. The engineer chiefly responsible for the sucessful completion of the project was Colonel GEORGE W. GOETHALS. The canal is 50 miles long, 110 feet wide, and 41 feet deep. It is a lake and lock type canal, having 12 locks. The line of the Canal is northwest-southeast, the Pacific end being 27 miles west of the Atlantic end. In 1950 the Canal carried 30,000,000 long tons of cargo. The Canal is the biggest economic asset of the Republic of Panama, with roughly one-third of the latter's national income derived from the wages of Panamanians working in the CANAL ZONE, or from funds spent by United States personnel in the Zone. The Canal is administered by the Panama Canal Company, organized in 1951 to replace the former Panama Railroad Company. The Company is an autonomous federally-chartered CORPORATION, and operates the Canal and its associated business enterprises including the Panama Railroad, commissaries, MOTION PICTURE houses, and stores.

Panama Canal Company. See Panama Canal.

Panama Canal Treaty. In January 1964 Panamanian riots protesting 1903 and 1955 treaties resulted in negotiations for a new treaty. Agreement was reached in August, 1977 on a proposed treaty giving Panama increasing control of the canal with complete transfer of control December 31, 1999. The U.S. to retain primary responsibility for defense and administration until that date. The proposed treaty became a controversial issue in the U.S. and by early 1978 the required ratification by two-thirds senate majority seemed to be far from certain.

Panama Canal Zone. A federal government area administered by the Canal Zone Government, headed by a presidentially-appointed governor. The TERRITORY was leased to the United States in perpetuity, in 1904, for $10,000,000 plus an annual payment of $250,000, increased in 1936 to $430,000. In 1951 the Canal Zone Government and the former Panama Railroad Company were reorganized, the latter incorporating the operation of the Canal and its related business enterprises into a single administrative organ known as the Panama Canal Company. Those units of the Canal Zone concerned exclusively with political functions, health, and sanitation constitute the Canal Zone Government. The Zone's POPULATION of 53,000 consists largely of civilian employees and personnel of the United States military forces and their dependents. Its area is 648 square miles. Geographically the Zone extends five miles on either side of the axis of the PANAMA CANAL, but excludes the cities of Panama and Colón which, with the exceptions of sanitation and quarantine, remain under the jurisdiction of the Republic of Panama. The Caribbean port is the city of Cristobal and the Pacific entrance is at the port of Balboa. No private individual is allowed to acquire land in the Zone.

Panama, Declaration of. Number XIV of a series of 16 resolutions adopted in 1939 at Panama City by the "Consultative Meeting of Foreign Ministers of the American Republics." This specific declaration, consisting of four parts, stated that American waters must be kept free of any hostile act by a non-American belligerent power, that the American republics would take joint action to obtain compliance with this statement, that they would consult further if necessary, and that individual or collective patrols by the members of the waters adjacent to their coast would be undertaken whenever the need arose. The meeting itself was called to deal with conditions created by the outbreak of war in Europe on Sept. 1, 1939.

Panama Revolt. Following the refusal of the Colombian legislature to ratify the HAY-HERRAN TREATY of 1903, a band of

475

rebels seized control of Panama on November 3, 1903, proclaiming the Republic of Panama. Colombian military forces, stationed at Colon on the other side of the Panamanian Isthmus, attempted to reach Panama, but were prevented from doing so by the *U.S.S. Nashville* which had been dispatched to the area. President T. ROOSEVELT justified this action under the terms of the Treaty of 1846, arguing that the United States was empowered to intervene to maintain free transit across the Isthmus. On November 6th the President recognized the Republic of Panama. The new government appointed the French engineer, Bunau-Varilla, minister to the United States. On November 18th the HAY-BUNAU-VARILLA TREATY was negotiated, granting the United States the right to build a canal. Subsequent attempts by Colombia to suppress the rebellion were prevented by United States marines. President Roosevelt and Secretary of State HAY consistently denied Colombia's accusation that the revolt had been instigated by the United States and that American military intervention had been illegal. Similar charges made in Congress and in the American press were answered by Roosevelt who argued the necessity of prompt action to safeguard United States interests in the area. Nevertheless, Congress appropriated $25,000,000 in 1921 as a payment to Colombia.

Pan-American Conferences. A series of meetings of delegates of the United States and the 20 Latin American nations, held from time to time. The first true conference was the Congress of Panama called in 1826 at the request of Simon Bolívar, and attended by the United States. Formally entitled the First International Conference of American States, the first modern Congress was held in Washington, D.C. in 1889, and was attended by the representatives of 18 nations. Its agenda comprised programs for the promotion of peace, the creation of an American TARIFF union, the establishment of a uniform system of customs laws, the adoption of uniform weights and measures, the development of an ARBITRATION plan, and the mutual protection of property, PATENT rights, copyright, and trade marks. This Conference established the PAN-AMERICAN UNION, formally called the Commercial Bureau of American Republics. The Second Conference convened at Mexico City in 1901-02, followed by a Third Conference at Rio de Janeiro in 1906. The Fourth Conference met at Buenos Aires in 1910, the Fifth Conference at SANTIAGO, Chile in 1923, the Sixth Conference at HAVANA in 1928, the Seventh Conference at MONTEVIDEO in 1933, and the Eighth Conference at LIMA in 1938. *Ad hoc* conferences have been called at BUENOS AIRES in 1936 to draw up plans for a NEUTRALITY pact among the American nations, at PANAMA in 1939 to establish sea safety zones and to issue a Declaration of Neutrality at the opening of World War II, and at Havana in 1940 to formulate plans for a joint TRUSTEESHIP over European colonies in the western hemisphere. Other special problems dealt with at such congresses have included ARBITRATION, sanitation, international law, narcotics control, international TRADE, child welfare, women's rights, and educational problems.

Pan-Americanism. A movement to improve the political and commercial relations of the American nations. Its genesis goes back to the invitation of Simon Bolívar in 1824 to the Latin American nations for a congress in Panama. In the United States HENRY CLAY set forth its principles in 1826, advocating a Pan-American system of which the United States would be the center. In 1881 Secretary of State JAMES G. BLAINE revived the idea of Pan-American amity by inviting the Latin American nations to attend a conference the following year. The death of President GARFIELD prevented the meeting, and the invitations were renewed in 1888 for a conference at Washington. This first PAN-AMERICAN CONFERENCE met in the national capital from October, 1889 to April, 1890.

Pan-American Union. The organization of the 21 republics of North and South America which was established on April 14, 1890 by the first Pan-American Conference. Originally known as the International Bureau of American Republics, it took its present name in 1910. The Union exercises the functions of an executive committee, preparing agendas for the PAN-AMERICAN CONFERENCE, arranging these conferences, and undertaking to execute the conferences' decisions. Its governing board is composed of the Secretary of State of the United States and the ambassadors and ministers in Washington, D.C. of the 20 Latin American republics. It is prohibited from engaging in political activities, having been created for the purpose of fostering the commercial and cultural relations of its members. Its headquarters are located in Washington, D.C.

Panay Incident. The sinking by Japanese bombers on December 12, 1937 of the United States GUNBOAT *Panay* and three American OIL supply vessels. The attack took place on the Yangtze River in China resulting in three deaths and other casualties. The incident aroused great public resentment in the United States in a period when Japanese-American relations were already strained as a result of the Japanese attack on China that year. The demand by the United States government for redress brought a formal Japanese apology, punishment for those responsible for the attack, and an indemnity of approximately $2,250,000.

Panic of 1837. An economic DEPRESSION whose fundamental causes included overspeculation in western lands, an unfavorable TRADE balance, the growth of "WILDCAT" BANKING, and the mounting state debts resulting from extensive loans and grants to CANAL, TURNPIKE, and RAILROAD companies. The issuance of the SPECIE CIRCULAR in 1836 and the calling of loans by British investors precipitated the panic in May, 1837. The depression lasted until 1843, and was severely felt in the West and South. Public works were suspended, UNEMPLOYMENT became widespread, and the purchasing power of the FARMER declined.

Panic of 1857. A cyclical DEPRESSION whose causes were overspeculation in RAILROADS, land speculation, and the unregulated growth of STATE BANKING. The depression was precipitated by the failure of the Ohio Life Insurance Company of Cincinnati, in August, 1857. It was most serious in the northern and eastern industrial sections of the nation, and was felt only slightly in the South. The depression was characterized by the customary phenomena of UNEMPLOYMENT, BANK FAILURES, decline in the national income, and deflation.

Panic of 1873. An economic DEPRESSION precipitated by the collapse on September 18th of several eastern financial institutions, the most important of which was Jay Cooke and Company. The fundamental causes of the depression were the currency INFLATION of the post-Civil War period, governmental extravagance, overexpansion of credit, an unfavorable TRADE balance, and overexpansion in RAILROADS and general commercial enterprises. The depression was part of a world wide economic decline that strongly affected the major European nations as a consequence of the Austro-Prussian, Franco-Prussian, and other European Wars, as well as of international speculation and overexpansion of business. This Panic was the severest up to that time, resulting in more than 22,000 business failures, the UNEMPLOYMENT of 500,000 workers, widespread wage cuts, and the general impoverishment of large sections of the industrial labor population. By 1878 general recovery had begun to take place.

Panic of 1893. A financial crisis resulting from the recall of European securities investments from the United States after 1890. The stock market collapse in New York City was accompanied by increased gold exports, the decline of the Treasury's gold reserve, and the falling off of the prices of gold, silver, and commodities. Important RAILROADS and business enterprises failed after the collapse of the Philadelphia and Reading Railroad in February and the National Cordage Company in May. The winter and summer of 1893 and 1894 represented the depths of the DEPRESSION, being characterized by widespread UNEMPLOYMENT, STRIKES and violence, continued business failure, and deflation. Recovery by 1897 resulted from an increased European demand for American exports, followed by price rises and gold imports that stabilized national finances.

Panic of 1907. A minor economic DEPRESSION brought on by the failures of the Knickerbocker Trust Company of New York City and the Westinghouse Electric and Manufacturing Company on October 22nd and 23rd respectively. The resulting stock market collapse caused banks to suspend activities all over the nation and business enterprises to close their doors. By the spring of 1908 recovery had already begun.

Panic of 1929. The severest STOCK MARKET and financial crash in American history. The great crash on October 29th was the culmination of a seven month decline of securities' prices whose causes

were traceable to the unusual overspeculation in stocks since 1924. On that day 16,410,030 shares of stock were traded. The causes included an easy money policy authorized by the FEDERAL RESERVE Board, low money rates on commercial loans, low discount rates of the Federal Reserve System, speculative securities purchases on margin, and extensive bank loans to brokers. Within 12 months stock values declined from $87,000,000,000 to $55,000,000,000. Prices continued to decline until they reached their lowest point in July, 1933, with a three and one half year loss of $74,000,000,000, representing five-sixths of the value of stocks in September, 1929.

Panics. Refers to economic DEPRESSIONS occuring periodically in the downswing of the BUSINESS CYCLE. Panics are characterized by UNEMPLOYMENT, BANK FAILURES, bankruptcies, deflation, falling profits, wage declines, reduction in foreign TRADE, and decline in agricultural production. Outstanding panics in American history occurred in 1819, 1837, 1857, 1873, 1893, 1907, 1921, and 1929. There have been minor panics, popularly called "RECESSIONS", in other years such as 1937 and 1949.

Paper Industry. The first paper mill in America was established in 1690 near Philadelphia by William Bradford and William Rittenhouse. Rittenhouse and his descendants built other mills and carried on their work until the late 19th century. Progress in paper making was slow until the introduction of the pulp engine from Holland in 1766. In 1794 a mill was established at Fairhaven, Vermont by Matthew Lyon for the production of wrapping paper from basswood bark. By 1810 the bulk of the paper used in the United States was domestically manufactured, most of it from rags. The problem of rag shortage was gradually solved by mixing it with ground wood pulp. The LUMBER resources of the New England and middle Atlantic states stimulated the establishment of paper mills in that area. Massachusetts, New York, and Pennsylvania became the center of the industry in the first third of the 19th century. Its principal products were writing and wrapping paper, wallpaper, and pasteboard. The first steam paper mill was erected in Pittsburgh in 1816, and was followed the next year by the first cylinder machine, an invention of Thomas Gilpin. The introduction of the Fourdrinier machine in 1820 for MANUFACTURING paper on an endless cloth web initiated the replacement of hand work by machine work. By the end of the century only three handmade paper plants remained in the United States. Other materials utilized in the manufacture of paper in the 19th century were straw and grass. These were widely used in the manufacture of books and NEWSPAPERS until the 1870's when woodpulp supplanted them in newsprint production. In the 20th century there has been a huge increase in the variety of products made of paper. These include liquid containers, cups, boxes, packaging materials, and many others. In 1949 there were 4,200 firms in the industry, employing 377,000 workers who added a value of $2,777,000,000 to paper and allied products by manufacturing. In 1963 the industry produced 29,436,000 short tons of wood pulp and 39,012,000 short tons of paper and paper board.

Paper Money. In American history this has comprised three types of CURRENCY: fiat money, certificates based on coin or bullion, and bank notes. Massachusetts issued bills in 1690, and was followed by the other colonies. During the Revolution, Congress issued $241,000,000 in FIAT CURRENCY between 1775-79 while the states authorized an additional sum of $210,000,000. Until 1861 when Congress authorized $450,000,000 of GREEN-

BACKS, the federal government issued no paper money with the exception of a small issue of treasury notes in 1815. During this period the paper currency circulating in the United States were bank notes issued by state-chartered institutions. In 1890 treasury certificates were authorized for the purchase of silver under the terms of the SHERMAN SILVER PURCHASE ACT of that year. Until 1893 when the law was repealed, the Treasury put into circulation $156,000,-000 of these notes. Gold certificates were authorized in 1863, the same year that national bank notes were authorized by the NATIONAL BANKING ACT. In 1878 the BLAND-ALLISON ACT provided for the issuance of silver certificates, a paper money which was again issued by the SILVER PURCHASE ACT of 1934. Other forms of bank notes in the history of American paper money were those of the two BANKS OF THE UNITED STATES between 1791-1811 and 1816-36. These and the bank notes of the state-chartered banks constituted more than one-half of the circulating currency. The FEDERAL RESERVE ACT of 1914 provided for the issuance of Federal Reserve notes, supplemented by Federal Reserve Bank Notes provided by amending legislation. The latter were withdrawn in 1934. In 1964 Federal Reserve notes, National bank notes and others amounted to nearly $56,000,000,-000.

Parcel Post. See postal system.

Paris, Treaty of, 1763. Ended the Seven Years' War. By its terms France ceded to England, Canada and the area east of the Mississippi, except for New Orleans. France retained the islands of St. Pierre and Miquelon. New Orleans and French TERRITORY west of the Mississippi were given to Spain. To France, England ceded most of the former French-held islands of the WEST INDIES, retaining Florida. Spain also acquired Havana and

Manila, holding these territories until the Spanish-American War. France ceded all her territorial interests in India to England. The result of the TREATY was to reduce the French empire to a secondary status, remove the French and Indian menace to the colonial FRONTIER, and provide valuable military experience for the English colonists. It also produced a revision in British imperial policy, England renouncing the POLICY OF "SALUTORY NEGLECT" in favor of firmer control of the empire.

Paris, Treaty of, 1783. Ended the American Revolution. Negotiated by American commissioners, FRANKLIN, JAY, and ADAMS. The terms included England's recognition of the independence of the United States, establishment of the Mississippi River as the western boundary of the United States, England's grant of full American rights in the Newfoundland fisheries, and promise by the United States to recommend to the states the restoration of property and payment of American debts to LOYALISTS.

Paris, Treaty of, 1898. Ended the Spanish-American War. Under its terms Spain ceded to the United States PUERTO RICO, GUAM, and the PHILIPPINES, agreed to withdraw from CUBA, and was indemnified in the sum of $20,000,000. The results of the TREATY were to establish the United States as a world power and to reduce Spain to the rank of a second class power.

Parity price. The price of a farm commodity which would make the purchasing power of a unit of that commodity equal to its purchasing power in the period from July, 1909 to July, 1914. The AGRICULTURAL ADJUSTMENT ACT OF 1933 was designed to raise the prices of WHEAT, corn, COTTON, milk and other farm products to a point where they would bear a fair relationship to the prices the farmer had to pay for the

goods he bought. The period of 1909-1914 was fixed as the standard. The DEPARTMENT OF AGRICULTURE was authorized to pay farmers, who signed contracts to reduce their acreage, the difference between the market price and the parity price. The AGRICULTURAL ADJUSTMENT ACT OF 1938 established a commodity loan program which provided loans to participants in production-control agreements when the market price was below 52 percent of parity for wheat and cotton, and below 75 percent of parity for corn. When the estimated corn crops exceeded estimated market by 25 percent, the minimum percentage for corn could decline to 52 percent. For loans on other commodities the minimum was subject to the discretion of the COMMODITY CREDIT CORPORATION. Loans were to be made at a figure equal to or above this percentage of the parity price. For complying with the plan of fixing marketing quotas for particular crops farmers could receive parity payments up to 90 percent of the parity value of the crops. The act of Congress of July 18, 1952 continued the prices of basic farm crops at 90 percent of parity for the 1953 and 1954 crop years. By 1965, most major crops were included in the various price support programs.

PARKER, Alton Brooks. 1852-1926. Jurist. b. New York. Admitted to the bar and practiced in Kingston, N.Y.; judge, N.Y. court of appeals (1889-96); appellate division of supreme court (1896-97); chief justice, court of appeals (1898-1904); unsuccessful Democratic candidate for the presidency (1904); practiced law in N. Y. City (from 1904); defended the A.F. OF L. in DANBURY HATTER'S CASE and GOMPERS and other labor leaders in contempt proceedings.

PARKER, Francis Wayland. 1837-1902. Educator. Superintendent of schools,

Quincy, Massachusetts (1875-80); important for contributions to progressive EDU-CATION in the United States; served throughout the Civil War, retiring as colonel; principal, Chicago Institute (1899) which became part of the school of education, University of Chicago.

PARKER, Theodore. 1810-1860. Unitarian clergyman. b. Massachusetts. Extremely liberal preacher whose ideas were condemned by many members of his congregation; leader in antislavery agitation, member of secret committee helping JOHN BROWN and his raid at Harpers Ferry.

Parker vs. Davis. See Legal Tender Cases.

PARKMAN, Francis. 1823-1893. Historian. b. Boston, Massachusetts. Graduated, Harvard; made trip over the old OREGON TRAIL (1846). Author of *The California and Oregon Trail* (1849), *History of the Conspiracy of Pontiac* (2 vols. 1851), *The Discovery of the Great West* (1869), *A Half-Century of Conflict* (2 vols. 1892) etc.; elected to HALL OF FAME (1915).

Parson's Cause, The. A conflict arising in Virginia in the mid-18th century over two laws passed by Parliament in 1755 and 1758 changing salary payments to ministers from TOBACCO to money at a discounted rate. Ministers' salaries had been fixed in 1748 at 17,200 pounds of tobacco annually, a rate not fully compensated for by the two subsequent laws. Many ministers began law suits for the difference between their money payment and the value of their tobacco quota at current market prices. Their attacks against the laws brought a royal VETO in 1759 which was in turn assailed by PAT-RICK HENRY on the grounds that vetoes against the public good were improper. The net result of the litigation, which

was ultimately appealed to the Privy Council in England, was the passage of a third law in 1769 satisfying the ministers.

PARSONS, Theophilus. 1750-1813. Jurist. b. Massachusetts. Graduated, Harvard (1769); practiced law (from 1774); outstanding lawyer in New England and leader of the ESSEX JUNTO (1778); important in securing the RATIFICATION OF THE FEDERAL CONSTITUTION in Massachusetts (1788); chief justice, Massachusetts supreme court (1806-13).

PARSONS, William Barclay. 1859-1932. Civil engineer. b. New York City. Graduated, Columbia University. (1879); designed and built the first sections of New York's SUBWAY system (1899-1904); built East River Tunnel, N.Y. City; member, Isthmian Canal Commission (1904); served in France with the 11th U.S. Engineers (1917-18) as colonel.

Party Government. The assumption by the victorious POLITICAL PARTY of the responsibility for the conduct of government. Although it is the legally elected officers who govern, as members of the party they work through the party in exercising their governmental functions. In the executive and legislative branches they coordinate the activities of the agencies of government and administration of law through a wide variety of conferences, CAUCUSES, committees, and governmental positions. The elected party leaders are appointed by these caucuses and conferences to committee memberships and chairmanships and as party whip, majority leader, SPEAKER, and other positions. The national and state committees of the party exercise great influence in integrating the executive and legislative branches into a harmoniously operating organism. The elected officials are beholden to these committees for political and financial support. The appointed governmental officers are even more indebted to the party leadership for their offices 'and support.

Party "Machines." That organization of the POLITICAL PARTIES which composes the management of the parties. It consists of the leaders and members of party committees and of party workers. The head of the "machine" is the "boss" who frequently utilizes his power for personal profit. The "machine" is often the personal property of the "boss" or of a "ring" consisting of insiders who use their positions for purposes of illegal profit and power. Party "bosses" and "rings" have flourished more frequently at the local and state level than in the federal government. The "machine" may use a variety of methods in achieving its goals. In the past these have included bribery, violence, trickery, padded voting, and propaganda. Notable illustrations of party "bosses" and "machines" in the United States have included William M. Tweed of TAMMANY HALL in the 1870's, Senator Boies Penrose of Pennsylvania from 1904 to 1921, Charles F. Murphy of Tammany Hall from 1902 to 1922, A. C. Townley of North Dakota from 1916 to 1921, and Mayor Frank Hague of Jersey City in the 1930's and 1940's. The party "machine" is distinguished from the organized party machinery although they may sometimes be the same. The Tammany "machine" in New York City has always been the Democratic organization and the Republican "machine" in Philadelphia is the Republican organization in that city.

Parties, Political. Organizations developed for the purpose of carrying on political activities such as nominating candidates, conducting election campaigns, expressing political issues, and carrying on party leadership within government. Other services claimed by parties to be valuable contributions to American life are PATRONAGE, social

services (picnics, outings, lunches, etc.), EDUCATION, and political organization. Political parties sprang up originally over the ratification struggle of the Constitution in the creation of the FEDERALIST PARTY and the ANTI-FEDERALIST PARTY in 1781. Since then parties have played a significant role in the American political scene. Typical aspects of the American party system have been the two party system, the THIRD PARTY MOVEMENT, party government, bi-partisan actions, and occasional merging of party lines. The two major parties in 1952 were the Democratic party and the Republican party.

Party System. See parties, political.

Patent Office, the United States. Created in 1836. Previously PATENTS had been registered with the STATE DEPARTMENT. The Patent Office remained a bureau c the State Department until 1839 whe it was transferred to the DEPARTMENT O THE INTERIOR. Since 1925 it has been es tablished in the DEPARTMENT OF COM MERCE. It has the power of granting o denying patent applications, keeps speci fications, models, and patent records, anc interprets patent law in light of judicia decisions. Although financed from the annual BUDGET, its receipts from patent fees often net a surplus above expenditures. Its average annual patent registrations numbered above 40,000. Its executive chief is the Commissioner of Patents, located in Washington, D.C.

Patents. In the accepted sense patents were first granted by the states after the Revolution, although MONOPOLY rights were conferred in charters granted by colonial legislatures to manufacturers. Under its constitutional authority, Congress enacted legislation in 1790 to protect authors and inventors. The law was liberalized by an AMENDMENT in 1793

482

and contributed greatly to the development of INVENTIONS in this country. The United States Patent Bureau was created in 1836 to administer all patent legislation. Later legislation provided for the protection of improvements on existing inventions as well as new inventions. These amendments were instrumental in stimulating inventions and modifications of equipment in new industries such as ALUMINUM, PETROLEUM, CHEMICALS, TRANSPORTATION, and plastics. The volume of patents steadily increased throughout the 19th and 20th centuries. Whereas the Patent Office issued approximately 1,000 patents in 1840, and 6,500 patents between 1840 and 1850, the annual number increased to over 95,000 in 1929. By 1940 more than 2,000,000 patents had been issued, almost half of these in the two preceding decades. Applications for patents are passed upon by the Commissioner of Patents in the order of receipts, and are granted for a term of 17 years to any person who has invented or discovered any new or useful ART, machine, manufacture, or matter, as well as any new or useful improvement thereof.

Paterson Plan. Also called the New Jersey Plan. A plan submitted by WILLIAM PATERSON, the head of the New Jersey delegation, to the CONSTITUTIONAL CONVENTION in 1787. It reflected the demands of the small states for equal representation in the legislature of the new government then being organized. It was in opposition to the VIRGINIA PLAN, and provided for the creation of executive and judicial departments and an equal number of delegates from all states to the proposed UNICAMERAL LEGISLATURE, as representatives of the states, not of the nation. The conflict between the Paterson and Virginia plans was ultimately reconciled by the CONNECTICUT COMPROMISE.

PATERSON, William. 1745-1806. Jurist and statesman. b. Ireland. Graduated, Princeton University. (1763); practiced law (from 1769); attorney general of New Jersey (1776-83); member, CONSTITUTIONAL CONVENTION (1787); supported the small states in his New Jersey plan; U.S. Senator (1789-90); governor (1790-93); associate justice, U.S. Supreme Court (1793-1806). See Paterson Plan.

Patriot Army. See Continental Army.

Patriots. Those persons devoted to the cause of independence during the Revolution. Formerly called WHIGS, they opposed the LOYALISTS. Generally they consisted of members of the middle class and lower class although many representatives of wealth were recruited to their cause.

Patrons of Husbandry. See Granger Movement.

Patronage. The non-merit political appointment of party supporters to CIVIL SERVICE positions. On April 10, 1952 President TRUMAN incorporated appointment reforms in Reorganization Plans Numbers 2, 3, and 4. These were aimed at shifting a large bloc of officers, formerly filled by patronage appointments, to promotion of career employees from the ranks. The offices included all postmasters, customs officers, and United States marshals whose positions were henceforth to be selected on the basis of merit and fitness rather than by political appointment. In the past these positions have been filled on recommendation of members of Congress or party leaders. The only important group of federal officers still subject to political appointment would be judges and District Attorneys. Of all groups postmasters, numbering 21,034 for the entire nation, constituted the largest single group of political appointees. Also included were 94 marshalls and 54 Customs Bureau officials. The Reorganization Plans effected recommendations that had been made in 1912 by the TAFT Commission on Economy and Efficiency, in 1937 by the President's Committee on Administrative Management, and in 1949 by the HOOVER COMMISSION.

Patroons. The name applied to the upper class of large landholders in the Dutch colony of NEW NETHERLANDS. Its origin goes back to the grant by the DUTCH WEST INDIA COMPANY in 1629 of a Charter of Freedoms and Exemptions which conferred great estates called patroonships upon members of the company who established settlements of 50 persons within four years after notifying the company. Such members, called patroons, were to own the land as a "perpetual fief of inheritance" with complete rights to all timber, minerals, crops, waterways, and other NATURAL RESOURCES. Within the century important patroon families had been established, including the Van Rensselaers, Glommaerts, Burghs, and Pauws. These families exercised the typical powers of a feudal lord, charging tenants substantial rents, requiring dues and services of them and in general wielding complete legal and political power over their estates.

PATTON, George Smith, Jr. 1885-1945. World War II General. b. California. Graduated, U.S.M.A., West Point (1909); commanded a tank brigade in World War I; commanded the U.S. 2nd Corps in North Africa and the 7th Army in Sicily during World War II (1942-43); considered a brilliant tactician; lost his command in 1944 for slapping a soldier in a fit of temper; given command of the 3rd army which led the forces of the United States from Normandy through Northern France, driving the Germans from Bastogne (December 1944); crossed the Rhine (March, 1945); drove through Germany and into Czechoslovakia; made military governor of Bavaria and criticized for leniency to the Nazis; removed (October, 1945) and placed in charge of the 15th Army; killed in an automobile accident in Germany. Author of an autobiography, *War As I Know It* (1947).

Pawnee Indians. Living on the Platte in Nebraska, the Pawnee Indians had a Plains culture. They were expert horsemen. They raised and lived on corn, beans, and squash. They were constantly at war with the SIOUX who almost wiped them out completely. They were friendly to the Americans, and in 1833 ceded all their lands south of the Platte to the United States. They finally surrendered all their lands and moved into INDIAN TERRITORY near the CHEROKEE strip.

Payne-Aldrich Tariff Act. Passed by Congress in 1909. Although it started out as a TARIFF reform act in conformance with the Republican party's platform pledge of 1908, many rates were increased in the House version of the bill. When it came to the Senate, the pressure of Senator NELSON W. ALDRICH resulted in high duties on IRON ore, COAL, and hides plus increases in other commodities. Despite pressure by President TAFT and the supporters of THEODORE ROOSEVELT in the Congress, it became a distinctly protective measure and was a contributing cause to the defeat of the party in the congressional elections of 1910. The failure of TARIFF REFORM constituted a partisan political issue during the next presidential election which the party lost to the Democratic candidate WOODROW WILSON. The average rate was 40.73 percent.

PAYNE, Sereno Elisha. 1843-1914. Lawyer and political leader. b. New York. Graduated, University of Rochester

(1864); admitted to the bar and began practice (1866); leading Republican; member, U.S. House of Representatives (1883-87; 1889-1914); chairman WAYS AND MEANS COMMITTEE (1899-1910); helped draft the MC KINLEY TARIFF ACT (1890) and the PAYNE-ALDRICH TARIFF ACT (1909).

Peace Corps. In 1961, President Kennedy set up an organization of volunteers to aid underdeveloped countries. Appropriations for fiscal 1965 totaled $115,-000.000. This budget provided for 14,000 volunteers.

"Peace" Democrats. See Copperheads.

Peace Treaties of 1947. A series of treaties signed on February 10, 1947 by the United States, Great Britain, France, and the Soviet Union on the one hand and Italy, Hungary, Rumania, Bulgaria, and Finland on the other. Between August and October, 1946 delegates from 21 of the UNITED NATIONS met in Paris to discuss the peace treaties with the defeated AXIS POWERS, Germany and Japan excepted. The treaties were thereafter drafted by the COUNCIL OF FOREIGN MIN-ISTERS in New York City in November and December, 1946. By their terms the defeated nations were required to pay REPARATIONS in the sum of $70,000,000 (Bulgaria), $300,000,000 (Rumania and Hungary), and $360,000,000 (Italy). The armies of these nations were limited to small police forces of 55,000 to 185,-000 men. Italy was stripped of all her African colonies, their control going to Great Britain pending ultimate United Nations disposal. Trieste was made a free TERRITORY. Small border areas were transferred from Italy to France and Yugoslavia and the Dodecanese Islands were ceded to Greece. Transylvania was ceded by Hungary to Rumania and the latter also confirmed the prior cession of Bessarabia to the Soviet Union. Hungary lost additional territory to Czechoslovakia. Limits were placed upon the navies, air forces, and armed divisions of the defeated nations. All the treaties limited border fortifications and prohibited the use of torpedo boats. The free right of all nations to navigate on the Danube River was recognized. Discrimination against races and religions was forbidden. Equal trading rights to all countries were provided for and the defeated powers agreed to repay CITIZENS of the United Nations two-thirds of the value of property lost in those countries as a result of the war. The United States did not sign the peace TREATY with Finland, not having been at war with that nation.

PEALE, Charles Wilson. 1741-1827. Portrait painter. Studied with COPLEY and WEST; served as an officer in Revolution; became an engraver in Philadelphia (1781?-90); helped found the Pennsylvania Academy of Fine Arts (1805); best known for his many portraits of GEORGE WASHINGTON, FRANKLIN, JEFFERSON, CLAY, etc.

Pearl Harbor. American naval base acquired on lease from Hawaii in 1889. It was the scene of the attack on 86 ships of the fleet stationed there by 100 Japanese planes and several SUBMARINES, on December 7, 1941, which brought the United States into World War II. The losses suffered were extreme, including 177 planes, five battleships, and five other vessels lost, and damage to three battleships, three cruisers, and two other vessels. American casualties were 2343 dead, 960 missing, and 1272 wounded. The Japanese lost 48 planes and three submarines.

"Pearl of the Antilles." See Cuba.

PEARY, Robert Edwin. 1856-1920. Arctic explorer. b. Pennsylvania. Graduated,

Bowdoin (1877); draftsman, U.S. Coast and Geodetic Survey, Washington, D.C. (1879-81); civil engineer, U.S. Navy (from 1881); many voyages to Greenland and on third trip tried to reach the North Pole, but failed (1893-95); on his fourth trip he reached the farthest north in the American arctic (1898-1902); reached the North Pole (1909); retired from navy as rear admiral (1911). Author of several books on his arctic explorations.

Pendleton Act. Enacted in 1883 as the first significant CIVIL SERVICE REFORM measure. The law established a bi-partisan CIVIL SERVICE COMMISSION of three members charged with the duty of administering a partial MERIT SYSTEM in the federal service. The Act resulted from the public pressure engendered by the assassination of President GARFIELD by a disappointed office seeker. Under its provisions the federal service was to be partially classified into grades to which appointments were to be made on the basis of success in competitive examinations. These classifications have subsequently been extended to encompass virtually all positions below that of CABINET or agency head rank. The bill also forbade political assessment on office holders or removals from office for failure to make voluntary contributions to political campaigns.

PENDLETON, Edmund. 1721-1803. Jurist. b. Virginia. Important leader in pre-Revolutionary activities in Virginia; member, House of Burgesses (from 1752); member, COMMITTEE OF CORRESPONDENCE (1773); member, CONTINENTAL CONGRESS (1774-5); president, COMMITTEE OF SAFETY (1775); governor of Virginia (1774-76); presiding judge, Virginia supreme court of appeals (1779-1803).

PENDLETON, George Hunt. 1825-1889. Lawyer and political leader. b.

Ohio. Admitted to the bar, Cincinnati (1847); member, U.S. House of Representatives (1857-65); U.S. Senator (1879-85); largely responsible for CIVIL SERVICE bill (1883) requiring competitive examinations;. U.S. Minister to Germany (1885-89).

PENFIELD, William Lawrence. 1846-1909. Jurist. b. Michigan. Studied law and practiced in Indiana; solicitor, U.S. DEPARTMENT OF STATE (1897-1905); important for handling of various State Department negotiations after the Spanish-American War and representing the United States before international arbitral tribunals; well-known authority on international law.

Peninsular Campaign. A series of battles which began on March 17, 1862, when the ARMY OF THE POTOMAC, under General MC CLELLAN, began its embarkation from Alexandria, Virginia, and ended on July 1st. The campaign was part of McClellan's plan to advance on Richmond by way of the peninsula formed by the junction of the York and James Rivers. The first battle was fought as a siege of Yorktown which was surrendered to McClellan on May 3rd. By May 20th he had succeeded in pushing to the Chickahominy River where he was faced by General JOSEPH E. JOHNSTON. The Battle of Fair Oaks on May 31st and June 1st ended without victory for either army and led to mutual withdrawals for the building up of reserves. Ultimately reinforced, McClellan planned to resume the offensive but was frustrated by LEE's attack at Mechanicsville on June 26th. The Seven Day's Battle which followed was marked by McClellan's steady retreat to his base at Harrison's landing, with intermittent battles at Gaines' Mill, Allen's Farm, Glendale, and Maleverne Hill. The unsuccessful Union campaign ended on July 1st with McClellan's withdrawal to his base. With the appointment of General HALLECK on July 11 to command the army, the withdrawal of the Army of the Potomac from the peninsula began. Union casualties totalled 15,000 while Confederate casualties were estimated at 20,-000.

PENN, William. 1644-1718. Founder of Pennsylvania colony. b. London. Studied law at Oxford; joined the SOCIETY OF FRIENDS; imprisoned in the Tower of London; preached RELIGIOUS TOLERATION and entered into various political campaigns (1675-80); when made a trustee and manager of the West Jersey colony he played an important part in the writing of the charter and the Concessions and Agreements (1677); in payment of a debt owed to his father by the crown, he was granted Pennsylvania (1681); successful governor of the colony granting a government that met the demands of the colonists; made peace TREATIES with the Indians; directed the building and general planning of Philadelphia; ordered the first public grammar school in Philadelphia (1689); granted a liberal charter to the colony (1701); considered an outstanding colonial leader.

PENNELL, Joseph. 1860-1926. Etcher and illustrator. b. Philadelphia, Pennsylvania. Outstanding American graphic artist represented in ART collections all over the world.

Pennsylvania. The 33rd state in size, with an area of 45,333 square miles. Entered the Union on December 12, 1787 as the second state. Harrisburg is the capital. In 1950 Pennsylvania's POPULATION of 10,498,012 made it third in rank. Its largest cities are Philadelphia, Pittsburgh, and Erie. Pennsylvania is one of the most important heavy industry states in the union. It produces almost one half of the nation's IRON and STEEL, most of it centered around Pittsburgh which is the focus of the greatest metal produc-

tion of one locality in the world. Other important manufactures are engines, locomotives, electrical machinery, TEXTILES, automotive equipment, silk products, blast furnaces, and knit goods. The state contains virtually the entire anthracite COAL deposits of the nation. Leading farm crops include buckwheat, potatoes, corn, WHEAT, barley, hay, TOBACCO, apples, and peaches. Pennsylvania is rich in Americana, having been the site of the NATIONAL CAPITAL, the signing of the DECLARATION OF INDEPENDENCE and Constitution, and important Revolutionary and Civil War battles. The state was discovered by HENRY HUDSON in 1609. Its nickname is the "Keystone State."

Pennsylvania Railroad. The principal railroad linking the Atlantic seaboard with the mid-West. It was begun in 1846 for the extension of lines from Philadelphia and Harrisburg to Pittsburgh. The line between Philadelphia and Pittsburgh was completed in 1852. The railroad provided outstanding service in transporting troops and equipment during the Civil War. After the war it grew rapidly, aiding the development of Philadelphia by linking it to the wealth of the West. In 1952 the system operated almost 12,000 miles of track under some 60 CORPORATIONS. It serves 13 states.

"Penny Press." The NEWSPAPERS of the 1830's-1850's which came into existence "to lay before the public, at a price within the means of everyone, all the news of the day." The quotation is from the announcement of Benjamin H. Day who published the *New York Sun* on September 3, 1833, to sell for a penny. The widespread educational movement and increased literacy of the Jacksonian era demanded a cheap press with a broad popular appeal. The headlines, lively news stories, and powerful editorials were characteristic of the "penny press." By 1836 the *Sun* was selling 27,-

487

000 copies daily as compared with a circulation of 1,700 copies for the most successful of the six-penny papers in New York City. Almost immediately other penny papers came into existence under the editorship of some of the nation's most prominent journalists. These included the *New York Herald* (1835, JAMES GORDON BENNETT), *New York Tribune* (1841, HORACE GREELEY), *New York Times* (1851, HENRY J. RAYMOND), *Chicago Tribune* (1855, Joseph Medill), and the *Philadelphia Press* and *Springfield (Massachusetts) Republican.*

Penology. See prison reform.

Pension Grabs. Attempts by Congress in the 1870's and 1880's to satisfy individual Civil War veterans whose applications for PENSIONS had been, or were likely to be, rejected by the Bureau of Pensions. Whereas, in 1866, expenditures for federal pensions totalled only $15,-450,000, in 1895 this amount had risen to $139,812,000. Between 1866 and 1917 Congress had appropriated more than $5,000,000,000 for Civil War veterans. The first law of 1862, and its AMENDMENTS, had provided pensions for disabled veterans and for dependents of those who had been killed or injured in service. In 1879 this amount aggregated $29,000,000. From 1864 to 1904 Congress attempted amendments virtually every year for the purpose of increasing disability benefits. The success of these amendments raised the pension rolls from 126,722 in 1866 to 933,529 in 1900. During CLEVELAND's first administration economy programs led him to VETO 233 pension bills on the grounds that most of them would provide a list for "imposters" rather than a "roll of honor." Cleveland, however, signed more private bills than he vetoed and during his first administration the annual appropriation for pensions was increased from $56,000,000 to $81,000,000. He reorganized the Bureau of Pensions and carefully examined all private pension bills referred to him by Congress. The loosest of all the pension laws was that passed in 1879, providing that all payment could be made in arrears from the day of death or discharge from military service. Such back payments could be made on all pensions already allowed and on those to be granted later. This was revised in March, 1879, because of public disapproval, allowing arrears to be paid only on applications filed before July 1, 1880. Pension grabs virtually ended with the Act of 1904 which transformed all previous legislation into a straight service pension measure by allotting monthly payments of six to 12 dollars, depending on age, to all Civil War veterans of 90 days service and over 62 years of age.

Pensions, Old Age. See Social Security Act.

Pensions, Veterans. Financial payments to veterans of the United States who have served in all wars including the Indian wars. These allowances are also granted to members of the regular armed services in peace time. They vary according to length of service, disability, and indigence. At one time pensions were also offered as an inducement to enlistment. The first pension law was passed by Congress in 1818 and the first pension for widows of Revolutionary veterans in 1836. Pension costs to the federal government have increased enormously. Before 1861 the total payment had exceeded $90,000,000 but by 1918 the cost was almost $5,500,000,000. By 1937 the figure was $12,883,000,000. In 1952 it was not yet possible to determine the aggregate pension costs arising out of World War II. In 1951 Congress' Pension Act provided for the payment of $120 a month to veterans disabled by non-service injuries.

People's Party. See Anti-Monopoly Party.

PEPPERELL, Sir William. 1696-1759.

General. b. Maine. Successful merchant; member of governor's council (1727-59); chief justice of Massachusetts (1730); cooperated with British in attack on French fortress at Cape Breton and made a colonel (1745); created a baronet, the first American to receive this honor (1746); raised regiment for French and Indian War and made lieutenant general (1759).

Pequot Indians. A tribe of Indians in New England who frequently fought against the colonists. Although they negotiated a TREATY with the colonists in Boston in 1634 they waged war against them. The Pequots originated as a former ALGONQUIN tribe in Connecticut, but later merged with the Mohegans. When the settlers came to New England a band, under UNCAS, seceded, retaining the name Mohegan. In 1637 they were nearly annihilated and many of them were sold as slaves. The remainder were dispersed. There are about 3,000 Pequots today.

PERKINS, Frances. 1882-1965. Social worker and cabinet officer. b. Boston, Massachusetts. Graduated Mt. Holyoke College (1902); Columbia University (M.A. 1910); executive secretary, New York Consumer's League (1910-12); New York Committee of Safety (1912-17); authority on industrial hazards and hygiene; lobbyist in Albany for better factory conditions; appointed chairman, New York State Industrial Board (1926-29); Industrial Commission of N. Y. State (1921) to enforce factory and labor laws; appointed U.S. Secretary of Labor, by F. D. ROOSEVELT (1933), the first woman cabinet member; supported UN-EMPLOYMENT INSURANCE, CHILD WEL-FARE, and better labor conditions; her appointment was met with opposition, but she administered her position with great efficiency; member, U. S. CIVIL SERVICE COMMISSION (1946). Author of books on labor problems and *The Roosevelt I Knew* (1946).

Perkins vs. Elg. A decision of the United States Supreme Court in 1939 establishing the doctrine that natural born citizens may not be involuntarily denaturalized. Miss Elg had been born in the United States of a Swedish mother and a NATURALIZED American father both of whom returned with her to Sweden where the father renounced his American CITIZENSHIP. After returning to the United States in 1939 she was notified by Secretary of Labor PERKINS that she was an alien illegally in the United States, and subject to deportation. The court upheld Miss Elg's claim to citizenship under the FOURTEENTH AMENDMENT and argued that since she had not voluntarily relinquished her natural born citizenship she could not involuntarily be deprived of it.

Permanent Court of Arbitration. Also known as the Hague Tribunal. Established by the first HAGUE CONFERENCE in 1899. Each of the 45 member nations of the convention may choose not more than four individuals as members of the Court. These members constitute a panel from which the nations signing an agreement to arbitrate may choose as many as they desire. Thus a special tribunal is chosen for each case. Unless specified to the contrary all tribunals meet at the Hague. Administration of the Court is supervised by a permanent Counsel and a Bureau of Registry. By the opening of World War I the Hague Tribunal had decided 14 cases although the enforceability of its decisions was constantly in question.

Permanent Court of International Justice. Popularly known as the World Court. The international tribunal established by Article XIV of the Covenant of the LEAGUE OF NATIONS. The functions of the court were to hear and determine international disputes and to render advisory opinions in matters referred to it by the Council or Assembly of the League. The statute of the Court was principally drawn up by ELIHU ROOT, former Secretary of War and Secretary of State of the United States. Although the United States never became a member of the Court four prominent Americans served it as judges; John Bassett Moore, CHARLES EVANS HUGHES, FRANK B. KELLOGG, and Manley O. Hudson. The opposition of irreconcilable ISOLATIONIST Senators, using the argument that membership was "the backdoor to the League," prevented entry. In 1926 the Senate voted adherence to the Court with five reservations. The last and the most serious of these declared that the Court could not without the consent of the United States "entertain any request for an advisory opinion touching any dispute or question in which the United States has or claims an interest." The Court refused to accept this reservation. In 1929 an attempt was made to amend the statute of the Court to meet the objections of the United States. The ROOT PROTOCOL was accepted by the other members but the Senate nevertheless voted down American entry.

PERRY, Matthew Calbraith. 1794-1858. Naval officer. b. Rhode Island. Strong supporter of naval steamships; superintended the building of the *Fulton*, one of the first naval steamships which he commanded with the rank of captain (1837); served during the Mexican War; sent on mission to open trade with Japan and succeeded (1854).

PERRY, Oliver Hazard. 1785-1819. Naval officer. b. Rhode Island. Commissioned to build, equip and man a fleet at Lake Erie; fought battle of Lake Erie (1813); forced surrender of British fleet; famous for his dispatch to General HARRISON; "WE HAVE MET THE ENEMY AND THEY ARE OURS."

PERSHING, John Joseph. 1860-1948. Army commander. b. Missouri. Graduated, U.S.M.A., West Point (1886);

served in CUBA (1898); PHILIPPINES (1899-1903); brigadier general (1906); commanded force sent into Mexico to capture FRANCISCO (PANCHO) VILLA (1916); major general (1916); commander in chief, A.E.F. (1917-19); general (1917); chief of staff, U.S. Army (1921-24).

Personal Liberty Laws. Enacted by 10 northern state legislatures after the passage of the COMPROMISE ACT OF 1850. The aim of the laws was to overcome the effects of the fugitive slave provisions of the federal act. They attempted to accomplish this by forbidding their officers to aid in the arrests of fugitive slaves, denying the use of their jails for the detention of such fugitives, and ordering their courts to provide jury trials for all seized Negroes.

"Pet Banks." The state-chartered banks into which President JACKSON placed the federal funds after their withdrawal from the BANK OF THE UNITED STATES in 1833. By 1836, 89 "pet banks" acted as depositories for these funds.

Petroleum Administration for War. An agency established by EXECUTIVE ORDER on December 2, 1942 for the purpose of coordinating the government's PETROLEUM policies and seeing to it that oil was provided for the prosecution of the war and other essential purposes. HAROLD ICKES was appointed Administrator and given extreme authority concerning the conservation, RATIONING and TRANSPORTATION of petroleum.

Petroleum Industry. See oil industry.

Philadelphia. The fourth largest city in the United States. Its 1960 population of more than 2,000,000 occupies a combined land and water area of 135 square miles. Philadelphia, popularly known as the "City of Brotherly Love," was first settled in 1681 by Captain William Markham, leading a group of colonists sent by WILLIAM PENN. By 1685 the city

490

had a population of 7,000, and was already developing its physical properties on the basis of a general plan laid out by Penn. Up to the American Revolution it surpassed all other colonial cities in industry, COMMERCE, EDUCATION, and the ARTS and SCIENCES. The TWO CONTINENTAL CONGRESSES met there in 1774-76, and it was the capital of the United States under the ARTICLES OF CONFEDERATION from 1781 to 1783. In 1790 it became the second capital of the United States under the present Constitution, remaining the seat of its government until 1800. Philadelphia is one of the important industrial areas of the world, producing important quantities of ships, rolling stock, electronic equipment, and textiles. It produces more than half of the surgical instruments manufactured in the United States. A suburb is the site of the Baldwin Locomotive Plant, the largest in the world. Its important historical landmarks include INDEPENDENCE HALL, the LIBERTY BELL, and the Congress Hall.

Philadelphia Orchestra. One of the most famous symphonic organizations in the United States. It was founded in 1900 by Fritz Scheel. It gave its first public concert on November 16, 1900. Among its famous conductors have been Felix Weingartner, Willem Mengelberg, Fritz Reiner, Alexander Smallens, ERNST BLOCH, Vincent D'Indy, Sergei Rachmaninoff, and Igor Stravinsky. Its most notable permanent conductor was LEOPOLD STOKOWSKI who served from 1912-38. The Philadelphia Orchestra gave its 5,000th concert in 1949.

Philadelphia Plan. In 1969 the federal government reacting to criticism that Blacks and other minorities were not being hired into construction jobs passed a law requiring all federal construction contractors to hire Blacks and other minorities. This plan, known as the Philadelphia Plan, sparked a good deal of controversy. Philip Davis,

Director of the Labor Department Office of Federal Contract Compliance, felt that the plan resulted in significant gains in minority construction employment. On the other hand, George Meany, President of the AFL-CIO, denounced the Philadelphia Plan and its trend-setting approach to increasing minority employment in the construction industry.

PHILIP, King. Indian name Metacomet. d. 1676. Indian chief. Son of MASSASOIT. Leader of the WAMPANOGAS (from 1662); led Indians against the English settlers; responsible for KING PHILIP'S WAR (1675-76) against the New England colonies; burned many towns and slaughtered many colonists before being killed in a raiding party (Aug. 12,1676).

Philippine Commission. See Taft Commission.

Philippine Independence Act. See McDuffie-Tydings Act.

Philippine Islands. A republic established in 1946 by the MCDUFFIE-TYDINGS ACT of 1934. It is the northeastern part of the Malayan Archipelago, comprising all large and several thousand smaller islands. Its population of 19,-500,000 people lives in an area of 114,-400 square miles, and consists of a mixture of native Filipinos, Chinese, Japanese, Americans, and others. Manila, the capital and chief port, has a population of 1,000,000. Other important cities are Cebu, Davao, and Zamboanga. The principal languages are Tagalog, Spanish and English, although 64 other languages and dialects are spoken. Roughly 80 per cent of the people are Roman Catholic, the remainder being Mohammedan and Protestant. The Archipelago was first discovered by Magellan in 1521 and claimed for Spain. It was ceded to the United States in 1898 under the terms of the TREATY OF PARIS. A civil-military government was established for the Islands in 1901 which was modified by the JONES ACT OF 1916 and the Mc-Duffie-Tydings Act of 1934. During World War II a commonwealth government-in-exile carried on the struggle against the Japanese until the recapture of the Islands by the United States in 1944. The outstanding president of the Philippine Islands was MANUEL QUEZON.

PHILLIPS, David Graham, 1867-1917. Novelist. b. Indiana. Author of many books dealing with the problems and evils of society which he tried to reform including *The Cost* (1904), *The Conflict* (1911) and *Susan Lenox: Her Fall and Rise* (1917).

PHILLIPS, Samuel. 1752-1802. Industrialist, political leader and philanthropist. b. Massachusetts. Graduated, Harvard (1771); manufactured powder for the Continental army (from 1771); member, Massachusetts provincial congress (1775-80); state senator (1780-1801); known as the founder and benefactor of Phillips Academy, Andover (1778) the first endowed academy in America; lieutenant governor of Massachusetts (1802).

PHILLIPS, Wendell. 1811-1884. Orator and reformer. b. Boston, Massachusetts. Graduated, Harvard (1831); admitted to the bar (1834); important ABOLITIONIST associated with GARRISON; president, Anti-Slavery Society (1865-70); prominent orator ranking with WEBSTER in ability; worked for penal reforms, and WOMAN SUFFRAGE.

Philosophy. Colonial philosophy was controlled by Calvinist theology which in New England was expressed in the writings of JOHN COTTON and JOHN WINTHROP. Calvinist orthodoxy, based on rigid discipline, a state church, theocratic government, and the Puritan ideals was challenged in the latter third of the 18th century by the religious philosophy of Deism. The scientific and natural law concepts of 18th century French Rationalism were incorporated into the thinking of BENJAMIN FRANKLIN, THOMAS JEFFERSON, JAMES MADISON, and THOMAS PAINE. After the Revolution, rationalism became dominant and the writings of W. E. CHANNING and BENJAMIN RUSH. The HUMANITARIAN REVOLT of the Jacksonian era revealed itself strongly in the philosophy of TRANSCENDENTALISM whose most distinguished spokesmen were RALPH WALDO EMERSON, THEODORE PARKER, and HENRY DAVID THOREAU. The intellectual life of the GILDED AGE was the most profound in American culture. Charles S. Pierce, WILLIAM JAMES, and JOSIAH ROYCE pioneered new philosophical schools. Idealism received its fullest expression in Royce's *Religious Aspects of Philosophy* and *The World and the Individual*. Pierce's *How to Make our Ideas Clear* (1878) laid the groundwork for the philosophy of Pragmatism, elevated by William James into the most significant philosophical advance in 20th century America in his *Pragmatism* (1907). The first third of the 20th century witnessed the development of pragmatic thinking in the Instrumentalism of JOHN DEWEY who upheld the use of logic and scientific method as an instrument of reform of social evils. In the latter part of this period GEORGE SANTYANA and Irwin Edman contributed important analyses of aesthetics.

Phonograph. Although experiments in reproducing machines had been conducted as early as 1807 the first practical phonograph was patented in 1877 by THOMAS A. EDISON. Edison exhibited his machine at Menlo Park, New Jersey to thousands of interested observers. It was not generally available because of its costliness. Whereas Edison had used cylinders for recording, the disc was introduced in 1888 by Emil Berliner. Some years later Edison changed over to this method of recording. The appearance of the phonograph in public amusement places stimulated a growing public interest.

PHYFE, Duncan. 1768-1854. Cabinetmaker. b. Scotland. Came to America (1783?); apprenticed to cabinetmaker in Albany (1784); had shop in New York City (from about 1792); famous for his chairs, tables, sofas, settees, and sideboards.

PICKENS, Andrew. 1739-1817. Revolutionary general. b. Pennsylvania. Lived in South Carolina (1763); served at Cowpens (1781) during the Revolution; brigadier general (1781); captured Augusta, Georgia (1781); fought against the CHEROKEES; member, U.S. House of Representatives (1793-95).

PICKENS, Francis Wilkinson. 1805-1869. Statesman. b. South Carolina. Lawyer; member, U.S. House of Representatives (1834-43); supported NULLIFICATION; U. S. Minister to Russia (1858-60); governor of South Carolina (1860-62) supported SECESSION.

PICKERING, Edward Charles. 1846-1919. Astronomer and physicist. b. Massachusetts. Graduated, Lawrence Scientific School, Harvard; professor of physics, Massachusetts Institute of Technology; professor of astronomy and director of observatory, Harvard (1877-1919); known for his investigations in photographic photometry and spectroscopy; famous for his "photographic library of the sky."

PICKERING, Timothy. 1745-1829. Statesman. b. Massachusetts. Graduated, Harvard (1763); admitted to the bar (1768); member, COMMITTEE OF CORRESPONDENCE (1774-75); adjutant general of Continental army (1777-78); quartermaster general (1780-83); member, CONSTITUTIONAL CONVENTION (1789-90); U.S. Postmaster General (1791-95); U.S. Secretary of War (1795);

U.S. Secretary of State (1795-1800); chief justice, court of common pleas, Massachusetts (1802-3); U.S. Senator (1803-11); member U.S. House of Representatives (1811-17); leader of ESSEX JUNTO; strong FEDERALIST.

PICKERING, William Henry. 1858-1938. Astronomer. b. Massachusetts. Graduated, Massachusetts Institute of Technology; member, staff of Harvard Observatory (1887); known for discovery of Phoebe, 9th satellite of Saturn and predicted the existence and location of Pluto the 9th planet (1919).

Picketing. The concerted patrolling of a business establishment by workers on STRIKE. Its purpose is to dissuade persons from entering and carrying on business with the struck firm. Picketing has ranged from peaceful persuasion to violence. Historically, unions have always picketed as an economic weapon in carrying on strikes. The Philadelphia cordwainers employed the picket line in its strike in the first decade of the 19th century. Picketing came under the ban of the conspiracy doctrine until that principle was eliminated from LABOR RELATIONS in 1842. Many state and United States court decisions have established the law of picketing. In 1952 the basic judicial doctrines laid down held that peaceful picketing was legal, but prohibited violence or other illegal activities.

PICKETT, George Edward. 1825-1875. Confederate general. b. Virginia. Graduated, U.S.M.A., West Point (1846); served in the Mexican War; entered Confederate service (1861); brigadier general (1862) major general (Oct. 1862); served brilliantly at FREDERICKSBURG and at GETTYSBURG where "Pickett's charge" was the outstanding military feat of the war.

Pick-Sloan Plan. A plan authorized by Congress in 1944 for the exploitation of the water, soil, and land resources of the 10 states in the Missouri River Valley. It coordinated the programs of the Army Corps of Engineers and the BUREAU OF RECLAMATION in the development of the 529,000 square mile valley. The program had as its objectives the development of soil and water CONSERVATION work to supplement the soil, flood control, and conservation operations of other federal agencies. The plan has been opposed as inadequate. A HOOVER COMMISSION report dismissed it as "in no sense an integrated development plan for the (Missouri) Basin." When the disastrous Missouri River flood of April, 1952 struck, President TRUMAN, after a visit to the area, blamed Congress for its refusal to appropriate funds for this and other valley projects.

"Piece of party perfidy, a." See Wilson-Gorman Tariff Act.

Piedmont region. The area of the eastern colonies in the foothills of the easternmost Appalachian Mountains. Known as the back country it was connected to the coastal TIDEWATER AREA by the FALL LINE and was the first western region into which immigrants from the tidewater moved at the beginning of the 18th century. Basically these immigrants were small farmers, fur traders, hunters, and small merchanst who left the aristocratic influence of the coast to seek more democratic opportunities in the foothills. It is generally acknowledged that the characteristics of the American personality which are attributed to frontier existence first derived from life in the Piedmont.

PIERCE, Franklin. 1804-1869. Fourteenth President of the United States. b. New Hampshire. Graduated, Bowdoin College (1824); admitted to the bar (1827); practised in New Hampshire, strong JACKSONIAN democrat; member, U.S. House of Representatives (1833-37); U.S. Senator (1837-42); rose to rank of brigadier general in Mexican War (1847); elected President of the United States (1853-57); during his term of office the GADSDEN PURCHASE was made and the KANSAS-NEBRASKA BILL passed (1854); did not support LINCOLN during the Civil War and faded from the political scene.

PIERPONT, Francis Harrison. 1814-1899. Statesman. b. Virginia. Strong anti-SLAVERY WHIG who led Unionist forces in Western Virginia when Virginia seceded; elected governor at Wheeling Convention (1861-68).

PIKE, Albert. 1809-1891. Freemason. b. Massachusetts. Studied at Harvard; practised law in Arkansas; commanded Indians in Confederate army; brigadier general; practised law in Memphis and Washington, D.C.; known for writings on subject of freemasonry.

PIKE, Zebulon Montgomery. 1779-1813. Army officer and explorer. b. New Jersey. First lieutenant, U.S. Army (1799); led expedition to headwaters of the Mississippi River (1805-06); explored the old Southwest; discovered peak in Colorado now named Pike's Peak in his honor; pioneered the Sante Fe Trail; brigadier general (1813); killed while commanding troops in Canada (1813).

Pilgrims. Name given to the SEPARATISTS who fled from England to Leyden, Holland in the 17th century in their search for religious freedom. In 1620 they set sail for the New World on the *Mayflower*, landing in the area subsequently called Plymouth. The Pilgrims formed the basis of the Massachusetts Colony. Their migration to the New World was financed by London merchants to whom were turned over for a period of seven years, the products of their labor.

PINCHOT, Gifford. 1865-1946. Political leader and forester. b. Connecticut. Studied forestry in Europe; first professional forester in this country; chief Forest Service, U.S. DEPARTMENT OF AGRICULTURE (1898-1910); involved in the BALLINGER-Pinchot controversy; professor of forestry, Yale (1903-36); founder (with brother Amos) of Pinchot School of Forestry, Yale; commissioner of forestry, Pennsylvania (1920-22); governor of Pennsylvania (1923-27, 1931-35); tried to settle the COAL STRIKE (1923).

PINCKNEY, Charles. 1757-1824. Legislator. b. South Carolina. Served in the Revolution; member, CONTINENTAL CONGRESS (1784-87); submitted draft of "Pinckney Draught" a plan for a constitution at the federal CONSTITUTIONAL CONVENTION (1787) parts of which were used in the final CONSTITUTION; governor of South Carolina (1789-92, 1796-98, 1806-08); U.S. Senator (1798-1801); U.S. Minister to Spain (1801-05); member, U.S. House of Representatives (1819-21); made famous speech opposing the MISSOURI COMPROMISE.

PINCKNEY, Charles Cotesworth. 1746-1825. Statesman. b. South Carolina. Educated in England and admitted to the bar; member, COUNCIL OF SAFETY (1776); served in Revolution; captured by British and exchanged (1782); brevetted brigadier general (1783); member, federal CONSTITUTIONAL CONVENTION (1787); assisted in drafting the Constitution; U.S. Minister to France (1796); part of XYZ mission to France and reputed to have said "Millions for defense, sir, but not one cent for tribute!"; unsuccessful FEDERALIST candidate for Vive-President (1796) and for President (1804-1808).

PINCKNEY, Thomas. 1750-1828. Diplomat and statesman. b. South Carolina. Educated at Oxford and admitted to English and American bar (1774); served on GATES' staff during the Revolution; wounded and captured at Camden; governor of South Carolina (1787-89); U.S. Minister to Great Britain (1792-94); sent as special commissioner to Spain to negotiate treaty settling boundary disputes and NAVIGATION rights on the Mississippi River; unsuccessful FEDERALIST candidate for the vice-presidency (1796); member, U.S. House of Representatives (1797-1801).

Pinckney Treaty. Also known as the Treaty of San Lorenzo. A treaty between the United States and Spain in 1795 settling the long standing problems of the Florida-United States boundary and the navigation of the Mississippi River. By its terms Spain accepted the boundary claims of the United States, reopened trade relations with the United States, and provided for the free navigation of the Mississippi by American citizens with the right of deposit at New Orleans. The Treaty also provided for the establishment of a mixed commission to settle claims arising over Spain's capture of American neutral vessels during the wars of the French Revolution.

PINKNEY, William. 1764-1822. Statesman. b. Annapolis, Maryland. Admitted to the bar (1786); commissioner to England under JAY'S TREATY (1796-1804); with MONROE sent on special mission to England (1806); U.S. Minister to England (1806-11); U.S. Attorney General (1811-14); participated in the War of 1812; U.S. Minister to Russia (1816-18); prominent lawyer; U.S. Senator (1819-22).

Pioneers. Also called frontiersmen. Those who first migrated westward into the wilderness and established themselves in sparsely settled outlying communities. The economic motivation which stimulated this early WESTWARD MOVEMENT was principally fur-trading and secondarily farming and the search for gold. The Germans and Scotch-Irish who migrated into the Pennsylvania and Virginia backcountry were among the first pioneers. Other settlers moved into the FALL LINE and PIEDMONT AREAS and, as these became settled, migrated farther westward into the Ohio country and the Mississippi Valley. The drives which stimulated this advance movement arose from economic dissatisfaction, the desire for freedom, and motives of adventurism. Cheap land and the opportunity for trade drew thousands of settlers. The life of the pioneers was dangerous and devoid of the comforts of the TIDE-WATER AREA. The LOG CABIN with its rudimentary furniture and housewares was the typical abode. The day was filled with arduous labor which produced only the barest necessities of life. Loneliness, Indian attacks, economic scarcity, and the ravages of nature permitted only the hardiest to survive. Epidemics of disease destroyed populations of entire communities. Social life took the forms of cooperative cabin construction, quilting parties, weddings, camp meetings, and log-rollings. As contributors to the development of a native American culture the pioneers were of the greatest significance.

PITCHER, Molly. Real name Mary McCauley. 1754?-1832. Revolutionary heroine. b. New Jersey. During the BATTLE AT MONMOUTH (June 28, 1778) she carried water to the weary and wounded soldiers in a pitcher and was given the name Molly Pitcher. She is reputed to have taken her husband's place at his gun, but the story has not been verified.

Pittsburgh. The largest iron, steel, and aluminum producing city in the world. Pittsburgh manufactures 25 percent of the steel and 20 percent of the glass of the United States. The city also has the world's largest cork manufacturing factory and pickling and preserving business. Originally Pittsburgh was established as Fort Duquesne in 1754 by Virginia troops. It was subsequently seized by the French and recaptured by the British in 1758, being renamed Fort Pitt. The Department of Fine Arts of the Carnegie Institute conducts an annual exhibition of paintings of international fame. The Carnegie Museum contains more than 5,000,000 objects of scientific, ethnological, and artistic interest. Pittsburgh was incorporated in 1816. In 1950 its population of 676,806 made it 12th in rank among the cities in the United States. It has a combined land and water area of 59.3 square miles, located at the junction of the Allegheny and Monongahela Rivers in western Pennsylvania.

Pittsburgh Landing, Battle of. See Shiloh, Battle of.

"Pittsburgh of the South." The reference to Birmingham, Alabama which became the center of the IRON AND STEEL INDUSTRY in the South after the Civil War. Non-existent in 1861 it was incorporated 10 years later, and began its industrial development with the establishment there in 1886 of the De-Bardeleben Coal and Iron Company. Its 1900 population of 38,000 had grown by 1950 to 326,027. Birmingham's huge steel mills and blast furnaces successfully utilized its resources of coal, iron ore, and limestone. Like its namesake, Birmingham also produces quantities of cars, cement, machinery, stoves, and TEXTILES.

Plantations. In the 17th century the planting of a new settlement either as a colony or as part of one. The system originated in Virginia and spread to the New England colonies. In the 16th century efforts of Gilbert and RALEIGH to establish plantations in the Islands and in the New World had failed. Many such plantations were established under charters granted by the King to JOINT-STOCK TRADING COMPANIES or to individuals. The word also refers to a system of farming on huge landed estates.

Plantation System. The name applied to the division of a colony in the 17th century into smaller units under private ownership. This was done because of the impractical and uneconomic operation of an entire chartered colony. Originating in Virginia, the system had grown as a unit of well-developed independent farms and private plantations when it was transfered to the crown in 1624. The production of staple crops such as TOBACCO, RICE, SUGAR, NAVAL STORES, and COTTON was adaptable to the plantation system, and early showed the need for large LABOR masses. The result was the importation of slaves which by the middle of the 17th century had developed into a flourishing industry. Many plantations were over 1,000 acres in area and employed 100 or more slaves under the direction of a central authority, making it the dominant force in Southern economic life in the era prior to the Civil War. The plantation was a self-supporting community with orchards and fields, slave quarters, barns, tools, work houses, livestock, and domiciles. Determined largely by climate, soil, and topography the plantation system developed in the southern colonies and states, deriving the name the "BLACK BELT" from the wide-spread use of slave labor. Because of their economic dominance, the planters wielded great political and social authority. The plantation system was destroyed by the Civil War and the Reconsrtuction difficulties that followed.

Planters. The class of southern landed slave-holding aristocrats before the Civil War. Basically they constituted the TOBACCO planters, the RICE magnates of South Carolina, and the COTTON growers of the lower south. Their number was small in proportion to the total white population of the south. Of the total southern white population of 8,099,760 in 1860 only 384,000 owned slaves of whom only 10,780 owned 50 or more, and 1733 owned 100 or more. The wealth of the South was concentrated in the hands of this latter group. In 1850 it is estimated that 1,000 families received an income of $50,-000,000 while the remaining 666,000 families received only $60,000,000. Upon this wealth was built a superstructure of social prestige and political power that made the South the balance wheel of national politics through the 1850's. Centered on the imposing southern colonial mansion, was a life of luxury and grandeur which was unmatched elsewhere in the nation at the time. The southern planter rode, hunted, drank, and entertained elaborately. The work of the plantation was supervised by the overseer, a system which permitted the planter and his family to vacation for long periods at fashionable resorts.

Platt Amendment. Comprises a series of clauses drawn up by Senator ORVILLE H. PLATT of Connecticut and added as an amendment to the Cuban constitution in 1902. The amendment provided that CUBA makes no treaties impairing her independence or granting concessions to foreign powers without American consent, that she contract no debts whose service charges could not be met out of current revenues, that she grant the United States two naval stations, and that the United States be permitted to intervene whenever necessary to preserve her independence. Under the "GOOD-NEIGHBOR POLICY" of F. D. ROOSEVELT the Platt amendment was repealed in 1934.

PLATT, Orville Hitchcock. 1827-1905. Lawyer and legislator. b. Connecticut. Studied law; served in Connecticut legislature; U.S. Senator (1879-1905); important Republican; known for PROTECTIVE TARIFF measures; opposed "CHEAP MONEY" schemes; best known for the PLATT AMENDMENT.

Plattsburgh, Battle of. See Lake Champlain, Battle of.

PLATT, Thomas Collier. 1833-1910. Political leader. b. New York. Studied at Yale; banker; became associated with CONKLING; member, U.S. House of Representatives (1873-77); U.S. Senator (1881); resigned over disagreement with President GARFIELD over civil service appointment in New York; powerful Republican leader and largely responsible for election of T. ROOSEVELT as governor of New York (1898).

Pledge of Allegiance. The standard Pledge of Allegiance as set forth in the United States Code was first published in 1892 and is attributed to Francis Bellamy, a Baptist Minister. In the late 1960's some students in the nation's public schools refused to salute the flag and recite the pledge. The United States Second Circuit Court of Appeals in 1973 upheld the right of a high school student to remain seated silently while the pledge was recited.

"Plumbers". In 1971 under the Nixon administration there was organized a Special Investigations Unit within the White House which was given the name "The Plumbers" because they were designed to stop national security leaks. In one of the missions undertaken by this group, the office of the psychiatrist for Daniel Ellsberg was burglarized. This action was planned by G. Gordon Liddy and E. Howard Hunt, Jr. Both of these men were also involved in the break-in of Democratic National Headquarters and in a trial were found guilty.

Plumb Plan. A Plan suggested by Glenn E. Plumb, counsel for the RAILROAD BROTHERHOODS, advocating public ownership of the RAILROADS. The plan was proposed in 1919 as one of the solutions for settling the railroad problem after World War I. The railroads had been taken over and operated by the federal government during the war. The plan suggested their purchase by the government and their operation through a National Railway Operating Corporation. This agency was to be composed one third of railway employees, one third of railway managers, and one third of members appointed by the President. It would pay the government a rental of five per cent out of railroad income, and half of any excess would go to the employees. The Plumb Plan received the official endorsement of the AMERICAN FEDERATION OF LABOR as well as considerable public support. It was opposed by railroad management and by other business groups as being dangerously like socialism. This opposition succeeded in defeating the Plan.

Plymouth Colony. Sometimes called the New Plymouth Colony. The first settlement in Massachusetts. On November 11, 1620, a party of 108 SEPARATISTS from England, called the PILGRIM Fathers, arrived in the harbor of what has since become known as Plymouth, Massachusetts. JOHN CARVER was the first colonial governor. Although the colony existed for almost 70 years, no royal charter was ever granted, the colonists binding themselves to legal obedience by agreement. In 1643 the colony became a member of the NEW ENGLAND CONFEDERATION. By the charter granted to Massachusetts in 1691 it was united with the MASSACHUSETTS BAY COLONY.

Plymouth Rock. The place where the PILGRIMS are believed to have landed in November, 1620. The evidence is controversial, but historians generally accept

498

the authenticity of this story. The Rock has been moved inland from its original spot for greater protection.

POCAHONTAS. Indian name Matoaka. 1595?-1617. Indian princess. Daughter of POWHATAN; known for having saved the life of Captain JOHN SMITH near JAMESTOWN, Virginia; captured by the British and held as hostage at Jamestown; converted to Christianity and married to JOHN ROLFE (1614); went to England and was presented to the King and Queen; died while planning to return to America.

POE, Edgar Allan. 1808-1849. Poet and author. b. Boston, Massachusetts. Adopted by John Allan, a merchant at Richmond, Virginia upon the death of his mother; studied in England and Scotland and for a short time at the University of Virginia (1826); ran away from home (1827); enlisted in the army (1827-29); studied at U.S.M.A., West Point (1830-31); published *Poems* (1831); worked for magazines and wrote many well-known stories such as *The Murders in the Rue Morgue, The Fall of the House of Usher,* and the poems *The Raven, Annabel Lee, The Bells, El Dorado* and many others. Lived in poverty and despondency most of his life. Elected to the American HALL OF FAME (1910).

Poetry. See Literature.

Point Four Program. A plan announced by President TRUMAN in his inaugural address on January 20, 1949 as a "bold new program for making the benefits of our scientific advances available for the improvement and growth of underdeveloped areas." In May, 1950 Congress appropriated $35,000,000 for the first year's program of technical assistance. On June 12-14, 1950, 50 nations in the UNITED NATIONS Economic and Social Council pledged to spend $20,012,500 for programs of soil conservation, IRRI-GATION, technical aid, public health, and associated purposes by December, 1951. The United States declared its policy of granting 60 percent of the amount raised by the U.N. organization. In January, 1951 President Truman recommended to Congress a $900,000,000 program in American investments in Asia, Africa, and Latin America during 1951. Simultaneously, Gordon Gray, head of the Point Four Program, promised economic aid through a modified United States farm price-support system, reduced SUBSIDIES to the maritime industry, TARIFF reductions, and extension of reciprocal trade agreements, all designed to free international trade. In March, 1952 President Truman requested that Congress appropriate $650,000,000 to finance Point Four aid during the fiscal year 1953. In April, Eric Johnston, chairman of the International Development Advisory Board, told a national conference on Point Four problems that the United States was operating technical assistance programs in 33 countries around the globe.

Police Powers. The powers of the state governments in the United States which are designed to protect the public welfare, safety, health, and morals. Their constitutional basis lies in the Tenth Amendment of the federal document which reserves these powers to the states. Although Congress is not given any specific authority to exercise police powers it legislates in the fields of health, welfare, EDUCATION, RECREATION, public works, and LABOR RELATIONS. By the exercise of the "ELASTIC CLAUSE" the effect of this legislation is the same as that of the states' police powers.

Political Action Committee. Also known as the PAC. A political organization established in 1944 by the CONGRESS OF INDUSTRIAL ORGANIZATIONS. SIDNEY HILL-

MAN was its first chairman. In 1952 its national headquarters were located in Washington, D.C. under the leadership of its director Jack Kroll. Although it is theoretically unaffiliated with any POLITICAL PARTY it has consistently endorsed the policies and candidates of the Democratic party. In 1944 it supported FRANKLIN D. ROOSEVELT for re-election and in 1948 it supported HARRY S. TRUMAN. Its program comprises activities for political education and the organization of drives to get voters to register and vote on election day.

Political Activities Act of 1939. See Hatch Act of 1939.

Political Campaign. The activities undertaken by POLITICAL PARTIES in the two or three month period preceding ELECTION DAY. Having nominated their candidates for public office, the parties attempt to influence the voters to support them. The activities include publication and distribution of campaign literature extolling the virtues of their candidates and platforms, the undertaking of radio and television broadcasts, the organization of neighborhood meetings and demonstrations, the house to house canvassing of voters, the placing of newspaper and magazine advertisements, and the direct mailing of political literature to voters.

Political Platforms. The statement of purposes and promises which are drafted as planks at the NATIONAL CONVENTIONS of the POLITICAL PARTIES during presidential election years. It is generally acknowledged that platforms are "not something you stand on, but something you git in on" and are not too seriously accepted by the public as pledges to be fulfilled.

Political Warfare. See Committee of Public Information and Office of War Information.

POLK, James Knox. 1795-1849. Eleventh President of the United States. b. Mecklenburg County, North Carolina. Studied at the University of North Carolina and was admitted to the bar (1820); practised in Tennessee; member, U.S. House of Representatives (1825-39); Speaker of the House (1835-39); supported Jacksonian program; governor of Tennessee (1839-41); was successful "DARK HORSE" candidate for the presidency when VAN BUREN and CALHOUN factions split; President of the United States (1845-49); pushed the ANNEXATION OF TEXAS and supported the Mexican War; more territory was added to the UNITED STATES during his administration than any President with the exception of JEFFERSON; he favored a LOW TARIFF; responsible for the reestablishment of the INDEPENDENT TREASURY SYSTEM which the WHIGS had abolished.

Pollock vs. Farmers' Loan and Trust Company. A decision of the United States Supreme Court in 1895 in which it declared unconstitutional the INCOME TAX law enacted the previous year. This five to four vote held that an income tax, like a property tax, is a direct tax and must therefore be apportioned among the states according to POPULATION. The passage of the 16th amendment in 1913 reversed the effect of this decision.

Poll Tax. Also known as capitation or head tax. It is a tax levied upon a person rather than upon his property and is equal in assessment, thus bearing no relation to the ability to pay. During the colonial period poll taxes were levied in all the British colonies at one time or another. Although the poll tax has been and is collected for many purposes, it is generally associated in the public mind with the right to vote. In 1962 some 35 states imposed poll taxes for various purposes among which was a tax ranging from $1 to $2 per person in the states of Alabama, Arkansas, Mississippi, Texas, and Virginia as a condition for voting. California, Ohio, and Maryland forbid the imposition of such taxes by constitutional provision. The twenty-fourth amendment to the Constitution (1964) outlawed the poll tax as a requisite for voting.

Pomeroy Circular, the. A document sent out early in 1864 by a Republican committee chaired by Senator Pomeroy of Kansas. Its purpose was the solicitation of support within the party for the candidacy of Secretary of the Treasury SAL-MON P. CHASE for President. The move arose out of the split between the conservative Republicans who supported LINCOLN and the Radicals who united in support of Chase. On February 25, 1864 Ohio declared its support for Lincoln, and Chase's hopes for the nomination vanished.

PONCE de LEON, Juan. 1460?-1521. Spanish explorer, discoverer of Florida. b. Leon, Spain; to America with COLUM-BUS on second voyage (1493); helped conquer PUERTO RICO (1508); made governor (1510); founded San Juan (1511); became wealthy from the discovery of gold and the slave trade; searched for the island of Bimini where the Fountain of Youth was supposed to be located and discovered Florida on Easter Sunday (1513); on second expedition to Florida (1521) in an attempt to settle a colony there he was driven off by the natives and fatally wounded; died in CUBA.

POND, Peter. 1740-1807. Fur trader and explorer. b. Connecticut. Served in last of the French and Indian Wars; went to Northwest as fur trader (1765); explored the Upper Mississippi country, Wisconsin and the Lake Superior region, making well-known maps of this territory

which were sent to Congress, copied and supplied to England, France and Russia; joined the Northwest Organization (1783); journeyed into Western Canada.

PONTIAC. d. 1769 OTTAWA INDIAN chief; led Pontiac's War or Conspiracy as it is often called against the British in an attack on Detroit (1763); made peace with the British (1766) and remained friendly.

Pony Express. A method of carrying the overland mail through the Far West in the early 1860's. The system developed into a giant relay in which as many as 80 riders and 420 horses participated in carrying the mail from station to station. At each of the 190 stations the rider was given two minutes in which to transfer his saddle bags to a fresh pony. After a given distance he would hand the mail to another rider, and so on, until his destination was reached. The adventure and glory of carrying the mail in all seasons, over dangerous mountain paths, through hostile Indian lands, have furnished the source material of much native American folk lore. The original contract was granted in September 1857 to John Butterfield and his Overland Mail on a 1980 mile route emanating from St. Joseph, Missouri to Sacramento, California. The first mail was carried on April 6, 1860. The original charge of $5 per letter was later reduced to $1. Alexander Majors, the manager, pledged his riders under strict obligations of gentlemanly conduct and kindness to the horses. With the sending of the first telegram through to California on October 24, 1861 the pony express disappeared.

Pool. Also known as "gentlemen's agreement." A form of MONOPOLY organization in the 1860's and 1870's. Pooling in the cordage industry can be traced back to 1861, but its greatest era of growth was the 15 year period after the PANIC OF

1873. Pools in RAILROADS, salt, whiskey, COAL, and TOBACCO were particularly noteworthy. Under this system companies in the same industry divided the market by agreement, placed all profits in a common treasury, and divided them according to the business assigned to each company. By this method competition was effectively stifled. Pooling was frequently unsuccessful because the members of the pool violated the agreement. The INTERSTATE COMMERCE ACT forbade pools in railroads, and by the end of the 1880's this type of monopoly was already being replaced by the TRUST.

POORE, Benjamin Perley. 1820-1887. Journalist. b. Massachusetts E d i t e d *Southern Whig* (1838-41); traveled in Europe; Washington correspondent for a group of New England newspapers including the Boston *Journal* (from 1854); well known for stories under the by-line "Perley"; edited the *Journal of Agriculture* (1857-62); edited the first issue of the *Congressional Directory* (1869); author of biographies and historical works.

"Poor Whites." White persons in the South before the Civil War who did not own slaves and who were beneath farmers, artisans, and frontiersmen in the social scale. It applied generally as a term of stigma to those who lived on the poorest lands in the back country. Their conditions were economically unsound and they were subject to impoverishment and disease.

Popular Sovereignty. In American history this refers to the doctrine that the people of a territory have the right to decide for themselves whether they wish the territory to be admitted to the Union as a slave or free state. As first formulated by Senator LEWIS CASS of Michigan and supported by Senator STEPHEN A. DOUGLAS of Illinois this was to be done by writing a slave or anti-slave clause into the terri-

torial constitution in the petition for admission. The principle was included for the territories of New Mexico and Utah in the COMPROMISE ACT OF 1850 and for the territory of Kansas in the KANSAS-NEBRASKA ACT OF 1854. In political science it refers to the principle that sovereignty of the state resides within the people who therefore possess the revolutionary right to alter a government considered detrimental to the interests of the people. The political philosophy of John Locke, Jean Jacques Rousseau, and THOMAS JEFFERSON expresses this doctrine. In the United States the principle was first stated in the DECLARATION OF INDEPENDENCE.

Popular vote. The BALLOTS cast by the voters for members of the ELECTORAL COLLEGE. Constitutionally the popular vote is of no significance since the President and Vice-President are elected by a majority of the ELECTORAL VOTE. Nevertheless the popular vote is generally important in that the party whose electoral candidates receive a plurality or majority of the popular vote in each state carries that state and is given its total electoral vote. Occasionally candidates with a majority of the popular vote have not been elected. This occurred in 1876 with the election of HAYES, although TILDEN had a popular majority, and again in 1888, when BENJAMIN HARRISON was elected although CLEVELAND had a popular majority. Similarly candidates with a minority of the popular vote have been elected as in the cases of J. Q. ADAMS in 1824, LINCOLN in 1860, WILSON in 1912, and TRUMAN in 1948.

Population. The population of the United States has grown from less than 500 in 1610 (British colonies) to 193,000,000 in 1965. At the outbreak of the Revolution there were approximately 2,500,000 people in the colonies, increasing to 5,308,000 by the end of the 18th century. The census of 1900 showed a population of 75,995,000. The population of the United States has increased both because of the increase in the natural birth rate and, until 1920, of a virtually unlimited IMMIGRATION. For the two centuries preceding the Civil War the rate of growth was 35 percent per decade, declining to about 15 percent each decade after 1910. This rate of increase has been almost the highest in the world. The shift of population has consistently been from rural to urban areas. In the pre-Revolutionary period 95 percent of the American people lived on farms. According to the census of 1960 70 percent now live in urban communities.

Populist Party. Organized as a THIRD PARTY MOVEMENT in 1891 by farmers, westerners, workers and small businessmen. The platform of the party advocated the free and unlimited coinage of silver, the abolition of NATIONAL BANKS, public ownership of RAILROADS, steamship lines, and TELEPHONE and TELEGRAPH SYSTEMS, direct election of United States Senators, and a graduated INCOME TAX. The movement was part of the vast upheaval of agrarian discontent in the post-Civil War period. In the election of 1892 its candidate, JAMES W. WEAVER, received over 1,000,000 POPULAR VOTES and 22 ELECTORAL VOTES, carrying four states. In the mid-term elections of 1894 the party received 1,400,000 votes and elected six Senators and seven Representatives. The party did not run independent candidates in the election of 1896, supporting the Democratic party's candidates.

"Pork Barrel" Legislation. Federal appropriations laws which provide funds for local improvements such as post offices, public buildings, and river and harbor installations. These improvements are of particular benefit only to the districts of those congressmen who sponsor such legislation. The term arises from the custom on the old southern plantation to prepare a specific portion of pork for slaves. "Pork barrel" laws provide an opportunity for "LOG-ROLLING."

PORTER, David. 1780-1843. Naval officer. b. Boston, Mass. Served as commander of the *Essex* in War of 1812, first United States naval vessel used in Pacific waters; he was captured off Valparaiso, Chile (1814); commander-in-chief, squadron in the WEST INDIES to suppress piracy (1823-25); court-martialled and suspended from duty for actions contrary to government wishes in PUERTO RICO (1825-26); resigned from U.S. Navy (1826); served as rear admiral in Mexican Navy (1826-29); resigned to become U.S. consul general to Algiers (1830); U.S. charge d'affaires at Constantinople.

PORTER, Horace. 1837-1921. Army officer and diplomat. b. Pennsylvania, Graduated, U.S.M.A., West Point (1860); served through the Civil War; aide-de-camp to General GRANT (1864-65); received the CONGRESSIONAL MEDAL OF HONOR for heroism at CHICKAMAUGA; served as military secretary to President Grant (up to 1872); vice-president of Pullman Palace Car Company and executive for other railroads (1872-97); U.S. Ambassador to France (1897-1905); delegate to the HAGUE CONFERENCE (1907).

Porter, William Sydney. See O. Henry

Port Folio, The. Sometimes spelled *Portfolio.* One of the earliest scholarly magazines in the United States. It was a monthly established by Joseph Dennie at Philadelphia in 1801. Its contributors included some of the most distinguished writers of the early 19th century. It was the first American periodical to last more than 10 years, being published until 1825.

Port of New York Authority. An independent bi-state CORPORATION created in 1921 by an interstate compact between New Jersey and New York. The agency was established to plan and develop the terminal and TRANSPORTATION facilities, and to improve the COMMERCE of the port area of New Jersey and New York. The Port Authority is administered by a board of 12 commissioners, six from each state, appointed by the governors for six year terms. The agency maintains branch offices in Washington, Chicago, and Cleveland to promote the movement of commerce through the Port of New York. Its representatives appear before the INTERSTATE COMMERCE COMMISSION, CIVIL AERONAUTICS BOARD, and Federal Maritime Board in its efforts to improve traffic conditions in the port area. The agency operates the Lincoln and Holland tunnels, and the George Washington, Bayonne, and Goethals Bridges, as well as the Outerbridge Crossing. It has engaged in a vast program of construction of feeder tunnels, crossings, parkways, and viaducts to accelerate traffic conditions. Its airport facilities include La Guardia Airport, New York International Airport, Newark Airport, and Teterboro Airport. It leases and operates piers, and has constructed terminal buildings in the region.

Portsmouth, Treaty of. At the intercession of President T. ROOSEVELT this treaty ended the Russo-Japanese War on September 5th, 1905. Its terms gave formal approval to Japan's interests and political influence in Korea and southern Manchuria. Areas ceded to Japan included those in which Russia had formerly held special rights such as the Liaotung Peninsula lease, the South Manchurian railway, and the southern half of Sakhalin. As a result of Roosevelt's intercession and contribution to world peace, he was awarded the Nobel Peace Prize in 1906. Japanese resentment against the United States arose out of her inability to obtain an indemnity.

Postal Savings System. Created by Congress in 1910 as a division of the POST OFFICE DEPARTMENT. It receives savings deposits from individuals at specified post offices, paying an interest rate of two percent on such savings. The original maximum deposit of $1,000 was subsequently raised to $2500. The funds of the system are deposited in banks or invested in United States government securities. In 1951 the system had approximately $3,000,000,000 in deposits. Accounts may be opened with as little as one dollar by any person 10 years of age or over.

Postal System. When President WASHINGTON was inaugurated in 1789 there were in the United States only 2,400 miles of post roads and 76 post offices producing annual revenues under $25,000. All rural areas and much of the rest of the country were served only by private postal means. A great expansion of official post roads took place in the Jeffersonian period, after the War of 1812. Stage coaches, first employed as the carriers of mail, were supplemented by railroad service and express companies after 1835. The POST OFFICE DEPARTMENT, established in 1789, has, since that time, supervised the operations of the entire postal system. Through the first half of the 19th century there was considerable opposition to the Post Office Department as a MONOPOLY, a good deal of business going to the express companies. A "cheap postage" therefore was instituted by Congress in 1845, eliminating the competition of the express companies. The Railway Mail Service was inaugurated in 1865 for mail distribution on board trains. Ocean mail contracts were authorized in 1845 and the money order system in 1864, the latter providing a safe and convenient system of transferring funds. Free delivery service was inaugurated in 1863, special delivery service in 1885, rural free delivery in 1896, postal savings in 1910, and parcel post in 1913.

An experimental air mail line was inaugurated in 1918 between Washington, D.C. and New York, being expanded into a transcontinental system by 1920. Transoceanic air mail service was begun over the Pacific Ocean in 1935 and over the Atlantic in 1939.

Post Office Department. On July 1, 1971 after almost two centuries the Post Office Department was reorganized as an independent agency within the executive branch. It is headed by an 11-member board of governors, including a Post Master General. Rate increases are recommended by the Postal Rate Commission.

Potomac, Army of the. See Army of the Potomac.

Potsdam Conference. A meeting of President TRUMAN, Prime Minister Attlee, and Premier Stalin in Potsdam, Germany in July 1945. The Declaration issued on July 26th contained the following provisions: the promise that the UNITED NATIONS would utterly devastate Japan unless she immediately surrendered, the authority and influence of the Japanese leaders who had begun the war were to be eliminated, Japan was to be occupied until a new peaceable government under complete guarantees were established, Japan was to be disarmed, war criminals were to stand trial, freedom of speech, religion, thought, and fundamental HUMAN RIGHTS including democratic principles, were to be permitted in Japan, and Japanese industries for peacetime production were to be allowed for the purpose of producing REPARATIONS in kind. The Declaration ended by the reiteration upon UNCONDITIONAL SURRENDER. The territorial provisions of the CAIRO DECLARATION were repeated in the Potsdam Declaration. The following day the Japanese government broadcast her refusal to accept these terms of surrender, but the dropping of the ATOMIC BOMBS on HIRO-

SHIMA and Nagasaki rendered it unnecessary to invade the Japanese home islands.

POUND, Ezra Loomis. 1885-1972. Poet. b. Idaho. Graduated, Hamilton College and the University of Pennsylvania (1906); traveled in Europe; wrote both prose and poetry for various magazines. Author of *Cathay* (1915), *A Lume Spento* (1908), *Personae* (1909), *Canzoni* (1911), *Ripostes* (1912), *Cantos* (1925-40), and *Polite Essays* (1936). Lived in Italy during the Second World War; became controversial figure as the winner of the Pulitzer Prize for Poetry (1950).

POWDERLY, Terence Vincent. 1849-1924. Labor leader. b. Pennsylvania. Worked as a machinist; joined the KNIGHTS OF LABOR (1874); aided in obtaining alien contract-labor law (1885); instrumental in the establishment of labor bureaus and arbitration and mediation systems in many states; mayor of Scranton, Pa. (1878-84); U.S. Commissioner General of Immigration (1897-1902); chief, Division of Information in the Bureau of Immigration (1907-21). Author of *Thirty Years of Labor*, 1859-1889 (1889).

"Power of the Purse." The power of a legislature to control the executive branch of government by having the exclusive authorization of appropriations and revenues. This doctrine originated in medieval England and was brought to the British colonies where colonial legislatures rapidly gained control over the royal governor. The principle was embodied in the federal Constitution in 1787 in that provision which assigns to the House of Representatives the power to originate revenue legislation.

"Power to tax involves the power to destroy, the." The famous quotation from the opinion of Chief JUSTICE JOHN MARSHALL in the case of MC CULLOCH VS. MARYLAND in 1819. The phrase expresses the court's opinion that no state has the power to tax a federal instrumentality in this instance the BANK OF THE UNITED STATES.

Powhatan Confederacy. A confederation of 30 Indian tribes south of the Potomac River. It was created by Powhatan, its chief, in the first decade of the 17th century at the time of the settlement of JAMESTOWN. The Confederacy numbered 8,000 Indians who were in constant conflict with the settlers under Captain JOHN SMITH. In retaliation for the attempt by Smith to capture him he planned the destruction of the Jamestown settlement, but was prevented from accomplishing this by the warning of his daughter POCAHONTAS to the settlement.

"Prairie Schooner". See Wagon Train.

Preemption. The settling on the PUBLIC LANDS in the pre-Civil War period before such land was purchased or surveyed, with the privilege of purchasing it afterward. For a long time such preemptions were illegal and potentially unprofitable because of the possibility of forceable removal of the squatter and consequent loss of the value of his improvements upon it. Constant pressure by squatters upon Congress brought about the enactment of a series of Preemption Acts between 1801 and 1841 providing legal title to the settled land. See Preemption Acts.

Preemption Acts. A series of 19 land laws passed by Congress between 1801 and 1841 affecting the sale and distribution of the PUBLIC LANDS. All laws prior to 1841 were special acts with the exception of the Preemption Act of 1830 which was the first general land law. The most important of these Acts was the Preemption Act of 1841 which provided for the grant of 160 acres of public lands to any SQUATTER over 21 years of age upon considerations of residence and improvements. The period allowed for payment ranged from 12 to 33 months, the amount varying with the value and location of the tract. The Act was valuable because it allowed squatters to purchase the land upon which they had settled at the minimum price of $1.25 per acre before it was put up for public auction.

Presbyterians. Those who support a system of church government by presbyters, or elders. Originating in Scotland in the 16th century, Presbyterians migrated to the colonies where they established their first church in 1640. Internal conflicts produced schisms in the ensuing years. Questions arose over the issues of revivalism, SLAVERY, and doctrinal interpretation. All groups have been distinguished by their representative form of government and Calvinist philosophy. Among the many dissident organizations were the Cumberland Presbyterian Church (1806), Presbyterian Church in the United States of America (1640), Presbyterian Church in the United States (1861), Reformed Presbyterian (Covenanter) Church (1643), Associate Presbyterian (Seceder) Church (1733), and United Presbyterian Church (1858). In 1965 there were more than 4,383,000 Presbyterians in the United States.

President Pro-Tempore. The presiding officer of the United States Senate, selected by that body when the Vice President assumes the office of the presidency. The president *pro-tempore*, sometimes abbreviated to president pro-tem, serves out the remainder of the Vice President's term.

PRESCOTT, William. 1726-1795. Revolutionary soldier. b. Massachusetts. Colonel of regiment of MINUTEMEN (1775); directed the fortification of Breed's Hill and commanded the troops there the next day at what is called the BATTLE OF BUNKER HILL; served at the evacuation of New York (1776).

506

Presidency. The executive branch of the federal government. It is established in Article II of the Constitution. The chief executive is charged with seeing to it that the laws be faithfully executed. These EXECUTIVE POWERS, however, form merely the nucleus of a widely expanded set of powers which today include administrative, appointive, military, diplomatic, legislative, and judicial functions. Unlike the office of the chief executive in parliamentary systems the American President exercises vast powers combining within his office the political and prestige functions normally divided in the European system. In addition to the above listed authority the American President is also the party head, and the dispenser of PATRONAGE. Through the media of the PRESS CONFERENCE, RADIO, TELEVISION, and the MOTION PICTURE the American President has become the most widely known public figure in the country.

Presidency Terms of Office. The twenty-second amendment stated that no person shall be elected to the Presidency more than twice, and no person who has served as President for more than two years of a term to which some other person was elected shall be elected President more than once. The Amendment was ratified on February 26, 1951.

President and Vice President Replacement. This amendment established that the Vice President shall become President in case of the removal of the President from office or upon his death or resignation. Whenever there is a vacancy in the office of Vice President the President shall nominate a Vice President subject to confirmation by a majority of both Houses of Congress. In addition, there is established a procedure for the Vice President to assume the office of Acting President should the President become disabled. The amendment was used in 1973 when Spiro Agnew resigned from the Vice Presidency and President Nixon nominated Gerald Ford, Congressman from Michigan, to replace Agnew. This amendment was ratified on February 10, 1967.

Presidential Succession Acts. Laws passed by Congress providing for the order of succession to the presidency in the event of the removal, resignation, death, or inability of the President to serve. Constitutionally the Vice-President replaces the President in any of the above instances. The first law of 1792 provided for the succession, after the Vice-President, of the president PRO-TEMPORE of the Senate and the Speaker of the House of Representatives in that order. The Act of 1886 devolved the succession upon the heads of the EXECUTIVE DEPARTMENTS, after the Vice-President. The Act of 1947 revised this to provide for the succession of the Speaker of the House, the president PRO-TEMPORE of the Senate, and the heads of the executive departments in the order of their establishment. The thinking behind the 1947 revision was the belief that a popularly chosen figure rather than a presidentially appointed officer should succeed to the presidency in the event of the deaths of the President and Vice-President.

President, The. A 44 gun frigate completed in New York in 1800. Its initial prominence resulted from its reply with a broadside to the firing of a shot in 1811 by the British vessel *Little Belt*. This action received public acclaim because of the indignities to which the British navy had been subjecting American merchant ships. *The President* fired the first shot in the War of 1812, but gained no decisive victories thereafter. After being blockaded in New York harbor for a year it escaped in January 1815 but was surrounded by several British frigates which compelled her to

507

surrender. Its commander, STEPHEN DE-CATUR, was twice wounded in this battle. Ultimately *The President,* captured by the British in this struggle, was taken by them to Bermuda, but she never served in the British navy.

Press Conference. The meeting of prominent public figures with the press. Its purpose is the solicitation by the newspapermen of the current views and plans of the person interviewed. The press conference was raised to a position of political importance by President F. D. ROOSEVELT who held 988 such meetings, an average of nine every six weeks. In these conferences the President explained his program, illuminated complex political problems, and submitted himself to the critical questioning of the reporters. In his first six years of office President TRUMAN held 256 press conferences.

Press, Freedom of the. Guaranteed in the first amendment of the Constitution. Until 1925 this guarantee was generally considered to apply against infringement by the Congress. As a result of the Supreme Court's decision in 1925 in the case of Gitlow vs. New York, the free press clause of the first Amendment has since been applied against the states as well. The principle of the freedom of the press was originally set down in North America in 1734 in the famous trial of PETER ZENGER.

Press, the. See newspapers.

Price Administration and Civilian Supply, Office of. An agency established by EXECUTIVE ORDER in April, 1941 to administer a limited program of PRICE CONTROL over essential war commodities, allocations of civilian goods, and rationing. The overlapping functions between it and the OFFICE OF PRODUCTION MANAGEMENT led to its abolition in August, 1941 when its price and rationing functions were assumed by the OF-FICE OF PRICE ADMINISTRATION. Civilian supply was transferred to the Office of Production Management.

Price Administration, Office of. An agency established by EXECUTIVE ORDER in August, 1941 as a reorganization of the former OFFICE OF PRICE ADMINISTRATION AND CIVILIAN SUPPLY. It was authorized to issue price schedules on critical commodities such as copper, hides, silk, and steel scrap. Limited in its jurisdiction and enforcement power, the OPA did not succeed in halting overall price increases. In January, 1942 Congress enacted the EMERGENCY PRICE CONTROL ACT, conferring upon the OPA strong powers to impose price ceilings on retail and wholesale commodities and services and on rents not yet controlled. To it was transferred the rationing program which had been a function of the OPACS. The agency was dissolved in June, 1946. See Economic Stabilization Act and Emergency Price Control Act.

Price Control. The attempt of the federal or state governments to halt inflationary price increases by legislating specific commodity price ceilings. The first national effort in this direction was the establishment of the OFFICE OF PRICE ADMINISTRATION AND CIVILIAN SUPPLY IN 1941. See Inflation, Price Administration and Civilian Supply, Office of, Price Administration, Office of, and Price Stabilization, Office of.

Price Stabilization, Office of. An agency established on September 9, 1950 under the authority of the DEFENSE PRODUCTION ACT. It was empowered to stabilize prices during the INFLATION resulting from the Korean War. The agency's first mandatory PRICE CONTROLS were the imposition of a freeze on new automobile prices at the December 1, 1950 level. Subsequently, it announced "voluntary pricing standards" for business and INDUSTRY, asking nationwide compliance so that mandatory price ceilings would be unnecessary. It requested that prices be voluntarily held at their December 1, 1950 levels. On January 26, 1951 it was ordered by the ECONOMIC STABILIZA-TION AGENCY to impose a general price freeze for all commodities and services, on the basis of prices in 'effect from December 19, 1950 to January 25, 1951. On July 31, 1951 the amended Defense Production Act was criticized by President TRUMAN as a measure that would result in increased prices. Subsequently the OPS lifted ceilings on the prices of specific goods and services. The agency was headed by an Administrator under the supervision of the Director of the OFFICE OF ECONOMIC STABILIZATION.

Primary Election. A method by which the voter selects the nominees for office. This preliminary election is conducted from March to September of every year. The first primary "the Crawford County plan," was adopted by Republican party leaders in 1868. Ohio and Pennsylvania safeguarded primaries by law in 1871. By 1952 46 states had adopted the primary election in some form. Primary elections may be either closed or open, the former being restricted only to enrolled party members. Other classifications of primaries include partisan or non-partisan, mandatory or optional, direct primaries, and run-off primaries. Primary elections are used in the nominations of state and municipal officials or delegates to national NOMINATING CONVENTIONS. The direct primary in presidential nominations was introduced in Wisconsin in 1903.

Primogeniture. The English legal principle which held that only the eldest son could inherit the property and estates of his parent. The system existed in all 13 British colonies, although opposition caused it to disappear by the end of the

Revolution. JEFFERSON attacked it as undemocratic. In 1798 Rhode Island was the last state to abolish primogeniture.

Princeton, Battle of. See Trenton, Battle of.

Princeton University. Originally known as the College of New Jersey. It was established by a group of PRESBYTERIANS and chartered in 1746, opening in Elizabethtown, New Jersey, the following year. In 1757 it moved to its present site at Princeton, New Jersey. Many of its graduates contributed to the later founding of the United States and to the writing of many of the most distinguished documents of American history. Among them were its president JOHN WITHERSPOON, RICHARD STOCKTON, and BENJAMIN RUSH all of whom signed the DECLARATION OF INDEPENDENCE. Nine of its alumni including, JAMES MADISON, WILLIAM PATERSON, and OLIVER ELLSWORTH were delegates to the CONSTITUTIONAL CONVENTION in 1787. The College took its present name in 1896 by which time it had established graduate faculties in many fields of scholarly study. Although it was founded by a church group it has nevertheless remained a non-sectarian institution for instruction "in the learned languages, and in the liberal arts and sciences." Its most notable alumnus was President WOODROW WILSON who had previously been a professor of political science and its president.

Printing Industry. Although the first printing press was used in Mexico City in the early 16th century, it was not introduced into English colonies until STEPHEN DAY used one in 1638 to produce a calendar and the BAY PSALM BOOK in Cambridge, Massachusetts. In 1685 WILLIAM BRADFORD employed a printing press in Philadelphia in the production of the KALENDARIUM PENNSILVANIENSE. The early Massachusetts printed matter was basically religious, culminating in the printing of the Bible in 1663. The pre-Revolutionary presses were a flat platen making impressions with a screw against type assembled on a flat bed. The capacity was 50 impressions per hour. In 1810 the revolving cylinder was substituted for the platen, increasing the capacity to 1,000 per hour. Although the printing industry was devoted to the production of legal matter including statutes, proclamations, and other governmental documents, the printing of NEWSPAPERS became important by the opening of the Revolution. In 1756 a complete newspaper was printed in New Hampshire, followed by papers in Georgia in 1763 and the District of Columbia in 1789. The New York SUN introduced a steam printing press in 1835. This new form of power plus the inventions of RICHARD MARSH HOE in 1828 and 1847 increased printing capacity to 20,000 impressions per hour. Further improvements were made by other inventions of Hoe and in the introduction of the WALTER and BULLOCK presses after the Civil War. These presses employed stereotype curved to fit cylinder parts. They became important in the production of newspapers. The speed of printing was further accelerated by the development of methods of forming sheets of paper of desired lengths for feeding to cylinder presses from rolls. Later machines were invented for folding newspapers. In the late 19th and 20th centuries new types of printing surfaces were provided in the form of etchings, steel engravings, photogravure, rotogravure, and lithography. Printing in color was developed by applying inks of different colors to the surface. In 1949 the printing and publishing industry employed 460,000 workers in approximately 29,000 establishments. The value of the product added by MANUFACTURING was $4,659,000,000.

Prison Reform. Prison conditions in colonial America retained medieval characteristics. Punishments included whipping, the stocks, pillories, and ducking. Prisoners were confined in unsanitary quarters and not segregated as to sex or age. In 1787 the Quakers in Philadelphia organized the Society for Alleviating the Miseries of Public Prisons, the first reform organization in America. In 1791 the first penitentiary was established in Philadelphia. Overcrowded conditions, nevertheless, prevented any serious reforms. It was not until the HUMANITARIAN REVOLT of the Jacksonian period that fundamental prison reform was undertaken. In 1824 the Auburn System of silent confinement was established as part of a new system of prison management in Auburn, New York. Correction houses and reform SCHOOLS were founded to meet the special needs of juvenile offenders. By the opening of the Civil War, Auburn-type prisons had been established in all the states except New Jersey and Pennsylvania. The American Prison Association was founded in 1870 to carry out the ideas of such reformers as Enoch C. Wines and Zebulon R. Brockway. These leaders had been strongly influenced by the Irish penal system which maintained the importance of rehabilitation rather than punishment as the aim of imprisonment. In 1877 the New York State Reformatory at Elmira was opened under Brockway's administration to further this experiment. Youthful offenders were separated from hardened criminals and encouraged to reduce their terms through good conduct. Parole and probation were introduced to provide continuing supervision after release. The Elmira plan was quickly adopted in many northern and western states. In the 20th century, psychology, psychiatry, sociology, and MEDICINE have contributed to reform concepts in penology. These new ideals have emphasized occupational therapy, psychiatric care, social work, classification of inmates, the suspended sentence, and compensated labor. Post-release supervision has stressed adjustment to society through the means of employment services, hospitalization, and family care.

Privateering. The preying of private vessels upon enemy naval or merchant ships in time of war. In past periods such vessels were commissioned by the issuance of letters of marque and reprisal. The authority to issue such commissions is vested in Congress by Article I Section VIII of the Constitution. This power is specifically denied to the states in Article I Section X. PRIVATEERING was abolished by the Declaration of Paris in 1856. Although the United States government observed this declaration it did not sign it and thus could not effectively protest against Confederate PRIVATEERING during the Civil War.

Proclamation of 1763. A parliamentary law which organized the government of the provinces of Quebec, East Florida, and West Florida, and laid down the policy to be followed with reference to the Indians and western lands. It placed Indian trade under royal control and provided for the licensing of traders. Colonial governers were prohibited from granting PATENTS for lands beyond the sources of the rivers which flow into the ATLANTIC OCEAN. Private purchases of land from the Indians or settlement beyond the river sources was forbidden. The Proclamation was strongly opposed by the colonists. Land speculators and FRONTIERSMEN attacked the PROHIBITION upon westward migration. Veterans of the French and Indian War, who had been promised western lands, were incensed at the withdrawal from public sale of these territories. Powerful colonists of Virginia and Maryland opposed the curtailment of TRADE provided by the law.

Proclamation of Neutrality. See Neutrality, Proclamation of.

PROCTOR, Redfield. 1831-1908. Lawyer and politician. b. Vermont. Graduated, Dartmouth (1851); practiced law in Boston; served as colonel of Vermont regiment at GETTYSBURG (July, 1863) during the Civil War; as president of Vermont Marble Co. (from 1880) he became well known for his progressive treatment of employees; governor of Vermont (1878-80); U.S. Secretary of War (1889-91) appointed by HARRISON; U.S. Senator (1891-1908) supported strong action at CUBA.

Production Management, Office of. An agency established by EXECUTIVE ORDER on January 7, 1941 to supervise the production and allocation of raw materials in the defense effort. It succeeded the COUNCIL OF NATIONAL DEFENSE, and assumed that agency's authority. Until January, 1942, when it was succeeded by the WAR PRODUCTION BOARD, it shared this responsibility with the SUPPLY, PRIORITIES, AND ALLOCATIONS BOARD. The resulting division of responsibility and overlapping functions interfered with its efficiency. After the attack on PEARL HARBOR, it was, therefore, abolished, and replaced by the WPB. During its life it was led by WILLIAM S. KNUDSEN and SIDNEY HILLMAN as co-chairmen. See Council of National Defense, World War II.

Progressive Citizens of America. A political and lobbying organization created in 1946 for the avowed purpose of carrying on the policies of the NEW DEAL which, as alleged by this group, had been abandoned by the TRUMAN administration. It formed the nucleus of the PROGRESSIVE PARTY OF 1948 which ran HENRY WALLACE as its candidate for the presidency. Among its proposals were the establishment of more amicable relationships with the Soviet Union, the strengthening of the UNITED NATIONS, an improvement in social security legislation, and widespread CIVIL LIBERTIES reform. Its leaders included JO DAVIDSON, the sculptor, Congressman Vito Marcantonio, former governor of Minnesota, Elmer Benson, and former Assistant Attorney General, O. John Rogge.

Progressive Era. Also known as the Age of Reform. The period from 1890 to World War I during which a concerted attempt was made to establish basic reforms in political, economic, and social affairs. The failure to realize the potential of American DEMOCRACY in the preceding century was clearly revealed by the evils and abuses of industrialism by the end of the 19th century. Such evils as child and woman labor, SLUMS, SWEAT SHOPS, concentration of economic power, lobbying, maldistribution of wealth, limited suffrage, city political machines and bosses, bribery and corruption of political officials, labor strife, business MONOPOLIES, anti-Negro prejudice and discrimination, inequitable tax laws, agrarian discontent, and wasteful consumption of the nation's resources aroused widespread national protest. This protest took the form of the writings of the MUCKRAKERS, the development of critical scholarship in the nation's universities, and the passage of federal, state, and local reform legislation. The reforms included the 16TH and 17TH AMENDMENTS, the PURE FOOD AND DRUGS ACT, the MEAT INSPECTION ACT, the FEDERAL RESERVE ACT, the SHERMAN ANTI-TRUST ACT, the CLAYTON ANTI-TRUST ACT, the FEDERAL TRADE COMMISSION ACT, the ADAMSON ACT, the LA FOLLETTE SEAMAN'S ACT, the UNDERWOOD-SIMMONS ACT, the FEDERAL FARM LOAN ACT, and a vast body of state and municipal laws providing for WOMAN SUFFRAGE, the INITIATIVE, the REFERENDUM, the RECALL, the direct PRIMARY,

the SHORT BALLOT, PROPORTIONAL REPRESENTATION, and HOUSING, educational, labor, social security, and welfare reforms. Among the outstanding leaders of the Progressive Era were WOODROW WILSON, THEODORE ROOSEVELT, JOHN ALTGELD, EUGENE V. DEBS, JOHN DEWEY, WILLIAM JAMES, ROBERT M. LA FOLLETTE, GEORGE NORRIS, and the muckrakers.

Progressive Party of 1912. Also known as the Bull Moose party. Organized as a THIRD PARTY MOVEMENT in 1912. It consisted of Republicans under the leadership of former President THEODORE ROOSEVELT, who had broken with the TAFT leadership of that party. The party platform, drawn up at the "Bull Moose" convention, advocated measures of direct government such as the REFERENDUM, RECALL, INITIATIVE, direct PRIMARY, the SHORT BALLOT, WOMAN SUFFRAGE, and the direct election of United States Senators. It approved strong ANTI-TRUST LEGISLATION, TARIFF REFORM, and social measures such as PROHIBITION of CHILD LABOR, the elimination of over-work and night work for women, the protection of factory workers against industrial accidents, and fairer hiring and firing practices for labor. It also advocated the establishment of a federal DEPARTMENT OF LABOR in the CABINET and the liberal extension of credit to FARMERS. Its nominees for the presidency and vice-presidency were Roosevelt and HIRAM JOHNSON of California, respectively. The party received 4,126,020 POPULAR VOTES and 88 ELECTORAL VOTES, running ahead of the Republican party candidates. Its showing so split the Republican vote as to bring about the election of the Democratic candidate WOODROW WILSON.

Progressive Party of 1924. An important minor party which broke away from the

Republican party during the campaign of 1924. Its presidential candidate, Senator ROBERT LA FOLLETTE of Wisconsin, polled 4,822,000 POPULAR VOTES and caried his own state of Wisconsin. Its platform advocated more intensive MONOPOLY control, the ABOLITION of the Supreme Court's power of JUDICIAL REVIEW, extended farm relief, and adoption of such popular political reforms as the INITIATIVE, the RECALL, the REFERENDUM, and the direct election of United States senators. The party also advocated public ownership of utilities, RAILROADS, and water power, the election of federal judges for limited terms, and public referenda on questions of war and peace. It received the support of the AMERICAN FEDERATION OF LABOR and of the SOCIALIST PARTY.

Progressive Party of 1948. A minor party which ran HENRY A. WALLACE and Glen H. Taylor as its candidates for the presidency and vice-presidency. Its membership consisted generally of Democrats who opposed the policies of the TRUMAN administration, radical urban labor groups, and professionals. Its program demanded CIVIL RIGHTS legislation, repeal of the TAFT-HARTLEY ACT, and legislation for HOUSING, welfare, EDUCATION, and public works. Its foreign policy program was based on opposition to the TRUMAN DOCTRINE and MARSHALL PLAN. The party demanded a reconciliation of Soviet-American conflicts. It polled 1,157,-172 votes.

Prohibition. The policy of forbidding the manufacture, TRANSPORTATION, or sale of beverages for intoxicating purposes. Prior to 1920 many states had enacted such legislation, being known thereby as "dry" states. In that year the adoption of the 18TH AMENDMENT authorized Congress to legislate federal prohibition. The passage of the VOLSTEAD ACT in 1919 represented the exercise by

Congress of this power even before the adoption of the 18th amendment. The resulting flagrant violations leading to gangsterism, RACKETEERING, and bootlegging created a wave of public protest and in 1933 the 21ST AMENDMENT repealed the prohibition amendment. Oklahoma and Mississippi were the only two remaining states with prohibition laws in 1956.

Prohibition Party. Still in existence, it is the oldest of the minor parties in the United States. It was organized in 1869 as a result of more than 70 years of TEMPERANCE agitation. Its first campaign took place in 1872 when it nominated James Black of Pennsylvania for the presidency. Its early strength lay in Ohio and New York although nowhere has it been able to win any presidential electors for its candidates. Its greatest success was obtained in 1892 when it polled 271,000 votes. In the election of 1948 its candidate, Claude A. Watson, polled 103,216 POPULAR VOTES. Its program has had the primary object of securing the PROHIBITION of the manufacture and sale of intoxicating liquors. It has also advocated many political, economic, and social reforms, some of which were subsequently adopted by the major parties. Its influence h.. spread principally through educational activities and its appeal to the moral thinking of the American people.

Property Rights. As developed in English common law and in the political philosophy of Thomas Hobbes and John Locke it refers to the right of ownership of private property against public restraint. Property rights, in the evolution of Anglo-American law, have become subject to public control when necessary to protect the PUBLIC WELFARE. This has become particularly recognized in the area of PUBLIC UTILITIES such as TRANSPORTATION, power, COM-

MUNICATION, and water-works. Public restraints are based on a reconciliation of the POLICE POWER and DUE PROCESS doctrines.

Proportional Representation. An electoral reform seeking to give minority parties a share of legislative seats proportional to their VOTING power. By instituting voting-at-large to replace district voting, and giving the voter the opportunity to indicate preferences listed numerically, minority parties are able to elect candidates. In the United States the Hare system has proved the most popular, and has been adopted in many cities.

Proprietary Colony. A type of British colony in North America in the 17th and 18th centuries. Its basis of government was the patent employed by the king in granting lands. The patentee, or proprietor, exercised virtually complete powers in governing the colony, limited only by the terms of the patent, or charter. In relation to the inhabitants the proprietor stood in the same position that the king held in relation to the royal colony. Although the colonists elected the members of the lower house, the proprietor appointed the members of the upper house as well as the governor and administrative officials. Maryland and Georgia were prominent examples of proprietary colonies. From 1664 to 1689 New York was of this type as were the early settlements in New Hampshire and Maine.

Protectionism. The TARIFF policy based on the belief that high tariffs are necessary to protect "infant industries." Until 1816, the United States tariff policy was almost wholly revenue in purpose. The tariff of that year introduced a policy of protectionism that lasted until 1846. The MORILL TARIFF ACT resumed a policy of high tariffs which, with the sole exception of the UNDERWOOD-SIMMONS TARIFF, endured until the TRADE AGREEMENT ACT of the NEW DEAL administration.

Protective Tariff. Refers to a purpose of customs collection. The objective of this form of TARIFF is to protect "infant industries" against the competition of well-established foreign industries. The TARIFF OF 1816 was the first protective tariff in American history. The HAWLEY-SMOOT TARIFF ACT of 1930 was the highest protective tariff. Protectionism was the established policy of the United States from the passage of the MORILL TARIFF of 1861 to 1930 with the brief exception of the period from the passage of the UNDERWOOD-SIMMONS ACT of 1913 to the FORDNEY-MCCUMBER ACT OF 1922.

Protestant Episcopal Church. A religious group in the United States representing Anglican theology. It was introduced into the JAMESTOWN colony in 1607. Shortly afterwards it was made autonomous, and adopted its present name in 1789. Although it declined in strength at the beginning of the 19th century, it resumed its growth by the opening of the Civil War. In this period it established church seminaries, missionary societies, and Sunday schools. The Civil War caused a schism between the ABOLITIONISTS and SLAVERY groups within the church. The split was not healed until after the war. Doctrinal conflicts caused subsequent splits which culminated in the organization of the Reformed Episcopal Church in 1873 by seceding groups. In the 20th century the church adopted a moderate liberal program with respect to social and LABOR PROBLEMS and a conservative attitude towards theological questions. In 1965 there were almost 3,500,000 Protestant Episcopalians in the United States.

PRYOR, Roger Atkinson. 1828-1919. Lawyer, legislator, army officer and jurist. b. Virginia. Graduated, University of Virginia Law School (1848) admitted to the bar (1849); worked as editor for several papers; member, U.S. House of Representatives (1859-61); served with the Confederate Army during the Civil War; staff writer, N. Y. *Daily News* (1866); practiced law in New York City (1866-90); judge, court of common pleas of N.Y. (1890-94); justice, N.Y. supreme court (1894-99).

Public Administration. The management and operation of governmental business. The various fields of public administration include finance, personnel, organization and structure, administrative procedure, inter-governmental relationships, internal management and control, administrative adjudication, judicial sanctions, political control and enforcement, planning and policy formulation, and public relations. The study of public administration is concerned with the transactions of all public business, including municpal, state, federal, and international, in all their aspects. The administration of the public business may be exercised by the EXECUTIVE DEPARTMENTS, independent establishments, or a large group of miscellaneous bodies including boards, agencies, councils, authorities, CORPORATIONS, administrations, and commissions. Some of these, like the executive departments, National Housing and Home Finance Agency, and FEDERAL SECURITY AGENCY are headed by a single executive. Most of the others are directed by boards of three to 11 persons. Their powers vary from the relatively controlled functions of a minor bureau in an executive department to the sweeping quasi-judicial powers of the INTERSTATE COMMERCE COMMISSION, FEDERAL TRADE COMMISSION, and NATIONAL LABOR RELATIONS BOARD. In the United States the systematic study of public administration is of relatively recent development. The first serious analysis was made by WOODROW WILSON in 1887 and carried forward by Frank Goodnow at the beginning of the 20th century. Distinguished scholars and public figures in the field of public administration have included Paul Appleby, Frederick Blachly, Marshall E. Dimock, Herbert Emmerich, John M. Gaus, James M. Landis, Arthur W. MacMahon, John D. Millett, Fritz Morstein-Merx, Miriam E. Oatman, John Pfiffner, William J. Ronan, Wallace S. Sayre, Sterling D. Spero, Donald C. Stone, Harvey Walker, and Leonard D. White.

Public Health Service, U. S. Formerly an independent agency known by that title since 1912. Under presidential EXECUTIVE ORDER it was transferred from the Treasury Department to the FEDERAL SECURITY AGENCY in 1939. It has provided for medical service and examinations in the MERCHANT MARINE since 1798. The principal work of the Public Health Service is the conduct of research in the causes and prevention of disease and the publication of its reports for the use of state and municipal departments of health and hospitals. The Service also enforces quarantine laws at ports of entry, cooperates with state and local agencies in public health programs, provides hospitalization for certain categories of patients under federal law, makes sanitary rules regarding shipment of animals and food in INTER-STATE COMMERCE, and enforces federal laws forbidding the TRANSPORTATION of animals and persons with certain designated diseases. By the Public Service Health Act of 1944 its activities in arranging close working relationships with state and local public health officials were extended in the matters of personnel training, standardized reports, and a unified national public health program. In 1953 the Surgeon General, as administrative head of the U. S. Public

Health Service, reported to the Secretary of the newly created Department of Health, Education, and Welfare.

Public Housing Administration. An agency created on July 27, 1947 by Reorganization Plan Number 3 within the NATIONAL HOUSING AND HOME FINANCE AGENCY. It took over the work formerly performed by the UNITED STATES HOUSING AUTHORITY and the FEDERAL PUBLIC HOUSING AUTHORITY. It was authorized to administer the program of federal loan and SUBSIDY assistance to municipal low-rent SLUM clearance projects under the WAGNER-STEAGALL ACT and its AMENDMENTS. Under the supervision of the NHHFA the agency managed and disposed of federally-owned war and veteran HOUSING and also the federally-owned subsistence homesteads, labor camps, and "Greenbelt" towns built by the RESETTLEMENT ADMINISTRATION. Under these various programs the PHA, in 1948, had interest in 800,000 housing units, three-quarters of them war and veteran's emergency housing and the rest under low-rent programs.

Public Lands. Formally known by the term "original public domain." They embrace all the area, the title to which was originally vested in the United States government as a sovereign power. In continental United States this area involved 1,442,200,320 acres of land and 20,232,320 acres of water area. These figures were determined in 1912 by the calculation made by a committee representing the General Land office and the Geological Survey of the DEPARTMENT OF THE INTERIOR, and the Bureaus of Statistics and the Census in the DEPARTMENT OF COMMERCE AND LABOR. In its history the United States has disposed of the "original public domain" by granting 224,000,000 acres to the states, 285,000,000 acres as homesteads, 95,000,000 acres as military bounties and private land claims, 91,-000,000 acres as grants to railroads, and 334,000,000 acres in cash sales and other disposals. The total remaining territory to which the United States has title comprises an area of 720,000,000 acres plus 50,000,000 acres of federal mineral rights in patented lands.

Public Service Commissions. State agencies authorized to regulate the practices of PUBLIC UTILITIES engaged in intrastate commerce. In 1952 every state except Delaware had a public service commission. The functions and powers of these agencies are based on those exercised by the INTERSTATE COMMERCE COMMISSION. See Interstate Commerce Commission.

Public Service Health Act of 1944. See Public Health Service, U.S.

Public Utility. A privately owned corporation affected with a public interest. Examples include water works, electric companies, HYDRO-ELECTRIC POWER companies, gas plants, RAILROADS, TELEPHONES, telegraphs, cables, radio, and television. Public utility corporate organizations in the 20th century took the form of the HOLDING COMPANY through which MONOPOLY control was practised. Not until the passage of the FEDERAL POWER ACT of 1920 did Congress provide for regulatory control. Previously, and since, regulation has been exercised by the states under their POLICE POWERS.

Public Utility Doctrine. The legal principle which upholds the right of government to regulate a private enterprise which affects the public interest. Under this principle the western states established agencies after the Civil War to control the operations of RAILROADS and other industries.

Public Utility Holding Company Act. See Wheeler-Rayburn Act.

Public Welfare. The term as such does

not appear in the federal Constitution. The preamble refers to the necessity of promoting the "general welfare" and Article I, Section 8 authorizes Congress to tax to "provide for the common defense and general welfare of the United States." Since the preamble is not considered part of the Constitution proper and provision by Congress for the general welfare is limited to the tax power, there is no power of Congress to protect the public welfare as such. This power has developed out of its DELEGATED POWERS and those implied by the "ELASTIC CLAUSE." Through this evolution Congress has succeeded in steadily enlarging its powers in those fields which were earlier considered to be properly within the domain of the states. The result has been federal laws in the areas of HOUSING, EDUCATION, RECREATION, LABOR RELATIONS, UNEMPLOYMENT INSURANCE, old age annuities, HIGHWAY construction, health, relief, public works, AGRICULTURE, and the regulation of various aspects of business activities. Simultaneously, the states, acting under the authorization of the 10TH AMENDMENT, have developed increasingly important public welfare programs. These have included those described above and, in addition, programs in police and fire protection, park development, CITY PLANNING, TRANSPORTATION, fiscal reform, and PENOLOGY.

Public Works Administration. An agency established as the Federal Emergency Administration of Public Works by Title II of the NATIONAL RECOVERY ACT in 1933. The President was authorized, through the Administrator of the PWA, to spend $3,300,000,000 for various public works projects. The funds could be granted to states, municipalities, or other public bodies upon such terms as the President might set down for the construction, repair, or improvement of any projects. The Administrator was em-

powered to purchase or otherwise acquire any property necessary to the construction of any such project. The Act limited grants for the cost of labor and materials to 30 percent, the rest being extended as loans. The recipient bodies posted their bonds to the PWA and were required to draw up plans for PWA approval before embarking on projects. By June, 1934 the agency had distributed its entire fund to 13,266 federal projects and 2,407 non-federal projects. The "PUMP-PRIMING" objective of the public works program thus created was not realized because of the various restrictions described, and public employment did not succeed in significantly reducing the army of unemployed. Subsequent appropriations added $2,291,000,000 to PWA funds for construction of public buildings, dams, sewage works, bridges, HOUSING, RAILROADS, water works, power stations, and AVIATION. In 1939 the PWA was incorporated into the FEDERAL WORKS AGENCY.

Pueblo Affair. The USS Pueblo, an intelligence ship, was captured by North Korean naval forces in January 1968. North Korea claimed that the ship was within the 12 mile limit and was using listening devices to spy on military installations. The United States denied that the Pueblo had been in territorial waters and brought the seizure before the UN Security Counsel. Negotiations lasted for 11 months when the 83 man crew was finally released. One crew member was killed in the capture.

Puerto Rico. An island 95 miles long and 35 miles wide at the northeast end of the Caribbean Sea. It was discovered by Christopher Columbus 1493. Its POPULATION of 2,250,000 in an area of 3,435 square miles makes it one of the most densely populated sections in the world. Its capital and largest city is San Juan. Its principal products are cane SUGAR and rum, other important

517

crops being TOBACCO, pineapples, coffee, rope, and fruits. The United States acquired Puerto Rico from Spain in 1898 as a result of the Spanish-American War. It was governed by the military until 1900 when it was furnished with a civil government. In 1917 its CITIZENS were made American citizens by the JONES ACT. The Act of Congress in 1947 made the governor a popularly elected official who now has the power to appoint six of the seven administrative heads of departments. The auditor and island judges are appointed by the President of the United States. A Resident Commissioner in Washington, D.C., with a four year term, has a voice in the House of Representatives but no vote. In 1951 the native population voted for a constitution with local autonomy which will go into effect upon approval by the United States Congress. Although Puerto Ricans are American citizens they do not enjoy all the CIVIL LIBERTIES or suffrage privileges that continental Americans exercise. This situation has been determined by several decisions of the United States Supreme Court which has declared that Congress may legislate for American territories as it sees fit. In 1952 the governor of the island was Luis Munoz Marin, chosen in 1948 as the first popularly elected governor. On July 23, 1952, Congress approved the Constitution of Puerto Rico as adopted March 3, 1952.

Pujo Committee. Created by Congress in 1912 to investigate the "MONEY TRUST." The committee, in its report to Congress, substantiated the frequently asserted charges of financial manipulation and control exercised by BANKING combinations. The report further described at length the evils which had resulted from such activities. The intervention of World War I, however, drew public attention away from this situation. The passage of the GLASS-OWEN ACT in 1914 did not directly attack the evils revealed in the report, but rather attempted to deal with financial matters in other areas.

PULASKI, Casimir. 1748?-1779. Polish nobleman who served in the American Revolution. b. Poland. With a letter of introduction to General WASHINGTON from BENJAMIN FRANKLIN he arrived in America (1777); served at BRANDYWINE and GERMANTOWN; organized, with the authority of Congress, a cavalry unit (1778); killed at the siege of Savannah (1779).

PULITZER, Joseph. 1847-1911. Journalist. b. Hungary. To United States (1864); served in the Civil War for a year; served as a reporter on CARL SCHURZ's paper, *Westliche Post*, St. Louis (1868); became a naturalized American CITIZEN (1867); served in the Missouri legislature (1869); supported GREELEY (1872) and TILDEN (1876); studied law and admitted to the bar (1876); became owner of the St. Louis *Post-Dispatch* (1878); moved to New York City and purchased the New York *World* (1883); member, U.S. House of Representatives (1885-86); established the N.Y. *Evening World* (1887); founded and endowed the School of Journalism, Columbia University (1903); established PULITZER PRIZES "for the encouragement of public service, public morals, American LITERATURE, and the advancement of EDUCATION."

Pulitzer Prizes. Annual awards granted for meritorious work in the fields of JOURNALISM and letters. The prizes were established by JOSEPH PULITZER in 1912 in a bequest to Columbia University. They are awarded by the University trustees on the recommendations of the Advisory Board of the School of Journalism at the University. Prizes are awarded for work done in the preceding year.

PULLMAN, George Mortimer. 1831-

518

1897. Inventor. b. New York. CABINET maker (1848-55); worked as contractor in Chicago (1855-59); with Ben Field he designed the first Pullman car with folding upper berth (patented 1864) and extensible seats which became lower berths (patented 1865); organized Pullman Palace Car Co. (1867); made a fortune; later designed dining cars (1868), chair cars (1875), etc.

Pullman Strike. Broke out in Chicago in 1894 as the result of a reduction in wages to the workers of the Pullman Palace Car Company. The refusal by the company of an offer of ARBITRATION by the American Railway Union precipitated the strike. The. union forbade its members to handle Pullman cars and the STRIKE spread to 27 states and territories from Ohio to California. The strike is notable because of the dispatch of federal troops by President CLEVELAND and the issuance of one of the most wide-spread injunctions in American labor history. Attorney-General RICHARD OLNEY sought the INJUNCTION under the provisions of the SHERMAN ANTI-TRUST ACT and was bitterly condemned as a result. The violation of the injunction by EUGENE V. DEBS, president of the union, resulted in his imprisonment. This plus the firing by federal troops on workers for the first time in American labor history resulted in much labor antagonism to government and management.

Pulp Industry. See paper industry.

"Pump Priming." In the early NEW DEAL period the public spending of large sums to stimulate the private economy and expansion of INDUSTRY. Beginning with the PUBLIC WORKS ADMINISTRATION and continuing with other agencies in the fields of AGRICULTURE, HOUSING, utilities, and public works, the federal government spent an average of $250,000,000 a month in 1934 and 1935. By 1937 the marked upswing in the nation's economy had reduced federal spending to $50,000,000 a month.

Pure Food, Drug, and Cosmetic Act. See Pure Food and Drugs Act.

Pure Food and Drugs Acts. A series of laws passed by Congress for the purpose of establishing federal control over adulterated foods and drugs moving in INTERSTATE COMMERCE. The original Act of June 30, 1906 was in large degree a consequence of the public anger aroused by the revelations of UPTON SINCLAIR'S THE JUNGLE and the articles of Doctor Harvey W. Wiley which showed the conditions of filth existing in the STOCKYARDS and slaughterhouses of the nation. This law attempted to prevent the adulteration or misbranding of food or drugs. Poisonous color flavor, or other ingredients detrimental to health were barred. Food composed of filthy or decomposed animal matter or material added to conceal inferior goods was defined as adulterated. The narcotic and stimulants content of proprietary medicines had to be labelled. Misleading statements concerning the composition or purity of packaged foods or drugs subjected the distributor or manufacturer to federal prosecution. Amendments in 1912, 1913, 1919, and 1923 strengthened the law by providing penalties against false statements regarding the healing qualities of drugs, and against the fraudulent stamping or marking of the weight of packaged goods. On March 21, 1938 the Wheeler-Lea Act extended the original law by providing for the prosecution of persons or groups participating in the furnishing of false or misleading statements concerning foods, drugs, diagnostic and therapeutic devices, and cosmetics. The portions of the Act dealing with advertising were made enforceable by the FEDERAL TRADE COMMISSION, although the misbranding was left to the jurisdiction of the PURE FOOD AND DRUG ADMINISTRATION. The

Copeland Act, also known as the Pure Food, Drug, and Cosmetic Act of 1938, added cosmetics and therapeutic devices to foods and drugs. The Pure Food and Drug Administration administers the entire program with the above noted exception. Originally located within the DEPARTMENT OF AGRICULTURE, it was transferred to the FEDERAL SECURITY AGENCY on April 11, 1940.

Pure Food and Drugs Administration. See Pure Food and Drugs Act.

Puritans. Those in England who wanted to purify the Anglican Church of the remaining Catholic rites after the Reformation in the early 16th century. The Puritans were opposed to Papal control, clerical vestments, certain church ceremonies, and hierarchical organization. Their migration to the new world resulted in the settlement of the MASSACHUSETTS BAY COLONY in 1629. There and in Connecticut the colonial governments and society were rigidly controlled by the Puritans. Their impact on theology, LITERATURE, social manners, politics, and the economy of New England endured until the Revolution.

Purple Heart, Order of the. A military award established in 1782 by General GEORGE WASHINGTON. It was a reward for meritorious action and fidelity. It was revived as General Order Number 3 of the War Department on February 22, 1932 as an award to recipients of the Meritorious Services Citation Certificate and to troops wounded in action. It is reserved only for services performed in time of war. The medal is heart shaped with a gold border and a purple enamel center on which is a bust of Washington and the inscription "For Military Merit."

PUTNAM, Israel. 1718-1790. General in American Revolution. b. Massachusetts. Served through French and Indian War (1754-63); major general, Continental Army (1775); served at BUNKER HILL; commander in chief at New York and in BATTLE OF LONG ISLAND (1776); in command at Philadelphia (1776); in charge of recruiting in Connecticut (1778-79); his service was cut short when he suffered a paralytic stroke (1779).

"Putting Out" System. See colonial manufacturing.

PYNCHON, William. 1590?-1662. Colonist. b. England. Settled at Dorchester, Mass. (1630); treasurer, MASSACHUSETTS BAY COLONY (1632-34); member, Massachusetts Board of Assistants (1642-51); published a tract The Meritorious Price of our Redemption (1652); declared a heretic; returned to England.

Q

Quakers. Known as the Society of Friends. A religious, pacifist group emanating from England where it was founded by George Fox in 1647. The earliest Quakers arrived in Boston in 1656 whence they were deported by the PURITAN government which prohibited further Quaker IMMIGRATION. The Quakers were persecuted and banished from the MASSACHUSETTS BAY COLONY and other colonies, until finally they were able to establish themselves in Pennsylvania in 1681 under the sponsorship of WILLIAM PENN, who was himself converted to Quakerism. Pennsylvania became a haven for the exiled Quakers from the British Isles as well as from the other colonies spreading to the hospitable colonies of Delaware and New Jersey. Basic Quaker tenets include democracy in church government, equality of opportunity for religious expression, the renunciation of ritual and the sacraments, simple sermons or prayers, plainness of speech and apparel, rigid discipline and punishment for breaches of the faith, and widespread humanitarian activities. The Quakers were among the first ABOLITIONISTS in American history, attacking the slave trade and SLAVERY in the late 18th century. They made distinguished contributions in the fields of Indian relations, penal reform, temperance, care of the indigent and unbalanced, and EDUCATION. During the two World Wars they contributed much in relief and good will work in the United States and abroad. In 1965 there were over 127,000 Quakers in the United States.

Quarantine. The inspection of incoming ships and crews and the medical inspection of aliens at the ports of entry of the United States. Quarantine was formerly administered by state and municipal governments, but is now under the supervision of the United States Public Health Service. Since 1924 medical inspection of prospective alien immigrants has been conducted at American consulates in foreign nations.

"Quarantine the Aggressor." A quotation from the famous speech of President F. D. ROOSEVELT in Chicago in October, 1937 in which he likened war to a disease which requires that a quarantine be set up. In this speech the President, foreseeing the spread of war in Asia and Europe, attempted to place the American people on guard and awaken it to the danger of attack. Calling for collective action against the aggressor, he asked for a "concerted effort in opposition" to treaty-breaking nations.

Quartering Acts. Two laws passed by Parliament in 1765 and 1774. The first Act, known as the Mutiny Act, authorized colonial governors to requisition certain buildings for the use of British troops. The second Act, passed in re-

521

sponse to the BOSTON TEA PARTY, provided that colonial authorities must furnish quarters for British troops when no barracks were available. Upon failure to do so, the colonial governors were authorized to demand the use of inns or uninhabited buildings. In Boston the PATRIOTS flouted the law by refusing to permit laborers to recommission wineries and other empty buildings for the use of the troops. The troops therefore were compelled to remain camped on the British Common. It was their presence in Boston which provoked the BOSTON MASSACRE of 1774.

QUAY, Matthew Stanley. 1833-1904. Politician. b. Pennsylvania. Admitted to the bar (1854); served through Civil War; served at FREDRICKSBURG and awarded the CONGRESSIONAL MEDAL OF HONOR for bravery; became boss of the Republican party in Pennsylvania; elected to U.S. Senate (1887-99; 1901-1904); chairman, Republican National Committee, largely responsible for success of HARRISON's campaign; had exceptional ability as political organizer.

Quebec Act. Passed by Parliament in 1774. It provided for the recognition of the Roman Catholic religion in Quebec and extended the boundary of that province southward to the Ohio River. The law was interpreted by the New England colonists as an act of hostility as part of the anti-colonial legislation known as the INTOLERABLE ACTS passed in the same year. It served therefore to aggravate English-colonial relations in the period leading up to the American Revolution.

Quebec Conference. A conference between President F. D. ROOSEVELT and Prime Minister Churchill, held in Quebec, Canada, between August 11-24, 1943. In the declaration issued at the conclusion of the conference, the two heads of state announced important

progress in limiting German SUBMARINE activity. They also stated that the two powers had surveyed the "whole field of world operations." At the second Quebec Conference held between September 11-16, 1944, Roosevelt and Churchill announced that comprehensive plans had been drawn up for carrying on the war in Europe and in the Pacific, and for creating the peace.

Queen Anne's War. The name by which the War of the Spanish Succession was known in North America. It was fought between 1701 and 1714. The fundamental causes were Anglo-French colonial rivalry, dynastic quarrels, and economic competition. It was precipitated by a struggle over the succession to the Spanish throne and, in Europe, involved France in a war against England, Holland, and Spain. In America battles were fought in the West Indies, the Carolinas, and New England. In 1702 the English captured the island of St. Christopher. Military activities in the West Indies took the form of naval skirmishes by PRIVATEERS. In 1702 St. Augustine was taken by colonists from South Carolina. In 1706 a combined Spanish-French fleet was driven from Charleston. The French and their Indian allies ravaged the New England frontier until 1709 when a British force was dispatched to aid colonial expeditions against Quebec and Montreal. In 1710 Port Royal was captured but the principal attacks on Quebec and Montreal failed the following year. The Treaty of Utrecht concluded the war in 1713 leaving most of the issues unsolved.

QUEZON, Manuel Luis. 1878-1944. Philippine statesman. b. Balen, PHILIPPINE ISLANDS. Graduated Santo Tomàs University and studied law in Manila; admitted to the bar (1903); served with AGUINALDO during the Revolution; delegate to first Philippine assembly (1907-09); president of Philippine Senate

(1916-35); spoke before the Congress of the United States in an appeal for Philippine Independence (1910); opposed the administration of Governor-General LEONARD WOOD (1921-27); in constant opposition to THEODORE ROOSEVELT; president of the Commonwealth of the Philippines (1935-44); strongest political leader of the Philippines in their history; leader of Philippine government in exile after the Japanese overran the Islands, with headquarters in Australia (Mar.-May, 1942) and in the United States (from May, 1942).

QUINCY, Josiah. 1744-1775. Lawyer and political leader. b. Boston, Massachusetts. Graduated, Harvard (1763); studied law and practiced in Boston; wrote anonymous letters for the Boston *Gazette* opposing the STAMP ACT and other British pre-Revolutionary legislation; went to England to plead the colonial cause (1774-75); died at sea on his return trip to the colonies (April 26, 1775).

QUINCY, Josiah. 1772-1864. Educator, statesman and reformer. b. Massachusetts. Graduated, Harvard (1790); studied law and admitted to the bar, Boston (1793); member, U.S. House of Representatives (1805-13); FEDERALIST leader in opposition to the policies of JEFFERSON and MADISON; opposed the War of 1812; argued violently for rights of the individual states; member, Massachusetts state senate (1804-05, 1813-20); mayor of Boston (1823-29); instituted many needed reforms; made president of Harvard (1829-45); author of two volume *History of Harvard University* (1840) and other histories.

QUITMAN, John Anthony. 1798-1858. General, lawyer and political leader. b. New York. Studied law in Ohio and admitted to the bar (1821); practiced law in Natchez, Mississippi; served as brigadier general under TAYLOR in the Mexican War; appointed governor of Mexico City by SCOTT during its occupation by Americans (1847); commissioned major general (1847); governor of Mississippi (1850-51); member, U.S. House of Representatives (1855-58).

Quitrent. A permanent payment in money or kind as a condition for holding land in the British colonies. It originated in the British feudal practice of commuting food and work debts into an established sum. The right to charge quitrents was generally included in colonial charters, but rapidly disappeared in Plymouth and Massachusetts where title was given to the freeholder. Quitrents soon disappeared from New England but were strongly enforced in Pennsylvania and the southern colonies. The amounts varied from two to four shillings per 100 acres. Forfeiture of the land was the means of enforcement, and furnished a prolific source of discontent. The state assemblies abolished the quitrent during the Revolution.

Quota Act of 1921. Passed by Congress in 1921. It is also known as the Emergency Quota Act. The law limited IMMIGRATION in any year to three percent of each country's nationals in the United States as established by the 1910 census. It applied to all nations except those in the western hemisphere and was to operate for one year. In 1922 it was renewed with several changes for an additional two year period. Its objective, in addition to restricting immigration, was to select immigrants from northern and western European countries and limit those from southern and eastern Europe. Although total immigration was severely reduced its secondary purpose was not accomplished. The result was the passage by Congress in 1924 of the JOHNSON-REED ACT.

Quota Act of 1924. See Johnson-Reed Act.

R

Racketeering. That phase of crime based on the illegal collection of fees for presumed protection. In the 20th century racketeering became an established criminal activity in large cities in the fields of prostitution, gambling, the sale of liquor, and narcotics. Sharp practices such as swindling schemes, the coercive collection of tolls from reputable business men, hi-jacking, "protection" rackets, slot machine control, and bookmaking were developed in the "easy money" efforts of gangsters. The high point was reached during the PROHIBITION era when national gangster syndicates ruled over large empires of crime extending to the control of government, LABOR UNIONS, and industry. Important rackets arose in poultry, laundries, milk, and other industries. The accompaniments of racketeering were bribes, bombings, assassinations, and corruption. Alphonse Capone was the recognized "king" of the underworld. Other prominent racketeers were "Legs" Diamond, "Dutch Schultz," "Waxey" Gordon, Frank Yale, "Lucky" Luciano, "Nocky" Johnson, and Frank Costello. From time to time public drives against racketeering have been undertaken, generally with little success. Among these campaigns have been those of special prosecutor THOMAS E. DEWEY in New York County, William O'Dwyer in Kings County, and the national investigation of the Kefauver Committee. See Kefauver Investigation.

Radical Republicans. Extremists in the Republican party during and after the Civil War who advocated a punitive Reconstruction policy in the South. They were strongly anti-slavery in sentiment, and opposed LINCOLN's policies of moderation. They claimed Reconstruction to be properly a legislative, not executive, function. Employing the device of congressional investigation, the Radical Republicans attacked Lincoln's military appointments, urged their own candidates for high posts, denounced the moderates in the party, and bitterly opposed the policies of Lincoln and JOHNSON. With their electoral success in 1866, they introduced a series of Reconstruction measures designed to punish the South. Among their leaders were CHARLES SUMNER, THADDEUS STEVENS, ZACHARIAH CHANDLER, HENRY W. DAVIS, and BENJAMIN WADE.

Radio Act of 1927. See Federal Radio Commission.

Radio Industry. Stems from the inventions of Marconi in 1898 and LEE DEFOREST in 1906. Before World War I radio was principally used for experimental and commercial purposes. The first major radio corporation, the Radio Corporation of America, was chartered in Delaware in 1919. Between the World Wars the industry was notable for improvements in transmission, the increased number of receivers, the development of broadcasting chains, the growth of international broadcasting, and its rapidly increasing use as a medium for publicity, education, and public purposes. The first announced broadcast in the United States was made by station KDKA in Pittsburgh on November 2, 1920. Federal regulation of the industry was initiated in 1912, although the first basic statute was not passed by Congress until 1927 when it enacted the Federal Radio Act. In 1934 the Federal Communications Act supplanted the earlier law. Unlike its counterpart in European nations, the industry is almost wholly privately owned in the United States. Notable exceptions include municipally operated stations such as Station WNYC in New York City. There are four major broadcast networks in the United States, the American Broadcasting Company, Columbia Broadcasting System, Mutual Broadcasting System and National Broadcasting Company. These networks owned, operated, or were affiliated with 1335 stations in 1962. At that time the total number of stations including those under construction was 5072, including frequency modulation stations. In 1964 there were approximately 111 million radio sets in almost 57 million homes in the United States, almost half of the world's total.

Railroad Abuses. A series of malpractices after the Civil War which included overcapitalization, rebates, discriminatory rates, charging more for a short haul than a long haul, free passes, favors to preferred shippers, and non-posting of rates. These abuses redounded against the small farmer who sought relief in state legislation. In the 1870's the western states passed the GRANGER LAWS aimed at curbing these abuses.

Railroad Brotherhoods. The name applied to the four largest unions of railroad workers. The Brotherhood of Locomotive Engineers was founded in 1863, Conductors in 1868, Firemen and Enginemen in 1873, and Railway Trainmen in 1883. These were originally organized as benefit societies, rather than as LABOR UNIONS, to provide their members with life insurance. LABOR RELATIONS activities were later added to their functions, and today they are among the most powerful national labor organizations. They have remained independent, although cooperating with other national unions for common purposes. Although loathe to strike, the Brotherhoods have, from time to time, engaged in important railroad STRIKES. Customarily they engage in conciliation, mediation, and ARBITRATION activities within the terms of federal law. The Brotherhood of Locomotive Engineers, since 1920, has expanded its non-labor functions by the creation of the Engineers Cooperative National Bank of Cleveland. In 1952 the aggregate membership of the four Brotherhoods was over 430,000.

Railroad Disputes Act. See Crosser-Dill Act.

Railroad Labor Board. See Railroad Transportation Act.

Railroad Retirement Acts. Federal laws providing annuities for railroad workers. The Act of 1934 granted retirement allowances for certain railroad employees to be administered by a three man Railroad Retirement Board. Two thirds of the cost was borne by the carriers and the balance by the workers. It was opposed by the carriers who resented their large contribution to the plan. The Act was declared unconstitutional in March, 1935, but was followed by two laws in August. These established a new plan to be financed by special taxes. Again opposed by the RAILROADS, further efforts were made to provide a satisfactory retirement program. In May, 1937 a new Railroad Retirement Act was passed with little opposition. In 1951 the Act was amended to increase benefits of pensioners and annuitants by 15 percent, survivor's benefits by 33 and one third percent, and spouse's benefits up to 50 percent of retired employee's benefit. It guaranteed that no beneficiary should receive less than social security system employees. In 1964 the Railroad Retirement Board collected and disbursed about $600,000,000.

Railroads. Tramways in quarries and kilns, at the beginning of the 19th century, were the first railroads in the United States. Early suggestions in 1786 and 1811 for the application of steam to carriages did not materialize. In 1820 a narrow-gauge railroad was built by JOHN STEVENS in Hoboken. The first major railroad was begun in 1828 when South Carolina chartered the BALTIMORE AND OHIO COMPANY. Its carriages were pulled by horses. Three years later steam locomotives were introduced from England and in 1830 steam engines, manufactured in New York, were installed on the B & O and on the Charleston and Hamburg Railroads. The development of the New York Central System linked the middle Atlantic and New England states and ultimately connected them to the mid-west. The firms of Matthias, Baldwin and Thomas Rogers began constructing locomotives in Philadelphia and Patterson, New Jersey respectively after 1830, although railroads were still horse drawn. The earliest passenger cars were modifications of stagecoaches. Tracks were fabricated of iron-covered wood, and were subject to rapid wear. Accidents were frequent and travel time long. Scheduling was poorly administered, and many hours and even days were spent waiting for trains. By the opening of the Civil War there were 30,000 miles of railroad in the United States, two-thirds of it in the North. The success of industrial capitalism in the war opened the nation to the greatest era of railroad construction in its history. The transcontinental railroads, begun in 1864, opened the Far West to IMMIGRATION and economic exploitation. Financial assistance by the states and the federal government spurred this activity so that by the turn of the 20th century the United States already had over 200,000 miles of rail. The railroads were seized by the federal government in 1917 and operated at a net loss of almost $1,000,000,000 until their return to private ownership in 1920. The competition of motor and air transportation has placed the railroad industry in an unfavorable financial situation. Attempts to overcome this have included improvement of service, introduction of superior equipment, and financial reorganization. In recent years the railroads have introduced streamlined trains, the Diesel engine, air-conditioning, improved sleepers, luxury appointments, double-deck cars, and other refinements to attract the traveller. Attempts have been made to reduce elapsed time between points, and otherwise improve service. In 1962 there were 217,552 miles of railroad in the United States, with an estimated capital investment in road and equipment of approximately $35,513,-000,000. There were 711,000 railroad employees. The industry carried more than 313,000,000 passengers and 2,400,-000,000 tons of freight in that year.

Railroads, Aid To. Assistance to private carriers by federal and state governments in the form of land grants, loans, right of way, tax exemption, liberal charter provisions, and monopoly rights. Although land grants were the most substantial form of public aid to railroads in the period up to 1871, direct financial aid in the form of loans and liberal credit terms was also extended by Congress. The Union and Central Pacific Railroads and their subsidiaries received a total of more than $60,000,000 in such loans. Illinois, Minnesota, Texas, and

Wisconsin granted over 50,000,000 acres of land. Municipalities in Kentucky and Illinois alone incurred debts of well over $41,000,000 in direct SUBSIDIES and loans to western railroads, while an additional sum of $165,000,000 was openly granted by Kansas, Nebraska, and Wisconsin. See land grants to railroads.

The Railroad Retirement Act as amended in 1939 and 1946 provides benefits substantially the same as under the Old Age Insurance title of the Social Security Act. The Act is administered by the Railroad Retirement Board. The federal government makes grants to the states to help provide financial assistance to the aged, blind or disabled. Also dependent children because of the death, disability, absence or unemployment of a parent. The states and the national government manage jointly unemployment insurance programs. The waiting period, weekly amounts, and number of payments vary from state to state.

Railroad Strike of 1877. The first major railroad strike in American history. Its immediate cause was a 10 percent wage reduction, the last of a series of wage cuts resulting from the general economic depression after the PANIC OF 1873. Trainmen struck the BALTIMORE AND OHIO RAILROAD in Martinsburg, West Virginia. At the request of the governor, President HAYES dispatched 200 federal troops. The strike spread throughout the country and led to conflicts between the strikers and troops in Baltimore, Pittsburgh, and Philadelphia. Sympathetic STRIKES sprang up in other centers. The strike was broken, but it left a heritage of distrust by labor against the federal government for its use of troops.

Railroad Transportation Act. Also known as the Esch-Cummins Act. Passed by Congress in 1920. It solved the controversial problem of disposing of the federally operated RAILROADS after World War I. Its principal provisions were the enlargement of the INTERSTATE COMMERCE COMMISSION from seven to 11 members, the conferral upon the Commission of the power to fix rates so as to yield a return of six percent on the estimated value of the railroads, and to control the issue of railroad securities. The Act created a Railway Labor Board of nine members appointed by the President, three each from railroad management, labor, and the public, to settle labor disputes. It appropriated $200,000,-000 to aid the railroads in reestablishing their pre-war status, and a $300,000,000 "revolving fund" for loans to financially weak railroads. All rate and wage adjustments were prohibited before September 1, 1920. The Act also provided that no man should serve as a director of more than one road after December 31, 1921. The Commission was given the power to fix minimum as well as maximum rates and to divide the nation into rate districts for evaluation purposes. The feature known as the recapture clause compelled the carriers to turn back to the Commission one half of the excess earnings above six percent, these funds to be placed into the "revolving fund." The Commission was also authorized to work out plans for the consolidation of railroads into not less than 20 or more than 35 systems. The labor features of the Act proved unworkable and the Railroad Labor Board, powerless to enforce its decisions, was abolished in 1926. Other features of the Act proved weak because of decisions of the Supreme Court and the opposition of railroad management.

Railway Labor Act of 1926. See Watson-Parker Act.

Railway Labor Act of 1934. See Crosser-Dill Act.

RALEIGH, Sir Walter. 1552?-1618. English courtier, navigator, and statesman. Studied at Oxford; favorite in the Court of Queen Elizabeth; given land grant in America; sent expedition of exploration and named the northern part of

Florida "Virginia" after the Virgin Queen (1584); sent a group of settlers to Roanoke Island, North Carolina, but the colony failed (1585); introduced potatoes and tobacco into England; wrote many poems; lost favor at court and imprisoned; tried a few more times to establish colonies in America but failed; went on unsuccessful expedition to seek gold along the Orinoco; beheaded.

Ranching. The breeding and raising of cattle, horses, or sheep on grazing lands known as ranches. The ranch consists of the land, domiciles, work quarters, and stockades. With the development of the CATTLE INDUSTRY after the Civil War, ranching in the far western states became a major industry. Ranches vary in size from a few acres to the 1,000,000 acres of the King Ranch in Texas. Many of them extend over into government land. The COWBOY is the labor mainstay of the ranch, not only caring for the stock but also carrying on the routine work of maintenance and repair.

RANDALL, Alexander Williams. 1819-1872. Lawyer, political leader and governor. b. New York. Studied law and moved to Wisconsin Territory (1840); delegate to state constitutional convention; important in state assembly; governor of Wisconsin (1857-61); strong supporter of the Union cause; U.S. Minister to Italy; appointed by JOHNSON, U.S. Postmaster-General.

RANDALL, Samuel Jackson. 1828-1890. Legislator. b. Philadelphia, Pennsylvania. Served in the Union Army; member, U.S. House of Representatives as Democrat from Pennsylvania (1863-90) serving as Speaker of the House (1876-81); presided during disputed election of 1876; known for having codified the rules of the House and granting more power to the Speaker.

RANDOLPH, Edmund Jennings. 1753-1813. Statesman. b. Virginia. Graduated,

William and Mary College; studied law and practiced in Williamsburg; served as aide-de-camp to General WASHINGTON during the Revolution (1775-76); member Virginia constitutional convention helping to draft the document (1776); attorney general of Virginia (1776-1786); member, CONTINENTAL CONGRESS (1779-82); governor of Virginia (1786-88); delegate to CONSTITUTIONAL CONVENTION (1787) presenting the VIRGINIA OR RANDOLPH PLAN; opposed the Constitution as drafted and refused to sign it; later he advocated its acceptance at the ratifying convention in Virginia (1788); appointed first U.S. Attorney-General by Washington (1789-94); U.S. Secretary of State (1794-95) succeeding JEFFERSON; returned to private practice and was chief counsel for AARON BURR at the time of his treason trial (1807).

RANDOLPH, John. 1773-1833. Statesman. b. Virginia. Known as Randolph of Roanoke. Studied at the College of New Jersey (now Princeton—1787-88) and at Columbia College (1788-89); member, U.S. House of Representatives (1799-1813, 1815-17, 1819-25, 1827-29); and U.S. Senate (1825-27); served as chairman of the House WAYS AND MEANS COMMITTEE; bitterly opposed MADISON and Northern Democrats and was in opposition to JEFFERSON (after 1805); opposed the War of 1812, MISSOURI COMPROMISE; excellent orator; opposed CLAY and fought harmless duel with him (April 8, 1826); member, Virginia constitutional convention (1829-30); appointed by JACKSON, U.S. Minister to Russia (1830) resigning because of ill health; denounced Jackson's NULLIFICATION DOCTRINE; died insane.

RANDOLPH, Peyton. 1721? - 1775. Statesman. b. Virginia. Graduated, William and Mary College; studied law in London and admitted to the bar; was made king's attorney for Virginia (1748-66); member, Virginia House of Burgesses (1748-49, 1752-75); member Virginia COMMITTEE OF CORRESPONDENCE (1759-67); chairman (1773); first president, CONTINENTAL CONGRESS (1774, 1775).

Randolph Plan. Also known as the Virginia Plan. The plan submitted by EDMUND RANDOLPH on behalf of the Virginia delegation at the CONSTITUTIONAL CONVENTION in 1787. It provided for a lower house to be elected by the people and an upper house elected by the lower. This legislature was to choose the executive and judiciary.

RANDOLPH, Thomas Jefferson. 1792-1875. Financier and statesman. b. Virginia. Grandson of THOMAS JEFFERSON. Studied in Philadelphia; managed Jefferson's financial affairs and at his death managed the estate (1816-26); member, Virginia constitutional convention; chairman, Democratic national convention (1872); published *Memoir, Correspondence, and Miscellanies from the Papers of Thomas Jefferson* (4 vols., 1829).

Rasmussen vs. United States. See Insular Cases.

Rathbun vs. United States. See Humphrey's Executor vs. United States.

Ratification of the Constitution. Provided for by Article VII of the document in which it was declared that the Constitution would go into effect upon the ratification of nine states, for the states so ratifying. The ratification struggle between the strong STATES RIGHTS' and strong central government groups brought into being the first political parties of American history. The FEDERALIST party supported ratification and the ANTI-FEDERALIST party opposed it. The dispute over ratification went on from September 1787 to June 1788 by which time the necessary nine states had ratified it. New Hampshire was the ninth state. North Carolina did not ratify until No-

vember 1789, by which time the new government had been in existence for six months. Rhode Island, the 13th state, did not ratify until the Spring of 1790, doing so only as the result of threats of commercial and financial retaliation against her.

Ratifying Conventions. State conventions consisting of popularly elected delegates who vote on proposed amendments. Article VII of the Constitution of 1787 provided that the document would come into existence upon the ratification of conventions in nine states. Although the amendment process of the federal Constitution permits the ratification of amendments by state conventions, this procedure was adopted only in the ratification of the 21ST AMENDMENT.

Rationing. The system of allocating scarce raw materials and finished products to INDUSTRY and the civilian population. Rationing began shortly after Japan's conquest of the East Indies when the WAR PRODUCTION BOARD froze existing RUBBER stocks and rationed tires in the Spring of 1942. In May, 1942 gasoline was rationed on the east coast by the OFFICE OF PRICE ADMINISTRATION under the instructions of the WPB. Immediately thereafter the OPA expanded the list of rationed goods to include AUTOMOBILES, tubes, and other products. By December 1st, gasoline rationing was extended throughout the nation. Fuel oil was rationed and, after shortages had begun to appear in meat, butter, canned goods, and other food stuffs, rationing was extended to these commodities. An organized system began in May, 1942 when the OPA required civilians to register for stamp books necessary for the purchase of SUGAR. Rationing was extended to coffee in November. The following month the Secretary of Agriculture declared that rationing would cover many types of processed goods early in 1943. By the end of that year 95 percent of the shoe, tire, COAL, OIL, gasoline, and food production was being rationed to civilians. The OPA was authorized to extend or limit the list of rationed goods as the need arose. Portions of the program were weakened by the development of a "black market," particularly in meat and gasoline.

RAYMOND, Henry Jarvis. 1820-1869. Journalist and political leader. b. New York. Founded (with George Jones) the New York *Times* (1851); editor of the paper (1851-69) making it an outstanding newspaper; lieutenant governor of New York (1855-57); helped to found the Republican party (1856); supported LINCOLN during the Civil War; member, U.S. House of Representatives (1865-67). Author of several biographies.

READ, George. 1733-1798. Lawyer and Revolutionary leader. b. Maryland. Admitted to the bar (1753); practiced in Philadelphia; member, CONTINENTAL CONGRESS (1774-77); signer of DECLARATION OF INDEPENDENCE; presiding officer Delaware constitutional convention (1776); elected by Congress, Judge, U.S. Court of Appeals in admiralty cases (1782-86); as a delegate to the CONSTITUTIONAL CONVENTION (1787) he was a leader of the fight for the rights of the smaller states; important in getting Delaware to be the first state to RATIFY THE CONSTITUTION; U.S. Senator (1789-93); chief justice of Delaware (1793-98).

REAGAN, John Henninger. 1818-1905. Statesman. b. Tennessee. Participated in the campaigns against the CHEROKEE INDIANS (1839); studied law, admitted to the bar (1848), and practiced in Texas; member, U.S. House of Representatives (1857-61); appointed by JEFFERSON DAVIS postmaster general of the CONFEDERATE STATES (March 1861); while imprisoned after war in Boston, he advocated CIVIL RIGHTS and suffrage for the Negro in Texas; helped draft the Texas

constitution; member, U.S. House of Representatives (1875-87); U.S. Senator (1887-91); joint author of INTERSTATE COMMERCE ACT OF 1887.

Rebate. A discriminatory practice of the RAILROADS in the post-Civil War era. A rebate was a refund of a portion of the rate charged for TRANSPORTATION. It was granted to favored shippers during the rate wars of that period in an effort by the carriers to maintain their traffic without resorting to general rate reductions. Rebates were often the result of secret agreements with the favored shipper and therefore bitterly resented by the public and by the shipper who paid the published rate. The INTERSTATE COMMERCE ACT forbade rate discrimination but was unable to prevent the practice because of the difficulty of proving that a rebate actually resulted in discrimination. THE ELKINS ACT finally succeeded in eliminating rebates by declaring it illegal to charge any but the published rates.

Recall. A method of popular IMPEACHMENT whereby the voters may remove a public officer before his term of office has expired. A recall petition is drafted by interested individuals and circulated among the qualified voters, the requisite number of signatures ranging from 10 to 35 percent, depending upon the state. If a scheduled election is not imminent a special election is called within a month or so in which this officer runs for the position against other candidates. If he fails of reelection he is considered recalled. The recall was introduced in 1908 in Oregon and has since been adopted by a total of 11 states. This procedure is available to the electorate only in state and municipal governments.

Recapture Clause. See Railroad Transportation Act.

Recession. A minor business DEPRESSION. The recession of 1937 was marked by a decline of 27 percent in business activity between the summer and end of the year. Slow recovery began in the spring of 1938. The typical characteristics of a depression appeared, although in less severe proportions. Stock prices fell, production declined, and there was an upswing in UNEMPLOYMENT until recovery set in. From the spring of 1949 until winter of 1949-1950, when there was another recession, characterized by the same trends.

Reciprocal Tariff. See Reciprocity.

Reciprocal Trade Agreements. See Trade Agreements Act.

Reciprocity. Agreements in international commerce involving concessions in tariff rates in return for similar concessions from other nations. This system has generally been practiced in European countries but has appeared in United States history only occasionally. The first reciprocity experience was with Canada from 1854 to 1866 under the ELGIN-MARCY TREATY, dealing with fisheries and navigation on the St. Lawrence River. A treaty with HAWAII in 1875, renewed in 1887, dealt with the raw sugar and molasses trade. The first basic reciprocity measure was inaugurated by Secretary of State JAMES G. BLAINE in 1881 and later promoted into the Pan-American movement. The MC KINLEY TARIFF ACT of 1890 included a reciprocity provision under which such treaties were negotiated with a number of Latin-American and European nations. The WILSON-GORMAN TARIFF ACT of 1894 virtually repealed these provisions although they were reaffirmed in the DINGLEY TARIFF ACT of 1897. They were once more repealed by the PAYNE-ALDRICH TARIFF ACT of 1909 although an ad hoc treaty with Canada was negotiated in 1911. The TRADE AGREEMENTS ACT OF 1934 revived the movement which has lasted to date.

Reclamation Act of 1902. See Newlands Reclamation Act.

Reclamation, Bureau of. Located within the DEPARTMENT OF THE INTERIOR. It is responsible for the construction and functioning of many public works designed to supply water for IRRIGATION purposes, to generate electric power, and to engage in flood control projects. The bulk of its work is carried on in the western states.

Recognition of the U.S.S.R. The establishment of diplomatic relationships between the United States and the Soviet Union on November 16, 1933. The Hull-Litvinoff Agreement included Soviet assurances of non-interference with affairs within the United States, a Soviet pledge to refrain directly or indirectly from agitation or propaganda within the United States or its territories, and a further pledge not to allow the formation within its jurisdiction of any revolutionary group aimed against the United States. The Soviet government also promised to secure freedom of conscience and religious liberty for American CITIZENS within its jurisdiction and to grant the right of fair trial for American citizens accused of crimes in the Soviet Union. Both nations agreed to negotiate all existing claims. The Soviet government waived all claims arising out of United States intervention in eastern Siberia and agreed to respect the past and future acts of the United States regulating the property of the Soviet government or its nationals. In 1934 ambassadors were duly exchanged.

Reconstruction. Refers to the attempts after the Civil War to bring back into the Union those states which had seceded. Also applies to the efforts at physical, financial, and political rehabilitation of these states. Under this program various plans were advanced by President LINCOLN, President JOHNSON, moderate congressional Republicans, and the RADICAL REPUBLICANS. It is generally considered that the reconstruction movement was terminated by President HAYES in 1877. The period of Reconstruction is often called the "TRAGIC ERA" because of the bitter sectional hatred between the North and the South, the Negro-White clashes in the South, and the political animosity between the Democratic and the Republican parties.

Reconstruction Acts of 1867. A series of congressional acts passed over President JOHNSON'S VETO. The Act of March 2, 1867 divided the South into five military districts, each under a major general. This officer was authorized to maintain the civil officers and courts or supplant them by military tribunals. New elections were to be held in each state with Negroes participating. When the newly elected legislature had ratified the 14TH AMENDMENT and adopted a new Constitution providing for Negro suffrage, it could apply to Congress for readmission. If acceptable to Congress, the state would be readmitted to the Union. By supplementary acts Congress authorized the military commanders to register the voters and supervise the elections. A more rigid oath of allegiance was enacted that resulted in the disfranchisement of 200,000 southern whites. As a result of these laws 703,000 Negro and 627,000 white voters were registered, elections held, new constitutions adopted, and the former Confederate states readmitted. By 1870 the last of these states had returned to the Union.

Reconstruction Finance Corporation. A federal corporation chartered by Congress in 1932. Its purpose was the alleviation of financial difficulties by lending funds to banks, mortgage companies, insurance companies, RAILROADS, states, municipalities, and other public agencies. The unusual number of bank failures in the preceding three years of the GREAT DEPRESSION, accompanied by the insolvency of other institutions and large withdrawals of deposits, moved the federal government to this solution. The ultimate objectives were the revival of industry, the restoration of credit, and the inducement of private financial institutions to increase their lending capacities. Its original life of 10 years was extended until June 30, 1956 by amending legislation. The R.F.C.'s original working capital of $500,000,000 had been reduced by 1952 to $325,000,000 and its initial authorization to borrow over $20,-000,000,000 had been reduced by 90 percent. During World War II the corporation established other public agencies for the purchase, storage, and sale of critical materials. Scandals involving unauthorized, illegal, or improper loans were exposed during 1952 and brought about a reorganization of the agency. Congress voted abolishment of R.F.C. to be effective June 30, 1954.

Reconstruction Finance Corporation Scandals. A series of scandals involving directors of the RECONSTRUCTION FINANCE CORPORATION, the President's personal assistant, and the Democratic National Committee chairman. The first revelation, in February, 1951, was made by a Senate investigating committee which discovered that a $9,540 mink coat had been given to Mrs. E. Merl Young, a White House stenographer whose husband was suspected of having influenced the RFC in expediting loans, including a $175,000 loan to the furrier. William E. Boyle Jr., Democratic chairman, resigned in October after he had been named as intermediary between RFC director Walter L. Dunham and other RFC clients. Dunham, director William E. Willett, and five others were named on February 2nd in a report of the Senate subcommittee on BANKING as having been influenced by personal and political pressure in extending RFC loans. President TRUMAN called the Senate's report "asinine" on February 8th and declared that all loans had been made in the public interest. Improper loans were later charged against the RFC to the Sorrento Hotel in Miami Beach.

Senator James E. Murray of Montana was named before the Senate committee as interceding on behalf of the $1,000,000 loan to the hotel while his son James A. Murray was declared to have received a fee of $21,000 for this and other cases. In May, 1951 and in the following months the RFC administrator announced the removal of incumbent personnel and their replacement by new appointments. Those removed had been charged with improper influence in securing loans for the American Lithofold Company, Texmass Petroleum Company, Central Iron and Steel Company, Lustron Corporation, and other borrowers.

Reconstruction Plans. See Congress' Reconstruction Plan, Johnson's Reconstruction Plan, and Lincoln's Reconstruction Plan.

Recreation. Colonial recreation differed among the economic and social classes. In the back country drinking, outdoor sports, and militia training provided relaxation from work. Communal activities such as the construction of a home or the launching of a ship offered opportunity for recreation. All the colonists hunted and fished. The wealthy seaboard groups entertained themselves with horse racing, cock fighting, and gambling. Oftentimes these pursuits were frowned upon by the PURITANS, QUAKERS, and other sects. Dancing was probably the most common and popular form of relaxation. Among the wealthy formal dances were frequently extended affairs, a typical dance being one at a wedding in Connecticut which witnessed 92 jigs, 52 country dances, 45 minuets, and 17 hornpipes. Through the 19th century the American farmer relaxed at his church picnic, a husking bee, the county fair, or a trip to town. The drama appeared only occasionally. Reading was restricted to the educated urban population, although the publication of a rural press and the improvement of TRANSPORTATION increased

reading in the outlying areas in the latter part of the century. MUSEUMS, THEATRES, LIBRARIES, and "world fairs" developed as important recreational sources in the late 19th century. The urbanization of the nation produced commercial sports and indoor amusement for most classes. Gymnasiums and tennis courts appeared all over the nation. By 1900 golf, BASKETBALL, BASEBALL, football, boxing, track sports, swimming, and other outdoor sports had become professionalized. Clubs and leagues sprang up throughout the nation and attracted millions of participants and spectators. The amusement park with its games and sideshows had become internationally famous by the 20th century. In Coney Island every type of amusement could be found. By this period the professional theatre and MOTION PICTURE house had opened new recreational opportunities to the American people. In the mid-20th century the American people spent huge sums for RADIO and TELEVISION receivers which gained remarkable popularity in millions of homes. Vacation resorts in mountain, lake, and seashore regions attracted large numbers of enthusiasts. For children puppet shows, children's theatres, the motion picture, and summer camps opened new avenues for combined recreational and educational activities.

Redemptioner. See Indentured Servant.

RED JACKET. Indian name Sagoyewatha. 1758?-1830. Seneca Indian chief. b. New York. Supported the British during the Revolution; famous as an orator; opposed deeding of lands to white men; one of the chiefs of the Six Nations to visit President WASHINGTON (1792); given a medal by the President which he wore; influenced his tribe to support the United States in the War of 1812.

Reed-Bulwinkle Act. A federal law enacted in 1948. It exempted the RAILROADS from the provisions of the ANTI-

533

TRUST LAWS. The law provided that regulation of all MONOPOLY business practices and restraints of trade be transferred to the jurisdiction of the INTERSTATE COMMERCE COMMISSION.

REED, Joseph. 1741-1785. Revolutionary commander and statesman. b. New Jersey. Graduated, College of New Jersey (now Princeton) (1757); studied law and admitted to the bar (1763); studied law in London; practised in New Jersey and was active in pre-Revolution activities; moved to Philadelphia and became president, second Provincial Congress there (1775); military secretary to General WASHINGTON (1775), adjutant general of Continental Army (1775); served in many important battles; member CONTINENTAL CONGRESS (1777, 1778); president, supreme executive council of Pennsylvania (1778-81) and during his administration SLAVERY was abolished in the state; a founder and trustee of the University of Pennsylvania (1782-85).

REED, Thomas Brackett. 1839-1902. Lawyer and legislator. b. Maine. Graduated, Bowdoin College; admitted to the bar (1865); Republican member, U.S. House of Representatives (1877-99); excellent speaker and party leader, he was Speaker of the House (1889-91, 1895-99); known as "Czar Reed" because of Reed's Rules (1890) which increased the Speaker's power in the House and generally favored the majority party; opposed the Spanish-American War and American imperialistic aims; retired to private law practice in New York City.

REED, Walter. 1851-1902. Army surgeon. b. Virginia. Studied medicine at the University of Virginia (M.D. 1869) and Bellevue Medical College (1870); studied bacteriology at Johns Hopkins; entered Army medical corps (1875); investigated yellow fever in CUBA with Carrol and Agramonte (1900) discovering that the disease is carried by a mosquito;

curator, Army Medical Museum, and professor of bacteriology and microscopy at Army Medical College, Washington, D. C. (1893), promoted major (1893). The Walter Reed Hospital, Washington, D. C. was named for him.

Referendum. A method of popular legislation by which a bill or constitutional amendment is submitted to the voters for their approval after having been passed by the legislature. The referendum was introduced in 1898 in South Dakota and has since been adopted by 21 states. In 16 states from five to 10 percent of the voters must sign a referendum petition, and in four other states the number of signatures varies from 7,000 to 15,000. Referenda may be compulsory or optional, depending upon the state and legislative subject. This procedure is available to the electorate only in state and municipal governments.

Reforestation. Organized reforestation goes back to the opening of the 20th century, although some attempts were made in the colonial period. President T. ROOSEVELT'S CONSERVATION program included reforestation on a broad scale. A program was begun by the Forest Service in 1905. By 1914 10,000 acres had been planted. Federal SUBSIDIES and other aid under the TIMBER CULTURE ACT, NEWLANDS ACT, and CLARKE-MC-NARY ACT expanded this program to larger proportions. Simultaneously the states undertook reforestation programs, purchasing and planting millions of acres of neglected farm land. In 1933 the establishment of the CIVILIAN CONSERVATION CORPS carried forward a broad program based on federal funds. The National Park Service and National Forest Service contribute valuable work through the operation of nurseries which annually produce about 100,000,000 trees.

Reformed Church in America. Also

534

known as the Dutch Reformed Church. It was established as the Reformed Protestant Dutch Church in 1628 by the Dutch settlers in NEW AMSTERDAM. They spread throughout New York and New Jersey and became the strongest sect in this region for a century. Although controlled by the Reformed Church of Holland, the movement became independent after the Revolution. In the 19th century it attained strength in the trans-Mississippi region, attracting adherents in Wisconsin, Minnesota, and Michigan. It assumed its present name in 1867. In 1965 there were about 230,000 members of the Reformed Church in America.

Regionalism. A contemporary development in PUBLIC ADMINISTRATION concepts emphasizing the need for planned organization, exploitation, and utilization of the NATURAL RESOURCES, topography, and manpower of large geographic regions. The objectives of regionalism include the elimination of interstate political and economic barriers and the reduction of interstate conflicts and casts for the mutual profit of the POPULATION of such areas. The proponents of the regional idea have long recognized the impracticability of the state boundaries with reference to political and economic relations. They have considered that the United States is devided into six or seven natural regions whose development would be of mutual benefit to the populations of all the states contained therein. The most conspicuous examples of regional development are the TENNESSEE VALLEY AUTHORITY, the COLUMBIA RIVER PROJECT, and the COLORADO RIVER AUTHORITY. Contemplated regional developments include the Missouri Valley and St. Lawrence River programs.

Regulating Act. See Massachusetts Government Act.

Regulators, Uprising of the. A revolt of the frontier and back country people in North Carolina between 1768 and 1771. Heavy taxes, inequitable representation, and improper judicial administration were among the causes that led the FRONTIERSMEN to take up arms against Governor TRYON. In 1771, after three years of wide-spread rebellion on the border, Tryon defeated the Regulators at the battle of Alamance. His successor, Governor Martin, compromised with the rebels.

REID, Whitelaw. 1837-1912. Journalist and diplomat. b. Ohio. Graduated, Miami University, (1856); staff writer, Cincinnati *Gazette* (1861-65); became known for excellent reporting of Civil War; librarian, House of Representatives (1863-66); on staff, New York *Tribune* (1868); managing editor (1869); editor (1872-1905); increased the circulation and power of the paper; appointed U.S. Minister to France (1889-92); Republican vice-presidential candidate (1892); member, U.S. commission to negotiate peace with Spain (1898); special representative at coronation of Edward VII (1902); U.S. Ambassador to Great Britain (1905-12).

Religious Freedom. The liberty of communicants of all churches to observe their faith without restraint by the state. This principle signifies the existence of churches on a footing of equality, with no church enjoying special governmental privileges or exemptions. The first amendment to the federal Constitution established the SEPARATION OF CHURCH AND STATE in the United States. Each state constitution contains a similar clause. In the British colonies state churches existed but were strongly opposed by the Baptists and QUAKERS. The principle of religious freedom was established for the first time in Rhode Island and spread slowly to the other colonies. See separation of church and state.

Religious Toleration. The right of communicants of all churches to practice their faith even though there is an established state religion. Despite the fact that the established church enjoys certain privileges and exemptions other churches remain free from persecution. In the American colonies this principle was first laid down in Maryland. See religious freedom and separation of church and state.

"Remember the Maine." See *Maine, U.S.S.*, sinking of.

REMINGTON, Frederic. 1861 - 1909. Painter. b. New York. Worked and traveled in the West; artist-correspondent in CUBA during the Spanish-American War; famous for his paintings and sculptures of COWBOYS, and scenes of the early West. He was author and illustrator of several books including *Pony Tracks* (1895) and *The Way of an Indian* (1906).

Rendition. The act of returning a fugitive from justice to the state in which he has been accused of a crime and from which he has fled. In international law this is known as EXTRADITION. Rendition is imposed upon the chief executive of the state to which the accused person has fled by Article IV, Section 2 of the federal Constitution. As it has evolved in interstate relationships, state governors frequently refuse to observe this constitutional reading, relying upon a decision of the United States Supreme Court declaring that rendition is morally, but not legally, obligatory.

"Reoccupation of Oregon and Reannexation of Texas." The slogan raised by the Democratic party in the campaign of 1844. The demand was based on the belief that Texas had been included in the TERRITORY of the LOUISIANA PURCHASE and had thus been annexed in 1803. The claim on Oregon was founded on the thinking that Oregon had already been heavily settled by Americans. The slogan was an expression of the expansionist sentiment of the South in this period.

Reorganization Act of 1939. See executive reorganization.

Reorganization Act of 1949. See Hoover Commission.

Reparations. Financial or material compensation for loss or damage, generally applicable to the payment by a defeated nation to a victorious nation. Also known as indemnity. After World War I the TREATY OF VERSAILLES contained the requirement that Germany pay such reparations to the victorious allies and thereby raised serious international economic problems. The former allied powers declared themselves unable to pay their debts to the United States because of their inability to collect German reparations. This insistence in relating war debt payments to reparations was never recognized by the United States government. The failure of the HOOVER MORATORIUM in 1931 resulted in the ultimate forfeiture of debt payments. THE LAUSANNE AGREEMENT of 1932 established the final reparations payments by Germany.

Reparations Commission. Established by the TREATY OF VERSAILLES for the purpose of setting the amount of REPARATIONS to be paid by Germany to the victorious ALLIED POWERS. In 1921 the commission reduced the amount of reparations, tentatively set at $56,000,000,000, to $32,000,000,000 plus payments of materials such as shipping, machinery, coal, and railroad rolling stock.

Repeal Amendment. The 21st amendment to the Constitution, adopted in 1933. It repealed the PROHIBITION amendment (18TH AMENDMENT). This is the only one of the 22 amendments adopted by a ratification of state conventions rather than state legislatures. With its ratification the control over the manufacture and sale of intoxicating liquors was returned to the states. There are today two states with prohibition regulations.

Republican Party. Also known as the G.O.P. (Grand Old Party). Established at Ripon, Wisconsin in 1854 as an amalgamation of former WHIGS and FREE-SOILERS to which adhered business groups, workers, and the professional class. Its first presidential candidate in the election of 1856 was JOHN C. FREMONT. Its first successful candidate was ABRAHAM LINCOLN, elected in 1860. The party achieved national political success in the period from the Civil War to 1932, electing its candidates at every election with the exceptions of Grover Cleveland and Woodrow Wilson in 1884, 1892, 1912, and 1916. It is generally considered to represent the interests of "BIG BUSINESS" and the upper middle class. Historically, it had been identified with an isolationist foreign policy. Domestically the party argued for high tariffs and hard money; and against the welfare state concept and governmental regulation of business. In recent years, however, the liberal elements in both major parties agree substantially in their political philosophies.

Research and Development Board. An agency established by the NATIONAL SECURITY ACT of 1947 to direct the search for new military weapons. It administers a research program on new weapons such as guided missiles, rockets, atomic and HYDROGEN BOMBS, and AVIATION. Congress appropriates, for its use, $500,000,000 annually.

Reserve Officers Training Corps. Popularly known as the R.O.T.C. An organization for the training of military officers in the secondary SCHOOLS and colleges of the United States. It was created by the NATIONAL DEFENSE ACT of 1916 and reestablished in 1920 after having been interrupted by World War I. This system graduates approximately 6,000 students annually with commissions as second lieutenants in the Officers Reserve Corps. As students, they have undergone four years military training under regular army officers subsequent to which they attend a six weeks summer camp.

Reserve Powers. As provided in the Tenth Amendment of the Constitution of the United States these are the powers not delegated to the Congress nor prohibited by it to the states. The number of powers thus reserved is apparently unlimited. They are known as the "POLICE POWERS" inasmuch as they concern themselves with the protection of the public health, welfare, safety, and morals. The bulk of these powers are exercised in the fields of EDUCATION, welfare, public works, RECREATION, health, hospitalization, traffic, and similar matters.

Resettlement Administration. Established in 1935 to administer a program of land retirement, and to resettle displaced FARMERS in other communities. It was given the authority to enable farm tenants to become home owners. The situation which brought this agency into being arose out of the wasteful and destructive use to which much of the farm land of the United States had been put, and the consequent adoption of a program of soil erosion control, land reclamation, reforestation, and the restoration of retired and submarginal lands. In 1937 the Resettlement Administration was reorganized into the FARM SECURITY ADMINISTRATION within the DEPARTMENT OF AGRICULTURE.

Residual Powers. See police powers and state powers.

Restraining Acts. See Intolerable Acts.

Resumption of Specie Payment Act. A law of Congress passed in 1875. It provided that, beginning on January 1, 1879,

537

the Treasury would redeem GREEN-BACKS in gold. The amount redeemed subsequent to the effective date plus the prior redemption of greenbacks reduced the total amount in circulation from $450,000,000 to approximately $346,-000,000. These greenbacks are part of the CURRENCY in circulation today. The act was part of the sound money program of the Republican party in the post-Civil War period and was bitterly condemned by FARMER, DEBTOR, and western groups who sought an easy money program.

"Return to Normalcy." A slogan of the Republican party in the campaign of 1920 by which it sought to return to political power. It was raised to capture votes because of nationwide resentment against the hardships of the war and because of declining prices, UNEMPLOYMENT, overproduction of farm crops, and a fall in industrial production. Charging WILSON with dictatorial powers, Senator WARREN G. HARDING employed the phrase in an address on May 14, 1920 before the Home Market Club in Boston. In the campaign that followed normalcy expressed a program of PROTECTIONISM, open shoppism, subsidies to INDUSTRY, FREE ENTERPRISE, and a reduction of taxes.

REUTHER, Walter Phillip. 1907-1970. Labor leader. b. West Virginia. Started as a tool and die maker and became foreman in an automobile plant in Detroit, Michigan; studied at college at night; discharged from his job in an attempt to organize the plant into a union; travelled in Europe and China (1932-35); returned to the United States (1935) and joined the CIO in organizing the automobile industry; director of GENERAL MOTORS Department of the United Automobile Workers of America; physically assaulted and hospitalized while picketing FORD plant (1940); vice president of the CIO (1946); author of plan to con-vert peacetime industry to war materials production (1941-42); strongly anti-Communist and led movement to expel them from the UAW and CIO; now Vice Pres. of AFL-CIO.

Revenue Act of 1764. See Sugar Act.

revenue sharing. The main thrust of the State and Local Assistance Act of 1972 which provided for more than $30 billion to be given to state and local governments over a five year period was to aid local and state governments in financing public services. The Act mandated local governments to use their share of the money received to improve such areas as public safety, public transportation, health, recreation; and to provide additional social services to the aged and indigent. The basic theory behind revenue sharing is that the federal government can raise money more readily than local governments.

Revenue Tariff. Refers to a purpose of customs collection. The objective of this form of TARIFF is merely to raise revenue as in the case of any tax. The first United States tariff, the Revenue TARIFF OF 1789, was such an act.

REVERE, Paul. 1735-1818. Patriot, silversmith, and engraver. b. Boston, Massachusetts. Took part in capture of Crown Point during the French and Indian Wars (1756); member SONS OF LIBERTY; took part in BOSTON TEA PARTY (1773); official courier, Massachusetts Provincial Assembly and COMMITTEE OF CORRESPONDENCE (1774); rode from Boston to Philadelphia to announce passage of BOSTON PORT BILL (May, 1774); rode to LEXINGTON carrying information to ADAMS and HANCOCK about the British actions (April 16, 1775) stopped at Charlestown to arrange for light signals in church steeple (for which he is famous); most famous ride from Charlestown to Lexington (April 18, 1775) to announce the approach of British troops; this ride was made famous by LONG-

538

FELLOW in a poem, *The Midnight Ride of Paul Revere;* designed and printed the first issue of Continental money; designed and engraved first official seal for the colonies and the state seal for Massachusetts; opened powder mill at Canton; invented process for rolling sheet copper and owned a foundry at Canton for copper rolling and brass casting; assisted Governor SAMUEL ADAMS in laying the corner stone of Massachusetts State House (1795); founder and first president of the Massachusetts Charitable Mechanic Association. Revere is well known for his famous ride but too little known for his excellent engravings and works in silver and copper.

"Revolution of 1800." The term applied to the election of THOMAS JEFFERSON and AARON BURR in 1800. This election marked the end of the FEDERALIST PARTY's power and signalled a victory of the DEMOCRATIC REPUBLICAN's that was to last for a generation. It is considered a "revolution" because it supplanted the power of the aristocratic classes by that of a party whose program was based on the needs and desires of the common people. The various political, economic, and social reforms achieved during the administrations of Jefferson, MADISON, and MONROE emphasized the meaning of this term. These reforms included: the final ABOLITION of PRIMOGENITURE and ENTAIL, the LAND ACT OF 1820, the repeals of the Judiciary Act of 1801, the Whiskey Tax, and the ALIEN AND SEDITION LAWS, the LOUISIANA PURCHASE, the pardoning of the whiskey rebels, the extension of the franchise, the expansion of public EDUCATION, and penal reform.

"Revolution of 1828." The term applied to the election of ANDREW JACKSON in 1828. It signified the radical change in national policies and the transfer of political control from the propertied eastern bankers and manufacturers to the western FARMER and FRONTIERSMAN. See Jacksonian Democracy.

"Revolution of 1910." See Cannon, Joseph Gurney.

REYNOLDS, John Fulton. 1820-1863. Union general. b. Pennsylvania. Graduated, U.S.M.A., West Point (1841); served with General TAYLOR in the Mexican War; brigadier general of volunteers (Aug. 1861); major general (Nov. 1862); military governor of Fredericksburg (1862); captured by Confederate Army and later exchanged; given a command with Army of Potomac and served at FREDERICKSBURG and Chancellorsville; sent by MEADE to capture GETTYSBURG, he was killed during the first day of battle (July 1, 1863).

RHETT, Robert Barnwell. 1800-1876. Statesman. b. South Carolina. Lawyer; served in state legislature (1826); member, U.S. House of Representatives (1837-49); split with CALHOUN, whom he had supported, over state action on TARIFFS; U.S. Senator (1851); known as one of the most ardent "FIREATERS," and advocated SECESSION of South Carolina; member of lower house of Confederate Congress.

Rhode Island. The smallest state in size with an area of 1,214 square miles. Entered the Union on May 29, 1790 as the 13th state. Providence is the capital. In 1950 Rhode Island's POPULATION of 791,896 made it 36th in rank. Its largest cities are Providence, Pawtucket, and Cranston. Rhode Island has the greatest density of population of any state in the nation, yet boasts the greatest per capita industrial production. Ninety percent of the population lives in cities from which come leading manufactures of TEXTILES, jewelry, and silverware. Important minerals include sand, gravel, quartz, granite, and soapstone. Farm crops are apples, corn, hay, oats, and potatoes. The Naval War College is located at Newport which was the summer capital of wealthy society in the late 19th century. Rhode Island was discovered by Verrazano in 1524. Its nickname is "Little Rhody."

RHODES, James Ford. 1848-1927. Historian. b. Ohio. Studied in New York, Paris, and Berlin; in IRON and COAL business in Cleveland (1874-85); after acquiring a fortune he retired to Cambridge, Massachusetts to devote the rest of his life to historical research and writing; he is best known for his work *History of the United States from the Compromise of* 1850 (7 vols. 1893-1906); also wrote *History of the Civil War,* 1861-1865 (1917)..

Rice. Rice production became important in the Carolinas after 1700. For most of the 18th century it remained the greatest source of farm income, spreading to Georgia and Southern Virginia. The necesary water supply for its culture was obtained by IRRIGATION and tidal-flowing. The construction of CANALS, ditches, and sluices on tidal lands was undertaken widely. After the War of 1812 steam power was introduced for threshing. The emancipation of the slaves after the Civil War struck a blow at rice cultivation from which the INDUSTRY did not recover until the institution of labor saving machinery during the AGRICULTURAL REVOLUTION. By the 20th century the Carolinas, Georgia, and Louisiana had restored rice production as a major source of income. In 1955 the production of rice totalled approximately 60,000,000 bushels.

Richmond, fall of. In the last weeks of the Civil War the Confederate capital, defended by General LEE, faced an army three times the size of his own. With General SHERMAN moving north toward the city and General GRANT

pressing south Richmond was evacuated on April 2, 1865. On April 9th Lee was compelled to surrender at Appomattox Courthouse, some 80 miles west of the capital. This marked the end of the war.

RICKENBACKER, Edward Vernon. 1890-1973. Aviator. b. Ohio. Participated in AUTOMOBILE racing before entering the U.S. Army as an aviator (August 25, 1917); commanded 94th Aero Pursuit squadron; considered the outstanding American ace and winner of the CONGRESSIONAL MEDAL OF HONOR; associated with various automotive and aviation companies. Rose to chairman- of- the- board at Eastern Air Lines; lost at sea while on a special mission for the government and rescued after three weeks on a raft in the PACIFIC OCEAN (Nov. 1942). Author o *Seven Came Through* and other book: about his experiences.

Rider. A clause added to a legislative bill bearing no relation to the substance of that bill. Riders are generally AMENDMENTS to appropriations measures. The bill itself is enacted because of its legislative importance, and thus ensures the passage of the rider. The reluctance of the executive to VETO the appropriations measure guarantees the success of the amendment which otherwise would not be passed on its own merits.

"Right of Deposit." The right of American FARMERS in the West in the 1790's to land their goods at New Orleans free of duty, while awaiting trans-shipment on ocean going vessels. The right was recognized by the Spaniards in the PINCKNEY TREATY and suspended by them in 1802. The purchase of the LOUISIANA TERRITORY, the following year, settled the problem permanently.

Right of Way. The right of road, TURNPIKE, and RAILROAD companies to the use of PUBLIC LANDS for a specified distance on both sides of their construction. The right brought with it the privilege to construct buildings and exploit the resources of the site. The distance varied but was generally 100 feet.

Right to Vote. Refers to the presumed right of Americans to cast BALLOTS in elections. Constitutionally no such right to vote exists. As decided by the United States Supreme Court in 1874 in the cases of United States vs. Anthony and Minor vs. Happersett not even CITIZENS have this right. VOTING is a privilege conferred upon either citizens or ALIENS of any age by state legislatures or state constitutions. Thus until 1926 Arkansas conferred the franchise upon aliens with first papers, and Georgia has permitted citizens over 18 to vote since 1943 even though the minimum age is 21 in every other state. The 15TH AMENDMENT prohibits the United States or any state from denying or abridging the suffrage on account of race, color, or previous condition of servitude. The 19TH AMENDMENT contains the same provisions with respect to sex. Neither confers a right to vote upon anybody.

RIIS, Jacob August. 1849-1914. Journalist and philanthropist. b. Denmark. To United States (1870); staff writer, New York *Tribune* (1877-88); writer New York *Sun* (1888-99); close friend of T. ROOSEVELT; did much to improve the SCHOOLS and tenements of lower New York City; suggested the building of parks and playgrounds in SLUM areas; established the Jacob A. Riis Neighborhood House for social work (1888-89); author of many books on social work and best known for his book *The Making of an American* (1901).

RILEY, James Whitcomb. 1853-1916. Poet. b. Indiana. Known as the "Hoosier Poet." Staff writer, Indianapolis *Journal* (1877-85); became famous for poems

written for the paper under the name Benjamin F. Johnson, of Boone. His poems are full of human warmth and understanding, sincerity of purpose, a dry humor, and sentimental pathos. His best known books of poems are *The Old Swimmin' Hole and 'Leven More Poems* (1883), *Old Fashioned Roses* (1888), *Rhymes of Childhood* (1890), *The Little Orfaul (Annie Boat)* (1908), and *When the Frost is on the Punkin* (1911).

Rio Grande River. One of the major rivers of the United States. It flows 1,800 miles from San Juan County in Colorado to the Gulf of Mexico. It is the boundary between Texas and Mexico. It was the belief of many Americans that the LOUISIANA TERRITORY extended to the Rio Grande River, and the treaty by which Florida was purchased in 1819, establishing the Sabine River as the boundary, was deeply resented. The Republic of Texas maintained that the Rio Grande was the legal boundary between it and Mexico. These claims were advanced by the United States after the ANNEXATION OF TEXAS, and were the immediate cause of the Mexican War. The TREATY OF GUADALUPE-HIDALGO established the Rio Grande as the present boundary.

RIPLEY, George. 1802-1880. Literary critic and social reformer. b. Massachusetts. Graduated, Harvard (1832); ordained as a Unitarian minister (1826); joined the TRANSCENDENTALISTS (from 1836); founded and with MARGARET FULLER edited the *Dial* (1840); organized and was leader of the BROOK FARM experiment (1841-47); edited the *Harbinger,* a magazine of the FOURIER movement (1845-49); literary critic, New York *Tribune* (1849-80); founded and was literary editor of the *Harper's New Monthly Magazine;* translated European LITERATURE in *Foreign Standard*

Literature (14 vols. 1838-42); with CHARLES A. DANA, edited *New American Cyclopaedia* (16 vols. 1858-63).

RITTENHOUSE, David. 1732-1796. Astronomer. b. Pennsylvania. Skilled maker of mathematical instruments; built two orreries, one at Princeton University and one for the University of Pennsylvania; built what was believed to be the first telescope in America to observe the transit of Venus (1769); best known for invention of a collimating telescope which introduced the use of spider lines on the focus (1785); served as a member of Pennsylvania assembly and a member of the convention that framed the state's constitution; (1776) president of the COMMITTEE OF SAFETY (1777); treasurer of the state (1777-89); first director, U.S. Mint (1792-95); ardent ANTI-FEDERALIST; succeeded BENJAMIN FRANKLIN as president of the AMERICAN PHILOSOPHICAL SOCIETY (1791-96).

Rivers. Rivers were the principal medium of TRANSPORTATION and COMMUNICATION in colonial America and during the early decades after independence. Along their banks, settlements were founded and grew into important towns and cities. They connected the BACK COUNTRY with the TIDEWATER area, furnishing relatively cheap and efficient traffic arteries. In New England and the middle states the Hudson, Merrimac, Connecticut, Kennebec, Potomac, and Susquehanna Rivers were pre-eminent. They stimulated the WESTWARD MOVEMENT, provided a source of power, and furnished the sites for logging and sawmill operations. In the West, the Ohio and its tributaries, and later the Missouri and Mississippi with their feeder rivers, opened the most fertile area of the United States to habitation and economic exploitation. In the South, great PLANTATIONS were established along the York, James, Roanoke, and Rappahannock Rivers. After the War of 1812 the introduction of the STEAMBOAT replaced the barge and flatboat on the western rivers, providing the greatest stimulus to migration. In the Far West the Sacramento and San Joaquin Rivers brought the "FORTY-NINERS" efficiently into California. The Columbia River and its tributaries became the highway to the Northwest before the Civil War. In recent times the development of large river valleys, such as the Tennessee, Columbia, Colorado, St. Lawrence, and Missouri valleys have pointed the way to new and valuable economic uses.

RIVES, William Cabell. 1793-1868. Political leader and diplomat. b. Virginia. Graduated, William and Mary College (1809); admitted to the bar (about 1814); delegate, state CONSTITUTIONAL CONVENTION (1816); member, U.S. House of Representatives (1823-29); appointed by President JACKSON, U.S. Minister to France (1829-32); U.S. Senator (1832-34, 1836-39, 1841-45); again U. S. Minister to France (1849-53); member of peace commission in Washington which attempted to prevent Civil War (1861); member, Confederate Congress (1861-62).

Roads. In American history roads have been jointly constructed and maintained by the federal, state, and municipal governments. In the first third of the 19th century the federal government advanced funds for the construction of roads as part of a broad program of INTERNAL IMPROVEMENTS. National interest declined in the 1830's. Federal aid was revived in the 20th century as a result of the tremendous growth of the AUTOMOBILE INDUSTRY. By the Rural Post Roads Act of 1916, amended by legislation of 1919 and 1924, federal policy reverted to the aid of the states in building primary interstate roads and secondary connecting links. Like most grant-in-aid arrangements in this and

542

subsequent periods the SUBSIDIES were extended on a matching basis, the states contributing an amount equal to that granted by the Congress. With federal aid, roughly 130,000 miles of roads had been built by 1935 at which time an annual expenditure by all governments on roads was estimated to range up to $3,000,000,000 per annum. By the Federal-Aid Highway Act of 1944 Congress appropriated $500,000,000 a year for three years to establish a national system of interstate highways. By 1965 there were over 1,500,000 miles of streets, roads and highways administered by the state governments. The federal government is financing 40,000 miles of interstate expressways to the extent of 90%; a program expected to be completed in 1972.

Roanoke Settlements. After the failure of the two exploration expeditions of Sir Humphrey Gilbert in 1578 and 1583, his half brother Sir Walter Raleigh spent the rest of his life and his private fortune in an attempt to plant a settlement in Virginia. In 1584 Raleigh was given Gilbert's patent by Queen Elizabeth. In July of that year the expedition landed at Roanoke Island from which its leaders returned to England in a few months with news of its geography and NATURAL RESOURCES. The new land was named Virginia. Raleigh sent over a second expedition in 1585 which became involved in wars with the Indians the following year. The settlement proved a failure and its members returned to England in 1586. The third settlement reached Roanoke Island in 1587 and almost immediately met with difficulties with the Indians. On August 15, 1587 the birth of Virginia Dare in the colony marked the first English birth in North America. Ultimately all trace of the colony disappeared and when Governor John White returned to Roanoke in August, 1591 the only clue to the affairs

of the colony was the word "Croatoan" carved on a tree. Raleigh retired from active colonization, his wealth exhausted. To his credit, however, is the knowledge that he had succeeded briefly in establishing the first English colony in America.

ROBESON, Paul Bustell. 1898-1976. Actor-singer. b. Princeton, N. J. Son of a runaway slave who became a minister. Educated at Rutgers U. where he achieved highest scholastic average in the history of the school. Received law degree from Columbia Law School. Became outstanding concert singer and actor but gave up his career to become an activist for civil rights in the 1940s. For making pro-Soviet statements the State Dept. revoked his passport. In 1958 the Supreme Court restored his rights. He lived many years in the U.S.S.R. but returned to the U.S.

Robin Moor. An American merchant vessel sunk by a German SUBMARINE on May 21, 1941. In a message to Congress President F. D. ROOSEVELT charged the AXIS POWERS with an attempt to extend the area of war. Calling this sinking an act of piracy Roosevelt urged Congress and the people to prepare resistance against Germany's plan to control the seas and dominate the Western Hemisphere. The President's views were an open attack on ISOLATIONIST sentiment in Congress and a demand for a strategy to STRIKE the enemy before he could launch a direct attack upon the United States.

ROBINSON, Beverley. 1723-1792. Loyalist. b. Virginia. Served as major under Wolfe at Quebec; raised and became colonel of LOYALIST regiment in New York (1776); involved in ARNOLD'S TREASON and pleaded for life of MAJOR ANDRE; when British forces evacuated New York, he fled to Canada. Died in England.

543

ROBINSON, Charles. 1818-1894. PIONEER, journalist, and political leader. b. Massachusetts. Studied at Amherst College and graduated from Berkshire Medical School (1843); practiced in Massachusetts; to California (1849); founded and edited *Settlers' and Miners' Tribune* in Sacramento (1850); entered state legislature, he supported SQUATTER SOVEREIGNTY and opposed SLAVERY in California; back to Massachusetts to edit Fitchburg *Weekly News* (1853-54); to Kansas as agent for the NEW ENGLAND EMIGRANT AID SOCIETY to try to prevent that state from becoming a slave state (1854); leader of FREE STATE group; in command of Kansas Volunteers; member of Topeka Convention which adopted a free state constitution; elected governor of that TERRITORY (1856); first governor of the state of Kansas (1861-65); generously endowed the state university.

ROBINSON, Edwin Arlington. 1869-1935. Poet. b. Maine. Studied at Harvard and awarded honorary degrees from Yale and Bowdoin; known for work with summer group in Peterboro, N.H.; his known books are *The Children of the Night* (1897), *The Man against the Sky* (1916), *Lancelot* (1920), *Collected Poems*, which was awarded the Pulitzer Prize (1921); *The Man Who Died Twice* (1924-Pulitzer Prize), *Tristram* (Pulitzer Prize, 1927), and *The Glory of the Nightingales* (1930).

Robinson-Patman Act. Enacted by Congress on June 20, 1936 as an amendment to the CLAYTON ANTI-TRUST ACT. It is sometimes called the Anti-Chain Store Act. The law prohibited price discrimination against purchasers of commodities where such discrimination has the tendency to create MONOPOLY conditions or to reduce competition. It forbade special or concealed discounts to such purchasers and narrowed the exceptions allowed under the Clayton Act. It specifically outlawed certain methods by which price discriminations were accomplished other than through selling prices. These prohibitions included suspect middleman or advertising fees and concealed quality deterioration. The Act was designed to protect small independent dealers against the discount prices at which CHAIN STORES were able to purchase their goods because of their volume buying. The act is administered by the FEDERAL TRADE COMMISSION.

ROCHAMBEAU, Jean Baptist Donatien de Vimeur, Comte de. French general. Commanded French force sent to aid the American colonists during the Revolution (1780); joined WASHINGTON's CONTINENTAL ARMY at White Plains, N.Y. (July, 1781); was important in the defeat of CORNWALLIS forcing his surrender (Oct. 19, 1781); returned to France (1783).

Rockefeller Center. It is located in New York City and is the largest privately owned business and entertainment center in the United States. It consists of 15 buildings whose construction was begun in 1931. The surface area covers 549,856 square feet or more than 12½ acres. The Center is leased from Columbia University for an annual rental of $3,500,000. In 2015 the Center will revert to the ownership of the University. The estimated daily population of the Center is 160,000, including the 32,000 employees of its 1,100 tenants and 128,000 visitors. The largest indoor THEATER in the world, seating 6200 people, is located there. The studios of the National Broadcasting Company and the American Broadcasting Company are located in the 70 story R.C.A. building. In the Center are established many restaurants, garages, landscape gardens, special exhibitions, shops, a gymnasium, a skating rink, a U.S. POST OFFICE, a government passport bureau, and the consulates of 20 foreign nations.

Rockefeller Foundation. Established in 1913 "to promote the well-being of mankind throughout the world." Its program is the advancement of knowledge. It has engaged in vast research projects in the fields of MEDICINE, public health, social studies, and humanities. Its efforts are aimed at raising the general cultural level and at the promotion of cultural interchange among countries. It is not an operating organization, granting funds to universities and other agencies for the carrying on of its projects. Its main office is located in New York City.

ROCKEFELLER, John Davison. 1839-1937. Oil magnate, capitalist, philanthropist. b. New York. Moved to Cleveland, Ohio (1853); worked as bookkeeper, in produce commission business and later in OIL refinery; organized the STANDARD OIL COMPANY (1870); gained a MONOPOLY of the oil business (1882) with the formation of the Standard Oil Trust; the TRUST was ordered dissolved by the courts (1892); retired from leadership of company (1911); took part in organization of UNITED STATES STEEL CORPORATION; had interest in RAILROADS; established and endowed ROCKEFELLER FOUNDATION, General Education Board, Rockefeller Institute for Medical Research, University of Chicago, etc.

ROCKEFELLER, Nelson Aldrich (1908-)—Statesman. Grandson of John D. Rockefeller. After serving in the family business with Chase Manhattan Bank, Creole Petroleum Co., and Rockefeller Center, he entered a long career of government service: as Coordinator of Inter-American Affairs in 1940-44; Assistant Secretary of State for Latin Affairs in 1944-45; chairman of Development Advisory Board in 1950-51; Undersecretary of Department of Health, Education, and Welfare, and Special Assistant to President Eisenhower in 1954-55; chairman of the president's Advisory Committee on Government Organization 1953-58; governor of the State of New York in 1958 and served 4 terms. He was an unsuccessful candidate for presidential nomination in 1964 and 1968. After resigning as governor in December 1973 to direct his Commission on Critical Choices for Americans he accepted the nomination as vice-president under President Ford August 20, 1974. He announced well before the 1976 presidential campaign that he would not be a candidate for president or vice-president.

ROCKHILL, William Woodville. 1854-1914. Diplomat. b. Philadelphia, Pa. Graduated French military school and served in French army; served as U.S. secretary of the legation, Peking, China (1884-86); chargé d'affaires, Korea (1886-87); under the auspices of the SMITHSONIAN INSTITUTE he made important explorations into China, Mongolia, and Tibet (1888-89, 1891-92); appointed U.S. Assistant Secretary of State (1894-97); U.S. Minister to Greece, Rumania, and Serbia (1897-99); sent as special agent to China to settle difficulties after the BOXER REBELLION (1900); U.S. Minister to China (1905-09); U.S. Ambassador to Russia (1909-11); U.S. Minister to Turkey (1911-13); author of books on the Orient.

rock music. A mixture of country-western and blues, rock music developed in the mid-1950's and continued on into the 1960s and the 1970s. As a kind of music of revolt and social comment, it has been adopted by young people who link it to their life style. At Woodstock, New York and at Watkins Gien major festivals have taken place. Names associated with rock music are Mick Jagger, The Rolling Stones, Ray Charles, Elvis Presley and Bob Dylan.

ROCKWELL, Norman. 1894-   Artist b. New York City. Most famous as illustrator

545

especially for covers of magazine, Saturday Evening Post for over two generations. Depicted nostalgic episodes of American family life.

Rocky Mountains. The greatest mountain range in the United States. They were first discovered by Coronado in 1540, although the Mexican Rockies had been seen earlier. Their vast resources of metals furnished the greatest stimulus to their EXPLORATION. French and English explorers, following the Spaniards, sought the valuable resources of furs, game, and fish. Beaver, bear, buffalo, and deer abounded in the area. The LOUISIANA PURCHASE extended United States TERRITORY to the Rocky Mountains which were first officially explored by the LEWIS AND CLARK EXPEDITION. Subsequently the explorations of ZEBULON M. PIKE, JOHN C. FREMONT, and Major Long supplied a wealth of data about the flora and fauna of the region. Passes through the mountains became the gateways of the settlers under MARCUS WHITMAN, the MORMONS, and the gold miners before the Civil War. Melting snow from the high crests furnish the water for the IRRIGATION canals that make farming possible. The LUMBER resources of the mountainside forests have become one of the most important sources of the wealth of the West.

RODGERS, John. 1773-1838. Naval officer. Served as lieutenant in the first organized navy (1798); served against the Barbary pirates; in command of the *President* which was sent to stop the British ship *Guerriere* and its IMPRESSMENT of American seamen; he overhauled the British ship *Little Belt* and destroyed her; this was one of the incidents leading up to the War of 1812; president of the board of naval commissioners (1815-24, 1827-37); acting U.S. Secretary of War (1823).

RODNEY, Caesar. 1728-1784. Revolutionary statesman. b. Delaware. Delegate, STAMP ACT CONGRESS (1765); leader in Delaware; member, CONTINENTAL CONGRESS (1774-76, 1777-1778); signer of the DECLARATION OF INDEPENDENCE; major general, serving with Delaware militia during the Revolution; president of Delaware (1778-82).

ROEBLING, John Augustus. 1806-1869. Civil engineer and industrialist. b. Germany. Came to the United States (1831); became a naturalized citizen (1837); responsible for the success of steel cable, having organized the first wire rope factory in America (1841); famous for his building of suspension bridges including the one over Niagara River at Niagara Falls (1855) and his greatest achievement which was the designing and planning of the BROOKLYN BRIDGE.

ROEBLING, Washington Augustus. 1837-1926. Engineer. Son of JOHN ROEBLING. Graduated, Rensselaer Polytechnic Institute; served with the Union Army during the Civil War rising to the rank of colonel; working from his father's plans, he was largely responsible for directing the construction of the BROOKLYN BRIDGE. He served as chief engineer on the project at his father's death (1869) and carried the work to completion (1883).

Rogers Act. Passed by Congress in 1924. It provided for the consolidation of the American consular and DIPLOMATIC SERVICE into a single body. The transfer of personnel from the diplomatic to the consular corps and vice versa and the establishment of a personnel and salary classification system were also included.

ROGERS, Robert. 1731-1795. FRONTIERSMAN and soldier. b. Massachusetts. Served in French and Indian Wars; famous as the leader of "Rogers' Rangers" in their gallant raids against the Indians; during the Revolution he was thought to be a spy for the British and was imprisoned by WASHINGTON; escaped; organized the Queen's Rangers for the British but was defeated at White Plains, N.Y. He fled to England.

ROLFE, John. 1585-1622. British colonist. b. England. Settled in JAMESTOWN, Virginia (1610); important for discovery of method of curing TOBACCO so that it could be sold for export; tobacco became the staple crop of the colony; married POCAHONTAS, daughter of POWHATAN, the Indian chief; member, council of the VIRGINIA COLONY (1619).

"Roosevelt Corollary." The interpretation of the MONROE DOCTRINE made by President T. ROOSEVELT in his annual message on December 6, 1904. This interpretation justified United States' intervention in Latin-American nations to prevent European interference with their internal affairs. The result of the "Roosevelt Corollary" was intervention by the United States in CUBA, SANTO DOMINGO, HAITI, and NICARAGUA in subsequent years. It was officially repudiated by the United States in the DECLARATION OF LIMA in 1938.

ROOSEVELT, Eleanor. 1884-1962. First Lady and diplomat. b. New York City. Niece of T. ROOSEVELT and wife of F. D. ROOSEVELT (1905); active in social work, women's organizations, youth movements, and consumer groups; she has been interested in the rights of minority groups; held the first PRESS CONFERENCE ever held by a President's wife (1933); author of a syndicated newspaper column MY DAY (1935); assistant director of the OFFICE OF CIVILIAN DEFENSE (1941-42); appointed a delegate of the United States to the UNITED NATIONS (1945); chairman of the Commission on Human Rights (from 1946); lectured and traveled all over the world. Author of *This is My*

Story (1937), and *This I Remember* (1949).

ROOSEVELT, Franklin Delano. 1882-1945. Thirty-second President of the United States. b. Hyde Park, N.Y. Distant cousin of THEODORE ROOSEVELT. Graduated, Harvard University (1904); studied at Columbia Law School (1904-07); member of law firm of Roosevelt and O'Connor (1924-33); married distant cousin, Eleanor Anna Roosevelt (1905); member, New York state senate (1910-13); leader of independent Democrats; supported WILSON for the presidency; appointed by him, Assistant Secretary of the Navy (1913-20); unsuccessful candidate for Vice-President of the United States (1920); stricken with infantile paralysis; supported ALFRED E. SMITH for the presidency (1928); successful candidate for governor of New York (1929-33); supported social legislation, developed water power projects; supported regulation of PUBLIC UTILITIES; elected President (1933-45); he was the first President of the United States to be re-elected for a third term; declared a "BANK HOLIDAY" his second day in office; responsible for the legislative reforms known as the "NEW DEAL"; inaugurated a program of relief and public works; secured OLD AGE PENSIONS, UNEMPLOYMENT INSURANCE, SLUM clearance and HOUSING projects, ABOLITION of CHILD LABOR and better relations between management and labor; with Winston Churchill he wrote the ATLANTIC CHARTER (August 1941); granted emergency powers by Congress to determine the country's military production and civilian economy during World War II. Conferred with Churchill, Vargas, Camacho, Chiang Kai-shek, and Stalin on war strategy and international cooperation. Died of a cerebral hemorrhage at Warm Springs, Georgia (April 12, 1945). For his contribution to the social and economic advances of the United States, he will go down in history as an outstanding American President.

ROOSEVELT, Theodore. 1858-1919. Twenty-sixth President of the United States. b. New York City. Graduated, Harvard University (1880); studied law, Columbia University Law School (1880-81); member, New York State legislature (1882-84); appointed by President HARRISON member, U.S. CIVIL SERVICE COMMISSION (1889-95); president, New York City Board of Police Commissioners (1895-97) where he sponsored a reform program; appointed by President MC KINLEY, Assistant. Secretary of the Navy (1897-98) organized, with LEONARD WOOD, the "ROUGH RIDERS", the first volunteer cavalry unit of the Spanish-American War; served in CUBA as colonel (1898); elected governor of New York (1899-1900); elected Vice-President of the United States (1901), succeeding to the presidency on the death of McKinley (September 14, 1901); re-elected (1904); flamboyant in personality and aggressive in his policies, he made attempts to curb "BIG BUSINESS" and regulate "TRUSTS"; he fought for a strong CONSERVATION program; responsible for the "BIG STICK" policy in the Caribbean area which led to "DOLLAR DIPLOMACY"; he was responsible for the nomination of TAFT for the presidency; went on big game expedition to Africa (1909-10); nominated for the presidency on the "BULL MOOSE" ticket of the PROGRESSIVE PARTY and defeated by WILSON (1912); opposed Wilson's policies but unsuccessfully sought a military appointment (1917-18). Author of many books on game hunting, biographies cf other American personalities, and history.

ROOT, Elihu. 1845-1937. Lawyer and statesman. b. New York. Graduated, Hamilton College (1864); graduated, New York University Law School (1867); admitted to the bar; practiced in New York City, leading conservative Republican; appointed by MC KINLEY, U.S. Secretary of War (1899-1904); appointed by T. ROOSEVELT, Secretary of State (1905-09); known for attempt at better relations with Latin American countries and steps toward international peace and security; served as U.S. Senator from New York (1909-15); awarded NOBEL PEACE PRIZE (1912); served as counsel for the United States in North Atlantic Fisheries Arbitration (1910); member, HAGUE TRIBUNAL (1910); president, CARNEGIE ENDOWMENT FOR INTERNATIONAL PEACE; one of the founders of the WORLD COURT. Author of books on government and international relations.

Root Protocol. Also known as the Root Formula and World Court Protocol. Drawn up by ELIHU ROOT as a proposal to overcome objections of the United States Senate to American membership in the PERMANENT COURT OF INTERNATIONAL JUSTICE. The Protocol provided that in all matters involving advisory opinions the United States should be notified and given an opportunity to file objections. If the LEAGUE OF NATIONS desired such an opinion from the Court in spite of the objections to it, the United States could withdraw from the Court "without any imputation of unfriendliness." In spite of this attempt to amend the World Court statute the Senate in January, 1935 rejected the Protocol by a vote of 52 to 36.

Root-Takahira Agreement. Negotiated as an EXECUTIVE AGREEMENT between the United States and Japan in 1907. It provided for the mutual recognition of the OPEN-DOOR POLICY in China, the independence of China, and the recognition of each nation's territorial possessions in the Pacific. The agreement arose out of the political problems between the two nations following Japan's rise to power after the Russo-Japanese War.

ROPER, Daniel Calhoun. 1867-1943. Lawyer and political leader. b. South Carolina. Graduated, Duke University; studied law in Washington, D.C.; served in Census Bureau; clerk of WAYS AND MEANS COMMITTEE of the House of Representatives (1910-13); appointed by WILSON, First Assistant Postmaster General (1913-16); Commissioner of Internal Revenue (1917-20); appointed by F. D. ROOSEVELT, Secretary of Commerce (1933-38); Minister to Canada (1939).

ROSECRANS, William Starke. 1819-1898. Union general. b. Ohio. Graduated, U.S.M.A., West Point (1842); commissioned brigadier general in the U.S. Army at the outbreak of the Civil War; succeeded MC CLELLAN in command of the Department of the Ohio (1861); major general of volunteers (1862); commanded the army at Cumberland, MURFREES-BORO and was defeated at CHICKAMAUGA and relieved of his command (1863); commanded Department of the Missouri (1864); resigned (1867); U.S. Minister to Mexico (1868-69); member, U.S. House of Representatives from California (1881-85); U.S. Register of the Treasury (1885-93).

Rosenberg Case. Julius and Ethel Rosenberg were accused of giving information on the atomic bomb to the Soviets and were found guilty in a Federal Court on April 5, 1951. They were executed at Sing Sing on June 19, 1953. To the present many efforts are still being made to prove their innocence.

ROSS, Betsy. *Name in full,* Elizabeth Griscom Ross. 1752-1836. Flagmaker. b. Philadelphia, Pa. When the stars-and-stripes flag was adopted as a national emblem by a resolution of the CONTINENTAL CONGRESS (June 14, 1777); Mrs. Ross was commissioned to make the flag. It is believed that she was requested to do so by GEORGE WASHINGTON, ROBERT MORRIS and GEORGE ROSS.

ROSS, George. 1730-1779. Jurist. b. Delaware. Lawyer, Lancaster, Pennsylvania; member, colonial legislature; member, CONTINENTAL CONGRESS (1774-77); signer of the DECLARATION OF INDEPENDENCE.

ROSS, John. *Indian name* Coowescoowe or Kooweskoowe. 1790-1866. CHEROKEE Indian chieftain. b. Georgia. Son of Scotch father and Cherokee mother; educated in Tennessee; served with ANDREW JACKSON in wars against the CREEK INDIANS (1812); president, National Council of Cherokees (1819-26); chief, United Cherokee Nation (1839-66); fought policy of moving the Cherokee nation into INDIAN TERRITORY (1839) but led them west; 4,000 members of the tribe died enroute.

Rotation in Office. The principle which advocates short terms of public office and frequent changes of personnel. As interpreted by President JACKSON rotation in office signified a democratic method of giving all qualified persons the opportunity to work for the federal government. He maintained in his annual message in 1829 that the duties of public office should be made available to all and that new skills should be furnished to the public service. Jackson has been accused of furthering a SPOILS SYSTEM by his views.

R.O.T.C. See Reserve Officers Training Corps.

"Rough Riders." The name applied to the cavalry regiment led by Colonel LEONARD WOOD and Lieutenant Colonel THEODORE ROOSEVELT in the Spanish-American War. This widely advertised and flamboyant unit was recruited from CATTLE ranges, MINING camps, and western sheriffs, and after a short training period at San Antonio in the spring of 1898 they were officially designated as The First U.S. Cavalry Volunteers. When they left Tampa, Florida for the war area, their horses and half of their personnel were abandoned, the fragmentary remainder embarking for CUBA. Their charge up SAN JUAN HILL, although unconventional, was successful and the source of much subsequent dramatic and literary work.

ROWLAND, Henry Augustus. 1848-1901. Physicist. Studied at Rensselaer Polytechnic Institute, Troy, N.Y.; first professor of physics, Johns Hopkins (1875-1901); important for his invention of a grating (curved) for the spectroscope; determined *mechanical equivalent of heat and of the ohm;* did research in the solar spectrum and in alternating currents. One of the founders of the American Physical Society.

Royal Colony. A type of British colony in which the king ruled directly through an appointive governor. This type was first established in Virginia when its charter was revoked in 1624. By the opening of the Revolution all colonies were of this form with the exception of Connecticut, Maryland, Pennsylvania, and Rhode Island. In the royal colony the king governed without limitation, except for the "power of the purse" exercised by the COLONIAL ASSEMBLY. All colonial appointments were made by the king who also exercised a VETO power over the legislation of the assembly.

ROYCE, Josiah. 1855-1916. Philosopher. b. California. Professor of philosophy at Harvard (from 1892) who was noted as a metaphysician; he based his philosophy on the principle of individuality and will rather than the intellect. He wrote many books on the subject of philosophy.

Rubber Industry. Although first used commercially in England as early as 1820, rubber did not become important in the United States until CHARLES GOODYEAR developed his vulcanization process in 1839. The product was subsequently used in various commercial items but did not become important until the development of the AUTOMOBILE INDUSTRY in the 20th century. Today automobile tires consume approximately three-quarters of all commercial rubber produced. Until the 20th century, Brazil furnished over 99 percent of the total supply of world rubber, a figure rapidly declining thereafter as a result of the exploitation of rubber plantations in the East Indies, Africa, Central America, and India. From the beginning, the United States has assumed first place in the world's manufacture of rubber, producing more than the combined facilities of the rest of the world. Ohio produces more than 50 percent of all rubber products in this country. The industry exceeded $11 billion in volume in 1964. Synthetic rubber accounted for 25% of the total consumed in this country. The boom in automobile sales pushed the number of tires for new equipment to 43,000,000 and for replacements to about 100,000,000.

Rubber Reserve Company. A subsidiary CORPORATION of the RECONSTRUCTION FINANCE CORPORATION. It was established in June, 1940 and transferred to the DEPARTMENT OF COMMERCE in February, 1942. Its objective was the procurement at home and abroad of natural, synthetic, and scrap RUBBER for war purposes.

"Rugged Individualism." The term referring to the political, economic, and social principles which have historically been considered intrinsic to the American way of life. As developed in the theory of FREDERICK J. TURNER, individualism has developed out of the conditions of FRONTIER life in American history and has expressed the democratic and libertarian philosophy of the WESTWARD MOVEMENT. The phrase was used during the HOOVER administration as a justification for the LAISSEZ-FAIRE approach to government regulation of business.

"Rule of Reason." A constitutional doctrine established by the United States Supreme Court in 1911 in deciding the anti-trust prosecutions of the STANDARD OIL COMPANY and American Tobacco Company. The Court held that the restraints of TRADE by these two corporations were not unreasonable, and went on to argue that Congress' restrictions in the SHERMAN ANTI-TRUST ACT had been intended to apply only to unreasonable restraints of trade. The effect of the decision was to limit the application of the Act only to combinations considered by the Court to be unreasonable or in unreasonable restraint of trade.

Rule of Unanimity. The principle requiring the unanimous vote of the members of the Council of the LEAGUE OF NATIONS in carrying a measure. In the UNITED NATIONS the phrase has been applied to the requirement of a unanimous vote of the five great powers of the SECURITY COUNCIL in carrying substantive measures. In the latter situation the rule of unanimity is oftentimes referred to as the "great power veto." The Soviet Union's frequent exercise of this power, (51 vetoes by 1952), has lead to many demands for a modification of the Charter, designed to eliminate it. The principle virtually prevented action by the League of Nations against aggressors. It was generally recognized that major powers on the Council influenced minor power voting against a measure to ensure its defeat while simultaneously the major powers maintained "face" in terms of world public opinion. In the United Nations a procedural revision in 1950 enabled the General Assembly to act in certain areas after a great power veto in the Security Council.

Rule of 1756. Also known as the Rule of the War of 1756. A doctrine laid down by England at the opening of the Seven Years' War declaring that she would prohibit neutrals from engaging in any TRADE in time of war which was forbidden in time of peace. This rule was enforced by British prize courts. American effort to circumvent this limitation on neutral trade, by carrying French goods to United States ports for trans-shipment, was sustained in the *Polly* case in 1802 but was modified in the *Essex* case in 1805.

Rule of the War of 1756. See Rule of 1756.

Rum, Manufacture of. In the British colonies molasses was imported from the WEST INDIES in exchange for LUMBER and fish. New England, in the 17th century, became the leading manufacturer of rum from molasses. In Boston alone almost 1,500,000 gallons of rum were made from molasses purchased in the French West Indies. A profitable trade grew up by the sale of rum to Africa for slaves which were sold to the West Indies for molasses. This "triangular trade" was the mainstay of colonial prosperity through much of the 18th century. Since the colonists found this trade more profitable with the Dutch, French, and Spanish islands a good deal of COMMERCE was lost to Great Britain. Parliament's efforts to limit this trade by imposing the SUGAR ACT in 1733 failed because of the rise of SMUGGLING. Rum MANUFACTURING remained important throughout the 19th century. The expense of finer liquors prohibited their use by low income groups who found rum more available. In 1961, 1,706,000 gallons of rum were manufactured in the United States.

"Rum, Romanism, and Rebellion." A phrase contained in a speech by a New York minister, the Rev. S. D. Burchard, during the presidential campaign of 1884. Addressed to the Republican candidate, JAMES G. BLAINE, Burchard condemned the Democratic party in these terms. Although Blaine took no notice of this slur at the Catholic population, the phrase reacted against his success. CLEVELAND, the democratic candidate, carried New York by only 1149 votes, and was elected President. It is clear that the phrase, along with other factors, cost Blaine the election.

Rural Credits Act. Passed by Congress in 1916 in the period of preparedness before America's entry into World War I. The law established twelve Federal Farm Banks patterned after the FEDERAL RESERVE BANKS. These farm banks were authorized to lend funds on long term farm mortgages at a rate not exceeding six percent. Inasmuch as the prevailing interest rate was over 10 percent on a total of $3,500,000,000 worth of farm mortgages the Act was expected to relieve FARMERS of this financial burden and thus stimulate them to become more efficient producers.

Rural Electrification. The program, initiated on a large scale by the NEW DEAL administration, which attempted to bring the benefits of ELECTRIC power to the rural areas of the United States. Federal promotion of rural electrification began on May 11, 1935 with the creation of the Rural Electrification Administration by EXECUTIVE ORDER. Subsequently, Congress enacted the Rural Electrification Act, giving the R.E.A. statutory basis and appropriating $40,000,000 for each of the next 10 years. With these funds the Administration was to plan the electrification of the rural countryside, and grant loans to states and their subdivisions and to farm cooperative associations for the purpose of constructing electrification facilities. Under the terms of the statute, 25 year loans are granted for the erection of generating plants and lines. Short term loans are made to finance private investments in electrifying homesteads. By the end of World War II, the Administration's loans totalled over $370,000,000. Although more than 1,-000,000 homes had been electrified by this time, it was estimated that 7,000,-000 farmsteads still remained without electrical services. In 1939 the R.E.A. was transferred to the DEPARTMENT OF AGRICULTURE. By 1951 the R.E.A. had made loans of more than $2,350,000,000 to 1,076 borrowers, including 952 rural cooperatives. The latter have borrowed more than 95 percent of the agency's funds. Borrowers have constructed 1,-100,000 miles of line which serve nearly 3,500,000 rural consumers, of whom three-fourths are farmers. Of its loans the losses by 1951 were about $40,000.

Rural Electrification Act. See Rural Electrification.

Rush-Bagot Treaty. An agreement between the United States and Great Britain permanently settling the problems of American-Canadian relations. The TREATY provided for the disarmament of the FRONTIER between these two nations and thus tended to remove the causes of disputes. It also prohibited naval armament on the GREAT LAKES, except for policing purposes. This unusual example of an undefended and unfortified 3,000 mile frontier endures to this day.

RUSH, Benjamin. 1745?-1813. Physician and political leader. b. near Philadelphia, Pennsylvania. Graduated, Princeton; studied MEDICINE in Edinburgh, London and Paris; professor of chemistry, College of Philadelphia (1769-91); member, CONTINENTAL CONGRESS (1776, 1777); signer, DECLARATION OF INDEPENDENCE; Surgeon-General of the Continental Army; established the first dispensary in the United States (1786); member, Pennsylvania convention to ratify the Constitution (1786); successful in treatment of yellow fever during the epidemic (1793); appointed Treasurer, U.S. Mint (1797-1813); founder of the first AMERICAN ANTISLAVERY SOCIETY. Author of books on medicine.

552

RUSH, Richard. 1780-1859. Lawyer, statesman and diplomat. b. Philadelphia, Pennsylvania. Son of BENJAMIN RUSH. Graduated, Princeton; admitted to the bar (1800); attorney-general of Pennsylvania (1811); Comptroller, U.S. Treasury (1811); appointed U.S. Attorney General (1814-17); acting Secretary of State (1817); U.S. Minister to Great Britain (1817-25); believed to have persuaded MONROE and JOHN Q. ADAMS on the policy of the MONROE DOCTRINE; appointed by Adams, U.S. Secretary of the Treasury (1825-28); unsuccessful candidate for the vice-presidency; U.S. Minister to France (1847-49).

RUSH, William. 1756-1833. Sculptor. b. Philadelphia, Pennsylvania. Considered the first native-born American sculptor. Famous for his carved figureheads for the prows of ships; a life-size wood statue of WASHINGTON is in INDEPENDENCE HALL, Philadelphia; portraits of Voltaire, WILLIAM PENN, BENJAMIN FRANKLIN and others are done in wood and bronze. He was one of the founders of the Pennsylvania Academy of Fine Arts.

Rusk, Dean, 1909-   . Secretary of State. 1961-69, b. Georgia. Since 1934 has served in several important government posts in the State Department. Was special assistant Secretary of War (1946-1947).

RUSK, Thomas Jefferson. 1803-1857. Jurist and political leader. b. South Carolina. Studied law with JOHN C. CALHOUN; settled in Texas (1835); member, convention that declared Texas independent (1836); Secretary of War in the provisional government of Texas (1836); fought at SAN JACINTO; took over command of the army of Texas after HOUSTON was wounded; first chief justice, Texas supreme court (1838-42); president of the convention that confirmed the ANNEXATION OF TEXAS to the United States (1845) and aided in the drafting of the state constitution; served as U.S. Senator (1846-57).

RUSSELL, Lillian. 1861-1922. Actress and singer. Real name was Helen Louise Leonard. b. Iowa. Made debut as actress at Tony Pastor's in New York City in Gilbert and Sullivan operettas (1879); she made a great hit in these and later musical comedies; achieved outstanding triumphs at Weber and Fields Music Hall (1899); was famous for her beauty and fine singing voice.

Russell Sage Foundation. Established in 1907 by Mrs. RUSSELL SAGE as a memorial to her husband. The program of the Foundation is designed to improve social and living conditions in the United States and to increase the application in social work of the results of research in that field. Its office is located in New York City.

RUTLEDGE, Edward. 1749-1800. Jurist. b. South Carolina. Studied law; admitted to the bar and practised in South Carolina (1773); member, CONTINENTAL CONGRESS (1774-77); signer of the DECLARATION OF INDEPENDENCE; member, South Carolina legislature (1782-96); member, state CONSTITUTIONAL CONVENTION (1790); author of act that abolished the law of PRIMOGENITURE (1791); governor of South Carolina (1798-1800).

RUTLEDGE, John. 1739-1800. Jurist and statesman. b. South Carolina. Studied in South Carolina and in London; practised law in Charleston, S.C. (from 1761); delegate, STAMP ACT CONGRESS (1765); member, CONTINENTAL CONGRESS (1774-76; 1782-83); president and commander in chief, South Carolina (1776-78); governor of the state (1779-82); member of the state convention that ratified the Constitution (1788); Associate Justice, U.S. Supreme Court (1789-91); Chief Justice (1795) served one term but was not confirmed by Senate.

RYDER, Albert Pinkham. 1847-1917. Painter. b. Massachusetts. Best known for marines, landscapes, and figure paintings. Member of the National Academy. His most famous work is *Toilers of the Sea* which hangs in the Metropolitan Museum of Art, N.Y. Other well known works include *Moonlight at Sea, The Curfew Hour, The Bridge, and The Smuggler's Cove.*

S

SABIN, Florence Rena. 1871-1953. Anatomist. Graduated, Smith College (B.S. 1893); Johns Hopkins (M.D. 1900); gained recognition for a model she made of the brain stem of a newly born child which proved important in the teaching of neurology; associate professor of anatomy, Johns Hopkins (1902-17); professor of histology (1917-25); member of the staff of the Rockerfeller Institute for Medical Research (1925-38); winner, National Achievement Award (1932); well known for research in tuberculosis.

Sacco-Vanzetti Case. Refers to the arrest, trial, and ultimate execution of two anarchists accused of holding up and murdering a shoe factory paymaster at South Braintree, Massachusetts. The trial was conducted in an atmosphere of manifest prejudice, with the acceptance of evidence so inadequate as to convince American and world public pinion that the men were being tried f . their political and economic beliefs. The arrests of 1920 led to a trial extending over a period of seven years until they were ultimately executed in 1927. The case provoked world wide resentment manifested by demonstrations, meetings of protest, and international journalistic activity in their behalf. It has been acknowledged that the affair arose out of the anti-radical feeling of that period, also evidenced by the Palmer raids and alien deportations.

SAGE, Russell. 1816-1906. Financier. b. New York. Successful in grocery business (1839-57); member, New York STOCK EXCHANGE (1874); where he was associated with JAY GOULD; had extensive financial interests. His wife, Margaret, received his $70,000,000 estate at his death and established through a gift of $10,000,000 the Russell Sage Foundation for improving social and living conditions in the United States. This foundation has contributed to many institutions, universities and charities.

ST. CLAIR, Arthur. 1736?-1818. Revolutionary general. b. Scotland. Came to America and lived in western Pennsylvania; served as a brigadier general in the Continental army during the Revolution at the battles of TRENTON and Princeton; major general (1777); member, CONTINENTAL CONGRESS (1785-87); first governor of the NORTHWEST TERRITORY (1787-1802); defeated by Indians at Fort Wayne; resigned; removed from his governorship by JEFFERSON for criticism of the Congress for establishing the state of Ohio.

SAINT-GAUDENS, Augustus. 1848-1907. Sculptor. b. Ireland. Came to the United States as a child; worked in a studio in New York City (1873-85) and in Cornish, New Hampshire (1885-1907). He became the outstanding sculptor in the United States. He is well-known for

555

his many monuments and portraits. His statue of *Lincoln* is in Lincoln Park, Chicago; *Farragut*, Madison Square, New York; *General Sherman*, New York and many others.

St. Mihiel, Battle of. A battle of World War I fought September 12-16, 1918 as part of the last allied push of the War. Following the successful Aisne-MARNE drive the American First Army was organized to conduct operations between the Moselle River and the Argonne Forest. A total of 550,000 American and 70,000 French troops, under the command of General PERSHING, assaulted 60,000 German troops after a heavy artillery barrage. By September 16th the German salient was obliterated with a loss of only 7,000 Americans as compared with German casualties three times their number.

"Salary Grab" Act. A law of Congress in 1873 which raised the salaries of its members from $5,000 to $7,500 annually, making the increases retroactive to the date of that Congress' opening session. In effect this furnished a bonus of $5,000 for each member. Coming soon after the exposure of the CREDIT MOBILIER and other congressional scandals, this "back pay steal" became a political issue in that year's elections. Both parties denounced the measure, and many congressmen refused to accept the back pay or returned it to the Treasury. The 43rd Congress repealed the legislation in January, 1874 except for the clauses which had raised the President's salary from $25,000 to $50,000, the Chief Justice's salary from $8,500 to $10,500, and Associate Justices' salaries from $8,000 to $10,000.

Sales Tax. A tax paid by the consumer on retail purchases within the tax jurisdiction. Sales taxes today are collected only by state and municipal governments although many attempts have been made to enact federal sales tax legislation. The first state retail sales tax was enacted in Kentucky in 1930, but 11 additional states and many municipalities had adopted such legislation by 1933 to meet the financial costs of the GREAT DEPRESSION. Although originally adopted as emergency measures most of these laws have become part of the permanent statutes. The rates are generally two or three percent on sales. Sales taxes have been attacked as regressive taxation imposing a greater burden upon low income than on high income groups. In 1952 there were retail sales taxes in 28 states, general sales taxes in two states, gross receipts taxes in two states, and a gross income sales tax in Indiana. The state of Washington had a retail sales and a gross receipts tax.

SALK, Jonas 1914- . Dr. Salk, a virologist joined the staff of the University of Pittsburgh School of Medicine in 1947 as director of the Virus Research Laboratory. In 1951 he began work on developing a preventive for polio. In 1955 after a mass trial conducted by Dr. Thomas Francis, Jr., his vaccine was declared to be a safe and effective preventive for polio. In 1955, Dr. Salk received the first Medal for Distinguished Civilian Achievement awarded by Congress. He became the director of Salk Institute for Biological Studies. In 1977, President Carter presented him with the Medal of Freedom, the highest civilian award presented by the United States.

Salk Polio Vaccine. On the basis of results obtained from the mass test of 440,000 children in 1954, a vaccine, developed by Dr. Jonas E. Salk, was declared an effective preventative of paralytic poliomyelitis (1955). The National Foundation for Infantile Paralysis paid out millions of dollars in first, testing, and then making the vaccine available for immediate and widespread use. Congress authorized a special gold medal for Dr. Salk in recognition of his discovery (awarded, 1956).

Salt Lake Trail. Also known as the Mormon Trail. An old trail to the West which was reopened in the Spring of 1846 when BRIGHAM YOUNG led a band of Mormons westward from Nauvoo, Illinois. The group followed the north branch of the Platte River through the South Pass to Fort Laramie. Here they resumed their journey over the old OREGON TRAIL to Fort Bridger in Wyoming. A halt was made here while Young and a chosen few pushed over another range of mountains through Echo Canyon to make camp in Emigration Canyon. On July 24, 1847 the group emerged from Emigration Canyon into the vast plain that was the basin of the GREAT SALT LAKE.

SALT Talks. In Helsinki, Finland in 1970 there was initiated a series of sessions between the United States and the Soviet Union termed the Strategic Arms Limitation Talks, the purpose of which was to limit arms and to defuse the threat of a possible nuclear war.

Salutary Neglect, Policy of. The term applied to the disinterest of the British in enforcing the NAVIGATION ACTS and other mercantile laws of the 17th and 18th centuries. Great Britain pursued this policy because of the reciprocal economic benefits enjoyed by Anglo-Colonial business men which would have been prevented by the rigid enforcement of this legislation. With the unusual expenses of the SEVEN YEARS' WAR the British government repudiated this policy in an attempt to obtain additional colonial revenues and compel the colonies to pay their share of these expenses.

Salvation Army. An evangelist organization established by General William Booth in England and introduced into the United States in 1880. It is today an international organization conducting places of worship and rehabilitation centers in 89 countries and territories in the world. In the United States its 1,377 corps have a membership of 227,000 and

5,000 officers organized on a military basis. Its principal function is the religious enlightenment of the masses but its activities encompass social service operations, family welfare work, inquiry bureaus for missing persons, children's homes and nurseries, homes and hospitals for unmarried mothers, shelters for transients, and settlements. Its rehabilitation centers cater to the needs of the homeless, the alcoholic, the unemployed, and the ill. Its officers are authorized to perform all the functions of the clergy.

Samoa, American. A group of seven volcanic islands in the South Pacific, acquired by the United States by agreement with England and Germany in 1899. After World War I, New Zealand took possession of the German-held islands in the Samoan Group. In the 1900's the native chiefs of the American group assigned legal title of these seven islands to the United States. Until 1951 Samoa was administered by the United States Navy. Since that date it has been administered by the DEPARTMENT OF THE INTERIOR. In 1952 the population was approximately 20,000. The area of American Samoa is 76 square miles. The principal products are cocoanuts and copra. Samoa is important as a strategic naval and air base.

SAMOSET. Indian chief who was a friend of the Pilgrims in the Plymouth Colony.

SAMPSON, William Thomas. 1840-1902. Naval officer. b. New York. Graduated, U.S.N.A., Annapolis (1861); officer of the *Patapsco* when she was blown up in Charleston Harbor during the Civil War (1865); superintendent, Annapolis (1886-90); chief, Bureau of Ordnance (1893-97); president, Board of Inquiry into the destruction of the *Maine* (1898); comander in chief, North Atlantic Squadron, Spanish-American War; although he was not present for most of the battle, his plans were used in the destruction of the Spanish fleet in SANTIAGO harbor; SCHLEY was given credit for the victory. He was, however, hailed as a hero of the war; rear admiral (1899).

Sanborn Contracts. One of the scandals of the GRANT administrations. John D. Sanborn of Boston was given contracts by Secretary of the Treasury W. A. Richardson, in collusion with Representative BENJAMIN F. BUTLER, to collect unpaid revenue taxes at a commission of 50 percent. In May, 1874 the House WAYS AND MEANS COMMITTEE revealed that Sanborn had recovered $427,000 for which he had received the stipulated reward of $213,500. He declared that he had paid $156,000 to his assistants, a payment which was understood to support the Butler political machine in Massachusetts. The contracts could not be repudiated, and Sanborn went free. Richardson escaped a vote of censure by resigning, and Butler was defeated for reelection.

SANBORN, Franklin Benjamin. 1831-1917. Journalist, author, and humanitarian. b. New Hampshire. Graduated, Harvard University; active in Massachusetts Free Soil Association; associated with JOHN BROWN and although he knew of the plan to seize HARPER'S FERRY, he did not approve; editor, Boston *Commonwealth* (1863-67), Springfield, *Republican* (1868-72); with W. T. Harris, he established the Concord School of Philosophy (1879-88). Author of many excellent biographies of famous New Englanders.

SANDBURG, Carl. 1878-1967. Poet and author. b. Illinois. Served during the Spanish-American War in PUERTO RICO; staff writer for Chicago newspapers; won poetry awards which gained a national reputation for him as a poet of the people; known for his free verse in such works as *Chicago Poems* (1915), *Smoke*

and Steel (1920), *The People, Yes* (1936); also famous as a biographer of ABRAHAM LINCOLN. He was awarded the Pulitzer Prize in 1940 for his four-volume biography of Lincoln, *The War Years*, and again in 1951 for his *Complete Poems;* he received the gold medal of the American Academy of Arts and Letters for his achievements in history and biography in May 1952.

Sanctions. Punitive measures provided for by the Covenant of the LEAGUE OF NATIONS against aggressors. Sanctions included military intervention or economic embargo. The efforts of the League to apply sanctions against Italy for her invasion of Abyssinia in 1935 proved a failure. Although the United States, by its absence from the League, was not legally obligated to participate in such collective measures it took parallel action in the Chaco War in 1934 by a congressional embargo on arms and munitions to Bolivia and Paraguay.

San Francisco Conference. A meeting of 50 nations, officially known as the United Nations Conference on International Organization. They met at San Francisco, California between April 25 and June 26, 1945 to draw up the charter of the United Nations. The American delegation was headed by Secretary of State Edward L. Stettinius who was elected chairman of the conference. On June 26th the attending nations signed the charter. Poland, one of the original members, signed on October 15, 1945. The charter went into effect on October 24, 1945.

SANGER, Margaret. 1883-1966. Leader of the birth-control movement. Studied to be a trained nurse; also studied with Havelock Ellis (1914-15) and Dr. Marie Stopes in work for birth control; founded the American Birth Control League (1917); opened the first clinic in Brooklyn, N.Y. (1921); this clinic was closed by the police and Mrs. Sanger was jailed for 30 days; the first permanent clinic was opened in New York City (1923); author of many books and pamphlets on the subject.

San Jacinto, Battle of. The last important battle of the War for Texan Independence. It was fought on April 21, 1836. General HOUSTON, commanding 700 Texans, defeated 1536 Mexicans under SANTA ANNA. Houston's attack on the Mexican camp destroyed organized resistance in 20 minutes, and the remainder of the battle ending in a slaughter in which the Texans claimed to have killed 630 Mexicans, wounded 208, and taken 730 prisoners. Texan casualties included 16 killed and 24 wounded. Among the Mexican prisoners was Santa Anna who negotiated armistice terms to end the war.

San Juan Hill, Battle of. A famous battle of the Spanish-American War. It was fought on July 1, 1898 during the American advance on SANTIAGO. A division including the "ROUGH RIDERS", under the command of General Kent, captured the hill, thus placing the American army on high ground overlooking Santiago. On July 17th the city surrendered.

SANTA ANNA, Antonio Lopez de. 1795?-1876. Mexican general, political leader and President. b. Jalapa. Fought in the struggle to gain independence for Mexico (1821); led constant revolts against the government; President of Mexico (1833-35); in an attempt to stop the Texan revolution, he seized the ALAMO (1836); defeated by SAM HOUSTON at SAN JACINTO (1836); practically a dictator of Mexico (1844); deposed and exiled (1845); made provisional president (1847); led army against the United States but was defeated by General SCOTT and driven out of Mexico City; lived in the United States (1855-74); returned to Mexico City (1774); died in poverty.

SANTAYANA, George. 1863-1952. Poet, educator, and philosopher. b. Spain. Came to the United States (1872); studied at Harvard University and taught philosophy there (1889-1912); professor of philosophy (1907-1912). Has lived in Europe since 1912. Author of many books including *The Sense of Beauty* (1896), *The Life of Reason* (5 vols., 1905-06); *The Last Puritan* (1935), *Persons and Places* (1943) and many others.

Sante Fe Trail. An important route leading from Independence, Missouri to Sante Fe, New Mexico in the early 19th century. From 1822 to the opening of the Civil War it was the principal gateway to the American southwest over which passed a profitable wagon trade which furnished western trappers, hunters, and settlers with the goods of the East and mid-West. William Becknell, the "father of the Sante Fe Trail," opened this route when Mexico achieved her independence from Spain in 1821. In 1860 as many as 3,000 wagons, 9,000 men, 6,000 mules, and 28,000 oxen were employed in a trade that was valued at over $5,000,000. The construction of the Atchison, Topeka, and Sante Fe Railroad between 1868 and 1880 marked the end of the trail.

Santiago, Battle of. A major victory for the American navy in the Spanish-American War. Following the defeat of the Spaniards at San Juan Hill, on July 1, 1898 Admiral Cervera's fleet, blockaded in Santiago harbor by SAMPSON and SCHLEY, attempted to escape the blockade on July 3rd. The Army, fresh from its victory at San Juan Hill, decended upon the city from the rear. Within four hours the Spanish fleet of four cruisers and three destroyers had either surrendered or been destroyed. Spanish casualties totalled 600 killed as compared with one American killed and one wounded.

Santiago Conference. The fifth Pan-American Congress. It was held at Santiago, Chile in 1923. Its achievements were the adoption of the Gondra Convention for international mediation by providing a discussion period in international conflict. The Conference also attempted a reorganization of the PAN-AMERICAN UNION.

Santo Domingo. See Dominican Republic.

Saratoga, Battle of. The turning point of the Revolutionary War. The defeat of the British at BENNINGTON and at Fort Stanwix compelled their forces under General St. Leger to retreat to Canada, rendering BURGOYNE's position in the upper Hudson Valley untenable. In early September Burgoyne determined to take the offensive, crossing the Hudson toward Saratoga Springs. On September 19th he was met by the Continental Army of militia and regulars under General GATES, and was defeated on Freeman's Farm at Stillwater, New York. This was the farthest South Burgoyne reached. On October 7th, expecting reinforcements under CLINTON, moving northward along the Hudson, he was defeated again on Freeman's farm. With no word from Clinton, he accepted Gates' demand for surrender on October 15th, negotiating terms which provided that the British lay down their arms, march to Boston, and embark for England, never to serve against Americans again. This treaty is known as the Convention of Saratoga. On October 17th it went into effect, leading directly to France's decision to enter the war as an ally of the United States.

SARGENT, John Singer. Painter. b. Italy of American parents. Studied art in Europe; established a studio in Boston (1903); famous for portraits, murals, and landscapes. His paintings and murals are in outstanding museums and collections.

Satellites and Rockets. Russian scientists succeeded in firing the first unmanned satellite (Sputnik I) into an orbit around the earth on October 4, 1957. Less than a month later, the Russians fired a second satellite (Sputnik II) with the 11 pound dog, Laika, in its nose cone. On January 31, 1958, the first American artificial satellite was placed into orbit. Since then, both the Russians and the Americans have orbited additional earth satellites with as many as three occupants. In 1964 and 1965 the United States successfully launched Rangers 7, 8, and 9 which took nearly 17,500 pictures shortly before striking the surface of the moon.

Saturday Night Massacre. On Saturday night, October 20, 1973, a number of events took place that has been referred to as the "Saturday Night Massacre." Following Special Prosecutor Archibald Cox's televised news broadcast objecting to Nixon's refusal to turn over the controversial "Watergate" tapes and documents to Federal Judge John J. Sirica and declaring that he would ask the courts either to cite the president for contempt or to clarify why the President's out-of-court offer was unacceptable, Nixon ordered Attorney General Richardson to fire Cox. Richardson refused and resigned. Nixon then ordered Deputy Attorney General William Ruckelshaus to dismiss Cox. Ruckelshaus refused and he was fired by President Nixon, who then appointed Solicitor General Robert Bork Acting Attorney General. Bork was then directed to fire Cox and to abolish Cox's entire operation, including his full staff of attorneys who had been investigating the "Watergate" scandal for five months. Bork signed the letter that discharged Cox and the "massacre" was underscored by the FBI agents who showed up to guard Cox's files and to seal off the offices of the two top Justice Department men.

Sauk and Fox Indians. Indian tribes of the Algonquin groups who were originally separate tribes very closely related to each other. They joined forces about

560

1730. Driven west and south by the IROQUOIS, the Sauks settled in Illinois and Missouri. The Fox were friendly with the French and settled near Detroit. They were involved in the BLACK HAWK WAR in 1832. Ultimately they were forced to give up their lands and move into INDIAN TERRITORY.

"Scalawags." Name given to Southern politicans who, in the Reconstruction period, sought their own profit and political advancement. Working with northern "CARPETBAGGERS" they succeeded in achieving political power in many southern states. They supported the freedman, making promises to him which were unfulfilled. The result of the work of the "SCALAWAGS" was to plunge many southern states into debt, prevent economic rehabilitation, raise taxes to new heights, and create a feeling of antagonism by former Confederate leaders against the Republican Party whose policies created this situation. Nevertheless some of the work of the "scalawag" and "carpetbagger" governments included notable reforms in EDUCATION, VOTING, finance, and the physical rehabilitation of roads, bridges, and public buildings.

Schechter Poultry Corporation vs. United States. A unanimous decision of the United States Supreme Court in May, 1935 which held unconstitutional the NATIONAL RECOVERY ACT. The court's decision was based on the thinking that the Congress had unconstitutionally delegated legislative power to the President and that the law regulated business held not to be involved in INTERSTATE COMMERCE.

SCHLEY, Winfield Scott. 1839-1911. Naval officer. b. Maryland. Graduated, U.S.N.A., Annapolis (1860); served during the Civil War; commanded the third GREELEY rescue expedition in the Arctic (1884); second in command to SAMP-

SON in blockading of SANTIAGO, Cuba (1898); succeeded in the destruction of the enemy fleet; became involved in controversy with Sampson over credit for the victory; national hero; rear admiral (1899); retired (1901).

SCHOENBERG, Arnold. 1874-1951. Composer. Came to the United States (1933); professor of music and conductor at the University of Southern California; a member of the ultra-modern school; in his compositions he used a style of "atonality;" he has had a considerable influence on the young modern composer in the United States. He has written symphonic poems, chamber music, orchestral and piano works.

SCHOFIELD, John McAllister. 1831-1906. Union general. b. New York. Graduated, U.S.M.A., West Point (1853); brigadier general of volunteers (Nov. 1861); major general (1863); served with SHERMAN in Atlanta campaign (1864); commander, Department of North Carolina (1865); U.S. Secretary of War (1868-69); brevetted major general and placed in command of the army of Missouri (1869, 1883-86); superintendent, U.S.M.A., West Point (1876-81); succeeded SHERIDAN as general-in-chief, U.S. Army (1895); lieutenant general (1895). Author of autobiography *Forty-six Years in the Army* (1897).

SCHOOLCRAFT, Henry Rowe. 1793-1864. Ethnologist. Followed the Ohio River to the Mississippi (1817); explored mineral deposits of southern Missouri and Arkansas (1817-18); explored Lake Superior region and served as Indian agent there (1822-36); superintendent of Indian affairs for Michigan (1836-41); known for his excellent histories of the Indians.

Schools. Private and public schools date back to early colonial times. In 1638 the Dutch established the Collegiate School of New York, the oldest private school in the United States. Latin schools, grammar schools, country day schools, academies, and church schools were established in the mid-seventeenth century. Among those surviving today are the Roxbury Latin School (1645), Hopkins Grammar School of New Haven (1660), and Phillips Academy at Andover and Exeter, founded after the Revolution. The first country day school was the Gillman Country Day School established in Baltimore, Maryland in 1897. Catholic parochial schools were founded in Maryland in the 18th century. Public schools, namely those which are considered nonsectarian, compulsory, universal, tax supported, and open to all children without charge, were first established on an incomplete basis in Massachusetts in 1647. Such schools did not spread widely in the United States until the Jacksonian era and did not become national in scope until the end of the 19th century. By 1900 the principle of tax supported EDUCATION above the elementary grade had been firmly established. In 1949 there were approximately 148,000 public elementary schools and 26,000 public secondary schools in the United States. In that year there were 11,000 private elementary and 3400 private secondary schools and 630 public and 1160 private colleges, universities, and professional schools. These figures exclude residential schools for exceptional children, schools of nursing, and kindergartens. In 1952 the estimated public and private elementary school enrollment was 24,500,000 of which the public school registration was approximately 21,500,-000. The secondary school population was estimated at 6,200,000 of which the public secondary schools had registered approximately 5,500,000. University and college enrollment was estimated at 2,225,000. Additional students in private, commercial, nurse training, and unaffiliated schools brought the total enrollment in the schools of the United States in 1952 to 33,200,000.

Schurman Commission. A five man commission chaired by President J. G. SCHURMAN of Cornell University to investigate and report on political conditions in the PHILIPPINE ISLANDS. It was appointed by President MCKINLEY in 1899 to study the possibility of self-government in the Islands and to adopt a policy leading to that end. The Commission's report recommended that the Philippines be ruled by the United States because of the illiteracy of the people, their rudimentary knowledge of civil life, and the variety of languages spoken. In April, 1900 it was replaced by the TAFT COMMISSION.

SCHURMAN, Jacob Gould. 1854-1942. Educator and diplomat. b. Canada. Studied in England and Germany; professor of philosophy, Cornell University (1886-92); president (1892-1920); president, first United States Philippine Commission (1899); U.S. Minister to Greece and Montenegro (1912-13); Ambassador to China (1921-25); Ambassador to Germany (1925-30); conservative Republican who opposed ROOSEVELT's imperialism and supported TAFT. Author of books on philosophy and politics.

SCHURZ, Carl. 1829-1906. Union general and political leader. b. Germany. Forced to flee Germany when involved in revolutionary activities he came to the United States (1852); admitted to the bar (1859); practised in Milwaukee where he became involved in Republican politics; supported LINCOLN (1860); appointed U.S. Minister to Spain (1861-62); served in Civil War as brigadier general of volunteers (1862); served at SECOND BATTLE OF BULL RUN, Chancellorsville, and GETTYSBURG; major general (1863); was Washington correspondent for the New York *Tribune* and editor of Detroit *Post* (1865-68); U.S. Senator from Missouri (1869-75); U.S. Secretary of the Interior (1877-81); editor New York *Evening Post* (1881-83);

editorial writer, *Harper's Weekly* (1892-98). Author of *Life of Henry Clay* (2 vols., 1887) and other books.

SCHUYLER, Philip John. 1733-1804. Revolutionary general and statesman. b. New York. Attained rank of major during the French and Indian Wars (1755-60); member, provincial assembly (1768-75); delegate to CONTINENTAL CONGRESS (1775); commanded northern department of the Continental Army as major general; organized expedition to attack Canada (1775-76); after disagreements with GATES he was superceded by him (1777); resigned (1779); member, Continental Congress (1778-81); one of the first two Senators from New York (1789-91; 1797-98); strong supporter of the policies of ALEXANDER HAMILTON, who was his son-in-law.

SCHWAB, Charles Michael. 1862-1939. Steel magnate. b. Pennsylvania. Studied at St. Francis College; worked as a stake driver in an engineering gang at the Carnegie Steel Company plant; rose in the ranks to chief engineer and was finally recognized as CARNEGIE's chief assistant (1897); president, Carnegie Steel Company (1897-1901); chosen president of the newly organized United States Steel Company (1901-1903); resigned to become principal owner and president of Bethlehem Steel, which was the largest independent steel company (1903-13); chairman of the board (from 1913); served as director-general of shipbuilding for U.S. EMERGENCY FLEET CORP. (1918).

Science. More than any other field of intellectual activity, scientific research was notably inferior in colonial America. Mysticism and superstition were still firmly embedded in the colonial mind as was seen in the reading of horoscopes and the belief that eclipses were harbingers of natural catastrophes. Colonial medicine was still a potpourri of medieval dependence upon herbs, leeches, and incantation. Science and philosophy were considered in natural kinship and BENJAMIN FRANKLIN was clearly the exemplar of this concept. Early 19th century science showed particular interest in physiography and geology. Under the direction of Franklin's grandson, Alexander Dallas Bache, the Coast and Geodetic Service carried on research and EXPLORATION activity on the northwest coast and in the antarctic. Leaders in this activity included Charles Wilkes, JOHN C. FREMONT, and LOUIS AGASSIZ. In 1840 the American Society of Geologists was founded. In the biological sciences Asa Gray and J. J. AUDUBON classified American plants and birds respectively. The development of Darwinian thought produced a great conflict in religious groups in the United States, although liberal clergymen like Abbott and Gladden insisted that Darwin's hypothesis clashed only with theology, not religion. In the era of the Civil War American technology came into its own through the work of SAMUEL F. B. MORSE (telegraph), CYRUS MCCORMICK (reaper), JOSEPH HENRY and CYRUS W. FIELD (transatlantic cable), and ALBERT A. MICHELSON (velocity of light). In 1824 the first school in the United States devoted entirely to science and engineering was established at Troy, New York by STEPHEN VAN RENSSELAER. In 1846 the Smithsonian Institution was chartered by Congress as a center for scientific research. The late 19th century is the age of science in the United States. The country's greatest contribution was in the field of practical or applied science. Whereas the decade 1840-1850 had seen only 6,480 patents issued, the number issued between 1890 and 1900 was 221,500. This is the period which witnessed the inventions of the self-binding reaper, cable, harvester, tractor, combine, typewriter, printing machinery, air brake, refrigerated car, electric railway, duplex telegraph, motion picture, electric light, phonograph, telephone, Pullman car, and automobile. The leaders of this movement included J. F. Appleby (farm machinery), ALEXANDER GRAHAM BELL (telephone), GEORGE EASTMAN (photography), the WRIGHT BROTHERS and SAMUEL LANGLEY (airplane), GEORGE WESTINGHOUSE, (airbrake), and THOMAS A. EDISON (phonograph, motion picture, incandescent lamp, and many others). Scholastic research in science rapidly improved through the work of such institutions as the Columbia School of Mines (1849), Massachusetts Institute of Technology (1865), and Worcester Polytechnic Institute (1865). The research in physics of J. WILLARD GIBBS, astronomy of SIMON NEWCOMB, experimental psychology of G. STANLEY HALL and WILLIAM JAMES, archaeology of OTHNIEL C. MARSH and Edward D. Cope, and of LEWIS D. MORGAN in anthropology gained international renown. In the early 20th century American science continued to emphasize the practical rather than the theoretical. Technologists and engineers improved upon European inventions in radio, internal combustion engine, electrical equipment, and aircraft. Well-equipped laboratories were established by government and industry. In these, research and invention became institutionalized and directed toward the interests of a specific business. Government scientists, industrial technologists, and college professors merged their talents in producing new and improved machines. New discoveries in chemistry, physics, and bacteriology produced remarkable changes in medical practice. Among the leaders were WALTER REED (yellow fever), Bailey K. Ashford (anemia), Charles W. Stiles (hookworm), Edward L. Trudeau (tuberculosis), W. O. ATWATER (food chemistry), and THOMAS B. OSBORNE, L. B. Mendel, and Henry C. Sherman (vitamins). Industrial chemistry succeeded in producing a great variety of commodities from coal and oil and their components. After World War I scientific expansion was characterized by the development of research organizations as well as the continued improvement of technology. Many Americans won Nobel awards for research in the absolute sciences. Among these were ROBERT A. MILLIKAN (1923, physics), ARTHUR H. COMPTON (1927, physics), and Karl Landsteiner (1930, medicine). In 1914 Theodore W. Richards won the prize in chemistry and two years earlier ALEXIS CARREL in physics. Private, public, and university research institutions were founded for the pursuit of knowledge in the pure sciences. These included the National Research Council, American Council of Learned Societies, and the various organizations of the university physicists, chemists, biologists, and astronomers. In the 1950's notable achievements were made in the fields of nuclear physics, chemistry, and medicine. New developments in the production of atomic energy and the discovery of new physical elements were reported almost daily. The leadership in this field came from such outstanding universities as the California Institute of Technology, Massachusetts Institute of Technology, Columbia University, Harvard University, University of California, and the University of Chicago. In medicine outstanding developments included the synthesization of cortisone, the making of artificial muscle, and remarkable advances in poliomyelitis and cancer research and the treatment of tuberculosis, arthritis, and rheumatic fever. In July, 1952 the Air Research and Development Command reported that, since 1941, the federal government had spent about $10,000,000,-000 for scientific research and development. In the calendar year 1952 Congress was scheduled to spend $1,600,-000,000 for scientific research, more than one-half the total national expenditure for such purposes. Of the 22 federal agencies designated to spend this sum the most important were the ATOMIC ENERGY COMMISSION, DEPARTMENT OF

564

AGRICULTURE, UNITED STATES PUBLIC HEALTH SERVICE, and DEPARTMENT OF DEFENSE.

Scientific Management. The application of scientific techniques to the organization of industrial production. The development of the ^INDUSTRIAL REVOLUTION in the 19th century, based on the utilization of machines and specialized labor, provided the rudiments of management procedures in MANUFACTURING. The second industrial revolution after the Civil War furnished the fundamental impetus to scientific management as a result of the development of automatic machinery, specialized labor, ASSEMBLY LINE methods, the use of standardized parts, and the techniques of MASS PRODUCTION. The first ground was spaded by Frederick W. Taylor, an assistant foreman in the Midvale Steel Company in Philadelphia in the 1880's who undertook time and motion studies on machine workers. In 1903 he discussed his system in a dissertation before the American Society of Mechanical Engineers. Taylor's methods included the maintenance of records, analysis of work, establishment of standards, objective hiring of labor, and EDUCATION. These were designed to increase labor productivity. In later years similar studies of machines, distributing processes, materials flow, work traffic, labor specialization, and labor pooling were made. Programs were developed to accomplish adjustments in these factors to achieve the greatest production of quality merchandise in the shortest time. Accounting methods were introduced to determine unit costs based on carefully charted processes. Out of this there evolved on-the-job training programs for workers and supervisors in the effort to apply and develop ever-improving techniques. In the era before World War I the contributions of Henry L. Gantt added the developments in PSYCHOLOGY and EDUCATION to the program of scientific management. The "Gantt Chart" was the result of an effort to establish sound human relations in industrial production based on bonus payments. Production was organized around the use of psychological tests. Promotions and careful placements were based on these tests. Out of this area of work came the development of the field of personnel management and LABOR RELATIONS with the establishment of new departments in large CORPORATIONS to administer scientifically conceived programs in these fields. In this period Frank B. Gilbreth contributed a method of motion study in factory labor. By the time of World War II all of these developments had created new areas of managerial activities in such fields as worker benefits, social security, group insurance, and grievance machinery.

Scientific Research and Development, Office of. An agency established by EXECUTIVE ORDER in June, 1941 to recruit scientists for work on military problems. It drafted and circulated questionnaires to universities, public agencies, and private institutions in the preparation of a National Roster of Scientific and Professional Personnel from which were drawn trained individuals to carry on the agency's work. Vannevar Bush was appointed its director. The two most important contributions it made were the development of atabrine and the ATOMIC BOMB. It was absorbed into the United States ATOMIC ENERGY COMMISSION in 1946.

Scopes Trial. Occured in 1925 as a result of the teaching by J. T. Scopes of the theory of evolution in violation of a Tennessee law of that year. The law prohibited the teaching of any theory which denied the story of the divine creation of man as taught in the Bible. The affair received world wide publicity because of the spectacle of the former Democratic

presidential candidate WILLIAM JEN-
NINGS BRYAN, representing the state of
Tennessee, against the famous liberal
lawyer CLARENCE DARROW, defending
the obscure Tennessee village school
teacher. The case was a reflection of
the revival of religious conservatism popularly known as "fundamentalism" in the
era following World War I.

SCOTT, Hugh Lenox. 1853-1934. Army
General. b. Kentucky. Graduated, U.S.-
M.A., West Point (1876); served in the
West; friendly with the SIOUX Tribe, he
learned Indian sign language and led
many expeditions into the INDIAN TER-
RITORY making treaties with the Indian
tribes; superintendent of West Point
(1906-10); brigadier-general (1913);
chief of staff, U.S. Army (1914-17); retired (1919).

SCOTT, James Brown. 1866-1943. Lawyer and educator. b. Canada. Expert in
international law having studied at Harvard, in Germany and Paris; organized
law department at the University of
Southern California; dean (1896-99);
dean, University of Illinois Law School
(1899-1903); solicitor, U.S. DEPART-
MENT OF STATE (1906-1910); trustee
and secretary, CARNEGIE ENDOWMENT
FOR INTERNATIONAL PEACE (from 1910);
editor in chief, *American Journal of International Law* (1907-24); president,
American Society of International Law.
Author of several books.

SCOTT, Winfield. 1786-1866. General of
the Army. b. Virginia. Served through
War of 1812; brevetted major general
(1814); served with distinction in Indian
Wars; General in Chief, U.S. Army
(1841); commander during Mexican War;
after taking Vera Cruz (March, 1847) he
headed toward Mexico City; he defeated
the Mexicans at Cerro Gordo (April,
1847); succeeded in occupying Mexico
City (September, 1847); lieutenant general (1852); declared a hero; WHIG candidate for the presidency (1852) but

defeated by PIERCE; although born in
the South, he remained loyal to the
Union during the Civil War; but was
forced to retire from active service due
to ill health and was succeeded by MC
CLELLAN (1851).

Scottsboro Cases. A series of trials between 1931 and 1938 involving eight
Negroes who had been charged with the
rape of two white women in Scottsboro,
Alabama. After conviction and sentence
of death at the first trial the case remained pending for six years as a result
of nationwide protest. The evidence at
the trial was clear that the defendents
were innocent of the charges, and many
groups and individuals sought retrials on
the basis of new evidence. A second trial
was ordered by the United States Supreme Court on November, 1932 and
again in 1934 on the grounds respectively that the defendents had been denied adequate counsel and that Negroes
had been excluded from the juries at the
three preceding trials. Continued appeals
led to a decision in 1938 by the Court
denying new trials for four of the defendents. The other four had been released in 1947.

SCRIPPS, Edward Syllis. 1854-1926.
Newspaper publisher. b. Illinois. Organized the Cleveland *Penny Press* (1878);
founded other papers and set up Scripps-
McRae League; supported labor causes
and was politically liberal; established
the UNITED PRESS (1907); organized the
Newspaper Enterprise Association as a
syndicate for supplying featured articles,
cartoons, and pictures to his papers; contributed widely to scholarly research;
founded Scripps Institution of Oceanography at the University of California;
retired (1922).

"Scrub Race." A term applied to the
presidential election of 1824 because the
principal candidates were not nominated
in the customary manner by congressional
CAUCUSES. WILLIAM CRAWFORD was put

566

forth by a group of Georgia congressmen. JOHN QUINCY ADAMS was nominated by delegates from the New England states while HENRY CLAY was chosen by the states of Kentucky, Louisiana, Missouri, Illinois, and Ohio. ANDREW JACKSON was nominated by Tennessee. Although Jackson received the largest popular vote, his lack of an electoral majority threw the presidential choice into the House of Representatives which, strongly influenced by Clay, selected Adams.

Sculpture. Colonial sculpture revealed itself principally in simple building ornamentation. WILLIAM RUSH was a pioneer in woodcarving. In the early 19th century European classical influence was strong, showing itself in the *Greek Slave* of Hiram Powers. In this period American sculpture was inferior to painting. The "GILDED AGE" saw a revival of sculpture in the work of AUGUST SAINT-GAUDENS, DANIEL CHESTER FRENCH, and GEORGE GREY BARNARD. The transition to modern ideals was seen in the work of Gaston Lachaise. In the first ten years of the 20th century the United States produced more fine sculpture than during its entire previous history. The contemporary sculptors of note include Chaim Gross, Alexander Archipenko, Jose deCreeft, and Alexander Calder.

Seabury Investigation. An inquiry into municipal politics in New York City in 1931 and 1932 by a commission appointed by Governor F. D. ROOSEVELT and chaired by SAMUEL SEABURY. As a result of Seabury's investigation and report, Mayor James Walker resigned his office, and the reform Fusion movement under the leadership of former Representative FIORELLO H. LaGUARDIA defeated TAMMANY HALL in the election of 1933.

SEABURY, Samuel. 1873-1958. Jurist. b. New York City. Studied and practised law in New York City; Justice Supreme Court of New York (1907-14); associate judge, N.Y. Court of Appeals (1914-16); as chairman of an investigating committee which uncovered crime in New York City politics, he gained a national reputation; as a result of his investigations, Mayor James J. Walker was forced to resign, and LA GUARDIA on a reform Fusion ticket was elected in the following mayorality campaign.

Sea Witch, The. The famous CLIPPER SHIP which completed the ocean passage in 1850 around Cape Horn to San Francisco in 97 days, reducing the elapsed time for this trip from the average passage of 159 days of the sailing vessels in previous years. The voyage of the *Sea Witch* showed the possibilities of the clipper ship trade not only in intercoastal but also in foreign commerce. It inaugurated the famous clipper ship era.

Secession. The act of a state leaving the Union. Following the election of LINCOLN a South Carolina convention unanimously passed an ordinance of secession on December 20, 1860. Within six weeks the states of Mississippi, Florida, Alabama, Louisiana, Georgia, and Texas followed South Carolina out of the Union. Following the FIRING ON FORT SUMTER in April of 1861 and President Lincoln's call for volunteers the states of Virginia, North Carolina, Arkansas, and Tennessee seceded. These 11 states comprised the Confederate States of America. The constitutionality of secession had been vigorously argued prior to the Civil War but was not established until the Supreme Court in the case of Texas vs. White, 1869 declared it unconstitutional. Lincoln always felt that the states had not constitutionally seceded, and that he was therefore merely dealing with individuals who had rebelled against the authority of the United States. The RADICAL REPUBLICAN CONGRESS, in the Reconstruction era, argued that the southern states had seceded from the Union, and thus should be dealt with as conquered entities, to be readmitted only on the terms set down by Congress.

Secondary Boycott. See boycott.

Second Child Labor Law. A federal law passed in 1919 which attempted to limit child labor. Under its terms Congress imposed a tax of 10 percent on the profits of factories employing children under the age of 14, and of mines and quarries employing children under the age of 16. This law was an attempt by Congress to control child labor by the use of its tax power, following the Supreme Court's invalidation of its first effort in the KEATING-OWEN ACT of 1916. The law was declared unconstitutional by the court in 1922 in the case of BAILEY VS. DREXEL FURNITURE COMPANY.

Second Industrial Revolution. See manufacturing.

Second War Powers Act. See war powers of the President.

Secret Service. A division of the TREAS-URY DEPARTMENT whose principal function is the investigation of crimes against that Department. At its inception in 1864 its special function was the detection of counterfeiters, smugglers, and illegal liquor manufacturers. Following the death of President LINCOLN the Secret Service was entrusted with the protection of the persons of the President and his family at the WHITE HOUSE and elsewhere. During the two World Wars it was active in investigating plots designed to interfere with the manufacture and shipment of munitions. It has, as part of its work, collected photographs of well-known international criminals, which today number over 5,000. The organization was originally established in 1864 with a brigadier general in charge of a volunteer force.

Secret Treaties. International agreements secretly negotiated and not revealed to the world. Also secret clauses of known treaties. From 1880 to the opening of World War I European nations negotiated secret treaties containing military and colonial clauses. It has generally been accepted that they were a contributing cause of the War. At the VER-SAILLES PEACE CONFERENCE, President WILSON attacked the secret treaties, after they had been revealed by the Soviet government, and reiterated the plea for "OPEN COVENANTS, OPENLY ARRIVED AT" which he had made in his FOURTEEN POINTS.

Sectionalism. The term applied to the political and economic clashes between geographical sections of the United States. Historically sectional issues have included SLAVERY, democracy, internal improvements, CIVIL LIBERTIES, LABOR RELATIONS, the TARIFF, BANKING, CUR-RENCY, Negro voting, land policy, and states rights doctrines. Before the Civil War sectional groupings generally were acknowledged to comprise the East, West, and South. In the East commercial, industrial, and financial interests predominated. In the West and South agriculture was the dominant economy. For two decades the expansionist drive of the South and West, in the desire to acquire English, Spanish, and Mexican territory, involved these sections in political struggle with the East. This issue was joined with those of the tariff and internal improvements at federal expense, both of which they opposed. Since the Civil War, the East has been the dominant section. Its hard money program was bitterly opposed by the West's farmers, miners, and debtors. In contemporary times CIVIL LIBERTIES and the status of the Negro have furnished the principal issues cf conflict between the South and the East. Foreign policy issues of isolationism tended to range the West against the East in the period between the two World Wars.

Section 7a. The famous section of the NATIONAL INDUSTRIAL RECOVERY ACT which provided that employees have "the right to organize and bargain collectively through representatives of their own choosing." Other provisions of Section 7a granted rights to workers to join unions, forbade COMPANY UNIONS, and prohibited certain unfair labor practices. Inadequate enforcement plus the loose wording of the clause prevented the full realization of its objective. It is important, however, as the first general statute defining the rights of labor in its organization and membership in unions. Section 7a, as part of the NIRA, was invalidated in 1935 by the Supreme Court.

Securities Act. Also known as the Federal Securities Act. A law of Congress in 1933 designed to protect prospective investors by making available to them certain information concerning new securities sold in INTERSTATE COMMERCE. The Act required a company, offering securities, to file detailed information with the FEDERAL TRADE COMMISSION in the form of a registration statement. The company was also required to send a prospectus to an intended purchaser, in which it would specify such data as the names of oi `ɔers, nature of the securities offered, and the company's financial position. After complying with the requirements the company could offer its securities for sale. False statements in the registration and/or prospectus could be punished by civil or criminal suits. The weaknesses of the act lay in its lack of definition and in the absence of any control over stock markets and brokers.

Securities Exchange Act. Enacted in 1934 as a supplement to the SECURITIES ACT of 1933. The law established the SECURITIES AND EXCHANGE COMMISSION. The provisions of the Act included a require-

ment for registration of all STOCK EXCHANGES, a statement defining the functions of securities, dealers, and brokers, a list of standards of credit, registrations with full information of all established securities prior to their issuance, the prohibition of manipulation designed to control prices artificially, and a clause regulating margins and brokers credit by the Commission and the FEDERAL RESERVE BOARD of Governors. The Act was passed to fill the gaps of the 1933 legislation and to provide a full program of regulatory control over both securities and exchanges, designed to prevent a recurrence of the STOCK MARKET CRASH of October, 1929.

Securities and Exchange Commission. Established by the SECURITIES EXCHANGE ACT in 1934 to administer the Act. It is a bi-partisan independent regulatory agency of five members with five year terms. The Commission enforces the requirement of publication of stock prospectuses and the regulation of exchange practices. It also has the power to dissolve uneconomic portions of PUBLIC UTILITIES structures, to require the registration of and to regulate investment trusts, and to supervise the financial activities among public utility holding companies subsidiaries. It is one of the many independent regulatory commissions with strong quasi-judicial powers.

Security Council. The principal organ of the UNITED NATIONS. It is, in effect, the executive agency of that organization, exercising the responsibility for maintaining international peace and security. It consists of one delegate from each of 11 nations. The permanent members comprise China, France, the Soviet Union, the United Kingdom, and the United States. Six non-permanent members are elected for two year terms by the General Assembly. The Council is authorized to investigate disputes which threaten international peace and security. Decisions on procedural questions are made by a vote of seven members. On all other issues the Council decides by a vote of seven members, including the concurring votes of the permanent members. A party to a dispute may not vote. The chief officer of the Security Council is a president who sits for one month. The monthly rotation is done in accordance with the English alphabet. The agency sits in continuous session and has the authority to consider all situations which threaten peace. Its powers encompass diplomatic and economic sanctions against a nation guilty of breaching the peace, including the "complete or partial interruption of economic relations and of rail, sea, air, postal, telegraphic, RADIO, and other means of COMMUNICATION, and the severance of diplomatic relations." Its military measures may include demonstrations, BLOCKADE, and other operations by the military forces of members of the United Nations. Each member of the Council has one vote. As a result of the frequent vetoing of Council action by the Soviet Union the "Little Assembly" was voted into existence on November 7, 1947 for the purpose of considering questions and making recommendations for action without submitting these to the Security Council. Reporting to the Security Council are the Military Staff Committee, ATOMIC ENERGY COMMISSION, and Commission for Conventional Armaments.

SEDGWICK, Theodore. 1746-1813. Jurist. b. Connecticut. Practised law in Massachusetts; served in American Revolution; member, CONTINENTAL CONGRESS (1785-88); active in suppression of SHAYS' REBELLION; member, Massachusetts convention which ratified the Constitution (1788); member, U.S. House of Representatives (1789-96, 1799-1801); Speaker of the House (1799-1801); U.S. Senator (1796-99); Justice,

Massachusetts Supreme Court (1802-13); famous for having freed a Negro slave under the Massachusetts Bill of Rights.

Sedition Act. Passed by Congress in 1918 as a supplement to the ESPIONAGE ACT of the previous year. The law made it a crime to criticise by speech or writing the government or the Constitution. The penalties of the Espionage Act were extended to those obstructing the sale of United States Bonds, inciting insubordination, discouraging recruiting, or willfully uttering, printing, writing, or publishing "any disloyal, profane, scurrilous, or abusive language about the form of government of the United States or the Constitution." Under these two laws over 1500 persons were arrested for disloyalty.

Segregation (See Desegregation).

Selective Service Act. The second compulsory military draft law in American history. It was enacted by Congress in 1917. The law provided for an increase in the pay of soldiers from $15 to $30 per month and authorized the President to raise a volunteer infantry force of not more than four divisions. All males between the ages of 21 and 30 were required to register for military service on June 5th. Over 4,648 registration districts were established throughout the nation to register over nine and one half million males on that date. As a result of this and amending legislation approximately 4,000,000 men were ultimately drafted into the armed services, of whom approximately one half were overseas by the end of the war. Administration of the Act was supervised by civilian boards established in the registration districts. Under the four calls of June 5, 1917, June 5, 1918, August 24, 1918, and September 12, 1918 a total of 23,908,576 were registered. See Man Power Act.

Selective Service System. See Selective Service and Training Acts.

570

Selective Service and Training Acts. A series of laws passed by Congress in 1940, and subsequent years. The Act of 1940 known as the BURKE-WADSWORTH ACT, established the Selective Service System headed by a Director with 40,000 local selective service civilian boards distributed throughout the nation and its territories. Its national headquarters are located in Washington, D.C. A total of 56 state and territorial headquarters and boards of appeal were established to carry on the work of registering all males between the ages of 18 and 64 and of classifying them for various kinds of military duty. The Act of 1948 succeeded the original law which had expired on March 31, 1947, and was amended by the Act of 1951 which established a commission to study and report to Congress on a UNIVERSAL MILITARY TRAINING program for men 18 to 19 years of age. This Act also extends selective service indefinitely, but established July 1st, 1955 as the terminal date for the induction of men into the armed forces, excepting those deferred by selective service regulations. The draft age was lowered to 18½ years although persons between 18 and 26 must register. Liability for service lasts until age 35 for persons deferred for any reason. Those between 18½ and 25 are liable for immediate military service. The draft service period was extended to 24 months. A ceiling of 5,000,000 men was placed on the armed forces until July 31, 1955. In 1955 the Act was extended to July, 1959.

Selective Veto. Also known as item VETO. The power of an executive to veto portions of a bill. The President of the United States does not have the power of selective veto. The result is that riders to an appropriations bill are passed because of his reluctance to veto the entire measure. State governors generally have this power.

Selectmen. The members of the council of town and township governments in the United States. This council ordinarily bears the name of Board of Selectmen. This agency of municipal government is provided for by the state constitutions and exercises executive, administrative, and legislative functions.

Seminole Indians. They were mostly CREEK INDIANS who had settled in Florida. They helped the British during the War of 1812. Defeated by General ANDREW JACKSON, their homes and lands were destroyed in 1818. After Florida became a part of the United States they lived in peace with the settlers. However, trouble started when, in 1832, they were forced to move into INDIAN TERRITORY in the West. Under the leadership of a young chieftain, Osceola, the Seminole War, one of the costliest in all American history, began. This war with the Seminoles lasted for 10 years and when they were finally defeated they agreed to move to the west. They became one of the five civilized tribes in Indian Territory. Some Seminole Indians still live on a reservation in the Everglades of Florida.

Seminole Wars. Two wars between Seminole tribes in Florida and the United States. Prior to the purchase of Florida in 1819, it was the haven of escaped slaves and criminals from the United States. With the tacit approval of Spain, the Indians, Negroes, and Englishmen created strongholds in Northern Florida which proved a constant peril to Georgia. In 1817 there were many skirmishes and massacres against which General GAINES accomplished little. In January, 1818 General ANDREW JACKSON was given command, and within six months had reduced the Seminoles, burning their villages in the almost daily defeats. During this campaign two English adventurers, Ambrister and Arbuthnot, were arrested and hanged by Jackson, Pensacola was taken, and the whole of East

571

Florida was occupied. The second war broke out in 1835 because of the Seminole resistance, under their chief Osceola, to removal westward into the INDIAN TERRITORY. Osceola was arrested and jailed in 1835, and after his release the Indians renewed the warfare. Until 1842, skirmishes, bargaining, and harassing actions went on. By treaty in 1845 the Seminoles were removed west of the Mississippi, and in 1856 were assigned lands west of the CREEKS.

Senate Crime Committee. See Kefauver Investigation.

Senate, United States. The upper chamber of the United States Congress. Its members must be 30 years of age, reside in the state from which they are elected, and be American citizens. The Senate acts jointly with the House of Representatives in the enactment of all legislation, either originating or voting on House legislation with the exception of revenue bills which must originate in the House. The Senate enjoys exclusive power in the choice of the Vice-President if there is a tie or lack of majority in the ELECTORAL COLLEGE. It alone has the function of ratifying presidential treaties (by a two-thirds vote of those present) and of confirming presidential appointments (by a simple majority vote of those present). Under its constitutional power to make its own rules of procedure the Senate has consistently declined to limit debate, giving rise to the political institution known as the FILIBUSTER. The Senate is a stepping-stone to the presidency. Each state is entitled to two senators, a number which may not be changed by Congress. Prior to 1913 they were selected by the state legislatures. The passage of the 17TH AMENDMENT in that year provided for the direct election of senators by popular vote. The term is six years, one-third of the Senate being elected every two years. The Vice-President of the United States is the presiding officer of the Senate, but casts a vote only in cases of ties. The Senate acts as the court in the trial of IMPEACHMENT cases, conviction requiring a two-thirds vote.

Senatorial Courtesy. The tradition by which the President submits the name of a proposed nominee to the senators of the state in which he resides for their approval prior to the nomination. In the event of their disapproval senatorial courtesy prompts the Senate to refuse confirmation of the nomination. The effect of senatorial courtesy is to place the distribution of PATRONAGE into the hands of the Senate.

Senators, popular election of. The direct election of United States Senators by POPULAR VOTE. Article I, Section 3 of the federal Constitution provided for the appointment of Senators by the state legislatures. For more than a century afterwards vigorous campaigns for constitutional AMENDMENT were conducted to permit the popular election of Senators. POLITICAL PARTIES, such as the POPULIST PARTY and PROGRESSIVE PARTY OF 1912, contained such planks in their platforms. The adoption of the 17th Amendment finally produced this change. See Seventeenth Amendment.

Seneca Falls Convention. See feminism.

Separation of Church and State. Also known as disestablishment. The severing of official relationships between the state and the ESTABLISHED CHURCH. In the American colonies, where nine established churches existed, the struggles by the independent churches (Baptist, Catholic, Lutheran, Methodist, Presbyterian) had proceeded vigorously for a century before the American Revolution. In 1779 the Anglican Church was disestablished in Virginia although separation of the Congregational Church in New England followed slowly. The leadership of the Baptist Church in that area was supported by the Methodists and Episcopalians at the turn of the

18th century, and was successful in achieving disestablishment in Connecticut in 1818, in New Hampshire in 1819, and in Massachusetts in 1833.

Separation of powers. As developed by the French political philosopher Montesquieu and other European writers, it is the system of alloting the different powers of government to separate branches. Under this theory EXECUTIVE POWERS are exercised only by an executive branch, LEGISLATIVE POWERS by a legislative branch, and JUDICIAL POWERS by a judicial branch. The result is an absence of concentration of powers within one body, and thus a more democratic government. Montesquieu erroneously attributed this system to the contemporary British government. The Constitution of the United States reserved these specific powers to the legislature, executive, and judiciary in Articles I, II, and III. It should be noted that the theory is not completely applied inasmuch as these constitutional provisions permit each of the various branches to exercise certain powers more properly within the jurisdiction of the others.

Separatists. Also known as Independents. A radical group which broke away from the Puritans in England in the mid-sixteenth century. Their theology included doctrines proposing autonomous congregations democratically controlled by an elective leadership. Each congregation was to be self-governing, its authority being based upon a formal covenant. Persecution in England drove the Separatists to the New World where they settled in Massachusetts in the 1620's. The doctrinal opposition of the Separatists carried over into an attack against the conservative religious and political policies of the Presbyterians as well as the Anglicans and Puritans. In New England Separatist ministers preached free interpretation of the gospel and administration of the sacraments "without idolatrous gear." Many of the Pilgrim Fathers belonged to this sect. Their prominent leaders in Plymouth included JOHN CARVER and WILLIAM BRADFORD. By the period of the Revolution the Separatists had disappeared from American life. See Congregationalists.

Servicemen's Readjustment Act. See G.I. Bill of Rights.

"Service State." See "welfare state."

SETON, Elizabeth Bailey. Mother Elizabeth Bailey Seton was born on August 28, 1774. On September 14, 1975 she was canonized the Catholic church's first U.S.-born saint by Pope Paul VI.

Settlement Houses. Local associations established in large urban centers to assist the poor and develop friendly relations between the uneducated and the educated. The settlement house movement was a reaction to the labor unrest and evils of urban congestion and poverty after the Civil War. The University Settlement in New York City was begun as the Neighborhood Guild in 1886 by Stanton Coit and Charles B. Stover. Others followed soon afterwards in large cities. These included Hull House in Chicago, founded in 1889 by JANE ADDAMS, Henry Street Settlement, founded in 1893 in New York City by LILLIAN WALD, the Hudson Guild in New York in 1895, the University of Chicago Settlement in 1894, and Greenwich House in New York in 1902. In 1911 a national organization of settlement houses was founded which, by 1930, had 130 members. Most of the non-member institutions were sectarian. The work of the settlement houses has included group participation in handicrafts, MUSIC, ART, and LITERATURE. They have also provided home nursing service, playgrounds and camps for children, and employment services for their members.

Seventeenth Amendment. Adopted in

1913. It provided for the direct popular election of United States Senators. State governors were authorized to fill vacancies in the Senate.

Seventh-Day Adventists. A religious sect which developed out of the Adventist movement in 1833. Its members followed Ellen G. White in their belief in the imminent personal return of Jesus Christ and the observance of the seventh day sabbath. Other theological tenets included immersion, immortality through Christ, and the unchangeability of the decalogue. The Seventh-Day Adventists carry on their work through missionary activities, publications, and EDUCATION. In 1863 they organized a general conference. Their membership in 1956 was approximately 307,000.

"Seven-Thirties." Treasury notes of the United States authorized by Congress on July 17, 1861 to help finance the Civil War. By the end of the war, $830,000,-000 of these notes had been issued, bearing an interest rate of 7.30 percent.

Seventh of March Speech. Generally considered one of DANIEL WEBSTER's most brilliant and moving speeches in the Senate. It was made during the debates over the COMPROMISE ACT OF 1850. In it, Webster powerfully advocated adoption of the Act. In opposition to the vigorous ABOLITIONIST sentiment of the area which he represented, he declared that his love of the Union transcended his hatred of SLAVERY. He implored the South to dismiss the thought of SECESSION, and asked for the reestablishment of peace between the two sections. Webster was denounced by the antislavery groups of the North for his stand on this measure.

Seven Years' War. See French and Indian War.

SEVIER, John. 1745-1815. FRONTIERSMAN, soldier and political leader. b. Virginia. Member, COMMITTEE OF SAFETY (1776); served against the CHEROKEE INDIANS; led force to victory against the British at battle of King's Mountain (1780); governor of the temporary state of Franklin which was formed after North Carolina gave the TERRITORY to the government (1785-88); member, U.S. House of Representatives as first representative from the territory "south of the Ohio River" (1789-91); first governor of Tennessee (1796-1801, 1803-09); re-elected to House of Representatives (1811-15).

SEWALL, Samuel. 1652-1730. Colonial jurist. b. England. Came to America (1661); settled in Massachusetts; graduated, Harvard (1671); studied divinity; gave up the ministry to enter public career; member, governor's council (1684-86, 1689-1725); responsible for condemning 19 persons to death during the Salem WITCHCRAFT trials (1692); later repented and confessed publicly that he had sinned (1697); justice, Massachusetts Superior Court (1692-1728); chief justice (1718-28). His diary is an excellent source book for a picture of his time.

SEWARD, William Henry. 1801-1872. Statesman. b. New York. Graduated, Union College (1820); practiced law in Auburn, N.Y.; governor of New York (1839-43); U.S. Senator (1849-61); important WHIG; strong opponent of SLAVERY; opposed the COMPROMISE OF 1850 and the KANSAS-NEBRASKA BILL; joined the Republican party and became an outstanding leader of the party; appointed by LINCOLN, U.S. Secretary of State (1861-69); handled the difficult problems of the Civil War years with great skill; responsible for the purchase of ALASKA from Russia (1867).

"Seward's Icebox." See Alaska.

Sewing Machine. Improving the INVEN-

574

TIONS of sewing machines in the United States and Europe, ELIAS HOWE, Allen B. Wilson, and I. M. Singer obtained patent rights in the 1850's. In that decade three companies were organized to manufacture sewing machines on a commercial basis. The introduction of automatic machinery and replaceable standardized parts stimulated a rapid increase in production. By 1870 the United States was producing more than 500,-000 machines. The invention and its improvements radically changed the routine of the housewife by permitting the rapid and efficient fabrication and repair of the family's CLOTHING and furnishings.

S.H.A.E.F. The abbreviation for the Supreme Headquarters of the Allied Expeditionary Forces in World War II. Under the command of General DWIGHT D. EISENHOWER its headquarters were originally established in London. After the successful invasion of France the headquarters were transferred to Versailles. In England S.H.A.E.F. planned and organized the great task of invading Normandy.

Shakers. A colonial religious sect which originated as a schismatic group of Quakers. By 1830 there were 18 Shaker communities in New York, New England, and the states of the Ohio valley. Their strongest period of growth occurred during the democratic revivalism of the Jacksonian era and reflected the radical thinking of the UTOPIAN SOCIALISTS. The Shakers combined religious independence with social and economic reform. Their beliefs included communal ownership of property, high moral standards, equality of the sexes, the need to work, and celibacy. Their communities were organized into bishoprics administered by a headquarters ministery at New Lebanon, New York. The Shakers

virtually disappeared by the 20th century.

S.H.A.P.E. Abbreviation for Supreme Headquarters, Allied Powers in Europe. The headquarters of the allied command in Europe which was established in April, 1951 by the NORTH ATLANTIC TREATY Organization to build up the military forces of its 12 member nations. In his first report to the NATO Standing Group on April 2, 1951, General Dwight D. Eisenhower, the Supreme Commander, declared that NATO troop strength in Europe had been doubled since his appointment, and three subsidiary commands had been established for northern, central, and southern Europe, each with its own air and sea arm and supply organization. He declared that, by the end of 1952, the pledges made at the Lisbon conference in February, 1952 would be fullfilled.

SHAPLEY, Harlow. 1885-   . Astronomer. Graduated, University of Missouri and Princeton; astronomer at Mt. Wilson Observatory, California (1914-21); professor of astronomy at Harvard and director of their observatory (from 1921). An outstanding figure in the field known for his research work in photometry, spectroscopy, and cosmogony.

Sharecroppers. Negroes and poor whites who acquired small parcels of land as a result of the break-up of large estates in the South after the Civil War. Unable to pay cash for their land, they received farm equipment, seed, livestock, and other aid from landlords in return for a third or a half of the crops they grew. Sharecroppers were also those, who during the GREAT DEPRESSION, were foreclosed off their land and acquired the right to work it by the payment of shares to the mortgagor. With the TENANT FARMER and the MIGRATORY FARM LABORER, he was at the bottom of the economic scale, eking out a subsistence livelihood in permanent debt to the landowner with whom he was required to share his crop. In the 1930's more than 1,000,000 sharecroppers became public relief recipients. In 1937 the BANKHEAD-JONES ACT provided a means for sharecroppers to own their farms. The FARM SECURITY ADMINISTRATION spent $75,-000,000 by 1940 to enable 13,000 sharecropper and farm tenant families to purchase their own FARMS. By 1950, 1,000,000 families had received loans to purchase machinery, equipment, livestock, seed, fertilizer, and other supplies.

Share-The-Wealth Movement. A program to bring about the equal distribution of wealth. It was begun by Governor HUEY LONG of Louisiana in the early years of the GREAT DEPRESSION and included advocacy of a 100 percent inheritance tax, higher wages, and heavy taxes on the wealthy. Supporters of the idea established share-the-wealth clubs throughout the nation but the movement died out after Long's assassination in 1935.

SHAW, Anna Howard. Woman suffrage leader. b. England. Came to the United States (1851); became a licensed Methodist Minister (1878) and graduated, Boston University Medical School (M.D. 1886); worked with SUSAN B. ANTHONY for the cause of WOMAN'S SUFFRAGE for the rest of her life; became famous as a speaker; president, National American Woman Suffrage Association (1904-15).

SHAWNEE PROPHET. *Indian name* Tenskwatawa. 1768-1837. Famous Indian leader of the Shawnee tribe. Brother of TECUMSEH. After a rather dissolute life, he claimed to have received a message from the spirits to help the Indians return to their native ways and fight against the white man. Planned a confederation of Indian tribes which led to

the CREEK War (1813); aided the British during War of 1812 and was retired to Canada on a pension; returned to his tribe (1826) and went with them into INDIAN TERRITORY where he died.

SHAYS, Daniel. 1747?-1825. Revolutionary leader. b. Massachusetts. Fought in the Revolution at BUNKER HILL and in other major battles, being commissioned a captain (1777); leader of the insurrection in the western part of Massachusetts known as SHAYS' REBELLION (1786-87); fled to Vermont; captured and condemned to death (1788) but pardoned. Moved to New York State.

Shays' Rebellion. An uprising in Massachusetts in 1786 of 1,500 men under Captain DANIEL SHAYS in protest against a legislative act requiring the payment of all debts in specie. The rebellion reflected the opposition of farmers and debtors to a hard money program and was part of a similar movement of insurrection in other areas of the state. The inability of the Congress to muster an army to suppress the rebellion (which was put down by a force of 4,000 state militia) was an expression of the weakness of the government of the ARTICLES OF CONFEDERATION. It resulted in a demand by the property owners, businessmen, and conservatives for a convention to amend the Articles for the purpose of strengthening the government. This took the form of the Constitutional CONVENTION at Philadelphia the following year.

SHEELER, Charles. 1883-1965. Photographer and painter. b. Philadelphia, Pennsylvania. Studied with WILLIAM CHASE; studied in Europe and influenced by cubists; interested in the American scene and in portraying the development of industrial America; worked with STIEGLITZ in photography.

SHEPPARD, Morris. 1875-1941. Lawyer

and legislator. b. Texas. Studied and practised law in Texas; member, U.S. House of Representatives (1902-13); elected U.S. Senator on a prohibition platform (1913-41); co-sponsor of Sheppard-Towner Act (1921) which provided for federal and state aid in maternal and infant welfare and hygiene; also helped to draw up WEBB-KENYON ACT controlling interstate liquor shipments; guiding figure behind the VOLSTEAD ACT.

SHERIDAN, Philip Henry. 1831-1888. Union general. b. New York. Graduated, U.S.M.A., West Point (1853); appointed colonel of a Michigan cavalry regiment (1862); brigadier general (1862) after service at Booneville; major general (1862) serving with the ARMY OF THE POTOMAC; made famous ride (called Sheridan's Ride) from Winchester to Cedar Creek (1864); by leading his army across the Confederate line of retreat from APPOMATTOX he forced LEE to surrender (1865); lieutenant general (1869); served with German armies in Europe (1870-71); succeeded SHERMAN as Commander-in-Chief, U.S. Army (1884); general (1888). Author of *Personal Memoirs of P. H. Sheridan* (2 vols., 1888).

Sherman Anti-Trust Act. The first of several ANTI-TRUST LAWS designed to curb the growth of monopolies and MONOPOLY practices. It was passed in 1890 and provided that every contract, combination in the form of trust or otherwise, or conspiracy in restraint of trade among the several states or with foreign nations was illegal. Penalties for violation included $5,000 fine, a year's imprisonment, or both. The act has been administered by the Anti-Trust Division of the DEPARTMENT OF JUSTICE. From its inception the law has been ineffective in achieving its objectives. The reasons for its ineffectiveness were the absence of a strong idependent com-

mission for its enforcement, the lack of definition of its terms, and Supreme Court interpretation in various cases which virtually removed manufacturing and "reasonable" monopolies from its jurisdiction. The cases involved were THE UNITED STATES VS. E. C. KNIGHT, 1895, and the American Tobacco and Standard Oil Cases, 1911, in latter two of which the court laid down the "RULE OF REASON" principle.

SHERMAN, John. 1823-1900. Statesman. b. Ohio. Studied law and was admitted to the bar in Ohio (1844); prominent WHIG; member, U.S. House of Representatives (1855-61) and U.S. Senator (1861-77); chairman, Senate Finance Committee (1867-77); helped to organize the Republican party in Ohio; important in passage of MORRILL TARIFF ACT (1860); appointed by MC KINLEY, Secretary of the Treasury (1877-81); supported LEGAL TENDER ACT and a national banking system; pushed plan for resumption of specie payments; supported JOHNSON; unsuccessful candidate for Republican nomination for the presidency; again Senator (1881-97); author of the SHERMAN ANTI-TRUST ACT (1890); and SHERMAN SILVER PURCHASE ACT; appointed U.S. Secretary of State (1897-98). He was a brother of WILLIAM T. SHERMAN.

SHERMAN, Roger. 1721-1793. Jurist and statesman. b. Massachusetts. Moved to Connecticut (1743); became a county surveyor and studied law; member of Connecticut legislature (1755, 56, 58-61, 1764-66); member of state senate (1766-85); judge Conn. Superior Court (1766, 1767, 1773-88); member, CONTINENTAL CONGRESS (1774-81, 1783 and 1784); helped draft and signed DECLARATION OF INDEPENDENCE; also helped draft and signed the ARTICLES OF CONFEDERATION and the Federal Constitution; mayor, New Haven (1784-93); member, CON-

STITUTIONAL CONVENTION, Philadelphia (1787); member, U.S. House of Representatives (1788-91); U.S. Senator (1791-93).

Sherman Silver Purchase Act. Enacted in 1890 it provided for the purchase by the Treasury of 4,500,000 ounces of silver per month at the market price, to be paid by legal tender treasury notes redeemable in gold. The law was passed as a result of the continuing pressure of silver miners, westerners, debtors, and farmers following the enactment of the BLAND-ALLISON ACT OF 1878. The latter statute had not succeeded in preventing the decline in the price of silver. The Sherman Act did not achieve its aim of halting this decline while simultaneously the decrease in the gold stocks of the government went on. Between 1890 and 1893 the Treasury's gold reserves fell by $132,000,000 because of the redemption of the treasury certificates. Because of this and other reasons the Congress repealed the Act in 1893.

SHERMAN, William Tecumseh. 1820-1891. Union general. b. Ohio. Graduated, U.S.M.A., West Point (1840); served in California and the Mexican War; brigadier general of volunteers (August, 1861); fought at BULL RUN; served with GRANT at SHILOH; major general (1862); served at the capture of VICKSBURG (1863); placed in command of the Army of the Tennessee (1863); in his famous march to the sea he started from CHATTANOOGA (May 6, 1864) to Atlanta and reached there (September 2, 1864); he continued to Savannah (December 21, 1864); he marched northward through the Carolinas causing JOHNSTON to surrender (April 26, 1865); lieutenant general (1866); succeeded Grant as general and Commander of the Army (1869); retired (1884).

Shield Laws. In 1972 in the classic Caldwell Case the Supreme Court ruled that the first amendment does not give journalists the right to conceal the identity of their sources from a grand jury. Earl Caldwell was a reporter who had gained access to the revolutionary Black Panther Party. Caldwell felt that his coverage of this organization came to an end the day that he was subpoenead to produce documents and tapes because the members of the Black Panthers were afraid that he would become an unwilling agent of the government. Caldwell refused to honor the subpoena. In the Caldwell case Justice White wrote the majority decision in which reporters were required to reveal their sources.

SHIELDS, James. 1810-1879. Union general and political leader. b. Ireland. Came to the United States (1823); settled in Illinois; studied law and practised there; judge, State Supreme Court (1843-45); served under TAYLOR as brigadier general of volunteers during the Mexican War (1846) brevetted major general for heroism at Cerro Gordo; governor of Oregon territory (1849); U.S. Senator from Illinois (1849-55); moved to the Minnesota Territory and then to California (1859); volunteered for service and served as a brigadier general of volunteers in the Shenandoah Valley campaign of the Civil War; resigned (1863); moved to Missouri and became U.S. Senator from that state (1879).

Shiloh, Battle of. One of the most important and bloodiest battles of the Civil War. The Battle was fought at Pittsburgh Landing in Tennessee on April 6 and 7, 1862. The Union army of 33,000, under the command of General GRANT, was attacked by 40,000 Confederate troops under General JOHNSTON, retreating with great loss in the afternoon of the first day of battle. The wounding of Johnston brought General BEAUREGARD into command of the Southern army. On April 7th, Grant, reinforced by 7,000 troops under General BUELL, assumed the offensive. A charge, led by Grant himself, began the rout which ended in a full Confederate retreat. The Union casualties totalled 13,047. The Confederate losses were reported at about 10,700.

Shipbuilding. One of the most important INDUSTRIES in colonial America. In New England FISHING and COMMERCE called shipbuilding into being. The abundance of forest land and a ready foreign market stimulated a large construction program. The increasing IMMIGRATION of the 19th century provided a supply of shipbuilding labor. American ships were soon being purchased throughout the world. Although the first shipyards were located on the Atlantic coast, the post-Civil War period saw a movement of shipyards to the Gulf of Mexico and the Pacific coast. In the half-century preceding World War I American shipbuilding declined because of high construction costs. The requirements of the war stimulated the greatest period of shipbuilding in American history. In the five years after the United States entered the war more than 12,000,000 tons were constructed as compared with 225,000 tons in 1915. The post-war period witnessed another decline in shipbuilding activity until the extension of federal SUBSIDIES under the various MERCHANT MARINE ACTS. Before the outbreak of World War II the MARITIME COMMISSION had provided for a ship construction program of 500 ships in 10 years. During the war this program was accelerated to 5,300 vessels and 54,000,-000 deadweight tons. Modern dry cargo ships, tankers, Liberty ships, Victory ships, and transports were constructed. By the end of the war the United States MERCHANT MARINE had become the greatest in the world. See Merchant Marine.

Shipping. Colonial shipping was carried on principally in the WEST INDIES trade and with British ports in Europe. After the Revolution, the West Indies trade declined because of the British NAVIGATION ACTS and Congress' restrictions. TARIFFS in 1789 and 1790 imposed discriminatory duties favoring American ships, leading to an increase of American tonnage. In 1790 more than 41 percent of all American trade was carried in foreign vessels. By 1795 this had fallen to 9.7 percent. In 1807 American tonnage was eight times as great as in 1789 and by the end of the War of 1812 was carrying more than 77 percent of this nation's foreign trade. The American trader was primarily a merchant who bought and sold cargo, and occasionally his vessel. For a long time piracy, lack of capital, and unfavorable legislation hindered the growth of shipping. The rise of the common carrier after the War of 1812 saw the disappearance of the merchant trader. COMMERCE and carriage became independent transactions. The organization of the Black Ball Line in 1816 instituted the chartered system in American shipping. The tramp line became important after the Civil War as the second type of common carrier. The post-war period witnessed a decline from 65.2 percent to 27.7 percent in the value of United States foreign commerce carried by American vessels. Steam propulsion and steel vessels brought to the British merchant marine a virtual MONOPOLY of the TRANSPORTATION of American goods in foreign trade. Restrictive legislation by Congress, with respect to registry of American vessels and tariff barriers, accelerated this movement. In the 20th century industrial carriers operated by large trading houses became important in transporting general cargo in much the same way as the colonial and early American merchant trader. World War I brought a huge increase in United States foreign trade. By 1920 American vessels were carrying almost 43 percent of this country's goods as compared to less than 10 percent at the beginning of the War. World War II encouraged an increase in American shipping, the greatest stimulus resulting from the passage of the LEND-LEASE ACT in 1941. See commerce, and shipbuilding.

Ship Purchase Act. Also known as Merchant Marine Act of 1916. Passed by Congress in 1916. It established the United States Shipping Board of five members with power to build, purchase, lease, and operate vessels during and for a five year period after World War I. In April, 1917 the board was reorganized into the U.S. EMERGENCY FLEET CORPORATION which embarked on a vast program of ship construction. It spent approximately $1,000,000,000 in building ships more rapidly than they were lost in enemy action. By 1921, it had succeeded in raising the tonnage of American vessels in foreign trade from approximately 3,000,000 to 11,000,000. Under its stimulation the number of shipyards increased from 61 in 1917 to 341 by 1919, employing 380,000 workers, an increase of 335,000.

Ship Subsidy Act. See Maritime Commission, United States.

SHIRLEY, William. 1694-1771. Colonial governor. b. England. Came to America (1731); settled in Boston; appointed commissioner to settle the Rhode Island boundary dispute; governor of Massachusetts (1741-49); planned capture of Louisburg (1745); succeeded in stabilizing financial situation in the colony; member of commission that went to Paris to settle boundary dispute between New England and French North America (1749-53); governor (1753-56); at outbreak of the French and Indian war he was appointed major general (1755); failed in attack on Niagara (1755); succeeded BRADDOCK as commander in chief of British forces in America but was soon relieved of duty; recalled and deprived of governorship; governor of Bahama Islands (1761-67).

SHOLES, Christopher Latham. 1819-1890. Inventor. b. Pennsylvania. Famous as the inventor of the typewriter, having experimented with numbering and lettering machines (from 1864).

Short Ballot. A political reform which seeks to reduce the number of elective offices presented to the voter. Prior to its adoption by the states it was customary for the voter to choose from among 100 or more candidates for as many as 40 offices. By lengthening the tenure of the elected officers and eliminating many offices from the BALLOT, it has been hoped to improve the quality of VOTING.

Short Haul, Long Haul Abuse. A RAILROAD abuse of the post-Civil War period by which a higher rate was charged for a short haul under MONOPOLY conditions than for a long haul under conditions of competition. The INTERSTATE COMMERCE ACT forbade this practice.

SIBLEY, Henry Hastings. 1811-1891. Pioneer and governor. b. Michigan. Agent for AMERICAN FUR COMPANY in trading with SIOUX INDIANS (1830); became partner (1834); became prominent in Minnesota and served as territorial delegate to Congress; member of convention that drafted a state constitution; became first governor of Minnesota (1858); succeeded in controlling Indians in his territory.

Sicily, Invasion of. On July 10, 1943 the United States 7th Army, commanded by General PATTON, and the British 8th Army, commanded by General Montgomery, invaded southern Sicily after a strong air bombardment on July 9th and 10th. The United States forces were unopposed in their landing between Licata and Scoglitti, the Italian defenders having fled northward. On July 22nd the

7th Army reached Palermo, but the British were held up on the east coast by strong German artillery fire in the area south of Mt. Etna. On August 16th the 7th Army reached Messina on the north coast and caused the Germans to withdraw on the British front. The successful campaign laid the groundwork for the invasion of Italy.

SICKLES, Daniel Edgar. 1825-1914. Union general, politician, and diplomat. b. New York City. Studied at University of the City of New York (now New York University); admitted to the bar (1846); served as state senator (1856-57); member, U.S. House of Representatives (1857-61); acquitted in the killing of the son of FRANCIS SCOTT KEY who he claimed was too attentive to Mrs. Sickles; commissioned major general after raising several regiments at the outbreak of the Civil War; served in the Peninsular campaign, at Chancellorsville and GETTYSBURG; appointed military governor of the Carolinas (1865-67); U.S. Minister to Spain (1869-73); took part in the *Virginus* case; chairman, N.Y. Civil Service Commission (1888-89); again member, U.S. House of Representatives (1893-95); largely responsible for obtaining Central Park for New York City.

SIKORSKY, Igor. 1889-1972. Aeronautical engineer. b. Russia. Came to the United States (1919); became a naturalized citizen (1928); built and flew the first multimotored airplane (1913); organized companies to manufacture planes of his own design which were merged into the United Aircraft Manufacturing Corporation; best known for his multimotored amphibian.

SILLIMAN, Benjamin. 1779-1864. Chemist and geologist. Professor, Yale (1802-53); founded and edited *The American Journal of Science and Arts,* also referred to as *Silliman's Journal*

(1818); one of the founders of the National Academy of Science; played an important part in the organization of Yale Medical School. His son, Benjamin Silliman (1816-1885), organized the Sheffield School of Science at Yale.

Silver Purchase Act. Passed by Congress in 1934. It provided for the nationalization of all domestic silver and its purchase by the TREASURY DEPARTMENT until the price should reach $1.2929 per ounce or until the amount held would equal one third of the value of the federal government's gold stocks. The purpose of the law was to increase the price of silver which had fallen to new lows as a result of the DEPRESSION of the 1930's, to issue silver certificates for the purpose of accelerating general price increases, and to establish a mixed gold and silver standard. Under the Act the Treasury Department purchased $1,000,-000,000 worth of silver abroad at prices above the market value of 45 cents per ounce paying for it with silver certificates irredeemable in gold. All the purchased bullion has been deposited in vaults at West Point, New York. The aims of the law were not achieved, despite the huge purchases, because the large increase in gold holdings has prevented the silver stocks from approaching one third of the value of the gold.

SIMONSON, Lee. 1888-1967. Scenic designer. Associated with the Washington Square Players and the Theatre Guild; he designed the sets for many outstanding productions including *The Goat Song, The Road to Rome, Marco's Millions* and *Elizabeth the Queen.* He is the author of several books on the theater.

Sims Case. A famous FUGITIVE SLAVE case which exemplified a typical procedure surrounding the arrest and return of a slave. In 1851 Sims, the slave, was

581

seized in Boston on a false charge and immediately claimed as the property of a Mr. Potter of Virginia. He was returned to his alleged master by United States commissioner who signed a certificate to that effect despite the intense protests of th Boston population. So high was this indignation that the courthouse in Boston was surrounded and guarded by troops subsequently referred to as "Sims Brigade."

SINCLAIR, Upton Beall. 1878-1968. Novelist and social reformer. b. Maryland. Graduated, College of the City of New York (1897); prominent SOCIALIST; moved to California; Socialist candidate for the U.S. House of Representatives (1920); and for governor of California (1926, 1930); ran on Democratic ticket for governor on a platform to end poverty in California and old-age assistance (1934); founder of the AMERICAN CIVIL LIBERTIES UNION in California. Author of well-known novels including *The Jungle* (1906), *King Coal* (1917), *Oil* (1927), and a "Lanny Budd" series including *World's End* (1940), *Between Two Worlds* (1941) and *Wide Is the Gate* (1943) for which he was awarded the Pulitzer Prize.

Sinking Fund. A fund set aside from profits or reserves by governments or business organizations to amortize outstanding bonded obligations. The first federal sinking fund was established by Congress in 1790 to apply the net surplus income from customs duties to the reduction of the public debt. An amending law in 1795 placed the fund and the debt under the administration of the Commissioners of the Sinking Fund.

Sioux Indians. Also called Dakota Indians. The Sioux lived in the northern plains section, near the headwaters of the Mississippi River, as far north as Canada and south into South Carolina. The largest number lived in Wisconsin, Minnesota, North Dakota, and South Dakota. The Sioux were friendly to the British and supported them against the Americans during the Revolution and, with the exception of Chief Tohami or Rising Moose, in the War of 1812. They were consistently hostile against American settlers and troops, and were led by such outstanding chiefs as SITTING BULL, Red Cloud, CRAZY HORSE, and Rain-in-the-Face. It was the Sioux who massacred CUSTER at Little Big Horn River in 1876. They were a superior tribe, both physically and mentally, with a typical Plains culture. They depended largely on the buffalo for food, clothing, skins, and other uses. They were sun worshippers.

Sister Kenny Foundation. Named after Elizabeth Kenny who, in 1943, established this organization to combat poliomyelitis by the diagnostic and treatment methods she had developed. The Foundation also performs research into the nature and prevention of this desease. It maintains a wide-spread medical and public information program and grants scholarships for the training of qualified registered professional nurses and physical therapists. It maintains treatment centers which carry on their work through authorized local chapters. Its entire program is financed by public contributions. The office of the Foundation is located in Minneapolis, Minnesota.

Sit-Down Strikes. Strikes in which the workers remain within a plant forcing it to shut down. This type of strike was first used by the United Automobile Workers in 1936. It spread rapidly to other MASS PRODUCTION industries which the CONGRESS OF INDUSTRIAL ORGANIZATIONS was attempting to organize in 1936 and 1937. The sit-down strike was denounced as illegal and revolutionary. In the General Motors strike in January, 1937 in Michigan the state militia was sent to prevent violence while COLLECTIVE BARGAINING negotiations were undertaken between union and management. In February, 1939 the United States Supreme Court, in deciding the legality of a sit-down strike against the Fansteel Metallurgical Corporation, declared the sit-down strike to be illegal. The right of the employer to discharge sit-down strikers was sustained by the Court.

SITTING BULL. 1834?-1890. Sioux Indian chief. b. South Dakota. Leader of the SIOUX tribe and in the many Sioux wars; served with CRAZY HORSE at the battle of Little Big Horn where the massacre of CUSTER and his men took place (1876); fled to Canada; returned and surrendered; placed on Indian reservation but was constantly in rebellion until he was finally shot by Indian police. He was famous as a leader and medicine man and plays a prominent part in many legends.

Sixteenth Amendment. The income tax AMENDMENT to the Constitution of the United States. It provides that Congress shall have power to lay and collect taxes on incomes, without apportionment among the several states, and without regard to the POPULATION of the states. The amendment was adopted in 1913, a number of years after the invalidation of the income tax provision of the WILSON-GORMAN TARIFF ACT of 1894.

"Skinners." Refers to irregular bands of colonial PATRIOTS in the American Revolution who harried the British in New York State. Between 1779 and 1783 they marauded in Westchester County, plundering, burning, and destroying property belonging both to loyalists and patriots. Although officially disowned by both belligerents their services were frequently employed by both as scouts and spies. They were named after General Cortland Skinner's Brigade of New Jersey Volunteers. An opposing group of Loyalist irregulars were known as "cowboys."

Slavery. The first slaves were introduced into Virginia by a Dutch ship in 1619. In succeeding years slavery gradually spread into the other colonies under the impetus of a SLAVE TRADE which was favored by England during the 18th century. Slavery did not find favor among all groups in the colonies. In 1688 the Germantown Quakers prepared a memorial against it. In 1701 a Boston town meeting voted opposition to slavery. Although more numerous in the South, slavery was an important economic institution in northern colonies until the mid-eighteenth century. The importation of Negro slaves from Africa became particularly important after the unsuccessful attempts by the colonists to enslave the Indians. With INDENTURED SERVANTS these slaves formed the nucleus of the labor supply of the colonies up to the Revolution. In the South the PLANTATION SYSTEM stimulated this movement because of the obvious advantages of unpaid mass labor on large areas. In 1700 slaves numbered five percent of the colonial POPULATION. At the outbreak of the Revolution there were 500,000 slaves, 20 percent of the total colonial population. Three-quarters of these were in the South where they constituted 40 percent of the population. Although used principally in farm production, slaves were employed in household MANUFACTURING and commercial activities in the northern colonies. The expense of slave labor in an agricultural economy based on small scale production of truck crops for a local market rapidly brought about emancipation in many of the New England and middle colonies. ABOLITION was effected in Rhode Island (1774), Vermont (1777), Pennsylvania (1780), Massachusetts (1781), New Hampshire (1783), Connecticut (1784), New York (1799), and New Jersey (1804). By 1846 slavery had disappeared from the North. In the South moral, economic, religious, and intellectual principles were under constant scrutiny in the effort to determine the righteousness of the institution of slavery. Through the 17th and 18th century, distinguished figures like JAMES E. OGLETHORPE, ROGER WILLIAMS, JOHN ELIOT, HENRY LAURENS, and THOMAS JEFFERSON attacked slavery on humanitarian grounds. Its economic importance prevented emancipation, although in certain states legislation provided for individual manumission. The Founding Fathers seriously questioned the issue, but decided to leave slavery and its problems to the states. The Constitution recognized and protected slavery and the slave trade. Between the Revolution and the Mexican War the issue of slavery was generally not raised in political controversy. The Missouri petition for ADMISSION TO THE UNION in 1818 temporarily raised the question. In this period abolition societies and abolitionist agitation slowly engendered a sectional hostility that was to culminate in the political conflicts of the 1850's. By this time the invention of the cotton gin and the development of the great English market had fixed cotton culture and its slave labor upon the South. The expansionist tendencies of the plantation slave-holder brought the nation into war with Mexico. The decade before the Civil War witnessed the most profound struggle over the issue of slavery. Begun in the debates over the OMNIBUS BILL, this struggle continued over the KANSAS-NEBRASKA ACT, Kansas War, DRED SCOTT DECISION, LINCOLN-DOUGLAS Debates, JOHN BROWN'S RAID, PERSONAL LIBERTY LAWS. and UNDERGROUND RAILROAD. The election of LINCOLN culminated the divisive hatreds of the decade and was accepted by the South as proof that its claims were to be disregarded. SECESSION and Civil War followed. Meanwhile the conditions of the slave on the southern farm and plantation became the focal point of social and ethical controversy. Supporters defended slavery as necessary to the economy of the South. They argued that slaves were given food, shelter, and clothing, and were cared for in illness and need. They pointed to the high status of domestic slaves and to the maintenance of the religious and moral well-being of all slaves. Opponents attacked the institution as a violation of ethical and humanitarian ideals. They denounced the oppression of cruel overseers in the field and denied the right of slave-holders to keep human beings in bondage. Their opposition included denunciation of the traffic in human beings, the destruction of families, the violation of constitutional provisions relating to freedom, slave breeding, and the uneconomic use of slave labor. On the plantation slaves were divided into three general classifications: field hands, domestic servants, and mechanics. Among the latter was a labor supply of carpenters, plasterers, bricklayers, and workers of all kinds. By the opening of the Civil War there were approximately 4,000,000 slaves out of a southern population of 12,000,000. Slave ownership was concentrated in a handful of the white population. Slaves were owned by only 384,000 whites, of whom 107,957 owned more than 10, 10,781 owned 50 or more, and but 1,753 owned 100 or more. Two-thirds of the white population had no direct interest in slavery.

Slave Trade. The sale of slaves in established markets. In many states prior to the Civil War the breeding of slaves for sale was practiced. Following the introduction of slaves into the British colonies in 1619 a flourishing trade between Africa and these colonies grew up. The Constitution of 1787 provided that the importation of slaves could not be prohibited for 20 years. Upon the expiration of this period in 1808, Congress forbade this aspect of the slave trade. Domestic trade went on until the Civil War although it was abolished in the District of

Columbia by the COMPROMISE ACT OF 1850.

SLIDELL, John. 1793-1871. Diplomat and political leader. b. New York City. Graduated, Columbia College; practised law in New Orleans (1819-35); member, U.S. House of Representatives (1843-45); U.S. Senator (1853-61); unsuccessful in attempt to deal with Mexico in the purchase of California and New Mexico and the ANNEXATION OF TEXAS; played an important part in the nomination and election of BUCHANAN (1856); after his withdrawal from the Senate, he joined the Confederacy and was sent by them on a mission to France (1861); with MASON he was taken from the British steamer, *Trent,* and taken to Boston; released after much protest and returned to the British ship; he was unsuccessful in his attempt to gain aid and recognition for the Confederacy from France; lived in England after the war.

SLOAN, John. 1871-1952. Painter, etcher and illustrator. b. Pennsylvania. Famous as a teacher and a leader of the "Ash Can School" of American realism. Many of his paintings and prints are in the Metropolitan Museum of Art, N.Y. as well as in other leading museums throughout the country. His etchings and paintings of scenes under the "el" in New York City have great strength and originality and are an important contribution to American art.

SLOAT, John Drake. 1780-1867. Naval officer. b. New York City. In command of the Pacific squadron (1844); successful in wresting California from Mexico at the outbreak of the Mexican War (1845); commanded the Norfolk Navy Yard (1847-51); promoted to commodore (1862) rear admiral (1866).

SLOCUM, Henry Warner. 1827-1894. Union general. b. New York. Graduated, U.S.M.A., West Point (1852); brigadier general of volunteers (1861); major general (1862); commanded extreme right line of Union forces at GETTYSBURG (July 2-4, 1863); commanded the left wing in SHERMAN's march to the sea and back northward through the Carolinas (1864-65); resigned his commission to practice law in Brooklyn, N.Y. (1866); member, U.S. House of Representatives (1869-73; 1883-85).

Slums. The congested areas of urban communities which are characterized by unsanitary living conditions, sub-standard housing, poverty, and disease. Slum areas developed around factory sections which solicited the employment of newly arrived immigrants. The exploitation of immigrant labor by underpayment of wages in SWEATSHOPS helped perpetuate slum conditions. Inadequate income made for sub-standard living in tenement buildings which were fire hazards. Such conditions perpetuated poverty and bred crime, delinquency, and broken homes. Gang warfare, political corruption, and graft marked the growth of slums in the United States. The east-side of New York gained international notoriety for its slum conditions. Similar slums in Chicago, Boston, Philadelphia, and Washington, D.C. developed by the close of the 19th century. A report of the Commissioner of Labor in 1894 revealed that in Chicago and New York less than three percent of all families had bathtubs. In New York almost 7,000 families lived in rooms without windows. It was not until the opening of the 20th century that tenement laws attempted to rectify these conditions. See tenement laws.

Small Defense Plants Administration. An agency established in 1950 by the DEFENSE PRODUCTION ACT. Its purpose was to recommend to the RECONSTRUCTION FINANCE CORPORATION loans for small business concerns for defense and essential civilian activities. These loans could be granted up to a maximum of $100,-000,000 outstanding at any one time. Such loans were authorized under Section 714 of the Act. By May, 1952 the agency had received 462 loan applications from small business firms, totalling $208,000,000. Of these it had acted on 133 applications aggregating $87,-000,000.

Smith Act. Also known as the ALIEN REGISTRATION ACT. A law of Congress passed on June 29, 1940. Title I of the Act contained anti-sedition provisions for the first time in peacetime since the ALIEN AND SEDITION ACTS of 1798. These provisions included prohibitions against interference with the morale of the armed forces through advice or the distribution of written or printed matter, the advocacy, abetting, or teaching the desirability of overthrowing any government in the United States by force or violence, and the dissemination of matter or organization of any group aimed at this end. On October 14, 1949, after a nine month trial, 11 leaders of the Communist party were convicted of violation of the Smith Act. After appeal to the Court of Appeals and the United States Supreme Court the latter held on June 4, 1951 that their conviction was legal and that the Smith Act was constitutional. This decision was followed on June 20, 1951 by the arrests of 21 more Communists and in July and August of 25 other leaders of the party. The law also required all alien residents in the United States over 14 years of age to file a comprehensive statement of their personal and occupational status and a record of their political beliefs. Such aliens were registered and fingerprinted and were thereafter required to keep the proper federal authorities informed of their address and occupation. Within four months a total of 4,741,971 aliens had registered.

SMITH, Alfred Emanuel. 1873-1944. Political leader. b. New York City. Member, New York State legislature (1903-15); became Democratic leader of the Assembly (1911), speaker (1913); delegate to State constitutional convention (1915); sheriff of New York County (1915-17); president, New York Board of Aldermen (1917); extremely forceful and popular governor of New York for four terms (1919-20; 1923-28); defeated for the presidency (1928) on the Democratic ticket largely because of his religion and his opposition to PROHIBITION; president, Empire State, Inc., which managed the Empire State Building in New York. He was a leader of TAMMANY HALL and a strong supporter of F. D. ROOSEVELT in the early part of his career. He was an honest and sincere man who tried to help the people of his state.

Smith-Connally Act. Also known as War Labor Disputes Act. An act of Congress passed in May, 1943 for the purpose of reducing the number of STRIKES during World War II. It declared illegal any strike in a government operated mine or plant, and required a cooling-off period of 30 days, followed by a secret vote of the employees, before a strike could be called in any mine or plant. It conferred upon the WAR LABOR BOARD the right to subpoena the parties to a labor dispute. Because of organized labor's protests and the general hasty drafting and undemocratic features of the law it was vetoed by the President but enacted over his VETO. The law also gave a statutory basis to the War Labor Board.

SMITH, Edmund Kirby. Also known as Edmund Kirby-Smith. 1824-1893. Confederate general. b. Florida. Graduated, U.S.M.A., West Point (1845); served in the Mexican War; became a major general in the Confederate army (1861); lieutenant general (1862); general (1864); he commanded the department which was made up of the states west of the

Mississippi; he is best known because he was the last Confederate general to surrender (May 26, 1865); president, Atlantic and Pacific Telegraph Company; president, University of Nashville (1870-75); professor of mathematics, University of South Tennessee.

SMITH, Erminnie Adelle. 1836-1886. Ethnologist. b. New York. Best known for her work with the IROQUOIS INDIANS; wrote an Iroquois-English dictionary which is of importance in the field; wrote *Myths of the Iroquois* (1883); first woman fellow of the New York Academy of Sciences.

SMITH, Gerrit. 1797-1874. Philanthropist. b. New York. Graduated, Hamilton College (1818); became associated with WILLIAM LLOYD GARRISON in the ABOLITIONIST MOVEMENT; helped JOHN BROWN; gave large sums of money to various causes and campaigned for various social reforms including WOMAN'S SUFFRAGE and prison reform; during the Civil War he gave liberally to the northern cause; was one of the signers of the bail bond for JEFFERSON DAVIS.

SMITH, Hoke. 1855-1931. Lawyer, journalist and politician. b. North Carolina. Moved to Georgia where he became a successful lawyer; owned the Atlanta *Journal* (1887-1900); appointed by CLEVELAND, U.S. Secretary of the Interior (1893-96); governor of Georgia (1907-09; 1911); U.S. Senator (1911-21); opposed WILSON's stand on the LEAGUE OF NATIONS.

Smith-Hughes Act. Passed by Congress in 1917. It established a Federal Board for Vocational Education for the enhancement of training in agriculture, home economics, vocational subjects, COMMERCE, and trades and industries. The Act operates on a grant-in-aid basis, federal SUBSIDIES being matched by the states. Amending legislation has extended the original activities to vocational rehabilitation.

SMITH, James. 1719?-1806. Lawyer and legislator. b. Ireland. Came to America as a child and settled in Pennsylvania; practised law; served in various provincial assemblies; member, CONTINENTAL CONGRESS (1776-78); signer of the DECLARATION OF INDEPENDENCE.

SMITH, Jedediah Strong. 1798-1831. Explorer. b. New York. Fur trader in St. Louis; traveled over 5,000 miles with two companions in the West on one expedition into INDIAN TERRITORY; made first crossing of the Sierra Nevadas and first overland by the Central Route to be recorded; was killed by COMANCHE INDIANS along the SANTE FE TRAIL; although he is little known he deserves to rank with LEWIS AND CLARK as a western explorer.

SMITH, John. 1580-1631. Colonist. b. England. Came to America (1606) and to JAMESTOWN, Virginia (May 24, 1607); a member of the governing council of the colony; was a leader of the colony and succeeded in establishing trade relations with the Indians; when captured by POWHATAN and condemned to death; he was, so the story goes, rescued by POCAHONTAS, daughter of the chieftain; explored the territory surrounding Chesapeake Bay; he was a forceful leader and managed to hold the colony together through very difficult times; returned to England (1609); explored the New England coast (1614) and wrote many books and drew maps of the entire TERRITORY.

SMITH, Joseph. 1805-1844. Founder of the Mormon Church. b. Vermont. Moved to New York; when 14 years of age he received a vision that told him to start a new sect based on the words found on golden plates; he based the Book of Mormon upon these plates which he dictated to others to write; organized his Church

587

of Jesus Christ of Latter-day Saints at Fayette, N.Y. (1830); moved his small congregation to Ohio, from there to Missouri and to Commerce, Illinois, which he renamed Nauvoo; arrested and jailed by non-Mormons; shot by a mob (June 27, 1844).

Smith-Lever Act. Enacted in 1914 for the purpose of extending correspondence and traveling school education in AGRICULTURE. The Act provided for the appropriation of $500,000 with additional appropriations of $500,000 increased annually until 1923 when the annual appropriation would reach $4,500,000. These funds were to be distributed equally among the states for extension and ADULT EDUCATION in agriculture. Provision was also made for the close cooperation of the DEPARTMENT OF AGRICULTURE with the land grant colleges established under the MORILL LAND GRANT ACT of 1862 and the agriculture experiment stations established under the HATCH ACT of 1887.

Smithsonian Institution. It is located in Washington, D.C., and was established in 1846 by the will of James Smithson, an Englishman, who bequeathed his fortune in 1826 to the United States to found an Institution for the "increase and diffusion of knowledge among men." The Institution conducts and encourages scientific researches, explorations, and investigations. It issues 13 series of scientific publications which it distributes gratis to LIBRARIES, learned societies, and educational institutions throughout the world. Its own library of 900,000 volumes consists principally of the work of learned societies and periodicals. Among its branches are the National Museum, the National Gallery of Art, the National Collection of Fine Arts, and the National Zoological Park.

SMOOT, Reed. 1862-1941. Senator and Mormon leader. b. Utah. Graduated,

Brigham Young University; banker: elected an apostle of the Mormon Church (1900); Senator (1903-33) being the first Mormon elected to the Senate; chairman of the Finance Committee of the Senate; member of World War Foreign Debt Commission (1922); conservative Republican who opposed the LEAGUE OF NATIONS; sponsored the SMOOT-HAWLEY TARIFF ACT (1930).

SMITH, Theobald. 1859-1934. Pathologist. b. New York. Professor, Harvard (1896-1915); director, Department of Animal Pathology, Rockefeller Institute for Medical Research (1915-29); famous for his discovery of Texas cattle serum to cure cattle fever (1906); he proved that the disease may be carried by ticks and developed a method of immunization against the disease.

Smuggling. In the British colonies smuggling developed as an important economic activity because of the lack of enforcement of the NAVIGATION ACTS. Colonial geography made smuggling relatively easy since it was difficult to patrol the extended coastline and the many hidden bays and inlets. Forged accounts and bribery of British customs officials abetted smuggling. The goods smuggled included rum, tobacco, molasses, and manufactured goods. Most of this trade was carried on with the French, Spanish, and Dutch Islands in the West Indies. It was not until the abandonment of the policy of "salutary neglect" after the French and Indian War that Parliament made any serious attempts to enforce the Navigation Acts and prevent smuggling.

Snelling, Fort. Established in 1819 as part of our frontier defense. Its site was selected in 1805 by Lt. Z. M. Pike. It was originally named Fort St. Anthony but in 1825 it was changed to Fort Snelling in honor of Col. Josiah Snelling who became commandant in 1820. Located at the junction of the Mississippi and Missouri Rivers it was abandoned in 1858 and re-occupied in 1861.

Social Democratic Party. The original name of a group formed in 1897 of left wing political thinkers, labor leaders, Marxist philosophers, and sections of the American Railroad Union. Their founder and leader EUGENE V. DEBS whose "colonization" plan of concentrating socialist forces upon the political capture of the state of Colorado was repudiated the following year by a group including himself, VICTOR BERGER, and Jesse Cox. This group renamed itself the Social Democratic Party of America and in elections of that year sent two assemblymen to the Massachusetts legislature. In 1901 they merged with a moderate wing of the SOCIALIST LABOR PARTY to form the Socialist Party of America. See Socialist Party.

Socialism. The economic system which provides for the public ownership of the means of production. Socialism argues that its production is based on use not profit and that in a socialist society class warfare and BUSINESS CYCLES will be eliminated, resulting in a more equitable distribution of the products of society. In the United States various socialist groups have advocated democratic or coercive measures in achieving their aim. Among these have been the Utopian Socialists of the Jacksonian era, the SOCIAL DEMOCRATIC PARTY, the SOCIALIST LABOR PARTY, SOCIALIST PARTY, the COMMUNIST PARTY, and the various organizations of the Trotzkyite movement.

Socialist Labor Party. A minor party organized in 1874 as the WORKINGMEN'S PARTY of the United States. It adopted its present name in 1877, becoming the first American socialist party on a national scale. Its program became strongly Marxist after it fell under the revolutionary philosophy of DANIEL DE LEON in the 1890's. Its primary aim was the overthrow of capitalism by strict syn-dicalist methods, the trade unions to provide the leadership of this movement. Its greatest political strength was reached during the elections of 1898 after which its popularity declined.

Socialist Party. A minor party organized in 1897 by EUGENE V. DEBS. The following year a secessionist group established itself as the SOCIAL DEMOCRATIC PARTY winning minor political successes in state and local elections. In 1901 it merged with the moderate wing of the SOCIALIST LABOR PARTY to form the Socialist Party. Its presidential candidate, Debs, received 919,799 votes in 1920 while serving a term in the Atlanta Penitentiary on a war-time espionage charge. The party's program has obtained the support of moderate groups seeking to establish a system of SOCIALISM in the United States through evolutionary means. Pending this achievement the party has advocated reform programs such as SOCIAL SECURITY, improved labor conditions, housing and welfare legislation, extended educational opportunities, an increase in the suffrage, and a more widely expanded program of federal and local control over business practices. Its outstanding leader through the 1930's and 1940's was NORMAN THOMAS

Social Security Act. Passed by Congress in 1935 and amended several times up to 1965. Old Age and Survivors' Insurance provides for compulsory savings for wage earners so that annuities may be paid to them upon retirement. Deductions are made from each employee's pay at 3⅝% of the first $4800 of his yearly wages. An equal amount is charged to the employer. At 62 the wage earner may retire on a monthly annuity, the amount of which is determined by the amount contributed in prior years and the number of dependents. At present, persons who retire at 65 may receive monthly sums as high as $127.50 for a single person and

$190.50 for a married couple. By 1965 nearly 15,000,000 checks were being distributed each month. Full benefits under the law are available to workers who have one quarter of work for every year after 1950 up to but not including the year in which they become 65 (for women, 62). For disability benefits the worker must also have credit for five out of ten years before incurring disability. Men may now retire at 62, but with reduced benefits. For a worker, age 65, retiring in 1967, for example, he must have four full years of credit to qualify for maximum benefits. As this book goes to press, additional amendments to the Act are being discussed in the Congress. The House has overwhelmingly passed a bill (1965) which would provide extensive medical care for the aged through increased contributions to the Social Security fund.

Social Security Administration. The agency which administers the SOCIAL SECURITY ACT of 1935 as amended in 1939, 1950, 1954, 1956, 1958, 1960, 1961 and 1962. It is part of the FEDERAL SECURITY AGENCY which was established on July 1, 1939, under the authority of the REORGANIZATION ACT of April 3, 1939. Under the supervision of the Commissioner for Social Security, the agency consists of various bureaus administering the programs authorized under the statute. These include the Bureau of Old-Age and Survivors Insurance, Bureau of Public Assistance, Bureau of Employment Security, and Bureau of Federal Credit Unions. Formerly the Act was administered by a three-man Social Security Board established in 1935 and incorporated into the Federal Security Agency in 1939. The Social Security Administration's principal office is located in Washington, D.C. It manages 12 regional offices in which are located 613 local field offices.

Social Work. Organized social service in the United States originated in the es-

tablishment of the Society for Prevention of Pauperism in New York City, in 1818. In the 1840's the Association for Improving the Condition of the Poor was established, followed by the Charity Organization Movement in the 1870's. In 1873 the National Conference of Charities and Corrections was founded. In 1904 the New York School of Philanthropy was established, growing by 1939 to almost 40 schools, all members of the American Association of Schools of Social Work. In early years social work was conducted as a philanthropic venture by volunteers, and was financed generally by contributions of wealthy merchants and socialites. By the end of the nineteenth century the need for coordination and planning of social work led to the wider intervention of government. Twentieth century trends have developed out of advances in psychology, sociology, and MEDICINE, and include intensive work in psychiatry, psychology, housing reform, EDUCATION, preventive programs, rehabilitation, and the professionalization of the social worker.

Society of Friends. See Quakers.

Society of Jesus. See Jesuits.

Sod House. Adaptation of Indian habitats by white men during the western expansion period beginning about 1810. In the area beyond the Missouri River nearly 90% of the people lived in sod houses at one time or another. Three-foot sod walls provided warmth in the winter and coolness in the summer.

Soil Conservation and Domestic Allotment Act. Passed in 1936 for the purpose of carrying out the objectives of the AGRICULTURAL ADJUSTMENT ACT which was declared unconstitutional in that year. To overcome the court's objections, the Act provided that the Secretary of Labor would distribute to the states $500,000,000 annually drawn from the general treasury, to be allotted by the states up to $10 per acre to those farmers who substituted the planting of soil conserving for soil depleting crops. Such crops included peas, beans, clover, rye, and alfalfa. Under the law $1,500,-000,000 were distributed by the Secretary of Agriculture. The law was sustained by the Supreme Court.

Soldier Vote, the. The provision by the United States and the states for absentee balloting by members of the armed services. In 1952 some states made no such allowance, some required registration by servicemen in person, and some did not provide for the mailing of absentee ballots in time for counting. The result was that a large proportion of the 2,500,000 eligible servicemen at home and overseas were not expected to participate in that year's election unless remedial legislation were enacted. President TRUMAN requested a federal law to insure voting rights, pointing out that "although the most effective way ° ° ° is through state action," Congress has a prime responsibility in the matter. He recommended the revival of the 1944 federal BALLOT with modifications and improvements.

Soledad brothers. Three black prisoners of the Soledad Correctional Facility, a California prison, were accused of murdering a prison guard during an attempt to break out of the prison in 1970. During the court trial, guns were provided to the accused and during the escape attempt the judge as well as three convicts were killed. It was at this time that Angela Davis, a black militant, who had been fired from her post at the University of California, was charged with supplying the guns. She was later acquitted by an all-white jury in June 1972, two months after the two remaining prisoners, called by the press the "Soledad Brothers" were also found innocent.

Solid Fuels Administration for War. An agency established by EXECUTIVE ORDER on April 19, 1943 for the purpose of maintaining a sufficient supply of COAL and coke for armament production and for general industrial and civilian use. Secretary of the Interior ICKES was appointed Administrator and clothed with the authority to conserve, allocate, and ship solid fuels.

"Solid South." The name applied to the consistent voting of the Democratic Party ticket by the South. The origins of this political phenomenon lie in the problems of the Reconstruction period which southern political leaders have always attributed to Republican leadership. Among these problems were the protection of Negro rights, the military control of the South during the post-Civil-War period, the financial and economic chaos in southern states and the political disabilities imposed upon former Confederate officers by the Republican controlled Congress during this era. Only occasionally has the "Solid South" voted for Republicans. In 1896 one Kentucky ELECTORAL VOTE was cast for MCKINLEY and in 1920 Tennessee cast its electoral votes for HARDING. In 1928 the most widespread break occurred when the issues of Protestantism and PROHIBITION split the Solid South, the Republican candidate HOOVER carrying not only the BORDER STATES but also Virginia, North Carolina, Florida, Tennessee, and Texas.

Solomon Islands Campaign. A series of air, land, and sea battles in the southwest Pacific which was fought from August to November, 1942. The Solomon Islands were taken by Japan on March 13, 1942. On August 23, 1942 a fleet commanded by Admirals Ghormley, Fletcher, Noyes, and Turner, and including an Australian cruiser squadron, launched the attack. For six weeks scattered actions continued until the climax was reached when Admiral HALSEY's command moved in. On October 11th the Japanese lost four vessels. On October 26th they lost 130 planes while the United States lost 74 planes, a carrier, and a destroyer. On November 1st the recapture of the Islands was virtually completed with the landing on Bougainville Island, although one of the most furious naval battles in history was fought on November 11th and 12th. The American victory led to the encirclement and neutralization of the Japanese base on Rabaul, New Britain. The United States loss in the Battle of Savo Island was the only naval defeat in World War II.

Sons of the American Revolution. A patriotic organization consisting of males who claim descent from those who fought in the American Revolution. Organized in San Francisco in 1875 as the Sons of Revolutionary Sires it was reorganized in 1889 under its present title in New York City. It was incorporated in 1906.

Sons of Liberty. An organization of radicals in the English colonies created in 1765 to express colonial opposition to the STAMP ACT. Its members carried on demonstrations throughout the colonies and intimidated English agents who tried to sell stamps. Some of them performed acts of violence culminating in the destruction of the home of the Massachusetts Lieutenant Governor Hutchinson. The name was first used by an English member of Parliament who supported the colonial point of view in a speech on the floor which ended with his reference to the colonists as "these sons of liberty." SAMUEL ADAMS and PATRICK HENRY were among the leaders of the organization.

Sooners. A term applied to persons who illegally entered specified areas in the Indian Territory before the precise hour set for these lands to be settled. Originally the term was used during the settlement of the "Oklahoma Lands" (April 22, 1889, at noon).

SOUSA, John Philip. 1854-1932. Known as the "March King." Bandleader and composer. b. Washington, D.C. Bandmaster of the U.S. Marine Band at the WHITE HOUSE (1880-92); organized his own band; wrote songs and toured the United States and many foreign countries with unusual success. Among his better known marches are *Semper Fidelis* (1888), *Stars and Stripes Forever* (1897), and *Hands Across the Sea* (1899). He also wrote comic operas.

South Carolina. The 40th state in size, with an area of 31,055 square miles. Entered the Union on May 23, 1788 as the eighth state. Seceded on December 20, 1860 and readmitted on July 18, 1868. Columbia is the capital. In 1950 South Carolina's POPULATION of 2,117,027 made it 27th in rank. Its largest cities are Columbia, Charleston, and Greenville. Although long an agricultural state South Carolina's cotton textile mills and other industries now produce manufactured goods double the value of its farm production. Other manufactures are asbestos, wood pulp, and steel products. Farm products include cotton, tobacco, hay, sweet potatoes, corn, peanuts, oats, and peaches. South Carolina was the NULLIFICATION, STATES RIGHTS, and SECESSION leader in the pre-Civil War period. It was the first state to secede and the first to open military hostilities. In Charleston Harbor the first submarine was used in naval warfare. South Carolina was discovered by Vasquez de Ayllon. Its nickname is the "Palmetto State."

South Carolina Exposition. See Exposition and Protest.

South Dakota. The 16th state in size,

with an area of 77,047 square miles. Organized as a TERRITORY in 1861 and admitted as the 40th state on November 2, 1889. Pierre is the capital. In 1950 South Dakota's POPULATION of 652,740 made it 40th in rank. Its largest cities are Sioux Falls, Rapid City, and Aberdeen. South Dakota's principal industry is AGRICULTURE, the production being devoted to rye, corn, wheat, oats, and barley. Cattle raising and dairying are important industries. The Homesake gold mine at Lead is the nation's richest. The Black Hills are the highest range east of the Rocky Mountains, and an important tourist attraction. On Mt. Rushmore were carved the likenesses of WASHINGTON, JEFFERSON, LINCOLN, and T. ROOSEVELT by GUTZON BORGLUM. General CUSTER and his troops were massacred in this state. Armstrong County, with a population of about 50 and a recorded vote of seven in the 1948 election, is the nation's smallest county. South Dakota was discovered in 1743 by Verendye, a French trader. Its nicknames are the "Sunshine State" and "Coyote State."

Southeast Asia Collective Defense Treaty. Initiated by the United States and signed at Manila (1954) by representatives of U. S., Great Britain, France, Australia, New Zealand, Philippine Republic, Thailand, and Pakistan. Provided for continuous self-help and mutual aid to develop capacity to resist armed attack and subversive activities; also, technical assistance and cooperation to strengthen equal rights and self-determination of all peoples.

Southern Farmers' Alliance. See Farmers' Alliances.

space shuttle. During the first half of 1977, there were completed long duration tests involving human subjects to help researchers prepare for life and work aboard the "space shuttle." The tests are the Life Sciences Spacelab Mission Development Test which involved more than twenty biomedical experiments; Assess II, the second Airborne Science/Spacelab Equipment System Simulation, which had as its goal the involvement of the NASA and ESA management teams in the same roles they will have during an actual Spacelab flight; and tests of human tolerances to reentry acceleration after prolonged weightlessness. Nasa holds that such tests as these are important since many of the passengers on the space shuttle will be scientists and engineers and not professional astronauts.

Spanish-American War. The war declared against Spain on April 25, 1898. The causes were the desire to protect American investments of $50,000,000 in CUBA, the public protest in the United States against the Spanish cruelties imposed upon Cuba, the sinking of the U.S. battleship, *Maine,* in Havana harbor, the DE LOME LETTER, the pro-war publications of the "JINGO PRESS" in the United States, and the attempts of Americans to equip Cuban revolutionaries with arms and equipment. The war was relatively inexpensive in the cost of men and materials and thus was popularly received. Nevertheless there was a body of opposition which, in organized and unorganized form, attacked it as an imperialist war. The Anti-Imperialist League was one such anti-war organization. Notable public figures opposing the war included MARK TWAIN, WILLIAM JENNINGS BRYAN, and CARL SCHURZ. The War was ended by the TREATY OF PARIS of December 10, 1898. The most important consequence of the war was the projection of the United States into the arena of world politics as a major power. Of the 306,760 United States forces engaged total deaths of 2,926 were suffered, including 361 battle deaths, and 1,580 were wounded.

SPARKS, Jared. 1789-1866. Historian. b. Connecticut. Graduated, Harvard (1815); owner and publisher of the *North American Review* (1823-29); professor of history, Harvard (1839-49); president of Harvard (1849-53); author of many books including *The Diplomatic Correspondence of the American Revolution* (12 vols., 1829-30); *The Writings of George Washington* (12 vols., 1834-37); and the *Library of American Biography*.

Speaker of the House. The presiding officer of the House of Representatives in the United States Congress. His office is provided for by Article I Section 2 of the Constitution. He is always a member of the majority party, and although nominally elected by the entire House at its first session, is generally chosen by the majority party leaders. The speaker at one time exercised autocratic control, appointing members of the standing committees, being himself chairman of the Committee on Rules, determining the agenda and methods of debate, and controlling floor activity by his powers of recognition. The congressional "revolution of 1910" against "Czar" CANNON eliminated much of this power although he still recognizes speakers, refers bills to committee, rules on points of order, and has the customary powers of any member of the House. Outstanding speakers in American history have been HENRY CLAY, THOMAS REED, JOSEPH CANNON, and Sam Rayburn. Until 1950 Henry Clay enjoyed the distinction of having been Speaker more often than any other in congressional history, a total of six terms. With the selection of Sam Rayburn of Texas for his seventh term as speaker in 1951 this record was broken. He then served until 1961.

"Speak Softly and Carry a Big Stick." See "Big Stick."

Specie Circular. Issued by President JACKSON in 1836 this document forbade the Treasury to accept any money, but gold and silver or bank notes based on these metals in payment for PUBLIC LANDS. The document was issued for the purpose of inhibiting the decline in the value of paper CURRENCY. This decline resulted from its virtually unlimited printing by the western state banks following Jackson's withdrawal of federal funds from the BANK OF THE UNITED STATES and their deposit in such banks. This currency was being used in payment for federal lands. The effect of the Specie Circular was to bring on the disastrous PANIC OF 1837 which had been maturing for the previous two years as the result of overspeculation in western lands.

Specific Tariff. Refers to a method of collecting customs. This form applies a specific dollar amount per commodity of imports, e.g. $100 per automobile. The specific duty is applied on all such commodities irrespective of their value.

SPEED, James. 1812-1887. Jurist and statesman. b. Kentucky. Graduated, St. Joseph's College, Kentucky (1828); studied law and practised in Louisville; member of state legislature and state senate; opposed Kentucky's SECESSION and helped organize Union troops in his state; U.S. Attorney-General (1864-66); resigned in opposition to JOHNSON's policies; professor of law, University of Louisville (1856-58, 1875-79).

SPENCER, Anna Garlin. 1851-1931. Educator and feminist. Served as Unitarian minister in Rhode Island (1893); associate leader of the New York Society of Ethical Culture; associate director of the New York School of Philanthropy (1903-13); lectured at University of Wisconsin (1908-11) and at Columbia (from 1918); wrote on social problems and education.

594

SPENCER, John Canfield. 1788-1855. Jurist and statesman. b. New York. Graduated, Union College (1806); member, U.S. House of Representatives (1817-19); practised law in Albany (from 1837); superintendent of schools of New York (1839-40); U.S. Secretary of War (1841-43); U.S. Secretary of the Treasury (1843-44); resigned because he opposed the ANNEXATION OF TEXAS.

SPERRY, Elmer Ambrose. 1860-1930. Electrical engineer and inventor. b. New York. His most important contribution to American science was his adaptation of the gyroscope for the stabilization of ships, airplanes and aerial torpedoes; he invented an improved dynamo, a gyroscope compass and a high-intensity arc searchlight; organized the Sperry Gyroscope Company (1910).

Sphere of Influence. A territory in which another nation exercises strong political and economic influence. Such influence generally includes EXTRATERRITORIALITY.

SPINGARN, Joel Elias. 1875-1939. Author and literary critic. b. New York City. A founder of Harcourt, Brace & Co., publishers (1919-32); chairman of the board of directors of the NATIONAL ASSOCIATION FOR THE ADVANCEMENT OF COLORED PEOPLE (1913-19); created the Spingarn Medal award which is given annually to a Negro of outstanding achievement (from 1913). Author of many books on literature and literary criticism.

Spoils System. A phrase coined by a New York Senator in 1832 to justify the discharge of public office holders of the defeated party and the employment of faithful adherents of the victorious party. This political stratagem marked the beginnings of the "party machine" and "party boss" politics which have endured to the present. The phrase has been erroneously interpreted in its application to Jackson's administrations. To JACKSON it meant "ROTATION IN OFFICE," for more democratic and efficient administration of government.

Spooner Act. Passed by Congress in 1902. The Act authorized the President to acquire the French canal concession in Panama for $40,000,000 on the proviso that the Republic of Colombia should cede a strip of land across the Isthmus of Panama "within a reasonable time" and upon reasonable terms. If Colombia refused, the President was authorized to open negotiations with NICARAGUA for the construction of a canal. Under its authority the President purchased the French concession and the HAY-HERRAN TREATY with Colombia was negotiated.

"Squatter Sovereignty." See Popular Sovereignty.

Stagecoach. A vehicle drawn by four or six horses which were changed at the stations along the route. These stations were known as stages. Stagecoaches were not widely used until the 19th century bcause of poor road conditions prior to that time. In 1785 the first stagecoach connection in the United States was established beween New York and Albany as a substitute for travel on horseback. Thereafter the increased use of the stagecoach stimulated improved road construction. The average travel by stagecoach was 15 hours per day, the vehicle covering 40 miles a day in summer and 25 miles a day in winter. Its capacity ranged up to 14 passengers plus baggage, the mail, and the driver. The development of RAILROAD TRANSPORTATION after the 1840's signalled the end of the stagecoach.

"Stalwarts." The name applied by the "HALF-BREEDS" to the professional politicians and spoilsmen of the Republican party during the administration of President HAYES. Led by ROSCOE CONKLING,

595

SIMON CAMERON, MORTON, and LOGAN they supported the policies of former President GRANT against the independent reformers under Hayes. The "stalwarts" sought a third term for Grant in 1880, opposed CIVIL SERVICE reform, favored a strong reconstruction policy, and advocated HIGH TARIFFS.

Stamp Act. Passed by Parliament in 1765. The law required the purchase of stamps by the payment of a tax for all documents such as NEWSPAPERS, MAGAZINES, and legal and commercial papers of all kinds. The opposition to the Stamp Act grew immediately leading to the famous speech of PATRICK HENRY in the VIRGINIA HOUSE OF BURGESSES, rioting, destruction of property, and the calling of the STAMP ACT CONGRESS. See Stamp Act Congress.

Stamp Act Congress. A meeting of 27 delegates from nine colonies in New York in September, 1765. It was convened as a result of a call for such a meeting by the House of Representatives of the Massachusetts colony. The Congress drew up a declaration of rights and grievances for presentation to the King and Parliament declaring that the STAMP ACT had "a manifest tendency to subvert the rights and liberties of the colonies." The Congress was the first example of united colonial action in the developing struggle against Great Britain. It was successful in bringing about a repeal of the Stamp Act.

Standard Oil Company. The largest OIL company in the United States. It was organized in Ohio in 1870 with a capital investment of $1,000,000 by six individuals headed by JOHN D. and William ROCKEFELLER and Henry Flagler. At that time its 600 barrel per day capacity represented only four percent of the refining capacity of the United States. Immediately thereafter the corporation expanded its control by swallowing rival refineries in the Cleveland area by 1872,

in the New York City and Louisville area by 1873, and in the Pittsburgh and Philadelphia areas by 1876. By 1879 the company with its subsidiary and associate firms, controlled 90 to 95 percent of the refining capacity of the United States. It also operated pipeline, storage tank, and marketing systems domestically and abroad and was the most powerful industrial organization in the country. In 1882 it established the Standard Oil Trust Agreement as the first MONOPOLY in the United States, all control of its 40 component companies being vested in a board of nine trustees headed by John D. Rockefeller. The trust certificates issued had a par value of $70,000,000. In 1892 this trust was dissolved by the Ohio courts, and the separate establishments were reorganized into 20 companies. Nevertheless, the unity of these corporations was maintained by informal arrangements, INTERLOCKING DIRECTORATES, and HOLDING COMPANY techniques. The Standard Oil Company of New Jersey organized in 1899, is today the leader and the largest of all Standard Oil holdings.

Standing Committee. A permanent committee of either house of Congress. As established by the LEGISLATIVE REORGANIZATION ACT of 1946 there were, in 1952, 19 standing committees in the House of Representatives and 15 in the Senate. The functions of the standing committee include consideration of all bills, resolutions, and other legislative matters. Among the more important standing committees are those on WAYS AND MEANS, Finances, LABOR and EDUCATION, FOREIGN AFFAIRS, and AGRICULTURE.

STANDISH, Miles or Myles. 1584?-1656. Colonist. b. England. Came to America with the PILGRIMS on the *Mayflower* (1620); military leader of the colony in charge of defenses and relations with the Indians; went to England as an

596

agent for the colonists (1625-26) to negotiate for supplies and ownership of lands; served as treasurer of the colony and a member of the governor's council; founded Duxbury (1631) with JOHN ALDEN; immortalized in LONGFELLOW'S poem *The Courtship of Miles Standish* which actually has no historical basis in fact. During his fight with Thomas Morton of Merriemount, he was called by Morton "Captaine Shrimpe," but despite his small stature he was a strong leader of the Pilgrims.

STANFORD, Leland. 1824-1893. Railroad builder and politician. b. New York. Settled in California (1852); governor of California (1861-63); strong supporter of LINCOLN and the Union; a founder and president of the Central Pacific Railroad Company; president of Southern Pac: fic Railroad; U.S. Senator (1885-93); in memory of his son, he founded and endowed Stanford University.

STANTON, Edwin McMasters. 1814-1869. Jurist, politician and statesman. b. Ohio. Attended Kenyon College; admitted to the bar (1836); appointed by BUCHANAN, U.S. Attorney-General (1860-61); U.S. Secretary of War (1862-68) in LINCOLN'S cabinet, although he was a Jacksonian Democrat; opposed JOHNSON'S RECONSTRUCTION POLICY and when asked to resign he refused and was supported by the Senate; when Johnson was not IMPEACHED because of his action on Stanton, the latter resigned (May 1868); appointed Associate Justice of the Supreme Court, but died before he could serve.

STANTON, Elizabeth Cady. 1815-1902. Woman-suffrage leader and reformer. b. New York. Organized the first woman's rights convention at Seneca Falls, N.Y. (1848); associated with SUSAN B. ANTHONY and LUCRETIA MOTT in the WOMAN'S SUFFRAGE movement; an editor of *Revolution,* a militant feminist magazine (1868-70); she was an excellent journalist and a brilliant orator; she was the first president of the National Woman Suffrage Association (1869-90); with Susan Anthony and Matilda Gage she compiled the *History of Woman Suffrage* (3 vols. 1881-86).

Staple Act of 1663. A law of Parliament passed for the purpose of making England the depot for goods shipped to the Colonies. The Act provided that all European goods going to the colonies must first land in England. Exemptions from its provisions included salt coming from the Cape Verde Islands, servants, provisions from Scotland and Ireland, wines from the Azores and Madeira, and horses. The Act was aimed at enhancing the TRADE of English merchants against the interests of the colonists who would have profited by direct purchases from nations producing these goods. The Act was often violated by SMUGGLING and by direct TRANSPORTATION of ENUMERATED ARTICLES to Dutch and German markets without landing them in England. Similarly, European manufactured goods would be brought to the colonies without transshipment through England.

Staple Crops. Crops grown in large quantities on the southern colonial plantation. Such crops were generally grown for the European export market. The most important staple crops were TOBACCO, RICE, indigo, sugar, and COTTON. In 1775 the southern colonies exported 1,150,662 pounds of indigo. By 1754 Charleston alone exported 104,680 barrels of rice, a figure rising to 125,000 barrels by the opening of the Revolution. Tobacco was the single greatest export crop up to the Revolution. In 1616 the colonies produced 20,000 pounds. This was increased to 500,000 in 1627 and to 130,000,000 pounds in 1790.

STARK, John. 1728-1822. Revolutionary general. b. New Hampshire. Fought in

597

French and Indian Wars; led the charge at BUNKER HILL (1775); served at Princeton and TRENTON and resigned; commissioned as major general and served against BURGOYNE in Vermont; defeated him at BENNINGTON (1777); made a brigadier general of the Continental army and commanded the Northern Department; member of court-martial that found MAJOR ANDRE guilty.

Star Route Frauds. Frauds in the granting of contracts by the POST OFFICE DEPARTMENT for the TRANSPORTATION of mail over the "star routes." These routes were western roads where the mail was carried by wagons and horses under contract. The newly appointed Postmaster General, Thomas L. James of New York, began an investigation in 1881 which revealed that Senator Dorsey of Arkansas and second assistant postmaster general Brady had conspired with mail contractors on the star routes to defraud the government by extravagant prices and the multiplication of services. Other departmental officials were engaged in the conspiracy which imposed worthless securities on the post office and required large unnecessary expenditures on contractors and sub-contractors on these routes. Republican party politicians actively aided the defendants who became the subject of 25 indictments after investigations by Congress. The trials in 1882 and 1883 revealed frauds on 93 routes. The total government loss was $4,000,000. No convictions were obtained.

Star-Spangled Banner. The name applied to the national anthem of the United States. The text was inspired by the British attack on Fort McHenry during the War of 1812. It was written by a young Baltimore lawyer, FRANCIS SCOTT KEY, who visited the British admiral on the eve of the attack seeking the release of a prominent physician who had been captured by the British. Key and the friends who had accompanied him were detained on board a British vessel in the harbor during the bombardment of the fort. When the light of dawn revealed the American flag still flying, Key, who had believed the attack successful, was stirred to write the poem on the back of an envelope. The words were adapted to a popular drinking song "To Anacreon in Heaven." The complete draft later written by Key is now in a private collection in Baltimore. In 1931 Congress officially recognized it as the national anthem.

State. One of the 50 component bodies in the federal structure of the United States government. The 10th Amendment of the federal Constitution reserves to it the powers not delegated to the United States by the Constitution nor prohibited by it to the states. The sovereignty of the state is limited by the above and consists generally of powers exercised for the protection of the public health, welfare, safety, and morals. The exercise by Congress of the "ELASTIC CLAUSE" and its interpretation by the United States Supreme Court has led to a steady diminution of STATE POWERS. The governmental structure of all states is generally alike and resembles that of the federal government. Each state is a republic, has a SEPARATION OF POWERS system, a bicameral legislature (Nebraska excepted), a governor, a JUDICIARY, a written constitution, a BILL OF RIGHTS, and a state MILITIA.

State Church. See established church.

State, Department of. The first EXECUTIVE DEPARTMENT established by Congress on July 27, 1789 under the name of Department of Foreign Affairs, being a carry over under that title from the government of THE ARTICLES OF CONFEDERATION of 1781. It took its present name on September 15, 1789. Its administrative head, the Secretary of State, has the chief responsibility, under the President, for the conduct of foreign affairs. He negotiates with his opposite numbers in foreign governments in matters pertaining to the protection of American rights and the promotion of beneficial intercourse between the United States and other nations. The Department's domestic duties include the custody of the United States Seal, the publication of federal laws, and the authentication of official documents. Other officers carry on work in foreign intelligence, research liaison with the UNITED NATIONS, and foreign information duties.

State Government. The government of any of the 50 states in the United States. It is provided for by the 10th amendment of the federal Constitution and closely resmbles the national government in organization and structure. Under the federal system a state government is a sovereign entity, its powers being limited only as specified in the federal and state constitutions. All state governments have a legislative, executive, and judicial branch. Their powers are set down in the state constitution and, generally, parallel those of their opposite number in the central government.

Statehood. The act of becoming a state within the federal system of the United States. Statehood may be acquired as a transition from a territorial status or directly by an act of Congress following annexation. An example of the latter is Texas.

State Powers. Those powers not delegated to the Congress nor denied to the states by the federal Constitution. They are residual powers reserved to the states by th 10th amendment. See police powers and reserve powers.

States' Rights. The political doctrine expressing various theories upholding the powers of the states within the United States as opposed to the central government. The doctrine evolved from the theory of STRICT CONSTRUCTION OF THE CONSTITUTION to the present day theory of opposition to concentration of power in the federal government. At various times it has included the theories of NULLIFICATION and SECESSION. STATES' RIGHTS doctrine has been expressed in the VIRGINIA AND KENTUCKY RESOLUTIONS, THE HARTFORD CONVENTION, the WEBSTER-HAYNE DEBATES, the ORDINANCE OF NULLIFICATION, the EXPOSITION AND PROTEST, and the DIXIECRAT MOVEMENT.

States' Rights Party. A minor party organized on July 17, 1948 by 6,000 rebellious southern Democrats who opposed the CIVIL RIGHTS program of the Democratic party. At its convention in Birmingham, Alabama, it nominated Governor J. Strom Thurmond as its presidential candidate and Fielding L. Wright as its vice-presidential candidate. Its program supported STATES RIGHTS in opposition to federal regulation and maintenance of the TAFT-HARTLEY ACT. It attacked FAIR EMPLOYMENT PRACTICES proposals. The party polled 1,169,021 popular votes and 39 ELECTORAL VOTES.

Statue of Liberty. A giant bronze female figure which is located on Bedloe's Island in New York harbor, facing the ocean. It weighs 225 tons and is 152 feet five inches in height, rising 305 feet above the water line. The right hand holds a torch representing the light of liberty. In the left hand is a tablet upon which is inscribed "July 4, 1776." The statue was designed by the French sculptor Frederic Auguste Bartholdi at the request of his government for presentation to the United States as a commemoration of the centennial of American independence. The pedestal, 151 feet one inch in height, was erected by the United States at a cost of 350 thousand dollars, met by popular subscription. The cornerstone was laid on August 5th, 1884, and the unveiling of the statue occurred on October 28, 1886. Inscribed on a tablet inside the main entrance is the famous poem by Emma Lazarus, "The New Colossus," a dedication to the United States as a land of liberty. Bedloe's Island is administered by the National Park Service which has opened the Statue to the visits of the public. The cost of the statue was estimated to be $450,000.

Steamboat. In 1787 JOHN FITCH constructed a steamboat on the Delaware River which he revealed to members of the CONSTITUTIONAL CONVENTION. ROBERT FULTON'S *Clermont* made the first successful extended steamboat trip up the Hudson River in 1807. Immediately thereafter, steamboats were constructed for ocean-going passage and for use on the western rivers. On September 11, 1811 the *New Orleans*, a 300 ton vessel, moved down the Ohio River from Pittsburgh to New Orleans. In 1820 one of the earliest steamboat lines was established between New York and New Orleans. Through the 19th century vessels were increased in size and improved in physical comforts, featuring orchestras, bars, restaurants, sleeping quarters, and a variety of personal services including tailoring and barbering. On May 26th, 1819 the *Savannah* left Savannah, Georgia for Liverpool, England in the first transatlantic passage of a steamship, although sails were used. In 1832 the Canadian *Royal William* crossed the ATLANTIC entirely under steam power. By 1834 there were 230 steamboats on western rivers. At the opening of the Civil War tonnage on Western waters surpassed steam tonnage in the British

merchant fleet. These vessels were carrying over 10,000,000 tons of freight annually. The great cities of Cincinnati, Pittsburgh, New Orleans, and St. Louis grew in economic importance as hubs of steamboat TRADE. Important steamboat CORPORATIONS were organized to capture the trade. With the advent of the RAILROAD after the Civil War the steamboat declined in importance in the West.

Steel Industry. Before the Civil War steel production in the United States revolved basically around the production of housewares and tools. The steel age did not begin until operations in 1865 under a patent granted to Henry Bessemer. In 1857 the United States Patent Office recognized the priority of a similar improvement in steel making by conferring patent rights upon WILLIAM KELLY of Kentucky. The first plant operating under Kelly's invention opened in Wyandotte, Michigan in 1864. Two years later the Bessemer and Kelly processes were merged, removing all legal obstacles to a rapidly expanding steel production. In 1868 the open hearth process was introduced. With the development of electric power at the end of the century crucible steel gave way to steel produced in electric furnaces. Although only 380,000 tons of steel were produced in 1875, the United States was producing 10,000,000 tons by the end of the century, a figure equal to the entire production of the rest of the world. In 1964 steel production reached 127,000,000 tons, the largest in American history. The organization of the steel industry has consistently moved toward centralization, the apex being reached in 1901 with the creation of the UNITED STATES STEEL CORPORATION, which today produces one quarter of the steel in the industry. Other important producers include Bethlehem Steel Company, Republic Steel Company, and Na-

600

tional Steel Company. Integration has included the organization of the industry on a vertical basis so that today the steel companies also operate furnaces, rolling mills, ovens, machine shops, foundries, by-product plants, shipping lines, harbor installations, and railroads. The center of the industry is still the Pittsburgh-Youngstown area, eastward to the coast, but in recent years geographical decentralization has moved the industry to Illinois, Indiana, and Alabama.

Steel Mills, Seizure of. On April 8, 1952 President TRUMAN issued an EXECUTIVE ORDER providing for the seizure and operation of 95 percent of the nation's steel mills. A pending STRIKE by the United Steel Workers of America was called off subject to negotiations between the union and the Secretary of Commerce who was authorized to operate the steel mills. The President's action was denounced by the steel operators as unconstitutional. He defended his action as a proper exercise of his EXECUTIVE POWER under the Constitution despite the absence of authorizing legislation. Subsequently, the mills initiated litigation to test the President's power. On April 29, the federal District Court of Washington, D.C. ruled that the government's seizure of the steel mills was illegal. Immediately after the decision was announced, the union's president, PHILIP MURRAY, ordered the 650,000 members of the union out on strike. The court's issuance of a temporary INJUNCTION prohibited Secretary Sawyer from granting a contemplated wage increase and ordered the plants returned to their owners. The decision was historic in that it overruled an action of a President of the United States for the first time. The Attorney-General immediately sought a stay in the Court of Appeals which granted it the following day. The plants were returned to the DEPARTMENT OF THE INTERIOR. On May

2nd the strike was called off at the President's request. On May 3rd the Supreme Court issued a writ of certiorari, agreeing to review the District Court's ruling. On June 2nd the Court handed down its historic decision in which it held the President's seizure of the mills unconstitutional. The decision was based on the Court's reasoning that the President had usurped Congress' LEGISLATIVE POWER and had seized the mills without legislative or constitutional sanction. The Court declared that presidential seizure power "must stem either from an act of Congress or from the Constitution itself." In the absence of both, in this case, the President's seizure had violated the SEPARATION OF POWERS principle by his exercise of a power properly within Congress' jurisdiction. The decision was the first in the history of the Court that applied explicit limits on the President's power to act on the allegation that an emergency endangered national security and that his action was taken under the constitutional mandate that he see to it that the laws be faithfully executed. On the same day the United Steel Workers called its members out on strike.

STEIN, Gertrude. 1874-1951. Author. b. Pennsylvania. Graduated, Radcliffe (1897); lived in Paris, France and became associated with the leading artists and writers who worked or visited there. Known for her unusual style and the use of repetition in her writing; author of *Three Lives* (1908), *Making of Americans* (1925), *The Autobiography of Alice B. Toklas* (1933), *Four Saints in Three Acts* (1934), *Picasso* (1938) and many other books.

STEINBECK, John Ernst. 1902- Novelist. b. California. Studied at Stanford University. Gained national recognition for his realistic novels of the life of the poor in America. Author of many novels including *Pastures of Heaven*

(1932), *Tortilla Flat* (1935), *In Dubious Battle* (1936), *Of Mice and Men* (1937) which was produced as a play and made into a movie, and *The Grapes of Wrath* which was also filmed.

STEINMETZ, Charles Proteus. 1865-1923. Electrical engineer. b. Germany. Came to the United States (1889); became a consulting engineer for the GENERAL ELECTRIC COMPANY, Schenectady, N. Y. (from 1893); considered a genius in the field of mathematics and electrical theory and research; professor of electrical engineering at Union College (from 1902); patented over 100 inventions; interested in SOCIALISM and was elected president of the Common Council of Schenectady on the Socialist ticket. Author of scientific books.

STEPHENS, Alexander Hamilton. 1812-1883. Political leader. b. Georgia. Practised law; served in Cerogia legislature; member, U.S. House of Representatives (1843-59); was a member of the WHIG party and later became a leading Democrat; though he did not approve SECESSION he joined the Confederacy and became Vice-President of the Confederate States of America (1861-65); headed HAMPTON ROADS CONFERENCE (1865); imprisoned at the end of the war, but was paroled; elected U.S. Senator, but was refused his seat; member, U.S. House of Representatives (1873-82); governor of Georgia (1883). Author of an important book, *A Constitutional View of the War Between the States* (2 vols., 1868-70).

STEUBEN, Friedrich Wilhelm Baron von. 1730-1794. German-American general. b. Prussia. Became friendly with BENJAMIN FRANKLIN and SILAS DEANE in Paris (1777) and agreed to come to America to train the Continental army; reported to WASHINGTON at VALLEY FORGE (Feb. 23, 1778); Congress appointed him inspector-general to reorganize and train the army which he did

with unusual success; became an adviser to Washington and served at YORKTOWN and MONMOUTH; honorably discharged (1784) and given a pension by Congress as he had spent his own fortune for the colonial cause; one of the organizers of the SOCIETY OF THE CINCINNATI; became a NATURALIZED American CITIZEN in Pennsylvania (1783) and in New York (1786); lived in New York and wrote a manual of regulations for the Troops of the United States (1778-89).

STEVENS, John. 1749-1838. Inventor and shipbuilder. b. New York City. Worked on the development of the STEAMBOAT (1788-98); in order to protect his own inventions he was largely responsible for securing the first United States patent laws (1790); secured patents for a vertical steam boiler and an improved steam engine; associated with Nicholas Roosevelt and ROBERT LIVINGSTON in experimentation in steam TRANSPORTATION and NAVIGATION; built the *Phoenix* and sent it from New York to Philadelphia (1809) the first successful trip on the sea by a steamboat; succeeded in building an IRONCLAD which was a forerunner of the *Monitor;* organized the Pennsylvania Railroad, but only succeeded in laying one track for a steam locomotive which he built (1826).

STEVENS, Thaddeus. 1792-1868. Lawyer and political leader. b. Vermont. Graduated, Dartmouth (1814); admitted to the bar and practised in Pennsylvania; member, U.S. House of Representatives (1849-53, 1859-68); strong opponent of SLAVERY disapproving CLAY's COMPROMISE OF 1850; chairman, House WAYS AND MEANS COMMITTEE; supported LINCOLN'S EMANCIPATION PROCLAMATION and backed the 14TH AMENDMENT; radical reconstructionist; approved administration's legal tender measures; led strong opposition to JOHNSON and advocated IMPEACHMENT proceedings; chairman of the committee that prepared the charges against Johnson; firm believer in racial equality and insisted that he be buried in a cemetery open to Negroes as well as whites.

STEVENSON, Adlai Ewing. 1900-1965. Political leader. b. California. Graduated, Princeton University (1922), Northwestern University Law School and admitted to the bar in Illinois (1926); worked as foreign correspondent in Russia for the International News Service; with various government agencies and was head of an economic mission to Italy (1943); delegate to the United Nations General Assembly (1947); elected governor of Illinois (1948); unsuccessful Democratic nominee for president (1952, 1956). United States Ambassador to the United Nations, 1960-1965.

STIEGLITZ, Alfred. 1864-1946. Photographer, editor, and art expert. b. New Jersey. Studied in New York and Berlin (1879-90); experimented with photography including the use of three colors in New York City; editor, *American Amateur Photographer* (1892-96); founder and editor of *Camera Notes* (1897-1903) and *Camera Work* (from 1903). Married Georgia O'Keefe, American artist. Is well-known not only for his excellent work in photography, but because he discovered and exhibited at his studio for the first time in this country, the work of young American artists, who he felt had great promise and deserved a chance to be seen. In this group are included MAX WEBER, JOHN MARIN, Charles Demuth, Georgia O'Keefe and others.

STILWELL, Joseph W. 1883-1946. General. b. Florida. Graduated, U.S.M.A., West Point (1904); served in France during World War I; served in China and learned to speak Chinese (1920-23; 1926-28; 1932-39); appointed by Chiang Kaishek as chief of staff in the China area; in command of all American forces in the

China-Burma-India theater of operations (1942-44); made a general (1944); commander of U.S. Army ground forces (1945); commander of U.S. 10th Army in Pacific (1945); The *Stilwell Papers* were edited by T. H. White (1948).

Stimson Doctrine. A statement by Secretary of State HENRY L. STIMSON, in 1931, expressing the opposition of the United States government to the conquest of Manchuria by Japan. The doctrine condemned Japanese aggression as a violation of the OPEN-DOOR POLICY, the KELLOGG-BRIAND PACT, and the NINE-POWER TREATY. It declared that the United States would not recognize any situation that had come into existence contrary to the obligations of the Pact of Paris. This policy has been adhered to by the United States since its enunciation.

STIMSON, Henry Lewis. 1867-1950. Statesman. b. New York City. Graduated, Yale (1888); admitted to the bar and practised in New York City (1891); appointed by TAFT, U.S. Secretary of War (1911-13); served as a colonel with the field artillery in France during World War I; appointed Governor General of the PHILIPPINE ISLANDS (1927-29); appointed by HOOVER, U.S. Secretary of State (1929-33); chairman of American delegates to the LONDON NAVAL CONFERENCE (1930-31); his policy in MANCHUKUO is known as the STIMSON DOCTRINE; appointed by F. D. ROOSEVELT, U.S. Secretary of War (1940-45); urged unification of the United States armed forces (1944). Author of autobiography *On Active Service in Peace and War* (1948).

St. Lawrence Seaway Project. Also known as the St. Lawrence Ship Canal Project. A plan recommended by Secretary of Commerce HOOVER in 1929 as a shorter and more economical route to northern Europe. The project was not adopted during his presidential administration. The Canadian-American Treaty

603

negotiated by President F. D. ROOSEVELT in 1933 was turned down by the Senate the following year but was revived as a defense measure agreement in 1941. In the 11 years that followed many attempts were made in Congress to enact legislation establishing the $800,000,000 seaway and power projects linking the GREAT LAKES with the Atlantic Ocean. In 1951 the Canadian Parliament established a company to build the seaway with or without United States cooperation. In February, 1952 a Senate bill was introduced authorizing such cooperation. It was opposed by many on the grounds that the waterway would be frozen five months of the year, that it could easily be destroyed by an ATOMIC BOMB, and that it was expensive to build. New England Senators denounced the bill on the grounds that it would encourage industrial dispersal from the eastern seaboard. Other opposition stemmed from the fear that it would divert traffic from the RAILROADS and the government would therefore have to subsidize them or raise their rates. Supporters of the bill argued the need of the seaway for defense purposes, cheap power, and quicker TRANSPORTATION. This bill was defeated in June, 1952. In May, 1954, however, Congress authorized the St. Lawrence Seaway Project and created the Development Corp. Canada was to build 4 locks at Montreal and 2 at Iroquois, Ont. U. S. agreed to build 2 locks near Massena, N. Y. Additional locks are already in position on the Welland and Ste. Marie Canals.

Stock Clearing Corporation. See Stock Exchange.

Stock Exchange. An organization occupying physical facilities where the sale and purchase of securities occur. In 1952 there were over 20 such organizations located in the principal cities of the United States. The New York STOCK EXCHANGE is the largest and oldest stock market in the United States, having been estab-

lished in Wall Street in 1792. In 1951 this Exchange listed 1472 stock issues aggregating 2,353,221,166 shares with a total market value of $93,807,269,175. The record high annual trading in the New York Stock Exchange took place in 1921 when 1,124,800,410 shares were traded. Membership in stock exchanges are called seats, which are bought at varying prices. Sale orders come to the floor of the exchanges from all over the United States by TELEPHONE, TELEGRAPH, and cable. The Stock Clearing Corporation, begun in 1920, is the clearing house for the settlement of all trading. These settlements are made after the second day of the transaction. Exchanges are now regulated under the SECURITIES AND EXCHANGE ACT of 1934.

Stock Market Crash. See Panic of 1929.

STOCKTON, Richard. 1730-81. Statesman. b. New Jersey. Graduated, College of New Jersey (now Princeton University) (1748); member, executive council of New Jersey (1768-76); associate justice, New Jersey supreme court (1774-76), member, CONTINENTAL CONGRESS (1776); signer of the DECLARATION OF INDEPENDENCE; captured by the British (1777) and died as a result of the harsh treatment he received as a prisoner.

Stockyards. The earliest stockyards were located in the eastern cities. By the opening of the Civil War railroad facilities had brought the industry to the midwest. At the railroad termini stockades were erected to accommodate cattle, commission merchants established brokerage facilities to expedite shipment, and processing plants were set up as the constituent elements of an important new industry. At that time many of the stockyards were owned by the RAILROADS. In 1865 the Illinois legislature chartered the Union Stockyards in Chicago to consolidate the operations of the individual companies. As the CATTLE INDUSTRY grew, stockyards were established farther westward in Kansas City, St. Louis, Omaha, and Denver, but Chicago remained the center of the industry because of its superior railroad facilities, earlier start, and desirable location. The rise of the packing houses made Chicago the largest live stock center in the world.

STOKOWSKI, Leopold. 1882-1977. Conductor. b. England. Graduated, Oxford University; studied in Paris; conducted in London; came to the United States to conduct the Cincinnati Symphony Orchestra (1909-12); conductor of the PHILADELPHIA SYMPHONY ORCHESTRA (1912-36); conductor on many outstanding recordings; has appeared in movies; known for his work with children, and for his knowledge and conducting of Bach.

STONE, Harlan Fiske. 1872-1946. Jurist. b. New Hampshire. Graduated, Amherst (1894) and Columbia Law School (1898); admitted to the bar and practised in New York City; professor of law (1902-05) and dean of the Columbia Law School (1910-23); U.S. Attorney General (1924-25); appointed by COOLIDGE Associate Justice, U.S. Supreme Court (1925-41); Chief Justice (1941-1946).

STONE, Lucy. 1818-1893. Woman suffragist and reformer. b. Massachusetts. Graduated, Oberlin (1847); worked for WOMAN SUFFRAGE movement; lectured against SLAVERY; was one of the founders of the American Woman Suffrage Association (1869). Known for retaining her maiden name after marrying Henry Blackwell, and all women who followed her example are known as "Lucy Stoners."

STONE, Thomas. 1743-1787. Lawyer and statesman. b. Maryland. Studied law at Annapolis and practised in Maryland; member, CONTINENTAL CONGRESS (1775-78); signer of the DECLARATION OF INDEPENDENCE; supported the ARTICLES OF CONFEDERATION; member of the Congress of the Confederation (1784-85).

STONE, Willim Joel. 1848-1918. Lawyer and political leader. b. Kentucky. Studied law and practised in Missouri (1869); member, U.S. House of Representatives (1885-91); governor of Missouri (1893-97); U.S. Senator (1903-18); leader of the Democratic party in his state; as chairman of the Senate Committee on Foreign Relations, he was one of the "LITTLE GROUP OF WILLFUL MEN" who blocked WILSON's armed-ship bill (1917).

STONEMAN, George. 1822-1894. Union general and political leader. b. New York. Graduated, U.S.M.A., West Point (1846); served with MCCLELLAN as brigadier general in charge of cavalry in the ARMY OF THE POTOMAC; served in the Peninsular campaign (1861-62); major general of volunteers serving at VICKSBURG (1862); served with SHERMAN in ATLANTA campaign (1864); captured and exchanged; led raids through Virginia, Tennessee and the Carolinas (1864-65); retired (1871); elected governor of California (1883-87).

STORY, Joseph. 1779-1845. Jurist. b. Massachusetts. Graduated, Harvard (1801); practised law in Salem; member, U.S. House of Representatives (1808-09); Associate Justice, U.S. Supreme Court (1811-45); professor of law, Harvard (1829-45); famous for American patent law and established the present system of equity jurisprudence in the United States; largely responsible for organizing Harvard Law School where he was a brilliant teacher. Author of important books including *Commentaries on the Constitution of the United States* (1833), *Commentaries on the Conflict of Laws* (1834), and *On Equity Jurisprudence* (2 vols., 1836). Elected to the HALL OF FAME.

STOUGHTON, William. 1630?-1701. Colonial statesman. b. England or MASS-

ACHUSETTS BAY COLONY. Graduated, Harvard (1650); fellow, New College, Oxford (1652-61); served as assistant on Massachusetts council (1671-1686); lieutenant governor (1692-1701); presided at Salem WITCHCRAFT TRIALS (1692); served on Governor ANDROS's council but opposed his ideas; an early benefactor of Harvard founding Stoughton Hall.

STOWE, Harriet Beecher. 1811-1896. Daughter of LYMAN BEECHER and sister of HENRY WARD BEECHER. Author. b. Connecticut. Ardent ABOLITIONIST; famous as the author of *Uncle Tom's Cabin* which was originally published in an antislavery paper in serial farm, the *National Era,* Washington, D.C. It was also published as a book by a Boston publisher. Although it sold many copies and is sometimes considered to have been a factor in causing the Civil War, Mrs. Stowe never benefited by the book financially. She was prominent in other reform movements.

Strategic Services, Office of. An agency established by EXECUTIVE ORDER in 1942 to coordinate the military intelligence and information services of existing organizations. Under the leadership of Major General William J. Donovan it was authorized to obtain intelligence through the work of agents abroad and through research and analysis programs. Its work was necessarily secret, and received little publicity during the war. After the war the nation recognized the significant contributions that it had made in assisting its partisan allies in France, Italy, and other European and Far Eastern countries. It was dissolved in 1945.

Strategic Trust Territory of the Pacific Islands. See United States Trusteeships.

STRAUS, Isidor. 1845-1912. Merchant and philanthropist. b. Bavaria. Came to the United States (1854); with his brother

NATHAN he took over ownership of R. H. Macy & Co. (1896); also owned Abraham & Straus in Brooklyn, N.Y.; member, U.S. House of Representatives (1894-95); declined post in CLEVELAND's cabinet to devote his life to philanthropy; lost in the *Titanic* disaster (April 15, 1912).

STRAUS, Nathan. 1843-1931. Merchant, philanthropist, and sportsman. b. Bavaria. Came to the United States (1854); with his brother, ISIDOR, he owned R. H. Macy & Co. (1896); became Park Commissioner, New York City (1889-93); president of the Board of Health (1898); led fight for pasteurized milk and established milk stations for the poor during the PANIC OF 1893; honored as first citizen of the city (1923).

STRAUS, Oscar Solomon. 1850-1926. Lawyer and diplomat. Graduated, Columbia College (1871); Columbia Law School (L.L.B. 1873); practised law (1873-81); entered the mercantile business of the family; appointed U.S. Minister to Turkey by CLEVELAND (1887-89) reappointed by MCKINLEY and T. ROOSEVELT (1898-1900); U.S. Secretary of Commerce in Roosevelt's cabinet (1906-09); member, WORLD COURT (1922-26); first American Ambassador to Turkey (1909-10). Author of many books on political economy.

Strict Construction of the Constitution. An interpretation of the federal Constitution which attempts to limit the powers of the national government by holding it to those powers specifically delegated to it in Article I, Section 8 of the document. This interpretation was advocated by the Democratic-Republican party of JEFFERSON in its political struggle against the Hamiltonian FEDERALISTS who supported a LOOSE CONSTRUCTION OF THE CONSTITUTION.

STRICKLAND, William. 1787?-1854. Engraver, architect and engineer. b. Philadelphia, Pennsylvania. Leader in the Greek revival in architecture in the United States; designed and superintended the construction of many important buildings; one of the organizers and first president of the American Institution of Architects (1857).

Strikebreakers. Popularly known as scabs and referred to with contempt by strikers as "finks", "goons", and "nobles." They are persons who are hired by the employer to replace strikers. In the past professional strikebreakers have been supplied by detective agencies like the Pinkerton, Burns, and Bergoff agencies. Since many strikebreakers were former criminals or persons hired for the specific purpose of intimidating strikers, violence frequently characterized their use. The HOMESTEAD STRIKE of 1892 was the first important labor dispute in which strikebreakers were used when the CARNEGIE Steel Company employed 300 Pinkerton detectives. Strikebreakers were also used in the great railroad STRIKES of 1877, the PULLMAN STRIKE of 1894, and the Ludlow Coal Strike in Colorado in 1914 which resulted in a pitched battle and the death of six men, two women, and 11 children. In 1938 Congress attempted to regulate the use of strikebreakers through the enactment of the BYRNES LAW.

Strikes. Voluntary cessations of work by organized LABOR. There have been many famous and important strikes in American history, called for higher wages, lower hours, improved working conditions, or for other reasons arising out of the failure of negotiations. Important strikes have been the RAILROAD STRIKES OF 1877 and 1894, the DANBURY HATTERS' STRIKE of 1903, the COAL STRIKE of 1902, the Steel Strike of 1919, the Coal Strike of 1923, the N.R.A. strikes, the Pacific Coast general strike of 1934, and the strikes following World War II. The year 1946 saw the greatest number of work stoppages in American history. There were 4,985

strikes involving 4,600,000 workers who were idle a total of 116,000,000 man days. The first strike in America was probably that of the printers in New York City who struck for higher wages in 1776, In 1805 the strike of the Philadelphia cordwainers invoked the first application of the CONSPIRACY DOCTRINE in American LABOR RELATIONS.

Strong Central Government. The principle of government which, as developed by HAMILTON, supported a concentration of powers in Congress and a consequent reduction of the powers of the state. The doctrine was based on the theory of IMPLIED POWERS by which Hamilton argued "that there are implied, as well as EXPRESSED POWERS, and that the former are as effectually delegated as the latter." The principle as later expanded by DANIEL WEBSTER and JOHN MARSHALL held that the Constitution was created by the people, not by the states, and was fundamentally opposed to the STATES' RIGHTS and compact doctrines.

STUART, Gilbert Charles. 1755-1828. Painter. b. Rhode Island. Studied with BENJAMIN WEST in London; famous as a portrait painter and best known for his many portraits of GEORGE WASHINGTON. He also painted JOHN and JOHN QUINCY ADAMS, JEFFERSON, MADISON, STORY, George III, Mrs. Siddons, and Sir Joshua Reynolds. Elected to the HALL OF FAME (1910).

STUART, James Ewell Brown. Known as Jeb Stuart. 1833-1864. Confederate general. b. Virginia. Graduated, U.S. M.A., West Point (1854); resigned from the army to join the Confederate army (1861); as brigadier general he surrounded MCCLELLAN'S army (1862); engaged in the SEVEN DAYS' Battles and was promoted to major general (1862); succeeded JACKSON at Chancellorsville; commanded the cavalry division at GETTYSBURG (1863); was wounded in battle and died (1864). He was an outstanding general and the leading cavalry leader of the Confederacy.

STUYVESANT, Peter. 1592-1672. Dutch administrator in America. b. Netherlands. Served in the Dutch Army; appointed by the Dutch West India Company, director-general of NEW NETHERLAND and surrounding regions (1646); ruled NEW AMSTERDAM in a dictatorial fashion causing great resentment against him; he managed to keep friendly relations with the Indians, but lost the colony to the British (1664); he returned to Holland to defend his actions; spent the rest of his life on his estate on Manhattan Island at the point which is the "Bowery." He was a man of remarkable appearance having a wooden leg decorated in silver. He was of a violent and bombastic nature.

Submarine. A naval vessel able to travel entirely submerged for extended periods of time. The first practical submarine was built by David Bushnell in 1776. This vessel made several attacks on British ships in New York harbor. ROBERT FULTON subsequently experimented with a metal submersible in 1801, but failed to sell his idea either to the American, British, or French governments. Submarines were used to a limited degree in the Civil War, but were not fully accepted by the United States Navy until 1895. The most distinguished name in submarine invention was SIMON LAKE who sold several of his vessels to Russia in the late 1890's. In 1958 the 8th nuclear powered submarine, *Triton,* was launched and the *Nautilus* and *Skate* made undersea crossings of the North Pole.

Subsidies. Also known as grants-in-aid. They are financial grants to states for redistribution to local governments to improve conditions in the fields of highway construction, welfare, public works, housing, and EDUCATION. From time to time Congress has appropriated such grants

for specific purposes such as aid to CANAL, RAILROAD, SHIPPING, and AIRCRAFT construction, and to AGRICULTURAL production for the purpose of maintaining farm prices. There have been other lesser industries which have profited by congressional subsidies. It has generally been accepted that the national grants-in-aid movement was initiated with the MORRILL LAND GRANT ACT of 1862. Other laws providing extensive aid have been the SMITH-LEVER ACT, the SMITH-HUGHES ACT, and the Public Roads Acts. It is the established policy of Congress to grant such public funds on a matching basis, the states contributing an equal amount. In some instances, however, the states match less or more than the amount contributed by Congress. During the DEPRESSION period of the 1930's Congress occasionally bypassed the state governments by granting its funds directly to the municipalities, acting as the "municipal banker."

Subversive Activities Control Act. See McCurran-Wood Act.

Subways. Underground municipal railways serving as rapid transit commuting links between the residential and business areas of a city. Preceded by elevated rapid transit facilities they nevertheless were considered in New York City as early as 1860, but the idea was dropped because of the engineering and financial problems involved. The first subway in the United States was completed in Boston in 1900 consisting of remodeled trolley car tracks. In New York City the Interborough Rapid Transit Company opened its first line in 1904 extending it under the East River to Brooklyn in 1908. By 1930 the company was operating 224 miles of subway and 139 miles of elevated lines by which time the Brooklyn-Manhattan Corporation was operating 258 miles of subway and elevated lines. In 1932 the city government opened its first line which ultimately was extended into a 50 mile system. By 1952 New York City was being served by the largest municipally owned and operated subway system in the United States. Other large cities having subway systems include Chicago, Philadelphia, Los Angeles, Newark, and St. Louis.

Suffolk Resolves. A series of resolutions denouncing the INTOLERABLE ACTS. Delegates from Boston and other towns in Suffolk County in Massachusetts met on September 6-9, 1774 at Dedham to declare that they would refuse obedience to the laws and urge non-payment of taxes and suspension of trade with England. The resolutions suggested a colonial congress to convene at Concord in October. The resolves were unanimously passed and transmitted to the CONTINENTAL CONGRESS at Philadelphia.

Suffrage, Extension of. See universal suffrage.

Sugar Act. Passed by Parliament in 1764 to discourage the SMUGGLING which had occurred under the old SUGAR AND MOLASSES ACT OF 1733. This Act cut the duty on foreign molasses in half. The additional purpose of the Act was to raise revenue in partial payment of the expenses incurred by the French and Indian War completed the year before. The Act aroused great resentment in the mainland colonies and contributed to the ultimate outbreak of the American Revolution. Also known as Revenue Act of 1764.

Sugar and Molasses Act. Enacted by Parliament in 1733 as a result of the pressure of the powerful sugar planters of the British WEST INDIES. The purpose of the Act was to protect them against the competition of the French and Dutch islands. The Act laid heavy duties on rum, molasses, and sugar exported from these French and Dutch West Indian colonies to the mainland British colonies.

The Act was not enforced. If it had been enforced it would have destroyed the trade of the northern colonies.

Sugar Industry. An industry that has grown in importance in the last half century. Prior to the LOUISIANA PURCHASE, the only sugar made in the United States was from maple sap. Cane sugar was imported from the WEST INDIES. By 1830 New Orleans had the largest sugar refinery in the world with an annual capacity of 6,000 tons. Today the maple and cane sugar industries are dominated by large corporations operating vast plants heavily financed for their production, refining, and marketing activities. Generally refineries are located adjacent to port cities with shipping and banking facilities. New York City is the nation's principal refining center. The per capita sugar consumption in the United States in 1962 was about 100 lbs. per year. In that year the nation produced approximately 4,880,000,000 pounds of beet sugar and over 1,716,000,000 pounds of cane sugar. Among the leading refiners in the industry are the American Sugar Refining Company, and the National Sugar Refining Company. These and other companies have organized the Sugar Research Foundation to sponsor research at leading universities and laboratories on the role of sugar in the diet, and in the field of chemistry, bio-chemistry, MEDICINE, and micro-biology.

"Sugar Trust." One of the earliest trusts. It was the consolidation of sugar refineries, established in 1887. After its invalidation in New York State the sugar trust was reorganized in 1891 under the control of the American Sugar Refining Company. The directors, officers, and trustees of the new corporation constituted virtually the same group as under the old organization. Within a year the trust had acquired a MONOPOLY of sugar refining in the country. Although prosecuted by the DEPARTMENT OF JUSTICE under the SHERMAN ANTI-TRUST ACT, the United States Supreme Court held, in the case of the UNITED STATES vs. E. C. KNIGHT, that the corporation's activities did not violate the law.

Sullivan Campaign. Planned by General WASHINGTON in 1779 to stem Indian and Tory attacks on the New York and Pennsylvania frontier. The command was given to General JOHN SULLIVAN who was ordered to repel the eastern IROQUOIS and Onondaga tribes. General JAMES CLINTON commanded the New York wing of the army against the latter tribes. Leading 2500 men in Pennsylvania Sullivan was joined by Clinton with 1,500 men in the late summer in an attack on a composite army of Tories, Cayugas, Senecas, and MOHAWKS. Forty Indian villages and 160,000 bushels of corn were destroyed although Sullivan broke off the campaign because of the late season.

SULLIVAN, John. 1740-1795. Revolutionary general. Practised law in New Hampshire; member of the CONTINENTAL CONGRESS (1774, 75, 80, 81); commissioned a brigadier general serving throughout the siege of Boston (1775-76); major general serving at the BATTLE OF LONG ISLAND where he was captured (1776); exchanged; spent the winter at VALLEY FORGE (1777-78); succeeded in defeating the Indians in upper New York State; resigned (1779); appointed attorney-general of New Hampshire (1782-86); president of New Hampshire (1786, 1787, 1789); U.S. District Judge in that state (1789-95); helped suppress SHAYS' REBELLION and was largely responsible for New Hampshire's RATIFICATION OF THE CONSTITUTION.

SULLIVAN, Louis Henri. 1856-1924. Architect. b. Boston, Massachusetts. Famous for his principle of adapting architectural design to the function for which the building is intended; designed the first steel-skeleton skyscraper; considered the father of modern ARCHITECTURE; designed m a n y important buildings throughout the country.

SULLY, Thomas. 1783-1872. Painter. b. England. Came to the United States as a child (1792); studied with several well-known artists; famous for his portraits of LAFAYETTE, JEFFERSON, MADISON and JACKSON and for his painting *Washington Crossing the Delaware* which hangs in the Boston Museum of Art. He was a very prolific painter and well-known for his capable portraits.

SUMNER, Charles. 1811-1874. Statesman. b. Boston. Graduated, Harvard (1830); Harvard Law School (1834); admitted to the bar and practised in Boston; strong opponent of SLAVERY; opposed the ANNEXATION OF TEXAS; FREE-SOIL candidate for Congress; U.S. Senator (1851-74); his violent attacks on slavery resulted in a physical attack upon him by Representative Brooks of South Carolina (1856); urged emancipation (1861); chairman, Committee on Foreign Affairs in the Senate (1861-71); strong supporter of LINCOLN; took part in IMPEACHMENT proceedings against JOHNSON; opposed GRANT, and his SANTA DOMINGO policy (1871); author of *The Works of Charles Sumner* (15 vols.).

SUMTER, Thomas. 1734-1832. Revolutionary general. b. Virginia. Served with BRADDOCK against Fort Duquesne(1755); moved to South Carolina where he was lieutenant colonel of South Carolina troops (1776-78); took part in the CHEROKEE War; commissioned a brigadier general and fought in various battles of the Revolution; became strong FEDERALIST and a member, U.S. House of Representatives (1789-93; 1797-1801); U.S. Senator (1801-1810); U.S. Minister to Brazil (1809-11); Fort Sumter named after him.

Supply Priorities and Allocation Board. A defense organization created in September, 1941 for the purpose of directing defense production. Operating co-evally with the OFFICE OF PRODUCTION MANAGEMENT it was authorized to grant priority ratings to manufacturers of raw materials and other goods necessary to the defense of the United States. The overlapping jurisdiction between it and the OPM produced inefficient results and divided responsibility, leading the President to abolish it in January, 1942. The SPAB was chaired by Vice President WALLACE, and consisted of the Secretaries of War and Navy, the OPM directors, the Price Administrators, and the Lend-Lease Supervisor.

Supreme Commander for Allied Powers. See Japan, occupation of.

Supreme Court, United States. The highest federal court in the United States. Its existence is provided for in Article III of the Constitution, although Congress is given the power to determine the size of the Court. In 1801 the number of justices was reduced to five, but was increased to seven in 1807, to nine in 1837, and to 10 in 1863. In 1869 the number was again reduced to nine, remaining there to date. The Court's jurisdiction is original and appellate, the latter being determined by Congress. In 1925 a law of Congress delegated to the Court the power to lay down the terms of its appellate jurisdiction. The Court's original jurisdiction is limited to cases or controversies to which a state or an ambassador, public minister, or consul is a party. In its early history the Court was held in low esteem, but with the chief justiceship of JOHN MARSHALL in the first third of the 19th century, its prestige and power became outstanding. Under Marshall the Court assumed the power of JUDICIAL REVIEW, maintaining it to this day. Although the Court does not have self-enforcing power, requiring enforcements of its decisions by the executive branch, its decisions have been ignored only three times by American Presidents. There are no constitutional qualifications for Court membership, and in its early history politicians and military figures with little legal or judicial training were appointed to it. It is curious to note that of the 12 chief justices only the last five have had prior judicial experience. Decisions of the court are rendered by a simple majority vote, although the majority opinion is frequently the work of one member whose thinking affects the Court's policy and doctrine. Members of the Court are appointed for life by the President. They may be removed only by death, resignation, or impeachment. Outstanding members of the Court have been John Marshall, JOSEPH STOREY, ROGER B. TANEY, SALMON P. CHASE, OLIVER WENDELL HOLMES, LOUIS D. BRANDEIS, WILLIAM HOWARD TAFT, CHARLES EVANS HUGHES, BENJAMIN CARDOZA, and HARLAN F. STONE.

Surplus Property Act. A law of Congress passed in 1944 authorizing the DEPARTMENT OF JUSTICE to administer the disposal of $16,000,000,000 worth of surplus plants after World War II. Safeguards were set up by the Attorney-General to insure the proper sale of these plants in order to prevent the enhancement of MONOPOLY conditions.

Sussex Pledge. A promise by the German government on May 4, 1916 that American merchant ships would not be destroyed without warning and without saving human lives. This pledge followed the sinking of the French passenger steamer *Sussex* in the English channel by a German submarine, with the loss of two American lives. The German statement yielded to an ultimatum by President WILSON that the United States would sever diplomatic relations with that government unless it would immediately declare an abandonment of its methods of submarine warfare against passenger and freight vessels. The violation of the Sussex Pledge in January

1917, contributed to American entry into the War three months later.

SUTTER, John Augustus. 1803-1880. California pioneer. b. Germany. Came to the United States (1834); traded in the far West, mostly in Santa Fe and Oregon; went to California and founded a colony called New Helvetia, which is now Sacramento (1839); became wealthy and powerful; however, when gold was discovered on his property the mad crowds killed his cattle, destroyed his land and he was completely ruined (1852); moved to Pennsylvania (1873); given a pension by the State of California (1864-78).

Sweatshop. A factory employing children and adults of both sexes under oppressive conditions of LABOR. Such conditions included the use of unguarded dangerous machinery, inadequate sanitary facilities, speed-up work, long hours, and improper light and ventilation. The term arose out of the device by which clothing was farmed out by manufacturers to contractors who often had the work done at low pay in his workers' homes. Attacks on this situation were led by private organizations, trade unions, and the United States DEPARTMENT OF LABOR. By the 1930's sweatshops had virtually disappeared from the clothing industry.

Swedish Settlements. The only Swedish colony in America was established in 1638 on the Delaware River. Twenty-five men erected a fort which became the basis of the settlement. The colonists purchased land from the Indians on the west shore of the Delaware, extending from the site of Trenton, New Jersey to the mouth of the Delaware Bay, claiming it for Sweden. New colonists came in 1640, 1641, and 1643. The first governor. was Peter Hollandaer. Domiciles and forts were erected along the river, forests cleared, and the land placed under cultivation. The colonial government was despotic, and in the hands of Governor Johan Printz was a combination of military and civil rule. In 1653 New Sweden captured a Dutch fort in the Delaware Valley, precipitating a war with Holland that resulted in Dutch victory in 1655.

Swing-Johnson Act. Also known as the Boulder Canyon Project Act. See Colorado River Compact.

T

Tabloid Press. Small-size picture NEWS-PAPERS whose mass appeal is based on sensational stories involving crime, scandal and sex. The *Illustrated Daily News* was the first successful tabloid in the United States. It was established in New York City in 1919 by Joseph M. Patterson. Within two years it had the largest circulation in the city, and by 1952 had an average daily circulation of almost 2,200,000 and a Sunday circulation of more than 4,000,000. In 1924 WILLIAM RANDOLPH HEARST published the *Daily Mirror* in New York. From 1924 to 1932 Bernarr MacFadden published the *New York Evening Graphic*. By 1952 there were more than 50 tabloid newspapers in the country.

Taft Commission. Also known as the Philippine Commission. A body reorganized from the SCHURMAN COMMISSION in April, 1900. WILLIAM H. TAFT succeeded J. G. Schurman as chairman. Authorized to provide for civil government in the PHILIPPINES, it established local governments, granted suffrage to capable Filipinos, and announced that a central civil government would be created as soon as a functioning local government was established. After a year and a half of this fundamental organization Taft was appointed the first civil governor of the island on June 21, 1901. Civil officials replaced the military in most provinces.

Taft-Hartley Act. Also known as the Labor-Management Relations Act. A law of Congress passed over President TRUMAN'S veto on June 23, 1947. It incorporated the NATIONAL LABOR RELATIONS ACT as Title I. The membership of the NATIONAL LABOR RELATIONS BOARD from three to five and the office of General Counsel was established with final power to determine the issuance or prosecution of a complaint. It declared illegal the CLOSED SHOP, preferential shop, and union hiring hall, and permitted the UNION SHOP only after a vote of a majority of the employees. On October 22, 1951, an amendment to the law permitted union shop contracts without first polling employees. The Act guaranteed to employers the right to express their opinions on unionism but without threat of reprisal or force against employees. It forbade jurisdictional strikes and SECONDARY BOYCOTTS, but permitted the check-off of union dues when employees authorized it in writing. Employers were prohibited from contributing to union help and welfare funds unless such contributions were held in trust on the basis of a written plan administered equally by employer and employee representatives. Employers were exempted from bargaining with unions of foremen or supervisors unless they wished to. The NLRB was authorized to obtain temporary restraining orders simultaneously with the issuance of complaints and to obtain five-day restraining orders on unlawful boycotts and jurisdictional strikes. Unions and employers were forbidden from coercing employees or each other. Union's refusal to bargain was declared an UNFAIR LABOR PRACTICE. Employers were permitted to file petitions for certification whenever a union claimed recognition and were authorized to sue unions in District Courts for breach of contract or for conducting unlawful boycotts or jurisdictional strikes. The United States Attorney General was empowered to obtain an 80-day INJUNCTION when a threatened or actual strike imperilled the national health or safety. The Act forbade unions from contributing to political campaigns and required union leaders to file an affidavit with the NLRB affirming that they were not Communists in order to obtain the services of the Board. On May 8, 1950 the Supreme Court upheld the non-Communist oath.

TAFT, Robert Alphonso. 1889-1953. Political leader. b. Ohio. Graduated, Yale (1910); Harvard (L.L.B. 1913); practised in Cincinnati; U.S. Senator from Ohio (from 1939); a conservative leader of the Republican party unsuccessfully aspiring to the nomination for the presidency.

TAFT, William Howard. 1857-1930. Twenty-seventh President of the United States. b. Cincinnati, Ohio. Graduated, Yale (1878); Cincinnati Law School (1880); admitted to the bar and practiced Cincinnati (1880); judge, Ohio Superior court (1887-90); U.S. Solicitor General (1890-92); U.S. Circuit Court Judge (1892-1900); first civil governor of the PHILIPPINE ISLANDS while under American control (1901-04); appointed by T. ROOSEVELT, U.S. Secretary of War succeeding ROOT (1904-08); at the suggestion of Roosevelt he was Republican nominee for the presidency and elected (1909-13); lost support of Roosevelt

over his dismissal of PINCHOT and his sponsoring of the PAYNE-ALDRICH TARIFF, and was defeated for a second term (1912); professor of constitutional law, Yale (1913-21); Chief Justice, U.S. Supreme Court (1921-30); supported the LEAGUE OF NATIONS.

TALBOT, Silas. 1751-1813. Naval officer. b. Massachusetts. Captain in the Continental navy (1779); captured by the British; named by WASHINGTON as a leading captain of the U.S. Navy (1794); supervised the construction of and commanded the *Constitution* during the war with France; resigned (1801).

Tallmadge Amendment. Submitted by Representative George Tallmadge of New York in 1819 as an amendment to the bill of petition for Missouri's entrance into the Union. It provided that the introduction of SLAVERY into the TERRITORY be prohibited and that all children born within the state after its admission be free at the age of 25 years. The amendment passed the House by a narrow margin, but was defeated in the Senate. It died with the expiration of Congress the following year.

TALLMADGE, Benjamin. 1754-1835. Revolutionary colonel. b. New York. Graduated, Yale (1773); joined the Connecticut regiment during the Revolution and saw service at BRANDYWINE, GERMANTOWN, MONMOUTH and VALLEY FORGE; as a colonel he won a victory in LONG ISLAND (1779); served as a FEDERALIST in Congress (1801-17).

TALLMADGE, James. 1778-1853. Statesman and Jurist. b. New York. Graduated, Brown (1798); studied law and practised in New York; commanded a group of New York volunteers during the War of 1812; member, U.S. House of Representatives (1817-19); opposed the extension of SLAVERY; lieutenant governor of New York (1825-26); one of the founders of the University of the City of New

York (now New York University) and was its council president for many years.

Tallmadge Resolution. See Tallmadge Amendment.

TALMAGE, Thomas de Witt. 1832-1902. Presbyterian clergyman and preacher. Editor, *Christian Herald* (1890-1902); served in notable pastorates; famous as a preacher and his sermons were widely published.

Tammany Hall. The popular name of the Tammany Society of New York. Actually it is the headquarters of the New York County Democratic Committee, situated in New York City. See Tammany Societies.

Tammany Societies. Local political organization founded in the second decade of the 19th century in Rhode Island and Ohio on the pattern of the New York City Society. In that city the Society of Tammany, also known as the Columbian Order, was founded in 1783. The name was borrowed from a Delaware tribal chief Tammany, or Tammanend. Its ritual is governed by Indian traditions and its organization headed by 13 sachem. In 1805 the Society was incorporated as a charity, meeting at Martling's Tavern. Although its early membership was strongly FEDERALIST, the success of JEFFERSON in 1800 brought about a change in its membership which became overwhelmingly Republican. It remained loyal to this party after it had become the Democratic Party in the Jacksonian era. The leadership of WILLIAM M. TWEED in 1860 made of it a well-organized, powerful, political machine which served as the model for the "big city" machines to follow. Other important leaders or beneficiaries of Tammany have been RICHARD CROKER, ALFRED E. SMITH, James J. Walker, and William O'Dwyer. The New York Society has oftentimes been charged with corrupt political practices, involving the services of gangster elements in its control of municipal politics. From time to time investigations have been undertaken by federal, state, and local groups. Foremost among these have been the SEABURY INVESTIGATION and the KEFAUVER INVESTIGATION.

Tampico Incident. See Vera Cruz Incident.

TANEY, Roger Brooke. 1777-1864. Jurist. b. Maryland. Graduated, Dickinson College (1795); admitted to the bar (1799); practised in Maryland; U.S. Attorney General (1831-33) adviser to President JACKSON; appointed by him, U.S. Secretary of the Treasury (1833-34); his appointment not confirmed by the Senate; also rejected by that body as Associate Justice of the Supreme Court (1835); finally nominated and confirmed (1836); Chief Justice, U.S. Supreme Court succeeding JOHN MARSHALL; famous for his decision in the DRED SCOTT CASE (1857); also handed down decision declaring that only Congress had the right to suspend the writ of *habeas corpus*.

TARBELL, Ida Minerva. 1857-1944. Author and lecturer. b. Pennsylvania. Associate editor of the *Chautauquan* (1883-91), *McClure's Magazine* (1894-1906) and *American Magazine* (1906-15); appointed by President WILSON a member of the Industrial Conference (1919) and by President HARDING to the Unemployment Conference. Author of *Life of Abraham Lincoln* (2 vols. 1900), *History of the Standard Oil Company* (2 vols. 1904), *The Business of Being a Woman* (1912), *Owen D. Young, A New Type of Industrial Leader* (1932) and many other books on historical and economic subjects.

Tariff of Abominations. Also known as the Tariff of 1828. JOHN RANDOLPH called it a tariff concerned with "the manufacture of a President" and with manufactures of no other kind. His reference was to the scheme of JACKSON's supporters to ensure his election in 1828 by introducing a tariff bill with such high rates on raw materials that New England would vote with the South for its defeat. Expecting New England to support JOHN QUINCY ADAMS in any case and the South to support Jackson, his followers would then call upon the protectionist elements of the middle-Atlantic states, whose votes, along with the South's, would obtain his election. Jackson's expectations were not fulfilled since enough New England votes were cast for the bill to obtain its passage. CALHOUN and the southern members of Congress attacked the measure as the Tariff of Abominations. The South Carolina legislature adopted Calhoun's EXPOSITION AND PROTEST in bitter opposition to the bill.

Tariff Board. See Tariff Commission.

Tariff Commission. An agency established by Congress from time to time to advise it or the President on recommended increases or decreases in tariff rates. The Revenue Commission of 1865 was the first such body, but it was abolished the following year. The first major Tariff Commission was established by Congress in 1916 as a non-partisan body of six members to investigate all questions with reference to tariffs, and to submit reports to Congress. Previously a Tariff Commission and a Tariff Board had been established in 1882 and 1909 respectively. Both were subsequently legislated out of existence. By the FORDNEY-MC CUMBER Act the Tariff Commission was authorized to recommend to the President an increase or reduction of duties not exceeding 50 percent. This power was retained by the HAWLEY-SMOOT ACT.

Tariff of 1789. The first tariff act of the new government. Although it recognized protectionism it was basically a revenue tariff. It listed 81 articles on 30 of which specific duties were imposed. *Ad valorem* rates ranging from seven and one half to 15 percent were placed on the remaining

51 articles. A five percent ad valorem tax was levied on all other imports. The average rate was eight and one half percent. Commodities particularly aided were steel, paper, beer, glass, iron, rum, nails, boots, shoes, clothing, tea, coffee, sugar, and wine. The rates were revised upwards by amendment in 1790, 1792, and 1794. The tariff produced 88 percent of the total receipts of the federal government.

Tariff of 1816. The first PROTECTIVE TARIFF in American history. It was introduced by JOHN C. CALHOUN and WILLIAM LOWNDES of South Carolina in the belief that the South would prosper as an industrial area as a result of the stimulus of the War of 1812. It was strongly opposed by DANIEL WEBSTER as the spokesman of New England which considered it a blow to the commercial supremacy of that section. The act imposed duties ranging from seven and one-half to 30 percent *ad valorem*, providing special protection to cotton, iron, woolens, and other manufactured goods stimulated by the war.

Tariff of 1818. A PROTECTIVE TARIFF increasing the rates of the 1816 measure. Duties on iron were increased, and the 25 percent rate on COTTON was extended until 1826.

Tariff of 1824. A general revision of the tariffs of 1816 and 1818. Woolen goods, glass, iron, and lead rates were increased, and a 25 percent rate applied to hemp. The act received the general support of the Pennsylvania iron interests, the wool interests of Ohio and the middle states, and the hemp growers of Kentucky. It was strongly opposed by the Northern merchant and the Southern planter.

Tariff of 1828. See Tariff of Abominations.

Tariff of 1832. A bill enacted to conciliate the South after the passage of the

616

TARIFF OF ABOMINATIONS. Although essentially protective it restored the tariff to the average rates of 1824. Nevertheless it incurred the stiff opposition of South Carolina which passed the ORDINANCE OF NULLIFICATION.

Tariff of 1833. See Compromise Tariff of 1833.

Tariff of 1842. An upward revision of rates resulting from a depletion of the income of the national government. The rates virtually restored the tariff to the level of 1832. Enacted by the WHIGS, it was repudiated by the Democrats after their election success in 1844. It was modified by the WALKER TARIFF ACT.

Tariff of 1857. A downward revision of the WALKER TARIFF. It enlarged the free list and reduced the rates of the Walker Act by five percent. These reductions were a result of increased treasury receipts produced by business expansion at that time.

Tariff Lobby. The TARIFFS from 1890 to 1930 contained items designed to give American business men commercial advantages over their foreign competitors. At various times it has been charged that these business men have exercised undue influence in obtaining favorable tariff provisions. In 1913, while the UNDERWOOD-SIMMONS TARIFF Bill was under consideration, there were reports that a powerful tariff lobby was attempting to influence House action. On May 13th President WILSON issued a statement declaring that "Washington has seldom seen so numerous, so industrious, or so insidious a LOBBY. There is every evidence that money without limit is being spent to sustain this lobby." The result was an investigation ordered by the Senate followed shortly afterward by one ordered by the House. The report of the House Committee led to the resignation of a member from Illinois. Although it was not possible to establish responsibility, the evidence adduced by the report clearly showed that tariff legislation of the preceding generation had been accompanied by questionable practices.

Tariff reform. The move for a reduction in tariff rates. From the end of the Civil War to WILSON's first administration the program for tariff reform was an integral part of most of the quadrennial platforms of the Democratic party. The failure of the MILLS BILL in 1888 postponed serious tariff reduction until the enactment of the UNDERWOOD-SIMMONS ACT.

Tariffs. Also known as customs or duties. They are taxes on imports. They may be classified from the viewpoint of method of collection or purpose. The former category includes specific and *ad valorem* tariffs. The latter includes revenue and protective tariffs. See Trade Expansion Act (1962).

TARKINGTON, Booth. *Name in full* Newton Booth. 1869-1946. Novelist. b. Indiana. Graduated, Princeton (1893); author of many popular novels on the American scene including *Monsieur Beaucaire* (1900), *Penrod* (1914), *Penrod and Sam* (1916), *Seventeen* (1917), *The Magnificent Ambersons* (1918) which was awarded the Pulitzer Prize; *Little Orvie* (1934) and many others.

Taxation. The act of levying an assessment against the residents of a given area. The proceeds of these assessments are generally used to defray the costs of maintaining the government of the area. Basically, taxes are of two kinds, direct and indirect. The former are paid by those upon whom the assessment is levied while the latter are paid by a second, third, or other party to the collecting authority. Among the various taxes in American experience have been customs, excises, property, inheritance, income, corporate, profits, franchise, sales, use, and poll taxes. Colonial taxation was limited, the bulk of colonial income being derived from fees and quitrents. Under the ARTICLES OF CONFEDERATION. Congress could not levy taxes upon people, being restricted to requesting the assessments from the states. The failure to raise adequate revenues by this method was one of the prime causes of the failure of that government. Thus it was that the Constitution of 1787 conferred upon Congress the specific power to lay and collect taxes.

"Taxation without Representation." The slogan raised by the colonists in the years preceding the American Revolution. It referred, theoretically, to their opposition to the payment of the taxes imposed by Parliament after the French and Indian War, and was raised with the design of arousing public support of this opposition. It was an excellent illustration of the effect of economics upon politics but did not actually reflect the feeling contained in the slogan. The colonists objected to TAXATION by anybody at any time. American representation in the English Parliament was an impossibility in the 18th century, and well known as such to colonial leaders. The slogan was a sharp propaganda weapon in the struggle against Great Britain leading up to the American Revolution.

Tax Frauds. Corruption in the Internal Revenue Bureau which came to public light in 1950-1952. In August, 1950 James P. Finnegan, St. Louis Collector of Internal Revenue was asked to resign by Secretary of Treasury Snyder when bribery and graft were revealed in his office. In November the Federal Bureau of Internal Revenue investigated accusation of connections between the Revenue Office and the underworld in California. On February 2, 1951 a House Ways and Means sub-committee chaired by Cecil R. King was established to investigate the federal tax laws. On April 24th Finnegan resigned and was subsequently indicted on charges of using his office for private gain. In June the Boston Collector of Internal Revenue was suspended, and later discharged and indicted for bribery. Following the King Committee's hearings in September the San Francisco Collector of Internal Revenue, James G. Smyth, and eight employees were suspended. Smyth was later indicted. In October, the Brooklyn Collector resigned under fire and on November 1st President TRUMAN requested that Congress enact legislation placing Internal Revenue Collectors under the MERIT SYSTEM. On November 17th T. Lamar Caudle, Assistant Attorney General in charge of the Justice Department's Tax Division, resigned at the President's request for engaging in "outside activities * * * incompatible with the duties of his office." On November 28th the President discharged 21 Revenue Bureau officials and employees. In December the King Committee was informed that Caudle and Charles Oliphant, Chief Counsel of the Revenue Bureau, had been involved in an offer to "fix" a tax delinquency of $500,000 for Abraham Teitlebaum, Chicago attorney. The next day, Oliphant resigned. Subsequently the Attorney General ordered grand jury investigations of Teitelbaum's charges of tax frauds. On April 14, 1952 the Bureau announced that internal "house cleaning" would be completed in three months. It declared that 175 workers had been discharged since January 1, 1951 for irregularities ranging from bribe-taking to alcoholism. It added that 1,500 employees had been checked for all kinds of reported misbehavior.

TAYLOR, Bayard. *Name in full* James Bayard. 1825-1878. Journalist and author. b. Pennsylvania. Wrote sketches and letters to the newspapers and magazines on his various trips to Europe; wrote *Eldorado* (1850) based on his trip to California during the GOLD RUSH;

traveled to the Near East and the Orient and wrote books on these trips; translated Goethe's *Faust* (2 vols., 1870-71); U.S. Minister to Germany (1878).

TAYLOR, Deems. *In full* Joseph Deems. 1885- . Music critic and composer. b. New York City. Graduated, New York University (1906); music critic, New York *World* (1921-25); editor, *Musical America* (1927-29); music critic, New York *American* (1931-32); music consultant for the Columbia Broadcasting System; composer of *The Siren Song* (1912); *Through the Looking Glass* (1918), *The King's Henchman* (1927) an opera with libretto by EDNA ST. VINCENT MILLAY; *Peter Ibbetson* and others.

TAYLOR, George. 1716-1781. Iron manufacturer and statesman. b. Ireland. Came to America (1736?); operated a large furnace in Bucks County, Pennsylvania; member of the COMMITTEE OF CORRESPONDENCE (1774-76); member, CONTINENTAL CONGRESS (1776-77); signer of the DECLARATION OF INDEPENDENCE; colonel in the Pennsylvania militia.

TAYLOR, John. 1753-1824. Known as "John Taylor of Caroline." Agriculturist, political philosopher and statesman. b. Virginia. Graduated, William and Mary (1770); practised law; served with the Continental Army (1775-98; 1781); became interested in AGRICULTURE and wrote *Arator* (1813) which is the first analytical work on agriculture in the country; member of the Virginia House of Delegates (1779-85, 1796-1800); supported the VIRGINIA RESOLUTIONS; U.S. Senator (1792-94; 1803; 1822-24); ardent Jeffersonian and opposed to FEDERALIST financial measures; supported MONROE; fought with JOHN MARSHALL; first one to really formulate the policies of "STATES' RIGHTS." Author of books on political science.

TAYLOR, John. 1808-1887. Mormon leader. b. England. Became an apostle of the Mormon Church (1838); strong supporter of JOHN SMITH and was wounded the day that Smith was killed; accompanied BRIGHAM YOUNG to Utah and succeeded him as head of the Church.

TAYLOR, Richard. Confederate general. Son of ZACHARY TAYLOR. b. New Orleans, Louisiana. Served with his father in the Mexican War; successful sugar planter in Louisiana; brigadier general, Confederate army (1861); served with STONEWALL JACKSON in Shenandoah Valley campaign; major general (1862); succeeded to command of General HOOD's army (1864); forced to surrender despite his personal victories at the fall of the Confederacy in Alabama.

TAYLOR, Zachary. 1784-1850. Twelfth President of the United States. b. Virginia. Rose to major in the army during the War of 1812. Served as commander of the army in Texas and defeated the Mexicans at Palo Alto (1846); brevetted major general and named in command of the army of the Rio Grande; defeated SANTA ANNA at Buena Vista (1847); elected as President of the United States on the WHIG party ticket (1849-50); died of typhus fever while in office. Nicknamed "Old Rough-and-Ready."

Tea Act. Enacted by Parliament in 1773. The Act conferred upon the East India Company a MONOPOLY importation of tea into the mainland colonies, thus eliminating the profits of the colonial importer and local shopkeeper. The fear of the colonists that Parliament's power to confer such a monopoly might be extended to other economic activities created a deep resentment among them. In the leadership of the opposition to the Act was the powerful class of importers in the seaport towns. JOHN HANCOCK was their outstanding leader. The Act contributed greatly to the developing revolutionary sentiment of the time, and brought about the BOSTON TEA PARTY.

Teapot Dome Scandal. One of the scandals of the HARDING administration. Former Secretary of the Interior ALBERT FALL was indicted for leasing naval oil reserve lands at Teapot Dome, Wyoming and Elk Hill, California to the Sinclair and Doheny interests. It was discovered that Secretary Fall had accepted loans and he and Doheny were tried in Washington on charges of conspiracy and bribery in 1926. Although they were acquitted on technical grounds, it has since been considered that they were guilty.

Technocracy. A movement of the early 1930's which proposed a plan for industrial recovery and permanent economic equilibrium on the basis of production control by technicians. The Technocrats declared that industry in the United States was underproducing in terms of capacity, and argued that only under the administration of professionally trained and qualified engineers could the nation's industrial plant be utilized to its maximum capacity. They further proposed the modification of the market economics of CAPITALISM, including particularly the use of money and the employment of manual LABOR in factories. The indefinite program of the Technocrats attracted little support even though their theories were widely discussed. By 1935 the group had vanished from the political scene.

TECUMSEH. 1768-1813. Shawnee Indian Chief. b. Ohio territory. Led the Indians against the whites claiming the land belonged to the Indian tribes; his brother, while he was away, was defeated at Tippecanoe (1811) by an American army force led by WILLIAM H. HARRISON; fought with the British during the War of 1812; killed in action. He was a great organizer and a great leader and is considered one of the outstanding Indians of American history.

Teheran Conference. A meeting at Teheran, Iran of President F. D. ROOSEVELT, Prime Minister Churchill, and Premier Stalin between November 28th and December 1st, 1943. The Declaration issued at the conclusion of the Conference included the agreement of Iran to facilitate the TRANSPORTATION of supplies to the Soviet Union in the mutual war effort and the continuing effort of these nations to assist Iran with raw materials and supplies. The BIG THREE announced that they had agreed on future war plans including specifically the scope and timing of operations. Agreement was also reached on the need for an international security organization after World War II.

Telegraph. The first successful telegraph line was constructed by SAMUEL F. B. MORSE between Washington and Baltimore in 1844. The congressional appropriation of $30,000 for its construction placed the line under public ownership. Morse's patent remained in abeyance until 1847 when Congress turned over the 44 mile line to the Magnetic Telegraph Company. Private companies soon built additional lines, availing themselves of technical improvements. In the early period unsubstantial construction and legal disputes inhibited the industry's growth. In the 1850's the WESTERN UNION Company began the consolidation of telegraph lines which, by the 20th century, had brought the nation's lines into the hands of two major companies. In the 1930's Western Union absorbed the Postal Telegraph System.

Telephone System. The important communication system which began with the granting of a patent to ALEXANDER GRAHAM BELL in 1876 over the protests of ELISHA GRAY, who had filed his invention the same day. Subsequent improvements were made by James W. McDonough, THOMAS EDISON, and Emil Berliner. The telephone quickly outranked the TELEGRAPH and RADIO as a communication medium, long distance service being developed as early as January 28, 1878. The first commercial telephone exchange was opened at New Haven, Conn. in 1892 between New York City and Chicago. In 1925 transatlantic telephone service was inaugurated. As early as 1910 Congress passed the MANN-ELKINS ACT to provide regulation of this growing and important industry. Of the 70,000,000 telephones in the world, the United States has over 47,000,000. The International Telephone and Telegraph Company owns or controls approximately 95.5 percent of the world's telephone systems. Its subsidiary the AMERICAN TELEPHONE AND TELEGRAPH COMPANY operates or controls the bulk of the industry in the United States.

Television Industry. The first practical television system was proposed in Germany in 1884 by Paul Nipkow whose mechanical system employed a disc with a pattern of holes punched in it and was vastly different from the electronic systems used today. In 1925 Charles Francis Jenkins conceived the idea of combining photography, optics, and RADIO to create a picture which could be transmitted electronically. His system was improved a few years later by the use of an electron tube, called a kinescope, designed in the United States by Vladimir Kosma Zworykin. An improvement in the electronic scanning system was conceived simultaneously by Philo T. Farnsworth. In 1928 the National Broadcasting Company opened an experimental television station in New York City, its operation based on the old mechanical scanning equivalent. In 1931 this system was supplemented with the kinescope receiver which had been developed by Zworykin. In the same year a television transmitter was installed in the Empire State Building in New York City. In 1933 the Radio Corporation of America installed a completely electronic system in Camden, New Jersey, using the iconoscope,

a developed form of Zworykin's early electron tube. The first commercial television broadcasts were begun in New York City on April 30, 1939. The advent of World War II halted the growth of the industry, although technical improvements in camera work and electronics were continued. At the end of the war the television industry emerged as a highly developed, technologically advanced industry, which by 1952 employed more than 250,000 people in MANUFACTURING, service, and sales. The industry in the United States has opened new fields in ART, SCIENCE, AND COMMERCE, providing constructive employment for actors, musicians, writers, artists, producers, directors, cameramen, and technicians. New vocational opportunities have been opened in such fields as scenic design, costuming, and public relations. In the early 1950's rapid advances in the technology of transmission led to coast-to-coast broadcasting, on-the-spot coverage of news events, color transmission, and the use of larger sized screens. In 1952 the FEDERAL COMMUNICATIONS COMMISSION established new channels for educational television which up to that time had been limited to experimental telecasts of surgical operations and a few classroom broadcasts. During 1964, the NATIONAL CONVENTIONS of the Republican and Democratic parties received the widest television coverage ever given to a historic event. In that year there were over 62,000,000 television sets in American homes. As a result of the lifting of restrictions by the Federal Communications Commission in 1952, 511 new very high frequency stations were permitted as compared with 108 in that year. The new regulation also provided for an additional 1,432 ultra-high frequency stations. Of this total of 2,051 stations, 242 were to be set aside for educational purposes. The potential number of cities with broadcasting stations was increased to 1,275.

Telstar. An experimental communication satellite developed by the American Telephone and Telegraph Co. and its subsidiary, Bell Telephone Laboratories. Television and other media of communication have been inaugurated via Telstar between the United States and Europe, thus setting a milestone in the industry.

Temperance Movement. An organized movement to bring about the enactment by federal and state legislatures of laws prohibiting the manufacture, sale, and distribution of intoxicating liquors. Its origins go back to 17th century colonial America, although the first Temperance Society was formed in 1808 in New York State by Dr. Billy J. Clark. The most important early organization was the Connecticut Society for the Reformation of Morals, established in 1813 for the suppression of drunkenness, vice, and general lawlessness. Subsidiary societies were soon organized in New England and New York. For a time thereafter Protestant evangelical groups carried on the temperance crusade. The American Temperance Union appeared in the 1930's as the largest organization at that time, carrying on a program of propaganda, meetings, lectures, and personal tours which had a widespread influence upon state and local legislatures. As early as 1838 regulatory legislation appeared in Massachusetts, followed shortly thereafter by other states. The creation of the PROHIBITION PARTY in 1869 was the political expression of the movement. See Prohibition Party.

Temporary National Economic Committee. A committee established by Congress in 1938 to make an intensive study of the American economy. It was created on the recommendation of President F. D. ROOSEVELT to Congress on April 29, 1938 for the purpose of offering "a program

to preserve private enterprise for profit by keeping it free enough to be able to utilize all our resources of capital and labor at a profit." The Committee was chaired by Senator Joseph C. O'Mahoney of Wyoming and consisted of members from the House, Senate, FEDERAL TRADE COMMISSION, SECURITIES AND EXCHANGE COMMISSION, and the DEPARTMENTS OF TREASURY, JUSTICE, COMMERCE, and LABOR. The TNEC recruited a large staff of consultants from the nation's universities and research institutions and from the public service, including experts in finance, accounting, COMMERCE, PUBLIC ADMINISTRATION, LABOR RELATIONS, AGRICULTURE and statistics. It held many hearings over a period of three years. On March 11, 1941, Senator O'Mahoney published the final statement of the Committee as an accompaniment to hundreds of monographs analyzing the individual problems of BANKING, insurance, MONOPOLY growth and control, concentrations of wealth, concentration of power. In these reports the Committee attempted to determine, in part, the range, causes, and results of the decline in business competition as well as the reasons for economic DEPRESSIONS under conditions of extensive NATURAL RESOURCES. The monographs indicated that large business units possess certain economic advantages that limit the entry of competitors. Few businessmen can enter industries characterized by large firms. The power of large industries over PATENTS has often given firms control over the development of an INDUSTRY, the prices charged, the production, and the entry of new firms. The Committee showed that the control of patents by two companies permitted them to dominate the GLASS container manufacturing industry. The Committee studied the problems of life insurance regulation and indicated the need for federal control, although it made no specific recommendations to this effect. It revealed the in-

622

terrelations between INSURANCE COM-PANIES and banking institutions, accomplished through INTERLOCKING DIRECTOR-ATES, insurance company deposits in associated banks, financial transactions through these banks, and materials and supplies purchased through these banks. It is reported that 49 of the legal-reserves life insurance companies had assets of over $26,000,000,000. In its monograph on the problems of BUREAUCRACY the Committee drew comparisons between management problems of business and government. In the final statement the chairman declared the Committee's faith in free enterprise and the preservation of "opportunity for all the people." He stated the government's desire to "foster and encourage private business" and its opposition to arbitrary control of economic activity. The Committee's recommendations were designed to keep the government free and responsive to the people, "but to keep business free also." The Committee further recommended cooperation and production for peace, more extensive anti-monopoly regulation, a return to freer competition, a return to the private enterprise system, national charters for national businesses, encouragement to small business, a more democratic economy, stronger enforcement of the existing ANTI-TRUST LAWS, revision of the tax laws for the purpose of encouraging new employment and new industry, and a national conference to be called by Congress of the various organizations of business, labor, agriculture, and consumers for discussion of all these problems. Few of the Committee's recommendations were later put into effect.

Tenant Farmers. Negroes and poor whites who rented FARMS in the South after the Civil War, unable financially to purchase them outright. They lived in dire poverty, controlled by the landlord whose income from excessive rents was supplemented by usurious interest rates in loans in anticipation of harvest. In the 1930's tenant farmers numbered 42 percent of all the FARMERS of the United States. In 1934 the RESETTLEMENT ADMINISTRATION, later the FARM SECURITY ADMINISTRATION, extended long term loans on easy terms to 17,000 farmers in 12 states. The Tenant Farmers Act (BANKHEAD-JONES ACT) of 1937 provided loans to tenant farmers, SHARECROPPERS, and farm laborers for the purchase of family-type farms. These loans were made at three percent interest for periods up to 40 years. Approximately 38,000 families were aided in acquiring farms by this law. Up to 1944 an aggregate sum of $250,000,000 had been lent for this purpose by 2,000 county offices.

Tenement Laws. State and municipal legislation enacted in the 20th century. These laws aimed at removing the fire and health hazards of tenement buildings in the slum areas. New York State passed a Tenement House Act in 1895, amended in 1901, which set the pace for similar laws elsewhere in the nation. These laws provided for rigid inspection and enforcement of new standards of plumbing, fireproofing, ventilation, and light. In Boston a series of laws required the provision of water to tenement buildings. Although great strides were taken old law tenements still dotted the major cities through the 1930's. At that time federal legislation provided grants-in-aid to state and municipal housing authorities for the replacement of slum domiciles by low rental housing projects.

Tennessee. The 34th state in size, with an area of 42,246 square miles. Entered the Union on June 1, 1796 as the 16th state. Seceded on June 24, 1861 and readmitted on July 24, 1866. Nashville is the capital. In 1950 Tennessee's population of 3,291,718 made it 16th in rank. Its largest cities are Memphis, Nashville, and Chattanooga. Tennessee's industrial products include aluminum, shoes, textiles, electrical equipment, books, paper, machinery, and chemicals. Minerals are coal, marble, zinc, phosphates, and pottery clay. Leading crops are corn, cotton, dairy products, eggs, live stock, and poultry. Tennessee is the home of the TVA, and won international renown for the ATOMIC BOMB made at Oak Ridge. The Tennessee River, by virtue of its control and development under the TVA program, is the most completely employed river in the world. The state was discovered in 1541 by DE SOTO. Its nickname is the "Volunteer State."

Tennessee Valley Authority. Popularly known as the T.V.A. A government corporation chartered by Congress in 1933 for various purposes including production of HYDRO-ELECTRIC POWER, manufacture of nitrates, flood-control, soil erosion control, and REFORESTATION. The corporation is administered by a three man board appointed by the President, and a general manager. Its operations cover a seven state area of 41,000 square miles with a population of 3,000,000. Its sale of electric power based on the "yard stick" theory has succeeded in demonstrating the possibility of competitive low prices inasmuch as it has consistently made a profit on the capital investment allocated to power production. Its original capital of $750,000,000 was appropriated by Congress and has since been supplemented by its operating revenues and its sale of bonds. Its power is distributed through local governments, cooperatives, and private utility companies. The TVA was extremely important in the original ATOMIC BOMB project. In 1952 the TVA was engaged in a program designed to increase its installed capacity from 3,-181,000 kilowatts to 6,800,000 kilowatts by 1954. It was committed to supply the ATOMIC ENERGY COMMISSION with as much electrical energy as was being used in New York City. The TVA, in recent years, has produced about six percent of the ELECTRICITY generated in the United States. Since 1933 electrified farms in the TVA region have risen to almost double

the national average, and retail rates are less than half the national average. As part of its health program the TVA had wiped out malaria by 1952, eliminating an incidence of 30 percent which had existed in some parts of the region in 1933.

"Tennis Cabinet". Name applied to the group of friends and agency heads who met with President THEODORE ROOSEVELT from time to time as his unofficial advisers. They may be likened to the "KITCHEN CABINET" of President ANDREW JACKSON and the "BRAIN TRUST" of President F. D. ROOSEVELT. They were so-called because they discussed political problems during their tennis games. Among the members were JAMES A. GARFIELD and GIFFORD PINCHOT.

Tenure of Office Act. Passed by Congress in 1867. It required senatorial approval for the removal of officers appointed by the President with senatorial consent. The dismissal by President ANDREW JOHNSON of Secretary of War EDWARD STANTON in 1867, in disregard of this law, was one of the causes of his IMPEACHMENT by the House of Representatives in that year. Although this statute's constitutionality was never tested a similar law of 1876 applying to postmasters was declared unconstitutional by the Supreme Court in 1926.

Territorial Government. As originally established by the Ordinance of 1787 territorial government provided political rule for the possessions of the United States, subject to congressional control. An elective territorial legislature was established, its laws subject to revision by Congress. The territorial governor and judges were appointed by the President. A territorial delegate sat in the House of Representatives with voice but no vote. This basic form was extended subsequently to the Southwest, Mississippi, and Indian territories organized in 1790, 1798, and 1800. As the WESTWARD

MOVEMENT *opened* new areas to settlement, modifications were made to increase the powers of territorial legislature, extend the rights of the courts. Basically the territorial governments in the last half of the 19th century provided for presidentially appointed governors, secretaries, and judges for four year terms. Two year terms were established for the elected legislature and congressional delegate. Acts of the governors and legislators were subject to congressional approval, and their powers extended to the organization of municipal government and general domestic affairs. A well established system of territorial courts was provided for. With the acquisition of overseas territories after the Spanish-American War drastic modifications were made in the governments of Hawaii, the Philippines, Puerto Rico, the Virgin Islands, and Alaska.

Territory. A possession of the United States which is not part of any state or the District of Columbia. A territory may be organized or unorganized, the former term referring to the establishment of a territorial government. Since 1836 the legislatures in all organized territories have been popularly elected. Under the doctrines of the Insular Cases territories have been recognized as incorporated or unincorporated. Unincorporated territories are those whose citizens possess only the substantive rights of the Constitution and any others which Congress may confer upon them by legislation. The citizens of an incorporated territory are citizens of the United States and enjoy all substantive and procedural rights under the Constitution.

TERRY, Alfred Howe. 1827-1890. Union general. b. Connecticut. Graduated, Yale Law School; served at the first BATTLE OF BULL RUN as a colonel; brigadier general (1862); served at Richmond and Petersburg (1864); brevetted major general of volunteers (1865); conducted a campaign against SITTING BULL; major general in the regular army (1886); resigned (1888).

TESLA, Nikola. 1856-1943. Electrician and inventor. b. Austria-Hungary. Came to the United States (1884); worked for EDISON; became a naturalized citizen; famous for his work in the field of high tension of ELECTRICITY and the development in the field of RADIO transmission; he invented a system of arc lighting, a transformer, wireless systems of communications and power transmission; he designed the great power system at NIAGARA.

Texan Independence, War for. The revolt of Texans against the Mexican government in 1835. Between 1821 and 1835, 25,000 Texans, mostly from the United States, had migrated to the province under the stimulus of a liberal Mexican land policy. The lure of free land suitable for COTTON culture attracted most of them from the southern slave states. A change in government in 1829 brought about a restriction of American IMMIGRATION and a change in land policy. Sporadic armed conflicts after 1832 altered the previous conditions of peace in Texas. On October 2, 1835 the first pitched battle broke out. By December the Mexican towns of Gonzales, Goliad, and San Antonio had fallen to the Texans. In March, 1836 the Mexican commander, SANTA ANNA, defeated the Texans at the ALAMO. Another Texan force of 400 men was captured near Goliad. By April a reorganized Texas army under General SAM HOUSTON decisively defeated Santa Anna, who was captured. A convention declared Texas to be independent on March 2, 1836.

Texas. The largest state in size, with an area of 267,339 square miles. Entered the Union on December 29, 1845 as the 28th state. Seceded on March 2, 1861 and readmitted on March 30, 1870. Austin is the capital. In 1950 Texas' POPULATION of 7,711,194 made it sixth in rank. Its largest cities are Houston, Dallas, and San Antonio. Texas constitutes one-twelfth of the area of the United States and is 220 times as large as Rhode Island, the smallest state. Its resources make it one of the richest political subdivisions in the world. Texas' leading products are oil, natural gas, cotton, and cattle. Other important crops are wool, onions, corn, oats, wheat, barley, rye, and sorghum. Helium and sulphur are important minerals. Amarillo has the only helium plant in the nation. The most elevated highway bridge in the world runs over the Nueces River at Port Arthur. The deepest hole in the world, an oil well 15,279 feet deep, is located in Pecos County. Texas was discovered by Cabeza de Vaca in 1528. Its nickname is the "Lone Star State."

Texas Rangers. A semi-military mounted police force first organized in 1836 as a local body of settlers with the purpose of defense against Indian attacks. During the Texas War they were reorganized by General HOUSTON who built up their strength to a force of 1,600 men. They served in the Civil War as an element of the Confederate Army and were reorganized in the 1870's. As a police force at this time, the Rangers protected hundreds of miles of the Texas frontier against Indians, hold-up men, rustlers, and bandits. They operated without uniforms or standard procedures, being authorized as roving commissions for specific duties. The Rangers were famous for their skill and ability, and exercised great moral influence in the state. Their exploits have served as a source of much dramatic and literary material.

Textile Industry. The introduction of automatic spinning and weaving machinery before the Civil War replaced homespun goods. Cotton displaced flax and wool as the principal textile, increasing enormously with the use of steam and then electric power by the end of the 19th century. Today the three leading fabrics manufactured in the United States are prints, cotton, and silk and rayon broad goods. In 1952 there were in this country approximately 24,000,000 cotton spinning spindles producing almost 10,000,000,000 linear yards of cotton broad woven goods. In that year almost 2,500,000,000 linear yards of rayon broad woven fabrics were produced and almost 12,500,000,000 yards of nylon, silk, and synthetic broad woven fabrics. The industry in that year had over 8,000 establishments which employed well over 1,000,000 workers in the production of textile mill products whose value was increased by manufacturing by almost $5,000,000,000.

Thanksgiving Day. Celebrated nationally on the fourth Thursday in November by act of Congress in 1941. The first such national proclamation was by President LINCOLN in 1863 on the urging of Mrs. Sarah J. Hale, editor of GODEY'S LADY BOOK. It has been generally believed that the holiday dates back to the day of thanks ordered by Governor BRADFORD of PLYMOUTH COLONY in 1621. Scholars, however, point out that days of thanks are biblical in origin and stem from ancient times.

THAYER, Eli. 1819-1899. Educator, ABOLITIONIST, and inventor. b. Massachusetts. Graduated from Brown University; after the passage of the KANSAS-NEBRASKA bill he organized the New England Emigrant Aid Society which sent anti-slavery settlers into that territory; Republican member, U. S. House of Representatives (1857-61); supported LINCOLN; invented a hydraulic elevator and a sectional safety steam boiler. Author of A HISTORY OF THE KANSAS CRUSADE (1889) and other books.

Theatre. The colonial theatre was hampered in its development by church opposition. Although amateur drama was performed in the 17th century, it was not until the opening of the 18th that professional performances became common. New York saw many plays after 1700. The first American theatre as such was built in Williamsburg, Virginia in 1716. In addition to religious prejudice, personal and professional rivalry brought about the statutory banning of stage performances in Massachusetts, Pennsylvania, and Rhode Island from 1750 to 1762. In the other colonies English companies furnished the principal source of talent and production. The John Street Theatre was opened in New York in 1767 and quickly became the most famous in the colonies. At the turn of the 19th century the theatre had scarcely progressed. In 1774 Congress had urged the colonists to discourage shows, plays, and other entertainments during the emergency. Debates in the newspapers and legislative halls thereafter had raised the question of continuing a professional theatre in the country. There were few American playwrights, and England still supplied the bulk of material. William Dunlap, the "Father of the American Drama", wrote, translated, adapted, and managed over 60 plays by 1832 when he published his famous *History of the American Theatre.* Touring companies brought the theatre to the West, traveling down the tributaries of the Ohio, Missouri, and Mississippi rivers. By 1830 theatres had been established in New Orleans, Mobile, St. Louis, and Chicago. San Francisco saw its first professional drama in 1850. By the opening of the Civil War Charlotte Cushman, Edwin Forrest, and Joseph Jefferson had attained national recognition as actors in the American theatre. After the war stars and professionals, rather than local amateur and school productions, characterized the growth of the theatre. Increasingly the thematic material reverted to American

scenes. The last two decades of the century witnessed repeated performances of Denman Thompson's *The Old Homestead,* Lottie Parker's *Way Down East,* and James A. Herne's *Shore Acres.* Comic opera was stimulated after the production in 1878 of Gilbert and Sullivan's *Pinafore.* REGINALD DE KOVEN and VICTOR HERBERT became internationally famous for their charming operettas. Stock companies, utilizing the rapidly expanding railroad system of the nation, brought the classics as well as light opera to the towns and hamlets of the United States. This era saw the rise of the melodrama, farce, and burlesque show. New York City became the center of American drama, conducting performances of great merit. After 1900 the American theatre reflected the currents of American life. The romanticism of the preceding era was replaced by the "problem play," muckraking, and psychological drama. The great names of John Drew, David Warfield, Mrs. Fiske, Mrs. Leslie Carter, the Barrymores, and Otis Skinner elevated the theatre of this time to its pinnacle of achievement. European importations enjoyed a revival until after World War I. The 1920's and 1930's witnessed a relative decline in the American theatre, emphasized by the lack of funds and patronage during the GREAT DEPRESSION. Attempts to offset this decline revolved around the development of the municipal theatre, the little theatre movement, amateur productions, and the theatre projects of the WPA. The period of World War II produced some of the greatest drama in American theatrical history. Before the war expressions of disillusionment with the smug conventions and tenets of success of American life were found in the plays of MAXWELL ANDERSON, Laurence Stallings, Sydney Howard, George S. Kaufman, and George Kelly. A return to realism was reflected in the work of EUGENE O'NEILL, Elmer Rice, Clifford Odets, and Jack Kirkland. Robert Sherwood became famous for his historical plays. Among the distinguished actors of the American stage between the world wars were Helen Hayes, Paul Muni, Katharine Cornell, Tullulah Bankhead, Basil Rathbone, Frederic March, Claude Rains, Joseph Schildkraut, Betty Field, Uta Hagen, Jose Ferrer, Judith Anderson, Walter Hampden, Lynn Fontaine, and Alfred Lunt.

Third Party Movements. The participation in presidential campaigns of minor parties. Although generally unsuccessful in achieving electoral victories, third parties have occasionally influenced the outcome of these elections. In 1848 the FREE-SOIL PARTY insured the election of the WHIG candidate by drawing votes from the Democratic party in New York State. In 1860 the Republican candidate was elected because of the split in the Democratic party, the DOUGLAS voters drawing enough ballots from BRECKENRIDGE to insure LINCOLN's election. In 1912 the PROGRESSIVE candidate, T. ROOSEVELT, drew enough votes from TAFT to accomplish WILSON's election. The third party movement has also been important in raising political issues and advancing programs which have later been adopted by the major parties and enacted by Congress or the States. Such planks as regulation of monopolies, direct election of United States Senators, WOMAN'S SUFFRAGE, the INCOME TAX, universal tax-supported education, regulation of business, and many labor and social welfare programs were originally included in third party platforms.

Third Term Tradition. The refusal of Presidents to run for a third term. The tradition was based on the declination of George WASHINGTON as expressed in his FAREWELL ADDRESS. There have been occasions when third terms were sought, but until the re-election of F. D. ROOSE-

VELT in 1940 the tradition had been kept intact. The 22ND AMENDMENT prohibits a third term.

Thirteenth Amendment. See abolition of slavery.

Thomas Alva Edison Foundation. Established in 1946. Its objectives are the promotion of the well-being of the people by conducting research and discovery in the arts, science, and industry. It also carries on charitable, scientific, literary, and educational activities within the United States and its possessions. Accessory functions include research in the conduct of public administration and government with particular emphasis in the fields in which Edison made notable contributions. Its principal office is located in West Orange, New Jersey.

Thomas Amendment. A section of the AGRICULTURAL ADJUSTMENT ACT of 1933 which conferred on the President discretionary power to inflate the CURRENCY in several ways. He was authorized to order the FEDERAL RESERVE BOARD to purchase additional United States obligations to issue $3,000,000,000 in FIAT CURRENCY, establish a BI-METALLIC standard, or proclaim a reduction in the gold content of the dollar by not more than 50 percent.

THOMAS, George Henry. 1816-1870. Union general. b. Virginia. Graduated, U.S.M.A., West Point (1840); served as brigadier general of volunteers; served with heroism at CHICKAMAUGA in defending his position when the rest of the army retreated and he was given the nickname of "the Rock of Chickamauga" (1863); commanded the Army of the Cumberland with Grant at the BATTLE OF CHATTANOOGA; took part in SHERIDAN's ATLANTA campaign (1864); defeated HOOD at Nashville (1864) and was made a major general in the regular army; commanded the Military Division of the Pacific (1869-70).

THOMAS, Norman Mattoon. 1884-1968.

628

Socialist leader. Graduated, Princeton University (1905); graduated, Union Theological Seminary (1911) and served in several Presbyterian churches in New York City; resigned from the ministry (1931); founder and editor, *The World Tomorrow* (1918-21); associate editor, *The Nation* (1921-22); well-known speaker on economic and political affairs; SOCIALIST candidate for governor of New York (1924), for mayor of New York City (1925 and 1929); and for the President of the United States (1928, 1932, 1936, 1940, 1944, and 1948). Author of many books on American politics and economics.

THOMAS, Theodore. 1835-1905. Violinist and conductor. b. Germany. Came to the United States (1845); conducted Chicago Symphony Orchestra (1891-1905) and the NEW YORK PHILHARMONIC SOCIETY; important for his knowledge and conducting of symphonic music; with LEOPOLD DAMROSCH, he was most important in furthering music appreciation in the United States.

THOMPSON, Jacob. 1810-1885. Politician. b. North Carolina. Practiced law in Mississippi; member, U.S. House of Representatives (1839-51); appointed by BUCHANAN, U. S. Secretary of the Interior (1857-61); resigned to join the Confederate army; served as inspector general and special agent in Canada; thought to be responsible for attacks on the United States from the Canadian border.

THOMPSON, Richard Wigginton, 1809-1900. Politician. b. Virginia. Studied and practiced law in Indiana; WHIG member of the House of Representatives (1841-43, 1847-49); an organizer of the CONSTITUTIONAL UNION PARTY; appointed by Hayes, U. S. Secretary of the Navy (1877-80). Author of a number of books on history and religion.

THOMPSON, Smith. 1768-1843. Jurist. b. New York. Graduated, Princeton (1788); practiced law; associate justice of supreme court of New York (1802-14); chief justice (1814-18); U.S. Secretary of the Navy (1819-23); Associate Justice, U.S. Supreme Court (1823-43).

THOMSON, Charles. 1729-1824. Revolutionary patriot. b. Ireland. Came to America (1739); settled in Delaware; became successful merchant in Philadelphia (from 1760); active in pre-Revolutionary activity; called by JOHN ADAMS the "SAMUEL ADAMS of Philadelphia"; first secretary of the CONTINENTAL CONGRESS (1774-89).

THOREAU, Henry David. 1817-1862. Naturalist and author. b. Massachusetts. Graduated, Harvard (1837); one of the original transcendentalists with EMERSON, MARGARET FULLER, HAWTHORNE, RIPLEY and ALCOTT; famous for living at a retreat, Walden Pond, Concord (July 4, 1845-September 6, 1847) and writing one of the outstanding books by an American: *Walden, or Life in the Woods* (1854); his letters, manuscripts and journals were published as *The Writings of Henry David Thoreau* (20 vols., 1906).

THORNTON, Matthew. 1714-1803. Revolutionary patriot and physician. b. Ireland. Came to America when young; practiced medicine in New Hampshire; chairman of COMMITTEE OF SAFETY; member of the CONTINENTAL CONGRESS (1776 and 1778); signer of the DECLARATION OF INDEPENDENCE; judge of the New Hampshire supreme court (1776-82).

THORNTON, William. 1759-1828. Architect. b. West Indies. Graduated Edinburgh as a doctor (1784); came to the United States (1788) and settled in Delaware; moved to Philadelphia; won competition for design of the National CAPITOL at Washington, D. C. (1792); design approved by President WASHINGTON; commissioner of the District of Columbia (1794-1802); designed a number of private homes in Washington, D. C.

629

Three-fifths Compromise. The reconciliation of southern and northern views on the counting of slaves for purposes of direct TAXATION and representation in the lower house of the Congress. The South desired that slaves be considered persons in determining population for representation, but as chattels in determining direct taxes. The North held the opposite viewpoint. The issue arose at the Constitutional Convention after decision had been reached that direct taxes should be apportioned among the states according to population and that representation in the lower house of Congress would be based on POPULATION. The compromise provided that "three-fifths of all other persons" should be added to the whole number of free persons in determining the population of a state for purposes of representation and direct taxes.

THURMAN, Allen Granberry. 1813-1895. Politician. b. Virginia. Admitted to the bar and practiced in Ohio; member, U.S. House of Representatives (1845-47); U.S. Senator (1869-81); outstanding Democratic leader and supporter of the Thurman Act concerning financing of the Pacific railroads; unsuccessful candidate for the presidential and vice-presidential nomination on the Democratic party ticket (1876, 1880, 1884, 1888).

Ticonderoga, Battle of. See Green Mountain Boys, Ethan Allen, Benedict Arnold, and General John Burgoyne.

"Tidal Wave." The term applied to the great political successes of the Democratic party in federal and state elections in 1872 and 1876. These successes resulted from the corruption of "CARPETBAGGER" and "SCALAWAG" governments generally understood to be under Republican domination.

Tideland Oil Dispute. A controversy between the United States government and the governments of Texas, California, and Louisiana. The dispute dates back to the 1930's when exploitation revealed the existence of huge quantities of OIL in the underwater land lying along the coasts of the three states. The oil content of these lands has been valued between $10,000,-000,000 and $100,000,000,000. The potential yield has been estimated at 250,-000 barrels a day, valued at $250,000,-000 annually. These deposits have been largely untapped because of the disputed ownership of the lands. Until 1947 the three states held undisputed control, but in that year the Supreme Court ruled that the federal government has "paramount rights." In 1950 the Court reinforced its earlier decision by another which declared that the federal government has dominion over the submerged land even though the states had always assumed ownership. The Court's decisions applied to a three-mile-wide belt paralleling the coast and known as the marginal seas. By 1950 the three states had leased these lands to various oil companies which had invested $500,000,000 in leases and equipment. As a result of the 1950 Court decision the federal government impounded the lease money which, by 1952, amounted to $8,000,000. On May 29, 1952 President TRUMAN vetoed a bill of Congress which would have restored title in these lands to the coastal states. The President's VETO was accompanied by a message in which he declared that his disapproval was based on the thinking that the income from these lands properly belongs to the federal government and that approval would have turned over "to certain states as a free gift, very valuable land and mineral resources of the United States as a whole." In May, 1953 Congress passed the Tidelands Oil Law which gave coastal states the rights to all minerals in submerged lands within their historic boundaries. Control of the remainder of the continental shelf was retained by the federal government.

Tidewater Section. That part of the Atlantic coastal plain spreading east of the river areas and touched by the ocean tides. This section was the first frontier in American history and was the seat of the mercantile, SHIPPING, and plantation wealth in the period before the American Revolution. The tidewater gentry's control of the economic and political power of colonial America developed serious conflicts which resulted in BACON'S REBELLION in 1676, the Paxton Riots of 1765, and the UPRISING OF THE REGULATORS in 1767. Their control of colonial legislatures brought them decided advantages in debt and tax matters at the expense of the back-country population.

TILDEN, Samuel Jones. 1814-1886. Political leader. b. New York. Graduated, Yale and New York University Law School; practiced law in New York City; leader of the Democrats known as the "BARNBURNERS" (1845); joined FREE-SOIL Movement and supported LINCOLN; became leader of Democratic party in New York State and led fight to break the TWEED RING (1868-72); governor of New York (1875-76); Democratic candidate against HAYES for the presidency of the United States (1876) and lost by one ELECTORAL VOTE; the results have often been contested; left his money to a Tilden Trust to be used for a free public library in New York City. He was an honest and outstanding leader.

TILDEN, William T. Jr. 1893-1953. Tennis champion. Better known as "Big Bill" Tilden. b. Philadelphia, Pa. Graduated, Pennsylvania (1922); tennis champion of the world (1920-25); member, U.S. Davis Cup Team; turned a professional tennis player (1931); famous exhibition player and teacher. Famous for his "cannon-ball" service.

TILLMAN, Benjamin Ryan. 1847-1918. Politician. b. South Carolina. Reform governor of South Carolina (1890-94); U. S. Senator (1895-1918); opposed

CLEVELAND and T. ROOSEVELT; supported BRYAN and his silver policies; supported WILSON and a naval expansion program.

Timber Culture. The activities involved in preserving and profitably utilizing the timberlands of the United States. At its beginnings half of the nation was forest land, the greatest portion of which was desired for agricultural purposes. This plus the abundance of timber resulted in the burning and other useless destruction of vast quantities of wood to permit farming. At the opening of the 20th century, organized land reclamation and REFORESTATION programs were instituted in an attempt to preserve the nation's forest resources. Particular attention has been paid to the 120,000,000 acres of "non-commercial, cut-over" forest land which is non-productive, unimproved, and not necessary for farm purposes. In 1873 Congress passed the Timber Culture Act, the first of several laws dealing with the problem. This Act granted 160 acres of treeless lands to settlers who were encouraged to plant trees on this TERRITORY.

Timber Culture Act. See timber culture.

"Tippecanoe and Tyler Too." A slogan raised by the WHIG party in the presidential election campaign of 1840. Its presidential candidate WILLIAM HENRY HARRISON had been the general in command at the defeat of TECUMSEH's Indian confederacy at the battle of Tippecanoe in 1811. See Tippecanoe, Battle of.

Tippecanoe, Battle of. Fought in 1811 between an Indian Confederacy organized by the two Shawnee chieftains TECUMSEH and his brother the PROPHET, and General WILLIAM HENRY HARRISON, the governor of Indiana Territory. Harrison, leading a force of 900 troops, destroyed the Indian village on Tippecanoe creek and put an end to the then existing Indian threat to westward migration in the Mississippi area. This victory also had the effect of breaking up the British incitation of Indian tribes to attack American settlements in this area.

Tobacco Industry. An important consumers' non-durable goods industry centered in the southern and southwestern states of the United States. North Carolina is the largest producer of tobacco and its products. In 1963 over 2,272,-000,000 pounds of tobacco were produced netting an income of approximately $1,252,000,000.

TOCQUEVILLE, Alexis de. 1805-1859. French writer. On a special mission to the United States for his government (1831) he toured the United States and wrote a book *Democracy in America* (1835) which has become a famous defense of democracy and an excellent picture of America at that time.

TODD, David. 1855-1938. Astronomer. b. New York. Graduated, Amherst College; professor of astronomy and higher mathematics at Amherst and Smith College; in charge of many solar eclipse expeditions to various parts of the world. First to photograph the solar corona from an airplane (1925); invented an automatic device for photographing eclipses. Author of many books on his subject.

"Toledo War." A series of minor border skirmishes in 1835 and 1836 between the militia of Michigan and Ohio. The boundary dispute, over a strip of land averaging six and one half miles in width, arose out of Michigan's claim as laid down in the ORDINANCE OF 1787 and Ohio's claim as laid down in its state constitution accepted by Congress upon Ohio's ADMISSION INTO THE UNION. Congress' acceptance of Michigan's application for admission to the Union in 1837 involved that state's agreement to a compromise boundary.

Toleration Acts. Laws of the colonial assemblies granting RELIGIOUS TOLERATION to persons not affiliated with established churches. In 1644 Rhode Island conferred freedom of religion. In 1682 the Pennsylvania charter allowed religious liberty to those who believed in God, a principle which was modified in 1706 by the denial of religious freedom to Jews and Catholics. The TOLERATION ACT OF 1649 in Maryland established religious toleration. The QUAKERS provided for religious freedom in Jersey in 1681 and 1683. An act of 1708 allowed freedom of worship in Connecticut, but did not relieve persons who were not members of the established church from paying taxes in support of that church.

TOMPKINS, Daniel D. 1774-1825. Political leader. b. New York. Graduated, Columbia and admitted to the bar(1797); leader of the Republican party in New York State; associate justice, New York State supreme court (1804-07); governor of New York (1807-17); opposed SLAVery; Vice-President of the United States during the two MONROE administrations (1817-25).

"Tom Thumb." The locomotive built by PETER COOPER for the BALTIMORE AND OHIO RAILROAD. It was the first steam locomotive on an American railroad, and in its test on August 28, 1830 raced a horse drawn car out of Baltimore. A mechanical defect prevented the Tom Thumb from beating the other vehicle.

TOOMBS, Robert Augustus. 1810-1885. Confederate statesman. b. Georgia. Successful lawyer; member, U.S. House of Representatives (1845-53); leader of the Southern faction defending STATES RIGHTS and SLAVERY; supported the COMPROMISE OF 1850; U.S. Senator (1853-61); joined the Confederate States of America having favored SECESSION (1861); served as Secretary of State in the Confederacy; served as brigadier general at the SECOND BATTLE OF BULL RUN and at ANTIETAM; resigned his commission (1863); did not support JEFFERSON DAVIS' policies and caused dissention in the Confederacy; fled to London (1865-67) spent time in CUBA and Europe returning to Georgia to resume his law practice; refused to ask pardon and regain his CITIZENSHIP, remaining a "FIRE-EATER" to the end.

Topeka Constitution. A free-state constitution drawn by a convention at Topeka, Kansas between October 23 and November 12, 1855. The convention was attended by 51 delegates of whom 37 signed the document. It endorsed the principle of POPULAR SOVEREIGNTY, included a bill of rights prohibiting SLAVERY, prohibited the service of free Negroes in the Militia, and provided for a REFERENDUM on the issue of Kansas' ADMISSION TO THE UNION. It allowed male white citizens and civilized male Indians to vote. The Constitution was ratified on December 15, 1855, and in January a governor and legislature were chosen. In March, 1856 the legislature elected United States Senators and applied for admission to the Union under this Constitution. The House of Representatives voted for admission in July, but the Senate rejected the petition. See Kansas-Nebraska Bill, "bleeding Kansas," and Lecompton Constitution.

TORBERT, Alfred Thomas Archimedes. 1833-1880. Union general. Graduated U.S.M.A., West Point (1855); served with the ARMY OF THE POTOMAC; saw action at BULL RUN and ANTIETAM; served as brigadier general at GETTYSBURG; served as commander of a cavalry unit with SHERIDAN and SHERMAN and brevetted major general (1865).

Tories. See Loyalists.

TOSCANINI, Arturo. 1867-1957. Italian cellist and conductor. Successful as a musician and conductor in Europe and South America; conducted opera at La Scala, Milan; conducted the NEW YORK PHILHARMONIC - SYMPHONY ORCHESTRA, PHILADELPHIA ORCHESTRA, and is well-known as the conductor of the National Broadcasting Company's Symphony Orchestra (from 1937). He is considered the outstanding conductor in the United States today. He is famous for his unusual memory, being able to conduct without a score. His many recordings have been an important contribution in the field of music.

Town Meeting. A meeting of the citizens of New England towns in the colonial period. These meetings were called for the purpose of legislating directly in matters of interest to the town. The town meeting is the only example of direct democracy in American history. Contemporary meetings of this sort are CITIZENS' meetings generally called for the purpose of discussing important political issues. Today the governments of towns are administered by boards of SELECT MEN and mayors.

Townsend Plan. A social security plan originated by Dr. Francis E. Townsend in 1934. It provided that all CITIZENS 60 years of age and over receive an annual pension from the United States Treasury, not exceeding $200 per month. The receipt of this annuity was contingent upon its expenditure within the United States not later than five days thereafter. The estimated annual cost of $20,000,000,-000, was to be financed by a two percent business transaction tax. The Plan's supporters argued that it would solve all the economic problems of the current DEPRESSION, but it was attacked as economically unsound and inflationary in effect. It was never adopted.

Townshend Acts. Legislated in 1767 by parliament under the sponsorship of the British Chancellor of the Exchequer, Charles Townshend. The Acts imposed duties upon glass, lead, paper, tea, and painters' colors. They were passed for the purpose of raising revenue lost by the repeal of the STAMP ACT and to demonstrate Townshend's insistence on the power of parliament to tax the British colonies. The legislation also provided for the revival of WRITS OF ASSISTANCE and for the establishment of a board of customs commissioners with jurisdiction extending from Labrador to Florida. The Acts aroused instant opposition in the colonies and contributed greatly to the onset of the American Revolution.

TRACY, Benjamin Franklin. 1830-1915. Lawyer and politician. b. New York. Admitted to the bar (1851); helped organize the Republican party in the state; brigadier general of volunteers during the Civil War; he served as counsel for HENRY WARD BEECHER in the TILDEN VS. Beecher trials (1875); judge, New York Court of Appeals (1881-82); U.S. Secretary of the Navy (1889-93); sometimes called the "Father of the American Navy" because he increased the construction of modern battleships and cruisers and generally reorganized the department and the standards of the service.

Trade. See commerce.

Trade Agreements Act. Passed by Congress in 1934. It gave the President the power for three years to negotiate tariff agreements with foreign governments and to increase or reduce rates by not more than 50 percent. Although the law did not repeal the HAWLEY-SMOOT TARIFF ACT of 1930 it put tariff revisions in the hands of the state department rather than Congress. Secretary of State HULL, who is generally considered to have been the father of the law, negotiated approximately 30 such tariff treaties by 1937. The most-favored-nation clause of the Act provided for the benefits of each agreement to be extended to those nations not discriminating against the United States in tariff matters. The objective of the law was to accelerate economic recovery, and official statistics showed that by 1940 trade had materially increased with agreement countries by a greater percentage than with non-agreement countries.

Trade Association. An organization of business firms within a given industry. Its objectives are the improvement of business relationships, increase of profits, lobbying for desired legislation, elimination of unfair competition,, and the enhancement of LABOR RELATIONS. Although trade associations appeared in the United States before the Civil War, it was not until the 20th century that they occupied a prominent role in American industry. The member firms generally agree to standardize their practices, engage in cooperative advertising, and negotiate with unions as a group. They have been denounced for MONOPOLY practices involving market control through unified price policies and sales practices. Among the important trade associations in the United States are the NATIONAL ASSOCIATION OF MANUFACTURERS, Association of American Railroads, National Electric Light Association, and National Retail Dry Goods Association.

Trade, Foreign. Refers to the exports and imports of the United States. The value of American foreign trade has progressively increased over the years, totaling in 1963 over $40,000,000,000. Excess of exports over imports was over $5,000,-000,000 in that year.

Trade Expansion Act (1962). Authorizes President to make agreements with other nations which could remove all import duties on a reciprocal basis. The law provides that workers, whose jobs are lost through foreign competition, will receive cash allowances up to $61.00 weekly for unemployment and retraining for as long as 78 weeks.

Trade Unions. Also known as craft or horizontal unions. Refers to a form of labor organization based on membership in a given trade or craft, generally skilled. In such a union non-skilled and semi-skilled employees are customarily but not always excluded from membership. The most important national trade union organization in American history has been the AMERICAN FEDERATION OF

LABOR. Its unions have organized the following crafts: teamsters, plumbers, electricians, typographers, printers, painters and decorators, etc. See AFL-CIO for recent merger.

Trading with the Enemy Act. A federal law of October 6, 1917 defining trade with the CENTRAL POWERS, prohibiting such trade, and providing severe penalties for violation. The act established a licensing system over imports and exports and a conservation list of non-exportable commodities. It established the WAR TRADE BOARD to assure the acquisition of essential raw materials. A blacklist of all firms suspected of carrying on commercial relations with the enemy was prepared and to such companies American exporters were denied the privilege of shipping goods. The Act also established the office of the ALIEN PROPERTY CUSTODIAN.

"Tragic Era." See Reconstruction.

Transcendentalism. A philosophical movement which derived its name from the philosophy of Schelling. It expressed the philosophy of belief in the objective realities of the world which could be best analyzed by questioning the subjective consciousness. As developed by Kant Transcendentalism held that the essential qualities and inborn character of man transcended experience. The philosophy became the nucleus of the liberal, social, and intellectual revival in New England in the 1830's and 1840's. In 1836 RALPH WALDO EMERSON founded the Transcendental Club before which the most prominent American cultural figures spoke. Transcendentalism exercised great influence on the Unitarian religion and advocated programs of social and economic reform including Utopian Socialist principles, community organization, and anti-slavery propaganda. Their leaders were Emerson, MARGARET FULLER, HENRY DAVID THOREAU, and THEODORE PARKER.

Trans-Mississippi West. Exploration and occupation of the trans-Mississippi West were encouraged by the LOUISIANA PURCHASE. As early as 1812 the population of Louisiana was large enough to warrant its admission as a state, followed by Missouri in 1820. The FRONTIER line, by 1830, moved across the western boundary of Arkansas, Louisiana, and Missouri. By the opening of the Civil War Iowa, Minnesota, and Texas had already been admitted into the Union, and the territories of Kansas and Nebraska had been settled. The earliest important explorations were those of the LEWIS AND CLARK EXPEDITION in 1804-1806. In 1806 ZEBULON M. PIKE explored the Mississippi to its source and later moved up the Arkansas and Red Rivers to the ROCKY MOUNTAINS. In 1811 JOHN JACOB ASTOR established a fur post at Astoria on the Columbia River and, under the influence of a COLONIZATION society organized by Hall J. Kelley, thousands of settlers moved into Oregon in the 1830's. Missionaries, led by MARCUS WHITMAN, brought many others into the Oregon country in the 1830's and 40's. Meanwhile hunters, fishermen, trappers, traders, explorers, FARMERS, and pioneers were moving southward along the SANTA FE TRAIL and westward into California. The Mormons settled near the GREAT SALT LAKE in 1847. The discovery of gold in California the following year attracted about 80,000 settlers to the west coast, an area that had previously been explored by JOHN C. FREMONT. By the Civil War the trans-Mississippi West was already producing great mineral and agricultural wealth for the American people.

Transportation. In the colonies water TRANSPORTATION on the coastal rivers and inlets furnished the most appropriate means of transportation. The vessels in use included schooners, sloops, barges, flatboats, and various forms of sailing boats. These methods were employed basically by the farmer to carry his goods to market. Travel on land was done by foot or on horseback, supplemented, by the end of the 18th century, by the STAGECOACH. In urban communities the stagecoach was preceded by two-wheeled vehicles drawn by a horse. Its various forms included the cart, the chaise, and the chariot. With the growth of the United States after the American Revolution and because of postal needs, road and highway improvement proceeded rapidly. The toll road, the turnpike, the surfaced highway, and improvements to bridges and internal waterways became the link between the East and the rapidly expanding West. Overland freight was moved for several decades before the Civil War in the Conestoga Wagon. The most striking transportation developments in American history were the RAILROAD and the STEAMBOAT. Following the launching of Fulton's *Clermont* in 1807 the steamboat replaced the barge and flatboat on western rivers. In the 1850's more than 1,000 steamboats plied the Mississippi River alone. The opening of the Baltimore and Ohio Railroad on July 4, 1828 set off the spectacular railroad construction program that has made the United States preeminent in this field. Before it conquered the West the railroad was preceded by the express companies which conducted trade between the Mississippi Valley and the west coast. By 1860 there were almost 270 such companies in California alone, their work in the field of postal transportation being supplemented by the PONY EXPRESS. The invention of the internal combustion engine and its application to wheeled vehicles by the opening of the 20th century inaugurated a new era in transportation. The automobile, truck, and motor bus have grown into major rivals of the railroad industry in the transportation of goods and persons. The invention and improvement of the airplane since 1900 has added a new and significant element to the transportation of goods and passengers.

Transportation Act of 1940. See Wheeler-Lea Transportation Act.

Treason. The definition of and method of conviction for treason are carefully set down in Article III, Section 3 of the federal Constitution. By removing from Congress the power of defining treason the founding fathers sought to guarantee that charges of this heinous crime would not be lightly made. Treason against the United States can consist only in making war against it or assisting its enemies. No person may be convicted of treason except on the testimony of two witnesses to an overt act or on confession in open court. Congress is given the power to declare punishment for treason.

Treasury Certificates. Notes issued by the TREASURY DEPARTMENT for the purchase of silver under the SHERMAN SILVER PURCHASE ACT. Treasury certificates were redeemable in gold. The result was a drain upon the federal government's gold holdings between 1890 and 1893 as silver vendors redeemed them after selling silver to the Treasury. At the request of President CLEVELAND, Congress repealed the Sherman Act in 1893 to prevent the further decline of the government's stock of gold.

Treasury, Department of. An EXECUTIVE DEPARTMENT established by Congress in 1789. Its head is the Secretary of the Treasury, appointed by the President and Senate of the United States. He is one of nine executive heads collectively known as the cabinet. The Treasury Department supervises the collection of customs duties and internal revenues, coins money, administers the narcotic laws, sells bonds, supervises the NATIONAL BANKS, and administers supplies and services for the general needs of the federal government. During peace time the U.S. Coast Guard is under its jurisdiction. The secret service division has the function of protecting the person of the President, investigating thefts of public property, and investigating violations of the revenue and counterfeit laws.

TREAT, Robert. 1622-1710. Colonial governor. b. England. Settled in the Connecticut colony as a child; went with a group of settlers to New Jersey where he was one of the leaders in the founding of the city of Newark (1666-71); commanded the forces of Connecticut during the KING PHILIP'S WAR; governor of Connecticut (1683); fought against the surrender of the Connecticut charter; served on ANDROS' council and when the latter was ousted he again became governor of Connecticut (until 1698); served as deputy governor (1698-1708).

Treaty. An agreement between two or more sovereign states designed to establish, change, or terminate certain rights or obligations. The subject matter of a treaty may include virtually anything of importance to the signatories, such as TRADE, IMMIGRATION, NATURALIZATION, war, and territorial adjustment. See Treaty Making Power.

Treaty-Making Power. The President of the United States is authorized under Article II, Section 2 of the federal Constitution to make treaties by and with the advice and consent of the Senate, provided two thirds of the Senators present concur. This power of the Senate has often been attacked. Secretary of State HAY referred to the Senate as "the graveyard of treaties." Although the House of Representatives is not directly concerned in treaty-making, its control over treaties lies in its power to refuse appropriations which may be necessary for their execution. In the actual process of treaty negotiations the Secretary of State customarily acts as the President's emissary.

Treaty of San Lorenzo. See Pinckney Treaty.

Trent Affair. Name applied to a dispute between the United States and Great Britain arising out of the stopping of the British mail steamer *Trent* at Havana by the Union war vessel *San Jacinto* in 1861. On the British ship were two Confederate emissaries MASON and SLIDELL, traveling to England and France respectively, in the attempt to obtain recognition of the Confederacy by these nations. Although Captain WILKES of the *San Jacinto* was hailed in the North, and congratulated formally by the Navy Department and the House of Representatives, this obvious violation of international law was recognized by President LINCOLN who ordered the release of the two Southerners.

Trenton, Battle of. Fought on Christmas night, 1776 when General WASHINGTON undertook to seize the British force of 1400 troops, including a large number of Hessians. Dividing his army into three columns, he ordered them across the Delaware River. Although two were turned back by obstacles, Washington led the third column eight miles through a sleet storm. In the ensuing battle the British commander Colonel Dall was killed and 1000 of his men captured. Nine days later, having recrossed the river, Washington defeated a strong British column at Princeton. The effects of the two victories were a revival of American hope, an increased enlistment of troops, and the ultimate successful solicitation of French, Spanish, and Dutch assistance.

"Triangular Trade." See rum, manufacture of.

Trident. The Polaris and Poseidon missile-launching submarines are expected to be replaced by the new Trident missiles with their range of 4,000 nautical miles. The Trident missiles and submarines are supposed to be less vulnerable to detection.

Tripartite Security Treaty. A treaty of alliance negotiated by the United States, Australia, and New Zealand on Septem-

637

ber 1, 1951. It provided for the peaceful settlement of disputes among the signatories, consultation among them whenever the territorial integrity, political independence, or security of any of them was threatened in the Pacific, recognition that an armed attack in the Pacific on any of them would be dangerous to the peace and safety of them all, and the establishment of a council of their foreign ministers to consider matters concerning the implementation of the Treaty.

Tripoli, Wars with. Two wars fought against the Barbary pirates in the western Mediterranean between 1801-1805 and in 1815. The first war arose when the Barbary states of Morocco, Algiers, Tripoli, and Tunis declared war on the United States because of the latter's refusal to pay the annual tribute which had been regularly granted since after the American Revolution. It was almost entirely a naval conflict, at first weakly prosecuted by the American navy. Many American ships were seized until a blockade of Tripoli was established in 1803. By the Treaty of 1805 the Tripoli governments agreed to abolish all annual payments, and the United States government paid a $60,000 ransom for the officers and crew of the *Philadelphia,* who had been captured two years earlier. Payments continued to the other three governments because of the inability of the American fleet to guarantee shipping in the Mediterranean in the era preceding the War of 1812. The dispatch of STEPHEN DECATUR to Algiers immediately after the war, in 1815, finally produced a treaty which abolished all future payments, and provided for the restitution of American property, the liberation of all Christian slaves who had fled to American vessels, guarantees of humane treatment to war prisoners, and the payment of a $10,000 indemnity for a merchant vessel recently seized. The imposition of equally severe terms upon Tunis and Morocco guaranteed the future of American commerce in this area.

TRIST, Nicholas Philip. 1800-1874. Lawyer and diplomat. b. Virginia. Served as secretary to President JACKSON; consul at Havana (1834-36); sent to Mexico to negotiate end of Mexican War (1847); signed TREATY OF GUADALUPE-HIDALGO (1848).

Truman Doctrine. The name given to the anti-communist principle of foreign policy enunciated by President TRUMAN in March, 1947. In a message to Congress at that time, the President declared it to be the policy of the United States that moral and financial assistance be granted to countries whose political stability was threatened by communism. He requested that Congress appropriate $400,000,000 for military and economic aid to Greece and Turkey to whom should be sent as well American military and economic advisers. This principle has remained the basic tenet of American foreign policy during the "COLD WAR," later supplemented by the principles of the MARSHALL PLAN, the NORTH ATLANTIC TREATY, the Military Arms Program, and the MUTUAL SECURITY PROGRAM.

TRUMAN, Harry S 1884-1973. Thirty-third President of the United States. b. Lamar, Missouri. Served in World War I as an artillery officer; studied law; presiding judge, Jackson County Court, Missouri (1926-34); U.S. Senator (1935-45); elected Vice-President of the United States on the Democratic ticket with F. D. ROOSEVELT as President (1945); at the death of Roosevelt (April 12, 1945) he became President; conferred with Stalin, Churchill, and Attlee at POTSDAM (1945) on the future security of the world; responsible for TRUMAN DOCTRINE (March, 1947); re-elected President (1948); called his administration FAIR DEAL in speech in 1948 campaign; promoted NORTH ATLANTIC TREATY (1949); and MUTUAL SECURITY PROGRAM (1952); vigorous supporter of South Korea when

Korean War broke out in 1950.

TRUMBULL, John. 1750-1831. Jurist and poet. b. Connecticut. Graduated Yale; practised law in Boston and Connecticut; judge of Connecticut superior court (1801-19) and the supreme court of errors (1808-19); a leader of the "Hartford Wits" he was famous for his satirical poems including *The Progress of Dullness* (1772-73), *M'Fingal* (1782), and *Hudibras*. Worked with NOAH WEBSTER in the preparation of his famous dictionary.

TRUMBULL, John. 1756-1843. Painter. b. Connecticut. Son of JONATHAN TRUMBULL (1710-1785). Aide-de-camp to WASHINGTON and adjutant general to GATES during the Revolutionary War; studied with BENJAMIN WEST in London; famous for his portraits of Washington, HAMILTON, and others and for his paintings of important American historical events such as *Battle of Bunker Hill*, *The Signing of Declaration of Independence*, *Surrender of Lord Cornwallis at Yorktown* and many others. There is a Trumbull Gallery at Yale and his works are also hanging in other museums.

TRUMBULL, Jonathan. 1710-1785. Colonial governor and statesman. b. Connecticut. Graduated, Harvard (1727); served as deputy governor and governor of Connecticut (1766-84); aided the Continental army with supplies and was in constant touch with WASHINGTON, the name for an American "Brother Jonathan" was first used by Washington in referring to Trumbull.

TRUMBULL, Jonathan. 1740-1809. Political leader. b. Connecticut. Son of JONATHAN TRUMBULL (1710-85). Served in the Connecticut legislature; was the first comptroller of the U.S. Treasury (1778-79); served as a secretary to WASHINGTON; member, U.S. House of Representatives (1789-95); Speaker of the House (1791-93); U.S. Senator (1795-96); governor of Connecticut (1797-1809). He was a leading FEDERALIST.

TRUMBULL, Lyman. 1813-1896. Jurist and political leader. b. Connecticut. Practised law in Illinois; Illinois supreme court justice (1848-54); U.S. Senator (1855-73); Republican leader who supported LINCOLN; supported JOHNSON even during IMPEACHMENT trial; supported CIVIL SERVICE REFORM legislation; served as counsel for TILDEN before the ELECTORAL COMMISSION (1876); best known for helping to draft the THIRTEENTH AMENDMENT to the federal Constitution.

Trust. A form of business combination in which stock holders of former competing corporations surrendered their shares to a board of trustees in return for trust certificates. The board of trustees exercised full voting powers including the grant of dividends to the holders of trust certificates. The trust is the second known form of MONOPOLY organization, succeeding the POOL which had been outlawed in TRANSPORTATION by the INTERSTATE COMMERCE ACT. The trust itself was declared illegal by the SHERMAN ANTI-TRUST ACT of 1890. The earliest and best known trust was the STANDARD OIL COMPANY agreements in 1879 and 1882 at which time it controlled 90 percent of the refining capacity of the nation. Other important trusts were the Whiskey Trust, 1887, Sugar Trust, 1887, and the American Tobacco Trust, 1901. By 1904, despite the restraints of the Sherman Act, a comprehensive survey listed 318 industrial monopolies with a total capitalization of over $7,000,000,000, representing consolidations of 5300 plants.

"Trust Buster." The nickname applied to President T. ROOSEVELT for his policy of reviving the SHERMAN ANTI-TRUST LAW and ordering the Attorney General to initiate suits against MONOPOLY corporations. Prosecution was begun against the Northern Securities Company, STANDARD OIL COMPANY, American Tobacco Com-

639

pany, and others. Although Roosevelt began 44 suits under the Sherman Act in his tenure of more than seven years as compared with 67 suits begun by President TAFT during his four year term, the phrase has remained associated with Roosevelt because of his showmanship.

TRYON, William. 1729-1788. Colonial governor. b. England. Served as governor of North Carolina (1765-71); suppressed the "UPRISING OF THE REGULATORS" (1771); governor of New York (1771-78); dealt in land speculation in western New York; served as leader of a force of LOYALISTS attacking Connecticut towns and intercepting supplies going to the Continental army.

TUBMAN, Harriet. 1821-1913. Slave leader. b. Maryland. Born a slave, she fled to Philadelphia (1849); responsible for leading more than 300 slaves to the northern states and to Canada on annual trips. She was suppled with money by the ABOLITIONISTS of New York and Boston; she was a confident of JOHN BROWN. Honored by BOOKER T. WASHINGTON, a tablet was erected in her honor in Albany, N. Y. (1914).

TUCKER, John Randolph. 1812-1883. Confederate naval commander. b. Virginia. Commanded the *Patrick Henry* in the BATTLE AT HAMPTON ROADS; commanded the wooden fleet during the battle between the *Merrimac* and the *Monitor* that attempted to defend Drewrys Bluff; commanded the ironclad *Checora* off CHARLESTON (1862); rear admiral in the Peruvian navy serving in the war against Spain; in charge of an expedition along the upper Amazon River (1873).

TUGWELL, Rexford Guy. 1891-
Economist. b. New York. Professor of economics, Columbia University (1920-37); a member of the famous F. D. ROOSE-VELT "BRAIN TRUST" called to Washington, D.C. to act as a consultant to the President (from 1933); Undersecretary of Agriculture (1934-37); co-author of the AGRICULTURE ADJUSTMENT ACT; governor of PUERTO RICO (1941); faculty member, University of Chicago (1946 to present). Author of books on political science and economics.

TURNER, Frederick Jackson. 1861-1932. Historian. b. Wisconsin. Graduated, University of Wisconsin, Harvard and Johns Hopkins (Ph.D. 1890) taught at the University of Wisconsin (1889-1910) and at Harvard (1910-24); famous for his studies of the frontier and the importance of the frontier in the growth of America. Author of *Rise of the New West* (1906), *The Frontier in American History* (1920), and *The Significance of Sections in American History* (1932) which won a Pulitzer Prize.

Turnpikes. Toll roads built by private companies after the American Revolution. Between 1792 and 1810, 170 turnpike companies spent $5,000,000 in building or repairing 3,000 miles of road in New England. In that period a total of 176 companies operated in New York and Pennsylvania, spending up to $13,000 per mile of turnpike. These roads were built over old public roads, in clearings, or over newly chartered paths to link cities and rural communities. Generally turnpikes were not surfaced until after the War of 1812, when gravel and macadam were applied. With the development of CANALS and RAILROADS, turnpike traffic declined. Severe business failures resulted, and by 1825 the securities of these companies were worthless. In the decades up to 1840 the turnpike companies steadily lost money, the majority suffering the loss of their entire investment.

Turner's Rebellion. See Nat Turner's Rebellion.

Tuscarora War. An Indian war fought in North Carolina in 1711-1713. Led by

640

Chief Hancock the Tuscarora Indians attacked the English settlers in September, 1711, almost conquering the entire colony. The Virginia colony negotiated a neutrality agreement with the upper Tuscarora tribe, keeping it from invading North Carolina. From South Carolina military assistance was extended when an expedition of 50 settlers and 350 Indian allies marched against Hancock in January, 1712. A second South Carolina expedition in 1713 brought about the defeat of the Tuscarora who, in the treaty of peace, moved northward. North Carolina's opportunity for WESTWARD EXPANSION was now open.

Tuskegee Institute. A negro institution of higher learning established by the Alabama legislature after the Civil War. Its first president was BOOKER T. WASHINGTON who opened the Institute's first session with 30 students on July 4, 1881. Its faculty is Negro. The Institute has an annual student enrollment of about 2,000 and has graduated more than 35,000. There are ten schools housed in 132 buildings.

TWAIN, Mark. *Pseudonym* of Samuel Clemens. 1835-1910. Humorist and author. b. Missouri. Worked as a journeyman printer, pilot on a Mississippi river boat and as a newspaper reporter; he took the name Mark Twain, which means two fathoms deep when used by leadsmen when taking soundings on the Mississippi; he wrote many books which have become American classics, including *The Jumping Frog of Calaveras County* (1865), *Roughing It* (1872), The *Adventures of Tom Sawyer* (1876), *Life on the Mississippi* (1883), *The Prince and the Pauper* (1882), *Huckleberry Finn* (1885), and *Connecticut Yankee in King Arthur's Court* (1889). He wrote many other works and in his last years when he was short of money he lectured on tour.

Tweed Ring. A political organization in New York City from 1860 to 1871. Ruled by "Boss" Tweed, the ring included A. Oakley Hall, Richard B. Connolly, and Peter B. Sweeney. Operating through bribery and other dishonest practices, it gained a control of TAMMANY HALL and through it dominated the government of the city in 1865. Hall became Mayor, Sweeney, City and County Treasurer, Connolly, City Comptroller, and Tweed, the Superintendent of the Street Department. A new charter forced through by the Ring insured its members of complete control of municipal finances. Due to the vigorous efforts of a reform Democrat, SAMUEL J. TILDEN, as well as an aroused public opinion, frauds on the taxpayers were revealed in the press, and the Ring was overthrown in 1871. It was discovered that the city debt had been increased from $20,000,000 to $101,000,-000. After many adventures, Tweed was ultimately arrested, and died in prison. The other three fled the jurisdiction of the United States.

Twelfth Amendment. Adopted in 1804. It provided that electors cast their ballots seperately for the President and Vice-President of the United States. In the event of a lack of majority in the ELECTORAL COLLEGE the House of Representatives was to choose the President from the candidates with the three highest ELECTORAL VOTES. If the House had not succeeded in doing so by the following March 4th, the Vice-President was to act as President. The Senate was to choose the Vice-President from the candidates with the two highest electoral votes in the event of a lack of majority in the electoral college. The Amendment was adopted as a result of the JEFFERSON-BURR tie in the election of 1800.

Twentieth Amendment. See "Lame Duck" Amendment.

Twentieth Century Fund. Founded in

1919 by the Boston merchant, Edward A. Filene. Its objective is the promotion of improved economic, industrial, civic, and educational conditions in the United States. Since 1937 all its resources have been applied to a program of scientific research and public education in the field of current economic problems. Its office is located in New York City.

Twenty-fifth Amendment. See President and Vice-President replacement.

Twenty-first Amendment. See Repeal Amendment.

Twenty-fourth Amendment. Adopted in 1964. Outlaws the poll tax as a requisite for voting. See Poll tax.

"Twenty-One Demands." A series of demands made by Japan upon China in 1915. Couched as an ultimatum, these demands gave Japan a complete protectorate over China. Since they violated the OPEN-DOOR POLICY and the ROOT-TAKA-HIRA AGREEMENT of 1908, Secretary of State BRYAN issued a vigorous protest. The protest declared that the United States would not recognize any impairment of American rights, the open-door policy, or the territorial and political sovereignty of China. Japan ignored this note and continued her move toward domination of the Far East. It was not until the Washington Naval Conference that the problems of Far Eastern policies were thoroughly negotiated.

Twenty-second Amendment. Adopted in 1951. It provided that no person shall be elected as President more than twice, and no person that has been President for more than two years of a term shall be elected President more than once. The amendment did not apply to President TRUMAN. See Presidency terms of office.

Twenty-sixth Amendment. See Right to vote.

Twenty-third Amendment. Adopted in 1961. Permits the District of Columbia to choose three presidential electors.

TWIGGS, David Emanuel. 1790-1862. Army officer. b. Georgia. Served as a major in the War of 1812; colonel serving with General ZACHARY TAYLOR during the Mexican War; brigadier general (1846); commanded the Department of Texas at the outbreak of the Civil War and surrendered to the Confederate general MC CULLOCH without resistance (1861); commissioned a major general in the Confederate army (1861).

Two-Party System. The political system of a nation in which two major political parties vie for control of the government, minor parties seldom or never succeeding to power. In the United States the two-party system has prevailed since 1787. Only once has a third party succeeded in capturing political power, when the Republican party won the national election of 1860. The first two parties were the FEDERALISTS and ANTI-FEDERALISTS, the latter evolving into the Democratic-Republicans by the mid-1790's. The Federalists were transformed into the National Republicans by 1824 and generally formed the basis of the WHIG PARTY by 1836. The Republican party in 1854 replaced the latter. The present Democratic party has evolved directly from the Democratic-Republicans of the early 19th century. The supporters of the two-party system have argued its necessity on the grounds that it is essential to stable government, exercises political discipline, simplifies VOTING problems, facilitates the creation and operation of legislative majorities, and provides a counter-balancing opposition which prevents the development of dictatorial movements.

TYLER, John. 1790-1862. Tenth President of the United States. b. Virginia. Graduated, William and Mary College (1807); admitted to the bar and practised in Virginia (1809); member, U.S. House of Representatives (1817-21); Jeffersonian Democrat, voted against MISSOURI COMPROMISE; governor of Virginia (1825-27); U.S. Senator (1827-36); became leader of the WHIG party; Vice-President of the United States (1841); succeeded to the presidency on the death of W. H. HARRISON (April 4, 1841); clashed with Whigs; supported the WEBSTER-ASHBUR-TON TREATY, ANNEXATION OF TEXAS, and other Democratic party measures but could not establish a following in that party either; played a small part in the secession of Virginia; lost political prominence.

"Typographical Crowd." See Kitchen Cabinet.

U

UFO. Unidentified flying objects, commonly called "flying saucers" have been the subject of a study by the U.S. Air Force in 1969. The result of the study was that there has been no evidence to show that there are extra-terrestrial space ships.

UMT. See Universal Military Training.

Un-American Activities Committee. A standing committee of the House of Representatives whose chairman in the 82nd Congress, as of December 1, 1951, was Representative John S. Wood of Georgia. It was formerly an ad hoc committee organized in 1937, becoming permanent in 1946. Its functions are the investigation of un-American and subversive activities in the United States. It recommends corrective legislation to the House. Under the original chairmanship of Martin Dies of Texas the committee was frequently denounced for its alleged recklessness in bringing accusation of Communism against various public figures including President F. D. ROOSEVELT. Its methods were also attacked as unconstitutional and arbitrary.

UNCAS. 1588?-1683. Mohegan Indian Chief. Son of a Pequot Chief. Fought with other tribes and succeeded in capturing Narragansett (1643); fought against MASSASOIT (1661); strong and successful leader. Many PEQUOTS joined his tribe during the Pequot War.

"Uncle Sam." The popular nickname for the United States Government. It usually takes the form of a tall male figure dressed in striped trousers, a jacket with stars, and a top hat with stars and stripes. The term came into prominence in the War of 1812, and was first applied scornfully.to troops by those opposed to the War.

Uncle Tom's Cabin. An anti-SLAVERY novel written by HARRIET BEECHER STOWE in 1852. It first appeared serially in 1851-1852 in the Washington *National Era.* The book condemned the slave system and sold over 300,000 copies in the first year. By the opening of the Civil War it had sold over 1,000,-000 copies. It was dramatized, reaching other millions who were roused to bitter resentment against the institution of slavery. Although it contained many inaccuracies it was one of the most powerful propaganda indictments against slavery. Its author was referred to by President LINCOLN as the "little lady" who caused the Civil War.

Unconditional Surrender. Refers to the demand by a military or political head upon an enemy during war to surrender without negotiating any terms. In American history the phrase was first used by General U. S. GRANT in his attack on Fort Donelson in 1861, as the sole terms of the Confederate surrender. It was again

644

used during World War II by President F. D. ROOSEVELT and Prime Minister Churchill in 1943 at the CASABLANCA CONFERENCE, with reference to the AXIS POWERS.

Unconstitutionality. A decision by a court of competent jurisdiction that a legislative enactment violates a fundamental constitutional provision. In the constitutional law of the United States the federal and state courts are empowered to declare federal and state laws and municipal ordinances unconstitutional. The United States Supreme Court is the final court of appeal in such a determination.

Undefended Frontier. See Rush-Bagot Treaty.

Underground. The name applied to the secret organization of nationalist, patriotic, TRADE UNION, working class, and defeated forces within a conquered nation. These groups, during World War II, carried on their activities for liberation by clandestine publications, meetings, and radio broadcasts. They frequently were aided by secret shipments of arms and materials into their nations by the United States, Great Britain, and other countries.

Underground Railroad. The name applied to the system by which escaped slaves were aided in their flight to the North and Canada. ABOLITIONISTS in the North and South established "stations" at which slaves would be given sanctuary. This system of providing food, shelter, and financial aid to runaway Negroes was especially strong in New York, Pennsylvania, and along the northern bank of the Ohio River. Prominent citizens engaged in this labor even though it violated the FUGITIVE SLAVE LAWS.

UNDERWOOD, Oscar Wilder. 1862-1929. Lawyer and Senator. b. Kentucky. Successful lawyer in Alabama; member, U.S. House of Representatives (1895-96; 1897-1915); U.S. Senator (1915-27);

chairman, House WAYS AND MEANS COMMITTEE, leader in Democratic party; co-sponsor of UNDERWOOD-SIMMONS TARIFF ACT (1913); supported WILSON and the LEAGUE OF NATIONS; was a candidate for nomination for the presidency on the Democratic ticket.

Underwood-Simmons Tariff Act. The first tariff reform measure since the Civil War. Fulfilling the Democratic party's election pledge of 1912, Congress enacted this law in 1913. It put iron, steel, raw wool, sugar (by amendment in 1916), and certain agricultural products on the free list, and reduced the rates on cotton and woolen goods. The rates were raised on chemicals. Although lower than its predecessors, the Underwood-Simmons Act remained essentially protectionist. All told there were 958 reductions and 86 increases. Rates were left unchanged in 307 items. The average rate of the act was 26.67 percent as compared with the rate of 40.73 per cent of the PAYNE-ALDRICH ACT.

Unemployment. The existence of a large number of employable workers unable to find jobs. It is a characteristic of the downswing of the BUSINESS CYCLE, reaching its height in DEPRESSION periods. In addition to cyclical unemployment technological and secular unemployment is recognized by economists. The greatest unemployment period in American history occurred between 1933 and 1936. Although the estimates vary, it is generally agreed that there were between 14,-000,000 and 17,000,000 unemployed persons in the United States. Unemployment is a serious sociological and economic institution, leading to broken homes, delinquency, loss of income, and CRIME. It is estimated that the United States lost a total production of more than $200,000,000,000 worth of goods between 1929 and 1937 because of unemployment.

Unemployment Insurance. Refers to monetary benefits paid by the states to

645

unemployed workers. Under the authority of the SOCIAL SECURITY ACT of 1935 48 states and three TERRITORIES have established unemployment insurance systems. Since these are state plans they vary amongst themselves in amount of benefits, duration of benefits, administrative practices, and eligibility requirements. Despite the general improvement in these laws since their inception it is acknowledged that the benefit payments and duration are inadequate in terms of living costs and considerable legislative and political pressure continues in the direction of further reform. In 1964 about 5,750,000 unemployed persons received benefits. These payments totaled $2,642,000,000 The average beneficiary drew benefits for 13 weeks at about $35.60.

UNESCO. Abbreviation for the UNITED NATIONS Educational, Scientific, and Cultural Organization, a formally constituted specialized agency of the Economic and Social Council. Its purposes are to encourage collaboration among the nations through EDUCATION, SCIENCE, and culture for the furtherance of justice, the rule of law, and HUMAN RIGHTS without distinctions as to race, sex, language, or religion. It was established in 1946 and has its headquarters in France. Its first Director-General was the world famous British biologist Julian S. Huxley.

Unfair Labor Practices. Activities of employers declared illegal under Section 8 of the NATIONAL LABOR RELATIONS ACT. These practices include the restraint, coercion, or interference with employees exercising the rights guaranteed in the law, employers' domination of unions, discrimination against any employee in regard to hire, tenure of employment, or any term or condition of employment because he has joined a labor organization, discharge or other discrimination against an employee for taking action under the law, and refusal by an employer to bargain collectively with the

representatives of his employees' own choosing. The NATIONAL LABOR RELATIONS BOARD administers the law and is empowered to take appropriate action to prevent and remedy the commission of unfair labor practices. The Taft-Hartley Act, in Section 8(b) defined unfair labor practices of labor organizations as: restraints against employees in the exercise of the rights guaranteed in Section 7, restraints against employers in the choice of collective bargaining representatives, refusal to bargain collectively, secondary boycotts, and certain kinds of strikes. See National Labor Relations Act, National Labor Relations Board, and Taft-Hartley Act.

"Unfair Methods of Competition." Trade practices which were forbidden by the FEDERAL TRADE COMMISSION ACT and supplementary legislation including the CLAYTON ANTI TRUST ACT and ROBINSON-PATMAN ACT. These practices include: misbranding, bribery, fraudulent advertising, tie-in contracts, misrepresentation, price discrimination, and exclusive dealer contracts. The Fedmeral Trade Commission was authorized to define and prohibit unfair methods of competition.

Unicameral Legislature. A legislative body with one chamber. In the United States municipal councils are generally unicameral. Among the states only Nebraska, since 1936, has had a unicameral legislature. It is argued that such a body is less costly, more efficient, eliminates political strife, and reduces duplication and overlapping of functions.

Union Army. At the opening of the Civil War the United States Army consisted of 16,000 men and officers, a number reduced by the resignation of those who supported the CONFEDERACY. On April, 15, 1861 President LINCOLN incorporated 75,000 MILITIA into the Army and on May 3rd called for 42,000 volunteers. On July 22nd Congress provided for a volunteer army of 500,000 men.

By April, 1861 the northern states had offered to the President 300,000 volunteer troops on three year enlistments. These forces remained the nucleus of the Union Army during the war, the Regular Army having been assigned to FRONTIER defense. As a result of the initial defeats, the volunteer army had been reduced in number Ly the second year of the war and the President called upon the governors to recruit and equip new forces. The payment by the federal, state, and local governments of bounties succeeded in increasing the size of the Army through the end of 1862. Nevertheless, the increasing number of desertions, limited enlistments, and casualties reduced the number of Union Army effectives, leading to the enactment of the first DRAFT law in American history on March 3, 1863. The law contained many objectionable features, including avoidance of service by the payment of a $300 fee, or the offer of a substitute. Although the fee was later abolished for all except CONSCIENTIOUS OBJECTORS, the system of substitution continued throughout the war. These features aroused considerable resentment and led to the DRAFT RIOTS in New York City in August, 1863. In the last two years of the war the Army was increased by more than 1,000-000 volunteers encouraged by bounties, 50,000 conscripts, and 120,000 substitutes. At the end of the war the Union Army totaled approximately 800,000 men.

Union Labor Party. A minor party organized in 1887 in an effort to merge the farmer remnants of the GREENBACK LABOR PARTY with workers. It achieved little success because of the reluctance of organized labor to support its farmer-dominated leadership. In the 1888 election, its candidate, Alson J. Streeter of Illinois, received 147,000 votes, the bulk of which were registered in the farming areas of the South and West. The party's platform contained demands for CUR-RENCY inflation, public regulation of RAILROADS and TRUSTS, direct election of United States Senators, an INCOME TAX, and other principles found in the platform of the KNIGHTS OF LABOR at that time.

Union Pacific Railroad. The first transcontinental railroad. It ran by the central route across the United States from the western border of Iowa to the California-Nevada line where it met the Central Pacific Railroad. The Union Pacific Railroad Company was chartered by Congress in 1862 and was granted 6,400 acres of PUBLIC LANDS and a loan of $16,000 to $48,000 for each mile completed. In 1864 Congress doubled the land grant to overcome business resistance to the plan. The famous race between the two railroads was concluded by their dramatic union at Promotory Point, Utah in 1869. The Railroad was of extreme importance to the development of Nebraska, Colordo, Wyoming, Nevada, and California, bringing in immigrants and providing marketing facilities for the West's cattle, lumber, mining, and farm products. It served as a link in the nation's railroads between the East with the West.

Union Party. A minor party organized in 1861 after the Union defeat at the BATTLE OF BULL RUN. Its objective was the preservation of the Union by the merging of all anti-slave forces in the North regardless of party affiliations. It pledged the prosecution of the War and ran its ticket in many state elections in 1861.

Union Shop. A plant which may hire either union or non-union workers. After a specified period of time, usually 30 days, all employees must join the union. The union shop was permitted by the TAFT-HARTLEY ACT, but only after approval by a majority of the employees in a vote conducted by the NATIONAL LABOR RELATIONS BOARD.

647

Unitarians. A religious group which maintains the unipersonality as opposed to the tripersonality of the Diety. It originated in Poland about 1600 and became strong there in Transylvania and Venetia. The Unitarians formed a schismatic group which broke away from the Congregationalists in New England in the 18th century. In 1819 they followed WILLIAM ELLERY CHANNING in a split from the doctrines of predestination and the Holy Trinity. The theology of the Unitarians included beliefs in salvation through charity, the Fatherhood of God, and the ultimate brotherhood of Man in the Kingdom of Heaven on earth. In 1825 the American Unitarian Association was organized as a merger of the Unitarian Societies of Pennsylvania, New York, and New England. In that period the most prominent Unitarians were RALPH WALDO EMERSON and Joseph Priestley. In the mid-nineteenth century Transcendentalist philosophy emerged from early Unitarianism into a liberal religion based on a belief in humanity and intellectual liberalism advocating methods and social reform. Their outstanding leaders were Emerson, THEODORE PARKER, and HENRY THOREAU. In 1900 the American Unitarian Association sponsored the founding of the International Association of Liberal Christian and Religious Freedom with an international membership of 20,000,000. This organization advocated a program of religious liberalism similar to that of the American group. In 1961 the Unitarians and the Universalist Church of America merged with a combined membership of nearly 170,000 (1964).

United Colonies of New England. See New England Confederation.

United Confederate Veterans. An organization established in New Orleans in 1889 for the purpose of collecting data for an objective history of the Civil War and for maintaining bonds of friendship and the protection of widows and orphans of Confederate soldiers.

United Daughters of the Confederacy. An organization established in Nashville, Tennessee in 1894. It was composed of the female relatives and descendents of men who had served in the armed forces of the Confederate States.

United Mine Workers. An INDUSTRIAL UNION organized in 1890 in Ohio. At its inception it consisted of local, state, and district unions of the KNIGHTS OF LABOR in the bituminous and anthracite coal fields. It grew slowly and was almost destroyed by the failure of its first strike in 1894. The leadership of JOHN MITCHELL preserved the union, and it was strengthened by successful STRIKES in the bituminous and anthracite fields in 1897 and 1902 respectively. The EIGHT HOUR DAY, THE CHECK OFF, union recognition, and improved wage and working conditions were gradually won. It soon became the strongest of the affiliated A.F. OF L. unions and by 1936 it formed the backbone of LABOR support for the candidacy of FRANKLIN D. ROOSEVELT. Its most famous president has been JOHN L. LEWIS, who succeeded to that position in 1920. Under his leadership the United Mine Workers seceded from the A.F. of L. in 1935 to help found the C.I.O. In 1940 the union left the C.I.O., remained independent for a period, then rejoined the A.F. of L. It departed from that organization for the last time in 1947, because of a conflict between Lewis and the A.F. of L. leadership over the non-Communist provision of the TAFT-HARTLEY ACT. In 1964 the Union claimed a membership of 450,000 miners, virtually all in the United States. Its national headquarters are located in Washington, D. C.

United Nations. A world organization established at San Francisco on June 26,

1945 for the purpose of maintaining international peace and security. The United States Senate ratified the charter on August 8, 1945. Fifty-one members drew up the U.N. charter to which 25 additional nations had adhered by 1956. The charter became effective on October 24, 1945 when the requisite ratifications by the five permanent members of the SECURITY COUNCIL, plus a majority of the other signatories, was attained. In addition to the basic objective mentioned above, other functions of the U.N. include economic and social research, scientific development, promotion of HUMAN RIGHTS, economic advancement of all peoples, settlement of DISPLACED PERSONS, health, EDUCATION, and general cultural activities. The principal organs of the U.N. are the Security Council, General Assembly, Secretariat, Economic and Social Council, International Court of Justice, Permanent Chiefs of Staff, and the Trusteeship Council. There are, in addition, scores of important committees and councils engaged in *ad hoc* activities. The organization has achieved notable successes in resolving international disputes. Among these have been the withdrawal of Soviet troops from Iran in 1946, the solution of the Indonesian problem in 1948, the partition and successful conclusion of the war in Israel in 1948 and 1949, and the repulsion of the North Korean invasion in 1950-52. The United Nations may not intervene in the internal affairs of member states except to apply enforcement measures which have been legally determined in accordance with the principles of the charter. Its permanent headquarters are located in the United Nations Building in New York City.

United Nations Human Rights Commission. See human rights.

Universalists. A religious reform group opposed to the preaching of perpetual damnation and predestination. It was begun in 1770 in Massachusetts by John Murray whose preaching was followed in Pennsylvania and New Hampshire. In 1790 these three Universalist sects united. Universalism became strong in New York State and the Mid-West, although its principal influence remained in New England where it had originated. In 1866 the Church was incorporated as the Universalist General Convention, but in 1942 it adopted the present name of Universalist Church of America. In 1961 the Universalists merged with the American Unitarian Association. The combined membership in 1964 was nearly 170,000.

UNRRA. Abbreviation for the United Nations Relief and Rehabilitation Administration. It was organized in 1945 wth a membershp of 44 nations agreed to concentrate on a program of supplying the populations of liberated countries with food, shelter, clothing, seeds, agricultural machinery, and other necessary assistance to restore industrial and agricultural production. Such aid was to be based on each member's national income. Its administration consisted of a steering committee of members of THE BIG FOUR (United States, Great Britain, Soviet Union, France) with HERBERT H. LEHMAN as Director-General. During its two year life the organization distributed $3,000,000,000 worth of supplies.

United States Air Force Academy. The bill establishing the Academy was signed by President Eisenhower on April 1, 1954. Temporary headquarters located at Lowry Air Force Base where the first 306 cadets were sworn in on July 11, 1955. Permanent headquarters at Colorado Springs, Colo., was expected to be completed in 1957. Enrollment of 2500 cadets has been planned.

United States Emergency Fleet Corporation. See Ship Purchase Act.

United States Employment Service. See Wagner-Peyser Act.

649

United States Food Administration. See Food and Fuel Control Act.

United States Geological Survey. An agency established in the DEPARTMENT OF THE INTERIOR on March 3, 1879 for the purpose of analyzing and recording the geological structure and mineral resources of the nation. It replaced the Geological and Geographical Survey of the Territories, Geographical and Geological Survey of the Rocky Mountain Region, and Geographical Surveys West of the 100th Meridian. The agency conducts its operations throughout the United States and its territories with a staff of professional geologists. Its reports include periodic monographs, occasional papers, and a variety of maps among which the most famous is the *Geologic Atlas of the United States.*

United States Housing Act. See Wagner-Steagall Act.

United States Housing Authority. Established under the WAGNER-STEAGALL HOUSING ACT of 1937 for the purpose of granting federal aid in slum clearance and low cost housing projects. By 1941 over 120,000 family dwelling units for low income groups had been completed.

United States-Japanese Security Treaty. Negotiated in San Francisco on September 8th, 1951. By its terms Japan grants to the United States the right to station land, air, and sea forces on or about her islands. These forces are designed to maintain the international peace and security of the Far East and the security of Japan against armed attack by a third party. The United States may also, at the request of Japan, suppress internal "riots and disturbances" instigated by an outside power. Japan is forbidden to grant bases, rights, powers, or authority to any third power without the consent of the United States. The Treaty will expire when, in the opinion of the governments of the signatory powers, the UNITED NATIONS shall have arranged satisfactory methods of providing for the peace and security of the Japanese area. The Senate ratified this treaty on March 20, 1952.

United States-Japanese Treaty. (Jan. 19, 1960). Affirms the obligation to settle disputes in a manner consistent with the U.N. Charter, to strengthen ties, and to resist armed attack individually and by mutual assistance.

United States Military Academy. Popularly known as West Point. Established by Congress in 1802 and situated at West Point in New York State. Its original enrollment of fewer than a dozen cadets has grown to its present body of 2,500. They are chosen from congressional districts, states, TERRITORIES, and on the basis of personal recommendations of political officers. Some membership also comes from veteran ranks. All appointments are made by the President upon recommendation of nominating authorities who include Congressmen, Senators, and the Vice-President of the United States. Graduates are commissioned as second-lieutenants in the U.S. Army where they must serve at least three years.

United States Naval Academy. Popularly known as Annapolis. It was established in 1845 at Annapolis, Maryland as the Naval School and was renamed five years later. Like the candidates at the United States Military Academy its membership consists of men choosen from congressional districts, states, territories, and on the basis of personal recommendation of political officers. Some membership also comes from veteran ranks. All appointments are made by the President upon recommendation of nominating authorities who include Congressmen, Senators, and the Vice-President of the United States. Under-graduates are called midshipmen. Graduates are commissioned as ensigns in the Navy or second-lieutenants in the Marine Corps. A limited number of graduates is at present commissioned as second lieutenants in the United States Air Force.

United States Railroad Administration. Also known as the Federal Railroad Administration. An agency created by EXECUTIVE ORDER in 1917 to administer the nation's RAILROADS after the United States entered World War II. Under the leadership of WILLIAM GIBBS MCADOO and, later, Walker D. Hines, the agency organized the railroads into seven geographic districts for operating purposes. Former railroad executives were appointed to positions as federal managers. Standard contracts were drawn by which the railroads were guaranteed an annual compensation equal to the average net income of the preceding three years. Congress was to pay all railroad expenses, including taxes and maintenance. During the period of operation the Railroad Administration pooled equipment, limited traffic through its power over priorities, unified the use of terminals, accelerated the handling of goods, and managed railroad LABOR RELATIONS. It obtained new supplies and equipment, pooled passenger service, standardized equipment, and eliminated duplicating functions. The Administration was also authorized to operate a barge line on the Mississippi and Warrior Rivers.

United States Shipping Board. See Ship Purchase Act.

United States Steel Corporation. The largest steel company in the United States. It was organized as the first "billion dollar corporation" in 1901 by J. P. MORGAN, with a total capitalization of $1,400,000,000. It was generally recognized at the time that half of this sum was "watered stock." Nevertheless by 1924 the company had earned total net profits of over $2,000,000,000, thus vindicating the original capital stock declaration. The consolidation was a merger of 11 companies representing the steel interests of such figures as ANDREW CARNEGIE, HENRY CLAY FRICK, Henry Phipps, CHARLES SCHWAB, and the Morgan group of J. Pierpont Morgan and ELBERT GARY. The corporation was a vertical trust, controlling not only steel mills but iron mines, steamship lines, and railroad lines. In 1964 the company had assets in excess of $5,200,000,000.

United States Trusteeships. The Strategic Trust Territory of the Pacific Islands, assigned to the United States by the UNITED NATIONS in 1947 as trusts. The TERRITORY consists of the Mariana Islands, Caroline Islands, and Marshall Islands. The entire group constitutes over 1,400 islands with a total land area of 846 square miles. The three groups were sold to Germany by Spain in 1899, occupied by Japan in 1914, and mandated to Japan in 1919 by the LEAGUE OF NATIONS. The assignment of the trust was approved by Congress on July 18, 1947, and its administration conferred upon the NAVY DEPARTMENT. On July 1, 1951 they were transferred to the DEPARTMENT OF THE INTERIOR.

United States vs. Butler. A decision of the United States Supreme Court in 1936 declaring the AGRICULTURAL ADJUSTMENT ACT of 1933 unconstitutional. The court held that Congress had violated the Tenth Amendment by legislating in the field of AGRICULTURE, an area constitutionally reserved to the states. It declared that the processing tax of the law was not a proper tax, but was a penalty designed to aid the farmer rather than provide for the general welfare as required by Article I, Section 8, Clause 1 of the federal Constitution.

United States vs. Darby Lumber Company. A decision of the United States Supreme Court in 1941 upholding the constitutionality of the FAIR LABOR STAND-

ARDS ACT. In its opinion the court explicitly over-ruled HAMMER VS. DAGENHART and thus sustained Congress' control over CHILD LABOR in industries engaged in or affecting INTERSTATE COMMERCE.

United States vs. E. C. Knight Company. A decision of the United States Supreme Court in 1895 involving the first test of the SHERMAN ANTI-TRUST ACT. The court held that the American Sugar Refining Company, which controlled 98 percent of the nation's output of sugar, did not constitute a combination in restraint of INTERSTATE COMMERCE as defined by the law. It maintained that sugar refining was "transformation," not "TRANSPORTATION," and thus did not come under the prohibitions of the Sherman Act. This decision virtually rendered the Sherman Act ineffective against all corporations not engaged in purely trade activities.

United States vs. Wong Kim Ark. A decision of the United States Supreme Court in 1898 which held that native born CITIZENS were all those whose parents were not either foreign diplomats residing in the United States or members of an army in hostile occupation of the United States. Under this decision Wong Kim Ark who had been born in San Francisco, and had been refused admission at that port after a trip to China on the grounds that he had lost his CITIZENSHIP, was admitted. The court held that inasmuch as Wong had not voluntarily relinquished his citizenship, and was not born of the categories of parents above defined, was subject to the jurisdiction of the United States, and therefore a citizen within the meaning of the FOURTEENTH AMENDMENT.

Universal Military Training. Popularly known as UMT. The establishment by law of a system of national induction into the armed forces of persons of specified age for military training during a limited time. After such training these persons are placed into the military reserves. In the United States demand for UMT has arisen since the conclusion of World War II. On June 19, 1951 Congress passed the Universal Military Training and Service Act which provided for a five man National Security Training Commission to study and report to Congress such a program for men 18 to 19 years of age. The UMT commission was appointed by the President shortly thereafter. The Law required that its report be submitted to Congress within four months from the date of confirmation and that no UMT program be made effective until Congress has acted and the President approved. On October 28th, 1951 the Commission submitted its recommendations to Congress. These provided for six months compulsory military training for all able-bodied young men 18 years of age. It was envisioned that 800,000 youths a year would ultimately be trained although the starting program called for only 60,000 per year. Upon completion of this training all youths would serve seven and one half years in one of the civilian reserve organizations. The annual cost was estimated at $2,-000,000,000 per year. Mrs. Anna Rosenberg was appointed Assistant Secretary of defense in charge of this program. The system will not go into operation until special enabling legislation is enacted by Congress. In March, 1952 a bill incorporating the Commission's recommendation was defeated in the House of Representatives. See Selective Service and Training Acts.

Universal Suffrage. VOTING restrictions in the colonies limited the number of voters to roughly five percent of the total POPULATION. These restrictions were based on property, religious, taxpaying, sex, residence, literacy, and other legal qualifications which by 1789 could be met by only 25 percent of the adult males. In Philadelphia, for example, the franchise was limited to those who possessed

50 English pounds, successfully disqualifying 90 percent of the men. The impetus of the Jacksonian reform movement succeeded in eliminating or modifying the restrictions based on property holding, religion, and tax payment. Whereas at the time of the Revolution only Vermont granted universal white suffrage, the entry of the new western states increased the suffrage by eliminating these qualifications. By 1840 only the constitution of Rhode Island contained the old property qualifications. As a result of the Reconstruction program after the Civil War almost 1,500,000 white and Negro voters were added to the lists. Before the Civil War Negroes had been permitted to vote only in Maine, Massachusetts, and Vermont. In these states Negroes constituted less than one half of one percent of the total population, but in the election of 1872 Negroes cast more than 600,000 votes for President GRANT. The Southern states nevertheless nullified the intent of the 15TH AMENDMENT by barring Negro voters through the devices of the POLL TAXES, LITERACY qualifications, and the "GRANDFATHER CLAUSES." The spread of WOMAN SUFFRAGE began with the grant of the general franchise in the TERRITORY of Wyoming in 1869 and was concluded by the adoption of the 19TH AMENDMENT. By the 1930's voters in the United States numbered 45 percent of the total population. In the 1950's eligible voters totalled approximately 63 percent of the population, although only 33 percent voted in the election of 1948.

Unknown Soldier, Tomb of. Located in Arlington National Cemetery on the Potomac River. The body that is buried beneath the tomb was carefully selected to avoid identification. It is the body of a soldier killed in World War I. The tomb, designed by Thomas Hudson Jones and Lorimer Rich, was dedicated in 1921 to the memory of all American soldiers and sailors who lost their lives in World War

I. The tomb was actually erected in 1931 to replace the uncompleted monument which had been established there earlier.

Unrestricted Submarine Warfare. On January 31, 1917 the German foreign minister, Von Bernstorff, informed the United States government that, on the following day, unrestricted SUBMARINE warfare would be resumed. He declared that German submarines would sink on sight all merchant vessels, whether armed or not, within a military zone around the British isles and the Mediterranean Sea. The German government offered to permit passage of one passenger vessel a week, plainly marked with red and white stripes on her hull and funnels and carrying a checkered flag at each masthead. This vessel was to carry no contraband and was to travel through a narrow lane of safety to the English coast. This violation of the SUSSEX PLEDGE was followed on February 3rd by the severance of diplomatic relations between the United States and Germany.

UNTERMEYER, Samuel. 1858-1940. Lawyer. b. Virginia. Graduated, Columbia Law School (1878); admitted to the bar and practised in New York City; helped in the formulation of the FEDERAL RESERVE SYSTEM; acted as counsel for the House of Representatives in PUJO money-trust investigation (1912); during World War I he was chairman of the board that wrote the INCOME TAX law and EXCESS PROFITS TAX legislation; largely responsible for the five-cent subway fare in New York City. A leader in the anti-Nazi campaign and in the Zionist movement.

"Unwritten Constitution." The body of political customs and traditions that has developed in the American political process although not provided for in the Constitution. Among the more notable principles of the "unwritten constitution" are SENATORIAL COURTESY, LOBBYING,

653

the federal BUDGET, the COMMITTEE SYSTEM, POLITICAL PARTIES, the CABINET system, and the rubber-stamp nature of the ELECTORAL COLLEGE.

Urbanization. The growth of towns and cities and the shift of POPULATION from the country to these urban areas. At the close of the Revolution 95 per cent of the American people lived in rural areas. In 1800, 10 percent lived in cities. By the opening of the Civil War this figure had risen to 16 percent. In 1900 one-third of the population lived in cities over 8,000 and 50 percent in urban centers with more than 2,500 people. In 1900 there were 547 cities in the United States with more than 8,000 people compared with 141 such in 1800. Urbanization had become so marked by 1930 that more than 56 percent lived in cities of more than 2,500 population. In that year 93 cities had a population over 100,000 and five over 1,000,000. This movement to the cities was a result of industrial expansion, increased IMMIGRATION, an upswing in the birth rate, and the opening of the West. Although temporarily halted by the GREAT DEPRESSION, the movement was accelerated during the defense and war period of the 1940's. In the 1960's the urban population constituted 70 percent of the American people. This shift has been made possible by the increasing mechanization and productivity of AGRICULTURE, enabling farm production to meet the food needs of the total population despite the radical decline in the farm population. The results of urbanization have been the concentration· of wealth in cities, the development of SLUMS, and the manifold problems of EDUCATION, HOUSING, HEALTH, and RECREATION.

UREY, Harold Clayton. 1893-
Chemist. b. Indiana. Assistant professor of chemistry at Johns Hopkins (1924-29) and Columbia (from 1929) full professor (from 1934); winner of the Nobel prize for chemistry for his discovery of heavy hydrogen or isotope of hydrogen that is present in heavy water; has done work on the structure of atoms and molecules, thermodynamic properties of gases and other projects; professor, University of Chicago (1945).

Utah. The 11th state in size, with an area of 84,916 square miles. Organized as a TERRITORY in 1850 and admitted as the 45th state on January 4, 1896. Salt Lake City is the capital. In 1950 Utah's POPULATION of 688,862 made it 38th in rank. Its largest cities are Salt Lake City, Ogden, and Provo. The mining of copper, gold, and silver is Utah's most important industry. Other important minerals are iron, manganese, coal, dolomite, lime, and fluorspar. In recent years uranium and vanadium mining has become the state's most important economic pursuit. IRRIGATION crops include hay, onions, potatoes, sugar beets, and WHEAT. Other farm products are beans, tomatoes, peas, apples, apricots, peaches, and pears. The practice of Mormonism prevented its ADMISSION INTO THE UNION upon six applications until polygamy was abolished in 1896. Utah was discovered by Spanish adventurers in 1540. Its nickname is the "Beehive State." See Great Salt Lake and Mormons, the.

Ute Indians. A member of the Shoshonean linguistic family. They formerly occupied areas in Colorado, New Mexico, and Utah. The Utes were nomadic and warlike, seldom establishing themselves in any community for long periods. At one time the 15 Ute tribes organized themselves into a confederacy and frequently made war upon the white settlers. Today there are approximately 2,000 Utes in the United States.

Utopian Communities. See Utopian Socialism.

Utopian Socialism. A social development in the first half of the 19th century. It took the form of organized cooperative and semi-socialist communities established in various eastern and mid-western states. The philosophy of the movement grew out of the belief in the innate goodness of men who would voluntarily relinquish their wordly wealth to the less fortunate, and accommodate themselves to cooperative living. This reform movement was an outgrowth and part of the social upheaval of the Jacksonian movement, reflecting the reform demands of the FRONTIER. Among the various experiments were the German Separatists movement at Zoar, Ohio in 1817, the ONEIDA COMMUNITY in New York organized by John Humphrey Noyes in 1847, the NEW HARMONY establishment in Indiana founded by ROBERT OWEN in 1825 and again in 1840, the BROOK FARM experiment originated by the members of the Transcendental Club of Boston including GEORGE RIPLEY, CHARLES A. DANA, and NATHANIEL HAWTHORNE, and the Icarian movement in Texas established by Étienne Cabet in 1848. These communities were uniformly unsuccessful, their failures resulting from improper administration, the visionary views of their founders, inadequate financing, public opposition, and the physical destruction of many of them by fire and storm.

V

V-E Day. Abbreviation for Victory-in-Europe Day. Refers to the UNCONDITIONAL SURRENDER of the German armies at Rheims headquarters on May 6th, 1945, and providing for the cessation of all military operations on May 8th.

V-J Day. Abbreviation for Victory-in-Japan Day. On August 14th, 1945 Japan formally surrendered, the papers being signed aboard the *U.S.S. Missouri* on September 2nd, 1945. On August 10th the Japanese had offered to accept the POTSDAM terms but had been rejected by the United Nations the following day. The UNCONDITIONAL SURRENDER followed.

V-Mail. A method of transmitting mail from the United States to members of the armed services abroad during World War II. Developed cooperatively between the STATE DEPARTMENT and the POST OFFICE DEPARTMENT, it consisted of special V-Mail forms, written by the sender, and transcribed to microfilm for TRANSPORTATION to overseas units. The purpose of V-Mail was to lessen the transportation burden during the War by reducing the physical bulk of mail.

Valley Forge. The camp in which WASHINGTON kept the 11,000 men of his army after the defeats at BRANDYWINE and GERMANTOWN. From December, 1777 to June, 1778 he occupied this strategically situated height which commanded the roads from Philadelphia to the north. Despite Washington's plans and preparations the unexpectedly early and severe winter prevented his receipt of supplies. The misery of the army was increased by the neglect of the CONTINENTAL CONGRESS, the failure of the quartermaster officers to dispatch food, clothing, and supplies, the outbreak of typhus and smallpox, the lack of medical supplies, the absence of transport service, and the mismanagement of Washington's subordinate officers. The period was used, however, to discipline and train the troops. Shortly after their departure from Valley Forge, the army fought the British at Monmouth on equal terms. Its contribution to the ultimate patriot victory lay in the morale provided by the heroism of the troops during the bitter winter of their stay at Valley Forge.

VAN BUREN, Martin. 1782-1862. Eighth President of the United States. b. Kinderhook, New York. Admitted to the bar (1803); attorney general of New York (1816-19); leader of the Democratic party of the state and part of the group known as the "Albany Regency;" U.S. Senator (1821-28); did not have an impressive record; supporter of JACKSON; governor of New York (1829) resigned to become U.S. Secretary of State (1829-31) and Jackson's right hand man; appointed U.S. Minister to Great Britain but the Senate refused to confirm his appointment, this being a political victory for CALHOUN a rival of Van Buren; elected Vice-President of the United States with Jackson as President (1833-37); at the suggestion of Jackson he was nominated for the presidency on the Democratic ticket and elected (1837-41); his administration was, unfortunately for Van Buren, one of financial problems; defeated (1840) for the presidency; became a leading "BARNBURNER"; unsuccessful as FREE-SOIL candidate for the presidency (1848) although his votes insured the election of the WHIG candidate TAYLOR over his political rival CASS; supported LINCOLN. Author of *Inquiry into the Origin and Course of the Political Parties in the United States* (1867).

VANCE, Cyrus. 1917- . He attended Yale University and majored in economics, receiving his B.A. degree in 1939. During World War II, he served for twenty months on a destroyer. In 1976 he was appointed Secretary of State by President James Carter.

VANCE, Zebulon Baird. 1830-1894. Lawyer and political leader. A leader of the WHIG party; served during the Civil War as a colonel; governor of North Carolina; U.S. Senator.

VAN CORTLANDT, Stephanus. 1643-1700. Real estate owner and politician. b. New Amsterdam (now New York). Famous as the first native born mayor of New York City (1677, 1686, 1687); judge of various courts; associate justice (1691-1700) chief justice (1700) of New York supreme court; received a patent from William III of a large tract of land which he turned into a manor; he owned 10 miles on the east bank of the Hudson River above Manhattan. Van Cortlandt Park is named after his family.

VANDENBERG, Arthur Hendrick. 1884-1951. Political leader. b. Michigan. Worked as a journalist and writer; appointed to fill a vacancy in the U.S. Senate (1928) and re-elected regularly until his death; leader of the ISOLATIONIST bloc of Republicans; opposed revision of the NEUTRALITY ACT (1939); changed his views on foreign policy (1945) and became leader of the internationalist wing of the Republicans; leader, with F. D. ROOSEVELT, of the bi-partisan program and supported the TRUMAN DOCTRINE and the MARSHALL PLAN; member of the Senate Committee on Foreign Relations and its chairman (1947-49). Author several biographies of ALEXANDER HAMILTON.

VANDERBILT, Cornelius. 1794-1877. Railroad and SHIPPING owner; capitalist. Known as "Commodore Vanderbilt." b. New York. Controlled ferry lines between Staten Island and New York City; established successful shipping service on the Hudson River; entered the railroad business at the outbreak of the Civil War; bought controlling interest in the NEW YORK CENTRAL RAILROAD; involved in battle with FISKE and DREW over control of the Erie Railroad; left a fortune to Vanderbilt University.

VAN DOREN, Carl. 1885-1950. Writer. b. Illinois. Graduated, Illinois University (1907); Columbia (Ph.D. 1911); assistant professor in the English Department at Columbia (1911-34); managing editor, *Cambridge History of American Literature* (1917-21); literary editor, *The Nation* (1919-22) and *Century Magazine* (1922-25); editor, The Literary Guild (1926-34); author of *The American Novel* (1921), *Swift* (1930), *Sinclair Lewis* (1933), *Benjamin Franklin* (1938) for which he won a Pulitzer Prize; *Secret History of the American Revolution* (1941) and others.

VAN DOREN, Earl. 1820-1863. Confederate general. b. Mississippi. Graduated,

657

U.S.M.A., West Point (1842); served in Mexican War; joined the Confederate Army (1861); colonel of cavalry successful in capturing Union forts in Texas (1861); promoted to major general and served in other campaigns but was defeated; murdered over private dispute (1863).

VAN RENSSELAER, Martha. 1864-1932. Home economist. b. New York. Served as a schoolteacher; joined Cornell University to organize extension courses in home economics for farm women (1900); professor, home economics, Cornell (1911); executive member of the staff of the U.S. FOOD ADMINISTRATION (1918-19); honored as one of the 12 outstanding women in the United States (1923).

VAN RENSSELAER, Stephen. 1764-1839. General and politician. b. New York City. Graduated, Harvard (1782); managed the great Van Rensselaer estate; major general of militia (from 1801); FEDERALIST, member, House of Representatives (1822-29); member canal commission for the GREAT LAKES; founded Rensselaer Polytechnic Institute; member and chancellor of the Board of Regents of New York State.

VAN SCHAICK, Goose. 1736-1789. Revolutionary general. b. New York. Served in the French and Indian War; colonel in the Revolution leading troops against the Onondaga Indians; served at Cherry Valley, Ticonderoga, and Monmouth; brevetted brigadier general (1783).

Vaudeville. A pattern of variety theatrical entertainment which developed in the United States as light THEATRE based on unconnected skits, playlets, songs, dances, juggling acts, gymnastics, and monologues. Each of these is considered a separate performance and there is no related story or plot line. In the 19th century vaudeville was scorned by the legitimate theatres and was performed principally in third-rate houses and saloons. At the turn of the 20th century it had achieved status and was being performed in established theatres. The most prominent of these was the Palace Theatre in New York City before World War I. Here the great stars of that day included Fred Allen, Eddie Cantor, George M. Cohan, the Marx Brothers, LILLIAN RUSSELL, Weber and Fields, and Mae West. Vaudeville suffered a temporary eclipse with the advent of the MOTION PICTURE and RADIO, but enjoyed a revival in the 1950's with the rise of TELEVISION INDUSTRY. The word comes from the French vau de vire, originating from old French love songs of the 15th century.

VEBLEN, Thorstein Bunde. 1857-1929. Social scientist. b. Wisconsin. Graduated, Yale (Ph.D.); taught at the University of Chicago (1892-1906), Stanford (1906-1909); University of Missouri (1911-18) and the New School for Social Research (1919). Had an important influence on the thinking of his time and is well-known for his writings including *The Theory of the Leisure Class* (1899), *The Place of Science in Modern Civilization* (1920), *Absentee Ownership and Business Enterprise in Recent Times* (1923), and many others.

Venezuela Boundary Dispute. A dispute between Great Britain and Venezuela over the boundary line between the latter nation and the British colony of Guiana. Great Britain claimed 23,000 square miles of Venezuelan territory, justifying the claim on old maps. The State Department offered to arbitrate the disputed boundary line but was rejected by Great Britain in 1887. In 1895 Secretary of State RICHARD OLNEY issued a sharp dispatch declaring the United States to be "practically sovereign on this continent", reasserting the principles of the MONROE DOCTRINE. Ultimately, sounder relations between the United States and Great Britain prevailed and a TREATY of 1897 provided for arbitration. A Paris tribunal conferred a verdict in 1899, favorable on the whole to Great Britain, fixing the line which had been in dispute for nearly 60 years.

Venezuela Claims. An incident in 1902 which resulted from the attempts of the German, British, and Italian governments to collect claims for debts and injuries suffered by their nationals in the past. A BLOCKADE and bombardment of the coast followed, and shortly afterwards Venezuela proposed ARBITRATION with the support of the United States. The claims were settled after investigations by mixed commissions. The importance of the incident lies in the reiteration by President T. ROOSEVELT of the MONROE DOCTRINE. The United States held that European nations were justified in protecting the lives and property of their nationals, but could not obtain territory in Latin America.

Vera Cruz Incident. Refers to the arrest of United States MARINES in Tampico in 1914, followed by the dispatch of an American fleet and the landing of troops at Vera Cruz on April 21st. The city was bombarded and captured with the loss of 17 American dead and 63 wounded. The order by President WILSON followed the refusal of the Mexican government to grant a 21 gun salute to the AMERICAN FLAG despite the fact that the Marines had been released and apologies offered.

Vermont. The 43rd state in size, with an area of 9,609 square miles. Entered the Union on March 4, 1791 as the 14th state. Montpelier is the capital. In 1950 Vermont's POPULATION of 377,747 made it 45th in rank. Its largest cities are Burlington, Rutland, and Barre. Vermont is the only New England state without a sea coast. Its DAIRY INDUSTRY is important, its cows bearing a greater ratio per population than in any other state. Farm crops include truck vegetables and fruits. Its minerals are granite, marble, and asbestos. Vermont leads the United States in the production of maple syrup, and is an important lumber produced. It was the first state to enter the Union after the formation of the United States on the basis of the Constitution of 1787. It was also the first state to abolish SLAVERY. In politics Vermont has been consistently Republican. It was discovered in 1609 by SAMUEL DE CHAMPLAIN. Its nickname is the "Green Mountain State."

VERRAZANO, Giovanni da. 1485?-1528. Italian navigator. Explored the coast of North America, it is believed, from North Carolina to Cape Breton and was the first to discover the Hudson River and Narragansett Bay.

Versailles Peace Conference. A meeting of the victorious Allies after World War I. The Conference met from January 18 to June 28, 1919 at Versailles, France, and produced the VERSAILLES TREATY. The Conference was attended by 32 nations, meeting in many committees to carry on its work. This cumbersome procedure was quickly abandoned in favor of meetings under the Big Five, WILSON, Lloyd George, Clemenceau, Orlando, and Saionji. The United States delegation consisted of President Wilson, Secretary of State LANSING, Colonel HOUSE, HENRY WHITE, and General TASKER H. BLISS.

Versailles, Treaty of. The treaty which ended World War I. It was signed in June, 1919 by 32 nations, and was submitted for German signature. It consisted of 440 articles. Among the important clauses were a statement of sole German war guilt, the demilitarization of the Rhineland, the cession of the Saar Valley coal mines to France, a limitation of the

German army to 100,000 men, the abolition of the German general staff, the prohibition of German naval and air forces, the repayment by Germany to the allies, ton for ton, of all Allied SHIPPING sunk during the war, the stripping from Germany of all her colonies, the imposition of an indemnity of $5,000,000,000 and of a future REPARATION bill of an indeterminate amount, and the loss of much territory in Europe. Among the latter were the cession of Alsace and Lorraine to France, the Sudetenland to Czechoslovakia, Lupen, Malmedy, and Moresnet to Belgium, the Polish Corridor to Poland, and the creation of the free city of Danzig to be administered by the League of Nations. The Covenant of the LEAGUE OF NATIONS was the last clause of the treaty. The Treaty was not ratified by the United States Senate, although it received a majority of the Senate votes on November 19, 1919 and on March 20, 1920. The Republican "irreconcilables" led by Senators LODGE, BORAH, and JOHNSON succeeded in defeating American ratification.

Vertical Union. See Industrial Union.

VESCO, Robert L. Robert L. Vesco was an international financier who had legal proceedings initiated against him in a New York Court by the Securities and Exchange Commission in March 1963. It was revealed that John Mitchell, the Attorney General, had arranged a meeting between Vesco and SEC officials to discuss a charge that he looted a mutual fund under his control. Testimony by Mitchell and Stans, financial agents for the Committee to Reelect President Nixon, revealed that much of Vesco's money had been used to pay the Watergate conspirators.

VESPUCCI, Amerigo. 1451-1512. Italian navigator. b. Florence, Italy. Made several voyages to the New World but most of his trips were confined to South America; a German geographer, Wald-seemuller, first suggested the new lands be called "America" taken from his first name.

Veterans' Administration. Established by Congress in 1930 to administer veterans' affairs. Its head is called the Veterans' Administrator, usually a general officer of the U. S. Army, and appointed by the President and Senate. The agency supervises and administers all laws dealing with veterans' pensions, retirement pay, care of veterans' or their dependents, and death benefit payments. The V. A. operates the largest chain of hospitals in the United States, a vast EDUCATION and training program, and one of the largest life insurance projects in the nation.

Veterans' Bureau Scandal. Corruption in the Veterans' Bureau in 1923. Colonel Charles R. Forbes, Director of the Veterans' Bureau, was accused of illegal sale of federal property, liquor, and narcotics, and charged with waste and misconduct in office. He was indicted, tried, and sentenced to a term in prison. It was discovered that $250,000,000, appropriated for veterans, had been wasted or stolen during his term in office.

Veterans of Foreign Wars. A veterans' organization founded in 1913 as a consolidation of the American Veterans of Foreign Service and the Army of the Philippines. Among other activities, it lobbies for legislation favorable to veterans, and conducts annual essay contests on the theme "Freedom's Open Door." Its national headquarters are located in Kansas City, Missouri. Its membership in 1965 was 1,575,000.

Veto. Refers to the refusal of a chief executive to sign a legislative bill which requires his signature to become law. In the federal government the Constitution requires the President's signature under certain conditions. His refusal to grant it constitutes a veto. In the state governments 38 governors have the power to veto items in appropriation bills, and in two states, sections of non-fiscal bills. A congressional bill becomes law without the President's signature after 10 days, provided Congress is in session. Presidential vetoes may be overridden by a 2/3 vote of both houses of Congress. In the states, governors' vetoes may be overridden by votes ranging from a majority to 2/3 of the elected members of the state legislatures. See veto, pocket.

Veto, Pocket. Refers to an indirect method of vetoing a bill of Congress. A bill which is sent to the President for his signature is considered pocket vetoed if he takes no action on it and Congress adjourns before the expiration of a 10 day period excluding Sundays.

Veto Power, United Nations. The right of one of the five permanent members of the SECURITY COUNCIL to refuse approval to a measure of that body. It is sometimes called the "rule of unanimity." The Soviet Union has more frequently exercised this veto power than other nations, having cast 51 vetoes by 1952.

Vice-President. The second highest executive in the federal government. He is elected by a majority vote of the ELECTORAL COLLEGE. In the event of a tie or lack of majority in the electoral college, his election is thrown into the Senate where a majority of the whole number of Senators is necessary to elect. The Senate chooses from between the two highest numbers on the electoral list. No person, constitutionally ineligible to the office of President, is eligible to that of the Vice-President. The Vice-President is presiding officer of the Senate except in cases involving IMPEACHMENT of the President. He votes only in case of ties. The Vice-President succeeds to the presidency in the event of the death, impeachment, resignation, or inability of

the President to serve. Seven Vice-Presidents have succeeded to the presidency.

Vicksburg, Battle of. A battle and siege of the Civil War. The battle was fought in front of Vicksburg, Mississippi on December 28 and 29, 1862. General SHERMAN'S attack on the Confederate Army under JOHNSTON, on the Yazoo River between Vicksburg and Haines Bluff, was repulsed with heavy Union losses. Between December, 1862 and May, 1863; four subsequent attempts to reach Vicksburg culminated in Union defeats. General GRANT decided to abandon the Union base at Memphis and move down the west bank of the Mississippi below Vicksburg. He crossed the river eastward, deciding to attack the city from the rear. The Union Army, originally numbering 30,000, was reinforced during the siege until it numbered 70,000 troops. Johnston was replaced by General Pemberton who commanded 25,000 Confederates in defense of the city on May 19, 1863 when Grant began the siege. Three assaults by Grant on May 22nd were repulsed with great loss. Finally, after 47 days of siege, the dwindling food and munitions resources of the defending army, aggravated by illness and mounting casualties, compelled Pemberton to initiate surrender negotiations. On July 4th the garrison surrendered, but was parolled as prisoners of war, and allowed to go free. The capture of Vicksburg opened the way to the march to the coast, and was an important turning point of the war.

"Victory Loan." See Liberty Loans.

Vietnam. During President Johnson's administration when American troops were sent to Viet Nam to aid the government of South Vietnam to achieve victory, the people of the United States were launched on a program that was to result in a dramatic polarization and resultant confrontations

661

between groups. In addition, the anger and confusion generated by the commitment of so many Americans to fight in Viet Nam and the expenditure of huge sums of money for the military, seemed to bring about a dramatic reversal in American foreign policy, a sentiment against global commitment. Those who sought to justify huge expenditures of money and human life did so on the grounds of seeking to check the spread of communism not only in South East Asia but throughout the world. Under President Nixon, peace was finally achieved in this troubled area after a decade of involvement.

Vietnam draft evaders. As his first presidential act, President Carter on January 21, 1977 pardoned about 10,000 Vietnam War draft evaders but made no decision about deserters. He announced that cases of those with less-than-honorable discharges would be reviewed.

Viking I. On July 20, 1976 the robot craft Viking I made the successful landing on Mars, transmitting back to earth black and white photographs. On July 21st color photographs taken revealed light blue skies above a reddish soil. A series of tests conducted on August 26 presented evidence supporting the possibility of life on the planet.

Viking II. On September 3, 1976 the Viking II space craft landed on the Utopia Plains on Mars and transmitted panoramic photographs. Scientific investigation resulting from this landing confirms that Mars may have had at one time a considerably denser atmosphere.

VILLA, Francisco. Known as Pancho. *Real name* Doroteo Arango. 1877-1923. Mexican revolutionary leader. Skillful and bold outlaw chief; often pictured as a modern Robin Hood whose interest was in helping the poor; fought against the government of Carranza (1914-15); crossed American border into New Mexi-

co; troops under PERSHING sent to pursue him into Mexico but were ordered out of the country by the President of Mexico; he was later murdered.

Village Government. A municipal government consisting of a legislative assembly generally called Board of Supervisors or Board of Trustees, a mayor and administrative officials including department heads, clerks, sheriffs, and judges. The village government is established by act of the state legislature or is provided for in the state constitution. The village acts as an administrative arm of the state in carrying out state legislation. There are over 10,000 villages in the United States.

VILLARD, Henry. 1835-1900. Journalist, railroad executive, and financier. b. Bavaria, Germany. Came to the United States (1853); changed his name from Hilgard; worked for various NEWSPAPERS in New York City; formed a pool and bought control of the Northern Pacific Railroad; chairman of the board (1888-93); although he did not establish a complete MONOPOLY as he had intended, he was a very powerful railroad magnate; helped THOMAS A. EDISON found the Edison GENERAL ELECTRIC CO. (1889); held controlling interest in the New York *Evening Post.* (1881).

VINSON, Frederick Moore. 1890-1953. Political leader and jurist. b. Kentucky. Graduated, Kentucky Normal College (1908); LL.B. (1911); member, House of Representatives (1923-29 and 1931-38); sponsored fiscal legislation and supported the NEW DEAL; judge, Court of Appeals of the District of Columbia (1938); director, OFFICE OF ECONOMIC STABILIZATION (1943-45); chief of the FEDERAL LOAN AGENCY (1945); director, OFFICE OF WAR MOBILIZATION AND RECONVERSION (1945); U.S. Secretary of the Treasury (1945-46); appointed by TRUMAN, Chief Justice of the Supreme Court

(1946).

Virginia. The 36th state in size, with an area of 40,815 square miles. Entered the Union on June 25, 1788 as the 10th state. Seceded on April 17, 1861 and re-admitted on January 27, 1870. Richmond is the capital. In 1950 Virginia's POPULATION of 3,318,680 made it 15th in rank. Its largest cities are Richmond, Norfolk, and Roanoke. Virginia was the home of the first permanent English settlement in America. SLAVERY was introduced into Virginia for the first time in America. The state has an important history, having given many Presidents to the nation and been the site of Revolutionary and Civil War battles. AGRICULTURE is the leading industry. Chief crops are TOBACCO, apples, COTTON, oats, barley, potatoes, WHEAT, and sweet potatoes. Virginia's hams are internationally famous. Richmond is the world's largest CIGARETTE MANUFACTURING center. The TEXTILE INDUSTRY is the most important manufacturing activity. Historical sites include MONTICELLO, MOUNT VERNON, and the ARLINGTON NATIONAL CEMETERY. Norfolk, Portsmouth, and Newport News are important ports. Virginia was discovered in 1584 by SIR WALTER RALEIGH. Its nicknames are the "Old Dominion" and "Cavalier State."

Virginia Company of London. See London Company.

"Virginia Dynasty". The term applied to the Presidents of the United States, in the first two decades of the nation's history, who were Virginians. These included WASHINGTON, JEFFERSON, MADISON, and MONROE.

Virginia House of Burgesses. The first representative assembly in North America. It was established in Virginia in 1619, having been called into existence by Governor Yeardley. It was a UNICAMERAL LEGISLATURE, consisting of the governor, his council, and two burgesses elected from each town and PLANTATION. In later years the units of representation were transferred in part to certain privileged towns, cities, and counties. In the latter part of the century an elected lower house separated from the parent assembly, resulting in a bicameral body. From its origins the House of Burgesses exercised the right to initiate legislation, and control the power of the purse. It was of extreme importance in establishing the principle of representation among the colonies, and was shortly followed by similar assemblies in Massachusetts, Rhode Island, and Connecticut.

Virginia and Kentucky Resolutions. A series of resolutions adopted by the Virginia and Kentucky legislatures as an expression of opposition to the ALIEN AND SEDITION LAWS. The Kentucky Resolutions were drafted by Vice-President JEFFERSON and introduced by JOHN BRECKENRIDGE on November 16, 1798. The Virginia Resolutions were drafted by JAMES MADISON on December 24, 1798. Both sets were alike in that they asserted that the Constitution was a compact between sovereign states and that it was their right to interpret it and determine the validity of laws passed under its authority. Both sets declared that the Alien and Sedition Laws had violated the Constitution, and called on the other states to join in denouncing them and preventing their execution. In 1799 the two states passed a second set of resolutions declaring that "the rightful remedy for a state was NULLIFICATION." It is clear that these Resolutions were in the nature of a political attack upon the FEDERALIST PARTY rather than a fundamental analysis by Jefferson and Madison of constitutional theory. Both authors later denied that the Resolutions were intended to advocate disunion and Madison specifically stated that they were written purely as campaign documents.

Virginia Plan. See Randolph Plan.

Virgin Islands. An archipelago in the Caribbean Sea consisting of nine large islands and 75 islets. They were discovered by COLUMBUS in 1493 and, with the exception of six of the main islands, were eventually obtained by Denmark, being renamed the Danish West Indies. They were purchased in 1917 by the United States for $25,000,000. Its POPULATION of 26,500 inhabits an area of 132 square miles. Its capital is Charlotte Amalie, formerly St. Thomas. Eighty percent of the population is of NEGRO descent. In 1927 Congress conferred American CITIZENSHIP upon the islanders and, by the Organic Act of 1936, granted universal suffrage to those who could read and write the English language. The legislative assemblies of the municipalities of St. Thomas, St. John and St. Croix meet jointly annually as a Legislative Assembly for the Islands as a whole. The governor, appointed by the President, has certain VETO powers. The overall administration of the Islands is under the jurisdiction of the DEPARTMENT OF THE INTERIOR. Their principal products and exports are RUM, SUGAR, molasses, hides, and livestock. An additional important source of income is the tourist trade.

Virginius Massacre. Refers to the capture of the filibustering ship *Virginius* by a Spanish war vessel in 1873 and the execution of nine members of its crew and 44 passengers. The *Virginius* was illegally flying the American FLAG on its mission to supply Cuba rebels with arms. The incident caused feeling to run high in the United States, and the government demanded the punishment of the officers, a salute to the American flag, and an indemnity. Spain proved that the vessel was not American but paid the indemnity. The salute was waived.

Vocational Education. Formal, organized training for work in factories or offices. Prior to 1917 such schooling was provided on a local basis, financed by state and municipal funds, and was limited in its objectives. Beginning in that year, federal SUBSIDIES have been granted to the states for vocational education under the supervision of the UNITED STATES OFFICE OF EDUCATION. The various laws by which Congress has furnished such aid were the MORRILL ACT of 1862, the Agriculture Extension Act of 1914, and the SMITH-HUGHES ACT of 1917.

Voice of America. An international short wave RADIO series established as the International Broadcasting Service in the DEPARTMENT OF STATE by congressional act of January 27, 1948. Its functions were to communicate with persons in occupied and hostile countries by daily broadcasts all over the world. In 1948 a new policy led to the discontinuance of the issuance of news reports in favor of more intensive and direct propaganda following protests against broadcasts to Latin America. In 1950 Congress' appropriations included $2,800,000 for the purchase and distribution of radio receivers in Communist countries and other important areas. In 1952 the Voice of America employed 1,700 people in its programs which originated in New York City, Washington, D. C., and Munich, Germany. The service operated relay stations in the United States and Europe in carrying broadcasts in 46 languages to a potential audience of 300,000,000 people in 35 countries. It transmitted 35 or more daily broadcasts. In that year the Voice of America received about 1,000 letters daily and mailed out 1,250,000 program schedules bi-monthly. It transmitted from 74 short-wave radios of which 36 were abroad. The service was established as part of the State Department's Information and Education Exchange.

Volstead Act. Also known as the National Prohibition Act. Passed by Congress in 1919. Its enactment was a result of the authorization conferred upon Congress by the 18TH AMENDMENT. The law prohibited the manufacture, TRANSPORTATION, and sale of beverages containing more than .5 percent alcohol. It fixed penalties for sales of liquor and provided for INJUNCTIONS against public places which dispensed liquor in violation of the law. Private stocks bought before the Act went into effect could be retained. The Act was roundly condemned by a large segment of the American people as an invasion of their constitutional rights. One of the most unfortunate consequences of its passage was the development of widespread violations accompanied by gangsterism and CRIME.

VOLSTEAD, Andrew Joseph. 1860-1947. Legislator. b. Minnesota. Practiced law; a leading Republican member, U.S. House of Representatives (1903-23); known for his authorship of the VOLSTEAD ACT (1919) and the Farmers' Co-operative Marketing Act.

VOORHEES, Daniel Wolsey. 1827-1897. Lawyer and political leader. b. Ohio. Graduated, Indiana Asbury College (1849); practiced law in Indiana; prominent as a criminal lawyer; member, U. S. House of Representatives (1861-65; 1869-73); U. S. Senator (1877-97).

Voorhis Act. Passed by Congress in 1940. It required the filing of information with the Attorney General by all organizations acting as agents of foreign governments. Those organizations were included which engaged in either political, civilian, or military activities.

Voting. The act of casting a ballot for a public officer. In the United States qualifications for voting are established by the state legislatures. Thus the states have enacted a total of about fifty barriers to voting including vagrancy, registration, age, literacy, felony convictions, insanity, receipt of poor relief, malfeasance in office, and poll tax payment. The average is six to seven per state. Of a total eligible voting POPULATION of approximately 95,000,000, only 49,600,000 voted in 1940, 47,600,000 in 1944, and 48,600,000 in 1948. In addition, factors such as inertia, illness, absence from the state, lack of faith in the two party system, and weakness of THIRD PARTY MOVEMENT have produced a decline in voting.

voting age. The twenty-sixth amendment franchised citizens 18 years of age and older. The amendment was ratified by Congress on June 30, 1971 and on November 2, 1971 over 11 million persons between the ages of eighteen and twenty cast their vote for the first time.

Voting Machine. A machine substituting for the paper BALLOT in various states. The voter casts his ballot by pulling down levers under the names of candidates listed by POLITICAL PARTIES. He closes the curtain as he steps into the booth, depresses the levers in the desired spaces, and then leaves the booth. The opening of the Curtain as he leaves the booth automatically registers his votes on a clock-wise mechanism and returns the levers to their original position ready for the next voter. The voting machine was, for a long time, opposed by the party "machine" and "boss" because of the difficulty of tampering with it.

665

W

Wabash, St. Louis, and Pacific Railway vs. Illinois. A decision of the United States Supreme Court in 1886 invalidating an Illinois law regulating RAILROADS. The Court held that the Illinois legislature had acted beyond its authority, since its statutes affected INTERSTATE COMMERCE, a function properly exercised "by the Congress of the United States under the commerce clause of the Constitution." This decision held unconstitutional the GRANGER LAWS which had been originally sustained by the court in the case of MUNN VS. ILLINOIS.

WADE, Benjamin Franklin. 1800-1878. Lawyer and political leader. b. Massachusetts. Studied and practiced law in Ohio; WHIG member, U.S. Senate (1851-69); leading ABOLITIONIST who opposed KANSAS-NEBRASKA BILL; joint author of the Wade-Davis Manifesto (1864) opposing LINCOLN'S RECONSTRUCTION POLICY; opposed JOHNSON and voted for his IMPEACHMENT.

Wade-Davis Bill. A Reconstruction bill sponsored by the RADICAL REPUBLICANS in Congress in opposition to LINCOLN'S RECONSTRUCTION PLAN. It provided for the administration of the affairs of southern states by provisional governors until the end of the war. Civil government was to be reestablished when half of the male white CITIZENS took an oath of loyalty to the Union. Restoration in the southern states should be undertaken by state conventions which would exclude those who had held office under the Confederacy or voluntarily fought for it. These conventions were required to amend their state constitutions to provide that Confederate officials, except in administrative offices and below the rank of colonel, should not vote for or be governors or legislative members. SLAVERY was to be prohibited and all Confederate debts repudiated. Upon popular ratification of these constitutions the states would be allowed representation in Congress. The Wade-Davis Bill passed on July 2, 1864 but was "POCKET VETOED" by LINCOLN.

Wages and Hours Law. See Fair Labor Standards Act.

Wagner Act. See National Labor Relations Act.

Wage Stabilization. The program of preventing unlimited wage and salary increases to preserve economic stability. Such a program was first instituted during and after World War II and again by the DEFENSE PRODUCTION ACT in 1950. The principles of wage stabilization allowed for increases to meet the cost of living, remove substandard wages, and eliminate gross inequities and inequalities. See NATIONAL WAR LABOR BOARD and WAGE STABILIZATION BOARD.

Wage Stabilization Board. An agency in the Economic Stabilization Administration authorized by the DEFENSE PRODUCTION ACT of 1950. It was empowered to lay down policy designed to stabilize wages and prevent INFLATION. It is an 18 man Board, consisting of six men each representing the public, labor, and management. Its principal office is located in Washington, D. C., and it maintains 14 regional offices throughout the United States. After a dispute over the Board's powers in 1951 the labor members resigned. President TRUMAN reorganized the Board, conferring upon it the power to deal with disputes. In March, 1952 the Board handed down a decision granting the union shop and wage increases to the steel workers. The decision was unacceptable to the steel operators and on April 8, 1952 President Truman ordered the SEIZURE OF THE STEEL MILLS to prevent a STRIKE. By AMENDMENT of June 30, 1952 to the Defense Production Act, the Board was forbidden to intervene in labor disputes and its members made subject to Senate confirmation. It was authorized, however, to give interpretations or advice at the request of employers, workers, or an interested federal agency. Its powers to regulate wage and salary increases were extended to April 30, 1953 subject to the discretionary authority to suspend such controls without leading to "dangerous unstabilizing effect." Its functions under the new law were to formulate and recommend to the ECONOMIC STABILIZATION ADMINISTRATOR "general policies and general regulations relating to the stabilization of wages, salaries, and other compensation." The Board was forbidden to issue any new regulations dealing with WAGE STABILIZATION policy.

Wagner-Lea Act. See Investment Trust Act.

Wagner-Peyser Act. A law of Congress in 1933 creating the United States Employment Service within the federal DEPARTMENT OF LABOR. In 1939, pursuant to a reorganization plan, this agency was transferred to the FEDERAL SECURITY AGENCY and combined with the Unemployment Insurance Division of the Social Security Board. The USES has established over 1500 employment offices in the United States, and by 1940 had accepted over 16,000,000 applications, making 5,200,000 placements of which 3,000,000 were in private employment. The Act provided for joint federal-state administration of the public employment services with a matching of federal and state funds. Federal payments are based on POPULATION. Merit system conditions are required for the administrative employees of the agencies and all plans must be approved by the USES.

WAGNER, Robert Ferdinand. 1877-1949. Lawyer and legislator. b. Germany. Came to the United States as a child. Graduated, College of the City of New York (1898), New York Law School (1900); practiced law in New York City; state senator (1909-18); supreme court justice in New York (1919-26); U. S. Senator (1927-1949); well-known for the liberal social legislation which he sponsored including the NATIONAL INDUSTRIAL RECOVERY ACT, SOCIAL SECURITY ACT, NATIONAL LABOR RELATIONS ACT (called the Wagner Act), Railway Pension Law, the U.S. HOUSING ACT of 1937, and many others; he resigned from the Senate because of ill-health.

Wagon Train. A caravan or train of wagons organized for the purpose of efficient travel and defense against Indians in the Far West. It is believed that the first mule drawn train over the OREGON TRAIL consisted of 10 wagons and was organized by the Rocky Mountain Fur Company in 1830 from St. Louis to Wind River. These trains consisted of the "prairie schooner," a canvas covered type of wagon drawn by mules, horses, or oxen. These caravans plied well-marked routes into the Southwest and Northwest, emanating from St. Joseph or St. Louis, Missouri. By 1849 more than 5,500 trains were passing annually into California or Oregon, carrying freight and passengers. The hazards which confronted them included Indian attacks, thefts, storms, attacks by buffalo herds, and stampedes. The trains traveled from 10 to 15 miles a day. The Union Pacific-Central Pacific Railway Line and the establishment of STAGECOACH lines after the Civil War, reduced the need for wagon trains, and by the mid-1880's they had virtually disappeared from the western scene.

WAITE, Morrison Remick. 1816-1888. Jurist. b. Connecticut. Graduated, Yale; practiced law in Ohio; leading WHIG; represented the United States at the Geneva arbitration of the *Alabama* claims (1871); succeeded SALMON CHASE as Chief Justice of the U.S. Supreme Court (1874-88).

Wake Island. A group of three islets Wake, Wilkes, and Peale, discovered by the British in 1796 and annexed by the United States in 1898. They are located in the PACIFIC OCEAN, halfway between Midway and GUAM. The group is four and one half miles long and one and a half miles wide, with an area of 2,600 acres. Utilized solely as a military base, the Island is uninhabited and is administered as part of Honolulu County, HAWAII. It was attacked by the Japanese at the outbreak of World War II, and conquered by them on December 23, 1941. The Japanese surrendered the Island to the United States on September 4, 1945. On October 15, 1950 it was the site of an important conference between President TRUMAN and General MAC ARTHUR, dealing with the Korean War.

WALD, Lillian. 1867-1940. Social worker. b. Ohio. Organized the Henry Street Settlement in New York City; sponsor of the Federal CHILDREN'S BUREAU which was established by Congress (1908); important in visiting nurses services in both rural and city areas. Author of several books about the Henry Street Settlement.

WALKE, Henry. 1808-1896. Naval officer. Served in the Mexican War; served under Commodore FOOTE on the upper Mississippi (1861-63); served against VICKSBURG (1863); commanded the steamer *Sacramento* in the Atlantic (1863-65); made a commodore (1866); rear admiral (1870).

WALKER, Francis Amasa. 1840-1897. Economist, statistician, and educator. Graduated, Amherst; studied law; served through the Civil War being brevetted a brigadier general by the end of the war; chief, U. S. Bureau of Statistics (1869-71); U. S. Commissioner of Indian Affairs (1871-72); professor of economics at Yale (1873-81); became president of the Massachusetts Institute of Technology (1881-97); best known for his economic theories on wages and profits and advocated international bimetallism.

WALKER, Mary Edwards. 1831-1919. Physician. b. New York. Graduated, Syracuse Medical School (1855); the first woman to be commissioned assistant surgeon in the U. S. Army; served through the Civil War with the Union Army (1861-65); in fighting for equal rights for women she first adopted the Bloomer costume and then male attire; part of the WOMAN SUFFRAGE movement.

WALKER, Robert James. 1801-1869. Political leader. b. Pennsylvania. Graduated, University of Pennsylvania (1819); practiced law in Pittsburgh, then moved to Mississippi where he became wealthy and successful; strong opponent of NULLIFICATION; U.S. Senator (1836-45); favored recognition and ANNEXATION OF TEXAS; appointed by POLK U.S. Secretary of the Treasury (1845-49); author of the

WALKER TARIFF which was a REVENUE TARIFF (1846); governor of the Kansas territory (1857-58); supported DOUGLAS and "POPULAR SOVEREIGNTY" and the North during the Civil War at which time he was sent as an agent to Europe to act for the United States in financial matters; played a part in the planning of the transcontinental railroad and in the purchase of the TERRITORY of ALASKA.

Walker Tariff Act. A downward revision of the rates established in the TARIFF OF 1842. It was enacted in 1846 and classified imports under schedules. Luxuries were put into Class A with a rate of 100 percent, semi-luxuries in Class B with a rate of 40 percent, and commercial products into remaining classes with duties ranging from five to 30 percent. The act introduced the warehousing system of storing goods until the duty was paid, a method retained to this day. It also changed the system from SPECIFIC to AD VALOREM duties. Although still protectionist the Walker Tariff greatly reduced duties, and set the pace for further reductions in 1857.

WALLACE (Attempted Assassination). George Wallace, governor of Alabama, was a strong contender for the democratic presidential nomination in 1972. On May 15, 1972, while he was campaigning in Laurel, Maryland, he was shot by an assassin, Arthur Bremer. Although he survived, Wallace was paralyzed from the waist down and withdrew from the presidential campaign.

WALLACE, Henry. 1836-1916. Agricultural editor and author. b. Pennsylvania. A pioneer in modern dairying, in raising pure-bred hogs and in growing clover in Iowa; owner and editor (1895-1906) *Wallace's Farmer* (formerly *Wallace's Farm and Dairy*), wrote *Uncle Henry's Letters to the Farm Boy* (1897) and others. He tried to set up programs of better farming in the West.

WALLACE, Henry Agard. 1888-1965.

Agriculturist and CABINET officer. Graduated, Iowa State College of Agriculture; associate editor (1910-24) and editor (1924-29) of the *Wallace's Farmer* and of *Iowa Homestead and Wallace's Farmer* (from 1929);appointed by F. D. ROOSEVELT, U. S. Secretary of Agriculture (1933-40); Vice-President of the United States (1941-45); head of the Economic Defense Board (1941); U.S. Secretary of Commerce (March 1945); PROGRESSIVE PARTY candidate for the presidency (1948), polling over 1,000,000 votes; broke with the party after Korean War began. Author of books on AGRICULTURE, economics, and politics.

WALLACE, Henry Cantwell. 1866-1924. Agricultural editor and cabinet officer. Co-editor of *Wallace's Farmer* with his father HENRY WALLACE and his brother John; appointed by HARDING, U.S. Secretary of Agriculture serving for a short time in COOLIDGE's administration as well (1921-24).

WALLACE, Lewis. Better known as Lew Wallace. 1827-1905. Lawyer, army officer, political leader and author. Practiced law in Indiana; adjutant general of Indiana at outbreak of the Civil War being commissioned a brigadier general (1861) and major general (1862) serving at SHILOH and Cincinnati; served at courtmartial of those tried for assassination of LINCOLN; governor of New Mexico Territory (1878-81); U.S. Minister to Turkey (1881-85). Author of popular *Ben Hur; A Tale of Christ* (1880) and other books.

Wall Street. The name of a street in lower New York City. It is best known as the financial center of the nation. It was so named from a wall constructed 300 years ago by the Dutch to protect themselves against Indian raids. In and around it are established the most powerful BANKING and brokerage houses in the world.

Walsh-Healey Act. Passed by Congress in 1936. It is also known as the Public

669

Contracts Act and is administered by the Wage and Hour and Public Contracts division of the U.S. DEPARTMENT OF LABOR. It provides that government contractors must pay not less than the prevailing minimum wage for comparable work, observe the eight hour day and 40 hour week, allow no perilous or unhealthful working conditions, employ no persons under 18 years of age, and hire no convict labor.

WALSH, Thomas James. 1859-1933. Lawyer and political leader. b. Wisconsin. Practiced law in Montana; served as U. S. Senator from that state (1913-33); worked for reform legislation; supported WILSON and the LEAGUE OF NATIONS; led in the exposure of the TEAPOT DOME SCANDAL; supported F. D. ROOSEVELT.

WALTER, Thomas Ustick. 1804-1887. Architect. b. Philadelphia, Pennsylvania. Leader of the classic school of ARCHITECTURE in the United States; designed many important buildings including the CAPITOL, Washington, D.C. (1851); appointed by President FILLMORE; designing and supervising construction of wings and the dome (1851-65).

"Waltham System." The concentration of spinning and weaving processes in one factory which took place in 1814 in Waltham, Massachusetts when FRANCIS CABOT LOWELL and Paul Moody designed and built a power loom which combined these techniques. It is believed that this is the first time that this method was introduced in a modern factory.

WALTON, George. 1741-1804. Lawyer and political leader. b. Virginia. Practiced law in Georgia; delegate to CONTINENTAL CONGRESS (1776-81); a signer of the DECLARATION OF INDEPENDENCE; and the ARTICLES OF CONFEDERATION; governor of Georgia (1779-80, 1789); chief justice of Georgia supreme court and judge of the superior court; U.S. Senator (1795-96).

Wampanoag Indians. A tribe of ALGONQUIN INDIANS who lived in Massachusetts. They were led by their chief MASSASOIT and were on friendly terms with the PILGRIMS. Massasoit was also very friendly in his dealings with ROGER WILLIAMS but resisted all efforts to convert him to Christianity. His son Philip was responsible for the disastrous King Philip's War in 1675. They were badly defeated and, although a few members of the tribe joined the NARRAGANSETTS, they were almost completely wiped out.

WANAMAKER, John. 1838-1922. Merchant. b. Philadelphia, Pennsylvania. Became owner of the largest retail men's clothing store in the United States; U. S. Postmaster General (1889-93); important in contributions to the Y.M.C.A. in the United States and other countries; sent two relief ships to Belgium at the outbreak of World War I.

War Assets Administration. An agency created by EXECUTIVE ORDER in 1946 to supervise the disposal of public goods and properties declared to be surplus after World War II.

War Claims Fund. See Alien Property Custodian.

War Crimes. During World War II the first statement by the UNITED NATIONS that WAR CRIMES would be punished after the war was made in the Moscow Declaration on October 30, 1943. Subsequently the United Nations Commission for the Investigation of War Crimes was established to compile lists of suspected war criminals. It classified two groups of crimes: those against the nationals of a state, the trial of which was to be held by national courts or military tribunals, and those international in scope, to be tried by special international courts under military law. In August, 1945 the United States, England, France, and the Soviet Union adopted a statute for trying the principal Nazi civil and military leaders. These nations established the

670

Nuremberg Tribunal which opened its hearings on November 20, 1945 for the trial of 24 top Nazi leaders. Associate Justice ROBERT H. JACKSON, on leave from the United States Supreme Court, was the prosecutor. War crimes had been defined as plotting aggressive war, atrocities against civilians, genocide, slave labor, looting of occupied countries, and the maltreatment and murder of war prisoners. Voluminous evidence was introduced to the trial, and sentence of death was imposed on October 1, 1946 upon Goering, Streicher, Ribbentrop, and eight others. Seven were sentenced to imprisonment. No convictions were handed down against Nazi organizations or the German general staff. On June 3, 1945 trial was opened in Tokyo by an 11 man international tribunal against 28 Japanese indicted as war criminals. On November 12, 1948, sentence was handed down against 25, and on December 23, 1948 former Premier Tojo and six others were hanged in Tokyo after the failure of their appeal to the United States Supreme Court. During this period concurrent trials were held in German and Japanese courts which, by 1950, had tried more than 8,000 war criminals and executed 2,000 of them. The number of trials declined thereafter, and by 1952 many appeals by the convicted had resulted in reversals.

WARD, Artemas. 1727-1800. Revolutionary general. b. Massachusetts. Jurist in Massachusetts; served at TICONDEROGA (1758); in command of American forces at LEXINGTON; commander in chief of Massachusetts forces; directed siege of Boston; second in command in WASHINGTON by order of Congress; major general (1775); resigned (1776); member CONTINENTAL CONGRESS (1780-81) and U.S. House of Representatives (1791-95).

War Debt Commission. Also known as the Debt Funding Commission. An agency created by Congress in February, 1922 for the purpose of funding the $12,000,000,000 war and postwar debt. During its five year tenure it negotiated agreements with Belgium, France, Great Britain, Italy, and other nations. These agreements fixed the total funded indebtedness owed to the United States, the interest rate, and the fixed annual amount to be paid. The annual payments were to be made over a period of 62 years. By considering the financial status of specific nations, the Commission reduced individual debts up to 50 percent.

War Debts. Refers to the funds lent by American bankers and businessmen to Great Britain, France, Italy, and 13 other Allied and successor nations in World War I. These funds totaled approximately $12,000,000,000 by 1920. The bulk of these loans was never repaid. Various attempts to readjust these loans were made through the Dawes Plan of 1924, the Young Plan of 1929, and the Hoover Moratorium of 1931. The Johnson Debt Act of 1934 forbade loans by any private Americans to those governments which were in default of previous debt payments.

War Democrats. Northern Democrats who supported the Union cause in the Civil War. STEPHEN A. DOUGLAS and ANDREW JOHNSON were among the leaders of the Democratic party who believed that the question of maintaining the Union overshadowed all other issues in the war crisis.

War, Department of. One of the EXECUTIVE DEPARTMENTS established by the first Congress in 1789. The first Secretary of War, appointed by the President and Senate, was General HENRY KNOX. Under the NATIONAL SECURITY ACT of 1947 it was renamed the Department of the Army, and merged with the Department of the Navy and the newly created Department of Air into the existing Department of Defense. See Army, Department of.

War Finance Corporation. An agency established by Congress in 1918 to promote credit facilities for war industries by making loans to financial institutions. After the war it granted substantial loans to RAILROAD companies and was the fiscal agent of the Treasury Department in purchasing bonds. In 1919 its powers were augmented to allow it to finance American exports. In 1921 it inaugurated a system of lending agencies to assist AGRICULTURE. It was abolished in 1924 after having lent $700,000,000.

War Food Administration. An autonomous agency set up by EXECUTIVE ORDER within the DEPARTMENT OF AGRICULTURE in 1943. The WFA was given the responsibility for ensuring an adequate supply of food during World War II. The Administrator was empowered to determine the direct and indirect military, civilian, and foreign needs for human and animal food and for food used in INDUSTRY. He was authorized to draft a program that would provide such food supplies as far as possible, and allocate these supplies as he deemed suitable. He recommended the allotment of materials and equipment to the WAR PRODUCTION BOARD, and exercised administrative control over the supply of farm laborers and over agricultural wage and salary stabilization.

"War Hawks." Western and southern members of the 12th Congress, elected in 1810, who campaigned for war against Great Britain. The westerners desired the annexation of Canada; the southerners wanted to annex Florida and Texas. As spokesmen for their sections they expressed the expansionist tendencies of the southern planter and western FRONTIERSMAN. They considered the British responsible for inciting the Indians in the Northwest, and sparked the drive which culminated in the War of 1812.

Among their leaders were HENRY CLAY, JOHN C. CALHOUN, and THOMAS HART BENTON.

War Industries Board. An agency established by Congress in 1917 to coordinate the efforts of American INDUSTRY in producing goods for the war effort. The overlapping functions of the Committee of National Defense and the War Department's procurement agencies compelled the creation of a board to unify the tasks of war procurement. On March 4, 1918 BERNARD BARUCH was appointed chairman of the War Industries Board with power to mobilize the industrial resources of the nation in the production of war materials. The Board was authorized to fix prices, increase munitions productions, and allocate raw materials. It was abolished on January 1, 1919.

War Information, Office of. An agency established by EXECUTIVE ORDER on June 13, 1942 to mobilize the press, RADIO, MOTION PICTURE, and MAGAZINE facilities of the United States in the war effort. Into it were placed all existing civilian information services. The agency supervised the writing and presentation of information reporting the role of the United States and its allies to the nation and to foreign countries. Part of its program involved POLITICAL WARFARE designed to demoralize the enemy. These efforts took the form of information leaflets, magazines, and radio broadcasts distributed clandestinely to the enemy. Although it was criticized in the United States and abroad for some of its methods, the Office of War Information carried on an extremely sensitive program that achieved notable successes. Elmer Davis was appointed its director. The agency was abolished in 1945.

War Labor Board. See National War Labor Board, World War I, and National War Labor Board, World War. II.

War Labor Disputes Act. See Smith-Connally Act.

War Manpower Commission. A war agency established by EXECUTIVE ORDER on April 18, 1942 to plan the recruitment of workers to meet the critical labor shortage. It was authorized to classify occupations as essential or non-essential and to grant releases to employees wishing to transfer to essential jobs. Its other functions included the organization of training programs, the classification of areas as critical from a labor standpoint, and the publication of materials designed to attract labor to such areas. To it was transferred the United States Employment Service. Unable to enforce its decisions, and opposed by organized labor, the War Manpower Commission did not fully succeed in achieving the desired results. Plans in 1945 for conferring upon it legal enforcement powers to draft labor were abandoned when the war ended in May of that year. In 1945 the WMC was incorporated into the DEPARTMENT OF LABOR.

War Mobilization and Reconversion, Office of. An administrative agency established as the Office of War Mobilization by EXECUTIVE ORDER on May 27, 1943 to coordinate the activities of all civilian war agencies. It was renamed by the law of October 3, 1944. As Director of War Mobilization former Supreme Court Justice, JAMES F. BYRNES, was authorized to unify and correlate the activities of all federal agencies, engaged in the civilian aspects of war mobilization. He was specifically directed "to resolve and determine all controversies between such agencies." He was empowered to settle controversies among federal agencies concerned with the production, purchase, distribution, and transportation of military or civilian supplies. As "Assistant President," the Director was clothed with virtually dictatorial powers in carrying out this program. In the postwar period the agency was charged with the duty of reconverting from military to civilian production. The agency was abolished by executive order on July 19, 1945.

WARNER, Seth. 1743-1784. Revolutionary general. b. Connecticut. Served with ETHAN ALLEN and BENEDICT ARNOLD at TICONDEROGA (1775); lieutenant colonel of a Vermont regiment and led them at the BATTLE OF BENNINGTON (1777); commissioned brigadier general (1778).

War of 1812. A war between the United States and Great Britain, declared by Congress on June 18, 1812 and concluded by the TREATY OF GHENT on December 24, 1814. The causes of the War included IMPRESSMENT of American seamen, seizures of American cargoes on the high seas, British encouragement of Indian attacks in the Northwest, and general commercial and economic restrictions imposed by the British government. Notable highlights of the War were the unsuccessful attempt by American troops to capture Toronto, the BURNING OF WASHINGTON by the British, the consistent military defeats of American units, the two outstanding naval victories by American fleets on LAKE ERIE and LAKE CHAMPLAIN, and the victory at the BATTLE OF NEW ORLEANS a month after the War was over. The War of 1812 is sometimes called the "Second War for Independence" or the "War for Economic Independence." Its results were significant, including the beginnings of industrialization, the development of NATIONALISM, the opening of the West, and territorial expansion. Casualties included 2,260 dead and 4,505 wounded.

war on poverty. The term "war on poverty" was used by President Johnson in his first State of the Union Address delivered in January, 1964. In order to wage a "war on poverty" he recommended a broadened food stamp program for the poor, increased aid to the Appalchian Mountain System, improved unemployment insurance and youth employment legislation. The anti-poverty program was furthered through the Economic Opportunity Act of 1964 enacted by Congress which emphasized assistance to youth through job training and remedial education in the Job Corps. Federal grants were given to communities to help the poor through additional opportunities for employment and through educational programs to help prepare people to lead economically worthwhile lives.

War Powers Act. On November 7, 1973, Congress overrode President Nixon's veto of the Act which set a limit of 60 days on commitment of troops by the president into hostilities abroad unless authorized by Congress with an additional 30 days allowed for troop withdrawal.

War Powers of the President. Emergency powers exercised by the President during wartime. They are exercised either in his capacity as chief executive and commander-in-chief of the armed forces or by specific delegation by Congress. Special legislation of World War I conferred upon the President a vast reservoir of emergency powers to increase the strength of the armed forces, suspend or amend the rules controlling radio and telegraphy COMMUNICATIONS, and take control over powerhouses, dams, and waterworks, necessary in munitions MANUFACTURING. By the opening of World War II the President's war powers extended to over 100 such emergency controls. The SELECTIVE TRAINING AND SERVICE ACT of 1940 and LEND LEASE ACT of 1941 granted additional emergency powers which were expanded by the First War Powers Act of December, 1941. This law revived and extended the President's powers of World War I by authorizing him to establish a censorship over all communications media, transfer war-related functions among executive agencies, modify defense contracts, and control alien financial transactions. In

March, 1942 the Second War Powers Act permitted the President to requisition machinery, tools, and materials for war production, and conferred power upon him to extend priorities to tools and machines, penalize violations of priorities. and regulate motor and water carriers. In 1951 Congress extended the power to modify existing defense contracts.

War Production Board. An agency established by EXECUTIVE ORDER on January 16, 1942 to replace the OFFICE OF PRODUCTION MANAGEMENT and the SUPPLY, PRIORITIES, AND ALLOCATIONS BOARD. It was given the responsibility for the production and distribution of raw materials and manufactured goods, and their allocation between military and civilian needs. Chaired by Donald Nelson, its other members included the Vice-President, the Secretaries of War and Navy, the Federal Loan Administrator, and the Price Administrator. It rapidly undertook the huge task of converting the nation's industrial plant to war production. By the end of the year the WPB was able to report that it had exceeded the President's goal of 8,000,000 tons of SHIPPING. By the end of 1942 the nation had produced 49,000 planes, 32,000 tanks and motorized artillery, and huge quantities of other munitions. It was absorbed by the CIVILIAN PRODUCTION ADMINISTRATION *on November* 3, 1945.

War Refugee Board. An agency established by EXECUTIVE ORDER on January 22, 1944 and abolished on September 15, 1945. It consisted of the Secretaries of State, Treasury, and War who were authorized to effect the immediate rescue from the Nazis of as many persons as possible of persecuted racial, religious, or political minorities. The agency's powers were limited to the aid of civilian victims of enemy barbarism. It was charged with the duty of rescuing, transporting, and maintaining such refugees and of seeking the cooperation of all public and private organizations in this work. Its staff coordinated its work with that of neutral countries and succeeded in moving thousands of persons from the Balkans to Palestine, from the Lowlands and France through Switzerland to Spain and Portugal, and from Norway to Sweden. It established refugee camps, one of which was located at Oswego, New York where 1,000 Italians were sheltered at the end of the war. By special act of Congress these refugees were permitted to remain in the United States.

War Relief Control Board. An agency established by EXECUTIVE ORDER on July 25, 1942. It was authorized to assure the efficient and economic administration of resources for war relief and welfare in the United States and abroad. It controlled the program of solicitation and collection of funds and contributions for war relief in allied belligerent countries. This included the sales, service, receipts, expenditures, and distribution of goods and money for charities working in foreign and domestic relief, rehabilitation, reconstruction, and welfare. It was also empowered to grant aid in refugee relief, relief of the civilian POPULATION of the United States affected by enemy action, and relief of the armed forces of the United States and their dependents. The Board was authorized to license and register persons and organizations in such work. By June 30, 1945, when it went out of existence, it had collected $253,-802,862 in cash and $224,409,787 in kind. It had disbursed $218,736,798 in cash and $183,863,496 in kind.

Warren Commission. Appointed in 1963 by President Johnson to investigate the assassination of President John F. Kennedy and the murder of Lee Harvy Oswald, the alleged assassin. Headed by Chief Juistice Earl Warren, the Commission included Allen W. Dulles, former head of the Central Intelligence Agency; John J. McCloy, former adviser to President Kennedy; Senators Russell and Cooper; and Representatives Boggs and Ford. A report released on September 27, 1964 concluded that Lee Harvey Oswald was solely responsible for the murder of President Kennedy on November 22, 1963. The Commission also recommended major changes in the methods used to protect the life of the president.

WARREN, Earl. 1891-   Political leader and jurist. b. California. Law degrees from Univ. of California, 1912, 1914. Attorney General of California, 1939-1943. Elected Governor, 1943, and served until appointment as Chief Justice of the Supreme Court, 1953. Received 59 votes as favorite son candidate for President in 1948, then nominated for vice president to run with Thomas E. Dewey. In 1952, received 81 votes for president on the first ballot at the Republican Convention. In historic ruling, 1954, Chief Justice Warren read unanimous decision of the Supreme Court declaring as unconstitutional racial segregation in the public schools.

WARREN, Gouverneur Kemble. 1830-1882. Union general and military engineer. b. New York. Graduated, U.S.M.A., West Point (1850); assigned to the engineer corps; commissioned colonel of volunteers (1861); brigadier general (1862); chief of engineers of the Army of the Potomac; served with distinction at GETTYSBURG and in many other important battles.

WARREN, John Collins. 1778-1856. Surgeon. Professor, Harvard Medical School (1808-47); first surgeon, Massachusetts General Hospital, Boston (1821); famous as the first surgeon to use ether as an ANESTHESIA in a public demonstration (1846), the ether being administered by W. T. G. MORTON.

WARREN, Joseph. 1741-1775. Physician and revolutionary officer. b. Massachusetts. Practiced MEDICINE in Boston; opposed the STAMP ACT (1765) and joined SAMUEL ADAMS group; wrote the SUFFOLK RESOLUTION: and presented them to the convention (1774); member, COMMITTEE OF CORRESPONDENCE; he sent PAUL REVERE on his famous ride to LEXINGTON; president pro tempore of provincial Congress (1775); major general (1775); killed at Breed's Hill during the BATTLE OF BUNKER HILL.

WARREN, Mercy Otis. 1728-1814. Author. b. Massachusetts. Her home was a meeting place for the patriots of her day and she corresponded with such important figures as THOMAS JEFFERSON, JOHN and SAMUEL ADAMS and ELBRIDGE GERRY. She wrote the *History of the Rise, Progress, and Termination of the American Revolution* (3 vols., 1805) and POETRY and plays.

War Shipping Administration. An administrative agency established by EXECUTIVE ORDER on February 7, 1942 for the purpose of coordinating wartime SHIPPING. All vessels owned by the United States MARITIME COMMISSION were turned over to it, and it was authorized to purchase, requisition, or control all vessels under the flag of the United States. The agency allocated vessels to the armed services and other government agencies as required. It worked closely with the WAR PRODUCTION BOARD in establishing priorities for the TRANSPORTATION of commodities and raw materials. The administrative staff was divided into units in control of specialized areas dealing with LABOR RELATIONS, construction, ship operations, and the use of vessels. As a result of its efforts, millions of tons of Liberty and Victory ships were constructed. By the end of the war the United States had become the greatest merchant nation in the world, possessing well over half the tonnage of the world.

War Trade Board. See Trading with the Enemy Act.

WASHBURN, Cadwallader Colden. 1818-1882. Lawyer, merchant, army officer, and politician. b. Maine. Admitted to the bar (1842) and practiced in Wisconsin; successful real estate operator; member, U. S. House of Representatives (1855-61, 1867-71); served as a major general in the Union Army during the Civil War; elected governor of Wisconsin (1872-74); organized a large milling firm; donated the Washburn Observatory to the University of Wisconsin.

WASHBURNE, Elihu Benjamin. 1816-1887. Lawyer, politician and diplomat. b. Maine. Admitted to the bar and practiced in Illinois; member, U. S. House of Representatives (1853-69) where as chairman of the commerce committee he earned the nickname of "the watchdog of the treasury." Appointed by GRANT U.S. Secretary of State, he resigned to become U.S. Minister to France (1869-77).

Washington. The 20th state in size, with an area of 68,192 square miles. Organized as a TERRITORY in 1853 and admitted as the 42nd state on November 11, 1889. Olympia is the capital. In 1950 Washington's POPULATION of 2,378,963 made it 23rd in rank. Its largest cities are Seattle, Spokane, and Tacoma. Washington is the nation's leading producer of LUMBER. Great stands of fir, pine, spruce, larch, and cedar cover the state. It is one of the largest apple growing states in the Union. GRAND COULEE DAM, on the Columbia River, has the world's most powerful hydro-electric plant. Ninety percent of the state's electric energy is produced by hydro-electric plants. The result is that Washington boasts more electric lights per capita than any other state in the nation. The Hanford Engineer Works, near Pasco, is the world's first ATOMIC

676

BOMB plant. Washington was discovered in 1775 by Bruno Heceta. Its nicknames are the "Evergreen State" and "Chinook State."

WASHINGTON, Booker Taliaferro. 1856-1915. Educator. Born a slave in Virginia. His father was a white man. By perseverance and hard work he studied for three years at the Hampton Institute (1872-75); chosen to organize a school for Negroes at Tuskegee, Alabama which he made into a very fine institution; he lectured widely and received honorary degrees from other universities. He also wrote many books and gained a reputation as the outstanding NEGRO leader in the United States.

WASHINGTON, Bushrod. 1762-1829. Jurist. b. Virginia. Nephew of GEORGE WASHINGTON. Graduated, William and Mary (1770); served in the Continental Army during the Revolution; practiced law in Virginia; member Virginia house of delegates; Associate Justice, U.S. Supreme Court (1798-1829); lived at MOUNT VERNON which he had inherited from George Washington along with his LIBRARY and papers.

Washington, D. C. The capital of the United States since 1800. Its area is 61.4 square miles, housing a population of more than 800,000 people. It consists of TERRITORY ceded to the federal government by the states of Maryland and Virginia in 1788 and 1789 respectively. It was created as a municipal CORPORATION in 1871. Its present form of government was established in 1878. A Board of Commissioners exercises jurisdiction over local matters, but laws for the city are passed directly by Congress. It is famous for the physical planning of the city, having been constructed on the same plan as Paris, namely in the form of a wheel with streets radiating from the center. Among the many famous buildings are the WHITE HOUSE, CAPITOL

Building, the LIBRARY OF CONGRESS, the Lincoln Memorial, Washington Monument, TOMB OF THE UNKNOWN SOLDIER, and the Pentagon.

Washington, D. C., Burning of. On August 24, 1814 a British army defeated the badly organized MILITIA outside Washington, D.C. The British entered the city by that evening, and throughout the following night a detachment of troops, commanded by General Robert Ross and Admiral George Cockburn, began the destruction of the city. They burned the CAPITOL building, the WHITE HOUSE, and Treasury building. Although interrupted by rain, they later set fire to private homes, some business establishments, and buildings HOUSING the DEPARTMENT OF STATE and Department of War. A considerable quantity of military equipment was also destroyed. The British did not leave the city until August 25th.

WASHINGTON, George. 1732-1799. First President of the United States. b. Westmoreland County, Virginia. Privately educated; worked as a surveyor for Lord Fairfax; served with BRADDOCK on his staff (1755); commissioned colonel and commander in chief of Virginia troops (1755); in command of defense of the FRONTIER during the French and Indian attacks; lived life of country gentleman at MOUNT VERNON; member, VIRGINIA HOUSE OF BURGESSES (1759-74); led opposition to the British in his colony; member, First and Second CONTINENTAL CONGRESSES (1774-75); assumed command of all Continental armies (1775); fought with courage and brilliance through the many difficult battles including New York, LONG ISLAND, TRENTON, PRINCETON, VALLEY FORGE, BRANDYWINE and GERMANTOWN; retired to Mount Vernon but recalled to preside at the convention in Philadelphia (1787); unanimously elected the first President of

677

the United States under the new Constitution (1789) and re-elected (1793); declined the offer of a third term and made his famous FAREWELL SPEECH (1796); when war with France threatened he was commissioned a lieutenant general and commander in chief of the army; the first name elected to the HALL OF FAME; known as the "Father of His Country."

WASHINGTON, Martha Dandridge. 1732-1802. b. Virginia. Famous as the wife of GEORGE WASHINGTON, she was a gracious and charming hostess.

Washington Naval Conference. A conference for the limitation of naval armaments which met in Washington, D. C. from November, 1921 to February, 1922. The participating nations were the United States, Great Britain, Japan, France, Italy, the Netherlands, Portugal, Belgium, and China. The results of the Conference included a series of treaties involving naval limitation, adjustment of Far Eastern problems, the status of China, and limitation of island fortifications in the Pacific. The Conference left Japan as the strongest naval and military power in the Far East. Although it preserved peace in the Pacific for a decade and relieved the United States from the exclusive support of the OPEN-DOOR POLICY, it provided the political and military means for future Japanese aggression. See "Naval Holiday," Four Power Treaty, Five Power Treaty, and Nine Power Pact.

Washington Naval Treaty. See Five Power Treaty.

Washington's Birthday. Observed on February 22nd, it commemorates the birth of GEORGE WASHINGTON. It is celebrated as a legal HOLIDAY in all states, territories, and the District of Columbia. The observance began in 1796, three years before Washington's death.

Washington's Farewell Address. The publication in the Philadelpia *Daily American Advertiser* of an address by President WASHINGTON written on September 19, 1796. In it Washington stated his reasons for refusing a third term and submitted his views on the need for a strong union of the states. He set forth the doctrines for achieving enduring domestic peace and the respect of foreign nations, and outlined the reasons for his NEUTRALITY in the wars of the French Revolution. The broad program he laid down involved a reconciliation of party conflict and the necessity of remaining aloof from the political struggles of Europe. See "non-entangling alliances."

Washington's Proclamation of Neutrality. See Neutrality, Proclamation of.

Watauga Settlement. The migration and settlement of FRONTIERSMEN from North Carolina and Virginia to the Watauga River in Tennessee. The first settler moved into the area in 1769, and by 1772 the settlement was sufficiently numerous to bring about a local charter known as the Watauga Association. In that year the settlers obtained a 10 year lease from the CHEROKEE INDIANS on all lands on the river. Patterned on the Virginia system, they established an assembly of five men. The Watauga Settlement was important as the nucleus of subsequent Tennessee and Kentucky settlements. At the outbreak of the Revolution these hardy pioneers defended the West against the British.

"Watchful Waiting." The phrase describing the policy of President JACKSON in 1836 in refusing to take diplomatic action on the question of Texan independence. Also applied to the policy pursued by President WILSON with the respect to the Mexican governments from 1913 to 1917. After the accession of Huerta to the Mexican presidency in 1913 and his rejection of Wilson's demands for a cessation of fighting in Mexico, a general amnesty, and free elections, Wilson issued a warning for American CITIZENS to leave Mexico. In his address to Congress on December 2, 1913 he described his policy as "watchful waiting."

Watergate. On June 17, 1972 five men were arrested in the Democratic National Headquarters located in the Watergate Hotel complex in Washington, D.C. These five and two others involved in the planning and carrying out of the break-in were hired by the Committee for Re-Election of the President (Nixon) and were found guilty of conspiracy, burglary, and eavesdropping. Extensive hearings on Watergate and the presidential campaign were conducted by Sen. Sam J. Erwin, Jr. (Dem., N.C.) who headed the Senate Select Committee on Presidential Campaign Activities. Such matters as bugging of offices, burglary, fraudulent leaflets, and sabotage of political opponents were uncovered. President Nixon maintained he had no prior knowledge of the break-in attempts to cover it up. Examination of tapes recording Nixon's discussions in the Oval offices revealed that he was aware of the involvement of his associates and that he did obstruct justice by participating in the coverup. He resigned on August 9, 1974 avoiding almost certain impeachment.

Water Power. A source of power obtained by damming up a moving body of water and then releasing the flow under controlled conditions against a wheel or mill. As a matter of PUBLIC WELFARE, water power was controlled early in American history. Colonial governments in New England granted franchises for power rights. The first important water power development was the tapping of the Blackstone River at Pawtucket, Rhode Island in 1790. Important industrial centers grew up around the development of the power of the Passaic River in New Jersey, Fall River in Massachusetts, Fox River in Wisconsin, and elsewhere in the United States. By 1894 the power from Niagara

Falls was utilized for the production of ELECTRICITY. The use of this "white coal" in this period, to turn generators in the production of electric power, spread rapidly. By 1900 18,000,000 horsepower were being developed in this way, many of the old waterpower systems at Paterson, Cohoes, Rochester, and others being converted into hydro-electric plants. In the 20th century the construction by the federal government of vast hydro-electric power projects enormously increased the total. These projects included MUSCLE SHOALS, the BOULDER DAM, the T.V.A., the BONNEVILLE and GRAND COULEE dams on the Columbia River, the Parker Dam on the Colorado River, and the Shasta Dam on the Sacramento River. The ultimate development of the MISSOURI VALLEY and ST. LAWRENCE VALLEY PROJECTS will increase the electric power potential of the United States tremendously. The water power industry is regulated by the FEDERAL POWER COMMISSION, established in 1920.

Watson-Parker Act. Also known as the Railway Labor Act of 1926. It was passed by Congress in 1926. It abolished the Railroad Labor Board which had been created by the ESCH-CUMMINS ACT, and substituted for it a National Board of Mediation. The Mediation Board was authorized to act in all disputes not settled by bipartisan boards of adjustment. In the event of failure to adjust disputes, the Board was to induce the parties to submit the controversy to a court of ARBITRATION. If this court failed, the President was empowered to set up an emergency board to investigate and report the situation to him. Railway labor was legally bound to accept the arbitration board's decision. The law did not deny the right to STRIKE. Because of the failure of the RAILROADS to set up bi-partisan boards of adjustment, the Act did not achieve its purpose. The Act was specifically aimed at encouraging COLLECTIVE BARGAINING and voluntary agreements in railroad LABOR RELATIONS by making railroad workers free to organize into unions without interference or coercion. It was weak, however, in that it provided no penalty for violation by the employer, but did furnish a public means of mediating public disputes if no agreement could be reached through collective bargaining. It also provided a temporary cooling-off period pending investigation by a fact-finding agency, during which no changes would be made in existing conditions, except by agreement.

WATSON, Thomas Edward. 1856-1922. Lawyer, political leader, and author. b. Georgia. Admitted to the bar (1875) and practiced in Georgia; elected Populist member of the U. S. House of Representatives (1890) on the FARMERS' ALLIANCE ticket; sponsored the first bill to introduce rural free delivery of mail; nominated as Vice-President (1896) and President (1904) on the POPULIST PARTY ticket; served as U.S. Senator (1921-22). He wrote several biographies and an attack on Catholicism in his last book.

WATTERSON, Henry. 1840-1921. Journalist and politician. b. Washington, D. C. Served with the Confederate Army during the Civil War; edited the Louisville *Courier-Journal* (1868-1918) in Kentucky; gained a national reputation as an editor; opposed CLEVELAND and BRYAN; was an opponent of T. ROOSEVELT; supported Wilson but opposed the LEAGUE OF NATIONS; member, U.S. House of Representatives (1876-77); won a PULITZER PRIZE for JOURNALISM; author of many books.

WAVES. Abbreviation for Women Appointed for Voluntary Emergency Service. It was auxiliary service for women troops connected with the United States Navy during World War II. It was later reorganized into the Women's Reserve of the U. S. Naval Reserve, which was abolished in 1948 when its members were permitted to join the regular navy and the naval reserve. All legal provisions relating to pay, leave, money allowances, and other emoluments, pertaining to male personnel of the navy, are applicable to women members. They are not assigned to duty in aircraft in combat missions or to any combat ships of the line except hospital ships and naval transports.

"Waving the Bloody Shirt." An expression employed in the campaigns of 1872 and 1876 by liberal Republicans who opposed the persistent attempts by radical Republicans to revive the sectional hatred arising out of the Reconstruction program. The phrase referred to the oratory of the followers of President GRANT who continued to attack the South bitterly at the end of the post-war decade.

WAYNE, Anthony. 1745-1796. Revolutionary General. b. Pennsylvania. Surveyor in Philadelphia; member of the COMMITTEE OF SAFETY; colonel in the Pennsylvania regiment in Continental Army (1776); placed in command at TICONDEROGA; brigadier general (1777); distinguished himself in the battles of Morristown, BRANDYWINE, GERMANTOWN, MONMOUTH, Stony Point, and YORKTOWN; brevetted major general (1783); member, from Georgia, U.S. House of Representatives (1791-92); WASHINGTON appointed him major general in command of American troops in the BATTLE OF FALLEN TIMBERS against the Indians (1794); successfully negotiated the TREATY OF GREENVILLE with the Indian tribes (1795). He was called "Mad Anthony" because of his daring and adventuresome spirit.

Ways and Means Committee. A STANDING COMMITTEE of the House of Representatives. It was established in 1795 to deal with all financial legislation. Since 1865 its jurisdiction has been limited to revenue raising bills. In 1952 it consisted of 25 members and its chairman was Robert E. Doughton.

Weather Bureau, U. S. Established by Congress in the DEPARTMENT OF AGRICULTURE in 1891. Previously, a national weather service had been established in 1870 under the Army Signal Corps. The work of the Bureau now extends in the fields of weather and climate to civil aeronautics, and general agricultural, commercial, industrial, and TRANSPORTATION services. The Bureau engages in research into the causes of weather and climate. Its central office is located in Washington, D.C. through which administrative control is exercised over 14 forecast centers and approximately 400 local offices. Its forecasts are published in practically all daily NEWSPAPERS and broadcast from most radio stations daily. By the Fourth Reorganization Plan of 1940 it was transferred to the DEPARTMENT OF COMMERCE.

WEATHERFORD, William. Known as Red Eagle. 1780?-1824. CREEK INDIAN Chief. b. Alabama. Led massacre at Fort Mims; finally defeated by Andrew JACKSON in the Battle of Horseshoe Bend (1814).

WEAVER, James Baird. 1833-1912. Lawyer and political leader. b. Ohio. Studied law and began practice in Iowa; brevetted brigadier general by the Union Army (1863) serving through the Civil War; GREENBACK PARTY member, U.S. House of Representatives (1879-81) and elected on a combined Democratic and GREENBACK LABOR PARTY ticket (1885-89); candidate for the presidency on the Greenback Labor party ticket (1880); presidential candidate, winning 22 electoral votes and over 1,000,000 popular votes on the POPULIST PARTY ticket (1892); backed BRYAN and the party became absorbed into the Democratic party.

WEBB, Alexander Stewart. 1835-1911. Union general and educator. b. New York City. Graduated, U.S.M.A., West Point (1855); served with the Army of the Potomac during the Civil War; repelled Pickett's charge at GETTYSBURG; served as chief-of-staff to General MEADE (1865); acted as military governor of Virginia; received MEDAL OF HONOR; taught at West Point; resigned from the army (1870); president, College of the City of New York (1869-1902).

Webb Export Act. See Webb-Pomerene Act.

WEBB, James Watson. 1802-1884. Journalist and diplomat. b. New York. Edited the *Morning Courier and New York Enquirer* (1829-61) which was the organ of the WHIG party; he revolutionized news gathering by establishing horse express and schooner service between New York and Washington; U.S. Minister to Brazil (1861-69).

Webb-Kenyon Act. A law of Congress in 1913 designed to foster a more effective enforcement of state PROHIBITION laws. It prohibited from INTERSTATE COMMERCE the TRANSPORTATION of liquor intended to be received, sold, or used in violation of laws of the state to which it was sent. The law was passed over President TAFT'S VETO and was subsequently sustained by the United States Supreme Court.

Webb-Pomerene Act. Also known as the Webb Export Act. A law of Congress passed on April 10, 1918. It exempted export trade associations from the provisions of the ANTI-TRUST LAWS by declaring legal all associations "entered into for the sole purpose of engaging in export trade and actually engaged solely in such trade." Such associations were required to file data with the FEDERAL TRADE COMMISSION relating to their organization, contracts and operations, but were permitted to function outside the jurisdiction of the Commission and the Anti-Trust Division of the DEPARTMENT OF JUSTICE provided that they did not attempt to restrain competition or restrain prices within domestic trade. The objective of the Act was to strengthen the position of American exporters. Although it resulted in a stimulation of foreign trade, it simultaneously increased the number of export trade combinations in the United States.

WEBER, Max. 1881-1961. Artist. b. Russia. Came to the United States (1891); studied in Paris and became a member of a group of modern artists who experimented with Cubism, Expressionism and other styles; his works hang in many Museums and he is considered one of the outstanding American artists of today.

Webster-Ashburton Treaty. A TREATY between the United States and Great Britain in 1842 fixing the Maine-Canadian boundary. Of the TERRITORY in dispute in Maine, the United States obtained 7,000 of the 12,000 square miles, including the fertile Aroostook Valley. Great Britain conceded about 200 square miles at the head of the Connecticut River and accepted in favor of the United States an early survey of the 45th parallel in Vermont and New York. This treaty established the present boundary line between Maine and Canada and settled a dispute which had existed since the birth of the United States.

WEBSTER, Daniel. 1782-1852. Lawyer, orator, and statesman. b. New Hampshire. Graduated, Dartmouth (1801); admitted to the bar in Boston (1805); practised in New Hampshire; member, U. S. House of Representatives (1813-17); member of the House from Massachusetts (1823-27); acted as lawyer for Dartmouth College trustees in the famous case (1818); U. S. Senator (1827-41); became famous as a brilliant orator; sup-

ported the TARIFF OF ABOMINATIONS; believed in strong federal government throwing him into opposition with CALHOUN; opposed JACKSON in NULLIFICATION and BANK OF THE UNITED STATES issues; U.S. Secretary of State under HARRISON and TYLER (1841-43) negotiated the WEBSTER-ASHBURTON TREATY with England (1842); U.S. Senator (1845-50); strong opponent of Mexican War and the ANNEXATION OF TEXAS; supported COMPROMISE OF 1850; served again as Secretary of State (1850-52); unsuccessful candidate for nomination for the presidency on WHIG ticket (1852). Considered an outstanding American orator and his speeches and debates with HAYNE (1830) on the Constitution are famous.

Webster-Hayne Debates. A month long series of debates in the United States Senate between Senators ROBERT Y. HAYNE of South Carolina and DANIEL WEBSTER of Massachusetts. It was initiated on January 19, 1830 when Hayne supported Senator BENTON's opposition to FOOTE's RESOLUTION in a brilliant speech accusing the North of a selfish sectional attitude. The following day Webster made his famous "Reply to Hayne" in which he laid down the strongest defense of federal supremacy in American legislative debate. Hayne's speeches contained the fullest analysis of the South's policies of strict construction, STATES' RIGHTS and NULLIFICATION up to that time. Webster's analysis powerfully defended the supremacy of Congress, attacking the nullification and compact doctrines of the South as an impractical absurdity and as a violation of the Constitution.

WEBSTER, Noah. 1758-1843. Lexicographer and author. b. Connecticut. Graduated, Yale (1778); served in the Revolution against BURGOYNE; admitted to the bar and established a successful practice in Hartford, Connecticut; taught, and wrote spellers that were popular for many years; strong advocate of copyright

law; FEDERALIST, favoring STRONG CEN-
TRAL GOVERNMENT; edited, *The American Magazine* (1787-88); president of
the first board of trustees of Amherst College; became chief authority on the English language in the United States and
published *An American Dictionary of the
English Language* (2 vols., 1828); also
compiled a *History of the United States*
(1832).

Wedemeyer Report. A report on Korea
submitted by General Albert C. Wedemeyer to President TRUMAN on September 9, 1947. The STATE DEPARTMENT was
charged with having suppressed the report on the alleged grounds that its con-
tents called the Department into question
on its handling of political conditions in
MANCHURIA and Korea. On May 1, 1951
the Senate published the Korean section
of the report. In it General Wedemeyer
discussed the stalemate in the negotiations between the United States and the
Soviet Union over a provisional government for Korea. He declared the military
situation "potentially dangerous" for the
United States and recommended the
training and equipment of a South Korean scout force under the United States
military commander. This force was to be
officered by Americans and be of sufficient strength to counteract the North
Korean Army and prevent the establishment of a COMMUNIST government in Korea. He advised moral and material support for China and South Korea to protect the strategic interests of the United
States, and suggested the UNITED NA-
TIONS as the appropriate instrument for
establishing a provisional Korean government under a four-power TRUSTEESHIP.

WEED, Thurlow. 1797-1882. Journalist
and political leader. b. New York. Served
in the War of 1812; edited Albany
Evening Journal (1830-62); opponent of
the famous Albany Regency politicians;
he was a power in the WHIG party; became leading Republican; associate with

SEWARD and GREELEY in New York politics; supported LINCOLN and the Civil
War effort; edited, New York *Commercial Advertiser* (1867) supporting strong
RECONSTRUCTION policies.

WEEKS, John Wingate. 1860-1926.
Broker and political leader. b. New
Hampshire. Graduated, U.S.N.A., An-
apolis (1881); joined large brokerage
house in Boston; member, U. S. House of
Representatives (1905-13); aided in adding FEDERAL RESERVE SYSTEM clause to
the ALDRICH-VREELAND ACT; U.S. Senator
(1913-19); appointed by HARDING and
COOLIDGE, U.S. Secretary of War (1921-
25).

**"We Have Met the Enemy and They Are
Ours."** The famous dispatch sent by
Commodore OLIVER H. PERRY to Major
General WILLIAM HENRY HARRISON, commander of the western army at Seneca,
during the War of 1812. Having compelled the surrender of the British flagship and three other vessels within 10
minutes on September 10, 1813, Perry
pursued and captured the remaining two
ships of the British fleet. He wrote the
message in pencil on an old envelope and
forwarded it to Harrison. The complete
wording was, "Dear Gen'l: We have met
the enemy and they are ours, two ships,
two brigs, one schooner and one sloop.
Yours with great respect and esteem.
O. H. Perry."

WEISER, Conrad. 1696-1760. Pioneer.
b. Germany; came to America (1710);
famous for establishing friendly relations
with the Indians in the Mohawk Country
of New York and in Pennsylvania; gained
allegiance of the IROQUOIS for the British
in the French and INDIAN WARS; a leader
in the founder of Reading, Pennsylvania;
commissioned colonel of forces west of
Susquehanna during the Revolution.

"Welfare Capitalism." The term applied
to the attempts of large CORPORATIONS in
the 1920's to weaken the LABOR MOVE-

MENT and develop a more loyal and stable employee force. These efforts took the form of profit sharing, stock subscription schemes, GROUP INSURANCE plans, PENSIONS, and a wide variety of welfare projects which included swimming clubs, company gardens, gymnasiums, day nurseries, athletic teams, dramatic shows, mutual aid societies, legal assistance, sewing circles, cafeterias, LIBRARIES, company orchestras, educational departments, kindergartens, and visiting nurses. Employees were encouraged to join and participate in these activities rather than join TRADE UNIONS. It is estimated that by 1927 group insurance, covering 4,700,-000 employees, had been taken out to the extent of $5,600,000,000. In 1926 at least 400 firms employing 4,000,000 had put pension plans into effect, of which 88 percent had been established in the preceding 15 years. Similar participation was noted in the other areas of this "Americanization of labor."

"Welfare State." Also called the "service state." The term applied to the wide extension of social services to the people by government. Traditionally government had supplied merely protective services in the form of military, fire, and police protection, plus minimum aid to the needy and aged. The development of technology which produced the complex industrial system in modern nations raised a host of serious problems concerned with the welfare of their people. In the United States cyclical depressions have given rise to serious UNEMPLOYMENT. This problem had paralleled the problems of old age, illness, workmen's disability, child welfare, HOUSING, EDUCATION, RECREATION, and poverty. The inability of private charity, state, and municipal assistance to cope with these problems has led to the development of a program of federal aid.

WELLES, Sumner. 1892-1961. Ambassador and statesman. b. New York City.
Graduated, Harvard (1914); served as career diplomat in many countries; supported F. D. ROOSEVELT and appointed Assistant Secretary of State for Latin-American affairs; U.S. Ambassador to CUBA (1933); again Assistant Secretary of State. Author of *The Time for Decision* (1944) and *Where are We Heading?* (1946).

WELLS, David Ames. 1828-1898. Economist. b. Massachusetts. Graduated, Williams (1847); edited, Springfield, *Republican*; invented the first machine that folded NEWSPAPERS as they left the press; published *Our Burden and Our Strength* (1864) a study of NATIONAL DEBT which gained a reputation for him as an economist; leading supporter of free-trade policies; he organized the Bureau of Statistics for the TREASURY DEPARTMENT. Author of many books on economics.

Wells, Fargo and Company. One of the famous express companies of the pre-Civil War period. It was organized in 1852 by Henry Wells and WILLIAM G. FARGO. The company divided the express service of the United States with the American Express Company. Within a decade it had attained a monopoly of the express business west of the Mississippi. In the two decades after the Civil War it was virtually the sole postal service in the MINING and LUMBER camps of the Far West. The company was the TRANSPORTATION agency in carrying gold and silver bullion to eastern markets. In later years it expanded its operations to ALASKA, Canada, Central America, HAWAII, and the WEST INDIES. In 1918 it was merged with the AMERICAN RAILWAY EXPRESS COMPANY, but maintained its identity as a separate CORPORATION.

WEST, Benjamin. 1738-1820. Painter. b. Pennsylvania. Self-taught. Worked in London and gained international recognition for his paintings of historical subjects; friend of Joshua Reynolds; presi-

684

dent of the Royal Academy (1792-1820). Among his best known works are *The Death of Wolfe, Death on the Pale Horse, Penn's Treaty with the Indians* and many others. His works are a part of the collections of many museums throughout the world.

Western Land Claims. The conflicting claims after the Revolution, of the 13 states to western lands based on royal charters. Virginia's claim extended to the TERRITORY including present day Kentucky, West Virginia, and the land east of the Mississippi and north of the Ohio River. Connecticut, Massachusetts, and New York claimed land in the northwestern part of this area. South of it were the claims of Georgia and North and South Carolina. The small states feared the power of these larger ones because of the ownership of such vast tracts, and Maryland declined to ratify the ARTICLES OF CONFEDERATION until all claims would be relinquished to the federal government. At the suggestion of the CONTINENTAL CONGRESS, New York and Virginia ceded their claims in 1781. In 1783 a second Virginia offer was accepted by the central government which had declined the original cession because of unacceptable qualifications laid down by the state. In 1785 Massachusetts ceded its claim. Connecticut ceded its claim in 1786 with the exception of the WESTERN RESERVE. In 1787 and 1790 South Carolina and North Carolina respectively relinquished their claims. The promise of the Continental Congress to organize new states out of these western lands was subsequently fulfilled in the LAND ORDINANCES of 1784, 1785, and 1787. The total amount of land ceded was 221,987,000 acres.

Western Reserve. Also known as the Connecticut Western Reserve. A large section of land west of Pennsylvania reserved by Connecticut in 1786 when it ceded its western lands to the federal government. The TERRITORY is today a section of northeastern Ohio on the south

shore of Lake Erie which was originally granted by charter in 1662. Connecticut's objective was the disposal of these western lands at profitable terms. In 1792 the state granted 500,000 acres on Long Island Sound to compensate for losses suffered by the residents during the Revolution. In 1795 the remaining portion of the Western Reserve, consisting of 3,000,000 acres, was sold to the Connecticut Land Company. In 1800 an agreement between Connecticut and the federal government provided for the transfer of the Western Reserve to the Ohio Territory.

Western Union. .A TELEGRAPH company organized in 1851 in New York State by Hiram Sibley and Samuel L. Selden. It took its present name in 1856. By 1860 its assimilation of competing companies brought its service to the Mississippi Valley. In 1881 the Western Union bought out JAY GOULD's Atlantic and Pacific Telegraph Company, doubling its assets and service. With the absorption, in 1928, of the Postal Telegraph Company by the International Telephone and Telegraph Corporation, the Western Union became virtually the sole provider of telegraph service in the country.

West Florida Controversy. A conflict which arose out of the problem of defining the boundaries of the LOUISIANA TERRITORY which had been purchased by the United States in 1803. The lack of a clear boundary definition made it possible for JEFFERSON to claim that west Florida was rightly part of the purchase. Neither Talleyrand, who negotiated the purchase on behalf of France, nor MONROE and LIVINGSTON, who represented the United States, believed that West Florida was rightfully part of the Territory. The TREATY of purchase itself merely provided that the Territory was of "the same extent that it now has in the hands of Spain and that it had when France possessed it." In 1804 Jefferson urged the Congress to enact the Mobile Act of

1804. This law created West Florida into a customs district as far as the Perdido River, and annexed it to the Mississippi Territory. The question of its rightful status was not settled until the purchase of Florida from Spain in 1819.

West Indies. The great archipelago which extends in a curve from Florida to the northern coast of South America, separating the Atlantic Ocean from the Gulf of Mexico and the Caribbean Sea. They were discovered by COLUMBUS in 1492. The islands include several groups, among them the Bahamas, Greater Antilles, Lesser Antilles, Trinidad-Tobago group, and the Keys. Their total area is 100,000 square miles. The most important group is the Greater Antilles, comprising CUBA, PUERTO RICO, HAITI, and Jamaica. AGRICULTURE is the chief industry. The leading crops are SUGAR, TOBACCO, and coffee. Although discovered and claimed by Spain, the West Indies have been owned at times by England, Holland, France, Denmark, and the United States. In the colonial period they were the most natural market for colonial merchandise, and a flourishing trade developed in RUM, SUGAR, manufactured goods, and slaves. British restrictions on this TRADE were among the causes of the American Revolution. In the 19th century various incidents involved the United States in serious diplomatic controversies and war. By the 20th century economic penetration, war, and purchase had brought Puerto Rico and the VIRGIN ISLANDS under direct ownership and Cuba, Haiti, and SANTO DOMINGO under varying conditions of political control.

WESTINGHOUSE, George. 1846-1914. Inventor and manufacturer. b. New York. Served in the Union Army and went to Union College; invented an AIR BRAKE and automatic signal devices for RAILROADS; was a pioneer in the introduction of a high-voltage alternating-current single-phase system for the transmission of ELECTRICITY; he held over 400 patents in his lifetime. Organized the Westinghouse Electric Company which manufactured the products of his many inventions.

West Point. See United States Military Academy.

West Point Scandal. On September 8, 1976, 65 U.S. Military Academy cadets made statements that many of their classmates had engaged in cheating in academic courses, had lied to officers, and had even manipulated student honor boards so as not to obtain guilty verdicts. These affidavits depicted pervasive dishonest practices at the Academy and the "honor system" was challenged. Cadets were dismissed with the right to apply for readmission after one year.

West Virginia. The 41st state in size, with an area of 24,181 square miles. Entered the Union on June 20, 1863 as the 35th state. Charleston is the capital. In 1950 West Virginia's POPULATION of 2,-005,552 made it 29th in rank. Its largest cities are Huntington, Charleston, and Wheeling. West Virginia is the nation's COAL MINING leader. It has been estimated that its coal alone could supply the nation for 250 years. Other important minerals are OIL, quarry products, and natural gas. LUMBER is a notable product. Farm crops include corn, hay, fruit, oats, TOBACCO, and WHEAT. The state came into being as a secessionist movement from Virginia when that state left the Union at the outbreak of the Civil War. Its many spas draw a large tourist trade. The most famous is White Sulphur Springs. West Virginia was discovered in 1671 by Thomas Batts. Its nickname is the "Mountain State."

Westward Movement. The movement of the POPULATION from the eastern seaboard to the Pacific Coast from the colonial period to the end of the 19th century. Unique to the United States this movement has always been considered to have strongly affected American history in the fields of economics, finance, culture, political reform, and the characteristics of the American personality. Specific periods stand out as the eras of greatest expansion, e.g. the periods following the War of 1812 and the Civil War. Celebrated historians who have dealt with the problems of the westward movement have been FREDERICK JACKSON TURNER and Frederick L. Paxson. See Frontier and Frontier, Effects of.

"Wetbacks." Mexican laborers who come into the United States illegally by swimming the Rio Grande River. Each year more than 1,000,000 border-jumpers enter the country and disperse to the fruit and vegetable farms of California and to the farm regions of Texas, Colorado, Arizona, and New Mexico. In 1951 more than 518,000 arrests were made along the 1,800 mile Mexican border in an effort by the United States Immigration and Naturalization Service to stem this migration. The "wetback" traffic has been appraised as a major factor in the farm labor situation. Underpaid, exploited, housed under unsanitary conditions, and lacking medical care, they have become a public health menace. Organized labor has charged unfair competition and the consequent decline of wage levels. In 1952 legislation pending in the Congress proposed sanctions against those who abet the traffic, and provided for increased budgetary allowances to the Immigration Service. There was a proposal for the negotiation of an agreement with Mexico under which 144,000 Mexicans would be legally allowed into the United States each year and by which the Mexican government would exercise greater efforts to halt the "wetback" traffic.

Whaling. In colonial times whaling was the principal source of fuel and tallow for lighting and cooking. The New Eng-

land area, before and after the Revolution, became the center of the world's whaling industry. Important whale fisheries were established in the Gulf of St. Lawrence, the Strait of Belle Isle, and Davis' Strait. The search for whales soon spread southward to the equator, and New England seamen sailed under the French and British flags. The first whale-ship to sail around Cape Horn left London in 1797 manned by Massachusetts seamen. After the War of 1812 whaling developed on the Pacific coast. By 1850 there were more than 700 whaling ships afloat, the bulk centering on New Bedford, Massachusetts. In the decade before the Civil War, the Arctic Ocean grew in importance as a whaling area. In the 1870's San Francisco became the most important whaling port on the Pacific. The growth of the railroad industry furnished a rapid and efficient means of transporting oil, bone, and other whaling products to the eastern market. By the opening of World War I, the growth of the PETROLEUM INDUSTRY virtually brought whaling to an end.

WHARTON, Edith Newbold. 1862-1937 Novelist. b. New York City. Studied and lived in Europe; greatly influenced by HENRY JAMES. Author of many novels including The Valley of Decision (1902), The House of Mirth (1905), Ethan Frome (1911), The Age of Innocence (1920) which was awarded the PULITZER PRIZE; books of short stories, travel, and an autobiography.

Wheat. Wheat was introduced into Virginia from England in 1618 but was not immediately successful. In that colony and in Maryland it achieved some importance, but became one of the basic crops in the "BREAD COLONIES" of Connecticut, New York, and Pennsylvania. By the end of the 17th century, wheat was the chief export from this region which yielded an average of 20 to 30 bushels per acre greater than was common in England. After the Revolution wheat production spread to the mid-West, the crop reaching 85,000,000 bushels by 1840. The chief stimulus to the production of wheat and other cereals in this period was the demand for animal feed and liquor. With the development of CANAL and RAILROAD TRANSPORTATION in the second third of the 19th century wheat was milled at Cincinnati, Louisville, and St. Louis for local and southern markets and in Buffalo and Pittsburgh for Eastern and foreign markets. In 1850 the middle Atlantic states were still producing a larger crop than the North Central, but by the opening of the Civil War wheat production in the latter area increased 125 percent. By 1870 the nation's production of wheat totalled 194,764,000 bushels. Within a decade the center of production had shifted from the North Central states to the Great . Plains. By the opening of World War II almost half of the nation's production was raised in Kansas, Montana, North Dakota, Oklahoma, and Washington. In 1930 the national production reached 886,470,000 bushels, making the United States the world's leader. In 1915, stimulated by the needs of World War I, production exceeded 1,000,000,000 bushels, the largest in American history up to that point. In the 1950's wheat was grown in 40 states, with Kansas and North Dakota the two leaders. In 1951 the production reached 998,000,000 bushels with a market price ranging from $2.066 to $2.44 as compared to the PARITY PRICE of $2.42. In 1952 the United States was the largest exporter of wheat in the world. In that year it was estimated that the crop would exceed 1,300,000,000 bushels and come close to the record of 1947. The United States Treasury spent more than $400,000,000 in SUBSIDIES to maintain wheat prices. It was estimated that, when the international wheat agreement of 1950 expires in July, 1953, the cost will have exceeded $600,000,000. In May, 1952 the wheat subsidy averaged 65 cents a bushel.

WHEATON, Henry. 1785-1848. Jurist and diplomat. b. Rhode Island. Graduated, Brown University (1802); admitted to the bar and practised in Providence (1807-12); moved to New York City where he continued his practice; justice of marine court of New York City (1815-19); member, New York constitutional convention (1821); U. S. Minister to Prussia (1837-46). Author of many books including the important *Elements of International Law* (1836).

WHEELER, Burton Kendall. 1882-1975. Lawyer and politician. b. Massachusetts. Studied law at the University of Michigan and practised in Montana; U. S. Senator (from 1923-47); unsuccessful candidate for Vice-President of the United States on the PROGRESSIVE PARTY ticket headed by LA FOLLETTE (1924); became an ISOLATIONIST in later years and an opponent of F. D. ROOSEVELT.

Wheeler-Howard Act. An act of Congress in 1934 designed to improve the status of American Indians. It permitted tribes on reservations to adopt self-governing constitutions by majority vote or to obtain corporate charters from the Secretary of the Interior upon petition of one-third of the adult Indians on such reservations. Qualified Indians became eligible for appointment to administrative posts. Congress provided for the appropriation of $250,000,000 annually for the establishment of vocational and trade schools, secondary schools, and colleges. A revolving fund of $10,000,000 was established from which annual loans of 250,000 could be made to the Indian chartered corporations. Surplus lands were withdrawn from public sale and restored to the tribes for CONSERVATION and development in the name of the United States as trust for the tribes.

WHEELER, Joseph. 1836-1906. Confed-

688

erate general. b. Georgia. Graduated, U.S.M.A., West Point (1859); joined the Confederate army and commanded the cavalry unit of the Army of the Mississippi; served at SHILOH, CHICKAMAUGA, Knoxville, CHATTANOOGA and other battles, becoming a lieutenant general (1865); member, U.S. House of Representatives (1881-82; 1883; 1885-1900); believed in a peaceful settlement and cooperation between the North and South; major general during the Spanish-American War; brigadier general of the U.S. Army; retired (1900).

Wheeler-Lea Transportation Act. Also known as the Transportation Act of 1940. It expanded the jurisdiction of the INTERSTATE COMMERCE COMMISSION over water carriers operating in coastal, interstate, and inter-coastal trade. Although maintaining the Commission's power over RAILROAD consolidations it relieved the Commission of the need of proposing such consolidations. Under the latter provision the Commission is required to consider the public interest and the needs of railroad labor on all proposals by the carriers for consolidation. The Commission was given power to investigate the business conduct of railroad, water, and motor carriers, and to recommend suitable legislation to Congress.

Wheeler-Rayburn Act. Also known as the Public Utility Holding Company Act. A law of Congress in 1935 which sought to eliminate the abuses of HOLDING COMPANY control of PUBLIC UTILITIES. It conferred upon the FEDERAL POWER COMMISSION the authority to regulate the rates and business practices of interstate utilities. It prohibited holding companies beyond the second degree, and required approval by the SECURITIES AND EXCHANGE COMMISSION for the issuance of securities, acquisition of properties, and the conduct of business. A clause required holding companies, after 1938, to limit their operations to single integrated systems and to business operations directly related to the sale of power. The Act was bitterly denounced by power companies as a "death penalty," and they sought its invalidation by the courts. Its constitutionality was ultimately sustained by the United States Supreme Court.

WHEELER, William Almon. 1819-1887. Lawyer and political leader. b. New York. Admitted to the bar (1845); Republican member, U. S. House of Representatives (1861-63; 1869-77); interested in banking and RAILROADS; author of the Wheeler Compromise to settle a political dispute in Louisiana (1875); elected Vice-President of the United States with HAYES as President in the disputed election of (1876) serving a term (1877-81).

Whig Party. An anti-JACKSON coalition organized in 1834 at the suggestion of the *New York Courier and Inquirer*. The name was adopted on the thinking that the forces within the party were opposed to "executive tyranny" with which Jackson was charged. The nucleus of the party was the NATIONAL REPUBLICANS of HENRY CLAY and JOHN QUINCY ADAMS but to it adhered all political elements opposed to Jackson. These included Southerners who resented his tariff and nationalist policies, former FEDERALISTS, personal enemies, those who opposed his bank policies, and all others who resented his personal conduct of the government by means of the "KITCHEN CABINET." The party did not run a candidate until 1840 when it succeeded in electing WILLIAM HENRY HARRISON. The only other President it elected was ZACHARY TAYLOR in 1848. The party disintegrated following its refusal to take a stand on the free-soil and slave issues in the controversies arising out of the MEXICAN CESSION. Its elements generally migrated to the newly created Republican Party in 1854.

WHIPPLE, William. 1730-1785. Revolutionary leader. b. Maine. Sea captain and merchant in New Hampshire; mem-

ber, CONTINENTAL CONGRESS (1776-79);
signer of the DECLARATION OF INDEPEND-
ENCE; brigadier general in charge of
militia at BATTLE OF SARATOGA (1777);
associate justice of the superior court in
New Hampshire (1782-85).

Whiskey Rebellion. A rebellion in 1794
of 3,000 west Pennsylvania farmers opposed to the payment of the whiskey excise tax. The tax on whiskey rendered
unprofitable the distilling of liquor from
grain, a previous practice developed to
reduce TRANSPORTATION costs to eastern
markets. The President's proclamation
calling out the militia of four states to
suppress the rebellion was indicative of
the strength of the new government established five years earlier. Peculiar to
the situation was the marching of the
Secretary of the Treasury ALEXANDER
HAMILTON at the head of these 15,000
troops to accomplish the capture of 18
rebels. Of these only two were convicted
after trial and they were soon pardoned
by the President. The result of the incident was to turn the frontier area to the
JEFFERSONIAN REPUBLICANS.

Whiskey Ring. A group of revenue officials in the TREASURY DEPARTMENT who
defrauded the government of the whiskey
tax revenue. The Ring involved the former Secretary of the Treasury BOUTWELL
and President GRANT's private secretary,
General Babcock. The Ring was exposed
in 1774 by Secretary of the Treasury,
BENJAMIN H. BRISTOW. It had been de-
frauding the government of $100,000 an-
nually until its exposure. This scandal
was part of a series of corrupt activities
in the two Grant administrations including the CREDIT MOBILIER scandal, a "SAL-
ARY GRAB" scandal, the "BLACK FRIDAY"
gold corner, and others.

WHISTLER, James Abbott McNeill.
1834-1903. Artist. b. Massachusetts.
Studied at U.S.M.A., West Point (1851-
54); served as a draughtsman in the
Coast Survey Department; went to Paris

(1855) to study; also lived and studied
in London; great individuality of style
and personality; excellent etcher best
known for his *Thames Series* (1871);
famous for his painting *Portrait of My
Mother* (1872) which hangs in the Lou-
vre and caused great consternation when
first exhibited, which he called a study
in black and gray; he sued Ruskin for
slander and won a verdict of one farth-
ing; his many paintings, etchings, and
lithographs are in important collections
throughout the world.

WHITE, Andrew Dickson. 1832-1918.
Educator and diplomat. b. New York.
Graduated, Yale (1853); studied abroad;
taught at the University of Michigan
(1857-63); persuaded EZRA CORNELL to
organize and endow Cornell University
which opened in 1868 with White as
president (1868-85); U.S. Minister to
Germany (1879-81); U.S. Minister to
Russia (1892-94); U.S. Ambassador to
Germany (1897-1902); chairman of the
United States delegation to the HAGUE
PEACE CONFERENCE (1899); prominent
Republican supporter of BLAINE; he
wrote several books.

WHITE, Clarence Cameron. 1880-1960.
Violinist and composer. Studied at the
Oberlin Conservatory and in England;
arranged many Negro spirituals for the
violin; composed the *Negro Rhapsody*
for orchestra and a book of 40 spirituals;
became head of the music department of
Hampton Institute (1932).

WHITE, Edward Douglas. 1845-1921.
Jurist. b. Louisiana. Studied at Georgetown College; served with the Confederate army during the Civil War (1861-
63); U. S. Senator (1891-94); appointed
Associate Justice, U. S. Supreme Court
by CLEVELAND (1894-1910) and Chief
Justice (1910-21) by TAFT.

WHITE, Henry. 1850-1927. Diplomat
b. Maryland. The first "career diplomat"
in the United States; served at various le-

690

gations before becoming U. S. Ambassador at Rome (1905-07) and to France (1907-09); headed the American delegation at the ALGECIRAS CONFERENCE; appointed by WILSON, American commissioner to the Peace Conference at Paris; supported the LEAGUE OF NATIONS and tried to get the United States to join.

WHITE, Horace. 1834-1916. Journalist. b. New Hampshire. Covered the famous LINCOLN-DOUGLAS debates for the Chicago *Tribune* while on the staff there (1857-74), editor in chief (1865-74); editorial writer and part owner, New York *Evening Post* (1881-99) and editor in chief (1899-1903). Well-known journalist and authority on BANKING and CURRENCY problems.

White House, The. The official home of the President of the United States. Although it has been painted white since 1817, it was not designated by its present name until 1902 when Congress so titled it at the request of President T. ROOSEVELT. Before then it was called the President's Palace, the President's House, or the Executive Mansion. It is situated on Pennsylvania Avenue in Washington, D.C. and includes a main building, a three story office building, and an executive office building, covering about 16 acres (including grounds). The White House was the first public building started in Washington, D.C., the cornerstone being laid on Oct. 13, 1792. President JOHN ADAMS, in June 1800, was the first President to occupy the still partially completed building. On August 24, 1814, during the War of 1812, the British set the building afire, leaving only blackened walls. Its rebuilding was completed in 1817 when President MONROE moved in.

"White Man's Burden." The term applied to the objectives of missionary work among the backward colonial areas of the world. It came into prominence after 1870 as a justification for the colonial expansion of the time.

White Slave Act. See Mann Act.

WHITE, Stanford. 1853-1906. Architect. b. New York City. Studied in Europe and the United States; organized firm of McKim, Mead & White with C. F. McKim and W. R. Mead (1879); designed many famous buildings in New York City as well as the Battle Monument at U.S.M.A., West Point; murdered by Harry K. Thaw in Madison Square Garden Roof.

WHITE, William Allen. 1868-1944. Journalist. b. Kansas. Educated at the University of Kansas; editor and owner of the Emporia *Gazette* which gained national recognition through his editorials; he was a liberal; supported T. ROOSEVELT and his PROGRESSIVE PARTY; influential Republican; supported HOOVER. Author of *The Real Issue and Other Stories* (1896), *A Puritan in Babylon* (1938) and many others. He was called the "Sage of Emporia."

WHITLOCK, Brand. 1869-1934. Diplomat and journalist. b. Ohio. Worked as a writer for the Chicago *Herald;* admitted to the Illinois bar (1894); U.S. Minister to Belgium (1913-22); gained international reputation for his handling of the difficult problems in Europe and his attempt to save the life of Nurse Edith Cavell. Supported HOOVER in the administration of the American Relief Committee. Author of several books including *Belgium: A Personal Record* (2 vols. 1919).

WHITMAN, Marcus. 1802-1847. Missionary and pioneer. b. New York. Served as a medical missionary in the Oregon territory; led settlers into that TERRITORY and considered important in gaining that territory for the United States; massacred with his family and party by the Indians.

Whitman Massacre. The murder of Reverend and Mrs. Marcus Whitman on November 29, 1847 by Indian tribes at the present site of Walla Walla, Washington. The rapid settlement of the Oregon TERRITORY as a result of Whitman's many missionary journeys had aroused Indian suspicions about the danger of white domination of the territory. During the attack 53 women and children were captured and held until ransomed by the Hudson's Bay Company. The Massacre brought on the Cayuse War in the Pacific Northwest.

WHITMAN, Walt. 1819-1892. Poet. b. New York. Lived in Brooklyn and worked as an editor of the Brooklyn *Eagle* (1846-48); served as a clerk in the U.S. DEPARTMENT OF THE INTERIOR (1865) but was dismissed because of the radical implications in his poetry *Leaves of Grass;* famous for poems *O Captain! My Captain!* referring to LINCOLN; *When the Lilacs Last in the Dooryard Bloom'd* and many books of poetry the greatest being *Leaves of Grass.*

WHITNEY, Eli. 1765-1825. Inventor. b. Massachusetts. Graduated, Yale (1792); famous for his invention of the cotton gin (1793); manufactured arms for the government being the first to produce interchangeable parts in the production of guns. Elected to the American HALL OF FAME (1900).

WHITNEY, William Collins. 1841-1904. Financier and political leader. b. Massachusetts. Graduated, Yale and Harvard Law School and admitted to the bar (1865); successful corporation counsel, New York City (1875-82); was able to save the city millions of dollars in the handling of the street-railway system court cases; served as U. S. Secretary of the Navy (1885-89) in CLEVELAND'S cabinet; organized railroad and electric light, heat, and power companies; owned famous racing stable of horses.

WHITTIER, John Greenleaf. 1807-1892. Poet. b. Massachusetts. Self-educated; supported GARRISON and the ABOLITIONISTS; famous as writer of the poems *The*

Barefoot Boy, Barbara Frietchie, **and** books of poetry including *The Voices of Freedom* (1846); *Snow-Bound* (1866), *At Sundown* (1890) and many others.

Wickersham Commission on Law Observance. A commission under the chairmanship of former Attorney-General GEORGE W. WICKERSHAM to canvass the entire question of law observance and enforcement, with specific reference to the PROHIBITION laws. The Commission was appointed by President HOOVER in 1929 as a result of the widespread disrespect for law, the increased willingness of the public to condone graft and corruption, and the deficiency in enforcement of the prohibition laws. The report and findings of the Commission confirmed the current impression that enforcement had proved wholly inadequate, that the law was unsupported by public opinion, that it was freely violated, that the general conduct of enforcement agencies dealing with this and other laws was lax and even "lawless", and that corruption was operating in a novel and greater area than ever before. The Commission, however, did not recommend the repeal of the 18TH AMENDMENT, a step which was not taken until the adoption of the 21ST AMENDMENT in 1933.

WICKERSHAM, George Woodward. 1858-1936. Lawyer and political leader. b. Pennsylvania. Graduated, University of Pennsylvania (1880); admitted to the bar and practised in Philadelphia, and in New York City (from 1882); appointed by TAFT, U.S. Attorney General (1909-13); prosecuted several cases under the SHERMAN ANTI-TRUST ACT; president of the International Arbitral Tribunal (1932-36); trustee of the University of Pennsylvania.

WILBUR, Ray Lyman. 1875-1949. Physician, political leader, and educator. b. Iowa. Graduated, Stanford University (1896, M.A. 1897), Cooper Medical College (1899); professor of medicine and dean of the medical school, Stanford University; president of Stanford University (from 1916); president, American Academy of Medicine (1912-13); appointed by HOOVER, U.S. Secretary of the Interior (1929-33).

Wild Bill Hickok. See Hickok, James.

"Wild Cat Banks." The nickname applied to STATE BANKS chartered in the West in tremendous numbers between 1829 and 1837. Following JACKSON's withdrawal of federal funds from the BANK OF THE UNITED STATES in 1833 state banks found themselves in a position to secure liberal state charters, increase their loans, and add to the circulation of CURRENCY. The West's demand for easier credit and land speculation led to an increase of wildcat banks from 329 in 1829 to 1788 in 1837. Their note circulation leaped from $48,-000,000 to $149,000,000 and their loans from $137,000,000 to $525,000,000, during this period. By disregarding sound banking principles and offering easy loans for land speculation and the construction of HIGHWAYS, CANALS, and RAILROADS, they spurred a currency inflation that ultimately collapsed in the Panic of 1837. They were called "wildcat banks" because they were established in the "woods where the wildcat roamed."

Wilderness, Battle of the. A sanguinary battle in Virginia during the Civil War between the ARMY OF THE POTOMAC, commanded by General GRANT, and the Army of Northern Virginia, commanded by General LEE. The northern army of 118,000 men met the Confederate Army of 61,000 men on March 6th and 7th, 1864. The dense and impenetrable forest and brush rendered artillery and cavalry almost useless, leaving the bulk of the fighting to the infantry. After two days of bloody fighting, marked by Lee's brilliant tactical maneuvers, the battle remained undecided. Grant removed his forces from the flank, driving towards Richmond in an attempt to compel Lee to meet him. There were heavy losses on both sides.

Wilderness Road, The. A trans-Appalachian road that ran from eastern Virginia through the Cumberland Gap to Kentucky, and ultimately to the Ohio River. The early trail which existed in 1775 had been carved out by DANIEL BOONE and other FRONTIERSMEN as a pack-horse trail. For 50 years thereafter it was the principal road for the movement of immigrants to the Ohio country. Today it constitutes an important interstate highway as part of U.S. 25. It is sometimes referred to as the "Dixie Highway."

WILDER, Thornton Niven. 1897-1975. Novelist and playwright. b. Wisconsin. Graduated, Yale (1920); taught English at the Lawrenceville School and at the University of Chicago (until 1939); author of *The Bridge of San Luis Rey* (1927) which was awarded the Pulitzer Prize; *Heaven's My Destination* (1935) and others; and the plays *Our Town* (1938), *The Skin of Our Teeth* (1942) also awarded the Pulitzer Prize and others.

WILKES, Charles. 1798-1877. Union admiral and explorer. b. New York City. In command of an expedition sent to explore the antarctic island of the Pacific (1838-42); his experiences are published in his *Narrative of the United States Exploring Expedition* (5 vols., 1844); best known for his part in the *"Trent* Affair" when he commanded the *San Jacinto* (1861) which halted the *Trent* and captured MASON and SLIDELL the Confederate commissioners.

WILLKIE, Wendell. 1892-1944. Industrialist and political leader. b. Indiana. Graduated, Indiana University (1913), LL.B. (1916); practised law in Ohio (1914-23) and in New York City (1923-33); president, Commonwealth and Southern Corporation, PUBLIC UTILITY company (1933); was a Democrat but denounced the NEW DEAL and became a Republican; Republican candidate for President polling more than 22,000,000 votes but defeated (1940); supported F. D. ROOSEVELT's foreign policy, but opposed his domestic policies; appointed by F. D. Roosevelt his personal representative and visited England, the Near and Far East (1941-42); attempted to liberalize the Republican party; opposed ISOLATIONISM; ignored by the party in nominations of 1944. Author of *One World* (1943) and *An American Program* (1944). He was an outstanding and sincere leader.

WILKINSON, James. 1757-1825. General. b. Maryland. Served as a captain in the Continental Army at TRENTON; lieutenant general (1777); brigadier general involved in CONWAY CABAL; became ranking officer of the army at General WAYNE's death (1796); represented the United States in the LOUISIANA PURCHASE (1803); tried for his part in the BURR CONSPIRACY but acquitted; unsuccessful leader of campaign against Montreal (1813); honorably discharged (1815).

WILLARD, Frances Elizabeth Caroline. 1839-1898. Educator and reformer. b. New York. Important in her work for the TEMPERANCE MOVEMENT; president, National W.C.T.U. (1879); one of the organizers of the PROHIBITION PARTY (1882). Elected to the HALL OF FAME (1910).

WILLETT, Marinus. 1740-1830. Revolutionary officer. b. New York. Served against Fort TICONDEROGA; leader of the SONS OF LIBERTY of New York; served under WASHINGTON and commanded the New York troops in the Mohawk Valley; mayor of New York City (1807-11); negotiated peace treaty with the CREEK INDIANS (1792).

William and Mary, College of. The second institution of higher learning established in the English colonies. It was chartered in 1693 at Williamsburg, Virginia as an Episcopalian school. It became a university in 1779. The college conducts a wide program of undergraduate and graduate studies in liberal arts and sciences, social work, EDUCATION, law, public health nursing, government, and politics. The College of William and Mary is noted for possessing the oldest college building in the United States (1697), for having established the honor fraternity, Phi Beta Kappa (1776), and for having introduced the elective system (1779) originally sponsored by THOMAS JEFFERSON. Among its distinguished students were Jefferson, JOHN MARSHALL, JAMES MONROE, and GEORGE WASHINGTON.

WILLIAMS, Roger. 1603?-1683. Founder of Rhode Island colony. b. Wales. Came to America (1630); served as an assistant in the Pilgrim Church at Salem, Massachusetts; banished from the colony for his outspoken criticism of those in power (1635); with a group of followers he travelled to what is now Providence, Rhode Island and founded a colony there; made friends with the NARRAGANSETT INDIANS; famous for his RELIGIOUS TOLERANCE and his insistence on a democratic and liberal form of government; went to England and secured a charter for the Providence Plantations in Narragansett Bay (1644); QUAKERS were allowed in his colony. He wrote many letters and pamphlets that were published.

WILLIAMS, William. 1731-1811. Merchant and political leader. b. Connecticut. Graduated, Harvard (1751); member, COMMITTEE OF SAFETY; member, CONTINENTAL CONGRESS (1776-78; 1783, 1784); signer of the DECLARATION OF INDEPENDENCE; member of the governor's council (1784-1803); member, Connecticut Convention that ratified the Constitution.

WILLING, Thomas. 1731-1821. Merchant, financier, jurist, political leader. b. Philadelphia, Pa. Educated in England; supplied the government during the Revolution; mayor of Philadelphia (1763); associate justice of the Pennsylvania supreme court (1767-74); member, CONTINENTAL CONGRESS (1775-76); first president of the BANK OF THE UNITED STATES (1791).

WILMOT, David. 1814-1868. Political leader. b. Pennsylvania. Lawyer; member, U. S. House of Representatives (1845-51); famous as the author of the WILMOT PROVISO; a founder of the Republican party; U.S. Senator (1861-63); supported LINCOLN and the Union during the Civil War; judge, U.S. Court of Claims.

Wilmot Proviso. Introduced into the House of Representatives in 1846 by Representative DAVID WILMOT of Pennsylvania as an amendment to an appropriations bill. It provided that neither SLAVERY nor involuntary servitude should ever exist in any part of the TERRITORY that might be acquired from Mexico as a result of the war then in progress. The House passed the resolution several times, but it was always defeated in the Senate. The resolution provided a rallying principle for the FREE SOIL forces in that period and pointed the way to a new political alignment for those in the North and Northwest who were opposed to the further extension of slavery.

Wilson-Gorman Tariff Act. A bill designed to bring about TARIFF REFORM. It was introduced in the House in December, 1893 by William L. Wilson, as a fulfillment of President CLEVELAND's pledge of tariff reform. It placed lumber, wool, coal, and iron ore on the free list and reduced the duties on silks, woolens, cottons, glass, and crockery. To offset the decline in federal revenues it increased the tax on liquors and imposed a two percent tax on incomes over $4,000. When it

went to the Senate it was bitterly opposed by the manufacturers of the commodities on the free list. Louisiana Senators submitted amendments placing a 40 percent AD VALOREM duty on raw sugar, and, under the leadership of Senator Gorman of Maryland, the Senate revised the House bill by putting duties on coal and iron. In all, the Senate made 334 changes in the House bill. When it came to the President for signature Cleveland denounced it as "a piece of party perfidy," charging that the Democratic Senators Gorman, Hill, Murphy, Smith, and Brice had betrayed the party's pledge. He refused to sign the measure, and it became law without his signature. The average rate was 41.29 percent.

WILSON, Henry. *Name changed from* Jeremiah Jones Colbath. 1812-1875. Political leader. b. New Hampshire. Successful shoe manufacturer. Opponent of SLAVERY and one of the WHIGS who left the party to form the FREE-SOIL PARTY (1848); edited the Boston *Republican* (1848-51) the party organ; joined the KNOW-NOTHING PARTY (1854) but left the party after disagreeing with its policies; U.S. Senator from Massachusetts (1855-73); a founder of the Republican party; leading ABOLITIONIST; opposed JOHNSON; elected Vice-President of the United States on the ticket with GRANT as President (1873).

WILSON, James. 1742-1798. Jurist and Political leader. b. Scotland. Studied in Scotland; came to New York and then settled in Philadelphia (1766); studied law; wrote important pamphlet for the patriot cause; member, CONTINENTAL CONGRESS (1775-77); signer of the DECLARATION OF INDEPENDENCE; again in Congress (1782, 83, 85-87); delegate from Pennsylvania to the CONSTITUTIONAL CONVENTION; and to the Pennsylvania convention for the RATIFICATION OF THE CONSTITUTION (1788); Associate Justice, U.S. Supreme Court (1789-98); first professor of law, Philadelphia College (1790) and in the University of Pennsylvania (when they were joined).

WILSON, James. 1836-1920. Agriculturist and political leader. b. Scotland. Came to the United States and settled in Connecticut (1851); became a farmer in Iowa (1855); served in the U.S. House of Representatives (1873-77; 1883-85); professor of AGRICULTURE and director of the experimental station at Iowa Agricultural College, Ames (1890-97); appointed U.S. Secretary of Agriculture by Presidents MC KINLEY and ROOSEVELT and also served under TAFT (1897-1913); under his administration the Department became an outstanding one.

"Wilsonian Democracy." See New Freedom.

WILSON, William Bauchop. 1862-1934. Labor leader. b. Scotland. Came to the United States and worked in the coal mines of Pennsylvania 1871); president of the district union and an organizer of the UNITED MINE WORKERS of America (1890) serving as secretary of the organization (1900-08); member, U.S. House of Representatives (1907-13); appointed by President WILSON the first Secretary of Labor when the Department was created (1913-21); important in the establishment of the Department, in creating mediation in labor disputes, and in advocating COLLECTIVE BARGAINING for LABOR.

WILSON, Woodrow. Full name Thomas Woodrow. 1856-1924. Twenty-eighth President of the United States. b. Staunton, Virginia. Graduated, Princeton University (1879); admitted to the bar and practiced in Georgia (1882); studied political science and jurisprudence at Johns Hopkins (Ph.D. 1886); after teaching at Bryn Mawr, Wesleyan and Princeton he was made president of the latter (1902-10); elected governor of New Jersey

(1911-13); supported important reform legislation including a CORRUPT PRACTICES ACT, WORKINGMEN'S COMPENSATION, and the direct PRIMARY; with the support of WILLIAM J. BRYAN, he was nominated for the presidency on the Democratic ticket and elected President of the United States (1913-21); during his administration many important Acts were passed including the CLAYTON ANTI-TRUST ACT, Workmen's Compensation Act, FEDERAL CHILD LABOR LAW and three amendments to the Constitution (17TH, 18TH, and 19TH); although he attempted to keep the United States neutral during the period leading up to World War I he finally directed mobilization and led the country to victory; outlined the FOURTEEN POINTS for Peace; participated in the Peace Conference and accepted the covenant of the LEAGUE OF NATIONS; he fought a losing battle for the United States to join the League; awarded the Nobel Peace Prize (1919); attempted to campaign throughout the country for his position but suffered a nervous collapse (Sept. 1919) and never fully recovered. Author of many books on political science and world affairs. He was an important, liberal, and honest President.

WINDOM, William. 1827-1891. Lawyer and political leader. b. Ohio. Studied law and admitted to the bar (1850); practised in Minnesota; member, U. S. House of Representatives (1859-69); U. S. Senator (1870-81; 1881-83); served for a time as Secretary of the Treasury in GARFIELD's cabinet (1881); again appointed Secretary of the Treasury and served with HARRISON (1889-91).

WINSLOW, Edward. 1595-1655. A Founder of the Plymouth Colony. b. England. Came to America aboard the *Mayflower* (1620); served as agent to England for the colony (1623-24); leader and founder of the colony serving as a member of the governor's council (1624-46); also served as governor (1633,

1636, 1644); went to England to defend the colony; sent on mission to the WEST INDIES by Cromwell and died on the return voyage. Wrote important pamphlets in defense of the New England colonies.

WINTHROP, John. 1588-1649. Colonial governor. b. England. Educated at Cambridge and practised law in London; deprived of his office in England because of his PURITAN beliefs he was granted a charter for the MASSACHUSETTS BAY COLONY and elected its governor; arrived in Salem with approximately 700 settlers (1630); served as governor for 12 terms; banished ANNE HUTCHINSON; organized the CONFEDERATION OF NEW ENGLAND and was its first president (1645); he was an able leader. His *Journals,* sometimes called the *History of New England from* 1630 *to* 1649 (1853) is an important historical document.

WINTHROP, Robert Charles. 1809-1894. b. Boston, Massachusetts. Graduated Harvard (1828); studied law with DANIEL WEBSTER and was admitted to the bar (1831); WHIG member, U.S. House of Representatives (1840-50); U.S. Senator (1850-51); unsuccessful Whig candidate for governor; famous as an orator; opposed SLAVERY and believed in a compromise between the North and the South. He was a descendant of JOHN WINTHROP (1588-1649).

Wireless. The first wireless set in the United States was installed on the American vessel ST. PAUL in 1899. Its limited range of 75 miles was increased by 1901 to 500 miles when a message from that distance was received on the *Philadelphia.* Marconi's invention was modified and improved in the United States by the work of E. F. W. Alexanderson, E. H. Armstrong, LEE DE FOREST, and R. A. Fessenden. DeForest's invention of the electronic tube in 1906 has remained one of the signal inventions in wireless. In 1903 a Marconi Company stationed on Cape Cod broadcast a message across the Atlantic. Five years later another station on Cape Breton Island began commercial service. The United States Navy installed wireless transmitters and receivers on its ships, and throughout the nation private amateur and commercial sending expanded. In 1912 Congress provided for the licensing and regulation of wireless.

WIRT, William. 1772-1834. Lawyer and political leader. b. Maryland. Practised law in Virginia; famous for his prosecution of AARON BURR (1807); U.S. Attorney General (1817-29) involved in many famous cases including MC CULLOCH VS. MARYLAND and GIBBONS VS. OGDEN; a Jeffersonian Democrat who later joined forces with CLAY, he was the unsuccessful ANTI-MASONIC PARTY candidate for the Presidency (1832).

Wisconsin. The 26th state in size, with an area of 56,154 square miles. Organized as a TERRITORY in 1836 and admitted as the 30th state on May 29, 1848. Madison is the capital. In 1950 Wisconsin's POPULATION of 3,434,575 made it 14th in rank. Its largest cities are Milwaukee, Madison, and Racine. Wisconsin is the nation's leading dairy state. Its chief products are dairy cattle, cheese, butter, and milk. Although partially exhausted its lumber resources are still important. Manufactures include paper, beer, machinery, furniture, and automobiles. Farm crops include cranberries, hemp, oats, rye, and tobacco. Wisconsin is famous for its progressive social and labor legislation, having pioneered in pensions for the blind (1907), aid to dependent children (1913), and pensions to the aged (1925). In 1932 it led the nation in the enactment of an unemployment compensation measure. The state has also broken ground in lobby regulation and legislation leading to popular control of government. The state was discovered in 1634 by Jean Nicolet. Its nickname is the "Badger State."

WISE, Stephen Samuel. 1874-1949. Reform Rabbi and Jewish leader. b. Hungary. Served as a rabbi in New York and Oregon; founded and served as rabbi of the Free Synagogue, New York City from (1907); leader of the Zionist movement; president of the American Jewish Congress; leader in international peace, child-labor reform, improved labor laws and progressive Judaism.

WISTAR, Caspar. 1761-1818. Physician. b. Philadelphia, Pennsylvania. Graduated, University of Edinburgh (M.D. 1786); professor of anatomy, University of Pennsylvania (1808-18); wrote the first American anatomy textbook, *System of Anatomy* (1811); succeeded THOMAS JEFFERSON as president of the AMERICAN PHILOSOPHICAL SOCIETY (1818).

WISTER, Owen. 1860-1938. Author. b. Philadelphia, Pennsylvania. Graduated with honors in music from Harvard (1882); graduated Harvard Law School and admitted to the bar (1889); best known for his novel *The Virginian* (1902).

Witchcraft. The belief that human beings could consort with evil spirits and thus develop the power to defy natural laws and bring harm to other people. The belief in witchcraft was practiced in the British colonies where it was frequently perverted by accusations against innocent persons for personal reasons. The first case of execution for witchcraft is noted in Boston in 1648, and was thereafter succeeded by repeated instances of accusations, trials, and executions. Between 1684 and 1693 more than 100 women were tried and convicted in Massachusetts, many of them being hanged. Governor PHIPPS established special courts for the trial of witches. The greatest outbreak occurred in Salem in 1692 when a group of girls who became victims of a hysteria neurosis, not susceptible to diagnosis by the village physician, accused many persons of having bewitched them. The ensuing hysteria caused the arrest of several hundred per-

sons of whom 19 were hanged between May and September of that year. The resistance of many educated, courageous leaders finally brought an end to the terror until finally the assembly passed a resolution in 1696 in which the mistakes of the preceding period were admitted. Examples of witchcraft persecution also occurred in Virginia in 1706 and in North Carolina in 1712, but virtually disappeared from the American scene as a result of the Salem outbreak. There is no record that witches were ever burned in Salem. It is known that learned men like INCREASE MATHER believed in witchcraft.

WITHERSPOON, John. 1723 - 1794. Clergyman, educator and author. b. Scotland. Presbyterian clergyman in Scotland; came to America to be President, College of New Jersey (now Princeton) (1768-94); member, CONTINENTAL CONGRESS (1776-79; 1789-82); a signer of the DECLARATION OF INDEPENDENCE and the ARTICLES OF CONFEDERATION; member of the New Jersey convention that RATIFIED THE CONSTITUTION; an organizer of the Presbyterian Church along national lines; author of many books.

"Wobblies." See Industrial Workers of the World.

WOLCOTT, Oliver. 1726-1797. Colonial leader. b. Connecticut. Graduated Yale (1747); served in the French and Indian Wars; member, CONTINENTAL CONGRESS (1775-78; 1780-84); a signer of the DECLARATION OF INDEPENDENCE; served in command of the Connecticut militia during the Revolution and as a brigadier general against BURGOYNE (1777); major general (1779); lieutenant governor of Connecticut (1787-96); governor (1796-97).

WOLCOTT, Oliver. 1760-1833. Lawyer and political leader. b. Connecticut. Graduated, Yale (1778); auditor of the U. S. Treasury (1789-91); comptroller (1791-95); U. S. Secretary of the Treasury (1795-1800) succeeding HAMILTON; governor of Connecticut (1817-27).

WOLCOTT, Roger. 1679-1767. Colonial administrator. b. Connecticut. Served in French and Indian Wars; deputy governor of Connecticut (1741-50); as major general he took part in the capture of Louisburg from the French (1745); governor of Connecticut (1751-54); wrote the first book of poetry published in Connecticut, *Poetical Meditations* (1725).

WOLFE, Thomas Clayton. 1900-1938. Novelist. b. North Carolina. Graduated, North Carolina (1920); studied under Baker at Harvard; teacher at New York University; famous as the author of *Look Homeward, Angel* (1929), *Of Time and the River* (1935), *The Web and the Rock* (1939) and many others which are by and large powerful and realistic autobiographical novels.

WOLLE, John Frederick. 1863-1933. Musician and conductor. b. Pennsylvania. Studied in Germany and became organist in church in Bethlehem (1885-1905); famous for his interpretation of Bach; founded and conducted the famous Bethlehem Bach Choir which gave the first performance of the complete B-minor Mass (March, 1900); professor of music, University of California (1905-11); conducted Bach festivals in Bethlehem and at Lehigh University (1912-32).

Women's Army Corps. Popularly known as the WACS. A permanent branch of the regular army, established on June 12, 1948. It grew out of the Women's Army Auxiliary Corps (WAAC) which was created in 1942 as an adjunct of the Army of the United States to relieve manpower problems. Enlistment is open to women between 18 and 34 who are CITIZENS of the United States, high school graduates, single, and with no dependents. Its functions today are to form a nucleus for expansion into an established body of specialists from which may be drawn troops in jobs for which they are suited. With the exception of combat duty, the training of WACS is parallel to that for men. In 1951 there were approximately 11,000 WACS in the army.

Women's Bureau. An agency in the United States DEPARTMENT OF LABOR which is charged with studying and improving the conditions of women workers. It was established in 1920. It has conducted conferences and made investigations into the problems relating to the employment of women. Among its studies have been those dealing with piece workers, state hour laws and MINIMUM WAGE rates, part-time work in retail work, and the potential earning power of southern mountaineer handicraft.

Woman's Christian Temperance Union. An organization founded in 1874 in Cleveland, Ohio for the purpose of curbing excessive liquor consumption, and seeking the enactment of PROHIBITION legislation in the states. As a result of its propaganda efforts, it succeeded by 1900, in bringing about temperance instruction in public schools, and in achieving widespread publication of its program in the press, periodicals, and in books. The organization also supported a program advocating the abolition of prostitution, the improvement of prison conditions, moral education, WOMEN'S SUFFRAGE, equal rights between men and women, and the elimination of the sale of drugs. Under the outstanding leadership of its second president, FRANCES E. WILLARD (1879-1898), the organization flourished and became the nucleus of the World Women's Christian Temperance Union which was founded in 1883.

Women's Clubs. Political and social organizations of women coming into existence in the late 19th century as a result of the women's rights movement. They were devoted to philanthropic, reform, suffrage, and educational programs. Many of them associated with the temperance and settlement house groups, merging their activities with these in their common objectives. The establishment of the Women's Home Mission Board in 1877 and the YOUNG WOMEN'S CHRISTIAN ASSOCIATION in 1906 reflects the interest of these groups in religion and morals. The General Federation of Women's Clubs was an amalgamation in 1889 of many cultural societies. Patriotic organizations which had existed since the early 19th century were reorganized into the DAUGHTERS OF THE AMERICAN REVOLUTION and the Colonial Dames of America in 1890. The spread of co-education in the nation's colleges and universities stimulated the growth of sororities which were brought together in 1891 in the National Pan-Hellenic Association.

Women's Suffrage. Minor local voting by women in the English colonies disappeared after the Revolution except in New Jersey which abolished it in 1807. From then until 1834 women voted in no state until the Kentucky legislature authorized women's suffrage in local elections that year. It was not until the adoption of the women's suffrage plank in the platform of the Women's Rights Convention at Seneca Falls in 1848 that a concerted movement was undertaken to achieve this right on a national basis. Under the leadership of ELIZABETH CADY STANTON, LUCY STONE, JULIA WARD HOWE, and SUSAN B. ANTHONY, the American Equal Rights Association championed this cause for the next generation. In 1869 the TERRITORY of Wyoming conferred this right upon women, to be retained after its admission as a state in 1889. The movement gained impetus by this innovation, and the franchise was conferred upon women in Colorado (1893). Utah and Idaho (1896), Washington (1910), California (1911), Arizona, Kansas, and Oregon (1912), Illinois (limited suffrage, 1913), Nevada and Montana (1914), and New York (1917). Since the turn of the 20th century the leadership of CARRIE CHAPMAN CATT, ANNA HOWARD SHAW, and Alice Paul succeeded in bringing about the adoption of the 19TH AMENDMENT in 1919. Although not directly conferring the right to vote upon women this amendment prohibits the states or the United States from restricting this right on account of sex.

WOOD, Grant. 1892-1942. Painter. b. Iowa. Taught art in Iowa; studied in Paris; artist in residence, School of Fine Arts, University of Iowa; well-known for his highly individual style that is best seen in his paintings *American Gothic, Daughters of the Revolution,* and his murals at Iowa State College.

WOOD, Leonard. 1860-1927. Physician, general, and colonial administrator. b. New Hampshire. Graduated Harvard with a medical degree and practised in Boston; entered the army as an assistant surgeon (1885); captain at the outbreak of the Spanish-American War; leader of the "ROUGH RIDERS" with T. ROOSEVELT; colonel; became mlitary governor of Cuba (1899-1902); commanded U.S. forces in the PHILIPPINES (1906-08); chief of staff of the U.S. Army (1910-14); Republican candidate for the presidential nomination (1916 and 1920); governor-general of the Philippines (1921-27); he did not believe in granting the natives self-rule and a later report of the Thompson Commission. was critical of his administration. Awarded the CONGRESSIONAL MEDAL OF HONOR.

WOODIN, William Hartman. 1868-1934. Industrialist, financier and political official. b. Pennsylvania. Studied engineering at Columbia; president, American Car and Foundry Co. (from 1916); U. S. Secretary of the Treasury (1933) appointed by F.D. ROOSEVELT; handled the bank crisis during the early days of the NEW DEAL with great efficiency; resigned for reasons of ill health and died shortly thereafter.

Woolens Act of 1699. An Act of Parliament designed to prevent the development of colonial manufactures which might be in competition with British goods, and to encourage the colonies to produce goods needed by England. It forbade the export of wool and woolens from the colonies to Great Britain and foreign nations, and among the colonies. The law did not prohibit the sale within a colony of woolens which had been manufactured there. The intercolonial market was thus preserved for the English woolen manufacturers. The following year an AMENDMENT removed the export duties on wool shipped from England to the colonies, its objective being the maintenance of low prices of British woolens in America and thus making it possible for these goods to compete with colonial manufactures.

Wool Industry. An important industry in the United States closely associated with TEXTILE MANUFACTURING. The first sheep in America were brought to the colonies in 1609 as a result of colonial laws fostering the wool trade. The introduction of superior breeds after the American Revolution, at a time when the industrialization of England and France created a considerable demand for fine wools, provided the greatest stimulus to the wool industry up to the Civil War. Sheep breeding spread rapidly throughout New England and the middle colonies, moving, for a time, as far south and west as Kentucky and Ohio. After the Civil War, sheep grazing spread to the trans-Mississippi west creating, for a decade, the famous range wars with the cattle men. In 1950 the value of wool manufactures in the United States was $76,000,000. In 1946 the nation consumed 746,000,000 pounds of wool, the highest in its history, although this figure dropped to 196,000,-000 pounds in the first third of 1951, a rate of 588,000,000 pounds for the year.

WOOLMAN, John. 1720-1772. QUAKER ABOLITIONIST. b. New Jersey. Visited the colonies preaching the faith of the Quakers and against the owning of slaves. Famous for his *Journal*.

WOOLWORTH, Frank Winfield. 1852-1919. Merchant. b. New York. Famous as the organizer of the five-and-ten-cent stores which became nationwide; amassed a huge fortune; built the Woolworth Building in New York City, then the tallest in the world (1913).

Worcester vs. Georgia. A decision of the United States Supreme Court in 1832 in which the court held that the CHEROKEE INDIAN tribe was a nation under the protection of the United States and therefore free from the jurisdiction of the state of Georgia. The Court overruled a decision of the Georgia courts which had resulted in the imprisonment of Samuel A. Worcester and 10 others for living in the Cherokee country in violation of a state law requiring a prior oath of allegiance and permit. President JACKSON'S opposition to Chief Justice JOHN MARSHALL resulted in the non-enforcement of the Court's decision.

WORK, Hubert. 1860-1942. Physician and politician. b. Pennsylvania. Graduated University of Pennsylvania (M.D. 1885); practised in Colorado; prominent in Republican politics and appointed U. S. Postmaster General (1922-23); U. S. Secretary of the Interior (1923-28); president, American Medical Association.

Works Progress Administration. Popularly known as the WPA. In 1937 its name was changed to Works Projects Administration. It was established by EXECUTIVE ORDER on May 6, 1935 with an initial appropriation of $4,880,000,000 to be expended for relief work, loans, and grants on non-federal projects, HIGHWAYS, rural rehabilitation, REFORESTATION, flood control, soil erosion work, RURAL ELECTRIFICATION, health and sanitation projects, and student aid. The purpose of the legislation was to provide work for the unemployed, to stimulate private business, and to inaugurate much needed reforms. At its height the WPA employed 3,800,000 persons, roughly a third of the then unemployed. In its eight year life it provided jobs for a total of 8,500,000 persons. It spent a total of $10,500,000,000 plus $2,700,000,000 contributed by sponsors, notably local governments. Among its accomplishments was the construction of 122,000 public buildings, 664,000 miles of roads, 77,000 bridges, 285 airports, and innumerable parks, playgrounds, and reservoirs. It achieved outstanding results in its cultural projects, as in the fields of the drama, writing, ART, and the professions. On December 4, 1942 it was abolished, its work being absorbed by the FEDERAL WORKS AGENCY.

Workingman's Party. A minor party founded in New York City in 1829 under the leadership of FRANCES WRIGHT and ROBERT DALE OWEN. Its program included demands for the abolition of imprisonment for debt and for a sound worker's lien law. As a purely local organization it never exercised national political influence, and because of public opposition to the religious views of its leaders, as well as the successful legislation fulfilling its program, the party declined in the 1830's. Its forces joined the WHIGS.

Workmen's Compensation. Payment of funds by the employer to workers who are injured in the course of their employment. See Workmen's Compensation laws.

Workmen's Compensation Laws. Also known as employers liability laws. A series of state and federal laws designed to protect industrial workers against the financial burdens of accident and disability arising out of their work conditions. Before their adoption in the early 20th century the burden rested on the

injured worker who was entitled to damages only upon proof that his employer had not provided reasonable care in his protection, that the accident had not resulted from the negligence of a "fellow-servant", that there had not been "contributory negligence" on his part, and that the risk assumed had been extraordinary. These laws were part of the wave of reform of the "PROGRESSIVE ERA" from 1890 to 1920. In 1906 Congress passed the EMPLOYERS LIABILITY ACT to protect railroad workers, and reanacted the law two years later as a result of its invalidation by the Supreme Court. Maryland passed the first state workmen's compensation law in 1918. New York passed a broad law in 1910, which was declared unconstitutional in 1911, but was reinforced by state constitutional amendment in 1914. By 1942 a total of 47 states (all except Mississippi) and all the territories had adopted such legislation. Congress has protected federal employees by such laws, and in 1927 extended their benefits to longshoremen and harbor workers. It is estimated that injured workers receive a total of $250,000,000 annually in compensation benefits.

World Bank. See International Bank for Reconstruction and Development.

World Court. See Permanent Court of International Justice.

World Court Protocol. See Root Protocol.

World Disarmament Conference. A conference of 57 nations which was convened by the LEAGUE OF NATIONS at Geneva, Switzerland in February, 1932 to discuss general DISARMAMENT. The United States was one of the non-member nations which participated. It was the first world conference in history to take up the limitation of armaments of every kind. To it were submitted peace memorials signed by 8,500,000 persons in 45 countries. For almost two years the nations bickered over the terms of proposed disarmament treaties. Germany demanded the right to armed equality. The Soviet delegation proposed that disarmament be complete and reasonably prompt. The French plan suggested COLLECTIVE SECURITY agreements and an international police force. President HOOVER proposed an immediate reduction of one third in existing national armaments and the outlawing of chemical warfare, bombing planes, heavy artillery, and tanks. On May 27, 1933 the United States delegate declared that his government was willing "to consult the other States" in the event of a threat to peace. The Japanese invasion of Manchuria in 1931, the accession of the Nazis to political power in Germany in January, 1933, and the withdrawal of Germany from the Conference in October, 1933 made all disarmament proposals impossible.

World Monetary and Economic Conference. See London Economic Conference.

"World Must Be Made Safe for Democracy, The." The famous phrase from President WILSON's message to Congress on April 4, 1917 in which he called for a declaration of war against Germany. In his war message the President declared that "it is a fearful thing to lead this great peaceful people into war . . . But the right is more precious than the peace . . . The world must be made safe for democracy."

World War I. The causes of World War I go back to 19th century European politics. National and economic conflicts developed antagonisms that finally resulted in war. These causes included: exaggeration of NATIONALISM, denial of nationalism, militarism, armaments, secret treaties, military alliances, and IMPERIALISM. Although President WILSON called upon the American people to be neutral

in thought as well as in action when the war broke out in Europe in 1914, many factors made this impossible. The large German-American and Irish-American population was fundamentally anti-British. Historical conflicts between the United States and Great Britain impelled many Americans to look with favor upon the German point of view. On the other hand traditional ties with Great Britain, arising out of the common language, culture, and political institutions, developed a considerable anti-German sentiment. Successful British propaganda enhanced this feeling, and many Americans were led to believe that the German army was guilty of atrocities and the German government a despotic power. Diplomatic issues arising from American neutral TRADE, involved the United States in conflict with England in the first year of the war. In 1915 German SUBMARINE warfare and the increasing pace of British propaganda turned the sympathy of the American people to Great Britain. The sinking of the *Lusitania* on May 7, 1915, the *Arabic* in August, 1915, and the *Sussex* in March, 1916, caused the United States to protest vigorously. On February 1, 1917 Germany announced the resumption of UNRESTRICTED SUBMARINE WARFARE. On February 24th the ZIMMERMAN NOTE was published. On February 26th President Wilson requested Congress for power to arm American merchant ships. On April 2nd he read his war message to a special session of Congress which four days later declared war against Germany. Meanwhile, in 1914, the firm of J. P. Morgan & Company had been appointed the official purchasing agent of the British and French governments in the United States. This company and other banking houses had lent huge sums to these governments, which, by 1917, totaled $2,500,-000,000. The charge has often been made that the administration was influenced by the desire to maintain economic prosperity in the United States and protect these loans. The war had brought a rise in foreign trade. The trade balance of $435,800,000 in June, 1914 had risen by 1917 to $3,567,800,000. From a debtor nation the United States had become the great creditor nation of the world. Secretary of State BRYAN had held that "money is the worst of all contrabands" and that loans to belligerent powers were "inconsistent with the spirit of NEUTRALITY." It was recognized, however, that the administration's position was compatible with the principles of international law. After its entry into the war the United States sent a token force to France in June, 1917. In the last year of fighting American armies assisted in the great allied counteroffensive, participating in the second BATTLE OF THE MARNE and the MEUSE-ARGONNE, ST. MIHIEL, and CHATEAU-THIERRY battles. The war was brought to an end by the ARMISTICE of November 11, 1918. President Wilson personally represented the UNITED STATES at 'he VERSAILLES CONFERENCE in January, 1918. The financial cost of World War I has been estimated at $35,000,000,000. One-third of this was raised by taxes and the remainder through the sale of bonds. Of the 4,609,190 personnel engaged, United States armed forces suffered casualties of 130,921 dead, including 53,403 battle deaths, and 202,261 wounded.

World War II. The causes of World War II may be traced to the conditions in Europe left by the peace treaties after World War I. Economic dislocation combined with political rivalries and national hatreds to sow the seeds of war. High TARIFFS, economic NATIONALISM, and the drive for autarchy brought about a decline in international TRADE in the 1930's. Financial distress and business bankruptcies in Germany and Austria laid the groundwork for the rise to power of the National Socialist Movement. The international DEPRESSION of the 1930's

brought chaos to the economies of all major nations. The result was mass UNEMPLOYMENT, a decline in the value of CURRENCIES, business failures, and trade wars. The fascist and nazi governments in Italy, Germany, and Japan geared those nations for war. Exaggerated nationalism led to racial doctrines that resulted in the persecutions of minority peoples and economic classes. Based specifically on a hatred for DEMOCRACY and LIBERALISM, these dictator governments prepared for war. A long series of aggressions began with the invasion of MANCHURIA by Japan in 1931. In 1934 Italy invaded Ethiopia. In 1936 Italy and Germany assisted General Franco in his revolt against the republican government of Spain. In 1938 Germany annexed Austria and in 1939 Czechoslovakia and Memel. Meanwhile Japan had invaded China in 1937 and was moving southward toward French Indo-China, Burma, and the Southwest Pacific. In 1939 Germany threatened Poland. In that year Italy occupied Albania. The failure of the LEAGUE OF NATIONS to prevent or punish these repeated aggressions was culminated in the unsuccessful negotiations in 1939 for a military alliance among England, France, and the Soviet Union. The invasion of Poland on September 1, 1939 brought on World War II. Meanwhile the United States had taken certain precautions against the outbreak of war in Europe. President F. D. ROOSEVELT attempted to prevent war by repeated appeals to Germany, Italy, and Japan against continued aggression. Within the country many Americans denounced Germany's barbarous treatment of the Jews. Organizations protested and raised funds for the care of refugees. In 1939 a poll taken by the American Institute of Public Opinion indicated that 69 percent of the American people favored supporting Britain and France by every' means "short of war." When the war broke out President Roosevelt convened Congress in special session to repeal the ARMS EMBARGO which had been imposed by the NEUTRALITY ACTS. A "CASH AND CARRY" program was instituted on November 3, 1939. A PAN-AMERICAN CONFERENCE at Panama City in September, 1939 brought the 21 Latin-American Republics into close harmony on necessary defense measures. Within the neutral zone, extending 1,250 miles out to sea, clashes between Allied and German ships subsequently occurred. Sharp diplomatic protests were sent to Germany. Within the United States the European war effected an upswing of business. Securities gained, prices rose, and production increased. Neutral and pro-German elements scoffed at the possibility of German attack against the United States. In the Hearst Press, SATURDAY EVENING POST, and Patterson-McCormick press, denunciations of the administration appeared with increasing frequency. In the government, Representative Hamilton Fish and Senators Nye, TAFT, and WHEELER attacked the President's program. In June, 1940 the President asked Congress to legislate a broad national defense program. In September Congress followed up this plan by authorizing loans of $1,500,000,000 to Latin-American nations. A coordinated program of defense with Mexico and Canada was worked out in 1940 and 1941. In September the President effected the exchange with England of 50 old-model destroyers for eight naval and air bases in the Atlantic. In April, 1941 the United States assumed the military protection of Greenland with the consent of the Danish minister at Washington. In July American troops were sent to Iceland to prevent German encroachment. In November, 1940 the President had announced that England would be allotted half the nation's production of military equipment. A few months later he declared that the United States must become the "ARSENAL OF DEMOCRACY."

This program was reorganized and expanded by the LEND-LEASE ACT of March, 1941. In September, 1940 the first peacetime compulsory DRAFT program was set up by the BURKE-WADSWORTH ACT. To expedite industrial mobilization the President created the Advisory Commission on National Defense on May 28, 1940. Congress increased tax rates in almost every category. In August, 1941 President Roosevelt and Prime Minister Churchill drew up the ATLANTIC CHARTER. Meanwhile a "bridge of ships" fed supplies from the United States to England, safeguarded by a naval patrol on the high seas by American forces based on Greenland and Iceland. American-owned vessels were sunk. After the attack on the GREER, Roosevelt ordered naval vessels and planes to shoot on sight. In October, the KEARNY and the REUBEN JAMES were sunk. In November, Congress authorized the arming of merchant ships. In the meantime Japan had moved down into southeast Asia. In the United States demands for an embargo on scrap steel were finally effective when the President forbade such exports in October, 1940. The formation of the Rome-Berlin-Tokyo Axis brought the realization of war close to the American people. In August, 1941 Roosevelt notified Japan that further aggression would compel this nation to take steps necessary for the protection of American rights. In November, 1941 Japan sent Saburo Kurusu to assist the Japanese ambassador in negotiations with Secretary of State HULL in an attempt to reconcile outstanding diplomatic controversies. While the talks were in progress news came of the Japanese attack on PEARL HARBOR on December 7th. On December 8th, Congress declared war on Japan, with but one dissenting vote. On December 11th Germany and Italy declared war on the United States and Congress responded with a unanimous vote on the same day. Congress and the President immediately mobilized the military and civilian defense agencies and provided for the establishment of new ones in the fields of production, economic stabilization, armed forces, finances, TRANSPORTATION, POLITICAL WARFARE, LABOR RELATIONS, food supply, and SHIPPING. A new and increased tax program was put into effect which, by 1944, raised 46 percent of the cost of the war. In February, 1946 the Treasury stated that the direct cost of the war up to that time was $330,500,000,000. It was estimated that by 1975 the total cost of the war, including veteran's allowances, would be $375,000,000,000. The first United States offensive was an attack on GUADALCANAL in August, 1942. This began the "ISLAND HOPPING" campaign which culminated in the atomic bombing of HIROSHIMA and Nagasaki in August, 1945. With the invasion of NORTH AFRICA in November, 1942, the offensive in western Europe began, reaching its climax in the invasion of France in June, 1944. In less than one year the allies had penetrated western Germany in conjunction with the invasion of eastern Germany by the armed forces of the Soviet Union. On May 8, 1945 the war was over in Europe. The war in the Far East came to an end four months later, on September 2, 1945. As a result of the development of the "COLD WAR" peace treaties were not negotiated until 1951 and 1952. On December 31, 1946, however, President TRUMAN formally proclaimed the termination of hostilities. On September 8, 1951 the JAPANESE PEACE TREATY was signed. The GERMAN PEACE CONTRACT was signed on May 26, 1952. Of the total army and air force personnel of 10,420,000, casualties included 237,049 killed in action, 69,000 deaths from other causes, and 139,703 wounded. All branches of the navy suffered casualties including 89,117 killed and 105,953 wounded. It has been estimated that the financial cost of the war was $350,000,000,000 of which 56 per-

cent was financed by loans and the remainder by taxes.

World Peace Foundation. Established in 1910 to promote peace, justice, and good will among the nations of the world. It seeks to improve public understanding of international problems by an impartial presentation of materials dealing with international relations. Its office is located in Boston, Massachusetts.

World's Columbian Exposition. An international exhibition in Chicago in May-November, 1893. It was authorized by Congress in 1890 to celebrate the 400th anniversary of the discovery of America. The main buildings, constructed of a composition resembling marble, gave the Exposition the name "White City." Their architecture was Greek, Romanesque, and Rennaissance, and was designed by DANIEL H. BURNHAM and John W. Root.

World's Fair. An international exposition opened in New York City in 1939 to commemorate the 150th anniversary of GEORGE WASHINGTON'S inauguration. Publicized as "The World of Tomorrow" the fair displayed exhibits of outstanding tools, architecture, industrial processes, and machinery. Hundreds of buildings were erected at a cost of more than $155,000,000, financed by bond issues. Sixty foreign nations and 23 American states participated. The fair was visited by 32,786,521 persons.

WORTH, William Jenkins. 1794-1849. General. b. New York. Served in the War of 1812; against the SEMINOLE INDIANS; Mexican War; brevetted major general being the first to enter Mexico City; in command of the department of Texas (1848); Fort Worth named in his honor.

WRIGHT, Silas. 1795-1847. Lawyer and political leader. b. Massachusetts. Graduated, Middlebury College, Vermont (1815); admitted to the bar (1819); practised in New York; served in state senate; member of the Albany Regency and a power in state politics; member, U. S. House of Representatives (1827-29); comptroller, New York (1829-33); U. S. Senator (1833-44); supported Jackson and the ANNEXATION OF TEXAS; supported VAN BUREN; chairman, Senate Finance Committee (1836-41); governor of New York (1845-47); opposed calling of state constitutional convention (1846); during the anti-rent riots in the state he called out the MILITIA.

WRIGHT, Wilbur. 1867-1912. Aviation pioneer. b. Indiana. With his brother, Orville who was born in Ohio, he ran a bicycle shop; they became interested in AVIATION and first experiment with kites and gliders (1896-1903); at Kitty Hawk, North Carolina, they tried out their motor-powered airplane which made its first successful flight (1903); granted PATENT for their machine (1906); organized the American Wright Company to manufacture airplanes (1909) which had undergone successful army tests.

WRIGHT, Frances. 1795-1852. Better known as Fanny Wright. Reformer. b. Scotland. Toured the United States with LAFAYETTE (1824); lived in New York Ciy (from 1829); became a champion of antislavery movement and established a colony at Nashoba, Tennessee (1827) which failed; gained national reputation as a lecturer on religious freedom, women's rights, progressive EDUCATION, and reforms needed in marriage laws.

WRIGHT, Frank Lloyd. 1869-1959. Architect. b. Wisconsin. Worked in Chicago with Adler and SULLIVAN; famous as the leader of the modern school of ARCHITECTURE; planned and designed modern functional homes and buildings. Author of many books on the subject.

WRIGHT, Horatio Gouverneur. 1820-1899. General. b. Connecticut. Graduated, U.S.M.A., West Point (1841);

served as brigadier general of volunteers at BULL RUN; commanded in Florida and the Department of Ohio; served at GETTYSBURG, in the WILDERNESS campaign; major general (1864); served with SHERIDAN in the Shenandoah Valley; chief of engineers (1879); retired (1884).

WRIGHT, Patience Lovell. 1725-1785. Sculptor. Her portraits in wax were the first attempts at SCULPTURE in the colonies; worked in England (after 1772); aided the American cause by acting as a spy during the Revolution and forwarding plans of the British to the Colonies.

Writ of Mandamus. An equity writ ordering an administrative officer to perform a function normally expected of his office. Under Anglo-American law the writ of mandamus is an order to perform a ministerial function not considered within the discretion of the officer to refuse.

Writs of Assistance. General search warrants issued by colonial courts to customs officers. They were first issued in 1751 in Massachusetts but did not create any difficulty. Their re-issue 10 years later was opposed as unconstitutional by JAMES OTIS, acting as counsel for eastern merchants; Otis' opposition was unsuccessful and, accepting advice from England as to their legality, the Massachusetts assembly authorized their issue in 1762. Their revival in the Townshend Revenue Act of 1767 produced the first major controversy concerning their legality, and by 1772 the courts of eight colonies, including the largest ones like New York, Pennsylvania, and Virginia, had refused to issue Writs of Assistance. In some of these refusals specific assertion was made as to their UNCONSTITUTIONALITY. By this time the conflict had spread to all the British colonies and had become one of the contributing factors leading to the Revolution. JEFFERSON speci-

fied the Writs of Assistance in the DECLA-
RATION OF INDEPENDENCE, as a grievance
common to all the colonies.

WYETH, Nathaniel Jarvis. 1802-1856.
Explorer. b. Massachusetts. Successful
merchant from Boston who travelled into
Far Northwest and explored the Oregon
territory in the hope of establishing trading posts there; he is one of the char-
acters in WASHINGTON IRVING's *Adventures of Captain Bonneville.*

WYLIE, Elinor Hoyt. 1885-1928. Poet
and novelist. b. New Jersey. Contributor to many reviews and periodicals; associate editor of Vanity Fair; winner of
POETRY prizes and recognized as an outstanding talent. Author of *Nets to Catch
the Wind* (1921), *Black Armour* (1923),
Last Poems (1923), and the novels *Jen-
nifer Lorn* (1923), *The Orphan Angel*
(1926) and others.

Wyoming. The ninth state in size,
with an area of 97,914 square miles. Organized as a TERRITORY in 1868 and admitted as the 44th state on July 10,
1890. In 1950 Wyoming's POPULATION
of 290,529 made it 47th in rank. Its
largest cities are Cheyenne, Casper, and
Laramie. Wyoming's principal products
are CATTLE, COAL, OIL, and wool. There
are also important stands of LUMBER. In
1869 Wyoming pioneered WOMAN SUF-
FRAGE in national elections. In 1925
Wyoming elected the first woman governor in American history. The state is
outstanding in its scenic splendor, containing notable NATIONAL PARKS AND
MONUMENTS, among them world famous
YELLOWSTONE NATIONAL PARK. The state
was first settled in 1812 by fur trappers,
but had been reached in 1807 by a
member of the LEWIS AND CLARK EXPE-
DITION. Its nickname is the "Equality
State."

X

XYZ Affair. A diplomatic controversy between the United States and France in 1797-1798. In an attempt to restore harmonious relations between the two nations, MARSHALL, PINCKNEY, and GERRY were sent to France in 1797 to relieve the tension between the two nations that had arisen out of the GENET AFFAIR. Unable to confer with the French foreign minister Talleyrand, they met instead with three emissaries, Bellamy, Hauteval, and Hottinguer. In dispatches to the United States its three commissioners designated these agents as "X", "Y", and "Z". The affair is notable because the three Frenchmen proposed that the United States grant to France the loan of a large sum of money as a condition for France's renunciation of the Treaty of Alliances of 1778. Considered as a bribe by the United States government, it indignantly rejected the proposal which simultaneously aroused intense feeling among the American people against France. Recognizing the deterioration of Franco-American relations and the possibility of war, the Congress established the Navy Department in 1798 and prepared for such an eventuality. The NAVAL WAR WITH FRANCE followed shortly thereafter.

Y

Yale University. One of the oldest institutions of higher learning in the United States. It was founded in 1701 at Killingworth, Connecticut, and moved in 1716 to New Haven, its present site. A gift by Elihu Yale, an East India merchant, in 1718, impelled the institution to take his name. By 1771 faculties had been established in astronomy, divinity, mathematics, and physics. Today the University consists of 12 undergraduate and graduate schools including faculties in liberal arts and sciences, engineering, MEDICINE, law, fine arts, MUSIC, forestry, and nursing. In 1861 it achieved the distinction of becoming the first American university to grant the degree of Doctor of Philosophy. The *Yale Literary Magazine* is the oldest periodical of its kind in the United States and the *Yale Daily News* the oldest college daily.

Yalta Conference. A meeting of President F. D. ROOSEVELT, Prime Minister Churchill, and Premier Stalin between February 4 and 11, 1945 at Yalta, Crimea, in the Soviet Union. The agreement provided for the following: common understanding to enforce UNCONDITIONAL SURRENDER on Germany, a four power OCCUPATION OF GERMANY after the war (to include France which would be invited to participate), the destruction of militarism and Nazism, the DISARMAMENT of German armed forces and the destruction of its general staff, the control of German INDUSTRY to prevent rearmament, the trial and punishment of all war criminals, a program of REPARATIONS, the elimination of Nazi and militarist influence from German society, and other measures to insure that Germany would thenceforth be prevented from embarking on war. The agreement also included a provision dealing with the terms under which the Soviet Union would enter the war against Japan, and arranged for the disposition of Japanese territories. Among these were Soviet consent to make war upon Japan not later than three months after Germany's surrender, and certain territorial adjustments which provided that the status quo be maintained in outer Mongolia, southern Sakhalin be restored to the Soviet Union, and that Dairen be internationalized with the recognition of the preeminent interests of the Soviet Union safeguarded by a lease of Port Arthur as a Soviet naval base. The Kurile Islands were to be returned to the Soviet Union, and the Chinese-Eastern and Southern-Manchurian railroads were to be jointly operated by a Soviet-Chinese Company.

YANCEY, William Lowndes. 1814-1863. Lawyer and political leader. b. Georgia. Practiced law in Alabama; member, U. S. House of Representatives (1844-46); leader in secessionist movement and a southern "FIRE-EATER"; member of the

710

Confederate Senate (1862-63); attempted to get help in Europe for the Southern cause, but failed.

Yankee. The name applied by the Confederate army to a Union soldier. Since the Civil War it has been applied to all northerners by the South. Although its origin is obscure it is believed to have been a corruption by the Massachusetts Indians of either the word "English" or the French word "Anglais."

"Yankee Doodle." A song of uncertain origin which was known in England as early as the mid-eighteenth century. Today it is the best known national march and is believed to have been introduced to the colonies about 1750. In the following generation it was played by English bands although it was not published in the United States until 1794. Scores of versions of the song from as many pens, have appeared in American history.

"Yankee Imperialism." The term expressing the opposition of Latin-American nations to the control by the United States of customs, finances, and elections in HAITI, SANTA DOMINGO, CUBA, and NICARAGUA. The phrase came into prominence in the first decade of the 20th century as a result of the application of the ROOSEVELT COROLLARY.

Yap Treaty. A TREATY between the United States and Japan negotiated on February 11, 1922. By its terms the United States consented to the provisions of the Japanese mandate over the island of Yap, and secured from Japan those rights which, under the mandate, had been granted to the members of the LEAGUE OF NATIONS. The most important right obtained was that giving the United States equal cable facilities.

YATES, Richard. 1815-1873. Lawyer and political leader. b. Kentucky. Graduated, Illinois College (1838); studied law and admitted to the bar and practiced in Illinois (1838); WHIG member, U.S. House of Representatives (1851-55); became a Republican governor of Illinois (1861-64); supporting LINCOLN and the Union cause throughout the Civil War; U.S. Senator (1865-71) served as chairman, Committee on Claims and Territories. He was considered an outstanding Civil War governor.

Yazoo Land Frauds. The successful bribing in 1795, of every member, except one of the Georgia legislature, by four land companies organized that year under the name of the Yazoo Companies. In consideration of the bribe, the legislature granted the companies a tract of land containing 35,000,000 acres for the nominal payment of $500,000. The frauds created strong feeling throughout the state, and in every county, except two, grand juries, established for the purpose, declared the legislature's act unconstitutional. The creation of an Anti-Yazoo party brought about the revocation of the sale on February 13, 1796 when that party captured the state legislature. The resulting invalidation of land claims led Congress to appoint MADISON, GALLATIN, and Lincoln as commissioners to investigate these claims. In 1802 Georgia ceded all western lands to the United States but the claims arising from the frauds were not settled until 1814, when Congress paid the claimants $4,282,-151.12.

"Yellow Dog Contract." An agreement between an employee and his employer by which the former states he will not join any union during his period of employ. Before the passage of the NORRIS-LA GUARDIA ANTI-INJUNCTION ACT in 1932 such contracts were enforceable in federal and state courts.

"Yellow Press." See "jingo press."

Yellowstone National Park. An area of 2,213,207 square acres in Wyoming, Montana, and Idaho owned and administered by the United States as a national park. It was established as such

711

by Congress in 1872 in response to the proposal of the Washburn-Langford-Doane party which had explored the area two years earlier. Its most famous natural wonder is the 120 identified geysers and 4,000 hot springs, most of which are located in the park's western portion. This number is greater than the number of geysers in the rest of the world. The park's other natural wonders include roaming herds of buffalo, elk, deer, antelope, and sheep, as well as the famous grizzly bear. It contains canyons, forest trails, great forests, lake and stream fishing, and the 20 miles long Yellowstone Lake.

YORK, Alvin Cullum. 1887-1964. Soldier. b. Tennessee. Hero of World War I and known by all as Sergeant York. During the battle for the ARGONNE (1918) he was credited with having killed 25 Germans and destroying enemy machine guns. He received the highest decorations of both the American and French governments. He was given a farm in Tennessee and a York Foundation was established to support schools for the mountain children of his state. His life was made into a MOTION PICTURE.

Yorktown, Battle of. The final battle of the American Revolution. After his defeat in the Carolinas by Generals GREENE and MORGAN. General CORNWALLIS moved north to Virginia. Failing to persuade General CLINTON to move down from New York, Cornwallis fortified himself at Yorktown, available to reinforcements from the sea if Clinton should decide to sail. Instead, he was attacked from the sea by the French fleet under de Grasse while WASHINGTON, leaving a decoy force to hold Clinton in New York, rapidly moved south with Rochambeau. In the early days of October, 1781 the combined Franco-American army moved in on Cornwallis, whose retreat by water was blocked off. Cornwallis' counterattack failed, and on October 17th he initiated surrender negotiations. Two days later he surrendered his 7247 troops to Washington in the last engagement of any consequence in the war.

Yosemite National Park. A United States owned area of 757,201 acres in California which was established as a national park in 1890. Its scenic beauty has been internationally famous since the discovery of the area in 1851. The Park contains inspiring gorges and waterfalls, and the world famous sequoia forests. Other objects of natural beauty include glaciers, hundreds of lakes, steep waterfalls, and hundreds of streams.

YOUNG, Brigham. 1801-1877. Mormon leader. b. Vermont. Joined JOSEPH SMITH and became a MORMON (1832); directed the Mormon settlement in Nauvoo, Illinois; succeeded Smith as head of the Church; directed the mass migration of Mormons to the Great Salt Lake Valley in Utah; organized and elected first governor of the Territory of Utah (1849-57); practiced polygamy in opposition to the wishes of the federal government; removed from his governorship by President BUCHANAN but retained leadership in the community; a great leader, he was an outstanding example of the pioneer spirit of early America.

YOUNG, Ewing. d. 1841. Trapper and guide. b. Tennessee. Famous as a guide in the West and for leading KIT CARSON from Sante Fe across the Mojave Desert to California (1829); leader in the exploration and settlement of Oregon (1834).

YOUNG, John Russell. 1840-1899. Journalist. b. Ireland. Famous as a news correspondent for the Philadelphia *Press* during the Civil War; worked for other newspapers until his appointment as U.S. Minister to China (1882-85); foreign correspondent for the New York *Herald* in Europe; librarian of Congress (1897-99). Author of *Around the World with General Grant* (2 vols., 1879).

Young Men's Christian Association. Popularly known as the Y.M.C.A. An organization founded in London in 1844 by George Williams. Its early objectives were the development of friendly contacts for its members, and religious activities. By 1894 the movement had spread throughout the world. In the United States the first Y.M.C.A. appeared in Boston in 1851 and rapidly spread throughout the nation. Among its many activities are training for CITIZENSHIP, sports, leadership training, education in public affairs, health and physical education, religious training, and individual services in vocational guidance counseling, camping, and related activities. In 1955 there were 1800 associations comprising 3,000,000 members. About two-thirds of these are under 25 years of age. The Y's carry on a publication program, and administer approximately 25 schools which conduct over 2600 informal EDUCATION programs. During both World Wars the YMCA supplied scores of thousands of special workers and millions of dollars to provide American troops with LITERATURE, entertainment, and residence accommodations. The national headquarters of the organization is located in New York City.

YOUNG, Owen D. 1874-1962. Lawyer. b. New York. Graduated, University of Boston Law School (1896) practised in Boston; counsel for large corporations; associated with CHARLES G. DAWES as American representatives to the Reparations Conference (1924); famous for the YOUNG PLAN involving German REPARATION *payments;* chairman of the board, Radio Corporation of America; chairman, General Electric, he was responsible for such innovations as a system of employee stock plans, UNEMPLOYMENT INSURANCE and a "cultural wage"; chairman, American Youth Commission (1936-42); appointed by F. D. ROOSEVELT head of a committee to survey the nation's TRANSPORTATION problems; member, New York regional committee of the WAR MANPOWER COMMISSION (1942); resumed duties of acting chairman of General Electric, from which he had retired in 1940, to supervise manufacture of more than $1,000,000,000 worth of war orders (1942); retired (1944) becoming honorary chairman of the board of the company.

Young Plan. A plan of debt and REPARATIONS payment recommended in June, 1929 by a committee chaired by OWEN D. YOUNG. The Plan established a schedule of annual payments of reparations by Germany considered to be within her financial capacity. It established the BANK FOR INTERNATIONAL SETTLEMENTS as the intermediary for acceptance and transfer of these payments. Under the Plan the total reparations bill was reduced to $27,000,000,000 and payment spread over a period of 59 years. It recognized the connection between reparations and allied war debts by providing that reparations payments could be reduced in the future in the same proportion that the United States reduced the war debts. The onset of the international DEPRESSION led to default by Germany, and in 1931 President HOOVER issued the Hoover Moratorium.

Young Women's Christian Association. Popularly known as the Y.W.C.A. An organization established in Boston in 1866 to work for the moral and religious welfare of young women. Similar associations were soon established elsewhere in the United States. In 1886 a National Association of Y.W.C.A.'s was organized. Its works has included education and training for nurses, residence accommodations for transients, training in leadership, and EDUCATION in public affairs. It parallels among women the work carried on by the Y.M.C.A. See Young Men's Christian Association.

Z

ZANE, Ebenezer. 1747-1812. Pioneer. b. Virginia. Created the first permanent settlement on the Ohio River (1770); acquired more land which is now called Zanesville, Ohio; led the fight against hostile Indians in that TERRITORY during the Revolution.

ZENGER, John Peter. 1697-1746. Printer, journalist, and publsher. b. Germany. Came to America (1710); learned trade of printer and published *New York Weekly Journal* (1733); famous for his part in the trial which established in America the principle of FREEDOM OF THE PRESS; he was sued for libel, defended by ANDREW HAMILTON, and acquitted.

Zenger, Peter Case. A famous colonial trial in 1734 establishing the principle of freedom of the press. JOHN PETER ZENGER, a German immigrant, published the *New York Weekly Journal* in which appeared articles claiming that actions of the governor of New York were arbitrary and tyrannical. Zenger was arrested and tried for libel. Despite an un-friendly judge, his attorney, ANDREW HAMILTON, convinced the jury of the truth of Zenger's accusations and of the application to the colonies of the British Bill of Rights. Zenger's acquittal firmly established this important doctrine.

Zimmerman Note. A message from the German foreign minister, Alfred Zimmerman, to the German minister in Mexico in 1917, giving orders that the latter seek to enlist Mexican support for Germany in the event the United States entered World War I. Mexico was offered an alliance with Germany, financial aid, and the restoration of "the lost territory of New Mexico, Texas, and Arizona." The Mexican president was urged to seek Japan's renunciation of her alliance with the ALLIED POWERS and her joining the CENTRAL POWERS. The note was intercepted by the British secret service and was turned over to the STATE DEPARTMENT which released it on March 1, 1917. The nation was deeply shocked by the Zimmerman note, and was well prepared to accept Congress' declaration of war a month later.

THE CONSTITUTION
OF THE
UNITED STATES

We the people of the United States, in order to form a more perfect union, establish justice, insure domestic tranquillity, provide for the common defense, promote the general welfare, and secure the blessings of liberty to ourselves and our posterity, do ordain and establish this Constitution for the United States of America.

ARTICLE I

Section 1. All legislative powers herein granted shall be vested in a Congress of the United States, which shall consist of a Senate and House of Representatives.

Section 2. 1. The House of Representatives shall be composed of members chosen every second year by the people of the several States, and the electors in each State shall have the qualifications requisite for electors of the most numerous branch of the State legislature.

2. No person shall be a representative who shall not have attained to the age of twenty-five years, and been seven years a citizen of the United States, and who shall not, when elected, be an inhabitant of that State in which he shall be chosen.

3. Representatives and direct taxes[1] shall be apportioned among the several States which may be included within this Union, according to their respective numbers, which shall be determined by adding to the whole number of free persons, including those bound to service for a term of years, and excluding Indians not taxed, *three-fifths of all other persons.*[2] The actual enumeration shall be made within three years after the first meeting of the Congress of the United States, and within every subsequent term of ten years, in such manner as they shall by law direct. The number of representatives shall not exceed one for every thirty thousand, but each State shall have at least one representative; and until such enumeration shall be made, the State of New Hampshire shall be entitled to choose three, Massachusetts eight, Rhode Island and Providence Plantations one, Connecticut five, New York six, New Jersey four, Pennsylvania eight, Delaware one, Maryland six, Virginia ten, North Carolina five, South Carolina five, and Georgia three.

4. When vacancies happen in the representation from any State, the executive authority thereof shall issue writs of election to fill such vacancies.

5. The House of Representatives shall choose their speaker and other officers; and shall have the sole power of impeachment.

1. See the 16th Amendment.
2. See the 14th Amendment.

Section 3. 1. The Senate of the United States shall be composed of two senators from each State, *chosen by the legislature thereof*,[3] for six years; and each senator shall have one vote.

2. Immediately after they shall be assembled in consequence of the first election, they shall be divided as equally as may be into three classes. The seats of the senators of the first class shall be vacated at the expiration of the second year, of the second class at the expiration of the fourth year, and of the third class at the expiration of the sixth year, so that one third may be chosen every second year; and if vacancies happen by resignation, or otherwise, during the recess of the legislature of any State, the executive thereof may make temporary appointments until the next meeting of the legislature, which shall then fill such vacancies.[3]

3. No person shall be a senator who shall not have attained to the age of thirty years, and been nine years a citizen of the United States, and who shall not, when elected, be an inhabitant of that State for which he shall be chosen.

4. The Vice President of the United States shall be President of the Senate, but shall have no vote, unless they be equally divided.

5. The Senate shall choose their other officers, and also a president *pro tempore*, in the absence of the Vice President, or when he shall exercise the office of the President of the United States.

6. The Senate shall have the sole power to try all impeachments. When sitting for that purpose, they shall be on oath or affirmation. When the President of the United States is tried, the chief justice shall preside: and no person shall be convicted without the concurrence of two thirds of the members present.

7. Judgment in cases of impeachment shall not extend further than to removal from office, and disqualifications to hold and enjoy any office of honor, trust or profit under the United States: but the party convicted shall nevertheless be liable and subject to indictment, trial, judgment and punishment, according to law.

Section 4. 1. The times, places, and manner of holding elections for senators and representatives, shall be prescribed in each State by the legislature thereof; but the Congress may at any time by law make or alter such regulations, except as to the places of choosing senators.

2. The Congress shall assemble at least once in every year, and such meeting shall be on the first Monday in December, unless they shall by law appoint a different day.

Section 5. 1. Each House shall be the judge of the elections, returns and qualifications of its own members, and a majority of each shall constitute a quorum to do business; but a smaller number may adjourn from day to day, and may be authorized to compel the attendance of absent members, in such manner, and under such penalties as each House may provide.

2. Each House may determine the rules of its proceedings, punish its members for disorderly behavior, and, with the concurrence of two thirds, expel a member.

3. Each House shall keep a journal of its proceedings, and from time to time publish the same, excepting such parts as may in their judgment require secrecy; and the yeas and nays of the members of either House on any question shall, at the desire of one fifth of those present, be entered on the journal.

4. Neither House, during the session of Congress, shall, without the consent of the other, adjourn for more than three days, nor to any other place than that in which the two Houses shall be sitting.

Section 6. 1. The senators and representatives shall receive a compensation for their services, to be ascertained by law, and paid out of the Treasury of the United States. They shall in all cases, except treason, felony, and breach of the peace, be privileged from arrest during

3. See the 17th Amendment.

their attendance at the session of their respective Houses, and in going to and returning from the same; and for any speech or debate in either House, they shall not be questioned in any other place.

2. No senator or representative shall, during the time for which he was elected, be appointed to any civil office under the authority of the United States, which shall have been created, or the emoluments whereof shall have been increased during such time; and no person holding any office under the United States shall be a member of either House during his continuance in office.

Section 7. 1. All bills raising revenue shall originate in the House of Representatives; but the Senate may propose or concur with amendments as on other bills.

2. Every bill which shall have passed the House of Representatives and the Senate, shall, before it becomes a law, be presented to the President of the United States; if he approves he shall sign it, but if not he shall return it, with his objections to that House in which it shall have originated, who shall enter the objections at large on their journal, and proceed to reconsider it. If after such reconsideration two thirds of that House shall agree to pass the bill, it shall be sent, together with the objections, to the other House, by which it shall likewise be reconsidered, and if approved by two thirds of that House, it shall become a law. But in all such cases the votes of both Houses shall be determined by yeas and nays, and the names of the persons voting for and against the bill shall be entered on the journal of each House respectively. If any bill shall not be returned by the President within ten days (Sundays excepted) after it shall have been presented to him, the same shall be a law, in like manner as if he had signed it, unless the Congress by their adjournment prevent its return, in which case it shall not be a law.

3. Every order, resolution, or vote to which the concurrence of the Senate and the House of Representatives may be necessary (except on a question of adjournment) shall be presented to the President of the United States; and before the same shall take effect, shall be approved by him, or being disapproved by him, shall be repassed by two thirds of the Senate and House of Representatives, according to the rules and limitations prescribed in the case of a bill.

Section 8. The Congress shall have the power

1. To lay and collect taxes, duties, imposts, and excises, to pay the debts and provide for the common defense and general welfare of the United States; but all duties, imposts, and excises shall be uniform throughout the United States;

2. To borrow money on the credit of the United States;

3. To regulate commerce with foreign nations, and among the several States, and with the Indian tribes;

4. To establish a uniform rule of naturalization, and uniform laws on the subject of bankruptcies throughout the United States;

5. To coin money, regulate the value thereof, and of foreign coin, and fix the standard of weights and measures;

6. To provide for the punishment of counterfeiting the securities and current coin of the United States;

7. To establish post offices and post roads;

8. To promote the progress of science and useful arts, by securing for limited times to authors and investors the exclusive right to their respective writings and discoveries;

9. To constitute tribunals inferior to the Supreme Court;

10. To define and punish piracies and felonies committed on the high seas, and offenses against the law of nations;

11. To declare war, grant letters of marque and reprisal, and make rules concerning captures on land and water;

12. To raise and support armies, but no appropriation of money to that use shall be for a longer term than two years;

13. To provide and maintain a navy;

14. To make rules for the government and regulation of the land and naval forces;

15. To provide for calling forth the militia to execute the laws of the Union, suppress insurrections and repel invasions;

16. To provide for organizing, arming, and disciplining the militia, and for governing such part of them as may be employed in the service of the United States, reserving to the States respectively, the appointment of the officers, and the authority of training the militia according to the discipline prescribed by Congress.

17. To exercise exclusive legislation in all cases whatsoever, over such district (not exceeding ten miles square) as may, by cession of particular States, and the acceptance of Congress, become the seat of the government of the United States, and to exercise like authority over all places purchased by the consent of the legislature of the State in which the same shall be, for the erection of forts, magazines, arsenals, dockyards, and other needful buildings; and

18. To make all laws which shall be necessary and proper for carrying into execution the foregoing powers, and all other powers vested by this Constitution in the government of the United States, or in any department or officer thereof.

Section 9. 1. The migration or importation of such persons as any of the States now existing shall think proper to admit, shall not be prohibited by the Congress prior to the year one thousand eight hundred and eight, but a tax or duty may be imposed on such importation, not exceeding ten dollars for each person.

2. The privilege of the writ of *habeas corpus* shall not be suspended, unless when in cases of rebellion or invasion the public safety may require it.

3. No bill of attainder or *ex post facto* law shall be passed.

4. No capitation, or other direct, tax shall be laid, unless in proportion to the census or enumeration hereinbefore directed to be taken.[4]

5. No tax or duty shall be laid on articles exported from any State.

6. No preference shall be given by any regulation of commerce or revenue to the ports of one State over those of another: nor shall vessels bound to, or from, one State be obliged to enter, clear, or pay duties in another.

7. No money shall be drawn from the treasury, but in consequence of appropriations made by law; and a regular statement and account of the receipts and expenditures of all public money shall be published from time to time.

8. No title of nobility shall be granted by the United States: and no person holding any office of profit or trust under them, shall, without the consent of the Congress, accept of any present, emolument, office, or title, of any kind whatever, from any king, prince, or foreign State.

Section 10. 1. No State shall enter into any treaty, alliance, or confederation; grant letters of marque and reprisal; coin money; emit bills of credit; make anything but gold and silver coin a tender in payment of debts; pass any bill of attainder, *ex post facto* law, or law impairing the obligation of contracts, or grant any title of nobility.

2. No State shall, without the consent of the Congress, lay any imposts or duties on imports or exports, except what may be absolutely necessary for executing its inspection laws: and the net produce of all duties and imposts laid by any State on imports or exports, shall be for the use of the treasury of the United States; and all such laws shall be subject to the revision and control of the Congress.

3. No State shall, without the consent of the Congress, lay any duty of tonnage, keep troops, or ships of war in time of peace, enter into any agreement or compact with another State, or

4. See the 16th Amendment.

with a foreign power, or engage in war, unless actually invaded, or in such imminent danger as will not admit of delay.

ARTICLE II

Section 1. 1. The executive power shall be vested in a President of the United States of America. He shall hold his office during the term of four years, and, together with the Vice President, chosen for the same term, be elected as follows:

2. Each State shall appoint, in such manner as the legislature thereof may direct, a number of electors, equal to the whole number of senators and representatives to which the State may be entitled in the Congress: but no senator or representative, or person holding an office of trust or profit under the United States, shall be appointed an elector.

The electors shall meet in their respective States, and vote by ballot for two persons, of whom one at least shall not be an inhabitant of the same State with themselves. And they shall make a list of all the persons voted for, and of the number of votes for each; which list they shall sign and certify, and transmit sealed to the seat of the government of the United States, directed to the president of the Senate. The president of the Senate shall, in the presence of the Senate and House of Representatives, open all the certificates, and the votes shall then be counted. The person having the greatest number of votes shall be the President, if such number be a majority of the whole number of electors appointed; and if there be more than one who have such majority, and have an equal number of votes, then the House of Representatives shall immediately choose by ballot one of them for President; and if no person have a majority, then from the five highest on the list the said House shall in like manner choose the President. But in choosing the President, the votes shall be taken by States, the representation from each State having one vote; a quorum for this purpose shall consist of a member or members from two thirds of the States, and a majority of all the States shall be necessary to a choice. In every case, after the choice of the President, the person having the greatest number of votes of the electors shall be the Vice President. But if there should remain two or more who have equal votes, the Senate shall choose from them by ballot the Vice President.[5]

3. The Congress may determine the time of choosing the electors, and the day on which they shall give their votes; which day shall be the same throughout the United States.

4. No person except a natural born citizen, or a citizen of the United States, at the time of the adoption of this Constitution, shall be eligible to the office of President; neither shall any person be eligible to that office who shall not have attained to the age of thirty-five years, and been fourteen years a resident within the United States.

5. In case of the removal of the President from office, or of his death, resignation, or inability to discharge the powers and duties of the said office, the same shall devolve on the Vice President, and the Congress may by law provide for the case of removal, death, resignation, or inability, both of the President and Vice President, declaring what officer shall then act as President, and such officer shall act accordingly, until the disability be removed, or a President shall be elected.

6. The President shall, at stated times, receive for his services a compensation, which shall neither be increased nor diminished during the period for which he shall have been elected, and he shall not receive within that period any other emolument from the United States, or any of them.

7. Before he enter on the execution of his office, he shall take the following oath or affirmation:—"I do solemnly swear (or affirm) that I will faithfully execute the office of President of the United States, and will to the best of my ability, preserve, protect and defend the Constitution of the United States."

5. Superseded by the 12th Amendment.

Section 2. 1. The President shall be commander in chief of the army and navy of the United States, and of the militia of the several States, when called into the actual service of the United States; he may require the opinion, in writing, of the principal officer in each of the executive departments, upon any subject relating to the duties of their respective offices, and he shall have power to grant reprieves and pardons for offenses against the United States, except in cases of impeachment.

2. He shall have power, by and with the advice and consent of the Senate, to make treaties, provided two thirds of the senators present concur; and he shall nominate, and by and with the advice and consent of the Senate, shall appoint ambassadors, other public ministers and consuls, judges of the Supreme Court, and all other officers of the United States, whose appointments are not herein otherwise provided for, and which shall be established by law: but the Congress may by law vest the appointment of such inferior officers, as they think proper, in the President alone, in the courts of law, or in the heads of departments.

3. The President shall have power to fill up all vacancies that may happen during the recess of the Senate, by granting commissions which shall expire at the end of their next session.

Section 3. He shall from time to time give to the Congress information of the state of the Union, and recommend to their consideration such measures as he shall judge necessary and expedient; he may, on extraordinary occasions, convene both Houses, or either of them, and in case of disagreement between them with respect to the time of adjournment, he may adjourn them to such time as he shall think proper; he shall receive ambassadors and other public ministers; he shall take care that the laws be faithfully executed, and shall commission all the officers of the United States.

Section 4. The President, Vice President, and all civil officers of the United States, shall be removed from office on impeachment for, and conviction of, treason, bribery, or other high crimes and misdemeanors.

ARTICLE III

Section 1. The judicial power of the United States shall be vested in one Supreme Court, and in such inferior courts as the Congress may from time to time ordain and establish. The judges, both of the Supreme and inferior courts, shall hold their offices during good behavior, and shall, at stated times, receive for their services, a compensation, which shall not be diminished during their continuance in office.

Section 2. 1. The judicial power shall extend to all cases, in law and equity, arising under this Constitution, the laws of the United States, and treaties made, or which shall be made, under their authority;—to all cases affecting ambassadors, other public ministers and consuls;—to all cases of admiralty and maritime jurisdiction;—to controversies to which the United States shall be a party;—to controversies between two or more States; between a State and citizens of another State;[6]—between citizens of different States;—between citizens of the same State claiming lands under grants of different States, and between a State, or the citizens thereof, and foreign States citizens or subjects.

2. In all cases affecting ambassadors, other public ministers and consuls, and those in which a State shall be party, the Supreme Court shall have original jurisdiction. In all the other cases before mentioned, the Supreme Court shall have appellate jurisdiction, both as to law and to fact, with such exceptions, and under such regulations as the Congress shall make.

3. The trial of all crimes, except in cases of impeachment, shall be by jury; and such trial shall be held in the State where the said crimes shall have been committed; but when not committed within any State, the trial shall be at such place or places as the Congress may by law have directed.

6. See the 11th Amendment.

Section 3. 1. Treason against the United States shall consist only in levying war against them, or in adhering to their enemies, giving them aid and comfort. No person shall be convicted of treason unless on the testimony of two witnesses to the same overt act, or on confession in open court.

2. The Congress shall have power to declare the punishment of treason, but no attainder of treason shall work corruption of blood, or forfeiture except during the life of the person attainted.

ARTICLE IV

Section 1. Full faith and credit shall be given in each State to the public acts, records, and judicial proceedings of every other State. And the Congress may by general laws prescribe the manner in which such acts, records and proceedings shall be proved, and the effect thereof.

Section 2. 1. The citizens of each State shall be entitled to all privileges and immunities of citizens in the several States.[7]

2. A person charged in any State with treason, felony, or other crime, who shall flee from justice, and be found in another State, shall on demand of the executive authority of the State from which he fled, be delivered up to be removed to the State having jurisdiction of the crime.

3. No person held to service or labor in one State under the laws thereof, escaping into another, shall in consequence of any law or regulation therein, be discharged from such service or labor, but shall be delivered up on claim of the party to whom such service or labor may be due.[8]

Section 3. 1. New States may be admitted by the Congress into this Union; but no new State shall be formed or erected within the jurisdiction of any other State, nor any State be formed by the junction of two or more States, or parts of States, without the consent of the legislatures of the States concerned as well as of the Congress.

2. The Congress shall have power to dispose of and make all needful rules and regulations respecting the territory or other property belonging to the United States; and nothing in this Constitution shall be so construed as to prejudice any claims of the United States, or of any particular State.

Section 4. The United States shall guarantee to every State in this Union a republican form of government, and shall protect each of them against invasion; and on application of the legislature, or of the executive (when the legislature cannot be convened) against domestic violence.

ARTICLE V

The Congress, whenever two thirds of both Houses shall deem it necessary, shall propose amendments to this Constitution, or, on the application of the legislature of two thirds of the several States, shall call a convention for proposing amendments, which in either case, shall be valid to all intents and purposes, as part of this Constitution when ratified by the legislatures of three fourths of the several States, or by conventions in three fourths thereof, as the one or the other mode of ratification may be proposed by the Congress; Provided that no amendment which may be made prior to the year one thousand eight hundred and eight shall in any manner affect the first and fourth clauses in the ninth section of the first article; and that no State, without its consent, shall be deprived of its equal suffrage in the Senate.

7. See the 14th Amendment, Sec. 1.
8. See the 13th Amendment.

ARTICLE VI

1. All debts contracted and engagements entered into, before the adoption of this Constitution shall be as valid against the United States under this Constitution, as under the Confederation.[9]

2. This Constitution, and the laws of the United States which shall be made in pursuance thereof; and all treaties made, or which shall be made, under the authority of the United States, shall be the supreme law of the land; and the Judges in every State shall be bound thereby, anything in the Constitution or laws of any State to the contrary notwithstanding.

3. The senators and representatives before mentioned, and the members of the several State legislatures, and all executive and judicial officers, both of the United States and of the several States, shall be bound by oath or affirmation to support this Constitution; but no religious test shall ever be required as a qualification to any office or public trust under the United States.

ARTICLE VII

The ratification of the conventions of nine States shall be sufficient for the establishment of this Constitution between the States so ratifying the same.

Done in Convention by the unanimous consent of the States present the seventeenth day of September in the year of our Lord one thousand seven hundred and eighty-seven, and of the independence of the United States of America the twelfth.. In witness whereof we have hereunto subscribed our names. [Names omitted]

Articles in addition to, and amendment of, the Constitution of the United States of America, proposed by Congress, and ratified by the legislatures of the several States pursuant to the fifth article of the original Constitution.

AMENDMENTS
First Ten Amendments passed by Congress Sept. 25, 1789.
Ratified by three-fourths of the States December 15, 1791.

ARTICLE I

Congress shall make no law respecting an establishment of religion, or prohibiting the free exercise thereof; or abridging the freedom of speech, or of the press; or the right of the people peaceably to assemble, and to petition the government for a redress of grievances.

ARTICLE II

A well regulated militia, being necessary to the security of a free State, the right of the people to keep and bear arms, shall not be infringed.

ARTICLE III

No soldier shall, in time of peace be quartered in any house, without the consent of the owner, nor in time of war, but in a manner to be prescribed by law.

ARTICLE IV

The right of the people to be secure in their persons, houses, papers, and effects, against unreasonable searches and seizures, shall not be violated, and no warrants shall issue, but upon probable cause, supported by oath or affirmation, and particularly describing the place to be searched, and the persons or things to be seized.

9. See the 14th Amendment, Sec. 4.

ARTICLE V

No person shall be held to answer for a capital, or otherwise infamous crime, unless on a presentment or indictment of a grand jury, except in cases arising in the land or naval forces, or in the militia, when in actual service in time of war or public danger; nor shall any person be subject for the same offense to be twice put in jeopardy of life or limb; nor shall be compelled in any criminal case to be a witness against himself, nor be deprived of life, liberty, or property, without due process of law; nor shall private property be taken for public use without just compensation.

ARTICLE VI

In all criminal prosecutions, the accused shall enjoy the right to a speedy and public trial, by an impartial jury of the State and district wherein the crime shall have been committed, which district shall have been previously ascertained by law, and to be informed of the nature and cause of the accusation; to be confronted with the witnesses against him; to have compulsory process for obtaining witnesses in his favor, and to have the assistance of counsel for his defense.

ARTICLE VII

In suits at common law, where the value in controversy shall exceed twenty dollars, the right of trial by jury shall be preserved, and no fact tried by a jury shall be otherwise reëxamined in any court of the United States, than according to the rules of the common law.

ARTICLE VIII

Excessive bail shall not be required, nor excessive fines imposed, nor cruel and unusual punishments inflicted.

ARTICLE IX

The enumeration in the Constitution of certain rights shall not be construed to deny or disparage others retained by the people.

ARTICLE X

The powers not delegated to the United States by the Constitution, nor prohibited by it to the States, are reserved to the States respectively, or to the people.

ARTICLE XI
Passed by Congress March 5, 1794. Ratified January 8, 1798.

The judicial power of the United States shall not be construed to extend to any suit in law or equity, commenced or prosecuted against one of the United States by citizens of another State, or by citizens or subjects of any foreign State.

ARTICLE XII
Passed by Congress December 12, 1803. Ratified September 25, 1804.

The electors shall meet in their respective States, and vote by ballot for President and Vice President, one of whom, at least, shall not be an inhabitant of the same State with themselves; they shall name in their ballots the person voted for as President, and in distinct ballots, the person voted for as Vice President, and they shall make distinct lists of all persons voted for as President and of all persons voted for as Vice President, and of the number of votes for each, which lists they shall sign and certify, and transmit sealed to the seat of the government of the United States, directed to the President of the Senate;—The President of the Senate shall, in the presence of the Senate and House of Representatives, open all the certificates and the votes shall then be counted;—The person having the greatest number of votes for President, shall be the President, if such number be a majority of the whole number of electors appointed; and if no person have such majority, then from the persons having the highest numbers not exceeding three on the list of those voted for as President, the House of Representatives shall choose immediately, by ballot, the President. But in choosing the President, the votes shall be taken by States, the representation from each State having one vote; a quorum for this purpose shall consist of a member or members from two thirds of the States, and a majority of all the States shall be necessary to a choice. And if the House of Representatives shall not choose a President whenever the right of choice shall devolve upon them, before the fourth day of March next following, then the Vice President shall act as President, as in the case of the death or other constitutional disability of the President. The person having the greatest number of votes as Vice President shall be the Vice President, if such number be a majority of the whole number of electors appointed, and if no person have a majority, then from the two highest numbers on the list, the Senate shall choose the Vice President: a quorum for the purpose shall consist of two thirds of the whole number of Senators, and a majority of the whole number shall be necessary to a choice. But no person constitutionally ineligible to the office of President shall be eligible to that of Vice President of the United States.

ARTICLE XIII
Passed by Congress February 1, 1865. Ratified December 18, 1865.

Section 1. Neither slavery nor involuntary servitude, except as punishment for crime whereof the party shall have been duly convicted, shall exist within the United States, or any place subject to their jurisdiction.

Section 2. Congress shall have power to enforce this article by appropriate legislation.

ARTICLE XIV
Passed by Congress June 16, 1866. Ratified July 23, 1868.

Section 1. All persons born or naturalized in the United States, and subject to the jurisdiction thereof, are citizens of the United States and of the State wherein they reside. No State shall make or enforce any law which shall abridge the privileges or immunities of citizens of the United States; nor shall any State deprive any person of life, liberty, or property, without due process of law; nor deny to any person within its jurisdiction the equal protection of the laws.

Section 2. Representatives shall be apportioned among the several States according to their respective numbers, counting the whole number of persons in each State, excluding Indians not taxed. But when the right to vote at any election for the choice of electors for President and Vice President of the United States, representatives in Congress, the executive and judicial officers of a State, or the members of the legislature thereof, is denied to any of the male inhabitants of such State, being twenty-one years of age, and citizens of the United States, or in any way abridged, except for participation in rebellion, or other crime, the basis of representation therein shall be reduced in the proportion which the number of such male citizens shall bear to the whole number of male citizens twenty-one years of age in such State.

Section 3. No person shall be a senator or representative in Congress, or elector of President and Vice President, or hold any office, civil or military, under the United States, or under any State, who having previously taken an oath, as a member of Congress, or as an officer of the United States, or as a member of any State legislature, or as an executive or judicial officer of any State, to support the Constitution of the United States, shall have engaged in insurrection or rebellion against the same, or given aid or comfort to the enemies thereof. But Congress may by a vote of two thirds of each House, remove such disability.

724

Section 4. The validity of the public debt of the United States, authorized by law, including debts incurred for payment of pensions and bounties for services in suppressing insurrection or rebellion, shall not be questioned. But neither the United States nor any State shall assume or pay any debt or obligation incurred in aid of insurrection or rebellion against the United States, or any claim for the loss or emancipation of any slave; but all such debts, obligations, and claims shall be held illegal and void.

Section 5. The Congress shall have power to enforce, by appropriate legislation, the provisions of this article.

ARTICLE XV
Passed by Congress February 27, 1869. Ratified March 30, 1870.

Section 1. The right of citizens of the United States to vote shall not be denied or abridged by the United States or by any State on account of race, color, or previous condition of servitude.

Section 2. The Congress shall have power to enforce this article by appropriate legislation.

ARTICLE XVI
Passed by Congress July 12, 1909. Ratified February 25, 1913.

The Congress shall have power to lay and collect taxes on incomes, from whatever source derived, without apportionment among the several States, and without regard to any census or enumeration.

ARTICLE XVII
Passed by Congress May 16, 1912. Ratified May 31, 1913.

The Senate of the United States shall be composed of two senators from each state, elected by the people thereof, for six years; and each senator shall have one vote. The electors in each State shall have the qualifications requisite for electors of the most numerous branch of the State legislature.

When vacancies happen in the representation of any State in the Senate, the executive authority of such State shall issue writs of election to fill such vacancies: *Provided*, That the legislature of any State may empower the executive thereof to make temporary appointments until the people fill the vacancies by election as the legislature may direct.

This amendment shall not be so construed as to affect the election or term of any senator chosen before it becomes valid as part of the Constitution.

ARTICLE XVIII
Passed by Congress December 17, 1917. Ratified January 29, 1919.

After one year from the ratification of this article, the manufacture, sale, or transportation of intoxicating liquors within, the importation thereof into, or the exportation thereof from the United States and all territory subject to the jurisdiction thereof for beverage purposes is hereby prohibited.

The Congress and the several States shall have concurrent power to enforce this article by appropriate legislation.

This article shall be inoperative unless it shall have been ratified as an amendment to the Constitution by the legislatures of the several States, as provided in the Constitution, within seven years from the date of the submission hereof to the states by Congress.

ARTICLE XIX
Passed by Congress June 5, 1919. Ratified August 26, 1920.

The right of citizens of the United States to vote shall not be denied or abridged by the United States or by any State on account of sex.

The Congress shall have power by appropriate legislation to enforce the provisions of this article.

ARTICLE XX
Passed by Congress March 3, 1932. Ratified January 23, 1933.

Section 1. The terms of the President and Vice President shall end at noon on the 20th day of January, and the terms of Senators and Representatives at noon on the 3d day of January, of the years in which such terms would have ended if this article had not been ratified; and the terms of their successors shall then begin.

Section 2. The Congress shall assemble at least once in every year, and such meeting shall begin at noon on the 3d day of January, unless they shall by law appoint a different day.

Section 3. If, at the time fixed for the beginning of the term of President, the President-elect shall have died, the Vice President-elect shall become President. If a President shall not have been chosen before the time fixed for the beginning of his term, or if the President-elect shall have failed to qualify, then the Vice President-elect shall act as President until a President shall have qualified; and the Congress may by law provide for the case wherein neither a President-elect nor a Vice President-elect shall have qualified, declaring who shall then act as President, or the manner in which one who is to act shall be selected, and such person shall act accordingly until a President or Vice President shall have qualified.

Section 4. The Congress may by law provide for the case of the death of any of the persons from whom the House of Representatives may choose a President whenever the right of choice shall have devolved upon them, and for the case of the death of any of the persons from whom the Senate may choose a Vice President whenever the right of choice shall have devolved upon them.

Section 5. Sections 1 and 2 shall take effect on the 15th day of October following the ratification of this article.

Section 6. This article shall be inoperative unless it shall have been ratified as an amendment to the Constitution by the legislatures of three-fourths of the several States within seven years from the date of it's submission.

ARTICLE XXI
Passed by Congress February 20, 1933. Ratified December 5, 1933.

Section 1. The Eighteenth Article of amendment to the Constitution of the United States is hereby repealed.

Section 2. The transportation or importation into any State, Territory, or possession of the United States for delivery or use therein of intoxicating liquors in violation of the laws thereof, is hereby prohibited.

Section 3. This article shall be inoperative unless it shall have been ratified as an amendment to the Constitution by conventions in the several States, as provided in the Constitution, within seven years from the date of the submission thereof to the States by the Congress.

ARTICLE XXII
Passed by Congress March 24, 1947. Ratified February 26, 1951.

Section 1. No person shall be elected to the office of the President more than twice, and no person who has held the office of President, or acted as President, for more than two years of a term to which some other person was elected President shall be elected to the office of the President more than once. But this article shall not apply to any person holding the office of President when this article was proposed by the Congress, and shall not prevent any person who may be holding the office of President, or acting as President, during the term within which this article becomes operative from holding the office of President or acting as President during the remainder of such term.

Section 2. This article shall be inoperative unless it shall have been ratified as an amendment to the Constitution by the legislatures of three-fourths of the several States within seven years from the date of its submission to the States by the Congress.

ARTICLE XXIII
Passed by Congress June 16, 1960. Ratified Mar. 29, 1961.

Section 1. The district constituting the seat of Government of the United States shall appoint in such manner as the Congress may direct:

A number of electors of President and Vice President equal to the whole number of Senators and Representatives in Congress to which the District would be entitled if it were a State, but in no event more than the least populous State; they shall be in addition to those appointed by the States, but they shall be considered, for the purposes of election of President and Vice President, to be electors appointed by a State; and they shall meet in the District and perform such duties as provided by the twelfth article of amendment.

Section 2. The Congress shall have the power to enforce this article by appropriate legislation.

ARTICLE XXIV
Passed by Congress Aug. 27, 1962. Ratified Jan. 23, 1964.

Section 1. The right of citizens of the United States to vote in any primary or other election for President or Vice President, for electors for President or Vice President, or for Senator or Representative in Congress, shall not be denied or abridged by the United States or any State by failure to pay any poll tax or other tax.

Section 2. The Congress shall have the power to enforce this article by appropriate legislation.

ARTICLE XXV
Passed by Congress July 6, 1965. Ratified February 10, 1967.

Section 1. In case of the removal of the President from office or of his death or resignation, the Vice President shall become President.

Section 2. Whenever there is a vacancy in the office of the Vice President, the President shall nominate a Vice President who shall take office upon confirmation by a majority vote of both Houses of Congress.

Section 3. Whenever the President transmits to the President pro tempore of the Senate and the Speaker of the House of Representatives his written declaration that he is unable to discharge the powers and duties of his office, and until he transmits to them a written declaration to the contrary, such powers and duties shall be discharged by the Vice President as Acting President.

Section 4. Whenever the Vice President and a majority of either the principal officers of the executive departments or of such other body as Congress may by law provide, transmit to the President pro tempore of the Senate and the Speaker of the House of Representatives their written declaration that the President is unable to discharge the powers and duties of his office the Vice President shall immediately assume the powers and duties of the office as Acting President.

Thereafter, when the President transmits to the President pro tempore of the Senate and the Speaker of the House of Representatives his written declaration that no inability exists, he shall resume the powers and duties of his office unless the Vice President and a majority of either the principal officers of the executive department or of such other body as Congress may by law provide, transmit within four days to the President pro tempore of the Senate and the Speaker of the House of Representatives their written declaration that the President is unable to discharge the powers and duties of his office. Thereupon Congress shall decide the issue, assembling within forty-eight hours for that purpose if not in session. If the Congress, within twenty-one days after receipt of the latter written declaration, or, if Congress is not in session, within twenty-one days after Congress is required to assemble, determines by two-thirds vote of both Houses that the President is unable to discharge the powers and duties of his office, the Vice President shall continue to discharge the same as Acting President; otherwise, the President shall resume the powers and duties of his office.

ARTICLE XXVI
Passed by Congress March 23, 1971. Ratified June 30, 1971.

Section 1. The right of citizens of the United States, who are eighteen years of age or older, to vote shall not be denied or abridged by the United States or by any State on account of age.

Section 2. The Congress shall have power to enforce this article by appropriate legislation.